Psychological Science

FOURTH EDITION

Psychological Science

FOURTH EDITION

Michael S. Gazzaniga
UNIVERSITY OF CALIFORNIA, SANTA BARBARA

Todd F. Heatherton
DARTMOUTH COLLEGE

Diane F. Halpern
CLAREMONT MCKENNA COLLEGE

W. W. NORTON & COMPANY
NEW YORK • LONDON

W. W. NORTON & COMPANY has been independent since its founding in 1923, when William Warder Norton and Mary D. Herter Norton first published lectures delivered at the People's Institute, the adult education division of New York City's Cooper Union. The Nortons soon expanded their program beyond the Institute, publishing books by celebrated academics from America and abroad. By mid-century, the two major pillars of Norton's publishing program—trade books and college texts—were firmly established. In the 1950s, the Norton family transferred control of the company to its employees, and today—with a staff of four hundred and a comparable number of trade, college, and professional titles published each year—W. W. Norton & Company stands as the largest and oldest publishing house owned wholly by its employees.

Editor: Sheri L. Snavely
Developmental Editor and Project Editor: Kurt Wildermuth
Managing Editor, College: Marian Johnson
Manuscript Editor: Janet Greenblatt
Editorial Assistants: Mary Dudley, Catherine Rice, and Carson Russell
Production Manager: Chris Granville
Art Director: Rubina Yeh
Book Designer: Lissi Sigillo
Photo Editors: Stephanie Romeo and Michael Fodera
Photo Researcher: Julie Tesser
Marketing Manager: Andrea Matter
Emedia Editor: Patrick Shriner
Associate Editors: Callinda Taylor and Matthew Freeman
Illustrators: Dragonfly Media Group
Compositor: Prepare, Emilcomp Inc.
Manufacturer: Transcontinental, Inc.

Library of Congress Cataloging-in-Publication Data

Gazzaniga, Michael S.
   Psychological science / Michael S. Gazzaniga, Todd F. Heatherton, Diane F. Halpern. — 4th ed.
      p. cm.
   Includes bibliographical references and index.

ISBN 978-0-393-91157-2 (hardcover)

   1. Psychology. I. Heatherton, Todd F. II. Halpern, Diane F. III. Title.
BF121.G393 2013
150—dc23
                              2011043532

W. W. Norton & Company, Inc., 500 Fifth Avenue, New York, N.Y. 10110
                    www.wwnorton.com

W. W. Norton & Company Ltd., Castle House, 75/76 Wells Street, London W1T 3QT

3 4 5 6 7 8 9 0

We dedicate this book to
Lilly, Emmy, and Garth Tretheway
Sarah Heatherton and James Heatherton
Sheldon, Evan, Karen, Amanda, and Jason Halpern
and Jaye, Danny, and Belle Halpern-Duncan.

Contents in Brief

About the Authors

MICHAEL S. GAZZANIGA (Ph.D., California Institute of Technology) is Distinguished Professor and Director of the Sage Center for the Study of the Mind at the University of California, Santa Barbara. He founded and presides over the Cognitive Neuroscience Institute and is founding editor-in-chief of the *Journal of Cognitive Neuroscience.* He is past president of the American Psychological Society and a member of the American Academy of Arts and Sciences, the Institute of Medicine, and the National Academy of Sciences. He has held positions at the University of California, Santa Barbara; New York University; the State University of New York, Stony Brook; Cornell University Medical College; and the University of California, Davis. In his career, he has introduced thousands of students to psychology and cognitive neuroscience. He has written many notable books, including, most recently, *Who's in Charge?: Free Will and the Science of the Brain.*

TODD F. HEATHERTON (Ph.D., University of Toronto) is the Lincoln Filene Professor in Human Relations in the Department of Psychological and Brain Sciences at Dartmouth College. His recent research takes a social brain sciences approach, which combines theories and methods of evolutionary psychology, social cognition, and cognitive neuroscience to examine the neural underpinnings of social behavior. He is associate editor of the *Journal of Cognitive Neuroscience* and serves on many editorial boards and grant review panels. He was elected president of the Society of Personality and Social Psychology in 2011 and has served on the executive committees of the Association of Researchers in Personality and the International Society of Self and Identity. He received the Award for Distinguished Service on Behalf of Social-Personality Psychology in 2005, was named to Thompson Reuters' ISI HighlyCited for Social Sciences in 2010, and received the Carol and Ed Diener Award for Outstanding Mid-Career Contributions to Personality Psychology in 2011. He received the Petra Shattuck Award for Teaching Excellence from the Harvard Extension School in 1994, the McLane Fellowship from Dartmouth College in 1997, and the Friedman Family Fellowship from Dartmouth College in 2001. He is a fellow of the American Psychological Association, the Association for Psychological Science, the Society of Experimental Social Psychology, and the Society for Personality and Social Psychology. He teaches introductory psychology every year.

DIANE F. HALPERN (Ph.D., University of Cincinnati) is the Trustee Professor of Psychology and Roberts Fellow at Claremont McKenna College. She is past president of the American Psychological Association, the Western Psychological Association, the Society for General Psychology, and the Society for the Teaching of Psychology. She has won many awards for her teaching and research, including the 2002 Outstanding Professor Award from the Western Psychological Association, the 1999 American Psychological Foundation Award for Distinguished Teaching, the 1996 Distinguished Career Award for Contributions to Education from the American Psychological Association, and the California State University's State-Wide Outstanding Professor Award. She has written many books, including *Thought and Knowledge: An Introduction to Critical Thinking and Sex Differences in Cognitive Abilities.* Her edited book, *Undergraduate Education in Psychology: A Blueprint for the Future of the Discipline* (APA Books), was published in 2009. She teaches introductory psychology every year.

Why Teach with *Psychological Science*?

Our Book Delivers What Students Need to Know

From the moment the original author team, Mike Gazzaniga and Todd Heatherton, conceived the first edition of *Psychological Science,* our primary motivation was to create a textbook that captured ongoing revolutionary changes in the field. Instead of an encyclopedic and homogenized compendium that dutifully covered worn themes and tired topics, we wanted to create a readable book that captured the excitement of contemporary research and yet respected the rich tradition of scientific research accumulated by the field. We sought and received excellent advice from countless colleagues about what was most important to them in introductory psychology courses and what they believed was of greatest value to students. It became clear that most instructors wanted a textbook that focused on material that students really needed to know at the introductory level. They did not want a book that burdened readers with unnecessary details.

In revising the book for each subsequent edition, we have kept students foremost in mind. We worked hard on hitting the right level of detail and also on keeping the material accessible, relevant, and interesting. We retained our ask and answer thematic approach, which captures the reader's interest, and our declarative prose style, which focuses on the answers to current scientific questions.

Our Book Crosses Levels of Analysis and Embraces Diverse Approaches

Although Mike came to the book with a strong background in cognitive neuroscience and Todd in social and personality psychology, our early goal was to feature research that crossed levels of analysis, from cultural and social context to genes and neurons. To really understand basic cognitive and perceptual processes, researchers need to appreciate that social contexts shape what people think about and how they perceive the world around them. Moreover, important differences in personality mean that people have unique interactions with those social environments.

Our focus on contemporary research extends well beyond brain science to include new thinking in social, personality, and developmental psychology as well as contemporary approaches to understanding psychological disorders and their treatment. Each subfield has made great progress over the last decade, and our goal in each edition has been to highlight how contemporary research is providing new insights into the brain, behavior, and psychological disorders. The unified approach to each topic has been to concentrate on what we have learned from scientific study, such as research over the past decade on the empirical basis of psychological treatment.

Students Will Succeed with Our Science of Learning Approach

For the third edition, the renowned critical thinking expert Diane Halpern joined the team. Diane shared our interest and vision in creating a highly accessible, scientifically grounded textbook. What she added, and we very much desired, was her expertise on the science of learning. Although we (Mike and Todd) had spent considerable time in the classroom and received awards for our teaching, Diane's empirical approach to the science of learning resonated for us. That, after all, is the point of our book: We learn how things work through careful scientific study.

Our book seeks to be the perfect union between the science of psychology and the science of learning. Through careful empirical research into the cognitive, individual, and environmental factors that influence active learning, psychologists have discovered the best practices for teaching. Researchers have studied the way people think, learn, and remember, yet this knowledge is not often applied to student learning. Our pedagogical framework is based on what researchers have learned about how students learn. Thanks to Diane's expertise, we incorporated many new science-based learning features into the third edition: an enhanced ask and answer approach; Learning Objectives, which focus students on the central questions they should be able to answer after reading a chapter; Summing Up/Measuring Up interim assessments, which are explicitly tied to the Learning Objectives and give students take-home messages as well as questions to test their understanding; Practice Tests, at the end of the chapters and on the student Web site, which help students consolidate their learning; and Critical Thinking sections, which show students how to put critical thinking into action. These features provide students with many opportunities to practice retrieval and use higher-order thinking, both of which increase the building of durable, transferable knowledge.

We also used a science of learning approach to design the visual art program. Because we value a scientific approach, we consulted with one of the world's leading educational psychologists, Richard Mayer, whose research focuses on how people can learn more effectively using visual materials. Rich helped us conceptualize new presentations of visual information that encourage active learning. For instance, we sought to help visual learners with clear, attractive graphics that stimulated students' thinking skills and drove home their understanding of key concepts. We introduced the "Try for Yourself" features, which encourage students to engage in demonstrations on their own. We introduced the "Scientific Method" illustrations, which carefully and consistently lead students through the steps of some of the most interesting experiments and studies in psychological science. In the chapter on sensation and perception, we created "How We" figures, which help students understand the complex processes involved in sensing and perceiving the world. These step-by-step figures enable students to see processes in action and to view the material from both micro perspectives and macro perspectives.

In this new edition, we continued our innovation by adding questions at the end of at least two captions in each chapter. These caption questions facilitate deeper understanding by encouraging students to connect the photos and figures to the concepts presented in the text.

New to This Edition: SmartWork Takes the Science of Learning Online

An exciting new development for the fourth edition is the creation of SmartWork, a sophisticated, flexible online homework system developed by W. W. Norton. For

Psychological Science, SmartWork is integrated with the fourth-edition art program and pedagogy, using interactive questions and activities to reinforce core concepts. We are very fortunate to have Sarah Grison and her team of psychologists authoring SmartWork for our book. Sarah has 17 years of teaching experience and has taught introductory psychology to thousands of students at the University of Illinois at Urbana-Champaign. Sarah's research examines how psychological research can be applied to teaching and learning.

Students Care about What They Learn in Our Book

A major goal of the fourth edition is encouraging students to care about psychology. As engaged readers, students will learn more deeply, understand themselves and others more fully, and become better critical thinkers and decision makers. And by acquiring skills and knowledge that they remember long after the course is finished, these engaged readers will come away with a richer appreciation of our field. As noted, Diane Halpern's vast experience has led to our popular Critical Thinking Skills sections, which address topics such as regression to the mean and drug bias in research. New to the fourth edition are "Psychology: Knowledge You Can Use" features, which keep students engaged and thinking. One per chapter, these applications address the question of what students might immediately do with the information they learn. "Psychology: Knowledge You Can Use" topics include the relationship between sleep and study habits, how psychology can help a person navigate in his or her romantic life, and how to help a friend who seems suicidal. By making clear how psychological concepts can have real-time usefulness, these applications provide additional motivation for students to engage with the material.

Have You Read It Lately?

Our adopters regularly praise our clear and inviting writing style. This feedback warms our hearts and makes the effort of writing a textbook worthwhile. However, instructors who have not adopted *Psychological Science* often indicate that they respect our book but think it is "too high-level" for their students. For the fourth edition, we decided to face this challenge head-on. After all, students should be focusing on the concepts, not the reading. With the help of reviewers, advisors, and our developmental editor, we found ways to maintain the integrity of content but make the explanations even clearer and more accessible. We cut unnecessary terms, examples, and digressions, shortening some chapters by as much as 10 percent. We reworked complex sentences and long paragraphs to maximize student understanding. We revised even the shortest sentences to engage introductory readers more colloquially. In addition, we further enhanced the already strong relationship between the art and the narrative to help students form lasting associations.

Throughout the book, we scrutinized the discussions of neuroscience to make their connections with the chapters' major concepts as meaningful as possible. Consider Chapter 7, "Attention and Memory." In the third edition, readers encountered the section "What Brain Processes Are Involved in Memory?" in the middle of the chapter, between discussions of long-term memory and forgetting. In the fourth edition, that material has been reduced to essentials, titled "Memory Is the Result of Brain Activity," and incorporated into "What Is Memory?", a brand-new, reader-friendly opening section that establishes the major themes of the chapter.

The Content Reflects Our Global, Multicultural Society

For the third edition, we reached our goal of increasing the inclusivity of our discussions. In every chapter, we added more material related to gender, culture, and international issues. For the fourth edition, we have continued our efforts to represent the world in its diversity: the young and the middle-aged and the elderly, blacks and whites, Asians and Middle Easterners, southerners and northerners, gays and straights, women and men and people in between. For example, the third-edition's discussion of Mary Whiton Calkins and Margaret Flay Washburn has been expanded to a subsection, "Women Have Helped Shape the Field," which acknowledges the historical and modern roles of women in countless areas of psychology. And for the first time, our human development chapter discusses the concept of *transgender*.

Meanwhile, it is unfortunate that many psychology textbooks focus almost completely on research from North America, because a tremendous amount of exciting psychological research takes place around the world. After all, the rich history of psychological science reflects contributions from scholars around the globe, such as Wundt's original work in Germany. Students should learn about the best psychological science, no matter where it originates. Our goal has always been to present the best psychological research regardless of country, and in the fourth edition each chapter includes new important research from many corners of the globe. For example, we discuss the fascinating work of researchers in Belgium and England who have been able to communicate with people who are in comas. We describe research from Australia that provides an elegant description of how working memory is updated to take into account new information. We describe cross-cultural work on self-perception. Such research from outside North America will not only help students learn more about psychology. It will also bring them new perspectives, encouraging a sense of themselves as global citizens.

The Content Reflects Our Colleagues and Our Students

The three of us hope that the revisions we have made to our textbook will greatly appeal to students and instructors. We conducted focus sessions of adopters, friends, and potential users to canvass their thoughts, and the text has been greatly improved because of their advice and experience in the classroom. In making major changes to every chapter, we feel that we have hit the perfect balance between fundamentals and the excitement that drives our science. As we have noted in previous editions, the present is an exciting time to work in psychological science, and we hope that our excitement is contagious to our readers and our students. We are energized and inspired by the many undergraduate and graduate students we have the pleasure to interact with each day. This book is written for them, with our respect for their intelligence and our admiration for their inquisitiveness.

Acknowledgments

We begin as always by acknowledging the unwavering support we have received from our families. Writing a textbook is a time-consuming endeavor, and our family members have been generous in allowing us the time to focus on writing. We are also extremely grateful to the many colleagues who gave us constructive feedback and advice. Some individuals deserve special recognition. First and foremost is our good friend Margaret Lynch, who read every sentence of the revised edition and made valuable comments throughout. Margaret is an amazing advocate for students and reminds us never to take them for granted or underestimate them. She has been a valuable partner throughout. Debra Mashek, recent recipient of an APA teaching award, has been an invaluable member of the team for two editions. For the third edition, Debra helped us create parts of the pedagogical system. For the fourth edition, Debra wrote the "Psychology: Knowledge You Can Use" features. Thanks in large part to Debra's engaging, insightful voice, students will love applying the findings of psychological science to their own lives. Also for the fourth edition, Sarah Grison and her talented team of psychologists—Angela Isaacs, Genevieve Hendricks, and Crystal Carlson—joined the team to guide the development of our SmartWork program. Sarah's teaching experience and her empirical research on the science of learning provide unparalleled expertise in how students best learn, and we are delighted that she has shared her expertise with us.

Sunaina Assanand graciously read each chapter, provided valuable critiques, and guided us in revising the chapter pedagogy to reflect the revision. Sunaina was especially valuable for making sure the details were accurate, and her insights often helped us frame the material to maximize student understanding. Insightful teacher/researcher Tasha R. Howe helped us revise the development chapter substantially, adding a new section on adolescence and bringing a more contemporary approach.

Throughout the planning process, we sought expert advice on many aspects of the textbook and the ancillary package. A talented group of individuals gave us tough-minded, thoughtful critiques that helped shape the ancillaries, helped launch SmartWork, and provided wisdom for the fourth edition revision. We would like to give special recognition to the following:

George Alder, *Simon Fraser University*

Sunaina Assanand, *University of British Columbia–Vancouver*

Karen Brebner, *St. Francis Xavier University*

Kathleen H. Briggs, *University of Minnesota*

Michele R. Brumley, *Idaho State University*

Patrick Carroll, *University of Texas*

Sarah P. Cerny, *Rutgers University–Newark*

Heidi L. Dempsey, *Jacksonville State University*

Renee Engeln-Maddox, *Northwestern University*

Clifford D. Evans, *Miami University of Ohio*

Kimberly Fenn, *Michigan State University*

Sarah Grison, *University of Illinois at Urbana-Champaign*

Jeffrey Henriques, *University of Wisconsin*

Tasha R. Howe, *Humboldt State University*

Howard C. Hughes, *Dartmouth College*

Sheila M. Kennison, *Oklahoma State University*

Lisa Kolbuss, *Lane Community College*

Dianne Leader, *Georgia Institute of Technology*

Jeff Love, *Pennsylvania State University*

Margaret F. Lynch, *San Francisco State University*

Corrine L. McNamara, *Kennesaw State University*

Kevin E. Moore, *DePauw University*

David Payne, *Wallace County Community College*

Steve Prentice-Dunn, *University of Alabama*

Gabriel Radvansky, *Notre Dame University*

Alan C. Roberts, *Indiana University–Bloomington*

David A. Schroeder, *University of Arkansas*

John W. Wright, *Washington State University*

Producing a textbook requires a small army of people who are crucial at each step of the way. Our ancillary team was instrumental in producing first-rate materials that will assist students and instructors in having a rich experience with the material. David Payne wrote the new Visual Summaries and authored a brand-new Study Guide with our longtime friends and colleagues from Bloomsburg University: Brett Beck, Eileen Astor-Stetson, and Jennifer Johnson. Brett, Eileen, and Jennifer also authored superb new content for the student StudySpace Web site, and Christa Padovano lent her creativity to design the Visual Summaries. Pat Carroll once again assembled wonderful video offerings that contribute so much to classroom instruction. Sue Franz wrote a spectacular Instructor's Manual, which is adapted to the new Interactive Instructor's Guide online format. For each chapter, Kimberly Fenn wrote a terrific set of class-tested "clicker questions" that will make instructors look like superstars. We are so grateful to all these individuals, who lent their talent and time to create a strong support package for the fourth edition.

We need to make special mention of the Test Bank, which, as every instructor knows, is crucial to a successful course. Inadequate test banks with uneven or ambiguous items can frustrate students and instructors alike. For the fourth edition, the Test Bank was again compiled using the science of learning approach to assessment designed by Valerie Shute and Diego Zapata-Rivera. The highly accomplished team of Nikole Diane Huffman, Matthew Isaak, Natasha Tokowicz, Todd McKerchar, and Roxana Conroy authored the new fourth edition Test Bank, aided by reviews from Joseph Etherton, Emily Stark, and Rachel Messer. We cannot express the depth of our appreciation for their efforts.

The Norton Team

In the modern publishing world, where most books are produced by large multinational corporations, W. W. Norton stands out as a beacon to academics and authors. Its employees own the company, and therefore every individual who worked on our book has a vested personal interest in its success; it shows in the great enthusiasm they bring to their work. Two individuals deserve special recognition for this new edition. Sheri Snavely took over as editor during the third edition and played a central role in shaping this new edition. Sheri is an amazingly talented and insightful editor who brought not only many years of expertise in science editing, but also a profound dedication to getting the word out on how we have revised the book and making sure the marketing message clearly articulated the strengths of our book. She has been a rock for us and has also become our good friend. There is not a better editor in psychology, and we are grateful for the attention she has given our book even as she has built one of the best overall lists in psychology today. Roby Harrington was a genius for hiring her, and we also express our gratitude to Roby for his support of the book.

There will always be a special place in our hearts for Kurt Wildermuth. In the third edition, we noted that Kurt is a wordsmith of the highest order. For the fourth edition, we capitalized on his talents by having him help us consider every single sentence in the book to make sure the writing was crisp and accessible. Kurt threw himself into this project and was crucial for every step of the revision, from overseeing the schedule to helping craft the chapter opening vignettes. Words fail to fully capture our admiration for his contributions to this revision and for his loyalty to the textbook.

Many others also provided crucial support. Mary Dudley was an extraordinary editorial assistant until she was promoted to traveler, where she will use her talents to help market the book in her new Texas territory. Catherine Rice has stepped into the editorial assistant role and helped us keep organized as all the final details came together. Our associate editor, Callinda Taylor, efficiently and creatively brought the best authors to our ancillaries program. Patrick Shriner, our media editor and a veteran when it comes to science media, has worked tirelessly to pull together our groundbreaking media program for the new edition and the Smart-Work online homework system for psychology. Photo editors Stephanie Romeo and Michael Fodera did a wonderful job of researching and editing all the photos in our book and finding the captivating faces that begin each chapter.

We are grateful for our marketing manager, Andrea Matter, who has created a cutting-edge and informative marketing campaign. She truly understands "better learning through science" and is doing a marvelous job of making sure our message reaches travelers and professors. A big thank you to the psychological science specialists Peter Ruscitti and Heidi Shadix, who travel across North America and have probably racked up enough frequent flier points traveling for our book that they could fly to the moon and back. Indeed, the entire sales force at W. W. Norton, led by Michael Wright and his legendary team of managers, has supported our book, and they continue to get the word out and develop key relationships in psychology departments. The Norton travelers are distinguished by the time they take to learn about the psychology in our book so that they can present it in the best way to professors. A special thank you to the senior travelers who have represented several editions of the book and know it almost as well as we do. They are Scott Cook, John Darger, John Kelly, Doris Oliver, Yovanny Pulcini, and Mary Helen Willett.

Finally, we acknowledge the president of Norton, Drake McFeely, for inspiring a workforce that cares so deeply about publishing and for having continuing faith in us.

Psychological Science Reviewers and Consultants

George Alder, *Simon Fraser University*

Rahan Ali, *Pennsylvania State University*

Gordon A. Allen, *Miami University of Ohio*

Mary J. Allen, *California State University, Bakersfield*

Ron Apland, *Malaspina College*

Christopher T. Arra, *Northern Virginia Community College*

Sunaina Assanand, *University of British Columbia, Vancouver*

Alan Baddelay, *Bristol University*

Lori Badura, *State University of New York, Buffalo*

Mahzarin Banaji, *Harvard University*

David H. Barlow, *Boston University*

Carolyn Barry, *Loyola College*

Scott Bates, *Utah State University*

Holly Beard, *Midlands Technical College*

Bernard C. Beins, *Ithaca College*

Lisa Best, *University of New Brunswick*

Joan Bihm, *University of Colorado Denver*

Joe Bilotta, *Western Kentucky University*

Colin Blakemore, *Oxford University*

Karen Brebner, *St. Francis Xavier University*

Kathleen H. Briggs, *University of Minnesota*

John P. Broida, *University of Southern Maine*

Michele R. Brumley, *Idaho State University*

Randy Buckner, *Washington University*

William Buskist, *Auburn University*

Tara Callaghan, *St. Francis Xavier University*

Elisabeth Leslie Cameron, *Carthage College*

Katherine Cameron, *Washington College*

Jennifer Campbell, *University of British Columbia*

Timothy Cannon, *University of Scranton*

Tom Capo, *University of Maryland*

Charles Carver, *University of Miami*

Michelle L. Caya, *Trident Technical College*

Sarah P. Cerny, *Rutgers University, Newark*

Jonathan Cheek, *Wellesley College*

Stephen Clark, *Keene State College*

Dennis Cogan, *Texas Tech University*

Martin Conway, *Bristol University*

Michael Corballis, *University of Auckland*

Brent Foster Costleigh, *Brookdale Community College*

Graham Cousens, *Macalester College*

Dale Dagenbach, *Wake Forest University*

Haydn Davis, *Palomar College*

Suzanne Delaney, *University of Arizona*

Heidi L. Dempsey, *Jacksonville State University*

Joseph Dien, *Tulane University*

Michael Domjan, *University of Texas at Austin*

Wendy Domjan, *University of Texas at Austin*

Jack Dovidio, *Colgate University*

Dana S. Dunn, *Moravian College*

Howard Eichenbaum, *Boston University*

Naomi Eisenberger, *University of California, Los Angeles*

Renee Engeln-Maddox, *Northwestern University*

James Enns, *University of British Columbia*

Clifford D. Evans, *Miami University of Ohio*

Raymond Fancher, *York University*

Valerie Farmer-Dougan, *Illinois State University*

Greg Feist, *University of California, Davis*

Kimberly M. Fenn, *Michigan State University*

Fernanda Ferreira, *University of South Carolina*

Vic Ferreira, *University of California, San Diego*

Holly Filcheck, *Louisiana State University*

Joseph Fitzgerald, *Wayne State University*

Trisha Folds-Bennett, *College of Charleston*

Margaret Forgie, *University of Lethbridge*

Howard Friedman, *University of California, Riverside*

David C. Funder, *University of California, Riverside*

Christopher Gade, *University of California, Berkeley*

Christine Gancarz, *Southern Methodist University*

Wendi Gardner, *Northwestern University*

Preston E. Garraghty, *Indiana University*

Margaret Gatz, *University of Southern California*

Caroline Gee, *Saddleback College*

Peter Gerhardstein, *Binghamton University*

Katherine Gibbs, *University of California, Davis*

Bryan Gibson, *Central Michigan University*

Rick O. Gilmore, *Pennsylvania State University*

Jamie Goldenberg, *University of South Florida*

Laura Gonnerman, *Lehigh University*

Peter Graf, *University of British Columbia*

Leonard Green, *Washington University*

Raymond Green, *Texas A&M–Commerce*

Sarah Grison, *University of Illinois at Urbana-Champaign*

James Gross, *Stanford University*

Tom Guilmette, *Providence College*

John Hallonquist, *University of the Caribou*

Thomas W. Hancock, *University of Central Oklahoma*

Erin E. Hardin, *Texas Tech University*

Brad Hastings, *Mount Aloysius College*

Linda Hatt, *University of British Columbia Okanagan*

Mikki Hebl, *Rice University*

Steven Heine, *University of British Columbia*

John Henderson, *Michigan State University*

Norman Henderson, *Oberlin College*

Mark Henn, *University of New Hampshire*

Terence Hines, *Pace University*

Sarah Hodges, *University of Oregon*

Cynthia Hoffman, *Indiana University*

Don Hoffman, *University of California, Irvine*

James Hoffman, *University of Delaware*

Mark Holder, *University of British Columbia Okanagan*

Tasha R. Howe, *Humboldt State University*

Howard C. Hughes, *Dartmouth College*

Jay Hull, *Dartmouth College*

Jake Jacobs, *University of Arizona*

Thomas Joiner, *Florida State University*

Steve Joordens, *University of Toronto–Scarborough*

William Kelley, *Dartmouth College*

Dacher Keltner, *University of California, Berkeley*

Lindsay A. Kennedy, *University of North Carolina–Chapel Hill*

Sheila M. Kennison, *Oklahoma State University–Stillwater*

Mike Kerchner, *Washington College*

Rondall Khoo, *Western Connecticut State University*

Lisa Kolbuss, *Lane Community College*

Gabriel Kreiman, *Harvard University*

Gert Kruger, *University of Johannesburg*

Gerard La Morte, *Rutgers University, Newark*

Lori Lange, *University of North Florida*

Mark Laumakis, *San Diego State University*

Natalie Kerr Lawrence, *James Madison University*

Steven R. Lawyer, *Idaho State University*

Benjamin Le, *Haverford College*

Dianne Leader, *Georgia Institute of Technology*

Mark Leary, *Wake Forest University*

Ting Lei, *Borough of Manhattan Community College*

Charles Leith, *Northern Michigan University*

Carol Lemley, *Elizabethtown College*

Gary W. Lewandowski Jr., *Monmouth University*

Christine Lofgren, *University of California, Irvine*

Liang Lou, *Grand Valley State University*

Jeff Love, *Pennsylvania State University*

Monica Luciana, *University of Minnesota*

Margaret F. Lynch, *San Francisco State University*

Neil Macrae, *University of Aberdeen*

Karl Maier, *Salisbury University*

Mike Mangan, *University of New Hampshire*

Gary Marcus, *New York University*

Leonard Mark, *Miami University (Ohio)*

Debra Mashek, *Harvey Mudd College*

Tim Maxwell, *Hendrix College*

Ashley E. Maynard, *University of Hawaii*

Dan McAdams, *Northwestern University*

Doug McCann, *York University*

Paul McCormack, *St. Francis Xavier University*

David McDonald, *University of Missouri–Columbia*

Bill McKeachie, *University of Michigan*

Patricia McMullen, *Dalhousie University*

Corrine L. McNamara, *Kennesaw State University*

Paul Merritt, *George Washington University*

Peter Metzner, *Vance Granville Community College*

Dennis K. Miller, *University of Missouri*

Hal Miller, *Brigham Young University*

Judy Miller, *Oberlin College*

Douglas G. Mook, *University of Virginia, Emeritus*

Kevin E. Moore, *DePauw University*

Joe Morrisey, *State University of New York, Binghamton*

Todd Nelson, *California State University–Stanislaus*

Julie Norem, *Wellesley College*

Maria Minda Oriña, *University of Minnesota–Twin Cities*

Dominic J. Parrott, *Georgia State University*

Lois Pasapane, *Palm Beach State College*

David Payne, *Wallace Community College*

James Pennebaker, *University of Texas at Austin*

Zehra Peynircioglu, *American University*

Brady Phelps, *South Dakota State University*

Elizabeth Phelps, *New York University*

Jackie Pope-Tarrance, *Western Kentucky University*

Steve Prentice-Dunn, *University of Alabama*

Gabriel Radvansky, *Notre Dame University*

Patty Randolph, *Western Kentucky University*

Catherine Reed, *Claremont McKenna College*

Lauretta Reeves, *University of Texas at Austin*

Jennifer Richeson, *Northwestern University*

Alan C. Roberts, *Indiana University–Bloomington*

Caton Roberts, *University of Wisconsin–Madison*

William Rogers, *Grand Valley State University*

Alex Rothman, *University of Minnesota*

Paul Rozin, *University of Pennsylvania*

Sharleen Sakai, *Michigan State University*

Juan Salinas, *University of Texas at Austin*

Laura Saslow, *University of California, Berkeley*

Heather Schellink, *Dalhousie University*

Richard Schiffman, *Rutgers University*

Lynne Schmetter-Davis, *Brookdale Community College*

David A. Schroeder, *University of Arkansas*

Constantine Sedikedes, *University of Southampton*

Ines Segert, *University of Missouri*

Allison Sekuler, *McMaster University*

Margaret Sereno, *University of Oregon*

Andrew Shatte, *University of Pennsylvania*

J. Nicole Shelton, *Princeton University*

Arthur Shimamura, *University of California, Berkeley*

Rebecca Shiner, *Colgate University*

Jennifer Siciliani-Pride, *University of Missouri–St. Louis*

Scott Sinnett, *University of Hawaii at Manoa*

Reid Skeel, *Central Michigan University*

John J. Skowronski, *Northern Illinois University*

Andra Smith, *University of Ottawa*

Dennison Smith, *Oberlin College*

Ashley Smyth, *South Africa College of Applied Psychology*

Mark Snyder, *University of Minnesota*

Sheldon Solomon, *Skidmore College*

Sue Spaulding, *University of North Carolina, Charlotte*

Faye Steur, *College of Charleston*

Dawn L. Strongin, *California State University–Stanislaus*

James Sullivan, *Florida State University*

Lorey K. Takahashi, *University of Hawaii at Manoa*

George Taylor, *University of Missouri–St. Louis*

Lee Thompson, *Case Western Reserve University*

Diane Tice, *Case Western Reserve University*

Rob Tigner, *Truman State College*

Peter Tse, *Dartmouth College*

David Uttal, *Northwestern University*

Robin R. Vallacher, *Florida Atlantic University*

Kristy L. vanMarle, *University of Missouri–Columbia*

Simine Vazire, *Washington University*

Shaun Vecera, *University of Iowa*

Athena Vouloumanos, *New York University*

Benjamin Walker, *Georgetown University*

Elaine Walker, *Emory University*

Brian Wandell, *Stanford University*

Kenneth A. Weaver, *Emporia State University*

Kevin Weinfurt, *Duke University*

Rajkumari Wesley, *Brookdale Community College*

Doug Whitman, *Wayne State University*

Gordon Whitman, *Tidewater Community College*

Nicole L. Wilson, *University of California, Santa Cruz*

Maxine Gallander Wintre, *York University*

Clare Wiseman, *Trinity College*

Al Witkofsky, *Salisbury University*

Vanessa Woods, *Santa Barbara City College*

John W. Wright, *Washington State University*

Jill A. Yamashita, *Saint Xavier University*

Dahlia Zaidel, *University of California, Los Angeles*

Media & Print Resources for Instructors and Students

Instructor Resources

Lecture Presentation Resources

Presentation Resources come in four varieties designed to help you build your lecture in the way that best suits your course needs:

- **Art:** Every figure, photo, and table from the textbook in JPEG and PowerPoint files enhanced for optimal viewing when projected.

- **Lecture Slides:** PowerPoint slides for each chapter with lecture outlines, key figures, and ideas and teaching suggestions in the notes field.

- **Beyond the Textbook Material:** PowerPoint slides that present research studies and applications for each chapter that are not included in the textbook.

- **Clicker Questions:** Authored by Kimberly Fenn, Michigan State University. Each chapter offers at least ten questions in PowerPoint that will engage your students by actively involving them in your lectures.

Lecture Presentation Resources are available on the Instructor's Resource Disc and downloadable on the Interactive Instructor's Guide.

Norton Psychology Video Resources

Patrick Carroll, *University of Texas, Austin*

Norton's popular video clips series has been updated and revitalized both with additional clips and by a new system of streaming video delivery.

The *Norton Psychology in the News DVD* features nearly 200 clips profiling recent psychological research.

Norton now offers instructors streaming video through its new **Interactive Instructor's Manual.** Patrick Carroll has selected a mix of classical and contemporary research studies, as well as videos that show applications of psychological concepts in the real world. New clips will be added through the academic year.

Test Bank

Nikole Diane Huffman, *Ohio State University*
Matthew Isaak, *University of Louisiana at Lafayette*
Natasha Tokowicz, *University of Pittsburgh*
Todd McKerchar, *Jacksonville State University*
Roxana Conroy, *Jacksonville State University*

With the goals of promoting a higher level of understanding for the student and a more targeted system of assessment for the professor, the *Psychological Science* test questions have been completely revised using an evidence-centered approach designed by Valerie Shute of Florida State University and Diego Zapata-Rivera from the Educational Testing Service. Using the chapter Learning Objectives and Bloom's taxonomy of cognitive skills, question creation has been fully integrated with the elements of the student study package, including SmartWork and the Study Guide.

The Test Bank is available in print, on disc in the ExamView Assessment Suite, and downloadable on the Interactive Instructor's Guide.

Instructor's Resource Manual

Sue Frantz, *Highline Community College*

The IRM is a rich resource for enhancing lectures and adapting *Psychological Science* for your course. It includes sample lectures, discussion questions, demonstrations, handouts, and suggested film/video, printed, and Web resources—all designed to make lectures more active, engaging, and informative.

Coursepacks

Available at no cost to professors or students, Norton coursepacks for online or hybrid courses are available in a variety of formats, including all versions of Blackboard and WebCT. With just a simple download from our instructor's Web site, an adopter can bring high-quality Norton digital media into a new or existing online course (no extra student passwords required), and it's theirs to keep forever. Coursepacks for *Psychological Science* draw on content from StudySpace, but go beyond it. Features include test bank, StudySpace quizzes, animations, Critical Thinking exercises, Studying the Mind videos, discussion questions, Learning Objectives exercises, and video exercises. Available in Blackboard, WebCT, ANGEL, Desire2Learn, and Moodle.

NEW—Interactive Instructor's Guide ties it all together online

The new IIG Web site makes it easy for instructors to integrate all the resources from the IRM, PowerPoint files, and video clips into their courses. Flexible searching and browsing tools help instructors find just the right resources to enhance their lectures and serve as a central hub for finding introductory psychology materials.

Integrated Study Package Helps Students Focus

The integration of the *Psychological Science* study package means that students will hear a single voice regardless of where they go to study—in the book, online, or beyond.

Study support starts in the textbook:

> Like the Summing Up/Measuring Up boxes for chapter sections, the **Summary** and **Practice Test** features at the end of each chapter boil down the key ideas and then test student comprehension of them.

Student review continues online with our free (no password or registration code) StudySpace Web site.

> Our new **Visual Summaries** tie it all together and expand students' understanding of concepts by helping them see how core ideas relate to one another.

Other **StudySpace** features include chapter **Study Plans** to help students get organized, **Flashcards** to aid in their mastery of key terms, and **Quiz+** chapter review quizzes that guide student learning. **Video Exercises** help students connect concepts to the world beyond the classroom.

Study Guide

David Payne, *Wallace Community College*
with Brett Beck, Eileen Astor Stetson, and Jennifer Johnson, *Bloomsburg University*

Our print Study Guide offers students a "guided approach" through the chapter content. Each section presents a reading schedule, priming questions, sets of quiz questions with hints and suggestions of where in the textbook to learn about particular concepts, and study-skills "best practices."

How Can Psychology Help You Learn?

In this increasingly fast-paced world, we are constantly bombarded with information: News stories reach us in minutes from around the globe, new technologies replace old ones, and groundbreaking scientific studies alter long-held beliefs about the physical world. To succeed in college and in your career, you will need to develop powerful learning strategies that produce durable and flexible learning—learning that lasts well into the future and that you can transfer to new situations. The following study skills, based on psychological research, will help you work more productively, learn more efficiently, and apply in a variety of settings what you have learned. (You will find more about learning in several chapters in this book, especially in Chapter 7, "Attention and Memory," and Chapter 8, "Thinking and Intelligence.")

1. The Right Goals Lead to Success

Throughout your life, you will set countless short-term and long-term goals for yourself: to get that enormous pile of laundry done, to run an eight-minute mile, to have a family, to succeed in your career. It is important to choose goals that are challenging yet attainable. If your goals are unrealistically high, you set yourself up for failure and discouragement, but if they are too low, you will not achieve your greatest potential. Divide each goal into specific, achievable steps, or sub-goals, and reward yourself when you reach a milestone. Even a small achievement is worth celebrating!

2. A Little Stress Management Goes a Long Way

Stress is a fact of life. A moderate amount of stress can improve your performance by keeping you alert, challenged, and focused. However, too much stress has the opposite effect and can diminish your productivity, interfere with your sleep, and even take a toll on your health. When the pressure is on, seek healthy ways to manage your stress, such as exercising, writing in a journal, spending time with friends, practicing yoga, or meditating.

3. Cramming Is a Crummy Way to Learn

You have a busy life, and it is always tempting to postpone studying until the night or two before an exam. But in all of your classes, there is too much to learn to cram your learning into a few days or late nights. You might be able to remember enough information to get a passing grade on an exam the following day, but plenty of research has shown that cramming does not produce learning that lasts. To make learning stick, you need to space out your study sessions over the semester and build in plenty of time for active reviews.

4. Learning Is Not a Spectator Sport

The more effort you put into your studying, the more benefit you will receive. Merely rereading a chapter or your class notes is not as effective as actively trying to remember what you have learned. Every time you learn something, you create "memory traces" in your brain. By retrieving the information that was learned, you strengthen the memory traces so that you will be more likely to recall the memory in the future. In this book, to encourage active studying, every major section heading is in the form of a question. When you go back to study each section, begin by writing out an answer to the question in the heading without looking at the book. Then check the accuracy and completeness of what you wrote.

5. Explaining Enhances Understanding and Memory

As you learn, focus on trying to explain and describe complicated topics in your own words, as opposed to just memorizing terms and definitions. For example, simply using flashcards to learn about visual perception may help you memorize individual parts of the eye and their functions, but doing so will not help you put the pieces together to understand the incredible process of how we see and recognize objects in the world. Memorizing isolated bits of information is also likely to result in shallow learning that is easily forgotten. A deeper level of learning based on explanation and description would give you a more holistic understanding and a greater ability to generalize the information.

6. There Is More Than One Way to Learn

As you will read in Chapter 7, people process information in two channels—visual and verbal. Another strategy for creating durable learning is to use both of these information formats. Try to supplement the notes you take with visual and spatial displays such as concept maps, graphs, flowcharts, and other types of diagrams. Doing so not only makes you more likely to remember the information but also helps you gain a better understanding of the big picture by emphasizing the connections among important ideas.

A knowledge of psychology can be useful to you in many ways, even if you do not pursue a career in the field. For this reason, we have tried to make all the material in *Psychological Science* accessible and interesting for you as well as directly applicable to your life. As you gain an integrated grounding in traditional and new approaches within psychological science, we hope that this book spurs your curiosity about psychological phenomena. We hope that, by thinking critically about issues and themes in psychological science and in aspects of your life, you will develop a greater understanding of yourself and others.

Mike, Todd, and Diane

Contents

Chapter 1 The Science of Psychology 1

This chapter provides a broad introduction to psychology. The authors review the primary schools of thought and latest developments in psychology. They attempt to make the content personally relevant to the reader.

Chapter 2   Research Methodology................29

This chapter reviews research methods in psychology. The authors discuss descriptive, correlational, and experimental studies; describe methods of data collection; and introduce the reader to basic statistical concepts.

Chapter 3 Biology and Behavior...........................73

This chapter reviews contemporary theory and research related to the brain and behavior. The authors discuss neurophysiology, neurotransmitters, neuroanatomy, the endocrine system, and neurodevelopment.

Chapter 4 Sensation and Perception...............131

This chapter discusses taste, smell, touch, hearing, and vision. For each of these phenomena, the authors review the processes associated with sensation and perception. At the end of the chapter, a section on visual perception illustrates the complexity of human perceptual processes.

Chapter 5 Consciousness..181

This chapter reviews theory and research related to consciousness. The authors discuss our contemporary understanding of consciousness and variations in consciousness, sleep, methods of altering consciousness, and drugs that influence consciousness.

Chapter 8 Thinking and Intelligence 317

This chapter reviews theory and research on thinking and intelligence. The authors discuss mental representations, reasoning, decision making, problem solving, and aspects of intelligence such as assessment and group differences.

Chapter 9 Human Development 365

This chapter presents the major stages and series of changes that constitute the human life span, from conception through childhood and adolescence to adulthood and old age. The authors discuss topics such as attachment, language acquisition, the sense of self, and the need to belong.

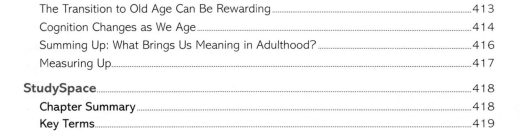

Chapter 10 Emotion and Motivation 421

This chapter presents classic theories of emotion, together with contemporary work on the neurological basis of emotional experience, emotional expression, and the functions of emotion. It then presents classic research on motivation, eating, and sexual behavior, together with contemporary work on each of these topics.

Chapter 11 Health and Well-Being....................469

This chapter reviews a substantial body of work related to health and well-being. The authors begin by discussing classic work on stress and coping, then progress to contemporary ideas from positive psychology.

Chapter 12 Social Psychology 513

This chapter reviews research related to social psychology. The authors consider topics such as conformity, compliance, obedience, aggression, and love.

Chapter 13 Personality...567

This chapter presents theory and research in personality psychology. The authors discuss psychological perspectives on personality, the assessment and significance of personality, biological bases of personality, and personality in relation to the sense of self.

Chapter 14   Psychological Disorders...................617

This chapter reviews psychological disorders identified by the DSM–IV–TR. The authors also present contemporary research and controversies associated with a number of these disorders.

Chapter 15 Treatment of Psychological Disorders....673

This chapter reviews contemporary treatments for a wide array of psychological disorders. The authors discuss the comparative effectiveness of treatments.

Psychological Science

FOURTH EDITION

The Science of Psychology

1.1 Why Study Psychology?

Psychology Is about *You* and about *Us*

Why is psychology one of the most popular majors at many colleges and universities? One reason is people's fascination with their own mental activity. After all, this field can help you understand your personality, your motives, and even why you remember some things and forget others. Yes, reader, this means *you*. Because most psychological research occurs at colleges and universities in North America and Europe, many of the participants in psychological studies and experiments have been college and university students (Henrich, Heine, & Norenzayan, 2010).

Yet psychology is more than personally relevant. In helping us understand our thoughts, feelings, and actions, psychology offers many insights that can be

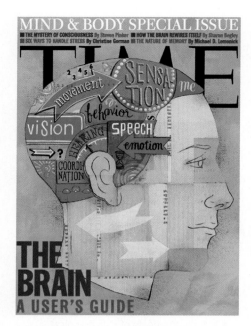

FIGURE 1.1 Psychology in the News Most people consume scientific research without even being aware of it. For example, research might be a major part of an intriguing news story. People will tend to focus on the story, however, not on the research.

generalized across societies and even cultures. It can help us be better parents, help us work more effectively in groups, and help us relieve chronic pain, to name just a few examples. Around the world, the popular press covers the topics you will learn about in this book: the brain, genetics, the senses, memory, sexuality, aging, psychological disorders, and much more (**Figure 1.1**). The information you will take away from the study of psychology is vital for helping people lead happier and healthier lives by understanding themselves and others.

Psychologists Explain Human Behaviors in Real-Life Contexts

Most of us have a strong desire to figure out other people. We want to understand their motives, thoughts, desires, intentions, moods, actions, and so on. We want to know whether they are friends or foes, leaders or followers, likely to reject us or fall in love with us. Through our social interactions, we form impressions of others. We use those impressions to categorize others and to make predictions about their intentions and actions. We want to know why they remember some details and conveniently forget others or why they engage in self-destructive behaviors. Essentially, we try to figure out what makes other people tick. People who do this for a living are *psychologists*.

Psychological science is the study of mind, brain, and behavior. But what exactly does each of these terms mean? *Mind* refers to mental activity. The perceptual experiences we have while interacting with the world (sight, smell, taste, hearing, and touch) are examples of the mind in action. The mind is also responsible for our memories, thoughts, and feelings. Mental activity results from biological processes within the brain. In other words, the physical brain enables the mind: The "mind is what the brain does" (Kosslyn & Koenig, 1995, p. 4).

The term *behavior* describes a wide variety of observable actions. These actions range from the subtle to the complex. Some of them occur exclusively in humans; others occur in all organisms. For many years, psychologists focused on behavior rather than on mental states. They did so largely because they had few objective techniques for assessing the mind. The advent of technology to observe the working brain in action has allowed psychologists to study mental states and has led to a fuller understanding of human behavior. Although psychologists make important contributions to understanding and treating mental illness, most psychological science has little to do with therapeutic clichés such as couches and dreams. Instead, the goals of psychology are to understand mental activity, social interactions, and how people acquire behaviors.

SURPRISING RESULTS This material is just common sense, right? The answer is no. The results of psychological research are often surprising and often run counter to common beliefs. For example, many people at least initially reject the idea that some of their thoughts, feelings, and actions may be determined by unconscious influences. However, hundreds of studies show that such influences happen. John Bargh and colleagues (Bargh, 2006; Bargh & Chartrand, 1999) have referred to these unconscious influences as the "automaticity of everyday life" because they occur automatically—without our effort or intent.

In a pair of studies (Dijksterhuis & van Knippenberg, 1998), Dutch participants were divided into three groups. Each group was asked to consider a stereotype: One group thought about professors (usually seen by most people as high in intelligence), a second group thought about secretaries (usually seen

psychological science The study of mind, brain, and behavior.

as neutral in intelligence), and a third group thought about soccer hooligans (usually seen as low in intelligence). After this exercise, all three groups were asked to play a modified game of Trivial Pursuit. Quite remarkably, those participants who thought about professors got more of the trivia answers correct than did those who thought about secretaries. The latter, in turn, performed better than those who thought about soccer hooligans. Once ideas regarding intelligence were *primed,* or activated, people seemed to have different levels of confidence in their own knowledge. These levels affected the ways they remembered. In a later study (Williams & Bargh, 2008), research participants held a cup of coffee for the researcher while he juggled an armful of textbooks, clipboards, and so on. Half the participants held a cup of hot coffee, and half held a cup of iced coffee. None of the participants believed that just holding the cup would affect their thoughts, feelings, or actions, but it did: The participants who held the hot coffee rated a third person as "warmer" and less selfish than did those who held the iced coffee. Throughout this book, you will read many such examples of the surprising nature of our psychological processes.

Psychological Knowledge Is Used in Many Professions

Some students become so fascinated by psychological science that they devote their lives to studying mind, brain, and behavior (**Figure 1.2**). As they discover, psychological science is an exciting field. Researchers around the globe are providing new insights into issues that great scholars of the past sought to understand. In fact, they are helping explain the very nature of what it means to be human.

If you are thinking about a career in psychology or a related field, there is good news. According to the U.S. Department of Labor (U.S. Bureau of Labor Statistics, 2009), opportunities for people with graduate degrees in psychology are expected to grow approximately 12 percent between now and 2018. The outlook is equally positive in many countries around the world. Developing countries, for example, are increasingly addressing the psychological well-being of their citizens. These efforts are providing hands-on opportunities for people trained in psychology to use their knowledge and skills.

If you are wondering what you can do with an undergraduate degree in psychology, the answer is "almost everything." Prospective employers want their employees to have data analysis skills, communication skills, critical thinking skills, and the abilities to learn and to get along with others. These skills are all developed in psychology curricula. One survey of college graduates with bachelor's degrees in psychology found that they held a wide range of positions. Jobs that require psychological knowledge include research assistant, attorney's assistant, police officer, social worker, personnel director, hospital counselor, and store manager (Morgan, n.d.).

Psychological science is equally useful for anyone whose career involves understanding people. To persuade jurors, lawyers need to know how groups make decisions. Advertisers need to know how attitudes are formed or changed and to what extent people's attitudes predict their behavior. Politicians use psychological techniques of impression

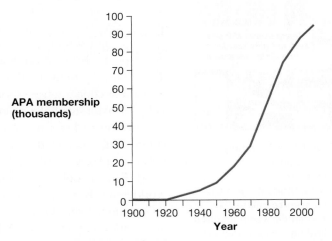

FIGURE 1.2 Growth of the Field This graph, adapted from data published by the American Psychological Association (APA), shows the great increase in this professional organization's membership from 1900 to 2010.

critical thinking Systematically evaluating information to reach reasonable conclusions.

management to make themselves attractive to voters. Physicians need to know how to relate to their patients, how patients' behaviors are linked to health, and what motivates or discourages patients from seeking medical care or following treatment protocols. Understanding the aging brain and how it affects visual perception, memory, and motor movement is vital for those who treat elderly patients. Basically, as humans dealing with other humans, we need knowledge of psychology.

Psychological Science Teaches Critical Thinking

Humans are intuitive psychologists. That is, they try to understand and predict others' behavior. For example, people choose marriage partners they expect will best meet their emotional, sexual, and support needs. Defensive drivers rely on their intuitive sense of when other drivers are likely to make mistakes. People try to predict whether others are kind, are trustworthy, will make good caretakers, will make good teachers, and so on. But people cannot intuitively know if many of the claims related to psychology are fact or fiction. For example, will taking certain herbs increase memory? Will playing music to newborns make them more intelligent? Does mental illness result from too much or too little of a certain brain chemical?

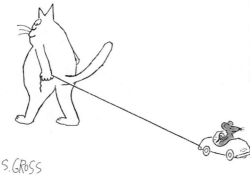

S. GROSS

"For God's sake, think! Why is he being so nice to you?"

One of this textbook's most important goals is to provide a basic, state-of-the-art education about the methods of psychological science. Even if your only exposure to psychology is through the introductory course for which *Psychological Science* is the textbook, you will become psychologically literate. With a good understanding of the field's major issues, theories, and controversies, you will also avoid common misunderstandings about psychology. You will learn how to separate the believable from the incredible. You will learn to spot badly designed experiments, and you will develop the skills necessary to critically evaluate claims made in the popular media. The media love a good story, and findings from psychological research are often provocative. Unfortunately, media reports can be distorted or even flat-out wrong. Throughout your life, as a consumer of psychological science, you will need to be skeptical of overblown media reports of "brand-new" findings obtained by "groundbreaking" research (**Figure 1.3**).

One of the hallmarks of a good scientist—or a savvy consumer of scientific research—is *amiable skepticism*. This trait combines openness and wariness. An amiable skeptic remains open to new ideas, but is wary of new scientific findings when good evidence and sound reasoning do not seem to support them. An amiable skeptic develops the habit of carefully weighing the facts when deciding what to believe. The ability to think in this way—systematically evaluating information to reach reasonable conclusions—is often called **critical thinking.** Being a critical thinker involves looking for holes in evidence, using logic and reasoning to see whether the information makes sense, and considering alternative explanations. It also involves considering whether the information might be biased, such as by personal or political agendas. Critical thinking involves healthy questioning and keeping an open mind. Most people are quick to question information that does not fit with their worldviews. But as an educated person, you also need to think critically about all information. Even when you "know" something, you need to keep refreshing that information in your mind. Ask yourself: Is that fact still true? What led me to believe it? What other facts support it? This exercise is important because you may be least motivated to think critically about information that verifies your preconceptions.

FIGURE 1.3 "Brand-New" Findings
Media reports seek to grab attention. Their claims can be based on science, but they can also be hype. **What methods do you use to figure out when science-related announcements in the media seem justified by the research findings, when they are overblown or misleading, and when they are outlandish?**

HOW CRITICAL THINKING WORKS Does eating too much sugar cause children to become hyperactive? Many people believe this connection has been established scientifically, but in fact a review of the scientific literature reveals that the relationship between sugar consumption and hyper-activity is essentially zero (Wolraich, Wilson, & White, 1995). Many people will argue that they have seen with their own eyes what happens when children eat large amounts of sweets. But consider the contexts of such firsthand observations. Might the children have eaten lots of sweets when they were at parties with many other children? Might the gatherings, rather than the sweets, have caused the children to be very excited and active? People often let their beliefs and their biases determine how they label observations. The highly active children's behavior, viewed in connection with the eating of sweets,

FIGURE 1.4 The Mozart Effect? Many products play on the assumption that babies benefit from hearing music. This Baby Einstein rocking chair, manufactured by Disney, can connect to CD players or iPods, enabling parents to develop music programs for their children. In 2009, following the publication of research revealing that Baby Einstein products do not foster intellectual development, Disney agreed to refund the purchase price of some of these products. **What other products promise to enhance their user's intelligence? What evidence supports their effectiveness?**

becomes an example of sugar-induced hyperactivity. A critical thinker would consider alternative explanations for such behavior and seek quality research that takes such possibilities into account.

Consider the validity of the "Mozart effect." In 1993, a research team found that playing Mozart to research participants led the participants to score higher on a test related to intelligence. The media jumped onto the so-called Mozart effect with abandon. Web sites made bold claims about the power of Mozart, including wild assertions that listening to Mozart could cure neurological illness and other maladies. As a result, many parents played Mozart to young infants and even to fetuses (**Figure 1.4**). Two U.S. states provided free Mozart CDs to every newborn. What is the true power of Mozart for the developing mind? To see the claims more clearly, we need to step back and critically evaluate the research underlying the Mozart effect.

The psychologists Frances H. Rauscher, Gordon L. Shaw, and Katherine N. Ky played the first 10 minutes of the Mozart Sonata for Two Pianos in D Major (K. 448) to a group of college students. Compared with students who listened to relaxation instructions or who sat in silence, those who heard Mozart performed slightly better on a task that involved folding and cutting paper. This task was part of a larger overall measure of intelligence. The modest increase lasted for about 10 to 15 minutes (Rauscher, Shaw, & Ky, 1993). However, subsequent research largely failed to get the same results, even when it used a similar research design. Having carefully reviewed the studies testing the Mozart effect, the psychologist Christopher Chabris (1999) concluded that listening to Mozart is unlikely to increase intelligence among listeners. According to Chabris, listening to Mozart appears to enhance only certain types of motor skills, not measures more commonly associated with intelligence.

Another important question from a critical thinking perspective is whether it was the music or some other aspect of the situation that led to better performance on the folding and cutting task. A team of researchers has shown that the effect may occur simply because listening to music is more uplifting than sitting in silence or relaxing; that is, the increase in positive mood may be largely responsible for better performance (Thompson, Schellenberg, & Husain, 2001).

Also note that all the studies to date have been conducted with college students as participants. Do you see the problem? All the publicity focused on whether listening to Mozart increases *infants'* intelligence! Of course, experiences during early life are important to later development. However, most of the claims about music go way beyond the data.

Before they have taken a psychology course, many students have false beliefs, or misconceptions, about psychological phenomena. In an exemplary study, the psychologists Patricia Kowalski and Annette Kujawski Taylor (2004) found that students who employ critical thinking skills will complete an introductory course with a more accurate understanding of psychology than that of students who complete the same course but do not employ critical thinking skills. As you read this book, you will benefit from paying close attention to the critical thinking skills. You can apply these skills in your other classes, your workplace, and your everyday life.

Summing Up

Why Study Psychology?

The findings of psychological science are relevant to every person's life, and they are of value to many professions. Perhaps for these reasons, psychology is one of the most popular majors at many colleges. While most of us function as intuitive psychologists, many of our intuitions and beliefs are wrong. To improve the accuracy of our own ideas, we need to think critically about them. We also need to think critically about research findings, and doing so means understanding the research methods that psychologists use.

Measuring Up

1. Psychology is relevant _____.
   a. in those parts of the world where it is a well-developed science
   b. in all aspects of life
   c. for people who are naturally inquisitive
   d. for the mentally ill but not for people who are mentally healthy

2. Critical thinking is _____.
   a. criticizing the way other people think
   b. systematically assessing information to reach reasonable conclusions
   c. questioning everything you read or hear and refusing to believe anything you have not seen for yourself
   d. becoming an authority on everything so you never have to rely on other people's judgments

2. b. systematically assessing information to reach reasonable conclusions.

Answers: 1. b. in all aspects of life.

Learning Objectives

■ Trace the development of psychology since its formal inception in 1879.

■ Define the nature/nurture debate and the mind/body problem.

■ Identify the major schools of thought that have characterized the history of experimental psychology.

1.2 What Are the Scientific Foundations of Psychology?

Psychology originated in philosophy. For example, the ancient Chinese philosopher Confucius emphasized human development, education, and interpersonal relations, all of which remain contemporary topics in psychology around the world (Higgins & Zheng, 2002; **Figure 1.5**). Some scholars claim that Western notions of psychology can be found in the works of early Muslim philosophers and scientists (Haque, 2004), such as the first-century writings by Al-Kindi about sorrow, grief, and depression.

In nineteenth-century Europe, psychology developed into a discipline. As that discipline spread throughout the world and developed into a vital field of science and a vibrant profession, different ways of thinking about the content of psychology emerged. These ways of thinking are called *schools of thought*. As is true in every science, one school of thought would dominate the field for a while. There would be a backlash. Then a new school of thought would take over the field. The following sections consider the major themes and schools of thought in the history of psychology.

The Nature/Nurture Debate Has a Long History

Since at least the times of ancient Greece, people have wondered why humans think and act in certain ways. Greek philosophers such as Aristotle and Plato debated whether the individual's psychology is attributable more to *nature* or to *nurture*. That is, are psychological characteristics biologically innate? Or are they acquired through education, experience, and **culture** (the beliefs, values, rules, norms, and customs existing within a group of people who share a common language and environment)?

The **nature/nurture debate** has taken one form or another throughout psychology's history. Psychologists now widely recognize that both nature and nurture are important to humans' psychological development. Psychologists study, for example, the ways that nature and nurture influence each other in shaping mind, brain, and behavior. In examples throughout this book, nature and nurture are so enmeshed that they cannot be separated.

The Mind/Body Problem Also Has Ancient Roots

The **mind/body problem** is perhaps the quintessential psychological issue: Are the mind and body separate and distinct, or is the mind simply the physical brain's subjective experience?

Throughout history, the mind has been viewed as residing in many organs of the body, including the liver and the heart. The ancient Egyptians, for example, elaborately embalmed each dead person's heart, which was to be weighed in the afterlife to determine the person's fate. They simply threw away the brain. In the following centuries, especially among the Greeks and Romans, recognition grew that the brain was essential for normal mental functioning. Much of this change came from observing people with brain injuries. At least since the time of the Roman gladiators, it was clear that a blow to the head often produced disturbances in mental activity, such as unconsciousness or the loss of speech.

Nonetheless, scholars continued to believe that the mind is separate from and in control of the body. They held this belief partly because of the strong theological belief that a divine and immortal soul separates humans from nonhuman animals. Around 1500, the artist Leonardo da Vinci challenged this doctrine when he dissected human bodies to make his anatomical drawings more accurate. (These experiments offended the Roman Catholic Church because they violated the presumed sanctity of the human body.) Da Vinci's dissections led him to many conclusions about the brain's workings. For example, da Vinci theorized that all sensory messages (vision, touch, smell, etc.) arrived at one location in the brain.

FIGURE 1.5 Confucius Ancient philosophers such as Confucius studied topics that remain important in contemporary psychology.

culture The beliefs, values, rules, and customs that exist within a group of people who share a common language and environment and that are transmitted through learning from one generation to the next.

nature/nurture debate The arguments concerning whether psychological characteristics are biologically innate or acquired through education, experience, and culture.

mind/body problem A fundamental psychological issue: Are mind and body separate and distinct, or is the mind simply the physical brain's subjective experience?

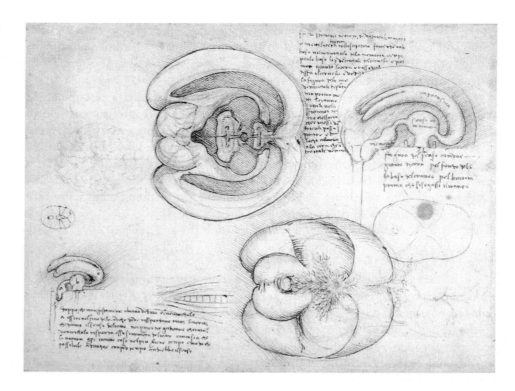

FIGURE 1.6 Da Vinci and the Brain This drawing by Leonardo da Vinci dates from around 1506. Using a wax cast to study the brain, da Vinci found that the various sensory images arrived in the middle region of the brain. He called this region the *sensus communis*.

He called that region the *sensus communis,* and he believed it to be the home of thought and judgment; its name may be the root of the modern term *common sense* (Blakemore, 1983). Da Vinci's specific conclusions about brain functions were not accurate, but his work represents an early and important attempt to link the brain's anatomy to psychological functions (**Figure 1.6**).

In the 1600s, the philosopher René Descartes promoted the first influential theory of *dualism.* This term refers to the idea that the mind and the body are separate yet intertwined (**Figure 1.7**). In earlier views of dualism, mental functions had been considered the mind's sovereign domain, separate from body functions. The way Descartes connected mind and body was at the time quite radical. The body, he argued, was nothing more than an organic machine governed by "reflex." Many mental functions—such as memory and imagination—resulted from body functions. Deliberate action, however, was controlled by the rational mind. And in keeping with the prevailing religious beliefs, Descartes concluded that the rational mind was divine and separate from the body.

Experimental Psychology Began with Introspection

In the mid-1800s in Europe, psychology arose as a field of study built on the experimental method. In *A System of Logic* (1843), the philosopher John Stuart Mill declared that psychology should leave the realms of philosophy and of speculation and become a science of observation and of experiment. Indeed, he defined psychology as "the science of the elementary laws of the mind" and argued that only through the methods of science would the processes of the mind be understood. As a result, throughout the 1800s, early psychologists increasingly studied mental activity through careful scientific observation. Like the shift from philosophy to experimentation, rapid increases in knowledge about basic physiology were central to the development of psychological science.

FIGURE 1.7 René Descartes According to Descartes' theory of dualism, the mind and the body are separate yet intertwined. As discussed throughout this book, psychologists now reject that separation.

In 1879, Wilhelm Wundt established the first psychology laboratory and institute (**Figure 1.8**). At this facility, in Leipzig, Germany, for the first time students could earn advanced academic degrees in psychology. Wundt trained many of the great early psychologists, many of whom then established psychological laboratories throughout Europe, Canada, and the United States.

Wundt realized that psychological processes, the products of physiological actions in the brain, take time to occur. Therefore, he would present each research participant with a simple psychological task and a related but more complex one. He would time each task. He would then perform a mathematical operation: subtracting the time a participant took to complete the simple task from the time the participant took to complete the more complex task. This method enabled Wundt to infer how much time a particular mental event took to occur. The event would be the common factor between the two tasks. Researchers still widely use *reaction time* to study psychological processes, but their equipment is of course more sophisticated than Wundt's.

Wundt was not satisfied with simply studying mental reaction times, however. He wanted to measure conscious experiences. To do so, he developed the method of **introspection,** a systematic examination of subjective mental experiences that requires people to inspect and report on the content of their thoughts. Wundt asked people to use introspection in comparing their subjective experiences as they contemplated a series of objects—for example, by stating which one they found more pleasant.

FIGURE 1.8 Wilhelm Wundt Wundt founded modern experimental psychology.

Introspection and Other Methods Led to Structuralism

Edward Titchener, a student of Wundt's, used methods such as introspection to pioneer a school of thought that became known as **structuralism.** This school is based on the idea that conscious experience can be broken down into its basic underlying components. Titchener believed that an understanding of the basic elements of conscious experience would provide the scientific basis for understanding the mind. He argued that one could take a stimulus such as a musical tone and, through introspection, analyze its "quality," "intensity," "duration," and "clarity." Wundt ultimately rejected such uses of introspection, but Titchener relied on the method throughout his career.

The general problem with introspection is that experience is subjective. Each person brings to introspection a unique perceptual system, and it is difficult for researchers to determine whether each participant in a study is employing introspection similarly. Additionally, the reporting of the experience changes the experience. Over time, psychologists largely abandoned introspection because it was not a reliable method for understanding psychological processes. Nonetheless, Wundt, Titchener, and other structuralists were important owing to their goal of developing a pure science of psychology with its own vocabulary and set of rules.

FIGURE 1.9 William James In 1890, James published the first major overview of psychology. Many of his ideas have passed the test of time. In theorizing about how the mind works, he moved psychology beyond structuralism and into functionalism.

Functionalism Addressed the Purpose of Behavior

One critic of structuralism was William James, a brilliant scholar whose wide-ranging work has had an enormous, enduring impact on psychology (**Figure 1.9**). In 1873, James abandoned a career in medicine to teach physiology at Harvard University. He was among the first professors at Harvard to openly welcome questions from students rather than having them listen silently to lectures. James's personal interests were more philosophical than physiological. He was captivated by the nature of conscious experience. In 1875, he gave his first lecture on

introspection A systematic examination of subjective mental experiences that requires people to inspect and report on the content of their thoughts.

structuralism An approach to psychology based on the idea that conscious experience can be broken down into its basic underlying components.

stream of consciousness A phrase coined by William James to describe each person's continuous series of ever-changing thoughts.

functionalism An approach to psychology concerned with the adaptive purpose, or function, of mind and behavior.

evolutionary theory A theory presented by the naturalist Charles Darwin; it views the history of a species in terms of the inherited, adaptive value of physical characteristics, of mental activity, and of behavior.

adaptations In evolutionary theory, the physical characteristics, skills, or abilities that increase the chances of reproduction or survival and are therefore likely to be passed along to future generations.

natural selection In evolutionary theory, the idea that those who inherit characteristics that help them adapt to their particular environments have a selective advantage over those who do not.

FIGURE 1.10 Charles Darwin Introduced in *On the Origin of Species,* Darwin's theory of evolution has had a huge impact on how psychologists think about the mind.

psychology, and he later quipped that it was also the first lecture on psychology he had ever heard. To this day, psychologists find rich delight in reading James's penetrating analysis of the human mind, *Principles of Psychology* (1890). It was the most influential book in the early history of psychology, and many of its central ideas have held up over time.

In criticizing structuralism's failure to capture the most important aspects of mental experience, James argued that the mind was much more complex than its elements and therefore could not be broken down. For instance, he noted that the mind consisted of an ever-changing, continuous series of thoughts. This **stream of consciousness** could not be frozen in time, according to James, so the structuralists' techniques were sterile and artificial. Psychologists who used the structural approach, he said, were like people trying to understand a house by studying each of its bricks individually. More important to James was that the bricks together formed a house and that a house has a particular function. The mind's elements mattered less than the mind's usefulness to people.

James argued that psychologists ought to examine the functions served by the mind—how the mind operates. According to his approach, which became known as **functionalism,** the mind came into existence over the course of human evolution. It works as it does because it is useful for preserving life and passing along genes to future generations. In other words, it helps humans *adapt* to environmental demands.

EVOLUTION, ADAPTATION, AND BEHAVIOR One of the major influences on functionalism was the work of the naturalist Charles Darwin (**Figure 1.10**). In 1859, Darwin published his revolutionary study *On the Origin of Species,* which introduced the world to **evolutionary theory.** By observing the variations in species and in individual members of species, Darwin reasoned that species change over time. Changes come about through random genetic mutations in individuals. Some of these changes—physical characteristics, skills, and abilities—increase individuals' chances of surviving and reproducing. Surviving and reproducing in turn ensure that these changes, in the form of the mutated genes, will be passed along to future generations. Changes passed along in this way are called **adaptations.**

Earlier philosophers and naturalists—including Darwin's grandfather, Erasmus Darwin—had discussed the possibility that species might evolve. But Charles Darwin first presented the mechanism of evolution, which he called **natural selection:** the process by which random mutations that are adaptive (i.e., facilitate survival and reproduction) are passed along and random mutations that are not adaptive (i.e., hinder survival and reproduction) are not. In other words, species struggle to survive. Those species that are better adapted to their environments will survive and reproduce, their offspring will survive and reproduce, and so on. This idea has come to be known as the *survival of the fittest.*

Darwin's ideas have profoundly influenced science, philosophy, and society. Rather than being a specific area of scientific inquiry, evolutionary theory is a way of thinking that can be used to understand many aspects of mind and behavior (Buss, 1999).

Many functionalists argued that if a behavior serves a purpose, that purpose ought to be reflected in daily human life. Thus, for example, James applied the functional approach to the study of phenomena such as the nature of religious experience. The educator John Dewey tested functionalist theories in his classrooms, teaching according to how the mind processes information. This *progressive* approach to education emphasized divergent thinking and creativity rather than the repetitive drill learning of conventional knowledge (knowledge that might, after all, be incorrect; Hothersall, 1995). Yet the broad-ranging subjects to which functionalism was applied led to criticism that this school was not sufficiently rigorous, and functionalism slowly lost momentum as a movement in psychology. Within the past few decades, however, the functional approach has returned to psychological science as more and more researchers consider the adaptiveness of the behaviors and mental processes they study.

Gestalt Psychology Emphasized Patterns and Context in Learning

Another school of thought that arose in opposition to structuralism was the *Gestalt* school, founded by Max Wertheimer in 1912 and expanded by Wolfgang Köhler, among others. According to **Gestalt theory,** the whole of personal experience is not simply the sum of its constituent elements. In other words, *the whole is different from the sum of its parts.* So, for example, if a researcher shows people a triangle, they see a triangle—not three lines on a piece of paper, as would be the case for the introspective observations in one of Titchener's structural experiments. (When you look at **Figure 1.11,** do you see the parts or the whole?) In

---

FIGURE 1.11   Try for Yourself: What Do You See?

The fragments make up a picture of a dog sniffing the ground.

Explanation: The mind organizes the picture's elements automatically to produce the perception of the dog. The picture is processed and experienced as a unified whole. Once you perceive the dog, you cannot choose to not see it.

*Many principles of psychological science are easy to experience. In each chapter of this book, **Try for Yourself** features will present you with the chance to be your own research participant.*

FIGURE 1.12 **Try for Yourself: What Do You See?**

This drawing by the psychologist Roger Shepard can be viewed as either a face behind a candlestick or two separate profiles.

Explanation: The mind organizes the scene into one or another perceptual whole, so the picture looks a specific way each time it is viewed. It is difficult to see both the single face and the two profiles at the same time.

FIGURE 1.13 Mary Whiton Calkins Calkins was an important early contributor to psychological science, despite having been denied the doctorate she earned in psychology.

experimentally investigating subjective experience, the Gestalt psychologists did not rely on the reports of trained observers. They sought out ordinary people's observations.

The Gestalt movement reflected an important idea that was at the heart of criticisms of structuralism. Namely, the perception of objects is subjective and dependent on context. Two people can look at an object and see different things. Indeed, one person can look at an object and see it in completely different ways. (When you look at **Figure 1.12,** how many possible views do you see?) The Gestalt perspective has influenced many areas of psychology, including the study of vision and our understanding of human personality.

Women Have Helped Shape the Field

Women have made substantial contributions to psychology throughout its history. Often, however, women with credentials in the field have had to fight sexism and other barriers to career success. One of the early contributors to psychology was Mary Whiton Calkins (**Figure 1.13**). At Wellesley College, Calkins was hired on a temporary basis as a Greek instructor. She then was invited to become a professor of the new field of philosophical psychology, but this appointment depended on her completing advanced training in psychology. At the time, her options were quite limited because psychology was relatively new to North America. After considering the possibilities, she decided that studying with William James at Harvard University would provide her with the best training. James was enthusiastic about having her as a student. Unfortunately, Harvard's president, Charles Eliot, did not believe in coeducation. After great pressure from James, Calkins's father, and the president of Wellesley, Eliot let Calkins enroll in the seminar as a guest. The male students withdrew from the seminar in protest, leaving Calkins with a private tutorial.

Calkins continued her psychological studies with several other mentors at Harvard, including the famous psychophysicist Hugo Munsterberg. In 1895, she completed all the requirements for a Ph.D. Although she scored higher than her male classmates on the qualifying exam, Harvard denied her the degree, offering instead a Ph.D. from Radcliffe, the women's school affiliated with Harvard. Calkins refused the degree, bristling at the unequal treatment she received and describing the differential education of men and women as artificial and illogical. Efforts to have Harvard overturn its earlier decision continue to this day, as does Harvard's refusal to grant her the degree she earned. (Harvard did not grant a Ph.D. to a woman until 1963.)

Calkins had a productive career as a professor at Wellesley and wrote an introductory psychology textbook in 1901. She was the first woman to set up a psychology laboratory, published more than 100 articles, and in 1905 was elected the first woman president of the American Psychological Association. Calkins's major research interest was the self, which she believed could be studied using the methods of science. She made several other important contributions to the early science of psychology, although in her later years she became somewhat disenchanted by the rise of behaviorism and its dismissal of the concept of self.

Margaret Floy Washburn was the first woman to be officially granted a Ph.D. in psychology (**Figure 1.14**). She was awarded her doctorate in 1894 at Cornell University, where she studied with Edward Titchener. In 1921, Washburn became the second woman president of the American Psychological Association. She spent most of her career at Vassar College, which she had attended as an undergraduate. Her passion for teaching was rewarded by her students, who raised $15,000 as a gift to celebrate her 25 years at Vassar. In keeping with her devotion to students, Washburn used the gift to set up a scholarship fund for women.

Through the first half of the twentieth century, societal forces continued to limit women's participation in psychology. For example, from 1920 to 1974, most women obtained their degrees in developmental psychology and school psychology. This focus reflected social stereotypes of the "women's world." Women were relatively underrepresented in other areas of psychological science. Indeed, fewer than 1 in 4 U.S. Ph.D.s in experimental, physiological, social, and clinical psychology went to women (Russo & Denmark, 1987). Despite these limitations, women made outstanding contributions to the field. Among these women were Nancy Bayley, who conducted groundbreaking research in developmental psychology and intelligence testing. In 1966, Bayley became the first woman to receive the American Psychological Association's Distinguished Scientific Contribution Award. The second person to receive this award, Eleanor Gibson, made major contributions to the study of perceptual learning. Dorothea Jameson advanced the understanding of color vision. Mary Cover Jones developed important techniques for behavioral therapy. Brenda Milner made vital contributions to understanding brain function. Janet Spence conducted important research on the effects of anxiety on learning. Spence was also the first person to be elected president of both the American Psychological Association and the more science oriented Association for Psychological Science.

Women's participation in psychology rapidly expanded in the 1970s. Their increased presence also spurred interest in how the earlier male domination of psychology had affected the content of psychology. For example, researchers had neglected many important topics, such as relationships and definitions of masculinity and femininity. In addition, researchers had used only men as research subjects, and that limitation had naturally affected the field's knowledge about human nature. As you will see in Chapter 10, Shelley Taylor and colleagues (Taylor, 2006; Taylor et al., 2002) studied psychology's longstanding view of how people react to stress. That view, they have shown, might be wrong because for many years only men were research participants. There are important differences in how men and women respond to stress.

In 1974, Eleanor Maccoby and Carol Jacklin published their landmark volume *The Psychology of Sex Difference*. Since then, psychologists have been more diligent in trying to understand when and why sex differences occur for psychological activity. For instance, scholars such as Sandra Bem have emphasized that many of these differences are due to societal conceptions of what it means to be masculine or feminine. The full participation of women, both as researchers and as research participants, has enriched the science of psychology (**Figure 1.15**). Today the majority of Ph.D.s granted in psychology are awarded to women.

FIGURE 1.14 Margaret Floy Washburn In 1894, Washburn became the first woman to receive a Ph.D. in psychology. She went on to a distinguished teaching career.

FIGURE 1.15 Contemporary Women in Psychology Throughout the history of psychology, women have contributed to the field even as they struggled against sexism. Barriers sometimes remain to career success for women in psychology, but women generally participate fully—and increasingly—as researchers and research participants. Here a diverse group of psychologists participates in a panel discussion at the National Multicultural Conference and Summit in January 2011. **Left to right:** Laura Brown, a private practitioner; Fred Leong, of Michigan State University; Jennifer Manly, of Columbia University; and Doug McDonald, of the University of North Dakota.

FIGURE 1.16 Sigmund Freud The father of psychoanalytic theory, Freud hugely influenced psychology in the twentieth century.

FIGURE 1.17 John B. Watson For most of his adult life, Watson worked in advertising. At the same time, he developed and promoted behaviorism. His views were amplified by thousands of psychologists, including B. F. Skinner.

unconscious The mental processes that operate below the level of conscious awareness.

psychoanalysis A method developed by Sigmund Freud that attempts to bring the contents of the unconscious into conscious awareness so that conflicts can be revealed.

behaviorism A psychological approach that emphasizes the role of environmental forces in producing behavior.

Freud Emphasized the Power of the Unconscious

Twentieth-century psychology was profoundly influenced by one of its most famous thinkers, Sigmund Freud (**Figure 1.16**). Freud was trained in medicine, and he began his career working with people who had neurological disorders, such as paralysis of various body parts. He found that many of his patients had few medical reasons for their paralysis. Soon he came to believe their conditions were caused by psychological factors.

Psychology was in its infancy at the end of the nineteenth century, when Freud deduced that much of human behavior is determined by mental processes operating below the level of conscious awareness, at the level of the **unconscious.** Freud believed these unconscious mental forces, often sexual and in conflict, produced psychological discomfort and in some cases even apparent psychological disorders. According to Freudian thinking, many of these unconscious conflicts arose from troubling childhood experiences that the person was blocking from memory.

From his theories, Freud pioneered the clinical case study approach (discussed in Chapter 2, "Research Methodology") and developed **psychoanalysis.** In this therapeutic approach, the therapist and the patient work together to bring the contents of the patient's unconscious into the patient's conscious awareness. Once the patient's unconscious conflicts are revealed, the therapist helps the patient deal with them constructively. For example, Freud analyzed the apparent symbolic content in a patient's dreams in search of hidden conflicts. He also used *free association,* a technique in which a patient would talk about whatever he or she wanted to for as long as he or she wanted to. Freud believed that through free association, a person eventually revealed the unconscious conflicts that caused the psychological problems.

Freud's influence was considerable. His work and his image helped shape the public's view of psychology. However, many of his ideas, such as the meaning of dreams, are extremely difficult to test using the methods of science. Contemporary psychologists no longer accept much of Freudian theory, but Freud's idea that mental processes occur below the level of conscious awareness is now widely accepted in psychological science.

Behaviorism Studied Environmental Forces

In 1913, the psychologist John B. Watson challenged, as inherently unscientific, psychology's focus on conscious and unconscious mental processes (**Figure 1.17**). Watson believed that if psychology was to be a science, it had to stop trying to study mental events that could not be observed directly. Scorning methods such as introspection and free association, he developed **behaviorism.** This approach emphasizes observable environmental effects on behavior.

The intellectual issue most central to Watson and his followers was the nature/nurture question. For Watson and other behaviorists, nurture was all. Heavily influenced by the work of the physiologist Ivan Pavlov (discussed further in Chapter 6, "Learning"), Watson believed that animals—including humans—acquired, or learned, all behaviors through environmental factors. Therefore, people needed to study the environmental *stimuli,* or triggers, in particular situations. By understanding the stimuli, people could predict the animals' behavioral *responses* in those situations. Psychologists greeted Watson's approach with great enthusiasm. Many had grown dissatisfied with the ambiguous methods used by those studying mental processes. They believed that psychologists would not be taken seriously as scientists until they studied observable behaviors.

B. F. Skinner became famous for taking up the mantle of behaviorism. Like Watson, Skinner denied the existence of mental states. In his provocative book

Beyond Freedom and Dignity (1971), Skinner argued that concepts about mental processes were of no scientific value in explaining behavior. In fact, Skinner believed that mental states were an illusion. He wanted to understand how repeated behaviors were shaped or influenced by the events or consequences that followed them. For instance, an animal would learn to perform a behavior if doing so in the past had led to a positive outcome, such as receiving food.

Behaviorism dominated psychological research well into the early 1960s. In many ways, these times were extremely productive for psychologists. Many of the basic principles established by behaviorists continue to be viewed as critical to understanding the mind, the brain, and behavior. At the same time, sufficient evidence has accumulated to show that thought processes influence outcomes. Few psychologists today describe themselves as strict behaviorists.

Cognitive Approaches Emphasized Mental Activity

During the first half of the twentieth century, psychology was largely focused on studying observable behavior. Evidence slowly emerged, however, that learning was not as simple as the behaviorists believed it was. Perceptions of situations could influence behavior. In the late 1920s, the Gestalt theorist Wolfgang Köhler found that chimpanzees could solve the problem of how to get a banana that was out of reach. The chimpanzees had to figure out how to connect two sticks to form a longer stick. This longer stick would then enable them to reach the banana and draw it close. The animals tried various methods, until suddenly they seemed to have insight: They used the two-stick strategy to reach the banana and then used that strategy perfectly on subsequent tasks.

At around the same time, learning theorists such as Edward Tolman were showing that animals could learn by observation. This finding made little sense (according to behaviorist theory) because the observing animals were not being rewarded. The connections were all being made in their minds. Other research was being conducted on memory, language, and child development. These studies showed that the simple laws of behaviorism could not explain, for example, why culture influences how people remember a story, why grammar develops systematically, and why children interpret the world in different ways during different stages of development. All of these findings suggested that mental functions were important for understanding behavior.

In 1957, George A. Miller and colleagues launched the *cognitive revolution* in psychology (**Figure 1.18**). Ulric Neisser integrated a wide range of cognitive phenomena in his classic book *Cognitive Psychology* (1967), which named and defined the field.

Cognitive psychology is concerned with mental functions such as intelligence, thinking, language, memory, and decision making. Cognitive research has shown that the way people think about things influences their behavior.

Several events in the 1950s set the stage for the rise of cognitive science. Perhaps the most important development was the growing use of computers. Computers operate according to software programs, which dictate rules for how information is processed. Cognitive psychologists such as Alan Newell and the Nobel laureate Herbert Simon applied this process to their explanation of how the mind works. These *information processing* theories of cognition viewed the brain as running the mind, or mental processes. In other words, the brain was the hardware, and the mental processes were the software. The brain took in information as a code, processed it, stored relevant sections, and retrieved stored information as required.

FIGURE 1.18 George A. Miller In 1957, Miller launched the cognitive revolution by establishing the Center for Cognitive Science at Harvard University.

cognitive psychology The study of how people think, learn, and remember.

FIGURE 1.19 Kurt Lewin Lewin founded modern social psychology. He pioneered the use of experimentation to test psychological hypotheses and thus to form theories about how people influence each other.

Some early cognitive psychologists recognized that the brain was important to cognition, but many cognitive psychologists focused exclusively on the software and had little interest in the specific brain mechanisms involved. In the early 1980s, cognitive psychologists joined forces with neuroscientists, computer scientists, and philosophers to develop an integrated view of mind and brain. During the next decade, **cognitive neuroscience** emerged. This field studies the neural mechanisms (mechanisms involving the brain, nerves, and nervous tissue) that underlie thought, learning, and memory.

Social Psychology Studies How Situations Shape Behavior

During the mid-twentieth century, many psychologists came to appreciate that people's behaviors were affected by the presence of others. This occurred partly because people sought to understand the atrocities committed in Europe before and during World War II. Why had apparently normal Germans, Poles, and Austrians willingly participated in the murders of innocents—men, women, and children? Was evil an integral part of human nature? If so, why did some people in these countries resist and put their own lives at risk to save others? Researchers focused on topics such as authority, obedience, and group behavior. Many of these psychologists were still influenced by Freudian ideas. For example, they believed that children absorb the values of authority figures as a result of unconscious conflicts. They concluded that certain types of people, especially those raised by unusually strict parents, displayed a slightly greater willingness to follow orders.

Almost everyone is strongly influenced by social situations, however. With this idea in mind, pioneering researchers such as Floyd Allport, Solomon Asch, and the Gestalt-trained Kurt Lewin rejected Freudian theorizing (**Figure 1.19**). Instead, they emphasized a scientific, experimental approach to understanding how people are influenced by others. The field that emerged from this work, **social psychology,** focuses on the power of situation and on the way people are shaped through their interactions with others.

In the 1950s, the civil rights movement encouraged social psychologists to try to understand stereotypes and prejudice. Many contemporary social psychologists examine the cognitive processes involved in how people evaluate and understand others: First, how do people form their identities through interactions with their social groups? Second, how do these social identities affect how people interact with members of other groups?

Science Informs Psychological Therapy

In the 1950s, psychologists such as Carl Rogers and Abraham Maslow pioneered a humanistic approach to the treatment of psychological disorders. This approach emphasized how people can come to know and accept themselves in order to reach their unique potentials. Some of the techniques developed by Rogers, such as specific ways of questioning and listening during therapy, are staples of modern treatment. Only in the last four decades, however, has a scientific approach to the study of psychological disorders emerged.

Throughout psychology's history, the methods developed to treat psychological disorders mirrored advances in psychological science. For instance, behaviorism's rise led to a group of therapies designed to modify behavior rather than address underlying mental conflicts. Behavioral modification methods continue to be highly effective in a range of situations, from training those with

cognitive neuroscience The study of the neural mechanisms (mechanisms involving the brain, nerves, and nervous tissue) that underlie thought, learning, and memory.

social psychology The study of how people are influenced by their interactions with others.

intellectual impairments to treating patients who are especially anxious and fear-ful. The cognitive revolution in scientific thinking led therapists to recognize the important role of thought processes in psychological disorders. Pioneers such as Aaron T. Beck developed therapies to correct faulty cognitions (faulty beliefs about the world). While these cognitive therapies are effective for treating many conditions, the most effective treatments for other conditions are drugs that alter brain chemistry. However, drugs can produce side effects and be addictive. In many situations, a combination of drugs and cognitive-behavioral therapy is the best treatment plan.

The nature/nurture debate is also central to the current understanding of psychological disorders. Psychologists now believe that many psychological disorders result as much from the brain's "wiring" (nature) as from how people are reared and treated (nurture). However, some psychological disorders are more likely to occur in certain environments, and this fact suggests that dis-orders can be affected by context. People's experiences change their brain struc-tures, which in turn influence people's experiences within their environments. Recent research also indicates that some people inherit genetic predispositions to developing certain psychological disorders—in this case, nurture activates nature. The social environment also plays an important role in whether treat-ment for these and other disorders is successful. For example, family members' negative comments tend to decrease a treatment's effectiveness.

In short, rapid advancements in understanding the biological and environmen-tal bases of psychological disorders are leading to effective treatments that allow people to live normal lives. Scientific research has made clear that—contrary to the thinking of the early giants such as Freud, Skinner, and Rogers—no universal treatment or approach fits all psychological disorders (Kazdin, 2008).

Summing Up

What Are the Scientific Foundations of Psychology?

Although people around the world have pondered psychological questions for thousands of years, the formal discipline of psychology began in Wilhelm Wundt's laboratory in Germany in 1879. Wundt believed it necessary to reduce mental processes into their constituent, "structural" parts. His approach was known as structuralism. Other early psychologists—functionalists—argued that it was more important to understand how the mind functions than to identify its constituent ele-ments. Early research in psychology was largely aimed at understanding the sub-jective mind. For example, the Gestalt movement focused on people's perceptions, and Freud emphasized the unconscious mind. With the rise of behaviorism, many psychologists claimed that the study of the mind had been too subjective and therefore unscientific. This view resulted in an emphasis, during the first half of the twentieth century, on the study of observable behavior. The cognitive revolution in the 1960s returned the mind to center stage, and research on mental processes such as memory, language, and decision making blossomed. The latter half of the twentieth century was also marked by an increased interest among psychologists in the influence of social contexts on behavior and on mental activity. As women's participation in psychology increased, researchers became interested in how the earlier male domination of psychology had affected the content of psychology. The advances in psychological science over the last century have informed the treat-ment of psychological disorders.

Identify the school of thought that each of the following statements character-izes. The options here are behaviorism, cognitive psychology, functionalism, Gestalt psychology, psychoanalysis, social psychology, and structuralism.

- **a.** To be a respectable scientific discipline, psychology should be concerned with what people and other animals do—in other words, with observable actions.
- **b.** Psychology should be concerned with the way behavior helps people adapt to their environments.
- **c.** Psychology should be concerned with the way in which people's thoughts affect their behavior.
- **d.** To understand behavior, psychologists need to understand the social con-texts in which people act.
- **e.** Because the sum is greater than the parts, psychologists should study the entirety of how we make sense of the world.
- **f.** Psychologists should study the "pieces" that make up the mind.
- **g.** To understand behavior, psychologists should study people's unconscious mental processes.

Answers: a. behaviorism; b. functionalism; c. cognitive; d. social; e. Gestalt; f. structuralism; g. psychoanalysis.

- Identify recent developments in psychological science.
- Distinguish between subfields of psychology.

FIGURE 1.20 Biological Bases We like to think that we choose our actions, from our romantic involvements to our career moves. **How much are these psychological phe-nomena influenced or even determined by our biology?**

1.3 What Are the Latest Developments in Psychology?

Biology Is Increasingly Important

The last three decades have seen tremendous growth in our understanding of the biological bases of mental activities (**Figure 1.20**). The field is only now drawing on biology's full power to explain psychological phenomena.

BRAIN CHEMISTRY Psychologists have made tremendous progress in understanding brain chemistry. It was long believed that only a handful of chemicals were involved in brain function, but in fact hundreds of substances play critical roles in mental activ-ity and behavior. Why, for instance, do we have more-accurate memories for events that happened when we were aroused than for events that happened when we were calm? Brain chemistry is different when we are aroused than when we are calm, and those same chemicals influence the neural mechanisms involved in memory.

NEUROSCIENCE Since the late 1980s, researchers have been able to study the working brain as it performs its vital psychological functions. The progress in un-derstanding the neural basis of mental life has been rapid and dramatic (Posner & DiGirolamo, 2000). For good reason, the 1990s were declared the decade of the brain by the U.S. federal government. Knowing where in the brain some-thing happens does not by itself reveal much. However, when consistent patterns of brain activation are associated with specific mental tasks, the activation appears to be connected with the tasks. For over a century, scientists had disagreed about whether psychological processes are located in specific parts of the brain or distrib-uted throughout the brain. We now know that there is some *localization* of func-tion. That is, some areas are important for specific feelings, thoughts, and actions. But many brain regions work together to produce behavior and mental activity.

THE HUMAN GENOME Scientists have also made enormous progress in understanding the influence of genetic processes on life. Genetic researchers have mapped the *human genome:* the basic *genetic code,* or blueprint, for the human body. For psychologists, this map represents the foundational knowledge for studying how specific genes—the basic units of hereditary transmission—affect thoughts, actions, feelings, and disorders. By identifying the genes involved in memory, for example, researchers soon may be able to develop therapies, based on genetic manipulation, that will assist people who have memory problems. Decades from now, at least some genetic defects might be corrected.

Meanwhile, the scientific study of genetic influences has made clear that very few single genes cause specific behaviors. Almost all biological and psychological activity is affected by the actions of multiple genes. Nonetheless, many physical and mental characteristics are inherited to some degree. In addition, scientists are beginning to understand how situational contexts, such as the presence or absence of specific environmental factors, influence how genes are expressed and therefore how they affect behavior.

Evolution Is Increasingly Important

As William James and his fellow functionalists knew, the human mind has been shaped by evolution. Modern evolutionary theory has driven the field of biology for years, but it has only recently begun to inform psychology. From this perspective, the brain has evolved over millions of years. The evolutionary changes to the brain have occurred in response to our ancestors' solving of problems related to survival and reproduction. In addition, there is accumulating evidence that the mind—the experience of the brain—also adapts. That is, while the brain adapts biologically, the contents of the mind adapt to cultural influences. In this way, the mind helps us overcome our particular challenges, but it also provides a strong framework for our shared social understandings of how the world works. Those understandings, of course, vary from place to place and from culture to culture.

SOLVING ADAPTIVE PROBLEMS Evolutionary theory is especially useful for considering whether behaviors and physical mechanisms are adaptive—in other words, whether they affect survival and reproduction. Through evolution, specialized mechanisms and adaptive behaviors have been built into our bodies and brains. For instance, a mechanism that produces calluses has evolved, protecting the skin from the abuses of physical labor. Likewise, specialized circuits or structures have evolved in the brain that solve adaptive problems, such as dealing with other people (Cosmides & Tooby, 1997). For example, people who lie, cheat, or steal may drain group resources and thereby decrease the chances of survival and reproduction for other group members. Some evolutionary psychologists believe humans have "cheater detectors" on the lookout for this sort of behavior in others (Cosmides & Tooby, 2000).

A classic example of the way adaptive mechanisms develop involves the "visual cliff" (**Figure 1.21**). When infants old enough to crawl are placed on top of a clear piece of plastic that covers both a firm surface (such as a table) and a dropped surface (where the clear plastic extends over the edge of the table), the infants may pat the surface that extends over the cliff and even accidentally back onto it. However, they will not willingly crawl over the cliff, even if their mothers are standing on the other side of the cliff encouraging them to do so. Infants become wary of heights at about the same age they learn to crawl, even though they have little personal experience with heights or gravity. This fear of heights is surely an adaptive mechanism that will enhance their chances of survival.

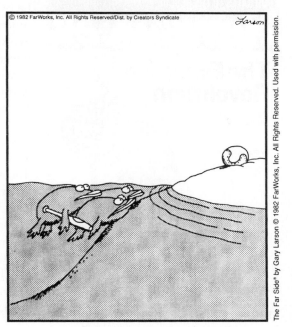

THE FAR SIDE® **BY GARY LARSON**

Great moments in evolution

FIGURE 1.21 Adaptive Mechanism
Despite the plastic covering over the visual cliff, infants will not crawl over the cliff even if their mothers call to them from the other side.

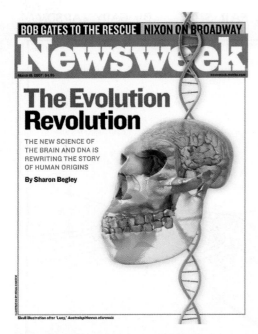

FIGURE 1.22 Evolution in the Present
To understand who we are as individuals, we need to understand who we are as a species. **Which of your own behaviors can you see as being influenced by 100,000 years of evolution? How about 5 million years?**

OUR EVOLUTIONARY HERITAGE According to evolutionary theory, we need to be aware of the challenges our early ancestors faced if we want to understand much of our current behavior, whether adaptive or maladaptive. Humans began evolving about 5 million years ago, but modern humans (*Homo sapiens*) can be traced back only about 100,000 years, to the Pleistocene era. If the human brain slowly adapted to accommodate the needs of Pleistocene hunter–gatherers, scientists should try to understand how the brain works within the context of the environmental pressures humans faced during the Pleistocene era (**Figure 1.22**).

For instance, people like sweet foods, especially those high in fat. These foods are high in calories, and in prehistoric times, eating them would have had great survival value. In other words, a preference for sweet, fatty foods was adaptive. Today, many societies have an abundance of foods, many of them high in fat and sugar. We still enjoy them and eat them, sometimes to excess, and this behavior may now be maladaptive in that it can produce obesity. Nonetheless, our evolutionary heritage encourages us to eat foods that had survival value when food was relatively scarce. Many of our current behaviors, of course, do not reflect our evolutionary heritage. Reading books, driving cars, using computers, texting, and watching television are among the human behaviors that we have displayed only recently. (Further complexities in the evolutionary process are discussed in Chapter 3, "Biology and Behavior.")

Culture Provides Adaptive Solutions

For humans, many of the most demanding adaptive challenges involve dealing with other humans. These challenges include selecting mates, cooperating in hunting and in gathering, forming alliances, competing for scarce resources, and even warring with neighboring groups. This dependency on group living is not unique to humans, but the nature of interactions among and between ingroup and outgroup members is especially complex in human societies. The complexity of living in groups gives rise to culture, and culture's various aspects are transmitted from one generation to the next through learning. For instance, our musical and food preferences, our ways of expressing emotion, and our tolerance of body odors are strongly affected by the cultures we are raised in. Many of a culture's "rules" reflect adaptive solutions worked out by previous generations.

Human cultural evolution has occurred much faster than human biological evolution. The most dramatic cultural changes have come in the last few thousand years. Although humans have changed only modestly in physical terms in that time, they have changed profoundly in regard to how they live together. Even within the last century, there have been dramatic changes in how human societies interact. The flow of people, commodities, and financial instruments among all regions of the world, often referred to as *globalization,* has increased in velocity and scale over the past century in ways that were previously unimaginable. Even more recently, the Internet has created a worldwide network of humans, essentially a new form of culture with its own rules, values, and customs.

Over the past decade, recognition has grown that culture plays a foundational role in shaping how people view and reason about the world around them—and that people from different cultures possess strikingly different minds. For example, the social psychologist Richard Nisbett and his colleagues (2001) have demonstrated that people from most European and North American countries are much more analytical than people from most Asian countries. Westerners break complex ideas into simpler components, categorize information, and use logic and rules to explain behavior. Easterners tend to be more holistic in their thinking, seeing everything in front of them as an inherently complicated whole, with all elements affecting all other elements (**Figure 1.23**). Moreover, the psychologist Steven Heine (2003) has found that Westerners are more likely to emphasize their personal strengths, whereas Easterners are more likely to emphasize their need for self-improvement. As psychologists come to better understand the relationship between culture and behavior, they make clear the importance of considering behavioral phenomena in their cultural contexts.

The culture in which we live shapes many aspects of daily life. Pause for a moment and think about the following questions: How do we decide what is most important in our lives? How do we want to relate to members of our families? Our friends? Our colleagues at work? How should we spend our leisure time? How do we define ourselves in relationship to our own cultures—or across cultures? For instance, the increased participation of women in the workforce has changed the nature of contemporary Western culture in numerous ways, from a fundamental change in how women are viewed to more practical changes, such as people marrying and having children later in life, a greater number of children in day care, and a greater reliance on convenient, fast foods. Culture shapes beliefs and values, such as the extent to which people should emphasize their own interests versus the interests of the group. This effect is magnified when we compare phenomena across cultures. Cultural rules are learned as *norms,* which specify how people ought to behave in different contexts. For example, norms tell us not to laugh uproariously at funerals and to keep quiet in libraries. There are also material aspects of culture, such as media, technology, health care, and transportation. Many of us find it hard to imagine life without computers, televisions, cell phones, and cars. We also recognize that each of these inventions has changed the fundamental ways in which people interact. Psychologists have played a significant role in our understanding of the complex relationship between culture and behavior.

Our social interactions, which vary among cultures (and subcultures and individuals), are reflected in the ways our brains are organized. *Cultural neuroscience* studies the ways that cultural variables affect the brain, the mind, genes, and behavior. This subdiscipline is necessarily multidisciplinary. It brings together information about brain functions (i.e., methods and data from brain imaging), analyses of social and emotional processes (e.g., recognizing faces, deciding whom to trust), and examinations of perceptual processes. It exemplifies the way that psychological science works across multiple levels of analysis.

(a)

(b)

FIGURE 1.23 Cultural Differences
(a) Westerners tend to be "independent" and autonomous, stressing their individuality. **(b)** Easterners—such as this Cambodian family—tend to be more "interdependent," stressing their sense of being part of a collective.

Psychological Science Now Crosses Levels of Analysis

Throughout the history of psychology, studying a phenomenon at one level of analysis has been the favored approach. Only recently have researchers started to explain behavior at several levels of analysis. By crossing levels in this way, psychologists are able to provide a more complete picture of mental and behavioral processes.

Four broadly defined levels of analysis reflect the most common research methods for studying mind and behavior (**Figure 1.24**). The *biological level of analysis* deals with how the physical body, including the brain, contributes to mind and behavior (as through the chemical and genetic processes that occur in the body). The *individual level of analysis* focuses on individual differences in personality and in the mental processes that affect how people perceive and know the world. The *social level of analysis* involves how group contexts affect how people interact and influence each other. The *cultural level of analysis* explores how people's thoughts, feelings, and actions are similar or different across cultures. Differences between cultures highlight the role that cultural experiences play in shaping psychological

LEVEL	FOCUS	WHAT IS STUDIED?
Biological	Brain systems	Neuroanatomy, animal research, brain imaging
	Neurochemistry	Neurotransmitters and hormones, animal studies, drug studies
	Genetics	Gene mechanisms, heritability, twin and adoption studies
Individual	Individual differences	Personality, gender, developmental age groups, self-concept
	Perception and cognition	Thinking, decision making, language, memory, seeing, hearing
	Behavior	Observable actions, responses, physical movements
Social	Interpersonal behavior	Groups, relationships, persuasion, influence, workplace
	Social cognition	Attitudes, stereotypes, perceptions
Cultural	Thoughts, actions, behaviors—in different societies and cultural groups	Norms, beliefs, values, symbols, ethnicity

FIGURE 1.24 Levels of Analysis

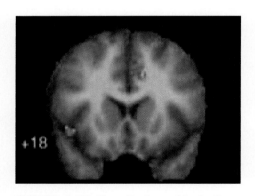

FIGURE 1.25 Your Brain on Music Certain regions of the brain are associated more with organized sounds than with scrambled sounds. The highlighted region on the left becomes more active when you hear spoken language or music. Noise does not activate that region.

processes, whereas similarities between cultures reveal evidence for universal phenomena that emerge regardless of cultural experiences.

To understand how research is conducted at the different levels, consider the many ways psychologists have studied listening to music, a pastime enjoyed by most people (Renfrow & Gosling, 2003). Why do you like some kinds of music and not others? Do you prefer some types of music when you are in a good mood and other types when you are in a bad mood? If you listen to music while you study, how does it affect how you learn? Does music help pick you up when you are tired or carry you away so that you momentarily forget your discomforts? Music has many important effects on the mind, brain, and behavior, and psychologists examine these effects using the methods of science. They examine how musical preferences vary among individuals and across cultures, how music affects emotional states and thought processes, and even how the brain perceives sound as music rather than noise.

At the biological level of analysis, for instance, researchers have studied the effects of musical training. They have shown that training can change not only how the brain functions but also its anatomy, such as changing brain structures associated with learning and memory (Herdener et al., 2010). Listening to pleasant music appears to increase the activation of brain regions associated with positive experiences (Koelsch, Offermanns, & Franzke, 2010). In other words, music does not affect the brain exactly the way other types of sounds, such as the spoken word, do. Instead, music recruits brain regions involved in a number of mental processes, such as those involved in mood and memory (Levitin & Menon, 2003; Peretz & Zatorre, 2005). Music appears to be treated by the brain as a special category of auditory information (**Figure 1.25**). For this reason, patients with certain types of brain injury become unable to hear tones and melody but can hear speech and environmental sounds perfectly well. One 35-year-old woman who had brain damage lost the ability to recognize even familiar tunes—a condition known as *amusia*—even though other aspects of her memory system and language system were intact (Peretz, 1996).

In studies conducted at the individual level of analysis, researchers have used laboratory experiments to study music's effects on mood, memory, decision making, and various other mental states and processes (Levitin, 2006). In one study, music from participants' childhoods evoked specific memories from that period (Janata, 2009). Moreover, playing certain types of music puts people into particular moods and magnifies their feelings (Baumgartner, Lutz, Schmidt, & Jäncke, 2006). Listening to sad background music leads young children to interpret a story negatively, whereas listening to happy background music leads them to interpret a story much more positively (Ziv & Goshen, 2006).

A study of music at the social level of analysis might compare the types of music people prefer when they are in groups with the types they prefer when alone, or how group preferences for some types of music influence individuals' preferences when they are not in a group. Recently, psychologists have sought to answer the question of whether certain types of music promote negative behaviors among listeners. For instance, researchers in Quebec found that certain types of rap music, but not hip-hop, were associated with more deviant behaviors, such as violence and drug use (Miranda & Claes, 2004). Likewise, a recent study from the Netherlands found that people who prefer heavy metal, punk, reggae, and techno music are more likely to use alcohol, drugs, and tobacco than are people who prefer pop or classical music (Mulder et al., 2009). Of course, such associations do not mean that listening to music causes the behaviors studied. It could just as easily be that those who practice the behaviors then develop the musical preferences. Listening to music with prosocial lyrics, however, led research participants to be more empathic and increased their helping behavior (Greitemeyer, 2009).

The cross-cultural study of music preferences has developed into a separate field, *ethnomusicology*. For example, one finding from this field is that African music has rhythmic structures different from those in Western music (Agawu, 1995), and these differences in turn may reflect the important role of dancing and drumming in African folktales. Because cultures prefer different types of music, some psychologists have noted that our attitudes about outgroup members can color our perceptions of their musical styles. For example, researchers from the United States and the United Kingdom found that the societal attitudes toward rap and hip-hop music revealed subtle prejudicial attitudes against blacks and a greater willingness to discriminate against them (Reyna, Brandt, & Viki, 2009).

As these examples show, research at different levels of analysis is creating a greater understanding of the psychology of music. Adding to that understanding is innovative research combining two or more levels of analysis. More and more, psychological science emphasizes examining behavior across multiple levels in an integrated fashion. Often psychologists collaborate with researchers from other scientific fields, such as biology, computer science, physics, anthropology, and sociology. Such collaborations are called *interdisciplinary*. For example, psychologists interested in understanding the hormonal basis of obesity might work with geneticists exploring the heritability of obesity as well as social psychologists studying human beliefs about eating. Crossing the levels of analysis usually provides more insights than working within only one level. The Gestalt psychologists were right in asserting that the whole is different from the sum of its parts. Throughout this book, you will see how this multilevel approach has led to breakthroughs in understanding psychological activity.

SUBFIELDS IN PSYCHOLOGY FOCUS ON DIFFERENT LEVELS OF ANALYSIS The term *psychologist* is used broadly to describe someone whose career involves predicting behavior or understanding mental life. Psychologists work in many different settings. Often the setting depends on whether the psychologist's primary focus is on research, teaching, or applying scientific findings to improving the quality of daily living. Researchers who study the brain, the mind, and behavior may work in schools, businesses, universities, or clinics. There are also psychological practitioners, who apply the findings of psychological science to do things such as help people in need of psychological treatment, design safe and pleasant work environments, counsel people on career paths, or help teachers design better classroom curricula. The distinction between science and practice can be fuzzy, since many researchers are also practitioners. For example, many clinical psychologists both study people with psychological disorders and treat those people.

A scientist will choose to study at a particular level of analysis—or more than one level—based on that scientist's research interests, general theoretical

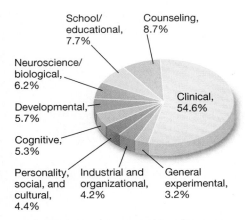

School/educational, 7.7%

Counseling, 8.7%

Neuroscience/biological, 6.2%

Developmental, 5.7%

Cognitive, 5.3%

Clinical, 54.6%

Personality, social, and cultural, 4.4%

Industrial and organizational, 4.2%

General experimental, 3.2%

FIGURE 1.26 Doctoral Degrees This pie chart shows doctoral degrees awarded for the 2007–2008 academic year. The degrees are divided by psychology subfields.

approaches, and training. Because the subject matter of psychology is vast, most psychologists focus within relatively large subfields (**Figure 1.26**). Many of the subfields in psychology are represented by specific chapters of this book.

Neuroscience/biological psychologists are particularly interested in examining how biological systems give rise to mental activity and behavior. They may study, for example, how certain chemicals in the brain control sexual behavior, how damage to certain brain regions disrupts feeding, or how different environments lead different genes to be expressed.

Cognitive psychologists study processes such as thinking, perceiving, problem solving, decision making, using language, and learning. Today, many of them study images of the brain to understand how the brain accomplishes these processes.

General *experimental psychologists* study basic psychological processes such as sensation and perception, movement, and learning. For instance, they might examine how people see in color, how expert dancers differ from novices, or how animals can be taught new behaviors.

Developmental psychologists study how people change across the life span, from infancy through old age. For example, they are interested in how children learn to speak and how they become moral beings, how adolescents form their identities, and how older adults can maintain their mental abilities in the face of typical age-related declines in those abilities.

Personality psychologists seek to understand enduring characteristics that people display over time and across circumstances, such as why some people are shy, whereas others are outgoing. They examine how genes, circumstances, and cultural context shape personality.

Social psychologists focus on how people are affected by the presence of others and how they form impressions of others. For instance, they might study what people believe about members of other groups, when people are influenced by others to behave in certain ways, or how people form or dissolve intimate relationships.

Cultural psychologists seek to understand how people are influenced by the societal rules that dictate behavior in the cultures in which they are raised. For example, they study how societal rules shape self-perception, how they influence interpersonal behavior, whether they produce differences in perception, and whether they produce differences in cognition.

Clinical psychologists are interested in the factors that cause psychological disorders and the methods best used to treat them. For example, they might study the factors that lead people to feel depressed, the types of therapy that are most effective for alleviating depression, and how the brain changes as a result of therapy.

Counseling psychologists have overlap with clinical psychologists. They seek to improve people's daily lives, but they work more with people facing difficult circumstances than with people who have serious mental disorders. For example, they provide marital and family counseling, provide career advice, and help people manage stress.

School psychologists work in educational settings. They help students with problems that interfere with learning, design age-appropriate curricula, and conduct assessment and achievement testing.

Industrial and organizational psychologists are concerned with various factors in industry and the workplace. They develop programs to motivate workers by building morale and improving job satisfaction, design equipment and workspaces so that workers can easily perform their duties and avoid accidents, and assist with identifying and recruiting talented workers.

These are the major categories of psychology, but psychologists pursue many more specialties and research areas. For instance, *forensic psychologists* work in legal settings, perhaps helping choose juries or identifying dangerous offenders. *Sports psychologists* work with athletes to improve their performance, perhaps teaching athletes how to control their thoughts during pressure situations. *Health psychologists* study the factors that promote or interfere with physical health, such as how stress may cause disease. A number of careers in psychology are predicted to grow substantially over the next decade. The growth areas include advising programs that aim to tackle societal problems (e.g., the Bill and Melinda Gates Foundation); working with older adults, since older adults will make up an increasing proportion of the population; working with soldiers returning from Iraq and Afghanistan; working with homeland security to study terrorism; consulting with industry; and advising on legal matters based on courtroom expertise (DeAngelis, 2008). Because psychologists are concerned with nearly every aspect of human life, what they study is remarkably diverse, as you will soon discover in the following chapters.

Summing Up

What Are the Latest Developments in Psychology?

Four themes characterize the latest developments in psychological science: (1) Biology is increasingly important. A biological revolution has energized psychological research into how the brain enables the mind. Among the revolutionary developments are increasing knowledge of brain chemistry, the use of technologies that allow researchers to observe the brain in action, and the mapping of the human genome. (2) Evolution is increasingly important. Psychological science has been influenced heavily by evolutionary psychology, which argues that the brain has evolved in response to our ancestors' solving of adaptive problems. (3) Culture provides adaptive solutions. Contemporary psychology is characterized by an increasing interest in cultural norms and their influence on thought processes and behavior. Cultural norms reflect solutions to adaptive problems that were worked out by previous generations and transmitted to successive generations through learning. (4) Psychological science now crosses levels of analysis. Psychologists share the goal of understanding mind, brain, and behavior. In approaching that goal, however, psychologists focus on the same problems at different levels of analysis: biological, individual, social, and cultural. Most problems in psychology require studies at each level. There are diverse subfields in psychology, and the subfields focus on different levels of analysis.

Measuring Up

Which recent development in psychological science is reflected by each example below?

Examples:

    a. In a study of prejudice, psychologists used an attitudes test and brain imaging when participants looked at pictures of African Americans' faces and of European Americans' faces.

    b. When psychologists study a disorder of the mind, they frequently look at genetic factors that might be involved in causing the disorder.

    c. To understand contemporary human behavior, psychologists often consider the environmental challenges that our ancestors faced.

    d. In a study of immigrants, psychologists examined the customs and practices that the immigrants adopted when they migrated to their new country.

Recent developments:

    1. Biology is increasingly important.

    2. Evolution is increasingly important.

    3. Culture provides adaptive solutions.

    4. Psychological science now crosses levels of analysis.

Answers: a. 4; b. 1; c. 2; d. 3.

Chapter Summary

1.1 Why Study Psychology?

■ **Psychology Is about *You* and about *Us*:** Psychology can help us better understand ourselves and others, and it can help us improve the quality of our lives. The field has broad applications to all areas of life.

■ **Psychologists Explain Human Behaviors in Real-Life Contexts:** Psychological science is the study of the mind, the brain, and behavior. Although psychological science explains behavior in real-life contexts, the results of psychological research are often surprising and run counter to common beliefs.

■ **Psychological Knowledge Is Used in Many Professions:** Because psychology focuses on human behavior, it is of interest to many students and professionals and is used in virtually every profession.

■ **Psychological Science Teaches Critical Thinking:** The use of critical thinking skills improves how we think. Skepticism, an important element of science, requires a careful examination of how well evidence supports a conclusion. Using critical thinking skills and understanding the methods of psychological science are important for evaluating research reported in the popular media.

1.2 What Are the Scientific Foundations of Psychology?

■ **The Nature/Nurture Debate Has a Long History:** Nature and nurture depend on each other. Their influences cannot be separated.

■ **The Mind/Body Problem Also Has Ancient Roots:** Older dualist notions about the separation of the brain and mind have been replaced with the idea that the (physical) brain enables the mind. Brain and mind cannot be separated.

■ **Experimental Psychology Began with Introspection:** Psychology's intellectual history dates back thousands of years. As a formal discipline, psychology began in 1879, in Wilhelm Wundt's laboratory in Germany. Using the technique of introspection, scientists attempted to understand conscious experience.

■ **Introspection and Other Methods Led to Structuralism:** Structuralists used introspection to identify the basic underlying components of conscious experience. Structuralists attempted to understand conscious experience by reducing it to its structural elements.

■ **Functionalism Addressed the Purpose of Behavior:** According to functionalists, the mind is best understood by examining its functions and purpose, not its structure.

■ **Gestalt Psychology Emphasized Patterns and Context in Learning:** Gestalt psychologists asserted that the whole experience (the gestalt) is greater than the sum of its parts. As a result, they emphasized the subjective experience of perception.

■ **Women Have Helped Shape the Field:** Women's early contributions to psychological science have been underacknowledged. Through the first half of the twentieth century, women in psychology struggled against sexism and other barriers to career success. Since then, women's participation in psychology has continued to increase and has affected the content of psychology.

■ **Freud Emphasized the Power of the Unconscious:** Freud advanced the idea that unconscious processes are not readily available to our awareness but nevertheless influence our behavior. This understanding had an enormous impact on psychology.

■ **Behaviorism Studied Environmental Forces:** Discoveries that behavior is changed by its consequences caused behaviorism to dominate psychology until the 1960s.

■ **Cognitive Approaches Emphasized Mental Activity:** The cognitive revolution and the computer analogy of the brain led to information processing theories. Cognitive neuroscience, which emerged in the 1980s, is concerned with the neural mechanisms that underlie thought, learning, and memory.

■ **Social Psychology Studies How Situations Shape Behavior:** Work in social psychology has highlighted how situations and other people are powerful forces in shaping behavior.

■ **Science Informs Psychological Therapy:** Psychological disorders are influenced by both nature (biological factors) and nurture (environmental factors). Scientific research has taught psychologists that no universal treatment exists for psychological disorders. Instead, different treatments are effective for different disorders.

1.3 What Are the Latest Developments in Psychology?

■ **Biology Is Increasingly Important:** Tremendous advances in neuroscience have revealed the working brain. Mapping of the human genome has furthered the role of genetics in analyzing both behavior and disease. These advances are changing how we think about psychology.

■ **Evolution Is Increasingly Important:** Evolution of the brain has helped solve survival and reproductive problems and helped us adapt to our environments. Many modern behaviors reflect adaptations to environmental pressures faced by our ancestors.

■ **Culture Provides Adaptive Solutions:** Cultural norms specify how people should behave in different contexts. They reflect solutions to adaptive problems that have been worked out by a group of individuals, and they are transmitted through learning.

■ **Psychological Science Now Crosses Levels of Analysis:** Psychologists examine behavior from various analytical levels: biological (brain systems, neurochemistry, genetics), individual (personality, perception, cognition), social (interpersonal behavior), and cultural (within a single culture, across several cultures). Psychology is characterized by numerous subfields. Within each subfield, psychologists may focus on one or more levels of analysis.

Key Terms

adaptations, p. 10
behaviorism, p. 14
cognitive neuroscience, p. 16
cognitive psychology, p. 15
critical thinking, p. 4
culture, p. 7
evolutionary theory, p. 10

functionalism, p. 10
Gestalt theory, p. 11
introspection, p. 9
mind/body problem, p. 7
natural selection, p. 10
nature/nurture debate, p. 7
psychoanalysis, p. 14

psychological science, p. 2
social psychology, p. 16
stream of consciousness, p. 10
structuralism, p. 9
unconscious, p. 14

Practice Test

1. When you mention to your family that you enrolled in a psychology course, your family members share their understanding of the field. Which comment best reflects the nature of psychological science?
   a. "You're going to learn how to get in touch with your feelings."
   b. "The concept of 'psychological science' is such an oxymoron. It is impossible to measure and study what goes on in people's heads."
   c. "I think you'll be surprised by the range of questions psychologists ask about the mind, the brain, and behavior, not to mention the methods they use to answer these questions."
   d. "By the end of the class, you'll be able to tell me why I am the way I am."

2. Match each definition with one of the following ideas from evolutionary theory: adaptations, natural selection, survival of the fittest.
   a. Gene mutations that endow physical characteristics, skills, and abilities can increase an organism's chances of survival and of reproduction.
   b. Individuals better adapted to their environment will leave more offspring.
   c. Organisms' adaptive random mutations are passed along, and mutations that hinder both survival and reproduction are not.

3. Titles of recent research articles appear below. Indicate which of the four levels of analysis—cultural, social, individual, or biological—each article likely addresses.
   a. Achievement motivation in adolescents: The role of peer climate and best friends (Nelson & DeBacker, 2008)
   b. Circadian affective, cardiopulmonary, and cortisol variability in depressed and nondepressed individuals at risk for cardiovascular disease (Conrad, Wilhelm, Roth, Spiegel, & Taylor, 2008)
   c. Schooling in Western culture promotes context-free processing (Ventura, Pattamadilok, & Fernandes, 2008)
   d. Severity of physical aggression reported by university students: A test of the interaction between trait aggression and alcohol consumption (Tremblay, Graham, & Wells, 2008)

4. Indicate which school or schools of thought each of the following scholars is associated with: John Dewey, William James, Wolfgang Köhler, Kurt Lewin, George Miller, B. F. Skinner, Edward Titchener, Edward Tolman, John B. Watson, Max Wertheimer, Wilhelm Wundt.
   a. Structuralism
   b. Functionalism
   c. Gestalt psychology
   d. Behaviorism
   e. Cognitive psychology
   f. Social psychology

5. Match each description with one of the following theoretical ideas: dualism, information processing theory, introspection, localization, stream of consciousness.
   a. A systematic examination of subjective mental experience that requires people to inspect and report on the contents of their thoughts
   b. The notion that the mind and the body are separate and distinct
   c. Some psychological processes are located in specific parts of the brain
   d. A continuous series of ever-changing thoughts
   e. The view that the brain takes in information as a code, processes it, stores relevant bits, and retrieves stored information as required

6. Imagine you have decided to seek mental health counseling. You mention this to a few of your friends. Each friend shares an opinion with you. Based on your understanding of psychological science, which friend offers the strongest advice?
   a. "I wouldn't bother if I were you. All therapy is a bunch of psychobabble."
   b. "I know a therapist who uses this really cool method that can fix any problem. Seriously, she knows the secret!"
   c. "That's great! Psychologists do research to figure out which interventions are most helpful for people with different concerns."
   d. "Well, I guess if you like relaxing on couches and talking, you might get a lot out of therapy."

The answer key for the Practice Tests can be found at the back of the book. It also includes answers to the green caption questions.

Research Methodology

VIONIQUE VALNORD-KASSIME WAS 32 YEARS OLD when she was killed by a drunk driver (**Figure 2.1a**). This tragedy happened at 1 AM on a Sunday in late September 2009. Having just left a friend's wedding reception in Brooklyn, New York, Valnord-Kassime was in the street trying to hail a cab. It was rainy and foggy. Andrew Kelly, a 30-year-old off-duty police officer, was driving his sport utility vehicle on that street (**Figure 2.1b**). Another off-duty cop was among the passengers in the vehicle, which struck Valnord-Kassime and threw her body several feet away. She died on the scene.

Andrew Kelly pled guilty to vehicular manslaughter and driving while intoxicated. His guilty plea helped him avoid the maximum prison sentence of seven years, but it ended his eight-year career in the police department. His official punishment? Kelly's driver's license was suspended for a year. He was ordered to complete an alcohol treatment program and install an ignition lock on

(a)

(b)

FIGURE 2.1 Avoidable Tragedy (a) Vionique Valnord-Kassime lost her life because she was standing in the street at the wrong time. Here she is shown in a photo held by her father. **(b)** Andrew Kelly accidentally killed Valnord-Kassime because he got behind the wheel when he was drunk.

scientific method A systematic procedure of observing and measuring phenomena (observable things) to answer questions about *what* happens, *when* it happens, *what causes* it, and *why;* involves a dynamic interaction between theories, hypotheses, and research.

his car. And he was sentenced to 90 days in jail. In a courtroom, Valnord-Kassime's father, a pastor, accepted an apology from Kelly. Still, her family filed a wrongful-death civil lawsuit against Kelly and the NYPD. The woman died for nothing, and lives connected with hers have been changed for the worse. Her family members and friends are left to deal with their loss.

What will it take to convince people not to drive after drinking? Will news stories like this one do the trick?

You know the facts. We all know the facts. Alcohol is a potent drug that slows down the nervous system. It changes how the brain operates. It can keep us from being able to think straight, speak properly, or even walk a straight line. It certainly can keep us from having the perceptual abilities, coordination, and motor skills necessary to operate machinery safely. People should not be drinking and then driving cars, riding motorcycles, piloting boats, flying planes, using power tools, or attempting any other activity that endangers their lives or the lives of others.

What if those facts are not enough to stop the problem? What if you read yet another story about someone injured or killed by a drunk driver, about a family ruined by a drunk driver's selfishness, and you become fed up? You happen to be a psychologist. For you, facts are not facts—they are simply *theories*—until they are supported empirically. Perhaps, you hope, by providing scientific evidence about the effects of alcohol on driving skills, you might be able to convince some people not to drink and drive. You might help prevent at least one tragedy.

How do you start? You begin with an idea: Alcohol probably impairs motor skills and coordination. This idea might seem obvious. In fact, it might seem so obvious that it would not need to be shown scientifically. If you are really going to understand how alcohol impairs driving, however, you need to move beyond a simple commonsense view. Think of a scientific understanding as being like a scale on which an increasing amount of evidence tips the balance in one direction.

To build up evidence around your particular idea, you need to test a specific way that alcohol affects behavior. And to begin this investigation, you set up a research study in which you give people alcohol and measure some behavioral response that you believe is related to driving skill. For example, you might want to see how well a person under the influence can see something in her or his visual field or how quickly the person can respond to a command to press a brake pedal. Basically, you are designing an *experiment* in which you alter, or *manipulate,* the situation to see how the change affects mental state or behavior. To see if the manipulation changes behavior, you must also measure the same behavior when your research participants have not been drinking. Alternatively, you could compare your group's behavior after drinking with that of another group of people who did not consume alcohol. You are measuring the effects seen in your experiment against a baseline, a condition that does not involve your manipulation.

Once you have collected the performance information, you evaluate it. You sift through it, draw conclusions from it, and put it into a form that you can share with other people. You need to share it with other psychologists for review. Ultimately, you want to see it published, so that your research becomes part of the scientific literature on drinking and driving. Only then can the facts, as developed scientifically, make their way into the public's consciousness.

Of course, an idea is not true just because you think it is. What if your research indicates that alcohol probably does *not* impair motor skills and coordination? Welcome to the world of scientific inquiry. ■

2.1 What Is Scientific Inquiry?

Learning Objectives

- Describe the scientific method.
- Differentiate between theories, hypotheses, and research.

This chapter will introduce you to the science and the art of psychological research methods. You will learn the basics of collecting, analyzing, and interpreting the data of psychological science. In this way, you will come to understand how psychologists study behavior and mental processes: describing *what* happens, predicting *when* it happens, controlling *what causes* it to happen, and explaining *why* it happens. Using these same research methods, you can test your own best guesses about people's thoughts and actions. With some practice, you can even contribute to the field of psychological science.

Contributions of this kind are collectively known as *scientific inquiry*. That term boils down to careful scientific research, nothing more and nothing less. Careful scientific research is a way of finding answers to empirical questions, meaning questions that can be answered by observing the world and measuring aspects of it. To be confident in the conclusions drawn from their observations, researchers in the various fields of science use a general approach known as the **scientific method.** This method is more objective than casual observations. It is more objective, in part, because it is *systematic*. To answer research questions, scientists use objective procedures in orderly steps that are carefully planned. An objective procedure is free from bias. If another researcher uses the same procedure with the same sample of people, he or she would expect to receive the same results.

The Scientific Method Depends on Theories, Hypotheses, and Research

The scientific method reflects a dynamic interaction between three essential elements: theories, hypotheses, and research (**Figure 2.2**). A **theory** is an explanation or model of how a *phenomenon*—an observable thing—works. The theory consists of interconnected ideas or concepts. It is used to explain prior observations and to make predictions about future events.

A good theory should generate a **hypothesis** (or multiple hypotheses). A hypothesis is a specific, testable prediction about the outcome that would best support the theory. If the theory is reasonably accurate, the prediction framed in the hypothesis should be supported. To see how theories lead to testable hypotheses, imagine you have begun your study of alcohol intoxication. You have spent some time observing people as they drank alcohol, and your observations indicate that people who drink alcohol tend to stumble, drop things, have impaired language, and show poor social judgment. What theory might you derive from these observations? Because you want to limit your research so that you can easily control its conditions, you probably would focus your theory on only some of those behaviors. For example, you might theorize that drinking alcohol impairs driving ability. What hypothesis might you derive from that theory? You might hypothesize that people who consume alcohol will tend to display poorer coordination and poorer motor control than will people who do not consume alcohol.

Once you have developed hypotheses to test your theory, you must do **research.** The research process involves the systematic and careful collection of **data.** The data consist of objective information that indicates whether the hypothesis—and ultimately the theory—is likely to be supported. In other words, the data provide a way to test the hypothesis, just as the hypothesis provides a way to test the theory. To test the hypothesis about alcohol's effects on coordination and motor skills, you would arrange for research participants to work with you. You might have some of

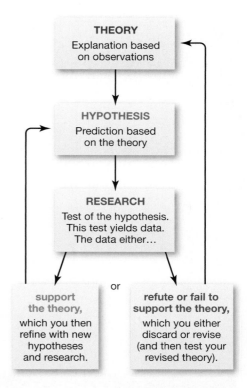

FIGURE 2.2 The Scientific Method The scientific method reflects a cyclical relationship: First the scientist formulates a theory. From the theory, the scientist derives one or more testable hypotheses. The scientist then conducts research to test the hypothesis. Findings from the research might prompt the scientist to re-evaluate and adjust the theory. A good theory evolves over time, and the result is an increasingly accurate model of some observable thing.

theory A model of interconnected ideas or concepts that explains what is observed and makes predictions about future events.

hypothesis A specific prediction of what should be observed if a theory is correct.

research A scientific process that involves the systematic and careful collection of data.

data Objective observations or measurements.

replication Repetition of an experiment to confirm the results.

the participants drink enough alcohol to bring their blood alcohol levels to the legal definition of drunkenness. You might have others drink tonic water. Or you might have all the participants drink tonic water as part of the first phase of the research, then have them drink alcohol as part of the second phase. You would systematically record the participants' behavior as they performed specific, carefully defined tasks.

Once the research findings are in, you would return to the original theory to evaluate the implications of the data you collected. The findings either support your theory or require that your theory be modified or discarded. Then the process starts all over again. Yes, the same sort of work needs to be performed repeatedly. You might consider the repetition unfortunate, but it is necessary. Good research reflects the cyclical process shown in Figure 2.2. In other words, a theory is continually refined by new hypotheses and tested by new research methods (**Figure 2.3**).

Often, more than one theory can explain human behavior. For this reason, no single study can provide a definitive answer about any phenomenon. In general, we can have more confidence in scientific findings when research outcomes are replicated. **Replication** involves repeating a study and getting the same (or similar) results. When the results from two or more studies are the same, or at least support the same conclusion, confidence in the findings increases.

THEORIES SHOULD GENERATE HYPOTHESES How can we decide whether a theory is good? When we talk about a good theory, we do not mean that it is likely to be supported by research findings. Instead, a good theory produces a wide variety of *testable* hypotheses. For instance, in the early twentieth century, the developmental psychologist Jean Piaget proposed a theory of infant and child development (see Chapter 9, "Human Development"). According to Piaget's theory, cognitive development occurs in a fixed series of "stages," from birth to adolescence. From a scientific standpoint, this theory was good because it led to a number of hypotheses. These hypotheses concerned the specific kinds of behaviors that should be observed at each stage of development. In the decades since its proposal, the theory has generated thousands of scientific papers. Our understanding of child development

---

FIGURE 2.3 The Scientific Method in Action

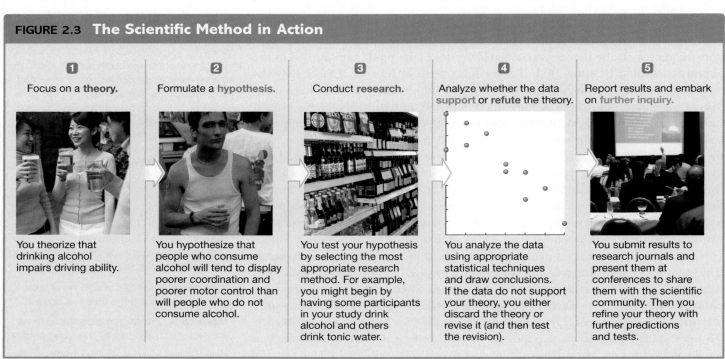

1 Focus on a **theory.**

You theorize that drinking alcohol impairs driving ability.

2 Formulate a **hypothesis.**

You hypothesize that people who consume alcohol will tend to display poorer coordination and poorer motor control than will people who do not consume alcohol.

3 Conduct **research.**

You test your hypothesis by selecting the most appropriate research method. For example, you might begin by having some participants in your study drink alcohol and others drink tonic water.

4 Analyze whether the data **support** or **refute** the theory.

You analyze the data using appropriate statistical techniques and draw conclusions. If the data do not support your theory, you either discard the theory or revise it (and then test the revision).

5 Report results and embark on **further inquiry.**

You submit results to research journals and present them at conferences to share them with the scientific community. Then you refine your theory with further predictions and tests.

has been enhanced both by studies that supported Piaget's stage theory and by those that failed to support it.

In contrast, Piaget's contemporary Sigmund Freud, in his famous treatise *The Interpretation of Dreams,* outlined the theory that all dreams represent the fulfillment of an unconscious wish. From a scientific perspective, Freud's theory was not good, because it generated few testable hypotheses regarding the actual function of dreams. Researchers were left with no way to evaluate whether the wish fulfillment theory was either reasonable or accurate. After all, unconscious wishes are, by definition, not known to anyone, including the person having the dreams. Indeed, on being presented with a patient's dream that clearly contained no hint of wish fulfillment, Freud went so far as to claim that the dreamer's unconscious wish was to prove his theory wrong!

Unexpected Findings Can Be Valuable

Research does not always proceed in a neat and orderly fashion. On the contrary, many significant findings are the result of *serendipity.* In its general sense, serendipity means unexpectedly finding things that are valuable or agreeable. In science, it means unexpectedly discovering something important.

For example, in the late 1950s, the physiologists Torsten Wiesel and David Hubel recorded the activity of nerve cells in cats' brains. Specifically, they were measuring the activity of cells in brain areas associated with vision. Wiesel and Hubel were studying how information travels from the eye to the brain (a process explored extensively in Chapter 4, "Sensation and Perception"). They had hypothesized that certain cells in the visual portion of the brain would respond when the cats looked at dots. To test that hypothesis, they showed slides of dot patterns to the cats. After much disappointing work that produced no significant activity in the brain cells being observed, the projector suddenly jammed between slides. The cells in question began to fire at an astonishing rate! What had caused this firing? Wiesel and Hubel realized that the jammed slide had produced a visual "edge" on the screen. Because of this little accident, they discovered that the cells do not respond to simple dots. Wiesel and Hubel eventually received a Nobel Prize for the serendipitous finding that these brain cells respond to lines and edges. Although their discovery is an example of serendipity, these researchers were not just lucky. They did not stumble onto a groundbreaking discovery that led straight to a Nobel Prize. Rather, they followed up on their unexpected finding. After a lifetime of hard work, they understood the implications of the rapid firing of brain cells in response to straight lines but not to other types of visual stimuli.

Summing Up

What Is Scientific Inquiry?

Our subjective beliefs, such as intuitions, can be useful in suggesting research questions. They are often biased, however, or based on limited information. To explain behavior, researchers use the scientific method. That is, researchers use objective, systematic procedures to measure behavior. The empirical process is based on the use of theories to generate hypotheses that can be tested by collecting objective data through research. Theories, in turn, must be adjusted and refined as new findings confirm or disconfirm the hypotheses. Good theories will generate several testable hypotheses. Unexpected findings can suggest new theories.

1. How are theories, hypotheses, and research different?
   a. Theories ask questions about possible causes of thoughts, emotions, and behaviors; hypotheses provide the empirical answers; and research is used to examine whether theories are correct.
   b. Theories are broad conceptual frameworks; hypotheses are derived from theories and are used to design research that will support or fail to support a theory; and research is a test of the hypotheses.
   c. Theories are assumed to be true; hypotheses need to be tested with appropriate experiments; and research is the final step.
   d. Theories do not require data for their verification because they are abstract; hypotheses depend on experimental findings; and research uses human participants to test theories and hypotheses.

2. How does psychological research differ from relying on personal experience or intuition as a way of understanding thoughts, emotions, and behaviors?
   a. Personal experience is the most objective method for understanding thoughts, emotions, and behaviors.
   b. Carefully designed research is the most objective method for understanding thoughts, emotions, and behaviors.
   c. Research provides theoretical answers that are best verified through individual experience.

Answers: 1. b. Theories are broad conceptual frameworks; hypotheses are derived from theories and are used to design research that will support or fail to support a theory; and research is a test of the hypotheses. 2. b. Carefully designed research is the most objective method for understanding thoughts, emotions, and behaviors.

2.2 What Types of Studies Are Used in Psychological Research?

Once a researcher has defined a hypothesis, the next issue to be addressed is the type of study design to be used. There are three main types of designs: *descriptive, correlational,* and *experimental.* These designs differ in the extent to which the researcher has control over the variables in the study. The amount of control over the variables, in turn, determines the type of conclusions the researcher can draw from the data.

All research involves variables. A **variable** is something in the world that can vary and that the researcher can measure. The term can refer to something that the researcher manipulates, something the researcher measures, or both. For instance, some of the variables you might use in your study of alcohol and driving would be: amount of alcohol consumed, level of intoxication, coordination, motor control, and balance.

Researchers must define variables precisely and in ways that reflect the methods used to assess them. They do this by using *operational definitions.* This phrase might seem intimidating, but it simply means identifying variables and *quantifying* them so they can be measured. In other words, each variable is specified in a way that makes it possible to record its *quantity.* For example, if you choose to study how coordination is affected by alcohol, how will you quantify "coordination" so you can judge whether it is affected by alcohol? One option might be to measure how easily people can touch their fingers to their noses with their eyes

variable Something in the world that can vary and that a researcher can measure.

closed. In this case, the operational definition could be the number of inches by which people miss their noses. The concrete definition would help other scientists know precisely what you measured. That knowledge would make it possible for them to replicate your research.

Descriptive Studies Involve Observing and Classifying Behavior

Descriptive studies are sometimes called *observational studies*. They involve observing and noting behavior to analyze that behavior objectively (**Figure 2.4**). For instance, an observer might take notes on the types of foods that people eat in cafeterias, measure the time that people spend talking during an average conversation, count the number and types of mating behaviors that penguins engage in during their mating season, or tally the number of times poverty or mental illness is mentioned during a presidential debate. Some researchers observe behavior at regular time intervals. These intervals span durations from as short as seconds to as long as entire lifetimes and across generations. In this manner, the researchers can keep track of what research participants do at particular points in time. They can study behaviors that may take years to unfold, as in tracking the job histories of college graduates.

There are two basic types of descriptive studies. In **naturalistic observation,** the observer remains separated from the situation and makes no attempt to change it. By contrast, in **participant observation,** the researcher is involved in the situation. An example of the latter was conducted by social psychologists who joined a doomsday cult to see how the cult members would respond when the world did not end on the date that was predicted by the cult. (The members made sense of this nonevent by deciding that their faith saved the world; Festinger, Riecken, & Schachter, 1956.) One possible problem with participant observation is that the observer might lose objectivity. Another is that the participants might change

descriptive studies A research method that involves observing and noting the behavior of people or other animals to provide a systematic and objective analysis of the behavior.

naturalistic observation A type of descriptive study in which the researcher is a passive observer, making no attempt to change or alter ongoing behavior.

participant observation A type of descriptive study in which the researcher is actively involved in the situation.

Descriptive studies involve observing and classifying behavior, either with no intervention by the observer (naturalistic observation) or with intervention by the observer (participant observation).

Advantages	Especially valuable in the early stages of research, when trying to determine whether a phenomenon exists. Takes place in a real-world setting.
Disadvantages	Errors in observation can occur because of an observer's expectations (observer bias). Observer's presence can change the behavior being witnessed (reactivity).

Naturalistic observation

Participant observation

FIGURE 2.4 Descriptive Studies (left) Employing naturalistic observation, the primatologist Jane Goodall observes a family of chimpanzees. Animals are more likely to act naturally in their native habitats than in captivity. **(right)** The evolutionary psychologist and human behavioral ecologist Lawrence Sugiyama has conducted fieldwork in Ecuadorian Amazonia among the Shiwiar, Achuar, Shuar, and Zaparo peoples. Here, hunting with a bow and arrow, he is conducting a particularly active form of participant observation.

Longitudinal studies involve observing and classifying developmental changes that occur in the same people over time, either with no intervention by the observer or with intervention by the observer.

Advantages Provide information about the effects of age on the same people, allowing researchers to see developmental changes.

Disadvantages Expensive, take a long time, and may lose participants over time.

FIGURE 2.5 Longitudinal Studies The *Up* series of documentary films is an ongoing longitudinal study that since 1964 has traced the development of 14 British people from various socioeconomic backgrounds. New material has been collected every seven years, starting when the participants were 7 years old. Here, three participants—Jackie, Sue, and Lynn—are pictured from the latest film, *49 Up*.

longitudinal studies A research method that studies the same participants multiple times over a period of time.

cross-sectional studies A research method that compares participants in different groups (e.g., young and old) at the same time.

observer bias Systematic errors in observation that occur because of an observer's expectations.

their behavior if they know they are being observed. You can imagine how bar patrons would respond if researchers entered the bar and announced they were studying the behavior of people who go to bars to meet potential dates. Such an announcement would interfere with the normal interactions that occur in bars. It might even eliminate those interactions. Thus observers need to keep their objectivity and minimize their impact on a situation.

Descriptive techniques are especially valuable in the early stages of research. At that point, researchers are trying to see whether a phenomenon exists. They can learn a great deal about behavior by just watching and taking careful notes. Even the simplest observations can prove valuable. Imagine you are observing seating patterns during lunch at two high schools. You find that at one school the lunch tables are racially segregated but at the other school students sit in mixed-race groups. With this finding, you have learned something valuable about racial behaviors at these two schools. You would need different types of research designs to understand what causes student groups to be segregated or integrated, but description would have proved a good first step in documenting this phenomenon.

Researchers sometimes design studies to examine developmental changes that occur over time. Sometimes the researchers want to watch changes unfold naturally, as in a descriptive design. Other times they want to see how different interventions affect future development. **Longitudinal studies** are one type of developmental design (**Figure 2.5**). If you wanted to know how intellectual abilities change over the adult years, you could begin by assessing the abilities of a group of young adults. You would then reassess the same participants every five years, as they progressed toward old age. Alternatively, you could assess the intellectual abilities of young adults and old adults and compare their scores on various measures of intellectual ability. Research designs of this type, comparing different groups to make inferences about both, are known as **cross-sectional studies** (**Figure 2.6**).

Like all research design choices, each of these methods has advantages and disadvantages. Longitudinal designs provide information about the effects of age on the same people, but they are expensive, they take a long time, and they can be jeopardized when (not if) some participants drop out of the experiment over time. By contrast, cross-sectional designs are faster and less expensive, but they include the possibility that some unidentified variable is responsible for any difference between the groups. In the example just given, the older people might not have received the same amount or type of education as the younger people, or differences between the age groups might be due to changes in societal norms. This potential difference is known as a *cohort effect*.

OBSERVER BIAS In conducting observational research, scientists must guard against **observer bias.** This flaw consists of systematic errors in observation that occur because of an observer's expectations. Observer bias can especially be a problem if cultural norms favor inhibiting or expressing certain behaviors. For instance, in many societies women are freer to express sadness than men are. If observers are coding men's and women's facial expressions, they may be more likely to rate female expressions as indicating sadness because they believe that men are less likely to show sadness. Men's expressions of sadness might be rated as annoyance or some other emotion. Likewise, in many societies women are generally expected to be less assertive than men. Observers therefore might rate women as more assertive when exhibiting the same behavior as men. Cultural norms can affect both the participants' actions and the way observers perceive those actions.

There is evidence that observer expectations can even change the behavior being observed. This phenomenon is known as the **experimenter expectancy effect.** In a classic study conducted in the 1960s by the social psychologist Robert Rosenthal, college students trained rats to run a maze (Rosenthal & Fode, 1963). Half the students were told their rats were bred to be very good at running mazes. The other half were told their rats were bred to be poor performers. In reality, there were no genetic differences between the groups of rats. Nonetheless, when students believed they were training rats that were bred to be fast maze learners, their rats learned the task more quickly! Thus these students' expectations altered how they treated their rats. This treatment in turn influenced the speed at which the rats learned. The students were not aware of their biased treatment, but it existed. Perhaps they supplied extra food when the rats reached the goal box. Or perhaps they gave the rats inadvertent cues as to which way to turn in the maze. They might simply have stroked the rats more often. This study exemplifies the idea that some aspects of our own behavior are not under our conscious control. We are not always aware of the many factors that affect how we think, feel, and act (**Figure 2.7**).

*As discussed extensively in this chapter, different types of research methods play important roles in the stories of psychological science. In each chapter of the book, **Scientific Method** features will lead you through the steps of some of the most interesting experiments and studies discussed in the text.*

FIGURE 2.7   Scientific Method: Rosenthal's Study of Observer Bias

Hypothesis: Research participants' behavior will be affected by experimenters' biases.

Research Method:

1 One group of college students was given a group of rats and told to train them to run a maze. These students were told their rats were bred to be very poor at running mazes.

2 A second group of college students was given a group of rats to train that were genetically the same as the first group of rats. These students were told their rats were bred to be very good at running mazes.

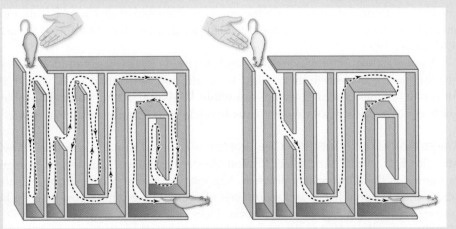

Results: The rats trained by the students who believed their rats were bred to be fast maze learners did learn the task more quickly.

Conclusion: The results for the two groups of rats differed because the students' expectations caused them to give off subtle cues that changed the rats' behavior.

Source: Rosenthal, R., & Fode, K. L. (1963). The effect of experimenter bias on the performance of the albino rat. *Behavioral Science, 8*, 183–189.

Cross-sectional studies involve observing and classifying developmental changes that occur in different groups of people at the same time.

Advantages Faster and less expensive than longitudinal studies.

Disadvantages Unidentified variables may be involved (cohort effect).

FIGURE 2.6 Cross-Sectional Studies
Together, the young adults on the top and the older adults on the bottom might participate in a cross-sectional study.

experimenter expectancy effect Actual change in the behavior of the people or nonhuman animals being observed that is due to the expectations of the observer.

FIGURE 2.8 Correlational Studies There may be a correlation between the extent to which parents are overweight and the extent to which their children are overweight. A correlational study cannot demonstrate the cause of this relationship, which may include biological propensities to gain weight, lack of exercise, and high-fat diets.

correlational studies A research method that examines how variables are naturally related in the real world, without any attempt by the researcher to alter them or assign causation between them.

directionality problem A problem encountered in correlational studies; the researchers find a relationship between two variables, but they cannot determine which variable may have caused changes in the other variable.

How do researchers protect against experimenter expectancy effects? It is best if the person running the study is *blind* to, or unaware of, the study's hypotheses. For example, the study just described seemed to be about rats' speed in learning to run through a maze. Instead, it was designed to study experimenter expectancy effects. The students believed they were "experimenters" in the study, but they were actually the participants. Their work with the rats was the subject of the study, not the method. Thus the students were led to expect certain results so that the researchers could determine whether the students' expectations affected the results of the rats' training. For these reasons, the researchers would not have told the person running the test (i.e., the true experimenter) that all the rats in the study were more or less the same genetically. That way, the person did not have knowledge that might have influenced the behavior of the students.

Correlational Studies Examine How Variables Are Related

There is a rather unfortunate twist to the case discussed at the opening of this chapter. According to news reports, Andrew Kelly reeked of booze at the scene of the fatal accident. He refused a Breathalyzer test. The off-duty cop in the SUV with him and the cop who arrived on the scene gave him chewing gum and water. By the time he underwent a blood alcohol test, seven hours later, Kelly's body was alcohol free. This drunk driver seems to have understood very well the connection between his physiological state and his actions behind the wheel. He understood the connection well enough to try to hide it.

Other drunk drivers do not have Kelly's options, however, so records exist of their physiological states. To study the effects of alcohol intoxication on behavior, you might sift through police records of alcohol-related accidents. Your goal would be to match the reported intoxication levels of drunk drivers with some measure of their driving performance, such as the severity of the drivers' accidents. Research of this kind consists of **correlational studies.** These studies examine how variables are naturally related in the real world, without any attempt by the researcher to alter them or assign causation between them (**Figure 2.8**). For example, researchers have established a correlation between the amount of alcohol available in a community and the likeliness of late-night, single-vehicle accidents in that community (Gruenewald et al., 1996).

Your data on intoxication levels and driving performance would enable you to compare how intoxication *might* have affected performance. It would not, however, enable you to show the causation. Why not? A few potential problems prevent researchers from drawing causal conclusions from correlational studies.

DIRECTIONALITY PROBLEM One problem with correlational studies is in knowing the direction of the cause/effect relation between variables. This sort of ambiguity is known as the **directionality problem.** Suppose you survey a large group of people about their sleeping habits and their levels of stress. Those who report sleeping little also report having a higher level of stress. Does lack of sleep increase stress levels, or does increased stress lead to shorter and worse sleep? Both scenarios seem plausible:

The Directionality Problem

Sleep (A) and stress (B) are correlated.

- Does less sleep cause more stress? (A → B)

or

- Does more stress cause less sleep? (B → A)

THIRD VARIABLE PROBLEM Another drawback with all correlational studies is the **third variable problem.** Instead of variable A causing variable B, as a researcher might assume, it is possible that a third variable, C, causes both A and B. Consider the relationship between drinking and driving. It is possible that people who are really stressed in their daily lives are more likely to drink before driving. It is also possible that they are likely to be distracted while driving. Thus the cause of both drinking and bad driving is the third variable, stress:

third variable problem A problem that occurs when the researcher cannot directly manipulate variables; as a result, the researcher cannot be confident that another, unmeasured variable is not the actual cause of differences in the variables of interest.

The Third Variable Problem

Drinking before driving (A) is correlated with being distracted while driving (B).

• Stress (C) causes some people to drink before driving. (C → A)

and

• Stress (C) causes some people to be distracted while driving. (C → B)

Sometimes the third variable is obvious. Suppose you were told that the more churches there are in a town, the greater the rate of crime. Would you conclude that churches cause crime? In looking for a third variable, you would realize that the population size of the town affects the number of churches and the frequency of crime. But sometimes third variables are not so obvious and may not even be identifiable. For instance, we have all heard that smoking causes cancer. Is the connection that simple for everyone? Evidence indicates that a particular gene predisposes some smokers to develop lung cancer (Paz-Elizur et al., 2003). In addition, a genetic predisposition—a built-in vulnerability to smoking—combines with environmental factors to increase the probability that some people will smoke *and* that they will develop lung cancer (Thorgeirsson et al., 2008). This connection is one of the countless ways that nature and nurture work together inseparably.

Sometimes, however, people mistakenly believe there is a causal relationship between two variables when there is a correlation. Suppose the newspaper reports that children who attend preschool are better readers in first grade than those who do not. It is tempting to conclude that children are better readers in first grade *because* they learned prereading skills in preschool. This explanation of the data might be true. Another explanation might also be true: Children who attend preschool have parents who are concerned with their academic success. Such parents probably read to their children and monitor their schoolwork more than parents who are less concerned with academic success.

ETHICAL REASONS FOR USING CORRELATIONAL DESIGNS Despite such potentially serious problems, correlational studies are widely used in psychological science. Some research questions require correlational research designs for ethical reasons. For example, suppose you want to know if soldiers who experience severe trauma during combat have more difficulty learning new tasks after they return home than soldiers who have experienced less-severe trauma during combat. Even if you theorize that severely traumatic combat experiences *cause* later problems with learning, it would be unethical to induce trauma in some soldiers so that you could compare soldiers who had experienced different degrees of trauma. (Likewise, most research on psychopathology uses the correlational method, because it is unethical to induce mental disorders in people to study the effects.) For this research question, you would need to study the soldiers' ability to learn a new task after they had returned home. You might, for example, observe soldiers who were attempting to learn computer programming. The participants in your study would have to include some soldiers who had experienced severe trauma during combat and some who had experienced less-severe trauma during combat. You would want to see which group, on average, performed less well when learning the task.

MAKING PREDICTIONS Correlational studies can be used to determine that two variables are associated with each other. In the example just discussed, the variables would be trauma during combat and learning difficulties later in life. By establishing such connections, researchers are able to make predictions. If you found the association you expected between severe trauma during combat and learning difficulties, you could predict that soldiers who experience severe trauma during combat will—again, on average—have more difficulty learning new tasks when they return than soldiers who do not experience severe trauma during combat. Because your study drew on but did not control the soldiers' wartime experiences, however, you have not established a causal connection.

By providing important information about the natural relationships between variables, researchers are able to make valuable predictions. For example, correlational research has identified a strong relationship between depression and suicide. For this reason, clinical psychologists often assess symptoms of depression to determine suicide risk. Typically, researchers who use the correlational method use other statistical procedures to rule out potential third variables and problems with the direction of the effect. Once they have shown that a relationship between two variables holds even when potential third variables are taken into account, researchers can be more confident that the relationship is meaningful.

An Experiment Involves Manipulating Conditions

In experimental research, the investigator has maximal control over the situation. An **experiment** is a study in which the researcher manipulates one variable to examine that variable's effect on a second variable. In studying how alcohol intoxication affects people's ability to drive, you could manipulate the extent to which participants were intoxicated and then measure their driving performance using a driving simulator. You might also incorporate a **control group** (a comparison group). This group might consist of participants who did not consume alcohol or participants who drank tonic water instead of alcohol. This way, you could compare two or more **experimental groups** (treatment groups) with the control condition. In this example, one experimental group might consist of participants who had just reached the legal measure of intoxication. Another group might consist of participants whose blood alcohol levels were double the legal measure of intoxication (**Table 2.1**). Two experimental groups and one control group is just one possible research design for this question. The variable that is manipulated (the amount of intoxication) is the **independent variable.** The variable that is measured (driving performance) is the **dependent variable.**

The benefit of an experiment is that the researcher can study the causal relationship between the two variables. If the independent variable (such as intoxication state) consistently influences the dependent variable (such as driving performance), then the independent variable is assumed to cause the change in the dependent variable.

ESTABLISHING CAUSALITY A properly performed experiment depends on rigorous control. Here *control* means the steps taken by the researcher to minimize the possibility that anything other than the independent variable will affect the experiment's outcome. A **confound** is anything that affects a dependent variable and that may unintentionally vary between the study's different experimental

experiment A study that tests causal hypotheses by measuring and manipulating variables.

control group A comparison group; the participants in a study that receive no intervention or receive an intervention that is unrelated to the independent variable being investigated.

experimental groups Treatment groups; the participants in a study that receive the intervention.

independent variable In an experiment, the variable that is manipulated by the experimenter to examine its impact on the dependent variable.

dependent variable In an experiment, the variable that is affected by the manipulation of the independent variable.

confound Anything that affects a dependent variable and may unintentionally vary between the experimental conditions of a study.

TABLE 2.1 Blood Alcohol Content and Its Effects

In the United States, blood alcohol content is measured by taking a sample of a person's breath or blood and determining the amount of alcohol in that sample. The result is then converted to a percentage. For example, in many states the legal limit is .08 percent. To reach this level, a person's bloodstream needs to have 8 grams of alcohol for every 100 milliliters of blood.

Different blood alcohol levels produce different physical and mental effects. These effects also vary from person to person. This table shows typical effects.

BAC Level	Effects
.01–.06	Feeling of relaxation Sense of well-being Thought, judgment, and coordination are impaired.
.06–.10	Loss of inhibitions Extroversion Reflexes, depth perception, peripheral vision, and reasoning are impaired.
.11–.20	Emotional swings Sense of sadness or anger Reaction time and speech are impaired.
.21–.29	Stupor Blackouts Motor skills are impaired.
.30–.39	Severe depression Unconsciousness Breathing and heart rate are impaired.
>.40	Breathing and heart rate are impaired. Death is possible.

SOURCE: BloodAlcoholContent.Org (2007–2010).

conditions. When conducting an experiment, a researcher needs to ensure that the only thing that varies is the independent variable. Control thus represents the foundation of the experimental approach, in that it allows the researcher to rule out alternative explanations for the observed data (**Figure 2.9**). For example, in

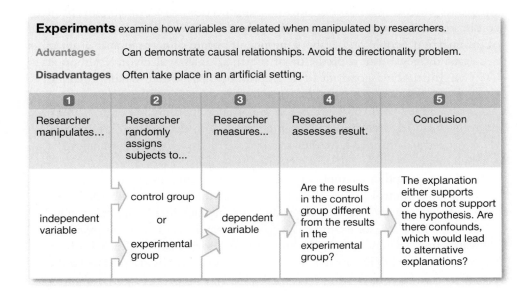

Experiments examine how variables are related when manipulated by researchers.

Advantages Can demonstrate causal relationships. Avoid the directionality problem.

Disadvantages Often take place in an artificial setting.

1 Researcher manipulates...	2 Researcher randomly assigns subjects to...	3 Researcher measures...	4 Researcher assesses result.	5 Conclusion
independent variable	control group or experimental group	dependent variable	Are the results in the control group different from the results in the experimental group?	The explanation either supports or does not support the hypothesis. Are there confounds, which would lead to alternative explanations?

FIGURE 2.9 Experiments

Identifying the Need for Control Groups

The two critical thinking skills for this chapter—identifying the need for control groups and recognizing that large samples provide more reliable data than small samples (see p. 46)—are essentially applications of research methods to everyday life. The idea that the principles of research methods can inform critical thinking was expressed by George (Pinky) Nelson, a leading U.S. astronaut who is deeply concerned with enhancing the critical thinking abilities of students as a way of preparing them for their future in the information age. Nelson said:

> Most people seem to believe that there is a difference between scientific thinking and everyday thinking. Clearly, most people haven't developed the capacity to think [scientifically]. Otherwise, they wouldn't buy lottery tickets that they can't afford. They wouldn't consistently fall for cheap promises and easy answers from politicians. They wouldn't become victims of medical quackery or misinformation from tobacco companies. They wouldn't keep employing the same failed strategies, both in their personal lives and in society at large, just because that's what they've always done.... But, the fact is, these same scientific thinking skills can be used to improve the chances of success in virtually any endeavor. (1998, April 29, p. A 14)

When designing an experiment, a researcher needs to include a control group that does not receive the treatment or experience being investigated. It is usually easy to recognize the need for such a comparison when planning a research project. It can be difficult to spot the need for control groups, however, when thinking about the many research results that we are bombarded with in newspapers, on the Web, in everyday conversation, and in advertisements.

Suppose you read in the newspaper that 75 percent of couples who are going through a divorce argue about money. You might conclude that disputes about money are a major cause of divorce. You might even conclude that more marriages would be saved if couples learned how to handle financial disputes. Missing from this analysis is a comparison figure for couples who do not divorce. Suppose you learn that 80 percent of those couples argue about money. Such a result would mean that almost all married people argue about money. It would also mean that arguing about money is not a predictor of which couples will divorce. Although it might still be a good idea for couples to learn how to handle financial disputes, nothing in these data supports the conclusion that money woes cause couples to divorce. You need to consider appropriate control groups to evaluate research findings meaningfully. When the controls are missing, you need to consider how they might have altered your understanding of the research.

Here is another example that requires critical thinking to recognize the need for a control group. Parents of young children are bombarded with advertisements for educational products to enhance their children's intelligence. There are, for example, special (and expensive) DVDs for infants to watch immediately after birth. Suppose you learn that toddlers who have watched these DVDs are able to talk in two- and three-word phrases by the time they are 18 months old. You might infer that the toddlers are communicating at such a young age because of the DVDs. However, you are missing data about toddlers who do not watch this material. At what age do they talk in two- and three-word phrases? In fact, studies show that the age at which toddlers begin talking does not depend on the use of specific learning programs. The National Academy of Pediatricians recommends that toddlers younger than 2 watch *no* DVDs, videos, or television. Without a control group, it would not be possible for you—as a researcher, concerned citizen, or parent—to know if particular programs had an effect on children's language development or any aspect of development.

your hypothetical study of alcohol and driving performance, what if a car with an automatic transmission is simulated to assess driving when participants are sober, but a car with a manual transmission is simulated to assess performance when participants are intoxicated? Given that manual transmissions require greater dexterity to operate than automatic transmissions, any apparent effect of intoxication on driving performance might actually be caused by the type of car. In this example, the drivers' skills might be *confounded* with the type of transmission, making it impossible to determine the true effect of the alcohol.

Other potential confounds include changes in the sensitivity of the measuring instruments, such as a systematic change in a scale so that it weighs things more heavily in one condition than in another. Changes in the time of day or the season when the experiment is conducted can also confound the results. The more confounds and thus alternative explanations that can be eliminated, the more confident a researcher can be that the change in the independent variable is causing the change (or effect) in the dependent variable. For this reason, researchers have to watch vigilantly for potential confounds. As consumers of research, we all need to think about confounds that could be causing particular results.

Random Sampling and Random Assignment Are Important for Research

An important issue for any research method is how to select participants for the study. Psychologists typically want to know that their findings *generalize,* or apply, to people beyond the individuals in the study. In studying the effects of alcohol on motor skills and coordination, you ultimately would not focus on the behavior of the specific participants. Instead, you would seek to discover general laws about human behavior. If your results generalized to all people, they would enable you, other psychologists, and the rest of humanity to predict, in general, how intoxication would affect driving performance. Other results, depending on the nature of the study, might generalize to all college students, to students who belong to sororities and fraternities, to women, to men over the age of 45, and so on.

The group you want to know about is the **population.** To learn about the population, you study a subset from it. That subset, the people you actually study, is the **sample.** *Sampling* is the process by which you select people from the population to be in the sample. The sample should represent the population, and the best method for making this happen is *random sampling.* This method gives each member of the population an equal chance of being chosen to participate.

population Everyone in the group the experimenter is interested in.

sample A subset of a population.

Most of the time, a researcher will use a *convenience sample*. As the term implies, this sample consists of people who are conveniently available for the study. Even if you wanted your results to generalize to all students in your country or in the world, you would, realistically, probably use a sample from your own college or university and hope that this sample represented all students in your country and beyond. It is important for researchers to assess how well their results generalize to other samples (Henrich, Heine, & Norenzayan, 2010). For many topics studied in psychology—for example, sex differences in some mating preferences (discussed in Chapter 10) and the structure of personality (in Chapter 13)—the findings appear highly similar regardless of the sample studied. For many other topics studied—for example, the Mueller-Lyer illusion (in Chapter 4) and the self-concept (in Chapter 13)—the results obtained from samples of North American university students do not apply to other populations. Indeed, they often look quite different from population to population.

Even with random sampling, one likely confound in a study is preexisting differences between groups that are assigned to different conditions. For example, in your study of drinking and driving, what happens to the results if the people assigned to have many drinks just happen to be heavier drinkers and therefore are less affected by alcohol? Some heavy drinkers develop such a tolerance to alcohol that they show few outward signs of intoxication even when they have blood alcohol levels that would knock out or even kill a typical person (Chesher & Greeley, 1992; tolerance to drugs such as alcohol, especially tolerance as a component of addiction, is discussed in Chapter 5, "Consciousness"). Alternatively, some participants might become intoxicated on very small amounts of alcohol. Unless you have assigned participants randomly to the various conditions, the possibility always exists that any difference you find derives from preexisting differences between the groups. Research design often involves a series of choices: It means balancing the problems of taking people as they come with the problems of creating an artificial environment for the experiment. In fact, although experiments allow us to infer cause, they are often criticized for being artificial. In real life, for example, people decide for themselves how much alcohol they can drink and still drive safely. Assigning different levels of impairment may be so artificial that you end up studying something you had not intended, such as how people react when they are told how many drinks they can have. If the experiment creates a greatly artificial situation, the experiment is said to be low in **external validity.** This term refers to the degree to which the findings of an experiment can be generalized outside the laboratory. (*Internal validity* is discussed later in this chapter.)

SELECTION BIAS When the groups are not equivalent because participants in different groups differ in unexpected ways, the condition is known as **selection bias.** Suppose you have two of the experimental conditions described earlier: a group assigned to drink tonic water and a group assigned to reach a blood alcohol level twice the legal definition of intoxication. What happens if the group assigned to drink tonic water includes many small-bodied young women with little drinking experience and the other group includes many overweight older men with strong tolerances for alcohol? How would you know if the people in the different conditions of the study are equivalent? You could match each group for age, sex, weight, drinking habits, and so on, but you can never be sure that you have assessed all possible factors that may differ between the groups.

external validity The degree to which the findings of an experiment can be generalized outside the laboratory.

selection bias In an experiment, unintended differences between the participants in different groups.

RANDOM ASSIGNMENT The only way to make it more likely that the groups are equivalent is to use **random assignment.** This method gives each potential research participant an equal chance of being assigned to any level of the independent variable. For your study, there might be three levels: drinking tonic water, reaching the blood alcohol level that is the legal definition of intoxication, and reaching the blood alcohol level that is double the legal definition of intoxication. First, you would gather participants by taking either a random sample or a convenience sample from the population. Then, to randomly assign those participants, you might have them draw numbers from a hat to determine who was assigned to the control group (tonic water) and to each experimental group (legal definition of intoxication and double the legal definition). Of course, individual differences are bound to exist among participants. For example, any of your groups might include some people with low tolerance for alcohol and some people with high tolerance, some people with excellent coordination and some people with comparably poor coordination. But these differences will tend to average out when participants are assigned to either the control or experimental groups randomly, so that the groups are equivalent *on average*. Random assignment balances out known and unknown factors (**Figure 2.10**).

random assignment Placing research participants into the conditions of an experiment in such a way that each participant has an equal chance of being assigned to any level of the independent variable.

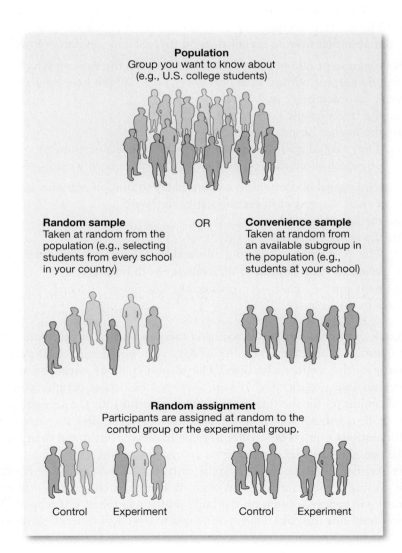

Population
Group you want to know about
(e.g., U.S. college students)

Random sample
Taken at random from the population (e.g., selecting students from every school in your country)

OR

Convenience sample
Taken at random from an available subgroup in the population (e.g., students at your school)

Random assignment
Participants are assigned at random to the control group or the experimental group.

Control　　Experiment　　　　　　Control　　Experiment

FIGURE 2.10 Sampling For the results of an experiment to be considered useful, the participants should be representative of the population. The best method for making this happen is random sampling, but most of the time researchers are forced to use a convenience sample. Random assignment is used when the experimenter wants to test a *causal* hypothesis.

Recognizing That Large Samples Generate More Reliable Results Than Small Samples

Given a thimbleful of facts, we rush to make generalizations as large as a tub.
— Gordon Allport (1954, p. 8)

A general critical thinking skill related to sampling from populations is considering the size of the sample, or the number of participants in the study. As consumers of research, we need to understand which studies provide strong evidence and which are poor science. The number of participants in a sample is one critical difference between the two types of studies. The importance of sample size can be difficult to understand when you think about it one way, but it can be easy to understand when you think about it a different way. First, read the following information and answer the questions:

A certain town is served by two hospitals. In the larger hospital, about 45 babies are born each day, and in the smaller hospital, about 15 babies are born each day. As you know, about 50 percent of all babies are boys. The exact percentage of baby boys, however, varies from day to day. Sometimes it may be higher than 50 percent and sometimes lower.

1. For a period of one year, each hospital recorded the days on which more than 60 percent of the babies born were boys. Which hospital do you think recorded more such days?
   a. the larger hospital
   b. the smaller hospital
   c. They would each record approximately the same number of days on which more than 60 percent of the babies born were boys.

2. Which hospital do you think is more likely to find on any one day that more than 60 percent of babies born were boys?
   a. the larger hospital
   b. the smaller hospital
   c. The probability of having more than 60 percent of babies born being boys on any day is the same for both hospitals.

(Sedlmeier & Gigerenzer, 1997, p. 34; original problem posed by Kahneman & Tversky, 1972)

Look carefully at both questions and the way you answered them. The first question is about the number of days you would expect 60 percent or more of the births to be boys. The second is about what you would expect on one specific day. If you answered like most people, you selected option (c) for the first question and option (b) for the second question. Both questions are about sample sizes, however, and the answer to both questions is (b). The smaller hospital has fewer births and therefore a smaller sample size, and small samples are more variable.

It may help to think about a similar situation that you are more familiar with: tossing a coin. Suppose you want to know if a coin is fair—that is, if heads will appear as often on the "up" side as tails when it is flipped. To demonstrate that the coin is fair, you would toss it a few times to show that heads and tails each come up about half the time. Suppose you flip it 4 times. Might you get 3 heads and 1 tail in 4 flips of a fair coin when there is an equal chance of getting a head or tail on each flip? It is not hard to see how heads and tails might not appear equally if you flip a coin a few times. Now suppose you flip the same coin 100 times. You probably would not get exactly 50 heads and 50 tails, but just by chance you would get close to 50 for each. With only 4 flips, it is quite possible that 75 percent of the flips could be all heads or all tails just by chance. With 100 flips, that same 75 percent is very unlikely.

Can you see how this is the same problem as in the hospital scenario? The smaller hospital is more likely to have some days when the percentage of boys (or girls) is higher than 60 percent, even when the true number of girl and boy babies in the population is approximately equal. It is easier to understand this principle when thinking about any single day (question 2) than about the number of days (question 1), although the reasoning is the same. Variability is discussed in more detail later in this chapter, but for now, just remember that small samples are more variable than large samples.

The *law of large numbers* states that you get more accurate estimates of a population from a large sample than from a small one. To apply this law in an everyday context, suppose you are deciding which of two colleges to attend. To help make this decision, you spend one day at each college and attend one class at each. You like the professor you meet at one of the colleges much better than the professor you meet at the other. Should this small sample of classes and professors influence your decision about which college to attend? Can you see how results from such a small sample could be very misleading? In planning a research project, as in deciding how you feel about a place, you must consider the size of the sample you are generalizing from (**Figure 2.11**).

FIGURE 2.11 Large Samples or Small Samples? Suppose you want to compare how many women go to the beach versus how many men do. Why might your results be more accurate if you use a large sample (such as the big picture here) rather than a small sample (such as the detail)?

Summing Up

What Types of Studies Are Used in Psychological Research?

There are three main types of studies in psychological research: descriptive, correlational, and experimental. In descriptive and correlational designs, researchers examine behavior as it naturally occurs. These types of studies are useful for describing and predicting behavior, but they do not allow researchers to assess causality. Correlational designs have limitations, which include directionality problems (knowing whether variable A caused variable B or the reverse) and the third variable problem (the possibility that a third variable is responsible for variables A and B). In an experiment, a researcher manipulates the independent variable to study how it affects the dependent variable. An experiment enables a researcher to establish a causal relationship between the independent and dependent variables. It also enables the researcher to avoid the directionality problem when trying to understand how one variable might affect another. An experiment gives the researcher the greatest control, so that the only thing that changes is the independent variable. If the goal is to conclude that changes in one variable cause changes in another variable, the researcher must assign participants at random to different groups to make the groups as equal as possible (on average) on all variables except the one being studied. The researcher wants to know about a population. Because it is usually impossible for everyone in the population to be a research participant, the researcher uses a representative sample of the population and then generalizes the findings to the population. Random sampling, in which everyone in the population has an equal chance of being a research participant, is the best way to sample. Since this is usually not possible, most researchers use a convenience sample. Among the most important factors in whether the results from a particular sample can be generalized back to the population is sample size. In general, large samples provide more accurate results than small ones.

Measuring Up

1. The main reason researchers randomly assign participants to different groups in an experiment is that _____.
   a. it is easier to assign participants to different conditions than it is to find people who naturally fit into different conditions
   b. random assignment controls for any intuitions the participants may have at the start of the experiment
   c. random assignment is used when there are ethical reasons for not using observational or correlational research designs
   d. random assignment is the only way to ensure that the experimental groups are (on average) equal and that any difference in the dependent variable is due to the participants' being in different experimental groups

2. Match each of the main methods of conducting research with the advantages and disadvantages listed below. Write in "descriptive," "correlational," "experimental," "longitudinal," or "cross-sectional" next to its advantage or disadvantage.
   a. _____ Allows the researcher to conclude that one variable causes a change in another variable.
   b. _____ Allows for a detailed description in a real-world setting.
   c. _____ Allows the researcher to understand if two or more variables are related, without demonstrating a causal relationship.
   d. _____ Measures people of different ages to learn about developmental changes.
   e. _____ Data are most likely to be biased (reflect the thoughts and beliefs of the person collecting the data).
   f. _____ The same people are repeatedly measured over time to understand developmental changes.
   g. _____ The research conditions are most likely to be artificial (because this method is often used in a laboratory).
   h. _____ It is always possible that a third variable not considered by the researcher causes the results.

What Are the Data Collection Methods of Psychological Science?

Learning Objectives

- Distinguish between five methods of data collection.

- List the advantages and disadvantages of different methods of data collection.

- Discuss the use of animal models in psychological research.

- Identify ethical issues associated with psychological research.

Once the researcher has established the best design for a particular study, the next task is to choose a method for collecting the data. The researcher's ultimate goal for the study, of course, is to answer an empirical question by observing and measuring some aspects of the world. A fundamental principle of psychological research is that the question the researcher wants to answer dictates the appropriate method for doing the observing and the measuring. In short, you start with a theory, derive a hypothesis from your theory, and phrase your hypothesis in the form of a question. Then you ask yourself: What sort of data will best answer my question? What collection method will best provide that data?

Recall from Chapter 1 the four major research categories that span the levels of analysis: biological, individual, social, and cultural. The first step in selecting a data collection method is determining the level of analysis a particular question is addressing. The data collection method used in the study must be appropriate for questions at that level of analysis.

When the research question is aimed at the biological level of analysis, researchers measure things such as brain processes and changes in body chemistry. For instance, they might record how the brain responds when people look at pictures of scary faces, or they might compare whether people secrete more testosterone when their favorite team wins than when the team loses. At the individual level of analysis, researchers are looking for individual differences among participants' responses. To find those differences, researchers might question participants directly. They might also use indirect assessments, such as observing how quickly participants respond to a particular question or whether they accurately discriminate between stimuli. At the social level of analysis, researchers often collect data by observing people within a single culture and seeing how they interact. Most work at the cultural level of analysis compares groups of people from different cultures as a way of studying the effect of culture on some variable. For example, cross-cultural studies might examine beliefs about appropriate roles for women and men or attitudes toward pornography. The various methods for studying this latter topic might include attitudinal measures, such as noting cultural differences in defining pornography; behavioral measures, such as observing who buys pornographic materials in different countries; and archival measures, such as examining legislative summary documents that collect differences in the laws regarding pornography.

One difficulty in comparing people from different cultures is that some ideas and practices do not translate easily across cultures, just as some words do not translate easily into other languages. Apparent differences between cultures may reflect such differences in language, or they may reflect participants' relative willingness to report things about themselves publicly. A central challenge for cross-cultural researchers is to refine their measurements to rule out these kinds of alternative explanations (**Figure 2.12**).

Some psychological traits are the same across all cultures (e.g., care for the young). Others differ widely across cultures (e.g., behaviors

Cross-cultural studies compare groups of people from different cultures.

Advantages Examine the effect of culture on some variable of interest. In this way, they help make psychology more applicable around the world.

Disadvantages Some situations and some specific words do not convey the same meaning when translated across cultures. These cultural differences can leave room for alternate explanations (other than culture per se). For example, misunderstandings can occur during the research process.

FIGURE 2.12 Cross-Cultural Studies (top) The living space and treasured possessions of a family in Japan, for example, differ from **(bottom)** those of a family in Mali. Cross-cultural researchers might study how either family would react to crowding or to the loss of its possessions.

culturally sensitive research Studies that take into account the role that culture plays in determining thoughts, feelings, and actions.

observational techniques A research method of careful and systematic assessment and coding of overt behavior.

expected of adolescents). **Culturally sensitive research** takes into account the significant role that culture plays in how we think, feel, and act (Adair & Kagitcibasi, 1995; Zebian, Alamuddin, Mallouf, & Chatila, 2007). Scientists use culturally sensitive practices so that their research respects—and perhaps reflects—the "shared system of meaning" that each culture transmits from one generation to the next (Betancourt & Lopez, 1993, p. 630). In cities with diverse populations, such as Toronto, London, and Los Angeles, cultural differences exist among different groups of people living in the same neighborhoods and having close daily contact. Researchers therefore need to be sensitive to cultural differences even when they are studying people in the same neighborhood or the same school. Researchers must also guard against applying a psychological concept from one culture to another without considering whether the concept is the same in both cultures. For example, Japanese children's attachment to their parents looks quite different from the attachment styles common among North American children (Miyake, 1993).

Observing Is an Unobtrusive Strategy

Observational techniques (see Figure 2.4) involve the systematic assessment and coding of overt behavior. Coding involves determining what previously defined category the behavior fits into. For example, researchers might watch and note people's gestures during social interactions, or they might code the behavior of nonhuman animals that have been injected with drugs that affect brain function.

Using observational techniques to collect data requires researchers to make at least three decisions. First, should the study be conducted in the laboratory or in a natural environment? The answer to that question will depend on the behavior being studied. Must it occur as it would in the real world? Might the laboratory setting lead to artificial behavior? For example, suppose you hypothesize that people greet friends and family more effusively at airports than at train stations (perhaps because people think of air travel as more dangerous than rail travel, or perhaps because travelers tend to make longer trips by air and so are likely to have been apart longer from the people greeting them). To begin your study, you most likely would decide that it is very important for your participants to exhibit such behavior naturally. Therefore, you would observe the behavior at airport gates and train platforms. It would not make sense for you to re-create the experience of arrival and greeting in a laboratory.

Second, how should the data be collected? Observers can write descriptions of what they see, or they can keep running tallies of prespecified categories of behavior. For your study of arrival and greeting, you would need to operationally define different categories of effusive greetings. You might rate hugging and kissing as more effusive than hand shaking or head nodding. Then, while observing each episode of greeting at the airport gate or train platform, you could check off the appropriate category on a tally sheet. Researchers generally prefer preestablished categories as being more objective. However, badly chosen categories can lead observers to miss important behavior. For example, how would you classify the two-cheek air kiss, a more popular greeting in some countries than in others? The extent to which such a greeting is "effusive" depends on the cultural context. Likewise, a kiss on the mouth is a standard greeting between men in some parts of the world, but it suggests a romantic relationship in other parts of the world. Any greeting would need to be rated and interpreted in its cultural context.

Third, should the observer be visible? The concern here is that the presence of the observer might alter the behavior being observed. Such an alteration is called **reactivity.** People may feel compelled to make a positive impression on an observer, so they may act differently when they believe they are being observed. An example of this happened in a series of studies on workplace conditions and productivity. Specifically, the researchers manipulated working conditions and then observed workers' behavior at the Hawthorne Plant, a Western Electric manufacturing plant in Cicero, Illinois, between 1924 and 1933 (Olson, Hogan, & Santos, 2006; Roethlisberger & Dickson, 1939). The conditions included different levels of lighting, different pay incentives, and different break schedules. The main dependent variable was how long the workers took to complete certain tasks. Throughout the studies, the workers knew they were being observed. Because of this awareness, they responded to changes in their working conditions by increasing productivity. The workers did not speed up continuously throughout the various studies, however. Instead, they worked faster at the start of each new manipulation, regardless of the nature of the manipulation (longer break, shorter break, one of various changes to the pay system, and so on). The *Hawthorne effect* refers to changes in behavior that occur when people know that others are observing them (**Figure 2.13**).

How might the Hawthorne effect operate in other studies? Consider a study of the effectiveness of a new reading program in elementary schools. Say that the teachers know they have been selected to try out a new program. They also

reactivity When the knowledge that one is being observed alters the behavior being observed.

FIGURE 2.13   Scientific Method: The Hawthorne Effect

Hypothesis: Being observed can lead participants to change their behavior.

Research Method:

1 During studies of the effects of workplace conditions, the researchers manipulated several **independent variables,** such as the levels of lighting, pay incentives, and break schedules.

2 The researchers then measured the **dependent variable,** the speed at which workers did their jobs.

Results: The workers' productivity increased when they were being observed, regardless of the change to the independent variable.

Conclusion: Being observed can lead participants to change their behavior because people often act in particular ways to make positive impressions.

Source: Roethlisberger, F. J., & Dickson, W. J. (1939). *Management and the worker: An account of a research program conducted by the Western Electric Company, Hawthorne Works, Chicago.* Cambridge, MA: Harvard University Press.

case studies A research method that involves the intensive examination of unusual people or organizations.

know that their students' reading progress will be reported to the schools' superintendent. It is easy to see how these teachers might teach more enthusiastically or pay more attention to each child's reading progress than would teachers using the old program. One likely outcome is that the students receiving the new program of instruction would show reading gains caused by the teachers' increased attention and not by the new program. In general, observation should be as unobtrusive as possible.

Case Studies Examine Individual Lives and Organizations

Case studies involve the intensive examination of unusual people or organizations (**Figure 2.14**). An organization might be selected for intensive study because it is doing something very well (such as making a lot of money) or very poorly (such as losing a lot of money). The goal of an organizational case study is to determine which practices led to success or failure. Did the employees have flexible work schedules, or was an exercise program offered at work? As discussed in Chapter 1, many psychologists work in organizations, employed to study the variables that influence human behavior at work.

In psychology, case studies are frequently conducted with people who have brain injuries or psychological disorders. Case studies of people with brain injuries have provided a wealth of evidence about which parts of the brain are involved in various psychological processes. In one case, a man who was accidentally stabbed through the middle part of the brain with a fencing foil lost the ability to store new memories (Squire & Moore, 1979). Case studies of people with psychological disorders, or clinical case studies, are the type used most frequently in psychology. The major problem with these studies is that it is difficult to know whether the researcher's theory about the cause of the psychological disorder is correct. The researcher has no control over the person's life and is forced to make assumptions about the effects of various life events. The same problem applies to organizational case studies. The researcher cannot know why different work practices can have different outcomes for different organizations.

Case studies are a special type of observational/descriptive study that involves intensive examination of one person or a few individuals (clinical case studies) or one or a few organizations (organizational case studies).

Advantages	Can provide extensive data about one or a few individuals or organizations.
Disadvantages	Can be very subjective: If a researcher has a preexisting theory (for example, people who are loners are dangerous), this theory can bias what is observed and recorded. The results cannot be generalized from a single case study to the population.

FIGURE 2.14 Case Studies The tragic story of Virginia Tech student Seung-Hui Cho provides a case study of a severely disturbed individual. Cho sent photos of himself to news organizations right before he went on a deadly campus shooting spree in April 2007, and he left in his wake a devastated campus that had lost 27 students and 5 teachers.

Thus the interpretation of case studies is often very subjective. Another big problem with case studies is the sample size, which equals one.

Consider an event that provides a snapshot into the mind of a severely disturbed individual. In April 2007, Seung-Hui Cho, a student at Virginia Tech University, went on a campus shooting spree. On the day of the shooting, Cho first shot two students in their dorm, then returned to his room to write about his extreme loneliness and anger. Finally, he went to a nearby classroom building, where he shot at everyone within his range before killing himself. Ultimately, he killed 32 people and wounded many others. The horror of these events led many people to ask what had been known about Cho's mental health. In fact, campus officials knew that Cho was deeply troubled. His professors had been concerned about him because of the violent themes in his writing, especially a 10-page play that was filled with anger and extreme violence.

In hindsight, it is easy to see that Cho should have been put in a locked facility where he could not harm others and could get treatment. Before his rampage, however, there was not enough evidence to allow his involuntary commitment to an institution. No one could have predicted his actions with certainty. Fortunately, murderous outbursts like this one are extremely rare. Unfortunately, that rarity makes them almost impossible to predict. Cho's writing might make him seem like a typical character in a horror novel or Hollywood thriller. But because Cho is not representative of disturbed individuals in general, psychologists and law enforcement officials cannot use the data from this unique case to identify other people who might erupt in similar ways. Some lonely people write violent stories, but very few of those people commit violent crimes. In this way, a case study can reveal a lot about the person being examined, but it does not allow generalization to all similar people (lonely ones, violent ones, what have you). Thus its use as a research tool is limited.

Asking Takes a More Active Approach

Ideally, observation is an unobtrusive approach for studying behavior. By contrast, asking people about themselves, their thoughts, their actions, and their feelings is a much more interactive way of collecting data. Methods of posing questions to participants include surveys, interviews, and questionnaires. The type of information sought ranges from demographic facts (e.g., ethnicity, age, religious affiliation) to past behaviors, personal attitudes, beliefs, and so on. "Have you ever used an illegal drug?" "Should people who drink and drive be jailed for a first offense?" "Are you comfortable sending food back to the kitchen in a restaurant when there is a problem?" Questions such as these require people to recall certain events from their lives or reflect on their mental or emotional states.

A critical issue in question-based research is how to frame the questions. *Open-ended questions* allow respondents to provide any answers they think of and to answer in as much detail as they feel is appropriate. In contrast, *closed-ended questions* require respondents to select from a fixed number of options, as in a multiple-choice exam. Ultimately, the researcher decides what style of question will provide the most appropriate information for the hypothesis being investigated.

Like all methods of data collection, methods that require participants to answer questions have strengths and weaknesses. Consider the differences between asking respondents to fill out a survey and actually interviewing each person

self-report methods Methods of data collection in which people are asked to provide information about themselves, such as in questionnaires or surveys.

Interactive methods involve asking questions of participants. The participants then respond in any way they feel is appropriate (open-ended questions) or select from among a fixed number of options (closed-ended questions).

Advantages Self-report methods such as questionnaires can be used to gather data from a large number of people. They are easy to administer, cost-efficient, and a relatively fast way to collect data. Interviewing people face-to-face gives the researcher the opportunity to explore new lines of questioning. Experience sampling allows researchers to determine how responses vary over time.

Disadvantages People can introduce biases into their answers (self-report bias). They may not recall information accurately.

Surveys and questionnaires

Interviews

Experience sampling

FIGURE 2.15 Interactive Methods

with open-ended questions. **Self-report methods,** such as questionnaires or surveys, can be used to gather data from a large number of people in a short time (**Figure 2.15**). They can be mailed out to a sample drawn from the population of interest or handed out in appropriate locations. They are easy to administer and cost-efficient. Interviews, another type of interactive method, can be used successfully with groups that cannot be studied through questionnaires or surveys, such as young children. Interviews are also helpful in gaining a more in-depth view of a respondent's opinions, experiences, and attitudes. Thus the answers from interviewees sometimes inspire avenues of inquiry that the researchers had not planned. The interview setting can give researchers handy opportunities to explore new lines of questioning.

What if researchers want to understand how thoughts, feelings, and behaviors vary throughout the day, week, or longer? They turn to a relatively new method of data collection, *experience sampling.* As the name implies, researchers take several samples of the participants' experiences over time. By repeatedly getting answers to set questions, researchers can determine how the responses vary over time. Suppose you want to know what a typical day is like for a high school student. You might give each student-participant a notebook with labeled categories in which to fill in what is happening and how the participant feels about it. Or you might give each student-participant a personal digital assistant (PDA) to carry at all times. At random or predetermined times, the PDA would signal the participants to record what they are doing, thinking, or feeling at that moment. Studies with experience sampling have shown, by the way, that high school students are frequently bored in class; most likely not paying attention; and generally thinking about lunch, friends, or other topics unrelated to the course content (Schneider & Csikszentmihalyi, 2000).

SELF-REPORT BIAS A problem common to all asking-based methods of data collection is that people often introduce biases into their answers. These biases make it difficult to discern an honest or true response. In particular, people may not reveal personal information that casts them in a negative light. Consider the question *How many times have you lied to get something you wanted?* Although most of us have lied at some points in our lives to obtain desired outcomes or objects, few of us want to admit this, especially to strangers. Researchers therefore have to consider the extent to which their questions produce *socially desirable responding,* or *faking good,* in which the person responds in a way that is most socially acceptable. Imagine having an interviewer around your parents' age — or, if you are an older student, perhaps a 20-something interviewer — ask you to describe intimate aspects of your sex life. Would you be embarrassed and therefore not very forthcoming? Might you even lie to the interviewer?

Even when respondents do not purposely answer incorrectly, their answers may reflect less-than-accurate self-perceptions. Research has shown that, at least in some cultures, people tend to describe themselves in especially positive ways, often because people believe things about themselves that are not necessarily true. This tendency is called the *better-than-average effect.* For instance, most people believe they are better-than-average drivers. The tendency to express positive things about oneself is especially common in Western cultures, such as those of North America and Europe, but is less pronounced in Eastern cultures, such as those in Korea and Japan (as discussed in Chapter 13, "Personality"). Although East Asians tend to rate themselves as better than average on a wide range of variables, they do so less consistently than people from Canada and the United States (Heine & Hamamura, 2007).

Response Performance Measures the Processing of Information

As noted in Chapter 1, Wilhelm Wundt established the first psychology laboratory in 1879. Wundt and his students pioneered many of the methods for studying how the mind works. For example, they examined how participants responded to psychological tasks such as deciding whether two stimuli were the same or whether words flashed on a screen were the names of animals. Such tests represent a research method called **response performance.**

This method has three basic forms (**Figure 2.16**). First, the researcher can measure and interpret *reaction times*. The interpretation of reaction times is the most useful and dependable research method of cognitive psychology. It is based on the idea that the brain takes time to process information. The more processing a stimulus requires, the longer the reaction time to that stimulus. So research participants will make an easy decision, such as whether a figure flashed on a screen is red or blue, faster than a more difficult decision, such as whether that figure is red or blue *and* round or square. By manipulating what a participant must do with a stimulus and measuring reaction times, the researcher can gain much information about how the participant's brain processes information.

Reaction times for responding to simple stimuli are often measured in hundredths or thousandths of a second. For example, think of the time it takes to press one key on a computer keyboard if a red shape appears or a different key if a blue

response performance A research method in which researchers quantify perceptual or cognitive processes in response to a specific stimulus.

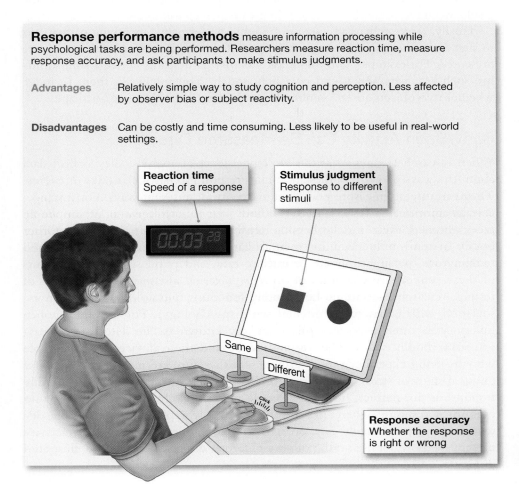

Response performance methods measure information processing while psychological tasks are being performed. Researchers measure reaction time, measure response accuracy, and ask participants to make stimulus judgments.

Advantages Relatively simple way to study cognition and perception. Less affected by observer bias or subject reactivity.

Disadvantages Can be costly and time consuming. Less likely to be useful in real-world settings.

Reaction time Speed of a response

Stimulus judgment Response to different stimuli

Same

Different

Response accuracy Whether the response is right or wrong

FIGURE 2.16 Response Performance Methods

FIGURE 2.17 Try for Yourself: The Stroop Effect

As quickly as you can, name the color of the ink each word is printed in. Do not read the words.

red	blue	green	red	blue	yellow	red	blue
blue	red	green	yellow	red	blue	green	red
yellow	blue	green	red	blue	yellow	red	green
green	yellow	red	yellow	blue	red	green	blue

If you are like most people, your reaction time for naming the ink colors in the bottom two rows was slower than your reaction time for naming the top two rows.

Explanation: The Stroop effect, named after the psychologist John Ridley Stroop, accounts for this phenomenon. Simply put, it takes longer to name the colors of words for colors when they are printed in conflicting colors. The tendency to automatically read the words interferes with the process of naming the ink colors.

shape appears. One reason psychologists use reaction times as dependent measures is that reaction times cannot be faked. If a participant tries to respond more slowly, for example, the reaction time will be much longer than what is expected (maybe two or three seconds instead of a fraction of a second). The experimenter will know immediately that the response was not a measure of actual processing time. Because people have very limited control over their reaction times, these measures again illustrate the idea that some psychological processes happen unconsciously. We have no conscious knowledge about what is happening in our brains as we use information, but measures of reaction time indirectly reflect brain processing (**Figure 2.17**).

A researcher can also measure *response accuracy*. For example, does paying attention to a visual stimulus improve a person's perception of that stimulus? To study this question, you might ask participants to pay attention to one side of a computer screen while keeping their eyes focused on the center of the screen. You would present a stimulus, such as by flashing a shape on either side of the screen. Then you would ask the participants whether the shape was a hexagon or an octagon. Suppose the participants answer more accurately when the stimulus appears on the side of the screen they are paying attention to than when it appears on the side they are ignoring. These results would indicate that attention improves perception of the stimulus.

Finally, a researcher can measure response performance by asking participants to make *stimulus judgments* regarding the different stimuli with which they are presented. For example, you might ask whether participants notice a faint stimulus, such as a very soft sound or a light touch. You might ask them to judge whether two objects are the same in some way, such as color, size, or shape.

Body/Brain Activity Can Be Measured Directly

When researchers operate at the biological level of analysis, they collect data about the ways people's bodies and brains respond to particular tasks or events. They can directly measure body/brain activity in different ways. For instance, certain emotional states influence the body in predictable ways. When people are frightened, their muscles become tense and their hearts beat faster. Other bodily systems influenced by mental states include blood pressure, blood temperature, perspiration rate, breathing rate, and pupil size. Measurements of these systems are examples of *psychophysiological assessment*. In this type of testing, researchers examine how bodily functions (physiology) change in association with behaviors or mental states (psychology). For example, police investigators often use *polygraphs,* popularly known as "lie detectors," to assess some bodily states. The assumption behind these devices is that people who are lying experience more arousal and therefore are more likely to show physical signs of stress. The correspondence between mental state and bodily response is not perfect, however. People who lie easily can show little or no emotional response when they lie during a polygraph recording, so lie detectors do not accurately measure whether someone is lying. (Brain activity methods—polygraphs and the other techniques discussed here—are illustrated in **Figure 2.18**.)

Body/brain activity methods measure body/brain responses to tasks or events.

Advantages Identify physical responses to external events. Polygraphs record changes in bodily activity. EEG measures electrical activity in the brain. PET, fMRI, and TMS identify brain regions involved in various tasks. MRI shows brain structure.

Disadvantages Deemphasize brain localization. Some methods are better for assessing how quickly the body or brain responds (polygraph, EEG) but not as good for identifying the brain regions that are active. Other methods (PET, fMRI, TMS) are better for localizing brain activity but not as good for examining the time course of that activity. All these data are correlational and thus have the disadvantage of the third variable problem; directionality problem.

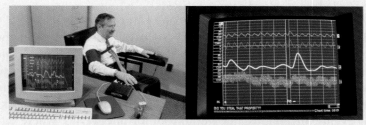

A polygraph (lie detector) measures changes in bodily functions (e.g., heart rate, perspiration rate, blood pressure) related to behaviors or mental states. These changes are *not* reliable measures of lying.

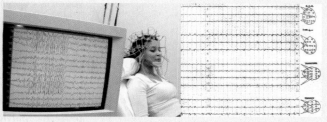

An electroencephalograph (EEG) measures the brain's electrical activity.

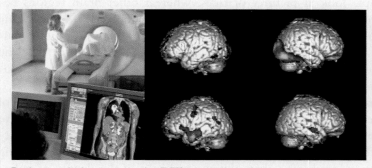

Positron emission tomography (PET) scans the brain's metabolic activity.

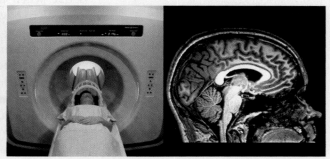

Magnetic resonance imaging (MRI) produces a high-resolution image of the brain.

Functional magnetic resonance imaging (fMRI) maps mental activity by assessing the blood's oxygen level in the brain.

Transcranial magnetic stimulation (TMS) momentarily disrupts brain activity in a specific brain region.

FIGURE 2.18 Body/Brain Activity Methods

ELECTROPHYSIOLOGY *Electrophysiology* is a data collection method that measures electrical activity in the brain. A researcher fits electrodes onto the participant's scalp. The electrodes act like small microphones that pick up the brain's electrical activity instead of sounds. The device that measures brain activity is an **electroencephalograph (EEG).** This measurement is useful because different behavioral states produce different and predictable EEG patterns. As Chapter 5 discusses further, the EEG shows specific, consistent patterns as people fall asleep.

electroencephalograph (EEG) A device that measures electrical activity in the brain.

It also reveals that the brain is very active even when the body is at rest, especially during dreams. As a measure of specific cognitive states, however, the EEG is limited. Because the recordings (*electroencephalograms*) reflect all brain activity, they are too "noisy" or imprecise to isolate specific responses to particular stimuli. A more powerful way of examining how brain activity changes in response to a specific stimulus involves conducting many trials and averaging across the trials. Because this method enables researchers to observe patterns associated with specific events, it is called *event-related potential (ERP)*.

BRAIN IMAGING The brain's electrical activity is associated with changes in the flow of blood carrying oxygen and nutrients to the active brain regions. *Brain imaging* methods measure changes in the rate, or speed, of the flow of blood to different regions of the brain. By keeping track of these changes, researchers can monitor which brain areas are active when people perform particular tasks or experience particular events. Imaging is a powerful tool for uncovering where different systems reside in the brain and how different brain areas interact to process information. For example, research has shown that certain brain regions become active when people look at pictures of faces, whereas other brain regions become active when people try to understand what other people are thinking. One brain imaging study—directly related to the impact of drinking on driving ability—found that alcohol leads to a one-third reduction in activity in areas of the brain concerned with vision (Levin et al., 1998). The major imaging technologies are *positron emission tomography* and *magnetic resonance imaging*.

Positron emission tomography (PET) is the computer-aided reconstruction of the brain's metabolic activity. After the injection of a relatively harmless radioactive substance into the bloodstream, a PET scan enables researchers to find the most active brain areas. The research participant lies in a special scanner that, by detecting the injected radiation, produces a three-dimensional map of the density of radioactivity inside the participant's brain. This map is useful because as the brain performs a mental task, blood flow increases to the most active regions. The increased blood flow carrying the radioactive material leads these regions to emit more radiation. The researchers have the participant perform some psychological task (such as looking at pictures of faces expressing fear). They scan the participant's brain during each phase of the task. By collating those scans, the researchers obtain a map of the brain's metabolic activity during the task. Since the entire brain is extremely metabolically active all the time, however, the researchers must also scan the participant's brain during the performance of another, closely related task (such as looking at pictures of faces with neutral expressions). The second task will differ from the first in only one way, and that difference will reflect the mental function being studied. Researchers are thus able to correlate brain regions with specific mental activities. One downside of PET is the need to inject a radioactive substance into the body. For safety reasons, researchers limit the use of this technology.

Magnetic resonance imaging (MRI) is the most powerful imaging technique. In MRI, a research participant lies in a scanner that produces a powerful magnetic field. Amazingly, this field is as strong as the kind used to pick up scrap metal at junkyards. The researchers momentarily disrupt the magnetic forces. During this process, energy is released from brain tissue in a form that can be measured by detectors surrounding the head. Because different types of brain tissue release energy differently, the researchers can produce a high-resolution image of the brain. (The amount of energy released is very small, so having an MRI is not dangerous. Nor is there any danger in being exposed to the magnetic field at the levels used in research.) MRI is extremely valuable for providing

positron emission tomography (PET)
A method of brain imaging that assesses metabolic activity by using a radioactive substance injected into the bloodstream.

magnetic resonance imaging (MRI)
A method of brain imaging that produces high-quality images of the brain.

information about the structure of the brain. It can be used to determine the location of brain damage or of a brain tumor. It can also be used to create images of other body parts, such as in determining hip and knee injuries.

Like a PET scan, **functional magnetic resonance imaging (fMRI)** makes use of the brain's blood flow to map the working brain. Again, the researchers have the participant perform a task (such as deciding whether a face looks happy or sad). During that task, the researchers scan the participant's brain. Whereas PET measures blood flow directly by tracking a radioactive substance, fMRI measures blood flow indirectly by assessing changes in the blood's oxygen level. As in all brain imaging methods, the participant then performs a task that differs from the first one in only one way and that reflects the particular mental function of interest. The researchers then compare images to examine differences in blood flow and therefore brain activity.

TRANSCRANIAL MAGNETIC STIMULATION One limitation of brain imaging is that the findings are necessarily correlational. We know that certain brain regions are active while a task is performed. We do not know whether each brain region is necessary for the task. As a correlational method, brain imaging has the conceptual problems, such as the third variable and directionality problems, discussed earlier. To see whether a brain region is important for a task, researchers ideally want to compare performances when that area is working effectively and when it is not. **Transcranial magnetic stimulation (TMS)** uses a very fast but powerful magnetic field to disrupt brain activity momentarily in a specific brain region. For example, placing the TMS coil over areas of the brain involved in language will disrupt a person's ability to speak. This technique has its limitations, particularly that it can be used only for short durations to examine brain areas close to the scalp. When used along with imaging, however, it is a powerful method for examining which brain regions are necessary for specific psychological functions.

Research with Animals Provides Important Data

Throughout the history of psychological science, many of the most important research findings have been obtained by studying the behavior of nonhuman animals. For instance, watching animals—usually rats—run through mazes or press levers to earn rewards led to the development of many principles about learning. Indeed, Ivan Pavlov's observation of a salivating dog inspired John B. Watson to launch the behaviorist movement (these topics are discussed further in Chapter 6, "Learning"). A central assumption underlying Watson's behaviorism was that humans are subject to the same laws of nature as other animals. Humans' behavior might seem more complex than that of rats or dogs. But the forces that control the behaviors of rats, dogs, and humans are in many ways the same. Indeed, those forces tend to control the behaviors of all animals—human and nonhuman—in very similar ways.

As our knowledge of the human genome increases, our interest increases in the way genes affect behaviors, physical illnesses, psychological disorders, and well-being. Psychologists working at the biological level of analysis manipulate genes directly to examine their effects on behavior. Of course, for ethical reasons, much of the genetic research cannot be conducted with humans, so researchers use other animals for this important work.

As Chapter 3 discusses in greater detail, specific genes can be targeted for manipulation. Researchers can delete genes to eliminate their effects or move genes to other locations to enhance their effects. For research purposes, *transgenic mice* are produced by manipulating the genes in developing mouse embryos—for

functional magnetic resonance imaging (fMRI) An imaging technique used to examine changes in the activity of the working human brain.

transcranial magnetic stimulation (TMS) The use of strong magnets to briefly interrupt normal brain activity as a way to study brain regions.

"WHAT IT COMES DOWN TO IS YOU HAVE TO FIND OUT WHAT REACTION THEY'RE LOOKING FOR, AND YOU GIVE THEM THAT REACTION."

example, by inserting strands of foreign DNA into the genes. The new genes are integrated into every cell of each mouse's body. This sort of research is providing new hope for curing and preventing many diseases (**Figure 2.19**).

There Are Ethical Issues to Consider

When scientists select a research method, they must make decisions with full knowledge of the ethical issues involved. They must also adhere strictly to the relevant ethical guidelines. Are they asking the participants to do something unreasonable? Are the participants risking physical or emotional harm from the study? Some ethical concerns are specific to the kind of method used, while others apply across all methods. Therefore, to ensure the participants' well-being, all colleges, universities, and research institutes have strict guidelines in place regarding research. **Institutional review boards (IRBs)** are the guardians of those guidelines. Convened at schools and other institutions where research is done, IRBs consist of administrators, legal advisers, trained scholars, and members of the community. They review all proposed research to ensure that it meets scientific standards. The research design must also put to rest any ethical concerns for the safety and well-being of participants.

PRIVACY One of the more prominent ethical concerns about research is participants' reasonable expectation of privacy. If behaviors are going to be observed, is it okay to observe people without their knowledge? This question obviously depends on what sorts of behaviors researchers might be observing. If the behaviors tend to occur in public rather than in private, researchers might be less concerned about observing people without their knowledge. For example, even without their knowledge, it would be okay to observe couples saying good-bye in a public place such as an airport. Without the couples' knowledge, it would be inappropriate to observe their private sexual behaviors. The concern over privacy is compounded by the ever-increasing technology for monitoring people remotely. Although it might be useful to compare men's and women's behaviors in public bathrooms, would it be acceptable to install discreet video cameras to monitor people in restrooms? (The answer is no!)

When people are asked for information, should some topics not be raised because they may be too personal or otherwise inappropriate? Say that researchers would like to understand how a physically and emotionally traumatic event affects people in the months and years after it occurs. Such issues must be explored to develop strategies for overcoming physical pain and emotional anguish. Still, researchers must consider how their lines of questioning will affect the individuals they are studying. They must also monitor the effects on the participants during the questioning.

ACCESS TO DATA No matter what research method they use, researchers must also consider who will have access to the data they collect. Participant confidentiality should always be guarded carefully so that personal information is not linked publicly to the study's findings. When participants are told that their information will remain confidential, the implicit promise is that their information will be kept secret or made available to only the few people who need to know it. Often the quality and accuracy of data depend on the participants'

FIGURE 2.19 Animal Research Researchers observe the behaviors of transgenic mice to understand how certain genes affect behavior.

certainty that their responses will be kept confidential. When emotionally or legally sensitive topics are involved, people are especially likely to provide valid data after they are promised confidentiality.

For studies concerning extremely sensitive topics, the participants' responses should remain anonymous. *Anonymity* is not the same as *confidentiality*, although these terms are often confused. Anonymity means that the researchers collect no personal information, so responses can never be traced to any individual. If you wanted to know how many college students in your sample had ever cheated on an exam, the students would have to be assured of anonymity so that they would be comfortable about responding honestly. An anonymous study might be conducted in the form of a written questionnaire that asked about cheating but did not ask for any identifying information. Participants would return the completed questionnaires to a large box so that no questionnaire could be linked to any individual.

INFORMED CONSENT Research involving human participants is a partnership based on mutual respect and trust. People who volunteer for psychological research have the right to know what will happen to them during the course of the study. Compensating people for their participation in research does not alter this fundamental right. Ethical standards require giving people all relevant information that might affect their willingness to become participants. *Informed consent* means that participants make a knowledgeable decision to participate. Typically, researchers obtain informed consent in writing. In observational studies of public behavior, the observed individuals remain anonymous to the researchers to protect their privacy, so informed consent is not required. Minors, the intellectually incapacitated, and the mentally ill cannot legally provide informed consent. If such an individual is to participate in a study, a legal guardian must grant permission.

It is not always possible to inform participants fully about a study's details. If knowing the study's specific goals may alter the participants' behavior, thereby rendering the results meaningless, researchers may need to use deception. That is, they might mislead the participants about the study's goals or not fully reveal what will take place. Researchers use deception only when other methods are not appropriate and when the deception does not involve situations that would strongly affect people's willingness to participate. If deception is used, a careful *debriefing* must take place after the study's completion. Here, the researchers inform the participants of the study's goals. They also explain the need for deception, to eliminate or counteract any negative effects produced by the deception.

RELATIVE RISKS OF PARTICIPATION Another ethical issue is the relative risk to participants' mental or physical health. Researchers must always remain conscious of what they are asking of participants. They cannot ask people to endure unreasonable amounts of pain or of discomfort, either from stimuli or from the manner in which data measurements are taken. Fortunately, in the vast majority of research being conducted, these types of concerns are not an issue. However, although risk is low, researchers have to think carefully about the potential for risk to specific participants. Again, any research conducted at a college, university, or research institute must be approved by an IRB familiar with the rules and regulations that protect participants from harm. Most IRBs look at the relative trade-off between risk and benefit. Potential gains from the scientific enterprise sometimes require asking participants to expose themselves to some risk to obtain important findings. The *risk/benefit ratio* is an analysis of whether the research is important enough to warrant placing participants at risk.

Should I Participate in Psychological Research?

Someday, perhaps even this term, you will be invited to participate in a psychological research study (**Figure 2.20**). Participating is a good idea for two reasons: It will help you contribute to scientific knowledge, and it will give you an insider's view of how psychological research works. Students in introductory psychology may worry that researchers will manipulate or trick them into doing something they do not want to do. Others may feel anxious because they have no idea what to expect once they walk through the doors of a psychology laboratory. Understanding the ethical principles that guide psychological research arms potential research participants, such as yourself, with insight about what to expect when participating in a study.

The research in which you participate might be conducted by professors or students at your college, or it might be conducted by researchers at another institution. Regardless of where the research takes place, psychologists in the United States conduct their studies according to a specific set of ethical principles, collectively known as the Belmont Report (http://www.hhs.gov/ohrp/policy/belmont.html). Psychologists outside the United States follow similar guidelines. The principles of the Belmont Report, a few of which are described below, guide many aspects of participants' experiences in research studies.

First, your participation is voluntary. No one can force you to participate in a study. Many psychology departments "require" students to participate in research as part of the students' course work, but the departments usually offer alternatives for fulfilling this requirement. For example, in some departments, students can read and write about articles published in journals in lieu of participating in research. Even once you agree to participate in a study, you have the right to discontinue your participation at any time, for any reason, and without penalty. And you can skip any questions you do not care to answer, perhaps because you find them intrusive or offensive. These freedoms mean that *you* are in the driver's seat when it comes to choosing if, and to what extent, you participate in a study.

Second, you are legally and ethically entitled to know what you are getting into so you can make an informed decision about participating. Researchers cannot reveal their exact research questions and hypotheses, because knowing that information might change the way you behave in the study. Researchers will be able to tell you, however, the general purpose of the study and the kinds of activities you will be asked to complete. You might, for example, be asked to answer questionnaires, solve math problems, or engage in moderate physical activity. Importantly, researchers must tell you about the risks and potential benefits faced by participants. A researcher studying eating disorders would inform volunteers about a possible risk: that some participants might experience psychological distress as a result of thinking about their health behaviors. A researcher studying the effectiveness of a new technique that might be used in psychological treatment would inform volunteers about a possible benefit: that participation might result in improved self-esteem. The point here is that you will actually know a good deal about the research study before the study even begins.

Third, after you complete the study, you can expect the researchers to provide a thorough explanation of the study, called a *debriefing*. During the debriefing, the researchers will tell you if they used deception in the study and why it was necessary. For example, if you participated in a study about first impressions, you might learn during the debriefing that the "person" you interacted with was actually a member of the research team chosen because he or she was very attractive and the researchers were interested

FIGURE 2.20 Student Participation in Psychological Research These students are enjoying the opportunity to contribute to scientific knowledge. Join them by participating in a study!

in how physical attractiveness affects how people are judged. If you had known in advance that the researchers were studying this idea, it might have affected how you evaluated the person you were judging. In addition, the researcher will likely describe the questions and hypotheses driving the study and will invite you to leave your contact information if you would like to learn the results of the investigation.

Finally, you can expect that the data you provide will remain confidential. Researchers take great pains to protect your confidentiality. For example, they remove all identifying information, such as your name, from any data submitted. They store consent forms separately from data, password-protect electronic files that contain sensitive information, and keep all files in a secured location. Then, when it comes time for researchers to share their results with others, they will do so while maintaining your privacy. For example, they will not show conference attendees a video clip of you discussing a problem in your romantic relationship (unless you provided consent for them to do so).

Just as researchers are governed by formal ethical guidelines (in addition to their own moral compasses), good study participants also engage in the research process respectfully. When you sign up to participate in a study, record the date, time, and location in your calendar. Jot down the researcher's contact information in case an emergency arises and you are unable to fulfill your commitment to attend the study session. Out of respect for the time of the researcher and any other participants, arrive at your session on time, and bring with you any paperwork your institution might require for you to receive class credit for your participation. Whether you are completing a study online or in a laboratory, make every effort to minimize potential distractions. Turn off your cell phone, iPod, and other devices that might divert your attention from the task at hand. And, importantly, ask questions! One of the benefits of volunteering in research is learning firsthand about the research process. Getting answers to your questions helps you fully derive this benefit.

Study participants are essential to the research enterprise, and researchers are grateful for the time and effort participants devote. The principles described here emerged out of concern for the well-being of these participants and in response to violations of human rights in early research studies. Understanding your rights prepares you to contribute meaningfully and confidently, without fear of trickery or unknown risks, to psychologists' efforts to understand and improve the human condition. On behalf of psychologists everywhere, thank you for joining us in this endeavor.

For a list of opportunities to participate in online research studies, see http://psych.hanover.edu/research/exponnet.html.

Summing Up

What Are the Data Collection Methods of Psychological Science?

In psychological science, there are five basic data collection methods. These methods operate at different levels of analysis. The choice of which to use is generally dictated by the research question. First, researchers can observe behaviors as they take place. They can either write down general descriptions of the behaviors or check off a tally sheet of prespecified behavior categories. Second, researchers may use case studies to examine unusual people or organizations. Third, researchers can ask people for information about their thoughts, feelings, and behaviors by using surveys, questionnaires, and interviews. Fourth, researchers can measure how quickly and accurately people respond to a stimulus. Fifth, researchers can directly measure the body's activity (e.g., psychophysiological reactions) and the brain's activity (e.g., electrical activity, blood flow), or they can disrupt ongoing brain processes. Psychological research has benefited from the use of animal models. Regardless of the method chosen, researchers must consider the ethical consequences of their data collection. They must carefully consider the use of deception and weigh the study's relative risks against its potential benefits.

Measuring Up

For each example below, indicate which data collection method would work best. Fill in the blank with one of the following: description/observation, case study, survey, interview, experience sampling, response performance (which includes accuracy and reaction time), EEG, brain imaging, or transcranial magnetic stimulation.

1. A researcher is investigating Adolf Hitler's childhood and teenage years to see if there are ways of recognizing the experiences that made Hitler evil as an adult. What data collection method is he using? _____

2. As discussed in Chapter 10, "Emotion and Motivation," Alfred Kinsey studied the sexual behaviors of large numbers of people from every walk of life. What data collection method or methods would you have suggested he use? _____

3. Fascinating new data reveal that the social lives of the great apes are surprisingly similar to human social systems. What method was probably used to obtain these data? _____

4. In a study of families, the researchers want to know when children and their parents feel stressed, happy, relaxed, and bored throughout the day. What data collection method should the researchers use? _____

5. If you wanted to study which parts of their brains longtime soccer players use when they perform spatial tasks, what method would you use? _____

6. Researchers are often interested in the similarities and differences between men's and women's brain processes. If you believed that women use both sides of their brains more equally when using language than men do, you could interrupt the brain processes and see what happens. What research method would be best for this proposed study? _____

Answers: 1. case study; 2. survey or interview; 3. description/observation [in the wild is best]; 4. experience sampling; 5. brain imaging; 6. transcranial magnetic stimulation.

Learning Objectives

- Identify three characteristics that reflect the quality of data.
- Describe measures of central tendency and variability.
- Describe the correlation coefficient.
- Discuss the rationale for inferential statistics.

2.4 How Are Data Analyzed and Evaluated?

So far, this chapter has presented the essential elements of scientific inquiry in psychology: how to frame an empirical question using theories, hypotheses, and research; how to decide what type of study to run; and how to collect data. This section focuses on the data. Specifically, it examines the characteristics that make for good data and the statistical procedures that researchers use to analyze data.

Good Research Requires Valid, Reliable, and Accurate Data

If you collect data to answer a research question, the data must address that question. **Internal validity** refers to whether the data you collect address your question. For data to be internally valid, they must measure what you want to measure. By doing so, they provide clear information you can use to evaluate your theory or hypothesis. Suppose you hypothesize that people in their 20s are more likely to channel surf (rapidly switch among television channels) than are people in their 50s. To test your hypothesis, you would need to study television-watching behavior and, in particular, the average length of time people stay tuned to each station they watch. To be internally valid, your data would need to reflect the independent variable (age) and the dependent variable (time spent watching stations). Say, for example, that participants in their 20s tended to do other things, such as sleeping or checking their Facebook status, while watching television. Because these participants were not paying attention during the study, the data would not reflect television watching and would not be internally valid. Likewise, say that a participant in his 50s was watching with children and trying to find programs that would appeal to those children. That participant's behavior would not reflect the television-watching experience of people in their 50s.

Another important aspect of data is **reliability,** the stability and consistency of a measure over time. If the measurement is reliable, the data collected will not vary substantially over time. One option for measuring the duration of each channel stay would be to have an observer use a stopwatch. There is likely to be some variability,

internal validity The extent to which the data collected in a study address the research hypothesis in the way intended.

reliability The extent to which a measure is stable and consistent over time in similar conditions.

however, in when the observer starts and stops the watch relative to when the surfer actually changes channels. As a consequence, the data in this scenario would be less reliable than data collected by a computer linked to each viewer's television remote.

The third and final characteristic of good data is **accuracy,** the extent to which the measure is error free. A measure may be valid and reliable but still not be accurate. Psychologists think about this problem by turning it on its head and asking, How do errors creep into a measure? Suppose that for the channel surfing study you use a stopwatch to measure the duration of each channel stay. The problem with this method is that each measurement will tend to overestimate or underestimate the duration (because of human error or variability in recording times). This is known as a *random error,* because although an error is introduced into each measurement, the value of the error differs each time. But suppose the stopwatch has a glitch, such that it always overstates the time measured by 2 seconds. This is known as a *systematic error,* because the amount of error introduced into each measurement is constant (**Figure 2.21**). Generally, systematic error is more problematic than random error because the latter tends to average out over time and therefore is less likely to produce inaccurate results.

Descriptive Statistics Provide a Summary of the Data

The first step in evaluating data is to inspect the *raw values.* This term refers to data that are as close as possible to the form in which they were collected. In examining raw data, researchers look for errors in data recording. For instance, they assess whether any of the responses seem especially unlikely (e.g., blood alcohol content of 50 percent or a 113-year-old participant). Once the researchers are satisfied that the data make sense, they summarize the basic patterns using **descriptive statistics.** These mathematical forms provide an overall summary of the study's results. For example, they might show how the participants, on average, performed in one condition compared with another.

The simplest descriptive statistics are measures of **central tendency.** This single value describes a typical response or the behavior of the group as a whole. The

accuracy The extent to which an experimental measure is free from error.

descriptive statistics Statistics that summarize the data collected in a study.

central tendency A measure that represents the typical response or the behavior of a group as a whole.

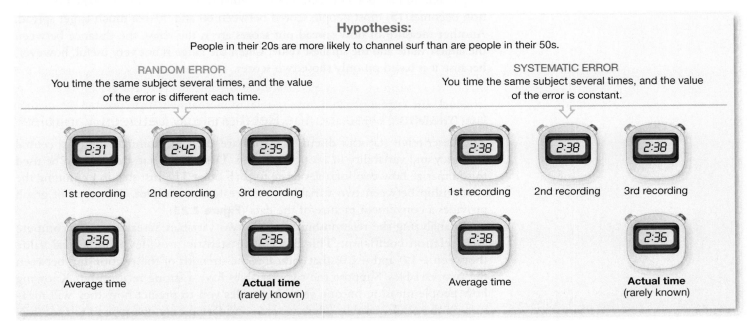

Hypothesis:
People in their 20s are more likely to channel surf than are people in their 50s.

RANDOM ERROR
You time the same subject several times, and the value of the error is different each time.

2:31   2:42   2:35
1st recording   2nd recording   3rd recording

2:36   2:36
Average time   Actual time (rarely known)

SYSTEMATIC ERROR
You time the same subject several times, and the value of the error is constant.

2:38   2:38   2:38
1st recording   2nd recording   3rd recording

2:38   2:36
Average time   Actual time (rarely known)

FIGURE 2.21 Data Accuracy Good data should be accurate (free from error). These examples illustrate how errors can creep into a measure. Random error occurs when the degree of error varies each time. Systematic error occurs when the measurement has the same degree of error each time.

mean A measure of central tendency that is the arithmetic average of a set of numbers.

median A measure of central tendency that is the value in a set of numbers that falls exactly halfway between the lowest and highest values.

mode A measure of central tendency that is the most frequent score or value in a set of numbers.

variability In a set of numbers, how widely dispersed the values are from each other and from the mean.

standard deviation A statistical measure of how far away each value is, on average, from the mean.

scatterplot A graphical depiction of the relationship between two variables.

most intuitive measure of central tendency is the **mean,** the arithmetic average of a set of numbers. The class average on an exam is an example of a mean score. Consider the hypothetical study of alcohol and driving performance. A basic way to summarize the data would be to calculate the means for driving performances: You would calculate one mean for when participants were sober and a second mean for when they were intoxicated. If alcohol affects driving, you would expect to see a difference in the means between sober and intoxicated driving performances.

A second measure of central tendency is the **median,** the value in a set of numbers that falls exactly halfway between the lowest and highest values. For instance, if you received the median score on a test, half the people who took the test scored lower than you and half the people scored higher. Sometimes researchers will summarize data using a median instead of a mean because if one or two numbers in the set are dramatically larger or smaller than all the others, the mean will give either an inflated or a deflated summary of the average. This effect occurs in studies of average incomes. Perhaps approximately 50 percent of Americans make more than $45,000 per year, but a small percentage of people make so much more (multiple millions or billions for the richest) that the mean income is much higher than the median and is not an accurate measure of what most people earn. The median provides a better estimate of how much money the average person makes.

A third measure of central tendency is the **mode,** the most frequent score or value in a set of numbers. For instance, the modal number of children in an American family is two, which means that more American families have two children than any other number of children. (For examples of how to calculate all three central tendency measures, see **Figure 2.22.**)

In addition to measures of central tendency, another important characteristic of data is the **variability** in a set of numbers. This term refers to how widely dispersed the values are about the mean. The most common measure of variability—how spread out the scores are—is the **standard deviation.** This measure reflects how far away each value is, on average, from the mean. For instance, if the mean score for an exam is 75 percent and the standard deviation is 5, most people scored between 70 percent and 80 percent. If the mean remains the same but the standard deviation becomes 15, most people scored between 60 and 90—a much larger spread. Another measure of how spread out scores are is the *range,* the distance between the largest value and the smallest value. Often the range is not very useful, however, because it is based on only those two scores.

Correlations Describe the Relationships between Variables

The descriptive statistics discussed so far are used for summarizing the central tendency and variability in a set of numbers. Descriptive statistics can also be used to summarize how two variables relate to each other. The first step in examining the relationship between two variables is to create a **scatterplot.** This type of graph provides a convenient picture of the data (**Figure 2.23**).

In analyzing the relationship between two variables, researchers can compute a correlation coefficient. This descriptive statistic provides a numerical value (between −1.0 and +1.0) that indicates the strength of the relationship between the two variables. Suppose the two variables have a strong relationship. Knowing how people measure on one variable enables you to predict how they will measure on the other variable. (Here we are considering only one type of relationship: a linear relationship, in which an increase or decrease in one variable is associated with an increase or decrease in the other variable.) What signifies a strong relationship? Consider the different scatterplots in **Figure 2.24.** If two variables

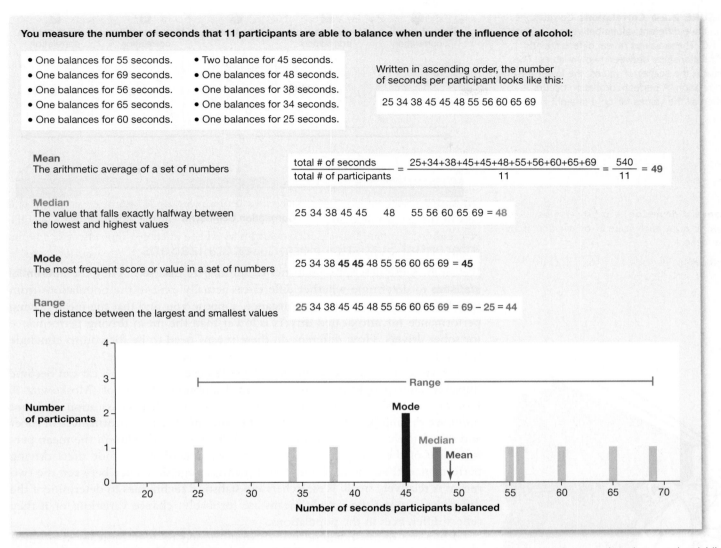

You measure the number of seconds that 11 participants are able to balance when under the influence of alcohol:

- One balances for 55 seconds.
- One balances for 69 seconds.
- One balances for 56 seconds.
- One balances for 65 seconds.
- One balances for 60 seconds.

- Two balance for 45 seconds.
- One balances for 48 seconds.
- One balances for 38 seconds.
- One balances for 34 seconds.
- One balances for 25 seconds.

Written in ascending order, the number of seconds per participant looks like this:

25 34 38 45 45 48 55 56 60 65 69

Mean
The arithmetic average of a set of numbers

$$\frac{\text{total \# of seconds}}{\text{total \# of participants}} = \frac{25+34+38+45+45+48+55+56+60+65+69}{11} = \frac{540}{11} = 49$$

Median
The value that falls exactly halfway between the lowest and highest values

25 34 38 45 45   48   55 56 60 65 69 = 48

Mode
The most frequent score or value in a set of numbers

25 34 38 **45 45** 48 55 56 60 65 69 = **45**

Range
The distance between the largest and smallest values

25 34 38 45 45 48 55 56 60 65 **69** = 69 − 25 = 44

FIGURE 2.22 Descriptive Statistics Descriptive statistics are used to summarize a data set and to measure the central tendency and variability in a set of numbers. The mean, median, and mode are different measures of central tendency. The range is a measure of variability. Which measure of central tendency provides the best summary for the data in this figure? Why is that measure more useful than the range?

have a positive correlation, they increase or decrease together. For example, the more people drink, the more likely they are to engage in risky behavior. This correlation is positive because the two parts increase together, not because either one is good or bad. A perfect positive correlation is indicated by a value of +1.0. If two variables have a *negative correlation,* as one increases in value, the other decreases in value. For example, as people become more intoxicated, they become less able to balance on one foot, so intoxication and balance have a negative correlation. A perfect negative correlation is indicated by a value of −1.0. If two variables show no apparent relationship, the value of the correlation will be a number close to zero (assuming a linear relationship for the purposes of this discussion).

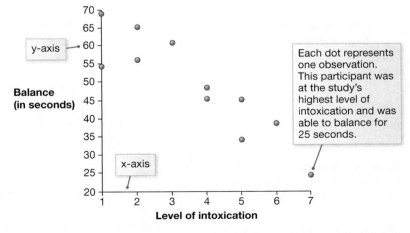

FIGURE 2.23 Scatterplots Scatterplots are graphs that illustrate the relationship between two variables. In general, according to this scatter plot, how was the ability to balance related to the level of intoxication?

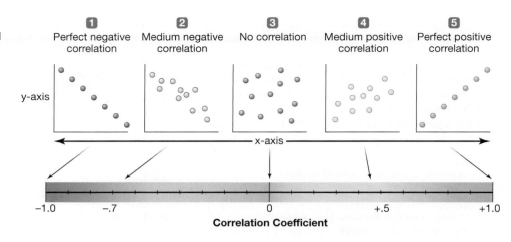

FIGURE 2.24 Correlations Correlations can have different values between −1.0 and +1.0. These values reveal different kinds of relationships between two variables. The greater the scatter of values, the lower the correlation. A perfect correlation occurs when all the values fall on a straight line.

Inferential Statistics Permit Generalizations

Researchers use descriptive statistics to summarize data sets. They use **inferential statistics** to determine whether differences actually exist in the populations from which samples were drawn. For instance, suppose you find that the mean driving performance for intoxicated drivers is lower than the mean driving performance for sober drivers. How different do these means need to be for you to conclude that drinking alcohol does in fact reduce people's ability to drive?

A review of 112 studies found that the skills necessary to drive a car can become impaired after people consume even small amounts of alcohol (Moskowitz & Fiorentino, 2000). Pretend for a moment, however, that intoxication does not influence driving performance. If you measure the driving performances of sober and drunk drivers, just by chance there will be some variability in the mean performance of the two groups. The key is that if alcohol does not affect driving performance, then the probability of showing a large difference between the two means is relatively small. Researchers use statistical techniques to determine if the differences among the sample means are (probably) chance variations or if they reflect differences in the populations.

When the results obtained from a study would be very unlikely to occur if there really were no differences between the groups of subjects, the researchers conclude that the results are *statistically significant*. According to generally accepted standards, researchers typically conclude there is a significant effect only if the obtained results would occur by chance less than 5 percent of the time.

META-ANALYSIS **Meta-analysis** is a type of study that, as its name implies, is an analysis of multiple analyses. (The plural of *meta-analysis* is *meta-analyses*.) In other words, it is a study of studies that have already been conducted. With meta-analysis, many studies that have addressed the same issue are combined and summarized in one "study of studies." Suppose, for example, that 10 studies have been conducted on men's and women's effectiveness as leaders. Among these 10 studies, 5 found no differences, 2 favored women, and 3 favored men. Researchers conducting a meta-analysis would not just count up the numbers of different findings from the research literature. Instead, they would weight more heavily those studies that had larger samples. After all, large samples are more likely to provide more accurate reflections of what is true in populations. The researchers would also consider the size of each effect. That is, they would factor in whether each study found a large difference, a small difference, or no difference between the groups being compared—in this case, between women and men. (The researchers who conducted such a meta-analysis on men's and

"I think you should be more explicit here in step two."

inferential statistics A set of procedures used to make judgments about whether differences actually exist between sets of numbers.

meta-analysis A "study of studies" that combines the findings of multiple studies to arrive at a conclusion.

women's effectiveness found no overall differences; Eagly, Karau, & Makhijani, 1995.) Because meta-analysis combines the results of separate studies, many researchers believe that meta-analysis provides stronger evidence than the results of any single study. As discussed earlier in this chapter, we can be more confident about results when the research findings are replicated. Meta-analysis has the concept of replication built into it.

Summing Up

How Are Data Analyzed and Evaluated?

Data analysis begins with descriptive statistics, which summarize the data. Measures of central tendency indicate the typical response or the behavior of a group as a whole. Measures of variability indicate how widely numbers are distributed about the mean or average score. A correlation coefficient describes the relationship between two variables: positive, negative, or none. Inferential statistics indicate whether the results of a study reflect a true difference between groups or are likely to be due to chance. Meta-analysis combines the results of several studies to arrive at a conclusion.

Measuring Up

1. When researchers want to summarize in a single number all the data they collect, they compute a measure of central tendency. Here are hypothetical data for a study in which 10 people in a sample consumed alcohol. The researchers measured the number of glasses of alcohol each person consumed and assessed her or his motor control after consuming the alcohol. The scores on motor control ranged from 1 (poor motor control) to 10 (good motor control). Compute the mean, median, and mode for the amount of alcohol consumed and the ratings of motor control.

Amount of Alcohol Consumed	Rating of Motor Control
3	4
1	9
5	1
2	7
3	5
3	3
1	8
4	2
5	1
2	6

2. Which is an accurate description of the rationale for inferential statistics?
   a. When the means of two sample groups are significantly different, we still need to compute a mean value for each population before we can conclude that the groups really are different.
   b. When the means of two sample groups are significantly different, we can be fairly certain that we did not make any mistakes in our research.
   c. When the means of two sample groups are significantly different, we can be certain that the data are not correlated.
   d. When the means of two sample groups are significantly different, we can infer that the populations the groups were selected from are different.

Answers: 1. Amount of alcohol consumed: mean = 2.9, median = 3, and mode = 3; rating of motor control: mean = 4.6, median = 4.5, and mode = 1. 2. d. When the means of two sample groups are significantly different, we can infer that the populations the groups were selected from are different.

Chapter Summary

2.1 What Is Scientific Inquiry?

■ **The Scientific Method Depends on Theories, Hypotheses, and Research:** Scientific inquiry relies on objective methods and empirical evidence to answer testable questions. Interconnected ideas or models of behavior (theories) yield testable predictions (hypotheses), which are tested in a systematic way (research) by collecting and evaluating evidence (data).

■ **Unexpected Findings Can Be Valuable:** Unexpected (serendipitous) discoveries sometimes occur, but only researchers who are prepared to recognize their importance will benefit from them.

2.2 What Types of Studies Are Used in Psychological Research?

■ **Descriptive Studies Involve Observing and Classifying Behavior:** Researchers observe and describe naturally occurring behaviors to provide a systematic and objective analysis.

■ **Correlational Studies Examine How Variables Are Related:** Correlational studies are used to examine how variables are naturally related in the real world, but cannot be used to establish causality or the direction of a relationship (which variable caused changes in another variable). Correlational reasoning occurs in many contexts, so readers need to be able to recognize correlational designs in everyday contexts, not just when reading research reports.

■ **An Experiment Involves Manipulating Conditions:** In an experiment, researchers control the variations in the conditions that the participants experience (independent variables) and measure the outcomes (dependent variables) to gain an understanding of causality. Researchers need a control group to know if the experiment has had an effect.

■ **Random Sampling and Random Assignment Are Important for Research:** Researchers sample participants from the population they want to study (e.g., drivers). They use random sampling when everyone in the population is equally likely to participate in the study, a condition that rarely occurs. To establish causality between an intervention and an outcome, random assignment must be used. When random assignment is used, all participants have an equal chance of being assigned to any level of the independent variable, and preexisting differences between the groups are controlled.

2.3 What Are the Data Collection Methods of Psychological Science?

■ **Observing Is an Unobtrusive Strategy:** Data collected by observation must be defined clearly and collected systematically. Bias may occur in the data because the participants are aware they are being observed or because of the observer's expectations.

■ **Case Studies Examine Individual Lives and Organizations:** A case study, one kind of descriptive study, examines an individual or an organization. An intensive study of an individual or organization can be useful for examining an unusual participant or unusual research question. Interpretation of a case study, however, can be subjective.

■ **Asking Takes a More Active Approach:** Surveys, questionnaires, and interviews can be used to directly ask people about their thoughts and behaviors. Self-report data may be biased by the respondents' desire to present themselves in a particular way (e.g., smart, honest). Culturally sensitive research recognizes the differences among people from different cultural groups and from different language backgrounds.

■ **Response Performance Measures the Processing of Information:** Measuring reaction times and response accuracy and asking people to make stimulus judgments are methods used to examine how people respond to psychological tasks.

■ **Body/Brain Activity Can Be Measured Directly:** Electrophysiology (often using an electroencephalograph, or EEG) measures the brain's electrical activity. Brain imaging is done using positron emission tomography (PET), magnetic resonance imaging (MRI), and functional magnetic resonance imaging (fMRI). Transcranial magnetic stimulation (TMS) disrupts normal brain activity, allowing researchers to infer the brain processing involved in particular thoughts, feelings, and behaviors.

■ **Research with Animals Provides Important Data:** Research involving nonhuman animals provides useful, although simpler, models of behavior and of genetics. The purpose of such research may be to learn about animals' behavior or to make inferences about human behavior.

■ **There Are Ethical Issues to Consider:** Ethical research is governed by a variety of principles that ensure fair and informed treatment of participants.

2.4 How Are Data Analyzed and Evaluated?

■ **Good Research Requires Valid, Reliable, and Accurate Data:** Data must be meaningful (valid) and their measurement reliable (i.e., consistent and stable) and accurate.

■ **Descriptive Statistics Provide a Summary of the Data:** Measures of central tendency and variability are used to describe data.

- **Correlations Describe the Relationships between Variables:** A correlation is a descriptive statistic that describes the strength and direction of the relationship between two variables. Correlations close to zero signify weak relationships; correlations near +1.0 or −1.0 signify strong relationships.

- **Inferential Statistics Permit Generalizations:** Inferential statistics allow us to decide whether differences between two or more groups are probably just chance variations (suggesting that the populations the groups were drawn from are the same) or whether they reflect true differences in the populations being compared. Meta-analysis combines the results of several studies to arrive at a conclusion.

Key Terms

accuracy, p. 65
case studies, p. 52
central tendency, p. 65
confound, p. 40
control group, p. 40
correlational studies, p. 38
cross-sectional studies, p. 36
culturally sensitive
    research, p. 50
data, p. 31
dependent variable, p. 40
descriptive statistics, p. 65
descriptive studies, p. 35
directionality problem, p. 38
electroencephalograph
    (EEG), p. 57

experiment, p. 40
experimental groups, p. 40
experimenter expectancy
    effect, p. 37
external validity, p. 44
functional magnetic resonance
    imaging (fMRI), p. 59
hypothesis, p. 31
independent variable, p. 40
inferential statistics, p. 68
institutional review boards
    (IRBs), p. 60
internal validity, p. 64
longitudinal studies, p. 36
magnetic resonance imaging
    (MRI), p. 58

mean, p. 66
median, p. 66
meta-analysis, p. 68
mode, p. 66
naturalistic observation, p. 35
observational techniques, p. 50
observer bias, p. 36
participant observation, p. 35
population, p. 43
positron emission tomography
    (PET), p. 58
random assignment, p. 45
reactivity, p. 51
reliability, p. 64
replication, p. 32
research, p. 31

response performance, p. 55
sample, p. 43
scatterplot, p. 66
scientific method, p. 31
selection bias, p. 44
self-report methods, p. 54
standard deviation, p. 66
theory, p. 31
third variable problem, p. 39
transcranial magnetic
    stimulation (TMS), p. 59
variability, p. 66
variable, p. 34

Practice Test

1. Which of the following is a technique that increases scientists' confidence in the findings from a given research study?
  a. amiable skepticism
  b. operationalization of variables
  c. replication
  d. serendipity

For the following five questions, imagine you are designing a study to investigate whether deep breathing causes students to feel less stressed. Because you are investigating a causal question, you will need to employ experimental research. For each step in the design process, indicate the most scientifically sound decision.

2. Which hypothesis is stronger? Why?
  a. Stress levels will differ between students who engage in deep breathing and those who do not.
  b. Students who engage in deep breathing will report less stress than those who do not engage in deep breathing.

3. Which sampling method is strongest? Why?
  a. Obtain an alphabetical list of all students enrolled at the college. Invite every fifth person on the list to participate in the study.

  b. Post a note to your Facebook and MySpace accounts letting friends know you would like their help with the study. Ask your friends to let their friends know about the study, too.
  c. Post fliers around local gyms and yoga studios inviting people to participate in your study.

4. Which set of conditions should be included in the study? Why?
  a. All participants should be given written directions for a deep-breathing exercise.
  b. Some participants should be given written directions for a deep-breathing exercise; some participants should be given a DVD with demonstrations of deep-breathing exercises.
  c. Some participants should be given written directions for a deep-breathing exercise; some participants should be given no instructions regarding their breathing.

5. How should participants be chosen for each condition? Why?
  a. Once people agree to participate in the study, flip a coin to decide if each will be in the experimental or control condition.
  b. Let participants select which condition they would like to be in.

The answer key for the Practice Tests can be found at the back of the book. It also includes answers to the green caption questions.

3

Biology and Behavior

LENORE WEXLER HAD SO LITTLE CONTROL OVER HER MOVEMENTS that she stumbled across the street. A policeman watched her. Then he asked her why she was drinking so early in the day. Wexler was not drinking, however. She was showing the first symptoms of Huntingon's disease. This genetic disorder affects the nervous system, specifically damaging parts of the brain (**Figure 3.1**). The damage results in mental deterioration, abnormal body movements, loss of control over all movement, dementia, and eventually death.

(a)

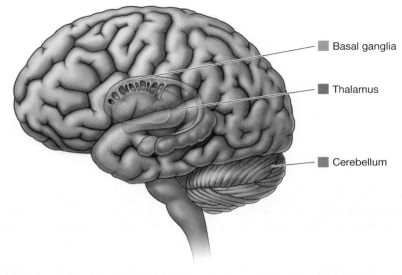

■ Basal ganglia

■ Thalamus

■ Cerebellum

FIGURE 3.1 Huntington's Disease as a Brain Disorder This diagram shows the areas of the brain damaged by Huntington's disease.

(b)

FIGURE 3.2 Huntington's Disease as an Inheritable Condition (a) One of the most famous people to have suffered from Huntington's disease is the folksinger Woody Guthrie, the writer and performer of classic songs such as "This Land Is Your Land." Guthrie died of Huntington's at age 55, in 1967. **(b)** Woody Guthrie fathered eight children. His most famous child is the folksinger Arlo Guthrie, the writer and performer of classic songs such as "Alice's Restaurant." Like his siblings, Arlo Guthrie has a 50/50 chance of inheriting Huntington's. Two of his siblings have inherited the disease, but he has not exhibited symptoms of it.

The first symptoms of Huntington's typically appear when people are middle-aged, but they can occur much earlier. The afflicted person develops a jerky walk and eventually loses the ability to walk, write, or speak. Emotional and personality changes occur, such as extreme anxiety and depression. Many people in the early stages of the disease commit suicide. No cure has been found.

Lenore Wexler was the mother of Nancy Wexler. At the time of her mother's illness, Wexler was a clinical psychologist. After her mother's death—from Huntington's, in 1978—she changed the nature of her scientific research. Moving from the clinical area of the field to the biological area, Wexler dedicated herself to finding the genetic marker for the progressive, degenerative disorder that had killed her mother. This dedication and love for her mother were rewarded when Wexler found the genetic marker for Huntington's.

If a parent has Huntington's, a biological child has a 50/50 chance of developing the disorder. Because symptoms often do not appear before the afflicted person is around 40, many of those with Huntington's have children before they realize they have a genetic disorder. Those who have relatives with Huntington's spend a good part of their lives wondering whether they will develop symptoms and whether it is safe for them to have children (**Figure 3.2**).

Thanks to the work of Nancy Wexler and her colleagues, people can now take a genetic test to determine whether they are going to develop the disease. But Wexler decided not to take the genetic test that she played an integral role in developing. Now in her early 60s, she shows no signs of the disease, and her chances of developing it are dropping each year.

If one of your immediate relatives showed symptoms of Huntington's, would you take the test? Suppose you tested positive for Huntington's—or any fatal illness. How might that knowledge affect your future? Would you live the rest of your life with the same goals? Would you stay in school, aim for the same career, keep working if you are already working? How might your personal relationships be affected? Would you remain hopeful?

To know what makes us who we are, we need to understand how physiological processes affect our thoughts, feelings, and behavior. We need to understand the genetic underpinnings of those physiological processes. We also need to understand how these aspects of our biology interact with the environment: How does nurture influence nature, and how does nature influence nurture? ∎

3.1 How Does the Nervous System Operate?

Over the past three decades, scientific understanding of the physiological foundations of psychological activity has increased dramatically. As technology has advanced, scientists have developed sophisticated tools to explore the biological bases of who we are. Researchers have learned a great deal about the biological basis of brain activity. For example, they have been able to study why particular drugs affect thoughts and emotions in specific ways. And as noted in the previous chapters, brain imaging has enabled psychologists to better understand the functions of different brain regions. In addition to examining people's genetic makeup—predicting who will develop specific disorders and understanding how certain diseases are passed from one generation to the next—researchers have also identified the functions of specific genes. For example, they know which combination of genes predisposes people to be outgoing or to be intelligent. In presenting such intimate yet far-ranging developments, this chapter will introduce you to the basics of some human biological systems. You are about to learn how psychological activity is related to the nervous system, the endocrine system, and genetics.

The nervous system is an amazing network, responsible for everything we think, feel, or do. Essentially, each of us *is* a nervous system. The basic units of this system are nerve cells, called **neurons (Figure 3.3)**. These cells receive, integrate, and transmit information in the nervous system. Complex networks of neurons sending and receiving signals are the functional basis of all psychological activity. Although the actions of single neurons are simple to describe, human complexity results from billions of neurons. Each of these billions makes contact with tens of thousands of other neurons. Neurons do not communicate randomly or arbitrarily, however. They communicate selectively with other neurons to form circuits, or *neural networks*. These networks develop through maturation and experience. In other words, permanent alliances form among groups of neurons.

The entire nervous system is divided into two functional units: The **central nervous system (CNS)** consists of the brain and the spinal cord, both of which contain massive numbers of nerve cells. The **peripheral nervous system (PNS)** consists of all the other nerve cells in the rest of the body. These two units are anatomically separate, but their functions are highly interdependent. The peripheral nervous system transmits a variety of information to the central nervous system. The central nervous system organizes and evaluates that information and then directs the peripheral nervous system to perform specific behaviors or make bodily adjustments.

Neurons Are Specialized for Communication

Neurons are specialized for communication. That is, unlike other cells, nerve cells are excitable: They are powered by electrical impulses and communicate with other nerve cells through chemical signals. During the reception phase, they

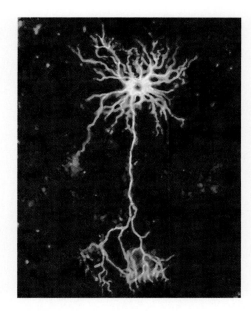

FIGURE 3.3 Human Nerve Cell Nerve cells, or neurons, like this one are the basic units of the human nervous system.

Learning Objectives

- Distinguish between the functions of distinct types of neurons.
- Describe the structure of the neuron.
- Describe the electrical and chemical changes that occur when neurons communicate.
- Identify the major neurotransmitters and their primary functions.

neurons The basic units of the nervous system; cells that receive, integrate, and transmit information in the nervous system. They operate through electrical impulses, communicate with other neurons through chemical signals, and form neural networks.

central nervous system (CNS) The brain and the spinal cord.

peripheral nervous system (PNS) All nerve cells in the body that are not part of the central nervous system. The peripheral nervous system includes the somatic and autonomic nervous systems (discussed later in this chapter).

sensory neurons One of the three types of neurons; these afferent neurons detect information from the physical world and pass that information to the brain.

motor neurons One of the three types of neurons; these efferent neurons direct muscles to contract or relax, thereby producing movement.

interneurons One of the three types of neurons; these neurons communicate only with other neurons.

take in the chemical signals from neighboring neurons. During integration, they assess the incoming signals. During transmission, they pass their own signals to yet other receiving neurons.

TYPES OF NEURONS The three basic types of neurons are *sensory neurons, motor neurons,* and *interneurons* (**Figure 3.4**). **Sensory neurons** detect information from the physical world and pass that information along to the brain, usually via the spinal cord. Sensory neurons are often called *afferent* neurons. This term means that they carry information to the brain. To get a sense of how fast that process can work, think of the last time you touched something hot or accidentally pricked yourself with a sharp object, such as a tack. Those signals triggered your body's nearly instantaneous response and sensory experience of the impact. The sensory nerves that provide information from the skin and muscles are referred to as *somatosensory nerves.* (This term comes from the Greek for "body sense." It means sensations experienced from within the body.)

Motor neurons direct muscles to contract or relax, thereby producing movement. Motor neurons are therefore *efferent* neurons. This term means that they transmit signals from the brain to the muscles throughout the body. **Interneurons** communicate within local or short-distance circuits. That is, interneurons integrate neural activity within a single area rather than transmitting information to other brain structures or to the body organs.

Together, sensory and motor neurons control movement. For instance, if you are using a pen to take notes as you read these words, you are contracting and relaxing your hand muscles and finger muscles to adjust your fingers' pressure on the pen. When you want to use the pen, your brain sends a message via motor neurons to your finger muscles so they move in specific ways. Receptors in both your skin and your muscles send back messages through sensory neurons to help determine how much pressure is needed to hold the pen. This symphony of neural communication for a task as simple as using a pen is remarkable, and yet most of us employ motor control so easily that we rarely think about it. In fact, our *reflexes,* automatic motor responses, occur before we even think about those responses. For each reflex action, a handful of neurons simply converts sensation into action.

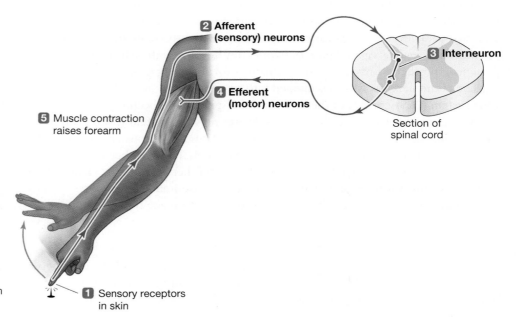

FIGURE 3.4 The Three Types of Neurons Receptors send afferent signals to the brain for processing. To produce a response, an efferent signal is then sent from the brain to the body via the spinal cord.

2 Afferent (sensory) neurons

3 Interneuron

Section of spinal cord

4 Efferent (motor) neurons

5 Muscle contraction raises forearm

1 Sensory receptors in skin

NEURON STRUCTURE In addition to performing different functions, neurons have a wide assortment of shapes and sizes. A typical neuron has four structural regions that participate in communication functions: the *dendrites,* the *cell body,* the *axon,* and the *terminal buttons* (**Figure 3.5**). The **dendrites** are short, branchlike appendages that increase the neuron's receptive field and detect chemical signals from neighboring neurons. In the **cell body,** also known as the *soma* (Greek for "body"), the information received from thousands of other neurons is collected and integrated.

Once the incoming information from many other neurons has been integrated in the cell body, electrical impulses are transmitted along a long, narrow outgrowth known as the **axon.** Axons vary tremendously in length, from a few millimeters to more than a meter. The longest axons stretch from the spinal cord to the big toe. You probably have heard the term *nerve,* as in "a pinched nerve." In this context, a nerve is a bundle of axons that carry information between the brain and other specific locations in the body. At the end of the axon are knoblike structures called **terminal buttons.** The site where chemical communication occurs between neurons is called the **synapse.** Because neurons do not touch each other, they communicate by sending chemicals into the **synaptic cleft,** a tiny gap between the axon of the "sending" neuron and the dendrites of the "receiving" neurons. Chemicals leave one neuron, cross the synapse, and pass signals along to other neurons' dendrites. Thus neurons in the chain of communication are referred to as *presynaptic* or *postsynaptic.*

The neuron's membrane plays an important role in communication between neurons: It regulates the concentration of electrically charged molecules that are the basis of the neuron's electrical activity. These electrical signals travel quickly down the axon because of the fatty **myelin sheath** that encases and insulates it like the plastic tubing around wires in an electrical cord. The myelin sheath is made up of *glial cells,* commonly called *neuroglia* or simply *glia* (Greek for "glue"). It grows along an axon in short segments. Between these segments are small gaps of exposed axon called the **nodes of Ranvier** (after the researcher who first described them). Located at these gaps are *ion channels.* These specialized pores allow negatively and positively charged molecules called *ions* to pass in and out of the cell when the neuron transmits signals down the axon.

THE RESTING MEMBRANE POTENTIAL IS NEGATIVELY CHARGED When a neuron is resting, not active, the inside and outside are different electrically. This phenomenon is called the **resting membrane potential.** The difference occurs because the ratio of negative to positive ions is greater inside the neuron than outside it. Therefore, the electrical charge inside the neuron is slightly more negative

dendrites Branchlike extensions of the neuron that detect information from other neurons.

cell body Site, in the neuron, where information from thousands of other neurons is collected and integrated.

axon A long narrow outgrowth of a neuron by which information is transmitted to other neurons.

terminal buttons Small nodules, at the ends of axons, that release chemical signals from the neuron into the synapse.

synapse The site at which chemical communication occurs between neurons.

synaptic cleft The gap between the axon of a "sending" neuron and the dendrites of a "receiving" neuron; it contains extracellular fluid.

myelin sheath A fatty material, made up of glial cells, that insulates the axon and allows for the rapid movement of electrical impulses along the axon.

nodes of Ranvier Small gaps of exposed axon, between the segments of myelin sheath, where action potentials are transmitted.

resting membrane potential The electrical charge of a neuron when it is not active.

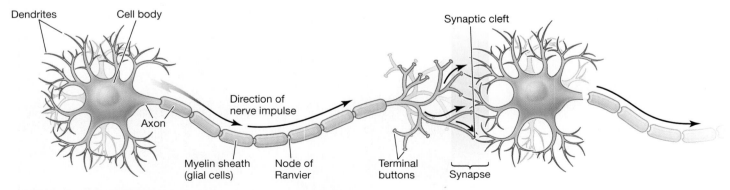

FIGURE 3.5 Neuron Structure Messages are received by the dendrites, processed in the cell body, transmitted along the axon, and sent to other neurons via chemical substances released from the terminal buttons across the synaptic cleft.

than the electrical charge outside. When the electrical charge inside a neuron is different from the electrical charge outside the neuron, this condition is known as *polarization*. Thus, when a neuron has more negative ions inside it than outside it, the neuron is described as being *polarized*. The polarized state of the resting neuron creates the electrical energy necessary to power the firing of the neuron.

THE ROLES OF SODIUM AND POTASSIUM IONS Two types of ions that contribute to a neuron's resting membrane potential are *sodium ions* and *potassium ions*. Although other ions are involved in neural activity, sodium and potassium are most important for this discussion. Ions pass through the cell membrane at the ion channels (**Figure 3.6**). Each channel matches a specific type of ion: Sodium channels allow sodium ions but not potassium ions to pass through the membrane, and potassium channels allow potassium ions but not sodium ions to pass through the membrane. The flow of ions through each channel is controlled by a gating mechanism. When a gate is open, ions flow in and out of the cell membrane. A closed gate will prevent their passage. Ion flow is also affected by the cell membrane's selective permeability. That is, much like a bouncer at an exclusive nightclub, the membrane allows some types of ions to cross more easily than others. Partially as a result of this selective permeability of the cell

FIGURE 3.6 Resting Membrane Potential A neuron at rest is polarized: It has a different electrical charge inside and outside. The passage of negative and positive ions inside and outside the membrane is regulated by ion channels located at the nodes of Ranvier.

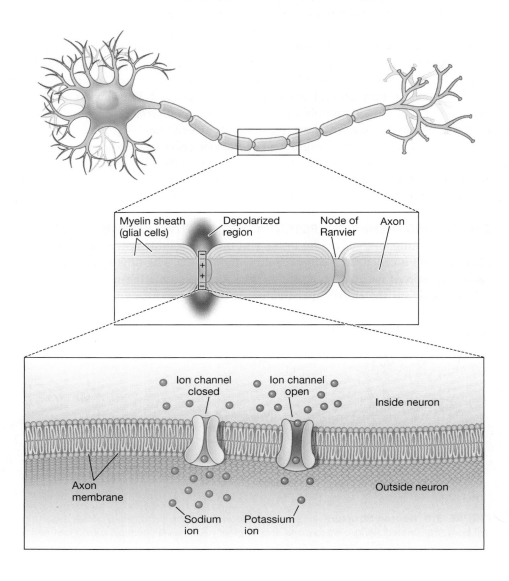

membrane, more potassium than sodium is inside the neuron. This imbalance contributes to polarization. Another mechanism in the membrane that contributes to polarization is called the *sodium-potassium pump*. This pump works to increase potassium and decrease sodium inside the neuron.

Action Potentials Cause Neural Communication

Neural communication depends on a neuron's ability to respond to incoming stimulation. The neuron responds by changing electrically and then passing along signals to other neurons. An **action potential,** also called *neural firing,* is the electrical signal that passes along the axon and causes the release of chemicals that transmit signals to other neurons. The following sections examine some factors that contribute to the firing of an action potential.

CHANGES IN ELECTRICAL POTENTIAL LEAD TO ACTION A neuron receives chemical signals from nearby neurons through its dendrites. By affecting polarization, these signals tell the neuron whether to fire. The signals arrive at the dendrites by the thousands and are of two types: *excitatory* and *inhibitory.* Excitatory signals depolarize the cell membrane (i.e., reduce polarization), increasing the likelihood that the neuron will fire. Inhibitory signals hyperpolarize the cell (i.e., increase polarization), decreasing the likelihood that the neuron will fire. Excitatory and inhibitory signals received by the dendrites are integrated within the neuron. If the total amount of excitatory input surpasses the neuron's threshold, an action potential is generated.

When a neuron fires, the sodium gates in the cell membrane open. The open gates allow sodium ions to rush into the neuron. This influx of sodium causes the inside of the neuron to become slightly more positively charged than the outside. A fraction of a second later, potassium channels open to allow the potassium ions inside the cell membrane to rush out. This change from a negative charge to a positive one inside the neuron is the basis of the action potential. As the sodium ion channels close, the sodium ions stop entering the cell. Similarly, as the potassium ion channels close, potassium ions stop exiting the cell. Thus, during this process, the electrical charge inside the cell starts out slightly negative in its initial resting state. As the cell fires and allows more positive ions inside, the charge becomes positive. Through natural restoration, the charge then returns to its slightly negative resting state (**Figure 3.7**).

action potential The neural impulse that passes along the axon and subsequently causes the release of chemicals from the terminal buttons.

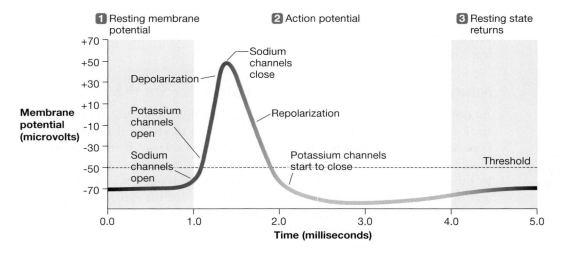

1 Resting membrane potential 2 Action potential 3 Resting state returns

Sodium channels close

Depolarization

Potassium channels open

Sodium channels open

Repolarization

Potassium channels start to close

Threshold

Membrane potential (microvolts)

+70, +50, +30, +10, -10, -30, -50, -70

Time (milliseconds): 0.0, 1.0, 2.0, 3.0, 4.0, 5.0

FIGURE 3.7 Action Potential The electrical charge inside the neuron starts out slightly negative (resting membrane potential). As the neuron fires, it allows more positive ions inside the cell (depolarization). Through natural restoration (repolarization), it then returns to its slightly negative resting state. This three-part process repeats at every node of Ranvier along the axon.

ACTION POTENTIALS SPREAD ALONG THE AXON When the neuron fires, the cell membrane's depolarization moves along the axon like a wave. This movement is called *propagation*. Sodium ions rush through their ion channels, causing adjacent sodium channels to open. Thus, like toppling dominoes, sodium ion channels open successively. The action potential always moves down the axon away from the cell body to the terminal buttons. Because of the insulation provided by the myelin sheath, the action potential skips quickly along the axon. It pauses briefly to be recharged at each node of Ranvier on the axon. The entire process takes about $1/_{1,000}$ of a second, permitting the fast and frequent adjustments required for coordinating motor activity.

To understand the importance of neural insulation, consider the disease multiple sclerosis (MS). The earliest symptoms can begin in young adulthood and often include numbness in the limbs and blurry vision. This especially tragic neurological disorder is characterized by deterioration of the myelin sheath. Because the myelin insulation helps messages move quickly along axons, demyelination slows down neural impulses. The axons essentially short-circuit, and normal neural communication is interrupted. Motor actions become jerky, as those afflicted lose the ability to coordinate motor movements. Over time, movement, sensation, and coordination are severely impaired. As the myelin sheath disintegrates, axons are exposed and may start to break down. The life expectancy of people with MS is 5 to 10 years less than that of people who are not afflicted.

ALL-OR-NONE PRINCIPLE Any one signal received by the neuron has little influence on whether the neuron fires. Normally, the neuron is barraged by thousands of excitatory and inhibitory signals, and its firing is determined by the number and frequency of those signals. If the sum of excitatory and inhibitory signals leads to a positive change in voltage that exceeds the neuron's firing threshold, an action potential is generated.

A neuron either fires or it does not. It cannot partially fire. The **all-or-none principle** dictates that a neuron fires with the same potency each time. In other words, it does not fire in a way that can be described as weak or strong. How often the neuron fires depends on the strength of stimulation.

For the sake of comparison, suppose you are playing a video game in which you fire missiles by pressing a button. Every time you press the button, a missile is launched at the same velocity as the previous one. It makes no difference how hard you press the button. If you keep your finger on the button, additional missiles fire in rapid succession. Likewise, if a neuron in the visual system, for example, receives information that a light is bright, it might respond by firing more rapidly and more often than when it receives information that the light is dim. Regardless of whether the light is bright or dim, however, the strength of the firing will be the same every time.

Neurotransmitters Bind to Receptors across the Synapse

As noted earlier, neurons do not touch one another. They are separated by a small space known as the synaptic cleft, at the site of chemical communication between neurons. Action potentials cause neurons to release chemicals from their terminal buttons. These chemicals travel across the synaptic cleft and are received by other neurons' dendrites. The neuron that sends the signal is called the *presynaptic neuron,* and the one that receives the signal is called the *postsynaptic neuron.*

How do these chemical signals work (**Figure 3.8**)? Inside each terminal button are vesicles (small packages) that contain **neurotransmitters.** Neurotransmitters are chemical substances that carry signals across the synaptic cleft. After an

all-or-none principle The principle whereby a neuron fires with the same potency each time, although frequency can vary; a neuron either fires or not—it cannot partially fire.

neurotransmitters Chemical substances that carry signals from one neuron to another.

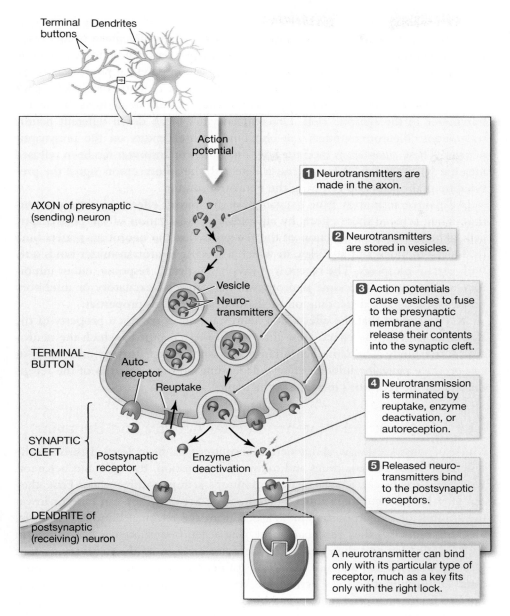

FIGURE 3.8 How Neurotransmitters Work

Terminal buttons **Dendrites**

Action potential

AXON of presynaptic (sending) neuron

1 Neurotransmitters are made in the axon.

2 Neurotransmitters are stored in vesicles.

Vesicle
Neuro-transmitters

3 Action potentials cause vesicles to fuse to the presynaptic membrane and release their contents into the synaptic cleft.

TERMINAL BUTTON
Auto-receptor
Reuptake

4 Neurotransmission is terminated by reuptake, enzyme deactivation, or autoreception.

SYNAPTIC CLEFT
Postsynaptic receptor
Enzyme deactivation

5 Released neuro-transmitters bind to the postsynaptic receptors.

DENDRITE of postsynaptic (receiving) neuron

A neurotransmitter can bind only with its particular type of receptor, much as a key fits only with the right lock.

action potential travels to the terminal button, it causes the vesicles to attach to the presynaptic membrane and release their neurotransmitters into the synaptic cleft. These neurotransmitters then spread across the synaptic cleft and attach themselves, or *bind,* to receptors on the postsynaptic neuron. **Receptors** are specialized protein molecules located on the postsynaptic membrane that specifically respond to the chemical structure of the neurotransmitter available in the synapse. The binding of a neurotransmitter with a receptor produces an excitatory or inhibitory signal for the postsynaptic neuron. An excitatory signal encourages the neuron to fire, whereas an inhibitory signal discourages it from firing.

NEUROTRANSMITTERS BIND WITH SPECIFIC RECEPTORS More than 60 chemicals convey information in the nervous system. Different neurotransmitters influence either emotion, thought, or behavior. In much the same way as a lock opens only with the correct key, each receptor can be influenced by only one type of neurotransmitter.

Once a neurotransmitter is released into the synaptic cleft, it continues to fill and stimulate that receptor. It also blocks new signals until its influence is terminated.

receptors In neurons, specialized protein molecules on the postsynaptic membrane; neurotransmitters bind to these molecules after passing across the synaptic cleft.

reuptake The process whereby a neurotransmitter is taken back into the presynaptic terminal buttons, thereby stopping its activity.

agonists Drugs that enhance the actions of neurotransmitters.

antagonists Drugs that inhibit the actions of neurotransmitters.

The three major events that terminate the neurotransmitter's influence in the synaptic cleft are *reuptake, enzyme deactivation,* and *autoreception.* **Reuptake** occurs when the neurotransmitter is taken back into the presynaptic terminal buttons. The cycle of reuptake and release repeats continuously. An action potential prompts terminal buttons to release the neurotransmitter into the synaptic cleft and then take it back for recycling. *Enzyme deactivation* then occurs when an enzyme destroys the neurotransmitter in the synaptic cleft. Different enzymes break down different neurotransmitters. Neurotransmitters can also bind with receptors on the presynaptic neuron. These *autoreceptors* monitor how much neurotransmitter has been released into the synaptic cleft. When excess is detected, the autoreceptors signal the presynaptic neuron to stop releasing the neurotransmitter.

All neurotransmitters have excitatory or inhibitory effects on action potentials. They achieve these effects by affecting the polarization of the postsynaptic cells. The effects are a function of the receptors that the neurotransmitters bind to. Recall the lock and key idea, in which a specific neurotransmitter binds only with certain receptors. The receptor always has a specific response, either inhibitory or excitatory. The same neurotransmitter can send excitatory or inhibitory postsynaptic signals, depending on the particular receptor's properties.

Keep in mind that the effects of a neurotransmitter are not a property of the chemical. Instead, the effects are a function of the receptor to which the neurotransmitter binds. The same neurotransmitter can be excitatory or inhibitory, or can produce radically different effects, depending on the properties of the receptor and on the receptor's location in the brain.

Neurotransmitters Influence Mental Activity and Behavior

Much of what we know about neurotransmitters has been learned through the systematic study of how drugs and toxins affect emotion, thought, and behavior. Drugs and toxins can alter a neurotransmitter's action in three ways: First, they can alter how a neurotransmitter is synthesized. Second, they can raise or lower the amount of a neurotransmitter released from the terminal buttons. Third, by blocking reuptake, they can change the way a neurotransmitter is deactivated in the synaptic cleft and therefore affect the concentration of the neurotransmitter. Drugs and toxins that enhance the actions of neurotransmitters are known as **agonists.** Drugs inhibiting these actions are known as **antagonists.** Drugs and toxins can also mimic neurotransmitters and bind with their receptors as if they were the real thing (**Figure 3.9**). Addictive drugs such as heroin and cocaine, for example, have their effects because they are chemically similar to naturally occurring neurotransmitters. The receptors cannot differentiate between the ingested drug and the real neurotransmitter released from a presynaptic neuron. That is, although a neurotransmitter fits a receptor the way a key fits a lock, the receptor-lock cannot tell a real neurotransmitter-key from a forgery—either will open it.

Researchers often inject agonists or antagonists into animals' brains to assess how neurotransmitters affect behavior. The goal is to develop drug treatments for many psychological and medical disorders. For instance, researchers can test the hypothesis that a certain neurotransmitter in a specific brain region leads to increased eating. Injecting an agonist into that brain region should increase eating. Injecting an antagonist should decrease eating.

TYPES OF NEUROTRANSMITTERS There are many kinds of neurotransmitters. Nine of them have been the focus of research in psychological science. These nine neurotransmitters are particularly important in understanding how we think, feel, and behave (**Table 3.1**).

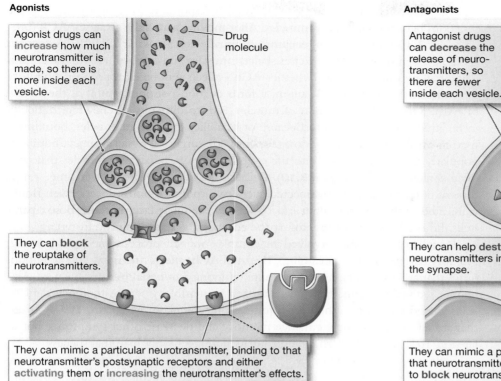

Agonists

Agonist drugs can **increase** how much neurotransmitter is made, so there is more inside each vesicle.

Drug molecule

They can **block** the reuptake of neurotransmitters.

They can mimic a particular neurotransmitter, binding to that neurotransmitter's postsynaptic receptors and either **activating** them or **increasing** the neurotransmitter's effects.

Antagonists

Antagonist drugs can **decrease** the release of neuro-transmitters, so there are fewer inside each vesicle.

Drug molecule

They can help **destroy** neurotransmitters in the synapse.

They can mimic a particular neurotransmitter, binding to that neurotransmitter's postsynaptic receptors enough to **block** neurotransmitter binding.

FIGURE 3.9 How Drugs Work

TABLE 3.1	Common Neurotransmitters and Their Major Functions
Neurotransmitter	**Functions**
Acetylcholine	Motor control over muscles Learning, memory, sleeping, and dreaming
Epinephrine	Energy
Norepinephrine	Arousal and vigilance
Serotonin	Emotional states and impulsiveness Dreaming
Dopamine	Reward and motivation Motor control over voluntary movement
GABA (gamma-aminobutyric acid)	Inhibition of action potentials Anxiety reduction Intoxication (through alcohol)
Glutamate	Enhancement of action potentials Learning and memory
Endorphins	Pain reduction Reward
substance P	Pain perception Mood and anxiety

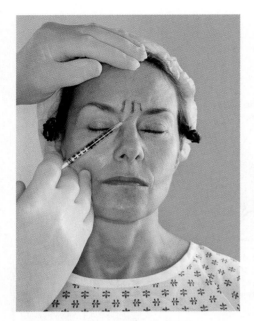

FIGURE 3.10 Acetylcholine and Botox Acetylcholine (ACh) is responsible for motor control between nerves and muscles. Botox inhibits the release of ACh, paralyzing muscles. Here, a woman receives a Botox injection to remove wrinkles in her forehead. **How do you feel about the practice of paralyzing muscles to change appearance? Why do you feel this way?**

acetylcholine (ACh) The neurotransmitter responsible for motor control at the junction between nerves and muscles; also involved in mental processes such as learning, memory, sleeping, and dreaming.

epinephrine A monoamine neurotransmitter responsible for bursts of energy after an event that is exciting or threatening.

norepinephrine A monoamine neurotransmitter involved in states of arousal and awareness.

serotonin A monoamine neurotransmitter important for a wide range of psychological activity, including emotional states, impulse control, and dreaming.

dopamine A monoamine neurotransmitter involved in motivation, reward, and motor control over voluntary movement.

The neurotransmitter **acetylcholine (ACh)** is responsible for motor control at the junctions between nerves and muscles. After moving across the synapses, ACh (pronounced A-C-H) binds with receptors on muscle cells, making the muscles contract or relax. For instance, ACh excites skeletal muscles and inhibits heart muscle. As is true of all neurotransmitters, whether ACh's effects will be excitatory or inhibitory depends on the receptors. Botulism, a form of food poisoning, inhibits the release of ACh. The resulting paralysis of muscles leads to difficulty in chewing, difficulty in breathing, and often death. Because of its ability to paralyze muscles, botulism is used in small, much less toxic doses for cosmetic surgery. Physicians inject botulism, popularly known as Botox, into the eyebrow region, paralyzing muscles that produce certain wrinkles (**Figure 3.10**). Because the effects wear off over time, a new dose of botulism needs to be injected every two to four months. If too much Botox is injected, however, the result can be an expressionless face, because Botox paralyzes the facial muscles we use to express emotions, as in smiling and frowning.

Acetylcholine is also involved in complex mental processes such as learning, memory, sleeping, and dreaming. Because ACh affects memory and attention, drugs that are ACh antagonists can cause temporary amnesia. In a similar way, Alzheimer's disease, a condition characterized primarily by severe memory deficits, is associated with diminished ACh functioning (Geula & Mesulam, 1994). Drugs that are ACh agonists may enhance memory and decrease other symptoms, but so far drug treatments for Alzheimer's have experienced only marginal success.

Four transmitters (epinephrine, norepinephrine, serotonin, and dopamine) are grouped together because each has the same basic molecular structure. Together they are called *monoamines*. Their major functions are to regulate arousal, regulate feelings, and motivate behavior.

The neurotransmitter **epinephrine** was initially called *adrenaline.* This name is the basis for the phrase *adrenaline rush,* a burst of energy caused by the release of epinephrine that binds to receptors throughout the body. This adrenaline rush is part of a system that prepares the body for dealing with threats from an environment (this fight-or-flight response is discussed in Chapter 11, "Health and Well-Being"). **Norepinephrine** is involved in states of arousal and alertness. It is especially important for vigilance, a heightened sensitivity to what is going on around you. Norepinephrine appears useful for fine-tuning the clarity of attention.

Serotonin is involved in a wide range of psychological activity. It is especially important for emotional states, impulse control, and dreaming. Low levels of serotonin are associated with sad and anxious moods, food cravings, and aggressive behavior. Drugs that block serotonin reuptake and thus leave more serotonin at the synapse to bind with the postsynaptic neurons are used to treat a wide array of mental and behavioral disorders, including depression, obsessive-compulsive disorders, eating disorders, and obesity (Tollesfson, 1995). One class of drugs that specifically target serotonin is prescribed widely to treat depression. These drugs, which include Prozac, are referred to as *selective serotonin reuptake inhibitors,* or *SSRIs.*

Dopamine serves many significant brain functions, especially motivation and reward. Many theorists believe dopamine is the primary neurotransmitter that communicates which activities may be rewarding. Eating when hungry, drinking when thirsty, and having sex when aroused, for example, activate dopamine receptors and therefore are experienced as pleasurable. At the same time, dopamine activation is involved in motor control and planning. It helps guide our behavior toward things—objects and experiences—that will lead to additional reward.

A lack of dopamine may be involved in problems with movement, and dopamine depletion is implicated in Parkinson's disease (PD). First identified by the physician James Parkinson in 1917, Parkinson's is a degenerative and fatal neurological disorder marked by muscular rigidity, tremors, and difficulty initiating voluntary action. It affects about 1 in every 200 older adults and occurs in all known cultures. The actor Michael J. Fox is one of the many famous people who have developed this disease. Most people with Parkinson's do not experience symptoms until after age 50, but as Fox's case makes clear, the disease can occur earlier in life. With Parkinson's disease, the dopamine-producing neurons slowly die off. In the later stages of the disorder, people suffer from cognitive and mood disturbances. Injections of one of the chief building blocks of dopamine, *L-DOPA*, help the surviving neurons produce more dopamine. When used to treat Parkinson's disease, L-DOPA often produces a remarkable, though temporary, recovery.

A promising development in Parkinson's research is the transplantation of fetal tissue into human brains in the hope that the new fetal cells will produce dopamine. The first American to undergo fetal neural transplantation, Donald Wilson, regained the ability to walk and returned to his hobby of woodworking. Research in Canada has found that transplanted dopamine neurons thrive and can last as long as 14 years (Mendez et al., 2008; **Figure 3.11**). At the same time, other clinical studies using random assignment have not found large differences between patients receiving fetal cell transplants and those undergoing sham surgery, which mimics the real surgery but does not involve transplantation (Olanow et al., 2003). These methods are still being developed, though, and researchers continue to explore how fetal cell transplants might be used to treat brain disorders.

A more promising approach is *deep brain stimulation*. The physician Alim Louis Benabid pioneered this method, in 1987. It involves surgically implanting electrodes deep within the brain and then using mild electrical stimulation in the regions affected by the disorder, much the way a pacemaker stimulates the heart. Deep brain stimulation of motor regions of the brains of Parkinson's patients reverses many of the movement problems associated with the disease (DeLong & Wichmann, 2008). Researchers have reported successful long-term results from this treatment, lasting as long as six years (Lozano et al., 2010).

GABA (gamma-aminobutyric acid) is the primary inhibitory neurotransmitter in the nervous system. It is more widely distributed throughout the brain than most other neurotransmitters. Without the inhibitory effect of GABA, synaptic excitation might get out of control and spread through the brain chaotically.

"I'LL HAVE TO GET DR. KENDRICK TO REDUCE HIS DOSAGE OF PROZAC."

GABA Gamma-aminobutyric acid; the primary inhibitory transmitter in the nervous system.

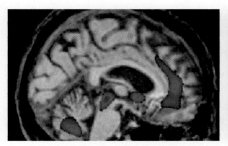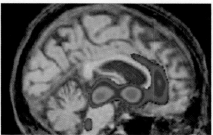

FIGURE 3.11 Hope for Parkinson's Patients In this study, neurosurgeons transplanted fetal tissue into two brain regions of a 48-year-old male. A brain scan using PET imaging indicates the survival and functioning of the transplanted dopamine neurons. (The areas in color show increased dopamine.)

glutamate The primary excitatory transmitter in the nervous system.

endorphins Neurotransmitters involved in natural pain reduction and reward.

substance P A neurotransmitter involved in pain perception.

Epileptic seizures may be caused by low levels of GABA (Upton, 1994). Drugs that are GABA agonists are widely used to treat anxiety disorders. For instance, people with nervous disorders commonly use benzodiazepines, which include drugs such as Valium, to relax. Ethyl alcohol—the type people drink—has similar effects on GABA receptors, which is why alcohol typically is experienced as relaxing. GABA reception also may be the primary mechanism by which alcohol interferes with motor coordination.

In contrast, **glutamate** is the primary excitatory transmitter in the nervous system and is involved in fast-acting neural transmission throughout the brain. Glutamate receptors aid learning and memory by strengthening synaptic connections.

Endorphins are involved in both natural pain reduction and reward (**Figure 3.12**). In the early 1970s, the pharmacology researchers Candace Pert and Solomon Snyder established that opiate drugs such as heroin and morphine bind to receptors in the brain, and this finding led to the discovery of naturally occurring substances that bind to those sites. Called *endorphins* (short for *endogenous morphine*), these substances are part of the body's natural defense against pain. Pain is useful because it signals to animals, human and nonhuman, that they are hurt or in danger and therefore should try to escape or withdraw. Pain can also interfere with adaptive functioning, however. If pain prevents animals from engaging in behaviors such as eating, competing, and mating, the animals fail to pass along their genes. Endorphins' painkilling, or analgesic, effects help animals perform these behaviors even when they are in pain. In humans, the administration of drugs, such as morphine, that bind with endorphin receptors reduces the subjective experience of pain. Apparently, morphine alters the way pain is experienced rather than blocking the nerves that transmit pain signals: People still feel pain, but they report detachment and do not care about the pain (Foley, 1993).

Substance P is another neurotransmitter involved in pain perception as well as mood states and anxiety. This mysterious-sounding substance was first identified in 1931 by the pharmacology researchers Ulf von Euler and John Gaddum, who referred to it in their notes simply by the initial *P*. Substance P helps transmit signals about pain to the brain. Probably the best evidence for it can be found at your local Mexican restaurant, where you can conduct your own experiment. Chili peppers such as jalapeños contain the substance capsaicin, which activates sensory neurons and leads to the release of substance P in the brain. This neural activity makes you feel your tongue and mouth burn, makes your eyes water, and makes your hand reach for the nearest pitcher of water. Water spreads capsaicin around, however, and causes the release of more substance P, which only intensifies the pain.

FIGURE 3.12 Exercise and Endorphins Endorphins are involved in both pain reduction and reward, and scientists think that endorphin production can be stimulated by strenuous exercise. An endurance event, such as a marathon or a speed skating competition, will yield an enormous endorphin rush. Here, the final leg runner in the Saudi men's 4 × 400 relay team, Yousef Ahmed Masrahi, celebrates after finishing first in the men's 4 × 400 relay final at the 16th Asian Games in Guangzhou on November 26, 2010.

Summing Up

How Does the Nervous System Operate?

Neurons are the nervous system's basic units. Their primary task is to take in information, integrate that information, and pass signals to other neurons. A neuron receives information at the dendrites and processes that information in its cell body. By firing, it passes signals down its axon and then to other neurons' dendrites. The insulating myelin sheath surrounding the axon allows the firing, or action potential, to travel, or propagate, rapidly. When a neuron is in a resting state, it is (slightly) negatively charged. Whether a neuron fires depends on the combination of excitatory and inhibitory signals the dendrites receive. Excitatory neurotransmitters make the postsynaptic neuron more likely to fire, and inhibitory neurotransmitters make the postsynaptic neuron less likely to fire. This firing results from the changes in the electrical charge across the cell membrane: Sodium ions rush in when the sodium channels open, and potassium ions rush out when the potassium channels open. When the channels close, sodium ions stop entering and potassium ions stop exiting, allowing the neuron to return to its resting state. The intensity of the excitatory signal affects the frequency of neural firing but not its strength—neurons fire on an all-or-none basis.

Action potentials cause vesicles to fuse to the presynaptic membrane and release neurotransmitters into the synaptic cleft. Neurotransmitters diffuse across the synaptic cleft and bind with specific postsynaptic receptors. These signals are terminated through reuptake, enzyme deactivation, or the actions of autoreceptors. Substances that enhance the actions of neurotransmitters are agonists. Substances that inhibit the actions of neurotransmitters are antagonists. The number of known substances that act as neurotransmitters is now more than 60 and growing, but certain neurotransmitters are especially important for psychological research: Acetylcholine is involved in motor control and several complex mental processes; epinephrine and norepinephrine are associated with energy, arousal, and attention; serotonin is important for emotional states, impulse control, and dreaming; dopamine is involved in reward, motivation, and motor control; GABA and glutamate are related to general inhibition and excitation; endorphins are important in pain reduction; and substance P is related to pain perception.

Measuring Up

1. Neurons communicate by firing. Put the following steps in the correct order so they describe this process.
   a. The presynaptic neuron "reuptakes" the neurotransmitter from the synapse.
   b. If the postsynaptic neuron receives a sufficient amount of excitatory input, it will respond by opening its sodium and potassium channels.
   c. Neurotransmitters bind with receptors on the postsynaptic neuron's dendrites.
   d. Excitatory and inhibitory messages are compared in the cell body of the postsynaptic neuron.
   e. Neurotransmitters are released into the synaptic cleft by a presynaptic neuron.
   f. The charge inside the cell goes from negative to positive.
   g. The channels open in succession as the information is passed along the axon away from the cell body and toward the terminal buttons.
   h. The sodium and potassium channels close, and the neuron returns to its resting potential.

2. Match each major neurotransmitter with its major functions.

Neurotransmitter	Major Functions
a. substance P	1. emotional states, impulse control, dreaming
b. glutamate	2. reward, motivation, voluntary muscle control
c. acetylcholine	3. enhancing action potentials, facilitating learning and memory
d. serotonin	4. pain perception, mood, and anxiety
e. endorphins	5. motor control, learning, memory, sleeping, dreaming
f. dopamine	6. reward, pain reduction
g. GABA	7. inhibiting action potentials, reducing anxiety, intoxication (through alcohol)

Answers: 1. e, c, d, b, f, g, h, a.
2. a. 4; b. 3; c. 5; d. 1; e. 6; f. 2; g. 7.

Learning Objective

■ Identify the basic structures of the brain and their primary functions.

3.2 What Are the Basic Brain Structures and Their Functions?

The first animals' nervous systems were probably little more than a few specialized cells with the capacity for electrical signaling. Today, an adult human brain weighs approximately 3 pounds (1.4 kilograms) and is considerably more complex. The brain is best viewed as a collection of interacting neural circuits that have accumulated and developed throughout human evolution. Through the process of adapting to the environments in which humans have lived, the brain has evolved specialized mechanisms to regulate breathing, food intake, sexual behavior, and body fluids, as well as sensory systems to aid in navigation and assist in recognizing friends and foes. Everything we are and do is accomplished by the brain and, for more rudimentary actions, the spinal cord (**Figure 3.13**). Early in life, overabundant connections form among the brain's neurons. Subsequently, life experiences help "prune" some of these connections to strengthen the rest, much as pruning weak or nonproductive branches will strengthen a fruit tree.

The brain's basic structures and their functions enable us to accomplish feats such as seeing, hearing, remembering, and interacting with others. Understanding these relationships also helps us understand psychological disorders.

By the beginning of the nineteenth century, anatomists understood the brain's basic structure reasonably well. But debates raged over how the brain produced mental activity. Did different parts do different things? Or were all areas of the brain equally important in cognitive activities such as problem solving and memory? (This idea is called *equipotentiality*.) In the early nineteenth century, the neuroscientist Franz Gall and his assistant, the physician Johann Spurzheim, proposed their theory of phrenology, based on the idea that the brain operates through functional localization. *Phrenology* is the practice of assessing personality traits and mental abilities by measuring bumps on the human skull. The theory of phrenology was so popular that in the 1930s an enterprising company manufactured 33 Psychographs. Psychographs were devices used to tell about participants' personalities based on the locations and sizes of bumps on their heads. The popularity of these machines at state fairs and amusement parks suggests that few people, if any, took the personality readings seriously (**Figure 3.14**). Phrenology was influential, however, because it was based on the seemingly scientific principle that brain functions were localized. At the time, the technology was not available to test this theory scientifically.

In the early decades of the twentieth century, the behavioral psychologist Karl Lashley built his research on the general idea of equipotentiality. Lashley believed that specific brain regions were involved in motor control and sensory experiences, whereas all other parts of the brain contributed equally to mental abilities. Today, Lashley's theory has been largely discredited. We now know that the brain consists of a patchwork of highly specialized areas.

The first strong evidence that brain regions perform specialized functions came from the work of the physician and anatomist Paul Broca (Finger, 1994). In 1861, Broca performed an autopsy on his patient Monsieur Leborgne. Before his death, Leborgne had lost the ability to say anything other than the word *tan* but could still understand language. When he examined Leborgne's brain, Broca found a large lesion (substantially damaged tissue) in a section of the front left side. This observation led him to conclude that this particular

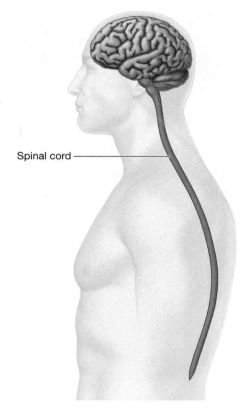

FIGURE 3.13 The Brain and the Spinal Cord This drawing illustrates the brain exterior and the brain's connection with the spinal cord. The view is from the left side of the body.

Spinal cord

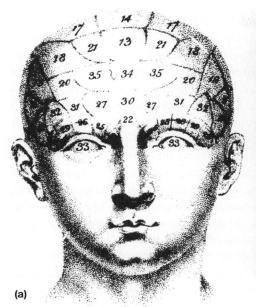

(a)

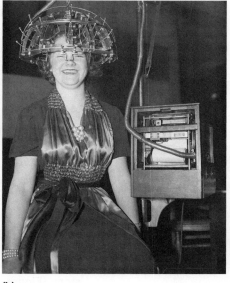

(b)

FIGURE 3.14 Phrenology and the Psychograph (a) In the early nineteenth century, Johann Spurzheim created phrenological maps of the skull. In this one, each numbered region corresponds to a different characteristic. (b) Psychographs, such as the one depicted here, were marketed as being able to "do the work of a psychoanalyst" by showing "your talents, abilities, strong and weak traits, without prejudice or flattery."

region was important for speech. Broca's theory has survived the test of time. This left frontal region, crucial for the production of language, became known as **Broca's area (Figure 3.15)**.

For most of human history, of course, theorists and researchers have not had methods for studying ongoing mental activity in the working brain. In the late 1980s, the invention of brain imaging methods changed that situation swiftly and dramatically. The new imaging techniques have advanced our understanding of the human brain the way the development of telescopes advanced our understanding of astronomy—and the brain's structures and functions may be as complex as distant galaxies. The following sections discuss specific brain areas. They explore how each area is linked with particular mental processes and particular behaviors.

Broca's area A small portion of the left frontal region of the brain, crucial for the production of language.

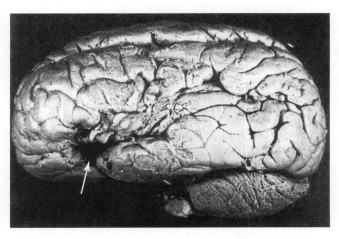

(a)

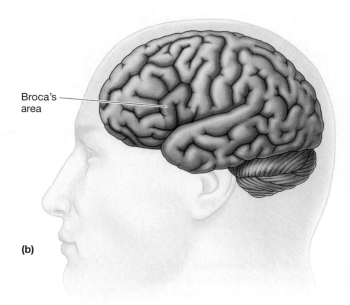

Broca's area

(b)

FIGURE 3.15 Broca's Area (a) Paul Broca studied Monsieur Leborgne's brain and identified the lesioned area as crucial for speech production. (b) This illustration shows the location of Broca's area.

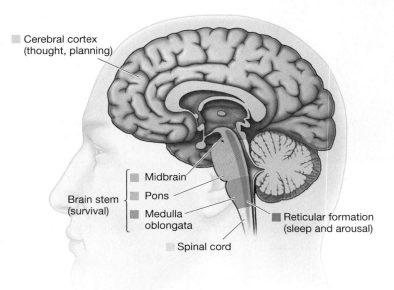

brain stem An extension of the spinal cord; it houses structures that control functions associated with survival, such as breathing, swallowing, vomiting, urination, and orgasm.

cerebellum A large, convoluted protuberance at the back of the brain stem; it is essential for coordinated movement and balance.

Cerebral cortex
(thought, planning)

Brain stem
(survival)

Midbrain

Pons

Medulla
oblongata

Spinal cord

Reticular formation
(sleep and arousal)

FIGURE 3.16 The Brain Stem This drawing shows the brain stem, and its parts, in relation to the cerebral cortex.

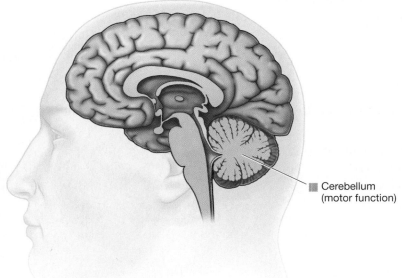

Cerebellum
(motor function)

FIGURE 3.17 The Cerebellum The cerebellum is located at the back of the brain: It is below the cerebral cortex and behind the brain stem.

The Brain Stem Houses the Basic Programs of Survival

The spinal cord is a rope of neural tissue. As shown in Figure 3.13, it runs inside the hollows of the vertebrae from just above the pelvis up into the base of the skull. One of its functions is the coordination of reflexes, such as the reflexive movement of your leg when a doctor taps your knee or the reflexive movement of your arm when you jerk your hand away from a flame. Its most important function is to carry sensory information up to the brain and carry motor signals from the brain to the body parts below to initiate action. In cross section, the cord is seen to be composed of two distinct tissue types: the *gray matter,* which is dominated by neurons' cell bodies, and the *white matter,* which consists mostly of axons and the fatty sheaths that surround them. Gray matter and white matter are clearly distinguishable throughout the brain as well.

In the base of the skull, the spinal cord thickens and becomes more complex as it transforms into the **brain stem** (**Figure 3.16**). The brain stem consists of the *medulla oblongata,* the *pons,* and the *midbrain.* It houses the nerves that control the most basic functions of survival, such as heart rate, breathing, swallowing, vomiting, urination, and orgasm. Thus a significant blow to this region can cause death. As a continuous extension of the spinal cord, the brain stem also performs functions for the head similar to those that the spinal cord performs for the rest of the body. Many reflexes emerge from here, analogous to the spinal reflexes; gagging is one example.

The brain stem also contains a network of neurons, known collectively as the *reticular formation.* The reticular formation projects up into the *cerebral cortex* (outer portion of the brain—discussed shortly) and affects general alertness. It is also involved in inducing and terminating the different stages of sleep (as discussed in Chapter 5, "Consciousness").

The Cerebellum Is Essential for Movement

The **cerebellum** (Latin, "little brain") is a large protuberance connected to the back of the brain stem (**Figure 3.17**). Its size and convoluted surface make it look like an extra brain. The cerebellum is extremely important for proper motor function, and damage to its different parts produces very different effects. Damage to the little nodes at the very bottom causes head tilt, balance problems, and a loss of smooth compensation of eye position for head movement. Try turning your head while looking at this book and notice that your eyes remain focused on the material. Your eyes would not be able to do that if an injury affected the bottom of your cerebellum. Damage to the ridge that runs up its back would affect your walking. Damage to the bulging lobes on either side would cause a loss of limb coordination, so you would not be able to perform tasks such as reaching smoothly to pick up a pen.

The cerebellum's most obvious role is in motor learning and motor memory. It seems to be "trained" by the rest of the nervous system and operates independently and unconsciously. For example, the cerebellum allows you to ride a bicycle effortlessly while planning your next meal. In fact, the cerebellum may be involved in cognitive processes such as making plans, remembering events, using language, and experiencing emotion. Researchers have observed the cerebellum's activation when a person experiences a painful stimulus or observes a loved one receiving that stimulus, so the cerebellum may be involved in the experience of empathy (Lamm, Batson, & Decety, 2007; Singer et al., 2004).

Subcortical Structures Control Emotions and Appetitive Behaviors

Above the brain stem and cerebellum is the *forebrain,* which consists of the two cerebral hemispheres (left and right; **Figure 3.18**). From the outside, the most noticeable feature of the forebrain is the cerebral cortex. Below this are the *subcortical* regions, so named because they lie under the cortex. Subcortical structures that are important for understanding psychological functions include the *hypothalamus,* the *thalamus,* the *hippocampus,* the *amygdala,* and the *basal ganglia.* Some of these structures belong to the *limbic system. Limbic* is the Latin word for "border," and this system serves as the border between the evolutionarily older parts of the brain (the brain stem and the cerebellum) and the evolutionarily newer part (the cerebral cortex). The brain structures in the limbic system are especially important for controlling appetitive behaviors, such as eating and drinking, and emotions (as discussed in Chapter 10, "Emotion and Motivation").

HYPOTHALAMUS The **hypothalamus** is the brain's master regulatory structure. It is indispensable to the organism's survival. Located just above the roof of the mouth, it receives input from almost everywhere in the body and brain, and it projects its influence to almost everywhere in the body and brain. It affects the functions of many internal organs, regulating body temperature, body rhythms, blood pressure, and blood glucose levels. It is also involved in many motivated behaviors, including thirst, hunger, aggression, and lust.

THALAMUS The **thalamus** is the gateway to the cortex: It receives almost all incoming sensory information, organizes it, and relays it to the cortex. The only exception to this rule is the sense of smell. The oldest and most fundamental sense, smell has a direct route to the cortex. During sleep, the thalamus partially shuts the gate on incoming sensations while the brain rests. (The thalamus is discussed further in Chapter 4, "Sensation and Perception.")

HIPPOCAMPUS AND AMYGDALA The **hippocampus** (Greek, "sea horse," for its sea horse shape) plays an important role in the storage of new memories. It seems to do this important work by creating new interconnections within the cerebral cortex with each new experience. Karl Lashley, in his research discussed earlier, failed to find the location of memory by removing parts of rats' cerebral cortices (plural of *cortex*). Had he damaged their hippocampal formations as well, his results would have been quite different.

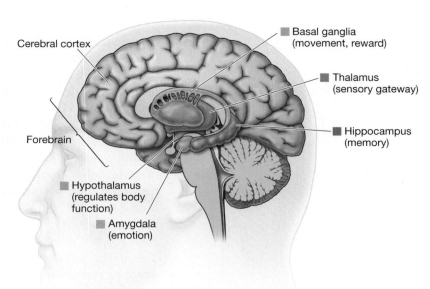

■ Basal ganglia
(movement, reward)

Cerebral cortex

■ Thalamus
(sensory gateway)

■ Hippocampus
(memory)

Forebrain

■ Hypothalamus
(regulates body
function)

■ Amygdala
(emotion)

FIGURE 3.18 The Forebrain and the Subcortical Regions The subcortical regions are below the forebrain. They are responsible for many aspects of motivation and emotion.

hypothalamus A brain structure that is involved in the regulation of bodily functions, including body temperature, blood pressure, and blood glucose levels; it also influences our basic motivated behaviors.

thalamus The gateway to the brain; it receives almost all incoming sensory information before that information reaches the cortex.

hippocampus A brain structure that is associated with the formation of memories.

The hippocampus has recently been shown to grow larger with increased use. This finding is consistent with the role of the hippocampus in memory formation. One hypothesis suggests that this structure may be involved in how we remember the arrangements of both places and objects in space, such as how streets are laid out in a city or how furniture is positioned in a room. The best study to support this theory focused on London taxi drivers. Maguire and colleagues (2003) found that one region of the hippocampus was much larger in London taxi drivers' brains than in most other London drivers' brains. Is a person with a large hippocampus more likely to drive a taxi? Or does the hippocampus grow as the result of navigational experience? London taxi drivers are well known for their expertise. To acquire a commercial license, a London taxi driver must take an exam testing knowledge of the city's streets. In this study, the volume of gray matter in the hippocampal region was highly correlated with the number of years of experience as a taxi driver. In other words, the hippocampus changes with experience. This phenomenon is just one of many examples of the way the brain's size and structure change in response to experiences. More examples are discussed at the end of this chapter.

The **amygdala** (Latin, "almond," for its almond shape) is located immediately in front of the hippocampus. It serves a vital role in our learning to associate things in the world with emotional responses, such as an unpleasant food with disgust. The amygdala thus enables us to overcome instinctive responses. It also intensifies the function of memory during times of emotional arousal. For example, a frightening experience can be seared into your memory for life, although (as discussed further in Chapter 7, "Attention and Memory") your memory of the event may not be completely accurate. Research also shows that emotional arousal can influence what people attend to in their environments (Schmitz, De Rosa, & Anderson, 2009).

The amygdala plays a special role in our responding to stimuli that elicit fear. The emotional processing of frightening stimuli in the amygdala is a hardwired circuit that has developed over the course of evolution to protect animals from danger. The amygdala is also involved in evaluating a facial expression's emotional significance (Adolphs et al., 2005). Imaging studies have found that the amygdala activates especially strongly in response to a fearful face (Whalen et al., 2001).

In addition, the amygdala is involved in the processing of more-positive emotions, including sexual arousal. Hamann and colleagues (2004) have found that activity within the amygdala increases when people view sexually arousing stimuli, such as nude photos or videos of sexual activity, and that the amygdala activates markedly higher in men. This finding suggests that the amygdala may be involved when men respond more strongly to visual sexual stimuli than women do.

THE BASAL GANGLIA The **basal ganglia** are a system of subcortical structures crucial for planning and producing movement. These structures receive input from the entire cerebral cortex. They project that input to the motor centers of the brain stem. Via the thalamus, they also project the input back to the motor planning area of the cerebral cortex. Damage to the basal ganglia can produce symptoms that range from the tremors and rigidity of Parkinson's disease to the uncontrollable jerky movements of Huntington's disease. In addition, there is evidence that damage to the basal ganglia can impair the learning of movements and habits, such as automatically looking for cars before you cross the street.

One structure in the basal ganglia, the *nucleus accumbens,* is important for experiencing reward and motivating behavior. As discussed in Chapter 6, nearly every pleasurable experience, from eating food you like to looking at a person you find attractive, activates dopamine neurons in the nucleus accumbens and

amygdala A brain structure that serves a vital role in our learning to associate things with emotional responses and in processing emotional information.

basal ganglia A system of subcortical structures that are important for the production of planned movement.

cerebral cortex The outer layer of brain tissue, which forms the convoluted surface of the brain.

occipital lobes Regions of the cerebral cortex—at the back of the brain—important for vision.

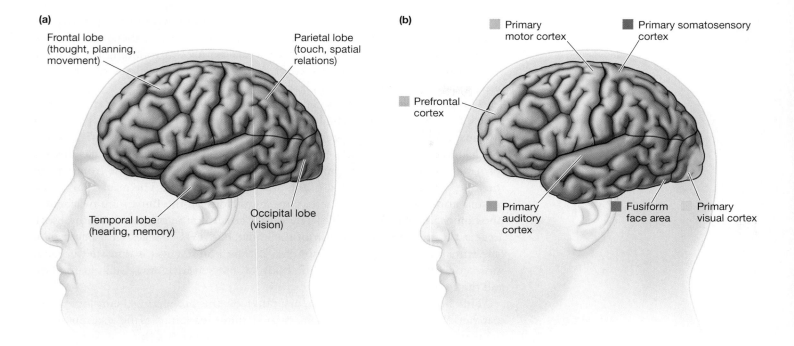

(a)

Frontal lobe
(thought, planning,
movement)

Parietal lobe
(touch, spatial
relations)

Temporal lobe
(hearing, memory)

Occipital lobe
(vision)

(b)

Primary
motor cortex

Primary somatosensory
cortex

Prefrontal
cortex

Primary
auditory
cortex

Fusiform
face area

Primary
visual cortex

FIGURE 3.19 The Cerebral Cortex (a) This diagram identifies the lobes of the cerebral cortex. **(b)** The colored areas mark important regions within those lobes.

makes you want the thing or person you are experiencing. One brain imaging study found that viewing expensive sports cars led to greater activation of the nucleus accumbens in men than did viewing less expensive economy cars (Erk, Spitzer, Wunderlich, Galley, & Walter, 2002). The more desirable objects are, the more they activate basic reward circuitry in our brains.

The Cerebral Cortex Underlies Complex Mental Activity

The **cerebral cortex** is the outer layer of the cerebral hemispheres and gives the brain its distinctive wrinkled appearance. (*Cortex* is Latin for "bark"—the kind on trees. The cerebral cortex does not feel like bark, however. It has the consistency of a soft-boiled egg.) In humans, the cortex is relatively enormous—the size of a large sheet of newspaper—and folded in against itself many times so as to fit within the skull. It is the site of all thoughts, detailed perceptions, and complex behaviors. It enables us to comprehend ourselves, other people, and the outside world. By extending our inner selves into the world, it is also the source of culture and communication. Each cerebral hemisphere has four "lobes": the *occipital, parietal, temporal,* and *frontal* lobes (**Figure 3.19**). The *corpus callosum,* a massive bridge of millions of axons, connects the hemispheres and allows information to flow between them (**Figure 3.20**).

The **occipital lobes** are at the back portion of the head. Devoted almost exclusively to vision, they include many visual areas. By far, the largest of these areas is the *primary visual cortex,* the major destination for visual information. As discussed further in Chapter 4, visual information is typically organized for the cerebral cortex in a way that preserves spatial relationships. That is, the image

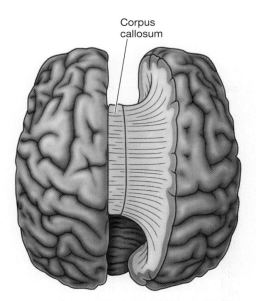

Corpus
callosum

FIGURE 3.20 The Corpus Callosum In this top view of the brain, the right cerebral hemisphere has been pulled away to expose the corpus callosum. This fibrous structure connects the two hemispheres of the cerebral cortex.

relayed from the eye is "projected" more or less faithfully onto the primary visual cortex. Two objects near one another in a visual image, then, will activate neurons near one another in the primary visual cortex. Surrounding the primary visual cortex is a patchwork of secondary visual areas that process various attributes of the visual image, such as its colors, forms, and motions.

The **parietal lobes** are devoted partially to touch. Their labor is divided between the left and right cerebral hemispheres. The left hemisphere receives touch information from the right side of the body, and the right hemisphere receives touch information from the left side of the body. In each parietal lobe, this information is directed to the *primary somatosensory cortex,* a strip in the front part of the lobe, running from the top of the brain down the sides. The primary somatosensory cortex groups nearby sensations: Sensations on the fingers are near sensations on the palm, for example. The result, covering the primary somatosensory area, is a distorted representation of the entire body: the *somatosensory homunculus* (the latter term is Greek for "little man"). The homunculus is distorted because more cortical area is devoted to the body's more sensitive areas, such as the face and the fingers (**Figure 3.21a**).

This homunculus is based on mappings by the pioneering neurological researcher Wilder Penfield. Penfield created these mappings as he examined patients who were to undergo surgery for epilepsy (**Figure 3.21b**). The idea behind this work was to perform the surgery without damaging brain areas vital for functions such as speech. After a local anesthetic was applied to the scalp and while the patient was awake, Penfield would electrically stimulate regions of the brain and ask the patient to report what he or she was experiencing (**Figure 3.21c**). Penfield's studies provided important evidence about the amount of brain tissue devoted to each sensory experience.

A stroke or other damage to the right parietal region can result in the neurological disorder *hemineglect.* Patients with this syndrome fail to notice anything on their left sides. Looking in a mirror, they will shave or put makeup on only the right sides of their faces. If two objects are held up before them, they will see only the one on the right. Asked to draw a simple object, they will draw only its right half (**Figure 3.22**).

The **temporal lobes** hold the *primary auditory cortex,* the brain region responsible for hearing. Also within the temporal lobes are specialized visual areas (for recognizing detailed objects such as faces), plus the hippocampus and the amygdala (both critical for memory, as discussed above). At the intersection of the temporal and occipital lobes is the *fusiform face area.* Its name comes from the fact that this area is much more active when people look at faces than when they look at other things. In contrast, other regions of the temporal lobe are more activated by objects, such as houses or cars, than by faces. Damage to the fusiform face area can cause specific impairments in recognizing people but not in recognizing objects.

The **frontal lobes** are essential for planning and movement. The rearmost portion of the frontal lobes is the *primary motor cortex.* The primary motor cortex includes neurons that project directly to the spinal cord to move the body's muscles. Its responsibilities are divided down the middle of the body, like those of the sensory areas: The left hemisphere controls the right arm, for example, whereas the right hemisphere controls the left arm. The rest of the frontal lobes consists of the **prefrontal cortex,** which occupies about 30 percent of the brain in humans. Scientists have long thought that what makes humans unique in the animal kingdom is our extraordinarily large prefrontal cortex. Recent evidence, however, indicates that what separates humans from other animals is not how much of the brain the prefrontal cortex occupies but rather the complexity and

parietal lobes Regions of the cerebral cortex—in front of the occipital lobes and behind the frontal lobes—important for the sense of touch and for conceptualizing the spatial layout of an environment.

temporal lobes Regions of the cerebral cortex—below the parietal lobes and in front of the occipital lobes—important for processing auditory information, for memory, and for object and face perception.

frontal lobes Regions of the cerebral cortex—at the front of the brain—important for movement and higher-level psychological processes associated with the prefrontal cortex.

prefrontal cortex The frontmost portion of the frontal lobes, especially prominent in humans; important for attention, working memory, decision making, appropriate social behavior, and personality.

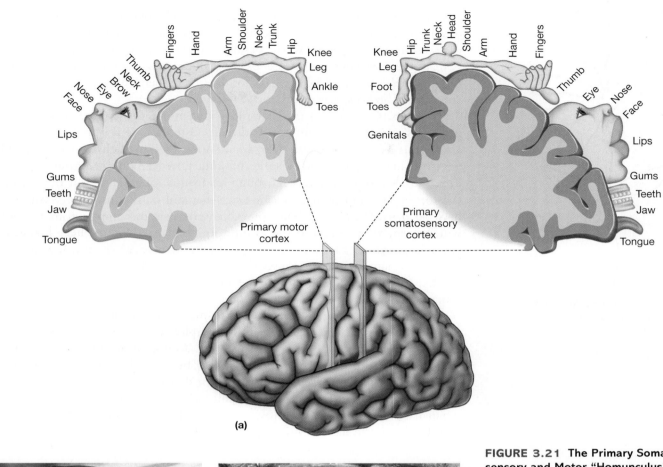

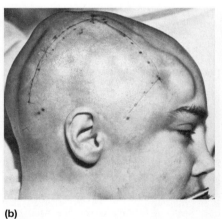

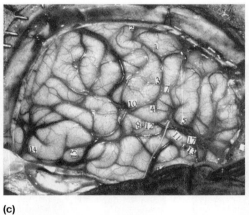

(a)

(b)

(c)

FIGURE 3.21 The Primary Somato-sensory and Motor "Homunculus"
(a) The cortical representation of the body surface is organized in strips that run down the side of the brain. Connected areas of the body tend to be represented next to each other in the cortex, and more-sensitive skin regions have more cortical area devoted to them. **(b)** Wilder Penfield's mappings of the brain provided the basis for our knowledge of the homunculus. This photograph shows one of Penfield's patients immediately before direct stimulation of the brain. **(c)** Here you can see the exposed surface of the patient's cortex. The numbered tags denote locations that were electrically stimulated.

organization of its neural circuits—the way it is put together (Bush & Allman, 2004; Schoenemann, Sheehan, & Glotzer, 2005).

Parts of the prefrontal cortex are responsible for directing and maintaining attention, keeping ideas in mind while distractions bombard us from the outside world, and developing and acting on plans. The entire prefrontal cortex is indispensable for rational activity. It is also especially important for many aspects of human social life, such as understanding what other people are thinking, behaving according to cultural norms, and contemplating our own existence. It provides both our sense of self and our capacity to empathize with others or feel guilty about harming them.

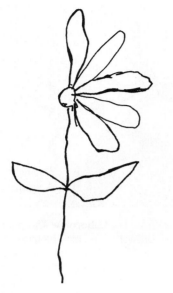

FIGURE 3.22 Hemineglect This drawing, made by a hemineglect patient, omits much of the flower's left side.

THE PREFRONTAL CORTEX IN CLOSE-UP Psychologists have learned a great deal of what they know about the functioning of different brain regions through the careful study of people whose brains have been damaged by disease or injury. Perhaps the most famous historical example of brain damage is the case of Phineas Gage. Gage's case provided the basis for the first modern theories of the prefrontal cortex's role in both personality and self-control.

In 1848, Gage was a 25-year-old foreman on the construction of Vermont's Rutland and Burlington Railroad. One day, he dropped a tool called a tamping iron, which was over a yard long and an inch in diameter. The iron rod hit a rock, igniting some blasting powder. The resulting explosion drove the rod into his cheek, through his frontal lobes, and clear out through the top of his head (**Figure 3.23**). Gage was still conscious as he was hurried back to town on a cart. Able to walk, with assistance, upstairs to his hotel bed, he wryly remarked to the awaiting physician, "Doctor, here is business enough for you." He said he expected to return to work in a few days. In fact, Gage lapsed into unconsciousness and remained unconscious for two weeks. Afterward, his condition steadily improved. Physically, he recovered remarkably well.

Unfortunately, Gage's accident led to major personality changes. Whereas the old Gage had been regarded by his employers as "the most efficient and capable" of workers, the new Gage was not. As one of his doctors later wrote, "The equilibrium or balance, so to speak, between his intellectual faculties and animal propensities seems to have been destroyed. He is fitful, irreverent, indulging at times in the grossest profanity . . . impatient of restraint or advice when it conflicts with his desires. . . . A child in his intellectual capacity and manifestations, he has the animal passions of a strong man." In summary, Gage was "no longer Gage."

(a)

(b)

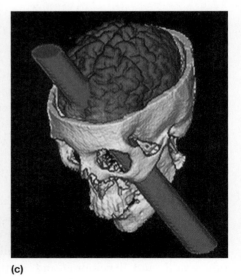
(c)

FIGURE 3.23 Phineas Gage Analysis of Gage's damaged skull provided the basis for the first modern theories about the role of the prefrontal cortex in both personality and self-control. **(a)** This recently discovered photo shows Gage holding the rod that passed through his skull. **(b)** Here you can see the hole in the top of Gage's skull. **(c)** This computer-generated image reconstructs the rod's probable path through the skull.

Unable to get his foreman's job back, Gage exhibited himself in various New England towns and at the New York Museum (owned by the circus showman P. T. Barnum). He worked at the stables of the Hanover Inn at Dartmouth College. In Chile, he drove coaches and tended horses. After a decade, his health began to decline, and in 1860 he started having epileptic seizures and died within a few months. Gage's recovery was initially used to argue that the entire brain works uniformly and that the healthy parts of Gage's brain had taken over the work of the damaged parts. However, the medical community eventually recognized that Gage's psychological impairments had been severe and that some areas of the brain in fact have specific functions.

Reconstruction of Gage's injury through examination of his skull has made it clear that the prefrontal cortex was the area most damaged by the tamping rod (Damasio, Grabowski, Frank, Galaburda, & Damasio, 1994). Recent studies of patients with similar injuries reveal that this brain region is particularly concerned with social phenomena, such as following social norms, understanding what other people are thinking, and feeling emotionally connected to others. People with damage to this region do not typically have problems with memory or general knowledge, but they often have profound disturbances in their ability to get along with others.

Beginning in the late 1930s, mental health professionals treated many patients by performing a procedure called *lobotomy,* a deliberate damaging of the prefrontal cortex (**Figure 3.24**). This form of brain surgery generally left patients lethargic and emotionally flat, and therefore much easier to manage in mental hospitals, but it also left them disconnected from their social surroundings. Most lobotomies were performed in the late 1940s and early 1950s. In 1949, António Egas Moniz received the Nobel prize for developing the procedure, which was phased out with the arrival of drugs to treat psychological disorders.

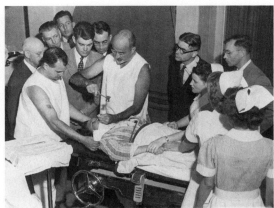

FIGURE 3.24 Lobotomy This photo shows Dr. Walter Freeman performing a lobotomy in 1949. Freeman is inserting an ice pick–like instrument under the upper eyelid of his patient to cut the nerve connections in the front part of the brain.

Summing Up

What Are the Basic Brain Structures and Their Functions?

Distinct functions are associated with the structures of the nervous system. The spinal cord carries sensory information from the body to the brain and motor information from the brain to the body. It also produces reflexes. The brain stem serves survival functions, such as breathing, swallowing, and urination. At the back of the brain stem is the cerebellum. This structure is associated with coordinated movement, balance, and motor learning. Beneath the cerebral cortex are a number of structures that serve unique functions: The hypothalamus regulates bodily functions; the thalamus serves as a way station through which sensory information travels to the cortex; the hippocampus is involved in memory formation; the amygdala influences our emotional states; and the structures of the basal ganglia are involved in the planning and production of movement. The cerebral cortex is the outer surface of the brain and is divided into lobes: The occipital lobes are associated with vision; the parietal lobes are associated with touch; the temporal lobes are associated with hearing, memory, facial perception, and object perception; and the frontal lobes, which contain the prefrontal cortex, are associated with movement, higher-level psychological processes, and personality.

3.3 How Does the Brain Communicate with the Body?

Recall that the nervous system consists of the central nervous system (the brain and the spinal cord) and the peripheral nervous system (all the other nerves in the rest of the body). The peripheral nervous system transmits a variety of information to the central nervous system. It also responds to messages from the central nervous system to perform specific behaviors or make bodily adjustments. In the production of psychological activity, however, both of these systems interact with a different mode of communication within the body, the *endocrine system*.

The Peripheral Nervous System Includes the Somatic and Autonomic Systems

The peripheral nervous system has two primary components: the *somatic nervous system* and the *autonomic nervous system* (**Figure 3.25**). The **somatic nervous system** transmits sensory signals to the central nervous system via nerves. Specialized receptors in the skin, muscles, and joints send sensory information to the spinal cord, which relays it to the brain. In addition, the central nervous system sends signals through the somatic nervous system to muscles, joints, and skin to initiate, modulate, or inhibit movement. The second major component of the peripheral nervous system, the **autonomic nervous system (ANS)** regulates the body's internal environment by stimulating glands (such as sweat glands) and by maintaining internal organs (such as the heart). Nerves in the autonomic nervous system also

somatic nervous system A component of the peripheral nervous system; it transmits sensory signals and motor signals between the central nervous system and the skin, muscles, and joints.

autonomic nervous system (ANS) A component of the peripheral nervous system; it transmits sensory signals and motor signals between the central nervous system and the body's glands and internal organs.

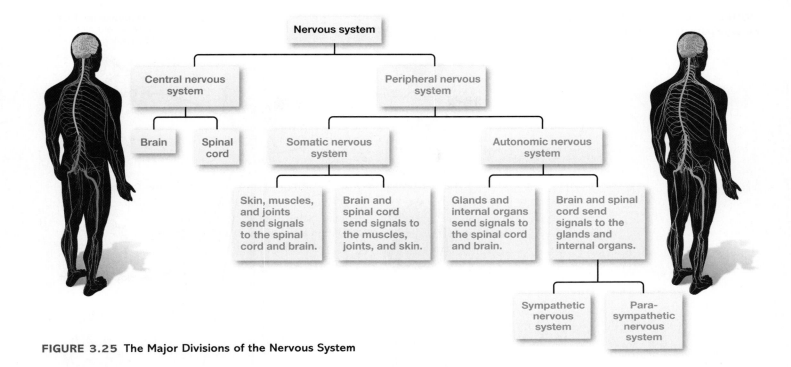

FIGURE 3.25 The Major Divisions of the Nervous System

carry somatosensory signals from the glands and internal organs to the central nervous system. These signals provide information about, for example, the fullness of your stomach or how anxious you feel.

SYMPATHETIC AND PARASYMPATHETIC DIVISIONS Two types of signals, *sympathetic* and *parasympathetic,* travel from the central nervous system to organs and glands, controlling their activity (**Figure 3.26**). To understand these signals, imagine you hear a fire alarm. In the second after you hear the alarm, signals go out to parts of your body that tell those parts to prepare for action. As a result, blood flows to skeletal muscles; epinephrine is released, increasing your heart rate and blood sugar; your lungs take in more oxygen; your digestive system suspends activity as a way of conserving energy; your pupils dilate to maximize visual sensitivity; and you perspire to keep cool. These preparatory actions are prompted by the autonomic nervous system's **sympathetic division.** Should there be a fire, you will be physically prepared to flee. If the alarm turns out to be false, your heart will return to its normal steady beat, your breathing will slow, you will resume digesting food, and you will stop perspiring. This return to a normal state will be prompted by the ANS's **parasympathetic division.** Most of your internal organs are controlled by inputs from sympathetic and parasympathetic systems. The more aroused you are, the greater the sympathetic system's dominance.

It does not take a fire alarm to activate your sympathetic nervous system. When you meet someone you find attractive, for example, your heart beats quickly, you perspire, you might start breathing heavily, and your pupils widen. Such signs of sexual arousal provide nonverbal cues during social interaction. These signs occur because sexual arousal has activated the ANS's sympathetic division. The sympathetic nervous system is also activated by psychological states such as anxiety or unhappiness. Certain people worry a great deal or do not cope well with stress. Their bodies are in a constant state of arousal. Important research

sympathetic division A division of the autonomic nervous system; it prepares the body for action.

parasympathetic division A division of the autonomic nervous system; it returns the body to its resting state.

FIGURE 3.26 The Sympathetic and Parasympathetic Divisions

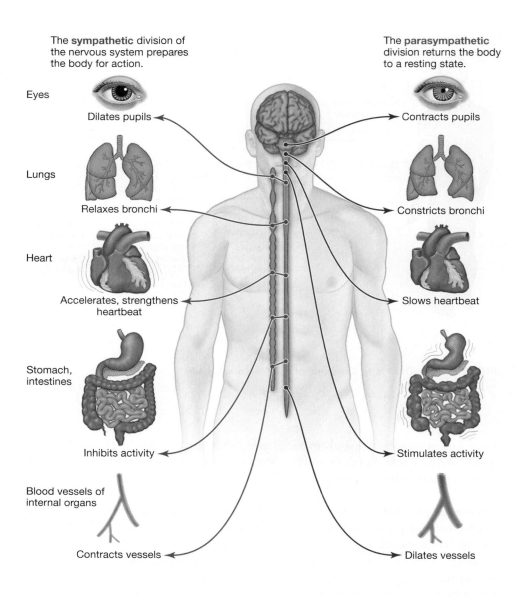

The **sympathetic** division of the nervous system prepares the body for action.

The **parasympathetic** division returns the body to a resting state.

Eyes — Dilates pupils / Contracts pupils

Lungs — Relaxes bronchi / Constricts bronchi

Heart — Accelerates, strengthens heartbeat / Slows heartbeat

Stomach, intestines — Inhibits activity / Stimulates activity

Blood vessels of internal organs — Contracts vessels / Dilates vessels

in the 1930s and 1940s by Hans Selye demonstrated that chronic activation of the sympathetic nervous system is associated with medical problems that include ulcers, heart disease, and asthma. Selye's work is discussed further in Chapter 11, "Health and Well-Being."

The Endocrine System Communicates through Hormones

Like the nervous system, the **endocrine system** is a communication network that influences thoughts, behaviors, and actions. Both systems work together to regulate psychological activity. For instance, from the nervous system the brain receives information about potential threats to the organism. The brain communicates with the endocrine system to prepare the organism to deal with those threats. (The threats could involve physical injury or be psychological, such as nervousness at having to talk in front of a group.) The main difference between the two systems is in their modes of communication: Whereas the nervous system uses electrochemical signals, the endocrine system uses *hormones*.

endocrine system A communication system that uses hormones to influence thoughts, behaviors, and actions.

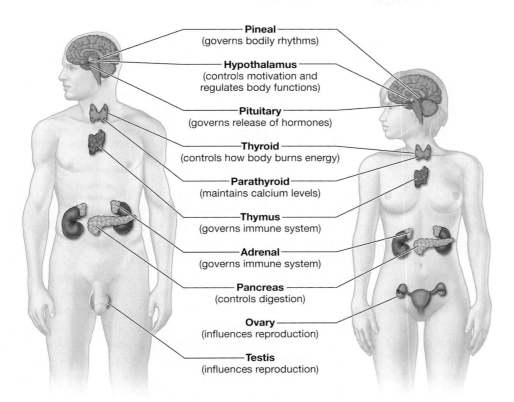

Pineal
(governs bodily rhythms)

Hypothalamus
(controls motivation and
regulates body functions)

Pituitary
(governs release of hormones)

Thyroid
(controls how body burns energy)

Parathyroid
(maintains calcium levels)

Thymus
(governs immune system)

Adrenal
(governs immune system)

Pancreas
(controls digestion)

Ovary
(influences reproduction)

Testis
(influences reproduction)

FIGURE 3.27 The Major Endocrine Glands

Hormones are chemical substances released into the bloodstream by the ductless *endocrine glands,* such as the pancreas, thyroid, and testes or ovaries (**Figure 3.27**). Once released, hormones travel through the bloodstream until they reach their target tissues, where they bind to receptor sites and influence the tissues. Because they travel through the bloodstream, hormones can take from seconds to hours to exert their effects. Once hormones are in the bloodstream, their effects can last for a long time and affect multiple targets.

HORMONES' EFFECTS ON SEXUAL BEHAVIOR An example of hormonal influence is in sexual behavior. The main endocrine glands influencing sexual behavior are the **gonads:** the testes, in males, and the ovaries, in females. Although many people talk about "male" and "female" hormones, the two major gonadal hormones are identical in males and females. What differs is the quantity: *Androgens* such as testosterone are more prevalent in males, whereas *estrogens* such as estradiol and progesterone are more prevalent in females. Gonadal hormones influence the development of secondary sex characteristics (e.g., breast development in females, growth of facial hair in males). Gonadal hormones also influence adult sexual behavior.

For males, successful sexual behavior depends on having at least a minimum amount of testosterone. Prior to puberty, surgical removal of the testes, or *castration,* diminishes the capacity for developing an erection and lowers sexual interest. Yet a man castrated after puberty will be able to perform sexually

"You've been charged with driving under the influence of testosterone."

hormones Chemical substances, released from endocrine glands, that travel through the bloodstream to targeted tissues; the tissues are subsequently influenced by the hormones.

gonads The main endocrine glands involved in sexual behavior: in males, the testes; in females, the ovaries.

if he receives an injection of testosterone. Testosterone injections do not increase sexual behavior in healthy men, however, and this finding implies that a healthy man needs only a minimum amount of testosterone to perform sexually (Sherwin, 1988).

In females, the influence of gonadal hormones is much more complex. Many nonhuman female animals experience a finite period, *estrus,* when the female is sexually receptive and fertile. During estrus, the female displays behaviors designed to attract the male. Surgical removal of the ovaries terminates estrus: No longer receptive, the female ends her sexual behavior. However, injections of estrogen reinstate estrus. Women's sexual behavior may have more to do with androgens than estrogens (Morris, Udry, Khan-Dawood, & Dawood, 1987). According to pioneering work by Barbara Sherwin (1994, 2008), women with higher levels of testosterone report greater interest in sex, and testosterone injections increase women's sexual interest after surgical removal of the uterus. Women's sexual activity is not particularly linked to the menstrual cycle (Breedlove, Rosenzweig, & Watson, 2007). When they are ovulating, however, heterosexual women find men who look and act masculine more attractive (Gangestad, Simpson, Cousins, Garver-Apgar, & Christensen, 2004), and they show greater activity in brain regions associated with reward while viewing attractive male faces (Rupp et al., 2009). In addition, women report having lower self-esteem when ovulating, and their greater motivation to find a mate during that time may increase their efforts to appear attractive (Hill & Durante, 2009). Indeed, one study found that when their fertility was highest, women showed up for a laboratory study wearing more-revealing clothing than they normally wore (Durante, Li, & Haselton, 2008).

Actions of the Nervous System and Endocrine System Are Coordinated

All the communication systems described in this chapter link neurochemical and physiological processes to behaviors, thoughts, and feelings. These systems are fully integrated and interact to facilitate survival. They use information from the organism's environment to direct adaptive behavioral responses. Ultimately, the endocrine system is under the central nervous system's control. The brain interprets external and internal stimuli, then sends signals to the endocrine system, which responds by initiating various effects on the body and on behavior.

Most of the central control of the endocrine system is accomplished by the hypothalamus (for the location of this gland, see Figure 3.27; for a more detailed look, see Figure 3.18). How does this central control work? At the base of the hypothalamus is the **pituitary gland,** which governs the release of hormones from the rest of the endocrine glands. Neural activation causes the hypothalamus to secrete a particular *releasing factor.* The releasing factor causes the pituitary to release a hormone specific to that factor, and the hormone then travels through the bloodstream to endocrine sites throughout the body. Once the hormone reaches the target sites, it touches off the release of other hormones, which subsequently affect bodily reactions or behavior. The pituitary is often referred to as the "master gland" of the body: By releasing hormones into the bloodstream, it controls all other glands and governs major processes such as development, ovulation, and lactation. This integration can be extremely finely tuned.

pituitary gland A gland located at the base of the hypothalamus; it sends hormonal signals to other endocrine glands, controlling their release of hormones.

Consider physical growth. *Growth hormone (GH),* a hormone released from the pituitary gland, prompts bone, cartilage, and muscle tissue to grow or helps them regenerate after injury. Since the 1930s, many people have administered or self-administered GH to increase body size and strength. Many athletes have sought a competitive advantage through GH. For example, the legendary baseball pitcher Roger Clemens has been accused of injecting GH to improve his performance. Clemens has long denied the accusation. In August 2010, however, a U.S. federal grand jury indicted him for lying to Congress during its 2008 hearings about the use of performance-enhancing drugs in major league baseball (**Figure 3.28**).

Similarly, GH has helped make the current generation of young adults in Japan considerably taller than their parents' generation (Murata, 2000). This increase has resulted from the increased availability and consumption of dietary protein in Japan after World War II. How is GH related to protein intake? *Growth hormone releasing factor (GRF)* stimulates the release of GH, which relies on protein to build bones and muscles. GRF also selectively stimulates the eating of protein but not of fats or carbohydrates, perhaps by making protein especially enjoyable (Dickson & Vaccarino, 1994). The area of the hypothalamus connected to GRF neurons is involved in sleep/wake cycles. Thus the bursts of GH, the need for protein, and the consumption of protein are controlled by the body's internal clock. All these connections illustrate how the CNS, the PNS, and the endocrine system work together to ensure the organism's survival: These systems prompt the behaviors that provide the body with the substances it needs when it needs them.

FIGURE 3.28 Growth Hormone and Baseball Growth hormone (GH) helps bone, cartilage, and muscle tissues to grow or to regenerate after injury. In February 2008, a bipartisan committee of the U.S. House of Representatives held hearings on the use of performance-enhancing drugs in major league baseball. The committee particularly addressed accusations that Roger Clemens **(lower left corner, in the blue suit, with his back to the camera)** had injected GH and steroids to improve his competitive advantage.

How Does the Brain Communicate with the Body?

The central nervous system, consisting of the brain and spinal cord, attends to the body and its environment, initiates actions, and directs the peripheral nervous system and endocrine system to respond appropriately. The peripheral nervous system is made up of the somatic nervous system and autonomic nervous system; the autonomic nervous system controls sympathetic and parasympathetic activity. The endocrine system consists of a number of endocrine glands. The central nervous system, peripheral nervous system, and endocrine system use chemicals to transmit their signals. Transmission in the nervous system occurs across synapses, whereas transmission in the endocrine system uses hormones that travel through the bloodstream. Gonadal hormones (estrogen, progesterone, and testosterone) are important in the development of secondary sex characteristics and in sexual behavior. The hypothalamus controls the endocrine system by directing the pituitary to release hormones that affect other endocrine glands. The various communication systems are integrated and promote behavior that is adaptive to the organism's environment.

Measuring Up

1. Complete each statement by choosing one or more of the following terms: peripheral nervous system (PNS); somatic nervous system; autonomic nervous system (ANS); sympathetic division; parasympathetic division.
   a. You are studying quietly in the library when a friend jumps out from behind a partition and scares you, making your heart race. Your _____ has been affected.
   b. When you calm down and return to your former (not scared) state, your _____ is affected.
   c. The _____ controls movement by carrying signals from the central nervous system to the muscles.
   d. The _____ has two primary components: the somatic nervous system and the autonomic nervous system.
   e. The _____ consists of two main divisions that regulate the body's internal environment.

2. Which of the following statements are true? Choose as many as apply.
   a. Only gays and lesbians secrete testosterone and estrogen.
   b. All (normal) people of both sexes secrete testosterone and estrogen.
   c. Men have gonads, and women have ovaries.
   d. The endocrine system acts more slowly than the nervous system.
   e. Hormones are secreted from several places in the body, including the brain.
   f. The pituitary gland is called the master gland.
   g. The central nervous system and the peripheral nervous system work together, whereas the endocrine system works independently.
   h. Women's sexual responsiveness is related more to androgens (such as testosterone) than to estrogen.

2. Choices b, d, e, f, and h are true.

nervous system (ANS).

nervous system; d. peripheral nervous system (PNS); e. autonomic

Answers: 1. a. sympathetic division; b. parasympathetic division; c. somatic

3.4 What Is the Genetic Basis of Psychological Science?

Learning Objectives

- Explain how genes are transmitted from parent to offspring.
- Discuss the goals and methods of behavioral genetics.
- Explain how both environmental factors and experience influence genetic expression.

So far, this chapter has presented the basic biological processes underlying psychological functions. The following section considers how genes and environment affect psychological functions. From the moment of conception, we receive the genes we will possess for the remainder of our lives, but do those genes determine our thoughts and behaviors? How do environmental influences, such as the cultures in which we are raised, alter how our brains develop and change?

Until the last few years, genetic research focused almost entirely on whether people possessed certain types of genes, such as genes for psychological disorders or for intelligence. Although it is important for us to discover the effects of individual genes, this approach misses the critical role of environmental factors in shaping who we are. While the term *genetics* is typically used to describe how characteristics such as height, hair color, and eye color are passed along to offspring through inheritance, it also refers to the processes involved in turning genes "on" and "off." This research reflects and reveals that environment affects our genes: how they are expressed and therefore how they influence our thoughts, feelings, and behavior. Genetic predispositions are often important in determining the environments we select for ourselves, so biology and environment mutually influence each other. All the while, biology and environment—in other words, our genes and every experience we ever have—influence the development of our brains.

All of Human Development Has a Genetic Basis

Within nearly every cell in the body is the genome for making the entire organism. The genome is the master blueprint that provides detailed instructions for everything from how to grow a gallbladder to where the nose gets placed on a face. Whether a cell becomes part of a gallbladder or a nose is determined by which genes are turned on or off within that cell, and these actions are in turn determined by cues from outside the cell. The genome provides the option, and the environment determines which option is taken (Marcus, 2004).

Within each cell are **chromosomes.** These structures are made of *deoxyribonucleic acid (DNA),* a substance that consists of two intertwined strands of molecules in a double helix shape. Segments of those strands are called **genes (Figure 3.29)**.

chromosomes Structures within the cell body that are made up of DNA. DNA consists of genes.

genes The units of heredity that help determine the characteristics of an organism.

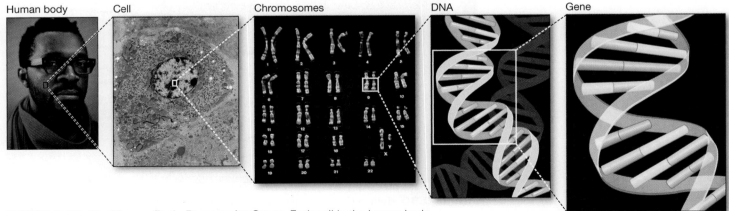

Human body | Cell | Chromosomes | DNA | Gene

FIGURE 3.29 The Human Body Down to Its Genes Each cell in the human body includes pairs of chromosomes, which consist of DNA strands. DNA has a double helix shape and is composed of genes.

In a typical human, nearly every cell contains 23 pairs of chromosomes. One member of each pair comes from the person's mother, the other from the person's father. In other words, each parent contributes half of a person's DNA, half of a person's genes.

Each gene—a particular sequence of molecules along a DNA strand—specifies an exact instruction to manufacture a distinct polypeptide. One or more polypeptides make up a protein. Proteins are the basic chemicals that make up the structure of cells and direct their activities. There are thousands of different types of proteins, and each type carries out a specific task. The environment determines which proteins are produced and when they are produced. For example, a certain species of butterfly becomes colorful or drab, depending on the season in which it is born. The environment during its development probably causes a gene sensitive to temperature to be expressed. Similarly, although each cell in the human body contains the same DNA, cells become specialized, depending on which of their genes are expressed. Gene expression determines the body's basic physical makeup, but it also determines specific developments throughout life. It is involved in all psychological activity. Gene expression allows us to sense, to learn, to fall in love, and so on.

In February 2001, two groups of scientists published separate articles that detailed the results of the first phase of the *Human Genome Project,* an international research effort. This achievement represents the coordinated work of hundreds of scientists around the world to map the entire structure of human genetic material. The first step of the Human Genome Project was to map the entire structure of DNA. In other words, the researchers set out to identify the precise order of molecules that make up each of the thousands of genes on each of the 23 pairs of human chromosomes (**Figure 3.30**).

FIGURE 3.30 Human Genome Project A map of human genes is presented by J. Craig Venter, president of the research company Celera Genomics, at a news conference in Washington on February 12, 2001. This map is one part of the international effort by hundreds of scientists to map the entire structure of human genetic material.

One of the most striking findings from the Human Genome Project is that we have fewer than 30,000 genes. That number means we have only about twice as many genes as a fly (13,000) or a worm (18,000), not much more than the number in some plants (26,000), and fewer than the number estimated to be in an ear of corn (50,000). Indeed, more-recent estimates indicate that the human genome may consist of just over 20,000 genes (Pennisi, 2007). Why are we so complex if we have so few genes? The number of our genes might be less important than subtleties in how those genes are expressed and regulated (Baltimore, 2001).

Heredity Involves Passing Along Genes through Reproduction

The first clues to the mechanisms responsible for heredity were discovered by the monk Gregor Mendel around 1866. At the monastery where Mendel lived, there was a long history of studying plants. For studying genetics, Mendel developed an experimental technique, *selective breeding,* that strictly controlled which plants bred with which other plants.

In one simple study, Mendel selected pea plants that had either only purple flowers or only white flowers. He then cross-pollinated the two types to see which color flowers the plants would produce. Mendel found that the first generation of pea offspring tended to be completely white or completely purple. If he had stopped there, he would never have discovered the basis of heredity. However, he then allowed each plant to self-pollinate into a second generation. This second generation revealed a different pattern: Of the hundreds of pea plants, about 75 percent had purple flowers and 25 percent had white flowers. This 3:1 ratio repeated itself in additional studies. It also held true for other characteristics, such as pod shape. From this pattern, Mendel deduced that the plants contained separate units, now referred to as genes, that existed in different versions (e.g., white and purple). In determining an offspring's features, some of these versions would be dominant and others would be recessive. We now know that a **dominant gene** from either parent is expressed (becomes apparent or physically visible) whenever it is present. A **recessive gene** is expressed only when it is matched with a similar gene from the other parent. In pea plants, white flowers are recessive, so white flowers occur only when the gene for purple flowers is not present. All "white genes" and no purple ones were one of the four possible combinations of white and purple genes in Mendel's experiments (**Figure 3.31**).

GENOTYPE AND PHENOTYPE The existence of dominant and recessive genes means that not all genes are expressed. The **genotype** is an organism's genetic makeup. That genetic constitution is determined at the moment of conception and never changes. The **phenotype** is that organism's observable physical characteristics and is always changing.

Genetics, or nature, is one of the two influences on phenotype. So, for instance, in Mendel's experiments, two plants with purple flowers had the same phenotype but might have differed in genotype. Either plant might have had two (dominant) genes for purple. Alternatively, either plant might have had one (dominant) purple gene and one (recessive) white gene. Environment, or nurture, is the second influence on phenotype. For instance, humans inherit their height and skin color; but good nutrition leads to increased size, and sunlight can change skin color. Another example of environmental influence on phenotype

dominant gene A gene that is expressed in the offspring whenever it is present.

recessive gene A gene that is expressed only when it is matched with a similar gene from the other parent.

genotype The genetic constitution of an organism, determined at the moment of conception.

phenotype Observable physical characteristics, which result from both genetic and environmental influences.

FIGURE 3.31 Genotypes and Phenotypes Mendel's experiments with cross-breeding pea plants resulted in purple flowers 75 percent of the time and white flowers 25 percent of the time.

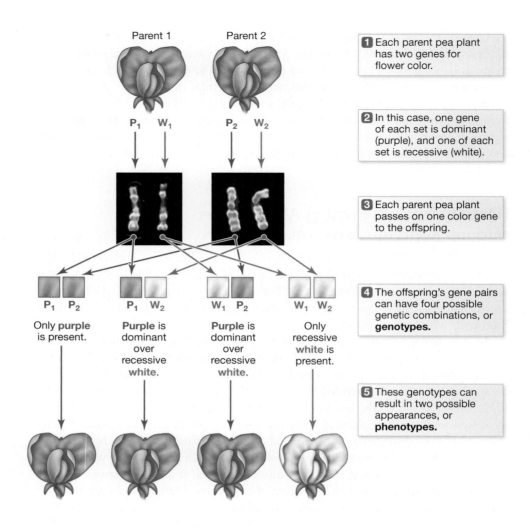

Parent 1   Parent 2

P₁   W₁   P₂   W₂

1 Each parent pea plant has two genes for flower color.

2 In this case, one gene of each set is dominant (purple), and one of each set is recessive (white).

3 Each parent pea plant passes on one color gene to the offspring.

P₁ P₂   P₁ W₂   W₁ P₂   W₁ W₂

Only **purple** is present.

Purple is dominant over recessive **white.**

Purple is dominant over recessive **white.**

Only recessive **white** is present.

4 The offspring's gene pairs can have four possible genetic combinations, or **genotypes.**

5 These genotypes can result in two possible appearances, or **phenotypes.**

is *phenylketonuria (PKU)*. Infants who have this rare genetic disorder are unable to break down phenylalanine (an enzyme that appears in dairy and other products, including aspartame, a sweetener in diet soft drinks). The resulting excess of phenylalanine can lead to severe brain damage. Fortunately, providing such children with a low-phenylalanine diet until they pass the critical stages of neural development greatly helps reduce brain damage. The phenotype, then, is modified by diet.

POLYGENIC EFFECTS Mendel's flower experiments dealt with single-gene characteristics. Such traits appear to be determined by one gene each. But when a population displays a range of variability for a certain characteristic, such as height or intelligence, the characteristic is *polygenic*. In other words, the trait is influenced by many genes (as well as by environment).

Consider human skin color. There are not just three or four separate skin colors. There is a spectrum of colors. The U.S. Census of 2000 allowed respondents to select more than one race for the first time. The data from that census showed that approximately 2.4 percent of the population (over 6.8 million people) identify themselves as multiracial (CensusScope, 2000). The huge range of skin tones among Americans alone shows that human skin color is not inherited the same way as flower color was in Mendel's research. The rich variety of skin colors (phenotype) is not the end product of a single dominant/recessive gene pairing (genotype). Instead, the variety shows the effects of multiple genes.

Genotypic Variation Is Created by Sexual Reproduction

Although they have the same parents, siblings may differ from each other in many ways, such as eye color, height, and personality. These differences occur because each person has a specific combination of genes, determined in part by random cell division before reproduction. Most cells in the human body contain 23 pairs of chromosomes. These pairs include the sex chromosomes, which are denoted X and Y due to their shapes. Females have two X chromosomes. Males have one X chromosome and one Y (**Figure 3.32**).

In each parent, reproductive cells divide to produce *gametes,* the egg and sperm cells. Each gamete contains half of every chromosome pair. After one sperm and one egg combine during fertilization, the resulting fertilized cell, known as a *zygote,* contains 23 pairs of chromosomes. In other words, half of each pair of chromosomes comes from the mother, and the other half comes from the father. From any two parents, 8 million different combinations of the 23 chromosomes are possible. The net outcome is that a unique genotype is created at conception, and this accounts for the genetic variation of the human species (**Figure 3.33**).

The zygote grows through *cell division*. This process has two stages: First the chromosomes duplicate. Then the cell divides into two new cells with an identical chromosome structure. Cell division is the basis of the life cycle and

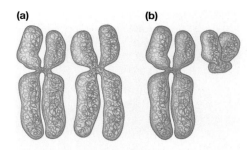

(a) **(b)**

FIGURE 3.32 Sex Chromosomes (a) In females, the 23rd pair of chromosomes consists of two X chromosomes. **(b)** In males, the 23rd pair consists of one X and one Y chromosome. The Y chromosome is much smaller than the X chromosome.

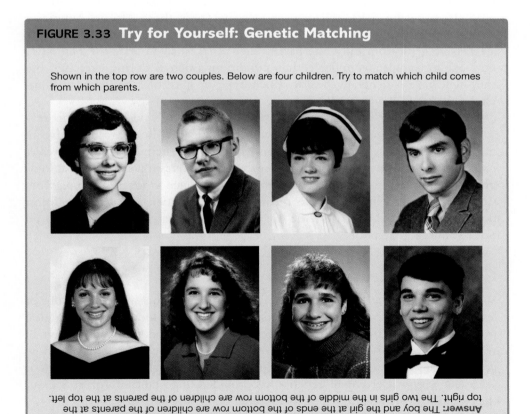

FIGURE 3.33 Try for Yourself: Genetic Matching

Shown in the top row are two couples. Below are four children. Try to match which child comes from which parents.

Answer: The boy and the girl at the ends of the bottom row are children of the parents at the top right. The two girls in the middle of the bottom row are children of the parents at the top left.

FIGURE 3.34 Mutations (a) These moths illustrate industrial melanism at work. As shown here, it is easier to spot light-colored insects against dark backgrounds. Because predators have an easier time catching insects they can spot, darker moths and darker butterflies are better able to survive in more-polluted areas. **(b)** Sickle-cell disease occurs when people receive recessive genes for the trait from both parents. It causes red blood cells to assume the distinctive "sickle" shape seen here in the left cell. Sickle-cell disease is most common among African Americans.

is responsible for growth and development. Errors sometimes occur during cell division and lead to *mutations,* most of which are benign and have little influence on the organism. Occasionally, a genetic mutation produces a selective advantage or disadvantage in terms of survival or reproduction. That is, mutations can be adaptive or maladaptive. The evolutionary significance of such a change in adaptiveness is complex. If a mutation produces an ability or behavior that proves advantageous to the organism, that mutation may spread through the gene pool. The mutation may spread because those who carry the gene are more likely to survive and reproduce.

Consider *industrial melanism.* This phenomenon accounts for the fact that in areas of the world with heavy soot or smog, moths and butterflies tend to be darker in color. What has created this dark coloration? Before industrialization, landscapes (trees, buildings, etc.) were lighter in color. Predators were more likely to spot darker insects against pale backgrounds, so any mutation that led to darker coloring in insects was eliminated quickly through natural selection. But with industrialization, pollution darkened the landscapes. Darker coloring in insects therefore became more adaptive because the darker insects were harder to see against the darker backgrounds (**Figure 3.34a**).

What about genetic mutations that are disadvantageous adaptively, such as by leading to disease? The dominance or recessiveness of a gene helps determine if it remains in the gene pool. For instance, *sickle-cell disease* is a genetic disorder that alters the bloodstream's processing of oxygen. It can lead to pain, organ and bone damage, and anemia. The disease occurs mainly in African Americans: Approximately 8 percent of African Americans are estimated to have the (recessive) gene for it (National Human Genome Research Institute, n.d.). Because the sickle-cell gene is recessive, only those African Americans who receive it from both parents will develop the disease. Those who receive a recessive gene from only one parent have what is called *sickle-cell trait.* They may exhibit symptoms under certain conditions (such as during exercise), but they will have a generally healthy phenotype in spite of a genotype that includes the trait (**Figure 3.34b**).

Recessive genes do not interfere with most people's health. For this reason, the recessive genes for diseases such as sickle-cell anemia can survive in the gene pool. This particular gene also has some benefit in that it increases resistance to malaria, a parasitic disease prevalent in certain parts of Africa. People with only one sickle-cell gene enjoy this resistance without suffering from sickle-cell disease. In contrast to recessive gene disorders like this one, most dominant gene disorders are lethal for most of their carriers and therefore do not last in the gene pool.

Genes Affect Behavior

What determines the kind of person you are? What factors make you more or less bold, intelligent, or able to read a map? Your abilities and your psychological traits are influenced by the interaction of your genes and the environment in which you were raised or to which you are now exposed. The study of how genes and environment interact to influence psychological activity is known as *behavioral genetics.* Behavioral genetics has provided important information about the extent to which biology influences mind, brain, and behavior.

Any research suggesting that abilities to perform certain behaviors are biologically based is controversial. Most people do not want to be told that what they can achieve is limited by something beyond their control, such as their genes.

It is easy to accept that genes control physical characteristics such as sex, race, eye color, and predisposition to diseases such as cancer and alcoholism. But can genes determine whether people will get divorced, how smart they are, or what careers they choose? Increasingly, science indicates that genes lay the ground-work for many human traits. From this perspective, people are born essentially like undeveloped photographs: The image is already captured, but the way it eventually appears can vary based on the development process. Psychologists study the ways in which characteristics are influenced by nature, nurture, and their combination—in other words, by the ways genes are expressed in distinct environments.

BEHAVIORAL GENETICS METHODS Most of us, at one time or another, have marveled at how different siblings can be, even those raised around the same time and in the same household. The differences are to be expected, because most siblings share neither identical genes nor identical life experiences. Within the household and outside it, environments differ subtly and not so subtly. Siblings have different birth orders. Their mother may have consumed different foods and other substances during pregnancies. They may have different friends and teach-ers. Their parents may treat them differently. It is difficult to know what causes the similarities and differences between siblings, who always share some genes and often share much of their environments. Therefore, behavioral geneticists use two methods to assess the degree to which traits are inherited: twin studies and adoption studies.

Twin studies compare similarities between different types of twins to deter-mine the genetic basis of specific traits. **Monozygotic twins,** or *identical twins,* result from one zygote (fertilized egg) dividing in two. Each new zygote, and therefore each twin, has the same chromosomes and the same genes on each chromosome. Interesting research indicates, however, that monozygotic twins' DNA might not be as identical as long thought, due to subtle differences in how the mother's and father's genes are combined (Bruder et al., 2008). **Dizygotic twins,** sometimes called *fraternal* or *nonidentical twins,* result when two separately fertilized eggs de-velop in the mother's womb simultaneously. The resulting twins are no more similar genetically than any other pair of siblings. To the extent that monozygotic twins are more similar than dizygotic twins, the increased similarity is considered most likely due to genetic influence. Even identical twins do not have the exact same environment (and in rare circumstances might even have some different genes due to random mutations), and therefore they have different phenotypes. Still, they are typically much more similar than dizygotic twins, who differ mark-edly in genotype.

Adoption studies compare the similarities between biological relatives and adoptive relatives. Nonbiological adopted siblings may share similar home en-vironments but will have different genes. Therefore, the assumption is that similarities among nonbiological adopted siblings have more to do with envi-ronment than with genes. Growing up in the same home turns out to have rela-tively little influence on many traits, including personality traits. Indeed, after genetic similarity is controlled for, even biological siblings raised in the same home are no more similar than two strangers plucked at random off the street. (This point is examined in greater detail in Chapter 9, "Human Development," and Chapter 13, "Personality.")

One way to conduct a behavioral genetic study is to compare monozygotic twins who have been *raised together* with ones who were *raised apart.* Thomas Bouchard and his colleagues at the University of Minnesota identified more than

monozygotic twins Also called *identical twins;* twin siblings that result from one zygote splitting in two and therefore share the same genes.

dizygotic twins Also called *fraternal twins;* twin siblings that result from two separately fertilized eggs and therefore are no more similar genetically than nontwin siblings.

FIGURE 3.35 Twins **(a)** Fraternal twins, such as this pair pictured during their 13th birthday party, result when two separate eggs are fertilized at the same time. **(b)** Identical twins result when one fertilized egg splits in two. Identical twins Gerald Levey and Mark Newman, participants in Dr. Bouchard's study, were separated at birth. Reunited at age 31, they discovered they were both firefighters and had similar personality traits. **What other factors might account for the similarities between twins raised apart?**

(a) Dizygotic (fraternal) twins

Two sperm fertilize two eggs...

which become two zygotes.

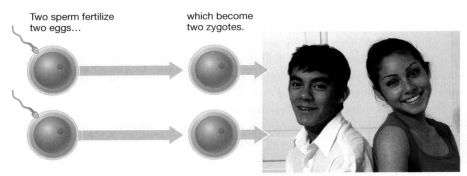

(b) Monozygotic (identical) twins

One sperm fertilizes one egg...

and the zygote splits in two.

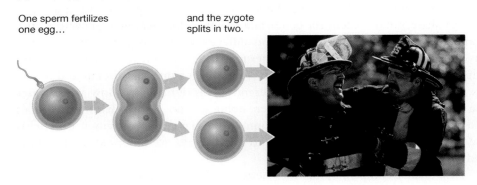

100 pairs of identical and nonidentical twins, some raised together and some raised apart (1990; **Figure 3.35**). The researchers examined a variety of these twins' characteristics, including intelligence, personality, well-being, achievement, alienation, and aggression. The general finding from the Minnesota Twin Project was that identical twins, raised together or not, were likely to be similar.

The "Jim twins" were among the most famous case studies to emerge from this project. These twin brothers were separated at birth and raised by different families. It is easy to guess about how each one was given the same name, but how is it possible that each James went on to marry a woman named Linda, divorce Linda and marry a woman named Betty, name a son James Alan (or James Allen), and name a dog Toy? In addition, both were part-time law enforcement officers who drove Chevrolets and vacationed in Florida. They were the same height and weight, chain-smoked the same brand of cigarettes, and drank the same brand of beer. Although no one would seriously suggest there are genes for naming dogs Toy or for marrying and divorcing women named Linda, the many similarities in the Jim twins' lives point to the strong genetic influences in shaping personality and behavior.

Some critics have argued that most of the adopted twins in the Minnesota study were raised in relatively similar environments. This similarity came about, in part, because adoption agencies try to match the child to the adoptive home. However, this argument does not explain the identical twins Oskar Stohr and Jack Yufe, who were born in Trinidad in 1933 (Bouchard, Lykken, McGue, Segal, & Tellegen, 1990). Oskar was raised a Catholic in Germany and eventually joined the Nazi Party. Jack was raised a Jew in Trinidad and lived for a while in Israel. Few twins have more-different backgrounds. Yet when they met, at an interview for the study, they were wearing similar clothes, exhibited similar mannerisms, and shared odd habits, such as flushing the toilet before using it, dipping toast in coffee, storing rubber bands on their wrists, and enjoying startling people by sneezing loudly in elevators. Some critics feel that nothing more than coincidence is at work in these case studies. They argue that if a researcher randomly selected any two people of the same age, many surprising similarities would exist in those people and their lives, just by coincidence, even if the people and their lives differed in most other ways. But twins and other relatives share similarities beyond coincidental attributes and behavior quirks. For instance, intelligence and personality traits such as shyness tend to run in families due to strong genetic components.

Moreover, some evidence suggests that twins raised apart may be more similar than twins raised together. This phenomenon might occur if parents encouraged individuality in twins raised together by emphasizing different strengths and interests as a way of helping each twin develop as an individual. In effect, the parents would actively create a different environment for each twin.

UNDERSTANDING HERITABILITY *Heredity* is the transmission of characteristics from parents to offspring by means of genes. A term that is often confused with *heredity* but means something different is **heritability.** This term refers to a statistical estimate of the genetic portion of the variation in some specific trait. The heritability for a trait depends on the *variation:* the measure of the overall difference among a group of people for that particular trait. That is, within a group of people (e.g., American women), how much do members vary in some trait (e.g., height)? Once we know the typical amount of variation within the population, we can see whether people who are related show less variation. For instance, do sisters tend to be more similar in height than unrelated women chosen at random?

Heritability refers to populations, not to individuals. If within a certain population a trait such as height has a heritability of .60, that means 60 percent of height variation among individuals within that population is genetic. It does not mean that anyone necessarily gets 60 percent of his or her height from genetics and 40 percent from environment. For instance, almost everyone has two legs. More people lose legs through accidents than are born without them. Thus the heritability value for having two legs is nearly zero, despite the obvious fact that the human genome includes instructions for growing two legs. The key lesson here is: Estimates of heritability are concerned only with the extent that people differ in terms of their genetic makeup within the group.

Social and Environmental Contexts Influence Genetic Expression

In a longitudinal study of criminality, Avshalom Caspi and his colleagues (2002) followed a group of more than 1,000 New Zealanders from their births in 1972–73 until adulthood. Every few years, the researchers collected enormous amounts of information about the participants and their lives. When the participants were 26 years old, the investigators examined which factors predicted who became a violent criminal. Prior research had demonstrated that children who are mistreated by their parents are more likely to become violent offenders. But not all mistreated children become violent, and these researchers wanted to know why not. They hypothesized that the enzyme monoamine oxidase (MAO) is important in determining susceptibility to the effects of mistreatment, because low levels of MAO have been implicated in aggressive behaviors (this connection is discussed further in Chapter 14, "Psychological Disorders"). The gene that controls MAO comes in two forms, one of which leads to higher levels of MAO and one of which leads to lower levels. Caspi and colleagues found that boys with

heritability A statistical estimate of the extent to which variation in a trait within a population is due to genetic factors.

the low-MAO gene appeared to be especially susceptible to the effects of early-childhood mistreatment. Those boys were also much more likely to be convicted of a violent crime than those with the high-MAO gene. Only 1 in 8 boys was mistreated *and* had the low-MAO gene. That minority, however, was responsible for nearly half of the violent crimes committed by the group (**Figure 3.36**). The New Zealand study is a good example of how nature and nurture together affect behavior—in this case, unfortunately, violent behavior. Nature and nurture are inextricably entwined.

Many other studies have provided evidence that genes and social contexts interact to affect the phenotype. Sandra Scarr and her colleagues have proposed a theory of development that stresses the interactive nature of genes and

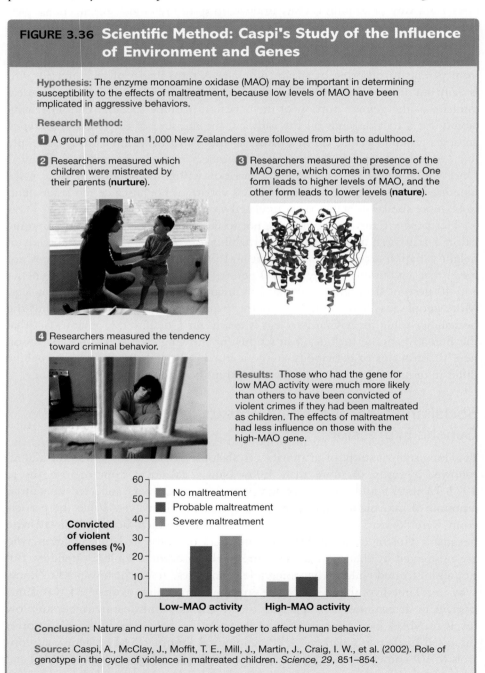

FIGURE 3.36 **Scientific Method: Caspi's Study of the Influence of Environment and Genes**

Hypothesis: The enzyme monoamine oxidase (MAO) may be important in determining susceptibility to the effects of maltreatment, because low levels of MAO have been implicated in aggressive behaviors.

Research Method:

1 A group of more than 1,000 New Zealanders were followed from birth to adulthood.

2 Researchers measured which children were mistreated by their parents (**nurture**).

3 Researchers measured the presence of the MAO gene, which comes in two forms. One form leads to higher levels of MAO, and the other form leads to lower levels (**nature**).

4 Researchers measured the tendency toward criminal behavior.

Results: Those who had the gene for low MAO activity were much more likely than others to have been convicted of violent crimes if they had been maltreated as children. The effects of maltreatment had less influence on those with the high-MAO gene.

Convicted of violent offenses (%)

- No maltreatment
- Probable maltreatment
- Severe maltreatment

Low-MAO activity   High-MAO activity

Conclusion: Nature and nurture can work together to affect human behavior.

Source: Caspi, A., McClay, J., Moffit, T. E., Mill, J., Martin, J., Craig, I. W., et al. (2002). Role of genotype in the cycle of violence in maltreated children. *Science, 29*, 851–854.

environment (Scarr & McCarthy, 1983). According to Scarr, early environments influence young children, but children's genes also influence the experiences they receive. For instance, children exposed to the same environment interpret and react to it in different ways. When teased, some children withdraw, others shrug it off without concern, and still others fight back. Because of differences in how they react to events, different children evoke different responses from others. A well-mannered, cuddly child prompts parents and caregivers to provide more nurturing than an irritable, fussy child does. Similarly, a child who seems to enjoy reading is likely to receive more books and be read to more often than a child who does not. And as children become older, they can choose their social situations. Some children prefer vigorous outdoor activities, others prefer quieter indoor activities, and so on. Thus genes predispose people to certain behaviors. Those behaviors prompt other people to respond in particular ways. Together, the behaviors, the responses, and subsequent actions shape people's phenotypes. Because genes and social contexts interact, separating their independent effects can be very difficult. Some argue that it is impossible.

Genetic Expression Can Be Modified

Researchers can employ various gene manipulation techniques to enhance or reduce the expression of a particular gene or even to insert a gene from one animal species into the embryo of another. The researchers can then compare the genetically modified animal with an unmodified one to test theories about the affected gene's function (**Figure 3.37**). Such techniques have dramatically increased our understanding of how gene expression influences thought, feeling, and behavior. For instance, some of the transgenic mice discussed in Chapter 2 are called *knockouts*. Within these research mice, particular genes have been "knocked out," or rendered inactive by being removed from the genome or disrupted within the genome. If a gene is important for a specific function, knocking out that gene should interfere with the function. This experimental technique has revolutionized genetics, and in recognition the 2007 Nobel Prize in Physiology or Medicine was awarded to the three scientists who developed it: Mario Capecchi, Oliver Smithies, and Sir Martin Evans.

One remarkable finding from genetic manipulation is that changing even a single gene can dramatically change behavior. Through various gene manipulations, researchers have created anxious mice, hyperactive mice, mice that cannot learn or remember, mice that groom themselves to the point of baldness, mice that fail to take care of their offspring, and even mice that progressively increase alcohol intake when stressed (Marcus, 2004; Ridley, 2003). In one study, a gene from the highly social prairie vole was inserted into the developing embryos of normally antisocial mice. The resulting transgenic mice exhibited social behavior more typical of prairie voles than of mice (Insel & Young, 2001). Another study found that knocking out specific genes led mice to forget mice they had previously encountered. These knockouts also failed to investigate new mice placed in their cages, though normal mice would do so readily. In essence, knocking out one gene led to multiple impairments in social recognition (Choleris et al., 2003). This finding does not indicate that mice have a specific gene for being social. It indicates that changing one gene's expression leads to the expression of a series of other genes. This effect ultimately influences even complex behaviors. In other words, genes seldom work in isolation to influence mind and behavior. Rather, complex interaction among thousands of genes gives rise to the complexity of human experience.

FIGURE 3.37 Genetic Modifications The two white mice and three brown mice in this photo are genetically normal. The sixth mouse is hairless because it has been genetically modified. Specifically, this mouse has received two *nu* genes, which cause the "nude" mutation. These genes also cause the mouse to have no thymus and therefore no T cells (an important part of the immune system). The lack of T cells makes the mouse a good laboratory subject, as its body cannot reject tumors or transplants of cells from other animals.

Seeking Disconfirming Evidence

Most of us tend to focus on information that confirms what we already believe. Suppose you believe that genetics plays only a small role in the way people think, feel, and act. How would you test this belief? If you are like most people, you would look for studies that show a small genetic effect and criticize studies that show a large one. But a better way to gather and study information would be to draw a 2 × 2 chart and fill in every cell (**Figure 3.38**).

On the left, you would list each position: your thesis (A) and its opposite, or antithesis (B). In the middle, you would supply at least one or two reasons that support each position, provide evidence for each reason, and evaluate the relative strength of each piece of evidence. (For example, how reliable is your source for this information? If a study was conducted, did it use appropriate control groups?) On the right, you would supply at least one or two reasons that contradict each position; provide evidence for each of these reasons; and, as with the supporting evidence, evaluate the relative strength of each piece of evidence. The table would force you to consider information that supports your beliefs. It would also force you to consider information that fails to support those beliefs.

Suppose you believe that vitamin C reduces your likelihood of getting a cold. If you acted on the natural tendency to consider only confirming information, you would look for studies in which people who took vitamin C had fewer colds. If you employed this table, you would also need to consider other possibilities, such as studies in which people took vitamin C and did not have fewer colds, or did not take vitamin C and had fewer colds, or did not take vitamin C and had more colds. To consider the subject thoroughly, you would include all four kinds of studies in your thinking. This critical thinking skill (or strategy) will not only keep you from ignoring disconfirming evidence. It will also increase your ability to gather disconfirming evidence, evaluate it, and thereby strengthen your arguments—for and against.

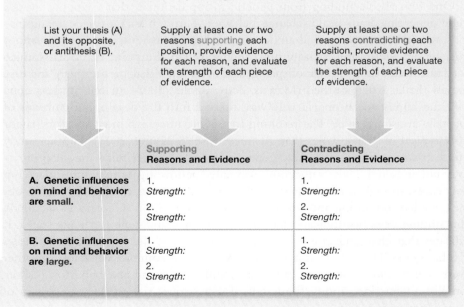

FIGURE 3.38 Supporting and Contradictory Evidence

3.5 How Does the Brain Change?

In a perfect illustration of how nurture can influence nature, the brain can reorganize itself based on which parts of it are used lightly and which are used heavily. In fact, despite the great precision and the specificity of its connections, the brain is extremely malleable. Over the course of development, throughout our constant stream of experience, and after injury, the brain continually changes. This property is known as **plasticity.**

Reptiles hatch from their leathery eggs ready to go; in contrast, human infants require lots of sleep and high-quality nutrition before they can function independently. As children's bodies grow and develop, their brains grow and develop, actively rewiring in major ways for many years. The brain's development follows set sequences. Different structures and abilities progress at different rates and mature at different points in life. In babies, for example, general vision develops before the ability to see depth. The prefrontal cortex is not anatomically fully mature until early adulthood. Each development is programmed in the genes. But even with these meticulously specified genetic instructions, environment plays a major role.

plasticity A property of the brain that allows it to change as a result of experience, drugs, or injury.

The Interplay of Genes and Environment Wires the Brain

Every life experience alters an individual brain's connections. In fact, gene expression is profoundly affected by environment. Which cells express which genes, and to what extent, depends to a large extent on environment. Through the constant interplay between nature and nurture, environment affects our DNA's activity and the products of that activity. Thus brain plasticity reflects the interactive nature of our biological and environmental influences.

CELL IDENTITY BECOMES FIXED OVER TIME In the developing embryo, each new cell receives signals, from its surroundings, that determine what type of cell it will become. If cells from one part of an embryo are surgically transplanted to another part, the transplant's success depends on how developed the cells' identity is. Tissue transplanted early enough completely transforms into whatever type is appropriate for its new location. As an embryo develops, each cell becomes more and more committed to its identity, so transplanting cells too late may disfigure the organism. Many people are therefore excited about the possibility of transplanting fetal cells. Because fetal cells are undeveloped enough to become any type of tissue, they might be used to cure diseases and even restore mobility to people who have lost some motor abilities. This work is in its infancy, so to speak, but it promises breakthroughs in how mental illness and other psychological conditions are treated. Neural cells transplanted early enough take on the identity appropriate to their new location, and the organism develops normally.

EXPERIENCE FINE-TUNES NEURAL CONNECTIONS Connections form between brain structures when growing axons are directed by certain chemicals that tell them where to go and where not to go. The major connections are established by chemical messengers, but the detailed connections are governed by experience. If a cat's eyes are sewn shut at birth, depriving the animal of visual input, the visual cortex fails to develop properly. If the sutures are removed weeks later, the cat is permanently blind, even though its eyes function normally. Adult cats that are similarly deprived do not lose their sight (Wiesel & Hubel, 1963). Evidently, ongoing activity is necessary in the visual pathways to refine the visual cortex enough for it to be useful. In general, such plasticity has *critical periods*. During these times, particular experiences must occur for development to proceed normally.

To study the effects of experience on development, researchers reared rats in two different laboratory environments. One group was raised in a normal environment for laboratory rats: featureless boxes with bedding at the bottom, plus dishes for food and water. The other group was raised in an enriched environment, with many interesting things to look at, puzzles to solve, obstacles to run, toys to play with, running wheels to exercise on, and even balance beams to hone athletic skills on. In the first environment, the rats suffered mental deprivation. The unused portions of their brains atrophied (failed to develop normally). In the second environment, the "luxury" items might simply have approximated rat life in the wild, allowing normal rat development. As a result, the second group developed bigger, heavier brains than the first group (Rosenzweig, Bennett, & Diamond, 1972). Thus experience is important for normal development and maybe even more so for superior development.

Culture Affects the Brain

Our cultural experiences help shape how we view the world and how we think. As a result, cultural differences contribute to different patterns of brain activity.

For instance, cultures differ slightly in how they express emotions. As discussed further in Chapter 10, evidence indicates that people are better at identifying emotional expressions from members of their own cultures than from members of other cultures. This effect occurs in part, it seems, because people have more experience in interpreting emotional expressions among those with whom they interact regularly. If so, this greater recognition should mean that people's brain responses are enhanced when they are interpreting emotional expressions within their own cultural groups than from other cultural groups. A recent brain imaging study involved one group of participants in Japan and another group in the United States (Chiao et al., 2008). The researchers showed pictures of both neutral and fearful facial expressions portrayed by Japanese and American faces. As noted earlier in this chapter, the amygdala shows increased activity when people view fearful expressions. In this study, activity in the amygdala was greatest when participants viewed fearful expressions within their own cultural group. Thus cultural experience appears to fine-tune the brain's responses to such important environmental cues (**Figure 3.39**).

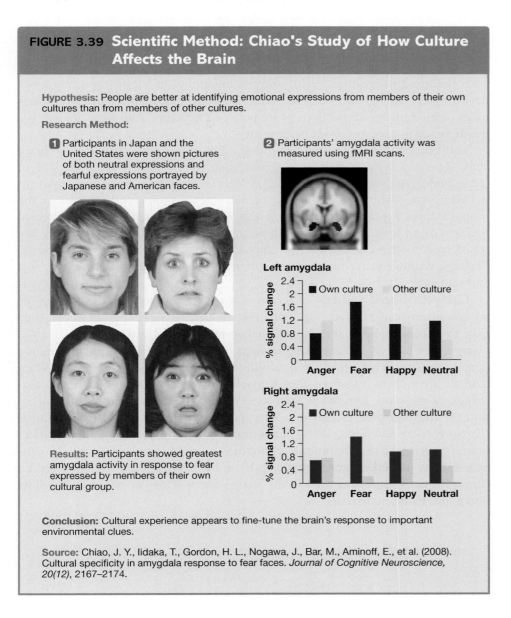

FIGURE 3.39 **Scientific Method: Chiao's Study of How Culture Affects the Brain**

Hypothesis: People are better at identifying emotional expressions from members of their own cultures than from members of other cultures.

Research Method:

1 Participants in Japan and the United States were shown pictures of both neutral expressions and fearful expressions portrayed by Japanese and American faces.

2 Participants' amygdala activity was measured using fMRI scans.

Left amygdala

Right amygdala

Results: Participants showed greatest amygdala activity in response to fear expressed by members of their own cultural group.

Conclusion: Cultural experience appears to fine-tune the brain's response to important environmental clues.

Source: Chiao, J. Y., Iidaka, T., Gordon, H. L., Nogawa, J., Bar, M., Aminoff, E., et al. (2008). Cultural specificity in amygdala response to fear faces. *Journal of Cognitive Neuroscience, 20(12),* 2167–2174.

The Brain Rewires Itself throughout Life

Brain plasticity decreases with age. Even into very old age, however, the brain can grow new connections among neurons and even grow new neurons. The rewiring and growth within the brain represents the biological basis of learning.

CHANGE IN THE STRENGTH OF CONNECTIONS UNDERLIES LEARNING In every moment of life, we gain memories: experiences and knowledge that are acquired instantaneously and may be recalled later, as well as habits that form gradually. All these memories are reflected in the brain's physical changes.

Psychologists widely accept that changes in the brain are most likely not in its larger wiring or general arrangement. The changes are mainly in the strength of existing connections. One possibility is that when two neurons fire simultaneously, the synaptic connection between them strengthens. The strengthened synaptic connection makes these neurons more likely to fire together in the future. Conversely, *not* firing simultaneously tends to weaken the connection between two neurons. This theory can be summarized by the catchphrase *Fire together, wire together*. First proposed in the 1940s, by the renowned psychologist Donald Hebb, it is consistent with a great deal of experimental evidence and many theoretical models. It accounts for both the "burning in" of an experience (a pattern of neural firing becomes more likely to recur, and its recurrence leads the mind to recall an event) and the ingraining of habits (repeating a behavior makes the repeater tend to perform that behavior automatically). Sometimes, entirely new connections grow between neurons. This new growth is a major factor in recovery from brain injury.

Until recently, scientists believed that adult brains produced no new brain cells. There is now evidence, however, that new neurons are produced in some brain regions (Eriksson et al., 1998). The production of new neurons is called *neurogenesis*. A fair amount of neurogenesis apparently occurs in the hippocampus. Recall from earlier in this chapter that memories are retained within (or at least require) the hippocampus initially. They eventually are transferred to the cortex, so the hippocampus is continuously overwritten. Perhaps, without disrupting memory, neurons in the hippocampus can be lost and replaced.

Elizabeth Gould and her colleagues have demonstrated that environmental conditions can play an important role in neurogenesis. For example, they have found that for rats, shrews, and marmosets, stressful experiences—such as being confronted by strange males in their home cages—interfere with neurogenesis during development and adulthood (Gould & Tanapat, 1999). When animals are housed together, they typically form dominance hierarchies that reflect social status. Dominant animals—those who possess the highest social status—show greater increases in new neurons than do subordinate animals (Kozorovitskiy & Gould, 2004). Thus social environment can strongly affect brain plasticity, a dynamic process we are only beginning to understand. Neurogenesis may underlie neural plasticity. If so, further research might enable us, through neurogenesis, to reverse the brain's natural loss of neurons and slow down age-based mental decline.

synesthesia Cross-sensory experience (e.g., a visual image has a taste).

CHANGES IN THE BRAIN The functions of portions of the cerebral cortex shift in response to their activity. Recall the somatosensory homunculus (see Figure 3.21a). As that representation makes clear, more cortical tissue is devoted to body parts that receive more sensation or are used more. Again, wiring in the brain is affected by amount of use. Another example of changes in cortical maps, discussed earlier, is the enlargement of hippocampi in experienced London taxi drivers.

Cortical reorganization can also have bizarre results. For example, an amputee can be afflicted with a *phantom limb,* the intense sensation that the amputated body part still exists. Some phantom limbs are experienced as moving normally, such as being used to gesture in conversation, whereas some are frozen in position. Moreover, a phantom limb often is accompanied by pain sensations, which may result from the misgrowth of the severed pain nerves at the stump. The cortex misinterprets the pain as coming from the place where those nerves originally came from. This phenomenon suggests that the brain has not reorganized in response to the injury and that the missing limb's cortical representation remains intact. The neurologist V. S. Ramachandran has discovered, however, that an amputee who has lost a hand may, when his or her eyes are closed, perceive a touch on the cheek as if it were on the missing hand (Ramachandran & Hirstein, 1998). Apparently, on the somatosensory homunculus the hand is represented next to the face. The unused part of the amputee's cortex (the part that would have responded to the now-missing limb) assumes to some degree the function of the closest group, representing the face. Somehow, the rest of the brain has not kept pace with the somatosensory area enough to figure out these neurons' new job, so the neurons are activated by a touch on the amputee's face (**Figure 3.40**).

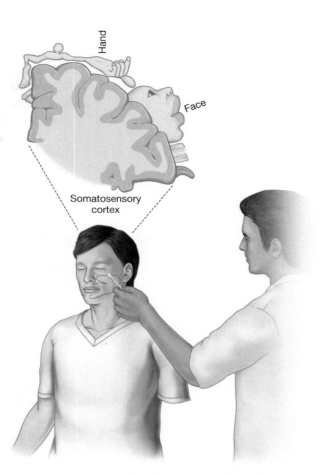

FIGURE 3.40 **Cortical Remapping Following Amputation** The participant felt a cotton swab touching his cheek as touching his missing hand. **What is the apparent reason for this effect?**

THE PUZZLE OF SYNESTHESIA People called *synesthetes* experience **synesthesia.** This kind of cross-sensory experience can take many forms. One man hates driving because the sight of road signs tastes to him like a mixture of pistachio ice cream and ear wax (McNeil, 2006). For another man, any personal name has a specific taste—for example, the name *John* tastes like cornbread (Simner et al., 2006). For yet another synesthete, each day of the week is colored (Monday is red, Tuesday is indigo), as is each month of the year (December is yellow, January is red; Ramachandran, 2003). For others, colors evoke smells, sights evoke sounds, and numbers come in colors (e.g., 5 is always red, 2 is always green; **Figure 3.41**). Such experiences are idiosyncratic. For one person, bread is always smooth in texture and silver in color, but for another person it sounds like a foghorn. For each person, the associations do not vary. If road signs have a taste, for example, they always taste the same.

Reports of people with synesthesia date as far back as ancient Greece (Ferry, 2002). Estimates of the percentage of the population that report these cross-sensory experiences range from 1 in 2,000 to 1 in 200. Since we cannot simply write these people off as "crazy," we need to understand their bizarre sensations.

Recent research into heredity and brain organization provides fascinating clues for understanding synesthesia. Because synesthesia tends to run in families,

FIGURE 3.41 **Synesthesia** For synesthetes, sensory experiences are crossed. For example, colors may evoke smells, sights may evoke sounds, and numbers may come in colors.

it appears to have a genetic basis. Thus it may help us understand how heredity affects the way we experience the world. Even more provocatively, brain research suggests that cross-sensory experiences could be related to creativity. Could the mixture of colors, words, and images by artists be the result of "special brain wiring" that they inherited (Blakeslee, 2001)? Can synesthesia explain why we call some smells "sharp" and some colors "loud"? Questions like these, and the scientific research being used to answer them, are radically changing how we think about all human experience and behavior.

V. S. Ramachandran, the neurologist who conducted many of the studies on phantom limbs (discussed in the previous section), has also conducted a series of experiments to better understand what is happening when someone reports, for example, that a sound is lime green or that chicken tastes pointy (Ramachandran & Hubbard, 2001). Ramachandran inferred that the genes involved in synesthesia were related to brain formation. Because the brain area involved in seeing colors is physically close to the brain area involved in understanding numbers, he theorized that in people with color/number synesthesia, these two brain areas have some connections or cross-wiring. The process of linking these areas would have resembled the process of linking areas of an amputee's brain (again, discussed earlier): One portion of the brain would have adopted another portion's role.

To test his hypothesis, Ramachandran examined MRIs taken of synesthetes when they looked at black numbers on a white background. He found evidence of neural activity in the brain area responsible for color vision. Control participants without synesthesia did not experience activity in this brain area when they looked at the same numbers (**Figure 3.42**).

FIGURE 3.42 Try for Yourself: Synesthesia Test

Two stimuli used by Ramachandran and Hubbard (2003) to study synesthesia:

Look first at the square on the left, and as quickly as possible count the number of 2s.

Now do the same task with the square on the right.

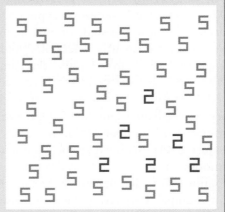

Explanation: Unless you have synesthesia and it causes you to see particular numbers in particular colors, you were much faster at counting the 2s on the right. They "popped out" at you because they are a different color from the 5s. Some synesthetes are equally fast at both tasks because they see the numbers in different colors. This test is one of many used to determine if someone has color-related synesthesia.

Recognizing Unstated Assumptions

All human interactions are based partly on unstated assumptions. For example, the participants in a conversation assume the parties have some knowledge in common but that they do not all have the same knowledge. When you enter a classroom, you assume the instructor will act differently than the students. In writing this textbook, the authors explained information they assumed would be new for most readers, but they did not define words they assumed most readers would know.

When you are trying to understand a complex topic, begin by recognizing your assumptions about that topic. Also consider other people's assumptions. Once you make those assumptions explicit, you can apply reason to them.

Consider, for example, common assumptions about genetic influences and the brain. Many people assume that if a trait or tendency is passed along genetically, then those who inherit that trait or tendency cannot change it in themselves. By this thinking, those who inherit shyness, intelligence, or boldness cannot change how shy, intelligent, or bold they are.

When people learn about sex differences in the brain, they often assume that the brain does not change and that it "causes" sex differences in behaviors. In reality, the brain reflects genetic inheritance and experience, and together these variables determine the size, function, and structure of the brain.

In fact, because nature is inextricably intertwined with nurture, no biological effects can occur independent of environment. Just as all learning is influenced by assumptions, all choices are influenced by past learning and its influence on both thoughts and feelings.

There is one major difference between a phantom limb and synesthesia, however. The phantom limb is caused primarily by environment (the loss of the limb), whereas synesthesia appears to be caused primarily by genetics. Why has this sensory anomaly remained in the gene pool? Ramachandran suggests that it confers an adaptive advantage: Synesthetes' brains are wired to connect seemingly disparate topics, and the ability to make remote associations is an important part of creativity. As an example, Ramachandran and his collaborator E. M. Hubbard ask us to consider Shakespeare's line "It is the East and Juliet is the sun." The likening of Juliet to the sun is a metaphor, but where did it come from? Its association of a woman and a bright light resembles a synesthetic experience. In fact, these authors conclude that creative people experience a higher incidence of synesthesia than do noncreative people (2003).

Females' and Males' Brains Are Similar and Different

The interplay of biological and environmental effects on the brain is reflected in the similarities and differences between females' and males' brains. Everything a person experiences alters his or her brain, of course, and females and males differ in their life experiences and hormonal makeups. Hormonal differences might affect brain development, and thus they might influence the way males and females differ on some cognition tasks, such as on the ease with which they mentally rotate objects or recall parts of a story (Kimura, 1999).

Sex differences in anatomy are referred to as *sexual dimorphism*. The study of the brain's sexual dimorphism has a long history. Many comparisons of males' and females' brains, especially the earliest comparisons, were questionable scientifically and mostly used to show that female brains were inferior (for a review, see Halpern, 2000). The unstated assumption was always that if two groups (in this case, females and males) were different, one had to be inferior. But people do not have to be the same to be equal. In fact, there is evidence that men and women may perform a task, such as remembering a recent occurrence, equally well but by using different parts of the brain. For example, Richard Haier and colleagues (2005) have found that females and males may solve some complex problems, such as items on IQ tests, differently. Females show greater use of language-related brain regions, and males show greater use of spatial-related brain regions, even when participants are matched for intelligence.

Males generally have larger brains than females, but larger is not necessarily better. In fact, one developmental process in the brain involves disconnecting neurons so that only the most useful connections remain. Jay Giedd and his colleagues (1997) at the U.S. National Institutes of Health concluded that among both sexes, the sizes of brain structures are highly variable. They reported that boys' brains are approximately 9 percent larger than girls' brains, with some differences in the rate of maturation for different parts of the brain for girls and boys.

As discussed in Chapter 5, to some extent the brain's two hemispheres are lateralized: Each hemisphere is dominant for different cognitive functions. A considerable body of evidence says that females' brains are more bilaterally organized for language. In other words, the brain areas important in processing language are more likely to be found in both halves of females' brains. The equivalent language areas are more likely to be in only one hemisphere, usually the left, in males' brains (**Figure 3.43**). One source of data that supports

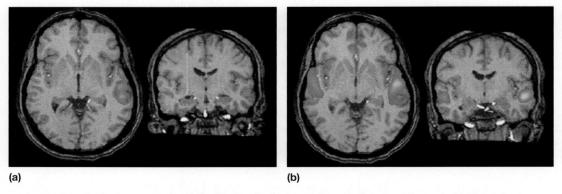

(a)   **(b)**

FIGURE 3.43 Male versus Female Brains A considerable body of evidence indicates that female brains are more bilaterally organized for language. For example, researchers studied men and women listening to someone reading aloud. As these fMRI images show, **(a)** the men listened with one side of their brains, whereas **(b)** the women tended to listen with both sides.

this distinction is people's experiences following strokes. Even when patients are matched on the location and severity of the brain damage caused by a stroke, women are less impaired in language use than men are (Jiang, Sheikh, & Bullock, 2006). A possible reason for women's better outcomes is that, because language is represented in both halves of women's brains, damage to half of a woman's brain will have less effect on that woman's ability to process language than it would if most of the language areas were in the damaged half of the brain. A related hypothesis, in accord with the idea that women's brains are more bilaterally organized, is that the halves of women's brains are connected by more neural fibers than men's are. Remember that a thick band of neurons, the corpus callosum, connects the brain's two halves (see Figure 3.20). Some researchers have found that a portion of this connective tissue is larger in women (Gur & Gur, 2004).

Before we can be confident about recent findings of sex differences in the brain, much more research is needed. We need to better understand normal, healthy brain development. We also need to better understand brain and behavior relationships before we can reason about human sex differences from our knowledge of brain structures (Halpern et al., 2007). Finally, although we tend to focus on the ways in which males and females are different, we need to keep in mind that their brains are similar in many (perhaps most) ways.

The Brain Can Recover from Injury

Just as the brain reorganizes in response to amount of use, it also reorganizes in response to brain damage. Following an injury in the cortex, the surrounding gray matter assumes the function of the damaged area, like a local business scrambling to pick up the customers of a newly closed competitor. This remapping seems to begin immediately, and it continues for years. Such plasticity involves all levels of the central nervous system, from the cortex down to the spinal cord.

Reorganization is much more prevalent in children than in adults, in accord with the sensitive periods of normal development. Young children afflicted with severe and uncontrollable epilepsy that has paralyzed one or more limbs sometimes undergo *radical hemispherectomy*, the surgical removal of an entire cerebral hemisphere. The remaining hemisphere eventually takes on most of the lost hemisphere's functions, and the children regain almost complete use of their limbs. This procedure is not possible in adults. If it were performed on adults, the lack of neural reorganization in their brains would lead to permanent paralysis and loss of function.

As discussed earlier in this chapter, one of the most exciting areas of current neurological research is the transplantation of human fetal tissue into the brain to repair damage. The transplanted tissue consists specifically of *stem cells*. These "master" cells can regenerate themselves. They also can develop into any type of tissue, such as muscle or nerve cells. This relatively new procedure is being explored as a possible treatment for strokes and degenerative diseases such as Parkinson's and Huntington's. The significant challenge is to get the newly introduced cells to make the proper connections so that the damaged circuits regrow. Many people oppose the use of fetal tissue for any type of research, however, on religious or other philosophical grounds. Fortunately, many new methods are emerging that allow researchers to create stem cells by reprogramming adult cells (Kim et al., 2008).

How Does the Brain Change?

Experience affects the circuitry of the brain. During development and across the life span, the circuitry of the brain is constantly reworked in response to experience. Culture, as context for experience, affects brain activity. An understanding of the brain's organization and plasticity has allowed researchers to better understand conditions such as phantom limb syndrome and synesthesia. Although there are many similarities between the brains of females and males, research suggests that females' and males' brains differ in some ways. Males' brains are larger. Females' brains are organized more bilaterally. The brain can reorganize after a brain injury; however, children demonstrate greater reorganization following brain injury than adults.

Measuring Up

1. A person's brain changes in response to environment, including all of that person's experiences. Place an X next to the statements below that support this idea.

    _____ a. The sizes of London taxi drivers' hippocampi were correlated with how long the participants had been London taxi drivers.

    _____ b. Some amputees can feel sensations in their amputated limbs when their eyes are closed and their faces are touched.

    _____ c. Many drugs can mimic neurotransmitters' actions.

    _____ d. Laboratory rats raised in enriched environments developed heavier brains than laboratory rats raised in standard environments.

    _____ e. Phineas Gage's personality changed profoundly after his frontal cortex was damaged.

    _____ f. Some brain responses to selected stimuli vary due to cultural influence.

2. Indicate whether the following statements, about the ways in which females' and males' brains differ, are true or false.

    _____ a. Males' brains generally are larger than females' brains.

    _____ b. Males' and females' brains have no differences.

    _____ c. Researchers have found that sex differences in the brain explain why males tend to hold executive positions more than females do.

    _____ d. Sex differences in the brain indicate that males and females have essentially different abilities.

    _____ e. A larger brain is a better brain—more advanced, plus more complex in its organization.

Answers: 1. Choices a, b, c, d, and f are all examples of environment's effect on the brain. Choice e is an extreme effect caused by a brain injury.
2. a. true; b. false; c. false; d. false; e. false.

Will My Learning Disability Prevent Me from Succeeding in College?

Have you been diagnosed with a learning disability? Do you suspect you might have one?

According to the National Center for Learning Disabilities (2009), a learning disability is a "neurological disorder that affects the brain's ability to receive, process, store, and respond to information." According to the U.S. government (1990), a learning disability "substantially limits one or more major life activities." One of the most common learning disabilities is dyslexia, which involves difficulties in acquiring and processing language (**Figure 3.44**). Typically, a person with dyslexia has trouble reading, spelling, or writing. Someone who has difficulty spelling or writing might, alternatively, have the learning disability dysgraphia, a disorder of written expression.

Learning disabilities often become apparent in childhood, but some people first realize they have one in adulthood. These individuals might excel academically all the way through high school. They are able to mask or make up for their learning disabilities through intelligence and effort. What happens, though, when people with learning disabilities enter college? The new academic and organizational challenges of college might help reveal

FIGURE 3.44 An Inspiring Example The celebrity chef Jamie Oliver suffers from dyslexia. His disability has hardly kept him from achieving his career goals. Here, in June 2010, Oliver is announcing Home Cooking Skills, a new and inspirational program he has cocreated to teach basic cooking skills to young people in England.

a person's learning disability. But that person is not therefore doomed to fail in college!

If you have a learning disability or suspect you have one, the first thing to do is get in touch with your campus's disability support services staff. Your campus may not have an entire office dedicated to disabilities. In that case, talk with a member of the Student Affairs staff (e.g., the dean of students, a director of residence life, or a mental health counselor on your campus). Someone at Student Affairs will be able to point you in the right direction. The earlier you contact the disability support office or Student Affairs, the sooner you will have access to the resources available on your campus. That way, you will be able to employ these resources if and when you need them (probably when the semester becomes most intense).

If your learning disability is verified, disability support office staff will work with you to determine the types of accommodations necessary to level the playing field for you. What does "level the playing field" mean? United States law requires colleges and universities to provide equal opportunity to the fruits of education for individuals with learning disabilities. Without accommodations of particular kinds, students with learning disabilities start off at a disadvantage.

Imagine if one football team had to play blindfolded while the opposing team was able to see perfectly. The "playing field" would be uneven, and thus the game would be unfair for the blindfolded team. While it is certainly *possible* to navigate college with a learning disability and with no formal support, it certainly is not fair. Students who go this route may not realize they have a learning disability or may feel that seeking the accommodations they are legally entitled to would be stigmatized by their peers, professors, and family. Thankfully, football players need not play blindfolded, and people with learning disabilities need not go through college wearing their own versions of blindfolds.

Given your particular strengths and weaknesses in processing information, some types of accommodations will be helpful, others will not. For example, a student with dyslexia might benefit from hearing exam questions read aloud. A student with dysgraphia might benefit from receiving notes from a classmate.

Disability support office staff will let your professors know you are entitled to a specific type of accommodation. Importantly, they will not tell your professors about the nature of your learning disability. They will simply note that you have a learning disability. For example, a disability support office staff member might send a note to your professors that reads "[Your name will go here], a student in your introductory psychology course, has provided evidence of a condition that requires academic accommodation. As a result, please provide [him or her] with time and a half on exams and on in-class writing assignments."

If you wish, you can also speak directly with individual professors about your learning disability and the kinds of resources likely to help you. Linda Tessler, a psychologist who works with persons with learning disabilities, writes:

> It must be clear that you are not asking for standards to be lowered. You are using tools to help you perform. To pass, you must perform the task that your classmates perform. You may, however, need to get there in a different way. Dyslexic students have to read the textbook just as nondyslexic students do. They may just do it differently through the use of books on tape. (Tessler, 1997)

Will a learning disability prevent you from succeeding in college? Not if you can help it, and you can help it by advocating for yourself. Line up the resources you need to ensure that you are able to reap the rewards of college.

Chapter Summary

3.1 How Does the Nervous System Operate?

- **Neurons Are Specialized for Communication:** Neurons are the basic building blocks of the nervous system. They receive and send chemical messages. All neurons have the same basic structure, but neurons vary by function and by location in the nervous system.

- **Action Potentials Cause Neural Communication:** Changes in a neuron's electrical charge are the basis of an action potential, or neural firing. Firing is the means of communication within networks of neurons.

- **Neurotransmitters Bind to Receptors across the Synapse:** Neurons do not touch; they release chemicals (neurotransmitters) into the synaptic cleft, a small gap between the neurons. Neurotransmitters bind with the receptors of postsynaptic neurons, thus changing the charge in those neurons. Neurotransmitters' effects are halted by reuptake of the neurotransmitters into the presynaptic neurons, by enzyme deactivation, or by autoreception.

- **Neurotransmitters Influence Mental Activity and Behavior:** Neurotransmitters have been identified that influence aspects of the mind and behavior in humans. For example, neurotransmitters influence emotions, motor skills, sleep, dreaming, learning and memory, arousal, pain control, and pain perception. Drugs and toxins can enhance or inhibit the activity of neurotransmitters by affecting their synthesis, their release, and the termination of their action in the synaptic cleft.

3.2 What Are the Basic Brain Structures and Their Functions?

- **The Brain Stem Houses the Basic Programs of Survival:** The top of the spinal cord forms the brain stem, which is involved in basic functions such as breathing and swallowing. The brain stem contains the reticular formation, a network of neurons that influences general alertness and sleep.

- **The Cerebellum Is Essential for Movement:** The cerebellum ("little brain"), the bulging structure connected to the back of the brain stem, is essential for movement and controls balance.

- **Subcortical Structures Control Emotions and Appetitive Behaviors:** The subcortical structures play a key part in psychological functions because they control vital functions (the hypothalamus), sensory relay (the thalamus), memories (the hippocampus), emotions (the amygdala), and the planning and producing of movement (the basal ganglia).

- **The Cerebral Cortex Underlies Complex Mental Activity:** The lobes of the cortex play specific roles in vision (occipital), touch (parietal), hearing and speech comprehension (temporal), and movement, rational activity, social behavior, and personality (frontal).

3.3 How Does the Brain Communicate with the Body?

- **The Peripheral Nervous System Includes the Somatic and Autonomic Systems:** The somatic system transmits sensory signals and motor signals between the central nervous system and the skin, muscles, and joints. The autonomic system regulates the body's internal environment through the sympathetic division, which responds to alarm, and the parasympathetic division, which returns the body to its resting state.

- **The Endocrine System Communicates through Hormones:** Endocrine glands produce and release chemical substances. These substances travel to body tissues through the bloodstream and influence a variety of processes, including sexual behavior.

- **Actions of the Nervous System and Endocrine System Are Coordinated:** The endocrine system is largely controlled through the actions of the hypothalamus and the pituitary gland. The hypothalamus controls the release of hormones from the pituitary gland. The pituitary gland controls the release of hormones from other endocrine glands in the body.

3.4 What Is the Genetic Basis of Psychological Science?

- **All of Human Development Has a Genetic Basis:** Human behavior is influenced by genes. Through genes, people inherit both physical attributes and personality traits from their parents. Chromosomes are made of genes, and the Human Genome Project has mapped the genes that make up humans' 23 chromosomal pairs.

- **Heredity Involves Passing Along Genes through Reproduction:** Genes may be dominant or recessive. An organism's genetic constitution is referred to as its genotype. The organism's observable characteristics are referred to as its phenotype. Many characteristics are polygenic.

- **Genotypic Variation Is Created by Sexual Reproduction:** An offspring receives half of its chromosomes from its mother and half of its chromosomes from its father. Because so many combinations of the 23 pairs of chromosomes are possible, there is tremendous genetic variation in the human species. Mutations resulting from errors in cell division also give rise to genetic variation.

- **Genes Affect Behavior:** Behavioral geneticists examine how genes and environment interact to influence psychological activity and behavior. Twin studies and research on adoptees provide insight into heritability.

- **Social and Environmental Contexts Influence Genetic Expression:** Genes and social contexts interact in ways that influence our observable characteristics.

■ **Genetic Expression Can Be Modified:** Genetic manipulation has been achieved in mammals such as mice. Animal studies using the technique of "knocking out" genes to determine their effects on behavior and on disease are a valuable tool for understanding genetic influences.

3.5 How Does the Brain Change?

■ **The Interplay of Genes and Environment Wires the Brain:** Chemical signals influence cell growth and cell function. Environmental experiences, particularly during critical periods, influence cell development and neural connections.

■ **Culture Affects the Brain:** The influence of experience on brain development is reflected in the different patterns of brain activity of people from different cultures.

■ **The Brain Rewires Itself throughout Life:** Although plasticity decreases with age, the brain retains the ability to rewire itself throughout life. This ability is the biological basis of learning. Anomalies in sensation and in perception, such as synesthesia, are attributed to the cross-wiring of connections in the brain.

■ **Females' and Males' Brains Are Similar and Different:** Females' and males' brains are more similar than different. They are different, however: Males' brains are larger than females' (on average), and females' verbal abilities are organized more bilaterally (more equally in both hemispheres).

■ **The Brain Can Recover from Injury:** The brain can reorganize its functions in response to brain damage, although this capacity decreases with age.

Key Terms

acetylcholine (ACh), p. 84
action potential, p. 79
agonists, p. 82
all-or-none principle, p. 80
amygdala, p. 92
antagonists, p. 82
autonomic nervous system (ANS), p. 98
axon, p. 77
basal ganglia, p. 92
brain stem, p. 90
Broca's area, p. 89
cell body, p. 77
central nervous system (CNS), p. 75
cerebellum, p. 90
cerebral cortex, p. 93
chromosomes, p. 105

dendrites, p. 77
dizygotic twins, p. 111
dominant gene, p. 107
dopamine, p. 84
endocrine system, p. 100
endorphins, p. 86
epinephrine, p. 84
frontal lobes, p. 94
GABA, p. 85
genes, p. 105
genotype, p. 107
glutamate, p. 86
gonads, p. 101
heritability, p. 113
hippocampus, p. 91
hormones, p. 101
hypothalamus, p. 91
interneurons, p. 76

monozygotic twins, p. 111
motor neurons, p. 76
myelin sheath, p. 77
neurons, p. 75
neurotransmitters, p. 80
nodes of Ranvier, p. 77
norepinephrine, p. 84
occipital lobes, p. 93
parasympathetic division, p. 99
parietal lobes, p. 94
peripheral nervous system (PNS), p. 75
phenotype, p. 107
pituitary gland, p. 102
plasticity, p. 117
prefrontal cortex, p. 94
receptors, p. 81

recessive gene, p. 107
resting membrane potential, p. 77
reuptake, p. 82
sensory neurons, p. 76
serotonin, p. 84
somatic nervous system, p. 98
substance P, p. 86
sympathetic division, p. 99
synapse, p. 77
synaptic cleft, p. 77
synesthesia, p. 121
temporal lobes, p. 94
terminal buttons, p. 77
thalamus, p. 91

Practice Test

1. Complete the following analogy: Genes are to chromosomes as _____ are to _____.
   a. recipes, ingredients
   b. seeds, vegetables
   c. bricks, walls
   d. feet, shoes

2. Which of the following statements are true regarding the relationship between genetic makeup and environment?
   a. Environmental factors can influence gene expression.
   b. The presence of certain genes can influence an organism's susceptibility to environmental stressors.
   c. Genes and environment can interact to affect phenotype.

3. Which *two* labels accurately describe neurons that detect information from the physical world and pass that information along to the brain?
   a. motor neuron
   b. sensory neuron
   c. interneuron
   d. efferent neuron
   e. afferent neuron

4. Who do you predict would have a larger hippocampus?
   a. someone who plays computer games requiring the exploration of complex virtual worlds
   b. someone who plays computer games requiring extraordinarily quick reflexes and body awareness

The answer key for the Practice Tests can be found at the back of the book. It also includes answers to the green caption questions.

4

Sensation and Perception

WHEN HELEN KELLER WAS 19 MONTHS OLD, she completely lost the senses of sight and hearing. Her life became dark and silent, and for her the world existed only through touch, smell, and taste. She recognized her parents, and determined her location, through touch and through smell. But otherwise she was completely isolated in a mental prison. Realizing that others could communicate but she could not, she became so enraged and frustrated that she threw daily tantrums. She later wrote, "Sometimes, I stood between two persons who were conversing and touched their lips. I could not understand, and was vexed. I moved my lips and gesticulated frantically without result. This made me so angry at times that I kicked and screamed until I was exhausted" (quoted by Diane Schuur in *Time* magazine, June 14, 1999).

When Keller was 6 years old, her parents sought assistance from Alexander Graham Bell. Bell was the inventor of devices such as the telephone, and he also taught a system called "Visible Speech" to

FIGURE 4.1 Keller and Sullivan Eight-year-old Helen Keller **(left)** sits with her teacher, Anne Sullivan, in Cape Cod in 1888.

to deaf children. He put the Kellers in touch with the Perkins School for the Blind, in Watertown, Massachusetts. Through the school, the Kellers hired a teacher, Anne Sullivan, to teach Helen to communicate through signs **(Figure 4.1)**. At first, Helen simply mimicked Sullivan's strange hand motions, making no sense. One day, Sullivan ran water over one of Helen's hands while spelling *w-a-t-e-r* in the other, and Helen made the connection. She grabbed some dirt and asked Sullivan to spell its name. By evening, Helen had memorized her first 30 words in sign language. She had begun a life of both passionate learning and social activism.

What would your life be like if you could not see or hear? What would it be like if you were not only blind and deaf but also unable to smell, taste, and feel pain or temperature? You would still feel hunger and other bodily sensations, such as being tired, but you would have no way of knowing about other people or an environment outside your body. No one could communicate with you, and you could communicate with no one. What would you do without sensation, your windows to the world? How would you do anything if you lacked perception, your ability to make sense of your sensory experiences? ■

sensation The sense organs' detection of external stimuli, their responses to the stimuli, and the transmission of these responses to the brain.

perception The processing, organization, and interpretation of sensory signals; it results in an internal representation of the stimulus.

4.1 How Do We Sense Our Worlds?

Psychologists often divide the way we experience the world into two distinct phases: *sensation* and *perception*. **Sensation** is our sense organs' detection of external stimulus energy, such as light, air vibrations, and odors. It is also our sense organs' responses to the external stimulus energy and the transmission of those responses to the brain. Sensation is an elementary experience, such as color or motion, without the more complex perceptual experience of what is being seen or what is moving. **Perception** is the brain's further processing of these detected signals. It results in internal representations of the stimuli, representations that form a conscious experience of the world. Whereas the essence of sensation is detection, the essence of perception is construction of useful and meaningful information about a particular environment.

Say that you drive up to a traffic signal as the light turns green. The light emits its particular photons. Those photons are detected by specialized neurons in your eyes, and those neurons transmit signals to your brain. As a result of these steps, you have sensed the energy (photons). When the brain processes the resulting neural signals, you experience the green light and register the meaning of that signal. As a result of these additional steps, you have perceived the light and the signal. (The basic movement from sensation to perception is depicted in **Figure 4.2**.)

This chapter will discuss how the sense organs detect various types of stimulus energy, how the brain constructs useful information about the world on the basis of what has been detected, and how we use this constructed information to guide ourselves through the world around us. An important lesson in this chapter is that our sensation and perception of the world do not work like a camera or digital recorder, faithfully and passively capturing the physical properties of stimuli we encounter. Rather, what we *sense* (what we see, hear, taste, touch, or smell) is the result of how we *perceive*. Brain processes actively construct perceptual experiences from sensory experiences.

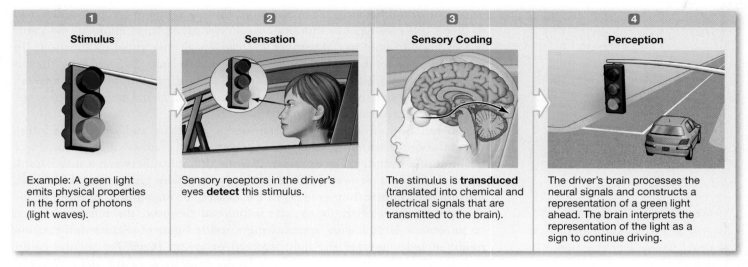

1 Stimulus	**2** Sensation	**3** Sensory Coding	**4** Perception
Example: A green light emits physical properties in the form of photons (light waves).	Sensory receptors in the driver's eyes **detect** this stimulus.	The stimulus is **transduced** (translated into chemical and electrical signals that are transmitted to the brain).	The driver's brain processes the neural signals and constructs a representation of a green light ahead. The brain interprets the representation of the light as a sign to continue driving.

FIGURE 4.2 From Sensation to Perception

This constant conversion of sensation to perception allows us to adapt to the details of our environments. But sometimes our sensory systems can get the details wrong. For example, they sometimes fill in information that an environment has not provided. Even when sensory systems do something like fill in information, they do so in an intelligent and efficient way that produces a meaningful understanding of what is and what happens. Perception is often based on our prior experiences, which shape our expectations about new sensory experiences. For example, you are unlikely to see a blue, apple-shaped object as a real apple because you know from past experience that apples are not blue. Because of the different adaptive challenges that humans and the various nonhuman animals have faced, humans are sensitive to different types of physical energy than nonhuman animals are. This chapter focuses on sensation and perception as they operate in humans.

Stimuli Must Be Coded to Be Understood by the Brain

Our sensory organs translate the physical properties of stimuli into patterns of neural impulses. This process is called *sensory coding*. The different features of the physical environment are coded by patterns of impulses in different neurons. Thus a green stoplight will be coded by a particular neural response pattern in the eye's retina before being read by other areas of the brain. (Technically, the retina is part of the brain. This point is discussed further in the section "In Vision, the Eye Detects Light Waves," later in this chapter.)

When a hand touches a hot skillet, neurons in the hand and in the brain will signal pain. The brain cannot process the physical stimuli directly, so the stimuli must be translated into chemical and electrical signals the brain can interpret. The translation of stimuli is called **transduction.** Through this process, specialized cells in the sense organs, called *sensory receptors,* receive physical or chemical stimulation and pass the resulting impulses to connecting neurons. Connecting neurons then transmit information to the brain in the form of neural impulses. Most sensory information first goes to the thalamus, a structure in the middle of the brain. Neurons in the thalamus then send information to the cortex, where incoming neural impulses are interpreted as sight, smell, sound, touch, or taste. Each sense

transduction A process by which sensory receptors produce neural impulses when they receive physical or chemical stimulation.

organ contains different types of receptor cells. Each type of receptor is designed to detect different types of stimulus energy. For example, receptors in the visual system respond only to light waves and can signal only visual information. (In Chapter 3, Figures 3.18 and 3.19 depict the brain regions discussed here. In this chapter, **Table 4.1** lists the stimuli, receptors, and pathways to the brain for each major sensory system. The brain's interpretation of neural impulses—perception—is discussed later in this chapter.)

To function effectively, the brain needs *qualitative* and *quantitative* information about a stimulus. Qualitative information consists of the most basic qualities of a stimulus. For example, it is the difference between a tuba's honk and a flute's toot. It is the difference between a salty taste and a sweet one. Quantitative information consists of the degree, or magnitude, of those qualities: the loudness of the honk, the softness of the toot, the relative saltiness or sweetness. If you were approaching a traffic light, qualitative information might include whether the light was red or green. Regardless of the color, quantitative information would include the brightness of the light. We can identify qualitative differences because different sensory receptors respond to qualitatively different stimuli. In contrast, quantitative differences in stimuli are coded by the rate of a particular neuron's firing. A more rapidly firing neuron is responding at a higher frequency to a more intense stimulus, such as a brighter light, a louder sound, or a heavier weight (**Figure 4.3**).

Sensory receptors—except, possibly, those involved in smell—provide *coarse coding*. The coding is called coarse because sensory qualities are coded by only a few different types of receptors. Each type of receptor responds to a broad range of stimuli. The combined responses by different receptors firing at different rates enable us to tell the difference between stimuli—between, for example, lime green and forest green or between a pinch on the arm and a shove. Sensation and perception result from a symphony of sensory receptors and the neurons those receptors communicate with. The receptors and neurons fire in different combinations and at different rates. As discussed in Chapter 5, the sum of this activity is consciousness, the huge range of perceptions that make up our experience of the world.

TABLE 4.1 The Stimuli, Receptors, and Pathways for Each Sense			
Sense	**Stimuli**	**Receptors**	**Pathways to the Brain**
Taste	Molecules dissolved in fluid on the tongue	Cells in taste buds on the tongue	Portions of facial, glossopharyngeal, and vagus nerves
Smell	Molecules dissolved in fluid on mucous membranes in the nose	Sensitive ends of olfactory neurons in the mucous membranes	Olfactory nerve
Touch	Pressure on the skin	Sensitive ends of touch neurons in skin	Cranial nerves for touch above the neck, spinal nerves for touch elsewhere
Hearing	Sound waves	Pressure-sensitive hair cells in cochlea of inner ear	Auditory nerve
Vision	Light waves	Light-sensitive rods and cones in retina of eye	Optic nerve

Qualitative Information
Sensory receptors respond to qualitative
differences by firing in different combinations.

Quantitative Information
Sensory receptors respond to quantitative
differences by firing at different rates.

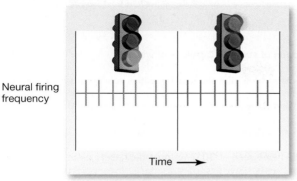

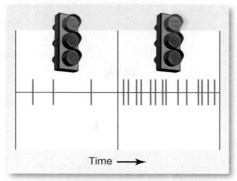

Neural firing
frequency

Time ⟶

Time ⟶

A green light is coded by different
receptors than a red light.

A bright light causes receptors to fire more
rapidly (at a higher frequency) than a dim light.

FIGURE 4.3 Qualitative versus Quantitative Sensory Information

Psychophysics Measures the Relationship between Stimuli and Perception

We have long understood that perceptual experience is constructed from information detected by the sense organs. For more than a century, psychologists have tried to understand the relationship between the world's physical properties and how we sense and perceive them. *Psychophysics,* a subfield developed during the nineteenth century by the researchers Ernst Weber and Gustav Fechner, examines our psychological experiences of physical stimuli. For example, how much physical energy is required for our sense organs to detect a stimulus? How much change is required before we notice that change? To test such things, researchers present very subtle changes in stimuli and observe how participants respond. They study the limits of humans' sensory systems.

SENSORY THRESHOLDS Your sensory organs constantly acquire information from your environment. You do not notice much of this information. The *absolute threshold* is the minimum intensity of stimulation that must occur before you experience a sensation. In other words, it is the stimulus intensity you would detect more often than by chance. The absolute threshold for hearing is the faintest sound a person can detect 50 percent of the time (**Figure 4.4**). For instance, how loudly must someone in the next room whisper for you to hear it? In this case, the absolute threshold for auditory stimuli would be the quietest whisper you could hear half the time. (**Table 4.2** lists some approximate minimum stimuli for each sense.)

A *difference threshold* is the just noticeable difference between two stimuli. In other words, it is the minimum amount of change required for a person to detect a difference. If your friend is watching a television show while you are reading and a commercial comes on that is louder than the show, you might look up, noticing that something has changed. The difference threshold is the minimum change in volume, the minimum quantitative change, required for you to detect a difference.

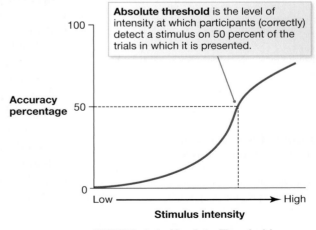

Absolute threshold is the level of intensity at which participants (correctly) detect a stimulus on 50 percent of the trials in which it is presented.

Accuracy percentage

Low ⟶ High

Stimulus intensity

FIGURE 4.4 Absolute Threshold

TABLE 4.2 Approximate Absolute Sensory Threshold (Minimum Stimulus) for Each Sense

Sense	Minimum Stimulus
Taste	1 teaspoon of sugar in 2 gallons of water
Smell	1 drop of perfume diffused into the entire volume of six rooms
Touch	A fly's wing falling on your cheek from a distance of 0.04 inch
Hearing	The tick of a clock at 20 feet under quiet conditions
Vision	A candle flame seen at 30 miles on a dark, clear night

SOURCE: Galanter, 1962.

There are four possible outcomes when a participant is asked whether something occurred during a trial:

Response given

Stimulus signal	Yes	No
On	Hit	Miss
Off	False alarm	Correct rejection

Those who are biased toward reporting a signal tend to be "yea-sayers":

Response given

Stimulus signal	Yes	No
On	89%	11%
Off	41%	59%

Those who are biased toward denying that a signal occurred tend to be "nay-sayers":

Response given

Stimulus signal	Yes	No
On	45%	55%
Off	26%	74%

FIGURE 4.5 Payoff Matrices for Signal Detection Theory Note that the percentages in this figure were invented to show representative numbers. Actual percentages vary from question to question.

The difference threshold increases as the stimulus becomes more intense. Pick up a 1-ounce letter and a 2-ounce letter, and you will easily detect the difference. But pick up a 5-pound package and a package that weighs 1 ounce more, and the difference will be harder, maybe impossible, to discern. The principle at work here is called *Weber's law.* This law states that the just noticeable difference between two stimuli is based on a proportion of the original stimulus rather than on a fixed amount of difference. That is, the more intense the stimulus, the bigger the change needed for you to notice.

SIGNAL DETECTION THEORY Classical psychophysics was based on the idea of a sensory threshold. That is, either you saw something or you did not. Your detection depended on whether the intensity of the stimulus was above or below the sensory threshold. As research progressed, however, it became clear that early psychophysicists had ignored an important variable: human judgment.

Imagine you are a participant in a study of sensory thresholds. You are sitting in a dark room, and an experimenter asks if you detect a faint light, hear a faint sound, or feel a very light touch on your arm. You might fail to detect a weak stimulus that is presented. Even if you do not detect this stimulus, you might ask yourself if you do or if you should, since someone has asked about it. You might even convince yourself you had sensed a weak stimulus that had not been presented. After realizing that their methods of testing absolute thresholds were flawed, researchers formulated **signal detection theory (SDT).** This theory states that detecting a stimulus requires making a judgment about its presence or absence, based on a subjective interpretation of ambiguous information (Green & Swets, 1966).

For example, SDT applies to the work of radiologists, who scan medical images to detect early signs of disease. A radiologist might be looking for the kind of faint shadow that signals an early-stage cancer and have difficulty judging whether an abnormality in the image is likely cancerous. The radiologist's knowledge of the patient (e.g., age, sex, family medical history) will likely affect this judgment. So, of course, will factors such as the radiologist's training, experience, motivation, and attention. Moreover, the knowledge of the consequences can influence a radiologist's judgment. Being wrong could mean missing a fatal cancer or, conversely, causing unnecessary and potentially dangerous treatment.

Any research study on signal detection involves a series of trials in which a stimulus is presented in only some trials. In each trial, the participant must state whether he or she sensed the stimulus. A trial of this kind, in which a participant judges whether an event occurs, can have one of four outcomes. If the signal is presented and the participant detects it, the outcome is a *hit*. If the participant fails to detect the signal, the outcome is a *miss*. If the participant "detects" a signal that was not presented, the outcome is a *false alarm*. If the signal is not presented and the participant does not detect it, the outcome is a *correct rejection* (**Figure 4.5**). The participant's sensitivity to the signal is usually computed by comparing the hit rate with the false alarm rate. This comparison corrects for any bias the participant might bring to the testing situation.

Response bias refers to a participant's tendency to report detecting the signal in an ambiguous trial. The participant might be strongly biased against responding and need a great deal of evidence that the signal is present. Under other conditions, that same participant might need only a small amount of evidence.

The context of a judgment made outside the research lab will affect the person's judgment (see "Critical Thinking Skill: Recognizing the Effects of Context on Judgments," p. 138). A radiologist checking a CAT scan for signs of a brain tumor might be extra cautious about accepting any abnormality as a signal (i.e., a tumor), since a positive response could lead to drastic and dangerous neurosurgery. A doctor checking an X-ray for signs of a broken bone might be more willing to make a positive diagnosis, since treatment, although uncomfortable, will most likely not endanger the life of the patient. People's expectations often influence the extent to which they are biased. For instance, a soldier expecting an imminent attack will likely err on the side of responding, such as by mistaking a dim shape as an enemy when in fact no one is there. The important point is that personal beliefs and expectations, as well as the situation, influence how a person experiences sensations from the environment.

SENSORY ADAPTATION Our sensory systems are tuned to detect changes in our surroundings. It is important for us to be able to detect such changes because they might require responses. It is less critical to keep responding to unchanging stimuli. **Sensory adaptation** is a decrease in sensitivity to a constant level of stimulation (**Figure 4.6**).

Imagine you are studying and work begins at a nearby construction site. When the equipment starts up, the sound seems particularly loud and disturbing. After a few minutes, however, the noise seems to have faded into the background. Researchers have often noticed that if a stimulus is presented continuously, the responses of the sensory systems that detect it tend to diminish over time. Similarly, when a continuous stimulus stops, the sensory systems usually respond strongly as well. If the construction noise suddenly halted, you would likely notice the silence.

signal detection theory (SDT) A theory of perception based on the idea that the detection of a faint stimulus requires a judgment—it is not an all-or-none process.

sensory adaptation A decrease in sensitivity to a constant level of stimulation.

FIGURE 4.6 Sensory Adaptation Because of sensory adaptation, people who live near constant noise eventually become less aware of the noise. Pictured here are homes near Heathrow Airport, in London. **If jets were flying this close over your home, how long do you think it would take for you to adjust? What other kinds of constant stimulation must people adjust to?**

Recognizing the Effects of Context on Judgments

Are you smart? Are you beautiful? Are you good in math? If you make such a judgment, to what or to whom would you be comparing yourself? Any judgment you make about yourself will depend on the context. Likewise, any judgment you make *about anything* will be affected to a large extent by the specific situation in which you make that judgment.

Imagine sitting in a windowless room illuminated with one small candle. If you light a second candle, the room will appear much brighter. Now imagine sitting in a room lit brightly by several 200-watt lightbulbs. If you light a small candle here, the room's brightness might not differ perceptually, as would be predicted by Weber's law (described earlier). In an analogous way, the subtle effects of context within a situation can become obvious when that situation is viewed from afar or later or in the abstract (**Figure 4.7**).

The effects of context extend beyond immediate sensations and perceptions and across a wide range of events. For example, people generally define their own social and physical characteristics by comparing themselves with others (Alicke, LoSchiavo, Zerbst, & Zhang, 1997). We often make such comparisons automatically and usually without being conscious that we are relying on some comparator (i.e., some basis for comparison).

Often without realizing they are doing it, many people compare themselves with the highly attractive and ultrathin models in advertising. Since the viewers cannot match the perfect, often digitally manipulated images they encounter, they experience negative feelings (Bower, 2001). If the viewers are prone to making immediate comparisons, their moods become more negative, and they feel more dissatisfied with their own bodies (Tiggermann & McGill, 2004). One study found that when male and female college students viewed beautiful models, they rated photos of average-looking people as less attractive than did a similar group of college students who did not see the models' photos (Kenrick, Montello, Gutierres, & Trost, 1993).

Research has shown that we do not completely control comparisons we make unconsciously. Gilbert, Giesler, and Morris (1995) have found, however, that we can control comparisons by either avoiding some encounters or rejecting conclusions we have come to in the past. Thus people prone to feeling bad about themselves after seeing advertisements with seemingly perfect models could stop reading magazines that carry such advertisements, or they could continue to read the magazines but remind themselves that these models set unattainable standards that do not apply to real people. In other words, people can define themselves as students, writers, scientists, artists, athletes, parents, or whatever else they choose. They can choose to reject fashion models as their standards for comparison. And understanding the basis for any comparison is the key to making a sound judgment related to that comparison.

FIGURE 4.7 Context Matters If you had seen just the detail, would you have guessed the bigger picture? The girl turns out to be crying because she is at a Justin Bieber performance.

How Do We Sense Our Worlds?

The study of sensation focuses on the ways our sense organs detect and respond to external stimulus energy. When sensory receptors receive physical or chemical stimulation, the stimuli are converted to neural impulses through transduction. Transduction allows the brain to perceive sensory stimuli. Sensory coding for the qualitative aspects of a stimulus, such as color and bitterness, depends on the combination of receptors activated by the stimulus. Sensory coding for the quantitative aspects of a stimulus, such as intensity and loudness, depends on the number of neurons that fire and the frequency with which they fire. Psychophysics enables scientists to study psychological reactions to physical events. Psychophysical methods can be used to determine thresholds for detecting stimuli and noticing change. These thresholds can be influenced by human judgment and situational factors. Sensory systems are most responsive to changes in stimulation. When exposed to constant stimulation, the responses of sensory systems diminish over time.

Measuring Up

1. Suppose you are designing an experiment to determine the absolute threshold for detecting a salty taste. You plan to give participants plain water that
   _____.
   a. always has a small amount of salt in it
   b. sometimes has a small amount of salt in it and sometimes has no salt

   You plan to have them sip a small amount of water and tell you _____.
   a. whether they taste salt or no salt
   b. how much salt is in each sip from different glasses of water

   You will use the participants' responses to calculate an absolute threshold for tasting salt by _____.
   a. comparing hits and false alarms
   b. calculating the amount of salt used in each sip of water

2. What is Weber's law?
   a. When participants are unsure whether they can detect a stimulus, they will guess about it.
   b. Some people are biased toward saying they detected something, and others are biased toward saying they detected nothing.
   c. We are especially tuned to detect changes in stimulation.
   d. The amount of physical energy needed to detect a change in sensation depends on the proportional change from the original stimulus.

Answers: 1. b. sometimes has a small amount of salt in it and sometimes has no salt; a. whether they taste salt or no salt; a. comparing hits and false alarms. 2. d. The amount of physical energy needed to detect a change in sensation depends on the proportional change from the original stimulus.

4.2 What Are the Basic Sensory Processes?

How does information about the world get into the brain? Remember that neurons in the brain receive signals from other neurons. As discussed at the opening of this chapter, Helen Keller's perceptual experiences were restricted because her sensory systems were damaged. The neurons in her brain that

FIGURE 4.8 **How We Taste**

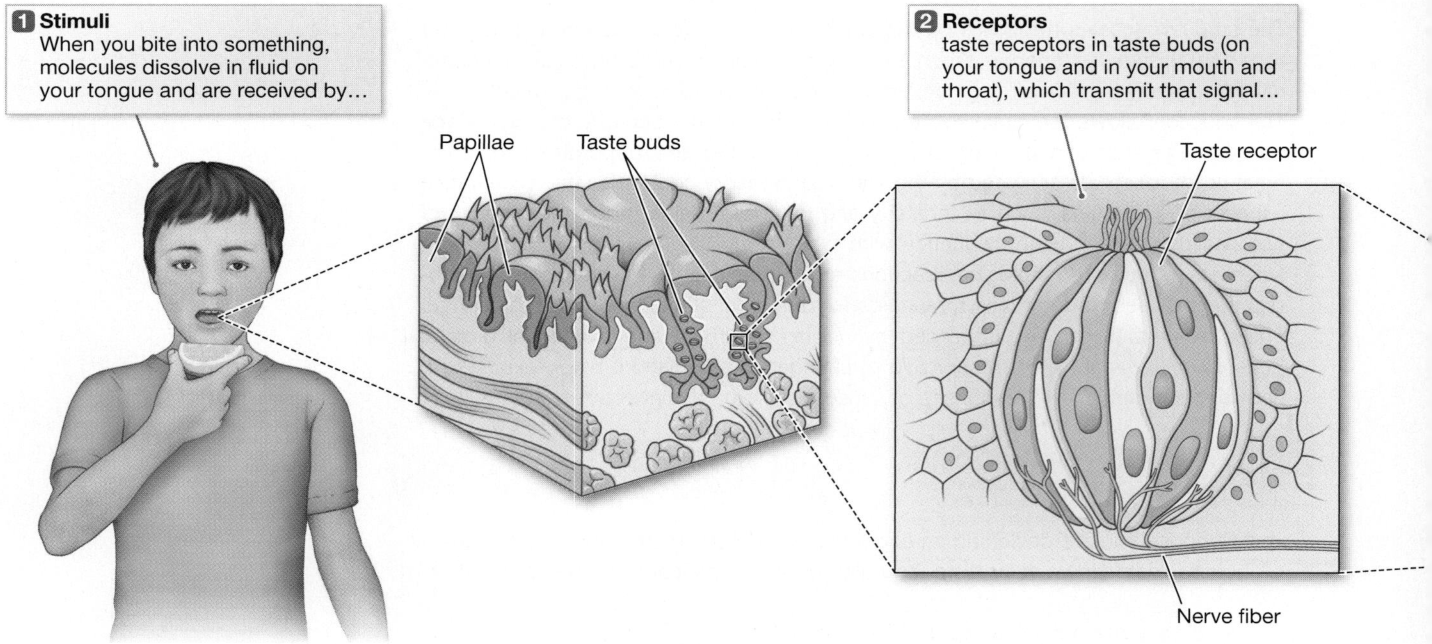

1 Stimuli
When you bite into something, molecules dissolve in fluid on your tongue and are received by...

2 Receptors
taste receptors in taste buds (on your tongue and in your mouth and throat), which transmit that signal...

Papillae

Taste buds

Taste receptor

Nerve fiber

constructed visual and auditory perceptions did not receive any sensory signals. This section discusses how each sense organ detects stimuli and how the resulting information is then sent to the brain for processing.

In Taste, Taste Buds Detect Chemicals

The job of **gustation,** our sense of taste, is to keep poisons out of our digestive systems while allowing good food in. The stimuli for taste are chemical substances from food that dissolve in saliva, though how these stimuli work is still largely a mystery. The taste receptors are part of the **taste buds.** These sensory organs are mostly on the tongue (in the tiny, mushroom-shaped structures called *papillae*) but are also spread throughout the mouth and throat. Most individuals have approximately 8,000 to 10,000 taste buds. When food, fluid, or some other substance (e.g., dirt) stimulates the taste buds, they send signals to the brain, which then produces the experience of taste (**Figure 4.8**).

In all the senses, a near-infinite variety of perceptual experiences arises from the activation of unique combinations of receptors. Scientists once believed that different regions of the tongue are more sensitive to certain tastes, but they now know that the different taste buds are spread relatively uniformly throughout the tongue and mouth (Lindemann, 2001). Every taste experience is composed of a mixture of five basic qualities: sweet, sour, salty, bitter, and *umami* (Japanese for "savory" or "yummy").

Only within the last decade have scientists recognized umami as the fifth taste sensation (Krulwich, 2007). This delicious taste was perhaps first created intentionally in the late 1800s, when the French chef Auguste Escoffier invented a veal stock that did not taste primarily sweet, sour, salty, or bitter. Independently of Escoffier, in 1908, the Japanese cook and chemist Kikunae Ikeda identified the taste as arising from the detection of glutamate, a substance that occurs naturally in foods such as

gustation The sense of taste.

taste buds Sensory organs in the oral cavity that contain the receptors for taste.

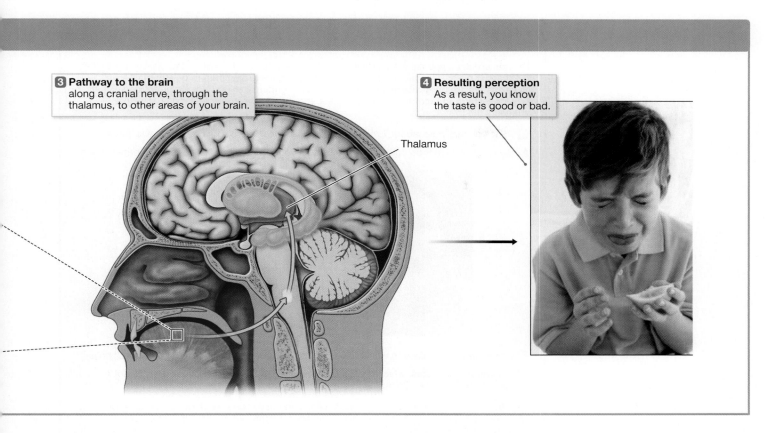

3 Pathway to the brain
along a cranial nerve, through the thalamus, to other areas of your brain.

Thalamus

4 Resulting perception
As a result, you know the taste is good or bad.

meat, some cheese, and mushrooms. Glutamate is the sodium salt in glutamic acid, and as *monosodium glutamate*—or *MSG,* which is commercially available under the brand name Accent—it can be added to various foods as a "flavor enhancer."

Taste alone does not affect how much you like a certain type of food. As you might know from having had colds, food seems tasteless if your nasal passages are blocked, since taste relies heavily on the sense of smell. A food's texture also matters: Whether a food is soft or crunchy, creamy or granular, tender or tough affects the sensory experience, as does the extent to which the food causes discomfort, as can happen with spicy chilies. The entire taste experience occurs not in your mouth but in your brain, which integrates these various sensory signals.

Some people experience especially intense taste sensations, a trait largely determined by genetics. These individuals, known as *supertasters,* are highly aware of flavors and textures and are more likely than others to feel pain when eating very spicy foods (Bartoshuk, 2000). First identified by their extreme dislike of bitter substances, supertasters have nearly six times as many taste buds as normal tasters. Although it might sound enjoyable to experience intense tastes, many supertasters are especially picky eaters because particular tastes can overwhelm them. When it comes to sensation, more is not necessarily better (**Figure 4.9**).

Each of us has individual taste preferences. For example, some people hate anchovies, while others love them. Some people love sour foods, while others prefer sweet ones. These preferences come partly from our different numbers of taste receptors. The same food can actually taste different, because the sensation associated with that food differs in different people's mouths. But cultural factors influence taste preferences as well.

Cultural influences on food preferences begin in the womb. In a study of infant food preferences, pregnant women were assigned to four groups: Some drank carrot juice every day during the last two months of pregnancy, then

drank carrot juice again every day during the first two months *after* childbirth; some drank a comparable amount of water every day during both of those periods; some drank carrot juice during the first period, then drank water during the second period; and some drank water during the first period, then drank carrot juice during the second period (Mennella, Jagnow, & Beauchamp, 2001). All the mothers breast-fed their babies, so the taste of what each mother ate was in the breast milk that constituted each newborn's sole food source during the first few months of life. When the babies were several months old, they were all fed carrot juice (either alone or mixed with their cereal). The infants whose mothers drank carrot juice during the two months before child-birth, the first two months after childbirth, or both periods showed a prefer-ence for carrot juice compared with the infants whose mothers drank only water during those same months. Thus, through their own eating behaviors before and immediately following birth, mothers apparently pass their eating preferences on to their offspring. Once again, as noted throughout this book, nature and nurture are inextricably entwined (**Figure 4.10**).

In Smell, the Nasal Cavity Gathers Odorants

Lacking vision and hearing, Helen Keller relied on her other senses. She called her sense of smell a "potent wizard" that guided her through life. In general, however, humans' sense of smell is vastly inferior to that of many animals. For example, dogs have 40 times more olfactory receptors than we do and are 100,000 to 1 million times more sensitive to odors. Our less developed sense of

FIGURE 4.10 Scientific Method: Infant Taste Preferences Affected by Mother's Diet

Hypothesis: Taste preferences in newborns are influenced by their mothers' food preferences during the months immediately before and after birth.

Research Method:

Pregnant women were assigned at random to one of four groups instructed to drink a certain beverage every day for two months before the baby's birth and two months after the baby's birth:

	Before birth	After birth
Group 1:	carrot juice	water
Group 2:	carrot juice	carrot juice
Group 3:	water	carrot juice
Group 4:	water	water

Results: Babies whose mothers were in Groups 1, 2, or 3 preferred the taste of carrot juice more than did babies whose mothers were in Group 4 and did not drink carrot juice.

Conclusion: Babies become familiar with the taste of foods their mothers consume around the time of their birth, and they prefer familiar tastes.

Source: Mennella, J. A., Jagnow, C. P., & Beauchamp, G. K. (2001). Prenatal and postnatal flavor learning by human infants. *Pediatrics, 107,* e88.

smell comes from our ancestors' reliance on vision. Yet smell's importance to us in our daily lives is made clear, at least in Western cultures, by the vast sums of money we spend on fragrances, deodorants, and mouthwash.

Of all the senses, smell, or **olfaction,** has the most direct route to the brain. It may, however, be the least understood sense. Like taste, it involves the sensing of chemicals that come from outside the body. We smell something when chemical particles, or *odorants,* pass into the nose and, when we sniff, into the nasal cavity's upper and back portions. In the nose and the nasal cavity, a warm, moist environment helps the odorant molecules come into contact with the **olfactory epithelium,** a thin layer of tissue embedded with smell receptors. These receptors transmit information to the **olfactory bulb,** the brain center for smell. From the olfactory bulb, which is just below the frontal lobes, smell information goes direct to other brain areas. Unlike other sensory information, smell signals bypass the thalamus, the early relay station. Information about whether a smell is pleasant or aversive is processed in the brain's prefrontal cortex. The smell's intensity is processed in brain areas also involved in emotion and memory (Anderson, Christoff, et al., 2003), so it is not surprising that olfactory stimuli can evoke feelings and memories (**Figure 4.11**). For example, many people find that the aromas of certain holiday foods cooking, the smell of bread baking, and/or the fragrances of particular perfumes generate fond childhood memories.

There are thousands of receptors in the olfactory epithelium, each responsive to different chemicals. It remains unclear exactly how these receptors

olfaction The sense of smell.

olfactory epithelium A thin layer of tissue, within the nasal cavity, that contains the receptors for smell.

olfactory bulb The brain center for smell, located below the frontal lobes.

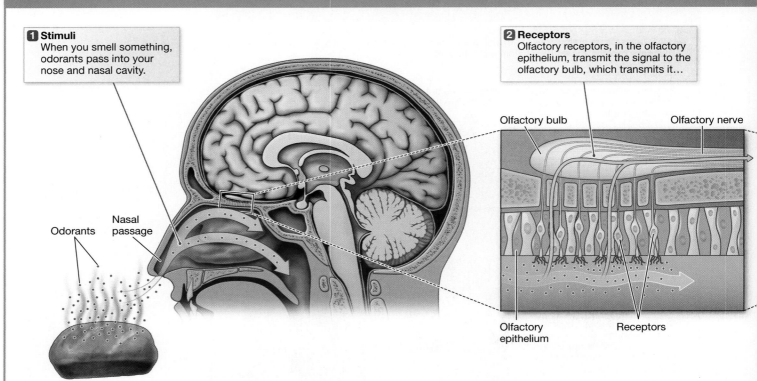

FIGURE 4.11 How We Smell

1 Stimuli
When you smell something, odorants pass into your nose and nasal cavity.

Odorants

Nasal passage

2 Receptors
Olfactory receptors, in the olfactory epithelium, transmit the signal to the olfactory bulb, which transmits it...

Olfactory bulb

Olfactory nerve

Olfactory epithelium

Receptors

encode distinct smells. One possibility is that each type of receptor is uniquely associated with a specific odor (for example, one type would encode only the scent of roses). This explanation is unlikely, however, given the huge number of scents we can detect. Another possibility, more likely to be correct, is that each odor stimulates several receptors and that the activation pattern across several types of receptors determines the olfactory perception (Lledo, Gheusi, & Vincent, 2005). In all sensory systems, sensation and perception result from the specificity of receptors and the pattern of receptor responses.

According to the researchers Yaara Yeshurun and Noam Sobel (2010), although humans can discriminate among thousands of different odors, most people are pretty bad at identifying odors by name. What humans can readily do is say whether an odor is pleasant or unpleasant. Many are often surprised to find out that people have difficulty naming odors, but you can test this claim by asking your friends or relatives to name familiar food items from the fridge. You will probably find that they are unable to name the smell of odorous household refrigerator items at least 50 percent of the time (de Wijk, Schab, & Cain, 1995). At the same time, the available evidence indicates that women are generally better than men at identifying odors (Bromley & Doty, 1995; Lehrner, 1993; Schab, 1991).

The sense of smell is also involved in an important mode of communication. *Pheromones* are chemicals released by animals, probably including humans, that trigger physiological or behavioral reactions in other animals. These chemicals do not elicit "smells" that we are conscious of, but they are processed in a manner similar to the processing of olfactory stimuli. Specialized receptors in the nasal cavity respond to the presence of pheromones. Pheromones play a major role in sexual signaling in many animal species, and they may affect humans in similar ways (as discussed in Chapter 10, "Emotion and Motivation"). For example,

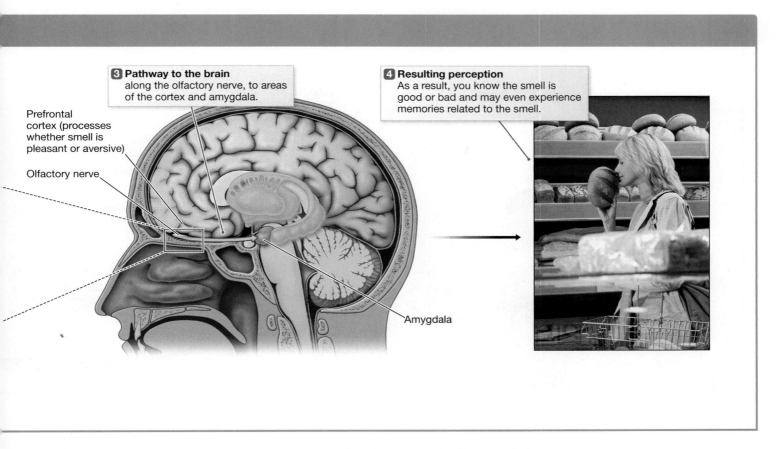

3 Pathway to the brain along the olfactory nerve, to areas of the cortex and amygdala.

4 Resulting perception As a result, you know the smell is good or bad and may even experience memories related to the smell.

Prefrontal cortex (processes whether smell is pleasant or aversive)

Olfactory nerve

Amygdala

pheromones may explain why the menstrual cycles of women who live together tend to synchronize (McClintock, 1971).

In Touch, Sensors in the Skin Detect Pressure, Temperature, and Pain

Touch, the **haptic sense,** conveys sensations of temperature, of pressure, and of pain. It also delivers a sense of where our limbs are in space. Anything that makes contact with our skin provides *tactile stimulation,* which gives rise to the experience of touch. In fact, skin is the largest organ for sensory reception.

The haptic receptors for both temperature and pressure are sensory neurons that reach to the skin's outer layer. Their long axons enter the central nervous system by way of spinal or cranial nerves. (Simply put, spinal nerves travel from the rest of the body into the spinal cord and then to the brain. By contrast, cranial nerves connect directly to the brain.) For sensing temperature, there appear to be receptors for warmth and receptors for cold. Intense stimuli can trigger both warmth and cold receptors, however. Such simultaneous activation can produce strange sensory experiences, such as a false feeling of wetness. Some receptors for pressure are nerve fibers at the bases of hair follicles. These receptors respond to movement of the hair. Four other types of pressure receptors are capsules in the skin. These receptors respond to continued vibration; to light, fast pressure; to light, slow pressure; or to stretching and steady pressure. Pain receptors, discussed in greater detail in the next section, are found throughout the body, not just in the skin. The integration of various signals and higher-level mental processes produces haptic experiences (**Figure 4.12**). For instance, stroking multiple pressure points can produce a tickling sensation, which can be pleasant or unpleasant, depending on the mental state of the person being tickled.

haptic sense The sense of touch.

FIGURE 4.12 **How We Experience Touch: The Haptic Sense**

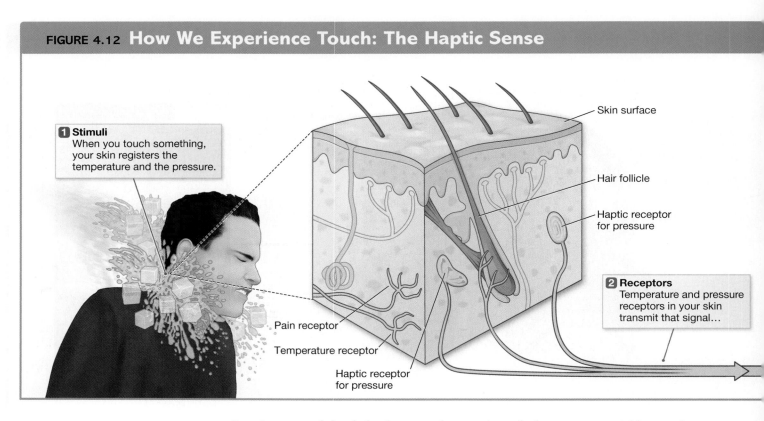

1 Stimuli
When you touch something, your skin registers the temperature and the pressure.

Skin surface

Hair follicle

Haptic receptor for pressure

2 Receptors
Temperature and pressure receptors in your skin transmit that signal…

Pain receptor

Temperature receptor

Haptic receptor for pressure

Imaging research has helped answer the question of why we cannot tickle ourselves: The brain areas involved in touch sensation respond less to self-produced tactile stimulation than to external tactile stimulation (Blakemore, Wolpert, & Frith, 1998).

TWO TYPES OF PAIN Pain is part of a warning system that stops you from continuing activities that may harm you. For example, the message may be to remove your hand from a jagged surface or to stop running when you have damaged a tendon. Children born with a rare genetic disorder that leaves them insensitive to pain usually die young, no matter how carefully they are supervised. They simply do not know how to avoid activities that harm them or to report when they are feeling ill (Melzack & Wall, 1982).

Like other sensory experiences, the actual experience of pain is created by the brain. For instance, a person whose limb has been amputated may sometimes feel phantom pain in the nonexistent limb (see Figure 3.40). The person really feels pain, but the pain occurs because of painful sensations *near* the site of the missing limb or even because of a nonpainful touch on the cheek. The brain simply misinterprets the resulting neural activity.

Most experiences of pain result when damage to the skin activates haptic receptors. The nerve fibers that convey pain information are thinner than those for temperature and for pressure and are found in all body tissues that sense pain: skin, muscles, membranes around both bones and joints, organs, and so on. Two kinds of nerve fibers have been identified for pain: *fast fibers* for sharp, immediate pain and *slow fibers* for chronic, dull, steady pain.

An important distinction between these fibers is the myelination or non-myelination of their axons, which travel from the pain receptors to the spinal cord. As also discussed in Chapter 3, myelination speeds up neural communication. Myelinated axons, like heavily insulated wire, can send information quickly. Nonmyelinated axons send information more slowly. Think of a time when you

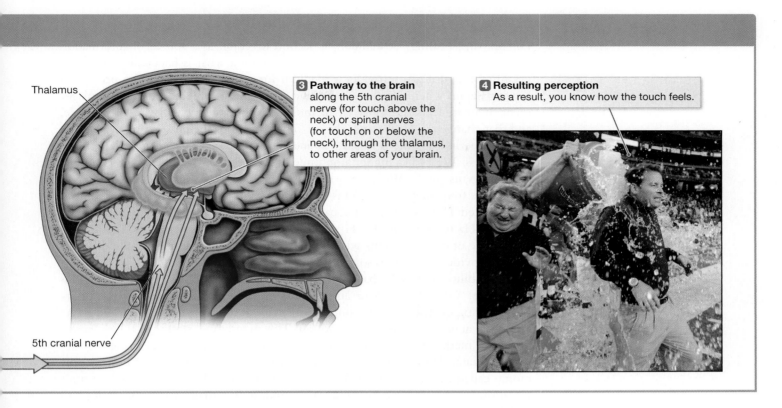

Thalamus

3 Pathway to the brain along the 5th cranial nerve (for touch above the neck) or spinal nerves (for touch on or below the neck), through the thalamus, to other areas of your brain.

4 Resulting perception As a result, you know how the touch feels.

5th cranial nerve

touched a hot object, such as a cooking pan. You probably can recall feeling two kinds of pain: a sharp, fast, localized pain at the moment your skin touched the pan, followed by a slow, dull, more diffuse burning pain. The fast-acting receptors are activated by strong physical pressure and temperature extremes, whereas the slow-acting receptors are activated by chemical changes in tissue when skin is damaged. In terms of adaptation, fast pain leads us to recoil from harmful objects and therefore is protective, whereas slow pain keeps us from using the affected body parts and therefore helps in recuperation (**Figure 4.13**).

FIGURE 4.13 How We Experience Touch: The Sense of Pain

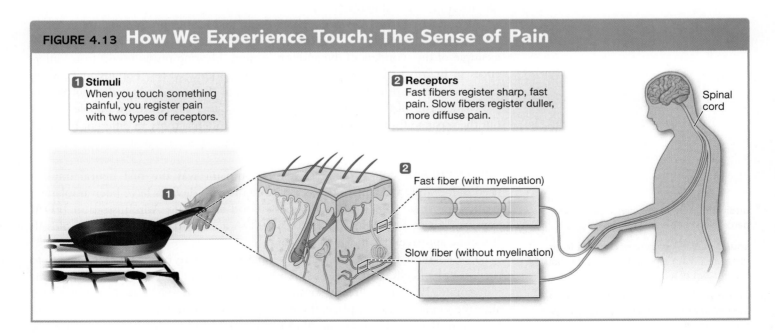

1 Stimuli When you touch something painful, you register pain with two types of receptors.

2 Receptors Fast fibers register sharp, fast pain. Slow fibers register duller, more diffuse pain.

Fast fiber (with myelination)

Slow fiber (without myelination)

Spinal cord

In Hearing, the Ear Detects Sound Waves

For humans, hearing, or **audition,** is second to vision as a source of information about the world. It is a mechanism for determining what is happening in an environment, and it also provides a medium for spoken language. The process of hearing begins when the movements and vibrations of objects cause the displacement of air molecules. Displaced air molecules produce a change in air pressure, and that change travels through the air. The pattern of the changes in air pressure during a period of time is called a **sound wave.** The wave's *amplitude* determines its loudness: We hear a higher amplitude as a louder sound. The wave's *frequency* determines its pitch: We hear a higher frequency as a sound that is higher in pitch. The frequency of a sound is measured in vibrations per second, called *hertz* (abbreviated *Hz*). Most humans can detect sound waves with frequencies from about 20 Hz to about 20,000 Hz. Like all other sensory experiences, the sensory experience of hearing occurs within the brain, as the brain integrates the different signals provided by various sound waves.

Our ability to hear is based on the intricate interactions of various regions of the ear. When changes in air pressure produce sound waves within a person's hearing distance, those sound waves arrive at the person's *outer ear* and travel down the auditory canal to the **eardrum.** This membrane, stretched tightly across the canal, marks the beginning of the *middle ear.* The sound waves make the eardrum vibrate. These vibrations are transferred to *ossicles,* three tiny bones commonly called the hammer, anvil, and stirrup. The ossicles transfer the eardrum's vibrations to the *oval window.* The oval window is actually a membrane located within the *cochlea,* in the *inner ear.* The cochlea is a fluid-filled tube that curls into a snail-like shape, with a membrane at the end called the *round window.* Running through the center of the cochlea is the thin *basilar membrane.* The oval window's vibrations create pressure waves in the cochlear fluid; these waves prompt the basilar membrane to oscillate. Movement of the basilar membrane stimulates *hair cells* to bend and to send information to the *auditory nerve.* These hair cells are the primary auditory receptors. Thus sound waves, mechanical signals, hit the eardrum and are converted to neural signals that travel to the brain along the auditory nerve. This conversion of sound waves to brain activity produces the sensation of sound (**Figure 4.14**).

As noted by Daniel Levitin, a psychologist and former professional musician, in his best-selling book *This Is Your Brain on Music* (2006), music provides an excellent example of the wonders of the auditory system. Hearing music results from differences in brain activity, not from differentiated sound waves. For instance, when you hear guitars, drums, and singing, nothing in the sound waves themselves tells you which part of the music is which. Yet it is rather easy for most people to pick out the separate features in a piece of music. Through activity in different brain regions, the features all come together to create the experience of music.

THE COCHLEAR IMPLANT The cochlear implant was the first neural implant used successfully in humans. Over 100,000 of these devices have been implanted worldwide since 1984, when the U.S. Food and Drug Administration (FDA) approved them for adults. (In 1990, the FDA approved them for 2-year-olds. It has since approved them for 1-year-olds.)

The cochlear implant has helped people with severe hearing problems due to the loss of hair cells in the inner ear. Unlike a hearing aid, the implant does not amplify sound. Rather, it directly stimulates the auditory nerve. The downside is that after the implant is put in place, the person who received it loses all residual normal hearing in that ear, because sound no longer travels along the ear canal and middle

audition Hearing; the sense of sound perception.

sound wave A pattern of changes in air pressure during a period of time; it produces the percept of a sound.

eardrum A thin membrane that marks the beginning of the middle ear; sound waves cause it to vibrate.

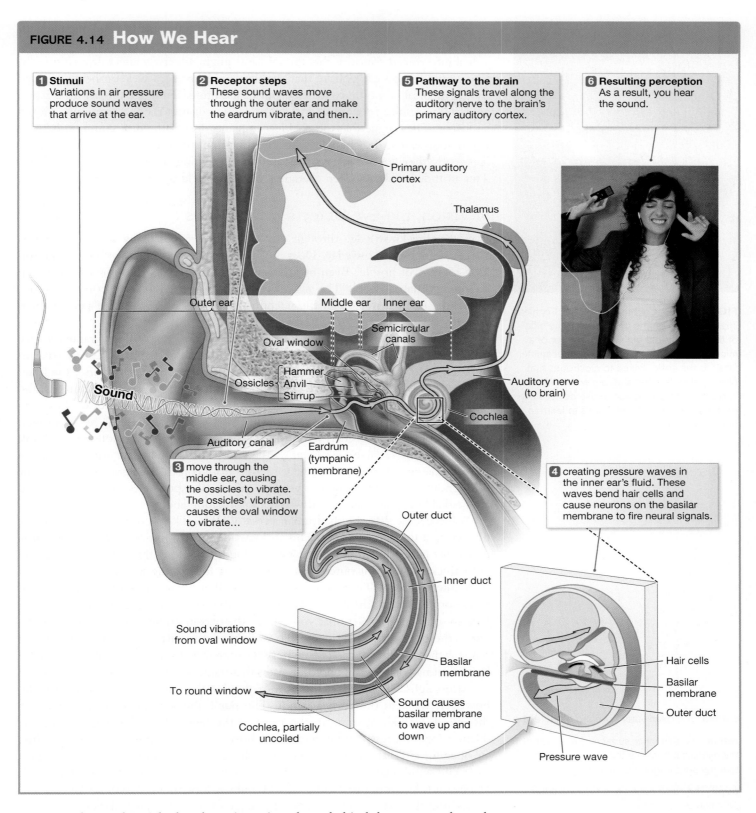

FIGURE 4.14 How We Hear

1 Stimuli Variations in air pressure produce sound waves that arrive at the ear.

2 Receptor steps These sound waves move through the outer ear and make the eardrum vibrate, and then...

5 Pathway to the brain These signals travel along the auditory nerve to the brain's primary auditory cortex.

6 Resulting perception As a result, you hear the sound.

Primary auditory cortex

Thalamus

Outer ear   Middle ear   Inner ear

Semicircular canals

Oval window

Hammer
Ossicles — Anvil
Stirrup

Sound

Auditory nerve (to brain)

Cochlea

Auditory canal

Eardrum (tympanic membrane)

3 move through the middle ear, causing the ossicles to vibrate. The ossicles' vibration causes the oval window to vibrate...

4 creating pressure waves in the inner ear's fluid. These waves bend hair cells and cause neurons on the basilar membrane to fire neural signals.

Outer duct

Inner duct

Sound vibrations from oval window

Basilar membrane

To round window

Sound causes basilar membrane to wave up and down

Cochlea, partially uncoiled

Hair cells

Basilar membrane

Outer duct

Pressure wave

ear. Instead, sound is picked up by a tiny microphone behind the ear, sent through a computer processor, and then transmitted to the implant's electrodes inside the cochlea. If the devices are implanted at a young enough age in a child born deaf (younger than 2 years being optimal), the child's hearing will be quite functional. He or she will learn to speak reasonably normally (**Figure 4.15**).

FIGURE 4.15 Cochlear Implants Cochlear implants, such as the one fitted on the side of this 10-year-old girl's head, consist of a microphone around the ear and a transmitter fitted to the scalp, linked to electrodes that directly stimulate the auditory nerve. When implanted at a young age, these devices can enable people with hearing loss to learn to hear and speak.

cornea The clear outer covering of the eye.

retina The thin inner surface of the back of the eyeball; it contains the photoreceptors that transduce light into neural signals.

pupil The small opening in the eye; it lets in light waves.

iris The colored muscular circle on the surface of the eye; it changes shape to let in more or less light.

The benefits of cochlear implants might seem indisputable to many people with normal hearing. In the 1990s, however, deaf people who do not consider deafness a disability voiced concerns that the implants might adversely affect deaf culture. In fact, some deaf people believe that cochlear implants are a weapon being wielded by the medical community to wipe out deaf culture. They see this effort as being an extreme result of prejudice and discrimination against them, commonly known as *audism*. They argue that the cochlear implants disrupt the deaf community's cohesiveness. While deaf people with cochlear implants can still use sign language, apparently they are not always welcome in the signing community (Chase, 2006). This attitude has slowly been changing, but is still held by many deaf signers.

In Vision, the Eye Detects Light Waves

If we acquire knowledge through our senses, then vision is by far our most important source of knowledge. Does a place look safe or dangerous? Does a person look friendly or hostile? Even our metaphors for knowledge and for understanding are often visual: "I see," "The answer is clear," "I'm fuzzy on that point." It is not surprising, then, that most of the scientific study of sensation and of perception is concerned with vision.

Sight seems so effortless, so automatic, that most of us take it for granted. Every time a person opens his or her eyes, though, nearly half of that person's brain springs into action to make sense of the energy arriving in the eyes. Of course, the brain can do so only based on sensory signals from the eyes. If the eyes are damaged, the sensory system fails to process new information. This section focuses on how energy is transduced in the visual system, but what we commonly call *seeing* is much more than transducing energy. As the psychologist James Enns notes in his book *The Thinking Eye, the Seeing Brain* (2005), very little of what we call seeing takes place in the eyes. Rather, what we see results from constructive processes that occur throughout much of the brain to produce our visual experiences. Seeing is therefore a remarkable process that produces useful information about our environments.

Some people describe the human eye as working like a crude camera, in that it focuses light to form an image. This analogy does not do justice to the intricate processes that take place in the eye, however. Light first passes through the **cornea,** the eye's thick, transparent outer layer. The cornea focuses the incoming light, which then enters the *lens*. There, the light is bent farther inward and focused to form an image on the **retina,** the thin inner surface of the back of the eyeball. If you shine a light in someone's eyes so that you can see the person's retina, you are in fact looking at the only part of the brain that is visible from outside the skull. In fact, the retina is the one part of the central nervous system that is located where we can see it. The retina contains the photoreceptors that transduce light into neural signals.

More light is focused at the cornea than at the lens. The lens is adjustable, however, whereas the cornea is not. The **pupil,** the dark circle at the center of the eye, is a small opening in the front of the lens. By contracting (closing) or dilating (opening), the pupil determines how much light enters the eye. The **iris,** an opaque, circular muscle, determines the eye's color and controls the pupil's size. The pupil dilates in dim light but also when we see something we like, such as a beautiful painting or a cute baby (Tombs & Silverman, 2004).

Behind the iris, muscles change the shape of the lens. They flatten it to focus on distant objects and thicken it to focus on closer objects. This process is called *accommodation*. The lens and cornea work together to collect and focus light rays reflected from an object, to form on the retina an upside-down image of the object. The world looks right-side up to us even though the image of the world projected on the retina is upside down (**Figure 4.16**).

RODS AND CONES The retina has two types of receptor cells: **rods** and **cones.** The name of each type comes from its distinctive shape. Rods respond at extremely low levels of illumination and are responsible primarily for night vision. They do not support color vision, and they resolve fine detail poorly. This is why, on a moonless night, objects appear in shades of gray. In contrast to rods, cones are less sensitive to low levels of light. They are responsible primarily for vision under high illumination and for seeing both color and detail. Within the rods and cones, light-sensitive chemicals called *photopigments* initiate the transduction of light waves into electrical neural impulses.

Each retina holds approximately 120 million rods and 6 million cones. Near the retina's center, cones are densely packed in a small region called the **fovea.** Although cones are spread throughout the remainder of the retina (except in the blind spot, as you will see shortly), they become increasingly scarce near the outside edge. Conversely, rods are concentrated at the retina's edges. None are in the fovea. If you look directly at a very dim star on a moonless night, the star will appear to vanish because its light will fall on the fovea, where there are no rods. If you look just to the side of the star, however, the star will be visible, because its light will fall just outside the fovea, where there are rods.

TRANSMISSION FROM THE EYE TO THE BRAIN The visual process begins with the generation of electrical signals by the photoreceptors in the retina. Immediately after light is transduced into neural impulses by the rods and cones, other cells in the retina perform on those impulses a series of sophisticated computations that help the visual system process the incoming information. The outputs from these *bipolar, amacrine,* and *horizontal cells* converge on about a million retinal *ganglion cells* (see Figure 4.16). Ganglion cells are the first neurons in the visual pathway with axons. During the process of seeing, they are the first neurons to generate action potentials.

The ganglion cells send their signals along their axons from inside the eye to the thalamus. These axons are gathered into a bundle, the *optic nerve,* which exits the eye at the back of the retina. The point at which the optic nerve exits the retina has no rods or cones, and this lack produces a blind spot in each eye. If you stretch out one of your arms, make a fist, and look at your fist, the size that your fist appears to you is about the size of your blind spot. The brain normally fills in this gap automatically, so you assume the world continues and are not aware that a blind spot exists in the middle of your field of vision. However, you can isolate your blind spot (**Figure 4.17**).

At the optic chiasm, half of the axons in the optic nerves cross. (The axons that cross are the ones that project from the portion of the retina nearest the nose.) This arrangement causes all information from the left side of visual space (i.e., everything visible to the left of the point of gaze) to be projected to the right hemisphere of the brain and vice versa. In each case, the information reaches the visual areas of the thalamus and then travels to the *primary visual cortex,* cortical areas in the occipital lobes, at the back of the head. The pathway from the retina to this region carries all the information that we consciously experience as seeing.

THE COLOR OF LIGHT IS DETERMINED BY ITS WAVELENGTH We can distinguish among millions of shades of color. An object appears to be a particular color because of the wavelengths it reflects. The color is not a property of the

rods Retinal cells that respond to low levels of illumination and result in black-and-white perception.

cones Retinal cells that respond to higher levels of illumination and result in color perception.

fovea The center of the retina, where cones are densely packed.

FIGURE 4.16 **How We See**

1 Stimuli
For you to see an image, its light waves have to strike your eye.

2 Receptor steps
The light waves then enter the eyeball through the pupil, which determines how much light enters. The size of the pupil is controlled by the iris.

4 Two types of photoreceptors on the retina, rods and cones, convert the light waves into electrical impulses. Those signals are processed by the bipolar, amacrine, and horizontal cells. Information from those cells is passed to ganglion cells, which generate action potentials that are transmitted by the optic nerve.

Ganglion cell   Amacrine cell   Bipolar cell   Horizontal cell   Rod   Cone

Retina
Fovea
Pupil
Light waves   Cornea   Lens   Iris
Optic nerve (to brain)
Blind spot
Optic nerve

3 The cornea focuses the incoming light. Then light rays are bent farther inward by the lens, which focuses the light to form an upside-down image on the retina.

FIGURE 4.17 **Try for Yourself: Find Your Blind Spot**

To find your blind spot using your right eye, hold this book in front of you and look at the dot, closing your left eye. Move the book toward and away from your face until the rabbit disappears.

You can repeat this exercise for your left eye by turning the book upside down.

Result: The optic nerve creates the blind spot, a small point at the back of the retina. There are no receptors at this spot because it is where the nerves leave the eye.

---

object. In fact, color is always a product of our visual system; there is no color in the physical world.

Visible light consists of electromagnetic waves ranging in length from about 400 to 700 nanometers (abbreviated *nm;* this length is about one billionth of a meter). In simplest terms, the color of light is determined by the wavelengths of the electromagnetic waves that reach the eye. In the center of the retina, the cone cells transduce light into neural impulses. According to the *trichromatic theory,* color vision results from activity in three different types of cones that are sensitive to different wavelengths. One type of cone is most sensitive to short wavelengths (blue–violet light), another type is most sensitive to medium wavelengths (yellow–green light), and the third type is most sensitive to long wavelengths (red–orange light; **Figure 4.18**). The three types of cones in the retina are therefore called "S," "M," and "L" cones because they respond maximally to short, medium, and long wavelengths,

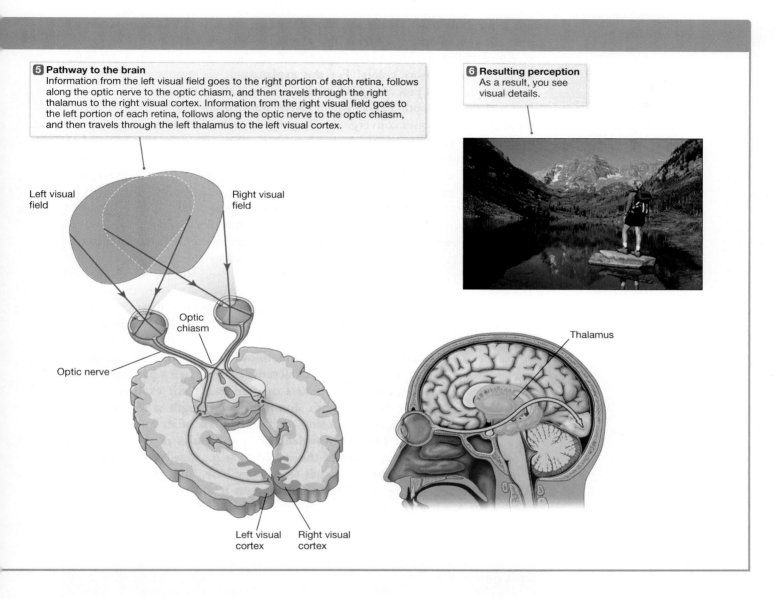

5 Pathway to the brain
Information from the left visual field goes to the right portion of each retina, follows along the optic nerve to the optic chiasm, and then travels through the right thalamus to the right visual cortex. Information from the right visual field goes to the left portion of each retina, follows along the optic nerve to the optic chiasm, and then travels through the left thalamus to the left visual cortex.

6 Resulting perception
As a result, you see visual details.

Left visual field

Right visual field

Optic chiasm

Optic nerve

Thalamus

Left visual cortex

Right visual cortex

respectively. For example, yellow light looks yellow because it stimulates the L and M cones about equally and hardly stimulates the S cones at all. In fact, we can create yellow light by combining red light and green light because each type of light stimulates the corresponding cone population. As far as the brain can tell, there is no difference between yellow light and a combination of red light and green light!

Our perception of different colors is determined by the ratio of activity among the three types of cone receptors. Some aspects of color vision, however, cannot be explained by the responses of three types of cones in the retina. For example, we have trouble visualizing certain color mixtures. It is easier to imagine reddish yellow or bluish green, say, than reddish green or bluish yellow. In addition, some colors seem to be "opposites." This perceptual effect is the basis of *opponent-process theory* (Hering, 1878/1964). When we stare at a red image for some time, we see a green afterimage when we look away; when we stare at a green image, we see a red afterimage. Likewise, when we stare at a blue

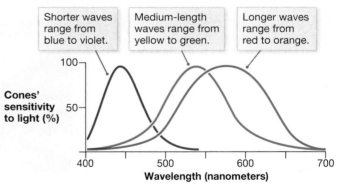

Shorter waves range from blue to violet.

Medium-length waves range from yellow to green.

Longer waves range from red to orange.

Cones' sensitivity to light (%)

FIGURE 4.18 The Experience of Color The color of light is determined by the wavelength of the electromagnetic wave that reaches the eye. This graph shows the percentage of light at different wavelengths that is absorbed by each kind of cone.

image for some time, we see a yellow afterimage when we look away; when we stare at a yellow image, we see a blue afterimage (**Figure 4.19**).

Since colors are themselves optical effects, how do we account for what appear to be opposite colors? For this explanation, we must turn to the second stage in visual processing. This stage occurs in the ganglion cells—the cells that make up the optic nerve, which carries information to the brain. Different combinations of cones converge on the ganglion cells in the retina. One type of ganglion cell receives excitatory input from L cones (the ones that respond to long wavelengths, which we see as red), but it is inhibited by M cones (medium wavelengths, which we see as green). Cells of this type create the perception that red and green are opposites. Another type of ganglion cell is excited by input from S cones (short wavelengths, which we see as blue), but it is inhibited by both L- and M-cone activity (when light includes long and medium wavelengths, we see yellow). These different types of ganglion cells, working in opposing pairs, create the perception that blue and yellow are opposites.

Ultimately, how the brain converts physical energy to the experience of color is quite complex and can be understood only by considering the response of the visual system to different wavelengths at the same time. In fact, when we see white light, our eyes are receiving the entire range of wavelengths in the visible spectrum (**Figure 4.20**).

We categorize color along three dimensions: *hue, saturation,* and *brightness.* Hue consists of the distinctive characteristics that place a particular color in the spectrum—the color's greenness or orangeness, for example, which will depend primarily on the light's dominant wavelength when it reaches the eye. Saturation is a color's purity, or the vividness of its hue. Saturation varies according to the unity of wavelengths in a stimulus or the mixture of those wavelengths. Basic colors of the spectrum (e.g., blue, green, red) have only one wavelength, whereas pastels (e.g., baby blue, lime green, and pink) have a mixture of many wavelengths. Brightness is the color's perceived intensity, or luminance. This characteristic is determined chiefly by the total

---

FIGURE 4.19 Try for Yourself: Afterimage

For at least 30 seconds, stare at this version of the Union Jack, flag of the United Kingdom. Then look at the blank space to the right.

Result: Because your receptors have adapted to the green and orange in the first image, the afterimage appears in the complementary colors red and blue. You can tell that afterimages are caused by events in the retina, because the afterimage moves with you as you move your eyes, as though it is "painted" on the retina.

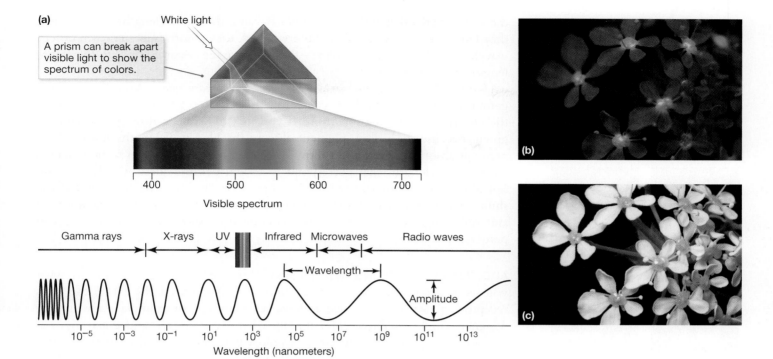

(a)

White light

A prism can break apart visible light to show the spectrum of colors.

400   500   600   700

Visible spectrum

Gamma rays   X-rays   UV   Infrared   Microwaves   Radio waves

|← Wavelength →|

Amplitude

10^{-5} 10^{-3} 10^{-1} 10^{1} 10^{3} 10^{5} 10^{7} 10^{9} 10^{11} 10^{13}

Wavelength (nanometers)

(b)

(c)

FIGURE 4.20 The Color Spectrum (a) When white light shines through a prism, the spectrum of color that is visible to humans is revealed. As shown here, the visible color spectrum is only a small part of the electromagnetic spectrum: It consists of electromagnetic wavelengths from just under 400 nm (the color violet) to just over 700 nm (the color red). By using night-vision goggles, humans are able to see infrared waves (i.e., waves below red in terms of frequency). **(b)** Some insects can see ultraviolet light (i.e., light greater than violet in terms of frequency). This ability helps them find nectar glands, which can appear fluorescent in UV illumination. **(c)** When humans view the same flowers under visible light, they do not see the same nectar patterns that the insects see.

amount of light reaching the eye — think of the difference between, say, a bright blue and a pale blue of the same shade (**Figure 4.21a**). However, do not confuse brightness with *lightness*. The lightness of a visual stimulus is determined by the brightness of the stimulus relative to its surroundings. Thus two examples of the same color — two grays with the same brightness, say — can differ in lightness. The lightness of each example will depend on the level of brightness that surrounds it. Because lightness is related to the context in which a color appears, it is more useful than brightness for describing appearance (**Figure 4.21b**).

SUBTRACTIVE COLOR MIXING A color is determined by the mixture of wavelengths from a stimulus. Depending on the particular stimulus, any given color can be produced through either the *subtractive* or the *additive* mixture of wavelengths. Mixing paints is one form of **subtractive color mixing,** because the mixture occurs within the stimulus and is a physical process (**Figure 4.22a**).

Paint colors are determined by pigments, which are chemicals on the surfaces of objects. Pigments absorb different wavelengths of light and prevent them from being reflected to the eye. Therefore, the color of a pigment is determined by

subtractive color mixing A process of color mixing that occurs within the stimulus itself; a physical, not psychological, process.

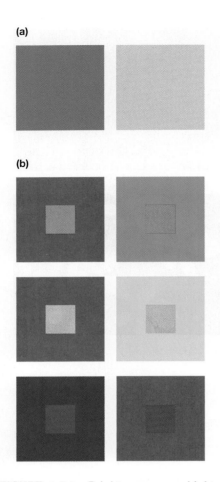

(a)

(b)

FIGURE 4.21 Brightness versus Lightness (a) Which blue is brighter? Why? (b) For each pair, which central square is lighter? In fact, the central squares in each pair are identical. Most people see the gray square that is surrounded with red, for example, as lighter than the gray square surrounded with green. Why do they look different?

additive color mixing A process of color mixing that occurs when different wavelengths of light interact within the eye's receptors; a psychological process.

kinesthetic sense Perception of the positions in space and movements of our bodies and our limbs.

vestibular sense Perception of balance.

the wavelengths that *it does not absorb*. Because these wavelengths are reflected, they enter the eye. When pigments are mixed, they absorb (subtract) each other's wavelengths. The resulting color—the color we see—corresponds to the wavelengths that are "left over."

Red, yellow, and blue are the *subtractive primary colors*. Mix all three together and you get black, because together these pigments absorb nearly all the colors of the visible spectrum. If you mix blue and yellow paints, you get green, because the yellow pigment absorbs the blue wavelengths and the blue pigment absorbs the red and yellow wavelengths. What remains to be reflected are the wavelengths that correspond to green, because these wavelengths are not absorbed. When you see a blue shirt, it is blue because the material the shirt is made from has absorbed medium and long wavelengths (yellow–green and red–orange). The material is reflecting only short wavelengths that you perceive as blue.

ADDITIVE COLOR MIXING When lights of different wavelengths are mixed, what you see is determined by the interaction of these wavelengths within the eye's receptors. This process is called **additive color mixing.** For example, stage lighting designers employ additive color mixing when they aim red and green lights at the same point on a stage to create a yellow light (**Figure 4.22b**). In fact, as laid out by the *three primaries law of color,* almost any color can be created by combining just three wavelengths, so long as one is from the long-wave end of the spectrum (red–orange), one is from the middle (yellow–green), and one is from the short end of the spectrum (blue–violet).

Psychologists consider the *additive primary colors* to be red, green, and blue. Whereas mixing red, yellow, and blue paint yields black paint, mixing red, green, and blue light yields white light. Because different wavelengths of light bend (refract) at different angles when they pass through a prism, white light entering a prism leaves it with all the colors of a rainbow (see Figure 4.20). Indeed, rainbows form in the sky because tiny water droplets in the air function as prisms, refracting sunlight in different directions.

We Have Other Sensory Systems

In his book *Sensory Exotica* (1999), the psychologist Howard Hughes points out that humans, like other animals, have several internal sensory systems in addition to the five primary senses. One such system is the **kinesthetic sense,** which some researchers group with the touch senses. Kinesthetic sensations come from receptors in muscles, in tendons, and in joints. This information enables us to pinpoint the positions in space and the movements of both our bodies and our limbs. Thus it helps us coordinate voluntary movement and is invaluable in avoiding injury.

The **vestibular sense** uses information from receptors in the semicircular canals of the inner ear. These canals contain a liquid that moves when the head moves, bending hair cells at the ends of the canal. The bending generates nerve impulses that inform us of the head's rotation. In this way, it is responsible for a sense of balance. It explains why inner-ear infections or standing up quickly can make us dizzy. The experience of being seasick or carsick results in part from conflicting signals arriving from the visual system and the vestibular system.

Questioning the "Evidence" for Extrasensory Perception (ESP)

Do you believe in the so-called *sixth sense,* the "unexplainable" feeling that something is about to happen? Our many sensory systems provide information about the world, but they are sensitive to only a small range of the energy available in any environment. For instance, dogs can hear much higher frequencies than we can, and many insects can sense energy forms that we cannot detect. Is it possible that other frequencies or energy forms exist and scientists simply have not discovered them? If so, might these undiscovered energy forces allow people to read other people's minds, predict the future by examining the stars, or communicate with ghosts? In other words, could people be able to perceive information beyond ordinary sensory information through *extrasensory perception,* or *ESP*?

Many reports of ESP are anecdotal. Scientists reject claims supported only by anecdotes, no matter how scientific the stories sound. Anecdotes are not valid evidence, because they are difficult to test in the laboratory and in the world outside the lab. In addition, many claims made about people's ability to predict events can be explained away through logic. For instance, if you see a couple fighting all the time, you might predict accurately that they will break up, but that does not make you a psychic. Much of our social perception requires us to be sensitive to the subtle cues that guide behavior in a situation. But the information we glean from social situations does not arrive from some "extra" sensory system.

Some evidence for ESP was obtained by the social psychologist Daryl Bem and his collaborator Charles Honorton (1994). In their studies, a "sender" in a soundproof booth focused on a randomly generated image. A "receiver" in another room tried to sense the sender's imagery. The receiver was then asked to choose among four alternatives, one of which was correct. By chance, the receivers should have been correct 25 percent of the time. Across 11 studies, however, Bem and Honorton found that receivers were right about 33 percent of the time. Is this evidence of ESP? Many psychologists say that other factors in the experiments might have affected the results. A statistical review of many such studies found little support for ESP (Milton & Wiseman, 2001). Moreover, numerous scientific organizations and government agencies have reviewed decades of research and have concluded that no such phenomenon exists.

In 2011, Bem published a paper that presented data from a series of studies that were purported to show evidence of ESP. In some of the studies, participants reportedly responded to stimuli that they had not yet encountered. For instance, participants were asked to predict where erotic pictures would appear on a computer screen. On each trial, the participant would identify a location before a computer program would independently present the picture. At a rate better than chance, participants were able to predict where the computer would present the erotic

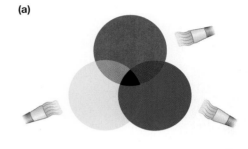

(a)

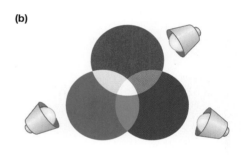

(b)

FIGURE 4.22 Subtractive and Additive Color Mixing (a) Subtractive color mixing is the physical process of color mixing that happens within the stimulus. The subtractive primary colors are red, yellow, and blue. **(b)** By contrast, additive color mixing happens when lights of different wavelengths are perceived by the eye. The additive primary colors are red, green, and blue.

images. The findings remain highly controversial, however. Many in the psychological community believe that extraordinary claims require extraordinary evidence, so they are concerned about the paper's lack of explanation for the findings. In addition, most of the positive results were quite small, and they may have been produced through an inappropriate use of statistical procedures. The only reasonable conclusion is that the evidence for ESP is currently weak and that healthy skepticism demands better evidence.

Summing Up

What Are the Basic Sensory Processes?

All the senses share similar processes. Each has receptors that respond to different physical or chemical stimuli by transducing them into some pattern of brain activity. Typically, different receptors respond to different types of stimuli, and most sensory systems integrate signals from these different receptors into an overall sensation. This system allows a relatively small number of receptors to code a wide variety of stimuli. For example, the entire range of colors is interpreted by three types of visual cones. These various sensory receptors help the perceptual system receive important information that assists in solving adaptive problems. Sensory information, although obtained from the outside world, is processed entirely in the brain to produce sensory experience through perception.

Measuring Up

1. The sensory systems _____.
   a. use all the available energy in their environment to create a true representation of both objects and events
   b. use only a small portion of the available energy in their environment

2. A general principle regarding sensation is that _____.
   a. the combined firing of many different receptors and the neurons they connect with creates our sensations
   b. each sensation (for example, seeing a blue color or hearing a high-pitch tone) is coded by one type of receptor, which is sensitive to only one type of stimulus

3. An intense stimulus, such as a loud sound or a heavy touch, is coded by
   _____.
   a. different sensory receptors that project to different areas of the brain
   b. an increase in the number of neurons that respond to the stimulation

Answers: 1. b. use only a small portion of the available energy in their environment. 2. a. the combined firing of many different receptors and the neurons they connect with creates our sensations. 3. b. an increase in the number of neurons that respond to the stimulation.

4.3 How Does Perception Emerge from Sensation?

The perceptual system is stunningly intelligent in its ability to guide each of us around. For example, right this minute your brain is making millions of calculations to produce a coherent experience of your environment. Despite the illusion that the objects and events you are experiencing exist in the space around you, your experience is a construction of your brain and resides inside your skull. Neurons inside your brain do not directly experience the outside world. Instead, they communicate with other neurons inside and outside your brain. Neurons talk to neurons in total darkness. Yet your conscious experience of the world emerges from this communication. This process happens in milliseconds.

If you lay this book flat and look at the pages as a whole, you will see one image. You will not see the thousands of images that dance across your retina to create a constant, perhaps static view. What you perceive, then, is vastly different from the pattern of stimulation your retina is taking in. If you were aware of what your brain was doing every moment, you would be paralyzed by information overload. Most of the computations the brain performs never reach your consciousness. Only important new outcomes do. How does the brain extract a stable representation of the world from the information the senses provide?

So far, you have seen how sensation happens: Sensory receptors transduce stimuli into electrical impulses, and nerves then transmit those impulses to the brain. Working with just the electrical impulses it receives from nerves, the brain creates a rich variety of perceptual experiences. With the exception of olfaction, all sensory information is relayed to cortical and other areas of the brain from the thalamus. Information from each sense is projected separately from the thalamus to a specific region of the cerebral cortex. In these *primary sensory areas,* the perceptual process begins in earnest (**Figure 4.23**). Because the brain regions involved in taste and smell are not well understood, these senses are not discussed in the following sections.

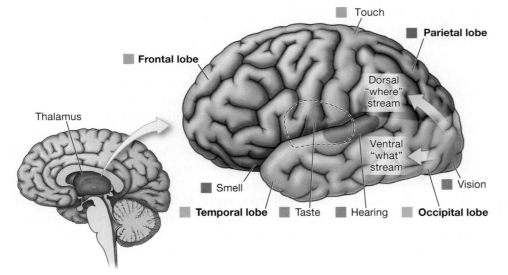

FIGURE 4.23 Primary Sensory Areas
These are the primary brain regions where information about taste, touch, hearing, smell, and vision are projected. Visual information travels in separate "streams"—what you see and where it is—from the occipital lobe (visual cortex) to different parts of the brain for further processing.

In Touch, the Brain Integrates Sensory Information from Different Regions of the Body

Touch information from the thalamus is projected to the *primary somatosensory cortex,* in the parietal lobe. In the 1940s, in a classic series of studies of patients undergoing brain surgery, the neurosurgeon Wilder Penfield discovered that electrical stimulation of the primary somatosensory cortex could evoke the sensation of touch in different regions of the body (Penfield & Jasper, 1954). Penfield found that neighboring body parts tended to be represented next to one another, so that the body is effectively mapped out there according to physical proximity. As shown in Chapter 3's drawing of the homunculus (see Figure 3.21a), sensitive body parts have large amounts of cortical tissue dedicated to them. The most sensitive regions of the body, such as lips and fingers, have a great deal of cortex devoted to them. Other areas, such as the back and the calves, have very little.

GATE CONTROL THEORY The brain regulates the experience of pain, sometimes producing it, sometimes suppressing it. Pain is a complex experience that depends on biological, psychological, and cultural factors. The psychologist Ronald Melzack did pioneering research in this area. For example, he demonstrated that psychological factors, such as past experiences, are extremely important in determining how much pain a person feels.

With his collaborator Patrick Wall, Melzack formulated the *gate control theory of pain,* which states that for us to experience pain, pain receptors must be activated and a neural "gate" in the spinal cord must allow the signals through to the brain (Melzack & Wall, 1965). This theory was radical in that it conceptualized pain as a perceptual experience within the brain rather than simply a response to nerve stimulation. According to this theory, pain signals are transmitted by small-diameter nerve fibers, which can be blocked at the level of the spinal cord (prevented from reaching the brain) by the firing of larger sensory nerve fibers. Thus sensory nerve fibers can "close a gate" and prevent or reduce the perception of pain. This is why scratching an itch is so satisfying, why rubbing an aching muscle helps reduce the ache, and why vigorously rubbing the skin where an injection is about to be given reduces the needle's sting (**Figure 4.24**).

CONTROLLING PAIN A number of cognitive states, such as distraction, can also close the gate. Athletes sometimes play through pain because of their intense focus on the game. Wounded soldiers sometimes continue to fight during combat, often failing to recognize a level of pain that would render them inactive at other times. An insect bite bothers us more when we are trying to sleep and have few distractions than when we are wide awake and active.

Conversely, some mental processes, such as worrying about or focusing on the painful stimulus, seem to open the pain gates wider. Research participants who are well rested rate the same level of a painful stimulus as less painful than do participants who are fearful, anxious, or depressed

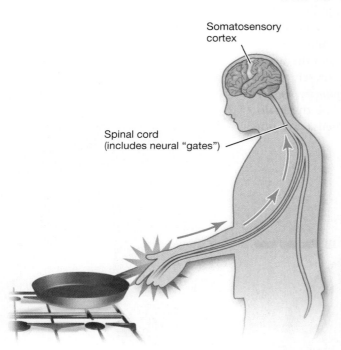

Somatosensory cortex

Spinal cord (includes neural "gates")

FIGURE 4.24 Gate Control Theory
According to the gate control theory of pain, neural "gates" in the spinal cord allow signals through. Those gates can be closed when information about touch is being transmitted (e.g., by rubbing a sore arm) or by distraction.

(Loggia, Mogil, & Bushnell, 2008; Sullivan et al., 2001). Likewise, positive moods help people cope with pain. In a systematic review of the literature, Swedish researchers found that listening to music was an extremely effective means of reducing postoperative pain, perhaps because it helps patients relax (Engwall & Duppils, 2009).

DeCharms and colleagues (2005) have pioneered techniques that offer hope for people who suffer from painful conditions. The researchers sought to teach people in pain—many of these people in chronic pain—to visualize their pain more positively. For example, participants were taught to think about a burning sensation as soothing, like the feeling of being in a sauna. As they tried to learn such techniques, they viewed fMRI images that showed which regions of their brains were active as they performed the tasks. Many participants learned techniques that altered their brain activity and reduced their pain.

Of course, there are more-traditional ways to control pain. Most of us have taken legal drugs, usually ibuprofen or acetaminophen, to reduce pain perception. If you have ever suffered from a severe toothache or needed surgery, you have probably experienced the benefits of pain medication. When a dentist administers Novocain to sensory neurons in the mouth, pain messages are not transmitted to the brain, so the mouth feels numb. General anesthesia slows down the firing of neurons throughout the nervous system, and the patient becomes unresponsive to stimulation (Perkins, 2007).

You can use your knowledge of pain perception anytime you need to reduce your own pain or to help others in pain. Distraction is usually the easiest way to reduce pain. If you are preparing for a painful procedure or suffering after one, watching an entertaining movie can help, especially if it is funny enough to elevate your mood. Music may help you relax, making it easier to deal with pain. Rapid rubbing can benefit a stubbed toe, for example, or a finger that was caught in a closing drawer. You will also feel less pain if you are rested, not fearful, and not anxious. Finally, try to visualize your pain as something more pleasant. Of course, severe pain is a warning that something in the body is seriously wrong. If you experience severe pain, you should be treated by a medical professional.

In Hearing, the Brain Integrates Sensory Information from the Ears

Auditory neurons in the thalamus extend their axons to the *primary auditory cortex,* which is located in the temporal lobe. Neurons in the primary auditory cortex code the frequency (or pitch) of auditory stimuli. The neurons toward the front respond best to higher frequencies, such as that of a train whistle. Those toward the rear respond best to lower frequencies, such as that of a foghorn.

Locating the origin of a sound is an important part of auditory perception. In audition, the sensory receptors cannot code where events occur. Instead, the

"Great! O.K., this time I want you to sound taller, and let me hear a little more hair."

brain integrates the different sensory information coming from each of our two ears. Much of our understanding of auditory localization has come from research with barn owls. These nocturnal birds have finely tuned hearing, which helps them locate their prey. In fact, in a dark laboratory, a barn owl can locate a mouse through hearing alone. A barn owl uses two cues to locate a sound: the time the sound arrives in each ear and the sound's intensity in each ear. Unless the sound comes from exactly in front or in back of the owl, the sound will reach one ear first. Whichever side it comes from, it will sound softer on the other side because the owl's head acts as a barrier. These differences in timing and magnitude are minute, but they are not too small for the owl's brain to detect and act on. Although a human's ears are not as finely tuned to the locations of sounds as an owl's ears are, the human brain uses information from the two ears similarly (**Figure 4.25**).

In Vision, the Brain Processes Sensory Information from the Eyes

The study of perception has focused to a large extent on the visual cortex and the multiple areas in which the retinal image is processed. The complexity of visual perception is underscored by the amount of cortical real estate dedicated to processing visual information. Some estimates suggest that up to half of the cerebral cortex may participate in visual perception in some way. As noted earlier, the *primary visual cortex* is in the occipital lobe.

WHAT VERSUS WHERE One important theory proposes that visual areas beyond the primary visual cortex form two parallel processing streams, or pathways. The lower, *ventral stream* appears to be specialized for the perception and recognition of objects, such as determining their colors and shapes. The upper, *dorsal stream* seems to be specialized for spatial perception—determining where an object is

(a)

(b)

2 Sound reaches right ear first.

3 Sound reaches left ear second, indicating the source is closer to the right ear.

1 Source of sound (here a cell phone)

FIGURE 4.25 Auditory Localization (a) Like barn owls, **(b)** humans draw on the intensity and timing of sounds to locate where the sounds are coming from.

and relating it to other objects in a scene. (Both streams are shown in Figure 4.23.) These two processing streams are therefore known as the *"what" stream* and the *"where" stream* (Ungerleider & Mishkin, 1982).

Damage to certain regions of the visual cortex provides evidence for distinguishing between these two streams of information. Consider the case of D.F. (Goodale & Milner, 1992). At age 34, this woman suffered carbon monoxide poisoning that damaged her visual system. Regions involved in the "what" pathway were particularly damaged. D.F. was no longer able to recognize the faces of her friends and family members, common objects, or even drawings of squares or of circles. She could recognize people by their voices, however, and objects if they were placed in her hands. Her condition—*object agnosia,* the inability to recognize objects—was striking in what she could and could not do. When presented with a drawing of, say, an apple, she could not identify or reproduce it. But if asked to draw an apple, she could do so from memory. Despite major deficits in her perception of objects, she could use visual information about the size, shape, and orientation of objects to control visually guided movements. In other words, her "where" pathway appeared to be intact. For instance, she could walk across a room and step around things adeptly. She could reach out and shake a person's hand. Most confounding, in laboratory tests, she could reach out and grasp a block. In performing this action, D.F. would put exactly the right distance between her fingers, even though she could not tell you what she was going to pick up or how large it was. Thus her conscious visual perception of objects—her "what" pathway—was impaired. She was not aware of taking in any visual information about objects she saw. Still, other aspects of her visual processing were unaffected. The intact regions of her visual cortex allowed her to use information about the size and location of objects despite her lack of awareness about those objects. As illustrated by D.F.'s case, different neurological systems operate independently to help us understand the world around us.

BLINDSIGHT Some research on visual awareness has examined **blindsight.** A person with this condition experiences some blindness because of damage to the visual system, but is unaware of having retained some sight. Typically, a blindsighted patient loses vision in only a portion of the visual field. For example, when looking forward, the person might not be able to see anything on his or her left. Researchers have discovered that when a stimulus is presented in this blind field, the patient can respond unconsciously to that stimulus. Say that a moving dot is presented in the blind field and the patient is asked to indicate the direction in which the dot is moving. Typically, the patient reports seeing nothing. When pressed to guess the direction of motion, however, more often than by chance the patient will guess correctly.

A 52-year-old physician became blind after two consecutive strokes destroyed his primary visual cortex (Pegna, Khateb, Lazeyras, & Seghier, 2005). Nothing was wrong with his eyes, but the visual regions of his brain could not process any information they received from them. Although alert and aware of his surroundings, the patient reported being unable to see anything, not even the presence of intense light. When the patient was shown a series of faces and was asked to guess their emotional expressions, he had no sense of having seen anything. Remarkably, however, he was able to identify the expressions at a level much better than by chance. He did not respond to other stimuli (such as shapes, animal faces, or scary stimuli).

blindsight A condition in which people who are blind have some spared visual capacities in the absence of any visual awareness.

4.4 What Factors Influence Visual Perception?

Object Perception Requires Construction

Within the brain, what exactly happens to the information the senses take in about an object's features? How does that information get organized?

Optical illusions are among the tools psychologists have for understanding how the brain uses such information. Many perceptual psychologists believe that illusions reveal the mechanisms that help our visual systems determine the sizes and distances of objects in the visual environment. In doing so, illusions illustrate how we form accurate representations of the three-dimensional world. Researchers rely on these tricks to reveal automatic perceptual systems that, in most circumstances, result in accurate perception (**Figure 4.26**).

GESTALT PRINCIPLES OF PERCEPTUAL ORGANIZATION As discussed in Chapter 1, Gestalt psychologists theorized that perception is more than the result of

FIGURE 4.26 Try for Yourself: Optical Illusions

(a) The Ouchi Illusion

Named for the Japanese artist Hajime Ouchi, who invented it, this illusion shows how we separate a figure from its background.

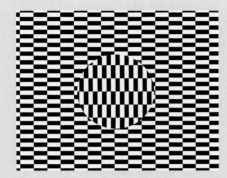

Result: The circle is made of lines offset from the rest of the display. Scrolling the image horizontally or vertically gives a much stronger effect. Some people report seeing colors and movement in this illusion.

(b) The McCollough Effect

This illusion was named for the vision researcher Celeste McCollough, who first described it. Alternate your gaze from the green stimulus with vertical lines to the magenta stimulus with horizontal lines, changing from one to the other approximately every second for 40 seconds.

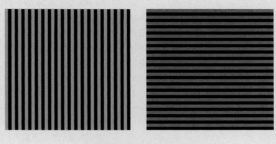

Then look at the black-and-white stimulus, composed of vertical and horizontal lines.

What do you see?

Result: You should see magenta vertical lines and green horizontal lines. Because the McCollough effect can last for hours or even a day, it cannot be explained by simple neural fatigue (where neurons reduce firing after repeated use). For this reason, the effect more likely occurs in higher brain regions, not in the eye. As noted in the text, the visual system is especially primed to process information about edges, and color-related edge perception may be involved.

accumulating sensory data. The German word *Gestalt* means "shape" or "form." As used in psychology, *Gestalt* means "organized whole." The founders of Gestalt psychology postulated a series of laws to explain how our brains group the perceived features of a visual scene into organized wholes. Gestalt psychology holds that our brains use innate principles to organize sensory information. These principles explain why we perceive, say, "a car" as opposed to "metal, tires, glass, door handles, hubcaps, fenders," and so on. For us, an object exists as a unit, not as a collection of features.

FIGURE AND GROUND One of the visual perception system's most basic organizing principles is distinguishing between figure and ground. A classic illustration of this is the *reversible figure illusion*. Look back at Figure 1.12, where you can see either a full face or two faces looking at each other—but not both at the same time. In identifying either figure—indeed, *any* figure—the brain assigns the rest of the scene to the background. In this illusion, the "correct" assignment of figure and ground is ambiguous. The figures periodically reverse (switch back and forth) as the visual system strives to make sense of the stimulation. In ways like this, visual perception is dynamic and ongoing.

As discussed in Chapter 1, Richard Nisbett and colleagues (2001) have demonstrated cultural differences between Eastern people's perceptions and Western people's perceptions. Easterners focus on a scene holistically, whereas Westerners focus on single elements in the forefront. Thus Easterners are more likely to be influenced by the (back)ground of a figure, and Westerners are more likely to extract the figure from its (back)ground.

Now look back at Figure 1.11. In this illusion, it is hard to see the Dalmatian standing among the many black spots scattered on the white background. This effect occurs because the part of the image corresponding to the dog lacks contours that define the dog's edges and because the dog's spotted coat resembles that of the background. Many observers find that they first recognize one part of the dog—say, the head—and from that are able to discern the dog's shape. Once you perceive the dog, it becomes very difficult to *not* see it the next time you look at the figure. Thus experience can inform shape processing.

PROXIMITY AND SIMILARITY Two of the most important Gestalt principles concern proximity and similarity. The *principle of proximity* states that the closer two figures are to each other, the more likely we are to group them and see them as part of the same object (**Figure 4.27a**). You might already be familiar with the *principle of similarity* as illustrated by the *Sesame Street* song and game "One of These Things Is Not Like the Others." We tend to group figures according to

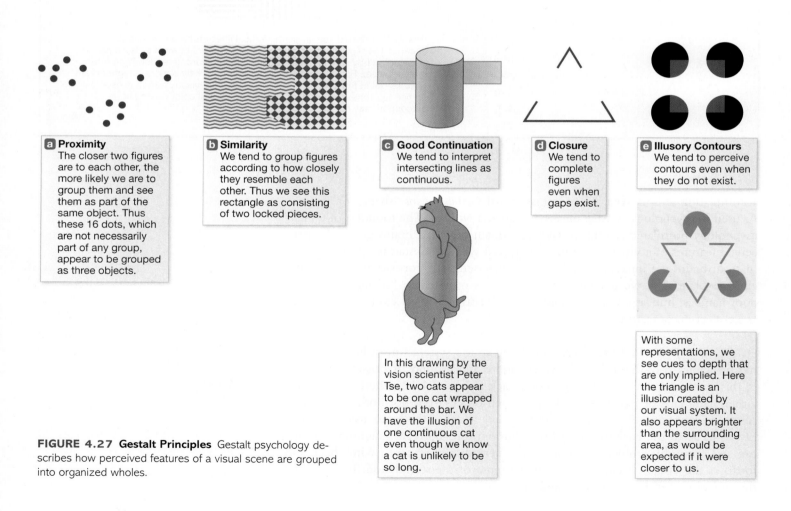

a Proximity
The closer two figures are to each other, the more likely we are to group them and see them as part of the same object. Thus these 16 dots, which are not necessarily part of any group, appear to be grouped as three objects.

b Similarity
We tend to group figures according to how closely they resemble each other. Thus we see this rectangle as consisting of two locked pieces.

c Good Continuation
We tend to interpret intersecting lines as continuous.

In this drawing by the vision scientist Peter Tse, two cats appear to be one cat wrapped around the bar. We have the illusion of one continuous cat even though we know a cat is unlikely to be so long.

d Closure
We tend to complete figures even when gaps exist.

e Illusory Contours
We tend to perceive contours even when they do not exist.

With some representations, we see cues to depth that are only implied. Here the triangle is an illusion created by our visual system. It also appears brighter than the surrounding area, as would be expected if it were closer to us.

FIGURE 4.27 Gestalt Principles Gestalt psychology describes how perceived features of a visual scene are grouped into organized wholes.

how closely they resemble each other, whether in shape, color, or orientation (**Figure 4.27b**). In accordance with both of these principles, we tend to cluster elements of the visual scene. Clustering enables us to consider a scene as a whole rather than as individual parts. For example, we often perceive a flock of birds as a single entity because all the elements, the birds, are similar and in close proximity.

THE "BEST" FORMS Other Gestalt principles describe how we perceive a form's features. *Good continuation* is the tendency to interpret intersecting lines as continuous rather than as changing direction radically. Good contour (boundary line) continuation appears to play a role in completing an object behind an *occluder,* which can be anything that hides from view a portion of an object or an entire object. For example, in **Figure 4.27c** the bar in the top illustration appears to be completely behind the occluder. Good continuation may operate over features that are more complex than contours, however. In the bottom illustration, two cats appear to be one extremely long cat wrapped around the pole, yet no continuous contours permit this completion. *Closure* refers to the tendency to complete figures that have gaps, as in **Figure 4.27d.** *Illusory contours* refers to the fact that we sometimes perceive contours and cues to depth even though they do not exist (**Figure 4.27e**).

BOTTOM-UP AND TOP-DOWN INFORMATION PROCESSING How do we assemble the information about parts into a perception of a whole object? According to most models of the process, pattern recognition is hierarchical. Specifically, pattern recognition occurs through **bottom-up processing.** This term means that data are relayed in the brain from lower to higher levels of processing. But perception is actually a combination of bottom-up and **top-down processing.** In top-down processing, information at higher levels of mental processing can influence lower, "earlier" levels in the processing hierarchy. For this reason, context affects perception: What we expect to see (higher level) influences what we perceive (lower level). Consider the Dalmatian illustration discussed earlier. Also consider the incomplete letters in **Figure 4.28.** The same shape appears in the center of each word, but you perceive the shape first as "H" and then as "A" (lower level). Your perception depends on which interpretation makes sense in the context of the particular word (higher level).

Knowing how information is processed can help us understand and avoid mistakes. For example, faulty expectations can lead to faulty perceptions. On November 28, 1979, Air New Zealand Flight 901 crashed into the slopes of Mount Erebus, on Ross Island in Antarctica, causing the deaths of the 237 passengers and 20 crew members. Because the aircraft's flight computer had been programmed incorrectly, the plane was far off course. In addition, the pilots had descended below the minimum altitude allowed for the flight. However, these factors do not explain why, until moments before impact, the flight crew failed to notice the 12,000-foot volcano looming in front of them (**Figure 4.29**).

Psychologists testifying at the commission of inquiry offered a possible, if startling, explanation: The pilots saw what they expected to see. One unique hazard of Antarctic aviation is "whiteout," in which the sky and the snow-covered terrain appear to merge and pilots are unable visually to distinguish the ground or the horizon. The pilots believed they were flying over the Ross Ice Shelf, hundreds of miles from their actual location. They did not expect to encounter mountains anywhere near their flight path. The psychologists argued that the few visual cues available to the pilots were sufficiently consistent with what they

bottom-up processing A hierarchical model of pattern recognition in which data are relayed from one level of mental processing to the next, always moving to a higher level of processing.

top-down processing A hierarchical model of pattern recognition in which information at higher levels of mental processing can also influence lower, "earlier" levels in the processing hierarchy.

THE CAT

FIGURE 4.28 Context Context plays an important role in object recognition. **How does context aid your interpretation of the shapes shown here?**

FIGURE 4.29 **Mount Erebus** Because the pilots on Air New Zealand Flight 901 did not expect to see this Antarctic volcano ahead of them, they failed to see it.

Participants were shown an array of faces and objects.

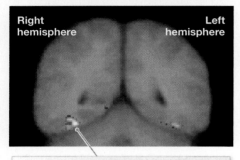

Right hemisphere   Left hemisphere

The visual perception of faces activated an area of the brain known as the fusiform gyrus. The right hemisphere responded more strongly than the left, especially when faces were presented among objects.

FIGURE 4.30 Perceiving Faces Brain imaging shows increased activity in the right hemisphere when faces are viewed.

expected to see that in their minds their expectations were confirmed. Since there appeared to be no danger, the pilots decided, fatally, to reduce altitude to give the passengers a better view of the spectacular Antarctic landscape. The combination of an unusually sparse visual environment and the pilots' beliefs conspired to fool their visual systems into seeing terrain that was not there—and failing to see the mountain that was.

FACE PERCEPTION One special class of object that the visual system is sensitive to is faces. As highly social animals, humans are well able to perceive and interpret facial expressions. Several studies support the idea that human faces reveal "special" information that is not available in any other way. For example, we can more readily discern information about a person's mood, attentiveness, sex, race, age, and so on by looking at that person's face than by listening to the person talk, watching the person walk, or studying his or her clothing (Bruce & Young, 1986).

People are better at recognizing members of their own race or ethnic group, however, than at recognizing members of other races or ethnic groups. There is some truth to the saying *they all look alike,* but the saying applies to all groups. This effect may occur because people have more exposure to people of their own race or ethnicity (Gosselin & Larocque, 2000). In the United States, where whites greatly outnumber blacks, whites are much better at recognizing white faces than at recognizing black faces (Brigham & Malpass, 1985).

Some people have particular deficits in the ability to recognize faces—a condition known as *prosopagnosia*—but not in the ability to recognize other objects (Farah, 1996). As discussed earlier in this chapter, patient D.F. has trouble with object recognition. Because D.F. also has prosopagnosia, she cannot tell one face from another. Still, she is able to judge whether something is a face or not and whether that face is upside down or not. This ability implies that facial recognition differs from nonfacial object recognition (Steeves et al., 2006).

Faces are so important that certain brain regions appear to be dedicated solely to perceiving them. As part of the "what" stream discussed earlier, certain cortical regions, and even specific neurons, seem to be specialized to perceive faces. A number of separate brain imaging studies have found that a region of the *fusiform gyrus,* in the right hemisphere, may be specialized for perceiving faces (Grill-Spector, Knouf, & Kanwisher, 2004; McCarthy, Puce, Gore, & Allison, 1997; **Figure 4.30**). Indeed, this brain area responds most strongly to upright faces, as we would perceive them in the normal environment (Kanwisher, Tong, & Nakayama, 1998).

People have a surprisingly hard time recognizing faces, especially unknown faces, that are upside down. We are much worse at this task than we are at recognizing other inverted objects. The inversion interferes with the way people perceive the relationship between facial features (Hancock, Bruce, & Burton, 2000). For instance, if the eyebrows are bushier than usual, this facial characteristic is obvious if the face is upright but not detectable when the face is inverted. One interesting example of the perceptual difficulties associated with inverted faces is evident in the Thatcher illusion, so called because the effect was first studied using photos of the former British prime minister Margaret Thatcher (Thompson, 1980; **Figure 4.31**).

Other brain areas are sensitive to facial expression and gaze direction. For example, a face's emotional significance appears to activate the amygdala, which is involved in calculating potential danger (Adams, Gordon, Baird, Ambady, & Kleck, 2003; Adolphs, 2003). As discussed in Chapter 10, one theory suggests that the amygdala processes visual information very crudely and quickly, to help identify potential threats. For example, the amygdala becomes activated when people observe subliminal presentations of faces expressing fear (Whalen et al., 2001). When the blind physician discussed earlier was shown a series of faces and was asked to guess their emotional expression, he had no sense of having seen anything, but he was able to identify the expression at a level much better than by chance. He did not respond to other stimuli (such as shapes, animal faces, or scary stimuli). A brain scanner showed that his amygdala became activated when he was presented with emotional faces but not with faces showing neutral expressions. Thus his amygdala might have processed the faces' emotional content despite his lack of awareness. This possibility raises the intriguing question of whether the physician was "seeing" the faces. It also may help illuminate how visual information reaches the amygdala when primary visual areas are damaged.

In a series of studies, researchers found that people more quickly and accurately recognize angry facial expressions than happy ones (Becker, Kenrick, Neuberg, Blackwell, & Smith, 2007). In addition, the researchers found that most people recognize anger more quickly on a man's face than on a woman's, and they found the reverse for happiness. The researchers think these results are due partly to people's beliefs that men express anger more often than women do and that women express happiness more often than men do (i.e., the beliefs would be contributing to top-down processing—we are more likely to "see" what we expect to see). They also think that female and male facial features drive the effect. For example, bushy eyebrows low on the face are more likely to be perceived as an expression of anger, and men typically have bushier and lower eyebrows than women. According to evolutionary psychology, there is an adaptive advantage to the detection of angry faces. Given that men in every society commit most violent crimes, it is adaptive to be especially fast and accurate at recognizing angry male faces. Thus facial recognition supports an idea emphasized throughout this book: The brain is adaptive.

FIGURE 4.31 Try for Yourself: The Thatcher Illusion

These two inverted pictures of Margaret Thatcher look normal. Turn your book upside down to reveal a different perspective.

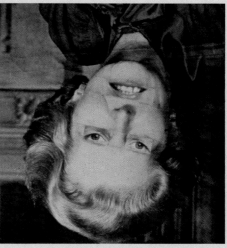

Result: Inversion of the whole face interferes with the perception of the individual components. This effect implies that we pay most attention to the eyes and mouth. As long as those features are oriented correctly, the rest of the face appears normal even if it is not.

Depth Perception Is Important for Locating Objects

One of the visual system's most important tasks is to locate objects in space. Without this capacity, we would find it difficult to navigate in the world and interact with things and people. One of the most enduring questions in psychological research is how we are able to construct a three-dimensional mental representation of the visual world from two-dimensional retinal input. Our ability to see depth in a photograph illustrates this point: A three-dimensional array of objects creates exactly the same image on the retina that a photograph of the same array of objects does. Despite this inherent ambiguity, we do not confuse pictures with the scenes they depict.

We are able to perceive depth in the two-dimensional patterns of photographs, movies, videos, and television images because the brain applies the same

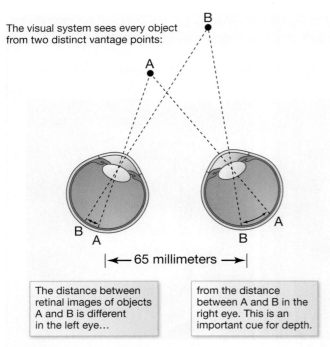

The visual system sees every object from two distinct vantage points:

B

A

|← 65 millimeters →|

B
A

B
A

The distance between retinal images of objects A and B is different in the left eye...

from the distance between A and B in the right eye. This is an important cue for depth.

FIGURE 4.32 Binocular Disparity To demonstrate your own binocular disparity, hold one of your index fingers out in front of your face and close first one eye and then the other. Your finger appears to move because each eye, due to its position relative to the finger, has a unique retinal image.

rules or mechanisms that it uses to work out the spatial relations between objects in the three-dimensional world. To do this, the brain rapidly and automatically exploits certain prior assumptions it has about the relationship between two-dimensional image cues and the three-dimensional world. Among these assumptions are cues that help the visual system perceive depth. These depth cues can be divided into two types: **Binocular depth cues** are available from both eyes together and contribute to bottom-up processing. **Monocular depth cues** are available from each eye alone and provide organizational information for top-down processing.

BINOCULAR DEPTH PERCEPTION One of the most important cues to depth perception is **binocular disparity** (or *retinal disparity*). This cue is caused by the distance between humans' two eyes. Because each eye has a slightly different view of the world, the brain has access to two different but overlapping retinal images. The brain uses the disparity between these two retinal images to compute distances to nearby objects (**Figure 4.32**). The ability to determine an object's depth based on that object's projections to each eye is called *stereoscopic vision.*

A related binocular depth cue is **convergence.** This term refers to the way that our eye muscles turn our eyes inward when we view nearby objects. The brain knows how much the eyes are converging, and it uses this information to perceive distance (**Figure 4.33**).

MONOCULAR DEPTH PERCEPTION Although binocular disparity is an important cue for depth perception, it is useful only for objects relatively close to us. Furthermore, we can perceive depth even with one eye closed, because of monocular depth cues. Artists routinely use these cues to create a sense of depth, so monocular depth cues are also called *pictorial depth cues*. The Renaissance painter,

binocular depth cues Cues of depth perception that arise from the fact that people have two eyes.

monocular depth cues Cues of depth perception that are available to each eye alone.

binocular disparity A depth cue; because of the distance between a person's eyes, each eye receives a slightly different retinal image.

convergence A cue of binocular depth perception; when a person views a nearby object, the eye muscles turn the eyes inward.

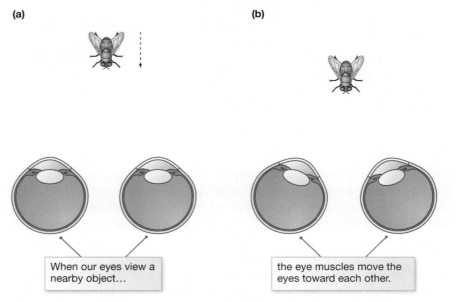

(a)

(b)

When our eyes view a nearby object...

the eye muscles move the eyes toward each other.

FIGURE 4.33 Convergence Hold one of your index fingers out in front of your face, about a foot away. Slowly bring your finger toward your eyes. Are you able to perceive your eyes converging?

FIGURE 4.34 Pictorial Depth Cues Using the bulleted list below as a reference, try to identify the six depth cues in Edvard Munch's painting *Evening on Karl Johan Street* (circa 1892).

sculptor, architect, and engineer Leonardo da Vinci first identified many of these cues, which include:

- *Occlusion:* A near object occludes (blocks) an object that is farther away.

- *Relative size:* Far-off objects project a smaller retinal image than close objects do, if the far-off and close objects are the same physical size.

- *Familiar size:* We know how large familiar objects are, so we can tell how far away they are by the size of their retinal images.

- *Linear perspective:* Seemingly parallel lines appear to converge in the distance.

- *Texture gradient:* As a uniformly textured surface recedes, its texture continuously becomes denser.

- *Position relative to horizon:* All else being equal, objects below the horizon that appear higher in the visual field are perceived as being farther away. Objects above the horizon that appear lower in the visual field are perceived as being farther away (**Figure 4.34**).

MOTION CUES FOR DEPTH PERCEPTION Motion is another cue for depth. *Motion parallax* is the relative movements of objects that are at various distances from the observer. For example, when you watch the scenery from a moving car, near objects such as mailboxes seem to pass quickly, far objects more slowly (**Figure 4.35**). If you fixate on an object farther away, such as a mountain, it appears to match your speed. If you fixate on an object at an intermediate distance, such as a house set back from the road, anything closer (e.g., the mailbox) moves opposite your direction relative to that object (e.g., house). Anything farther (e.g., mountain) moves in your direction relative to the object (e.g., house). Motion cues such as these help the brain calculate which objects are closer and which are farther away.

FIGURE 4.35 Motion Parallax Near objects seem to pass us more quickly in the opposite direction of our movement. Objects farther away seem to move more slowly.

Size Perception Depends on Distance Perception

The size of an object's retinal image depends on that object's distance from the observer. The farther away the object is, the smaller its retinal image. To determine an object's size, then, the visual system needs to know how far away it is. Most of the time, enough depth information is available for the visual system to work out an object's distance and thus infer how large the object is. Size perception sometimes fails, however, and an object may look bigger or smaller than it really is (**Figure 4.36**). This optical illusion arises when normal perceptual processes incorrectly represent the distance between the viewer and the stimuli. In other words, depth cues can fool us into seeing depth when it is not there. Alternatively, a lack of depth cues can fool us into *not* seeing depth when it *is* there. This section considers two phenomena related to both depth perception and distance perception: *Ames boxes* (also called *Ames rooms*) and the *Ponzo illusion*.

AMES BOXES Ames boxes were crafted in the 1940s by Adelbert Ames, a painter turned scientist. These constructions present powerful depth illusions. Inside the Ames boxes, rooms play with linear perspective and other distance cues. One such room makes a far corner appear the same distance away as a near corner (**Figure 4.37**). In a normal room and in this Ames box, the nearby child projects a larger retinal image than the child farther away. Normally, however, the nearby child would not appear to be a giant, because the perceptual system would take depth into account when assessing size. Here, the depth cues are wrong, so the nearby child appears farther away than he is, and the disproportionate size of his image on your retina makes him look huge.

THE PONZO ILLUSION The Ponzo illusion, first described by the psychologist Mario Ponzo in 1913, is another classic example of a size/distance illusion (**Figure 4.38**). The common explanation for this effect is that monocular depth cues make the two-dimensional figure seem three-dimensional (Rock, 1984). As noted earlier, seemingly parallel lines appear to converge in the distance. Here, the two lines drawn to look like railroad tracks receding in the distance trick your brain into thinking they are parallel. Therefore, you perceive the two

FIGURE 4.36 Distance Perception This picture, by Rebecca Robinson, captures what appears to be a tiny Sarah Heatherton standing on James Heatherton's head. This illusion occurs because the photo fails to present depth information: It does not convey the hill on which Sarah is standing.

FIGURE 4.37 The Ames Box Ames played with depth cues to create size illusions. For example, as illustrated here, he made a diagonally cut room appear rectangular by using crooked windows and floor tiles. When one child stands in a near corner and another (of similar height) stands in a far corner, the room creates the illusion that they are equidistant from the viewer. Therefore, the closer child looks like a giant compared with the child farther away.

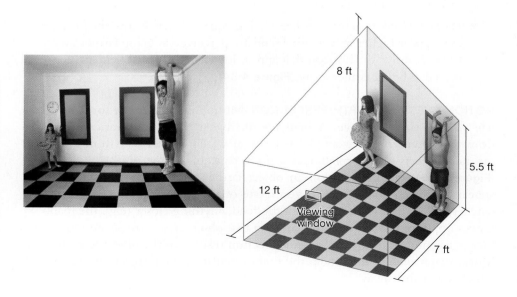

parallel lines in the center as if they are at different distances and thus different in size when they actually are the same size. This illusion shows how much we rely on depth perception to gauge size. The brain defaults to using depth cues even when depth is absent. Once again, the brain responds as efficiently as possible.

Motion Perception Has Internal and External Cues

We know how motion can cue depth perception, but how does the brain perceive motion? One answer is that we have neurons specialized for detecting movement. In other words, these neurons fire when movement occurs. But how does the brain know what is moving? If you look out a window and see a car driving past a house, how does your brain know the car is moving and not the house?

Consider the dramatic case of M.P., a German woman. After receiving damage to secondary visual areas of her brain—areas critical for motion perception—M.P. saw the world as a series of snapshots rather than as a moving image (Zihl, von Cramon, & Mai, 1983). Pouring tea, she would see the liquid frozen in air and be surprised when her cup overflowed. Before crossing a street, she might spot a car far away. When she tried to cross, however, that car would be right in front of her. M.P. had a unique deficit: She could perceive objects and colors but not continuous movement.

This section considers three phenomena that offer insights into how the visual system perceives motion: *motion aftereffects, compensation for head and eye motion,* and *stroboscopic motion perception.*

MOTION AFTEREFFECTS Motion aftereffects may occur when you gaze at a moving image for a long time and then look at a stationary scene. You experience a momentary impression that the new scene is moving in the opposite direction from the moving image. This illusion is also called the *waterfall effect,* because if you stare at a waterfall and then turn away, the scenery you are now looking at will seem to move upward for a moment.

Motion aftereffects are strong evidence that motion-sensitive neurons exist in the brain. According to the theory that explains this illusion, the visual cortex has neurons that respond to movement in a given direction. When you stare at a moving stimulus long enough, these direction-specific neurons begin to adapt to the motion. That is, they become fatigued and therefore less sensitive. If the stimulus is suddenly removed, the motion detectors that respond to all the other directions are more active than the fatigued motion detectors. Thus you see the new scene moving in the other direction.

COMPENSATION FOR HEAD AND EYE MOVEMENT The existence of motion-sensitive neurons does not completely explain motion perception. For instance, when you see what appears to be a moving object, how do you know whether the object is moving, you are moving, or your eyes are moving? Images move across your retina all the time, and you do not always perceive them as moving. Each slight blink or eye movement creates a new image on the retina. Why is it that every time you move your eye or your head, the images you see do not jump around? One explanation is that the brain calculates an object's perceived movements by monitoring the movement of the eyes, and perhaps also of the head, as they track a moving object. In addition, motion detectors track an image's motion across the retina, as the receptors in the retina fire one after the other (**Figure 4.39**).

FIGURE 4.38 The Ponzo Illusion The two horizontal lines appear to be different sizes but are actually the same length.

perceptual constancy Correctly perceiving objects as constant in their shape, size, color, and lightness, despite raw sensory data that could mislead perception.

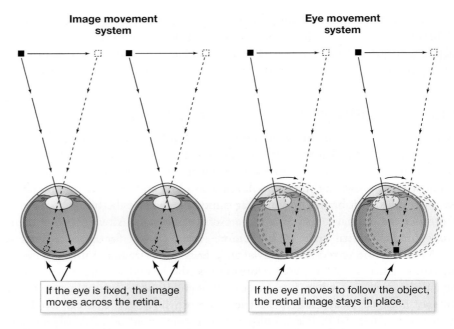

Image movement system

Eye movement system

If the eye is fixed, the image moves across the retina.

If the eye moves to follow the object, the retinal image stays in place.

FIGURE 4.39 Perceiving Movement These diagrams illustrate the two ways that the visual system detects movement.

STROBOSCOPIC MOTION PERCEPTION Movies are made up of still-frame images, presented one after the other to create the illusion of motion pictures. This phenomenon is based on stroboscopic movement, a perceptual illusion that occurs when two or more slightly different images are presented in rapid succession (**Figure 4.40**). The Gestalt psychologist Max Wertheimer conducted experiments in 1912 by flashing, at different intervals, two vertical lines placed close together. He discovered that when the interval was less than 30 milliseconds, subjects thought the two lines were flashed simultaneously. When the interval was greater than 200 milliseconds, they saw two lines being flashed at different times. Between those times, movement illusions occurred: When the interval was about 60 milliseconds, the line appeared to jump from one place to another. At slightly longer intervals, the line appeared to move continuously—a phenomenon called *phi movement*.

Perceptual Constancies Are Based on Ratio Relationships

Illusions occur when the brain creates inaccurate representations of stimuli. In the opposite situation, **perceptual constancy,** the brain correctly perceives objects as constant despite sensory data that could lead it to think otherwise. Consider your image in the mirror. What you see in the mirror might look like it is your actual size, but the image is much smaller than the parts of you being reflected. (If you doubt this claim, try tracing around the image of your face in a steamy bathroom mirror.) Similarly, how does the brain know that a person is 6 feet tall when the retinal image of that person changes size according to how near or far the person is (**Figure 4.41**)? How does the brain know

FIGURE 4.40 How Moving Pictures Work This static series would appear transformed if you spun the wheel. When the slightly different images were presented in rapid succession, the stroboscopic movement would tell your brain that you were watching a moving horse.

that snow is white and a tire is black, even when snow at night or a tire in bright light might send the same luminance cues to the retina?

For the most part, changing an object's angle, distance, or illumination does not change our perception of that object's size, shape, color, or lightness. But to perceive any of these four constancies, we need to understand the relationship between the object and at least one other factor. For *size constancy,* we need to know how far away the object is from us. For *shape constancy,* we need to know from what angle we are seeing the object. For *color constancy,* we need to compare the wavelengths of light reflected from the object with those reflected from its background. Likewise, for *lightness constancy,* we need to know how much light is being reflected from the object and from its background. In each case, the brain computes a ratio based on the relative magnitude rather than relying on each sensation's absolute magnitude. The perceptual system's ability to make relative judgments allows it to maintain constancy across various perceptual contexts. Although their precise mechanisms are unknown, these constancies illustrate that perceptual systems are tuned to detect changes from baseline conditions, not just to respond to sensory inputs.

By studying how illusions work, many perceptual psychologists have come to believe that the brain has built-in assumptions that influence perceptions. The vast majority of visual illusions appear to be beyond our conscious control—we cannot make ourselves not see illusions, even when we know they are not true representations of objects or events (**Figure 4.42**). Thus the visual system is a complex interplay of constancies, which allow us to see both a stable world and perceptual illusions that we cannot control.

(a)

(b)

FIGURE 4.41 Perceptual Constancy
When you look at each of these photos, your retinal image of the bearded man is the same. Why, then, does he appear larger in (a) than in (b)?

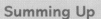

Summing Up

What Factors Influence Visual Perception?

Information first arrives in primary sensory regions. Multiple brain regions then contribute to our unified perceptual experience. The perceptual system uses cues from the perceiver's environment to help interpret sensory information. For example, the brain uses depth cues to determine the location of objects, and it uses ratio relationships to determine the perceptual constancy of objects. Contemporary theorists emphasize that perceptions are not faithful reproductions of the physical world. Instead, perceptions are constructed by the brain through multiple processes.

Measuring Up

1. Match each of the following monocular depth cues with its description: familiar size, linear perspective, occlusion, position relative to horizon, relative size, texture gradient.
   a. Seemingly parallel lines appear to converge in the distance.
   b. Near objects block those that are farther away.
   c. We use our knowledge of an object's size to judge the object's distance.
   d. Smaller objects are judged to be farther away.
   e. Uniform surfaces appear denser in the distance.
   f. Objects below the horizon that appear higher in the visual field are judged to be farther away.

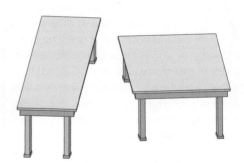

FIGURE 4.42 The Tabletop Illusion
Created by the psychologist Roger Shepard, this illusion demonstrates the brain's automatic perceptual processes. Even when we know the two tabletops are the same size and shape—even if we have traced one image and placed it on top of the other—perspective cues make us see them as different.

2. What is binocular disparity?
   a. a disorder in which a person loses depth perception
   b. a cue to depth caused by the formation of a slightly different retinal image in each eye
   c. the distance between our eyes
   d. the ability to see depth in a two-dimensional stimulus by defocusing our vision

3. Perceptual constancy _____.
   a. allows us to see objects as stable even when there are large fluctuations in the sensory information we receive
   b. allows us to understand how physical energy is transduced into neural activity
   c. is a misnomer because our perceptions are not constant
   d. was based on the idea that different parts of the brain underlie different perceptual experiences

How Can I Use Psychology to Improve My Next PowerPoint Presentation?

At some point in your college career, you will probably be asked to give a formal presentation. There is a good chance that you will be either expected or encouraged to use PowerPoint slides as part of that presentation. Good slides will support the audience's engagement with and comprehension of your talk. Poor slides will muddle your message, confuse your audience, and reflect negatively on you. If you are going to use slides in a presentation, you want those slides to sparkle. Psychology has a lot to say about how to make this happen.

The cognitive psychologist Stephen Kosslyn is an expert in how people process information. While attending many academic presentations, he noticed a trend, which he describes in his book *Clear and to the Point: 8 Principles for Compelling PowerPoint Pre-sentations* (2007): "I realized that virtually all of [the problems in PowerPoint presentations] occur because the presentations failed to respect the fundamental characteristics of how we humans perceive, remember, and comprehend information" (p. 2). Kosslyn has translated his observations into three principles that you can use to direct and hold the attention of your audience. These principles are *salience, discriminability, and perceptual organization*.

Salience Our brains pay attention to things that are prominent, or salient. For example, when you look at a line of people, you are likely to notice an especially tall or short person. When you walk through a parking lot, you might notice an especially old, dirty, or damaged car or an especially bright and shiny one. You notice, and you pay attention.

Of course, members of your audience have the same tendency. If you want the audience to pay attention to a particular point in your presentation, make that point salient. For example, use a larger font for the titles of slides than for the body of the slides. Use colored text to call attention to key words in a quote or diagram.

Be mindful of some pitfalls, however. First, if items are not centrally important, avoid making them salient. Avoid using a flashy animation to introduce a small piece of supporting evidence. Resist splashing a rainbow of colors across each slide. Be selective. Second, avoid many of the nifty backgrounds available in PowerPoint. Because they are loaded with bright colors and bold

**Now, on this slide, may I direct your attention
to the flashy animation and cool transition effects...
because I worked really, really hard on them.**

patterns, your audience may focus attention on the package of your presentation. You want them, instead, to focus on the content.

Discriminability As you learned earlier in this chapter, we are able to detect differences between two stimuli only if those differences exceed some threshold (see the discussions of difference threshold and Weber's law). As Kosslyn explains, "We need contrast to distinguish shapes, colors, or positions from each other and from the background" (2007, p. 123).

Suppose you want to create a bar graph that shows differences in religiosity between urban and rural participants. It would be unwise for you to represent urban participants using a teal bar and rural participants using a turquoise bar. The two colors are insufficiently different. In fact, audience members may not detect any difference between them and thus might not understand the slide. To vary the colors, you might make one bar teal and the second bar orange. These two colors will be easy for most audience members to discriminate.

By the way, a relatively common deficit in color vision makes it difficult for people to perceive distinctions between reds and greens. When preparing slides, you should avoid contrasting reds and greens.

Perceptual Organization Our brains like to group things. For example, we see *** *** as two groups of three and ** ** ** as three groups of two. Likewise, we see ♥■●♦♣♠ as two groups and ♥■●♦♣♠ as three groups. Why does this tendency matter? When creating PowerPoint slides, make all elements associated with a particular point one color. Make all elements associated with a different point another color. For example, in illustrating differences in religiosity between urban and rural participants, you might make the bar representing urban participants and the label that says "Urban Participants" the exact same color. You would then make the bar representing rural participants and the label that says "Rural Participants" a second color.

A cautionary note is warranted here, too. If you have used PowerPoint, you might know that you can use the animations tool to make pieces of text "fly in" at different times. For example, one bullet point might move quickly from the left margin to the center of the screen. A second bullet point might scoot up from the bottom of the screen. If you would like audience members to perceive two elements as part of the same group, be sure to bring those pieces onto the slide at the same time. For example, in creating the bar graph about religiosity, you might make the bar representing the religiosity of urban participants appear at the same time as a bullet point describing the mean and standard deviation of that variable. Shared motion, like shared color, signals group membership.

These are just a few of the many great ideas Kosslyn shares in his book. If you really want to make your next presentation shine, read his book and employ the many practices it recommends. And when you are up in front of the group, please remember not to chew gum.

Chapter Summary

4.1 How Do We Sense Our Worlds?

- **Stimuli Must Be Coded to Be Understood by the Brain:** Stimuli reaching the receptors are converted to neural impulses through the process of transduction.

- **Psychophysics Measures the Relationship between Stimuli and Perception:** By studying how people respond to different sensory levels, scientists can determine thresholds and perceived change (based on signal detection theory). Our sensory systems are tuned to both adapt to constant levels of stimulation and detect changes in our environment.

4.2 What Are the Basic Sensory Processes?

- **In Taste, Taste Buds Detect Chemicals:** The gustatory sense uses taste buds to respond to the chemical substances that produce at least five basic sensations: sweet, sour, salty, bitter, and umami (savory). The number and distribution of taste buds vary among individuals. Cultural taste preferences begin in the womb.

- **In Smell, the Nasal Cavity Gathers Odorants:** Receptors in the olfactory epithelium respond to chemicals and send signals to the olfactory bulb in the brain. Humans can discriminate among thousands of odors. Females are more accurate than males at detecting and identifying odors.

- **In Touch, Sensors in the Skin Detect Pressure, Temperature, and Pain:** The haptic sense relies on tactile stimulation to activate receptors for pressure, for temperature, and for distinct types of pain (immediate, sharp pain and chronic, dull pain).

- **In Hearing, the Ear Detects Sound Waves:** Sound waves activate hair cells in the inner ear. The receptors' responses depend on the sound waves' amplitude and frequency.

- **In Vision, the Eye Detects Light Waves:** Receptors (rods and cones) in the retina detect different forms of light waves. The lens helps the eye focus the stimulation on the retina for near versus far objects. Color is determined by wavelengths of light, which activate certain types of cones; by the absorption of wavelengths by objects; or by the mixing of wavelengths of light.

- **We Have Other Sensory Systems:** In addition to the five "basic" senses, humans and other animals have a kinesthetic sense (ability to judge where one's body and limbs are in space) and a vestibular sense (ability to judge the direction and intensity of head movements, associated with a sense of balance).

4.3 How Does Perception Emerge from Sensation?

- **In Touch, the Brain Integrates Sensory Information from Different Regions of the Body:** The primary sensory area for touch information is the primary somatosensory cortex in the parietal lobe. Neural "gates" in the spinal cord control pain. We can reduce pain perception by distracting ourselves, visualizing pain as more pleasant, being rested and relaxed, learning how to change the brain activity that underlies pain perception, and taking drugs that interfere with the neural transmission of pain.

- **In Hearing, the Brain Integrates Sensory Information from the Ears:** The primary sensory area for auditory information is the primary auditory cortex in the temporal lobe. The neurons at the front of the auditory cortex respond best to higher frequencies. The neurons at the rear of the auditory cortex respond best to lower frequencies. The brain localizes sound by comparing the times that a sound arrives at the individual ears and by comparing the magnitudes of the resulting sound waves at the ears.

- **In Vision, the Brain Processes Sensory Information from the Eyes:** The primary sensory area for visual information is the primary visual cortex in the occipital lobe. The visual system is characterized by a ventral stream that is specialized for object perception and recognition (what) and a dorsal stream that is specialized for spatial perception (where). Blindsight occurs when individuals who are blind retain some visual capacities of which they are unaware.

4.4 What Factors Influence Visual Perception?

- **Object Perception Requires Construction:** The Gestalt principles of organization account for some of the brain's perceptions of the world. The principles include distinguishing figure and ground, the grouping of objects on the basis of proximity and similarity, and the perception of "best" forms. Perception involves two processes: bottom-up processes (sensory information) and top-down processes (expectations about what we will perceive). Researchers have identified brain regions that are specialized for the perception of faces.

- **Depth Perception Is Important for Locating Objects:** The brain uses binocular cues, monocular cues, and motion cues to perceive depth. Binocular disparity and convergence are binocular depth cues. Pictorial depth cues such as occlusion, relative size, and linear perspective are monocular depth cues. Motion parallax is a motion depth cue.

- **Size Perception Depends on Distance Perception:** Illusions of size can be created when the retinal size conflicts with the known size of objects in the visual field, as in the Ames box illusion and the Ponzo illusion.

- **Motion Perception Has Internal and External Cues:** Motion detectors in the cortex respond to stimulation. The perceptual system establishes a stable frame of reference and relates object movement to it. Intervals of stimulation of repeated objects give the impression of continuous movement. Motion aftereffects, which are opposite in motion from things that have been observed, tell us about the fatigue of neural receptors that fire in response to motion in certain directions.

- **Perceptual Constancies Are Based on Ratio Relationships:** We create expectations about the world that allow us to use information about the shape, size, color, and lightness of objects in their surroundings to achieve constancy.

Key Terms

additive color mixing, p. 156
audition, p. 148
binocular depth cues, p. 170
binocular disparity, p. 170
blindsight, p. 163
bottom-up processing, p. 167
cones, p. 151
convergence, p. 170
cornea, p. 150
eardrum, p. 148

fovea, p. 151
gustation, p. 140
haptic sense, p. 145
iris, p. 150
kinesthetic sense, p. 156
monocular depth cues, p. 170
olfaction, p. 143
olfactory bulb, p. 143
olfactory epithelium, p. 143
perception, p. 132

perceptual constancy, p. 174
pupil, p. 150
retina, p. 150
rods, p. 151
sensation, p. 132
sensory adaptation, p. 137
signal detection theory (SDT), p. 136
sound wave, p. 148

subtractive color mixing, p. 155
taste buds, p. 140
top-down processing, p. 167
transduction, p. 133
vestibular sense, p. 156

Practice Test

1. Which answer accurately lists the order in which these structures participate in sensation and perception (except for smell)?
   a. specialized receptors, thalamus, cortex
   b. specialized receptors, cortex, thalamus
   c. cortex, specialized receptors, thalamus
   d. thalamus, specialized receptors, cortex

2. While listening to a string quartet, you find you can easily decipher the notes played by the violins, by the viola, and by the cello. When you focus on the viola, you find some of the notes especially loud and others barely discernable. Which of the following statements best describes your sensations of the quartet?
   a. You can decipher qualitative differences among the instruments because of the rate of firing of your sensory neurons, whereas you can make quantitative distinctions—recognizing variations in the notes' intensity—due to the involvement of specific sensory receptors.
   b. You can decipher quantitative differences among the instruments because of the rate of firing of your sensory neurons, whereas you can make qualitative distinctions—recognizing variations in the notes' intensity—due to the involvement of specific sensory receptors.
   c. You can decipher qualitative differences among the instruments because of the involvement of specific sensory receptors, whereas you can make quantitative distinctions—recognizing variations in the notes' intensity—due to the rate of firing of your sensory neurons.
   d. You can decipher quantitative differences among the instruments because of the involvement of specific sensory receptors, whereas you can make qualitative distinctions—recognizing variations in the notes' intensity—due to the rate of firing of your sensory neurons.

3. When the violist plays a solo, you cannot hear it. Which of the following statements is the most likely explanation?
   a. The differences in intensity between the notes of the solo are too small to be noticeable.
   b. The intensity of the auditory stimulation does not exceed the minimum threshold needed for you to detect a sensation.
   c. The quartet's playing has left your hearing receptors overstimulated and thus unable to process less intense stimuli.

4. Imagine you have a steady, radiating pain across your lower back. No matter how you position yourself, you cannot make the pain go away. Select the answer choices most relevant to this type of pain. More than one choice may be correct.
   a. activated by chemical changes in tissue
   b. activated by strong physical pressure of temperature extremes
   c. fast fibers
   d. myelinated axons
   e. nonmyelinated axons
   f. slow fibers

5. A 1-year-old girl skins her knees on a rough sidewalk. The girl cries in pain. Which of the following interventions will most likely calm her?
   a. Promising to give her a piece of candy if she stops crying.
   b. Quickly cleaning and bandaging the skinned knees.
   c. Looking intently into her eyes and saying, "Let's take some deep breaths together. Ready. . . . Breathe in. . . . Now breathe out."
   d. Directing the girl's hand on a quick touching tour of the nearby environment and saying things such as "Feel this tree's rough bark. Touch the grass; it tickles. Feel how smooth this rock is!"

The answer key for the Practice Tests can be found at the back of the book. It also includes answers to the green caption questions.

5

Consciousness

IN 2000, WHEN HE WAS 16 YEARS OLD, ERIK RAMSEY was involved in a car crash. His brain stem was damaged in the accident. Since then, as a result of that injury, Ramsey has suffered from *locked-in syndrome*. In this rare condition, all or nearly all of a person's voluntary muscles are paralyzed. Even when Ramsey is awake and alert, he cannot communicate with those around him except by moving his eyes up and down (**Figure 5.1**). As a psychological state, locked-in syndrome has been compared to being buried alive. Imagine that you see all the sights around you and hear every noise, but you cannot respond physically to these sights and noises. Imagine that you can feel every itch, but you cannot scratch yourself or move to gain relief.

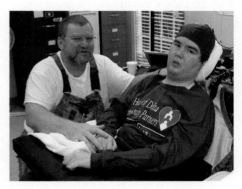

FIGURE 5.1 Conscious but Locked In Erik Ramsey (**right,** with his father, Eddie) suffers from locked-in syndrome. He has total awareness, but his condition leaves him almost completely unable to communicate.

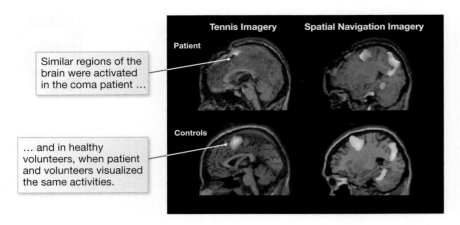

Tennis Imagery   Spatial Navigation Imagery

Patient

Similar regions of the brain were activated in the coma patient ...

Controls

... and in healthy volunteers, when patient and volunteers visualized the same activities.

FIGURE 5.2 In a Coma but Aware The brain images on the top are from the patient, a young woman in a coma who showed no outward signs of awareness. The images on the bottom are a composite from the control group, which consisted of healthy volunteers. Both the patient and the control group were told to visualize playing tennis and walking around. Right after the directions were given, the neural activity in the patient's brain appeared similar to the neural activity in the control group's brains.

Recent scientific advances have raised the possibility that Ramsey and patients like him will be able to communicate. That is, we might be able to "read" their thoughts by imaging brain activity in real time. Communication of this kind is the goal of researchers who, in 2004, planted electrodes in the speech region of Ramsey's left hemisphere. For the past several years, Ramsey has been listening to recordings of vowel sounds and mentally simulating those sounds. His simulation of each vowel sound should produce its own pattern of brain activity. Ultimately, the researchers hope to use this brain activity to create a voice synthesizer that will translate Ramsey's neural patterns into understandable speech (Bartels et al., 2008). So far, researchers working with Ramsey have demonstrated that he can produce numerous specific vowel sounds (Guenther et al., 2009).

Other researchers have obtained similarly promising results. A 23-year-old woman in an apparent coma was asked to imagine playing tennis or walking through her house (Owen et al., 2006). This woman's pattern of brain activity became quite similar to the patterns of control subjects who also imagined playing tennis or walking through a house (**Figure 5.2**). The woman could not give outward signs of awareness, but researchers believe she was able to understand language and respond to the experimenters' requests. The implications of this finding are extraordinary. Could the researchers' method be used to reach other people who are in comas, aware of their surroundings, but unable to communicate? Indeed, this research team has now evaluated 54 coma patients and found 5 who could willfully control brain activity to communicate (Monti et al., 2010). One 29-year-old man was able to answer five of six yes/no questions correctly by thinking of one type of image to answer yes and another type to answer no. The ability to communicate from a coma might allow some patients to express thoughts, ask for more medication, and increase the quality of their lives. These advances add up to one astonishing fact: Some people in comas are conscious! ∎

5.1 What Is Consciousness?

This chapter looks at consciousness and its variations. The cases discussed in the chapter opener highlight the chapter's two main points. First, people can be conscious of their surroundings even when they do not appear to be. Second, conscious experiences are associated with brain activity. To understand the relationship between the brain and consciousness, we need to consider how conscious experiences differ. As explored later in this chapter, there are natural variations in consciousness (e.g., sleep). Moreover, people manipulate consciousness through natural methods (e.g., meditation) as well as artificial methods (e.g., drugs). In addition, because of the very nature of consciousness, conscious experiences differ from person to person.

Consciousness Is a Subjective Experience

Consciousness refers to moment-by-moment subjective experiences. Paying attention to your immediate surroundings is one such experience. Reflecting on your current thoughts is another. You know you are conscious because you are experiencing the outside world through your senses and because you are aware that you are thinking. But what gives rise to your consciousness? Are you conscious simply because many neurons are firing in your brain? If so, how are the actions of these brain circuits related to your subjective experiences of the world?

An iPad's electrical circuits produce images and sound when they are energized, but gadgets such as iPads are neither conscious nor unconscious in the same way humans are. The difference is not simply that the circuitry in gadgets works one way and the circuitry in human brains works another way. Nor is the difference simply that humans are biological and gadgets are not. Your body includes many highly active biological systems, such as your immune system, that do not produce the sort of consciousness you are experiencing right now. At every minute, your brain is regulating your body temperature, controlling your breathing, calling up memories as necessary, and so on. You are not conscious of the brain operations that do these things. Why are you conscious only of certain experiences?

Philosophers have long debated questions about the nature of consciousness. As discussed in Chapter 1, the seventeenth-century philosopher René Descartes stated that the mind is physically distinct from the brain, a view called *dualism*. Most psychologists reject dualism. Instead, they believe that the brain and the mind are inseparable. According to this view, the activity of neurons in the brain produces the contents of consciousness: the sight of a face, the smell of a rose. More specifically, for each type of content—each sight, each smell—there is an associated pattern of brain activity. The activation of this particular group of neurons in the brain somehow gives rise to conscious experience.

But because each of us experiences consciousness personally—that is, subjectively—we cannot know if any two people experience the world in exactly the same way. What does the color red look like to you (**Figure 5.3**)? How does an apple taste? As discussed in Chapter 1, early pioneers in psychology attempted to understand consciousness through introspection, but psychologists largely abandoned this method because of its subjective nature. Conscious experiences exist, but their subjective nature makes them difficult to study empirically. When children play the game "I spy, with my little eye," the players might be looking at the same thing—say, "something that is red"—but they might be experiencing that thing differently. In other words, there is no way to know whether each player's experience of the thing (its shape, size, color, and so on) is the same or whether each player is using the same words to describe a different experience. The labels applied to experience do not necessarily do justice to the experience. When you experience heartbreak and a friend consoles you by saying, "I know how you feel," does your friend definitely know?

There Are Variations in Conscious Experience

Conscious experience can be seen as unified and coherent. In this view, the mind is a continuous stream and thoughts float on that stream. There is a limit, however, to how many things the mind can be conscious of at the same time.

For example, as you read this chapter, what are you conscious of, and how conscious are you? Are you focused intently on the material? Is your mind wandering, occasionally or often? You cannot pay attention to reading while doing

consciousness One's subjective experience of the world, resulting from brain activity.

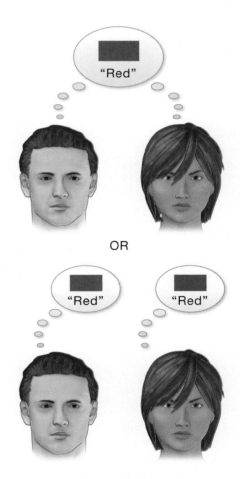

FIGURE 5.3 Seeing Red One difficult question related to consciousness is whether people's subjective experiences of the world are similar. For instance, does red look the same to everyone who has normal color vision?

THE BIRTH OF SELF-CONSCIOUSNESS

HOLY SMOKE—I'M STANDING HERE!

several other things, such as watching television or instant messaging. As you focus on developments in the show or in the messages, you might realize that you have no idea what you just read or what your friend just replied. Likewise, you can think about what you will do tomorrow, what kind of car you would like to own, and where you most recently went on vacation—but you cannot think about them all at the same time. While driving to a familiar destination, have you ever begun to think about something other than your driving? Before you knew it, you had arrived. But how did you get there? You knew you had driven, but you could not remember details of the drive, such as whether you stopped at traffic lights or passed other vehicles.

As you go through any day, you experience variations in consciousness. As discussed later, your level of consciousness varies naturally through the day in your sleep/wake cycle. It is also affected by your actions (such as eating or meditating) and by consciousness-altering substances you consume (such as caffeine or alcohol).

In general, all of us can execute routine or *automatic* tasks (such as driving, walking, or catching a baseball) that are so well learned that we do them without much conscious effort. Indeed, paying too much attention can interfere with these automatic behaviors. By contrast, difficult or unfamiliar tasks require greater conscious effort. Such *controlled* processing is slower than automatic processing, but it helps us perform in complex or novel situations. For example, if a rainstorm starts while you are driving, you will need to pay more attention to your driving and be very conscious of the road conditions.

Through such variations, consciousness serves at least three vital functions (Baumeister & Masicampo, 2010; Baumeister, Masicampo, & Vohs, 2011). First, consciousness lets us perform complex actions that may require input from several different brain regions. Second, consciousness helps us connect with one another by sharing our thoughts and feelings and even imagining ourselves in another person's situation. Third, consciousness is required for complicated thinking, such as understanding the development of a plot in a story, using logical reasoning, and performing mathematical calculations. Most of us are fortunate enough to take these functions for granted. But to understand the importance of these functions, consider cases in which the basic operations of consciousness are impossible or compromised.

EXTREME STATES As noted by the cognitive neuroscientist Steven Laureys (2007), medical advances are enabling a greater number of people to survive traumatic brain injuries. For example, doctors now save the lives of many people who previously would have died from injuries sustained in car accidents or on battlefields. A good example is the remarkable survival of Congresswoman Gabrielle Giffords, who was shot in the head by an assailant in 2011. Surviving is just the first step toward recovery, however, and many of those who sustain serious brain injuries fall into comas or, like Giffords, are induced into coma as part of medical treatment. The coma allows the brain to rest. Most people who regain consciousness after such injuries do so within a few days, but some people do not regain consciousness for weeks. In this state, they have sleep/wake cycles—they open their eyes and appear to be awake, close their eyes and appear to be asleep—but they do not seem to respond to their surroundings. When this condition lasts longer than a month, it is known as a *persistent vegetative state*. Evidence indicates that the brain sometimes can process information in this state (Gawryluk, D'Arcy, Connolly, & Weaver, 2010). But the persistent vegetative state is not associated with consciousness. Normal brain activity does not occur when a person is in this state, in part because much of the person's brain may be dead. The longer the persistent vegetative state lasts, the less likely it is that the person will ever recover consciousness or show normal brain activity. Terri Schiavo, a woman living in Florida, spent more than 15 years in a persistent vegetative state. Eventually, her husband wanted to terminate her life support, but her parents wanted to continue it. Both sides waged a legal battle. A court ruled in the husband's favor, and life support was terminated. After Schiavo's death, an autopsy revealed substantial and irreversible damage throughout her brain and especially in cortical regions known to be important for consciousness (**Figure 5.4a**).

Between the vegetative state and full consciousness is the *minimally conscious state*. In this state, people make some deliberate movements, such as following an object with their eyes. They may try to communicate. The prognosis for those in a minimally conscious state is much better than for those in a persistent vegetative state. Consider the case of the Polish railroad worker Jan Grzebski, who in June 2007, at age 67, woke up from a 19-year coma. He lived for another 18 months. Grzebski remembered events that were going on around him during his coma, including his children's marriages. There is some indication that he tried to speak on occasion but was not understood (Scislowska, 2007; **Figure 5.4b**). Differentiating between states of consciousness by behavior alone is difficult, but brain imaging may prove useful for identifying the extent of a patient's brain injury and likelihood of recovery.

Brain Activity Gives Rise to Consciousness

As psychological science is beginning to reveal, common brain activity may give rise to people's subjective experiences. Scientists cannot (yet) read your mind by looking at your brain activity, but they can identify objects you are seeing by looking at your brain activity (Kay, Naselaris, Prenger, & Gallant, 2008). For instance, researchers can use fMRI (see Chapter 2, "Research Methodology") to determine, based on your pattern of brain activity at that moment, whether the picture you are seeing is of a house, a shoe, a bottle, or a face (O'Toole, Jiang, Abdi, & Haxby, 2005). Similarly, brain imaging can reveal whether a person is looking at a striped pattern that is moving horizontally or vertically, whether a person is looking at a picture or a sentence, which of three categories a person is thinking about during a memory task, and so on (Norman, Polyn, Detre, & Haxby, 2006).

Philosophers have long debated what it means to be conscious of something. Psychologists now examine, even measure, consciousness and other mental states that were previously viewed as too subjective to be studied. For example, Frank Tong and colleagues (1998) studied the relationship between consciousness and neural responses in the brain. Participants were shown images in which houses were superimposed on faces. When participants reported seeing a face, neural activity increased within temporal lobe regions associated with face recognition. When participants reported seeing a house, neural activity increased within temporal lobe regions associated with object recognition. This finding suggests that different types of sensory information are processed by different brain areas: The particular type of neural activity determines the particular type of awareness (**Figure 5.5**).

THE GLOBAL WORKSPACE MODEL The *global workspace model* posits that consciousness arises as a function of which brain circuits are active (Baars, 1988; Dehaene, Changeux, Naccache, Sachur, & Sergent, 2006). That is, you experience your brain regions' output as conscious awareness. Studying people with brain injuries, who are sometimes unaware of their deficits (that is, the consciousness-related problems that arise from their injuries), supports this idea. For instance, a

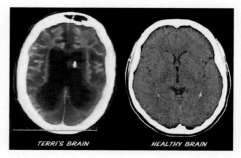

(a)

(b)

FIGURE 5.4 Persistent Vegetative State versus Minimally Conscious State (a) Terri Schiavo spent more than 15 years in a persistent vegetative state before she was taken off life support. Her parents and their supporters believed she showed some awareness. As the dark areas of the brain scan on the left indicate, however, there was no activity in Schiavo's brain because her cortex had deteriorated beyond recovery. By using imaging to examine the brain of a person in an apparent coma, doctors can determine whether the patient is a good candidate for treatment. **(b)** Jan Grzebski was in a minimally conscious state for 19 years before he awoke and reported that he had in fact been aware of events around him. **Suppose you were trapped in a minimally conscious state for even half that time. How might you respond to the world after regaining full consciousness?**

person who has vision problems caused by an eye injury will know about those problems because the brain's visual areas will notice something is wrong. But if that same person then suffers damage to the brain's visual areas so that they stop delivering output, the person may have no visual information to consider and thus will not be aware of vision problems. Of course, if the person suddenly becomes blind, that person will know he or she cannot see. But a person who loses part of the visual field because of a brain injury tends not to notice the gap in visual experience. This tendency appears with hemineglect, for example (see Figure 3.22). A hemineglect patient is not aware of missing part of the visual world. In one patient's words, "I knew the word 'neglect' was a sort of medical term for whatever was wrong but the word bothered me because you only neglect something that is actually there, don't you? If it's not there, how can you neglect it?" (Halligan & Marshall, 1998, p. 360). The hemineglect patients' unawareness of their visual deficits supports the idea that consciousness arises through the brain processes active at any point in time.

Most importantly, the global workspace model presents no single area of the brain as responsible for general "awareness." Rather, different areas of the brain deal with different types of information. Each of these systems in turn is responsible for conscious awareness of its type of information (**Figure 5.6**). From this perspective, consciousness is the mechanism that makes us actively aware of information and that prioritizes what information we need or want to deal with at any moment.

THE SPLIT BRAIN Studying people who have undergone brain surgery has given researchers a better understanding of the conscious mind. On rare occasions, for example, epilepsy does not respond to modern medications. Surgeons may then remove the part of the brain in which the epileptic seizures begin. Another strategy, pioneered in the 1940s and still practiced on occasion when other interventions have failed, is to cut connections within the brain to try to isolate the site where the seizures begin. After the procedure, a seizure that begins at that site is less likely to spread throughout the cortex.

The major connection between the hemispheres that may readily be cut without damaging the gray matter is the massive fiber bundle called the corpus callosum (see Figure 3.20). When the corpus callosum is severed, the brain's halves are almost completely isolated from each other. The resulting condition is called **split brain.** This surgical procedure has provided many important insights into the basic organization and specialized functions of each brain hemisphere (**Figure 5.7**).

What is it like to have your brain split in half? Perhaps the most obvious thing about split-brain patients after their operations is how normal they are. Unlike patients after other types of brain surgery, split-brain patients have no immediately apparent problems. In fact, some early investigations suggested the surgery had not affected the patients in any discernible way. They could walk normally, talk normally, think clearly, and interact socially. In the 1960s, this book's coauthor Michael Gazzaniga, working with the Nobel laureate Roger Sperry, conducted a series of tests on the first split-brain patients. The results were stunning: Just as the brain had been split in two, so had the mind!

As discussed in Chapter 4, images from the visual field's left side (left half of what you are looking at) go to the right hemisphere. Images from the visual field's right side go to the left hemisphere. The left hemisphere also controls the right hand, and the right hemisphere controls the left hand. With a split-brain patient, these divisions enable researchers to provide information to, and receive information from, a single hemisphere at a time (**Figure 5.8**).

Psychologists have long known that in most people the left hemisphere is dominant for language. If a split-brain patient sees two pictures flashed on a

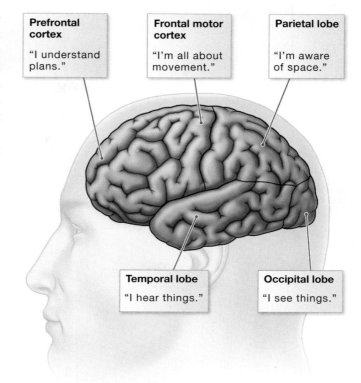

Prefrontal cortex
"I understand plans."

Frontal motor cortex
"I'm all about movement."

Parietal lobe
"I'm aware of space."

Temporal lobe
"I hear things."

Occipital lobe
"I see things."

FIGURE 5.6 Areas of Awareness A central theme emerging from cognitive neuroscience is that awareness of different aspects of the world is associated with functioning in different parts of the brain. This simplified diagram indicates major areas of awareness.

split brain A condition in which the corpus callosum is surgically cut and the two hemispheres of the brain do not receive information directly from each other.

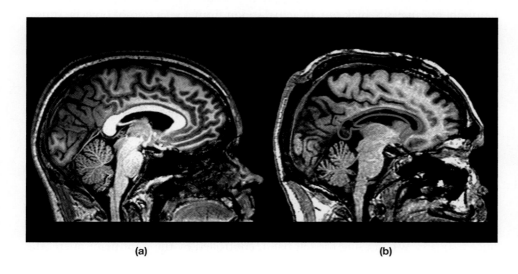

(a)   (b)

FIGURE 5.7 Split Brain (a) This image shows the brain of a normal person whose corpus callosum is intact. **(b)** This image shows the brain of a patient whose corpus callosum has been removed (as indicated by the red outline). With the corpus callosum removed, the two hemispheres of the brain are almost completely separated.

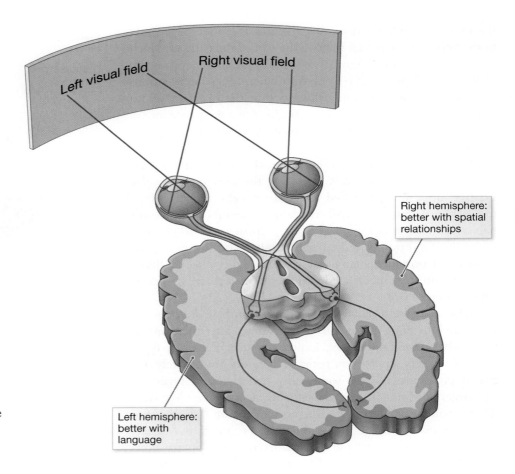

FIGURE 5.8 Visual Input Images from the left side go to the brain's right hemisphere. Images from the right side go to the left hemisphere.

Right hemisphere: better with spatial relationships

Left hemisphere: better with language

Left visual field

Right visual field

screen briefly and simultaneously—one to the visual field's right side and one to the left side—the patient will report that only the picture on the right was shown. Why is this? The left hemisphere (or "left brain"), with its control over speech, sees only the picture on the right side. It is the only picture a person with a split brain can talk about. In many patients, the right hemisphere has no discernable language capacity. The mute right hemisphere (or "right brain"), having seen the picture on the left, is unable to articulate a response. The right brain can act on its perception, however: If the picture on the left was of a spoon, the right hemisphere can easily pick out an actual spoon from a selection of objects. It uses the left hand, which is controlled by the right hemisphere. Still, the left hemisphere does not know what the right one saw. Splitting the brain, then, produces two half brains. Each half has its own perceptions, thoughts, and consciousness (**Figure 5.9**).

In some patients, the right hemisphere displays rudimentary language comprehension, such as the ability to read simple words. Such right hemisphere language capabilities tend to improve in the years following the split-brain operation. Presumably, the right hemisphere attains communication skills that were not needed when that hemisphere was connected to the fluent left brain.

Normally, the competencies of each hemisphere complement those of the other. The left brain is generally hopeless at spatial relationships. In one experiment, a split-brain participant is given a pile of blocks and a drawing of a simple arrangement in which to put them. For example, the participant needs to produce a square. When using the left hand, controlled by the right hemisphere, the

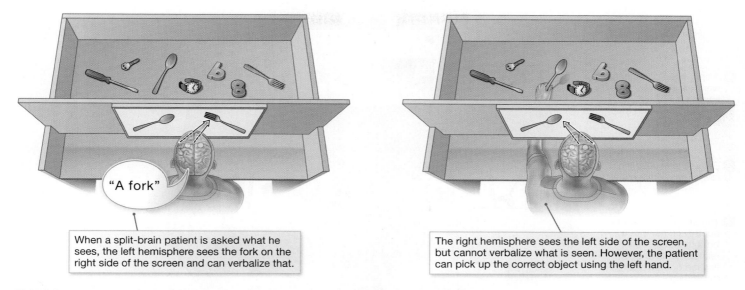

When a split-brain patient is asked what he sees, the left hemisphere sees the fork on the right side of the screen and can verbalize that.

"A fork"

The right hemisphere sees the left side of the screen, but cannot verbalize what is seen. However, the patient can pick up the correct object using the left hand.

FIGURE 5.9 Split-Brain Experiment: The Left Hemisphere versus the Right Hemisphere

participant arranges the blocks effortlessly. When using the right hand, controlled by the left brain, the participant produces only an incompetent, meandering attempt. During this dismal performance, the right brain presumably grows frustrated, because it makes the left hand try to slip in and help!

THE INTERPRETER Another interesting dimension to the relationship between the brain's hemispheres is how they work together to reconstruct our experiences. This collaboration can be demonstrated by asking a disconnected left hemisphere what it thinks about previous behavior that has been produced by the right hemisphere. In one such experiment, the split-brain patient sees different images flash simultaneously on the left and right sides of a screen. Below those images is a row of other images. The patient is asked to point with each hand to a bottom image that is most related to the image flashed on that side of the screen above. In one such study, a picture of a chicken claw was flashed to the left hemisphere. A picture of a snow scene was flashed to the right hemisphere. In response, the left hemisphere pointed the right hand at a picture of a chicken head. The right hemisphere pointed the left hand at a picture of a snow shovel. The (speaking) left hemisphere could have no idea what the right hemisphere had seen. When the participant was asked why he pointed to those pictures, he (or, rather, his left hemisphere) calmly replied, "Oh, that's simple. The chicken claw goes with the chicken, and you need a shovel to clean out the chicken shed." The left hemisphere evidently had interpreted the left hand's response in a manner consistent with the left brain's knowledge (**Figure 5.10**).

The left hemisphere's propensity to construct a world that makes sense is called the **interpreter.** This term means that the left hemisphere is interpreting what the right hemisphere has done (Gazzaniga, 2000). In this last example, the left hemisphere interpreter created a ready way to explain the left hand's action. The left hand was controlled by the disconnected right hemisphere. The left hemisphere's explanation, however, was unrelated to the right hemisphere's real reason for commanding that action. Yet to the patient, the movement seemed perfectly plausible once the action had been interpreted. Usually, the interpreter's

interpreter A term specific to the left hemisphere; refers to the left hemisphere's attempts to make sense of actions and ongoing events.

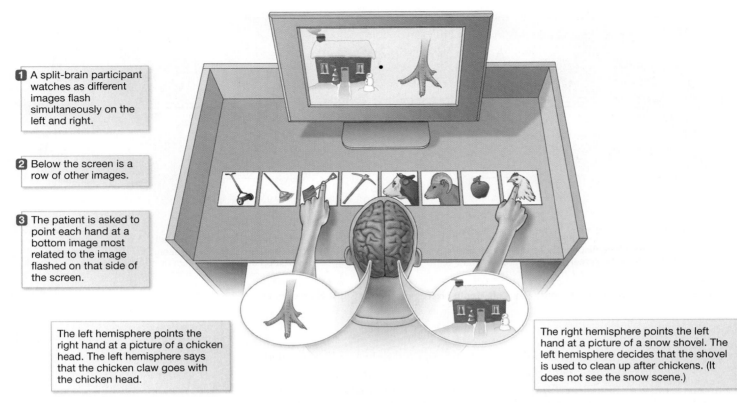

1 A split-brain participant watches as different images flash simultaneously on the left and right.

2 Below the screen is a row of other images.

3 The patient is asked to point each hand at a bottom image most related to the image flashed on that side of the screen.

The left hemisphere points the right hand at a picture of a chicken head. The left hemisphere says that the chicken claw goes with the chicken head.

The right hemisphere points the left hand at a picture of a snow shovel. The left hemisphere decides that the shovel is used to clean up after chickens. (It does not see the snow scene.)

FIGURE 5.10 The Left Hemisphere Interpreter On the basis of limited information, the left hemisphere attempts to explain behavior governed by the right hemisphere.

explanations come readily. In fact, Jeffrey Cooney and Michael Gazzaniga (2003) explain hemineglect by arguing that the left hemisphere interpreter can make sense only of available information. Even though normally sighted people might find the hemineglect patients' attitude bizarre, the hemineglect patients see their particular limited visual states as perfectly normal. To give another example: If the command *Stand up* is flashed to a split-brain patient's right hemisphere, the patient will stand up. But when asked why he or she has stood up, the patient will not reply, "You just told me to," because the command is not available to the (speaking) left hemisphere. Instead, unaware of the command, the patient will say something like, "I just felt like getting a soda." The left hemisphere is compelled to concoct a story that explains, or interprets, the patient's action after it has occurred.

Such interpretation does not always happen instantly. Sometimes it takes the patient's left hemisphere as long to figure out why the left hand is acting as it would take an outside observer. In one session, Gazzaniga and his colleagues presented the word *phone* to the right hemisphere of patient J.W. and asked him to verbalize what he saw. J.W. replied that he did not see anything. Of course, J.W. was speaking from his left hemisphere, which did not see the word *phone,* and his right hemisphere was mute. When a pen was placed in his left hand, however, and he was asked to draw what he saw, J.W. immediately started drawing a phone. Outside observers who had not seen the word *phone* took some time to make out what J.W. was drawing. J.W.'s left hemisphere had the same difficulty in interpreting the drawing. Fortunately, J.W. tended to articulate what he was thinking. He was initially confused by what he was drawing and started guessing about what it was. Not until the picture was almost complete did the outside observers, including J.W.'s left hemisphere, understand what his left hand was drawing. At that point, J.W. exclaimed, "Duh, it's a phone!" The communication between the hemispheres occurred on the paper and not within his head. J.W.'s right hemisphere drew what it saw. After viewing the drawing, his left hemisphere identified it as a phone. In the meantime, his interpreter struggled to guess what his hand was drawing.

THE INTERPRETER SPECULATES The interpreter strongly influences the way we view and remember the world. Say that normal participants are shown a series of pictures that form a story. Later, these same participants are shown another group of pictures and are asked to identify which pictures they had seen previously. They will have a strong tendency to falsely "recognize" pictures consistent with the theme of the original series and to reject those inconsistent with the theme. The left brain, then, tends to "compress" its experiences into a comprehensible story and to reconstruct remembered details based on the gist of that story. The right brain seems simply to experience the world and remember things in a manner less distorted by narrative interpretation.

Sometimes the left brain interpreter makes life more difficult than it needs to be. In one experiment, human or (nonhuman) animal participants must predict, on each trial, whether a red light or a green light will flash. A correct prediction produces some small reward. Both lights flash in a random sequence, but overall the red light flashes 70 percent of the time. Nonhuman participants, such as rats, pretty quickly notice that the red light comes on more often. So to receive the most reward, what strategy do they follow? After doing this task a number of times, most animals simply choose the red light—the most probable response—100 percent of the time. By doing so, they receive rewards on 70 percent of the trials. This strategy makes great sense in terms of adaptiveness, because it guarantees that the animals receive the maximum rewards. Humans do something much different, however. They try to figure out patterns in the way the lights flash, and they choose the red light about 70 percent of the time. That is, overall their choices match the frequency of how often red flashes. Because the lights flash randomly, humans may choose incorrectly on any given trial. Indeed, when humans choose the red light 70 percent of the time, they generally receive rewards on only 58 percent of the trials.

Why do humans not follow the optimal strategy, which even rats can figure out? According to George Wolford and colleagues (2000), the left hemisphere interpreter leads people to search for patterns that might not even exist. To test this idea, the researchers had two split-brain patients perform a version of the task described in the previous paragraph. The patients' right hemispheres tended to respond in the optimal way that animals did, choosing the same thing 100 percent of the time. The patients' left hemispheres chose red only 70 percent of the time. The left hemisphere interpreter's tendency to seek relationships between things may be adaptive in some contexts, but it can produce less-than-optimal outcomes when such relationships (e.g., patterns) do not exist.

The split brain is a rare condition, of course, and nearly all people have two hemispheres that communicate and cooperate on the tasks of daily living. The popular media have sometimes exaggerated the findings of this research. They have suggested that certain people are "left brain" logical types and others are "right brain" artistic types. It is true that the hemispheres are specialized for certain functions, such as language or spatial navigation. Still, most cognitive processes involve the coordinated efforts of both hemispheres.

Unconscious Processing Influences Behavior

Before reading further, think of your phone number. If you are familiar enough with the number, you probably remembered it quickly. Yet you have no idea how your brain worked this magic. That is, you do not have direct access to the neural or cognitive processes that lead to your thoughts and behavior. You thought about your phone number, and (if the magic worked) the number popped into your consciousness.

This brief exercise illustrates a central property of consciousness: We are aware of some mental processes and not aware of others. Over the last several decades, many researchers have explored different ways in which unconscious cues, or **subliminal perception,** can influence cognition. Subliminal perception refers to stimuli that get processed by sensory systems but, because of their short durations or subtle forms, do not reach consciousness.

Advertisers have long been accused of using subliminal cues to persuade people to purchase products (**Figure 5.11**). The evidence suggests that subliminal messages have quite small effects on purchasing behavior (Greenwald, 1992). Material presented subliminally can influence how people think, however, even if it has little or no effect on complex actions. (Buying something you did not intend to buy would count as a complex action.) That is, considerable evidence indicates that people are affected by events—stimuli—they are not aware of (Gladwell, 2005). In one study, participants exerted greater physical effort when large images of money were flashed at them, even though the flashes were so brief the participants did not report seeing the money (Pessiglione et al., 2007). The subliminal images of money also produced brain activity in areas of the limbic system, which is involved in emotion and motivation. Subliminal cues may be most powerful when they work on people's motivational states. For example, flashing the word *thirst* may prove more effective than flashing the explicit directive *Buy Coke*. Indeed, researchers found that subliminal presentation of the word *thirst* led participants to drink more Kool-Aid, especially when they were actually thirsty (Strahan, Spencer, & Zanna, 2002).

Other events can influence our thoughts without our awareness. In a classic experiment by the social psychologists Richard Nisbett and Timothy Wilson (1977), the participants were asked to examine word pairs, such as *ocean-moon,* that had obvious semantic associations between the words. They were then asked to free-associate on other, single words, such as *detergent.* Nisbett and Wilson wanted to find out the degree, if any, to which the word pairs would influence the free associations. And if the influence occurred, would the participants be conscious of it? When given the word *detergent* after the word pair *ocean-moon,* participants typically free-associated the word *tide.* However, when asked why they said "tide," they usually gave reasons citing the detergent's brand name, such as "My mom used Tide when I was a kid." They were not aware that the word pair had influenced their thoughts. Here again, the left hemisphere interpreter was at work, making sense of a situation and providing a plausible explanation for cognitive events when complete information was not available. We are,

subliminal perception The processing of information by sensory systems without conscious awareness.

FIGURE 5.11 Try for Yourself: Subliminal Perception

Try to pick out the subliminal message in the advertisement below.

Break out the frosty bottle

GILBEYS
LONDON DRY
GIN

and keep your
tonics dry!

Answer: The ice cubes spell out S-E-X.

of course, frequently unaware of the many different influences on our thoughts, feelings, and behaviors. Similar effects underlie the classic mistake called a *Freudian slip,* in which an unconscious thought is suddenly expressed at an inappropriate time or in an inappropriate social context.

To study the power of unconscious influences, John Bargh and colleagues (1996) supplied participants with different groups of words. Some of the participants received words associated with the elderly, such as *old, Florida,* and *wrinkles.* The participants were asked to make sentences out of the supplied words. After they had made up a number of sentences, they were told the experiment was over. But the researchers continued observing the participants. They wanted to know whether the unconscious activation of beliefs about the elderly would influence the participants' behavior. Indeed, participants primed with stereotypes about old people walked much more slowly than did those who had been given words unrelated to the elderly. When questioned later, the slow-walking participants were not aware that the concept of "elderly" had been activated or that it had changed their behavior.

Other researchers have obtained similar findings. For instance, Ap Dijksterhuis and Ad van Knippenberg (1998) found that people at Nijmegen University, in the Netherlands, were better at answering trivia questions when they were subtly presented with information about "professors" than when they were subtly presented with information about "soccer hooligans." The participants were unaware that their behavior was influenced by the information. Such findings indicate that much of our behavior occurs without our awareness or intention (Bargh & Morsella, 2008; Dijksterhuis & Aarts, 2010).

THE SMART UNCONSCIOUS Common sense tells us that consciously thinking about a problem or deliberating about the options is the best strategy for making a decision. Consider the possibility that *not* consciously thinking can produce an outcome superior to that of consciously thinking. In a study by Ap Dijksterhuis (2004), participants evaluated complex information regarding real-world choices. One situation involved selecting an apartment. In each case, the participants chose between alternatives that had negative features (e.g., high rent, bad location) and positive features (e.g., nice landlord, good view). Objectively, one apartment was the best choice. Some participants were required to make an immediate choice (no thought). Some had to think for 3 minutes and then choose (conscious thought). Others had to work for 3 minutes on a difficult, distracting task and then choose (unconscious thought). Across three separate trials, those in the unconscious thought condition made the best decisions. According to Dijksterhuis and Nordgren (2006), unconscious processing is especially valuable for complex decisions in which it is difficult to weigh the pros and cons consciously. Perhaps this is why, for very important decisions, people often choose to "sleep on it." (Chapter 8, "Thinking and Intelligence," will return to this idea in discussing problem solving strategies.)

Consider also the possibility that consciously thinking can undermine good decision making. The social psychologist Tim Wilson and the cognitive psychologist Jonathan Schooler (1991) asked research participants to rate jams. When the participants simply tasted the jams, their ratings were very similar to experts' ratings. However, when the participants had to explain their ratings jam by jam, their ratings differed substantially from the experts'. Unless the experts were wrong, the participants had made poorer judgments: Having to reflect consciously about their reasons apparently altered their perceptions of the jams.

Learning Objectives

- Describe the stages of sleep.
- Identify common sleep disorders.
- Discuss the functions of sleeping and dreaming.

circadian rhythms The regulation of biological cycles into regular patterns.

5.2 What Is Sleep?

At regular intervals, the brain does a strange thing: It goes to sleep. A common misconception is that the brain shuts itself down during sleep. Nothing could be further from the truth. Many brain regions are more active during sleep than during wakefulness. It is even possible that some complex thinking, such as working on difficult problems, occurs in the sleeping brain (Walker & Stickgold, 2006).

Sleep is part of the normal rhythm of life. Brain activity and other physiological processes are regulated into patterns known as **circadian rhythms.** (*Circadian* roughly translates to "about a day.") For example, body temperature, hormone levels, and sleep/wake cycles operate according to circadian rhythms. Regulated by a biological clock, circadian rhythms are influenced by the cycles of light and dark. Humans and nonhuman animals continue to show these rhythms, however, when removed from light cues.

Multiple brain regions are involved in producing and maintaining circadian rhythms and sleep. For instance, information about light detected by the eyes is sent to a small region of the hypothalamus called the *suprachiasmatic nucleus*. This region then sends signals to a tiny structure called the *pineal gland* (**Figure 5.12**). The pineal gland may then secrete *melatonin,* a hormone that travels through the bloodstream and affects various receptors in the body, including the brain. Bright light suppresses the production of melatonin, whereas darkness triggers its release. Researchers recently have noted that taking melatonin can help people cope with jet lag and shift work, both of which interfere with circadian rhythms. Taking melatonin also appears to help people fall asleep, although it is unclear why this happens.

The average person sleeps around 8 hours per night, but individuals differ tremendously in the number of hours they sleep. Infants sleep much of the day. People tend to sleep less as they age. Some adults report needing 9 or 10 hours of sleep a night to feel rested, whereas others report needing only an hour or two a night. It might be that your genes influence the amount of sleep you need, as researchers have identified a gene that influences sleep (Koh et al., 2008). Called *SLEEPLESS,* this gene regulates a protein that, like many anesthetics, reduces action potentials in the brain. Loss of this protein leads to an 80 percent reduction in sleep. But people's sleep habits can be quite extreme. When a 70-year-old retired nurse, Miss M., reported sleeping only an hour a night, researchers were skeptical. On her first two nights in a research laboratory, Miss M. was unable to sleep, apparently because of the excitement. But on her third night, she slept for only 99 minutes, then awoke refreshed, cheerful, and full of energy (Meddis, 1977). You might like the idea of sleeping so little and having all those extra hours of spare time, but most of us do not function well on so little sleep. And as discussed in later chapters, sufficient sleep is important for memory and good health and is often affected by psychological disorders, such as depression.

Sleep Is an Altered State of Consciousness

The difference between being awake and being asleep has as much to do with conscious experience as with biological processes. When you sleep, you are not fully conscious. Your conscious experience of the outside world is largely turned off. To some extent, however, you remain aware of your surroundings and your brain still processes information. Your mind is analyzing potential dangers, controlling body movements, and shifting body parts to maximize comfort. For this reason, people who sleep next to children or to pets tend not to roll over onto them. Nor do most people fall out of bed while sleeping—in this case, the brain is aware of at least the edges of the bed. (Because the ability to not fall out of bed when asleep is learned or perhaps develops with age, infant cribs have side rails and young children may need bed rails when they transition from crib to bed.)

Before the development of objective methods to assess brain activity, most people believed the brain went to sleep along with the rest of the body. In the 1920s, researchers invented the electroencephalograph, or EEG. As discussed in Chapter 2, this machine measures the brain's electrical activity. When people are awake, they

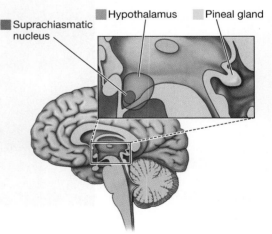

FIGURE 5.12 The Pineal Gland and the Sleep/Wake Cycle Changes in light register in the suprachiasmatic nucleus of the hypothalamus. In response, this region signals the pineal gland when the time for sleep or the time for wakefulness has come.

have many different sources of sensory activity. As a result, the neurons in their brains are extremely active. The EEG shows this activity as short, frequent, irregular brain signals known as *beta waves* (shown in **Figure 5.13**). When people really focus their attention on something or when they close their eyes and relax, brain activity slows and becomes more regular. This pattern produces *alpha waves*.

STAGES OF SLEEP As evidenced by changes in EEG readings, sleep occurs in stages (see Figure 5.13). When you drift off to sleep, you enter stage 1. Here, the EEG shows *theta waves*. You can easily be aroused from stage 1, and if awakened, you will probably deny that you were sleeping. In this light sleep, you might see fantastical images or geometric shapes. You might have the sensation of falling or that your limbs are jerking. As you progress to stage 2, your breathing becomes more regular, and you become less sensitive to external stimulation. You are now really asleep. Although the EEG continues to show theta waves, it also shows occasional bursts of activity called *sleep spindles* and large waves called *K-complexes*. Some researchers believe that these bursts are signals from brain mechanisms involved with shutting out the external world and keeping people asleep (Steriade, 1992). Two findings indicate that the brain must work to maintain sleep. First, abrupt noise can trigger K-complexes. Second, as people age and sleep more lightly, their EEGs show fewer sleep spindles.

The progression to deep sleep occurs through stages 3 and 4, which nowadays are typically seen as one stage because their brain activity is nearly identical (Silber et al., 2007). This period is marked by large, regular brain patterns called *delta waves*, and it is often referred to as *slow-wave sleep*. People in slow-wave sleep are very hard to wake and often very disoriented when they do wake up. People still process some information in slow-wave sleep, however, because the mind continues to evaluate the environment for potential danger. For example, parents in slow-wave sleep can be aroused by their children's cries. Yet they can blissfully

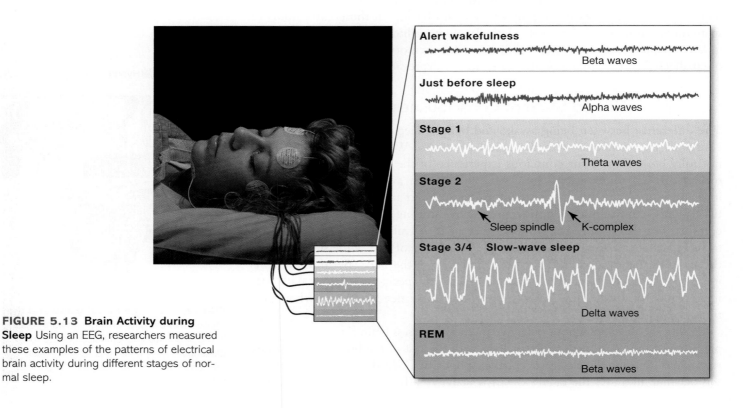

FIGURE 5.13 Brain Activity during Sleep Using an EEG, researchers measured these examples of the patterns of electrical brain activity during different stages of normal sleep.

ignore sounds, such as sirens or traffic noise, that are louder than the crying children but are not necessarily relevant.

REM SLEEP After about 90 minutes of sleep, the sleep cycle reverses, returning to stage 1. At this point, the EEG suddenly shows a flurry of beta wave activity that usually represents an awake, alert mind. The eyes dart back and forth rapidly beneath closed eyelids. Because of these *rapid eye movements,* this stage is called **REM sleep.** It is sometimes called *paradoxical sleep* because of the paradox of a sleeping body with an active brain. Indeed, some neurons in the brain, especially in the occipital cortex and brain stem regions, are more active during REM sleep than during waking hours. But while the brain is active during REM episodes, most of the body's muscles are paralyzed. At the same time, the body shows signs of genital arousal: Most males of all ages develop erections, and most females of all ages experience clitoral engorgement.

REM sleep is psychologically significant because of its relation to dreaming. About 80 percent of the time when people are awakened during REM sleep, they report dreaming, compared with less than half of the time during non-REM sleep (Solms, 2000). As discussed later, the dreams differ between these two types of sleep.

Over the course of a typical night's sleep, the cycle repeats about five times. The sleeper progresses from slow-wave sleep through to REM sleep, then back to slow-wave sleep and through to REM sleep (**Figure 5.14**). As morning approaches, the sleep cycle becomes shorter, and the sleeper spends relatively more time in REM sleep. People briefly awaken many times during the night, but they do not remember these awakenings in the morning. As people age, they sometimes have more difficulty going back to sleep after awakening.

SLEEP DISORDERS Sleep problems are relatively common throughout life. Nearly everyone occasionally has trouble falling asleep, but for some people the inability to sleep causes significant problems in their daily lives. **Insomnia** is a sleep disorder in which people's mental health and ability to function are compromised by their inability to sleep. Indeed, chronic insomnia is associated with diminished psychological well-being, including feelings of depression (Bootzin & Epstein, 2011; Hamilton et al., 2007). An estimated 12 percent to 20 percent of adults have persistent insomnia; it is more common in women than in men and in older adults than in younger adults (Espie, 2002; Ram, Seirawan, Kumar, & Clark, 2010). One factor that complicates the estimation of how many people have insomnia is that many people who believe

REM sleep The stage of sleep marked by rapid eye movements, dreaming, and paralysis of motor systems.

insomnia A disorder characterized by an inability to sleep.

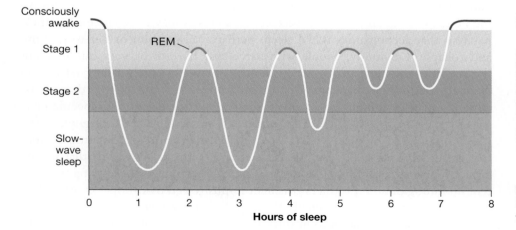

FIGURE 5.14 Stages of Sleep This chart illustrates the normal stages of sleep over the course of the night.

obstructive sleep apnea A disorder in which a person, while asleep, stops breathing because his or her throat closes; the condition results in frequent awakenings during the night.

narcolepsy A sleep disorder in which people experience excessive sleepiness during normal waking hours, sometimes going limp and collapsing.

FIGURE 5.15 Obstructive Sleep Apnea This man suffers from obstructive sleep apnea. Throughout the night, a continuous positive airway pressure device blows air into his nose or mouth to keep his throat open.

they are poor sleepers overestimate how long it takes them to fall asleep and often underestimate how much sleep they get on a typical night. For instance, some people experience *pseudoinsomnia,* in which they basically dream they are not sleeping. Their EEGs would indicate sleep. But if you roused them, they would claim to have been awake.

In an odd twist, a major cause of insomnia is worrying about sleep. When people experience this kind of insomnia, they may be tired enough to sleep. As they try to fall asleep, however, they worry about whether they will get to sleep and may even panic about how a lack of sleep will affect them. This anxiety leads to heightened arousal, which interferes with normal sleep patterns. To overcome these effects, many people take sleeping pills, which may work in the short run but can cause significant problems down the road. People may come to depend on the pills to help them sleep. Then if they try to stop taking the pills, they may lie awake wondering whether they can get to sleep on their own. According to research, the most successful treatment for insomnia combines drug therapy with *cognitive-behavioral therapy* (CBT, discussed in Chapter 15, "Treatment of Psychological Disorders"). CBT helps people overcome their worries about sleep and relieves the need for the drugs, which should be discontinued before the end of therapy (Morin et al., 2009). Other factors that contribute to insomnia include poor sleeping habits. Ways to improve sleeping habits are given in this chapter's "Psychology: Knowledge You Can Use" feature, "Can Sleep Deprivation Hurt Me?" (p. 201).

Another fairly common sleeping problem is **obstructive sleep apnea.** While asleep, a person with this disorder stops breathing for short periods. Basically, the sleeper's throat closes during these periods. In struggling to breathe, the person briefly awakens and gasps for air. Obstructive sleep apnea is most common among middle-aged men and is often associated with obesity, although it is unclear if obesity is the cause or consequence of apnea (Pack & Pien, 2011; Spurr, Graven, & Gilbert, 2008). People with apnea are often unaware of their condition, since the main symptom is loud snoring and they do not remember their frequent awakenings during the night. Yet chronic apnea causes people to have poor sleep, which is associated with daytime fatigue and even problems such as an inability to concentrate while driving. Moreover, apnea is associated with cardiovascular problems and stroke. For serious cases, physicians often prescribe a continuous positive airway pressure (CPAP) device. During sleep, this device blows air into the person's nose or nose and mouth (**Figure 5.15**).

A student who falls asleep during a lecture is likely sleep deprived, but a professor who falls asleep while lecturing is probably experiencing an episode of **narcolepsy.** In this rare disorder, excessive sleepiness occurs during normal waking hours. During an episode of narcolepsy, a person may experience the muscle paralysis that accompanies REM sleep, perhaps causing him or her to go limp and collapse. Obviously, people with narcolepsy have to be very careful about the activities they engage in during the day, as unexpectedly falling asleep can be dangerous or fatal, depending on the situation. Evidence suggests that narcolepsy is a genetic condition that affects the neural transmission of a specific neurotransmitter in the hypothalamus (Chabas, Taheri, Renier, & Mignot, 2003; Nishino, 2007). The most widely used treatments for this condition are drugs that act as stimulants. Researchers have found evidence, however, that narcolepsy may be an autoimmune disorder and that treating it as such (using the protein immunoglobulin) produces excellent results (Cvetkovic-Lopes et al., 2010).

REM behavior disorder is roughly the opposite of narcolepsy. In this condition, the normal paralysis that accompanies REM sleep is disabled. Sufferers act out their dreams while sleeping, often striking their sleeping partners. No treatment exists for this rare sleep disorder. The condition is caused by a neurological deficit and is most often seen in elderly males.

By contrast, sleepwalking is most common among young children. Technically called *somnambulism,* this relatively common behavior occurs during slow-wave sleep, typically within the first hour or two after falling asleep. During an episode, the person is glassy-eyed and seems disconnected from other people and/or the surroundings. No harm is done if the sleepwalker wakes up during the episode. Being gently walked back to bed is safer for the sleepwalker than being left to wander around and potentially get hurt.

Sleep Is an Adaptive Behavior

In terms of adaptiveness, sleep might seem illogical. Tuning out the external world during sleep can be dangerous and thus a threat to survival. Beyond that, humans might have advanced themselves in countless ways if they had used all their time productively rather than wasting it by sleeping. But people cannot override indefinitely the desire to sleep. Eventually, our bodies shut down and we sleep whether we want to or not.

Why do we sleep? Some animals, such as some frogs, never exhibit a state that can be considered sleep (Siegel, 2008). Most animals sleep, however, even if they have peculiar sleeping styles. (For example, some dolphin species have *unihemispherical sleep,* in which the cerebral hemispheres take turns sleeping.) Sleep must serve an important biological purpose. Researchers have proposed three general explanations for sleep's adaptiveness: *restoration, circadian rhythms,* and *facilitation of learning.*

RESTORATION AND SLEEP DEPRIVATION According to the *restorative theory,* sleep allows the body, including the brain, to rest and repair itself. Various kinds of evidence support this theory: After people engage in vigorous physical activity, such as running a marathon, they generally sleep longer than usual. Growth hormone, released only during deep sleep, facilitates the repair of damaged tissue. Sleep apparently enables the brain to replenish energy stores and also strengthens the immune system (Hobson, 1999).

Numerous laboratory studies have examined sleep deprivation's effects on physical and cognitive performance. Surprisingly, most studies find that two or three days of sleep deprivation have little effect on strength, athletic ability, or the performance of complex tasks. When deprived of sleep, however, people find it difficult to perform quiet tasks, such as reading. They find it nearly impossible to perform boring or mundane tasks.

A long period of sleep deprivation causes mood problems and decreases cognitive performance. People who suffer from chronic sleep deprivation may experience attention lapses and reduced short-term memory. Studies using rats have found that extended sleep deprivation compromises the immune system and leads to death. Sleep deprivation is also dangerous and potentially disastrous because it makes people prone to *microsleeps,* in which they fall asleep during the day for periods ranging from a few seconds to a minute (Coren, 1996).

Sleep deprivation might serve one very useful purpose: When people are suffering from depression, depriving them of sleep sometimes alleviates their depression. This effect appears to occur because sleep deprivation leads to increased activation of serotonin receptors, as do drugs used to treat depression

FIGURE 5.16 Sleeping Predator After a fresh kill, a lion may sleep for days.

(Benedetti et al., 1999; the treatment of depression is discussed in Chapter 15, "Treatment of Psychological Disorders"). For people who are not suffering from depression, however, sleep deprivation is more likely to produce negative moods than positive ones.

CIRCADIAN RHYTHMS The *circadian rhythm theory* proposes that sleep has evolved to keep animals quiet and inactive during times of the day when there is greatest danger, usually when it is dark. According to this theory, animals need only a limited amount of time each day to accomplish the necessities of survival, and it is adaptive for them to spend the remainder of the time inactive, preferably hidden. Thus an animal's typical amount of sleep depends on how much time that animal needs to obtain food, how easily it can hide, and how vulnerable it is to attack. Small animals tend to sleep a lot. Large animals vulnerable to attack, such as cows and deer, sleep little. Large predatory animals that are not vulnerable sleep a lot (**Figure 5.16**). We humans depend greatly on vision for survival. We are adapted to sleeping at night because our early ancestors were more at risk in the dark.

FACILITATION OF LEARNING Scientists have also proposed that sleep is important because it is involved in the strengthening of neural connections that serve as the basis of learning. The general idea is that circuits wired together during the waking period are consolidated, or strengthened, during sleep (Wilson & McNaughton, 1994). When research participants sleep after learning, their recall is better than in control conditions where participants remain awake (Drosopoulos, Schulze, Fischer, & Born, 2007). Robert Stickgold and colleagues (2000) conducted a study in which participants had to learn a complex task. After finding that participants improved at the task only if they had slept for at least 6 hours following training, the researchers argued that learning the task required neural changes that normally occur only during sleep. Both slow-wave sleep and REM sleep appear to be important for learning to take place, but people may be especially likely to perform better if they dream about the task while sleeping. In one study, participants learned how to run a complex maze. Those who then slept for 90 minutes went on to perform better on the maze. Those who dreamed about the maze, however, performed much better (Wamsley, Tucker, Payne, Benavides, & Stickgold, 2010).

Indeed, there is some evidence that students experience more REM sleep during exam periods, when a greater mental consolidation of information might be expected to take place (Smith & Lapp, 1991). The argument that sleep, especially REM sleep, promotes the development of brain circuits for learning is also supported by the changes in sleep patterns that occur over the life course. Infants and the very young, who learn an incredible amount in a few years, sleep the most and also spend the most time in REM sleep.

Findings linking sleep to learning should give caution to students whose main style of studying is the all-nighter. In one recent study, students who were sleep deprived for one night showed reduced activity the next day in the hippocampus, a brain area essential for memory (Yoo, Hu, Gujar, Jolesz, & Walker, 2007). These sleep-deprived students also showed poorer memory at subsequent testing. According to the investigators, there is substantial evidence that sleep does more than consolidate memories. Sleep also seems to prepare the brain for its memory needs for the next day.

Can Sleep Deprivation Hurt Me?

College students are incredibly busy. They juggle their academic work with extracurricular activities, jobs, volunteer positions, social calendars, and family commitments. Obligations seemingly expand beyond the available hours in a day. Not surprisingly, many students steal hours from their sleep in hope of making room for all the to-dos (**Figure 5.17**). Is cutting back on sleep a healthy strategy for fitting it all in? Psychological research says, emphatically, no.

Sleep deprivation poses risks to mind, body, and spirit. It undermines your ability to think and solve problems, interferes with memory, and makes it more difficult to concentrate. Sleep deprivation also interferes with your body's hunger signals, contributing to overeating and weight gain (late-night pizza run, anyone?). It impairs your motor abilities, contributing to accidents and injuries. Moreover, sleep deprivation increases anxiety, depression, and distress. In addition—to add insult to injury—others perceive us as less attractive when we are sleep deprived, compared with when we are well rested (Axelsson et al., 2010).

In short, if you restrict your amount of sleep so that you can study more, you are setting yourself up for poor mental health, poor physical health, and an academic struggle. Yet you have to do the work and accomplish all your other tasks. What are your options?

If you voluntarily skip sleep, think about the facts just presented. Perhaps just knowing the potential impact of your decision will help you modify your behavior. Then again, you might find these specific strategies helpful:

1. **Plan.** Create a weekly calendar. Use it to schedule your classes, study time, social time, exercise, down time, and so on. Honestly estimate the amount of time it will take you to complete tasks. Schedule sufficient time for each task in your calendar.

2. **Know your priorities.** There will be times when your schedule simply cannot accommodate all the to-dos. When you are so pressed for time, you will need to make decisions about what to cut. Knowing your priorities can help you make those decisions. If doing well on your biology exam is a top priority, consider skipping the party that weekend. Yes, your decision will have consequences (you might miss your friend's crazy antics), but knowing your priorities will make it easier to accept those consequences.

3. **Stick to the plan.** Procrastination can wreak havoc on your sleep. If you find yourself procrastinating on important tasks, consider working with a mental health practitioner to figure out why you procrastinate and how you might overcome this tendency.

4. **Practice saying no.** College is a great time to explore the activities available on your campus or in your community, but exploring all those options simultaneously is a recipe for disaster. Be selective.

Of course, sometimes sleep may elude you. Even when you long for sleep as you lie in bed, you may find yourself dog-tired but unable to doze off. In such cases, the strategies described below might help you develop better sleep:

1. **Establish a routine to help set your biological clock.** Every day (including weekends), go to bed at the same time and wake up at the same time. Changing the time you go to bed or wake up each day alters your regular nightly sleep cycle and can disrupt other physiological systems.

2. **Avoid alcohol and caffeine just before going to bed.** Alcohol might help you get to sleep more quickly, but it will interfere with your sleep cycle and most likely cause you to wake up early the next day. Caffeine is a stimulant: It interferes with a chemical (adenosine) that helps you sleep, so it will prevent you from falling asleep.

3. **Exercise regularly.** Regular exercise will help maintain your sleep cycle. Exercising creates arousal that interferes with sleep, however, so do not exercise right before going to bed. But a little stretching before bedtime can help your mind and body relax.

4. **Remember, your bed is for sleeping.** Most of us do not sleep in our kitchens, nor should we eat in our beds. Or watch TV. Or study. Your mind needs to associate your bed with sleeping. The best way to make that association is to use your bed exclusively for sleeping. And maybe a little cuddling.

FIGURE 5.17 Sleep Deprivation Students may try to avoid sleep. Sleep will catch up with them!

(continued)

People Dream while Sleeping

Because **dreams** are the products of an altered state of consciousness, dreaming is one of life's great mysteries. Indeed, no one knows if dreaming serves any biological function. Why does the sleeper's mind conjure up images, fantasies, stories that make little sense, and scenes that ignore physical laws and rules of both time and space? Why does the mind then confuse these conjurings with reality? Why does it sometimes allow them to scare the dreamer awake? Usually, only when people wake up do they realize they have been dreaming. Of course, dreams sometimes incorporate external sounds or other sensory experiences, but this happens without the type of consciousness experienced during wakefulness.

Although some people report that they do not remember their dreams, everyone dreams unless a particular kind of brain injury or a particular kind of medication interferes. In fact, the average person spends six years of his or her life dreaming. If you want to remember your dreams better, you can teach yourself to do so: Keep a pen and paper or a voice recorder next to your bed so you can record your dreams as soon as you wake up. If you wait, you are likely to forget most of them.

REM DREAMS AND NON-REM DREAMS Dreams occur in REM and non-REM sleep, but the dreams' contents differ in the two types of sleep. REM dreams are more likely to be bizarre. They may involve intense emotions, visual and auditory hallucinations (but rarely taste, smell, or pain), and an uncritical acceptance of illogical events. Non-REM dreams are often very dull. They may concern mundane activities such as deciding what clothes to wear or taking notes in class.

The activation and deactivation of different brain regions during REM and non-REM sleep may be responsible for the different types of dreams. During non-REM sleep, there is general deactivation of many brain regions; during REM sleep, some areas of the brain show increased activity, whereas others show decreased activity (Hobson, 2009). The contents of REM dreams result from the activation of brain structures associated with motivation, emotion, and reward (i.e., the amygdala); the activation of visual association areas; and the deactivation of the prefrontal cortex (Schwartz & Maquet, 2002; **Figure 5.18**). As discussed in Chapter 3, the prefrontal cortex is indispensable for self-awareness, reflective thought, and conscious input from the external world. Because this brain region is deactivated during REM dreams, the brain's emotion centers and visual

"Look, don't try to weasel out of this. It was my dream, but you had the affair in it."

dreams Products of an altered state of consciousness in which images and fantasies are confused with reality.

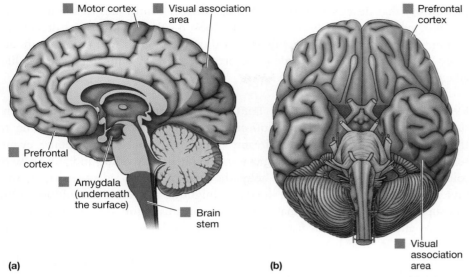

Motor cortex

Visual association area

Prefrontal cortex

Prefrontal cortex

Amygdala (underneath the surface)

Brain stem

Visual association area

(a)

(b)

FIGURE 5.18 Brain Regions and REM Dreams These two views of the brain show the regions that are activated and deactivated during REM sleep. **(a)** As seen here from the side, the motor cortex, the brain stem, and visual association areas are activated, as are brain regions involved in motivation, emotion, and reward (e.g., the amygdala). The prefrontal cortex is deactivated. **(b)** As shown here from below, other visual association areas are activated as well. (This view also reveals the full size of the prefrontal cortex.)

association areas interact without rational thought. Note, however, that REM and dreaming appear to be controlled by different neural signals (Solms, 2000). In other words, REM does not produce the dream state. REM is simply linked with the contents of dreams.

WHAT DO DREAMS MEAN? Sigmund Freud presented one of the first major theories of dreams. According to Freud, dreams contain hidden content that represents unconscious conflicts within the mind of the dreamer. The **manifest content** is the dream the way the dreamer remembers it. The **latent content** is what the dream symbolizes; it is the material disguised to protect the dreamer from confronting a conflict directly. Virtually no support exists for Freud's ideas that dreams represent hidden conflicts and that objects in dreams have special symbolic meanings. Daily life experiences do, however, influence the contents of dreams. For example, you may be especially likely to have dreams with anxious content while studying for exams.

Some dreams have thematic structures. They unfold as events or stories rather than as jumbles of disconnected images. Still, such structures apparently hold no secret meanings. Although most people think their dreams are uniquely their own, many common themes occur in dreams. Have you ever dreamed about showing up for an exam and being unprepared or finding that you are taking the wrong test? Many people in college have dreams like these. Even after you graduate and no longer take exams routinely, you probably will have similar dreams about being unprepared. Retired professors sometimes dream about being unprepared to teach classes!

ACTIVATION-SYNTHESIS THEORY The sleep researchers John Alan Hobson and Robert McCarley proposed a model that has dominated scientific thinking about dreaming. According to Hobson and McCarley's **activation-synthesis theory,** random brain activity occurs during sleep. This neural firing can activate mechanisms that normally interpret sensory input. The sleeping mind tries to make sense of the resulting sensory activity by synthesizing it with stored memories. From this perspective, dreams are the side effects of mental processes produced by random neural firing.

In 2000, Hobson and his colleagues revised the activation-synthesis theory to take into account recent findings in cognitive neuroscience. For instance, they included activation of the limbic regions, associated with emotion and motivation, as the source of dreams' emotional content. They also proposed (as mentioned

manifest content According to Sigmund Freud, the plot of a dream; the way a dream is remembered.

latent content According to Sigmund Freud, what a dream symbolizes; the material that is disguised in a dream to protect the dreamer from confronting a conflict directly.

activation-synthesis theory A theory of dreaming; this theory proposes that the brain tries to make sense of random brain activity that occurs during sleep by synthesizing the activity with stored memories.

previously) that deactivation of the frontal cortices contributes to the delusional and illogical aspects of dreams. Critics of Hobson's theory argue that dreams are seldom as chaotic as might be expected if they were based on random brain activity (Domhoff, 2003). Indeed, most dreams are fairly similar to waking life, albeit with some strange features.

EVOLVED THREAT-REHEARSAL THEORY The neuroscientist Antti Revonsuo (2000) has proposed an evolutionary account of dreaming. According to the *evolved threat-rehearsal theory*, dreams sometimes simulate threatening events so that people can rehearse strategies for coping. In providing individuals with solutions to problems, dreaming helps the human species adapt—that is, survive and reproduce. In this way, dreaming might be the result of evolution. One fact supporting this theory is that most of the dreams reported by people involve negative emotions, such as fear and anxiety. In addition, people tend to dream about threats in their lives and to have nightmares about even long-past traumas. Moreover, dreaming is associated with the activation of limbic structures, such as the amygdala, that are activated by real dangers.

Summing Up

What Is Sleep?

Most animals experience sleep. In this altered state of consciousness, the sleeper loses substantial contact with the external world. Sleep is characterized by stages. Each stage is associated with a unique pattern of electrical activity in the brain, as reflected in EEG readings. Insomnia, sleep apnea, and narcolepsy are among the sleep disorders that have been identified. Dreams occur in both REM sleep and non-REM sleep, but the content of dreams differs between these two types of sleep. This variation may be due to the activation and deactivation of different brain structures during REM sleep and non-REM sleep. A number of theories have been proposed to explain why we sleep and dream. The biological functions of sleeping and dreaming remain unknown.

Measuring Up

1. When people sleep, _____.
   a. the brain shuts down so it can rest
   b. brain activity goes through several cycles of different stages, and each stage has its own characteristic pattern of brain waves
   c. the brain goes into a random pattern of firing that causes dreaming; dreaming is the left hemisphere interpreter making sense of brain activity
   d. REM sleep occurs continuously throughout the sleep period as different types of brain waves determine how deeply we sleep

2. Select the hypothesized reasons why we dream. Select as many as apply.
   a. Dreams get rid of excessive energy that accumulates throughout the day.
   b. Dreams are a way of making sense of neural firing patterns.
   c. Dreams allow us to rehearse coping strategies for anxiety-producing events.
   d. Dreams help us forget information we no longer need to remember.
   e. Dreams restore natural brain waves to their original state.

Answers: 1. b. brain activity goes through several cycles of different stages, and each stage has its own characteristic pattern of brain waves. 2. b. Dreams are a way of making sense of neural firing patterns; c. Dreams allow us to rehearse coping strategies for anxiety-producing events.

5.3 What Is Altered Consciousness?

A person's consciousness varies naturally over the course of the day. Often this variation is due to the person's actions. Watching television might encourage the mind to zone out, whereas learning to play a piece on the piano might focus attention. The following sections discuss three ways of potentially reaching altered states of consciousness: *hypnosis, meditation, and immersion in an action.*

Hypnosis Is Induced through Suggestion

As part of an act, a stage performer or magician might hypnotize audience members and instruct them to perform silly behaviors, such as making animal noises. Has this hypnotist presented a real change in mental state or just good theater? What exactly is hypnosis?

Hypnosis involves a social interaction during which a person, responding to suggestions, experiences changes in memory, perception, and/or voluntary action (Kihlstrom, 1985; Kihlstrom & Eich, 1994). Psychologists generally agree that hypnosis affects some people, but they do not agree on whether it produces a genuinely altered state of consciousness (Jamieson, 2007).

During a hypnotic induction, the hypnotist makes a series of suggestions to at least one person (**Figure 5.19**). "You are becoming sleepy," the hypnotist might say. "Your eyelids are drooping. . . . Your arms and legs feel very heavy." As the listener falls more deeply into the hypnotic state, the hypnotist makes more suggestions. "You cannot move your right arm," "You feel warm," "You want to bark like a dog," and so on. If everything goes according to plan, the listener follows all the suggestions as though they are true. For example, the person really barks like a dog.

Sometimes the hypnotist suggests that, after the hypnosis session, the listener will experience a change in memory, perception, or voluntary action. Such a *posthypnotic suggestion* is usually accompanied by the instruction to not remember the suggestion. For example, a stage performer or magician serving as a hypnotist might suggest, much to the delight of the audience, "When I say the word *dog,* you will stand up and bark like a dog. You will not remember this suggestion." Therapists sometimes hypnotize patients and give them posthypnotic suggestions to help them diet or quit smoking, but evidence suggests that hypnosis has quite modest effects on these behaviors. Evidence clearly indicates, however, that posthypnotic suggestions can at least subtly influence behaviors.

Consider a study of moral judgment conducted by Thalia Wheatley and Jonathan Haidt (2005). Participants in this study received a posthypnotic suggestion to feel a pang of disgust whenever they read a certain word. The word itself was neutral (e.g., the word *often*). Subsequently, participants made more-severe moral judgments when reading stories that included the word, even when the stories were innocuous. Like split-brain patients, the participants were surprised by their reactions and sometimes made up justifications for their harsh ratings, such as saying that the lead character seemed "up to something." This result suggests that the left hemisphere interpreter might be involved in people's understanding their own behavior when that behavior results from posthypnotic suggestion or other unconscious influence.

To the extent that hypnosis works, it relies mostly on the person being hypnotized rather than the hypnotist: Most of us could learn to hypnotize other people, but most of us cannot be hypnotized. Why not? Standardized tests exist for

hypnosis A social interaction during which a person, responding to suggestions, experiences changes in memory, perception, and/or voluntary action.

FIGURE 5.19 Hypnotized? Are hypnotized people merely playing a part suggested to them by the hypnotist? What theory informs your conclusion?

hypnotic suggestibility, and hypnosis works primarily for people who are highly suggestible (Kallio & Revonsuo, 2003). What does it mean to be among the approximately 1 in 5 people who are highly suggestible? Researchers have a hard time identifying the personality characteristics of people who can or cannot be hypnotized. Suggestibility seems related less to obvious traits such as intelligence and gullibility than to the tendencies to get absorbed in activities easily, to not be distracted easily, and to have a rich imagination (Balthazard & Woody, 1992; Crawford, Corby, & Kopell, 1996; Silva & Kirsch, 1992). Furthermore, a person who dislikes the idea of being hypnotized or finds it frightening would likely not be hypnotized easily. To be hypnotized, a person must go along with the hypnotist's suggestions willingly. No reliable evidence indicates that people will do things under hypnosis that they find immoral or otherwise objectionable.

THEORIES OF HYPNOSIS Some psychologists believe that a person under hypnosis essentially plays the role of a hypnotized person. That person is not faking hypnosis. Rather, he or she acts the part as if in a play, willing to perform actions called for by the "director," the hypnotist. According to this *sociocognitive theory of hypnosis,* hypnotized people behave as they expect hypnotized people to behave, even if those expectations are faulty (Kirsch & Lynn, 1995; Spanos & Coe, 1992). Alternatively, the *dissociation theory of hypnosis* acknowledges the importance of social context to hypnosis, but it views the hypnotic state as an altered state. According to this theory, hypnosis is a trancelike state in which conscious awareness is separated, or dissociated, from other aspects of consciousness (Gruzelier, 2000).

It seems unlikely that a person could alter his or her brain activity to please a hypnotist, even if that hypnotist is a psychological researcher, and numerous brain imaging studies have supported the dissociation theory of hypnosis (Rainville, Hofbauer, Bushnell, Duncan, & Price, 2002). In one of the earliest such studies, Stephen Kosslyn and colleagues (2000) demonstrated that when hypnotized participants were asked to imagine black-and-white objects as having color, they showed activity in visual cortex regions involved in color perception. Hypnotized participants asked to drain color from colored images showed diminished activity in those same brain regions. This activity pattern did not occur when participants were not hypnotized. These results suggest that the brain follows hypnotic suggestions.

Another study used the Stroop test. As you may recall from Figure 2.17, this test involves naming the color in which a color's name is printed. For example, it takes longer to name the color of the word *red* when that word is printed in blue ink than when it is printed in red ink. Participants took the test having received the posthypnotic suggestion that they would be looking at meaningless symbols instead of words. The participants apparently followed that suggestion and therefore did not show the standard Stroop interference effect, which is believed to result from automatic cognitive processes that cannot be controlled (Raz, Shapiro, Fan, & Posner, 2002). In a subsequent imaging study, the same researchers found that their suggestion to view the words as meaningless was associated with less activity in brain regions typically activated when people read or perform the Stroop test. Thus these participants seem to have perceived the stimuli as nonwords. This alteration of brain activity would be hard for people to accomplish just to please a hypnotist—or a researcher (Raz, Fan, & Posner, 2005).

HYPNOSIS FOR PAIN One of the most powerful uses of hypnosis is *hypnotic analgesia,* a form of pain reduction. Laboratory research has demonstrated that this technique works reliably (Hilgard & Hilgard, 1975; Nash & Barnier, 2008). For instance, a person who plunges one of his or her arms into extremely cold water will feel great pain, and the pain will intensify over time. On average, a person can leave the arm in the water for only about 30 seconds, but a person given hypnotic analgesia can hold out longer. As you might expect, people high in suggestibility who are given hypnotic analgesia can tolerate the cold water the longest (Montgomery, DuHamel, & Redd, 2000).

There is overwhelming evidence that in clinical settings, hypnosis is effective in dealing with immediate pain (e.g., during surgery, dental work, burns) and chronic pain (e.g., from arthritis, cancer, diabetes; Patterson & Jensen, 2003). A patient can also be taught self-hypnosis to improve recovery from surgery (**Figure 5.20**). Hypnosis may work more by changing the patient's interpretation of pain than by diminishing pain. That is, the patient feels the sensations associated with pain, but feels detached from those sensations (Price, Harkins, & Baker, 1987). An imaging study confirmed this pattern by showing that while hypnosis does not affect the sensory processing of pain, it reduces brain activity in regions that process the emotional aspects of pain (Rainville, Duncan, Price, Carrier, & Bushnell, 1997). Findings such as these provide considerable support for the dissociation theory of hypnosis. It seems implausible that either expectations about hypnosis or social pressure not to feel pain could explain how people given hypnotic analgesia are able to undergo painful surgery and not feel it. Nor does it seem likely that either expectations about hypnosis or social pressure not to feel pain could result in the changes in brain activity seen during hypnotic analgesia.

Meditation Produces Relaxation

With a growing awareness of different cultural and religious practices and alternative approaches to medicine, people in the West have become more interested in examining Eastern techniques, including acupuncture and meditation. Different forms of meditation are popular in many Eastern religions, including Hinduism, Buddhism, and Sikhism. **Meditation** is a mental procedure that focuses attention on an external object or on a sense of awareness. Through intense contemplation, the meditator develops a deep sense of tranquility.

Mark Leary (2004) notes that one goal of meditation is to quiet the internal voices we experience as we go through the day or as we try to sleep. Do you ever find that while you are trying to concentrate on a lecture or carry on a conversation, an inner voice keeps interrupting you, perhaps reminding you of things you need to do or wondering what the other person thinks of you? Or perhaps, as you lie in bed at night, the inner voice chatters on about worries and concerns that you would prefer to forget so that you can get some sleep. During meditation, people learn to calm this inner voice, sometimes by simply letting it continue without paying attention to it.

There are two general forms of meditation. In *concentrative meditation,* you focus attention on one thing, such as your breathing pattern, a mental image, or a specific phrase (sometimes called a *mantra*). In *mindfulness meditation,* you let your thoughts flow freely, paying attention to them but trying not to react to them. You hear the contents of your inner voice, but you allow them to flow from one topic to the next without examining their meaning or reacting to them in any way. Why not take a break from reading and try one of these methods (**Figure 5.21**)?

FIGURE 5.20 Self-Hypnosis This advertisement promotes one way that patients can learn self-hypnosis.

meditation A mental procedure that focuses attention on an external object or on a sense of awareness.

FIGURE 5.21 Try for Yourself: Meditation

For at least 20 minutes, try meditating. To practice concentrative meditation, focus your attention on your breathing pattern, in and out. To practice mindfulness meditation, let your thoughts flow freely without reacting to them.

Result: The goal of meditation is to help people achieve a deep state of relaxation. How close did you come to that goal? What does this experience suggest to you about consciousness and its variations?

Religious forms of meditation are meant to bring spiritual enlightenment. Most forms of meditation popular in the West are meant to expand the mind, bring about feelings of inner peace, and help people deal with the tensions and stresses in their lives. These methods include *Zen, yoga,* and *transcendental meditation,* or *TM.*

Perhaps the best-known meditation procedure, TM involves meditating with great concentration for 20 minutes twice a day. Many early studies found a number of benefits from TM, including lower blood pressure, fewer reports of stress, and changes in the hormonal responses underlying stress. These studies have been criticized, however, because they had small samples and lacked appropriate control groups. In a more rigorous recent study, a large number of heart patients were randomly assigned to TM or an educational program. After 16 weeks, the patients performing TM improved more than the control group on a number of health measures, such as blood pressure, blood lipids, and insulin resistance (Paul-Labrador et al., 2006). Unfortunately, this study does not show which aspects of TM produced the health benefits. Was it simply relaxing, or was it the altered state of consciousness? (As discussed in Chapter 11, reducing stress, no matter how it is done, yields substantial health benefits.)

Psychologists also study how meditation affects cognitive processing and brain function (Cahn & Polich, 2006). In one study, participants were assigned randomly to five days of either intensive meditation training or relaxation training. Those who underwent the meditation training showed greater stress reduction and more significant improvement in attention than did the group that underwent relaxation training (Tang et al., 2007). When participants in another study were made to feel sad, those who had received meditation training felt less sad than those in a control group who did not receive meditation training (Farb et al., 2010; **Figure 5.22**). Some researchers argue that long-term meditation brings about structural changes in the brain that help maintain brain function over the life span. For instance, the volume of gray matter typically diminishes with age. One study found that this volume did not diminish in older adults who practiced Zen meditation (Pagnoni & Cekic, 2007). This finding suggests that Zen

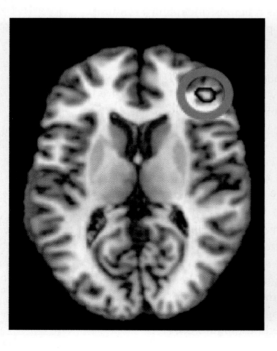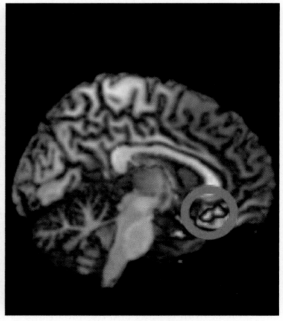

FIGURE 5.22 The Brain on Meditation In these fMRI scans, the circles indicate brain areas that typically show less activity when people are sad. After control subjects watched sad clips from movies, these areas of their brains were less active, as expected. In the brains of participants who had received eight weeks of meditation training, these areas remained active, indicating that these participants felt less sadness.

meditation might help preserve cognitive functioning as people age. But people who meditate may differ substantially from people who do not, especially in terms of lifestyle choices such as diet and a willingness to take care of their health. As Chapter 2 notes, such correlational data do not prove causation. Careful empirical research using the methods of psychological science should contribute significantly to our understanding of meditation's effects.

People Can Lose Themselves in Activities

Hypnosis and meditation involve doing something to alter consciousness. As noted throughout this chapter, however, a person's level of conscious awareness changes as a result of the time of day as well as the person's activities. For instance, when a person performs an automatic task, such as driving, that person's conscious thoughts might not include the experience of driving. Instead, the driver's brain shifts to "autopilot" and automatically goes through the process. During most of our daily activities, of course, we are consciously aware of only a small portion of both our thoughts and our behaviors.

EXERCISE, RELIGIOUS PRAYER, AND FLOW Why do many people listen to music while exercising? In offering a distraction from physical exertion, music can bring about an energizing shift in consciousness. Many people have had a similar but more extreme experience during exercise. One minute they are in pain and feeling fatigued, and the next minute they are euphoric and feeling a glorious release of energy. Commonly known as *runner's high,* this state is partially mediated by physiological processes (especially endorphin release; see Chapter 3, "Biology and Behavior"). It also occurs because of a shift in consciousness.

Shifts in consciousness that are similar to runner's high occur at other moments in our lives. Religious ceremonies often decrease awareness of the external world and create feelings of euphoria. Indeed, such rituals often involve chanting, dancing, and/or other behaviors as a way for people to lose themselves in *religious ecstasy.* Like meditation, religious ecstasy directs attention away from the self. In this way, it allows a person to focus on his or her spiritual awareness (**Figure 5.23**).

One psychological theory about such peak experiences is based on the concept of *flow,* "a particular kind of experience that is so engrossing and enjoyable [that it is] worth doing for its own sake even though it may have no consequence outside itself" (Csikszentmihalyi, 1999, p. 824). That is, a person might perform a particular task out of fascination with it rather than out of a desire for a reward. Flow is an optimal experience in that the activity is completely absorbing and completely satisfying. The person experiencing flow loses track of time, forgets about his or her problems, and fails to notice other things going on (Csikszentmihalyi, 1990). The person's skills are well matched with the task's demands; the situation is less like driving, where much of the work happens automatically, than like rock climbing, where every thought is on the next step and is concrete, not deep and abstract (Leary, 2004). Flow experiences have been reported during many activities, including playing music (O'Neil, 1999) or a moderately challenging version of the computer game *Tetris* (Keller & Bless, 2008), participating in sports (Jackson, Thomas, Marsh, & Smethurst, 2001), and simply doing satisfying jobs (Demerouti, 2006). In the view of the psychologist Mihaly Csikszentmihalyi (1999), flow experiences bring personal fulfillment and make life worth living.

FIGURE 5.23 Religious Ecstasy During a service at a Baptist church in Beulah, Mississippi, a woman is overcome with religious ecstasy. According to the photographer, the woman was speaking in tongues.

FIGURE 5.24 Escapist Entertainment
Simple entertainment can veer toward obsession. **What would you say are the possible benefits of devoting time to video games? What are the potential negative effects?**

ESCAPING THE SELF Our conscious thoughts can be dominated by worries, frustrations, and feelings of personal failure. Sometimes people get tired of dealing with life's problems and try to make themselves feel better through escapist pursuits. Potential flow activities such as sports or work may help people escape thinking about their problems, but people engage in such activities mainly to feel personally fulfilled. The difference is between escaping and engaging. Sometimes people choose to escape the self rather than engage with life: To forget their troubles, they drink alcohol, take drugs, play video games, watch television, surf the Web, text, and so on. The selective appeal of escapist entertainment is that it distracts people from reflecting on their problems or their failures, thereby helping them avoid feeling bad about themselves.

Some escapist activities—such as running or reading—tend to have positive effects; some tend to be relatively harmless distractions; and some tend to come at great personal expense. For example, people obsessively playing online games such as *World of Warcraft* have lost their jobs and even their marriages (**Figure 5.24**). They have even taken the lives of their offspring: In South Korea in 2010, Kim Jae-beom and his common-law wife, Kim Yun-jeong, neglected their 3-month-old daughter to the point that she died of starvation. The couple reportedly spent every night raising a virtual daughter as part of a role-playing game they engaged in at an Internet café. Some ways of escaping the self can also be associated with self-destructive behaviors, such as binge eating, unsafe sex, and, at the extreme, suicide. According to the social psychologist Roy Baumeister (1991), people engage in such behaviors because, to escape their problems, they seek to reduce self-awareness. The state of being in lowered self-awareness may reduce long-term planning, reduce meaningful thinking, and help bring about uninhibited actions. Chapter 12 further discusses the connections between behavior and self-awareness. The next section of this chapter looks at a common way people try to escape their problems—namely, using drugs or alcohol to alter consciousness.

Summing Up

What Is Altered Consciousness?

Altered states of consciousness may be achieved through hypnosis. Some people are more susceptible to hypnosis than others. Posthypnotic suggestions can alter how people react, even though they are not aware that a suggestion was given to them. Hypnosis can also be used to control pain. Patterns of brain activity suggest that individuals who are hypnotized are not simply faking their responses or engaging in theatrical tricks. Altered states of consciousness may also be achieved through concentrative or mindfulness meditation. The results of some studies suggest that meditation may contribute to improved health. Altered states of consciousness—in particular, flow states—may also occur as a consequence of extreme physical

exertion, profound religious experiences, or engaging in tasks that are deeply absorbing. Those who attempt to decrease self-awareness by escaping the self often
face devastating consequences.

Measuring Up

Mark each statement below with a T if it is true and an F if it is false.

a. Participants under hypnosis who were told that they would not see real words
did not show the Stroop effect. (To review the Stroop effect, see Figure 2.17.)

b. Brain imaging showed that hypnotized subjects really were asleep.

c. Brain imaging showed that hypnosis changes brain activity in ways inconsistent
with the idea that people are simply role-playing.

d. People who are hypnotized will do anything the hypnotist tells them to.

e. Hypnosis is not useful in reducing pain.

f. Hypnotized people are aware of the hypnotist's suggestions and simply go
along with what they are asked to do.

Answers: a. T; b. F; c. T; d. F; e. F; f. T

5.4 How Do Drugs Affect Consciousness?

Learning Objectives

- Describe the neurochemical, psychological, and behavioral effects of marijuana, stimulants, MDMA, opiates, and alcohol.

- Identify physiological and psychological factors associated with addiction.

Throughout history, people have discovered that ingesting certain substances can
alter their mental states in various ways. Some of those altered states, however
momentary, can be pleasant. Some, especially over the long term, can have negative consequences, including injury or death. According to the United Nations
Office on Drugs and Crime (2009), upward of 250 million people around the
globe use illicit drugs each year. Societal problems stemming from drug abuse are
well known. Most people probably know and care about someone addicted to
a commonly abused drug, such as alcohol, an illegal substance, or a prescription
medication. If we include nicotine and caffeine on that list, most people probably
are drug addicts. To investigate the biological, individual, and societal effects of
drug use, psychologists ask questions such as *Why do people use drugs? Why do some
people become addicted to drugs? Why do drug addicts continue to abuse drugs when doing
so causes turmoil and suffering?*

People Use—and Abuse—Many Psychoactive Drugs

Drugs are a mixed blessing. If they are the right ones, taken under the right circumstances, they can provide soothing relief from severe pain or a moderate headache. They can help people suffering from depression lead more satisfying lives.
They can help children who have attention deficits or hyperactivity disorders
settle down and learn better. But many of these same drugs can be used for "recreational" purposes: to alter physical sensations, levels of consciousness, thoughts,
moods, and behaviors in ways that users believe are desirable. This recreational use
sometimes can have negative consequences.

Psychoactive drugs are mind-altering substances. These drugs change the brain's neurochemistry by activating neurotransmitter systems. The effects of a particular drug depend on which neurotransmitter systems it activates. *Stimulants,* for example, are drugs that increase behavioral and mental activity. They include caffeine and nicotine as well as cocaine and amphetamines. These substances generally work by interfering with the normal reuptake of dopamine by the releasing neuron, allowing dopamine to remain in the synapse and thus prolonging its effects, although sometimes stimulants also increase the release of dopamine (Fibiger, 1993). Activation of dopamine receptors seems to be involved in drug use in two ways. First, the increased dopamine is associated with greater reward, or increased liking (Volkow, Wang, & Baler, 2011). Second, the increased dopamine leads to a greater desire to take a drug, even if that drug does not produce pleasure. Thus sometimes an addict *wants* a drug even if the addict does not *like* the drug when he or she uses it (Kringelbach & Berridge, 2009). The available evidence suggests that dopamine is particularly important for the wanting aspect of addiction. Stimulants activate the sympathetic nervous system, increasing heart rate and blood pressure. They improve mood, but they also cause people to become restless, and they disrupt sleep.

This section considers a few common psychoactive drugs. Some of them have legitimate medical uses, but all of these drugs are commonly abused outside of treatment.

MARIJUANA The most widely used illicit drug in the world is marijuana, the dried leaves and flower buds of the hemp plant. Many drugs can easily be categorized as a stimulant, a depressant, or a hallucinogen, but marijuana can have the effects of all three types. The psychoactive ingredient in marijuana is THC, or tetrahydrocannabinol. This chemical produces a relaxed mental state, an uplifted or contented mood, and some perceptual and cognitive distortions. Marijuana users report that THC also makes perceptions more vivid, and some say it especially affects taste. Most first-time users do not experience the "high" obtained by more experienced users. Novice smokers might use inefficient techniques, they might have trouble inhaling, or both, but users apparently must learn how to appreciate the drug's effects (Kuhn, Swartzwelder, & Wilson, 2003). In this way, marijuana differs from most other drugs. Generally, the first time someone uses a drug other than marijuana, the effects are very strong, and subsequent uses lead to tolerance, in which a person has to use more of the drug to get the same effect.

Although the brain mechanisms that marijuana affects remain somewhat mysterious, researchers have discovered a class of receptors that are activated by naturally occurring THC-like substances. Activation of these *cannabinoid* receptors appears to adjust and enhance mental activity and perhaps alter pain perception. The large concentration of these receptors in the hippocampus may partly explain why marijuana impairs memory (Ilan, Smith, & Gevins, 2004). Marijuana is also used for its medicinal properties, and this use is legal in many countries and American states. For instance, cancer patients undergoing chemotherapy report that marijuana is effective for overcoming nausea. Nearly 1 in 4 AIDS patients reports using marijuana to relieve nausea and pain (Prentiss, Power, Balmas, Tzuang, & Israelski et al., 2004). The medical use of marijuana is controversial because of the possibility that chronic use can cause health problems or lead to abuse of the drug.

COCAINE Cocaine is derived from the leaves of the coca bush, which grows primarily in South America. After inhaling (snorting) cocaine as a powder or smoking it in the form of crack cocaine, users experience a wave of confidence. They feel good, alert, energetic, sociable, and wide awake. Cocaine produces its stimulating effects by increasing the concentration of dopamine in the neural synapse. These short-term effects are especially intense for crack cocaine users. In contrast, habitual use of cocaine in large quantities can lead to paranoia, psychotic behavior, and violence (Ottieger, Tressell, Inciardi, & Rosales, 1992).

Cocaine has a long history of use in America. John Pemberton, a pharmacist from Georgia, was so impressed with cocaine's effects that in 1886 he added the drug to soda water for easy ingestion, thus creating Coca-Cola. In 1906, the U.S. government outlawed cocaine, so it was removed from the drink. To this day, however, coca leaves from which the cocaine has been removed are used in the making of Coke (**Figure 5.25**).

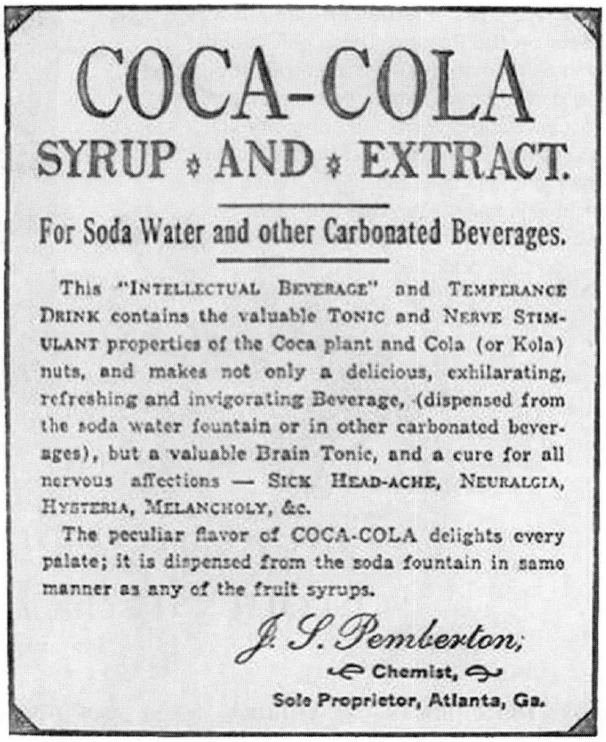

AMPHETAMINES Amphetamines are synthesized using simple lab methods. They go by street names such as *speed, meth* (for *methamphetamine*), *ice,* and *crystal*. Amphetamines have a long history of use for weight loss and staying awake. However, their numerous negative side effects include insomnia, anxiety, and heart, skin, and dental problems. In addition, people quickly become addicted to them. They are seldom used for legitimate medical purposes.

Methamphetamine is the world's second most commonly used illicit drug, after marijuana (Barr et al., 2006). It was first developed in the early twentieth century as a nasal decongestant, but its recreational use became popular in the 1980s. The National Institute of Drug Abuse (2006) estimates that around 4 percent of the U.S. population have tried methamphetamine at some point in their lives. The use of methamphetamine may have declined in recent years, however (Gonzales, Mooney, & Rawson, 2010). One factor that encourages the use of this drug and may explain its popularity over the past decade is that methamphetamine is easy to make from common over-the-counter drugs.

By blocking the reuptake of dopamine and increasing its release, methamphetamine yields much higher levels of dopamine in the synapse. In addition, methamphetamine stays in the body and brain much longer than, say, cocaine, so its effects are prolonged. Over time, methamphetamine damages various brain structures, including the frontal lobes (**Figure 5.26**). Ultimately, it depletes dopamine levels. The drug's effects on the temporal lobes and the limbic system may explain the harm done to memory and emotion in long-term users (Kim et al., 2006; Thompson et al., 2004). Methamphetamine also causes considerable physical damage (**Figure 5.27**).

MDMA MDMA, or ecstasy, has become popular since the 1990s. It produces an energizing effect similar to that of stimulants, but it also causes slight hallucinations. According to the National Institute of Drug Abuse (2010), MDMA use by high school students increased from 3.7 percent to 4.7 percent between 2009 and 2010. The drug first became popular among young adults in nightclubs and at all-night parties known as raves. Compared with amphetamines, MDMA is associated with less dopamine release and more serotonin release. The serotonin release may explain ecstasy's hallucinogenic properties. Although many users believe it to be relatively safe, researchers have documented a number of impairments from long-term ecstasy use, especially memory problems and a diminished ability to perform complex tasks (Kalechstein, De La Garza II, Mahoney III, Fantegrossi, & Newton, 2007). Because ecstasy also depletes serotonin, users

COCA-COLA SYRUP AND EXTRACT.

For Soda Water and other Carbonated Beverages.

This "INTELLECTUAL BEVERAGE" and TEMPERANCE DRINK contains the valuable TONIC and NERVE STIMULANT properties of the Coca plant and Cola (or Kola) nuts, and makes not only a delicious, exhilarating, refreshing and invigorating Beverage, (dispensed from the soda water fountain or in other carbonated beverages), but a valuable Brain Tonic, and a cure for all nervous affections — SICK HEAD-ACHE, NEURALGIA, HYSTERIA, MELANCHOLY, &c.

The peculiar flavor of COCA-COLA delights every palate; it is dispensed from the soda fountain in same manner as any of the fruit syrups.

J. S. Pemberton;
Chemist,
Sole Proprietor, Atlanta, Ga.

FIGURE 5.25 Early Coke Ad This advertisement's claim that Coca-Cola is "a valuable Brain Tonic" may have been inspired by the incorporation of cocaine into the drink before 1906.

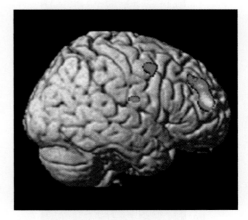

FIGURE 5.26 Methamphetamine's Effects on the Brain This image is a composite of brain scans from 29 methamphetamine addicts. The red and yellow areas represent the brain damage that typically occurs in the frontal cortex as a result of methamphetamine abuse (Kim et al., 2006). Such damage may explain the cognitive problems associated with methamphetamine use.

FIGURE 5.27 Methamphetamine's Effects on the Person These before-and-after photos dramatically illustrate how the physical damage from methamphetamine can affect appearance. When the photo on the left was taken, Theresa Baxter was 42 and not a methamphetamine addict. The photo on the right was taken 2 ½ years later, after Baxter was arrested for crimes she committed to support her addiction.

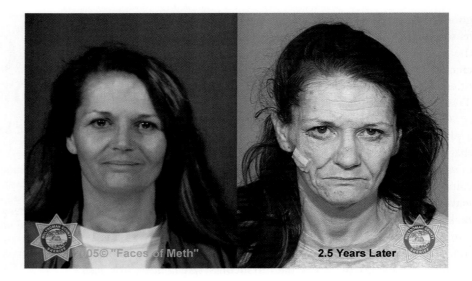

2005© "Faces of Meth"   2.5 Years Later

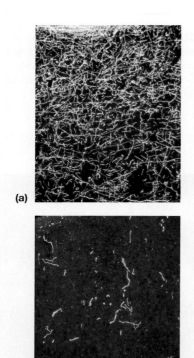

(a)

(b)

FIGURE 5.28 MDMA's Effects on the Brain **(a)** This image shows serotonin nerve fibers in the cortex of a normal monkey. **(b)** This image shows the same brain area of a monkey that received multiple doses of MDMA (ecstasy). Eighteen months after the monkey received the MDMA, the monkey's serotonin nerve fibers remain drastically reduced.

often feel depressed when the drug's rewarding properties wear off (Fischer, Hatzidimitriou, Wlos, Katz, & Ricaurte, 1995; **Figure 5.28**).

OPIATES Opiates are a type of depressant. They include heroin, morphine, and codeine. These drugs provide enormous reward value, producing feelings of relaxation, analgesia, and euphoria. Heroin provides a rush of intense pleasure that most addicts describe as similar to orgasm. This rush evolves into a pleasant, relaxed stupor. Heroin and morphine may be so highly addictive because they have dual physical effects: They increase pleasure by binding with opiate receptors and increase wanting of the drug by activating dopamine receptors (Kuhn et al., 2003).

Opiates have been used to relieve pain and suffering for hundreds of years. Indeed, before the twentieth century, heroin was widely available without prescription and was marketed by Bayer, the aspirin company (**Figure 5.29**). The benefits of short-term opiate use to relieve severe pain seem clear, but long-term opiate use to relieve chronic pain will much more likely lead to abuse or addiction than will short-term use (Ballantyne & LaForge, 2007). Moreover, long-term use of opiates is associated with a number of neurological and cognitive deficits, such as attention and memory problems (Gruber, Silveri, & Yurgelun-Todd, 2007). Therefore, clinicians need to be cautious in prescribing opiates, such as Vicodin, especially when the drugs will be used over extended periods.

Alcohol Is the Most Widely Abused Drug

Like other addictive drugs, alcohol may offer its rewards by activating dopamine receptors. But alcohol also interferes with the neurochemical processes involved in memory, and memory loss can follow excessive alcohol intake. Heavy long-term alcohol intake can cause extensive brain damage. *Korsakoff's syndrome,* a disorder sometimes caused by alcoholism, is characterized by both severe memory loss and intellectual deterioration.

Many societies have a love / hate relationship with alcohol. On the one hand, moderate drinking is an accepted aspect of social interaction and may even be good for one's health. On the other hand, alcohol is a major contributor to many societal problems, such as spousal abuse and other forms of violence. Although the percentage of traffic fatalities due to alcohol is dropping, alcohol is a factor in more than one-third of fatal accidents (Mayhew, Brown, & Simpson, 2002). One study found that approximately one-third of college students reported having had sex during a drinking binge, and the heaviest drinkers were likely to have had sex with a new or casual partner (Leigh & Schafer, 1993), thus increasing their risk for exposure to AIDS and other sexually transmitted diseases. The overall cost of problem drinking in the United States—from lost productivity due to employee absence, from health care expenses, and so on—is estimated to be more than $100 billion annually.

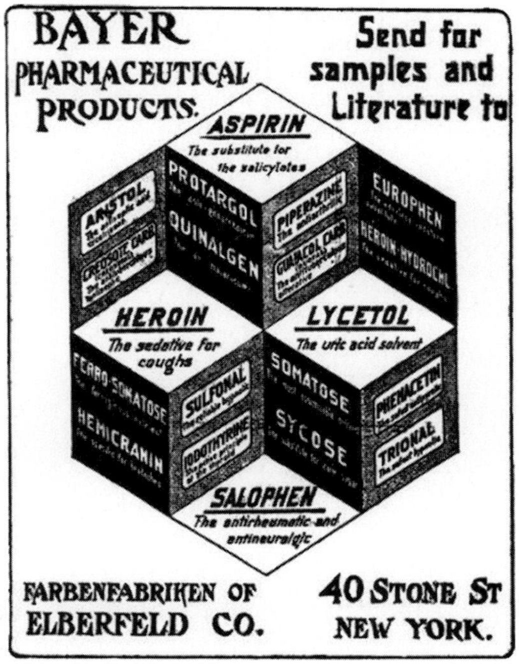

GENDER DIFFERENCES IN ALCOHOL CONSUMPTION ACROSS CULTURES

The World Health Organization conducts a massive international study of gender-related and culture-related differences in alcohol consumption (Obot & Room, 2005). The study's main premise is that to understand alcohol consumption worldwide, we need to study the various ways alcohol is used, by men and by women, across cultural and social contexts. The authors call the gap between men and women in alcohol consumption "one of the few universal gender differences in human social behavior" (Wilsnack, Wilsnack, & Obot, 2005, p. 1). Can you guess whether men or women consume more alcohol? In every region of the world, across a wide variety of measures (e.g., drinking versus abstinence, heavy drinking versus occasional drinking, alcohol-related disorders), men drink a lot more. Men are twice as likely to report binge drinking (drinking five or more servings in one evening), chronic drinking, and recent alcohol intoxication. Gender gaps in binge drinking may be smaller among university students, however.

What accounts for the large and universal difference between men's drinking and women's drinking? One possible explanation is that because women do not

FIGURE 5.29 **Early Heroin Ad!** Before 1904, Bayer advertised heroin as "the sedative for coughs."

CRITICAL THINKING SKILL

Recognizing Slippery Slope Thinking

What happens when you slip while walking down a slope? Might you fall to the bottom? A person making a *slippery slope argument* reasons that some first slippery step must lead down to a larger, more slippery step or even a large fall. For example, a slippery slope argument against all "recreational" drug use proposes that if you start using a drug that is not likely to have lasting effects (say, marijuana), this behavior will lead you to take "harder" drugs (say, cocaine), and soon you will be robbing to support your heroin habit. The "starter," less powerful drug is referred to as a *gateway drug* because it supposedly opens the gate to more-regular and more-dangerous drug use.

The data are mixed on whether using drugs such as marijuana is associated with later use of drugs such as heroin. Even if the relationship were strong, what might be wrong with these data? The conclusion that taking marijuana *causes* people to take harder drugs cannot be inferred from these data. There are many other possible explanations for this relationship. For example, people with a tendency to get addicted could start with any drug and generally do start with the cheapest and most available one, marijuana. It might or might not be true that a minor action will lead to a more serious one. There is no reason to assume, however, that this progression is always true or is even usually true.

metabolize alcohol as quickly as men do and generally have smaller body volumes, they consume less alcohol than men to achieve the same effects. Another possible explanation is that women's drinking may be more hidden because it is less socially accepted than men's drinking. According to this view, women's alcohol consumption may be underreported, especially in cultures where it is frowned upon or forbidden. In some cultures, "real men" are expected to drink a lot and prove they can "hold" their liquor, whereas women who do the same are seen as abnormal.

EXPECTATIONS   Alan Marlatt (1999), a leading researcher on substance abuse, has noted that people view alcohol as the "magic elixir," capable of increasing social skills, sexual pleasure, confidence, and power. They anticipate that alcohol will have positive effects on their emotions and behavior. For example, people tend to think that alcohol reduces anxiety, so both light and heavy drinkers turn to alcohol after a difficult day. Alcohol *can* interfere with the cognitive processing of threat cues, so that anxiety-provoking events are less troubling when people are intoxicated. This effect occurs, however, only if people drink *before* the anxiety-provoking events. In fact, according to the research, drinking after a hard day can increase people's focus on and obsession with their problems (Sayette, 1993). In addition, while moderate doses of alcohol are associated with more-positive moods, larger doses are associated with more-negative moods.

Expectations about alcohol's effects are learned very early in life, through observation. Children may see that people who drink have a lot of fun and that drinking is an important aspect of many celebrations. Teenagers may view drinkers as sociable and grown up, two things they desperately want to be. Studies have shown that children who have very positive expectations about alcohol are more likely to start drinking and become heavy drinkers than children who do not share those expectations (Leigh & Stacy, 2004).

According to the social psychologists Jay Hull and Charles Bond (1986), expectations about alcohol profoundly affect behavior. These researchers gave study participants tonic water with or without alcohol. Regardless of the drinks' actual

CRITICAL THINKING SKILL

Recognizing Circular Reasoning

Have you ever seen a cat chase its tail? It can be a pretty funny sight, as the cat never gets closer to its "prey." Similarly, a person who engages in circular reasoning moves around without truly reaching a conclusion. The argument ends up where it started, because the reason for believing the conclusion is just a restatement of the conclusion. Here is an example: "We need to raise the legal drinking age from 21 to 25 because 21-year-olds are too young to drink." Can you see what is wrong with this argument? Saying that 21-year-olds are too young to drink is just another way of saying "We need to raise the legal drinking age from 21." The argument does not explain *why* 21 is too young. If the speaker had said, "We need to raise the legal drinking age from 21 to 25 because research shows that 25-year-olds have half the number of traffic accidents that 21-year-olds do" or ". . . because the frontal areas of the brain mature between ages 21 and 25" or ". . . because 25-year-olds are more responsible," she or he would have provided a reason to support the conclusion.

contents, they told some participants they were drinking just tonic water and some they were drinking tonic water with alcohol. This balanced-placebo design allowed for a comparison of those who thought they were drinking tonic water but were actually drinking alcohol with those who thought they were drinking alcohol but were actually drinking tonic water. The researchers demonstrated that alcohol impairs motor processes, information processing, and mood, independent of whether the person thinks he or she has consumed it. In addition, the researchers demonstrated that the belief that one has consumed alcohol leads to disinhibition regarding various social behaviors, such as sexual arousal and aggression, whether or not the person has consumed alcohol. Thus some behaviors generally associated with drunkenness are accounted for by learned beliefs about intoxication rather than by alcohol's pharmacological properties. Sometimes the learned expectations and the pharmacology work in opposite ways. For instance, alcohol tends to increase sexual arousal, but it interferes with sexual performance.

(a)

(b)

Addiction Has Physical and Psychological Aspects

Addiction is drug use that remains compulsive despite its negative consequences. The condition consists of physical and psychological factors. Physical dependence on a drug is a physiological state associated with *tolerance,* whereby a person needs to consume more of a particular substance to achieve the same subjective effect. Failing to ingest the substance leads to symptoms of *withdrawal,* a physiological and psychological state characterized by feelings of anxiety, tension, and cravings for the addictive substance. The physical symptoms of withdrawal vary widely from drug to drug and from individual to individual, but they include nausea, chills, body aches, and tremors. A person can be psychologically dependent, however, without showing tolerance or withdrawal. This section focuses on addiction to substances that alter consciousness, but people can also become psychologically dependent on behaviors, such as shopping or gambling (**Figure 5.30**).

FIGURE 5.30 Physical Dependence versus Psychological Dependence Both types of dependence can force people to go to extremes. **(a) What does this scene, outside a restaurant in Germany, suggest about patrons such as this woman? (b) How do casinos, such as this one in Las Vegas, encourage patrons' "addiction" to gambling?**

ADDICTION'S CAUSES How do people become addicted? One central factor appears to be dopamine activity in the limbic system, because this activity underlies the rewarding properties of taking drugs (Baler & Volkow, 2006; Chapter 6, "Learning," further discusses dopamine's role in the experience of reward). A brain region called the *insula* seems to be important for craving and addiction (Goldstein et al., 2009), since this region becomes active when addicts view images of drug use (**Figure 5.31**). Patients with insula damage report that immediately after being injured, they quit smoking easily. In fact, they no longer experience conscious urges to smoke. One patient who had a stroke to his left insula commented that he quit smoking because his "body forgot the urge to smoke" (Naqvi, Rudrauf, Damasio, & Bechara, 2007, p. 534).

Only about 5 percent to 10 percent of those who use drugs become addicted. Indeed, more than 90 million Americans have experimented with illicit drugs, yet most of them use drugs only occasionally or try them for a while and then give them up. In a longitudinal study, Jonathan Shedler and Jack Block (1990) found that those who had experimented with drugs as adolescents were better adjusted in adulthood than those who had never tried them. Complete abstainers and heavy drug users had adjustment problems compared with those who had experimented. This finding does not suggest, however, that everyone should try drugs or that parents should encourage drug experimentation. After all, no one can predict just who will become addicted or know who is prepared to handle a drug's effects on behavior.

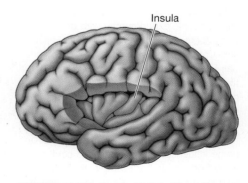
Insula

FIGURE 5.31 Insula This brain region appears to play a role in craving and addiction.

Some adolescents are especially likely to experiment with illegal drugs and to abuse alcohol. Children high in sensation seeking (a personality trait that involves attraction to novelty and risk taking) are more likely to associate with deviant peer groups and to use alcohol, tobacco, and drugs (Wills, DuHamel, & Vaccaro, 1995). These children and their parents tend to have poor relationships, which in turn promote the children's association with deviant peer groups. Does the family environment determine alcohol and drug use? Some theorists suggest that an inherited predisposition to sensation seeking may predict behaviors, such as affiliating with drug users, that increase the possibility of substance abuse.

Some evidence points to genetic components of addiction, especially for alcoholism, but little direct evidence points to a *single* "alcoholism" or "addiction" gene. Rather, what people inherit is a cluster of characteristics. These inherited risk factors might include personality traits such as risk taking and impulsivity, a reduced concern about personal harm, a nervous system chronically low in arousal, or a predisposition to finding chemical substances pleasurable. In turn, such factors may make some people more likely to explore drugs and enjoy them.

Social learning theorists have sought to account for the initiation of drug or alcohol use among either children or adolescents. They emphasize the roles of parents, the mass media, and peers, including self-identification with high-risk groups (e.g., "stoners" or "druggies"). Teenagers want to fit in somewhere, even with groups that society perceives as deviant. And as discussed further in Chapter 6, children imitate the behavior of role models, especially those they admire or with whom they identify. For children whose parents smoke, the modeling of the behavior may be continuous through early childhood and elementary school. When parents smoke, their children tend to have positive attitudes about smoking and to begin smoking early (Rowe, Chassin, Presson, & Sherman, 1996).

ADDICTION'S CONTEXT Some evidence suggests that context is important for understanding addiction. For example, in the late 1960s, drug abuse among U.S. soldiers, including the use of narcotics such as heroin and opium, appeared to be epidemic. The widespread drug use was not surprising. It was a time of youthful drug experimentation, soldiers in Vietnam had easy access to various drugs, and drugs helped the soldiers cope temporarily with fear, depression, homesickness, boredom, and the repressiveness of army regulations (**Figure 5.32**). The military commanders mostly ignored drug use among soldiers, viewing it as "blowing off steam."

Beginning in 1971, the military began mandatory drug testing of soldiers to identify and detoxify drug users before they returned to the United States. Amid speculation that a flood of addicted soldiers returning from Vietnam would swamp treatment facilities back home, the White House asked a team of behavioral scientists to study a group of returning soldiers and assess the extent of the addiction problem. Led by the behavioral epidemiologist Lee Robins, the research team examined a random sample of 898 soldiers who were leaving Vietnam in September 1971. Robins and her colleagues found extremely high levels of drug use among them (Robins, Helzer, & Davis, 1975). Over 90 percent reported drinking alcohol, nearly three-quarters smoked marijuana, and nearly half used narcotics such as heroin, morphine, and opium. About half the soldiers who used narcotics either had symptoms of addiction or reported believing they would be unable to give up their drug habits. The team's findings suggested that approximately 1 soldier in 5 returning from Vietnam was a drug addict. Given the prevailing view that addiction was a biological disorder with a low rate of recovery, these results indicated that tens of thousands of heroin addicts would soon be inundating the United States. But this did not happen.

(a)

(b)

FIGURE 5.32 The Sixties, Drugs, and Vietnam (a) By the late 1960s, youth culture had taken many new forms in the United States and elsewhere. In exploring the boundaries of society and consciousness, many young people experimented with drugs. Here, two people share drugs at the Shiva Fellowship Church Earth Faire at Golden Gate Park, San Francisco, in April 1969. **(b)** Through those years and beyond, the United States played a leading role in the Vietnam War, a military conflict that took place in the "faraway lands" of Vietnam, Laos, and Cambodia. Perhaps inevitably, the changes and conflicts at home influenced the changes and conflicts away from home. For example, many U.S. soldiers abused drugs. Here, two soldiers exchange vials of heroin in Quang Tri Province, South Vietnam, July 1971.

Robins and her colleagues examined drug use among the soldiers after they returned to the United States. Of those who were apparently addicted to narcotics in Vietnam, only half sought out drugs when they returned to the States, and fewer still maintained their narcotic addictions. Approximately 95 percent of the addicts no longer used drugs within months of their return—an astonishing quit rate considering that the success rate of the best treatments is typically only 20 percent to 30 percent. A long-term follow-up study conducted in the early 1990s confirmed that only a handful of those who were addicts in Vietnam remained addicts.

Why did coming home help the addicts recover? In the United States, they likely did not have the same motivations for taking the drugs as they did in Vietnam. No longer needing the drugs to escape combat's horrors, they focused on other needs and goals, such as careers and family obligations. An important lesson from this case study is that we cannot ignore environment when we try to understand addiction. Knowing drugs' physical actions in the brain may give us insights into addiction's biology, but that information fails to account for how these biological impulses can be overcome by other motivations.

Summing Up

How Do Drugs Affect Consciousness?

People have long ingested drugs that alter the way they think, feel, and act. Commonly used psychoactive drugs include marijuana, cocaine, amphetamines, MDMA, opiates, and alcohol. These drugs produce their psychological and behavioral effects by affecting neurotransmitter systems. The abuse of these drugs is costly to society, contributing to illness, violence, crime, and death. Excessive drug use can lead to addiction, a condition characterized by physical and psychological dependence. A brain region called the insula has been implicated in the experience of addiction. Addiction is influenced by personality factors, such as sensation seeking. Addiction is also influenced by the environment or context in which drug use occurs.

Measuring Up

1. All drugs work by _____.
   a. increasing neural firing in the cerebellum
   b. decreasing the amount of neurotransmitter affected by reuptake
   c. creating dizziness, which the interpreter translates as a drug state
   d. activating neurotransmitter systems

2. Match each of the following drugs or drug categories to the appropriate statement below: stimulants, MDMA, opiates, marijuana, alcohol.
   a. It is involved in more than one-third of fatal car accidents.
   b. It is the only drug that does not have its strongest effect on first-time users.
   c. They include heroin, morphine, and codeine.
   d. Its psychoactive ingredient is THC, or tetrahydrocannabinol.
   e. They include cocaine, nicotine, caffeine, and amphetamines.
   f. It is known as ecstasy.
   g. According to their reports, one-third of college students had sex while under its influence.
   h. One of them was used in Coca-Cola's original recipe.
   i. It is associated with Korsakoff's syndrome, a disorder characterized by severe memory loss and intellectual impairment.

Answers: 1. d. activating neurotransmitter systems.
2. a. alcohol; b. marijuana; c. opiates; d. marijuana; e. stimulants; f. MDMA; g. alcohol; h. stimulants; i. alcohol.

StudySpace: Your Place for a Better Grade

Visit StudySpace to access free review materials, such as:

■ complete study outlines   ■ vocabulary flashcards of all key terms   ■ additional chapter review quizzes

Chapter Summary

5.1 What Is Consciousness?

■ **Consciousness Is a Subjective Experience:** Consciousness is difficult to study because of the subjective nature of our experience of the world. Brain imaging research has shown that particular brain regions are activated by particular types of sensory information.

■ **There Are Variations in Conscious Experience:** Consciousness is each person's unified and coherent experience of the world around him or her. At any one time, each person can be conscious of a limited number of things. A person's level of consciousness varies throughout the day and depends on the task at hand. Whereas people in a persistent vegetative state show no brain activity, people in minimally conscious states show brain activity. That activity indicates some awareness of external stimuli.

■ **Brain Activity Gives Rise to Consciousness**: The global workspace model maintains that consciousness arises from activity in different cortical areas. The corpus callosum connects the brain's two sides; cutting it in half results in two independently functioning hemispheres. The left hemisphere is responsible primarily for language, and the right hemisphere is responsible primarily for images and spatial relations. The left hemisphere strives to make sense of experiences, and its interpretations influence the way a person views and remembers the world.

■ **Unconscious Processing Influences Behavior:** Research findings indicate that much of a person's behavior occurs automatically, without that person's conscious awareness. Thought and behavior can be influenced by stimuli that are not experienced at a conscious level.

5.2 What Is Sleep?

■ **Sleep Is an Altered State of Consciousness:** Sleep is characterized by stages that vary in brain activity. REM sleep is marked by rapid eye movements, dreaming, and body paralysis. Sleep disorders include insomnia, sleep apnea, and narcolepsy.

■ **Sleep Is an Adaptive Behavior:** Sleep allows the body, including the brain, to rest and restore itself. Sleep also protects animals from harm at times of the day when they are most susceptible to danger, and it facilitates learning through the strengthening of neural connections.

■ **People Dream while Sleeping:** REM dreams and non-REM dreams activate and deactivate distinct brain regions. Sigmund Freud believed that dreams reveal unconscious conflicts. Evidence does not support this view. Activation-synthesis theory posits that dreams are the product of the mind's efforts to make sense of random brain activity during sleep. Evolved threat-rehearsal theory maintains that dreaming evolved as a result of its adaptive value. That is, dreaming may have enabled early humans to rehearse strategies for coping with threatening events.

5.3 What Is Altered Consciousness?

■ **Hypnosis Is Induced through Suggestion:** Scientists have debated whether hypnotized people merely play the role they are expected to play or whether they experience an altered state of consciousness. Consistent with the latter view, brain imaging research has demonstrated changes in brain activity among hypnotized subjects.

■ **Meditation Produces Relaxation:** The goal of meditation, particularly as it is practiced in the West, is to bring about a state of deep relaxation. Studies suggest that meditation can have multiple benefits for people's physical and mental health.

■ **People Can Lose Themselves in Activities:** Exercise, religious practices, and other engaging activities can produce a state of altered consciousness called flow. In this state, people become completely absorbed in what they are doing. Flow is experienced as a positive state. In contrast to activities that generate flow, activities used to escape the self or reduce self-awareness can have harmful consequences.

5.4 How Do Drugs Affect Consciousness?

■ **People Use—and Abuse—Many Psychoactive Drugs:** Stimulants, including cocaine and amphetamines, increase behavioral and mental activity. THC (the active ingredient in marijuana) produces a relaxed state, an uplifted mood, and perceptual and cognitive distortions. MDMA, or ecstasy, produces energizing and hallucinogenic effects. Opiates produce a relaxed state, analgesia, and euphoria.

■ **Alcohol Is the Most Widely Abused Drug:** Alcohol impairs motor processes, informational processing, mood, and memory. Research has demonstrated that, across the globe, males consume more alcohol than females. A drinker's expectations can significantly affect his or her behavior while under the influence of alcohol.

■ **Addiction Has Physical and Psychological Aspects:** Physical dependence occurs when the body develops tolerance for a drug. Psychological dependence occurs when someone habitually and compulsively uses a drug or engages in a behavior, despite its negative consequences.

Key Terms

activation-synthesis theory, p. 203

circadian rhythms, p. 194

consciousness, p. 183

dreams, p. 202

hypnosis, p. 205

insomnia, p. 197

interpreter, p. 189

latent content, p. 203

manifest content, p. 203

meditation, p. 207

narcolepsy, p. 198

obstructive sleep apnea, p. 198

REM sleep, p. 197

split brain, p. 187

subliminal perception, p. 192

Practice Test

1. What is a key distinction between a person in a persistent vegetative state and a person in a minimally conscious state?
   a. The person in the minimally conscious state is less responsive to her or his surroundings.
   b. The person in the persistent vegetative state is more likely to regain full consciousness at some point in the future.
   c. The person in the minimally conscious state shows some degree of brain activity, whereas the person in the persistent vegetative state shows no brain activity.
   d. The person in the minimally conscious state is dreaming, whereas the person in the persistent vegetative state is in a coma.

2. A researcher asks study participants to play a word game in which they unscramble letters to form words. In Condition A, the unscrambled words are *outgoing, talkative,* and *smile.* In Condition B, the unscrambled words are *standoffish, silent,* and *frown.* After participants complete the word game, they meet and interact with a stranger. What do you predict participants' behavior during that interaction will reveal?
   a. Participants in Conditions A and B will behave nearly identically.
   b. Participants in Condition A will be more friendly toward the stranger than will participants in Condition B.
   c. Participants in Condition B will be more friendly toward the stranger than will participants in Condition A.

3. A study participant who has a severed corpus callosum is asked to focus on a dot in the middle of a computer screen. After a few seconds, a car appears on the left half of the screen while an automobile tire appears on the right half of the screen. How will the participant most likely respond if asked to describe the objects in the pictures?
   a. The participant will say he saw a tire and will draw a car.
   b. The participant will say he saw a car and will draw a tire.
   c. The participant will say he saw a car and a tire, but he will not be able to draw either object.
   d. The participant will draw a car and a tire, but he will not be able to name either object.

4. For each description below, name the sleep disorder: insomnia, apnea, narcolepsy, or somnambulism.
   a. _____ Despite feeling well rested, Marcus falls asleep suddenly while practicing piano.
   b. _____ Emma walks through the living room in the middle of the night, seemingly oblivious to those around her.
   c. _____ Sophia spends most of the night trying to fall asleep.
   d. _____ Ivan's roommate regularly complains that Ivan's snoring wakes him multiple times throughout the night.

5. Which of the following pieces of evidence suggest sleep is an adaptive behavior? Check all that apply.
   a. A few days of sleep deprivation do not impair physical strength.
   b. All animals sleep.
   c. It is impossible to resist indefinitely the urge to sleep.
   d. Sleep deprivation helps people feel less depressed.
   e. Animals die when deprived of sleep for extended periods.

6. Four students discuss a hypnotist's performance on campus. Which student's claim about hypnotism is most consistent with current evidence?
   a. "We just witnessed a bunch of people acting goofy solely because they thought they were supposed to act goofy."
   b. "I can't believe the hypnotist was able to make those people do things they would usually be so opposed to!"
   c. "What worries me is that someone could hypnotize me without my even knowing about it."
   d. "It's pretty cool that a hypnotist could help those people enter an altered state of consciousness."

7. Which of the following instruction sets would a yoga teacher trained in concentrative meditation be most likely to give?
   a. "Close your eyes while sitting in a comfortable position. Let your thoughts move freely through your mind, like clouds passing through the sky. Acknowledge them, but do not react to them."
   b. "Lying on your back, rest your hands gently on your abdomen. As you breathe in and out, focus attention on your breath. Notice the rhythmic rise and fall of your abdomen and the slow, deep movement of your chest."

The answer key for the Practice Tests can be found at the back of the book. It also includes answers to the green caption questions.

6

Learning

IN THE MID-1940s, BURRHUS FREDERIC SKINNER and his wife, Yvonne, were living in Minnesota. When their daughter Deborah was born, Skinner kept the infant in a box. After the magazine *Ladies' Home Journal* published an article about Skinner with a photo of the "Baby in a Box," Skinner's treatment of Deborah became notorious. Readers of the piece, and even people who only heard about it, were outraged. What kind of monster would deprive a child of human contact?

In fact, this incident was a perfect example of how the media can misrepresent facts. Skinner developed the sleeping chamber for Deborah so that she could remain comfortable during the cold winters in Minnesota without being constrained by clothing and blankets (**Figure 6.1**). He called the box a "baby tender," and it maintained an optimal temperature and provided a continuous supply of fresh linens. There was also a smaller, portable version. Each of these cribs had

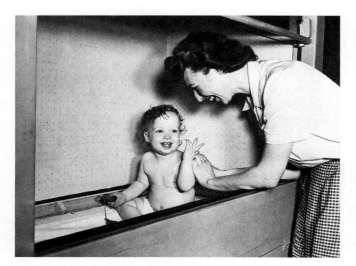

FIGURE 6.1 "Baby in a Box" B. F. Skinner developed this crib for his daughter in 1945. **If you were offered a contemporary version of Skinner's invention, would you accept it or reject it as a crib for one of your own children? Why?**

a safety-glass front that adults could open. Contrary to rumors, Skinner did not lock Deborah in the box. She did not grow up to be depressed, sue her father, or commit suicide. In fact, Deborah—a successful artist living in London, England—has denounced such rumors. She and her sister, Julie—an author and educator—had excellent relationships with their father until his death, in 1990.

Even at the time of the "Baby in a Box" incident, B. F. Skinner was a famous behavioral scientist. He is now seen as the person who arguably had the greatest influence on contemporary psychological science. He and Yvonne raised Deborah and Julie according to the ideas established through his research. Especially important to Skinner was emphasizing reward over punishment. He was not a cold, mad scientist or a child abuser.

As a young man, Skinner had wanted to be a novelist so that he could explore large questions about the human condition. Then he read two works of nonfiction that changed his life. The first was the 1924 book *Behaviorism,* by the psychologist John B. Watson. The second was a 1927 article in the *New York Times Magazine,* in which the novelist H. G. Wells expressed admiration for the work of the physiologist Ivan Pavlov. Increasingly, the behaviorists' perspective made sense to Skinner. He became convinced that psychology was his calling.

Skinner received his Ph.D. from Harvard University in 1931, but he differed with his professors about what psychologists should study. Many faculty members were concerned about his disregard for their efforts to analyze the mind through introspection, an approach then common at Harvard. As discussed in Chapter 1, introspection is the process of using verbal reports to assess mental states. After thinking about your own thoughts and feelings, you talk about them as a way of making them public and available for others to study. The main objection to using introspection as a research method is that it is not very reliable. Behaviorists such as Skinner believed that, to be scientists, psychologists had to instead study observable actions. In other words, psychologists needed to focus on the behaviors that people and nonhuman animals display.

Inspired by the work of Watson and of Pavlov, Skinner believed that he could dramatically change an animal's behavior by providing incentives to the animal for performing particular acts. For the next half century, he conducted systematic studies of animals, often pigeons or rats, to discover the basic rules of learning. His groundbreaking work led Skinner to form radical ideas about behaviorism. In the process, he outlined many of the most important principles that shape the behavior of animals, including humans. These principles remain as relevant today as they were more than 50 years ago. And as you will learn in this chapter, a device known as the Skinner box—a different Skinner box—played a major part in this scientist's work. ■

Learning Objectives

- Define classical conditioning.
- Differentiate between US, UR, CS, and CR.
- Describe the role of learning in the development and treatment of phobias and drug addiction.
- Discuss the evolutionary significance of classical conditioning.
- Describe the Rescorla-Wagner model of classical conditioning.

6.1 What Ideas Guide the Study of Learning?

B. F. Skinner's ideas have been enormously influential throughout society, from classrooms to clinics and beyond. Dismissing the importance of mental states and questioning philosophical concepts such as free will, Skinner believed that the application of basic learning principles could create a better, more humane world. In fact, he felt that his ideas could free the world of poverty and violence. In *Walden Two* (1948), a best-selling novel, he depicts a utopia in which children are raised only with praise and incentives, never with punishment. *Walden Two* has inspired many people. Entire communities, such as northern Mexico's Los Horcones and rural Virginia's Twin Oaks, were founded on the principles in it.

This chapter focuses on what Skinner and a number of other learning theorists have discovered about how learning takes place. This material represents some of psychology's central contributions to our understanding of behavior. Learning theories have been used to improve quality of life and to train humans and nonhuman animals to learn new tasks. They have also contributed to the other major areas of psychology. To understand what humans and nonhuman animals are, we need to know what learning is.

Learning Results from Experience

Learning is a relatively enduring change in behavior. That change results from experience. Learning occurs when an animal benefits from experience so that its behavior is better adapted to the environment. The ability to learn is crucial for all animals. To survive, animals need to learn things such as which types of foods are dangerous, when it is safe to sleep, and which sounds indicate potential dangers. Learning is central to almost all aspects of human existence. It makes possible our basic abilities (such as walking and speaking) and our complex ones (such as flying airplanes, performing surgery, or maintaining intimate relationships). Learning also shapes many aspects of daily life: clothing choices, musical tastes, social rules about how close we stand to each other, cultural values about either exploiting or preserving the environment, and so on.

The essence of learning is understanding how events are related. For example, you might associate going to the dentist with being in pain. You might associate working with getting paid. Associations develop through *conditioning,* a process in which environmental stimuli and behavioral responses become connected. Psychologists study two types of conditioning. The first, *classical conditioning, or Pavlovian conditioning,* occurs when you learn that two types of events go together. For example, you learn that certain music plays during scary scenes in a movie. Now you feel anxious when you hear that music. The second type, *operant conditioning, or instrumental conditioning,* occurs when you learn that a behavior leads to a particular outcome. For example, you grasp that studying leads to better grades. This latter type of learning was of greatest interest to B. F. Skinner. Other types include learning by observing others. For example, you might learn about new fashions by paying attention to what celebrities are wearing.

Learning theory arose in the early twentieth century. Its development was due partly to the dissatisfaction among some psychologists with the widespread use of introspection. At the time, Freudian ideas were at the heart of psychological theorizing. For their research, Freud and his followers used verbal report techniques, such as dream analysis and free association. They aimed to assess the unconscious mental processes that they believed were the primary determinants of behavior. John B. Watson, however, argued that Freudian theory was unscientific and ultimately meaningless. He rejected any psychological enterprise that focused on things that could not be observed directly, such as people's mental experiences. Although he acknowledged that thoughts and beliefs existed, he believed they could not be studied using scientific methods. According to Watson, observable behavior was the only valid indicator of psychological activity.

learning A relatively enduring change in behavior, resulting from experience.

As discussed in Chapter 1, Watson founded behaviorism on such principles. This school of thought was based on the belief that humans and nonhuman animals are born with the potential to learn just about anything. In formulating his ideas, Watson was influenced by the seventeenth-century philosopher John Locke. An infant, Locke argued, is a *tabula rasa* (Latin for "blank slate"). Born knowing nothing, the infant acquires all of its knowledge through sensory experiences. In this way, a person develops. Building on this foundation, Watson stated that environment and its associated effects on animals were the sole determinants of learning. Watson felt so strongly about the preeminence of environment that he issued the following bold challenge: "Give me a dozen healthy infants, well formed, and my own specified world to bring them up in and I'll guarantee to take any one at random and train him to become any type of specialist I might select—doctor, lawyer, artist, merchant-chief, and yes, even beggar-man and thief, regardless of his talents, penchants, tendencies, abilities, vocations and race of his ancestors" (Watson, 1924, p. 82). In North America, Watson enormously influenced the study of psychology. Behaviorism was the dominant psychological paradigm there well into the 1960s. It affected the methods and theories of every area of psychology.

Behavioral Responses Are Conditioned

Watson developed his ideas about behaviorism after reading the work of Ivan Pavlov, who had won a Nobel Prize in 1904 for his research on the digestive system. Pavlov was interested in the *salivary reflex*. This automatic, unlearned response occurs when a food stimulus is presented to a hungry animal, including a human. For his work on the digestive system, Pavlov created an apparatus that collected saliva from dogs. With this device, he measured the different amounts of saliva that resulted when he placed various types of food into a dog's mouth (**Figure 6.2**).

Like so many major scientific advances, Pavlov's contribution to psychology started with a simple observation. One day he realized that the laboratory dogs were salivating before they tasted their food. Indeed, the dogs started salivating the moment a lab technician walked into the room or whenever they saw the bowls that usually contained food. Pavlov's genius was in recognizing that this

(a)

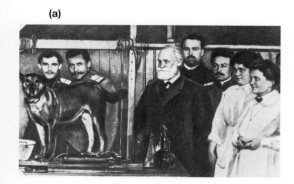

FIGURE 6.2 Pavlov's Apparatus and Classical Conditioning (a) Ivan Pavlov, pictured here with his colleagues and one of his canine subjects, conducted groundbreaking work on classical conditioning. **(b)** Pavlov's apparatus collected and measured a dog's saliva.

(b)

1 The dog is presented with a bowl that contains meat.

2 A tube carries the dog's saliva from the salivary glands to a container.

3 The container is connected to a device that measures the amount of saliva.

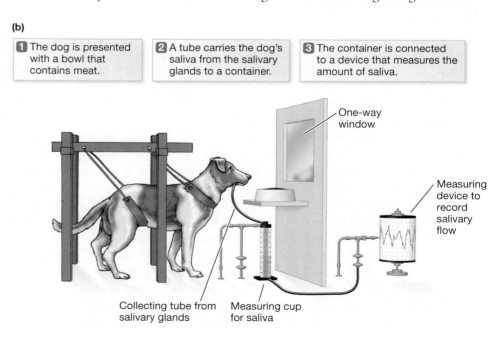

One-way window

Measuring device to record salivary flow

Collecting tube from salivary glands

Measuring cup for saliva

behavioral response was a window to the working mind. Unlike inborn reflexes, salivation at the sight of a bowl or of a person is not automatic. Therefore, that response must have been acquired through experience. This insight led Pavlov to devote the rest of his life to studying the basic principles of learning.

A researcher at the University of Pennsylvania, Edwin Twitmyer, independently made the same discovery of classical conditioning. Twitmyer studied the patellar (knee-jerk) reflex in humans. He informed his study participants that a bell would be rung when the knee tap was delivered. In one presentation, the bell accidentally rang without the tap occurring, and the knee-jerk response followed. The participants not only acquired the conditioned response. They also found it difficult or impossible to suppress the response. Twitmyer published this serendipitous discovery in his doctoral dissertation and presented it at the annual APA meeting a year before Pavlov's discovery, but he received little attention (Fernberger, 1943).

PAVLOV'S EXPERIMENTS Consider a typical Pavlovian experiment. A *neutral stimulus* unrelated to the salivary reflex, such as the clicking of a metronome, is presented along with a stimulus that reliably produces the reflex, such as food. The neutral stimulus can be anything that the animal can see or hear as long as it is not something that is usually associated with being fed. This pairing is called a *conditioning trial*. It is repeated a number of times. Then come the *critical trials*. Here, the metronome sound is presented alone and the salivary reflex is measured. Pavlov found that under these conditions, the sound of the metronome on its own produced salivation. This type of learning is now referred to as **classical conditioning,** or **Pavlovian conditioning.** In this type of conditioning, a neutral stimulus elicits a response because it has become associated with a stimulus that already produces that response.

Pavlov called the salivation elicited by food the **unconditioned response (UR).** The response is "unconditioned" because it occurs without prior training. It is an unlearned, automatic behavior, such as any simple reflex. Similarly, the food is the **unconditioned stimulus (US).** In the normal reflex response, the food (US) leads to salivation (UR). Because the clicking of the metronome produces salivation only after training, it is the **conditioned stimulus (CS).** That is, the clicking stimulates salivation only after learning takes place. The increased salivation that occurs when only the conditioned stimulus is presented is the **conditioned response (CR).** Both the unconditioned and the conditioned responses are salivation, but they are not identical: The conditioned response usually is weaker than the unconditioned response. Thus the metronome sound produces less saliva than the food does. (The process of conditioning is outlined in **Figure 6.3.**)

Suppose you are watching a movie in which a character is attacked. As you watch the attack scene, you feel tense, anxious, and perhaps disgusted. In this scenario, the frightening scene and your feelings occur naturally. That is, the stimulus and your response to it are unconditioned. Now imagine a piece of music that does not initially have much effect on you but that you hear in the movie just before each frightening scene. (A good example is the musical theme from the classic 1970s movie *Jaws.*) Eventually, you will begin to feel tense and anxious as soon as you hear the music. You have learned that the music, the conditioned stimulus, predicts scary scenes. Because of this learning, you feel the tension and anxiety, the conditioned response. As in Pavlov's studies, the CS (music) produces a somewhat different emotional response than the US (the scary scene). The response may be

classical conditioning (Pavlovian conditioning) A type of learned response; a neutral object comes to elicit a response when it is associated with a stimulus that already produces that response.

unconditioned response (UR) A response that does not have to be learned, such as a reflex.

unconditioned stimulus (US) A stimulus that elicits a response, such as a reflex, without any prior learning.

conditioned stimulus (CS) A stimulus that elicits a response only after learning has taken place.

conditioned response (CR) A response to a conditioned stimulus; a response that has been learned.

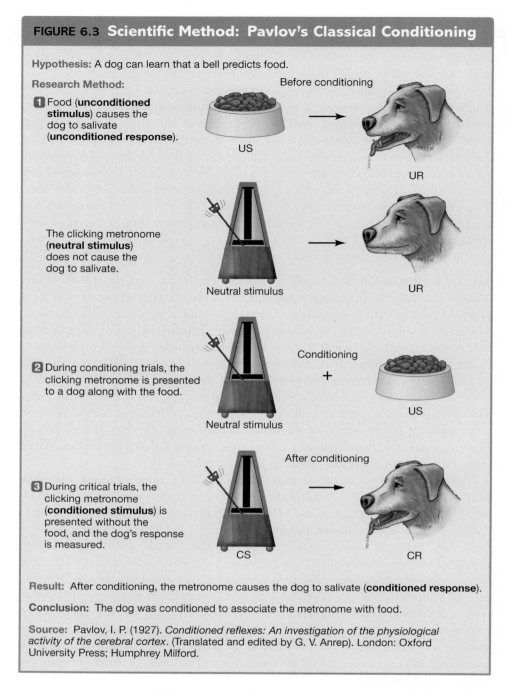

FIGURE 6.3 Scientific Method: Pavlov's Classical Conditioning

Hypothesis: A dog can learn that a bell predicts food.

Research Method:

1 Food (**unconditioned stimulus**) causes the dog to salivate (**unconditioned response**).

Before conditioning

US

UR

The clicking metronome (**neutral stimulus**) does not cause the dog to salivate.

Neutral stimulus

UR

2 During conditioning trials, the clicking metronome is presented to a dog along with the food.

Conditioning

Neutral stimulus

+

US

3 During critical trials, the clicking metronome (**conditioned stimulus**) is presented without the food, and the dog's response is measured.

After conditioning

CS

CR

Result: After conditioning, the metronome causes the dog to salivate (**conditioned response**).

Conclusion: The dog was conditioned to associate the metronome with food.

Source: Pavlov, I. P. (1927). *Conditioned reflexes: An investigation of the physiological activity of the cerebral cortex.* (Translated and edited by G. V. Anrep). London: Oxford University Press; Humphrey Milford.

weaker. It may be more a feeling of apprehension than one of fear or disgust. If you later hear this music in a different context, however, such as on the radio, you will again feel tense and anxious even though you are not watching the movie. You have been classically conditioned to be anxious when you hear the music. Because this association is learned, however, your anxious feeling from the music will always be weaker than your response to the scary scene was.

ACQUISITION, EXTINCTION, AND SPONTANEOUS RECOVERY Like many other scientists (of his time and subsequently), Pavlov was greatly influenced by Darwin's *On the Origin of Species.* Pavlov believed that conditioning is the basis for how animals learn to adapt to their environments. By learning to predict what objects

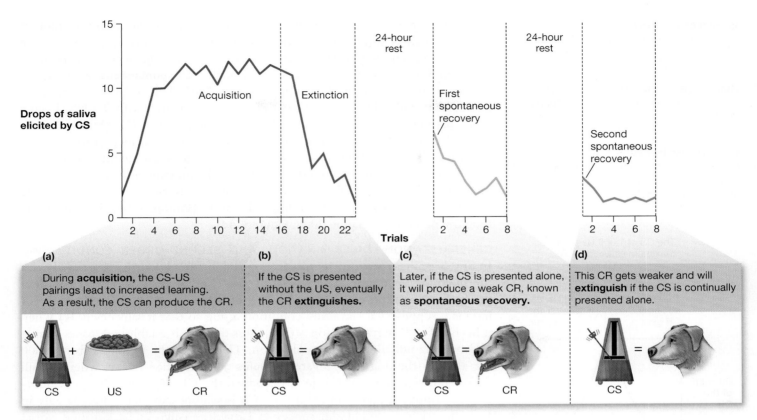

FIGURE 6.4 Acquisition, Extinction, and Spontaneous Recovery

bring pleasure or pain, animals acquire new adaptive behaviors. For instance, when an animal learns that a metronome beat predicts the appearance of food, this process of association is called **acquisition.** Acquisition is the gradual formation of an association between a conditioned stimulus (here, a metronome) and an unconditioned stimulus (here, food; **Figure 6.4a**).

From his research, Pavlov concluded that the critical element in the acquisition of a learned association is that the stimuli occur together in time. This bond is referred to as *contiguity.* Subsequent research has shown that the strongest conditioning occurs when there is a very brief delay between the conditioned stimulus and the unconditioned stimulus. Thus you will develop a stronger conditioned response to a piece of music if it comes just before a scary scene than if it occurs during or after the scary scene: The music's role in predicting the frightening scene is an important part of the classical conditioning. The next time you watch a horror movie, pay attention to the way the music gets louder just before a scary part begins.

Once a behavior is acquired, how long does it persist? For instance, what if the animal expects to receive food every time it hears the beat of the metronome, but after a long time no food appears? Animals sometimes have to learn when associations are no longer adaptive. Normally, after standard Pavlovian conditioning, the metronome (CS) leads to salivation (CR) because the animal learns to associate the metronome with the food (US). If the metronome is presented many times and food does not arrive, the animal learns that the metronome is no longer a good predictor of food. Because of this new learning, the animal's salivary response gradually disappears. This process is known as **extinction.** The conditioned response is *extinguished* when the conditioned stimulus no longer predicts the unconditioned stimulus (**Figure 6.4b**).

acquisition The gradual formation of an association between the conditioned and unconditioned stimuli.

extinction A process in which the conditioned response is weakened when the conditioned stimulus is repeated without the unconditioned stimulus.

spontaneous recovery A process in which a previously extinguished response reemerges after the presentation of the conditioned stimulus.

stimulus generalization Learning that occurs when stimuli that are similar but not identical to the conditioned stimulus produce the conditioned response.

stimulus discrimination A differentiation between two similar stimuli when only one of them is consistently associated with the unconditioned stimulus.

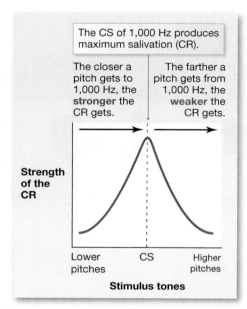

FIGURE 6.5 Stimulus Generalization

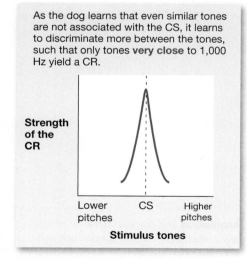

FIGURE 6.6 Stimulus Discrimination

Now suppose, a long time after extinction, the metronome is set in motion now and then. The adaptive response is to check back once in a while to see if the metronome is beating. Starting the metronome will once again produce the conditioned response of salivation. Through such **spontaneous recovery,** the extinguished CS again produces a CR (**Figure 6.4c**). This recover is temporary, however. It will fade quickly unless the CS is again paired with the US. Even a single pairing of the CS with the US will reestablish the CR, which will then again diminish if CS-US pairings do not continue. Thus extinction inhibits (reduces the strength of) the associative bond, but it does not eliminate that bond. Extinction is a form of learning that overwrites the previous association: The animal learns that the original association no longer holds true (e.g., the metronome no longer signals that it will be followed by meat; Bouton, 1994; Bouton, Westbrook, Corcoran, & Maren, 2006; **Figure 6.4d**).

GENERALIZATION, DISCRIMINATION, AND SECOND-ORDER CONDITIONING
In any learning situation, hundreds of possible stimuli can be associated with the unconditioned stimulus to produce the conditioned response. How does the brain determine which stimulus is—or which stimuli are—relevant? For instance, suppose we classically condition a dog so that it salivates (CR) when it hears a 1,000-hertz (Hz) tone (CS). After the CR is established, tones similar to 1,000 Hz will also produce salivation. The farther the tones are from 1,000 Hz, the less the dog will salivate. **Stimulus generalization** occurs when stimuli similar but not identical to the CS produce the CR (**Figure 6.5**). Generalization is adaptive, because in nature the CS is seldom experienced repeatedly in an identical way. Slight differences in variables—such as background noise, temperature, and lighting—lead to slightly different perceptions of the CS. As a result of these different perceptions, animals learn to respond to variations in the CS.

Of course, generalization has limits. Sometimes it is important for animals to distinguish among similar stimuli. For instance, two plant species might look similar, but one might be poisonous. In **stimulus discrimination,** animals learn to differentiate between two similar stimuli if one is consistently associated with the unconditioned stimulus and the other is not. Pavlov and his students demonstrated that dogs can learn to make very fine distinctions between similar stimuli. For example, dogs can learn to detect subtle differences in shades of gray or in tones (**Figure 6.6**).

Sometimes a conditioned stimulus does not become directly associated with an unconditioned stimulus. Instead, the conditioned stimulus becomes associated with other stimuli associated with the US. This phenomenon is known as *second-order conditioning*. In one of Pavlov's early studies, a CS-US bond was formed between a tone (CS) and food (US) so that the tone (CS) led to salivation (CR). In a second training session, a black square was repeatedly presented at the same time as the tone. There was no US (no presentation of the meat) during this phase of the study. After a few trials, the black square was presented alone. It too produced salivation.

Second-order conditioning helps account for the complexity of learned associations, especially in people. For instance, suppose a child has been conditioned to associate money with desirable objects, such as candy and toys. Now suppose that whenever the child's uncle visits, the uncle gives the child some money. Through second-order conditioning, the child will learn to associate the uncle with money. If the child feels affection for the uncle, some of that affection will come from the association with money (Domjan, 2003).

Phobias and Addictions Have Learned Components

Classical conditioning helps explain many behavioral phenomena. Among the examples are phobias and addictions.

PHOBIAS AND THEIR TREATMENT A **phobia** is an acquired fear out of proportion to the real threat of an object or of a situation. Common phobias include the fears of heights, of dogs, of insects, of snakes, and of the dark. According to classical-conditioning theory, phobias develop through the generalization of a fear experience, as when a person stung by a wasp develops a fear of all flying insects. (Phobias are discussed further in Chapter 14, "Psychological Disorders.")

Animals can be classically conditioned to fear neutral objects. This process is known as *fear conditioning*. In a typical study of fear conditioning, a rat is classically conditioned to produce a fear response to an auditory tone: Electric shock follows the tone, and eventually the tone produces fear responses on its own. These responses include specific physiological and behavioral reactions. One interesting response is *freezing,* or keeping still. Humans are among the many species that respond to fear by freezing. For example, as captured in video footage, right after a bomb exploded at the Atlanta Summer Olympics in 1996, most people froze for a few seconds. Immediately keeping still might be a hardwired response that helps animals deal with predators, which often are attracted by movement (LeDoux, 2002).

In 1919, John B. Watson became one of the first researchers to demonstrate the role of classical conditioning in the development of phobias. In this case study, Watson taught an infant named Albert B. to fear neutral objects. It is important to note Watson's motives for conditioning "Little Albert." At the time, the prominent theory of phobias was based on Freudian ideas about unconscious repressed sexual desires. Believing that Freudian ideas were unscientific and unnecessarily complex, Watson proposed that phobias could be explained by simple learning principles, such as classical conditioning. To test his hypothesis, Watson devised a learning study. He asked a woman he knew to let him use her son, Albert B., in the study. Because this child was emotionally stable, Watson believed the experiment would cause him little harm. When Albert was 9 months old, Watson and his lab assistant, Rosalie Rayner, presented him with various neutral objects, including a white rat, a rabbit, a dog, a monkey, costume masks, and a ball of white wool. Albert showed a natural curiosity about these items, but he displayed no overt emotional responses.

When Albert was 11 months old, Watson and Rayner began the conditioning trials. This time, as they presented the white rat and Albert reached for it, Watson smashed a hammer into an iron bar, producing a loud clanging sound. The sound scared the child, who immediately withdrew and hid his face. Watson did this a few more times at intervals of five days until Albert would whimper and cringe when the rat was presented alone. Thus the US (smashing sound) led to a UR (fear). Eventually, the pairing of the CS (rat) and US (smashing sound) led to the rat's producing fear (CR) on its own. The fear response generalized to other stimuli that Watson had presented along with the rat at the initial meeting. Over time, Albert became frightened of them all, including the rabbit and the ball of wool. Even a Santa Claus with a white beard produced a fear response. Thus classical conditioning was shown to be an effective method of inducing phobia (**Figure 6.7**).

Watson had planned to conduct extinction trials to remove the learned phobias. Albert's mother removed the child from the study, however, before Watson

phobia An acquired fear that is out of proportion to the real threat of an object or of a situation.

FIGURE 6.7 **Scientific Method: Watson's "Little Albert" Experiment**

Hypothesis: Phobias can be explained by classical conditioning.

Research Method:

1 Little Albert was presented with neutral objects that provoked a neutral response. These objects included a white rat and costume masks.

2 During conditioning trials, when Albert reached for the white rat (CS) a loud clanging sound (US) scared him (UR).

Results: Eventually, the pairing of the rat (CS) and the clanging sound (US) led to the rat's producing fear (CR) on its own. The fear response generalized to other stimuli presented with the rat initially, such as the costume masks.

Conclusion: Classical conditioning can cause people to fear neutral objects.

Source: Watson, J. B., & Rayner, R. (1920). Conditioned emotional reactions. *Journal of Experimental Psychology, 3,* 1–14.

could conduct those trials. For many years, no one seemed to know what had become of Little Albert. His fate was one of psychology's great mysteries. Finally, an investigative team led by the psychologist Hall Beck uncovered evidence that Little Albert was actually Douglas Merritte. Merritte died at age 6, likely of meningitis (a brain infection; Beck, Levinson, & Irons, 2009). Watson's conditioning of Albert has long been criticized as unethical. An ethics committee probably would not approve such a study today.

In his detailed plans for the reconditioning, Watson described a method of continually presenting the feared items to Albert paired with more pleasant things, such as candy. A colleague of Watson's used this method on a child who was afraid of rabbits and other furry objects. The behavioral pioneer Mary Cover Jones eliminated the fear of rabbits in a 3-year-old named Peter by bringing the rabbit closer as she provided Peter with a favorite food (Jones, 1924). Such classical-conditioning techniques have since proved valuable for developing very effective behavioral therapies to treat phobias. For instance, when a person is suffering from a phobia, a clinician might expose the patient to small doses of the feared stimulus while having the client engage in an enjoyable task. This technique, called *counterconditioning,* may help the client overcome the phobia.

The behavioral therapist Joseph Wolpe has developed a formal treatment based on counterconditioning (Wolpe, 1997). Wolpe's treatment is called *systematic desensitization*. First the client is taught how to relax his or her muscles. Then the client is asked to imagine the feared object or situation while continuing to use the relaxation exercises. Eventually, the client is exposed to the feared stimulus while relaxing. The general idea is that the CS → CR$_1$ (fear) connection can be broken by developing a CS → CR$_2$ (relaxation) connection. As discussed in Chapter 15, psychologists now believe that in breaking the fear connection, repeated exposure to the feared stimulus is more important than relaxation.

DRUG ADDICTION Classical conditioning also plays an important role in drug addiction. (Addiction is discussed fully in Chapter 5, "Consciousness.") Conditioned drug effects are common and demonstrate conditioning's power. For example, the smell of coffee can become a conditioned stimulus. The smell alone can lead coffee drinkers to feel activated and aroused—as though they have actually consumed caffeine. Likewise, for heroin addicts, the sight of the needle and the feeling when it is inserted into the skin become a CS. For this reason, addicts sometimes inject themselves with water to reduce their cravings when heroin is unavailable. Sometimes, the sight of a straight-edge razor blade, which is often used to "cut" heroin, can briefly increase a drug addict's cravings (Siegel, 2005). When former heroin addicts are exposed to environmental cues associated with their drug use, they often experience cravings. If such cravings are not satisfied, the addict may experience *withdrawal,* the unpleasant state of tension and anxiety that occurs when addicts stop using drugs. Addicts who quit using drugs in treatment centers often relapse when they return to their old environments because they experience conditioned craving.

In laboratory settings, researchers have presented heroin addicts or cocaine addicts with cues associated with drug ingestion. These cues have led the addicts to experience cravings and various physiological responses associated with withdrawal, such as changes in heart rate and blood pressure. Brain imaging studies have found that such cues lead to activation of the prefrontal cortex and various regions of the limbic system, areas of the brain involved in the experience of reward (Volkow et al., 2008). Seeing a tantalizing food item when you are hungry activates these same brain regions as you anticipate enjoying your tasty meal. In the same way, the sight of drug cues produces an expectation that the drug high will follow (**Figure 6.8**). According to the psychologist Shepard Siegel (2005), it is therefore important that treatment for addiction include exposing addicts to drug cues. Such exposure helps extinguish responses, in the brain and the rest of the body, to those cues. In this way, the cues are prevented from triggering cravings in the future.

Siegel and his colleagues have also conducted research into the relationship between drug tolerance and situation. As discussed in Chapter 5, tolerance is a process by which addicts need more and more of a drug to experience the same effects. Siegel's research has shown that tolerance is greatest when the drug is taken in the

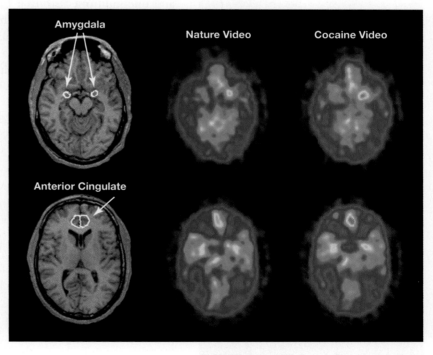

FIGURE 6.8 **PET Scans Showing Activation of Limbic System Structures** Cocaine addicts were shown videos of nature scenes and videos of cocaine cues. The cocaine-related videos sparked activation in brain regions associated with reward and emotion, such as the anterior cingulate and the amygdala. Watching nature videos did not lead to increased activity in these areas. (Areas with greatest activation are shown in orange and red.)

same location as previous drug use occurred in. Presumably, the body has learned to expect the drug in that location and then to compensate for the drug, such as by altering neurochemistry or physiology to metabolize it. For example, college students show greater tolerance to alcohol when it is provided with familiar cues (e.g., a drink that looks and tastes like beer) than when the same amount of alcohol is provided in a novel form (e.g., a blue, peppermint-flavored drink; Siegel, Baptista, Kim, McDonald, & Weise-Kelly, 2000). Tolerance can be so great that addicts regularly use drug doses that would be fatal for the inexperienced user. Conversely, Siegel's findings imply that if addicts take their usual large doses in novel settings, they are more likely to overdose. That is, because the addicts are taking drugs under different conditions, their bodies will not respond sufficiently to compensate for the drugs (Siegel, 1984; Siegel, Hinson, Krank, & McCully,1982).

Classical Conditioning Involves More Than Events Occurring at the Same Time

Pavlov's original explanation for classical conditioning was that any two events presented in contiguity would produce a learned association. Any object or phenomenon could be converted to a conditioned stimulus when associated with any unconditioned stimulus. Pavlov and his followers believed that the association's strength was determined by factors such as the intensity of the conditioned and unconditioned stimuli. For example, the more intense the stimuli were, the greater the learning would be. (A louder metronome or larger piece of meat would produce stronger associations than a quieter metronome or smaller piece of meat.) In the mid-1960s, a number of challenges to Pavlov's theory suggested that some conditioned stimuli were more likely than others to produce learning. Contiguity was not sufficient to create CS-US associations.

(a)

EVOLUTIONARY SIGNIFICANCE Research conducted by the psychologist John Garcia and colleagues showed that certain pairings of stimuli are more likely to become associated than others. For instance, when animals receive nonlethal amounts of poison in their food that make them ill, they quickly learn to avoid the tastes or smells associated with the food (Garcia & Koelling, 1966).

Likewise, most people can recall a time when they ate a particular food and then became ill with nausea, stomach upset, and vomiting. Whether or not the food caused the illness, most people respond to this sequence of events by demonstrating a *conditioned food aversion*. This response occurs even if the illness clearly was caused by a virus or some other condition. It is especially likely to occur if the food was not part of the person's usual diet. The association between eating a novel food and getting sick, even when the illness occurs hours after eating, is so strong that a food aversion can be formed in one trial (**Figure 6.9**). Some people cannot stand even the smell of a food they associate with a stomach-related illness.

(b)

FIGURE 6.9 Conditioned Food Aversion in Animals (a) After eating a monarch butterfly, **(b)** this blue jay vomited and thus learned to avoid eating anything that looks like the butterfly. **What evolutionary value do you see in this learned behavior?**

Conditioned food aversions are easy to produce with smell or taste, but they are very difficult to produce with light or sound. This difference makes sense, since smell and taste are the main cues that guide an animal's eating behavior. From an evolutionary viewpoint, animals that quickly associate a certain flavor with illness, and therefore avoid that flavor, will be more successful. That is, they will be more likely to survive and pass along their genes.

Contemporary researchers are interested in how classical conditioning helps animals learn adaptive responses (Hollis, 1997; Shettleworth, 2001). The adaptive value of a particular response varies according to the animal's evolutionary history. For example, taste aversions are easy to condition in rats but difficult to condition in birds. This difference occurs because in selecting food, rats rely more on taste and birds rely more on vision. Accordingly, birds quickly learn to avoid a visual cue they associate with illness. Different types of stimuli cause different reactions even within a species. Rats freeze and startle if a CS is auditory, but they rise on their hind legs if the CS is visual (Holland, 1977).

Such differences in learned adaptive responses may reflect the survival value that different auditory and visual stimuli have for particular animals in particular environments. Those meanings are of course related to the potential dangers associated with the stimuli. For example, monkeys can more easily be conditioned to fear snakes than to fear objects such as flowers or rabbits (Cook & Mineka, 1989). The psychologist Martin Seligman (1970) has argued that animals are genetically programmed to fear specific objects. He refers to this programming as *biological preparedness*. Preparedness helps explain why animals tend to fear potentially dangerous things (e.g., snakes, fire, heights) rather than objects that pose little threat (e.g., flowers, shoes, babies).

The threats may also come from within an animal's own species. For example, when people participate in conditioning experiments in which aversive stimuli are paired with members of their own racial group or members of a different racial group, they more easily associate the negative stimuli with outgroup members (Olsson, Ebert, Banaji, & Phelps, 2005). This finding indicates that people are predisposed to wariness of outgroup members. Presumably, this tendency has come about because outgroup members have been more dangerous over the course of human evolution. The tendency has sometimes been exploited to create or enhance prejudice toward outgroups during wars and other intergroup conflicts. For example, as the Nazis prepared for and conducted their extermination of Jews during World War II, they created films in which Jews' faces morphed into those of rats crawling in filth. By showing these images to the German population, the Nazis aimed to condition a national response of repulsion to facial features associated with being Jewish. (Videos of these films are cataloged at the Museum of Tolerance, in Los Angeles, California.)

Learning Involves Cognition

Until the 1970s, most learning theorists were concerned only with observable stimuli and observable responses. Since then, learning theorists have placed a greater emphasis on trying to understand the mental processes that underlie conditioning. An important principle has emerged from this work: Classical conditioning is a way that animals come to *predict* the occurrence of events. Psychologists' increasing consideration of mental processes such as prediction and expectancy is called the *cognitive perspective* on learning (Hollis, 1997).

The psychologist Robert Rescorla (1966) conducted one of the first studies that highlighted the role of cognition in learning. He argued that for learning to take place, the conditioned stimulus must accurately predict the unconditioned stimulus. For instance, a stimulus that occurs *before* the US is more easily conditioned than one that comes *after* it. Even though the two are both contiguous presentations with the US (close to it in time), the first stimulus is more easily learned because it predicts the US. Across all learning conditions, as mentioned earlier, some delay between the CS and the US is optimal for learning. The length of delay varies, depending on the natures of the conditioned and unconditioned stimuli. For instance, eyeblink conditioning occurs when a sound (CS) is associated with a puff of air blown into the eye (US), which leads to a blink. Optimal

FIGURE 6.10 Questioning Superstitions According to superstition, bad luck will come your way if a black cat crosses your path or if you walk under a ladder. **What misfortunes could actually occur in the situations shown here?**

Avoiding the Association of Events with Other Events That Occur at the Same Time

Do you have a lucky charm? Do you wear your "good luck" socks every time you take an exam? Do you try to blow out the candles on your birthday cake in just one breath so that your silent wish will come true? The list of people's superstitions is virtually endless. In North America and Europe, people avoid the number 13. In China, Japan, Korea, and Hawaii, they avoid the number 4. The basketball player Michael Jordan, a graduate of the University of North Carolina, always wore shorts with the North Carolina logo under his uniform for good luck. The baseball player Wade Boggs ate only chicken on the day of a game (Morrison, n. d.). Even pigeons *might* be superstitious. In conditioning pigeons' pecking behavior, Skinner found that, during each trial, a particular pigeon would swing its head in the same way before responding, while another would do a half turn before responding.

The tendency to associate events that occur together in time is incredibly strong. When a chance event happens to occur close in time to a second event, humans and nonhuman animals sometimes associate the chance event with the second event. People, and apparently other animals, have a strong need to understand what causes or predicts events. Their resulting associations can lead people, at least, to cling to superstitions.

Most superstitions are harmless, but some can interfere with daily living, as when people stay in bed on the 4th or 13th of every month or refuse to get off on the 4th or 13th floor of a building. As a critical thinker, be aware of the tendency to associate events with other events that occur, perhaps simply by chance, at the same time (**Figure 6.10**).

---

learning for eyeblink conditioning is measured in milliseconds. By contrast, conditioned food aversions often take many hours, since the ill effects of consuming poisons or food that has gone bad may not be felt for hours after eating.

The cognitive model of classical learning, published by Rescorla and his colleague Allan Wagner, profoundly changed our understanding of learning (Rescorla & Wagner, 1972). The **Rescorla-Wagner model** states that an animal learns an expectation that some predictors (potential CSs) are better than others. According to this model, the strength of the CS–US association is determined by the extent to which the US is unexpected or surprising. The greater the surprise of the US, the more effort an organism puts into trying to understand its occurrence so that it can predict future occurrences. The result is greater classical conditioning of the event (CS) that predicted the US.

Say you always use an electric can opener to open a can of dog food. Your dog associates the sound of the can opener (CS) with the appearance of food (US). The dog wags its tail and runs around in circles when it hears that sound. Now say the electric can opener breaks and you replace it with a manual one. Without hearing the sound of the electric can opener, your dog receives food. According to Rescorla and Wagner, when an animal encounters a novel

Rescorla-Wagner model A cognitive model of classical conditioning; it states that the strength of the CS-US association is determined by the extent to which the unconditioned stimulus is unexpected or surprising.

stimulus, it pays attention to it. This behavior is known as an *orienting response.* In other words, the unexpected appearance of the food (US) will cause your dog to pay attention to events in the environment that might have produced the food. Through this *orienting response,* your dog soon will learn to associate being fed with your use of the new can opener (**Figure 6.11**).

Other aspects of classical conditioning are consistent with the Rescorla-Wagner model. First, an animal will more easily associate an unconditioned stimulus with a novel stimulus than with a familiar stimulus. For example, a dog can be conditioned more easily with a smell new to it (such as that of almonds) than with a smell it knows (that of dog biscuits, perhaps). Second, once a conditioned stimulus is learned, it can prevent the acquisition of a new conditioned stimulus. This phenomenon is known as the *blocking effect.* For example, if a dog has learned that the smell of almonds (CS) is a good predictor of food (US), that dog will not look for other predictors, even if they now also predict the availability of food. Third, a stimulus associated with a CS can act as an *occasion setter,* or trigger, for the CS (Schmajuk, Lamoureux, & Holland, 1998). For example, a dog might

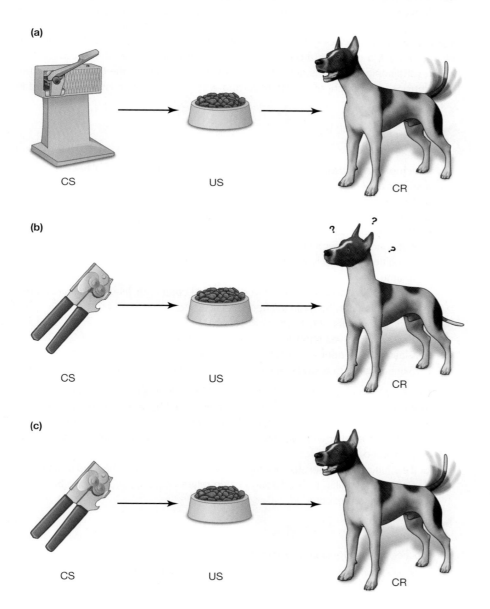

(a)

CS   US   CR

(b)

CS   US   CR

(c)

CS   US   CR

FIGURE 6.11 Rescorla-Wagner Model
The Rescorla-Wagner model of learning emphasizes the substitution of one stimulus for another. **(a)** Here a dog associates the sound of an electric can opener with the arrival of food. **(b)** With the substitution of a manual can opener for the electric one, the dog is initially surprised. What happened to the reliable predictor of the dog's food? **(c)** The orienting response causes the dog to check the environment for a new stimulus. When the dog comes to associate the manual can opener with the arrival of food, the new stimulus has become the better predictor of the expected event: time to eat!

learn that the smell of almonds predicts food only when the smell is preceded by a sound or by a flash of light. The sound or light lets the dog know whether the association between the smell of almonds and food is active.

Summing Up

What Ideas Guide the Study of Learning?

Behaviorism, founded by John B. Watson, focuses on observable aspects of learning. Ivan Pavlov developed classical-conditioning theory to account for the learned association between neutral stimuli and reflexive behaviors. Conditioning occurs when a conditioned stimulus becomes associated with an unconditioned stimulus. For learning to occur, the conditioned stimulus needs to reliably predict the unconditioned stimulus, not simply be contiguous with it. Classical conditioning explains the development of phobias and contributes to drug addiction. Accordingly, techniques based on classical conditioning may be used to treat phobias and drug addiction. Many psychologists believe that classical conditioning evolved because it helps animals learn adaptive responses—that is, responses that facilitate survival. The Rescorla-Wagner model, a cognitive model of classical conditioning, states that the degree to which conditioning occurs is determined by the extent to which the US is unexpected or surprising, with stronger effects occurring when a novel or unusual CS is used in conditioning.

Measuring Up

1. Which of the following are true statements about conditioning? Check as many as apply.
   a. Conditioning is one kind of learning.
   b. Only nonhuman animals can be conditioned.
   c. B. F. Skinner used rats and pigeons in most of his research because he was not concerned with human learning.
   d. Conditioning usually involves the association of two events that occur close in time.
   e. Conditioning does not meet the definitional criteria for learning because the association can be extinguished, or unlearned.
   f. Learning results only from experiences.
   g. Learning involves short-term changes in behavior.
   h. Classical and operant conditioning are the same.
   i. Skinner came to appreciate the introspection methods used by his professors.

2. John B. Watson had planned to extinguish Little Albert's conditioned response to the rat. Which of the following techniques would have achieved that goal?
   a. Repeatedly showing Little Albert the rat without making a loud sound.
   b. Making a loud sound every time a different and unrelated object was presented.
   c. Teaching Little Albert to strike the bar so he could make the loud sound.
   d. Repeatedly making a loud sound when related objects, such as the ball of wool, were presented.

Answers: 1. Choices a, d, and f are true. 2. a. Repeatedly showing Little Albert the rat without making a loud sound.

6.2 How Does Operant Conditioning Differ from Classical Conditioning?

Classical conditioning is a relatively passive process. In it, an animal learns predictive connections between stimuli, regardless of what the animal does beyond that. This form of conditioning does not account for the many times that one of the events occurs because the animal has taken some action.

Our behaviors often represent means to particular ends. They are *instrumental*—done for a purpose. We buy food to eat it, we study to get good grades, we work to receive money, and so on. We learn that behaving in certain ways leads to rewards, and we learn that not behaving in other ways keeps us from punishment. This type of learning is called **operant conditioning,** or **instrumental conditioning.** B. F. Skinner, the psychologist most closely associated with this process, chose the term *operant* to express the idea that animals *operate* on their environments to produce effects. Operant conditioning is the learning process in which an action's consequences determine the likelihood that the action will be performed in the future.

The study of operant conditioning began in the late nineteenth century, in Cambridge, Massachusetts, at the home of the Harvard psychologist William James. A young graduate student working with James, Edward Thorndike, took inspiration from Charles Darwin's painstakingly precise observations of animal behavior. In James's basement, Thorndike performed the first reported carefully controlled experiments in comparative animal psychology. Specifically, he studied whether nonhuman animals showed signs of intelligence. As part of his research, Thorndike built a *puzzle box,* a small cage with a trapdoor (**Figure 6.12a**). The trapdoor would open if the animal inside performed a specific action, such as pulling a string. Thorndike placed food-deprived animals, initially chickens, inside the puzzle box to see if they could figure out how to escape.

operant conditioning (instrumental conditioning) A learning process in which the consequences of an action determine the likelihood that it will be performed in the future.

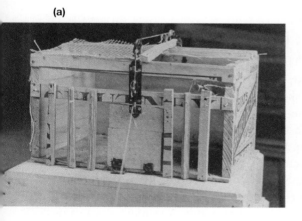

(a)

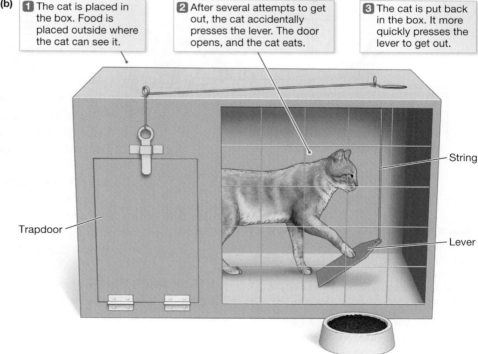

(b)

1. The cat is placed in the box. Food is placed outside where the cat can see it.
2. After several attempts to get out, the cat accidentally presses the lever. The door opens, and the cat eats.
3. The cat is put back in the box. It more quickly presses the lever to get out.

String

Lever

Trapdoor

FIGURE 6.12 Thorndike's Puzzle Box
(a) Thorndike used puzzle boxes, such as the one depicted here, **(b)** to assess learning in animals.

FIGURE 6.13 Law of Effect By studying cats' attempts to escape from a puzzle box, Thorndike was able to formulate his general theory of learning.

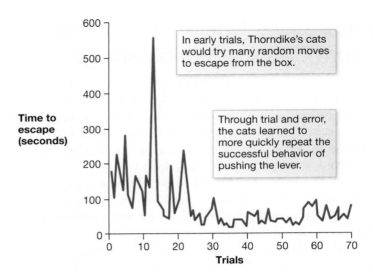

FIGURE 6.13 Law of Effect By studying cats' attempts to escape from a puzzle box, Thorndike was able to formulate his general theory of learning.

In early trials, Thorndike's cats would try many random moves to escape from the box.

Through trial and error, the cats learned to more quickly repeat the successful behavior of pushing the lever.

When Thorndike moved to Columbia University to complete his Ph.D., he switched from using chickens to using cats in his studies. To motivate the cats, he would place food just outside the box. When a cat was first placed in the box, it usually attempted to escape through numerous nonproductive behaviors. After 5 to 10 minutes of struggling, the cat would *accidentally* pull the string, and the door would open. Thorndike would then return the cat to the box and repeat the trial. The cat would pull the string more quickly on each subsequent trial. Soon, it would learn to escape from the puzzle box within seconds (**Figure 6.10b**). From this line of research, Thorndike developed a general theory of learning. According to this **law of effect,** any behavior that leads to a "satisfying state of affairs" is likely to occur again. Any behavior that leads to an "annoying state of affairs" is less likely to occur again (**Figure 6.13**).

Reinforcement Increases Behavior

Thirty years after Thorndike experimented with animals escaping puzzle boxes, another Harvard graduate student in psychology, B. F. Skinner, developed a more formal learning theory based on the law of effect. As discussed at the beginning of this chapter, Skinner had been greatly influenced by John B. Watson and shared his philosophy of behaviorism. He therefore objected to the subjective aspects of Thorndike's law of effect: States of "satisfaction" are not observable empirically. Skinner coined the term *reinforcer* to describe an event that produces a learned response. A **reinforcer** is a stimulus that occurs after a response and increases the likelihood that the response will be repeated. Skinner believed that behavior—studying, eating, driving on the proper side of the road, and so on—occurs because it has been reinforced.

THE SKINNER BOX To assess operant conditioning, Skinner developed a simple device. It consists of a small chamber or cage. Inside, one lever or response key is connected to a food supply, and a second lever or response key is connected to a water supply. An animal, usually a rat or pigeon, is placed in the chamber or cage. The animal learns to press one lever or key to receive food, the other

"Oh, not bad. The light comes on, I press the bar, they write me a check. How about you?"

law of effect Thorndike's general theory of learning: Any behavior that leads to a "satisfying state of affairs" is likely to occur again, and any behavior that leads to an "annoying state of affairs" is less likely to occur again.

reinforcer A stimulus that follows a response and increases the likelihood that the response will be repeated.

(a)

(b)

Lever

Food tray

FIGURE 6.14 **Skinner Box (a)** B. F. Skinner and one of his subjects demonstrate **(b)** the operant chamber, now known as the Skinner box.

lever or key to receive water. In his earlier research, Skinner had used a maze. There, a rat had to make a specific turn to get access to the reinforcer, usually a small piece of food in the goal box. After the rat completed a trial, Skinner had to return the rat to the beginning of the maze. He developed the *operant chamber,* as he called it, basically because he grew tired of fetching rats. With the device—which came to be known as the *Skinner box,* although he never used that term—he could expose rats or pigeons to repeated conditioning trials without having to do anything but observe (**Figure 6.14**). Skinner later built mechanical recording devices that allowed the experimenter to conduct trials without being present.

SHAPING When performing operant conditioning, you cannot provide the reinforcer until the animal displays the appropriate response. An animal inside the Skinner box has so little to do that it typically presses the lever or key sooner rather than later. One major problem with operant conditioning outside the Skinner box is that the same animal might take a while to perform the action you are looking for. Rather than wait for the animal to spontaneously perform the action, you can use an operant-conditioning technique to teach the animal to do so. This powerful process is called **shaping.** It consists of reinforcing behaviors that are increasingly similar to the desired behavior.

Suppose you are trying to teach your dog to roll over. You initially reward the dog for any behavior that even slightly resembles rolling over, such as lying down. Once this behavior is established, you reinforce behaviors more selectively. Reinforcing *successive approximations* eventually produces the desired behavior. In other words, the animal learns to discriminate which behavior is being reinforced.

Shaping has been used to condition animals to perform amazing feats: pigeons playing table tennis, dogs playing the piano, pigs doing housework such as picking up clothes and vacuuming, and so on (**Figure 6.15**). Shaping has also been used to teach appropriate social skills to mentally ill people; to teach language to children with autism; and to teach basic skills, such as dressing themselves, to mentally retarded individuals. More generally, parents and educators often use shaping to encourage appropriate behavior in children. For example, they praise children for their initial—often illegible—attempts at handwriting.

FIGURE 6.15 **Shaping** Shaping, an operant conditioning technique, consists of reinforcing behaviors that are increasingly similar to the desired behavior. This technique can be used to train animals to perform extraordinary behaviors. Here a trained dog water-skis for a boat show. **Suppose you wanted to teach yourself to do something. Which behavior would you choose, and how would you go about shaping it?**

REINFORCERS CAN BE CONDITIONED The most obvious reinforcers are those necessary for survival, such as food or water. Because they satisfy biological needs, they are called *primary reinforcers*. From an evolutionary standpoint, the learning value of primary reinforcers makes a great deal of sense: Animals that repeatedly perform behaviors reinforced by food or water are more likely to survive and pass along their genes. But many apparent reinforcers do not directly satisfy biological needs. For example, a compliment, money, or an A on a paper can be reinforcing. Events or objects that serve as reinforcers but do not satisfy biological needs are called *secondary reinforcers*. These reinforcers are established through classical conditioning, as described earlier in this chapter: We learn to associate a neutral stimulus, such as money (CS), with rewards such as food, security, and power (US). Money is really only pieces of metal or of paper, but these and other neutral objects become meaningful through their associations with unconditioned stimuli.

REINFORCER POTENCY Some reinforcers are more powerful than others. The psychologist David Premack (1959; Holstein & Premack, 1965) theorized about how a reinforcer's value could be determined. The key is the amount of time an organism, when free to do anything, engages in a specific behavior associated with the reinforcer. For instance, most children would choose to spend more time eating ice cream than eating spinach. Ice cream is therefore more reinforcing for children than spinach is. One great advantage of Premack's theory is that it can account for differences in individuals' values. For people who prefer spinach to ice cream, spinach serves as a more potent reinforcer.

A logical application of Premack's theory, now called the *Premack principle,* is that a more valued activity can be used to reinforce the performance of a less valued activity. Parents use the Premack principle all the time. They tell their children, "Eat your spinach and then you'll get dessert," "Finish your homework and then you can go out," and so on.

Both Reinforcement and Punishment Can Be Positive or Negative

Reinforcement and punishment have the opposite effects on behavior. Whereas reinforcement increases a behavior's probability, punishment decreases its probability. For example, feeding a rat after it presses a lever will increase the probability that the rat will press the lever. Giving a rat an electric shock after it presses a lever will decrease that action's probability. Both reinforcement and punishment can be positive or negative. The designation depends on whether something is given or removed, not on whether any part of the process is good or bad.

POSITIVE AND NEGATIVE REINFORCEMENT Through the administration of a stimulus, **positive reinforcement** increases the probability that a behavior will be repeated. Positive reinforcement is often called *reward*. Rewarded behaviors increase in frequency, as when people work harder in response to praise or increased pay. In contrast, **negative reinforcement** increases behavior through the *removal* of an unpleasant stimulus. For instance, when a rat is required to press a lever to turn off an electric shock, the pressing of the lever has been negatively reinforced. Negative reinforcement differs from punishment. If the rat were being punished, it would receive a shock *for* pressing the lever. The key point is that reinforcement—positive or negative—*increases* the likelihood of a behavior, whereas punishment *decreases* the likelihood of a behavior.

positive reinforcement The administration of a stimulus to increase the probability of a behavior's being repeated.

negative reinforcement The removal of a stimulus to increase the probability of a behavior's being repeated.

Negative reinforcement is quite common in everyday life. You take a pill to get rid of a headache. You close the door to your room to shut out noise. You change the channel to avoid watching an awful program. You pick up a crying baby. In each case, you are trying to avoid or escape an unwanted stimulus. If the action you take successfully reduces the unwanted stimulus, then the next time you have a headache, hear noise in your room, see an awful program, or are with a crying baby, the more likely you are to repeat the behavior that reduced the stimulus. The behavior has been negatively reinforced.

POSITIVE AND NEGATIVE PUNISHMENT Punishment reduces the probability that a behavior will recur. It can do so through positive or negative means. Again, "positive" or "negative" here means whether something is added or removed, not whether it is good or bad. **Positive punishment** decreases the behavior's probability through the administration of a stimulus. Usually the stimulus in positive punishment is unpleasant. When a rat receives a shock for pressing a lever, the rat has received positive punishment. **Negative punishment** decreases the behavior's probability through the removal of a usually pleasant stimulus. When a teenager loses driving privileges for speeding, the teenager has received negative punishment. If that same teen has received a speeding ticket, the ticket serves as a positive punishment. Here, the negative and positive forms of punishment may produce the same result: The teen will be less likely to speed the next time he or she gets behind the wheel.

In thinking about these terms, which can be confusing, consider whether the behavior is more likely to occur (reinforcement) or less likely to occur (punishment). A reinforcement or punishment is positive if something is applied or given and negative if something is removed or terminated. Likewise, you have to think in terms of which behavior is being reinforced or punished. Suppose a teacher gives students a special treat for being quiet in class. Subsequently, the students talk less. In this case, the treat is a positive punishment for talking because it reduces the probability that talking will occur again. At the same time, the treat is a reinforcement for being quiet. Giving the treat led to a decrease in talking and an increase in being quiet. (For an overview of positive and negative kinds of both reinforcement and punishment, see **Figure 6.16.**)

EFFECTIVENESS OF PARENTAL PUNISHMENT To make their children behave, parents sometimes use punishment as a means of discipline. Many contemporary psychologists believe that punishment is often applied ineffectively, however, and that it may have unintended and unwanted consequences. Research has shown that for punishment to be effective, it must be reasonable, unpleasant, and applied immediately so that the relationship between the unwanted behavior and the punishment is clear (Goodall, 1984; O'Leary, 1995). But considerable potential exists for confusion. For example, sometimes punishment is applied after a desired action. If a

positive punishment The administration of a stimulus to decrease the probability of a behavior's recurring.

negative punishment The removal of a stimulus to decrease the probability of a behavior's recurring.

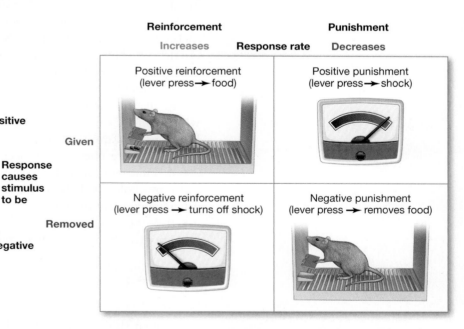

FIGURE 6.16 Negative and Positive Reinforcement, Negative and Positive Punishment Use this chart to help solidify your understanding of the terms in this section.

student is punished after admitting to cheating on an exam, the student may then associate the punishment with being honest rather than with the original offense. As a result, the student learns not to tell the truth. As Skinner once pointed out, one thing people learn from punishment is how to avoid it. Rather than learning how to behave appropriately, they may learn not to get caught.

Punishment can also lead to negative emotions, such as fear and anxiety. Through classical conditioning, these emotions may become associated with the person who administers the punishment. If a child thus learns to fear a parent or teacher, the long-term relationship between child and adult may be damaged (Gershoff, 2002). In addition, punishment often fails to offset the reinforcing aspects of the undesired behavior. In real life, any behavior can be reinforced in multiple ways. For instance, thumb sucking may be reinforced because it makes a child feel good, because it provides relief from negative emotions, and because it alleviates hunger. Punishment may not be sufficient to offset such rewards, but it may reinforce the child's secrecy about thumb sucking. For these and other reasons, most psychologists agree with Skinner's recommendation that reinforcement be used rather than punishment. A child complimented for being a good student is likely to perform better academically than one punished for doing poorly. After all, reinforcing good behavior tells the child what to do. Punishing the child for bad behavior does not tell the child how to improve.

One form of punishment that most psychologists believe is especially ineffective is physical punishment, such as spanking. Spanking is very common, however. Nearly three-quarters of American parents spank their children and thus apparently believe it is effective (Gallup, 1995). As noted by Alan Kazdin and Corina Benjet (2003), beliefs about the appropriateness of spanking involve religious beliefs and cultural views, as well as legal issues. Many countries (e.g., Austria, Denmark, Israel, Sweden, and Italy) have banned corporal punishment in homes or schools. Even the United Nations has passed resolutions discouraging it.

Some researchers have provided evidence of numerous negative outcomes associated with spanking, especially severe spanking (Bender et al., 2007). These problems include poor parent/child relations, weaker moral values, mental health problems, increased delinquency, and future child abuse. One concern is that physical punishment teaches the child that violence is an appropriate behavior for adults. (*Imitation learning* is discussed later in this chapter.) Although the extent to which mild forms of spanking cause problems is open to debate (Baumrind, Larzelere, & Cowan, 2002), the evidence indicates that other forms of punishment are more effective for decreasing unwanted behaviors (Kazdin & Benjet, 2003). Time-outs, small fines, and grounding can effectively modify behavior. Yet many psychologists believe that any method of punishment is less effective than providing positive reinforcement for "better" behaviors. By rewarding the behaviors they wish to see, parents are able to increase those behaviors while building more positive bonds with their children.

Operant Conditioning Is Influenced by Schedules of Reinforcement

How often should a reinforcer be given? For fast learning, behavior might be reinforced each time it occurs. This process is known as **continuous reinforcement.** In the real world, behavior is seldom reinforced continuously. Animals do not find food each time they look for it, and people do not receive praise each

continuous reinforcement A type of learning in which behavior is reinforced each time it occurs.

time they behave acceptably. The intermittent reinforcement of behavior is more common. This process is known as **partial reinforcement.** Partial reinforcement's effect on conditioning depends on the reinforcement schedule.

RATIO AND INTERVAL SCHEDULES Partial reinforcement can be administered according to either the number of behavioral responses or the passage of time. For instance, factory workers can be paid by the piece (behavioral responses) or by the hour (passage of time). A **ratio schedule** is based on the number of times the behavior occurs, as when a behavior is reinforced on every third or tenth occurrence. An **interval schedule** is based on a specific unit of time, as when a behavior is reinforced when it is performed every minute or hour. Ratio reinforcement generally leads to greater responding than does interval reinforcement. For example, factory workers paid by the piece are usually more productive than those paid by the hour, especially if the workers receive incentives for higher productivity.

FIXED AND VARIABLE SCHEDULES Partial reinforcement also can be given on a *fixed schedule* or a *variable schedule.* In a **fixed schedule,** the reinforcer is given consistently after a specific number of occurrences or after a specific amount of time. For example, whether factory workers are paid by the piece or by the hour, they usually are paid according to a fixed rate. They earn the same amount for each piece or for each hour, so the rate of reinforcement is entirely predictable. In a **variable schedule,** the reinforcer is given at different rates or at different times. The responder does not know how many behaviors need to be performed or how much time needs to pass before reinforcement will occur. One example of variable reinforcement is when a salesperson receives a commission only when a customer agrees to purchase a product. (The patterns of behavior typically observed under different schedules of reinforcement are illustrated in **Figure 6.17.**)

BEHAVIORAL PERSISTENCE The schedule of reinforcement also affects the persistence of behavior. Continuous reinforcement is highly effective for teaching a behavior. If the reinforcement is stopped, however, the behavior extinguishes quickly. For instance, normally when you put money in a vending machine, it gives you a product in return. If it fails to do so, you quickly stop putting your money into it. By contrast, at a casino you might drop a lot

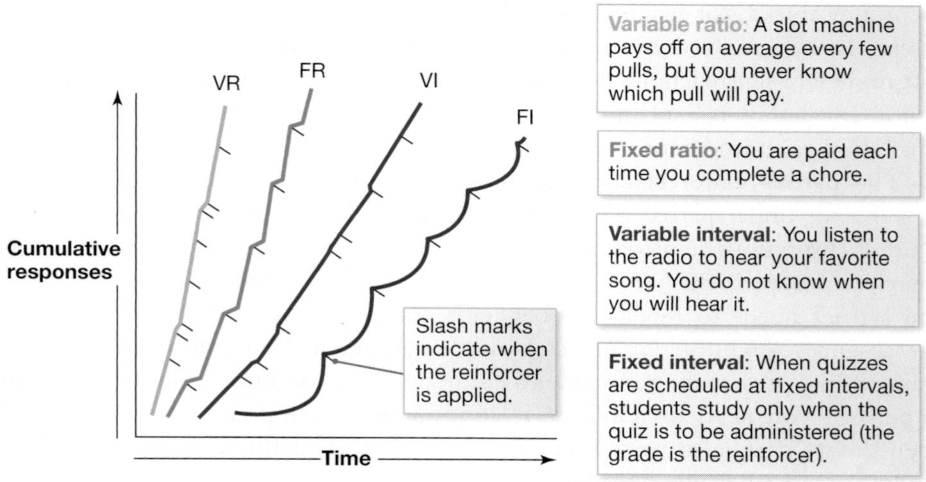

partial reinforcement A type of learning in which behavior is reinforced intermittently.

ratio schedule A schedule in which reinforcement is based on the number of times the behavior occurs.

interval schedule A schedule in which reinforcement is provided after a specific unit of time.

fixed schedule A schedule in which reinforcement is provided after a specific number of occurrences or after a specific amount of time.

variable schedule A schedule in which reinforcement is provided at different rates or at different times.

Variable ratio: A slot machine pays off on average every few pulls, but you never know which pull will pay.

Fixed ratio: You are paid each time you complete a chore.

Variable interval: You listen to the radio to hear your favorite song. You do not know when you will hear it.

Fixed interval: When quizzes are scheduled at fixed intervals, students study only when the quiz is to be administered (the grade is the reinforcer).

Slash marks indicate when the reinforcer is applied.

FIGURE 6.17 Behavior and Reinforcement The curves on this graph show cumulative responses under different schedules of reinforcement over time. The steeper the line, the higher the response rate. Ratio reinforcement leads to the highest rates of response.

Can Behavior Modification Help Me Stick with an Exercise Program?

The U.S. surgeon general recommends that each adult engage in at least 30 minutes of moderate physical activity daily, but most of us fail to achieve this goal (Centers for Disease Control and Prevention, 1999). Maybe you intend to exercise daily, then struggle to find the time to get to the gym. Or maybe you make working out a priority for a few weeks, then fall off the wagon. How can psychology help you stick with your exercise program (**Figure 6.18**)?

As you learned earlier in this chapter, experts regularly use the principles of operant conditioning to change the behaviors of animals, including humans. You do not have to be an expert, however, to condition yourself to perform healthful behaviors. Consider these steps:

1. **Identify a behavior you wish to change.** Before you begin a behavior modification program, you need to know which behavior you wish to modify. If your lack of physical activity is a concern, the behavior you need to target is being sedentary.

2. **Set goals.** Set goals that are realistic, specific, and measurable. If your current exercise program consists of a daily race to beat the closing elevator door, setting a goal to run 10 miles per day every day this month is not realistic. Likewise, a goal of "exercise more" will not do the trick, because it is too vague. Instead, you might set one of the following goals: Jog 1 mile on the treadmill at least four days this week, attend three yoga sessions this week, or walk at least 10,000 steps each day this week. Note that you can measure each of these goals objectively. You can use the treadmill's odometer to know whether you hit the 1-mile mark, or a calendar to indicate your performance of yoga, or the readout on a pedometer to track your daily steps.

Note, too, that these goals sit on a relatively short time horizon. Setting goals you can meet in short order allows for more opportunities for reinforcement. If your ultimate goal is to run a marathon 12 months from now, you need to set small, incremental subgoals that you can reinforce along the way.

3. **Monitor your behavior.** Monitor your behavior for a week or more before you begin your activity. Simply noting the behavior will likely move you toward your goal, since you will be more conscious of it. Keeping careful track will also enable you to get a sense of your baseline. By using this baseline as a point of comparison later, you will be able to assess your progress. Record your observations. If you have a smart phone, you might download an app for recording physical activity. Register at an exercise-tracking Web site. Or just use a paper notebook.

4. **Select a reinforcer and decide on a reinforcement schedule.** When you choose a reinforcer, pick something attainable that you genuinely find enjoyable. For example, you could buy one song from iTunes after every other yoga class. Alternatively, you could treat yourself to a movie each week that you meet your goal. Or you could give yourself one penny for every hundred

of money into a slot machine that rarely rewards you with a "win." Such behavior is not simply the result of an "addiction" to gambling. Rather, people put money in slot machines because the machines *sometimes* provide monetary rewards. Psychologists explain this persistent behavior as the effect of a *variable-ratio schedule* of reinforcement.

The **partial-reinforcement extinction effect** refers to the greater persistence of behavior under partial reinforcement than under continuous reinforcement. During continuous reinforcement, the learner easily can detect when reinforcement has stopped. But when the behavior is reinforced only some of the time, the learner needs to repeat the behavior comparatively more times to detect the absence of reinforcement. Thus the less frequent the reinforcement during training, the greater the resistance to extinction. To condition a behavior so that it persists, you need to reinforce it continuously during early acquisition and then slowly change to partial reinforcement. Parents naturally follow this strategy in teaching behaviors to their children, as in toilet training.

partial-reinforcement extinction effect
The greater persistence of behavior under partial reinforcement than under continuous reinforcement.

FIGURE 6.18 Behavior Modification in Action To see behavior modification in action, select a target behavior of your own that you wish to change. Maybe you feel that you should be studying more, exercising more, or watching less television. Any behavior will do, as long as it is specific and you have a realistic goal for changing it. Over time, as you successfully change the behavior, phase out the reinforcer and simply perform the behavior out of habit. For example, once you are used to exercising regularly, you will exercise regularly. The reinforced behavior may even become reinforcing on its own.

steps you take each day. Eventually, you could use the money to buy something you do not normally spend money on.

5. Reinforce the desired behavior. To cause the behavior change you want to see, you need to reinforce the desired behavior whenever it occurs. Be consistent. Suppose that if you work out at the gym

three times this week, you treat yourself by watching the new episode of *Glee*. This is important: If you do not work out at the gym three times this week, do not watch *Glee*. If you're a *Glee*k, it might be hard to resist streaming the newest episode (perhaps as you lounge on the couch instead of heading to the gym). But if you want the behavior modification to work, you have to

resist. If you do not behave appropriately, you do not receive the reinforcer! Allow yourself no exceptions.

6. Modify your goals, reinforcements, or reinforcement schedules, as needed. Once you begin consistently hitting your stated goals, make the goals more challenging. Add more days per week, more miles per run, or more laps per workout. If you find yourself getting bored with a reinforcer, mix it up a bit. Just be sure to select reinforcers that are genuinely appealing. And change the reinforcement schedule so you have to work harder to get the reward. For example, rather than reinforcing your good behavior after each workout, use reinforcement after you complete two workouts or after you work out consistently for a week.

Of course, you can use these principles to address other behaviors, such as procrastinating on your studies, neglecting to call your family, spending too much time on Facebook, and so on. For now, just pick one behavior you want to modify and try implementing the steps above. Once you get the hang of it, see if you can translate these steps to other areas of your life. Give it a try! You might amaze yourself with the power of behavior modification.

BEHAVIOR MODIFICATION **Behavior modification** is the use of operant-conditioning techniques to eliminate unwanted behaviors and replace them with desirable ones. The general rationale behind behavior modification is that most unwanted behaviors are learned and therefore can be unlearned. Parents, teachers, and animal trainers use conditioning strategies widely. People can be taught, for example, to be more productive at work, to save energy, and to drive more safely. Children with profound learning disabilities can be trained to communicate and to interact. As discussed in Chapter 15, operant techniques are also effective for treating many psychological conditions, such as depression and anxiety disorders.

Another widespread behavior modification method draws on the principle of secondary reinforcement. Chimpanzees can be trained to perform tasks in exchange for tokens, which they can later trade for food. The tokens thus reinforce behavior, and the chimps work as hard to obtain the tokens as they work to obtain food. Prisons, mental hospitals, schools, and classrooms often use *token economies,* in which people earn tokens for completing tasks and lose tokens for behaving

behavior modification The use of operant-conditioning techniques to eliminate unwanted behaviors and replace them with desirable ones.

badly. The people can later trade their tokens for objects or privileges. Here, the rewards not only reinforce good behavior but also give participants a sense of control over their environment. So, for instance, teachers can provide tokens to students for obeying class rules, turning in homework on time, and helping others. At some future point, the tokens can be exchanged for rewards, such as fun activities or extra recess time. In mental hospitals, token economies can encourage good grooming and appropriate social behavior and can discourage bizarre behavior.

Biology and Cognition Influence Operant Conditioning

Behaviorists such as B. F. Skinner believed that all behavior could be explained by straightforward conditioning principles. Recall from the beginning of this chapter that Skinner's *Walden Two* describes a utopia in which all of society's problems are solved through operant conditioning. In reality, however, reinforcement schedules explain only a certain amount of human behavior. Biology constrains learning, and reinforcement does not always have to be present for learning to take place.

FIGURE 6.19 Biological Constraints
Animals have a hard time learning behaviors that run counter to their evolutionary adaptation. For example, raccoons are hardwired to rub food between their paws, as this raccoon is doing. They have trouble learning *not* to rub objects.

BIOLOGICAL CONSTRAINTS Behaviorists believed that any behavior could be shaped through reinforcement. We now know that animals have a hard time learning behaviors that run counter to their evolutionary adaptation. A good example of biological constraints was obtained by Marian and Keller Breland, a husband-and-wife team of psychologists who used operant-conditioning techniques to train animals for commercials (Breland & Breland, 1961). Many of their animals refused to perform certain tasks they had been taught. For instance, a raccoon learned to place coins in a piggy bank, but eventually it refused to perform this task. Instead, the raccoon stood over the bank and briskly rubbed the coins in its paws. This rubbing behavior was not reinforced. In fact, it delayed reinforcement. One explanation for the raccoon's behavior is that the task was incompatible with innate adaptive behaviors. The raccoon associated the coin with food and treated it the same way: Rubbing food between the paws is hardwired for raccoons (**Figure 6.19**).

Similarly, pigeons can be trained to peck at keys to obtain food or secondary reinforcers, but it is difficult to train them to peck at keys to avoid electric shock. They can learn to avoid shock by flapping their wings, however, because wing flapping is their natural means of escape. The psychologist Robert Bolles has argued that animals have built-in defense reactions to threatening stimuli (Bolles, 1970). Conditioning is most effective when the association between the response and the reinforcement is similar to the animal's built-in predispositions.

ACQUISITION/PERFORMANCE DISTINCTION There is another challenge to the idea that reinforcement is responsible for all behavior. Namely, learning can take place without reinforcement. Edward Tolman, an early cognitive theorist, argued that reinforcement has more impact on performance than on learning. At the time, Tolman was conducting experiments in which rats had to learn to run through complex mazes to obtain food. Tolman believed that each rat developed a **cognitive map.** That is, during an experiment, each rat held in its brain a visual/spatial representation of the particular maze. The rat used this knowledge of the environment to help it find the food quickly.

To test his theory, Tolman and his students studied three groups of rats. The first group traveled through the maze but received no reinforcement: The rats reached the "goal box," found no food in the box, and simply wandered through the maze on each subsequent trial. The second group received reinforcement on every trial: Because the rats found food in the goal box, they learned to find the box quickly. The third group, critically, started receiving re-

cognitive map A visual/spatial mental representation of an environment.

FIGURE 6.20 Scientific Method: Tolman's Study of Latent Learning

Hypothesis: Reinforcement has more impact on performance than on learning.

Research Method:

1 One group of rats is put through trials running in a maze with a goal box that never has any food reward as reinforcement.

2 A second group of rats is put through trials in a maze with a goal box that always has food reinforcement.

3 A third group of rats is put through trials in a maze that has food reinforcement only after the first 10 trials.

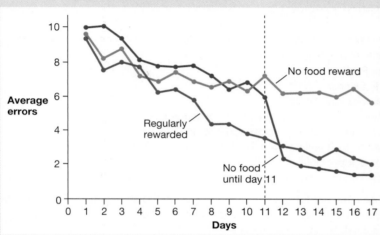

Results: Rats that were regularly reinforced for correctly running through a maze (blue) showed improved performance over time compared with rats that did not receive reinforcement (green). Rats that were not reinforced for the first 10 trials but were reinforced thereafter showed an immediate change in performance (red). Note that between days 11 and 12 the red group's average number of errors decreased dramatically.

Conclusion: Rats may learn a path through a maze but not reveal their learning. They do not reveal the learning because the maze running behavior has not been reinforced. Learning of this kind is called latent learning. It may be revealed once the behavior is reinforced. In other words, there is a distinction between acquisition of a behavior and performance of that behavior.

Source: Tolman, E. C., & Honzik, C. H. (1930). Introduction and removal of reward, and maze performance in rats. *University of California Publications in Psychology, 4,* 257–275.

inforcement only after the first 10 trials: At that point, the rats showed an amazingly fast learning curve and immediately caught up to the group that had been continuously reinforced (Tolman & Honzik, 1930). This result implies that the rats had learned a cognitive map of the maze and used it when the reinforcement began. Tolman's term **latent learning** refers to learning that takes place without reinforcement (**Figure 6.20**). For example, latent learning occurs when a person learns something simply by observing it. When most people drive for the first time, they do not need to be told that rotating the steering wheel turns the car. They already know that they need to rotate the steering wheel, even though they have never been reinforced for doing so.

Another form of learning that takes place without reinforcement is *insight learning.* In this form of problem solving, a solution suddenly emerges after either a period of inaction or contemplation of the problem. (Problem solving is discussed further in Chapter 8, "Thinking and Intelligence.") You probably have had this sort of experience, in which you mull over a problem for a while and then suddenly know the answer. The presence of reinforcement does not adequately explain insight learning, but it helps determine whether the behavior is subsequently repeated.

latent learning Learning that takes place in the absence of reinforcement.

How Does Operant Conditioning Differ from Classical Conditioning?

Whereas classical conditioning involves the learned association between two events, operant conditioning involves the learned association between a behavior and its consequences. B. F. Skinner developed the concept of operant conditioning to explain why some behaviors are repeated and others are not. Reinforcement increases a behavior's likelihood of being repeated. Punishment reduces that likelihood. Positive reinforcement and positive punishment involve the administration of a stimulus. Negative reinforcement and negative punishment involve the removal of a stimulus. Four schedules of reinforcement have been identified: variable ratio, fixed ratio, variable interval, and fixed interval. Each schedule has a distinct effect on behavior. Although Skinner maintained that operant conditioning could explain all behavior, contemporary theorists recognize that biological predispositions and cognitive processes influence organisms' ability to learn.

Measuring Up

1. Indicate whether each of the following people and phenomena is related to operant conditioning or classical conditioning.
   a. Ivan Pavlov
   b. B. F. Skinner
   c. behavior modification
   d. A behavior is associated with its consequences.
   e. Two events that occur close together in time are associated.
   f. used to train animals to perform tricks and useful tasks
   g. Premack principle
   h. Punishment's effects are explained by this type of conditioning.

2. Suppose a mother is trying to get her 8-year-old to stop cursing. Each time the child curses, the mother waits until the child's father is present before spanking the child. Select the better answers:
   a. The time interval between the cursing and the punishment is
      _____ too long for optimal learning.
      _____ fine as long as the punishment is administered on the same day as the cursing.
   b. One likely outcome to the continued use of this punishment is
      _____ the child will curse at times he or she is unlikely to be caught.
      _____ the child will gradually extinguish the cursing response.
   c. Generalization is likely to occur such that
      _____ the child curses only when the father is at work.
      _____ the child comes to fear the father and mother.
   d. What is the child likely to learn?
      _____ Do not get caught cursing.
      _____ Cursing is a nasty behavior that must be stopped.
   e. A more effective approach would be to
      _____ spank the child as soon as the cursing occurs.
      _____ provide rewards for not cursing.

Answers: 1. a. classical; b. operant; c. operant; d. operant; e. classical; f. operant; g. operant; h. operant. 2. a. __X__ too long for optimal learning; b. __X__ the child will curse at times he or she is unlikely to be caught; c. __X__ the child comes to fear the father and mother; d. __X__ Do not get caught cursing; e. __X__ provide rewards for not cursing.

6.3 How Does Watching Others Affect Learning?

Suppose you were teaching someone to fly an airplane. How might you apply the learning principles discussed in this chapter to accomplish your goal? Obviously, reinforcing arbitrary correct behaviors would be a disastrous way to train an aspiring pilot. Similarly, teaching someone to play football, eat with chopsticks, or perform complex dance steps requires more than simple reinforcement. We learn many behaviors not by doing them but by watching others do them. For example, we learn social etiquette through observation. We sometimes learn to be anxious in particular situations by seeing that other people are anxious. We often acquire attitudes about politics, religion, and the habits of celebrities from parents, peers, teachers, and the media.

Learning Can Be Passed On through Cultural Transmission

All humans belong to the same species and share the vast majority of genes. Around the world, however, there is enormous cultural diversity in what people think and how they behave. Would you be the same person if you had been raised in a small village in China, or in the jungles of South America, or in the mountains of Afghanistan? Probably not, since your religious beliefs, your values, and even your musical tastes are shaped by the culture in which you are raised. Each unit of cultural knowledge that is transmitted is a **meme.** Evolutionary psychologists view memes as analogous to genes. Like genes, memes are selectively passed on from one generation to the next. But unlike natural selection, which typically occurs slowly over thousands of years, memes can spread quickly, as in the worldwide adoption of the Internet. Although memes can be conditioned through association or reinforcement, many memes are learned by watching the behavior of other people. Some memes, however—such as fads—die out quickly.

One good example of the cultural transmission of knowledge is the case of Imo the monkey. In the 1950s, researchers who were studying monkeys in Japan threw some sweet potatoes onto a sandy beach for the monkeys there to eat. Imo developed the habit of washing her sweet potatoes in the ocean to remove the sand. Within a short time, other monkeys copied Imo, and soon many monkeys were washing their potatoes before eating them. Through social learning, this behavior has continued to be passed along from one generation to the next, and monkeys there still wash their potatoes (Dugatkin, 2004; **Figure 6.21**).

Learning Can Occur through Observation and Imitation

Observational learning is the acquisition or modification of a behavior after exposure to at least one performance of that behavior. This kind of learning is a powerful adaptive tool for humans and other animals. For example, offspring can learn basic skills by watching adults perform those skills. They can learn which things are safe to eat by watching what adults eat. They can learn to fear dangerous objects and dangerous situations by watching adults avoid those objects and situations. Children even acquire beliefs through observation. Young children are sponges, absorbing everything that goes on around them. They learn by watching as much as by doing.

FIGURE 6.21 Memes In the 1950s, a Japanese macaque named Imo developed and unwittingly passed along to her fellow monkeys the meme of washing sweet potatoes in the ocean. The descendants of these sweet potato–washing macaques continue the behavior, as shown here. **Think of an example of meme transmission in humans. How is it similar to the behavior of these monkeys? How is it different?**

meme A unit of knowledge transmitted within a culture.

observational learning The acquisition or modification of a behavior after exposure to at least one performance of that behavior.

BANDURA'S OBSERVATIONAL STUDIES The most thorough work on observational learning was conducted in the 1960s by the psychologist Albert Bandura. In a now-classic series of studies, Bandura divided preschool children into two groups. One group watched a film of an adult playing quietly with a large inflatable doll called Bobo. The other group watched a film of the adult attacking Bobo furiously: whacking the doll with a mallet, punching it in the nose, and kicking it around the room. When the children were later allowed to play with a number of toys, including the Bobo doll, those who had seen the more aggressive display were more than twice as likely to act aggressively toward the doll (Bandura, Ross, & Ross, 1961). These results suggest that exposing children to violence may encourage them to act aggressively (**Figure 6.22**).

MEDIA AND VIOLENCE On average, a television in the United States is on for 5 or 6 hours per day, and young children often spend more time watching television than doing any other activity, including schoolwork (Roberts, 2000). Worldwide, children consume an average of 3 hours per day of screen media (television, movies, and video games; Groebel, 1998). The most popular media, including Sat-

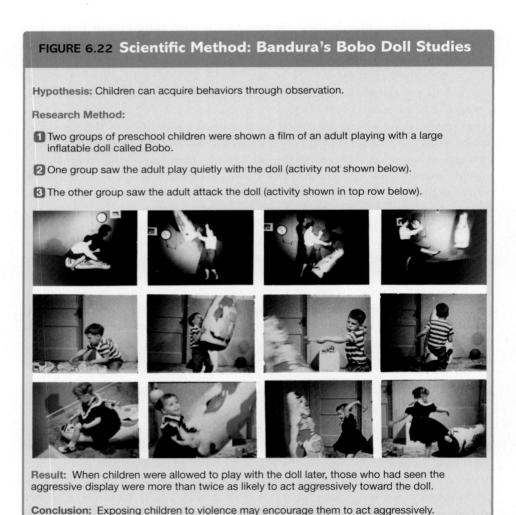

FIGURE 6.22 Scientific Method: Bandura's Bobo Doll Studies

Hypothesis: Children can acquire behaviors through observation.

Research Method:

1 Two groups of preschool children were shown a film of an adult playing with a large inflatable doll called Bobo.

2 One group saw the adult play quietly with the doll (activity not shown below).

3 The other group saw the adult attack the doll (activity shown in top row below).

Result: When children were allowed to play with the doll later, those who had seen the aggressive display were more than twice as likely to act aggressively toward the doll.

Conclusion: Exposing children to violence may encourage them to act aggressively.

Source: Bandura, A., Ross, D., & Ross, S. (1961). Transmission of aggression through imitation of aggressive models. *Journal of Abnormal and Social Psychology, 66*, 3–11.

urday morning cartoons, contain considerable amounts of violence (Carnagey, Anderson, & Bartholow, 2007).

Media violence has been found to increase the likelihood of short-term and long-term aggressive and violent behavior (Anderson et al., 2003). In one study, after children played a violent video game for only 20 minutes, they were less physiologically aroused by scenes of real violence. In other words, they had become desensitized to violence, showing fewer helping behaviors and increased aggression (Carnagey, Anderson, & Bushman, 2007; **Figure 6.23**). In another study, Leonard Eron and colleagues found that TV viewing habits at age 8 predicted, for age 30, amounts of both violent behavior and criminal activity (Eron, 1987). A 2002 meta-analysis of studies involving the effects of media violence—taking into account laboratory experiments, field experiments, cross-sectional correlational studies, and longitudinal studies—showed that exposure to violent media increases the likelihood of aggression (Gentile, Saleem, & Anderson, 2007).

FIGURE 6.23 Media and Violent Behavior Studies have shown that playing violent video games desensitizes children to violence.

A number of problems exist, however, with the studies on this topic. The social psychologist Jonathan Freedman (1984) has noted that many of the so-called aggressive behaviors displayed by children could be interpreted as playful rather than aggressive. A more serious concern is whether the studies generalize to the real world. Viewing a violent film clip in a lab is not like watching TV in one's living room. The film clips used in studies are often brief and extremely violent, and the child watches them alone. In the real world, violent episodes are interspersed with nonviolent material, and children often watch them with others, who may buffer the effect.

Even the longitudinal studies that assess childhood TV watching and later violent behavior fail to empirically support satisfactorily that TV caused the behavior. Extraneous variables, such as personality, poverty, or parental negligence, could have affected both TV viewing habits and violent tendencies. After all, not all of those who view violence on TV become aggressive later in life. Perhaps those who watch excessive amounts of TV, and therefore have fewer opportunities to develop social skills, act aggressively. Correlation does not prove causation (as discussed in Chapter 2, "Research Methodology"; see, for example, "Critical Thinking Skill: Identifying the Need for Control Groups," p. 42). Only through careful laboratory studies in which participants are randomly assigned to experimental conditions can we determine causality. Obviously, it is not practical to assign children randomly to experience different types of media, and it is ethically questionable to expose any children to violence if it might make them more aggressive.

Despite the problems with specific studies, most scientists see a relation between exposure to violence and aggressive behavior. How might media violence promote aggression in children? One possibility is that exposure to massive amounts of violence in movies, which misrepresent the prevalence of violence in real life, leads children to believe that violence is common and inevitable. Because in movies few people are punished for acting violently, children may come to believe that such behaviors are justified (Bushman & Huesmann, 2001). That is, the portrayal of violence in movies teaches children questionable social scripts for solving personal problems. By mentally rehearsing a violent scenario or observing the same violent scenario enacted many times and perhaps in different movies, a child might come to believe that engaging in brutality is an effective way to both solve problems and dispense with annoying people (Huesmann, 1998).

FIGURE 6.24 Scientific Method: Fear Response in Rhesus Monkeys

Hypothesis: Monkeys can develop phobias about snakes by observing other monkeys reacting fearfully to snakes.

Research Method:

1 Two sets of monkeys, one reared in the laboratory and one reared in the wild, had to reach past a clear box to get food.

2 When the clear box contained a snake, the laboratory-reared monkeys reached across the box, but the wild-reared monkeys refused to reach across the box.

Results: After watching wild-reared monkeys react, laboratory-reared monkeys no longer reached across the box.

Conclusion: Fears can be learned through observation.

Source: Mineka, S., Davidson, M., Cook, M., & Keir, R. (1984). Observational conditioning of snake fear in rhesus monkeys. *Journal of Abnormal Psychology, 93*, 355–372.

modeling The imitation of behavior through observational learning.

FIGURE 6.25 Early Modeling Babies frequently imitate expressions and behaviors.

SOCIAL LEARNING OF FEAR The psychologist Susan Mineka noticed that monkeys raised in laboratories do not fear snakes, whereas monkeys raised in the wild fear snakes intensely. She set out to explore whether monkeys, by observing other monkeys reacting fearfully to snakes, could develop a phobia of snakes. Mineka and colleagues set up an experiment with two groups of rhesus monkeys. One group was reared in the laboratory, and one group was reared in the wild. To obtain food, the monkeys had to reach beyond a clear box that contained either a snake or a neutral object. When a snake was in the box, the wild-reared monkeys did not touch the food. They also showed signs of distress, such as clinging to their cages and making threatening faces. The laboratory-raised monkeys reached past the box even if it contained a snake, and they showed no overt signs of fear. The researchers then showed the laboratory-raised monkeys the wild monkeys' fearful response, to see if it would affect the laboratory monkeys' reactions to the snake. The laboratory monkeys quickly developed a fear of the snakes, and this fear was maintained over a three-month period (Mineka, Davidson, Cook, & Keir, 1984; **Figure 6.24**).

Humans too can learn to fear particular stimuli by observing others. For example, a person might become afraid of a specific neighborhood after watching news video of a person being assaulted there. In fact, people can learn to fear particular things simply by hearing that the things are dangerous. Thus social forces play an important role in the learning of fear (Olsson & Phelps, 2007).

DEMONSTRATION AND IMITATION Because humans can learn through observation, they can be taught many complex skills through demonstration. For instance, parents use slow and exaggerated motions to show their children how to tie their shoes. Some nonhuman animals also appear to teach their offspring certain skills through demonstration, although this idea remains controversial among scientists (Caro & Hauser, 1992). For instance, cheetah mothers seem to facilitate the stages in which their young learn to hunt. At first, the mothers kill their prey. Later, they simply knock down the prey and let their cubs kill it, or they injure the prey to make it easier for the cubs to knock down and kill.

Humans readily imitate the actions of others. Within a few days (or even hours) of birth, human newborns will imitate facial expressions, and they will continue to imitate gestures and other actions as they mature (**Figure 6.25**). These forms of copying resemble the behavior of the monkeys, discussed earlier, who copied Imo the monkey's potato washing. Indeed, one study found that infant macaque monkeys also imitate facial expressions when they are 3 days old (Ferrari et al., 2006). But the issue of whether nonhuman animals engage in imitation in the same way that humans do is controversial. For example, pigeons will more quickly learn to step on bars to receive food pellets when they observe other pigeons receiving food this way (Zentall, Sutton, & Sherburne, 1996). It is possible, however, that in such situations, the animals are learning about features of their environment rather than imitating the particular actions. According to the most recent research, imitation is much less common in nonhuman animals than in humans.

The imitation of observed behavior is commonly called **modeling.** The term indicates that people are reproducing the behaviors of *models*—those being observed. Modeling in humans is influenced by numerous factors. Generally, we are more likely to imitate the actions of models who are attractive, have high status, and are somewhat similar to ourselves. In addition, modeling is effective only if the observer is physically capable of imitating the behavior. Simply watching Tiger Woods blast 300-yard drives does not mean we could do so if handed a golf club.

The influence that models have on behavior often occurs implicitly, without our being aware that our behaviors are being altered. People might not want to admit that they have changed their ways of speaking or dressing to resemble those of celebrities. Overwhelming evidence says, however, that we imitate what we see in others. We especially imitate the behaviors of people we admire. Adolescents whose favorite actors smoke in movies are much more likely to smoke (Tickle, Sargent, Dalton, Beach, & Heatherton, 2001). The more smoking that adolescents observe in movies, the more positive their attitudes about smoking become and the more likely they are to begin smoking (Sargent et al., 2005). Surprisingly, these effects are strongest among children whose parents do not smoke. Why would this be so? Perhaps what such children learn about smoking comes completely through the media, which tend to glamorize the habit. For example, movies often present smokers as attractive, healthy, and wealthy, not like the typical smoker. Adolescents do not generally decide to smoke after watching one movie's glamorous depiction of smoking. Rather, images of smokers as mature, cool, sexy—things adolescents want to be—shape adolescents' attitudes about smoking and subsequently lead to imitation (**Figure 6.26**). As adolescent viewers learn to associate smoking with people they admire, they incorporate the general message that smoking is desirable.

FIGURE 6.26 Imitation and Smoking This shot appears in the movie *The Killer Inside Me* (2010). The movie's title might be appropriate, because eye-catching images such as this one contribute to viewers' sense that smoking is a mature, cool, sexy behavior worth imitating. Notice how the character's pose is wrapped by the tight framing, the colors, and the swirls. These effects give the impression that the life of Lou Ford (played by Casey Affleck) depends on some mysterious power in his cigarette.

VICARIOUS REINFORCEMENT Another factor that determines whether observers imitate a model is whether the model is reinforced for performing the behavior. In one study, Bandura and colleagues showed children a film of an adult aggressively playing with a Bobo doll, but this time the film ended in one of three different ways (Bandura, Ross, & Ross, 1963). In the first version, a control condition, the adult experienced no consequences for the aggressive behavior. In the second version, the adult was rewarded for the behavior with candy and praise. In the third version, the adult was punished for the behavior by being both spanked and verbally reprimanded. When subsequently allowed to play with the Bobo doll, the children who observed the model being rewarded were much more likely to be aggressive toward the doll than were the children in the control group. In contrast, those who saw the model being punished were less likely to be aggressive than were those in the control group. Through **vicarious learning,** people learn about an action's consequences by watching others being rewarded or punished for performing the action.

These findings do not mean that the children who did not show aggression did not learn the behavior. Later, all the children were offered small gifts to perform the model's actions, and all performed the actions reliably. As noted earlier, a key distinction in learning is between the *acquisition* of a behavior and its *performance*. Here, all the children acquired the behavior. But only those who saw the model being rewarded performed the behavior—at least until the children themselves were rewarded. Direct rewards prompted the children in the control group to reveal the behavior they had acquired.

MIRROR NEURONS What happens in the brain during imitation learning? When a monkey observes another monkey reaching for an object, **mirror neurons** in the observing monkey's brain become activated (Rizzolatti, Fadiga, Gallese, & Fogassi, 1996). These same (mirror) neurons would be activated if the observing monkey

vicarious learning Learning the consequences of an action by watching others being rewarded or punished for performing the action.

mirror neurons Neurons that are activated when one observes another individual engage in an action and when one performs the action that was observed.

performed the behavior. Mirror neurons are especially likely to become activated when a monkey observes the target monkey engaging in movement that has some goal. For example, the target monkey might be reaching to grasp an object. Neither the sight of the object alone nor the sight of the target monkey at rest leads to activation of these mirror neurons.

Brain imaging techniques have identified similar mirror neurons in humans (Rizzolatti & Craighero, 2004). Thus every time you observe another person engaging in an action, similar neural circuits are firing in your brain and in the other person's brain. Scientists are debating the function of mirror neurons. This system may serve as the basis of imitation learning, but the firing of mirror neurons in the observer's brain does not always lead to imitative behavior in the observer. Therefore, some theorists speculate, mirror neurons may help us explain and predict others' behavior. In other words, mirror neurons may allow us to step into the shoes of people we observe so we can better understand those people's actions. One speculation is that mirror neurons are the neural basis for empathy, the emotional response of feeling what other people are experiencing.

Humans also have mirror neurons for mouth movements, and these neurons are stimulated when observers see a mouth move in a way typical of chewing or speaking (Ferrari, Gallese, Rizzolatti, & Fogassi, 2003). This phenomenon has led to speculation that mirror neurons are not just important for imitation learning. They may also play a role in humans' ability to communicate through language. Mirror neurons may be a brain system that creates a link between the sender of a message and the receiver of that message. Rizzolatti and Arbib (1998) have proposed that the mirror neuron system evolved to make language possible. Their theory relies on the idea that speech evolved mainly from gestures. Indeed, people readily understand many nonverbal behaviors, such as waving or thrusting a fist in the air. Evidence indicates that listening to sentences that describe actions activates the same brain regions active when those actions are observed (Tettamanti et al., 2005). Even reading words that represent actions leads to brain activity in relevant motor regions, as when the word *lick* activates brain regions that control tongue movements (Hauk, Johnsrude, & Pulvermüller, 2004).

The idea of mirror neurons has been expanded to include even our understanding of other people's mental states. There are a number of questions, however, about the meaning of brain activity observed during mirror neuron studies, such as whether brain activity reflects prior learning rather than imitation (Hickok, 2009). As the evidence accumulates, support grows for at least this idea: Mirror neurons in brain regions responsible for movement track the behaviors of targets as those behaviors unfold over time (Press, Cook, Blakemore, & Kilner, 2011).

Summing Up

How Does Watching Others Affect Learning?

Humans learn behavior by observing the behavior of others. We acquire basic and complex skills, beliefs, attitudes, habits, and emotional responses by observing others—for example, parents, peers, teachers, and individuals in popular media. We tend to imitate models who are attractive, who have high status, who are similar to ourselves, and whom we admire. Through vicarious learning, we learn about an action's consequences. We are more likely to perform a behavior when a model has been rewarded for the behavior than when a model has been punished for the behavior. Mirror neurons, which fire when a behavior is observed and performed, may be the neural basis of imitation learning.

6.4 What Is the Biological Basis of Learning?

Scientists have long understood the basics of learning: The brain undergoes relatively permanent changes as a result of exposure to environmental events. That is, your experience of the world changes your brain, and these changes reflect learning.

Over the past few decades, psychologists have made numerous discoveries about the biological basis of learning. For instance, researchers have explored the brain processes that underlie reinforcement. They have demonstrated that similar brain activity occurs for most rewarding experiences. Likewise, researchers have provided considerable information about how learning occurs at the neuronal level. This section discusses the findings regarding learning's biological basis that have emerged through the methods of psychological science.

Dopamine Activity Underlies Reinforcement

As noted earlier, people often use the term *reward* as a synonym for positive reinforcement. By contrast, Skinner and other traditional behaviorists defined reinforcement strictly in terms of whether it increased behavior. They were relatively uninterested in *why* it increased behavior. For instance, they carefully avoided any speculation about whether subjective experiences had anything to do with behavior. After all, they believed that mental states were impossible to study empirically.

Studies of learning have made clear, however, that positive reinforcement works in two ways: It provides the subjective experience of pleasure, and it increases wanting for the object or event that produced the reward. More generally, behaviors that have favorable outcomes create responses in the brain that support the recurrence of those behaviors. One important component of the neural basis of reinforcement is the neurotransmitter dopamine. As discussed in Chapter 5, dopamine is involved in addictive behavior, especially in terms of increased wanting for the addictive substance. Research over the past 50 years has shown that dopamine plays an important role in reinforcement (Schultz, 2010; Wise & Rompre, 1989).

PLEASURE CENTERS One of the earliest discoveries that pointed to the role of neural mechanisms in reinforcement came about because of a small surgical error. In the early 1950s, the brain researchers Peter Milner and James Olds were testing whether electrical stimulation to a specific brain region would facilitate learning. To see whether the learning they observed was caused by brain activity or by the aversive qualities of the electrical stimulus, Olds and Milner administered electrical stimulation to rats' brains only while the rats were in one specific location in the cage. The logic was that if the application of electricity was aversive, the rats would selectively avoid that location. Fortunately for science, Milner and Olds administered each shock to the wrong part of the brain. Instead of avoiding the area of the cage associated with electrical stimulation, the rats quickly came back. Apparently, they were looking for more stimulation!

Olds and Milner then set up an experiment to see whether rats would press a lever to self-administer shock to specific sites in their brains. This procedure was subsequently referred to as *intracranial self-stimulation* (*ICSS;* **Figure 6.27**). The rats self-administered electricity to their brains with gusto, pressing the lever hundreds of times per hour (Olds & Milner, 1954). Olds and Milner referred to brain regions that support ICSS as *pleasure centers.* Although behaviorists objected to the term *pleasure,* ICSS was a powerful reinforcer. In one experiment, rats that had been on a near-starvation diet for 10 days were given a choice between food and the opportunity to administer ICSS. They chose the electrical stimulation more than 80 percent of the time. Deprived rats also chose electrical stimulation over water or receptive sexual partners. They even crossed a painful electrified grid to receive ICSS. Rats will continue intracranial self-stimulation until they collapse from exhaustion. Monkeys tested in similar studies have been found to press a bar for electrical stimulation up to 8,000 times per hour (Olds, 1962)!

Most psychologists believe that ICSS acts on the same brain regions as those activated by natural reinforcers, such as food, water, and sex. When electrical stimulation is applied to the pleasure center in a rat and then turned off, the rat will engage in a naturally motivated behavior. For example, the rat might eat, drink, or copulate with an available partner. Also, depriving an animal of food or of water leads to increased ICSS. This finding is taken to indicate that the animal is trying to obtain the same reward experience it would obtain from drinking water or eating. Finally, the neural mechanisms underlying both ICSS and natural reward appear to use the same neurotransmitter, namely, dopamine. This evidence suggests that

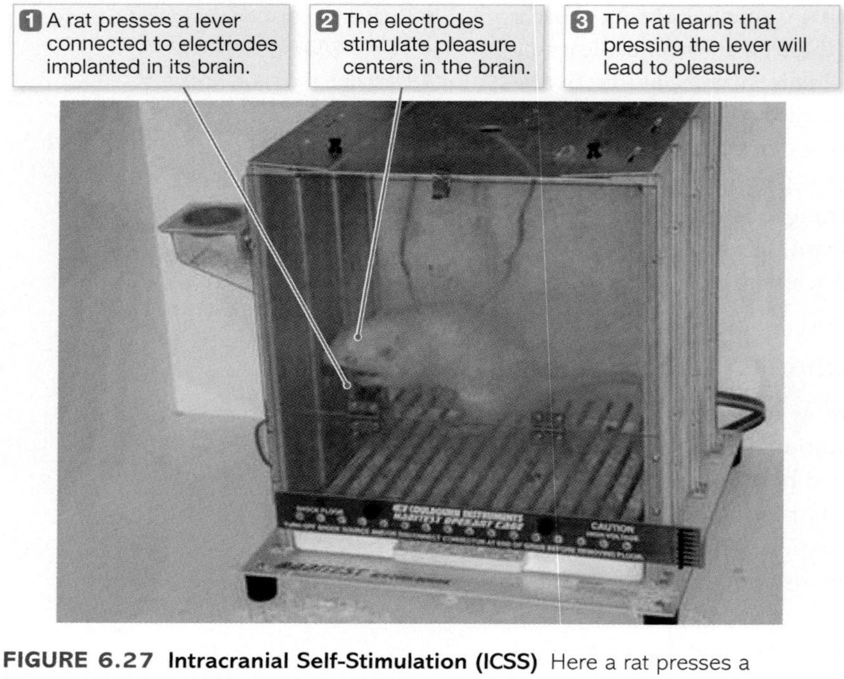

1 A rat presses a lever connected to electrodes implanted in its brain.

2 The electrodes stimulate pleasure centers in the brain.

3 The rat learns that pressing the lever will lead to pleasure.

FIGURE 6.27 **Intracranial Self-Stimulation (ICSS)** Here a rat presses a lever to administer ICSS.

dopamine serves as the neurochemical basis of positive reinforcement in operant conditioning. For instance, ICSS activates dopamine receptors. Interfering with dopamine eliminates self-stimulation as well as naturally motivated behaviors, such as eating, drinking, and copulating.

DOPAMINE AND REWARD The nucleus accumbens is a subcortical brain region that is part of the limbic system. Reward results from activation of dopamine neurons in the nucleus accumbens (**Figure 6.28**). Other brain regions, such as the amygdala and the prefrontal cortex, are involved, as are other neurotransmitters, such as endorphins (discussed in Chapter 3, "Biology and Behavior"). Still, dopamine plays a key role in reward (Volkow et al., 2011). When hungry rats are given food, they experience an increased dopamine release in the nucleus accumbens: the greater the hunger, the greater the dopamine release (Rolls, Burton, & Mora, 1980). Food tastes better when you are hungry, and water is more rewarding when you are thirsty, because more dopamine is released under deprived conditions than under nondeprived conditions. Even looking at funny cartoons activates the nucleus accumbens (Mobbs, Greicius, Abdel-Azim, Menon, & Reiss, 2003). Have you ever experienced the chills while listening to a favorite piece of music—a tingling sense that feels like a shiver down the spine and that might give you goose bumps? Using PET imaging and fMRI, researchers have shown that when people experience optimal pleasure while listening to music, there is dopamine activity in the nucleus accumbens (Salimpoor, Benovoy, Larcher, Dagher, & Zatorre, 2011).

In operant conditioning, dopamine release sets the value of a reinforcer. Drugs that block dopamine's effects disrupt operant conditioning. In one study, rats were taught to run a maze to receive electrical stimulation; but after being injected with a dopamine blocker, the rats would not run the maze until the electrical current was turned up (Stellar, Kelley, & Corbett, 1983). The blocker decreased the value of the reinforcement. Dopamine blockers are often given to individuals with Tourette's syndrome, a motor control disorder, to help them regulate their involuntary body movements. These individuals often have trouble staying on their drug regimens, however, because they feel the drugs prevent them from enjoying life. Conversely, as you might expect, drugs that enhance dopamine activation, such as cocaine and amphetamines, increase the reward value of stimuli.

Until recently, psychologists believed that rewards increased behavior primarily because of the pleasure those rewards produce. Robinson and Berridge (1993) introduced an important distinction between the *wanting* and *liking* aspects of reward. With drugs, for instance, wanting refers to the desire or craving a user has to take the substance. Liking refers to the subjective sense of pleasure the user receives from consuming the substance. Although wanting and liking often go together, there are circumstances under which wanting occurs without liking (Berridge et al., 2010; Kringelbach & Berridge, 2009). For example, a smoker may desire a cigarette but then not particularly enjoy smoking it. As mentioned in Chapter 5, dopamine appears to be especially important for the wanting aspect of reward.

SECONDARY REINFORCERS ALSO RELY ON DOPAMINE Natural reinforcers appear to signal reward directly. Primarily, they work through the activation of dopamine receptors in the nucleus accumbens. But what about secondary

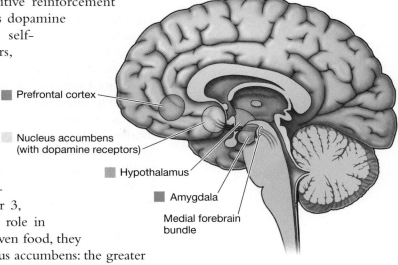

Prefrontal cortex

Nucleus accumbens
(with dopamine receptors)

Hypothalamus

Amygdala

Medial forebrain
bundle

FIGURE 6.28 **Pleasure Centers of the Brain**

reinforcers, such as money or good grades? Neutral stimuli that at first fail to trigger dopamine release may do so readily after they are paired with unconditioned stimuli. This association comes about through a classical-conditioning process.

In one study, monkeys were presented with a trapdoor that opened occasionally. The door opening did not activate dopamine activity. The experimenters then placed apples in the doorway. As a result of this placement, the monkeys associated the door opening with the unconditioned stimulus of eating a tasty food. After many conditioning trials, the door opening led on its own to increased activation of dopamine (Ljungberg, Apicella, & Schultz, 1992). Similarly, seeing a loved one, getting a good grade, or receiving a paycheck may be conditioned to produce dopamine activation. Money is an excellent example of a secondary reinforcer, as mentioned earlier, and anticipated monetary rewards have been found to activate dopamine systems (Knutson, Fong, Adams, Varner, & Hommer, 2001).

Habituation and Sensitization Are Simple Models of Learning

As noted earlier, learning involves relatively permanent changes in the brain, and these changes result from exposure to environmental events. The roots of this idea can be traced back to numerous scientists, including the researcher Richard Semon. In 1904, Semon proposed that memories are stored through changes in the nervous system. He called the storage of learned material an *engram,* a term later popularized by the psychologist Karl Lashley.

In 1948, the psychologist Donald Hebb proposed that learning results from alterations in synaptic connections. According to Hebb, when one neuron excites another, some change takes place that strengthens the connection between the two neurons. Subsequently, the firing of one neuron becomes increasingly likely to cause the firing of the other neuron. In other words, basically, "cells that fire together wire together" (a concept discussed in Chapter 3, "Biology and Behavior"). Hebb did not have the technology to examine whether his hypothesis was valid, but his basic theory has been confirmed.

What activity at the synapse leads to learning? One answer is found in research using simple invertebrates such as the aplysia, a small marine snail that eats seaweed (**Figure 6.29**). The aplysia is an excellent species to use in the study of learning because it has relatively few neurons, and some of its neurons are large enough to be seen without a microscope (Kandel, Schwartz, & Jessell, 1995). The neurobiologist Eric Kandel and colleagues have used the aplysia to study the neural basis of two types of simple learning: *habituation* and *sensitization.* As a result of this research, Kandel received a Nobel Prize in Physiology or Medicine in 2000.

Habituation is a decrease in behavioral response after repeated exposure to nonthreatening stimuli. As discussed earlier, an animal will orient, or pay attention, to a novel stimulus. Through the process of habituation, if the stimulus is neither harmful nor rewarding, the animal learns to ignore it.

We constantly habituate to meaningless events around us. For instance, sit back and listen to the background sounds wherever you are. Perhaps you can hear a clock, or a computer fan, or your roommates playing music in the next room. Had you really noticed this noise before being directed to or had you habitu-

FIGURE 6.29 Simple Model of Learning The aplysia, a marine invertebrate, is used to study the neurochemical basis of learning.

habituation A decrease in behavioral response after repeated exposure to a nonthreatening stimulus.

ated to it? Habituation can be demonstrated quite easily by repeatedly touching an aplysia. The first few touches cause it to withdraw its gills. After about 10 touches, it stops responding, and this lack of response lasts about 2 to 3 hours. Repeated habituation trials can lead to a state of habituation that lasts several weeks.

Sensitization is an increase in behavioral response after exposure to a threatening stimulus. For instance, imagine that while studying you smell something burning. You probably will not habituate to this smell. You might focus even greater attention on your sense of smell to assess the possible threat of fire, and you will be highly vigilant for any indication of smoke or of flames. In general, sensitization leads to heightened responsiveness to other stimuli. Giving a strong electric shock to an aplysia's tail leads to sensitization. Following the shock, a mild touch anywhere on the body will cause the aplysia to withdraw its gills.

Kandel's research on the aplysia has shown that alterations in the functioning of the synapse lead to habituation and sensitization. For both types of simple learning, presynaptic neurons alter their neurotransmitter release. A reduction in neurotransmitter release leads to habituation. An increase in neurotransmitter release leads to sensitization. Knowing the neural basis of simple learning gives us the building blocks to understand more-complex learning processes in both human and nonhuman animals.

Long-Term Potentiation Is a Candidate for the Neural Basis of Learning

To understand how learning occurs in the brain, researchers have investigated *long-term potentiation*. This phenomenon was first observed in a laboratory in Oslo, Norway, in the late 1960s. The word *potentiate* means to strengthen, to make something more potent. **Long-term potentiation (LTP)** is the strengthening of a synaptic connection, resulting in postsynaptic neurons that are more easily activated.

To demonstrate long-term potentiation, researchers first establish the extent to which electrically stimulating one neuron leads to neural firing in a second neuron. (Recall from Chapter 3 that neurons fire when they receive sufficient stimulation.) The researchers then provide intense electrical stimulation to the first neuron. For example, they might give it 100 pulses of electricity in 5 seconds. Finally, they readminister a single electrical pulse to measure the extent of the second neuron's firing. LTP occurs when the intense electrical stimulation increases the likelihood that stimulating one neuron leads to increased firing in the second neuron (**Figure 6.30**). In the aplysia, habituation and sensitization are each due to changes in the release of a neurotransmitter from the presynaptic neuron. LTP results from changes in the postsynaptic neuron that make it more easily activated.

Numerous lines of evidence support the idea that long-term potentiation is involved in learning and memory (Beggs et al., 1999; Cooke & Bliss, 2006). For instance, LTP effects are most easily observed in brain sites known to be involved in learning and memory, such as the hippocampus. Moreover, the same drugs that improve memory also lead to increased LTP, and those that block memory also block LTP. Finally, behavioral conditioning produces neurochemical effects nearly identical to LTP.

The process of long-term potentiation also supports Hebb's contention that learning results from a strengthening of synaptic connections between neurons that fire together. Hebb's rule—"cells that fire together wire together"—can be used to explain a variety of learning phenomena. Consider classical conditioning. Neurons that signal the unconditioned stimulus are active at the same time as those that

sensitization An increase in behavioral response after exposure to a threatening stimulus.

long-term potentiation (LTP) The strengthening of a synaptic connection, making the postsynaptic neurons more easily activated.

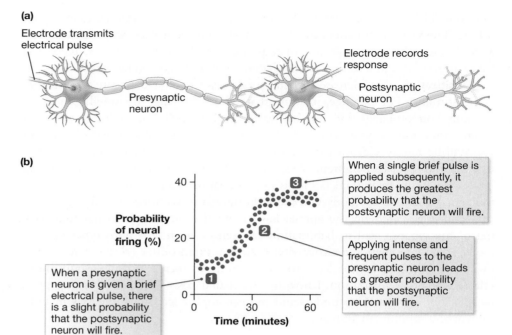

(a)

Electrode transmits electrical pulse

Presynaptic neuron

Electrode records response

Postsynaptic neuron

(b)

Probability of neural firing (%)

Time (minutes)

1 When a presynaptic neuron is given a brief electrical pulse, there is a slight probability that the postsynaptic neuron will fire.

2 Applying intense and frequent pulses to the presynaptic neuron leads to a greater probability that the postsynaptic neuron will fire.

3 When a single brief pulse is applied subsequently, it produces the greatest probability that the postsynaptic neuron will fire.

FIGURE 6.30 Long-Term Potentiation (LTP) (a) This diagram depicts the basic process used in testing for LTP between two neurons. **(b)** This graph shows the steps involved in LTP.

FIGURE 6.31 Doogie Mice Doogie mice (such as the one pictured here) and regular mice were given a test of learning and memory. In the first part, both kinds of mice had the chance to familiarize themselves with two objects. In the second part, the researchers replaced one of the objects with a novel object. The Doogie mice quickly recognized the change, but the normal mice did not recognize it.

signal the conditioned stimulus. Over repeated trials, the synapses that connect these two events become strengthened. As a result of this strengthened synaptic connection, when one neuron fires, the other fires automatically. In other words, the conditioned response results from the increased connection between the two neurons.

LTP AND THE NMDA RECEPTOR Over the last decade, researchers have made considerable progress in understanding how long-term potentiation works. The *NMDA receptor* (a type of glutamate receptor) is required for it and has a special property: It opens only if a nearby neuron fires at the same time. This phenomenon supports Hebb's rule.

The finding that the NMDA receptor is involved in LTP led researchers to examine genetic processes that might influence learning. For instance, the neuroscientist Joseph Tsien modified genes in mice to make the genes' NMDA receptors more efficient. When tested in standard learning tasks, these transgenic mice performed amazingly well, learning novel tasks more quickly and showing increased fear conditioning (Tsien, 2000). The mice were such great learners that Tsien named them "Doogie mice," after the prime-time television character Doogie Howser, a boy doctor (**Figure 6.31**).

Might we be able to modify human genes so that people learn more quickly? This fascinating question raises many ethical issues, but some pharmaceutical companies are exploring drugs that might enhance the learning process by manipulating gene expression or activating NMDA receptors. If successful, such treatments might prove valuable for treating patients with diseases such as Alzheimer's. This especially active area of research is increasing our understanding of how genes, neurotransmitters, and the environment interact to produce learning.

FEAR CONDITIONING Long-term potentiation was first observed in the hippocampus, but recent evidence indicates that fear conditioning may induce LTP in the amygdala (Kim & Jung, 2006). In fact, there is substantial evidence that the amygdala is crucial for fear conditioning. If a particular part of the amygdala is removed, an animal is unable to learn that one particular event (such as an electric shock) will follow another one (such as a tone; Davis, 1997). The neuroscientist Joseph LeDoux and his students have demonstrated that fear conditioning and the induction of LTP lead to similar changes in amygdala neurons. This finding suggests that fear conditioning might produce long-lasting learning through the induction of LTP (Rogan, Stäubli, & LeDoux, 1997; Sigurdsson, Doyère, Cain, & LeDoux, 2007).

As discussed earlier, fear learning can occur through observation. For example, monkeys can learn to fear objects by seeing other monkeys fear those objects. This social learning of fear likely relies on the amygdala. In one imaging study, research participants watched another person experience and display distress when receiving an electric shock paired with a conditioned stimulus. The observing participants subsequently were presented with the CS. To ensure that all their learning was vicarious, however, they did not receive a shock. During the observation period and during the trials when the observers were presented with the CS, the investigators found heightened activity in the amygdala (Olsson, Nearing, & Phelps, 2007). This finding suggests that similar mechanisms are involved in conditioned and observational fear learning.

Summing Up

What Is the Biological Basis of Learning?

Researchers are rapidly identifying the neurophysiological basis of learning. Research has demonstrated that activation of dopamine receptors in the nucleus accumbens is associated with the experience of reinforcement. Research has also supported Hebb's theory that neurons that fire together wire together. Kandel's work on the aplysia has shown that habituation and sensitization, two simple forms of learning, occur through alteration in neurotransmitter release. Through long-term potentiation, intense stimulation of neurons strengthens synapses, increasing the likelihood that one neuron's activation will increase the firing of other neurons. LTP occurs when NMDA receptors are stimulated by nearby neurons. LTP in the amygdala appears to play a role in fear conditioning.

Measuring Up

1. What can we learn from the superlearner Doogie mice?
   a. NMDA receptors are important in producing learning.
   b. A breed of extremely smart mice provides a good model for understanding how some people are able to become doctors at a young age.
   c. Neurons that fire together wire together.
   d. Animal models of human learning cannot account for mirror neurons' action.

2. What is the evidence that dopamine is a critical neurotransmitter for the effects of reinforcers on behavior?
   a. The increased administration of self-stimulation suppresses dopamine release.
   b. Rats will work continuously to deliver electrical stimulation to a portion of the brain that uses dopamine in its neural processes.
   c. When rats press a lever to self-administer dopamine directly into the brain, they stop eating and drinking.
   d. When rats receive dopamine, they increase the rate at which they deliver intracranial self-stimulation.

Answers: 1. a. NMDA receptors are important in producing learning. 2. b. Rats will work continuously to deliver electrical stimulation to a portion of the brain that uses dopamine in its neural processes.

Chapter Summary

6.1 What Ideas Guide the Study of Learning?

- **Learning Results from Experience:** Learning is a relatively enduring change in behavior that results from experience. Learning enables animals to better adapt to the environment, and thus it facilitates survival. Learning involves understanding the associations between events. These associations are acquired through classical conditioning and operant conditioning.

- **Behavioral Responses Are Conditioned:** Pavlov established the principles of classical conditioning. Through classical conditioning, associations are made between two stimuli, such as the clicking of a metronome and a piece of meat. What is learned is that one stimulus predicts another. Acquisition, extinction, spontaneous recovery, generalization, discrimination, and second-order conditioning are processes associated with classical conditioning.

- **Phobias and Addictions Have Learned Components:** Phobias are learned fear associations. Similarly, addiction involves a conditioned response, which can result in withdrawal symptoms at the mere sight of drug paraphernalia. Addiction also involves tolerance: the need for more of a drug, particularly when that drug is administered in a familiar context, to get a high comparable to the one obtained earlier.

- **Classical Conditioning Involves More Than Events Occurring at the Same Time:** Not all stimuli are equally potent in producing conditioning. Animals are biologically prepared to make connections between stimuli that are potentially dangerous. This biological preparedness to fear specific objects helps animals avoid potential dangers, and thus it facilitates survival.

- **Learning Involves Cognition:** Animals are predisposed to form predictions that enhance survival, such as judging the likelihood that food will continue to be available at one location. The Rescorla-Wagner model maintains that the strength of a CS-US association is determined by the extent to which the US is unexpected or surprising.

6.2 How Does Operant Conditioning Differ from Classical Conditioning?

- **Reinforcement Increases Behavior:** A behavior's positive consequences will make it more likely to occur. Shaping is a procedure in which successive approximations of a behavior are reinforced, leading to the desired behavior. Reinforcers may be primary (those that satisfy biological needs) or secondary (those that do not directly satisfy biological needs).

- **Both Reinforcement and Punishment Can Be Positive or Negative:** For positive reinforcement and positive punishment, a stimulus is delivered after the animal responds. For negative reinforcement and negative punishment, a stimulus is removed after the animal responds. Positive and negative reinforcement increase the likelihood that a behavior will recur. Positive and negative punishment decrease the likelihood that a behavior will recur.

- **Operant Conditioning Is Influenced by Schedules of Reinforcement:** Learning occurs in response to continuous reinforcement and partial reinforcement. Partial reinforcement may be delivered on a ratio schedule or an interval schedule. Moreover, partial reinforcement may be fixed or variable. Partial reinforcement administered on a variable-ratio schedule is particularly resistant to extinction. Behavior modification involves the use of operant conditioning to eliminate unwanted behaviors and replace them with desirable behaviors.

- **Biology and Cognition Influence Operant Conditioning:** An organism's biological makeup restricts the types of behaviors the organism can learn. Latent learning takes place without reinforcement. Latent learning may not influence behavior until a reinforcer is introduced.

6.3 How Does Watching Others Affect Learning?

- **Learning Can Be Passed On through Cultural Transmission:** Memes (units of knowledge transmitted within a culture) are analogous to genes in that memes are selectively passed on from generation to generation.

- **Learning Can Occur through Observation and Imitation:** Observational learning is a powerful adaptive tool. Humans and other animals learn by watching the behavior of others. The imitation of observed behavior is referred to as modeling. Vicarious learning occurs when people learn about an action's consequences by observing others being reinforced or punished for their behavior. Mirror neurons are activated when a behavior is observed and performed and may be the neural basis of imitation learning.

6.4 What Is the Biological Basis of Learning?

- **Dopamine Activity Underlies Reinforcement:** The brain has specialized centers that produce pleasure when stimulated. Behaviors that activate these centers are reinforced. The nucleus accumbens (a part of the limbic system) has dopamine receptors, which are activated by pleasurable behaviors. Through conditioning, secondary reinforcers can also activate dopamine receptors.

- **Habituation and Sensitization Are Simple Models of Learning:** Habituation is a decrease in behavioral response after repeated exposure to a nonthreatening stimulus. In contrast, sensitization is an increase in behavioral response after exposure to a new and threatening stimulus.

- **Long-Term Potentiation Is a Candidate for the Neural Basis of Learning:** Long-term potentiation refers to the strengthening of synaptic connections. Long-term potentiation has been observed in the hippocampus (learning and memory) and amygdala (fear conditioning). The receptor NMDA is involved in long-term potentiation.

Key Terms

acquisition, p. 229

behavior modification, p. 247

classical conditioning (Pavlovian conditioning), p. 227

cognitive map, p. 248

conditioned response (CR), p. 227

conditioned stimulus (CS), p. 227

continuous reinforcement, p. 244

extinction, p. 229

fixed schedule, p. 245

habituation, p. 260

interval schedule, p. 245

latent learning, p. 249

law of effect, p. 240

learning, p. 225

long-term potentiation (LTP), p. 261

meme, p. 251

mirror neurons, p. 255

modeling, p. 254

negative punishment, p. 243

negative reinforcement, p. 242

observational learning, p. 251

operant conditioning (instrumental conditioning), p. 239

partial reinforcement, p. 245

partial-reinforcement extinction effect, p. 246

phobia, p. 231

positive punishment, p. 243

positive reinforcement, p. 242

ratio schedule, p. 245

reinforcer, p. 240

Rescorla-Wagner model, p. 236

sensitization, p. 261

shaping, p. 241

spontaneous recovery, p. 230

stimulus discrimination, p. 230

stimulus generalization, p. 230

unconditioned response (UR), p. 227

unconditioned stimulus (US), p. 227

variable schedule, p. 245

vicarious learning, p. 255

Practice Test

1. Every night for a few weeks, you feed your pet rat while watching the evening news. Eventually, the rat learns to sit by its food dish when the news program's opening theme song plays. In this example of classical conditioning, what are the US, UR, CS, and CR?

2. At a psychology lecture, each student receives 10 lemon wedges. The professor instructs the students to bite into a lemon wedge anytime a large blue dot appears within her slide presentation. Nearly every time the students bite into lemons, their mouths pucker. The 11th time a blue dot appears on the screen, many students' mouths pucker visibly. In this case, what are the US, UR, CS, and CR?

3. A few minutes later in that same psychology lecture, the professor projects the image of a turquoise dot. How will the students likely respond to this image?
   a. The students will not experience puckering responses, because the conditioned association has been extinguished.
   b. The students will not experience puckering responses, because they are able to discriminate between the two dot colors.
   c. The students will experience puckering responses, because of stimulus generalization.

4. Which pairing of stimuli will most quickly create a learned association?
   a. Eating a box of raisins and experiencing extreme nausea at the same time.
   b. Eating a box of raisins and experiencing extreme nausea a few hours later.
   c. Seeing clouds in the sky and experiencing a severe rain shower a few minutes later.
   d. Seeing clouds in the sky and experiencing a severe rain shower a few hours later.

5. Identify each statement as an example of negative punishment, positive punishment, negative reinforcement, or positive reinforcement.
   a. Whenever a puppy barks, it gets its belly rubbed, so it barks more.
   b. A professor directs all questions to the student who arrives late to class.
   c. A person with a clean driving record receives a reduced insurance premium.
   d. Your date arrives an hour late, and you refuse to speak for the rest of the evening.

The answer key for the Practice Tests can be found at the back of the book. It also includes answers to the green caption questions.

Attention and Memory

HENRY MOLAISON, ONE OF THE MOST FAMOUS PEOPLE IN MEMORY RESEARCH, was born in 1926 and died in 2008. In vital ways, though, his world stopped in 1953, when he was 27.

As a young man, Molaison suffered from severe epilepsy. Every day, he had several grand mal seizures, an affliction that made it impossible for him to lead a normal life. Seizures are

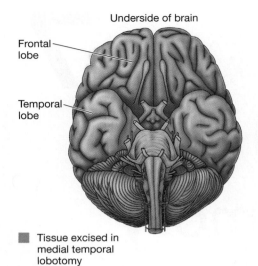

Underside of brain

Frontal lobe

Temporal lobe

■ Tissue excised in medial temporal lobotomy

FIGURE 7.1 A Drawing of H.M.'s Brain The portions of the medial temporal lobe that were removed from H.M.'s brain are indicated by the shaded regions.

FIGURE 7.2 Henry Molaison (H.M.) Known to the world only by his initials, Molaison became one of the most famous people in memory research by participating in countless experiments. He died at a nursing home on December 2, 2008.

Learning Objectives

■ Describe the three phases of memory.

■ Identify brain regions involved in learning and memory.

■ Describe the processes of consolidation and reconsolidation.

uncontrolled random firing of groups of neurons, and they can spread across the brain. Molaison's seizures originated in the temporal lobes of his brain and would spread from there. Because the anticonvulsive drugs available at that time could not control his seizures, surgery was the only choice for treatment. The reasoning behind this surgery was that if the seizure-causing portion of his brain was removed, he would stop having seizures. In September 1953, Molaison's doctors removed parts of his medial temporal lobes, including the hippocampus (Figure 7.1). The surgery quieted his seizures, but it had an unexpected and very unfortunate side effect: Molaison lost the ability to remember things over long periods of time.

Until his death, the larger world did not know Molaison's real name or what he looked like (Figure 7.2), because his privacy was guarded by the researchers who studied his memory. H.M., as he was known, never remembered the day of the week, what year it was, or his own age. Still, he could talk about his childhood, explain the rules of baseball, and describe members of his family, things he knew at the time of the surgery. According to the psychologists who tested him, his IQ was slightly above average. His thinking abilities remained intact. He could hold a normal conversation as long as he was not distracted, but he forgot the conversation in a minute or less. H.M.'s ability to hold a conversation showed that he was still able to remember things for short periods. After all, to grasp the meaning of spoken language, a person needs to remember the words recently spoken, such as the beginning and end of a sentence. But H.M. did not appear to remember any new information over time. People who worked with H.M. — such as the psychologist Brenda Milner, who followed his case for over 40 years — had to introduce themselves to him every time they met. As H.M. put it, "Every day is alone in itself." Because of his profound memory loss, he remembered nothing from minute to minute. But he knew that he remembered nothing. How could this have been the case? What did it mean for H.M. to have memory at all? ■

7.1 What Is Memory?

Memory Is the Nervous System's Capacity to Acquire and Retain Usable Skills and Knowledge

H.M. learned some new things, although he did not know he had learned them. Most impressively, he learned new motor tasks. In one series of tests, he was required to trace the outline of a star while watching his hand in a mirror. Most people do poorly the first few times they try this difficult task. On each of three consecutive days, H.M. was asked to trace the star 10 times. His performance improved over the three days, and this result indicated that he had retained some information about the task. On each day, however, H.M. could not recall ever performing the task previously. His ability to learn new motor skills enabled him to get a job at a factory, where he mounted cigarette lighters on cardboard cases. But his condition left him unable to describe the job or the workplace. Studies of H.M.'s strange condition have contributed many clues to how memories are stored — normally and abnormally — in the brain.

Normally, each of us remembers millions of pieces of information, from the trivial to the vital. Each person's entire sense of self, or identity, is made up of what that person knows from memories, from his or her recollections of personal experiences and of things learned from others. Thus **memory** is the nervous system's capacity to acquire and retain skills and knowledge. This capacity enables organisms to take information from experiences and store it for retrieval later.

Yet memory does not work like a digital video camera that faithfully captures and just as faithfully retrieves the events its operator experiences. Instead, memories are often incomplete, biased, and distorted. Two people's memories for the same event can differ vastly, because each person stores and retrieves memories of the event distinctively. We tend to remember personally relevant information and filter our memories through our various perceptions and our knowledge of related events. In other words, memories are stories that can be altered subtly by the process of recollection.

In addition, all experiences are not equally likely to be remembered. Some life events pass swiftly, leaving no lasting memory. Others are remembered but later forgotten. Still others remain for a lifetime. We have multiple memory systems, and each memory system has its own "rules." For example, some brain processes underlie memory for information we will need to retrieve in 10 seconds. Those processes operate differently from the processes that underlie memory for information we will need to retrieve in 10 years. The following section looks at psychologists' basic model of how the mind remembers: the *information processing model*.

Memory Is the Processing of Information

Since the late 1960s, most psychologists have viewed memory as a form of information processing. In this model, the ways that memory works are analogous to the ways computers process information. A computer receives information through the keyboard or modem, and software determines how the information is processed; the information may then be stored in some altered format on the hard drive; and the information may be retrieved when it is needed. Likewise, the multiple processes of memory can be thought of as operating over time in three phases (**Figure 7.3**). The **encoding** phase occurs at the time of learning, as information is acquired by being encoded. That is, the brain changes information into a neural code that it can use. Consider the process of reading this book. In the encoding phase, your brain converts the sensory stimuli on the page to meaningful neural codes. The **storage** phase is the retention of

memory The nervous system's capacity to acquire and retain skills and knowledge.

encoding The processing of information so that it can be stored.

storage The retention of encoded representations over time.

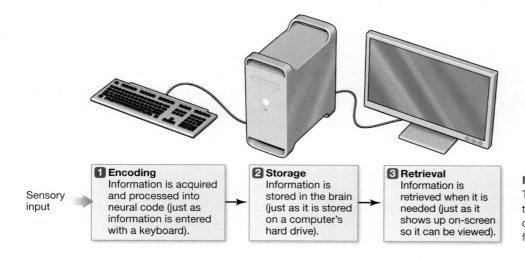

Sensory input →

1 Encoding
Information is acquired and processed into neural code (just as information is entered with a keyboard).

2 Storage
Information is stored in the brain (just as it is stored on a computer's hard drive).

3 Retrieval
Information is retrieved when it is needed (just as it shows up on-screen so it can be viewed).

FIGURE 7.3 Information Processing
The information processing model compares the working of memory to the actions of a computer. **How does human memory differ from a computer's memory?**

retrieval The act of recalling or remembering stored information when it is needed.

the coded representation. It corresponds to some change in the nervous system, a change that registers what you read as a memorable event. Storage can last a fraction of a second or as long as a lifetime. Think of this phase as being when you keep material you read in mind until test time or longer. There are at least three storage systems, which differ in how long they store information. These systems will be discussed in detail later in this chapter. **Retrieval,** the third phase of memory, consists of reaching into memory storage to find and bring to mind a previously encoded and stored memory when it is needed. Think of this phase as being when you draw on the material in your brain for use on the midterm, on the final, or sometime long after graduation when someone asks you a question about psychology.

Memory Is the Result of Brain Activity

What role does biology play in the processing of information? Memory researchers have made tremendous progress over the past two decades in understanding what happens in the brain when we acquire, store, and retrieve memories.

MEMORY'S PHYSICAL LOCATIONS As discussed in Chapter 3, Karl Lashley spent much of his career trying to figure out where in the brain memories are stored. Lashley's term *engram* refers to the physical site of memory storage—that is, the place where memory "lives." As part of his research, Lashley trained rats to run a maze, then removed different areas of their cortices. (For more information on the cortex and on other brain regions discussed here, such as the cerebellum and the amygdala, see **Figure 7.4.**) In testing how much of the maze learning the rats retained after the surgery, Lashley found that the size of the area removed was the most important factor in predicting retention. The location of the area was far less important. From these findings, he concluded that memory is distributed throughout the brain rather than confined to any specific location. This idea is known as *equipotentiality*. Lashley was right that memories are not stored in any one brain location. In many other ways, though, Lashley was wrong about how memories are stored.

The psychologist Donald Hebb built on Lashley's research. In Hebb's interpretation, memories are stored in multiple regions of the brain, and they are linked through memory circuits. As discussed in Chapter 6, Hebb proposed that when neurons "fire together," they "wire together." Through this firing and wiring, all learning leaves biological trails in the brain.

Not all brain areas are equally involved in memory, however. A great deal of neural specialization occurs. Because of this specialization, different brain regions are responsible for storing different aspects of information. Indeed, different memory systems use different brain regions. Lashley's failure to find the brain regions critical for memory is due to at least two factors. First, the maze task he used to study memory involved multiple sensory systems (such as vision and smell). The rats could compensate for the loss of one sense by using other senses. Second, Lashley did not examine subcortical areas, which are now known to be important for memory retention.

Over the past three decades, researchers have identified many brain regions that contribute to learning and memory. For instance, we know from studies of H.M. that regions within the temporal lobes, such as the hippocampus, are important for the

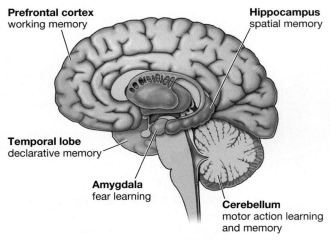

Prefrontal cortex
working memory

Hippocampus
spatial memory

Temporal lobe
declarative memory

Amygdala
fear learning

Cerebellum
motor action learning and memory

FIGURE 7.4 Brain Regions Associated with Memory

ability to store new memories. The temporal lobes are important for being able to say what you remember, but they are less important for motor learning and classical conditioning (discussed in Chapter 6, "Learning"). As noted in Chapter 3, the cerebellum plays a role in how motor actions are learned and remembered. The amygdala, in contrast, is especially important for one type of classical conditioning, fear learning. As noted in Chapter 6, an animal without an amygdala cannot learn to fear objects that signal danger. The take-home message here is that memory is distributed among different brain regions. Memory does not "live" in one part of the brain. If you lose a particular brain cell, you will not therefore lose a memory.

CONSOLIDATION OF MEMORIES Reading this chapter should be making some of your neural connections stronger. At the same time, new neural connections should be developing, especially in your hippocampus. Your brain is different than it was before you began reading the chapter. Neural connections that support memory have become stronger, and new synapses have been constructed (Miller, 2005). This process is known as **consolidation.** Through it, your immediate memories—memories acquired through encoding—become your lasting memories.

Most likely, the middle section of the temporal lobes (called the *medial temporal lobes*) are responsible for coordinating and strengthening the connections among neurons when something is learned. The medial temporal lobes are particularly important for the formation of new memories. The actual storage, however, occurs in the particular brain regions engaged during the perception, processing, and analysis of the material being learned. For instance, visual information is stored in the cortical areas involved in visual perception. Sound is stored in the areas involved in auditory perception. Thus memory for sensory experiences, such as remembering something seen or heard, involves reactivating the cortical circuits involved in the initial seeing or hearing (**Figure 7.5**). The medial temporal lobes form links, or pointers, between the different storage sites, and they direct the gradual strengthening of the connections between these links (Squire, Stark, & Clark, 2004). Once the connections are strengthened sufficiently, the medial temporal lobes become less important for memory. As discussed earlier, H.M.'s surgery removed parts of his medial temporal lobes. Without those parts, he could not make new memories (at least ones he could talk about), but he still was able to retrieve old memories.

To understand the basic consolidation process, consider that while reading this chapter you have come to understand that *medial* means middle. Now that you have acquired this information, you need to think about it over time so that it will be consolidated in your memory.

A good night's sleep might also contribute to this process. There is compelling evidence that sleep helps with the consolidation of memories and that disturbing

consolidation A process by which immediate memories become lasting (or long-term) memories.

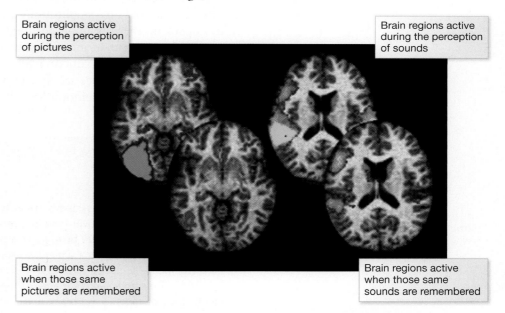

Brain regions active during the perception of pictures

Brain regions active during the perception of sounds

Brain regions active when those same pictures are remembered

Brain regions active when those same sounds are remembered

FIGURE 7.5 Brain Activation during Perception and Remembering These four horizontally sliced brain images were acquired using magnetic resonance imaging. In each pair, the top image shows the brain areas that are activated during a particular sensory-specific perception. The bottom image shows the regions of the sensory cortex that are activated when that sensory-specific information is remembered. Notice that the perceptions and the memories involve similar cortical areas.

FIGURE 7.6 Altering Memories In the 2004 movie *Eternal Sunshine of the Spotless Mind,* Joel Barish (played by Jim Carrey) undergoes a procedure that eliminates memories of his former girlfriend. **If this procedure were real, would you choose to undergo it? Why would you want to eliminate parts of your past from your memory? What drawbacks might there be from losing even bad memories?**

reconsolidation Neural processes involved when memories are recalled and then stored again for later retrieval.

sleep interferes with learning. Chronic sleep deprivation certainly will interfere with learning. (For more information on sleep, see Chapter 5, "Consciousness." Advice on improving your sleeping habits appears in that chapter's "Psychology: Knowledge You Can Use" feature, "Can Sleep Deprivation Hurt Me?")

RECONSOLIDATION OF MEMORIES An exciting theory developed by Karim Nader and Joseph LeDoux proposes that once memories are activated, they need to be consolidated again to be stored back in memory (LeDoux, 2002; Nader & Einarsson, 2010). These processes are known as **reconsolidation.** To understand how reconsolidation works, think of this image: A librarian returns a book to a shelf for storage so that it can be taken out again later.

When memories for past events are retrieved, those memories can be affected by new circumstances, and so the newly reconsolidated memories may differ from their original versions (Nader, Schafe, & LeDoux, 2000). In other words, our memories begin as versions of what we have experienced. Then they actually might change when we use them. In the library book analogy, this change would be like tearing pages out of the book or adding new pages or notes before returning it. The book placed on the shelf differs from the one taken out. The information in the torn-out pages is no longer available for retrieval, and the new pages or notes that were inserted alter the memory the next time it is retrieved.

The reconsolidation process repeats itself each time a memory is activated and placed back in storage, and it may explain why our memories for events can change over time. As you might imagine, this theory has received considerable attention. It not only has implications for what it means to remember something. It also opens up the intriguing possibility that bad memories could be erased by activating them and then interfering with reconsolidation. Recently, researchers have shown that using extinction (discussed in Chapter 6, "Learning") during the period when memories are susceptible to reconsolidation can be an effective method of altering bad memories (Schiller et al., 2010; **Figure 7.6**).

Summing Up

What Is Memory?

Memory is the nervous system's capacity to acquire and retain skills and knowledge. Memory operates over time in three phases: encoding, storage, and retrieval. Multiple brain regions have been implicated in memory, including the hippocampus, temporal lobes, cerebellum, amygdala, and the brain structures involved in perception. The medial temporal regions of the brain are particularly important for the consolidation of memories into storage. As memories are consolidated, neurons link into distributed networks in the brain, and these networks become linked. Reconsolidation refers to the processes that occur when memories are retrieved, altered, and placed back into storage. Reconsolidation may explain why memories for events change over time.

Measuring Up

1. Which of the following statements are true? Choose as many as apply.
   a. The hippocampus is particularly important in fear conditioning.
   b. Donald Hebb proposed the notion of equipotentiality.
   c. Encoding occurs before storage.

d. Reconsolidation is the first phase of memory.

e. The cerebellum is involved in the learning of motor actions.

f. Memory storage is limited to the parietal lobes.

2. What changes occur at the synapses when people learn and remember? Choose as many as apply.

a. Neural connections are strengthened.

b. Reuptake is enhanced.

c. Neurons make more synaptic connections.

d. Brain regions associated with learning and remembering become more sensitive to glucose.

e. The cerebellum grows larger.

Answers: 1. c. Encoding occurs before storage.; e. The cerebellum is involved in the learning of motor actions.
2. a. Neuronal connections are strengthened.; c. Neurons make more synaptic connections.

How Does Attention Determine What We Remember?

Learning Objectives

- Distinguish between parallel processing and serial processing.
- Describe filter theory.
- Define change blindness.

Many students say they have memory problems. Specifically, they have trouble remembering the material covered in class and in their textbooks. Their problems often have nothing to do with the way their brains work, however. Instead, they simply do not pay attention when they are supposed to be learning. For example, students who overload their systems by studying while checking e-mail, instant messaging, and watching television will do worse at all these tasks than they would if they focused on one task at a time (Manhart, 2004).

Your elementary school teachers probably had a basic understanding of the way memory works. For this reason, they demanded that you and your fellow students "pay attention." Good teachers know that to get information into memory, a person needs to *attend*. That is, the person needs to focus on the subject and be alert. Think about the difference between the words *see* and *look, hear* and *listen*. *Look* and *listen* are commands that tell you where to direct your attention. Each of us has the ability to direct something in ourselves, called *attention,* to some information. We do so at the cost of paying less attention to other information. In fact, the word *pay* indicates that costs are associated with attending to some forms of information and not to others. Attention is limited. When it is divided among too many tasks or the tasks are difficult, performance suffers.

Attention is an important part of your ability to function in your daily life. Imagine how awful it would be if you could not block out the irrelevant information that comes at you all the time. Throughout any day, you try to focus attention on the tasks at hand and ignore other things that might distract you. A task as simple as having a conversation requires paying focused attention. If the other speaker has unusual facial features or has food on his or her chin, the unusual features or food might capture your attention and make it difficult to comprehend what the person is saying. If the other speaker is boring, your mind might wander. You might find your own thoughts, or even a nearby conversation, more interesting to attend to than your long-winded companion. In short, your attention can be distracted by external sensory cues or by internal thoughts

parallel processing Processing multiple types of information at the same time.

and memories (Chun, Golomb, & Turk-Browne, 2011). The following section presents the basic principles of how human attention works.

Our Visual Attention Works Selectively and Serially

The psychologist Anne Treisman has made great advances in the study of attention. According to her theory about attention and recognition, we automatically identify "primitive" features within an environment. Such features include color, shape, size, orientation, and movement. Treisman has proposed that separate systems analyze the different visual features of objects. Through **parallel processing,** these systems all process information at the same time. We can attend selectively to one feature by effectively blocking the further processing of the others (Treisman & Gelade, 1980).

In studies that employ Treisman's *visual search tasks* (also called *feature search tasks*), participants look at a display of different objects on a computer screen. They search for *targets,* objects that differ from the others in only one feature. The other objects in the display are called *distractors.* A typical display might consist of a few red As (the targets) among many black ones (the distractors; **Figure 7.7**). In these conditions, the targets seem to pop out immediately, regardless of the number of distractors. Some features that seem to pop out when the targets differ from the distractors are color, shape, motion, orientation, and size (Wolfe & Horowitz, 2004). Suppose you are trying to find a friend of yours in a large crowd of people. This task will be fairly easy if your friend is wearing red and everyone else is wearing black, or if your friend is the only one waving, the only one standing up, or a much different size than everyone else.

As discussed in Chapter 3, a similar research paradigm was used to identify synesthetes, some of whom see particular numbers as printed in particular colors even when all the numbers are black. If you are not a synesthete, it might take you a while to find, for example, all the 2s in an array of 2s and 5s if all the numbers are black. A synesthete who sees 2s in one color and 5s in another color will be able to find the 2s very quickly.

Searching for a single feature, such as a red stimulus, is fast and automatic. Searching for two features is *serial* (you need to look at the stimuli one at a time) and *effortful* (takes longer and requires more attention). Imagine, for example, trying to find all the red Xs in a display of differently colored Xs and Ys. This effort would be called a *conjunction task* because the stimulus you are looking for is made up of two simple features conjoined (**Figure 7.8**).

Our Auditory Attention Allows Us to Listen Selectively

Because attention is limited, it is hard to perform two tasks at the same time. It is especially hard if the two tasks rely on the same sensory mechanisms or the same mental mechanisms. We easily can listen to music and drive at the same time, but it is hard to listen to two conversations at once. Think about driving along an open road, singing along with a song on the radio and perhaps even talking with a passenger. What happens when you see the brake lights of cars ahead of you? You need to stop singing or talking and direct your attention to the task of driving. Suddenly, the task becomes more difficult and requires additional attention. Driving and listening to the radio at the same time can even be hazardous, depending on what you are listening to. For example, a sports broadcast might engage your visual system if it inspires you to imagine a game in progress. The game in your imagination would divert your attention from the visual cues on the road ahead.

(a)

(b)

FIGURE 7.7 Parallel Processing
(a) Parallel processing allows us to process information from different visual features at the same time by focusing on targets instead of distractors. Here the targets are the red objects. **(b) In this photo, which details serve as targets?**

As you might imagine, behaviors such as reading, eating, talking on a cell phone, or texting are dangerous while driving because they distract the driver's attention. It is estimated that in the United States from 2005 to 2008, deaths from distracted driving increased by 28 percent (National Highway Traffic Safety Administration, 2009; Wilson & Stimpson, 2010). Simulated-driving experiments have shown that talking on a cell phone is especially dangerous. In fact, talking on a cell phone can impair driving skills nearly as much as alcohol. For instance, drivers' braking reactions are reduced, possibly because talking impairs visual processing (Strayer, Drews, & Johnston, 2003). Talking on a cell phone while driving is likely more hazardous than talking with a passenger in the car while driving. A cell phone conversation will not vary naturally with the driving conditions, because the person talking with the driver will not know what is happening. Suppose that traffic has become heavy or the car ahead has suddenly braked. A driver talking with a passenger can signal in many ways that the conversation needs to pause as situations demand (Drews, Pasupathi, & Strayer, 2008). Hands-free cell phones do not solve the attention problem. Because drivers using hands-free phones still have to divide their attentional resources among multiple tasks, hands-free cell phone use may be just as dangerous as talking while holding the phone (Ishigami & Klein, 2009).

In thinking about the power of distraction, consider the *cocktail party phenomenon*. In 1953, the psychologist E. C. Cherry described the process this way: You can focus on a single conversation in the midst of a chaotic cocktail party. A particularly pertinent stimulus, however—such as hearing your name mentioned in another conversation or hearing a juicy piece of gossip—can capture your attention. If you really want to hear the other conversation or piece of gossip, you can focus your attention on it. Of course, when you redirect your attention in this way, you probably will not be able to follow what the closer (and therefore probably louder) partygoer is saying. You will lose the thread of your original conversation.

Cherry developed selective-listening studies to examine what the mind does with unattended information when a person pays attention to one task. He used a technique called *shadowing*. In this procedure, a participant wears headphones that deliver one message to one ear and a different message to the other. The person is asked to attend to one of the two messages and "shadow" it by repeating it aloud. As a result, the person usually notices the unattended sound (the message given to the other ear), but will have no knowledge about the content of the unattended sound (**Figure 7.9**).

Imagine you are participating in an experiment about what happens to unattended messages. You are repeating whatever is spoken into one ear (shadowing) and ignoring the message spoken into the other ear. What would happen if your own name were spoken into the unattended ear? You would probably hear your own name but know nothing about the rest of the message. Some important information gets through the filter of attention. It has to be personally relevant information, such as your name or the name of someone close to you, or it has to be particularly loud or different in some obvious physical way.

Through Selective Attention, We Filter Incoming Information

In 1958, the psychologist Donald Broadbent developed *filter theory* to explain the selective nature of attention. He assumed that people have a limited capacity for

FIGURE 7.8 Try for Yourself: Conjunction Tasks

Count the blue squares as quickly as you can.

Result: This task is relatively difficult because you are searching for two features. You need to slow down and determine if each stimulus is blue *and* square.

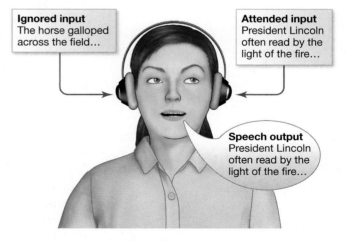

Ignored input
The horse galloped across the field...

Attended input
President Lincoln often read by the light of the fire...

Speech output
President Lincoln often read by the light of the fire...

FIGURE 7.9 Shadowing In this procedure, the participant receives a different auditory message in each ear. The participant is required to repeat, or "shadow," only one of the messages.

sensory information. They screen incoming information to let in only the most important material. In this model, attention is like a gate that opens for important information and closes for irrelevant information. But can we really close the gate to ignore some information? When and how do we close the gate?

Some stimuli demand attention and virtually shut off the ability to attend to anything else. Imagine you are focusing all your attention on reading this book, and suddenly you develop a muscle cramp. What will happen to your attention? The sharp jab of the cramp will demand your attention, and whatever you are reading will leave your consciousness until you attend to the muscle. Similarly, some stimuli, such as those that evoke emotions, may readily capture attention because they provide important information about potential threats in an environment (Phelps, Ling, & Carrasco, 2006). An object produces a stronger attentional response when it is viewed as socially relevant (e.g., an eye) than when it is viewed as nonsocial (e.g., an arrowhead; Tipper, Handy, Giesbrecht, & Kingstone, 2008).

Faces are a good example of stimuli that capture attention because they provide important social information. For example, a face indicates whether someone is a potential mate (i.e., has an attractive face) or may intend to cause physical harm (i.e., has an angry face). A series of studies found that the attentional system prioritizes faces, especially when they appear threatening, over less meaningful stimuli (West, Anderson, & Pratt, 2009). Indeed, threatening information receives priority over other stimuli within $\frac{1}{20}$ of a second after it is presented (West, Anderson, Ferber, & Pratt, 2011).

Studies such as the one just described indicate that decisions about what to attend to are made early in the perceptual process. At the same time, however, unattended information is processed at least to some extent. As discussed in Chapter 5, people are often influenced by information delivered subliminally or incidentally. Several selective-listening studies have found that even when participants cannot repeat an unattended message, they still have processed its contents. In one experiment, participants were told to attend to the message coming in one ear: *They threw stones at the bank yesterday.* At the same time, the unattended ear was presented with one of two words: *river* or *money.* Afterward, participants could not report the unattended words. However, those presented with the word *river* interpreted the sentence to mean someone had thrown stones at a riverbank. Those presented with the word *money* interpreted the sentence to mean someone had thrown stones at a financial institution (MacKay, 1973). Thus the participants extracted meaning from the word even though they did not process the word consciously.

To understand just how inattentive we can be, consider the phenomenon known as **change blindness.** Because we cannot attend to everything in the vast array of visual information available, often we are "blind" to large changes in our environments. For example, would you notice if the person you were talking to suddenly changed into another person? In two studies, participants were on a college campus when they were approached by a stranger. The stranger asked for directions. Then the stranger was momentarily blocked by a large object and replaced with another person of the same sex and race. Fifty percent of the people giving directions never noticed that they were talking to a different person. When giving directions to a stranger, we normally do not attend to the distinctive features of the stranger's face or clothing. If we are unable to recall those features later, it is not because we forgot them. More likely, it is because we never processed those features very much in the first place. After all, how often do we need to recall such information? (Simons & Levin, 1998; **Figure 7.10**).

change blindness A failure to notice large changes in one's environment.

Hypothesis: People can be "blind" to large changes around them.

Research Method:

1 A participant is approached by a stranger asking for directions.

2 The stranger is momentarily blocked by a larger object.

3 While being blocked, the original stranger is replaced by another person.

Results: Half the participants giving directions never noticed they were talking to a different person (as long as the replacement was of the same race and sex as the original stranger).

Conclusion: Change blindness results from inattention to certain visual information.

Source: Photos from Simons, D. J., & Levin, D. T. (1998). Failure to detect changes to people during a real-world interaction. *Psychonomic Bulletin and Review, 5,* 644–649. © 1998 Psychonomic Society, Inc. Figure courtesy Daniel J. Simons.

In the first study, older people were especially likely not to notice a change in the person asking them for directions. Younger people were pretty good at noticing the change. Are older people especially inattentive? Or do they tend to process a situation's broad outlines rather than its details? Perhaps the older people encoded the stranger as simply "a college student" and did not look for more-individual characteristics. To test this idea, Simons and Levin (1998) conducted an additional study. This time, the stranger was an easily recognizable type of person from a different social group. That is, the same experimenters dressed as construction workers and asked college students for directions. Sure enough, the college students failed to notice the replacement of one construction worker with another. This finding supports the idea that the students encoded the strangers as belonging to a broad category of "construction workers" without looking more closely at them. For these students, construction workers seemed pretty much all alike and interchangeable. Subsequent research has shown that people with a greater ability to maintain attention in the face of distracting information are less likely to experience a similar type of change blindness (Seegmiller, Watson, & Strayer, 2011).

As change blindness illustrates, we can attend to a limited amount of information. Large discrepancies exist between what most of us believe we see and what we actually see. Thus our perceptions of the world are often inaccurate, and we have little awareness of our perceptual failures. We simply do not know how much information we miss in the world around us. Every time we miss a piece of information, we run the risk of not storing it as a memory. Every time we fail to pay attention, in other words, we are likely to forget what just happened.

Recognizing When "Change Blindness Blindness" May Be Occuring

The main message from studies of change blindness is that we can miss obvious changes in what we see and hear. Despite this possibility, most of us believe that we will always notice large changes—that important events automatically draw our attention. This erroneous belief persists because we often do not find out about the things we fail to perceive (Simons & Ambinder, 2005). In addition, the phenomenon of change blindness is so counterintuitive that few of us believe how much we do not see. *Change blindness blindness* is our unawareness that we often do not notice apparently obvious changes in our environments.

Imagine you are driving up a hill. At the top of the hill, there is an intersection. When you reach the top, you see another car heading straight into your lane, and in a flash you swerve to avoid a collision. The other car hits yours, but your last-minute swerve convinces eyewitnesses that you caused the accident by driving erratically. Change blindness blindness could be a factor in their reports: Perhaps out of a desire to help, the eyewitnesses believe they saw the whole accident. They may have missed the critical moments, however, because they were attending to their own activities. Attention, of course, influences memory.

Being aware of change blindness blindness is a critical thinking skill. Thinking that we always notice large changes may lead us to perceive things incorrectly, such as in erroneously believing something did or did not happen. Recognizing the limitations of attention may help prevent us from misleading ourselves about our perceptions. Knowledge about change blindness should make us more humble about what we really see and what we remember.

Summing Up

How Does Attention Determine What We Remember?

Attention is the ability to focus on certain stimuli. This ability is adaptive in that it facilitates functioning by enabling us to block out irrelevant information. Using visual search tasks, researchers have found that we process basic features of stimuli (e.g., color, motion, orientation, shape, and size) through parallel processing. Parallel processing is fast and automatic. Using conjunction tasks, researchers have found that we process multiple features of stimuli (e.g., trying to find red Xs) serially and effortfully. Filter theory maintains that attention is selective. Consistent with this theory, we can choose the stimuli to which we attend. For example, we can ignore a nearby conversation in favor of a more interesting one farther away. To some extent, however, we process information contained in sensory stimuli to which we are not consciously attending. We commonly exhibit change blindness, failing to notice major changes in the environment. Change blindness illustrates that our perceptions can be inaccurate.

7.3 How Are Memories Maintained over Time?

Have you been paying attention to your reading? How well do you remember this chapter's opening discussions of memory? Recall from the start of the chapter that the information processing model is based on the model of the computer (**Figure 7.11a**). Information is encoded in the brain during learning, stored in memory, and then retrieved for later use. In 1968, the psychologists Richard Atkinson and Richard Shiffrin proposed a different model. Atkinson and Shiffrin's three-part model consists of *sensory memory, short-term memory,* and *long-term memory* (**Figure 7.11b**). Each of these terms refers to the length of time that information is retained in memory. In addition, the three parts of this model differ in their capacity for storage, with sensory memory having the least capacity and long-term memory having the most. The following sections will look at these parts in more detail.

Sensory Memory Is Brief

Sensory memory is a temporary memory system closely tied to the sensory systems. It is not what we usually think of when we think about memory, because it lasts only a fraction of a second. In fact, normally we are not aware that it is operating.

As discussed in Chapter 4, we obtain all our information about the world through our senses. Our sensory systems transduce, or change, that information into neural impulses. Everything we remember, therefore, is the result of neurons firing in the brain. For example, a memory of a sight or of a sound is created by intricate patterns of neural activity in the brain. A sensory memory occurs when a light, a sound, an odor, a taste, or a tactile impression leaves a vanishing trace

sensory memory A memory system that very briefly stores sensory information in close to its original sensory form.

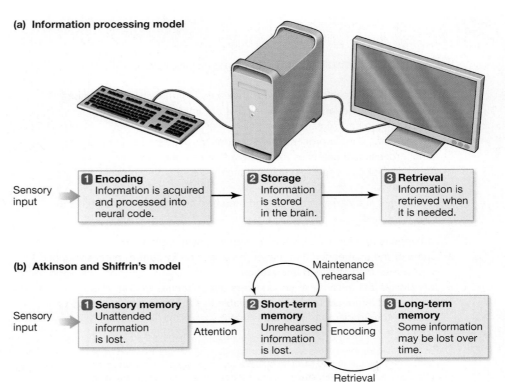

(a) Information processing model

| **1 Encoding** Information is acquired and processed into neural code. | → | **2 Storage** Information is stored in the brain. | → | **3 Retrieval** Information is retrieved when it is needed. |

Sensory input →

(b) Atkinson and Shiffrin's model

Maintenance rehearsal

Sensory input →

| **1 Sensory memory** Unattended information is lost. | — Attention → | **2 Short-term memory** Unrehearsed information is lost. | — Encoding → | **3 Long-term memory** Some information may be lost over time. |

Retrieval

FIGURE 7.11 Three-Part Memory Systems (a) Recall that the information processing model compares the working of memory to the actions of a computer. **(b)** By contrast, Atkinson and Shiffrin's model emphasizes that memory storage varies in duration and capacity.

on the nervous system for a fraction of a second. When you look at something and quickly glance away, you can briefly picture the image and recall some of its details. When someone protests, "You're not paying attention to me," you often can repeat back the last few words the person spoke, even if you were thinking about something else.

In 1960, the cognitive psychologist George Sperling provided the initial empirical support for sensory memory. In this classic experiment, three rows of letters were flashed on a screen for $\frac{1}{20}$ of a second. Participants were asked to recall all the letters. Most people believed they had seen all the letters, but they could recall only three or four. That is, in the time it took them to name the first three or four, they forgot the other letters. These reports suggested the participants had very quickly lost their memories of exactly what they had seen. Sperling tested this hypothesis by showing all the letters exactly as he had done before, but signaling with a high-, medium-, or low-pitched sound as soon as the letters disappeared. A high pitch meant the participants should recall the letters in the top row, a medium pitch meant they should recall the letters in the middle row, and a low pitch meant they should recall the letters in the bottom row. When the sound occurred very shortly after the letters disappeared, the participants correctly remembered almost all the letters in the signaled row. But the longer the delay between the letters' disappearance and the sound, the worse the participants performed. Sperling concluded that the visual memory persisted for about $\frac{1}{3}$ of a second. After that very brief period, the trace of the sensory memory faded progressively until it was no longer accessible (**Figure 7.12**).

Our sensory memories enable us to experience the world as a continuous stream rather than in discrete sensations. Thanks to visual memory, when you turn your head the scene passes smoothly in front of you rather than in jerky bits. Your memory retains information just long enough for you to connect one image with the next in a smooth way that corresponds to the way objects move in the

FIGURE 7.12 Scientific Method: Sperling's Sensory Memory Experiment

Hypothesis: Information in sensory memories is lost very quickly if it is not transferred for further processing.

Research Method:

1 Participants looked at a screen on which three rows of letters flashed for $\frac{1}{20}$ of a second.

2 When a high-pitched tone followed the letters, it meant the participants should recall the letters in the top row. When a medium-pitched tone followed the letters, it meant the participants should recall the middle row. And when a low-pitched tone followed the letters, it meant the participants should recall the bottom row.

3 The tones sounded at various intervals: .15, .30, .50, or 1 second after the display of the letters.

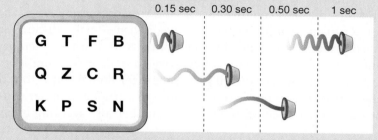

Results: When the tone sounded very shortly after the letters disappeared, participants remembered almost all the letters in the signaled row. The longer the delay between the disappearance of the letters and the tone, the worse the participants performed.

Conclusion: Sensory memory persists for about $\frac{1}{3}$ of a second and then progressively fades.

Source: Sperling, G. (1960). The information available in brief visual presentations. *Psychological Monographs, 74,* 1–29.

---

real world. In much the same way, a movie projector plays a series of still pictures that follow each other closely enough in time to look like continuous action.

Working Memory Is Active

Information attended to is passed from sensory stores to **short-term memory.** This memory system has a limited capacity, but it has more capacity than sensory memory. Researchers initially saw short-term memory as simply a buffer, or holding place, in which verbal information was rehearsed until it was stored or forgotten. Subsequently, however, researchers learned that short-term memory is not a single storage system. Instead, it is an active processing unit that deals with multiple types of information. A more contemporary model of the short-term retention of information is **working memory.** This storage system works on the information we have in memory, partly by combining information from different sources (Baddeley & Hitch, 1974; Baddeley, 2002). For example, working memory includes sounds, images, and ideas.

Information remains in working memory for about 20 to 30 seconds. It then disappears unless you actively prevent that from happening by thinking about or rehearsing the information. As an example, try to remember some new information: the meaningless three-letter string of consonants X C J. As long as you keep repeating the string over and over, you will keep it in working memory. But if

short-term memory A memory storage system that briefly holds a limited amount of information in awareness.

working memory An active processing system that keeps different types of information available for current use.

you stop rehearsing, you probably will soon forget the letters. After all, you are bombarded with other events that compete for your attention, and you may not be able to stay focused. Try again to remember X C J, but this time count backward in threes from the number 309. Most people find it difficult to remember the meaningless consonants after a few seconds of backward counting. The longer they spend counting, the less able they are to remember the consonant string. After only 18 seconds of counting, most people recall the consonants extremely poorly. This result indicates that working memory lasts less than half a minute without continuous rehearsing as a way to remember.

Researchers have recently demonstrated how working memory is updated to take into account new information (Ecker, Lewandowsky, Oberauer, & Chee, 2010). For instance, suppose a restaurant manager is told to expect 20 people for dinner. If subsequently told that 5 more people are coming, the manager needs to retrieve the original number, transform it by adding 5, and then substitute the new number for the old in working memory. These three processes—*retrieval, transformation,* and *substitution*—make distinct and independent contributions to updating the contents of working memory. Sometimes only one of the processes is necessary to update working memory. For instance, if the manager is expecting 20 people for dinner but is told there will be 25, the manager does not have to retrieve the original number or transform it. He or she just has to substitute the new number into working memory.

MEMORY SPAN AND CHUNKING Why do new items in working memory interfere with the recall of older items? Working memory can hold a limited amount of information. The cognitive psychologist George Miller has noted that the limit is generally seven items (plus or minus two). This figure is referred to as *memory span.* More-recent research suggests that Miller's estimate may be too high and that working memory may be limited to as few as four items (Conway et al., 2005). Memory span also varies among individuals. Indeed, some intelligence tests use memory span as part of the measure of IQ. Perhaps luckily for those of us whose memory spans may be tested, there is growing evidence that we can increase the capacity of working memory through exercises, such as working to maintain material in working memory in the face of interference or while performing other cognitive tasks (Morrison & Chein, 2011). The capacity of working memory increases as children develop (Garon, Bryson, & Smith, 2008) and decreases with advanced aging (McCabe et al., 2010).

Because working memory is limited, you might expect almost everyone to have great difficulty remembering a string of letters such as UTPHDNYUMAU CLABAMIT.

These 20 letters would tax even the largest memory span. But what if we organized the information into smaller, meaningful units? For instance, UT PHD NYU MA UCLA BA MIT.

Here the letters are separated to produce acronyms for universities and academic degrees. This organization makes them much easier to recall, for two reasons. First, memory span is limited to seven items, probably fewer, but the items can be letters or groups of letters, numbers or groups of numbers, words, or even concepts. Second, meaningful units are easier to remember than nonsense units. This process of organizing information into meaningful units is known as **chunking.** The term means that information is broken down into chunks. The more efficiently you chunk information, the more you can remember. Master chess players who glance at a scenario on a chessboard, even for a few seconds, later can reproduce the exact arrangement of pieces (Chase & Simon, 1973).

chunking Organizing information into meaningful units to make it easier to remember.

They can do so because they instantly chunk the board into a number of meaningful subunits based on their past experiences with the game. If the pieces are arranged on the board in ways that make no sense in terms of chess, however, experts are no better than novices at reproducing the board. In general, the greater your expertise with the material, the more efficiently you can chunk information and therefore the more you can remember (**Figure 7.13**).

Long-Term Memory Is Relatively Permanent

When people talk about memory, they usually are referring to the relatively permanent storage of information: **long-term memory.** In the computer analogy presented earlier, long-term memory is like the storage of information on a hard drive. When you think about long-term memory's capacity, try to imagine counting everything you know and everything you are likely to know in your lifetime. It is hard to imagine what that number might be, because you can always learn more. Unlike computer storage, human long-term memory is nearly limitless. It enables you to remember nursery rhymes from childhood, the meanings and spellings of words you rarely use (such as *aardvark* and *cantankerous*), what you had for lunch yesterday, and so on, and so on.

DISTINGUISHING LONG-TERM MEMORY FROM WORKING MEMORY Long-term memory is distinct from working memory in two important ways: It has a longer duration and a far greater capacity. A controversy exists, however, as to whether long-term memory represents a truly different type of memory storage from working memory. Initial evidence that long-term memory and working memory are separate systems came from research that required people to recall long lists of words. The ability to recall items from the list depended on the order of presentation. That is, items presented early or late in the list were remembered better than those in the middle. This phenomenon is known as the **serial position effect.** This effect actually consists of two separate effects: The *primacy effect* refers to the better memory people have for items presented at the beginning of the list. The *recency effect* refers to the better memory people have for the most recent items, the ones at the end of the list (**Figure 7.14**).

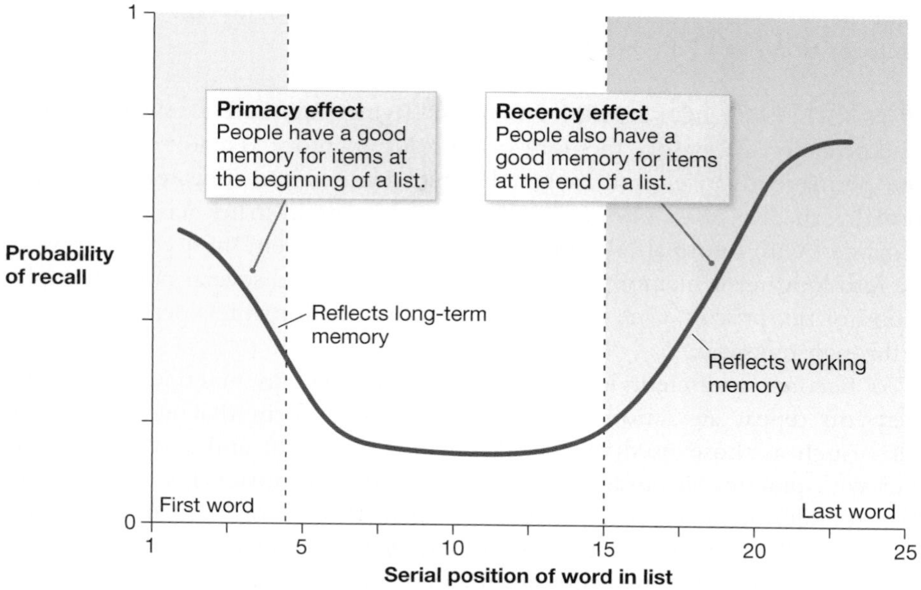

long-term memory The relatively permanent storage of information.

serial position effect The ability to recall items from a list depends on order of presentation, with items presented early or late in the list remembered better than those in the middle.

FIGURE 7.13 Memory Olympics Contestants in the Memory Olympics memorize names, faces, and even decks of cards, as shown here at the meet in Kuala Lumpur, October 2003. Almost all participants in such memory contests use strategies involving chunking. **What strategies do you use for remembering? Why do they work?**

Primacy effect
People have a good memory for items at the beginning of a list.

Recency effect
People also have a good memory for items at the end of a list.

Reflects long-term memory

Reflects working memory

Probability of recall

First word

Last word

Serial position of word in list

FIGURE 7.14 The Serial Position Effect This graph helps illustrate the primacy effect and the recency effect, which together make up the serial position effect. The serial position effect, in turn, helps illustrate the difference between long-term memory and working memory.

One explanation for the serial position effect relies on a distinction between working memory and long-term memory. When research participants study a long list of words, they rehearse the earliest items the most. As a result, that information is transferred into long-term memory. By contrast, the last few items are still in working memory when the participants have to recall the words immediately after reading them. The idea that primacy effects are due to long-term memory, whereas recency effects are due to working memory, is supported by studies in which there is a delay between the presentation of the list and the recall task. Such delays interfere with the recency effect but not the primacy effect. You would expect this result if the recency effect involves working memory and the primacy effect involves long-term memory. The recency effect might not be entirely related to working memory, however. After all, you probably remember your most recent class better than the classes you had earlier, even though you are not holding that material in working memory. If you had to recall the past presidents or past prime ministers of your country, you would probably recall the early ones and most recent ones best and have poorer recall for those in between, but it is unlikely that you maintain the information about presidents or prime ministers in working memory.

Perhaps the best support for the distinction between working memory and long-term memory comes from case studies such as that of H.M., the patient described at the beginning of this chapter. His working memory system was perfectly normal, as shown by his ability to keep track of a conversation as long as he stayed actively involved in it. Much of his long-term memory system was intact, since he remembered events that occurred before his surgery. He was unable, however, to transfer new information from working memory into long-term memory. In another case, a 28-year-old accident victim with damage to the left temporal lobe had extremely poor working memory, with a span of only one or two items. However, he had perfectly normal long-term memory: a fine memory for day-to-day happenings and reasonable knowledge of events that occurred before his surgery (Shallice & Warrington, 1969). Somehow, despite the bottleneck in his working memory, he was relatively good at retrieving information from long-term memory. These case studies demonstrate that long-term memory can be separated from working memory. Still, the two memory systems are highly interdependent, at least for most of us. For instance, to chunk information in working memory, people need to form meaningful connections based on information stored in long-term memory.

WHAT GETS INTO LONG-TERM MEMORY Paying attention is a way of storing information in sensory memory or working memory. To store information more permanently, we need to get that information into long-term memory. Normally, in the course of our daily lives, we engage in many activities and are bombarded with information. Some type of filtering system must constrain what goes into long-term memory. Researchers have provided several possible explanations for this process. One possibility is that information enters permanent storage through rehearsal.

To become proficient in any activity, you need to practice. The more times you repeat an action, the easier it is to perform that action. Motor skills—such as those used to play the piano, play golf, and drive—become easier with practice. Memories are strengthened with retrieval, so one way to make durable memories is to practice retrieval. Recent research in classrooms has shown that repeated testing is a good way to strengthen memories. In fact, it is even better than spending the same amount of time reviewing information you have already read (Roediger & Karpicke, 2006). In a recent study, one group of students read a passage and then took a test on it, a second group studied the information in depth for a week, and a third group made concept maps to organize the information by linking together different ideas (Karpicke & Blunt, 2011). One week later, the students that took the test remembered the information better.

When you practice retrieving information, you basically are doing what you will need to do on a test. So, for example, after reading a section in this or any other book, look back at the main section heading and, if it is not already a question, rephrase it as a question. Then be sure you can answer the heading's question without looking at the text. You might also practice retrieval by working with other students, quizzing each other so you can spot gaps in your knowledge. (In addition, remember to answer the Measuring Up questions at the end of every section in this book; take the Practice Test at the end of each chapter; and visit the book's Web site to take additional tests. The Web site provides feedback and explanations of the correct answers for the additional tests.)

The deeper the level of processing, the more likely you are to remember the material later (Craik & Lockhart, 1972). This fact is another reason that critical thinking skills are important. Rather than just reading the material, think about its meaning and how it is related to other concepts. Try to organize the material in a way that makes sense to you, putting the concepts into your own words. Making the material relevant to you is an especially good way to process material deeply and therefore to remember it easily.

With the material right in front of you, you may be overly confident that you will remember it later. But recognition is easier than recall, and information in a book might not be as accessible when the book is closed and you have to answer questions about what you read. Rehearse material even after you think you have learned it. Test yourself by trying to recall the material a few hours after studying. Keep rehearsing until you can recall the material easily. Distributing your study over time rather than cramming will help you retain the information for longer periods of time (Cepeda, Pashler, Vul, Wixted, & Rohrer, 2006). Six sessions of 1 hour each are much better for learning than one 6-hour marathon. The study sessions should be long enough to get a meaningful amount of information into memory, but they should be spread out over several days or weeks.

Rehearsal is a way to get some information into long-term memory, but simply repeating something many times is not a good method for making information memorable. After all, sometimes we have extremely poor memory for objects that are highly familiar (**Figure 7.15**). Merely seeing something countless times does not enable us to recall its details. For example, try covering a person's watch and then asking that person to describe the watch face. A surprising number of people will not know details such as whether all the numbers are on the face, even if they look at the watch many times a day. This loss of information in memory really shows how well attention and memory function: We attend just enough for the task at hand and lose information that seems irrelevant.

Generally, information about an environment that helps us adapt to that environment is likely to be transformed into a long-term memory. Of the billions of

FIGURE 7.15 Try for Yourself: The Penny Quiz

Can you tell which drawing of the U.S. penny is correct?

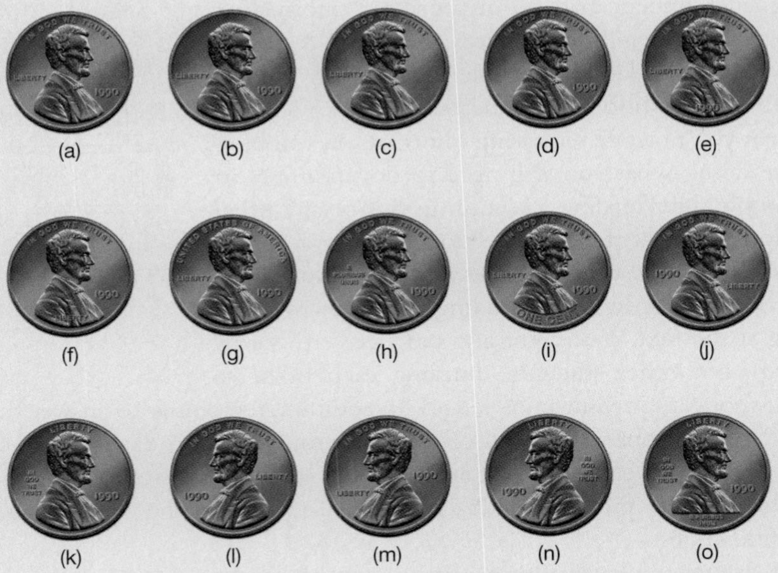

(a) (b) (c) (d) (e)

(f) (g) (h) (i) (j)

(k) (l) (m) (n) (o)

Answer: Even if you live in the United States and see pennies all the time, you might have had trouble identifying "(a)" as the accurate version. In any country, most people do not pay much attention to the specific details of their currency.

both sensory experiences and thoughts we have each day, we want to store only useful information so as to benefit from experience. Remembering that a penny is money and being able to recognize one when you see it are much more useful than being able to recall its specific features—unless you receive counterfeit pennies and have to separate them from real ones.

Evolutionary theory helps explain how we decide in advance what information will be useful. Memory allows us to use information in ways that assist in reproduction and survival. For instance, animals that can use past experiences to increase their chances of survival have a selective advantage over animals that

Summing Up

How Are Memories Maintained over Time?

Atkinson and Shiffrin's model maintains that memory has three components: sensory memory, short-term memory, and long-term memory. Sensory memory consists of brief traces on the nervous system that reflect perceptual processes. Material is passed from sensory memory to short-term memory, a limited system that briefly holds information in awareness. More recently, psychologists have come to think of short-term memory as working memory. Working memory may be limited to as few as four chunks of information. Long-term memory is a relatively permanent, virtually limitless store. The distinction between working memory and long-term memory has been demonstrated by studies that investigated the serial position effect and studies that investigated memory impairments. Information is most likely to be transferred from working memory to long-term memory if it is repeatedly retrieved, deeply processed, or helps us adapt to an environment.

Measuring Up

1. Indicate how long each of the three stages of memory holds information, and indicate its capacity.

   Stage:
   a. sensory memory
   b. short-term (working) memory
   c. long-term memory

   Duration:
   i. one week
   ii. a fraction of a second
   iii. about one day
   iv. between 20 and 30 seconds
   v. potentially as long as a person lives
   vi. until middle age

   Capacity:
   i. 20 chunks, plus or minus 10
   ii. 4 to 9 chunks
   iii. much of the visual world
   iv. almost limitless
   v. about 100,000 pieces of information
   vi. equal to the number of neurons in the brain

2. Which memory system is responsible for your ability to remember the first word in this question?
   a. sensory memory
   b. working memory
   c. long-term memory

Answers: 1. a. Duration: ii, capacity: iii; b. Duration: iv, capacity: ii; c. Duration: v, capacity: iv. 2. b. working memory.

fail to learn from past experiences. Recognizing a predator and remembering an escape route will help an animal avoid being eaten. Accordingly, remembering which objects are edible, which people are friends and which are enemies, and how to get home is typically not challenging for people with intact memory systems, but it is critical for survival.

7.4 How Is Information Organized in Long-Term Memory?

Imagine if a library put each of its books wherever there was empty space on a shelf. To find a particular book, a librarian would have to look through the inventory book by book. Just as this random storage would not work well for books, it would not work well for memories. When an event or some information is important enough, you want to remember it permanently. Thus you need to store it in a way that allows you to retrieve it later. The following section discusses the organizational principles of long-term memory.

Learning Objectives

- Discuss the levels of processing model.
- Explain how schemas influence memory.
- Describe spreading activation models of memory.
- Identify retrieval cues.
- Identify common mnemonics.

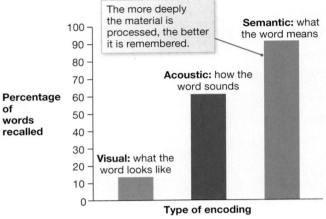

The more deeply the material is processed, the better it is remembered.

Semantic: what the word means

Acoustic: how the word sounds

Visual: what the word looks like

Percentage of words recalled

Type of encoding

FIGURE 7.16 Encoding This graph shows the results of a hypothetical study of encoding. Participants are asked to consider a list of words according to how the words are printed, how they sound, or what they mean. Later they are asked to recall the words.

schemas Cognitive structures that help us perceive, organize, process, and use information.

Long-Term Storage Is Based On Meaning

As discussed in Chapter 4, within our brains our perceptual experiences are transformed into representations. These representations are then stored in networks of neurons. For instance, when your visual system senses a shaggy, four-legged animal and your auditory system senses barking, you perceive a dog. The concept of "dog" is a *mental representation* for a category of animals that share certain features, such as barking and fur. You do not have a tiny picture of a dog stored in your head. Rather, you have a mental representation. The mental representation for "dog" differs from that for "cat," even though the two are similar in many ways. You also have mental representations for complex and abstract ideas, including beliefs and feelings.

Mental representations are stored by meaning. In the early 1970s, the psychologists Fergus Craik and Robert Lockhart developed an influential theory of memory based on depth of elaboration. According to their *levels of processing model,* the more deeply an item is encoded, the more meaning it has and the better it is remembered. Craik and Lockhart proposed that different types of rehearsal lead to different types of encoding. *Maintenance rehearsal* is simply repeating the item over and over. *Elaborative rehearsal* encodes the information in more meaningful ways, such as thinking about the item conceptually or deciding whether it refers to oneself. In other words, in this type of rehearsal, we elaborate on basic information by linking it to knowledge from long-term memory.

How does the levels of processing model work? Suppose you show research participants a list of words and then ask them to do one of three things. You might ask them to make simple perceptual judgments, such as whether each word is printed in capital or lowercase letters. You might ask them to judge the sound of each word, as in whether the word rhymes with *boat.* Or you might ask them about each word's semantic meaning, as in "Does this word fit the sentence *They had to cross the _____ to reach the castle*?" Once participants have completed the task (that is, processed the information), you might ask them to recall as many words as possible. You will find that words processed at the deepest level, based on semantic meaning, are remembered the best (**Figure 7.16**). Brain imaging studies have shown that semantic encoding activates more brain regions than shallow encoding and this greater brain activity is associated with better memory (Kapur et al., 1994).

Schemas Provide an Organizational Framework

If people store memories by meaning, how do they determine the meanings of particular memories? Chunking, discussed earlier, is a good way to encode groups of items for memorization. The more meaningful the chunks, the better they will be remembered. Decisions about how to chunk information depend on **schemas.** These structures in long-term memory help us perceive, organize, process, and use information. As we sort out incoming information, schemas guide our attention to an environment's relevant features. Thanks to schemas, we construct new memories by filling in holes within existing memories, overlooking inconsistent information, and interpreting meaning based on past experiences.

Although schemas help us make sense of the world, however, they can lead to biased encoding. This bias occurs in part because culture heavily influences schemas. In a classic demonstration conducted in the early 1930s, the psychologist Frederic Bartlett asked British participants to listen to a Native American folktale.

The story involved supernatural experiences, and it was difficult to understand for non–Native Americans unfamiliar with such tales. Fifteen minutes later, Bartlett asked the participants to repeat the story exactly as they had heard it. The participants altered the story greatly. They also altered it consistently, so that it made sense from their own cultural standpoint. Sometimes they simply forgot the supernatural parts they could not understand.

To understand the influence of schemas on which information is stored in memory, consider a study in which students read a story about an unruly girl (Sulin & Dooling, 1974). Some participants were told that the subject of the story was the famous blind girl Helen Keller. Others were told it was Carol Harris, a made-up name. One week later, the participants who had been told the girl was Helen Keller were more likely to mistakenly report having read the sentence *She was deaf, mute, and blind* in the story than those who thought the story was about Carol Harris. The students' schema for Helen Keller included her disabilities. When they retrieved information about Keller from memory, they retrieved everything they knew about her along with the story they were trying to remember.

To see how schemas affect your ability to recall information, read the following paragraph carefully:

> The procedure is actually quite simple. First arrange things into different bundles depending on makeup. Don't do too much at once. In the short run this may not seem important, however, complications easily arise. A mistake can be costly. Next, find facilities. Some people must go elsewhere for them. Manipulation of appropriate mechanisms should be self-explanatory. Remember to include all other necessary supplies. Initially the routine will overwhelm you, but soon it will become just another facet of life. Finally, rearrange everything into their initial groups. Return these to their usual places. Eventually they will be used again. Then the whole cycle will have to be repeated. (Bransford & Johnson, 1972, p. 722)

How easy did you find this paragraph to understand? Could you now recall specific sentences from it? It might surprise you to know that in a research setting, college students who read this paragraph found it easy to understand and relatively straightforward to recall. How is that possible? It was easy when the participants knew that the paragraph described washing clothes. Go back and reread the paragraph. Notice how your schema for doing laundry helps you understand and remember how the words and sentences are connected to one another. You will learn more about schemas in the next chapter.

Information Is Stored in Association Networks

One highly influential set of theories about memory organization is based on *networks of associations*. In a network model proposed by the psychologists Allan Collins and Elizabeth Loftus, an item's distinctive features are linked so as to identify the item. Each unit of information in the network is a *node*. Each node is connected to many other nodes. The resulting network is like the linked neurons in your brain, but nodes are simply bits of information. They are not physical realities. For example, when you look at a fire engine, all the nodes that represent a fire engine's features are activated. The resulting activation pattern gives rise to the knowledge that the object is a fire engine rather than, say, a car, a vacuum cleaner, or a cat.

An important feature of network models is that activating one node increases the likelihood that closely associated nodes will also be activated. As shown in

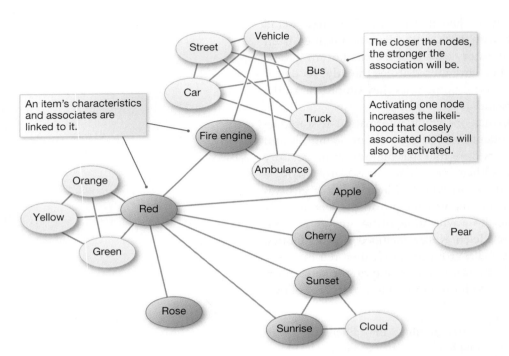

The closer the nodes, the stronger the association will be.

An item's characteristics and associates are linked to it.

Activating one node increases the likelihood that closely associated nodes will also be activated.

FIGURE 7.17 A Network of Associations In this semantic network, similar concepts are connected through their associations.

Figure 7.17, the closer the nodes, the stronger the association between them and therefore the more likely it is that activating one node will activate the other. Seeing a fire engine activates nodes that indicate other vehicles. Once your fire engine nodes are activated, you will more quickly recognize other vehicles than, for instance, fruits or animals.

The main idea here—that activating one node increases the likelihood of associated nodes becoming active—is central to *spreading activation models* of memory. According to these models, stimuli in working memory activate specific nodes in long-term memory. This activation increases the ease of access to that material and thus makes retrieval easier. Indeed, a recent study showed that retrieval of some items led to enhanced memory for related items even when participants were told to forget those items (Bäuml & Samenieh, 2010).

An associative network is organized by category. The categories are structured in a hierarchy, and they provide a clear and explicit blueprint for where to find needed information quickly. Given the vast amount of material in memory, it is amazing how quickly we can search for and obtain needed memories from storage. Each time you hear a sentence, you not only have to remember what all the words mean. You also have to recall all relevant information that helps you understand the sentence's overall meaning. For this process to occur, the information needs to be organized logically. Imagine trying to find a specific file on a full 40-gigabyte hard disk by opening one file at a time. Such a method would be hopelessly slow. Instead, most computer disks are organized into folders, within each folder are more-specialized folders, and so on. Associative networks in the brain work similarly.

Retrieval Cues Provide Access to Long-Term Storage

A **retrieval cue** can be anything that helps a person (or nonhuman animal) recall a memory. Encountering stimuli—such as the smell of turkey, a favorite song from years past, a familiar building, and so on—can trigger unintended memories. According to Endel Tulving's **encoding specificity principle,** any stimulus encoded along with an experience can later trigger a memory of the experience.

In one study of encoding, participants studied 80 words in either of two rooms. The rooms differed in ways such as location, size, and scent. The participants were then tested for recall in the room in which they studied or in the other room. When they studied and were tested in the same room, participants recalled an average of 49 words correctly. In contrast, when they were tested in the room in which they did not study, participants recalled an average of 35 words correctly (Smith, Glenberg, & Bjork, 1978). This kind of memory enhancement, when the recall situation is similar to the encoding situation, is known as

retrieval cue Anything that helps a person (or a nonhuman animal) recall information stored in long-term memory.

encoding specificity principle The idea that any stimulus that is encoded along with an experience can later trigger memory for the experience.

context-dependent memory. Context-dependent memory can be based on things such as physical location, odors, and background music, many of which produce a sense of familiarity (Hockley, 2008). In the most dramatic research demonstration of context-dependent memory, scuba divers learned information underwater, and they later recalled that information better underwater than on land (Godden & Baddeley, 1975; **Figure 7.18**).

Like physical context, internal cues such as mood can affect the recovery of information from long-term memory. When a person's internal states match during encoding and recall, memory can be enhanced. This effect is known as *state-dependent memory.* Research on this topic was inspired by the observation that alcoholics often misplace important objects, such as paychecks, because they store them in safe places while they are drinking but cannot remember where when they are sober. The next time they are drinking, however, they may remember where they hid the objects. Eric Eich and colleagues (1975) conducted a study of state-dependent memory and marijuana use. The participants best remembered items on a list when tested in the same state in which they had studied the list, either sober or high. Overall, however, they recalled the information best when they were sober during studying and testing. In a study involving alcohol, participants performed worst when they studied intoxicated and took the test sober (Goodwin, Powell, Bremer, Hoine, & Stern, 1969). They did worse than

---

FIGURE 7.18 Scientific Method: Godden and Baddeley's Study of Context-Dependent Memory

Hypothesis: When the recall situation is similar to the encoding situation, memory is enhanced.

Research Method:

1 One group of scuba divers learned a list of words on land.

2 Another group of scuba divers learned a list of words underwater.

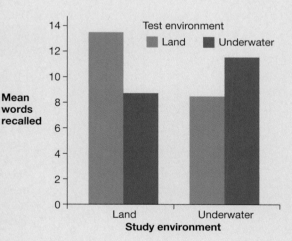

Results: The scuba divers who learned information underwater tested better underwater than on land. Those who studied on land tested better on land than underwater.

Conclusion: Information is best recalled in the same environment where it is learned.

Source: Godden, D. R., & Baddeley, A. D. (1975). Context-dependent memory in two natural environments: On land and underwater. *British Journal of Psychology, 66,* 325–331.

mnemonics Learning aids, strategies, and devices that improve recall through the use of retrieval cues.

participants who studied sober and took the test intoxicated. Participants who studied intoxicated and took the test intoxicated did much worse than those who were sober during study and test. It would be a mistake, then, to take an exam high or intoxicated. For the best results, study sober and take your tests sober.

MNEMONICS **Mnemonics** are learning aids or strategies that use retrieval cues to improve recall. People often find them helpful for remembering items in long lists, for example. One of the oldest methods dates back to the ancient Greeks, when the poet Simonides was able to recall who was killed by a ceiling collapse by visualizing where people were seated at the banquet table. Now referred to as the *method of loci* or the *memory palace*, this mnemonic consists of associating items you want to remember with physical locations. Suppose you want to remember the names of classmates you just met. First, you might visualize items from various places on your typical route across campus, or you might visualize parts of the physical layout of some familiar location, such as your bedroom. Then you would associate your classmates' names with the items or parts you have visualized. You might picture Sam climbing on your dresser, Latisha sitting on a chair, and Jerome hiding under the bed. When you later need to remember the names, you would visualize your room and retrieve the information associated with each piece of furniture.

The journalist Joshua Foer used this method when he competed in the U.S.A. Memory Championships in 2006 (Foer, 2011). During the contest, one of Foer's tasks was to memorize the order of two shuffled decks of playing cards. By imagining the cards in various locations in the house where he grew up, Foer was able to correctly remember the order of the cards in the two decks in just under 2 minutes. To keep from being distracted, he wore headphones and dark glasses. Strategies such as these enable people to excel at memory contests. The contest winners do not necessarily have better-functioning memories than most people. They are simply better able to use their memories.

Summing Up

How Is Information Organized in Long-Term Memory?

Human memory is stored according to meaning. The more an item is elaborated at the time of storage, the richer the later memory will be because more connections can serve as retrieval cues. Schemas help people perceive, organize, and process information. Thus schemas influence memory. Culture shapes our schemas. Hierarchical networks of associated nodes provide semantic links between related items. Activation of a node spreads throughout its network, enhancing memory of related items. Retrieval cues, including contextual cues and internal states, help us access stored information. Mnemonics, such as the method of loci and verbal mnemonics, involve the use of retrieval cues to improve recall.

Measuring Up

1. Which is the best way to teach scuba divers how to surface safely?
   a. Teach them in a classroom so they can use their declarative knowledge on a written test.

b. Teach them underwater because the situation will provide retrieval cues for when they need to use the knowledge.
   c. Teach them when they are on land and better able to pay attention.
   d. Have them learn from experience so the method becomes part of a schema.

2. One strategy for improving memory is to relate something you are learning to information you already know. Why would that strategy be effective?
   a. Because the known information can act as a retrieval cue to help you remember the new information when you need it.
   b. Because the known information will create a feeling of familiarity, which will make the new information similar to what you already know.
   c. Because new information is easier to remember than known information and can help you remember older memories by making them more distinct and exciting.
   d. Because old and new information need to mingle in memory so you are not confused when you implicitly try to retrieve information.

Answers: 1. b. Teach them underwater because the situation will provide retrieval cues for when they need to use the knowledge. 2. a. Because the known information can act as a retrieval cue to help you remember the new information when you need it.

7.5 What Are the Different Long-Term Memory Systems?

In the last few decades, most psychologists have come to view long-term memory as composed of several systems. The older view was that memories differed in terms of their strength (how likely something would be recalled) and their accessibility (the context in which something would be recalled). Generally, all memories were considered to be of the same type. In the late 1970s and early 1980s, cognitive psychologists began to challenge this view. They argued that memory is not just one entity. Rather, they saw it as a process that involves several interacting systems (Schacter & Tulving, 1994). The systems share a common function: to retain and use information. They encode and store different types of information in different ways, however. For instance, several obvious differences exist between your remembering how to ride a bicycle, your recalling what you ate for dinner last night, and your knowing that the capital of Canada is Ottawa. These are long-term memories, but they differ in how they were acquired (learned) and in how they are stored and retrieved. Remembering how to ride a bike requires a behavioral component. That is, it means integrating specific motor and perceptual skills that you acquired over time. You are not consciously aware of your efforts to maintain balance or to follow the basic rules of the road. By contrast, recalling a specific event you experienced or knowledge you learned from another source sometimes requires a conscious effort to retrieve the information from long-term memory.

Scientists do not agree on the number of human memory systems. For instance, some researchers have distinguished between memory systems based on how information is stored in memory, such as whether the storage occurs with or without deliberate effort. Other researchers have focused on the types of

Learning Objectives

- Distinguish between episodic, semantic, implicit, explicit, and prospective memories.
- Generate examples of each of these types of memory.

implicit memory The system underlying unconscious memories.

explicit memory The system underlying conscious memories.

declarative memory The cognitive information retrieved from explicit memory; knowledge that can be declared.

episodic memory Memory for one's personal past experiences.

information stored: words and meaning, particular muscle movements, information about a city's spatial layout, and so on. The following sections explore how the different memory systems work.

Explicit Memory Involves Conscious Effort

The most basic distinction between memory systems is a division of memories: On one hand are memories we are consciously aware of. On the other hand are memories we acquire without conscious effort or intention—memories we do not know we know. Remember that H.M., the memory loss sufferer described at the beginning of this chapter, improved at mirror tracing (tracing a pattern when only its mirror image is visible). He must have learned this motor task even without knowing he had. Peter Graf and Daniel Schacter (1985) referred to unconscious memory as **implicit memory.** They contrasted it with **explicit memory,** the processes we use to remember information we can say we know. The cognitive information retrieved from explicit memory is **declarative memory,** knowledge we can declare (consciously bring to mind).

For example, you use explicit memory when you recall what you had for dinner last night or what the word *aardvark* means. Declarative memories can involve words or concepts, visual images, or both. When you imagine the earth's orbit around the sun, you might also retrieve the images and names of the other planets. You could describe this knowledge in words, so it is declarative memory. Most of the examples presented in this chapter so far are of explicit memories. Every exam you ever took in school likely tested declarative memory.

In 1972, Endel Tulving found that explicit memory can be divided into *episodic memory* and *semantic memory*. **Episodic memory** refers to a person's past experiences and includes information about the time and place the experiences occurred (**Figure 7.19a**). If you can remember aspects of your 16th birthday, for example, such as where you were and what you did there, this information

(a)

(b)

FIGURE 7.19 Explicit Memory Explicit memory involves information that individuals are aware of knowing. **(a)** When these World War II veterans assembled aboard the USS *Intrepid* to reminisce on Memorial Day, they were drawing on episodic memory, which is based on past experiences. **(b)** Game shows such as *Jeopardy!* test semantic memory: the memory of facts independent of personal experience. In 2004, Ken Jennings (pictured here) became the longest-defending champion on *Jeopardy!* when he won 75 games in a row.

is part of your episodic memory. **Semantic memory** represents the knowledge of facts independent of personal experience. We might not remember where or when we learned it, but we know it (**Figure 7.19b**). For instance, people know what Jell-O is, they know the capitals of countries they have never visited, and even those who have never played baseball know that three strikes mean the batter is out.

Scientists have learned a great deal about normal memory by studying people such as H.M. and others who have impaired memory (Jacoby & Witherspoon, 1982). Evidence that episodic and semantic systems of explicit memory are separate can be found in cases of brain injury in which semantic memory is intact even though episodic memory is impaired. Researchers found this pattern of abnormal memory in three British people who had experienced brain damage (Vargha-Khadem et al., 1997). One child suffered the damage during a difficult delivery. The other two suffered it during early childhood (one had seizures at age 4; the other had an accidental drug overdose at age 9). Each of the three developed poor memory for episodic information. As children, they had trouble reporting what they had for lunch, what they were watching on television 5 minutes earlier, what they did during summer vacation. Their parents reported that the children had to be constantly monitored to make sure they remembered things such as going to school. Remarkably, these three children attended mainstream schools and did reasonably well. Moreover, when tested as young adults, their IQs fell within the normal range. They learned to speak and read, and they could remember many facts. For instance, when asked "Who is Martin Luther King Jr.?" one of the subjects, tested at age 19, responded, "An American; fought for Black rights, Black rights leader in the 1970s; got assassinated." These three, then, were able to encode and retrieve semantic information even though they could not remember their own personal experiences.

Implicit Memory Occurs without Deliberate Effort

Implicit memory consists of memories without awareness of them. In other words, you are not able to put these memories into words. Classical conditioning—discussed in Chapter 6, "Learning"—employs implicit memory. For example, if you always experience fear at the sight of a person in a white lab coat, you might have past associations (implicit memories) between a person in a white lab coat and pain.

Implicit memories do not require conscious attention. They happen automatically, without deliberate effort. Suppose that while driving you realize you have been daydreaming and have no episodic memory of the past few minutes. During that time, you employed implicit memories of how to drive and where you were going. Thus you did not crash the car or go in the wrong direction. This type of implicit memory is called **procedural memory,** or *motor memory*. It involves motor skills, habits, and other behaviors employed to achieve goals, such as coordinating muscle movements to ride a bicycle or following the rules of the road while driving (**Figure 7.20**). You remember to stop when you see a red light because you have learned to do so, and you might drive home on a specific route without even thinking about it. Procedural memories

semantic memory Memory for knowledge about the world.

procedural memory A type of implicit memory that involves motor skills and behavioral habits.

FIGURE 7.20 Implicit Memory The innate muscle memory for knowing how to ride a bicycle is procedural, or motor, memory. It is also an example of implicit memory—memory without the awareness of having the memory. Once you learn how to ride a bike, you can usually remember how to do it again, unconsciously, at any age.

are generally so unconscious that most people find that consciously thinking about automatic behaviors interferes with the smooth production of those behaviors. For instance, the next time you are riding a bicycle, try to think about each step involved in the process. These memories are also very resistant to decay. Once you learn to ride a bike, it is likely that, unless you suffer some brain damage, you will always be able to do so.

Implicit memory influences our lives in subtle ways, as when our attitudes are influenced by implicit learning. For example, you might like someone because he or she reminds you of another person you like, even if you are unaware of the connection. Advertisers rely on implicit memory to influence our purchasing decisions. Constant exposure to brand names makes us more likely to think of them when we buy products. If you find yourself wanting a particular brand of something, you might be "remembering" advertisements for that brand, even if you cannot recall the specifics.

Our implicit formation of attitudes can affect our beliefs about people, such as whether particular people are famous. Ask yourself: Is Richard Shiffrin famous? Try to think for a second how you know him. If you thought he was famous, you might have recalled that Shiffrin was one of the psychologists who introduced the model of sensory, short-term, and long-term memory (an accomplishment that might make him famous in scientific circles). Alternatively, you might have remembered reading his name before even if you could not remember where.

In studying what he called the *false fame effect,* the psychologist Larry Jacoby had research participants read aloud a list of made-up names (Jacoby, Kelley, Brown, & Jasechko, 1989). The participants were told that the research project was about pronunciation. The next day, Jacoby had the same people participate in an apparently unrelated study. This time, they were asked to read a list of names and decide whether each person was famous or not. The participants misjudged some of the made-up names from the previous day as being those of famous people. Because the participants knew they had heard the names before but probably could not remember where, implicit memory led them to assume the familiar names were those of famous people.

Prospective Memory Is Remembering to Do Something

"When you see Juan, tell him to call me, okay? And don't forget to bring the DVD tonight so we can watch the movie." Unlike the other types of remembering discussed so far in this chapter, **prospective memory** is future oriented. It means that a person remembers to do something at some future time (Graf & Uttl, 2001). As noted earlier in this chapter, paying attention has a "cost": The cognitive effort involved in attending to certain information makes us unable to attend closely to other information. Likewise, remembering to do something takes up valuable cognitive resources. It reduces either the number of items we can deal with in working memory or the number of things we can attend to (Einstein & McDaniel, 2005).

In a study of prospective memory, participants had to learn a list of words (Cook, Marsh, Clark-Foos, & Meeks, 2007). In one condition, they also had to remember to do something, such as press a key when they saw a certain word. The group that had to remember to do something took longer to learn the list than the control group that learned the same list of words but did not have to remember to do something.

prospective memory Remembering to do something at some future time.

Prospective memory involves both automatic and controlled processes. As discussed in Chapter 5, automatic processes happen without conscious awareness or intent (McDaniel & Einstein, 2000). Sometimes a retrieval cue occurs in a particular environment. For example, seeing Juan might automatically trigger your memory, so you effortlessly remember to give him the message. Sometimes particular environments do not have obvious retrieval cues for particular prospective memories. For example, you might not encounter a retrieval cue for remembering to fetch the DVD. Remembering to bring the disc might require some ongoing remembering as you head back to your room, even if you are not aware of that remembering. Prospective memory for events without retrieval cues is the reason sticky notes are so popular. In this case, you might stick a note that says "Bring DVD" on your notebook or on the steering wheel of your car. By jogging your memory, the note helps you avoid the effort of remembering. For an even more urgent reminder, you might set your cell phone alarm or electronic calendar (**Figure 7.21**).

FIGURE 7.21 Prospective Memory
Prospective memory involves remembering to do something in the future. When you use a device, such as this personal digital assistant (PDA), to remember appointments and deadlines, you are assisting your prospective memory.

Summing Up

What Are the Different Long-Term Memory Systems?

Long-term memory is composed of multiple systems. Fundamental differences exist among episodic and semantic memory, explicit and implicit memory, and prospective memory. Explicit memory involves the conscious storage and retrieval of declarative memories—these memories may be episodic or semantic. Episodic memory deals with personally experienced events, such as where and when the events occurred. For example, you might remember that you had eggs for breakfast at home this morning. Semantic memory deals with facts independent of personal experiences and does not include memory for where and when the facts were learned. Implicit memory does not require conscious attention. Examples of implicit memory include procedural (or motor) memory and attitudes influenced by implicit learning. Prospective memory involves remembering to do something at a future time. If a cue to remember is available in the person's environment, prospective memory can operate automatically. Without a retrieval cue, remembering requires conscious effort.

Measuring Up

Indicate whether each of the following examples of memory is prospective, implicit, or explicit. If it is explicit, also indicate whether it is episodic or semantic.

a. walking (for an adult)
b. the value of pi to six decimal places
c. writing a computer program
d. the fact that working memory is brief
e. the fact that you need to drive your sister home from school
f. the fact that the smell of eggs makes you sick and you do not know why

Answers: a. implicit; b. semantic and explicit; c. semantic and explicit; d. explicit and either semantic or episodic, depending on whether you remember when and where you learned it; e. prospective; f. implicit.

Learning Objectives

- List the seven sins of memory.
- Explain transience, blocking, and absentmindedness.
- Distinguish between retrograde and anterograde amnesia.
- Discuss methods to reduce persistence.

7.6 When Do People Forget?

In addition to remembering events and information, people fail to remember them. **Forgetting,** the inability to retrieve memory from long-term storage, is a perfectly normal, everyday experience. Ten minutes after you see a movie, you probably remember plenty of its details, but the next day you might remember mostly the plot and the main characters. Years later, you might remember the gist of the story, or you might not remember having seen the movie at all. We forget far more than we remember.

Most people bemoan forgetting. They wish they could better recall the material they study for exams, the names of childhood friends, the names of all seven dwarfs who lived with Snow White, what have you. But imagine what life would be like if you could not forget. Imagine, for example, walking up to your locker and recalling not just its combination but the 10 or 20 combinations for all the locks you have ever used. Consider the case of a Russian newspaper reporter who had nearly perfect memory. If someone read him a tremendously long list of items and he visualized the items for a few moments, he could recite the list, even many years later. But his memory was so cluttered with information that he had great difficulty functioning in normal society. Tortured by this condition, he eventually was institutionalized (Luria, 1968). Not being able to forget is as maladaptive as not being able to remember. It is therefore not surprising that we tend to best remember meaningful points. We remember the forest rather than the individual trees. Normal forgetting helps us remember and use important information.

The study of forgetting has a long history in psychological science. The late-nineteenth-century psychologist Hermann Ebbinghaus used the so-called *methods of savings* to examine how long it took people to relearn lists of nonsense syllables (e.g., vut, bik, kuh). Ebbinghaus provided compelling evidence that forgetting occurs rapidly over the first few days but then levels off. Most of us do not need to memorize nonsense syllables, but Ebbinghaus's general findings apply to meaningful material as well. You may remember very little of the Spanish or calculus you took in high school, but relearning these subjects would take you less time and effort than it took to learn them the first time. The difference between the original learning and relearning is "savings." In other words, you save time and effort because of what you remember.

Daniel Schacter (1999) has identified what he calls *the seven sins of memory* (**Table 7.1**). The first four sins—*transience, absentmindedness, blocking,* and *persistence*—are related to forgetting and remembering and are discussed here. The next three—*misattribution, suggestibility,* and *bias*—are discussed later in this chapter as distortions of memory. These so-called sins are very familiar to most people. Schacter sees them as by-products of otherwise desirable aspects of human memory. In fact, he argues that they are useful and perhaps even necessary characteristics for survival.

Transience Is Caused by Interference

Memory **transience** is forgetting over time. Ebbinghaus observed this pattern in his studies of nonsense syllables. Many early theorists argued that such forgetting results from the memory trace's *decay* in a person's nervous system. Indeed, some evidence indicates that unused memories are forgotten. Research over the last few decades, however, has established that most forgetting occurs because of *interference* from other information. Additional information can lead to forgetting

forgetting The inability to retrieve memory from long-term storage.

transience Forgetting over time.

TABLE 7.1 Seven Sins of Memory

Error	Type	Definition	Example
Transience	Forgetting	Reduced memory over time	Forgetting the plot of a movie
Blocking	Forgetting	Inability to remember needed information	Failing to recall the name of a person you meet on the street
Absentmindedness	Forgetting	Reduced memory due to failing to pay attention	Losing your keys or forgetting a lunch date
Persistence	Undesirable	The resurgence of unwanted or disturbing memories that we would like to forget	Remembering an embarrassing faux pas
Misattribution	Distortion	Assigning a memory to the wrong source	Falsely thinking that Richard Shiffrin is famous because his name is well known
Bias	Distortion	Influence of current knowledge on our memory for past events	Remembering past attitudes as similar to current attitudes even though they have changed
Suggestibility	Distortion	Altering a memory because of misleading information	Developing false memories for events that did not happen

SOURCE: Based on Schacter (2001).

proactive interference When prior information inhibits the ability to remember new information.

retroactive interference When new information inhibits the ability to remember old information.

through *proactive interference* or *retroactive interference*. In both cases, competing information displaces the information we are trying to retrieve.

In **proactive interference,** old information inhibits the ability to remember new information. For instance, if you study for your psychology test, switch to studying for your anthropology test, and then take the anthropology test, your performance on the test might be impaired by your knowledge about psychology (**Figure 7.22a**). In **retroactive interference,** new information inhibits the ability to remember old information. So once you take the psychology test, your performance might suffer because you recall the freshly reinforced anthropology material instead (**Figure 7.22b**).

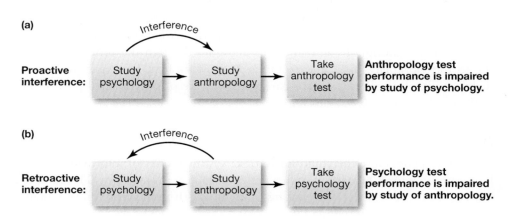

(a)

Interference

Proactive interference: Study psychology → Study anthropology → Take anthropology test **Anthropology test performance is impaired by study of psychology.**

(b)

Interference

Retroactive interference: Study psychology → Study anthropology → Take psychology test **Psychology test performance is impaired by study of anthropology.**

FIGURE 7.22 Proactive and Retroactive Interference (a) Proactive interference occurs when information already known (here, psychology material) interferes with the ability to remember new information (here, anthropology material). **(b)** Retroactive interference occurs when new information (anthropology material) interferes with memory for old information (psychology material).

blocking The temporary inability to remember something that is known.

absentmindedness The inattentive or shallow encoding of events.

amnesia A deficit in long-term memory, resulting from disease, brain injury, or psychological trauma, in which the individual loses the ability to retrieve vast quantities of information from long-term memory.

Blocking Is Temporary

Blocking occurs when a person is temporarily unable to remember something: You cannot recall the name of a favorite song, you forget the name of someone you are introducing, you "blank" on some lines when acting in a play, and so on. Such temporary blockages are common and frustrating. Roger Brown and David MacNeill (1966) described another good example of blocking: the *tip-of-the-tongue phenomenon,* in which people experience great frustration as they try to recall specific, somewhat obscure words. For instance, when asked to provide a word that means "patronage bestowed on a relative, in business or politics" or "an astronomical instrument for finding position," people often struggle (Brown, 1991). Sometimes they know which letter the word begins with, how many syllables it has, and even what it sounds like, but even with these partial retrieval cues they cannot pull the precise word into working memory. (Did you know the words were *nepotism* and *sextant*?) Blocking often occurs because of interference from words that are similar in some way, such as in sound or meaning, and that recur. For example, you might repeatedly call an acquaintance Margaret although her name is Melanie. The tip-of-the-tongue phenomenon increases with age, perhaps because older people have greater memories that might interfere.

Absentmindedness Results from Shallow Encoding

Absentmindedness is the inattentive or shallow encoding of events. The major cause of absentmindedness is failing to pay attention. For instance, you absentmindedly forget where you left your keys because when you put them down, you were also reaching to answer your phone. You forget the name of a person you are talking with because when you met, 5 minutes before, you were wondering where your keys went. You forget whether you took your vitamins this morning because you were deciding whether to study for your psychology test or your anthropology test (**Figure 7.23**).

Recall that when prospective memory fails, you fail to remember to do something. Often, this form of absentmindedness occurs because you are caught up in another activity. For instance, when you perform an automatic task, such as driving, your conscious thoughts might not include the driving experience. Your mind might wander to other ideas or memories.

There can be a negative side to this lack of attention: In the United States over the past decade, more than 300 children have died because they were left unattended in hot cars (49 in 2010 alone). In many cases, the parent forgot to drop the child off at day care on his or her way to work. It is easy to imagine forgetting your lunch in the car, but your child? Fortunately, such incidents are rare, but they seem to be especially likely when the parent's typical routine does not include day care drop-off duty. While the parent is driving, his or her brain shifts to "autopilot" and automatically goes through the process of driving to the workplace instead of stopping at day care first. During most of our daily activities, of course, we are consciously aware of only a small portion of both our thoughts and our behaviors.

FIGURE 7.23 Absentmindedness The major cause of absentmindedness is failing to pay sufficient attention when encoding memories. The celebrated musician Yo-Yo Ma is pictured here with his $2.5 million eighteenth-century cello, which was returned to him after he absentmindedly left it in a cab.

Amnesia Is a Deficit in Long-Term Memory

Sometimes people lose the ability to retrieve vast quantities of information from long-term memory. **Amnesia** is such a deficit in long-term memory. This kind of loss is not one of Schacter's "seven sins of memory." It results from disease, brain injury, or psychological trauma.

The two basic types of amnesia are *retrograde amnesia* and *anterograde amnesia*. In **retrograde amnesia,** people lose past memories for events, facts, people, and even personal information. Most portrayals of amnesia in the media are of retrograde amnesia, as when a character in a soap opera awakens from a coma and does not know who he or she is (**Figure 7.24a**). By contrast, in **anterograde amnesia,** people lose the ability to form new memories (**Figure 7.24b**). As discussed at the beginning of this chapter, H.M. had a classic case of anterograde amnesia. He could remember old information about his past, but after his surgery he lost the ability to form new memories. However, H.M. may have acquired some new semantic knowledge about things that occurred after 1953. For instance, when given a list of people who became famous or infamous after 1953, H.M. was able to provide some information about them (O'Kane, Kensinger, & Corkin, 2004). This new learning may have occurred through his extensive repetition of materials over a long time. Given the name Lee Harvey Oswald, H.M. described him as the man who "assassinated the president." Oswald is believed to have shot U.S. president John F. Kennedy to death, in 1963.

FIGURE 7.24 The Two Forms of Amnesia (a) Jeff Ingram, pictured here, developed retrograde amnesia after leaving his home, in Washington state. When he arrived in Denver, Colorado, four days later, he had no memory of his previous life. He was recognized two months later, when he appeared on the news pleading for help from anyone who knew who he was. Though he did not remember his three-year relationship with his fiancée (here seated next to him), the two eventually married. **(b)** Most portrayals of amnesia in the media are of retrograde amnesia. In the 2000 film *Memento,* however, Leonard Shelby (played by Guy Pearce) suffers from anterograde amnesia. In other words, he cannot form new memories and therefore cannot remember recent events. In search of his wife's killer, he tattoos words onto his body to remind himself of information he has discovered.

Persistence Is Unwanted Remembering

Sometimes you want to forget something but have difficulty doing so. **Persistence** occurs when unwanted memories recur in spite of the desire not to have them. Some unwanted memories are so traumatic that they destroy the life of the individual who suffers from them.

One prominent example of persistence occurs in posttraumatic stress disorder (PTSD; discussed further in Chapter 14, "Psychological Disorders"). PTSD is a serious mental health problem, with an estimated prevalence of 7.8 percent in the United States alone (Kessler, Sonnega, Bromet, Hughes, & Nelson, 1995). The most common triggers of PTSD include events that threaten people or those close to them. For example, the unexpected death of a loved one, a physical or sexual assault, a car accident, a natural disaster, or seeing someone badly injured or killed can be a source of PTSD. As mentioned earlier in this chapter, emotional events are associated with amygdala activity, which might underlie the persistence of certain memories.

Considerable research is under way to produce drugs that will erase unwanted memories. One drug, propranolol, blocks the postsynaptic norepinephrine receptors. If it is given before or right after a traumatic experience, the hormonally enhanced memories and fear response for that event are reduced, and the effect lasts for months (Cahill, Prins, Weber, & McGaugh, 1994; Pitman et al., 2002). Drugs such as propranolol might have side effects, however. Alternatively, as discussed earlier, extinction can be used during reconsolidation to yield the same or similar results, potentially without side effects (Schiller et al., 2010).

But erasing memories leads to many ethical questions. If we can erase traumatic memories, should we remove only the memories of traumas that were beyond the sufferer's control? Or should a person be treated for suffering a guilty conscience after an intentional malicious act? Will reducing memories to take the emotional sting out of life make us less human?

retrograde amnesia A condition in which people lose past memories, such as memories for events, facts, people, or even personal information.

anterograde amnesia A condition in which people lose the ability to form new memories.

persistence The continual recurrence of unwanted memories.

When Do People Forget?

Forgetting is the inability to retrieve memory from long-term storage. The ability to forget is as important as the ability to remember. Transience results from proactive or retroactive interference. That is, prior information inhibits the ability to remember new information, or new information inhibits the ability to remember old information. Blocking is a temporary inability to retrieve specific information, as exemplified by the tip-of-the-tongue phenomenon. Like transience, blocking results from interference during retrieval. Absentmindedness is caused by shallow encoding, which occurs when people fail to pay sufficient attention. Amnesia is a deficit in long-term memory. This condition results from disease, brain injury, or psychological trauma. Individuals with retrograde amnesia lose past memories. Individuals with anterograde amnesia lose the ability to form new memories. Persistence is the recurrence of unwanted memories. This problem is characteristic of posttraumatic stress disorder. Contemporary researchers are investigating methods to erase unwanted memories.

Measuring Up

Indicate whether each of the following is an example of retroactive interference or proactive interference or neither.

a. You learned Russian as a teenager, but now you speak Hungarian. You have forgotten much of the Russian you used to know.
b. According to an old Yiddish saying, you should never marry someone with a name similar to that of your last spouse. Although the expression loses a lot in translation, the idea is that you will forget and call your new spouse by the old spouse's name.
c. For years you took a bus home from work, and then you got a new car. One night after work, you take the bus home, forgetting that you drove your new car to work.

Answers: a. retroactive; b. proactive; c. proactive.

7.7 How Are Memories Distorted?

Most people believe that human memory is permanent storage. Research has shown clearly, however, that human memory is biased, flawed, and distorted. In this section, you will learn how the human memory systems provide less-than-accurate portrayals of past events.

People Reconstruct Events to Be Consistent

Memory bias is the changing of memories over time so that they become consistent with current beliefs or attitudes. As one of psychology's greatest thinkers, Leon Festinger (1987, p. 1), put it: "I prefer to rely on my memory. I have lived with that memory a long time, I am used to it, and if I have rearranged or distorted anything, surely that was done for my own benefit."

Consider students who take courses in study skills. Students often fail to heed the advice they receive in such courses, and there is only modest evidence that the courses are beneficial. Yet most students who take them describe them as extremely helpful. How can something that generally produces unimpressive outcomes be endorsed so positively? To understand this phenomenon, researchers randomly assigned students to either a genuine study skills course or a control group that received no special training. Students who took the real course showed few signs of improvement. In fact, their final-exam performances were slightly poorer than the control group's performances. Still, they considered the study skills program helpful. The experiment had one feature that helps explain why. At the beginning of the course, participants were asked to rate their studying skills. At the end of the course, they again rated themselves and were asked to recall how they had originally rated themselves. In describing their earlier ratings, students in the study skills course recalled themselves as having been significantly worse than they had rated themselves at the beginning. In this way, the students were "getting what they want[ed] by revising what they had" (Conway & Ross, 1984).

People tend to recall their past beliefs and past attitudes as being consistent with their current ones. Often, they revise their memories when they change attitudes and beliefs. People also tend to remember events as casting them in prominent roles or favorable lights. As discussed further in Chapter 12, people also tend to exaggerate their contributions to group efforts, take credit for successes and blame failures on others, and remember their successes more than their failures. Societies, too, bias their recollections of past events. Groups' collective memories can seriously distort the past. Most societies' official histories tend to downplay their past behaviors that were unsavory, immoral, and even murderous. Perpetrators' memories are generally shorter than victims' memories.

Flashbulb Memories Can Be Wrong

Some events cause people to experience what Roger Brown and James Kulik (1977) termed **flashbulb memories.** These vivid memories are of the circumstances in which people first learn of a surprising and consequential or emotionally arousing event. When in 1977 Brown and Kulik interviewed people about their memories of the assassination of U.S. president John F. Kennedy, they found that people described these 14-year-old memories in highly vivid terms. The details included who they were with, what they were doing or thinking, who told them or how they found out, and what their emotional reactions were to the event. In other words, flashbulb memories are an example of episodic memory. They do not reflect the problem of persistence, however, in that they are not recurring unwanted memories.

DO YOU REMEMBER WHERE YOU WERE WHEN . . . ? Do you remember where you were when you found out that the pop star Michael Jackson had died (**Figure 7.25a**)? Or when you first heard that the jihadist leader Osama bin Laden had been killed? An obvious problem affects research into the accuracy of flashbulb memories. Namely, researchers have to wait for a "flash" to go off and then immediately conduct their study. The explosion of the U.S. space shuttle *Challenger,* on January 28, 1986, provided a unique opportunity for research on this topic. Ulric Neisser and Nicole Harsch (1993) had 44 psychology students fill out a questionnaire the day the shuttle exploded. When they tested the students' memories three years later, only three students had perfect recall, and the rest were incorrect about multiple aspects of the situation (**Figure 7.25b**).

memory bias The changing of memories over time so that they become consistent with current beliefs or attitudes.

flashbulb memories Vivid episodic memories for the circumstances in which people first learned of a surprising, consequential, or emotionally arousing event.

(a)

(b)

(c)

FIGURE 7.25 Flashbulb Memories
Surprising and consequential or emotionally arousing events can produce flashbulb memories. For example, **(a)** the death of Michael Jackson, in 2009; **(b)** the explosion of the *Challenger,* in 1986; and **(c)** the resignation of Margaret Thatcher, in 1990, have left flashbulb memories of different kinds. The differences depend on how consequential the events were to the people remembering them.

Other researchers have documented better memory for flashbulb experiences. For example, Martin Conway and colleagues (1994) studied participants' responses to the news that the British prime minister Margaret Thatcher had resigned, in 1990. They found that participants who found the news surprising and felt the event was important had the strongest flashbulb memories. Thus students in the United Kingdom experienced stronger flashbulb memories for the Thatcher resignation than did students in the United States (**Figure 7.25c**).

For three years after the terrorist attacks on September 11, 2001, a study was conducted of more than 3,000 people across the United States (Hirst et al., 2009). Memories related to 9/11—such as where the person first heard about the attacks and the person's knowledge about the events—declined somewhat during the first year, but memory remained stable thereafter. As might be expected, people who were living in New York City on 9/11 had, over time, the most accurate memories of the World Trade Center attacks.

EMPHASIS AND MEMORY Although flashbulb memories are not perfectly accurate, they are at least as accurate as memory for ordinary events. Indeed, people are more confident about their flashbulb memories than they are about their ordinary memories (Talarico & Rubin, 2003). Any event that produces a strong emotional response is likely to produce a vivid, although not necessarily accurate, memory (Christianson, 1992). Or a distinctive event might simply be recalled more easily than a trivial event, however inaccurate the result. This latter pattern is known as the *von Restorff effect*, named after the researcher who first described it, in 1933. It is also possible that greater media attention to major events leads to greater exposure to the details of those events, thus encouraging better memory (Hirst et al., 2009).

People Make Source Misattributions

Source misattribution occurs when people misremember the time, place, person, or circumstances involved with a memory. A good example of this phenomenon is the false fame effect, discussed earlier. This effect causes people to mistakenly believe that someone is famous simply because they have encountered the person's name before. Another example is the *sleeper effect*. Here, an argument initially is not very persuasive because it comes from a questionable source, but it becomes more persuasive over time. Suppose you see an online ad for a way to learn French while you sleep. You probably will not believe the claims in the ad. Yet over time you might remember the promise but fail to remember the source. Because the promise occurs to you without the obvious reason for rejecting it, you might come to believe that people can learn French while sleeping, or you might at least wonder if it is possible.

SOURCE AMNESIA **Source amnesia** is a form of misattribution that occurs when a person has a memory for an event but cannot remember where he or she encountered the information. Consider your earliest childhood memory. How vivid is it? Are you actually recalling the event or some retelling of the event? How do you know you are not remembering either something you saw in a photograph or a story related to you by family members? Most people cannot remember specific memories from before age 3. The absence of early memories, *childhood amnesia*, may be due to the early lack of linguistic capacity as well as to immature frontal lobes.

source misattribution Memory distortion that occurs when people misremember the time, place, person, or circumstances involved with a memory.

source amnesia A type of amnesia that occurs when a person shows memory for an event but cannot remember where he or she encountered the information.

CRYPTOMNESIA An intriguing example of source misattribution is **cryptomnesia.** Here, a person thinks he or she has come up with a new idea, but really has retrieved an old idea from memory and failed to attribute the idea to its proper source (Macrae, Bodenhausen, & Calvini, 1999). For example, students who take verbatim notes while conducting library research sometimes experience the illusion that they have composed the sentences themselves. This mistake can later lead to an accusation of plagiarism. (Be especially vigilant about indicating verbatim notes while you are taking them; see **Figure 7.26.**)

George Harrison, the late former Beatle, was sued because his 1970 song "My Sweet Lord" is strikingly similar to the song "He's So Fine," recorded in 1962 by the Chiffons. Harrison acknowledged having known "He's So Fine," but vigorously denied having plagiarized it. He argued that with a limited number of musical notes available to all musicians, and an even smaller number of chord sequences appropriate for rock and roll, some compositional overlap is inevitable. In a controversial verdict, the judge ruled against Harrison.

People Are Bad Eyewitnesses

One of the most powerful forms of evidence is the eyewitness account. Research has demonstrated that very few jurors are willing to convict an accused individual on the basis of circumstantial evidence alone. But add one person who says, "That's the one!" and conviction becomes much more likely. This effect occurs even if it is shown that the witness had poor eyesight or some other condition that raises questions about the testimony's accuracy. Eyewitness testimony's power is troubling because witnesses are so often in error. When Gary Wells and colleagues (1998) studied 40 cases in which DNA evidence indicated that a person had been falsely convicted of a crime, they found that in 36 of these cases the person had been misidentified by at least one eyewitness (**Figure 7.27**). Why is eyewitness testimony so prone to error?

Recall the phenomenon of change blindness, discussed earlier. In studies of change blindness, people failed to notice that a person they were talking with had been replaced with a new person! Eyewitness testimony depends critically on a person's paying sufficient attention to an incident when it happens rather than after it happens. Therefore, the testimony is prone to error because often the eyewitness is not paying attention to the right details when the event happens.

CROSS-ETHNIC IDENTIFICATION One factor that contributes to poor eyewitness identification is that people are particularly bad at accurately identifying individuals of other ethnicities or races. This effect occurs among Caucasians, Asians, African Americans, and Hispanics. In brain imaging studies discussed in Chapter 4, African Americans and Caucasian Americans showed better memory for same-race faces. Apparently, people's superior memory for members of their own racial group is caused by greater activation in the fusiform face area (Golby, Gabrieli, Chiao, & Eberhardt, 2001). As discussed in Chapter 3, this area responds more strongly to faces than to other objects. Perhaps this area responds most strongly to same-race faces because people tend to have less frequent contact with members of other races and ethnicities. Or perhaps people encode race and ethnicity

FIGURE 7.26 Cryptomnesia The 2006 novel *How Opal Mehta Got Kissed, Got Wild, and Got a Life* turned into a possible case of cryptomnesia. The author, a student at Harvard University named Kaavya Viswanathan, admitted that several passages in the work were taken from books that she read in high school. As a result, *How Opal Mehta Got Kissed* had to be recalled from bookstores. Perhaps Viswanathan, thinking she had come up with new material, had retrieved other people's writing from memory.

FIGURE 7.27 Eyewitness Accounts Can Be Unreliable William Jackson **(left)** served five years in prison because he was wrongly convicted of a crime based on the testimony of two eyewitnesses. Note the similarities and differences between Jackson and the man on the right, the real perpetrator.

according to rules of categorization, and they do not notice much about individuals beyond this group description.

SUGGESTIBILITY AND MISINFORMATION During the early 1970s, a series of important studies conducted by Elizabeth Loftus and colleagues demonstrated that people can develop biased memories when provided with misleading information. This error is the "sin" of **suggestibility.** The general methodology of this research involved showing research participants an event and then asking them specific questions about it. The different wordings of the questions altered the participants' memories for the event. In one experiment, a group of participants viewed a videotape of a car—a red Datsun—approaching a stop sign (Loftus, Miller, & Burns, 1978). A second group viewed a videotape of that same scene but with a yield sign instead of a stop sign. Each group was then asked, "Did another car pass the red Datsun while it was stopped at the stop sign?" Some participants in the second group claimed to have seen the red Datsun stop at the stop sign, even though they had seen it approaching a yield sign (**Figure 7.28**).

In another experiment, Loftus and John Palmer (1974) showed participants a videotape of a car accident. When participants heard the word *smashed* applied to the tape, they estimated the cars to be traveling faster than when they heard *contacted, hit, bumped,* or *collided.* In a related study, participants saw a videotape of a car accident and then were asked about seeing the cars either *smash into* or *hit* each other. One week later, they were asked if they had seen broken glass on the ground in the video. No glass broke in the video, but nearly one-third of those who heard *smashed* falsely recalled having seen broken glass. Very few of those who heard *hit* recalled broken glass.

FIGURE 7.28 Scientific Method: Loftus's Studies on Suggestibility

Hypothesis: People can develop biased memories when provided with misleading information.

Research Method:

1 One group of participants was shown a videotape of a red Datsun approaching a stop sign.

2 Another group of participants was shown a videotape of a red Datsun approaching a yield sign.

3 Immediately after viewing the tapes, the participants were asked, "Did another car pass the red Datsun while it was stopped at the stop sign?"

Results: Some participants who had seen the yield sign responded to the question by claiming they had seen the car at the stop sign.

Conclusion: People can "remember" seeing nonexistent objects.

Source: Loftus, E. F., Miller, D. G., & Burns, H. J. (1978). Semantic integration of verbal information into a visual memory. *Journal of Experimental Psychology: Human Learning and Memory, 4,* 19–31.

Are these sorts of laboratory analogues appropriate for studying eyewitness accuracy? After all, the sights and sounds of a traffic accident, for example, impress the event on the witness's awareness. Some evidence supports the idea that such memories are better in the real world than in the laboratory. One study examined the reports of witnesses to a fatal shooting (Yuille & Cutshall, 1986). All the witnesses had been interviewed by the police within two days of the incident. Months afterward, the researchers found the eyewitness reports, including the details, highly stable. Given that emotional state affects memories, it makes sense for accounts from eyewitnesses to be more vivid than accounts from laboratory research participants. It remains unclear, however, how accurate those stable memories were in the first place. And by retelling their stories over and over again—to the police, to friends and relatives, to researchers, and so on—eyewitnesses might inadvertently develop stronger memories for inaccurate details. This alteration may occur due to reconsolidation.

EYEWITNESS CONFIDENCE How good are observers, such as jurors, at judging eyewitnesses' accuracy? The general finding from a number of studies is that people cannot differentiate accurate eyewitnesses from inaccurate ones (Clark & Wells, 2008; Wells, 2008). The problem is that eyewitnesses who are wrong are just as confident as (or *more* confident than) eyewitnesses who are right. Eyewitnesses who vividly report trivial details of a scene are probably less credible than those with poor memories for trivial details. After all, eyewitnesses to real crimes tend to be focused on the weapons or on the action. They fail to pay attention to minor details. Thus strong confidence for minor details may be a cue that the memory is likely to be inaccurate or even false. Some people are particularly confident, however, and jurors find them convincing. Taryn Simon, a photographer for the *New York Times,* created *The Innocents,* a photo essay of people who were wrongfully convicted of crimes they did not commit, most because of faulty eyewitness testimony (**Figure 7.29**). As Simon explained, "Police officers and prosecutors influence memory—both unintentionally and intentionally—through the ways in which they conduct the identification process. They can shape, and even generate, what comes to be known as eyewitness testimony" (Simon, 2003, para. 2). Simon described many compelling examples of memory's malleability. In one case, a victim, Jennifer Thompson, misidentified her attacker after being shown multiple images of possible assailants. According to Thompson, "All the images became enmeshed to one image that became Ron, and Ron became my attacker" (quoted in Simon, 2003, para. 3).

People Have False Memories

How easily can people develop false memories (**Figure 7.30**)? Think back to when you were 5. Do you remember getting lost in a mall and being found by a kind old man who returned you to your family? No? Well, what if your family told you about this incident, including how panicked your parents were when they could not find you? According to research by Elizabeth Loftus, you might then remember the incident, even if it did not happen.

In an initial study, a 14-year-old named Chris was told by his older brother Jim, who was part of the study, about the "lost in the mall" incident. The context was a game called "Remember when. . . ." All the other incidents narrated by Jim were true. Two days later, when asked if he had ever been lost in a mall, Chris began reporting memories of how he felt during the mall episode. Within two weeks he reported the following:

FIGURE 7.29 Fallibility of Memory For her photo essay *The Innocents,* Taryn Simon collaborated with members of the Innocence Project, an organization devoted to correcting errors in the criminal justice system. Here John Stickels **(right),** a member of the Innocence Project's board of directors, congratulates the exultant Patrick Waller on July 3, 2008, in a Dallas courthouse. Waller has just been told that he has been exonerated of a crime for which he had been wrongly convicted and sent to prison for 15 years. DNA evidence convinced the jury to reverse Waller's conviction.

FIGURE 7.30 Try for Yourself: Creating False Recognition

Read the following list out loud:

> *sour candy sugar bitter good taste tooth nice*
> *honey soda chocolate heart cake tart pie*

Now put your book aside and write down as many of the words as you remember.

Result: Researchers have devised tests such as this for investigating whether people can be misled into recalling or recognizing events that did not happen (Roedigger & McDermott, 1995). For instance, without looking back, which of the following words did you recall? *Candy, honey, tooth, sweet, pie.*

If you recalled *sweet* (or think you did), you have experienced a false memory, because *sweet* was not on the original list. All the words on that list are related to sweetness, though. This basic paradigm produces false recollections reliably. Moreover, people are often extremely confident in saying they have seen or heard the words they recollect falsely.

I was with you guys for a second and I think I went over to look at the toy store, the Kay-bee toy and uh, we got lost and I was looking around and I thought, "Uh-oh. I'm in trouble now." You know. And then I . . . I thought I was never going to see my family again. I was really scared you know. And then this old man, I think he was wearing a blue flannel shirt, came up to me. . . . [H]e was kind of old. He was kind of bald on top. . . . [H]e had like a ring of gray hair . . . and he had glasses. (Loftus, 1993, p. 532)

You might wonder if there was something special about Chris that made him susceptible to developing false memories. In a later study, however, Loftus and her colleagues used the same paradigm to assess whether they could implant false memories in 24 participants. Seven of the participants falsely remembered events that had been implanted by family members who were part of the study. How could this be so?

When a person imagines an event happening, he or she forms a mental image of the event. The person might later confuse that mental image with a real memory. Essentially, the person has a problem monitoring the source of the image. To Chris, the memory of being lost in the mall became as real as other events in childhood. Children are particularly susceptible, and false memories—such as of getting fingers caught in mousetraps or having to be hospitalized—can easily be induced in them. It is unlikely, however, that false memories can be created for certain types of unusual events, such as receiving an enema (Pezdek & Hodge, 1999).

CONFABULATION Some types of brain injury are associated with **confabulation,** the unintended false recollection of episodic memories. Morris Moscovitch, a memory research pioneer, has described confabulating as "honest lying," because the person does not intend to deceive and is unaware that his or her story is false. Moscovitch (1995) provides a striking example of confabulation in a patient he refers to as H.W. (not to be confused with H.M., the patient discussed at the opening of this chapter). The patient, a 61-year-old man, was the biological father of four children. All of his children were adults by the time H.W. experienced severe frontal lobe damage following a cerebral hemorrhage. Here is part of the clinical interview:

Q. Are you married or single?

confabulation The unintended false recollection of episodic memories.

Recognizing How the Fallibility of Human Memory Can Lead to Faulty Conclusions

Brooke Patterson (2004) refers to the *tyranny of the eyewitness*. This phrase means that people generally believe eyewitnesses even though, as memory researchers have shown, eyewitnesses are frequently wrong. Of course, beliefs often remain strong despite data showing those beliefs are unjustified. And when a person confidently reports what he or she heard or saw, other people tend to assume the report reflects an accurate memory.

Most people do not like to have their memories questioned. For the most part, however, there is little or no relationship between a person's confidence about a memory and the probability of that memory's accuracy (Weber & Brewer, 2004). Unless an independent party can verify the information, it is difficult to distinguish between a valid memory and a faulty one. An unknown number of innocent people have been imprisoned or even put to death because of memory errors. No doubt, guilty people have gone free because of either faulty memories or failure to believe valid memories.

As a critical thinker with an understanding of psychological science, you must recognize the fallibility of memories. Even when you believe your own memories are accurate, you must consider the possibility that they are not. When a memory is important to some outcome, consider that memory's likely accuracy. Whenever possible, check the memory against related objective facts, such as video or audio recordings.

H.W. Married.

Q. How long have you been married?

H.W. About four months.

Q. How many children do you have?

H.W. Four. (He laughs.) Not bad for four months!

Q. How old are your children?

H.W. The eldest is 32, his name is Bob, and the youngest is 22, his name is Joe.

Q. How did you get those children in four months?

H.W. They're adopted.

Q. Does this all sound strange to you, what you are saying?

H.W. (He laughs.) I think it is a little strange.

Patients such as H.W. confabulate for no apparent purpose. They simply recall mistaken facts. When questioned, they try to make sense of their recollections by adding facts that make the story more coherent. (Chapter 5 discusses Michael Gazzaniga's theory of the interpreter and how split-brain patients confabulate to make sense of conflicting information fed to each cerebral hemisphere.)

A dramatic example of confabulation occurs in *Capgras syndrome*. People with Capgras believe that their family members have been replaced by impostors. Even when confronted with contradictory evidence, they invent facts to support their delusions. No amount of evidence can convince them that their siblings, parents, spouses, children, and other relatives are real. This bizarre syndrome is devastating

How Can I Study More Effectively for Exams?

During your college years, you will likely take many exams. What sorts of tools does psychology offer to help you study more effectively for exams? As mentioned throughout this chapter, researchers have identified a number of methods that will help you remember information more easily. Here are some key methods. Because some of these methods are drawn from the material in this chapter, paying attention to this section will help reinforce in your mind some of the important concepts you have just read about.

1. **Distribute your learning.** Cramming does not work. Instead, distribute your study sessions. Six sessions of 1 hour each are much better for learning than one 6-hour marathon. By spreading your studying over multiple sessions, you will retain the information for longer periods of time.

2. **Elaborate the material.** Imagine you and two friends decide to engage in a little friendly competition. The challenge is to memorize a list of 20 words. Friend A simply reads the words. Friend B, after reading each word, copies the word's definition from a dictionary. You, after reading each word, think about how the word is relevant to you. For example, you

see the word *rain* and think, "My car once broke down in the middle of a torrential rainstorm." Who is most likely to remember that list of words later? You are. The deeper your level of processing, the more likely you are to remember material, particularly if you make the material personally relevant.

When you are learning something new, do not just read the material or copy down textbook descriptions. Think about the meaning of the material and how the concepts are related to other concepts. Organize the material in a way that makes sense to you, putting the concepts in your own words. Making the material relevant to you is an especially good way to process material deeply and therefore to remember it easily.

3. **Practice.** To make your memories more durable, you need to practice retrieving the information you are trying to learn. In fact, repeated testing is a more effective memory-building strategy than spending the same amount of time reviewing information you have already read. Most exams ask you to recall information. For example, you might be asked to provide a definition, apply a principle, or evaluate the relative strengths of two theories.

To be successful at any of those tasks, you need to recall the relevant information. Thus, to prepare for the exam, you should practice recalling that information over and over again.

After reading a section in this or any other book, look back to the main section heading. If that heading is not already a question, rephrase it as a question. Test yourself by trying to answer the heading's question without looking at the text. Make use of in-chapter or end-of-chapter test questions by answering these questions as you encounter them. Then answer them again a couple of days later.

You can also develop your own practice materials. Write quiz questions. Make flash cards on either pieces of card stock or on the computer (quizlet.com is a great Web site for creating and using flash cards). For example, on one side of the flash card, write a key term. On the other side, write the definition of that term. Then drill using the flash cards in both directions. Can you recall the term when you see the definition? Can you provide the definition when you see the term? A good way to drill is to study with another member of your class and take turns quizzing each other.

to the family members accused of being imposters. People with Capgras often have damage to the frontal lobes and the limbic brain regions. The most likely cause is that the brain region involved in emotions is separated from the visual input, so the images of family members are no longer associated with warm feelings. The visual image is the same, but the feeling is not. Because of the change in feeling, the sufferer concludes that the people are not his or her real relatives. Once we understand the underlying brain mechanisms, bizarre behaviors such as this become more understandable.

Repressed Memories Are Controversial

Over the past few decades, one of the most heated debates in psychological science has centered on repressed memories. On one side, some psychotherapists

4. Overlearn. With material in front of us, we are often overly confident that we "know" the information and believe we will remember it later. But recognition is easier than recall. Thus if you want to be able to recall information, you need to put in extra effort when encoding the material. Even after you *think* you have learned it, review it again. Test yourself by trying to recall the material a few hours (and a few days) after studying. Keep rehearsing until you can recall the material easily.

5. Use verbal mnemonics. Whatever their goals for remembering, people employ many types of mnemonics. For example, how many days are there in September? In the Western world, at least, most people can readily answer this question thanks to the old saying that begins *Thirty days hath September*. Children also learn *i before e except after c* and, along with that saying, *"weird" is weird*. By memorizing such phrases, we more easily remember things that are difficult to remember. Advertisers, of course, often create slogans or jingles that rely on *verbal mnemonics* so that consumers cannot help but remember them.

Students have long used acronyms to remember information, such as HOMES to remember the great lakes (Huron, Ontario, Michigan, Erie, and Superior). In studying Chapter 13, the acronym OCEAN will help you remember the major personality traits: openness to experience, conscientiousness, extraversion, agreeableness, and neuroticism. Even complex ideas can be understood through simple mnemonics. For example, the phrase *cells that fire together wire together* is a way to remember long-term potentiation, the brain mechanism responsible for learning (discussed in Chapter 6).

6. Use visual imagery. Creating a mental image of material is an especially good way to remember. Visual imagery strategies you can use include doodling a sketch to help you link ideas to images, creating a flow chart to show how some process unfolds over time, or drawing a concept map that shows the relationships between ideas (**Figure 7.31**).

To use all of these strategies, you need to remember them. As a first step toward improving your study skills, create a mnemonic to remember these strategies!

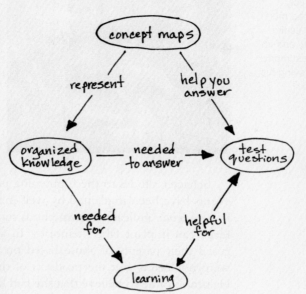

FIGURE 7.31 Concept Map as Memory Aid This concept map presents some ideas about—you guessed it—concept maps. When you need to visualize the relationships between different ideas about any subject, you can adapt this model. The ovals represent main ideas. The arrows indicate connections between ideas. A concept map can become far more complex. In fact, it can become as complex as you need it to be. For example, you might visually distinguish between main ideas and less important concepts by putting the main ideas in ovals and the less important concepts in triangles.

and patients claim that long-repressed memories for traumatic events can resurface during therapy. Recovered memories of sexual abuse are the most commonly reported repressed memories, and in the early 1990s there was a rash of reports about celebrities who had recovered memories of early childhood sexual abuse. On the other side, memory researchers such as Elizabeth Loftus point out that little credible evidence indicates that recovered memories are genuine or at least sufficiently accurate to be believable. Part of the problem is best summarized by a leading memory researcher, Daniel Schacter: "I am convinced that child abuse is a major problem in our society. I have no reason to question the memories of people who have always remembered their abuse, or who have spontaneously recalled previously forgotten abuse on their own. Yet I am deeply concerned by some of the suggestive techniques that have been recommended to recover repressed memories" (Schacter, 1996, p. 251).

FIGURE 7.32 Fallibility of "Repressed Memory" (a) Eileen Franklin **(center)** claimed to have recovered a previously repressed memory that her father had murdered a friend of hers two decades earlier. **(b)** George Franklin was found guilty and imprisoned based on his daughter's testimony. Evidence subsequently emerged proving his innocence, and he was released.

Schacter alludes to the frightening possibility that false memories for traumatic events have been implanted by well-meaning but misguided therapists. Convincing evidence indicates that methods such as hypnosis, age regression, and guided recall can implant false memories. In a few infamous examples, adults have accused their parents of abuse based on memories that the accusers later realized were not reality but the products of therapy (**Figure 7.32**). For instance, Diana Halbrook came to believe that she had been abused. She also believed that she had been involved in satanic ritualistic abuse, as part of which she had killed a baby. When she expressed doubts to her therapist and her "support" group about these events' veracity, they told her she was in denial and not listening to "the little girl" within. After all, the other members of the support group had recovered memories of being involved in satanic ritualistic abuse. After Halbrook left her therapy group, she came to believe she had not been abused and had not killed. Tellingly, "though thousands of patients have 'remembered' ritual acts, not a single such case has ever been documented in the United States despite extensive investigative efforts by state and federal law enforcement" (Schacter, 1996, p. 269).

Understandably, people on both sides of the debate about repressed memories hold strong and passionate beliefs. While research shows that some therapeutic techniques seem especially likely to foster false memories, it would be a mistake to dismiss all adult reports of early abuse. Some abuse certainly could have occurred and been forgotten until later, and we cannot ignore the memories of actual victims. In the latter half of the 1990s, the incidence of recovered memories fell dramatically, but we do not know whether this decline occurred because of less media attention to reports, because fewer people sought therapy to uncover their past memories, or because therapists stopped using these suggestive methods.

Neuroscience May Make It Possible to Distinguish between "True" and "False" Memories

Given the many advances in the neuroscience of how we learn and remember, can any neuroscientific techniques help us distinguish between "true" memories and "false" ones? That is, can we determine when memories refer to events as they really happened? Alternatively, can we determine when memories refer to events that did not happen or that happened very differently than remembered?

Recall that when we remember something, the brain areas activated are the same ones that were active when we first learned it. For example, auditory memories activate auditory areas of the brain. Retrieving a memory seems to require the same neural activity that was involved in the initial encoding. If the memory is "true," the brain areas activated should be the same as those active when the event occurred, but if the memory is "false," unrelated brain areas would be activated (Garoff-Eaton, Slotnick, & Schacter, 2006). Some preliminary data suggest that we can make this distinction, but this emerging area of research needs a great deal of further testing. One problem with this method is that false memories tend to be similar in many ways to true memories. For example, you might correctly recall an event that occurred in high school gym class but have a false memory about the teacher involved. In a case like this one, the area of the brain involved in true memory for similar events in high school would probably also be involved in the retrieval of the false memory. A totally unrelated memory, such as a song you heard earlier today, would involve different brain regions.

Summing Up

How Are Memories Distorted?

Memory is far from a faithful, objective recorder of facts and events. Instead, memory often includes biases and distortions. The mind has a general bias toward maintaining consistency between our memories, beliefs, and attitudes. Nevertheless, people display unjustified confidence in their personal memories, such as flashbulb memories. People frequently display source misattribution—misremembering the time, place, person, or circumstances involved in a memory. Examples of source misattribution include source amnesia and cryptomnesia. People tend to make poor eyewitnesses: They often fail to pay attention to the incidents and people they observe, and they are suggestible to misleading information. Memories can be distorted, or even implanted, by false information. Confabulation, or "honest lying," has been documented among individuals with Capgras syndrome, characterized by damage to the frontal lobes and limbic system. The legitimacy of repressed memories continues to be debated by contemporary psychologists, many of whom argue that such memories may be implanted by suggestive techniques. Neuroscientists are attempting to develop techniques to distinguish between true and false memories on the basis of patterns of brain activation.

Measuring Up

1. Flashbulb memories _____.
   a. are almost always true memories because they involve emotional events
   b. are likely to be wrong because people misattribute the source of information
   c. are often distorted in the same way as other memories, but "feel" true to the people whose memories they are
   d. are less important for men than for women because, on average, men are less emotional and have less need to remember emotional events

2. Suppose a teacher accuses you of plagiarizing a term paper. To back up his accusation, he shows you a published passage similar to one you wrote in your paper. Of course, you did not commit plagiarism—you would never do that. Which of the following phenomena might be cited in your defense?
   a. cryptomnesia
   b. social comparison
   c. absentmindedness
   d. temporary blocking

Answers: 1. c. are often distorted in the same way as other memories, but "feel" true to the people whose memories they are. 2. a. cryptomnesia.

Visit StudySpace to access free review materials, such as:

■ complete study outlines   ■ vocabulary flashcards of all key terms   ■ additional chapter review quizzes

Chapter Summary

7.1 What Is Memory?

■ **Memory Is the Nervous System's Capacity to Acquire and Retain Usable Skills and Knowledge:** Memory enables organisms to take information from experiences and store it for retrieval at a later time.

■ **Memory Is the Processing of Information:** Memory involves three phases. The first phase, encoding, is the processing of information so that it can be stored. The second phase, storage, is the retention of encoded information. The third phase, retrieval, is the recall of previously encoded and stored information.

■ **Memory Is the Result of Brain Activity:** Multiple brain regions have been implicated in memory, including the hippocampus, temporal lobes, cerebellum, amygdala, prefrontal cortex, and the brain structures involved in perception. Through consolidation, immediate memories become lasting memories. Through reconsolidation, memories may be altered.

7.2 How Does Attention Determine What We Remember?

■ **Our Visual Attention Works Selectively and Serially:** Simple searches for stimuli that differ in only one primary factor (e.g., shape, motion, size, color, orientation) occur automatically and rapidly through parallel processing. In contrast, searches for objects that are the conjunction of two or more properties (e.g., red and X shaped) occur slowly and serially.

■ **Our Auditory Attention Allows Us to Listen Selectively:** We can attend to more than one message at a time, but we cannot do this well. There is evidence that we weakly process some unattended information.

■ **Through Selective Attention, We Filter Incoming Information:** We often do not notice large changes in an environment because we fail to pay attention. This phenomenon is known as change blindness.

7.3 How Are Memories Maintained over Time?

■ **Sensory Memory Is Brief:** Visual, auditory, olfactory, gustatory, and tactile memories are maintained long enough to ensure continuous sensory experiences.

■ **Working Memory Is Active:** Working memory is an active processing system that keeps information available for current use. Chunking reduces information into units that are easier to remember. Research suggests that working memory may be limited to as few as four chunks of information.

7.4 How Is Information Organized in Long-Term Memory?

■ **Long-Term Memory Is Relatively Permanent:** Long-term memory is a relatively permanent, virtually limitless store. Information that is repeatedly retrieved, that is deeply processed, or that helps us adapt to an environment is most likely to enter long-term memory.

■ **Long-Term Memory Is Based on Meaning:** Maintenance rehearsal involves repetition. Elaborative rehearsal involves encoding information more meaningfully—for example, on the basis of semantic meaning. Elaborative rehearsal is more effective for long-term remembering than maintenance rehearsal.

■ **Schemas Provide an Organizational Framework:** Schemas are cognitive structures that help people perceive, organize, and process information. Thus schemas influence memory. Culture shapes schemas. As a result, people from distinct cultures process information in different ways.

■ **Information Is Stored in Association Networks:** Networks of associations are formed by nodes of information. The nodes are linked together and activated through spreading activation.

■ **Retrieval Cues Provide Access to Long-Term Storage:** According to the encoding specificity principle, any stimulus encoded along with an experience can later trigger the memory of the experience. Mnemonics are learning aids or strategies that use retrieval cues to improve recall. Examples include the method of loci and verbal mnemonics.

7.5 What Are the Different Long-Term Memory Systems?

■ **Explicit Memory Involves Conscious Effort:** Explicit, declarative memories that we consciously remember include personal events (episodic memory) and general, factual knowledge (semantic memory).

■ **Implicit Memory Occurs without Deliberate Effort:** Procedural (motor) memories of how to do things automatically are implicit.

■ **Prospective Memory Is Remembering to Do Something:** Prospective memory has "costs" in terms of reducing working memory capacity and reducing attention.

7.6 When Do People Forget?

■ **Transience Is Caused by Interference:** Forgetting over time occurs because of interference from old information and new information.

■ **Blocking Is Temporary:** The tip-of-the-tongue phenomenon is a person's temporary trouble retrieving the right word. This phenomenon is usually due to interference from a similar word.

■ **Absentmindedness Results from Shallow Encoding:** Inattentive or shallow processing causes memory failure.

- **Amnesia Is a Deficit in Long-Term Memory:** Disease, injury, or psychological trauma can result in amnesia. Retrograde amnesia is the inability to recall past memories. Anterograde amnesia is the inability to form new memories.

- **Persistence Is Unwanted Remembering:** Persistence is the recurrence of unwanted memories. This problem is common among individuals with posttraumatic stress disorder. Researchers are investigating methods to erase unwanted memories.

7.7 How Are Memories Distorted?

- **People Reconstruct Events to Be Consistent:** People exhibit memory bias. That is, over time they make their memories consistent with their current beliefs or attitudes.

- **Flashbulb Memories Can Be Wrong:** The strong emotional response that attends a flashbulb memory may affect the memory's strength and accuracy.

- **People Make Source Misattributions:** People can misremember the time, place, person, or circumstances involved with a memory (source misattribution). In source amnesia, a person cannot remember where she or he encountered the information associated with a memory. In cryptomnesia, a person believes that he or she came up with a new idea, but only retrieved the idea from memory.

- **People Are Bad Eyewitnesses:** Poor eyewitness recall occurs because people often fail to pay attention to events and are suggestible to misleading information. People are particularly poor at identifying those whose ethnicities are different from their own.

- **People Have False Memories:** False memories can be implanted. Children are particularly susceptible to false memories. Confabulation, or "honest lying," is associated with some forms of brain damage.

- **Repressed Memories Are Controversial:** Psychologists continue to debate the validity of repressed memories. Some therapeutic techniques are highly suggestive and may contribute to the occurrence of false repressed memories.

- **Neuroscience May Make It Possible to Distinguish between "True" and "False" Memories:** By examining brain activity during encoding and retrieval, researchers hope to distinguish between true and false memories. Further research is needed in this emerging area of neuroscience.

Key Terms

absentmindedness, p. 300
amnesia, p. 300
anterograde amnesia, p. 301
blocking, p. 300
change blindness, p. 276
chunking, p. 282
confabulation, p. 308
consolidation, p. 271
cryptomnesia, p. 305
declarative memory, p. 294
encoding, p. 269

encoding specificity
    principle, p. 290
episodic memory, p. 294
explicit memory, p. 294
flashbulb memories, p. 303
forgetting, p. 298
implicit memory, p. 294
long-term memory, p. 283
memory, p. 269
memory bias, p. 302
mnemonics, p. 292

parallel processing, p. 274
persistence, p. 301
proactive interference, p. 299
procedural memory, p. 295
prospective memory, p. 296
reconsolidation, p. 272
retrieval, p. 270
retrieval cue, p. 290
retroactive interference,
    p. 299
retrograde amnesia, p. 301

schemas, p. 288
semantic memory, p. 295
sensory memory, p. 279
serial position effect, p. 283
short-term memory, p. 281
source amnesia, p. 304
source misattribution, p. 304
storage, p. 269
suggestibility, p. 306
transience, p. 298
working memory, p. 281

Practice Test

1. The card game Set requires players to attend to four features (shape, color, shading, and number) across 12 cards in an effort to identify a "Set." A player has identified a Set when "any feature in the 'Set' of three cards is either common to all three cards or is different on each card" (directions from Set Enterprises, Inc.). Playing this game requires participants to engage in a _____, which is _____.
   a. conjunction task; effortful
   b. conjunction task; fast and automatic
   c. primitive features task; effortful
   d. primitive features task; fast and automatic

2. Sarah and Anna are chatting at a coffee shop. Anna notices that Sarah does not seem to be paying attention to what she, Anna, is saying. Which strategy could Anna use to effectively pull Sarah's attention back to the conversation?
   a. Anna should buy Sarah a fresh cup of coffee; more caffeine will help her pay attention.
   b. Anna should covertly modify something about her own appearance (e.g., remove her earrings); even subtle changes in a person's visual field draw attention.
   c. Anna should lower her voice to a near-whisper.
   d. Anna should use Sarah's name in a sentence.

The answer key for the Practice Tests can be found at the back of the book. It also includes answers to the green caption questions.

8

Thinking and Intelligence

ON THE MORNING OF SATURDAY, MAY 15, 2004, a steel girder fell from an overpass under construction on Interstate 70, west of Denver, Colorado. A 40-ton I-beam, the girder was apparently not secured properly. It dropped onto a car, cutting it in half. The impact killed all three passengers: William J. Post, 34; his 36-year-old wife, Anita; and their 2-year-old girl, Koby Ann (**Figure 8.1**).

In the news coverage of this story, two additional aspects added to the horror. First, about an hour before the collapse, a motorist with bridge construction experience had called 911 to report that the girder looked "structurally unsafe." The 911 operator, however, had mistakenly directed the maintenance crew to investigate a road sign. The maintenance crew never noticed the girder. Second, the Post family died in this freak accident because they were living in what they believed was a safe place. At the time of the terrorist attacks of September 11, 2001, William worked as a systems engineer near the World Trade Center. After the attacks, William left his job, and the Posts moved out of New York City to avoid personal danger. If the Posts had remained in New York, they might not have died three years later.

FIGURE 8.1 Tragic Accident After the Post family died, news coverage included photos of the crash site. Near the center of this shot, the crushed car is visible below the collapsed girder.

Throughout the world, people have repeatedly viewed the footage from 9/11: the two jets striking the World Trade Center towers, flames and smoke pouring out of the buildings' upper floors, office workers escaping the flames and smoke by leaping to their deaths, and the towers subsequently collapsing and showering debris on that part of lower Manhattan (**Figure 8.2a**). Those vivid images make it impossible not to think of the passengers in the hijacked planes and of the office workers in the World Trade Center and the Pentagon who died as a result of the hijackings. Another tragic consequence of 9/11 has rarely been discussed: the hundreds of people who died in automobile accidents because they chose to drive rather than fly in the years after the attacks. These additional deaths were not caused by terrorists' actions. They were caused by the way people commonly think about risks.

The psychologist Gerd Gigerenzer (2004) has written about fears that he calls *dread risks*. Gigerenzer has proposed that such fears can result when events with dire consequences receive a lot of publicity. Dread risks can result even when the publicized events have a low probability of recurring. These resulting fears can profoundly affect reasoning and decision making.

For example, after 9/11, many more people feared flying than normally do (**Figure 8.2b**). This fear arose even in countries, such as Canada, that were not likely targets for terrorists. In October, November, and December 2001, airline revenues in the United States dropped by 20 percent, 17 percent, and 12 percent, respectively, compared with those same months in 2000. Meanwhile, estimates for miles driven in the United States increased by almost 3 percent. The largest increase, 5.3 percent, was on interstate rural highways.

Thus hijacked planes may prompt people to avoid airline travel. But the number of people who die in car accidents every year far exceeds the number who die in airline disasters. It far, far exceeds the number of people who die in hijackings. In the three months following 9/11, the number of traffic fatalities was significantly above average: An estimated 350 Americans died during those months because they avoided flying. That number exceeds 266, the number of airplane passengers and crew members who died in all four hijackings on 9/11. And these numbers do not reflect the decisions of people, such as William and Anita Post, who did not just change their mode of travel. The Posts were, tragically, among the people who changed their whole lives in response to a dread risk. How do we explain decisions of this kind? ■

FIGURE 8.2 Dread Risks (a) The second plane strikes the World Trade Center on September 11, 2001. **(b)** For months after the attacks, airports around the United States were practically deserted. Here, Reagan National Airport in Washington, D.C., is pictured on November 1, 2001.

(a)

(b)

What Is Thought?

Learning Objectives

- Distinguish between analogical and symbolic representations.
- Describe the defining attribute, prototype, and exemplar models of concepts.
- Discuss the positive and negative consequences of using schemas and scripts.

Thinking Is the Manipulation of Mental Representations

For the most part, our thinking is adaptive. For example, we develop rules for making fast decisions because daily life demands we do so. Because our cognitive resources are limited, we need to use them efficiently. When reasoning about the right choices to make, however, we do not always weigh the actual probabilities of different actions. In fact, we can be influenced heavily by numerous factors that might not be considered rational. The prominence of events can affect our thinking. Images in our minds can overtake the facts.

Psychologists have identified some of the typical biases that enter into reasoning and decision making. Gigerenzer believes more attention should be paid to the biases that typically affect decision making after highly unlikely tragic events. Education about dread risks, he notes, might prompt people to reconsider choices that could result in additional negative consequences. As Gigerenzer suggests, the way we think about information affects the quality of our lives, both individually and collectively. This chapter therefore considers the nature of thought: How do we represent ideas in our minds? How do we use these ideas to solve problems and to make decisions? How do we explain differences in intelligence among people? Ultimately, how can exploring the nature of thought help us improve our thinking?

The field of cognitive psychology is the study of thought. It was originally based on two ideas: (1) The brain *represents* information. (2) **Thinking** is the mental manipulation of these representations. In other words, we use representations to understand objects we encounter in our environments. **Cognition** can be broadly defined to include thinking and the understandings that result from thinking.

Representations are all around us. For example, a road map represents streets. A menu represents food options. A photograph represents part of the world. The challenge for cognitive psychologists is to understand the nature of our everyday *mental* representations. When are such representations like maps or pictures, ones that happen to be in our minds? And when are they more abstract, like language?

Thinking Involves Two Types of Representations

In thinking, we use two basic types of representations: *analogical* and *symbolic*. Analogical representations usually correspond to images. Symbolic representations usually correspond to words. Together, both types of representations form the basis of human thought, intelligence, and the ability to solve the complex problems of everyday life.

Analogical representations have some characteristics of actual objects. Therefore, they are *analogous* to actual objects. Maps, for example, correspond to geographical layouts. Family trees depict relationships between relatives. A clock corresponds directly to the passage of time. A realistic drawing of a violin is an attempt to show that musical instrument from a particular perspective (**Figure 8.3a**).

In the mind's eye, we often see images without trying. For example, pause while reading this sentence and think about a lemon. What form did your "lemon" thought take? Did you pull up an image that resembled an actual lemon, with its yellow and waxy, dimpled skin? Did your month water (a different sort of mental image)? Not surprisingly, several lines of evidence support the notion that representations take on picturelike qualities.

Studies have shown that when you retrieve information from memory, as when you recall a picture you recently saw in a newspaper, the representation of that picture in your mind's eye parallels the representation in your brain the first time you saw the picture (Kosslyn, Thompson, Kim, & Alpert, 1995; Stokes, Thompson,

(a)   **(b)**

Violin

FIGURE 8.3 Analogical Representations and Symbolic Representations
(a) Analogical representations, such as this picture of a violin, have some characteristics of the objects they represent. **(b)** Symbolic representations, such as the word *violin*, are abstract and do not have relationships to the objects.

thinking The mental manipulation of representations of information (i.e., of objects we encounter in our environments).

cognition Mental activity that includes thinking and the understandings that result from thinking.

analogical representations Mental representations that have some of the physical characteristics of objects; they are analogous to the objects.

symbolic representations Abstract mental representations that do not correspond to the physical features of objects or ideas.

Cusack, & Duncan, 2009). In one study, participants were shown four objects (food, tools, faces, and buildings), or they were asked to recall such objects (Reddy, Tsuchiya, & Serre, 2010). In either case, the participants' brain activity was surprisingly similar for both seeing and remembering the specific objects. Neural activity occurs when we look at objects, and it can be reactivated when we recall the objects. This process is like having an eye that faces into the brain instead of outside to the world.

Of course, no "picture" exists inside your head. As explained in Chapter 3, neural activity consists of electrical impulses that cause groups of neurons to fire. The experience simply seems like viewing a picture inside your head. The mental image is not perfectly accurate. Instead, the image corresponds generally to the physical object it represents. By using mental images, you can answer questions about objects not in your presence. Manipulating mental images also allows you to think about your environment in novel and creative ways, helping you solve problems.

By contrast, **symbolic representations,** usually words or ideas, are abstract. They do not have relationships to physical qualities of objects in the world. For example, the word *violin* stands for a musical instrument (**Figure 8.3b**). There are no correspondences between what a violin looks like, what it sounds like, and the letters or sounds that make up the word *violin*. In Chinese, the word for violin is

小提琴

In Mandarin, it is pronounced *xiǎotíqín,* or *shiaw ti chin*. Like the English word *violin,* it is a symbolic representation because it bears no systematic relationship to the object it names. The individual characters that make up the word stand for different parts of what makes a violin, but they are arbitrary. You cannot "see" any part of a violin in their shapes.

MENTAL MAPS COMBINE REPRESENTATIONS Mental maps are an interesting case of this mixture. Most of us can pull up a visual image of Africa's contours even if we have never seen the actual contours with our own eyes. Mental maps of this kind include analogical and symbolic representations.

Consider the following question about two U.S. cities: *Which is farther east, San Diego, California, or Reno, Nevada?* If you are like most people (at least most Americans), you answered that Reno is farther east than San Diego. In fact, though, San Diego is farther east than Reno. Even if you formed an analogical representation of a map of the southwestern United States, your symbolic knowledge probably told you that a city on the Pacific Coast is always farther west than a city in a state that does not border the Pacific Ocean.

A symbolic representation can yield a wrong answer in this instance. While our general knowledge is correct, it does not take into account the way Nevada juts west

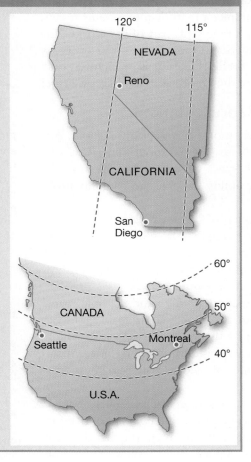

FIGURE 8.4 Try for Yourself: Conceptual Mental Maps

When asked whether San Diego or Reno is farther east, your symbolic knowledge probably informed you that California is farther west than Nevada.

So your conceptual mental map made you think that San Diego was west of Reno.

But this real map, showing location relative to uniform lines of longitude, shows that symbolic knowledge was inadequate in this case.

Explanation: Symbolic representations can lead to errors, because we can represent only a limited range of knowledge analogically and thus use memory shortcuts unconsciously. In this case, you probably were not taking into account the way northern Nevada juts west and southern California juts east.

Try for Yourself: Which is farther north, Seattle, Washington, or Montreal, Canada? You probably are picturing a mental map that looks like this, but be careful—consider the lines of latitude on a real map.

Answer: Seattle (47° north latitude) is north of Montreal (45° north latitude).

and the Pacific Coast near Mexico juts east. The regularization of irregular shapes in memory is a shortcut we use unconsciously for organizing and representing information in memory. While generally useful, such shortcuts can lead to errors (**Figure 8.4**).

Concepts Are Symbolic Representations

Much of our thinking reflects visual and verbal representations of objects in the world (as in answering the question above about San Diego versus Reno). It also reflects our general knowledge about the world. Say that you are shown a drawing of a small yellow object and asked to identify it. Your brain forms a mental image (analogical representation) of a lemon and provides you with the word *lemon* (symbolic representation). So far, so good. Still, in the real world your information would be incomplete. Picturing a lemon and knowing its name does not tell you what to do with a lemon. But knowing that parts of a lemon are edible helps you decide how to use the fruit. For example, you could make lemonade. Because you know that the lemon juice will taste strong and sour, you might dilute it with water and add sugar. In short, how you think about a lemon influences what you do with it.

One question of interest to cognitive psychologists is how we use knowledge about objects efficiently. As discussed in Chapter 7, our memory systems are organized so we can call up information quickly when we need it. The same principle holds true when we think about objects. For instance, if asked to say what a violin is, most people probably would begin by defining it broadly as a musical instrument. Grouping things based on shared properties, *categorization,* reduces the amount of knowledge we must hold in memory and is therefore an efficient way of thinking. We can apply a category such as "musical instruments"—objects that produce music when played—automatically to all members of the category. Applying a category spares us the trouble of storing this same bit of knowledge over and over for each musical instrument. We have to store unique knowledge for each member of a category, however. A violin "has four strings"; a guitar "has six strings" (**Figure 8.5**).

A **concept** is a category, or class, that includes subtypes and/or individual items. A concept can consist of mental representations (such as musical instruments or fruits). It can consist of a relation between representations (such as "violins are smaller than violas" or "watermelons are heavier than lemons"). Or it can consist of a quality or dimension (such as pitch or sweetness). By allowing us to organize mental representations around a common theme, a concept ensures that we do not have to store every instance of an object, a relation, or a quality or dimension individually. Instead, we store an abstract representation based on the properties that particular items or particular ideas share.

DEFINING ATTRIBUTE MODEL Consider the concept of a bachelor. If asked to, you probably could indicate whether each of your male acquaintances is a bachelor. According to the **defining attribute model** of concepts, each concept is characterized by a list of features that are necessary to determine if an object is a member of the category. The dictionary defines a bachelor as a male who has not married, so this concept's defining attributes would be *male* and *unmarried.* For a musical instrument, attributes would include *is a device that produces sound* (**Figure 8.6**).

Although the defining attribute model is intuitively appealing, it fails to capture many key aspects of how we organize things in our heads. First, the model suggests that membership within a category is on an all-or-none basis. In reality, we often make exceptions in our categorizations. We allow members into groups

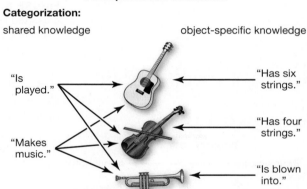

Concept: musical instruments

Categorization:

shared knowledge   object-specific knowledge

"Is played."

"Makes music."

"Has six strings."

"Has four strings."

"Is blown into."

FIGURE 8.5 Categorization We group objects into categories according to the objects' shared properties.

concept A mental representation that groups or categorizes objects, events, or relations around common themes.

defining attribute model A way of thinking about concepts: A category is characterized by a list of features that determine if an object is a member of the category.

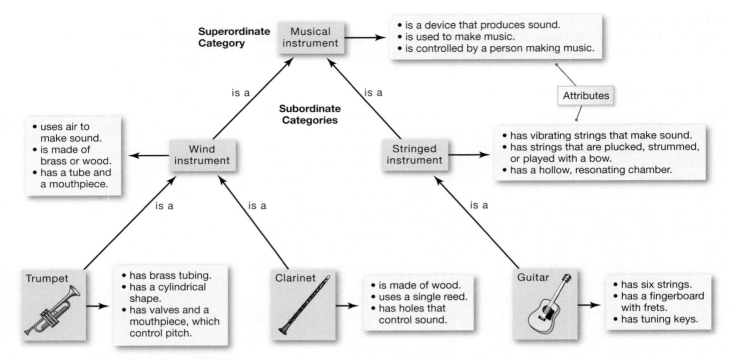

FIGURE 8.6 The Defining Attribute Model In the defining attribute model, concepts are organized hierarchically. That is, they can be subordinate or superordinate to each other. For example, horns and stringed instruments are subordinate categories of the superordinate category of musical instruments.

even if they do not have all the attributes, or we exclude them even if they have all the attributes. For instance, most people would include *can fly* as an attribute of *bird*. Yet some birds, such as penguins, cannot fly. Likewise, some people use spoons and even saws to play music, yet we do not usually categorize a spoon or a saw as a musical instrument.

Second, the defining attribute model suggests that all of a given category's attributes are equally important in defining that category. Some attributes, however, are more important for defining membership than others. In addition, the boundaries between categories are much fuzzier than the defining attribute model suggests. For example, *has wings* is generally considered a clear attribute of *bird*. But *is warm-blooded* does not come to mind as readily when we think of birds. Being warm-blooded is therefore not as important in how we think about birds. It remains important to the birds, just not to our thinking about them!

Third, the model posits that all members of a category are equal in category membership. In other words, no one item is a better fit than any other. Consider again the concept of a bachelor. According to the definition, a 16-year-old boy, a man who has been in a committed relationship for 25 years but never married, and a man in his 30s who goes on dates a few nights a week would equally exemplify the category *bachelor*. Do they seem the same to you? Or is the third example the best?

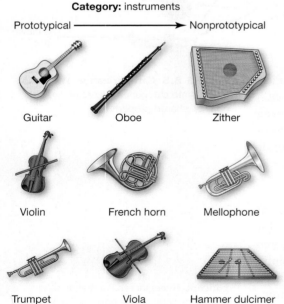

FIGURE 8.7 The Prototype Model
According to the prototype model, some items within a group or class are more representative (or prototypical) of that category than are other items within that group or class.

PROTOTYPE MODEL Among the alternatives to the defining attribute model is the **prototype model** of concepts (**Figure 8.7**). In thinking about a category, we tend to think in terms of a "best example," or *prototype,* for that category (**Figure 8.8**).

One positive feature of the prototype model is that it allows for flexibility in the representation of concepts. One drawback related to such flexibility is that a

FIGURE 8.8 Try for Yourself: The Prototype Model of Concepts

For each of the following categories, name the first member that comes into your mind (based on demonstration from Decyk, 1994):

a bird _____
a hero _____
a color _____
an animal _____
a motor vehicle _____

Result: For a bird, you likely named a robin or sparrow if you live in the United States. If you live in New Zealand, you might have named a kiwi. Wherever you live, you probably named a common bird in your country—a bird that seems to represent an idealized version of all birds.

For a hero, most people name a superhero such as Superman, Spiderman, or Mighty Mouse, or a police officer or firefighter. Few people will name a woman, a child, or an animal (such as Lassie, a hero dog from a popular television series), all of whom can be heroes.

 Robin (U.S.)    Kiwi (New Zealand)    Superman (U.S.)   Black Mask (China)

For a color, most people name red or blue—the primary colors are primary in human memory as well.

Despite regional differences in regard to animals, four legs and hair are the idealized attributes of an animal, and most people name a dog or cat.

For a motor vehicle, most people name a car or truck, except in the countries where the dominant motor vehicle is a motorbike.

Explanation: Even though there are countless birds we could name (penguin, chicken, dodo, etc.), we tend to think in terms of a "best example" of each category. The example will vary, depending on our life experiences, but within a culture people will be fairly consistent in the category members they name. The best example of a category is a prototype. For most people in the U.S., a robin is a better example of a bird than a penguin, so it becomes the prototype for the category.

prototype model A way of thinking about concepts: Within each category, there is a best example—a prototype—for that category.

exemplar model A way of thinking about concepts: All members of a category are examples (exemplars); together they form the concept and determine category membership.

particular prototype can be chosen for different reasons: Is it the most common example of that particular category? Is it a representation that all category members most resemble? Or does it represent a combination of typical attributes?

EXEMPLAR MODEL The **exemplar model** addresses this concern. It proposes that any concept has no single best representation. Instead, all the examples, or *exemplars,* of category members form the concept (**Figure 8.9**). For instance, your representation of dogs is made up of all the dogs you have encountered in your life. If you see an animal in your yard, you compare this animal with your memories of other animals you have encountered. If it most closely resembles the dogs you have encountered (as opposed to the cats, squirrels, rats, and other animals), you conclude it is a dog. How would you explain the difference between a dog and a cat to someone who has never seen either? Most dogs bark, but a dog is still a dog if it does not bark. It is still a dog if it loses its tail or a leg. The exemplar model assumes that, through experience, people form a fuzzy representation of a concept because there is no single representation of any concept. And the exemplar model accounts for the observation that some

FIGURE 8.9 The Exemplar Model The exemplar model holds that all members of a category are exemplars. For example, even this strange-looking feline is an exemplar of the category *cats.* (This cat happens to be a brown tortie white and tabby sphinx.)

(a)

(b)

FIGURE 8.10 Schemas Distorted by Stereotypes (a) In 2008, many reactions to the presidential candidacies of Hillary Clinton and Barack Obama reflected stereotypical schemas that exist in the United States.
(b) Different countries have different schemas concerning gender, race, leadership, and many other issues. Here, in January 2011, Brazil's first female president, Dilma Rousseff **(right)**, meets the South Korean prime minister, Kim Hwang-Sik.

stereotypes Cognitive schemas that allow for easy, fast processing of information about people based on their membership in certain groups.

category members are more prototypical than others: The prototypes are simply members we have encountered more often. This model points to one way in which our thoughts are unique and formed by personal experience.

Schemas Organize Useful Information about Environments

The defining attribute, prototype, and exemplar models explain how we classify objects we encounter and how we represent those objects in our minds. But in our daily lives, how do we use such classifications and representations?

When we think about aspects of the world, our knowledge extends well beyond a simple list of facts about the specific items we encounter every day. Instead, a different class of knowledge enables us to interact with the complex realities of our daily environments. As discussed in Chapter 7, schemas are cognitive structures that help us perceive, organize, and process information. As we move through various real-world settings, we act appropriately by drawing on knowledge of what objects, behaviors, and events apply to each setting. For example, at a casino blackjack table, it is appropriate to squeeze in between the people already sitting down. If a stranger tried to squeeze into a group of people dining together in a restaurant, however, the group's reaction would likely be quite negative. This kind of knowledge regarding situations and social contexts differs greatly from the knowledge associated with object classification. Here is a memorably concrete example: Suppose you see a picture of a finger and a picture of a nose. If the pictures are clear enough, you most likely will have no trouble classifying each object. If you have learned the appropriate schema, however, you will know that in public settings it is inappropriate to put a real finger into a real nose. This gross little example might seem trivial, but even simple schemas are important for guiding behavior in a complex world.

We can employ schemas for two reasons. First, common situations have consistent attributes (e.g., libraries are quiet and contain books). Second, people have specific roles within situational contexts (e.g., a librarian behaves differently in a library than a reader does). Unfortunately, schemas are like prototypes in that they sometimes have unintended consequences, such as reinforcing sexist or racist beliefs or other **stereotypes** (**Figure 8.10**). For example, when children and teens are asked to draw a scientist, very few draw women as scientists, because they unconsciously associate being a scientist with being male (Chambers, 1983).

Gender roles are the prescribed behaviors for females and males. They represent a type of schema that operates at the unconscious level. In other words, we follow gender roles without consciously knowing we are doing so. One reason we need to become aware of the way schemas direct our thinking is that they may unconsciously cause us to think, for example, that women lack assertiveness and therefore are generally unsuited for positions of leadership.

In his book *Blink: The Power of Thinking without Thinking* (2005), the journalist Malcolm Gladwell discusses an example of gender-related bias. In the past, orchestra conductors invariably chose men for principal positions in orchestras because the conductors believed that women did not play as well as men. The schema of women as inferior musicians interfered with the conductors' ability to rate auditioners objectively when the conductors knew the names and sexes of the musicians. After recognizing this bias, the top North American orchestras began holding auditions with the musicians hidden behind screens and their names withheld from the conductors. Since these methods were instituted, the number of women in orchestras has increased considerably (**Figure 8.11**).

(a)

(b)

FIGURE 8.11 Gender Roles Revised (a) As shown in this photo of the New York Philharmonic in 1960, stereotypes about men's and women's abilities to play musical instruments often fueled the formation of all-male orchestras. **(b)** Changes in attitudes and in audition procedures have contributed to the diversification of talent in contemporary orchestras.

One common type of schema helps us understand the sequence of events in certain situations. Roger Schank and Robert Abelson (1977) have referred to these schemas about sequences as *scripts*. A script is a schema that directs behavior over time within a situation. For example, *going to the movies* is a script most of us are familiar with (**Figure 8.12**).

Scripts dictate appropriate behaviors and the sequence in which they are likely to occur. What we view as appropriate is shaped by culture. The script for a heterosexual date, perhaps "dating" back to the automobile's invention, traditionally has involved the male driving and paying for dinner. In the 1950s, before the civil rights movement, a black person's script for boarding a bus in the southern United States involved going to the back of the bus.

(a)

(b)

(c)

FIGURE 8.12 Script Theory of Schemas According to this theory, we tend to follow general scripts of how to behave in particular settings. **(a)** At the movies, we expect to buy a ticket or print one if we bought it online. The cost of the ticket might depend on the moviegoer's age and the time of day. **(b)** Next, we might buy a snack before selecting a seat. Popcorn is a traditional snack at movie theaters. Caviar is not. **(c)** If we are part of a couple or group, we expect to sit with the other person in that couple or the people in the group. Although quiet talking might be appropriate before the movie, most of us expect talking to cease once the feature begins.

How Can Dating Scripts Help Me Navigate in My Romantic Life?

Many of us spend a good deal of time thinking about, pursuing, and participating in romantic relationships. Not surprisingly, our ideas about relationships guide the ways we engage in these activities. As you learned earlier in this chapter, we develop schemas about the sequences of events in certain situations, including dating. These schemas about events are called scripts. According to Amiraian and Sobal (2009), "Dating scripts are shared cognitive representations of likely sequences of dating events and sets of appropriate dating behaviors based on social norms and previous experiences that direct decisions and behavior on dates" (p. 226).

Knowing how a date is likely to unfold removes some of the ambiguity of an event that might already be laden with nervousness for you. Following a generally accepted script and behaving consistently with a set of culturally accepted rules helps manage the impressions that other people form about you. So, what scripts do college students hold about dating? How can awareness of common scripts about dating support your success in the dating scene?

The scripts college students hold about heterosexual dating seem to vary, depending on whether a man or a woman asks for the date, as well as on the location of the date (a keg party? a coffee shop?). In a clever study, Morr Serewicz and Gale (2008) asked the participants—all of whom were college students—to read a fictional scenario about a first date. The participants were then asked to imagine themselves as one of the people in the story and to describe the events they thought would occur just before and during the date.

Despite changing social norms and increasingly egalitarian beliefs in many areas of Western society, the dating scripts outlined by these modern-day college students tended to remain traditional. Women expected to be passive. They waited for dates to pick them up, allowed their dates to do the driving and pay the expenses, and responded to sexual advances rather than making them. Men expected to be active. They picked up their dates, did the driving and paying, and initiated sexual activity. Thus dating "rules" and scripts tended to remain consistent with the ones predominant in the 1950s!

Table 8.1 presents the typical story told by participants in the study. The actions listed here were mentioned by at least 25 percent of the participants. If at least 50 percent of the participants mentioned the action, it appears in ALL CAPS. If at least 40 percent of the participants who mentioned the action thought the action should be performed

TABLE 8.1 First Date Script Supplied by College Students
GET READY
PICK UP DATE (M)
Feel nervous
GO TO MOVIE
PAY (M)
TALK
Hold hands
GO TO CAFÉ/PARTY
Nonverbal closeness
TALK
Drink alcohol
Touch/hug
Deep conversation
Mingle with others
Talk
Leave party
Invite the other in
WALK/DRIVE HOME (M)
Polite leave-taking
KISS
FUTURE PLANS
Part for the night (M)

SOURCE: Morr Serewicz & Gale (2008).

by the male, an M appears after the action. (None of these actions were generally expected to be performed by the female.) For example, at least 25 percent of the participants thought alcohol would be consumed during the date. At least 50 percent of the participants thought the individuals would kiss before ending the date. Female and male participants anticipated more sexual activity when they had been asked for a date than when they had initiated a date. In addition, they anticipated more sexual intimacy when the date took place at a keg party than when it took place at a coffee shop.

Even if you have never been on a date, you probably have some sense of how to act. You probably know a date will include some small talk, some reciprocal self-disclosure, and probably some sort of activity, such as a movie, a concert, or a shared meal. You probably also know that the dating scripts of many college students include some sort of physical contact. Typically, a kiss is anticipated near the end of the date. Knowing about this expectation, you probably would not dare to try kissing someone within the first couple minutes of a first date. The person on the receiving end of that kiss would probably dodge the advance and might well walk away. The person might perceive you as socially awkward, creepy, inappropriate, or obnoxious. By contrast, if you ask questions about the other person, share your own perspectives, and avoid talking about someone else you have a crush on, you are likely to improve the chances that your date will think positively about you.

But what if a generally accepted script conflicts with your values or beliefs? For example, suppose you are not comfortable letting a relative stranger know where you live. Suppose you believe that someone who pays for a meal expects something in return, so you want to pay for your own meal on a first date. Suppose you do not drink alcohol. Or suppose you prefer to get to know someone before engaging in physical contact. If your date subscribes to the general script discussed here, must you let that person pick you up, pay for your meal, buy you drinks, and kiss you? No.

Instead, let your values and beliefs guide your behavior. Collaborate on a date that feels right to you. You can say, "I'll meet you at the coffee shop at 4." If your date pulls out a wallet to pay for the meal, you can say, "I appreciate the gesture, but I'll pay my share this time." If your date brings you a drink, you can say, "Oh, sorry. I don't drink alcohol. I'll take this back and get a soda." If your date leans in for a kiss, you can say, "I'd like to get to know you better before we kiss."

The goal—in dating as in so many other aspects of life—is to act in accord with the best version of yourself. If you ever feel compelled by cultural "oughts" or a pushy date to move away from your values or beliefs, stand up for yourself. After all, do you really want to date someone who does not think highly enough of you to respect your wishes?

The schemas and scripts that children learn are likely to affect their behavior when they are older. In one study, 120 children aged 2 to 6 were asked to use props and dolls to act out a social evening for adults (Dalton et al., 2005). As part of the role play, each child selected items from a miniature grocery store stocked with 73 products, including beer, wine, and cigarettes. Two of the most common items purchased were alcohol (by 62 percent) and cigarettes (by 28 percent). Children whose parents smoked or consumed alcohol were four times more likely to select these items. When the children were asked about the items they chose, alcohol and cigarettes were clearly included in most children's scripts for adult social life. One 4-year-old girl who selected cigarettes explained, "I need this for my man. A man needs cigarettes" (**Figure 8.13**). These examples

FIGURE 8.13 Scientific Method: Study of Preschoolers' Use of Cigarettes and Alcohol while Role-Playing as Adults

Hypothesis: Preschoolers' attitudes, expectations, and perceptions of alcohol and tobacco use will reflect scripts and schemas.

Research Method: Children used props and dolls to act out a social evening for adults. As part of the role play, each child selected items from a miniature grocery store stocked with 73 different products. The items on the shelves included beer, wine, and cigarettes.

Results: Out of 120 children, 34 (28 percent) "bought" cigarettes, and 74 (62 percent) "bought" alcohol. Children were more likely to buy cigarettes if their parents smoked. They were more likely to buy beer or wine if their parents drank alcohol at least monthly or if they viewed PG-13 or R-rated movies.

Conclusion: Children's play behavior suggests they are highly attentive to the use and enjoyment of alcohol and tobacco and have well-established expectations about how cigarettes and alcohol fit into social situations. Observation of adult behavior, especially parental behavior, may influence preschool children to view smoking and drinking as normative in social situations. These perceptions may relate to behaviors adopted later in life.

Source: Dalton, M. A., Bernhardt, A. M., Gibson, J. J., Sargent, J. D., Beach, M. L., Adachi-Mejia, A. M., Titus-Ernstoff, L. T., & Heatherton, T. F. (2005). "Honey, have some smokes." Preschoolers use cigarettes and alcohol while role playing as adults. *Archives of Pediatrics & Adolescent Medicine, 159*, 854–859.

highlight the need for us to think critically about whether our automatic beliefs and actions reflect the values we wish to hold. (This subject is discussed in greater detail in Chapter 12, "Social Psychology.")

If schemas and scripts are potentially problematic, why do they persist? Their adaptive value is that they minimize the amounts of attention required to navigate familiar environments. They also allow us to recognize and avoid unusual or dangerous situations. Mental representations in all forms assist us in using information about objects and events in adaptive ways.

Summing Up

What Is Thought?

Our thoughts consist of mental representations of the objects and information that we encounter in our environments. When we think of an object, we often bring to mind a visual image, or analogical representation, of the object. By contrast, a symbolic representation does not correspond to the object's physical features but to our knowledge about the object. Much of our knowledge of the world is based on concepts, or categories of items organized around common themes. Categories may be characterized by defining attributes, prototypes, or exemplars. Schemas are cognitive structures that help us perceive, organize, and process information. Scripts are schemas that direct our behavior. Schemas and scripts are adaptive in that they enable us to make quick judgments with little effort. Still, schemas and scripts may lead us to think and act in stereotypical ways.

Measuring Up

1. Indicate whether each of the following examples is an analogical or symbolic representation.
   _____ a. a watch with a standard watch face
   _____ b. a digital watch
   _____ c. a drawing of the information in a math problem
   _____ d. the word *rouge,* meaning "red" in French
   _____ e. a photograph of your best friend
   _____ f. a mental image of your best friend
   _____ g. a sketch of a football play

2. Which of the following is an advantage of scripts?
   a. They provide quick and almost effortless guides to behavior in different situations.
   b. They provide a flexible way of assessing different situations so each of us can decide how we want to behave in a given situation.

3. Which of the following is a disadvantage of scripts?
   a. They tend to reinforce stereotypical behaviors.
   b. Because they emphasize independent analysis of every situation, they take time.

Answers: 1. a. analogical; b. symbolic; c. analogical; d. symbolic; e. analogical; f. analogical; g. analogical. 2. a. They provide quick and almost effortless guides to behavior in different situations. 3. a. They tend to reinforce stereotypical behaviors.

The previous sections discussed how we represent and organize knowledge of the world. But how do we use that knowledge to guide our daily actions? Throughout each day we make decisions: what to eat for breakfast, which clothes to wear, which route to take to work or school, and so on. We scarcely notice making many of these decisions. Some decisions—such as which college to attend, whether to buy a house, and if it is time to commit to one's relationship partner—are much more consequential and require greater reflection. We also solve problems, as in figuring out how to break bad news or identifying the best way to study for a particular exam. Thinking enables us to do these things.

Sometimes the terms *reasoning, decision making,* and *problem solving* are used interchangeably. But they are not really the same. In **reasoning,** you determine if a conclusion is valid. To do so, you use information you believe is true. Consider the conclusion that human activities are responsible for the buildup of greenhouse gases in Earth's atmosphere. What information would you consider in judging whether that conclusion is valid? This thought process is analogous to the scientific process of using empirical evidence to test hypotheses to see if they are valid (see Chapter 2, "Research Methodology"). In **decision making,** you select among alternatives. Usually, you identify important criteria and determine how well each alternative satisfies these criteria. For example, if you can go to either Paris or Cancún for spring break, you need to choose between them. What criteria would you use in making this decision? In **problem solving,** you overcome obstacles to move from a present state to a desired goal state. For example, if you decide to go to Paris but do not have enough money for a plane ticket, you have a problem. In general, you have a problem when a barrier or a gap exists between where you are and where you want to be.

People Use Deductive and Inductive Reasoning

How do we evaluate evidence to draw conclusions? A police detective sifts through all the clues and tries to identify the right suspect. A parent listens to two children's conflicting stories and tries to figure out the truth. A scientist analyzes data to see if they support or refute a given hypothesis. Each situation requires reasoning: evaluating information, arguments, and beliefs to draw a conclusion. In **deductive reasoning,** you reason from the general to the specific. For example, if you have read that Parisians dress fashionably, you might expect your Parisian pen pal to dress fashionably. In **inductive reasoning,** you reason from the specific to the general. For example, since your Parisian pen pal is friendly, you might assume—or at least hope—that most Parisians are friendly. (Deductive reasoning, inductive reasoning, decision making, and problem solving are summarized in **Figure 8.14.**) Note, however, that even when you use deductive reasoning or inductive reasoning, you can still arrive at a false conclusion. After all, in employing one of these methods, you might commit errors in reasoning, such as making biased choices in what evidence to consider.

DEDUCTIVE REASONING In deductive reasoning, you use logic to draw specific conclusions under certain assumptions. Your assumptions are known as *premises.* For example, imagine you are deciding on a place to go for dinner and your

reasoning Using information to determine if a conclusion is valid or reasonable.

decision making Attempting to select the best alternative among several options.

problem solving Finding a way around an obstacle to reach a goal.

deductive reasoning Using general rules to draw conclusions about specific instances.

inductive reasoning Using specific instances to draw conclusions about general rules.

You use **deductive reasoning** to move from general to specific. You have read that Parisians are fashion conscious, so you expect your Parisian pen pal to be fashion conscious.

You use **inductive reasoning** to move from specific to general. Your Parisian pen pal is friendly, so you assume—or hope—that Parisians are friendly.

You use **decision making** to select between options. If you want to visit your pen pal, you might visit Paris instead of Cancún.

You use **problem solving** to overcome obstacles such as getting lost...

...or a delayed flight.

FIGURE 8.14 Deductive Reasoning, Inductive Reasoning, Decision Making, and Problem Solving

friend Bonnie tells you the new Thai restaurant is excellent. If you like Thai food (first premise) and if you think Bonnie has good taste (second premise), then choosing the place Bonnie has recommended (conclusion) might be a wise decision.

In research, a deductive reasoning task is often expressed as a syllogism: a logical argument that consists of a premise and a conclusion. For instance, If A is true, then B is true. The argument's conclusion depends on whether the premise is true. If you can assume the premise is true, then you can be certain about the conclusion. If Bonnie has good taste, then the new Thai restaurant she recommends will be excellent. If you like Thai cuisine, then you should choose this restaurant.

Another type of syllogism consists of two premises and a conclusion. Here, too, the conclusion can be judged as either valid or invalid.

All A are B.	All chimpanzees are primates.
All B are C.	All primates are mammals.
Therefore, all A are C.	Therefore, all chimpanzees are mammals.

Deductive reasoning allows us to determine a statement's validity given the premises. We can come up with a valid but incorrect conclusion, however, if the premises use terms inconsistently or ambiguously. Consider the following:

Nothing is better than a piece of warm apple pie.
A few crumbs of bread are better than nothing.
Therefore, a few crumbs of bread are better than warm apple pie.

As you can see, the ambiguity of the word *nothing* causes a logical error in this syllogism.

Deductive reasoning can be difficult because our prior beliefs (schemas) about typical events and typical situations influence the reasoning process (Klauer, Musch, & Naumer, 2000). Suppose you are told that *all foods made with spinach are delicious* and that *the cake is made with spinach*. The valid conclusion for you to draw would be that *the cake is delicious*. Still, you might have your doubts. After all, in the real world, we do not usually think of spinach as being a good ingredient for cake. Thus our beliefs can interfere with our ability to use logic.

INDUCTIVE REASONING In everyday life, we seldom go through the formality of using deductive reasoning. A more common approach is to determine general principles from specific instances. Suppose you have arranged to meet a new friend for lunch and your friend is late. You might conclude that special circumstances resulted in your new friend's tardiness. After a number of such instances, however, you might *induce* the general conclusion that your friend is usually tardy. In this way, you would draw a conclusion about your friend's behavior based on several separate instances.

INDUCTIVE AND DEDUCTIVE REASONING COMBINED Now suppose that one of your friends invites you to see a new movie that stars Nicolas Cage. You have seen some of Nicolas Cage's recent movies and hated them. Through inductive reasoning, you have come to believe that other movies Cage stars in will be terrible. In deciding whether to accept your friend's offer, you may combine inductive reasoning and deductive reasoning. Thus your belief that Nicolas Cage's latest movies are all terrible (premise based on inductive reasoning) leads you to expect that the new movie is not worth seeing (conclusion based on deductive reasoning).

REASONING AND THE SCIENTIFIC METHOD The use of the scientific method to discover general principles is one example of inductive reasoning. Say that a team of researchers hypothesizes that students involved in school clubs perform better academically. The researchers might select a random sample of students, half of whom participate in school clubs and half of whom do not. They might then compare the students' grade point averages. If they find that the students in school clubs have significantly higher GPAs, the researchers will conclude that, overall, students who participate in school clubs perform better academically. In other words, the researchers would induce a general principle from the specific instances of the students in the experiment.

As discussed in Chapter 2, the scientific method dictates that scientists meet certain standards when inducing general principles from several specific instances. These standards are designed to guard against biases in inductive reasoning. For example, researchers need an adequately large sample size to infer that a hypothesis is likely true. In day-to-day life, however, we may be more likely to reach inappropriate conclusions when reasoning about general principles from everyday circumstances. Say you are considering buying a car that was highly rated by a consumer magazine. A friend tells you that when his uncle had that type of car, it broke down all the time. Because it is based on a very small sample (one person's experience), this report should have little weight on your purchasing decision. People are strongly influenced by anecdotal reports, however. Physicians often lament that their patients reject therapies supported by science but readily accept ones supported by testimonials (Diotallevi, 2008).

Decision Making Often Involves Heuristics

Some cognitive psychologists focus on how we make decisions in everyday life. They especially want to know why many of our decisions do not match the predictions of "rational" behavior. In dealing with many real-world challenges, we often need to make decisions without taking time to consider all the possible pros and cons. Often, we rely on processes that allow us to make decisions quickly.

"I'll be happy to give you innovative thinking. What are the guidelines?"

In their research on decision making, psychologists have studied *normative models* and *descriptive models*. Normative models of decision making view people as optimal decision makers. In other words, according to these models, we always select the choice that yields the largest gain. Because these theories were developed from traditional economics, the largest gain usually means the most money. More recently, descriptive models have presented a more complicated view. According to these models, we tend to misinterpret and misrepresent the probabilities underlying many decision making scenarios. Even when we understand the probabilities, we have the potential to make irrational decisions.

Expected utility theory is one normative model of how we *should* make decisions (von Neumann & Morgenstern, 1947). According to this theory, we make decisions by considering the possible alternatives and choosing the most desirable one. To arrive at the most desirable alternative, we first rank the alternatives in order of preference: Is each alternative more desirable, less desirable, or equally desirable compared with each competing alternative? For example, if you were deciding what to do after graduation, you would list the alternatives. Suppose you were considering getting a job as a ski instructor, going to law school, or trying to make a living as a musician. The rational way to decide would be to rank-order these alternatives and select the one with the most *utility*, or value, to you. But do we always choose the most desirable alternative?

In the 1970s, Amos Tversky and Daniel Kahneman spearheaded descriptive research on both reasoning and decision making. Because of the importance of these topics in economic theory, Kahneman received the 2002 Nobel Prize in Economic Sciences for their research. (Tversky was deceased when the prize was awarded.) In examining how people make everyday decisions, Tversky and Kahneman identified several common **heuristics.** This term refers to mental shortcuts (rules of thumb, or informal guidelines) that we typically use to make decisions.

Psychologists distinguish between heuristics and algorithms. An *algorithm* is a procedure that, if followed correctly, will always yield the correct answer. If you wanted to know the area of a circle, for example, you could get the right answer by multiplying pi (3.1416) by the radius squared. This formula is an algorithm because it will always work. Similarly, if you follow a recipe exactly, it should always yield pretty much the same outcome. Suppose, however, you substitute one ingredient for another. Estimating the required sweetness, you use honey instead of the sugar the recipe calls for. Here, you are using a heuristic—an informed guide. Your result will likely be fine, but there is no guarantee. Heuristic thinking often occurs unconsciously: We are not aware of taking these mental shortcuts. Indeed, since the processing capacity of the conscious mind is limited, heuristic processing is useful partly because it requires minimal cognitive resources. Heuristics allows us to focus our attention on other things.

Heuristic thinking can be adaptive in that it allows us to decide quickly rather than weighing all the evidence each time we have to decide. Why do some people always want to buy the second-cheapest item, no matter what they are buying? They believe that by using this strategy, they save money but avoid purchasing the worst products. Other people want to buy only brand names.

heuristics Shortcuts (rules of thumb or informal guidelines) used to reduce the amount of thinking that is needed to make decisions.

Such quick rules of thumb often provide reasonably good decisions. As Tversky and Kahneman have demonstrated, however, heuristics can also result in biases, and biases may lead to errors or faulty decisions. Consider the commonly believed heuristic that a high price equals high quality. Although laboratory studies show that one type of soap is basically as good as any other, high prices have convinced many consumers that "fancy" soaps are superior.

In *Blink,* Malcolm Gladwell makes the case that the ability to use information rapidly is a critical human skill. When you encounter a person on the street who might pose a threat, you might change your route to avoid that person. Being able to size up whether a person is trustworthy allows you to avoid harm, and you do this sizing up instantly and without conscious awareness.

In illustrating how snap judgments can have important consequences, Gladwell describes a firefighter who led his colleagues in an effort to put out a kitchen fire. When they sprayed water on it, the fire did not respond in the expected way. Sensing that something was wrong, the firefighter quickly ordered everyone to leave the building. His decision turned out to be a good one because the fire was in the basement, under the kitchen, and the kitchen floor collapsed moments after the building was evacuated. The firefighter had known something was wrong but not what it was. If he had stopped to figure out the problem, he and his colleagues might have been killed. He saved himself and the others, but his snap decision was based on an intuition developed over years of experience in fighting fires.

Sometimes, however, snap decisions can be disastrous. Consider those cases in which a police officer has to make a split-second decision about whether to shoot a civilian. After a high-profile police shooting of an unarmed black person, for example, a community generally feels victimized and mistrustful toward the police (Correll et al., 2007). A quick choice can have many negative long-term ramifications.

FRAMING EFFECTS How information is presented can alter how people perceive it. This effect is known as **framing.** Framing a decision to emphasize the potential losses or potential gains of at least one alternative can significantly influence decision making (**Figure 8.15**).

FIGURE 8.15   Try for Yourself: Framing a Decision

Consider the following problem: Imagine that the United States is preparing for the outbreak of a disease that is projected to kill about 600 people. Two alternative programs are proposed to combat the disease. According to scientific estimates, if program A is chosen, 200 of the 600 people will be saved. If program B is chosen, there is a 1/3 probability that all 600 people will be saved and a 2/3 probability that nobody will be saved. Which program would you choose?

Result: When asked a question similar to this, 72 percent of respondents chose program A (Kahneman & Tversky, 1984). Each program potentially could save 200 people. Respondents clearly preferred program A's sure gain, however, as opposed to program B's chance of a larger gain and additional chance of no gain.

Now consider these alternatives: If program A is chosen, 400 people will die. If program B is chosen, there is a 1/3 probability that nobody will die and a 2/3 probability that 600 people will die.

Result: When asked a question like this one, 78 percent of respondents chose program B. In this case, most people felt that program A's certain death of 400 people was a worse alternative than program B's likely but uncertain death of 600 people. A sure loss was less appealing than an uncertain but possibly greater loss. The probabilities and outcomes in this second scenario are identical to those in the first, however. The difference is that the gains are emphasized in the first and the losses are emphasized in the second. Clearly, framing the decision to emphasize gains or losses affects the decision making.

framing The effect of presentation on how information is perceived.

Understanding How Heuristics Can Affect Your Thinking

The **availability heuristic** is the tendency to make a decision based on the answer that comes most easily to mind. In other words, when we think about events or make judgments, we tend to rely on information that is easy to retrieve. Recall the study on false fame discussed in Chapter 7, "Attention and Memory." Some participants read aloud a list of made-up names. The next day, those names were available in those participants' memories, even if the participants could not have said where they heard the names. Based on their familiarity with the names, the participants decided the people were famous. Similarly, as noted earlier in this chapter, prototypes come to mind when we think about certain categories. This connection tells us that prototypes are readily available in memory. Because of this ready availability, we tend to rely on prototypes in making decisions.

Consider this question: In most industrialized countries, are there more farmers or more librarians? If you live in an agricultural area, you probably said farmers. If you do not live in an agricultural area, you probably said librarians. Most people who answer this question think of the librarians they know (or know about) and the farmers they know (or know about). If they can retrieve many more instances in one category, they assume it is the larger category. In fact, there are many more farmers than librarians in most industrialized countries. Because people who live in cities and suburbs tend not to meet many farmers, they are likely to believe there are more librarians.

Now consider this example: You supervise two people. One of them is introverted, one is extraverted, but both of them do comparably outstanding work. If you can promote only one of them, which employee is more likely to come to mind first? For most of us, the extraverted person would come to mind first. Through more careful analysis, however, we would be able to overcome the availability heuristic and systematically consider the merits of each employee.

The **representativeness heuristic** is the tendency to place a person or object in a category if the person or object is similar to our prototype for that category. We use this heuristic when we base a decision on the extent to which each option reflects what we already believe about a situation. For example, say that Helena is intelligent, ambitious, and scientifically minded. She enjoys working on mathematical puzzles, talking with other people, reading, and gardening. Would you guess that she is a cognitive psychologist or a postal worker? Most people would employ the representativeness heuristic: Because her characteristics seem more representative of psychologists than of postal workers, they would guess that Helena is a cognitive psychologist.

But the representativeness heuristic can lead to faulty reasoning if you fail to take other information into account. One very important bit of information is the *base rate*. This term refers to how frequently an event occurs. People pay insufficient attention to base rates in reasoning. Instead,

availability heuristic Making a decision based on the answer that most easily comes to mind.

representativeness heuristic Placing a person or object in a category if that person or object is similar to one's prototype for that category.

they focus on whether the information presented is representative of one conclusion or another. For example, there are many more postal workers than cognitive psychologists, so the base rate for postal workers is higher than that for cognitive psychologists. Therefore, any given person, including Helena, is much more likely to be a postal worker. Although Helena's traits may be more representative of cognitive psychologists overall, they also likely apply to a large number of postal workers.

We cannot be aware of every heuristic we rely on. But we can be aware of frequently used ones, such as the availability and representativeness heuristics. Once we know that such shortcuts can lead us to make faulty judgments, we can use heuristics carefully as we seek to make rational decisions (**Figure 8.16**).

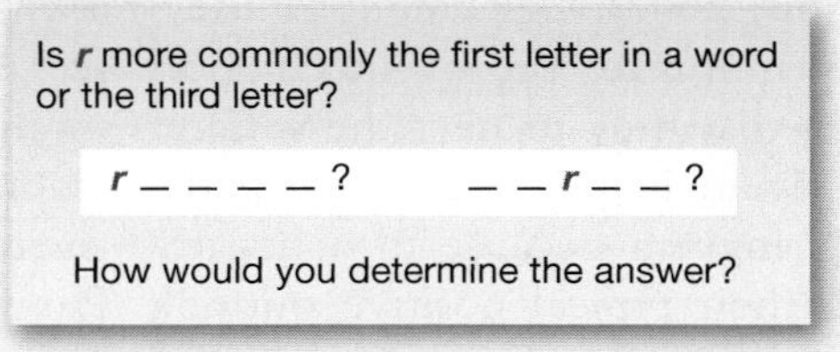

> Is *r* more commonly the first letter in a word or the third letter?
>
> *r* _ _ _ _ ?   _ _ *r* _ _ ?
>
> How would you determine the answer?

FIGURE 8.16 The Availability Heuristic at Work If you are like most people, you thought of words with *r* as the first letter (such as *right* and *read*). Then you thought of words with *r* as the third letter (such as *care* and *sir*). Because words with *r* at the beginning came most easily to mind, you concluded that *r* is more often the first letter of a word. *R* is much more likely, however, to be the third letter in a word.

To account for framing's effects, Kahneman and Tversky came up with *prospect theory*, a major theory in decision making. Their theory has two main components: (1) A person's wealth affects his or her choices. (2) Because losses feel much worse than gains feel good, a person will try to avoid situations that involve losses (Kahneman, 2007).

In most traditional studies of decision making, participants were presented with two choices. One choice was a "sure thing," such as winning $200. The other choice was associated with a probability, such as having a 20 percent probability of winning $1,000. These choices had the same "expected utility." That is, after numerous trials, the first choice would have yielded $200 each time. What about the second choice? After numerous trials, it too would have yielded an average of $200 each time (thanks to the 20 percent probability of winning $1,000). On those grounds, participants should have "preferred" the choices equally, since each choice would likely have yielded the same payoff. This choice was a one-time opportunity, however. Participants who selected the second option would not win an average amount from numerous trials—they would win either $1,000 or $0. Given that reality, would you expect poorer people to have made the same selection as richer ones? A student struggling to pay bills and working for $10 an hour would likely pick the sure $200. A student with a high income or with a rich and generous parent would likely pick the gamble, because $200 would have less utility for that student. In other words, all money does not have the same subjective value.

The second component of Kahneman and Tversky's prospect theory is called *loss aversion*. According to this principle, losing is much worse than gaining is good (**Figure 8.17**).

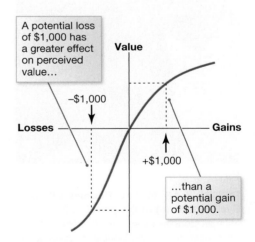

FIGURE 8.17 Loss Aversion How happy would you feel if someone walked over to you right now and handed you $1,000? How bad would you feel if someone took $1,000 from your checking account? Potential losses affect decision making more than potential gains do. In your opinion, why do people dislike losses so much?

(a)

(b)

FIGURE 8.18 Michael Douglas's Positive Outlook (a) At this point in 2010, Michael Douglas looked healthy. **(b)** After his cancer treatments, Douglas was reduced physically. In interviews, however, he expressed gratitude for the emotional benefits he received from the experience of battling a potentially terminal illness.

AFFECTIVE FORECASTING Daniel Gilbert and Timothy Wilson (2007) have found that people are not good at *affective forecasting*. That is, people are poor at predicting how they will feel about something in the future. Even more important, people generally do not realize how poor they are at predicting their future feelings. They tend to overestimate the extent to which negative events—such as breaking up with a romantic partner, losing a job, or being diagnosed with a serious medical illness—will affect them in the future (Gilbert, Pinel, Wilson, Blumberg, & Wheatley, 1998; Wilson & Gilbert, 2003). It seems that when we think about the death of a loved one, the loss of a limb, or some other tragic loss, we consider only the immediate, intense pain. Over time, however, life continues, with its daily joys and sorrows, so the pain of the loss becomes less prominent against the backdrop of everyday events.

After a negative event, people engage in strategies that help them feel better (Gilbert & Wilson, 2007). For example, they rationalize why the event happened, and they minimize the event's importance. These strategies are generally adaptive in that they protect the sufferers' mental health. After all, making sense of an event helps reduce its negative emotional consequences. Even after suffering anguish because of a negative event, most people will adapt and return to their typical positive outlook. People have an amazing capacity for manufacturing happiness. Consider the actor Michael Douglas. After undergoing severe treatments for throat cancer in 2010, Douglas said that he was grateful that the cancer made him realize the strength of his bonds with friends and family. This realization brought him great joy (Penacoli, 2011; **Figure 8.18**). Generally, however, people seem unaware that they can find positive outcomes from tragic events, so when asked to predict how they will feel following an aversive event, they overestimate their pain and underestimate how well they will cope with the event (Gilbert, Morewedge, Risen, & Wilson, 2004).

Affective forecasting can also influence our perceptions of positive events. How would you feel if you won an Olympic medal? Just about anyone would feel very good, right? Consider, however, the American tennis player Mardy Fish. As he prepared for his final match at the 2004 Athens Olympics, he fantasized about standing on the podium listening to "The Star-Spangled Banner" and having a gold medal placed around his neck. Fish's Olympic performance was amazing. He was an unseeded player who made it to the medal stand. But instead of a gold medal, he won a silver medal, and he cried tears of sadness rather than joy as he listened to the national anthem of Chile. The experience was bittersweet as he reflected on what he might have done differently to win the gold (**Figure 8.19**).

Perhaps ironically, Fish might have been happier if he had won a bronze medal instead of a silver one. According to research by the social psychologists Victoria Medvec, Scott Madey, and Thomas Gilovich, the subjective outcome of winning a silver medal can be more negative than that of winning a bronze. To test their hypothesis, Medvec and her colleagues (1995) studied videotapes of Olympic athletes' crucial moments. For instance, observers watched Jackie Joyner-Kersee complete her last long jump to win the bronze medal, Matt Biondi receive the silver medal for the 50-meter freestyle, and the Lithuanian men's basketball team receive bronze medals. They rated the athletes' facial expressions on a 10-point emotional scale, "from agony to ecstasy." The researchers found consistent evidence that, both at the moment of finding out how they did and when they were on the podium, bronze medal winners were happier than those who won silver.

When asked how you would feel if you won an Olympic medal, you probably compared winning a medal to winning no medal. But as discussed in Chapter 4, recognizing the context is crucial to determining the sort of comparison being made. Winning silver or bronze seems like quite an achievement next to winning no medal. For Olympic athletes, however, winning silver does not measure up to winning gold.

THE PARADOX OF CHOICE In modern society, many people believe that the more options they have, the better. But daily life presents an ever-widening array of choices. Major choices concern vital parts of life, such as which career path to follow and which health care plan to choose. Minor choices concern which cell phone to buy and how to have that cup of coffee (latte, cappuccino, or mocha? hot or iced? caffeinated or not? with skim or soy or regular milk?). Between the major choices and the minor ones, there exists a range of moderately important choices.

At least in Western cultures, not being able to choose violates our sense of freedom. As you will see in Chapter 9, when we are told what to do and what not to do, we react by wanting to do exactly what is forbidden to us. This response, *psychological reactance,* occurs even when we had no strong preferences before our choices were restricted. By contrast, feeling free to make our own choices generally gives us a sense of having control over our lives—something generally viewed as beneficial to mental health. But when too many options are available, especially when all of them are attractive, people experience conflict and indecision. Although some choice is better than none, some scholars note that too much choice can be frustrating, unsatisfying, and ultimately debilitating (Schwartz, 2004).

In a study by Sheena Iyengar and Mark Lepper (2000), shoppers at a grocery store were presented with a display of either 6 or 24 varieties of jam to sample. The shoppers also received a discount coupon for any variety of jam. The greater variety attracted more shoppers, but it failed to produce more sales: 30 percent of those with the limited choice bought jam, whereas only 3 percent with the greater variety did so (**Figure 8.20**). In a subsequent study, the same investigators found that people choosing among a small number of chocolates were more satisfied with the ones they selected than were people who chose from a wider variety.

FIGURE 8.19 Affective Forecasting
Mardy Fish **(left)** was disappointed when he won the silver medal for tennis at the 2004 Olympics. **At any point in your life, have you been disappointed by an outcome that someone else might have viewed as success? How did the circumstances contribute to your disappointment?**

(a)

(b)

FIGURE 8.20 Too Much Choice As part of Iyengar and Lepper's study, displays presented **(a)** 6 jams and **(b)** 24 jams. Bar-code labels on the jars indicated whether people bought more from one group of jams or the other. The results indicated that having many possibilities can make it difficult to choose one item.

According to the psychologist Barry Schwartz, having too much choice makes some people miserable. He divides the world into *satisficers* and *maximizers*. Satisficers live according to a philosophy of "good enough." Schwartz borrowed the term *satisficing* from the late Nobel laureate psychologist Herbert Simon, who described it as choosing an option that sufficiently satisfies needs. Satisficers do not lack standards. Rather, they look around until they find something that most closely matches what they want and then buy it, without worrying about whether better or cheaper products are available. They like good things, but they do not care if those things are not the best. They are the people at supermarkets who readily select their produce without going through every apple and tomato to find the very best ones.

By contrast, maximizers always seek to make the best possible choices. They devote time and effort to reading labels, checking consumer magazines, reading Internet reviews, considering alternatives, and comparing prices. They often are frustrated by the countless options available to them. They hesitate in making decisions, and they feel paralyzed by indecision when they have to select between equally attractive choices. For maximizers, making the wrong choice can have enormous consequences. Ordering the fish special for dinner means they will not have the pleasure of tasting the chicken special. What if the chicken is better than the fish? Even after they have made their selections, maximizers analyze and question their choices, often ruminating about those selections' negative features. As a result, they generally are more disappointed with their decisions and more likely to experience regret.

The paradox of choice might also be responsible for a cultural shift in the average age at which people are settling into jobs and marriage. Historically, people were set in their career paths well before age 25. Often, they were married and having children. A pattern emerging in industrialized nations is for young adults to delay decisions about these life stages for many years, as they explore their vast career options and seek mates who match their ideals (Grossman, 2005). In countries such as Canada, England, France, Germany, Italy, the United States, and Japan, the average age for marriage is approaching 30. One possible explanation for this phenomenon is that young adults are trying to maximize their life choices. They want just the right job and just the right marriage, to avoid the serious consequences of picking badly in either area.

According to Schwartz, the consequence of nearly unlimited choice may help explain the increase in clinical depression in modern countries: "If virtually every choice you make fails to live up to expectations and aspirations, and if you consistently take personal responsibility for the disappointments, the trivial looms larger and larger, and the conclusion that you can't do anything right becomes devastating" (2004, p. 215). Schwartz believes that when decisions are not crucial, people should restrict their options. They should settle for choices that meet their needs even if those choices might not be the absolute best. In addition, they should focus on the positive aspects of their decisions. Is Schwartz advising people to strive for mediocrity? If he is, perhaps picking mediocre produce is fine, especially if it saves an hour at the supermarket every time you shop (**Figure 8.21**).

FIGURE 8.21 Way Too Much Choice? Spam—a canned, precooked meat product—tends to divide people into lovers and haters. Haters of Spam would most likely not have a problem passing this display quickly. **Suppose you were a lover of Spam. How would Barry Schwartz recommend that you deal with the many varieties of Spam (and related products) offered here?**

Problem Solving Achieves Goals

Our thoughts are often focused on our goals and how to achieve them: How do you get into your car when you have locked the keys inside? How can you make enough money to spend your spring break somewhere nice? What do you have to do to get an *A* in this course? And so on. This section examines some of the best ways to solve problems. For the purposes of this discussion, a person has a problem when he or she has no simple and direct means of attaining a particular goal. To solve the problem, the person must use knowledge to determine how to move from the current state to the goal state. Often, the person must devise strategies to overcome obstacles. How the person thinks about the problem can help or hinder that person's ability to find solutions.

ORGANIZATION OF SUBGOALS One approach to the study of problem solving is to identify people's steps in solving particular problems. Researchers examine how people proceed from one step to the next, the typical errors people make in negotiating tricky or unintuitive steps, and how people decide on more efficient (or, in some cases, less efficient) solutions. For example, in the classic Tower of Hanoi problem, participants are given a board that has a row of three pegs on it. The peg on one end has three discs stacked on it in order of size: small on top, medium in the middle, large on the bottom. The task is to move the ordered stack of discs to the peg on the other end. Solving the problem requires breaking the task into *subgoals* (**Figure 8.22**).

Using subgoals is important for many problems. Suppose a high school senior has decided she would like to become a doctor. To achieve this goal, she needs first to attain the more immediate subgoal of being admitted to a good college. To get into a good college, she needs to earn good grades in high school. This additional subgoal would require developing good study skills and paying attention in class. Breaking down a problem into subgoals is an important component of problem solving. When you are facing a complex problem and the next step is not obvious, however, identifying the appropriate steps or subgoals and their order can be challenging. In a case like this, sometimes it is best to take a break from the problem. With a little distance, you may suddenly see an opening in what had looked like a solid wall. You experience *insight*.

SUDDEN INSIGHT As discussed in Chapter 5, unconscious processes can aid in solving complex problems. Indeed, unconscious processes sometimes lead to objectively better solutions than conscious processes do. How do we explain these mysterious results?

Often, a problem is not identified as a problem until it seems unsolvable and the problem solver feels stuck. For example, it is only when you spot the keys in the ignition of your locked car that you know you have a problem. Sometimes, as you stand there pondering the problem, a solution will pop into your head. **Insight** is the metaphorical mental lightbulb that goes on in your head when you suddenly realize the solution to a problem.

In 1925, the Gestalt psychologist Wolfgang Köhler conducted one of psychology's most famous examples of research on insight. Convinced that some nonhuman animals could behave intelligently, Köhler studied whether chimpanzees could solve problems. He would place a banana outside a chimp's cage, just beyond the chimp's reach, and provide several sticks that the chimp could use. Could the chimp figure out how to move the banana within grabbing distance? In one situation, neither of two sticks was long enough to reach the banana. One chimpanzee, who sat looking at the sticks for some time, suddenly grabbed the sticks and joined them together by placing one stick inside an opening in the other stick. With this longer stick, the chimp obtained the banana. Köhler argued that, after pondering the problem, the chimp had the insight to join the sticks into a tool long enough to reach the banana. Having solved

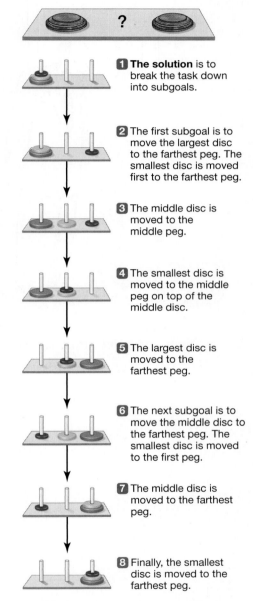

The task is to move the discs to the peg on the other end. You can move only one disc at a time. You cannot place a larger disc on top of a smaller disc.

The solution is presented below. Before you look at it, simulate the task by stacking three coins of unequal size. For example, if you have U.S. coins, use a penny, a nickel, and a quarter:

1 **The solution** is to break the task down into subgoals.

2 The first subgoal is to move the largest disc to the farthest peg. The smallest disc is moved first to the farthest peg.

3 The middle disc is moved to the middle peg.

4 The smallest disc is moved to the middle peg on top of the middle disc.

5 The largest disc is moved to the farthest peg.

6 The next subgoal is to move the middle disc to the farthest peg. The smallest disc is moved to the first peg.

7 The middle disc is moved to the farthest peg.

8 Finally, the smallest disc is moved to the farthest peg.

FIGURE 8.22 The Tower of Hanoi Problem

insight The sudden realization of a solution to a problem.

that problem, the chimp transferred this solution to similar problems and solved them quickly.

In another classic study of insight, Norman Maier (1931) brought participants, one at a time, into a room that had two strings hanging from the ceiling and a table in the corner. On the table were several random objects, including a pair of pliers. Each participant was asked to tie the strings together. However, it was impossible to grab both strings at once: If a participant was holding one string, the other string was too far away to grab. The solution was to tie the pliers onto one string and use that string as a pendulum. The participant could then hold the other string and grab the pendulum string as it swung by. Although a few participants eventually figured out this solution on their own, most people were stumped by the problem. After letting these people ponder the problem for 10 minutes, Maier casually crossed the room and brushed up against the string, causing it to swing back and forth. Once the participants saw the brushed string swinging, most immediately solved the problem, as if they had experienced a new insight. These participants did not report that Maier had given them the solution, however. It is possible that they did not even notice Maier's actions consciously. They all believed they had come up with the solution independently.

Maier's study also provides an example of how insight can be achieved when a problem initially seems unsolvable. In this case, most people had failed to see the pliers as a pendulum weight. To solve the problem, these people needed to reconsider the possible functions of the pliers and string. Thus how we view or represent a problem can significantly affect how easily we solve it. When a standard view does not work, the problem might be structured in less obvious ways. Sayings such as *think outside the box* and *think different* have become clichés (at least in Western cultures). These sayings embody ideas about insight that have been around a long time because they are of great value. Unfortunately, advice such as *think different*—or, to be grammatically correct, *think differently*—may not be very useful without hints for how to get started. In the following sections, we present a few such hints.

CHANGING REPRESENTATIONS TO OVERCOME OBSTACLES *Have you heard about the new restaurant that opened on the moon? It has great food but no atmosphere!* The premise of this joke is that *atmosphere* means one thing when interpreted in light of the restaurant schema but means something else in the context of the moon. Humor often violates an expectation, so "getting" the joke means rethinking some common representation. In problem solving, too, we often need to revise a mental representation to overcome an obstacle. This skill is exactly what we need to do crossword puzzles.

One strategy that problem solvers commonly use to overcome obstacles is **restructuring** the problem. This technique consists of representing the problem in a novel way. Ideally, the new view reveals a solution that was not visible under the old problem structure. The revelation leads to the sudden "Aha!" moment characteristic of insight. In one now-famous study, Scheerer (1963) gave each participant a sheet of paper that had a square of nine dots on it. As shown in **Figure 8.23a,** the task was to connect all nine dots using at most four straight lines, without lifting the pencil off the page. As shown in **Figure 8.23b,** one solution is truly to think outside the box: to see that keeping the lines within the

"Never, ever, think outside the box."

restructuring A new way of thinking about a problem that aids its solution.

(a) The task is to connect the dots by using at most four straight lines. Most participants consider only solutions that fit within the square formed by the dots.

(b) One solution is to extend the lines beyond the boundary formed by the dots.

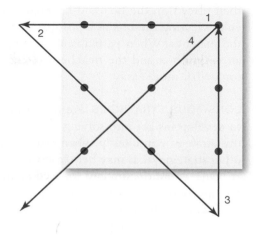

FIGURE 8.23 Scheerer's Nine-Dot Problem

box is not a requirement. People tend to think, however, that the problem includes that restriction. Another solution is to use one *very* fat line that covers all nine dots. Solving the problem requires restructuring the representation by eliminating assumed constraints.

In trying to solve a problem, we commonly think back to how we have solved similar problems. We tend to persist with previous strategies, or **mental sets.** These established ways of thinking are often useful, but sometimes they make it difficult to find the best solution.

In 1942, the Gestalt psychologist Abraham Luchins demonstrated a classic example of a mental set. He asked participants to measure out specified amounts of water, such as 100 cups, using three jars of different sizes. Say that jar A held 21 cups, jar B held 127 cups, and jar C held 3 cups. The solution to this problem was to fill jar B, use jar A to remove 21 cups from jar B's 127 cups, then use jar C to remove 3 cups of water twice, leaving 100 cups in jar B. The structure to the solution is $B - A - 2(C)$. Participants were given many of these problems. In each problem, the jar sizes and goal measurements differed, but the same formula applied. Then participants were given another problem: They were given jar A, which held 23 cups; jar B, which held 49 cups; and jar C, which held 3 cups. They were asked to measure out 20 cups. Even though the simplest solution was to fill jar A and use jar C to remove 3 cups from jar A's 23, participants usually came up with a much more complicated solution that involved all three jars. Having developed a mental set of using three jars in combination to solve this type of problem, they had trouble settling on the simpler solution of using only two jars. Surprisingly, when given a problem with a simple solution for which the original formula did not work, many participants failed to solve the problem most efficiently (**Figure 8.24**).

As demonstrated by Maier's experiment with strings and pliers, we also have mental representations about the typical functions of particular objects. Such *functional fixedness* can also create difficulties in problem solving. To overcome this kind of obstacle, the problem solver needs to reinterpret the object's potential function. One research example involves the candle problem, developed by Karl Duncker (1945). Participants are given a candle, a box of matches, a bulletin board, a box of tacks, and the following challenge: *Using only these objects, attach the candle to the bulletin board in such a way that the candle can be lit and burn*

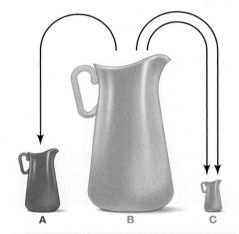

	Desired water	Jar A	Jar B	Jar C
Trial 1	100	21	127	3
Trial 2	8	18	48	11
Trial 3	62	10	80	4
Trial 4	31	20	59	4
Trial 5	29	20	57	4
Trial 6	20	23	49	3
Trial 7	25	28	76	3

FIGURE 8.24 Luchins's Mental Set

mental sets Problem solving strategies that have worked in the past.

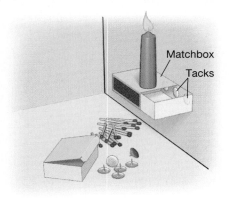

The task is to attach a candle to the bulletin board using only a box of matches and a box of tacks.

Matchbox

Tacks

The solution requires restructuring our concept of the matchbox by using it as a stand for the candle.

FIGURE 8.25 Overcoming Functional Fixedness

properly. Most people have difficulty in coming up with an adequate solution. If they reinterpret the function of the box, however, a solution emerges. The side of the box is tacked to the bulletin board so that it creates a stand. The candle is then placed on the box and lit (**Figure 8.25**). In general, participants have difficulty viewing the box as a possible stand when it is being used as a container for the matches. When participants are shown representations of this problem with an empty box and the matches on the table next to it, they solve the problem somewhat more easily.

CONSCIOUS STRATEGIES Restructuring mental representations is a valuable way to develop insight into solving a problem. Still, we often find it difficult to enact this strategy consciously when we are stuck. Fortunately, we can always apply other strategies that may help lead to a solution.

One common strategy for overcoming obstacles is *working backward*. When the appropriate steps for solving a problem are not clear, proceeding from the goal state to the initial state can help yield a solution. Consider the water lily problem (Fixx, 1978, p. 50):

> Water lilies double in area every 24 hours. On the first day of summer there is only one water lily on the lake. It takes 60 days for the lake to be completely covered in water lilies. How many days does it take for half of the lake to be covered in water lilies?

One way to solve this problem is to work from the initial state to the goal state: You figure that on day 1 there is one water lily, on day 2 there are two water lilies, on day 3 there are four water lilies, and so on, until you discover how many water lilies there are on day 60 and you see which day had half that many. But if you work backward, from the goal state to the initial state, you realize that if on day 60 the lake is covered in water lilies and that *water lilies double every 24 hours,* then on day 59 half of the lake must have been covered in water lilies.

Another common strategy for overcoming a problem solving obstacle is *finding an appropriate analogy* (Reeves & Weisberg, 1994). Say that a surgeon needs to use a laser at high intensity to destroy a patient's tumor. The surgeon must aim that laser so as to avoid destroying the surrounding healthy tissue. The surgeon remembers reading a story about a general who wanted to capture a fortress. The general needed to move a large number of soldiers up to the fortress, but all the roads to the fortress were planted with mines. A large group of soldiers would have set off the mines, but a small group could travel safely. So the general divided the soldiers into small groups and had each group take a different road to the fortress, where the groups converged and attacked together. Because her problem has constraints *analogous* to the general's problem, the doctor gets the idea to aim several lasers at the tumor from different angles. By itself, each laser will be weak enough to avoid destroying the living tissue in its path. But the combined intensity of all the converging lasers will be enough to destroy the tumor.

Transferring a problem solving strategy means using a strategy that works in one context to solve a problem that is structurally similar. To accomplish this kind of transfer, we must pay attention to the structure of each problem. For this reason, analogous problems may enhance our ability to solve each one. Some researchers have found that participants who solve two or more analogous problems develop a schema that helps them solve similar problems (Gick & Holyoak, 1983). Analogous solutions work, however, only if we recognize the similarities between the problem we face and those we have solved (Keane, 1987; Reeves & Weisberg, 1994).

Finding appropriate analogies can also help us achieve our goals. For example, recent immigrants often have difficulty navigating the customs and expectations of their new environment. For them, other immigrants with a similar background who have succeeded in the new country and culture provide examples of paths that lead to success. When we look to role models, we hope that their goals will enable us to achieve a similar outcome if we follow analogous paths.

Summing Up

How Do We Make Decisions and Solve Problems?

When drawing conclusions, we engage in deductive and inductive reasoning. Deductive reasoning involves reasoning from the general to the specific. Inductive reasoning involves reasoning from the specific to the general. When making decisions, we select among alternatives. Normative models of decision making were once assumed to be accurate; these model maintain that we are optimal decision makers. Research has demonstrated, however, that we are not rational in making decisions. Consistent with descriptive models of decision making, we often use heuristics when making decisions. The use of these mental shortcuts can lead to faulty outcomes. Research has also shown that decision making is influenced by how information is presented (framing) and our beliefs about how we will feel in the future (affective forecasting). When solving problems, we overcome obstacles to reach a goal. Insight often occurs suddenly, when we realize a solution to a problem. Problem solving may require that we break a problem down into subgoals, restructure the problem, work backward from the goal, or transfer an effective strategy from an appropriate analogy to the problem. Mental sets and functional fixedness inhibit our problem solving ability.

Measuring Up

1. For each of the following terms, identify the appropriate descriptions. Each term might have more than one description, and some descriptions might not apply to any term.

   _____ reasoning
   _____ decision making
   _____ problem solving

   a. There are multiple alternatives to select from.
   b. There is a barrier between the present state and the desired goal.
   c. Conclusions are deductively valid if they follow from the premises.
   d. Conclusions are true if they follow from the premises.
   e. There may be multiple ways to get around a barrier.
   f. If a premise is assumed to be correct, certain conclusions will follow.
   g. There is always only one solution.

2. In performing affective forecasting, _____.
   a. most people are poor judges of how they will feel about something in the future
   b. forecasters predict phenomena such as the weather and the stock market's performance
   c. most people underestimate the negative emotions they will experience as a result of their decisions
   d. scientists are more accurate in predicting their future emotions because they work with scientific principles

Answers: 1. reasoning—c, f, d; decision making—a; problem solving—b, e, g. 2. a. most people are poor judges of how they will feel about something in the future.

Learning Objectives

- Identify common measures of intelligence.

- Discuss the validity of measures of intelligence.

- Review theory and research related to general intelligence, fluid intelligence, crystallized intelligence, multiple intelligences, and emotional intelligence.

- Discuss the relationship between intelligence and cognitive performance.

- Summarize research examining genetic and environmental influences on intelligence.

- Discuss sex and race differences in intelligence.

- Define stereotype threat.

8.3 How Do We Understand Intelligence?

So far, this chapter has considered how we use knowledge when we think. Now it is time to consider what it means to think *intelligently*.

Sometimes our thought processes lead to great ideas and creative discoveries, but other times they lead to bad decisions and regret. Inevitably, some people seem to be better at using knowledge than others. When people are good at using knowledge, we say they are intelligent. Thus **intelligence** is the ability to use knowledge to reason, make decisions, make sense of events, solve problems, understand complex ideas, learn quickly, and adapt to environmental challenges.

Individuals differ in terms of intelligence just as they differ physically and in terms of their personalities. We observe people's physical differences. We also observe their personality differences, such as in how shy people are or how much they worry. But how do we know each person's level of intelligence? Psychologists consider two aspects of this question: They study the ways that knowledge and its applications in everyday life translate into intelligence, and they examine the degree to which intelligence is determined by genes and by environment (Neisser et al., 1996).

Intelligence Is Assessed with Psychometric Tests

The *psychometric* approach to measuring intelligence focuses on how people perform on standardized achievement tests. In other words: What do people know, and how do they solve problems? For much of the past century, the psychometric approach to intelligence has been the most dominant and influential. This approach has especially affected how we view intelligence in everyday life.

Some psychometric tests focus on *achievement*. That is, they assess people's current levels of skill and of knowledge. In the United States, millions of schoolchildren take these kinds of exams every three years as mandated by the federal government as part of the No Child Left Behind Act (2001). Other psychometric tests focus on *aptitude*. They seek to predict what tasks, and perhaps even what jobs, people will be good at in the future. For both kinds of tests, the stakes can be high. People's performances can hugely affect their lives.

The psychometric measurement of intelligence began just over a century ago. At the encouragement of the French government, the psychologist Alfred Binet developed the first method of assessing intelligence (**Figure 8.26**). Binet's goal was to identify children in the French school system who needed extra attention and special instruction. Binet proposed that intelligence is best understood as a collection of high-level mental processes. Accordingly, with the help of his assistant Théodore Simon, Binet developed a test for measuring each child's vocabulary, memory, skill with numbers, and other mental abilities. The result was the Binet-Simon Intelligence Scale. One assumption underlying the test was that each child might do better on some components by chance, but how the child performed on average across the different components would indicate his or her overall level of intelligence. Indeed, Binet found that scores on his tests were consistent with teachers' beliefs about children's abilities *and* with the children's grades.

A number of other intelligence tests have been developed. In 1919, the psychologist Lewis Terman, at Stanford University, modified the Binet-Simon test and established normative scores for American children (average scores for

FIGURE 8.26 Alfred Binet Binet launched the psychometric approach to assessing intelligence.

each age). This test—the Stanford Revision of the Binet-Simon Scale, known colloquially as the Stanford-Binet test—remains among the most widely used for children in the United States. In 2003, it was revised for the fifth time. In 1939, the psychologist David Wechsler developed a test for use among adults. The Wechsler Adult Intelligence Scale (WAIS)—the most current version being the WAIS-IV, released in 2008—has two parts. Each part consists of several tasks. The *verbal* part measures aspects such as comprehension, vocabulary, and general knowledge. The *performance* part involves nonverbal tasks, such as arranging pictures in proper order, assembling parts to make a whole object, and identifying a picture's missing features.

INTELLIGENCE QUOTIENT Binet noticed that some children seem to think like younger or older normal children. To assess a child's intellectual standing compared with the standing of same-age peers, Binet introduced the important concept of **mental age.** This measure is determined by comparing the child's test score with the average score for children of each chronological age. For instance, an 8-year-old who is able to read Shakespeare and do calculus might score as well as an average 16-year-old. This 8-year-old would have a mental age of 16. The **intelligence quotient (IQ),** developed by the psychologist Wilhelm Stern, is computed by dividing a child's estimated mental age by the child's chronological age and multiplying the result by 100. To calculate the IQ of the 8-year-old with a mental age of 16, we calculate 16/8 × 100. The result is 200, an extraordinarily high score.

The formula breaks down when used with adults, however, so the IQs of adults are measured differently. According to the formula, a 60-year-old would need to get twice as many test items correct as a 30-year-old to have the same IQ. Instead, IQ in the adult range is measured in comparison with the average adult and not with adults at different ages. Today, the average IQ is set at 100. Across large groups of people, the distribution of IQ scores forms a bell curve, or *normal distribution.* Most people are close to the average, and fewer and fewer people score at the tails of the distribution (**Figure 8.27**).

VALIDITY OF TESTING Are intelligence tests valid? That is, do they really measure what they claim to measure? To evaluate the tests, we need to consider what it means to be intelligent. If the word means doing well at school or at a complex career, intelligence tests perform reasonably well: The overall evidence indicates that IQ is a fairly good predictor of such life outcomes (Gottfredson, 2004b).

intelligence The ability to use knowledge to reason, make decisions, make sense of events, solve problems, understand complex ideas, learn quickly, and adapt to environmental challenges.

mental age An assessment of a child's intellectual standing compared with that of same-age peers; determined by comparing the child's test score with the average score for children of each chronological age.

intelligence quotient (IQ) An index of intelligence computed by dividing a child's estimated mental age by the child's chronological age, then multiplying this number by 100.

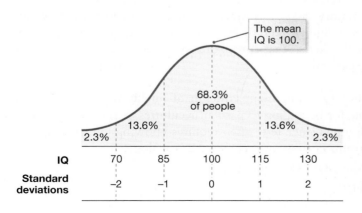

FIGURE 8.27 **The Distribution of IQ Scores** IQ is a score on a normed test of intelligence. That is, one person's score is relative to the scores of the large number of people who already took the test. And as discussed in Chapter 2, the statistical concept of standard deviation indicates how far people are from an average. The standard deviation for most IQ tests is 15. The average, or mean, is 100. As shown in this bell curve, approximately 68 percent of people fall within 1 standard deviation of the mean (they score from 85 to 115). Just over 95 percent of people fall within 2 standard deviations (they score from 70 to 130).

"I don't have to be smart, because someday I'll just hire lots of smart people to work for me."

To explore the validity of intelligence tests, researchers analyzed data from 127 different studies. In total, as part of these 127 studies, more than 20,000 participants took the Miller Analogy Test. This test is widely used for admissions decisions into graduate school as well as for hiring decisions in many work settings. It requires test takers to complete analogies such as "Fingers are to hands as toes are to ____." The researchers found that scores on the Miller Analogy Test predicted not only graduate students' academic performances but also individuals' productivity, creativity, and job performances in the workplace (Kuncel, Hezlett, & Ones, 2004). Similarly, people in professional careers—such as attorneys, accountants, and physicians—tend to have high IQs, while those who work as miners, farmers, lumberjacks, barbers, and so on tend to have lower IQs (Jencks, 1979; Schmidt & Hunter, 2004). These statistics refer to averages, of course, not to individuals. Still, the data suggest modest correlations between IQ and work performance, IQ and income, IQ and jobs requiring complex skills. Although higher IQ does not predict who will be a better truck driver, it predicts who will be a better computer programmer (Schmidt & Hunter, 2004).

When considering these findings, note that IQ scores typically predict only about 25 percent of the variation in performance at either school or work, so additional factors contribute to individuals' success (Neisser et al., 1996). For example, people from privileged backgrounds tend to have higher IQs, but they also tend to have other advantages. Family contacts, access to internships, and acceptance to schools that can cater to their needs may help determine their success. Moreover, people have greatly different amounts of motivation, and they differ greatly in how much time they are willing to spend to get ahead. One 20-year follow-up study of nearly 2,000 gifted 13-year-olds (those with IQs in the top 1 percent of their age group) revealed huge differences in how much people reported working as well as how much they were willing to work. At age 33, some individuals refused to work more than 40 hours per week, whereas others reported regularly working more than 70 (Lubinski & Benbow, 2000). Even with factors such as IQ and social background being more or less equal, a person working twice as many hours per week may have that much more chance of accomplishing his or her goals (Lubinski, 2004). Another study found that children's self-control, assessed through teacher and parent reports as well as laboratory tasks, was much better than IQ in predicting final grades (Duckworth & Seligman, 2005). In other words, IQ may be important, but it is only one of the factors that contribute to success in the classroom, the workplace, and life generally.

CULTURAL BIAS One important criticism of intelligence tests is that they may penalize people for belonging to particular cultures or particular groups. That is, doing well on intelligence tests often requires knowing the language and culture of the mainstream. For instance, consider this analogy:

STRING is to GUITAR as REED is to

a. TRUMPET

b. OBOE

c. VIOLIN

d. TROMBONE

To solve this analogy, you need specific knowledge of these instruments. In particular, you must know that an oboe uses a reed to make music. Unless you were exposed to this information and had an opportunity to learn it, you could not answer the question. In addition, some words mean different things to different groups, and how a person answers a test item is determined by the meaning of that item in his or her culture. When Randy Jackson on *American Idol* describes someone's performance as "da bomb," he does not mean she or he "bombed," or did badly. He means it was "cool," which does not mean it was cold. And so on. A person's exposure to mainstream language and mainstream culture affects which meaning of a word comes most quickly to mind, if the person knows the meaning at all.

What it means to be intelligent also varies across cultures. Most measures of IQ reflect values of what is considered important in modern Western culture, such as being quick-witted or speaking well. But what is adaptive in one society is not necessarily adaptive in others. One approach to dealing with cultural bias is to use items that do not depend on language. For example, the performance measures on the WAIS, discussed earlier, may be a fairer way to test intelligence. Other culture-neutral tests show a series of patterns and ask the test taker to identify the missing pattern (**Figure 8.28**). Still, most of the proposed substitutes for intelligence tests, such as interviews and ratings of job performance, are also biased. Sometimes it is difficult to detect and quantify the bias in intelligence assessments.

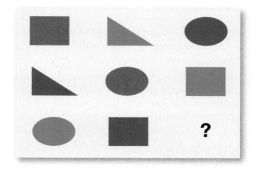

The task is to identify the missing shape in this sequence.

Choose from the eight shapes below to complete the sequence:

The solution is the first triangle in the bottom row.

FIGURE 8.28 Removing Bias from Tests According to the creators of this test, the task is not culturally biased. Do you agree? Why or why not?

Recognizing and Avoiding Reification

Reification is the tendency to think about complex traits as though they have a single cause and an objective reality. A good example of reification is the complex concept of intelligence. Because we measure intelligence with IQ scores, people tend to think intelligence can be understood with these numbers. As discussed earlier, IQ is a number derived from a normed intelligence test. If you score near the mean, your IQ is close to 100. If you score in the top 2 percent, your score is higher than 130. The number conveys how you scored relative to the people who were in the sample used to norm the test. It is not synonymous with intelligence. For example, if English is your native language but you speak enough Spanish to take an intelligence test in Spanish, you probably would not expect the resulting IQ to reflect your intelligence accurately. Intelligence is a multifaceted concept defined within a context, not just by a score in isolation.

Compare the concept of intelligence with that of weight. We can measure, gain, and lose weight. These qualities make weight seem similar to intelligence. Weight has a physical reality, however, that makes it unlike intelligence. When we think about intelligence as having physical reality, we are reifying the concept. Once we think about IQ as though it explains intelligence, we are ignoring all the problems with intelligence tests, including possible cultural biases. Critical thinkers avoid treating an abstract concept as though it has a tangible reality. They recognize the complexity in complex concepts.

It is also difficult to remove all forms of bias from testing situations. Doing well on tests, among them IQ tests, simply matters more to some groups than to others. Tests generally favor those who wish to do well.

General Intelligence Involves Multiple Components

Binet viewed intelligence as a general ability. We all know people, however, who are especially talented in some areas but weak in others. For example, some people write brilliant poems but cannot solve difficult calculus problems—or at least they feel more confident doing one than doing the other. The question, then, is whether intelligence reflects one overall talent or many individual ones. An early line of research examined the correlations among intelligence test items using *factor analysis*. In this statistical technique, items similar to one another are clustered, and the clusters are referred to as factors. Using this method, Charles Spearman (1904) found that most intelligence test items tended to cluster as one factor. People who scored highly on one type of item also tended to score highly on other types of items. In general, people who are very good at math are also good at writing, problem solving, and other mental challenges. Spearman viewed **general intelligence,** or **g,** as a factor that contributes to performance on any intellectual task (**Figure 8.29**). In a sense, providing a single IQ score reflects the idea that one general factor underlies intelligence.

general intelligence (g) The idea that one general factor underlies intelligence.

THE IMPORTANCE OF G Research has shown that g influences important life outcomes, such as by predicting performance in school and at work (Conway, Kane, & Engle, 2003; Deary, 2001; Garlick, 2002; Gray & Thompson, 2004; Haier, Jung, Yeo, Head, & Alkire, 2005). Low g is related to early death from causes including heart disease, diabetes, stroke, Alzheimer's disease, traffic accidents, and drownings (Gottfredson, 2004a; Gottfredson & Deary, 2004). One study followed Scottish people for 55 years, starting when they were schoolchildren, and examined the influence of intelligence and a personality variable related to emotional intelligence. Those who scored in the lower half on both measures were more than twice as likely to die over the next half century compared with those who scored in the top half on both measures (Deary, Batty, Pattie, & Gale, 2008).

These patterns might result from the different environmental forces at work on each of us. For example, people who do not perform well in academic settings may end up with dangerous jobs, people with less dangerous and/or better-paying jobs tend to have better access to health care, and so on. Indeed, it is possible that factors other than intelligence are responsible for early death. A study that followed people from age 10 until age 75 found that the more education people received, the longer they lived, independent of their IQ level (Lager, Bremberg, & Vågerö, 2009). Researchers from the United Kingdom and Finland found that lower socioeconomic status may be the most important predictor of early mortality (Jokela, Elovainio, Singh-Manoux, & Kivimäki, 2009).

According to Linda Gottfredson (2004a), however, g may directly affect health. People who score higher on intelligence tests may generally be more literate about health issues: accumulating greater health knowledge, better able to follow medical advice, better able to understand the link between behavior and health. As medical knowledge rapidly advances and becomes more complex, trying to keep up with and process all this new information is a challenge, and people who are higher in g have an advantage in doing so. This provocative idea warrants further investigation. If it is true, it has a number of important implications for the medical system and the way doctors communicate medical advice.

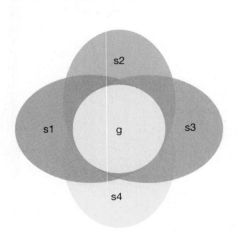

g = general intelligence

s1 = a specific ability
(e.g., math)

s2 = a second specific ability
(e.g., writing)

s3 = a third specific ability
(e.g., problem solving)

s4 = a fourth specific ability
(e.g., drawing)

FIGURE 8.29 General Intelligence as a Factor As depicted in this cluster of overlapping ovals and circle, Spearman viewed g as a general factor in intelligence. This underlying factor influences an individual's specific abilities related to intelligence.

A number of theorists have proposed that g's main value is in allowing people to adapt quickly to environmental challenges. The more complex the challenge, the greater g's importance. Satoshi Kanazawa (2004) suggests that general intelligence is relevant only in novel situations. He notes that for most of human evolution, our ancestors were hunter-gatherers who experienced few changes in their daily routines. Indeed, the lives of prehistoric hunter-gatherers remained pretty much the same as their ancestors' lives going back thousands of years. Only during the occasional novel event, such as a drought or other natural disaster, did those high in general intelligence have an advantage.

According to Kanazawa, one's level of intelligence does not matter for recurring adaptive challenges. For this reason, it has little influence over many aspects of daily human life, such as figuring out what to eat, finding mates, recognizing friends, and raising children. Indeed, people with high levels of intelligence have no advantage in these domains. For instance, there is no evidence that people with high g make better parents (Herrnstein & Murray, 1994). But today we encounter a multitude of phenomena that scarcely could be imagined even a century or two ago: automobiles, airplanes, electric appliances, high-rise buildings, televisions, computers, wireless telephones, international conglomerates, and so on. Such inventions and institutions increase the value of adapting to novel challenges and of thinking creatively. The overall evidence is consistent with the idea that g is most valuable for understanding novel, complex information (Lubinski, 2004). Although most psychologists agree that some form of g exists, however, they also recognize that intelligence comes in various forms.

FLUID VERSUS CRYSTALLIZED INTELLIGENCE Raymond Cattell (1971) proposed that g consists of two types of intelligence. **Fluid intelligence** involves information processing, especially in novel or complex circumstances, such as reasoning, drawing analogies, and thinking quickly and flexibly. It is often assessed in nonverbal, more culture-fair intelligence tests (such as the one in Figure 8.28). In contrast, **crystallized intelligence** involves knowledge we acquire through experience, such as vocabulary and cultural information, and the ability to use this knowledge to solve problems (Horn, 1968; Horn & McArdle, 2007). Distinguishing between fluid intelligence and crystallized intelligence is somewhat analogous to distinguishing between working memory (which is more like fluid intelligence) and long-term memory (which is more like crystallized intelligence). As would be expected because both types of intelligence are components of g, people who score highly on one factor also tend to score highly on the other. This finding suggests that a strong crystallized intelligence is likely aided by a strong fluid intelligence. As you will see in Chapter 9, crystallized intelligence grows steadily throughout the adult years, while fluid intelligence declines steadily.

MULTIPLE INTELLIGENCES Whereas Cattell argued that two types of intelligence contribute to g, Howard Gardner (1983) proposed a theory of **multiple intelligences.** Gardner identified different types of intellectual talents that are independent of one another. For example, he proposed that musical intelligence enables some people to discriminate subtle variations in pitch or in timbre and therefore to have an above-average appreciation of music (**Figure 8.30a**). Among the other intelligences Gardner proposed are bodily-kinesthetic (such as the forms that make athletes and dancers highly attuned to their bodies and able to control their motions with exquisite skill; **Figure 8.30b**), linguistic (excellent verbal skills), mathematical/logical, spatial (thinking in terms of images and pictures), intrapersonal (self-understanding), and interpersonal (social understanding).

fluid intelligence Intelligence that reflects the ability to process information, particularly in novel or complex circumstances.

crystallized intelligence Intelligence that reflects both the knowledge one acquires through experience and the ability to use that knowledge.

multiple intelligences The idea that there are different types of intelligence that are independent of one another.

(a)

(b)

FIGURE 8.30 One Theory of Multiple Intelligences Howard Gardner has theorized that intelligence can take many different forms. Here two types of intelligence—musical and bodily-kinesthetic—are represented by **(a)** the musician Yo-Yo Ma and **(b)** the athlete Mia Hamm.

FIGURE 8.31 A Second Theory of Multiple Intelligences Robert Sternberg has theorized that intelligence can take three forms. Here two types of intelligence—analytical and creative—are represented by **(a)** the scientist Shirley Jackson and **(b)** the artist Andy Warhol **(left front).**

Gardner's theory is important partly because it recognizes that people can be average or even deficient in some domains and outstanding in others. According to Gardner, each person has a unique pattern of intelligences and no one should be viewed as smarter than others, just differently talented. This view strikes some psychologists as a feel-good philosophy with little basis in fact. These critics have questioned whether being able to control body movements or compose music is truly a form of intelligence or should instead be considered a specialized talent. Is clumsiness or tone deafness a form of unintelligence? There are still no standardized ways to assess many of Gardner's intelligences. In fact, Gardner believes that standard testing methods are unable to capture the true essence of different types of intelligence. Thus, to support his theory, Gardner provides examples of people who have exhibited particular talents, such as the artist Pablo Picasso, the dancer Martha Graham, the physicist Albert Einstein, and the poet T. S. Eliot. Each of these figures was especially talented in his or her field, but they were also talented in many respects, and all were high in general intelligence (Gottfredson, 2004b).

Robert Sternberg (1999) has theorized that there are three types of intelligence. *Analytical intelligence* is similar to that measured by psychometric tests— being good at problem solving, completing analogies, figuring out puzzles, and other academic challenges (**Figure 8.31a**). *Creative intelligence* involves the ability to gain insight and solve novel problems—to think in new and interesting ways (**Figure 8.31b**). *Practical intelligence* refers to dealing with everyday tasks, such as knowing whether a parking space is large enough for your vehicle, being a good judge of people, being an effective leader, and so on. Evidence for the existence of such multiple intelligences is that many phenomenally successful public figures did not excel academically. For example, Bill Gates dropped out of college, yet he developed one of the world's largest companies, became the world's richest person, and has embarked on a second "career" as a philanthropist. Might Gates's talents not be measured on standardized intelligence tests?

EMOTIONAL INTELLIGENCE **Emotional intelligence (EI)** was conceived by the psychologists Peter Salovey and John Mayer and subsequently popularized by the science writer Daniel Goleman. This form of social intelligence consists of four abilities: to manage our own emotions, to use our own emotions to guide thoughts and actions, to recognize other people's emotions, and to understand emotional language (Salovey & Grewel, 2005; Salovey & Mayer, 1990). People high in EI recognize emotional experiences in themselves and others, then respond to those emotions productively. As you will see in Chapter 10, emotions sometimes overwhelm cognition and undermine motivation. For instance, when we are upset, we may act impulsively and thoughtlessly by lashing out at others, eating too much chocolate, or doing other things we later regret. Regulating our moods, resisting impulses and temptations, and controlling our behaviors are all important components of EI.

Emotional intelligence is correlated with the quality of social relationships (Reis et al., 2007). The idea of emotional intelligence has had a large impact in schools and industry, and programs have been designed to increase students' and workers' emotional intelligence. These efforts may be valuable, since emotional intelligence is a good predictor of high school grades (Hogan et al., 2010) and those high in emotional intelligence cope best with the challenges of college exams (Austin, Saklofske, & Mastoras, 2010). At the same time, some critics have questioned whether EI really is a type of intelligence or whether it stretches the definition of intelligence too far. A recent review found evidence that EI is correlated with more-traditional measures of intelligence, as well as academic performance among children and workplace performance among senior executives (Brackett, Rivers, & Salovey, 2011). The concept highlights the idea that many human qualities are important. Whether or not EI is a type of intelligence, it is advantageous for those who have it.

emotional intelligence (EI) A form of social intelligence that emphasizes the abilities to manage, recognize, and understand emotions and use emotions to guide appropriate thought and action.

Intelligence Is Associated with Cognitive Performance

In the late 1800s, the scientist Sir Francis Galton led one of the earliest efforts to study intelligence. Galton believed that intelligence was related to the speed of neural responses and the sensitivity of the sensory/perceptual systems. The smartest people, Galton believed, had the quickest responses and the keenest perceptions. Galton also speculated that intelligent people have larger, more efficient brains. According to Galton, intelligence is related to the efficiency of the brain as well as to keen perceptual skills. Other psychologists believe intelligence is supported by low-level cognitive processes, such as mental processing, working memory, and attention. But can we equate these types of cognitive performance with intelligence? What brain processes are involved in producing intelligence?

SPEED OF MENTAL PROCESSING People who are not very intelligent are sometimes described as "a bit slow." That description might be accurate, because people who score higher on intelligence tests respond more quickly and consistently on reaction time tests than those who score lower on intelligence tests (Deary, 2000). A test of *simple reaction time* might require a person to press a computer key as quickly as possible whenever a stimulus appears on the screen. For example, "Press the X key every time you see an X." A more difficult test might require a person to choose, again as quickly as possible, the right response

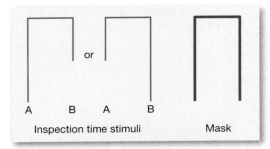

The task is to determine whether side A or side B of the stimulus is longer. The stimulus is presented and then quickly followed by a mask.

or

A   B   A   B

Inspection time stimuli   Mask

Judging the lengths is easy when you have enough time to view the stimulus but difficult when the mask decreases viewing time severely.

FIGURE 8.32 Inspection Time Tasks

for the stimulus presented. For example, "Press the X key every time you see an X, press the A key every time you see an A, and so on." Scores on intelligence tests are related even more strongly to this *choice reaction time* (Jensen, 1998). (For more information, see the discussion of reaction time measures in Chapter 2, "Research Methodology.")

Further support for the relation between general intelligence and speed of mental processing comes from *inspection time* tests. If a stimulus is presented and then covered up, how much viewing time does a particular person need to answer a question about the stimulus (**Figure 8.32**)? People who need very little time for this task tend to score higher on psychometric tests of intelligence (Deary, 2001). In addition, by measuring the electrical activity of brains in response to the presentation of stimuli, researchers have found that highly intelligent people's brains work faster than less intelligent people's brains.

The relation between general intelligence and mental speed appears to be correlated with the greater longevity of people with high IQs. According to a longitudinal study led by Ian Deary, those higher in intelligence and those who had faster reaction times at age 56 were much less likely to die in the next 14 years (Deary & Der, 2005). This outcome was true even after factors such as smoking, social class, and education were controlled for. The relationship between reaction time and longevity was somewhat stronger than the relationship between scores on standardized intelligence tests and longevity. Although the various response time measures lead to the conclusion that intelligence is associated with speed of mental processing, researchers are far from knowing what this finding means. Perhaps being able to process information quickly is just one of the many talents possessed by people high in general intelligence. This ability may allow them to solve problems, or make decisions, quickly when doing so is advantageous. The adaptive value of quick reaction time is obvious when you consider that lives hang on the snap judgments of firefighters (as in an example discussed earlier in this chapter), police officers, emergency room personnel, soldiers in combat, and so on.

WORKING MEMORY General intelligence scores are closely related to working memory (Conway et al., 2003). The two are not identical, however (Ackerman, Beier, & Boyle, 2005). As discussed in Chapter 7, working memory is the active processing system that holds information for use in activities such as reasoning, comprehension, and problem solving. In that capacity, working memory might be related to intelligence (Kyllonen & Christal, 1990; Süß, Oberauer, Wittman, Wilhelm, & Schulze, 2002). Many studies of the relationship between working memory and intelligence differentiate between simple tests of memory span and memory tests that require some form of secondary processing (**Figure 8.33**). Performance on a simpler test of memory, as in listening to a list of words and then repeating the list in the same order, is related weakly to general intelligence (Engle, Tuholski, Laughlin, & Conway, 1999). Memory tests that have dual components, however, show a strong relation between working memory and general intelligence (Gray & Thompson, 2004; Kane, Hambrick, & Conway, 2005; Oberauer, Schulze, Wilhelm, & Süß, 2005).

The link between working memory and general intelligence may be attention. In particular, being able to pay attention, especially while being bombarded with competing information or other distractions, allows a person to stick to a task until successfully completing it (Engle & Kane, 2004). The importance of staying focused makes great sense in light of the relationship, discussed earlier, between general intelligence and the accomplishment of novel, complex tasks. The question,

FIGURE 8.33 Memory Span Tasks

For a simple *word span task*, a participant listens to a short list of words and then repeats the words in order.

For a more difficult *secondary processing task*, a participant has to solve simple mathematical operations at the same time the words are presented. Once again, the person has to repeat the words in the order they are presented (adapted from Conway et al., 2003).

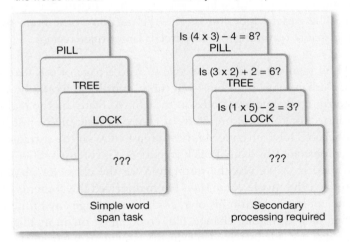

Simple word span task

Secondary processing required

then, is whether brain regions that support working memory are involved in general intelligence.

BRAIN STRUCTURE AND FUNCTION Intelligent people are sometimes called "brainy," but how are the brain and intelligence related? Many studies have documented a relationship between head circumference, which researchers use to estimate brain size, and scores on intelligence tests (Vernon, Wickett, Bazana, Stelmack, & Sternberg, 2000). Head circumference also predicts school performance, although the correlation is quite small (Ivanovic et al., 2004). Studies using magnetic resonance imaging have found a small but significant correlation between the size of selected brain structures and scores on intelligence tests (Johnson, Jung, Colom, & Haier, 2008; for information on MRI, see Chapter 2, "Research Methodology"). A meta-analysis with a total of over 1,500 participants found a connection between brain volume, as assessed by MRI, and about 10 percent of the differences in people's general intelligence (McDaniel, 2005). These findings are correlations, however, so we cannot infer that brain size necessarily causes differences in intelligence.

Instead, the situation is more complicated. Different kinds of intelligence seem to be related to the sizes of certain brain regions. These regions include ones associated with working memory, planning, reasoning, and problem solving. For example, studies have found that the volume of neuronal cell bodies (gray matter) in the frontal lobes and in other brain regions that support attentional control is related to fluid intelligence (Frangou, Chitins, & Williams, 2004; Haier et al., 2005; Wilke, Sohn, Byars, & Holland, 2003). Other studies have found no relation between the volume of those neuronal cell bodies and crystallized intelligence (Gong et al., 2005). Thus general intelligence appears to be associated mainly with increased cortex (Kamara et al., 2011). These findings are consistent with evidence that injury to the frontal lobes causes impairments in fluid intelligence but not in crystallized intelligence (Duncan, Burgess, & Emslie, 1995).

FIGURE 8.34 Extraordinary Brain
Sandra Witelson with Einstein's brain in her lab at McMaster University. **Does the size of Einstein's parietal lobe indicate that larger brains are smarter? Why or why not?**

Sandra Witelson, a Canadian neuroscientist at McMaster University, has her own personal collection of brains—125 of them, all from Canadians. She also has an enviable specimen from outside Canada: She is the official keeper of Albert Einstein's brain (**Figure 8.34**). (A pathologist at Princeton Hospital, where Einstein died, stole Einstein's brain and later gave it to Witelson to study. Although the pathologist lost his job for this famous theft, he reports not regretting his actions [Roberts, 2006].) Einstein's brain is rather unremarkable in overall size and weight. The parietal lobe, however—the portion of the brain used in visual thinking and spatial reasoning—is 15 percent larger than average.

SAVANTS How would you like to be able to read a page of this textbook in 8 to 10 seconds? Perhaps less useful but even more impressive would be the ability to recite all the zip codes and area codes in the United States by the region to which they are assigned, or to name hundreds of classical music pieces just by hearing a few notes of each. These amazing abilities are just a few of the extraordinary memory feats demonstrated by Kim Peek (Treffert & Christensen, 2006). Mr. Peek, a savant who died in 2008, was the inspiration for the character played by Dustin Hoffman in the 1988 movie *Rain Man*. He memorized the contents of over 9,000 books, but he could not button his own clothes or manage any of the usual chores of daily living, such as making change. He scored an 87 on an intelligence test, but this number did not adequately describe his intelligence. Mr. Peek was born, in 1951, with an enlarged head and many brain anomalies, including a missing corpus callosum, the thick band of nerves that connects the brain's two halves. He also had abnormalities in several other parts of his brain, especially the left hemisphere.

We know very little about *savants*. These people have minimal intellectual capacities in most domains, but at a very early age each savant shows an exceptional ability in some "intelligent" process. For example, a savant's exceptional ability may be related to math, music, or art. The combination of prodigious memory and the inability to learn seemingly basic tasks is a great mystery. Nonetheless, this rare combination adds a dimension to our understanding of intelligence.

Oliver Sacks (1995) recounts the story of Stephen Wiltshire, an artistic savant. Wiltshire has autism, a developmental disorder (discussed further in Chapter 14, "Psychological Disorders"). In childhood, it took him the utmost effort to acquire language sufficient for simple verbal communication. Years after a single glance at a place, however, Wiltshire can draw a highly accurate picture of it (**Figure 8.35**).

Genes and Environment Influence Intelligence

One of the most contentious battles in psychological science has been over the role of genes in determining intelligence. This battle exemplifies the nature/nurture debate: To what extent are individual differences in intelligence due to genes, and to what extent are they due to environment? As emphasized throughout this book, nature *and* nurture are important for all development. They are especially important for the development of intelligence.

As discussed in the previous section, head circumference is correlated with general intelligence. Now consider that the size of a child's head is correlated with the sizes of the parents' heads. The connection is clear, right? Intelligent parents with large heads produce intelligent children with large heads. Recall from Chapter 3, however, that gene expression is strongly influenced by external factors. One external factor, childhood nutrition, is closely related to head size. For example, malnourished children have smaller than expected head circumference and brain growth. Another external factor, education, may lead to

FIGURE 8.35 Stephen Wiltshire Despite his autism, Stephen Wiltshire had published a book of his remarkably accurate, expressive, memory-based drawings by the time he was a young teenager. Here, in October 2010, he holds his drawing of an architectural site in London, England. Wiltshire observed the site briefly, then completed the picture largely from memory.

selective increases in some brain regions. As discussed in Chapter 3, for example, driving a taxi in London seems to enlarge the hippocampus, the portion of the brain linked to spatial cognition. Perhaps more-intelligent individuals seek out mental challenges, which in turn increase the volume of their frontal lobes (Gray & Thompson, 2004).

Consider an even more familiar example of the way nature and nurture are inextricably entwined in the development of intelligence: The capacity for having a large vocabulary is considerably heritable, but every word in a person's vocabulary is learned in an environment (Neisser et al., 1996). Moreover, which words are learned is affected by the culture in which an individual is raised, the amount of schooling she or he receives, and the general social context. Thus even if intelligence has a genetic component, the way intelligence becomes expressed is affected by various situational circumstances. Instead of seeking to demonstrate whether nature or nurture is the more important factor, psychologists try to identify how each of these crucial factors contributes to intelligence.

BEHAVIORAL GENETICS As discussed in Chapter 3, behavioral geneticists study the genetic basis of behaviors and traits such as intelligence. They use twin and adoption studies to estimate the extent to which particular traits are heritable. That is, they try to determine the portion of particular traits' variance that can be attributed to genes. Numerous behavioral genetics studies have made clear that genes help determine intelligence—but the extent to which genes do so is difficult to determine (**Figure 8.36**). For example, studies show that twins raised apart are highly similar in intelligence. This finding seems to support the importance of genetics in the development of intelligence. That hasty conclusion, however, fails to consider the ways people interact with and alter their environments. Even when raised apart, twins who have inherited an advantage might receive some *social multiplier,* an environmental factor or an entire environment, that increases what might have started as a small advantage (Flynn, 2007). Suppose the twins have inherited a higher than average verbal ability. Adults who notice this ability might read to them more often and give them more books. The "intelligence gene" has eluded researchers, probably because thousands of genes contribute to intelligence and individually each has only a small effect (Plomin & Spinath, 2004).

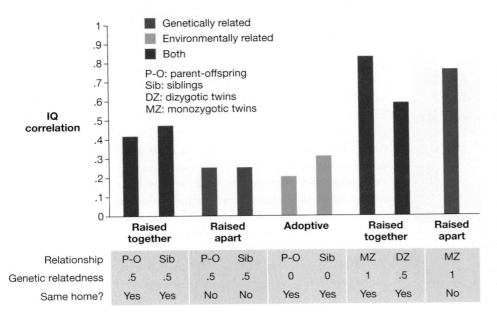

FIGURE 8.36 Genes and Intelligence This graph represents average IQ correlations from family, adoption, and twin study designs. As shown by the red and blue bars on the left, siblings raised together show more similarity than siblings raised apart. As indicated by the relations between parent and offspring (P-O) in the red and blue bars, a parent and child are more similar when the parent raises the child than when the child is raised by someone else. As shown by the red and blue bars on the right, the highest correlations are found among monozygotic twins, whether they are raised in the same household or not. Overall, the greater the degree of genetic relation, the greater the correlation in intelligence.

(a)

(b)

FIGURE 8.37 Environmental Impacts Within each of these planters, differences in the plants are likely due to genes. But note how different the plants are *as a whole* between one planter and the other. Those differences likely result from the environmental differences between the planters. **(a)** This planter has provided an impoverished environment. The poor conditions have negatively affected growth and development. **(b)** This planter has provided an enriched environment. The proper resources have contributed to robust growth and development.

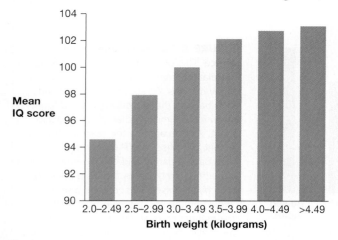

FIGURE 8.38 Birth Weight and Intelligence Among children of normal birth weight, mean IQ scores increase with weight.

ENVIRONMENTAL FACTORS Richard Lewontin (1976) has provided an excellent example of the difficulties of contrasting groups of people who differ in their circumstances. Consider seeds planted in two separate containers (**Figure 8.37**). In one container, the soil is rich, and the seeds receive regular watering, all the necessary nutrients, and abundant sunlight. In the other container, the soil is poor, and the seeds receive restricted water, few nutrients, and intermittent sunlight. Within each planter, differences between individual plants' growth can be attributed to the seeds' genetic differences. After all, the environment is identical, so only genes can explain the differences. But in addition, as groups, the plants in one container will differ from those in the other container because of their different environments. The enriched environment will help the seeds reach their potential, whereas the impoverished environment will stunt growth.

As mentioned earlier, poor nutrition can affect brain development and results in lower intelligence. Other environmental influences on human intelligence include prenatal factors (e.g., the mother's intake of substances, including toxins) and postnatal factors (e.g., family, social class, education, cultural beliefs about the value of intelligence, and the person's intake of substances, including toxins). Each factor is likely to exert an independent influence during development. For instance, breast-feeding during infancy has been shown to enhance cognitive development. Indeed, two large prospective studies—following more than 3,000 people from birth to age 18 or 27—found that breast-feeding for more than 6 months produced a 5- to 7-point difference in IQ, even after adjusting for all sorts of possible confounds, such as birth weight, mother's education, social status, and maternal smoking (Mortensen, Michaelsen, Sanders, & Reinisch, 2002). In an experimental study led by Michael Kramer, more than 17,000 infants from 31 Belarusian maternity hospitals were randomly assigned to either a control group or a group that received an intervention. Modeled on recommendations from the World Health Organization (WHO) and UNICEF, this intervention encouraged prolonged and exclusive breast-feeding. After 6.5 years, the children in the group receiving the intervention had higher means on standardized measures of intelligence (Kramer et al., 2008). There is also an apparent relation between birth weight and intelligence later in life. Even children of normal birth weight (so excluding children who are tiny because they are very premature) show a small positive association between birth weight and intelligence, although this effect is smaller than that of social class (Shenkin, Starr, & Deary, 2004; **Figure 8.38**).

As noted in Chapter 3, rats raised in enriched environments show more synaptic connections and larger neurons than those raised in impoverished environments. Research from numerous laboratories has shown that enriched environments enhance learning and memory as well (Lambert, Fernandez, & Frick, 2005; Tang, Wang, Feng, Kyin, & Tsien, 2001). The implication is that environment influences how genes involved in brain development are expressed. In one study, genetically identical mice were split into groups, which were then exposed to different levels of an enriched environment—given toys, tunnels, and the like. These researchers found that enrichment was associated with the activation of genes involved in a number of brain functions, including forming new synapses (Rampon et al., 2000). These results present clear evidence that our environments can affect properties associated with intelligence by influencing the expression of our genes. Research has shown that humans as well as mice gain clear advantages from living in stimulating environments and that these environmental effects can be seen in the brain.

The intellectual opportunities a child receives also affect intelligence. For instance, schooling makes an important contribution to intelligence. As Stephen Ceci (1999) notes, the longer children remain in school, the higher their IQs will be. In fact, students who start school early because of where their birth dates fall on the calendar have higher test scores than their same-age peers who start school a year later. Schooling not only builds knowledge but also teaches critical thinking skills, such as being able to think abstractly and learn strategies for solving problems (Neisser et al., 1996). Schooling encourages the development of children's brains and cognitive capacities and therefore fosters intelligence.

Taken together, the evidence is considerable that environmental factors contribute to intelligence. For example, IQ scores have risen dramatically during the last century of intelligence testing. This rise has been called the *Flynn effect* after James R. Flynn, the researcher who first described it (Flynn, 1981, 1987). (The various intelligence tests have been restandardized on numerous occasions over time so that the mean IQ score remains 100.) Since genes cannot have changed much during this period, the increase must be due to environmental factors. One possible explanation for the increase in IQ scores across generations is that, since every generation needs more education than the preceding one, and since work and leisure activities require more complex cognitive processing than in earlier years, cognitive abilities escalate within the span of one generation (Flynn, 2007). Other explanations include better nutrition, better health care, the refinement of education methods, longer school years, and smaller families with more intensive parenting, as well as exposure to technology such as computers.

Group Differences in Intelligence Have Multiple Determinants

SEX Which is the smarter sex—male or female? A great deal of research has addressed this commonly asked question. It might seem that the simplest way to answer the question is to determine whether females or males have the higher average IQ score. This solution does not work, however, because most of the commonly used intelligence tests were written in ways that would avoid creating an overall sex difference in IQ (Brody, 1992).

To study sex differences in intelligence, Arthur Jensen (1998) analyzed intelligence tests that "load heavily on g." Jensen used only tests that had not deliberately eliminated sex differences. Thus he was more likely to find evidence for sex differences in intelligence, if those differences existed. Jensen concluded, "No evidence was found for sex differences in the mean level of g or in the variability of g. . . . Males, on average, excel on some factors; females on others" (pp. 531–32). There are differences between females and males, on average, on some measures that presumably reflect intelligence. Females get better grades in school and tend to have the advantage on measures of writing and of language usage. By contrast, males tend to get higher scores on some standardized tests of math aptitude and of visuospatial processing (Halpern et al., 2007). Therefore, neither sex is "smarter."

RACE The most controversial aspect of intelligence testing over the last century has been the idea that genetics can explain overall differences in intelligence scores between racial groups. In particular, the debate continues about differences in African Americans' and white Americans' scores on measures of intelligence.

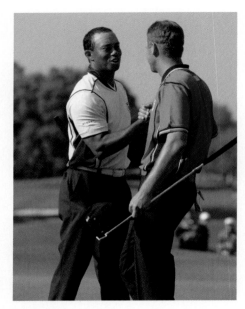

FIGURE 8.39 Tiger Woods as a Multiracial American Is the golfer Tiger Woods black or Asian? He refers to his multiracial identity as "Cablinasian," a term he invented to reflect his mother's being Thai and his father's being a mix of African American, Caucasian, and Native American. Most methods of classifying race depend on self-report, in which people group themselves into categories.

In a 1969 paper, Arthur Jensen created a firestorm of controversy by asserting that African Americans are, on average, less intelligent than European Americans. Multiple studies over the past 30 years have found that, while many African Americans have higher intelligence scores than most white Americans, whites score about 10 to 15 points higher on average than African Americans on most measures of intelligence. At issue is what causes the group difference, not whether the difference exists. Given the importance of intelligence to educational and career attainment, claims that some groups are superior to others require close scrutiny, and it is important to discuss controversial and sensitive topics with an eye to being as fair to all sides as possible.

What is the meaning of such differences, and why can it be so uncomfortable to talk about them? A finding that two or more groups differ with respect to some variable, such as scores on intelligence tests, does not mean the differences are inevitable or immutable. Here, the first issue to consider is whether "race" is a biologically meaningful concept. Many psychologists and anthropologists believe it is not. Indeed, a special issue of the flagship journal of the American Psychological Association, *American Psychologist* (January 2005), was devoted to the validity of race. In the issue, various authors noted that the vast majority of genes (perhaps as many as 99.9 percent) are identical among people. We differ in physical attributes such as hair color and skin color to varying degrees, depending on our entire ancestry, which raises troublesome issues of classification (**Figure 8.39**).

The increase in interracial relationships in the United States and many other countries means that a growing proportion of the population is racially mixed, and people increasingly identify themselves as biracial and multiracial to reflect their full racial and ethnic heritages. More and more people respond to questions of racial and ethnic identity by refusing to be pigeonholed into one category. For example, Barack Obama—the first "black" president of the United States—has described his family as "a little United Nations." Some genetically based biological differences exist between people who identify themselves as black and those who identify themselves as white. But are differences in biological attributes such as skin color related to the mental capacities that underlie intelligence?

Whether the effects of race are real or not, it is not scientifically appropriate to conclude that genes cause differences between groups if there are any environmental differences between those groups. Recall the earlier discussion of plants grown in different environments. On average, African Americans have very different life circumstances compared with white Americans. On average, African Americans make less money and are more likely to live in poverty. On average, they have fewer years of education and lower-quality health care, and they more likely face prejudice and discrimination. Around the world, minority groups that are the targets of discrimination—such as the Maori in New Zealand, the burakumin in Japan, and the Dalits, or "untouchables," in India—have lower intelligence scores on average. John Ogbu (1994) argues that poor treatment of minority-group members can make them pessimistic about their chances of success within their cultures, potentially making them less likely to believe that hard work will pay off for them. Such attitudes may lower their motivational levels and therefore their performances. This explanation is plausible, but it is not a clear-cut basis—indeed, at this time there is no clear-cut basis—for understanding the differences in test scores between African Americans and white Americans (Neisser et al., 1996).

Research over the past decade has provided an important reason that some racial groups may score lower on standardized tests of intelligence. **Stereotype threat** is the apprehension or fear that some people might experience if they believe that their performances on tests might confirm negative stereotypes about their racial group (Steele and Aronson, 1995; **Figure 8.40**). As noted by the psychologist Toni Schmader (2010), stereotype threat causes distraction and anxiety, interfering with performance by reducing the capacity of short-term memory and undermining confidence and motivation.

Stereotype threat applies to any group about which there is a negative stereotype. One negatively stereotyped group is women, who tend to perform less well than men on some standardized tests (such as those that involve math). Women tend to do more poorly than men when taking an exam on which they believe men typically outscore women, but they often perform as well as men on the same test if they do not hold such a belief (Schmader, Johns, & Forbes, 2008; Spencer, Steele, & Quinn, 1999). In an especially intriguing example of stereotype threat, Asian American women did well on a math test when the "Asians are good at math" stereotype was primed by having them respond to questions about racial identity, but they did poorly when the "women are bad at math" stereotype was primed by having them respond to questions about gender (Shih, Pittinsky, & Ambady, 1999). In this same study, however, women from Vancouver showed a slightly different pattern. The stereotype that Asians perform at a superior level is less strong in Canada than in the United States. In other words, the researchers had a two-part hypothesis: They predicted that being primed as women would reduce these women's test scores on math items. They also predicted that being primed as Asians would not lead to increased performance. Their findings supported both parts of the hypothesis. As a result, they demonstrate the power of sociocultural stereotypes on individual performance.

Steven Spencer is a leading researcher on stereotype threat. Spencer and his colleague Gregory Walton performed a meta-analysis on stereotype threat studies and reached two general conclusions. First, they examined 39 independent laboratory studies, which together included 3,180 participants from five countries (Canada, France, Germany, Sweden, and the United States). The participants came from a range of stereotyped groups (e.g., blacks, Latinos,

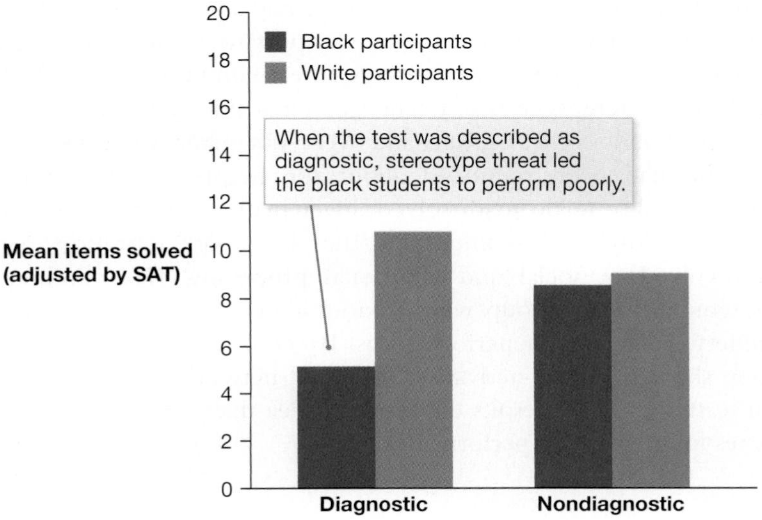

stereotype threat Apprehension about confirming negative stereotypes related to one's own group.

When the test was described as diagnostic, stereotype threat led the black students to perform poorly.

FIGURE 8.40 Stereotype Threat
Stereotype threat may lead black students to perform poorly on some standardized tests.

FIGURE 8.41 Stereotype Threat Counteracted Stereotype threat can be counteracted when people are warned about it.

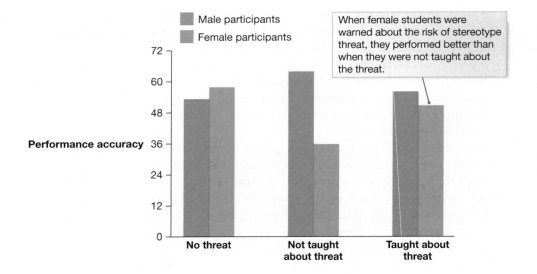

Turkish Germans, women). The researchers found that stereotyped groups perform worse than nonstereotyped groups in evaluative conditions, but this effect is reversed when the threat is reduced, such as when an exam is presented as nonevaluative (Walton & Spencer, 2009). Second, in studies that involved nearly 16,000 research participants, Walton and Spencer found that interventions to reduce stereotype threat effects are often successful. For instance, even simply informing people about the negative consequences of stereotype threat can inoculate them from the negative effects (Johns, Schmader, & Martens, 2005; **Figure 8.41**). In another study, encouraging African American students to write about important personal values appeared to protect them from stereotype threat, perhaps because it led them to focus on positive aspects of their lives rather than on stereotypes about their group (Cohen, Garcia, Apfel, & Master, 2006). Other studies have found that bolstering peer relations and social connections can help prevent stereotype threat. Indeed, school environments that provide opportunities to develop social skills and create friendships are associated with better academic performance among Canadian aboriginal children (Baydala et al., 2009).

A recent study used fMRI to examine the neural mechanisms underlying stereotype threat. Krendl, Richeson, Kelley, and Heatherton (2008) recruited a group of women who believed it was important to do well in math. Half the women were assigned to a stereotype threat condition in which they were reminded of the stereotype that women perform poorly in math, and half the women served as a control group and were not given these reminders. The women who had been reminded about the negative stereotypes concerning women's ability to do math solved fewer math problems correctly and responded more slowly. Most important, they had more activation in the brain regions involved in social and emotional processing. This finding suggests that the women in this group were anxious about their performances and that their anxiety led to poorer performances. By contrast, the women in the control group showed greater activation in neural networks associated with mathematical learning. These results confirm the idea that anxiety about confirming stereotypes interferes with performance.

How Do We Understand Intelligence?

Intelligence is our ability to reason, make decisions, solve problems, understand ideas, think quickly, and adapt to environmental challenges. Psychometric tests of general intelligence include the Stanford-Binet test, which measures intelligence using the intelligence quotient, or IQ score. The validity of such measures continues to be questioned, with some researchers arguing that intelligence tests are culturally biased. In contrast to the notion of general intelligence, some theorists have speculated that there are multiple intelligences. Cattell distinguished between fluid intelligence and crystallized intelligence. Fluid intelligence reflects the ability to process information, particularly in novel or complex circumstances. Crystallized intelligence reflects the knowledge that we acquire through experience and our ability to use that knowledge. Other theories of multiple intelligences include Gardner's theory of multiple intelligences; Sternberg's theory of analytical, practical, and creative intelligences; and Salovey and Mayer's theory of emotional intelligence. Intelligence is related to speed of mental processing and working memory. Small associations have emerged between intelligence and the size of the brain and specific brain structures. Both genes and environmental factors influence intelligence. Researchers are particularly interested in understanding how environmental factors lead to the differential expression of genes related to intelligence. Group differences in intelligence cannot be attributed to genetic differences when those groups have experienced environmental differences. Furthermore, group differences in intelligence, specifically by sex and race, may emerge as a consequence of stereotype threat—an apprehension or fear that one might confirm negative stereotypes about one's group. Research has demonstrated that stereotype threat may be reduced by informing people of the negative consequences of stereotype threat, having people focus on positive aspects of their lives, and bolstering people's peer relations and social connections.

Measuring Up

1. While discussing with his grandmother what he has been studying at college, Dave was impressed by how much she knows. When he showed her his new cell phone, she quickly understood its complexities. His grandmother's general knowledge exemplifies her _____ intelligence, whereas her ability to figure out the cell phone exemplifies her _____ intelligence.
   a. verbal, spatial
   b. crystallized, fluid
   c. fluid, spatial
   d. g, multiple

2. If you wanted to reduce the effects of stereotype threat, you could _____.
   a. make the assessment as difficult as possible to create a threat for all test takers
   b. include only information not taught in school
   c. use members of groups with which no negative stereotypes are associated
   d. tell test takers the upcoming test will not reflect group differences

Answers: 1. b. crystallized, fluid. 2. d. tell test takers that the upcoming test will not reflect group differences.

Chapter Summary

8.1 What Is Thought?

■ **Thinking Is the Manipulation of Mental Representations:** Cognitive psychology is the study of thought. Thinking involves the manipulation of mental representations of the objects that we encounter in our environments. Cognition includes thinking and the understandings that result from thinking.

■ **Thinking Involves Two Types of Representations:** Mental representations of objects may be analogical or symbolic. Analogical representations have some of the physical characteristics of objects; they usually correspond to images. Symbolic representations are abstract and do not have the physical features of objects; they usually correspond to words.

■ **Concepts Are Symbolic Representations:** Concepts are categories of items organized around common themes. Concepts may be characterized by defining attributes, prototypes, or exemplars.

■ **Schemas Organize Useful Information about Environments:** Schemas are cognitive structures that help us perceive, organize, and process information. Scripts are schemas that allow us to form expectations about the sequence of events in a given context. Schemas and scripts minimize the attention needed to navigate familiar environments, but they can lead to stereotypical ways of thinking and behaving.

8.2 How Do We Make Decisions and Solve Problems?

■ **People Use Deductive and Inductive Reasoning:** Reasoning involves the evaluation of information, arguments, and beliefs to draw a conclusion. Deductive reasoning proceeds from a general statement to specific conclusions. For example: If all psychology textbooks are fun to read and this is a psychology textbook, then this textbook will be fun to read. Inductive reasoning proceeds from specific statements to a general conclusion. For example: If you find this book interesting, you can infer that psychology books generally are interesting.

■ **Decision Making Often Involves Heuristics:** Decision making involves choosing between alternatives. Normative models assume people behave according to logical processes, such as always selecting the outcome that will yield the greatest reward. Descriptive models highlight reasoning shortcomings, specifically the use of heuristics (mental shortcuts) that sometimes lead to faulty decisions. The framing of information and our predictions (forecasts) of our future emotions can influence the decisions that we make.

■ **Problem Solving Achieves Goals:** Problem solving involves overcoming obstacles to reach a goal. Insight often comes suddenly, when we see elements of a problem in new ways. Breaking a problem down into subgoals, restructuring, working backward, and finding

appropriate analogies aid solutions; mental sets and functional fixedness inhibit solutions.

8.3 How Do We Understand Intelligence?

■ **Intelligence Is Assessed with Psychometric Tests:** The Binet-Simon Intelligence Test was the first modern test of mental ability and led to the concept of IQ as a ratio of mental age and chronological age. This test was later normed to a distribution with a mean of 100 and standard deviation of 15. Therefore, most people's IQ scores fall between 85 and 115. The validity of intelligence tests continues to be questioned. The validity of such tests among members of non-mainstream cultural groups is of particular concern, as intelligence tests may be culturally biased.

■ **General Intelligence Involves Multiple Components:** Charles Spearman concluded that a general intelligence component exists, known as g. Fluid intelligence refers to our ability to quickly process information. Crystallized intelligence refers to the knowledge that we have acquired through experience and our ability to apply this knowledge. Howard Gardner has proposed a theory of multiple intelligences that includes linguistic, mathematical/logical, spatial, bodily-kinesthetic, intrapersonal, and interpersonal abilities. Robert Sternberg has proposed a theory of three intelligences: analytical, creative, and practical. Emotional intelligence refers to the ability to manage, recognize, and understand emotions and use emotions to guide appropriate thought and action.

■ **Intelligence Is Associated with Cognitive Performance:** Intelligence is related to speed of mental processing (e.g., reaction time, inspection time) and working memory. The association between intelligence and working memory appears to involve attention. Intelligence may also be related to the size of the brain and specific brain regions, including the frontal lobes. Importantly, research examining the relation between intelligence and brain size is correlational. As a result, we cannot infer that brain size necessarily causes differences in intelligence

■ **Genes and Environment Influence Intelligence:** Behavioral genetics has demonstrated that genes influence intelligence. However, environmental factors—including nutrition, parenting, schooling, and intellectual opportunities—influence the expression of genes associated with intelligence.

■ **Group Differences in Intelligence Have Multiple Determinants:** One of the most contentious areas in psychology is group differences in intelligence. Females and males score similarly on measures of general intelligence, but some sex differences emerge on specific factors related to intelligence, such as writing ability and visuospatial processing. Race differences in intelligence are confounded with a multitude of environmental differences, including income, health care, and discrimination. Additionally, many scientists question the validity of race as a means by which to distinguish between groups of people.

Key Terms

analogical representations, p. 319
availability heuristic, p. 334
cognition, p. 319
concept, p. 321
crystallized intelligence, p. 349
decision making, p. 329
deductive reasoning, p. 329
defining attribute model, p. 321

emotional intelligence
    (EI), p. 351
exemplar model, p. 323
fluid intelligence, p. 349
framing, p. 333
general intelligence (g), p. 348
heuristics, p. 332
inductive reasoning, p. 329

insight, p. 339
intelligence, p. 344
intelligence quotient (IQ), p. 345
mental age, p. 345
mental sets, p. 341
multiple intelligences, p. 349
problem solving, p. 329
prototype model, p. 322

reasoning, p. 329
representativeness
    heuristic, p. 334
restructuring, p. 340
stereotypes, p. 324
stereotype threat, p. 359
symbolic representations, p. 320
thinking, p. 319

Practice Test

1. Which of the following statements reflect incorrect assumptions in the *defining attribute model* of concepts? Select all that apply.
   a. All attributes of a category are equally salient.
   b. All members of a category fit equally well into that category.
   c. An understanding of the category requires knowing a list of typical attributes of members of that category.
   d. An understanding of the category requires knowing the most common example of a member of that category.
   e. Membership within a category is on an all-or-none basis.

2. Which of the following fruits will most likely be considered prototypical? Which will least likely be considered prototypical?
   a. apple
   b. pineapple
   c. tomato
   d. strawberry

3. On the first day of the semester, students enter a new class. On each desk is a handout that lists a couple of thought-provoking questions with the instruction "Discuss in groups of 3 to 4 people." It is time for class to begin, yet the teacher is not there. If the students follow our cultural script for the first day of class, what will they most likely do?
   a. Students will settle into their seats and perhaps glance over the handout. People who already know each other might converse, but they most likely will not discuss the questions.
   b. Students will settle into their seats, quietly read the handout, and jot some ideas in their notebooks to prepare for the discussion they imagine will happen once class begins.
   c. Students will settle into their seats, read the handout, organize themselves into groups, and begin discussing the questions.

4. Label each of the following statements as an example of deductive reasoning or inductive reasoning.
   a. "I love my new pen! From now on, I'm going to buy all my pens from this company."
   b. "I'm not sure I'm in the mood for a concert. It's a ska band? Well, I do like ska. I'm sure I'll like the band."
   c. "She must be at least 18 years old, since she's in the club and the club only admits people who are over 18."
   d. "This restaurant is horrible. There's not a healthy item on this entire menu. Actually, we probably won't be able to find a decent meal in this entire town."
   e. "Yeah, I took a class from her last semester. It was pretty brutal. I bet all of her classes are tough."

5. Label each of the following scenarios as an example of affective forecasting, the availability heuristic, a framing effect, or the representativeness heuristic.
   a. Two candidates are running for office. One claims, "My administration will promote international trade and commerce." The other claims, "My opponent wants to send U.S. jobs—your jobs—overseas."
   b. Two friends come up with a hypothesis that married couples in their town seem much more likely to get divorced than couples in the United States in general. Their hypothesis seems bolstered when they quickly name five or six couples they know who got divorced over the past year.
   c. Jason, a sophomore at a state college in Nebraska, is tan and has blonde, shaggy hair. He spends a lot of time hanging out at the beach. When people meet him, they typically assume he is from California, although few Californians attend college in Nebraska.

6. _____ is an indicator of current levels of skill or knowledge, whereas _____ is an indicator of future potential.
   a. achievement, aptitude
   b. achievement, intelligence
   c. aptitude, achievement
   d. aptitude, intelligence

The answer key for the Practice Tests can be found at the back of the book. It also includes answers to the green caption questions.

Human Development

IN 1970, A MOTHER AND HER YOUNG DAUGHTER walked into a welfare office in Los Angeles. The mother was seeking help after escaping an abusive and mentally ill husband. The girl, later known as "Genie," appeared to be suffering from autism (**Figure 9.1**). When a social worker saw Genie, who was 4 feet 6 inches tall and weighed 59 pounds, she alerted her supervisor. Although Genie looked much younger, she turned out to be 13 years old. Having suffered severe neglect and abuse, she could not hop, skip, climb, or do anything that required the full extension of her limbs. After being admitted to a hospital, she was taken from her parents and placed in foster care.

Genie's early life had been a nightmare. For more than 10 years, her father had locked her in a tiny, dark room in an attic. Tied to a potty seat during the day and caged in a crib at night, she had been poorly fed and beaten for making any noise. In her barren room, she had no one to talk to, nothing to listen to, and nothing to look at. She was raised without normal human contact and stimulation from the external world. Her mother was legally blind and deathly afraid

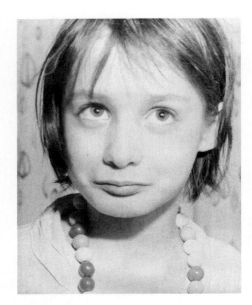

FIGURE 9.1 Genie This photo shows Genie in the early 1970s.

of her violent husband. When therapists first saw Genie, she had a strange gait, almost like a rabbit's, and held her hands out in front of her like a dog sitting up and begging. She understood just a few words and could form only brief phrases, such as *Stop it* and *No more.* For the next four years, scientists from Childrens Hospital Los Angeles (now Children's Hospital Los Angeles) examined Genie's development. The researchers hoped they would find evidence of Genie's overcoming at least some effects of her abuse. Genie's extreme case provided the opportunity to witness and record the potential consequences of extreme social isolation (Curtiss, 1977; Rymer, 1993).

Throughout the history of psychology, scientists have vigorously debated the contributions of nature and nurture to development. Nearly everyone now agrees that both are important, and current research focuses on how, exactly, genes and experiences might interact to make us who we are. As discussed in Chapter 3, environment determines which of a person's genes are expressed and how they are expressed. But how much of who we are as humans is hardwired in our genes, and how much is the result of experience? What is human nature when it is stripped of society and culture?

The scientists involved in Genie's case could not ethically conduct an experiment to examine these variables, but they hoped the case might provide insight into what makes us human. Would Genie develop normal social skills that would allow her to become a full member of society if she received the proper stimulation and nurturing so late in life? Would a warm, caring environment help her recover from her tragic past? Or had the years of abuse destroyed her capacities for cognition, language, and emotion?

After an extended stay in the hospital and some time at the home of her special-education teacher, Genie lived with her therapist and his family, which included his wife (a graduate student in human development) and their two children. She made some progress in forming social relationships, doing activities such as sewing, and acquiring minimal language. She learned many words, as well as some sign language, but she could not put words together into coherent sentences. When Genie turned 18, her mother regained custody of her and immediately cut off all contact with the professionals who had tried to help. She felt they were exploiting Genie and tried to sue the research team. Because her mother was legally blind and Genie was very difficult to care for, they lived together for only a short time before Genie was removed again and sent to a series of foster homes. In at least one home, she was again abused. Genie's mother was acquitted of child abuse, and her father committed suicide before he could stand trial for the abuse. Genie's mother died in 2003. Genie now lives in a small group home for adults who cannot look after themselves.

Unfortunately, we will never know whether her father's sadistic behavior and neglect caused Genie's developmental deficits. She could have been born with brain damage or other kinds of developmental delays. She could have been an irritable or hard to soothe infant, with whom her mentally ill father could not connect emotionally. The only certainty is that both nature and nurture played a role in Genie's developmental outcome, as they do in each person's. ■

Learning Objectives

- Describe how the prenatal environment can affect development.

- Explain how dynamic systems theory illuminates the ways biology and environment work together to shape development.

- Describe key processes in infant brain development and how these processes affect learning.

- Describe the types of attachment infants have to their caregivers.

- Explain how attachment and emotion regulation are related.

9.1 What Shapes Us during Childhood?

This chapter examines the ways biological and social forces combine to shape the path of human development. In doing so, it presents the findings of **developmental psychology.** As noted in Chapter 1, this subfield is concerned with changes, over the life span, in physiology, cognition, emotion, and social behavior. How do genes interact with early experiences to make each of us an individual? How do we, while remaining individuals, become members of society? How do we grow and adapt within our own cultures?

For the most part, human physical development follows a predictable progression. Physically, each human grows and matures at about the same periods in the life span: the *prenatal period,* which begins with conception and ends with birth; *infancy,* which begins at birth and lasts between 18 and 24 months; *childhood,* which begins at the end of infancy and lasts until somewhere between ages 11 and 14; *adolescence,* which begins at the end of childhood and lasts until somewhere between 18 and 21 years; and *adulthood,* which begins at the end of adolescence and lasts until death. The consistency of this pattern suggests that our genes set the order of development. For example, during the prenatal period, the body develops in a fixed sequence influenced by genes. That developmental journey is also influenced, however, by the environment in the mother's womb. For example, genes ordinarily tell the brain to develop two symmetrical hemispheres. If the mother drinks alcohol excessively during pregnancy, these hemispheres can become misshapen and not work properly. As a result, the child will experience cognitive delays later on. Thus, even in the prenatal period, the constant interplay between nature and nurture shapes who we are as we develop.

Development Starts in the Womb

From conception through birth approximately nine months later, remarkable developments occur (**Figure 9.2**). The process begins at the moment of conception, when the sperm from the male unites with the egg from the female to create the *zygote,* the first cell of a new life. At about 2 weeks after conception, the zygote is firmly implanted in the uterine wall, and the next stage of development begins. From about 2 weeks to 2 months, the developing human is known as an *embryo.* During this stage, the organs (such as the heart, lungs, liver, kidneys, and sex organs) and internal systems (such as the nervous system) begin to form. During this period, the embryo is critically vulnerable to insults to its development. Exposure to harm—such as toxins, drugs, extreme stress, or poor nutrition—can having lasting effects on developing organ systems.

After 2 months of prenatal development, the growing human is called a *fetus.* The whole body continues to grow into its infant form. No new structures emerge after prenatal month 2. The fetus simply grows larger, stronger, and fatter, as the body organs mature. With current medical technology helping out, many fetuses can now survive outside the womb after as little as 22 weeks of prenatal development. Most healthy full-term pregnancies, however, end with the birth of the baby between 38 and 42 weeks.

HORMONAL INFLUENCES DURING PRENATAL DEVELOPMENT Hormones that circulate in the womb influence the developing fetus. For instance, if the mother's thyroid does not produce sufficient amounts of hormones, the fetus is at risk for lower IQ and diminished intellectual development. The mother's emotional state can also affect the developing fetus. Pregnancy is often trying, but the fetuses of mothers who are unusually anxious or who experience chronic stress (such as through domestic violence) may be exposed to high levels of stress hormones. These hormones may interfere with normal development, producing low birth weight and negative cognitive and behavioral outcomes that can persist throughout life (Austin, Hadzi-Pavlovic, Leader, Saint, & Parker, 2005; Wadhwa, Sandman, & Garite, 2001).

developmental psychology The study of changes, over the life span, in physiology, cognition, emotion, and social behavior.

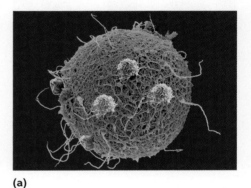
(a)

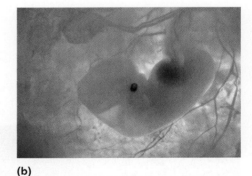
(b)

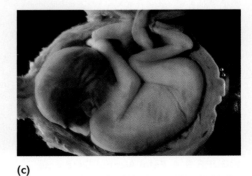
(c)

FIGURE 9.2 Development in the Womb (a) The union of egg and sperm forms a zygote. (b) The zygote develops into an embryo. (c) The embryo becomes a fetus.

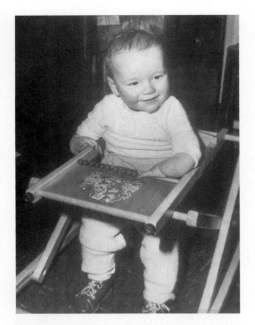

FIGURE 9.3 Birth Defects from a Teratogen Photos of this German infant's limb deformities were exhibited as evidence in a 1963 lawsuit, brought by distraught parents, against the makers of the drug thalidomide.

teratogens Environmental agents that harm the embryo or fetus.

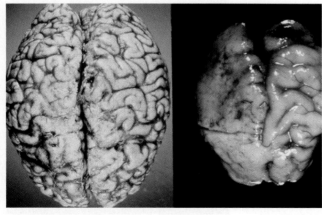

FIGURE 9.4 Fetal Alcohol Syndrome Compare (a) the brain of a normal 6-week-old baby with (b) the brain of a baby of the same age with FAS. What effects do you see of the interrupted brain development caused by FAS?

EXPOSURE TO TERATOGENS DURING PRENATAL DEVELOPMENT **Teratogens** are environmental agents that harm the embryo or fetus. (The word *teratogens* comes from the Greek for "monster makers.") Specifically, these agents can impair development in the womb, sometimes with terrible consequances. They include drugs, alcohol, bacteria, viruses, and chemicals. The physical effects of exposure to certain teratogens may be obvious at birth, but disorders involving language, reasoning, social behavior, or emotional behavior may not become apparent until the child is older. The extent to which a teratogen causes damage depends on when the fetus is exposed to it, as well as the length and amount of exposure. For instance, exposure to a teratogen at about 4 weeks' gestation can interfere with the proper development of basic brain structures. A tragic example of birth defects caused by teratogens occurred in the late 1950s and early 1960s, when women were prescribed the drug thalidomide to ease morning sickness accompanying pregnancy. Thalidomide caused various birth defects, especially limb deformities (**Figure 9.3**). The precise nature of the birth defects depended on when the mother took the drug, as the critical timing of embryonic development determines what systems and specific structures are affected by a teratogen.

After the revelation of its teratogenic effects, thalidomide was removed from the market. Still, other toxic substances continue to affect human development. For example, the most commonly used toxic substance is alcohol. Drinking alcohol during pregnancy can lead to a variety of defects that collectively are referred to as *fetal alcohol spectrum disorders (FASD)*. In fact, no minimal amount of alcohol has been determined to be safe for pregnant women and their developing babies. For this reason, many health workers recommend that women abstain from drinking alcohol when they are pregnant or trying to become pregnant (Mukherjee, Hollins, Abou-Saleh, & Turk, 2005).

The most severe form of FASD is *fetal alcohol syndrome (FAS)*. The symptoms of this disorder are low birth weight, face and head abnormalities, slight mental retardation, and behavioral and cognitive problems (Centers for Disease Control and Prevention, 2004; **Figure 9.4**). FAS is most likely to occur among infants of women who drink heavily during pregnancy, especially if they binge drink.

Alcohol interferes with normal brain development and can cause permanent brain damage, especially to the neocortex, hippocampus, and cerebellum. The resulting impairments can negatively affect learning, attention, the inhibition and regulation of behavior, memory, causal reasoning, and motor performance (Guerri, 2002). In the United States, the prevalence of FAS is estimated to be between 0.2 and 2.0 cases per 1,000 live births, though the actual numbers could be higher (Centers for Disease Control and Prevention, 2004).

The use of recreational drugs—such as opiates, cocaine, or cannabis—during pregnancy can also affect a child's development. Premature birth and other complications have been associated with the use of all these drugs during pregnancy (Gillogley, Evans, Hansen, Samuels, & Batra, 1990; Sherwood, Keating, Kavvadia, Greenough, & Peters, 1999). Infants of women taking opiates, particularly methadone, have two to three times greater risk for unexplained sudden death in infancy (Davidson Ward et al., 1990). Cocaine use has also been linked to sudden infant death (Hulse, Milne, English, & Holman, 1998; Kandall & Gaines, 1991). Among infants exposed to opiates in utero, 55 percent to 94 percent show symptoms of newborn withdrawal (American Academy of Pediatrics, 1998). These symptoms include irritability, high-pitched crying, tremors, vomiting, diarrhea, and rapid breathing.

Remember, however, that mothers are only half of the story when it comes to creating new humans. Men also play a role in the health and development of infants.

Far less research has been done on the effects of men's health and lifestyles on pre-natal development. There is evidence, however, that men should be just as cautious about their diets, exposure to toxins, and use of substances as women are, if there is a possibility that the men might father children. For example, paternal smoking is related to infant hydrocephalus, and paternal alcohol use is related to infant heart defects (Savitz, Schwingle, & Keels, 1991). In a fascinating study of veterans who fa-thered children after the first Gulf War, those veterans who served in battle positions were more likely to have infants with heart valve defects than were similar veterans who were never deployed (Araneta et al., 2003). This study points to the possible effects of toxins the men were exposed to in the war, the impact of chronic stress on fathers, or a complex combination of male and female partner stresses related to war and separation that might affect infant heart development. Much more research is needed on the male role in prenatal development because we do not know the precise mechanisms underlying such research findings, nor do we know how much stress or toxin exposure developing embryos can take.

An important point to remember is that some heavy substance users and some people exposed to toxins or stress have normal infants. Some people with only moderate exposure to teratogens have infants with serious developmental effects. Thus we cannot say with certainty that any given baby born to a drug user or to a person who works around chemicals will be impaired. Likewise, we cannot be assured that light drinking or teratogen exposure will allow for normal develop-ment. Thus all potential parents face the responsibility of caring for their own mental and physical health in order to increase the odds of being able to parent a healthy and robust newborn.

Biology and Environment Influence Developmental Milestones

No newborn talks immediately, nor does any baby walk before it can sit up. Virtually all humans make eye contact quickly after they are born, display a first social smile at around 6 weeks, and learn to roll over, to sit up, to crawl, to stand, to walk, and to talk, in that order. Occasionally, a child skips one of these steps or reverses a couple of them, but generally each child follows these steps within a predictable range of ages (**Figure 9.5**).

Meanwhile, each person's environment influences what happens through-out that person's development. For example, children often achieve develop-mental milestones at different paces, depending on the cultures in which they are raised. Consider that healthy Baganda children in Uganda were found to walk, on average, between 9 and 11 months of age, which was one month ear-lier than African American infants and about three months earlier than Euro-pean American infants (Kilbride, Robbins, & Kilbride, 1970). Such differences are due in part to different patterns of infant care across cultures. For example, Western infants spend a lot more time in cribs and playpens than African infants do. African infants are often strapped to their mothers' backs all day, practicing holding their heads up virtually from birth.

Kipsigi mothers living in the Kohwet village culture in western Kenya were found to put their babies in shallow holes in the ground so the babies could practice sitting upright (Super, 1976). The mothers then marched their babies around while placing their own arms under the babies' underarms, so the chil-dren could practice walking. These infants walked about one to two months earlier than American and European infants. When middle-class Kipsigi families

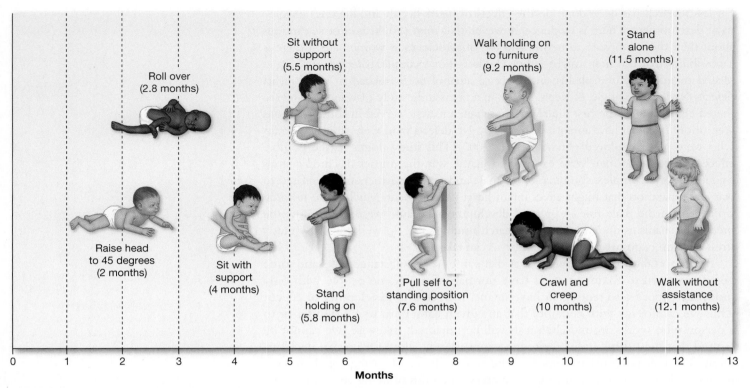

FIGURE 9.5 Learning to Walk Usually, a human baby learns to walk without formal teaching, in a sequence characteristic of all humans. The numbers of months given here are averages, however. A child might deviate from this sequence or these times but still be developing normally.

who had moved to a larger city were assessed in their Westernized homes, they still deliberately taught their infants motor skills. However, they also let their infants both sleep in cribs and lie in playpens like their European counterparts. These urban infants walked two weeks later than the rural infants in Kohwet but one week earlier than infants in Boston, Massachusetts. These findings illustrate the importance of socialization experiences and parental goals in the development of infant motor skills.

The aim of these early studies was to find out whether the development of walking was genetically or environmentally determined. Contemporary research has moved beyond such questions because we now know that every new development is due to complex and consistent interplays between biological and environmental forces. Developmental psychologists now consider new forms of development (such as when an infant is able to walk two weeks after not being able to walk) to be part of a *dynamic system*. **Dynamic systems theory** views development as a self-organizing process, where new forms of behavior emerge through consistent interactions between a biological being and his or her cultural and environmental contexts (Smith & Thelan, 2003; **Figure 9.6**).

From this perspective, developmental advances in any domain (physiological, cognitive, emotional, or social) occur through both the person's active exploration of an environment and the constant feedback that environment provides. For example, a child placed on a play mat may grow bored of the toys dangling above her on a mobile. She suddenly spies a very attractive stuffed unicorn about 10 feet away, far from the play mat where her mother placed her. Her physical body is strong enough to get herself off the mat, but because she cannot crawl,

dynamic systems theory The view that development is a self-organizing process, where new forms of behavior emerge through consistent interactions between a biological being and his or her cultural and environmental contexts.

FIGURE 9.6 Dynamic Systems Theory
Throughout life, every new form of behavior emerges through consistent interactions between a biological being and his or her cultural and environmental contexts.

she uses her own active strategizing in combination with feedback from the environment to figure out how to reach the toy. She rocks her body from side to side with her arm outstretched toward the toy. The environmental feedback tells her that after one more heavy roll, she will be on her stomach and possibly closer to the toy. She tries for over 10 minutes, and suddenly she rolls over. She continues to heave herself over and over until she has rolled 10 feet and can now grasp the unicorn. Her mother may walk into the room and think, "Wow, she just suddenly learned to roll around the room!" What her mother does not realize is that every new behavioral skill to emerge is the result of a complex and dynamic system of influences.

Brain Development Promotes Learning

To study how humans develop cognitive skills, developmental scientists have focused on age-related changes in psychological capacities such as perception, language, and thinking. They have discovered that the mind develops adaptively. That is, new, useful skills appear at appropriate times, even in the absence of specific training.

Newborns normally come into the world with fairly well-developed perceptual skills: smelling, hearing, tasting, and responding to touch. Although some of these skills are not fully developed at birth, the newborn is able to process a considerable range of sensory stimuli. For instance, 2-hour-old infants prefer sweet tastes to all other tastes (Rosenstein & Oster, 1988). Young infants also have a reasonably acute sense of smell, at least for smells associated with feeding. In a number of studies, infants turned their heads toward a pad containing their own mother's milk but not toward pads containing milk from other breast-feeding mothers (e.g., Winberg & Porter, 1998). The sense of hearing is also quite good shortly after birth: Infants are startled by loud sounds and often will turn their bodies toward the source of the sounds. Newborns' sense of hearing is much better than

synaptic pruning A process whereby the synaptic connections in the brain that are used are preserved, and those that are not used are lost.

their sense of vision, however. Their range of visual acuity is 8–12 inches. That is about the distance, during breast-feeding, between an infant's face and his or her mother's face. This limited visual range may be adaptive. Namely, it encourages the infant to focus on what is most important—the mother's breast and face—and promotes the beginnings of the child's social interaction. As discussed later in this chapter, newborns' perceptual skills increase tremendously over the first few months of life.

Although newborn infants cannot survive on their own, they are not completely helpless. Newborns have various basic reflexes that aid survival. Perhaps you have observed the *grasping reflex* when a baby held your finger. Some scholars believe this reflex is a survival mechanism that has persisted from our primate ancestors. After all, young apes grasp their mothers, and this reflex is adaptive because the offspring need to be carried from place to place. Also appearing at birth is the *rooting reflex,* the turning and sucking that infants automatically engage in when a nipple or similar object touches an area near their mouths. These reflexes pave the way for learning more-complicated behavior patterns, such as feeding oneself or walking. Thus at birth the brain is sufficiently developed to support basic reflexes, but further brain development appears necessary for cognitive development to occur.

MYELINATION AND NEURONAL CONNECTIONS Early brain growth has two important aspects. First, specific areas within the brain mature and become functional. Second, regions of the brain learn to communicate with one another through synaptic connections.

One important way that brain circuits mature is through myelination. This process begins on the spinal cord during the first trimester of pregnancy and on the neurons during the second trimester. As discussed in Chapter 3, myelination is the brain's way of insulating its "wires." Nerve fibers are wrapped with a fatty sheath, much like the plastic coating around electrical wire (see Figure 3.5). This wrapping increases the speed with which the fibers are able to transmit signals. Myelination occurs in different brain regions at different stages of development.

The myelinated axons form synapses with other neurons. Far more of these connections develop than the infant brain will ever use. This process allows every brain to adapt well to any environment in which it may find itself. The brain organizes itself in response to its environmental experiences, preserving connections it needs in order to function in a given context. In other words, "use it or lose it." When connections are used, they are preserved. Consider two children who learn to play the piano. One child learns to play reasonably well, and the other becomes a virtuoso. The virtuoso will have more dense synaptic connections in parts of the brain that process sound, recognize patterns, and relate to hand-eye coordination than will the child who can play reasonably well. When connections are not used, they decay and disappear. This process is called **synaptic pruning.**

Optimal stimulation of a child's developing brain can be achieved by talking to the child, reading books and singing to the child, providing physical contact, and generally helping the child explore his or her world—that is, humans, animals, and nature. When a child's brain is not stimulated by its environment, such as in the case of Genie (described in the chapter opener), very few synaptic connections will be made. The brain will be less sophisticated and less able to process complex information, solve problems, or allow the child to develop advanced language skills (Perry, 2002; **Figure 9.7**). As discussed in Chapter 3, rats raised in enriched environments also show evidence of greater brain development.

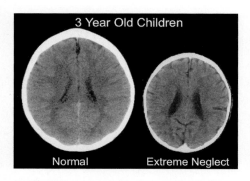

FIGURE 9.7 Environment and Synaptic Connections These images illustrate the impact of neglect on the developing brain. The CT scan on the left is from a healthy 3-year-old child with an average head size. The CT scan on the right is from a 3-year-old child following severe sensory-deprivation neglect (e.g., minimal exposure to language, to touch, and to social interaction) during early childhood. This brain is significantly smaller than average, and its cortical, limbic, and midbrain structures are abnormally developed.

Genetic instruction leads the brain to grow, but the organ is also highly "plastic." As already mentioned, the brain is hardwired to adapt to different environments. Though most neurons are already formed at birth, the brain's physical development continues through the growth of neurons and the new connections they make. By age 4, the human brain grows from about 350 grams (approximately 0.75 pound) to about 1,250 grams (2.75 pounds, or about 80 percent of the adult size). This size increase is due to myelination and to new synaptic connections among neurons.

Early childhood nutrition also affects aspects of brain development, including myelination. Malnourished children have less myelination, but they might also lack the energy to interact with objects and people in their environments. This lack of stimulation would further undermine brain development. The living conditions that tend to come with poverty are bad for the development of human brains; these deleterious effects begin at a young age—probably before birth—and continue through life (Farah et al., 2008; Farah et al., 2006). Thus, although genes provide instructions for the maturing brain, how the brain changes during infancy and early childhood is also very much affected by environment.

SENSITIVE LEARNING PERIODS Psychologists believe that the key to learning is the creation of connections among certain neurons. In addition, certain connections are made most easily during particular times in development, as long as the brain receives the right stimuli. During these specific points in development, people learn some skills or kinds of knowledge most easily. These periods are referred to as **sensitive periods.**

Language is one skill that is easier to learn during early sensitive periods than later on. It is much easier to learn two languages at once early in life when the brain is more plastic (the first 5 to 10 years) than it is to add a new language to an already fully developed language repertoire later in life, say at age 35. Another example of a developmental milestone most easily acquired in the early sensitive periods of infancy, rather than later in life, is the emergence of close emotional attachments with caregivers.

Children Develop Attachment and Emotion Regulation

Socioemotional development includes the maturation of skills and abilities that enable people to live successfully in the world with other people. The ability to understand one's own as well as other people's emotions builds an important foundation for socioemotional functioning later in life. People who can productively express and cope with emotions without hurting themselves or others have developed the skill of *emotion regulation*. For example, how did you learn not to lash out in anger in your professor's office while discussing a bad grade? It is likely that your caregivers taught you how to think about emotional experiences and talk about them (especially with people in power) in a rational and calm manner, without verbal or physical aggression. This skill likely took a lot of practice after many months or even years of temper tantrums and crying fits when things did not go your way.

Emotion regulation is not something we are born with. Children do come into the world with differences in how intensely they experience and express emotions. But each child's environment shapes how volatile or emotionally regulated the child will be later in life (Ramsden & Hubbard, 2002). Parents play a key role in helping their children regulate their emotions appropriately. The

sensitive periods Time periods when specific skills develop most easily.

attachment A strong emotional connection that persists over time and across circumstances.

bonds between parents and children motivate children to want to conform to adult expectations for emotional expression.

One of the fundamental needs infants have is to bond emotionally with those who care for them. Psychologists refer to the bond between caregivers and children as an **attachment.** An attachment is a strong, intimate, emotional connection between people that persists over time and across circumstances. These emotional bonds are the building blocks of a successful social life later on. The attachment process draws on humans' innate tendency to form bonds with others. This tendency to bond is, in fact, an adaptive trait. Forming bonds with others provides protection for individuals, increases their chances of survival, and thus increases their chances of passing along their genes to future generations (Bowlby, 1982).

Like all young primates, human infants need nurturance and care from adults to survive. Unlike horses and deer, which can walk and find food within hours after birth, humans are born profoundly immature. At that point, human infants cannot even hold up their own heads or roll over. But they are far from passive. Just minutes after birth, infants' cries cause psychological, physiological, and behavioral reactions in caregivers that compel the offering of food and comfort to the newborns. Even young infants have highly interactive social relationships. For example, within 10 weeks after birth, infants are profoundly affected by their caregivers' facial expressions and may become very upset when their primary caregivers fail to display emotional reactions (Cohn & Tronick, 1983). Caregivers shape much of an infant's early experience, from what the child eats to where the child sleeps to what social connections the child makes. These early interactions with people begin to shape the developing human. They are the first stages in which a person learns how to communicate with others, how to behave appropriately in various situations, and how to establish and maintain relationships. Ultimately, socialization also affects complex human characteristics such as gender roles, a sense of personal identity, and moral reasoning, each of which will be explored in this chapter.

Between 4 and 6 weeks of age, most infants display a first social smile. This expression of pleasure typically induces powerful feelings of love in caregivers. Infant attachment leads to heightened feelings of safety and security. According to the psychiatrist John Bowlby (1982), the architect of attachment theory, attachment motivates infants and caregivers to stay in close contact.

Bowlby argued that infants have an innate repertoire of attachment behaviors that motivate adult attention. For instance, they prefer to remain close to caregivers, act distressed when caregivers leave and rejoice when they return, and put out their arms to be lifted. Thus attachment is adaptive: Attachment is a dynamic relationship that facilitates survival for the infant and parental investment for the caregivers. Throughout the world, attachment behaviors begin during the first months of life, but normal attachment may vary somewhat, depending on cultural practices (Kappenberg & Halpern, 2006).

Adults generally seem predisposed to responding to infants, as in picking up and rocking a crying child. They also tend to respond to infants in ways that infants can understand, as in making exaggerated facial expressions and speaking in a higher-pitched voice. The next time you observe an adult talking to a baby, notice how even the gruffest men with deep voices change their voices to a higher pitch. Babies attend to high-pitched voices. In virtually every culture studied, men, women, and even children intuitively raise the pitch of their voices when talking to babies, and babies respond by maintaining eye contact (Fernald, 1989; Vallabha, McClelland, Pons, Werker, & Amano, 2007). Bowlby argued that these behaviors motivate infants and caregivers to stay in proximity.

ATTACHMENT IN OTHER SPECIES Attachment is important for survival in many other species as well. For instance, infant birds communicate hunger through crying chirps. In doing so, they prompt caregivers to find food for them. Some bird species seem to have a sensitive period in which fledgling chicks become strongly attached to a nearby adult, even one from another species. This pattern, first noticed in the nineteenth century, occurs for birds such as chickens, geese, and ducks. Because these birds can walk immediately after hatching, they are at risk of straying from their mothers. Therefore, within about 18 hours after hatching, these birds will attach themselves to an adult (usually to their mothers) and then follow the object of their attachment. The ethologist Konrad Lorenz called such behavior *imprinting*. He noted that goslings that became imprinted on him did not go back to their biological mothers when later given access to them (**Figure 9.8**). Such birds preferentially imprint on a female of their species if one is available, however.

FIGURE 9.8 Attachment Here Konrad Lorenz walks the goslings that had imprinted themselves on him. The little geese followed Lorenz as if he were their mother. **How is this form of attachment like attachment in humans? How is it different?**

During the late 1950s, the psychologist Harry Harlow began conducting research that later allowed him to discover one of the most striking examples of nonhuman attachment. At that time, psychologists generally believed an infant needed its mother primarily as a food source. For example, Freud viewed the attachment bond as being primarily motivated by the goal of drive reduction. He felt that infants attached to their mothers through having their oral needs met through breast-feeding. Thus the hunger drive was reduced. But Harlow saw explanations of attachment that were based on food as inadequate for explaining what he observed in infant monkeys. He recognized that infants need comfort and security in addition to food.

In a now-famous series of experiments, Harlow placed infant rhesus monkeys in a cage with two different "mothers" (Harlow & Harlow, 1966). One surrogate mother was made of bare wire and could give milk through an attached bottle. The second surrogate mother was made of soft terrycloth and could not give milk. Which of these two substitute mothers do you think the infant monkeys preferred—the wire one that provided milk or the soft and cuddly one that could not feed the baby?

The monkeys' responses were unmistakable: They clung to the cloth mother most of the day. They went to it for comfort in times of threat. The monkeys approached the wire mother only when they were hungry. Harlow tested the monkeys' attachment to these mothers in various ways. For example, he introduced a strange object, such as a menacing metal robot with flashing eyes and large teeth, into the cage. The infants always ran to the mother that provided comfort, never to the mother that fed them. Harlow repeatedly found that the infants were calmer, braver, and overall better adjusted when near the cloth mother. Once they clung to her, they would calm down and actually confront the feared object! Hence, the mother-as-food theory of mother/child attachment was debunked. Harlow's findings established the importance of *contact comfort*—the importance of physical touch and reassurance—in aiding social development (**Figure 9.9**).

Harlow performed thousands of studies along these lines, varying one variable at a time to be sure his hypotheses were correct. His experiments provided evidence that in this setting, infant monkeys could survive without a real mother. As long as food was available, the monkeys underwent normal physical growth

and development. Only the monkeys' physical aspects were normal, however. As Harlow observed these young, he noted that over the long term, these infants lacked very basic social skills. This effect occurred regardless of which types of surrogate mothers were available to the infants. For example, when the females reached reproductive age and had their own young, they were severely lacking in mothering skills. They showed no affection toward their offspring. They appeared to have no interest in touching and maintaining body contact with their offspring. In fact, they were often abusive toward their young—hitting them, biting them, and injuring them. In addition, those infants raised without biological mothers were generally not capable of getting along with other monkeys.

Harlow's experiments provided an understanding of the origins of social behavior. They also offered insights into abusive behaviors seen in humans. This pioneering research also showed that some key behaviors, such as mothering skills, are not genetically preprogrammed. Such behaviors are learned. Thus they require the presence of a caregiver who has been raised by a caregiver with the requisite skills. And thus the lack of nurturing skills has potentially long-term, intergenerational negative consequences.

ATTACHMENT STYLE If Bowlby and Harlow were correct in hypothesizing that attachment encourages proximity between infant and caregiver, then we might expect attachment responses to increase when children start moving away from caregivers. And indeed, just when infants begin to understand the difference between their attachment figures and strangers, and at the same time start to move away from them by crawling—at around 8 to 12 months—they typically display *separation anxiety*. That is, when the infants cannot see or are separated from their attachment figures or are left with babysitters, they may become very distressed. This pattern occurs in all human cultures.

To study attachment behaviors in humans, the developmental psychologist Mary D. Salter Ainsworth created the *strange-situation test*. The researchers observe the test through a one-way mirror in the laboratory. On the other side of the mirror is a playroom. There, the child, the caregiver, and a friendly but unfamiliar adult engage in a series of eight semi-structured episodes. The crux of the procedure is a standard sequence of separations and reunions between the child and each adult. Over the course of the eight episodes, the child experiences increasing distress and a greater need for caregiver proximity. The extent to which the child copes with distress and the strategies he or she uses to do so indicate the quality of the child's attachment to the caregiver. The researchers record the child's activity level and actions such as crying, playing, and paying attention to the mother and the stranger. Using the strange-situation test, Ainsworth identified infant/caregiver pairs that appeared *secure* as well as those that appeared *insecure,* or *anxious* (Ainsworth, Blehar, Waters, & Wall, 1978; **Figure 9.10**).

Secure attachment applies to approximately 60–65 percent of children. A secure child is happy to play alone and is friendly to the stranger as long as the attachment figure is present. When the attachment figure leaves the playroom, the child is distressed, whines or cries, and shows signs of looking for the attachment figure. When the attachment figure returns, the child usually reaches his or her arms up to be picked up and then is happy and quickly comforted by the caregiver. Then the child feels secure enough to return to playing. The key behavior to notice here, similar to what Harlow found with his monkeys, is the use of the caregiver as a source of security in times of distress. Just as a monkey would calm down when in contact with its cuddly cloth "mother," a securely attached human infant will be soothed immediately after a distressing separation when the caregiver picks up the infant.

Insecure attachment applies to the remaining 35–40 percent of children. Insecure attachments (sometimes referred to as *anxious* attachments) can take many forms, from an infant's completely avoiding contact with the caregiver during the strange-situation test to the infant's actively hitting or exhibiting angry facial expressions toward the caregiver (Ainsworth et al., 1978). Insecure attachments typically are of two types. Those with *avoidant* attachment do not get upset or cry at all when the caregiver leaves, and they may prefer to play with the stranger rather than the parent during their time in the playroom. Those with an *ambivalent* attachment style (sometimes called *anxious/ambivalent*) may cry a great deal when the caregiver leaves the room, but then be inconsolable when the caregiver tries to calm them down upon return. Insecurely attached infants have learned that their caregiver is not available to soothe them when distressed or is only inconsistently available. These children may be emotionally neglected or actively rejected by their attachment figures. Caregivers of insecurely attached infants typically have rejecting or inconsistently responsive parenting styles.

Keep in mind, however, that attachment is a complex developmental phenomenon. As in all relationships, both parties contribute to the quality or success of the interactions. For example, if a child has a disability such as autism—which may cause the infant to not cling to the caregiver or not make eye contact—the

secure attachment The attachment style for a majority of infants; the infant is confident enough to play in an unfamiliar environment as long as the caregiver is present and is readily comforted by the caregiver during times of distress.

insecure attachment The attachment style for a minority of infants; the infant may exhibit insecure attachment through various behaviors, such as avoiding contact with the caregiver, or by alternating between approach and avoidance behaviors.

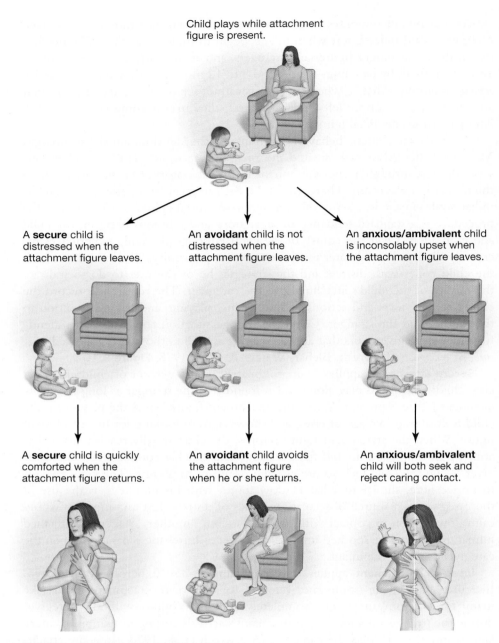

Child plays while attachment figure is present.

A **secure** child is distressed when the attachment figure leaves.

An **avoidant** child is not distressed when the attachment figure leaves.

An **anxious/ambivalent** child is inconsolably upset when the attachment figure leaves.

A **secure** child is quickly comforted when the attachment figure returns.

An **avoidant** child avoids the attachment figure when he or she returns.

An **anxious/ambivalent** child will both seek and reject caring contact.

FIGURE 9.10 The Strange-Situation Test

caregiver may have a more difficult time forming a secure emotional bond with the infant (Rutgers, Bakermans-Kranenburg, van Ijzendoorn, & van Berckelaer-Onnes, 2004). Similarly, if a parent is incapacitated by mental illness or extreme stress, he or she may not be able to exhibit warm or responsive behaviors to meet the baby's needs, thus reducing the likelihood of a secure attachment (Cicchetti, Rogosh, & Toth, 1998).

In cases of insecure (or anxious) attachment, it is important that early prevention efforts take place. The caregiver will need to build the skills necessary to increase the likelihood of secure attachments forming. As decades of research show, secure attachments are related to better socioemotional functioning in childhood, better peer relations, and successful adjustment at school (e.g., Bohlin, Hagekull, & Rydell, 2000; Granot & Mayseless, 2001). In contrast, insecure attachments have

Understanding That "Some" Does Not Mean "All"

As discussed in Chapter 2, researchers performing a longitudinal research study will test the same participants repeatedly over time. In a longitudinal study of attachment styles, researchers found that children who were rated as securely attached at 12 months of age (using the strange-situation test) were more socially competent in primary school and had healthier romantic relationships as young adults than those who were not securely attached (Simpson, Collins, Tran, & Haydon, 2007). These results show the importance of having positive attachments early in life: Such relationships are predictive of better attachment and adjustment over the next several decades of life.

What do these research findings say about a person who was not securely attached as an infant and did not develop a close and early bond with an adult? Should that person just give up now and forget about having positive romantic relationships? Of course not. Having a secure attachment in infancy makes it *more likely* that an adult will have healthy romantic attachments. But that attachment does not guarantee the result, nor does the lack of secure attachment to a caregiver in infancy mean that a person will not have strong romantic relationships later in life. Research is based on averages and probabilities, so research results do not imply that every person will develop in the way the results suggest.

In trying to apply these results to our own lives, however, we might misinterpret the take-home message as something like "If I was securely attached to my caregiver in infancy, I will have better romantic relationships as a young adult." That is, in thinking about such findings, we tend to change relative probabilities (e.g., "If securely attached as an infant, a person is *more likely* to have healthy romantic relationships later in life") to absolute statements (e.g., "If securely attached as an infant, a person *will* have healthy romantic relationships later in life" or the converse, "If not securely attached as an infant, a person *will not* have healthy romantic relationships later in life," which is equally wrong). The problem arises when we convert terms such as *some* and *more* into *all*. By focusing on the properly limited meanings of a study's terms, we can draw correct conclusions from that study's results.

"They got extinct because they didn't listen to their mommies."

been linked to poor outcomes later in life, such as depression and behavioral problems (e.g., Munson, McMahon, & Spieker, 2001).

CHEMISTRY OF ATTACHMENT Researchers have discovered that the hormone oxytocin is related to social behaviors, including infant/caregiver attachment (Carter, 2003; Feldman, Weller, Zagoory-Sharon, & Levine, 2007). Oxytocin plays a role in maternal tendencies, feelings of social acceptance and bonding, and sexual gratification. In the mother and the infant, oxytocin promotes behaviors that ensure the survival of the young. For instance, infant sucking during nursing triggers the release of oxytocin in the mother. This release stimulates biological processes in the mother that move milk into the milk ducts so the infant can nurse. This line of research provides a helpful reminder that phenomena that appear to be completely social in nature, such as the caregiver/child attachment, also have biological influences.

Summing Up

What Shapes Us during Childhood?

The human genome consists of instructions for building a functioning human being, but from the earliest moment of human development, environmental factors influence how each individual is formed. Throughout the prenatal period, various environmental agents, from the parents' hormones to substances they consume, can alter the formation of the fetus and its cognitive capacities. Once the child is born, learning is influenced by the development of both brain and body. Except in cases of abuse or some serious illnesses, children crawl and walk when their bodies develop the appropriate musculature and when their brains mature sufficiently to coordinate motor actions. These physical developments are also shaped by the internal motivation of the infant and the way he or she interprets feedback from the physical and social world. All new developmental skills emerge as a result of dynamic systems of influence, ranging from new synaptic connections to personality factors to cultural expectations. Humans are social creatures, and a young infant normally forms bonds of attachment with caregivers. The quality of these attachments, as well as the child's adjustment later in life, are shaped by interactions with the caregivers. Caregivers help infants to both regulate their emotional states and learn healthy ways to interact with others.

Measuring Up

1. Which of the following research findings would support the idea that humans have sensitive learning periods?
   a. Relative to many other animals, humans are almost helpless at birth.
   b. Genie could not learn to make coherent sentences, even after four years of therapy.
   c. Throughout the life span, the human brain reorganizes itself based on new experiences.
   d. There are individual differences in the rates of human physical development.

2. Which of the following statements is true regarding the research findings on attachment?
   a. Harlow's research on monkeys confirmed the idea that attachment is driven by biological needs such as hunger.
   b. Children with secure attachments will always grow up to be better adjusted than children with insecure attachments.
   c. If an infant cries as the caregiver leaves the room during the strange-situation test, the infant is probably insecurely attached.
   d. Warm, responsive, and supportive parenting helps children regulate their emotions, an essential skill for developing healthy adult relationships.

Answers: 1. b. Genie could not learn to make coherent sentences, even after four years of therapy. 2. d. Warm, responsive, and supportive parenting helps children regulate their emotions, an essential skill for developing healthy adult relationships.

As Children, How Do We Learn about the World?

Perception Introduces the World

To learn, children need to obtain information from the world. They do so principally through their senses. As noted earlier, newborns have all their senses at birth, although some of their senses are not fully developed. The development of their sensory capacities allows infants to observe and evaluate the objects and events around them. The infants then use the information gained from perception to try to make sense of how the world works.

INFANT RESEARCH TECHNIQUES How can we tell what a baby knows about the world? Psychologists have devised clever experiments for gauging what infants perceive about the objects and events in the infants' environments. Based on the observation that infants tend to look longer at stimuli that interest them, one type of experiment uses the *preferential-looking technique*. In using this technique, the researchers show an infant two things. If the infant looks longer at one of the things, the researchers know the infant can distinguish between the two and finds one more interesting.

Other experiments are based on the *orienting reflex*. This term refers to humans' tendency to pay more attention to new stimuli than to stimuli to which they have become habituated, or grown accustomed (Fantz, 1966). Even from birth, an infant will look away more quickly from something familiar than from something unfamiliar or puzzling. By using their knowledge of habituation, researchers can create a response preference in an infant for one stimulus over another.

For example, researchers might show the infant a picture or an object until the infant is familiar enough with it that the infant adapts to the stimulus or becomes bored. Thus the amount of time the infant looks at the stimulus declines. At that point, the researchers can measure whether the infant reacts to a change in the stimulus: If shown a new picture or new object, will the infant look longer at it? If so, the infant is noticing a difference between the old and new stimuli. If the infant looks at the new stimulus the same amount of time he or she looks at the old stimulus, the researchers assume the infant does not distinguish between the two. Such tests are used to gauge everything from infants' perceptual abilities—how and when they can perceive color, depth, and movement, for instance—to their understanding of words, faces, numbers, and laws of physics. So what do we know about infants' early perceptual abilities? What can they learn about their worlds?

VISION The ability to distinguish differences among shapes, patterns, and colors develops early in infancy. Developmental psychologists use the preferential-looking technique to determine how well an infant can see. That is, they measure the infant's *visual acuity*. Infants respond more to objects with high-contrast patterns, for example, than to other stimuli. In the early 1960s, Robert Fantz and other developmental psychologists observed infants' reactions to patterns of black-and-white stripes as well as patches of gray (**Figure 9.11**). In these studies, the mother or another caregiver was asked to hold the infant in front of a display of the two images. The experimenter, not knowing which image was on which side, would observe through a peephole to see where the infant preferred to look

FIGURE 9.11 Vision in Infancy Robert Fantz was the first scientist to determine that infants prefer patterns with high contrast. A more thorough understanding of infants' visual abilities has led parents to buy mobiles and toys that use some of Fantz's testing patterns.

A mother holds her infant in front of a display showing (left) a patch of gray and (right) a black-and-white pattern.

On the other side of the display, an experimenter looks through a peephole and notes whether the infant is looking left or right.

FIGURE 9.12 Testing Visual Acuity in Infants Which infant-research technique is being used here to test visual acuity?

(**Figure 9.12**). This research revealed that infants look at stripes with high contrast more readily than at gray images. The smaller the stripes are—that is, the less contrast between the images—the more difficult it becomes for infants to distinguish them from the gray patches.

Infants' visual acuity for distant objects is poor when they are first born, but it increases rapidly over the first six months (Teller, Morse, Borton, & Regal, 1974). They do not reach adult levels of acuity until they are about a year old. The increase in visual acuity is probably due to a combination of practice in looking at things in the world, the development of the visual cortex, and the development of the cones in the retina (as noted in Chapter 4, the cones are important for perceiving detail). Here again, development proceeds as a result of dynamic systems of interaction.

AUDITORY PERCEPTION When a newborn is presented with sounds, such as the shaking of a rattle in the right or left ear, the infant will turn her or his head in the direction of the sounds. This movement indicates both that the infant has perceived the sounds and that she or he knows where the sounds are coming from. The infant's abilities to recognize sounds and locate those sounds in space improve continuously as she or he gains experience with objects and people and as the auditory cortex develops. By the age of 6 months, the baby will have a nearly adult level of auditory function (DeCasper & Spence, 1986).

Infants also seem to have some memory and preference for sounds. To determine what sounds a 2-day-old infant can remember and whether that infant will prefer his or her mother's voice over other voices, Anthony DeCasper and William Fifer (1980) used operant conditioning (discussed in Chapter 6, "Learning"). By measuring an infant's rate of sucking on a rubber nipple, they determined if the infant was aroused in response to a specific sound. In their study, each infant wore earphones and was given a nipple linked to recordings of his or her mother's voice and a stranger's voice. If the infant paused for a longer time between sucking bursts, the mother's voice played. If the infant paused for a shorter time, the stranger's voice played. Even at this young age, the newborns learned to alter their sucking patterns to hear their mother's voices more often.

Memory Improves during Childhood

The development of memory helps children learn about the world around them. That is, children are able to use new information to build on what they already know. In two experiments, Carolyn Rovee-Collier (1999) revealed that from a very young age, infants possess some types of memory.

In one experiment, a mobile hanging over a crib was attached to an infant's ankle with a ribbon. The infant learned that he or she could move the mobile by kicking. The rate at which the infant kicked when the mobile was not attached served as the baseline. When the infant was tested later, the ribbon was attached to the ankle but not to the mobile, so the kicks no longer moved the mobile. If the baby recognized the mobile, presumably it would kick faster than the baseline rate to try to make the mobile move. Infants ranging in age from 2 months to 18 months were trained for two days on the mobile task and then tested after different lengths of time. The findings indicated, compared to younger infants, that older infants could retain their memories regarding the connection between the ankle kicking and the mobile movement for longer periods of time. By 18 months, the infants could remember the event even if they were tested several weeks after they learned the initial associations (**Figure 9.13**).

INFANTILE AMNESIA What is your earliest memory? Most adults remember few events that occurred before they were 3 or 4 years old. Freud referred to this inability to remember events from early childhood as **infantile amnesia.** Psychologists have offered various explanations for this phenomenon (Eacott, 1999). Some psychologists believe that children begin to retain memories after developing the ability to create autobiographical memory based on personal experience. For instance, a child might recall that "a cat scratched me" rather than "cats scratch." Other psychologists suggest that childhood memory develops with language acquisition because the ability to use words and concepts aids in memory retention. Still other psychologists theorize that children younger than 3 or 4 do not perceive contexts well enough to store memories accurately. They argue that improvements in children's abilities to encode new information, retain it for longer periods, and retrieve it deliberately underlie the decrease in infantile amnesia after the first five years of life (Hayne, 2004).

infantile amnesia The inability to remember events from early childhood.

FIGURE 9.13 Scientific Method: The Memory-Retention Test

Hypothesis: Very young infants have memory.

Research Method:

1 The rate at which an infant in a crib kicked under normal conditions was measured.

2 A mobile was hung over the crib and attached to the infant's ankle with a ribbon, so that when the infant kicked, the mobile moved.

3 The rate at which the infant kicked with the ribbon attached was measured against the normal rate of kicking.

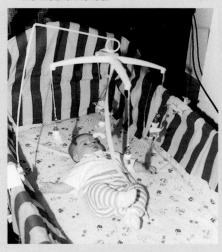

4 Later (at different delay intervals), each infant was placed in the crib, and the kicking rate was measured. A high rate of kicking indicated that the infant remembered that kicking moved the mobile.

Results: Among infants ranging from 2 months to 18 months old, older infants remembered the mobile for longer periods.

Conclusion: Very young infants have memory.

Source: Rovee-Collier, C. (1999). The development of infant memory. *Current Directions in Psychological Science, 8,* 80–85.

INACCURATE MEMORY Young children often have source amnesia (difficulty knowing where they learned something; discussed in Chapter 7, "Attention and Memory"). For example, even when tested immediately after being presented with information, 3-year-old children forget the source of the information faster than do 5-year-old children (Gopnik & Graf, 1988). Evidence from investigations of source amnesia suggests that many of our earliest memories come from looking at pictures in family albums, watching home movies, or hearing stories from our parents—not from actual memories of the events (Hyman & Pentland, 1996).

Children are also known to confabulate (make things up; also discussed in Chapter 7). The fact that children have underdeveloped frontal lobes may explain why they are more likely than adults to engage in this behavior. Confabulation happens most when children are asked about personal experiences rather than general knowledge. In one study, preschool children were interviewed repeatedly and asked to remember if their fingers had ever been caught in a mousetrap. They were asked to think hard about the event and to visualize the scene: who was with them, what they were wearing, and so on. After 10 weeks in which the children were to have thought about the event, a new interviewer repeated the question. Sixty percent of the children provided false narratives, telling a story about getting their fingers caught and behaving as if it really had happened. Many of the children developed very elaborate stories with numerous details about why their fingers had been caught and how it had felt (Bruck & Ceci, 1993). This research supports a point emphasized in Chapter 7: Memories can change based on later experience.

In your own experience, you might have noticed that people can have different memories of the same event. For example, siblings sometimes argue about memories. Each sibling may claim that the same event really happened to him or her. Researchers have found that most of the disputed events are for events that occurred during the preschool years, when source memory was still developing (Ikier, Tekcan, Gülgöz, & Küntay, 2003). Memory skills improve as cognitive abilities mature.

Piaget Emphasized Stages of Cognitive Development

Ultimately, how do we account for the differences between children's ways of thinking and adults' ways of thinking? Are children merely inexperienced humans? Do they simply not have the skills and knowledge that adults normally have learned over time? Or do children's minds work in qualitatively different ways from those of adults?

Through careful observations of young children, Jean Piaget devised an influential theory about the development of thinking (**Figure 9.14**; for more on Piaget, see Chapter 1, "Introduction"). Many of Piaget's ideas have consistently been found to be correct. As discussed here, however, researchers have challenged some of Piaget's assertions.

One crucial aspect of Piaget's research is that he paid as much attention to how children make errors as to how they succeed on tasks. These mistakes, illogical by adult standards, provide insights into how young minds make sense of the world. By systematically analyzing children's thinking, Piaget developed the theory that children go through four *stages of development,* which reflect different ways of thinking about the world. These stages are called *sensorimotor, preoperational, concrete operational, and formal operational* (**Figure 9.15**).

FIGURE 9.14 Jean Piaget Piaget introduced the idea that cognitive development occurs in stages.

From Piaget's perspective, it is not that children know less than adults. Rather, children's views of how the world works are based on different sets of assumptions than those held by adults. Contemporary researchers argue that such developmental "immaturity" in early-stage thinking actually serves very important functions for children's abilities to grow in their mental processes (Bjorklund, 2007).

Piaget proposed that we form new schemas during each stage of development. As defined and discussed in Chapter 7, schemas are ways of thinking—conceptual models of how the world works. Piaget believed that each stage builds on the previous one through two learning processes: Through **assimilation,** we place a new experience into an existing schema. Through **accommodation** (a different term than the one presented in Chapter 5), we create a new schema or dramatically alter an existing one, to include new information that otherwise would not fit into the schema.

assimilation The process by which we place new information into an existing schema.

accommodation The process by which we create a new schema or drastically alter an existing schema to include new information that otherwise would not fit into the schema.

Stage	Characterization	
1 Sensorimotor (birth–2 years)	• Differentiates self from objects • Recognizes self as agent of action and begins to act intentionally; for example, pulls a string to set a mobile in motion or shakes a rattle to make a noise • Achieves object permanence: realizes that things continue to exist even when no longer present to the senses 	
2 Preoperational (2–7 years)	• Learns to use language and to represent objects by images and words • Thinking is still egocentric: has difficulty taking the viewpoint of others • Classifies objects by a single feature; for example, groups together all the red blocks regardless of shape or all the square blocks regardless of color 	
3 Concrete operational (7–12 years)	• Can think logically about objects and events • Achieves conservation of number (age 7), mass (age 7), and weight (age 9) • Classifies objects by several features and can order them in a series along a single dimension, such as size 	
4 Formal operational (12 years and up)	• Can think logically about abstract propositions and test hypotheses systematically • Becomes concerned with the hypothetical, the future, and ideological problems 	

FIGURE 9.15 Piaget's Stages of Cognitive Development

For example, a 2-year-old might see a cow for the first time and shout, "Doggie!" After all, a cow has four legs and fur and is certainly not a human. Thus, based on a dog schema the child has developed, the label "doggie" can be considered logical. But the toddler's parent says, "No, honey, that's a cow! See, it doesn't say 'arf!' It says 'moo!' And it is much bigger than a dog." Because the child cannot easily fit this new information into the existing dog schema using the process of assimilation, the child must now create a new schema, cow, through the process of accommodation.

SENSORIMOTOR STAGE (BIRTH TO 2 YEARS) From birth until about age 2, according to Piaget, children are in the **sensorimotor stage.** During this period, they acquire information primarily through their senses and motor exploration. Thus very young infants' understanding of objects occurs when they reflexively react to the sensory input from those objects. For example, they learn by sucking on a nipple, grasping a finger, or seeing a face. They progress from being reflexive to being reflective, capable of mentally representing their world and experiences with increasingly complex schemas.

As infants begin to control their motor movements, they develop their first schemas. These conceptual models consist of mental representations of the kinds of actions that can be performed on certain kinds of objects. For instance, the sucking reflex begins as a reaction to the sensory input from the nipple: Infants simply respond reflexively by sucking. Soon they realize they can suck other things, such as a bottle, a finger, a toy, or a blanket. Piaget described sucking other objects as an example of assimilation to the schema of sucking. But sucking a toy or a blanket does not result in the same experience as the reflexive sucking of a nipple. The difference between these experiences leads the child to alter the sucking schema to include new experiences and information. In other words, the child must continually adjust her or his understandings of sucking. For example, the child may create a new schema of sucking a blanket, which includes using less force than sucking on a bottle. This new schema is created through the process of accommodation.

According to Piaget, one important cognitive concept developed in this stage is **object permanence.** This term refers to the understanding that an object continues to exist even when it is hidden from view. Piaget noted that until 9 months of age, most infants will not search for objects they have seen being hidden under a blanket. At around 9 months, infants will look for the hidden object by picking up the blanket. Still, their search skills have limits. For instance, suppose during several trials an 8-month-old child watches an experimenter hide a toy under a blanket and the child then finds the toy. If the experimenter then hides the toy under a different blanket, in full view of the child, the child will still look for the toy in the first hiding place. Full comprehension of object permanence was, for Piaget, one key accomplishment of the sensorimotor period.

Recall that two other major developments occur during this period: Parent/child attachments are forming, and synaptic connections in the brain are being rapidly solidified based on experience. How might these developments be related to the cognitive ability to recognize that objects continue to exist when not seen? Object permanence aids the child in developing attachments to a small set of consistent caregivers. It also contributes to the child's understanding of the world of objects. Once again, development proceeds as a function of dynamic systems of interaction.

PREOPERATIONAL STAGE (2 TO 7 YEARS) In the **preoperational stage,** according to Piaget, children can begin to think about objects not in their immediate view,

sensorimotor stage The first stage in Piaget's theory of cognitive development; during this stage, infants acquire information about the world through their senses and motor skills. Reflexive responses develop into more deliberate actions through the development and refinement of schemas.

object permanence The understanding that an object continues to exist even when it cannot be seen.

preoperational stage The second stage in Piaget's theory of cognitive development; during this stage, children think symbolically about objects, but they reason based on intuition and superficial appearance rather than logic.

and they have developed conceptual models of how the world works. During this stage, children begin to think symbolically. For example, they can pretend that a stick is a sword or a wand. Piaget believed that what children cannot do at this stage is think "operationally." That is, they cannot imagine the logical outcomes of performing certain actions on certain objects. They do not base their reasoning on logic. Instead, they perform intuitive reasoning based on superficial appearances.

For instance, children at this stage have no understanding of the law of conservation of quantity: that even if a substance's appearance changes, its quantity may remain unchanged. If you pour a short, fat glass of water into a tall, thin glass, you know the amount of water has not changed. However, if you ask children in the preoperational stage which glass contains more, they will pick the tall, thin glass because the water is at a higher level. The children will make this error even when they have seen someone pour the same amount of water into each glass or when they pour the liquid themselves. They are fooled by the appearance of a higher water line. They cannot think about how the thinner diameter of the taller glass compensates for the higher-appearing water level (**Figure 9.16**).

This lack of conservation skills is thought to be due to a key cognitive limitation of the preoperational period: *centration*. This limitation occurs when a preschooler cannot think about more than one detail of a problem-solving task at a time. The child "centers" on only one detail or aspect of the problem, limiting the child's ability to think logically.

Another cognitive limitation characteristic of the preoperational period is *egocentrism*. This term refers to the tendency for preoperational thinkers to view the world through their own experiences. They can understand how others feel, and they have the capacity to care about others. They tend, however, to engage in thought processes that revolve around their own perspectives. For example, a 3-year-old may play hide-and-seek by standing next to a large tree and facing it with his or her eyes closed. The child believes that if he or she cannot see other people, other people cannot see him or her. Instead of viewing this egocentric thinking as a limitation, modern scholars agree with Piaget that such "immature" skills prepare children to take special note of their immediate surroundings and learn as much as they can about how their own minds and bodies interact with the world. A clear egocentric focus prevents them from trying to expand their schemas too much before they understand all the complex information inside their own experience (Bjorklund, 2007).

CONCRETE OPERATIONAL STAGE (7 TO 12 YEARS) At about 7 years of age, according to Piaget, children enter the **concrete operational stage.** They remain in this stage until adolescence. Piaget believed that humans do not develop logic until they begin to think about and understand operations. In other words, once people understand operations, they can figure out the world by thinking about how events are related. A classic *operation* is an action that can be undone: A light can be turned on and off, a stick can be moved across the table and then moved back, and so on. Operations are a type of logical thought. Thus a preoperational child lacks logical thought. A concrete operational child is able to think logically. According to Piaget, the ability to understand that an action is reversible enables children to begin to understand concepts such as conservation of quantity. Children in this period are not fooled by superficial transformations in the liquid's appearance in conservation tasks. They can reason logically about the problem. And they begin to understand with much more depth how other people view the world and feel about things.

1 A 6-year-old understands that two identical short glasses of water contain the same amount of water.

2 She pours the water from one of the short glasses into a tall glass.

3 When asked which glass has more water, she points to the taller glass, even though she poured the water from the equivalent shorter glass.

FIGURE 9.16 The Preoperational Stage and the Law of Conservation of Quantity In the preoperational stage, according to Piaget, children cannot yet understand the concept of conservation of quantity. They reason intuitively, not logically.

concrete operational stage The third stage in Piaget's theory of cognitive development; during this stage, children begin to think about and understand logical operations, and they are no longer fooled by appearances.

formal operational stage The final stage in Piaget's theory of cognitive development; during this stage, people can think abstractly, and they can formulate and test hypotheses through deductive logic.

Although this development is the beginning of logical thinking, Piaget believed that children at this stage reason only about concrete things (objects they can act on in the world). They do not yet have the ability to reason abstractly, or hypothetically, about what might be possible. For example, if a teacher wanted a group of fifth-graders to understand an abstract concept such as democracy, the teacher would have to make the problem concrete for the students. He or she might break the class up into two groups: citizens and politicians. Together, these groups might need to simulate an election and manage it on a budget. By playing roles and solving problems in the classroom, the students could grapple with the advantages and disadvantages of a democratic political system. With concrete information, children in this stage can think in much more logical and less egocentric ways than children in the preoperational stage. According to Piaget, however, it is not until they reach adolescence that children can truly engage in sophisticated scientific and abstract thinking.

FORMAL OPERATIONAL STAGE (12 YEARS TO ADULTHOOD) Piaget believed that after about age 12, all people can reason in sophisticated, abstract ways. Thus the **formal operational stage** is Piaget's final stage of cognitive development. Formal operations involve critical thinking. This kind of thinking is characterized by the ability to form a hypothesis about something and test it through deductive logic. It also involves using information to systematically find answers to problems.

Piaget devised a way to study this ability. He gave teenagers and younger children four flasks of colorless liquid and one flask of colored liquid. He then explained that the colored liquid could be obtained by combining two of the colorless liquids. Adolescents, he found, can systematically try different combinations to obtain the correct result. Younger children just randomly combine liquids. Adolescents can form hypotheses and systematically test them. They are able to consider abstract notions and think about many viewpoints at once.

CHALLENGES TO PIAGET'S THEORY Piaget revolutionized the understanding of cognitive development. He was right about many things. For example, infants do learn about the world through sensorimotor exploration. Also, people do move from intuitive, illogical thinking to a more logical understanding of the world. Piaget also believed, however, that as children progress through each stage, they all use the same kind of logic to solve problems. His framework thus leaves little room for differing cognitive strategies or skills among individuals—or among cultures.

Some evidence supports Piaget's view. Still, many children move back and forth between stages if they are working on tasks that require varying skill levels. They may think in concrete operational ways on some tasks but revert to preoperational logic when faced with a novel task. Theorists believe that different areas in the brain are responsible for different skills and that development does not necessarily follow strict and uniform stages (Bidell & Fischer, 1995; Case, 1992; Fischer, 1980).

In addition, Piaget thought that all adults were formal operational thinkers. More-recent work has shown that without specific training or education in this type of thinking, many adults continue to reason in concrete operational ways, instead of employing critical and analytical thinking skills. These adults may think abstractly regarding topics with which they are familiar but not on new and unfamiliar tasks (De Lisi & Staudt, 1980).

Moreover, Piaget underestimated the age at which certain skills develop. For example, contemporary researchers have found that object permanence develops in the first few months of life, instead of at 8 or 9 months of age, as Piaget thought. With new scientific methods that do not require infants to physically search for hidden objects, researchers have found object permanence abilities in infants as early as 3.5 months of age (Baillargeon, 1987).

Consider the apple/carrot test devised by the developmental psychologist Renée Baillargeon (1995). The researcher shows an apple to an infant who is sitting on her or his parent's lap. The researcher lowers a screen in front of the apple, then raises the screen to show the apple. Then the researcher performs the same actions, but this time raises the screen to show a carrot—a surprising, impossible event. If the infant looks longer at the carrot than he or she had looked at the apple, the researcher can assume that the infant expected to see the apple. By responding differently to such an impossible event than to possible ones, infants demonstrate some understanding that an object continues to exist when it is out of sight. Thus, in his various testing protocols, Piaget may have confused infants' cognitive abilities with infants' physical capabilities.

UNDERSTANDING THE LAWS OF NATURE: PHYSICS Numerous studies conducted by the developmental psychologist Elizabeth Spelke and colleagues have indicated that infants even have a primitive understanding of some of the basic laws of physics. Consider one such example. Humans are born with the ability to perceive movement: A newborn will follow a moving stimulus with his or her eyes and head, and a newborn will also prefer to look at a moving stimulus than to look at a stationary one. As infants get older, they use movement information to determine if an object is continuous—that is, if it is all one object, even if the infant cannot see the entire thing because it is partially hidden (Kellman, Spelke, & Short, 1986).

In one experiment, the researchers showed 4-month-old infants a rod moving back and forth behind a block. Once habituated, the infants were shown two scenes: In one scene, the block was removed and there was a single rod. In the other scene, the block was removed and there were two small rods. The infants looked longer at the two small rods (**Figure 9.17**). This response indicated that they expected the rod moving behind the block to be one continuous object rather than two small ones.

Understanding the relation between the movement and the physical properties of the rod requires various cognitive skills. It requires the ability to see the rod as an object separate from the block and to surmise that since the two ends are moving together, they must be part of the same whole rod, even though part of the rod is hidden. If the experiment is conducted with a stationary rod, however, the infants do not look longer at the two small rods. Therefore, infants appear to use movement to infer that objects moving together are continuous, whereas for infants two stationary objects may or may not be continuous.

UNDERSTANDING THE LAWS OF NATURE: MATHEMATICS How much do you think infants and toddlers know about counting and other mathematical operations? Piaget believed that young children do not understand numbers and therefore must learn counting and other number-related skills through memorization. For some of his experiments in this area, he showed two rows of marbles to children from 4 to 5 years of age. Both rows had the same number of marbles, but in one row the marbles were spread out. The children usually said the longer row had more marbles (**Figure 9.18**). Piaget concluded that children understand quantity—the concepts *more than* and *less than*—in terms of length. He felt that children do not understand quantity in terms of number.

Challenging Piaget's view, Jacques Mehler and Tom Bever (1967) argued that children younger than 3 years of age can understand *more than* and *less than*.

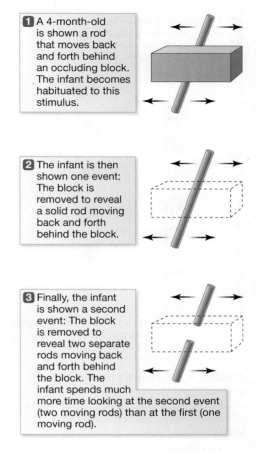

1 A 4-month-old is shown a rod that moves back and forth behind an occluding block. The infant becomes habituated to this stimulus.

2 The infant is then shown one event: The block is removed to reveal a solid rod moving back and forth behind the block.

3 Finally, the infant is shown a second event: The block is removed to reveal two separate rods moving back and forth behind the block. The infant spends much more time looking at the second event (two moving rods) than at the first (one moving rod).

FIGURE 9.17 The Perceptual Effect of Occlusions in Early Infancy As shown by this rod-and-block test, infants are able to perceive that objects moving together are continuous. Understanding the relation between movement and physical properties requires cognitive skills beyond those that Piaget expected 4-month-old infants to have.

1 A 4-year-old is shown two rows of marbles. Each row has the same number of marbles, but one row is spread out.

2 When asked which row has more marbles, the 4-year-old says the longer row.

FIGURE 9.18 Piaget's Marble Test This test led Piaget to conclude that very young children do not understand quantity in terms of number. They understand it in terms of length.

theory of mind The term used to describe the ability to explain and predict another person's behavior as a result of recognizing her or his mental state.

To demonstrate their point, they cleverly repeated Piaget's experiment using M&M's candy. They showed the children two rows of four M&M's each and asked if the rows were the same. When the children said yes, the researchers then transformed the rows. For instance, they would add two candies to the second row, but compress that row so it was shorter than the row with fewer candies. Then they would tell the children to pick the row they wanted to eat. More than 80 percent picked the row with more M&M's, even though it was the visually shorter row (**Figure 9.19**). This research indicated that when children are properly motivated, they understand and can demonstrate their knowledge of *more than* and *less than*. Despite Piaget's enormous contributions to the understanding of cognitive development, the growing evidence that infants have innate knowledge challenges his theory of distinct stages of cognitive development.

We Learn from Interacting with Others

According to current thinking among developmental psychologists, early social interactions between infant and caregiver are essential for understanding other people and communicating with them through language. In turn, these skills enable us to live in society. To interact with other people successfully, we need to be aware of other people's intentions, behave in ways that generally conform to others' expectations, develop moral codes that guide our actions, and so on. Consider a routine activity such as driving a car. To drive safely, we need to predict and respond to the actions of others: car drivers, truck drivers, motorcyclists, bicyclists, and pedestrians. Any of those people's actions can be erratic.

THEORY OF MIND In dealing with other people, we try to recognize each person's mental state. That is, we infer what the person is feeling or thinking. From that inference, we anticipate the other person's behavior. Predicting another person's behavior based on that person's mental state constitutes **theory of mind.**

Beginning in infancy, young children come to understand that other people perform actions for reasons (Gergely & Csibra, 2003; Sommerville & Woodward, 2005). The recognition that actions can be intentional reflects a capacity for theory of mind, and it allows people to understand, predict, and attempt to influence others' behavior (Baldwin & Baird, 2001).

In one study, an adult began handing a toy to an infant. On some trials, the adult became unwilling to hand over the toy (e.g., teasing the infant with the toy or playing with it himself or herself). On other trials, the adult became unable to hand it over (e.g., "accidentally" dropping it or being distracted by a ringing telephone). Infants older than 9 months showed greater signs of impatience—for example, reaching for the toy—when the adult was unwilling than when the adult was unable (Behne, Carpenter, Call, & Tomasello, 2005). This research shows that very young children understand other peoples' intentions, capabilities, and reasoning behind their actions.

Another study suggests that the ability to understand intentions is developed by 13 months of age. Here infants watched animations of a caterpillar as it searched behind a screen for food. On some trials, the caterpillar had information about whether a particular food was behind the screen. On other trials, the caterpillar did not have this information. To determine whether the infants expected the caterpillar to find the food, the researchers measured the amounts of time the infants looked at the screen. The infants' expectations appeared to depend on what they believed the caterpillar knew (Surian, Caldi, & Sperber, 2007). These studies and others (e.g., Onishi & Baillargeon, 2005) provide strong evidence that in the first year of life, children begin to read intentions and that by the end of the second year, perhaps even by 13 to 15 months of age, they become very good at reading them (Baillargeon, Li, Ng, & Yuan, 2009). In other words, even though preschool-age children tend to behave in egocentric ways and view the world through their own perspectives, mounting evidence suggests that they have the cognitive abilities to understand others' perspectives.

Children's development of theory of mind appears to coincide with the maturation of the brain's frontal lobes. The importance of the frontal lobes for theory of mind is also supported by research with adults. In brain imaging studies, prefrontal brain regions become active when people are asked to think about other people's mental states. People with damage to this region have difficulty attributing mental states to characters in stories (Stone, Baron-Cohen, & Knight, 1998). Brain imaging studies of theory of mind conducted in Canada, the United States, England, France, Germany, Japan, and Sweden have found similar patterns of activity in prefrontal regions (Frank & Temple, 2009). These findings support the idea that the ability is universal and biologically based. Unlike theory of mind, however, the way people understand morality and come to view moral judgments can vary widely based on socialization history and cultural experiences.

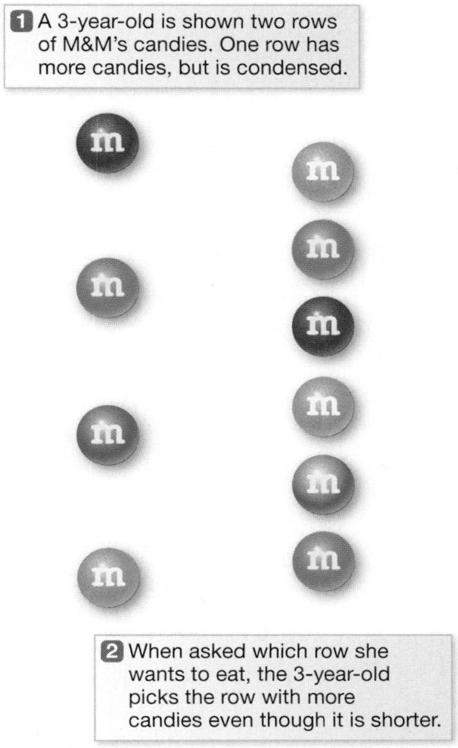

MORAL REASONING AND MORAL EMOTIONS Moral development is the way people learn to decide between behaviors with competing social outcomes. In other words, it involves the choices people make that affect others: When is it acceptable to take an action that may harm others or that may break implicit or explicit social contracts? Ideally, the ability to consider questions about morality develops during childhood and continues into adulthood. Theorists typically divide morality into *moral reasoning,* which depends on cognitive processes, and *moral emotions.* Of course, cognition and emotions are intertwined. Research has shown that if people lack adequate cognitive abilities, their moral emotions may not translate into moral behaviors (Tangney, Stuewig, & Mashek, 2007). Similarly, moral reasoning is enhanced by moral emotions (Moll & de Oliveira-Souza, 2007).

Psychologists who study the cognitive processes of moral behavior have focused largely on Lawrence Kohlberg's stage theory. Kohlberg (1984) tested moral-reasoning skills by asking people to respond to hypothetical situations in which a main character was faced with a moral dilemma. For example, the character had to steal a drug to save his dying wife because he could not afford the drug. Kohlberg was most concerned with the reasons people provided for their answers, rather than the answers themselves. He devised a theory of moral judgment that involved three main levels of moral reasoning.

At the **preconventional level,** people classify answers in terms of self-interest or pleasurable outcomes. For example, a child at this level might say, "He should steal the drug because then he will have it." At the **conventional level,** people's responses conform to rules of law and order or focus on others' disapproval. For example, a person at this level might say, "He shouldn't take the drug. You are not supposed to steal, so everyone will think he is a bad person." At the **postconventional level,** the highest level of moral reasoning, people's responses center around complex reasoning about abstract principles and the value of all life. For example, a person at this level might say, "Sometimes people have to break the law if the law is unjust. In this case, it's wrong to steal, but it's more wrong to charge too much money for a drug that could save a person's life." Thus Kohlberg

1 A 3-year-old is shown two rows of M&M's candies. One row has more candies, but is condensed.

2 When asked which row she wants to eat, the 3-year-old picks the row with more candies even though it is shorter.

FIGURE 9.19 The M&M's Version of Piaget's Marble Test This test enabled Mehler and Bever to show that very young children can in fact understand quantity in terms of number. **Children who might not have succeeded on Piaget's marble test were able to choose the row that contained more M&M's. Why?**

preconventional level Earliest level of moral development; at this level, self-interest and event outcomes determine what is moral.

conventional level Middle stage of moral development; at this level, strict adherence to societal rules and the approval of others determine what is moral.

postconventional level Highest stage of moral development; at this level, decisions about morality depend on abstract principles and the value of all life.

considered advanced moral reasoning to include a consideration of the greater good for all people, with less thought given to personal wishes or fear of punishment.

Moral-reasoning theories such as Kohlberg's have been faulted for emphasizing only the cognitive aspects of morality to the detriment of emotional issues that influence moral judgments, such as shame, pride, or embarrassment. Moreover, some theorists contend that moral reasoning fails to predict moral behavior because it excludes the complexities of morality. They believe instead that moral actions, such as helping others in need, are influenced more by emotions than by cognitive processes.

Research on the emotional components of moral behavior has focused largely on *empathy* and *sympathy*. These feelings are called moral emotions because they are related to moral behaviors. Empathy arises from understanding another's emotional state and feeling what the other person is feeling or would be expected to feel in the given situation. In contrast, sympathy arises from feelings of concern, pity, or sorrow for another (Eisenberg, 2000). In other words, empathy involves feeling *with* the other person. Sympathy involves feeling *for* the other person. Sympathy may produce different emotions from those experienced by the other person. Moral emotions, such as embarrassment and shame, are considered self-conscious emotions because they require comprehension of oneself as a causal agent and because they require an evaluation of one's own responses in comparison to other people.

Recent research has shown that parents' behaviors influence their children's level of both moral emotions and prosocial behavior. When parents are high in sympathy, promote an understanding of and focus on others, do not express hostility in the home, allow their children to express negative emotions in ways that do not harm others, and help their children cope with negative emotions, they tend to have children who are high in sympathy (Eisenberg, 2002; **Figure 9.20**). In contrast, when parents show frequent anger, are lax in discipline, and do not respond positively to the children's appropriate behavior, they tend to have children who are high in shame (Ferguson & Stegge, 1995).

Thus not all children progress through the stages of moral development at the same rate or in the same order. Research has shown that when a parent or guardian responds to a child's behavior, there is great value in displaying inductive reasoning, as in "You made Chris cry. It's not nice to hit because it hurts people." Adults' displays of inductive reasoning promote children's sympathetic attitudes, appropriate feelings of guilt, and awareness of others' feelings. The children's attitudes, feelings, and awareness then influence their moral reasoning and behavioral choices.

PHYSIOLOGICAL BASIS OF MORALITY Children develop their senses of morality through socialization, especially from interactions with their parents and members of their community and culture. Still, the moral emotions may be based in the physiological mechanisms that help people make decisions. As discussed in Chapter 10, Antonio Damasio's somatic marker theory states that people have a visceral response (they seem to feel it in the gut or stomach) to real or imagined outcomes and that this response aids decision making. People with damage to the prefrontal cortex fail to become emotionally involved in decision making because their somatic markers are not engaged.

Damasio and colleagues (Anderson, Bechara, Damasio, Tranel, & Damasio, 1999) studied two people who had experienced prefrontal damage during infancy. Both individuals showed severe deficiencies in moral and social reasoning. When given Kohlberg's moral-dilemma task, both patients scored at the preconventional level. These patients also neglected social and emotional factors in their

FIGURE 9.20 Parental Behavior Affects Children's Behavior Parents who are high in sympathy, and who allow their children to express negative emotions without shame or hostility, tend to have children who are high in sympathy.

life decisions. Both failed to express empathy, remorse, or guilt for wrongdoing, and neither had particularly good parenting skills. One engaged in petty thievery, was verbally and physically threatening (once to the point of physical assault), and frequently lied for no apparent reason. Thus the frontal lobes appear to support the capacity for morality.

Language Develops in an Orderly Way

As the brain develops, so does the ability to speak and form sentences. Thus as children develop social skills, they also improve their language skills. There is some variation in the rate at which language develops, but overall the stages of language development are remarkably uniform across individuals. According to Michael Tomasello (1999), the early social interactions between infant and caregiver are essential to understanding other people and being able to communicate with them through language. Research has demonstrated that infants and caregivers attend to objects in their environment together and that this joint attention facilitates learning to speak (Baldwin, 1991). The ability to speak can be disrupted by social isolation and lack of exposure to language, as illustrated by Genie's case (discussed in the chapter opener).

Language enables us to live in complex societies, because through language we learn the history, rules, and values of our culture or cultures. We are also able to communicate across cultures and to learn much more than other animals can. How does this remarkable ability, communication through language, develop?

FROM ZERO TO 60,000 Language is a system of using sounds and symbols according to grammatical rules. It can be viewed as a hierarchical structure, in that sentences can be broken down into smaller units, or *phrases*. Phrases can be broken down into words. Each word consists of one or more *morphemes* (the smallest units that have meaning, including suffixes and prefixes). Each morpheme consists of one or more *phonemes* (basic sounds; **Figure 9.21**). For example, the word *kissed* has two morphemes ("kiss" and "ed") and four phonemes (the sounds you make when you say the word). The system of rules that govern how words are combined into phrases and how phrases are combined to make sentences is a language's *syntax*. For example: *Stephanie kissed the crying boy*, not *kissed the crying boy Stephanie*.

Research has shown that newborns are already well on their way to learning how to use language (Kuhl, 2004; Werker, Gilbert, Humphrey, & Tees, 1981). Janet Werker and colleagues (Byers–Heinlein, Burns, & Werker, 2010) found that the language or languages spoken by mothers during pregnancy influenced listening preferences in newborns. Canadian newborns whose mothers spoke only English during pregnancy showed a robust preference for sentences in English compared with sentences in Tagalog, a major language of the Philippines. Newborns of mothers who spoke Tagalog and English during pregnancy paid attention to both languages. The latter finding implies that these newborns had sufficient bilingual exposure as fetuses to learn about each language before birth. Patricia Kuhl and colleagues (Kuhl, 2006; Kuhl et al., 2006; Kuhl, Tsao, & Liu, 2003) found that up to 6 months of age, a baby can discriminate all the speech sounds that occur in all languages, even if the sounds do not occur in the language spoken in the baby's home.

From hearing differences between sounds immediately after birth and then learning the sounds of their own languages, babies go on to develop the ability to speak. Humans appear to go from babbling as babies to employing a full vocabulary of about 60,000 words as adults without working very hard at it. Speech

FIGURE 9.21 Acquiring Spoken Language In learning to read, these children are combining phonemes into morphemes.

telegraphic speech The tendency for toddlers to speak using rudimentary sentences that are missing words and grammatical markings but follow a logical syntax and convey a wealth of meaning.

production follows a distinct path. During the first months of life, newborns' actions—crying, fussing, eating, and breathing—generate all their sounds. In other words, babies' first verbal sounds are cries, gurgles, grunts, and breaths. From 3 to 5 months, they begin to coo and laugh. From 5 to 7 months, they begin babbling, using consonants and vowels. From 7 to 8 months, they babble in syllables (*ba-ba-ba, dee-dee-dee*). By the first year, infants around the world are saying their first words. These first words are typically labels of items in their environment (*kitty, cracker*), simple action words (*go, up, sit*), quantifiers (*all gone! more!*), qualities or adjectives (*hot*), socially interactive words (*bye, hello, yes, no*), and even internal states (*boo-boo* after being hurt; Pinker, 1984). Thus even very young children use words to perform a wide range of communicative functions. They name, comment, request, and more.

By about 18 to 24 months, children begin to put words together. Their vocabularies start to grow rapidly. Rudimentary sentences of roughly two words emerge. Though they are missing words and grammatical markings, these mini sentences have a logic, or syntax. Typically, the words' order indicates what has happened or should happen: for example, *Throw ball*. "All gone" translates as *I threw the ball, and now it's gone*. The psychologist Roger Brown, often referred to as the father of child language for his pioneering research, called these utterances **telegraphic speech.** In other words, these children speak as if sending a telegram. They put together bare-bones words according to conventional rules (Brown, 1973).

As children begin to use language in more-sophisticated ways, one relatively rare but telling error they make is to overapply new grammar rules they learn. Children may start to make mistakes at ages 3 to 5 with words they used correctly at age 2 or 3. For example, when they learn that adding *-ed* makes a verb past tense, they then add *-ed* to every verb, including irregular verbs that do not follow that rule. Thus they may say "runned" or "holded" even though they may have said "ran" or "held" at a younger age. Similarly, they may overapply the rule to add *−s* to form a plural, saying "mouses" and "mans," even if they said "mice" and "men" at a younger age.

Like many "immature" skills children exhibit as they develop, such overgeneralizations reflect an important aspect of language acquisition. Children are not simply repeating what they have heard others say. After all, they most likely have not heard anyone say "runned." Instead, these errors occur because children are able to use language effectively by perceiving patterns in spoken grammar and then applying rules to new sentences they have never heard before (Marcus, 1996; Marcus et al., 1992). They make more errors with words used less frequently (such as *drank* and *knew*) because they have heard irregular forms of words less often. Adults tend to do the same thing, but adults are more likely to make errors on the past tenses of words they do not use often, such as *trod, strove,* or *slew* (saying "treaded," "strived," or "slayed"; Pinker, 1994).

ACQUIRING LANGUAGE WITH THE HANDS If the perception and production of sound are key determinants of early language acquisition, then babies exposed to signed languages should acquire these languages in fundamentally different ways than babies acquire spoken language. If, however, what makes human language special is its highly systematic patterns and the human brain's sensitivity to them, then babies should acquire signed language and spoken language in highly similar ways.

To test this hypothesis, Laura Ann Petitto and her students videotaped deaf babies of deaf parents in households using two entirely different signed languages: American Sign Language (ASL) and the signed language of Quebec, langue dessignes québécoise (LSQ). They found that deaf babies exposed to signed languages from birth acquire these languages on an identical maturational timetable as hearing babies acquire spoken languages (Petitto, 2000; **Figure 9.22**). For example, deaf babies will "babble" with their hands. Just as hearing infants will repeat sounds such as *da da da,* which are not actually spoken words, deaf infants will repeat imitative hand movements that do not represent actual signs in signed languages. In demonstrating that speech does not drive all human language acquisition, this research shows that humans must possess a biologically endowed sensitivity to perceive and organize aspects of language patterns. This sensitivity launches a baby into the course of acquiring language.

FIGURE 9.22 Acquiring Signed Language Deaf infants have been shown to acquire signed languages at the same rates that hearing infants acquire spoken languages.

UNIVERSAL GRAMMAR Much linguistic and psycholinguistic research is aimed at understanding the detailed steps by which language is assembled, produced, and understood. The linguist Noam Chomsky transformed the field when he argued that language must be governed by *universal grammar.* In other words, according to Chomsky, all languages are based on humans' innate knowledge of a set of universal and specifically linguistic elements and relations.

Until Chomsky came on the scene in the late 1950s, linguists had focused on analyzing language and identifying basic components of grammar. All languages include similar elements, such as nouns and verbs, but how those elements are arranged varies considerably across languages. In his early work, Chomsky argued that the way people combine these elements to form sentences and convey meaning is only a language's surface structure, the sound and order of words. He introduced the concept of *deep structure:* the implicit meanings of sentences. For instance, *The fat cat chased the rat* implies that there is a cat, it is fat, and it chased the rat. *The rat was chased by the fat cat* implies the same ideas even though on the surface it is a different sentence.

Chomsky believed we automatically and unconsciously transform surface structure to deep structure, the meaning being conveyed. In fact, research has shown that we remember a sentence's underlying meaning, not its surface structure. For example, you may not remember the exact words of someone who insulted you at a football game on campus, but you will certainly recall the deep structure behind that person's meaning. According to Chomsky, humans are born with a *language acquisition device,* which contains universal grammar. This hypothetical neurological structure in the brain allows all humans to come into the world prepared to learn any language. With exposure to a specific cultural context, the synaptic connections in the brain start to narrow toward a deep and rich understanding of one's native language over all others.

SOCIAL AND CULTURAL INFLUENCES Of course, environment greatly influences a child's acquisition of language. Indeed, the fact that you speak English rather than (or in addition to) Swahili is determined entirely by your environment.

The psychologist Lev Vygotsky developed the first major theory that emphasized the role of social and cultural context in the development of both cognition and language. According to Vygotsky, humans are unique because they use symbols and psychological tools—such as speech, writing, maps, art, and so on—through which they create culture. Culture, in turn, dictates what people need to learn and the sorts of skills they need to develop. For example, some cultures value science and rational thinking. Other cultures emphasize supernatural and mystical forces. These cultural values shape how people think about and relate to the world around them. Vygotsky distinguished between elementary mental functions (such as innate sensory experiences) and higher mental functions

FIGURE 9.23 Creole Language A creole language evolves from a mixing of languages. In Suriname, where this boy is reading a classroom blackboard, over 10 languages are spoken. The official language, Dutch, comes from the nation's colonial background. The other tongues include variants of Chinese, Hindi, Javanese, and half a dozen original creoles, among them Sranan Tongo (literally, "Suriname tongue").

(such as language, perception, abstraction, and memory). As children develop, their elementary capacities are gradually transformed. Culture exerts the primary influence on these capacities (Vygotsky, 1978).

Central to Vygotsky's theories is the idea that social and cultural context influences language development. In turn, language development influences cognitive development. Children start by directing their speech toward specific communications with others, such as asking for food or for toys. As children develop, they begin directing speech toward themselves, as when they give themselves directions or talk to themselves while playing. Eventually, children internalize their words into inner speech: verbal thoughts that direct both behavior and cognition. From this perspective, your thoughts are based on the language you have acquired through your society and through your culture, and this ongoing inner speech reflects higher-order cognitive processes.

Interaction across cultures also shapes language. The term *creole* describes a language that evolves over time from the mixing of existing languages (**Figure 9.23**). For example, a creole language may develop when a culture colonizes a place, as when the French established themselves in southern Louisiana and acquired slaves who were not native French speakers. The creole develops out of rudimentary communications, as populations that speak several languages attempt to understand each other. Often, the colonists and natives mix words from each other's languages into a *pidgin,* an informal creole that lacks consistent grammatical rules.

The linguist Derek Bickerton (1998) has found that the colonists' children impose rules on their parents' pidgin, developing it into a creole. Bickerton argues that this is evidence for built-in, universal grammar: The brain changes a nonconforming language by applying the same basic rules to it. Bickerton also has found that creoles formed in different parts of the world, with different combinations of languages, are more similar to each other in grammatical structure than to long-lived languages.

ANIMAL COMMUNICATION Nonhuman animals have ways of communicating with each other, but no other animal uses language the way humans do. Scientists have tried for years to teach language to chimpanzees, one of our nearest living relatives. Chimps lack the vocal ability to speak aloud, so studies have used sign language or visual cues to determine whether they understand words or concepts such as causation. Although chimpanzees can learn some words and have some sense of causation, other research challenges the idea that this learning means they have innate language abilities. Consider the work of the psychologists Herbert Terrace, Laura-Ann Petitto, and Tom Bever. To test Noam Chomsky's assertion that language is a uniquely human trait, these researchers attempted to teach American Sign Language to a chimpanzee. In honor of Chomsky, they named the chimp Neam Chimpsky. His nickname was Nim (**Figure 9.24**).

After years of teaching Nim, the team admitted that Chomsky might be right. Like all other language-trained chimps, Nim consistently failed to master key components of human language syntax. While he was quite adept at communicating with a small set of basic signs ("eat," "play," "more"), he never acquired the ability to generate creative, rule-governed sentences. He was like a broken record, talking about the same thing over and over again in the same old way. As previously discussed, a young child can name, comment, request, and more with his or her first words. Nim and all the ASL-trained chimps used bits and pieces of language almost exclusively to make requests. They wanted things (food, more food) from their caretakers, but otherwise they were not able to express meanings, thoughts, and ideas by generating language (Petitto & Seidenberg, 1979).

FIGURE 9.24 Laura-Ann Petitto with Nim Chimpsky

Summing Up

As Children, How Do We Learn about the World?

Through dynamic systems of interaction, children acquire information by perceiving and by actively engaging with their environments. Research, drawing on the fact that young infants look longer at novel stimuli than at familiar stimuli, indicates that infants are capable of learning at very young ages. A developing memory system helps children build a store of useful knowledge. Children's memory skills are not as sophisticated as adults' memory skills, and children think in egocentric ways. Still, children's developmental "immaturity" serves important purposes for ensuring they acquire the cognitive abilities they need to participate meaningfully in society. Piaget emphasized that most young children's cognitive development occurs in consistent stages, each of which builds on previous stages. Though his theory was influential in establishing typical developmental patterns of complex thought, recent evidence suggests that infants understand much more about objects' physical properties than Piaget believed and that he underestimated infants' innate and early knowledge. For instance, infants can use laws of physics and even demonstrate a basic understanding of addition and subtraction. An important part of learning occurs through social interaction, as young children develop the ability for empathy, a theory of mind, and moral reasoning. These capacities allow people to live in human society. The human capacity for language is innate, as there appear to be built-in methods of acquiring words and forming them into sentences. Although language development occurs in an orderly fashion, the specific language a child develops is influenced by environmental and cultural factors. These processes develop together to enable young children to learn and survive as they become members of society.

Measuring Up

1. Match each of Piaget's stages of cognitive development with its description. The stages are concrete operational, formal operational, preoperational, and sensorimotor.

   _____ **a.** Children can think about objects they cannot see and can play symbolically.
   _____ **b.** Children can think abstractly and form hypotheses.
   _____ **c.** Object permanence develops along with first schemas.
   _____ **d.** Children show evidence of logical thinking, but still cannot think about abstract concepts.

2. Which of the following statements about children's development is false?

   a. Deaf children proceed through different stages of language development than hearing children.
   b. Children's memories for events can be altered through later experiences in their environments.
   c. Moral behavior occurs due to the combined influence of emotional and cognitive factors.
   d. Shortly after birth, infants demonstrate preferences for specific visual patterns, sounds, and tastes.

Answers: 1. a. preoperational; b. formal operational; c. sensorimotor; d. concrete operational. 2. a. Deaf children proceed through different stages of language development than hearing children.

- Describe the key challenges faced in each of Erik Erikson's first five stages of psychosocial development.

- Understand how biology and environment interact to influence puberty.

- Explain key factors that influence gender identity development and gender-specific behaviors.

- Describe how parents, peers, and cultural forces shape the sense of self.

9.3 How Do We Progress from Childhood to Adolescence?

As a child develops and learns more about the world, the child begins creating a sense of identity. That is, the child starts to establish who he or she is. Identity formation is an important part of social development, especially in Western cultures, where individuality is valued. After all, who a person is has an enormous effect on how that person interacts with others.

The psychologist Erik Erikson proposed a theory of human development that emphasized age-related psychosocial challenges and their effects on social functioning across the life span. Erikson thought of identity development as composed of eight stages, which ranged from an infant's first year to old age (**Table 9.1**).

Erikson further conceptualized each stage as having a major developmental "crisis," or development challenge to be confronted. Each of these crises is present throughout life, but it takes on special importance at a particular stage. While each crisis provides an opportunity for psychological development, a lack of progress may impair further psychosocial development (Erikson, 1980).

For example, the psychosocial challenge in infancy is *trust versus mistrust*. This challenge coincides with the infant's development of attachment to key caregivers. During the crisis, the infant responds to feedback from her or his environment. On the one hand, if that environment comforts the infant when he or she cries, feeds the infant, and generally cares for essential needs, the infant will develop a sense of trust. That sense will build a foundation for the child's further exploration of identity issues and connections to others. On the other hand, if the infant's environment is not supportive or conducive to safety and security,

TABLE 9.1 Erikson's Eight Stages of Human Development

STAGE	AGE	MAJOR PSYCHOSOCIAL CRISIS	SUCCESSFUL RESOLUTION OF CRISIS
1. Infancy	0–2	Trust versus mistrust	Children learn that the world is safe and that people are loving and reliable.
2. Toddler	2–3	Autonomy versus shame and doubt	Encouraged to explore the environment, children gain feelings of independence and positive self-esteem.
3. Preschool	4–6	Initiative versus guilt	Children develop a sense of purpose by taking on responsibilities, but also develop the capacity to feel guilty for misdeeds.
4. Childhood	7–12	Industry versus inferiority	By working successfully with others and assessing how others view them, children learn to feel competent.
5. Adolescence	13–19	Identity versus role confusion	By exploring different social roles, adolescents develop a sense of identity.
6. Young adulthood	20s	Intimacy versus isolation	Young adults gain the ability to commit to long-term relationships.
7. Middle adulthood	30s to 50s	Generativity versus stagnation	Adults gain a sense that they are leaving behind a positive legacy and caring for future generations.
8. Old age	60s and beyond	Integrity versus despair	Older adults feel a sense of satisfaction that they have lived a good life and developed wisdom.

he or she may develop a sense of mistrust. The infant may also develop a fear of seeking out independence, and that search is the key psychosocial challenge of the next stage in Erikson's theory.

Each challenge provides skills and attitudes that the child will need to face the next challenge successfully. Successful resolution of these challenges depends on the supportive nature of the child's environment as well as the child's active search for information about his or her own competence. According to Erikson's theory, adolescents face perhaps the most fundamental crisis: how to develop an adult identity.

What shapes the sense of personal identity? All aspects of the self are changing as a child approaches adolescence. Physical changes occur during the entrance into puberty, social changes emerge as part of the renegotiation of relationships with parents and peers, cognitive changes arise as part of the potential emergence of critical and analytical thinking, and psychological changes accompany the child's development of a firm understanding of his or her gender and cultural identity. Earlier sections of this chapter explored cognitive development. This section will present the other influences on identity development.

Physical Changes and Cultural Norms Influence the Development of Identity

Biologically, adolescence is characterized by the onset of sexual maturity and the ability to reproduce. Remember going through *puberty?* What happened to your body during that time, and how did those changes make you feel? This roughly two-year developmental period marks the beginning of adolescence. It typically begins between 8 and 14 years for females and between 10 and 14 years for males. Most girls complete pubertal development by the age of 16, with boys ending by the age of 18 (Lee, 1980; **Figure 9.25**).

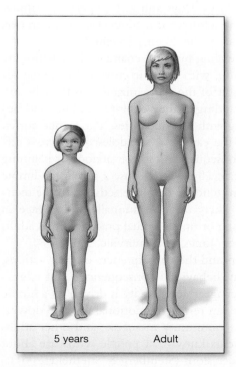
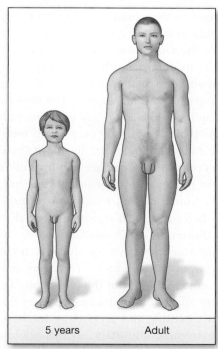

| 5 years | Adult | 5 years | Adult |

FIGURE 9.25 Physical Development during Adolescence These images show the major physical changes that occur as girls and boys mature into young adults.

"Do you know its sexual identity?"

During puberty, hormone levels increase throughout the body. The increased hormones stimulate physical changes. For example, the clear dividing line between childhood and the start of puberty is the *adolescent growth spurt,* a rapid, hormonally driven increase in height and weight. Puberty also brings the development of the *primary sex characteristics:* maturation of the male and female sex organs; in females, the beginning of menstruation; in males, the beginning of the capacity for ejaculation. Also developing at this time are the *secondary sexual characteristics,* including pubic hair, body hair, muscle mass increases for boys, and fat deposits on the hips and breasts for females. Boys' voices deepen and their jaws become more angular. Girls lose baby fat on their bellies as their waists become more defined (Lee, 1980).

Puberty may appear to be a purely biological phenomenon. Like all aspects of human development, however, it is affected by a complex and dynamic interaction between biological systems and environmental experiences. For example, when girls live in homes with nongenetically related adult males (such as the mother's boyfriend or a stepfather), they tend to start puberty months earlier than girls who live in homes with only genetically related males. Also, girls who live in extremely stressful environments or have a history of insecure attachments to caregivers begin menstruating earlier than girls in peaceful or secure environments (Wierson, Long, & Forehand, 1993). These findings suggest that the body responds to cues of threat (in the form of stress or family changes). Evolutionarily speaking, these threat cues increase a female's need to reproduce sooner to increase her chances of continuing her gene pool. Thus hormonal changes are triggered by environmental forces, which allow the girl to enter puberty (Belsky, Houts, & Fearon, 2010).

Because boys do not have an easily identifiable pubertal event like the initiation of menstruation in girls, we know less about environmental impacts on the timing and experience of puberty in boys. Boys and girls experience similar changes in their brain development during adolescence, however, so researchers are able to identify a few key characteristics of the "teenage brain."

At the same time teenagers are experiencing pubertal changes, their brains are also in an important phase of reorganization, with synaptic connections being refined and gray matter increasing. As a result of the reorganization in their brains, teenagers need extra support and understanding as they explore thinking and behaving more like adults and experimenting with new identities. The frontal cortex of the brain is not fully myelinated until the early 20s, so adolescents have a difficult time thinking critically about the consequences of their actions or planning for eventualities. They are *able* to think critically. But because a teenager's limbic system (the emotional center of their brain) tends to be more active than the teenager's frontal cortex, teenagers are more likely to act irrationally and engage in risky behaviors, such as drinking and driving or unsafe sexual practices, than adults are (Blakemore & Choudhury, 2006; Casey, Jones, & Somerville, 2011).

Because they have the ability to understand the consequences of their actions, it is important to educate teenagers about behavioral consequences. But education alone will not put the brakes on. Teenagers' impulsivity is driven by a limbic system affected by hormonal changes that can result in emotional ups and downs. Thus parenting and support by teachers, community members, and other adults are extremely important, so that adolescents know that people who care about them will help them avoid making poor decisions (Steinberg & Sheffield, 2001).

The research on such physiological changes points to an important fact about adolescence: It is not necessarily a stressful period of life, full of turmoil. For those kids who have already stressful home lives, experience many family changes, or display attachment difficulties, adolescence may be difficult. But for most kids, pubertal and brain changes can be a bit annoying, but they do not necessarily lead to the high rates of depression or anger that many in the general public associate with teenagers. In fact, if adolescents receive warm, supportive parenting with the proper guidance and discipline, and if they are allowed to express themselves openly for who they are, adolescence can be a positive time of growth and change, solidifying the youth's sense of identity (Steinberg & Sheffield, 2001).

Most people believe that gender—being female or male—is a major component of who they are. Now try to imagine yourself as the same person but a member of the other sex. For many of us this is hard to do. But how different are females and males (**Figure 9.26**)? Certain physical differences are obvious, but how do females and males differ psychologically? According to evolutionary theory, sex differences ought to reflect different adaptive problems males and females have faced, and this notion is generally supported by research (Buss, 1995). Since males and females have faced similar adaptive problems, however, they are similar on most dimensions (Hyde, 2005).

Many differences between males and females have as much to do with socialization as with biology. Some psychologists use the term *sex* to refer to biological differences and the term *gender* for differences between males and females that result from socialization. This distinction is not always easy to make, because the biological and psychosocial aspects of being female or male are usually so entwined that we cannot separate them (Hyde, 2005). Each person is treated in certain ways based on his or her biological sex, and each person's behaviors reflect both biological components and social expectations. For example, as discussed in Chapter 3, researchers have identified some differences between the brains of men and of women. They have not determined whether these differences are the result of genetics, of the way girls and boys are treated during development, or, more likely, of genetics (nature) combined with treatment (nurture). Nor do we know how or if sex-related brain differences translate into thoughts and actions.

CULTURAL INFLUENCES Whether you think of yourself as female or male is your **gender identity.** This set of beliefs—a major part of your sense of self—shapes how you behave. Children as young as 2 years old can indicate whether they are boys or girls. Once children discover that they are boys or girls, they seek out activities that are culturally appropriate for their sex (Bem, 1981). **Gender roles** are culturally defined norms that differentiate behaviors, and attitudes, according to maleness and femaleness. In North American culture, for example, most parents and teachers discourage girls from playing too roughly and boys from crying. The separation of boys and girls into different play groups is also a powerful socializing force. Most boys and girls strive to fulfill the gender roles expected of them by their cultures. **Gender schemas** are cognitive structures that reflect perceived appropriate behaviors for females and males. They play powerful roles in establishing gender identity. That is, these schemas act as lenses through which people see the world. For example, if a person has a gender schema that says nurses are women, that person might snicker, look surprised, or express amusement upon meeting a male nurse and learning of his profession. Gender schemas affect both how we process information in the social world and how we interact with other people.

Children develop their expectations about gender through observing their parents, peers, and teachers, as well as through media. Most high-level politicians and firefighters are male, most nurses and secretaries are female, and so on. Children learn to extrapolate from these statistical facts which jobs are "appropriate"

FIGURE 9.26 Try for Yourself: Girl or Boy?

Can you determine the sex of each infant?

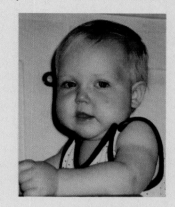

Answer: The infant on the top is a girl. The infant on the bottom is a boy.

gender identity Personal beliefs about whether one is male or female.

gender roles The characteristics associated with males and females because of cultural influence or learning.

gender schemas Cognitive structures that reflect the perceived appropriateness of male and female characteristics and behaviors.

for the sexes. As mentioned in Chapter 8, for example, when young children are asked to draw a picture of a scientist, most draw a man (Chambers, 1983). In addition, children's toys often reflect stereotyping. The next time you visit a toy store, inventory which toys' packages depict boys and which depict girls. You will find that boys are rarely shown with baby dolls or doll houses and girls are rarely shown in contact sports gear. Dolls for boys are even termed differently: *action figures*. These messages and many others provide information for children about how they should and should not behave.

Situational factors can also contribute to gender-specific behavior. Consider a study of young women talking on the telephone with either their boyfriends or their casual male friends (Montepare & Vega, 1988). When the women talked with their boyfriends, their voices changed to higher pitches and became softer and more relaxed than when they talked with their male friends. The way they spoke to their boyfriends was also more babyish, feminine, and absentminded, as rated by objective judges. When asked, the women said they knew they had spoken in two different ways and that they did so to communicate affection for their boyfriends. How do you imagine the boyfriends' behavior differed from the male friends' behavior during these phone conversations? Would the results have differed if the young women were lesbians talking with their girlfriends or gay men talking with their boyfriends?

BIOLOGICAL INFLUENCES On April 27, 1966, Janet and Ron Reimer brought their 7-month-old twins, Bruce and Brian, to St. Boniface Hospital in Winnipeg, Canada, for routine circumcision. Bruce was operated on first, and his penis was badly damaged in a very rare accident during this common and usually minor procedure. The penis deteriorated over the next several days, and within the week it had shriveled up and disappeared. (After what happened to Bruce, no attempt was made to circumcise Brian.) The accident and the events that followed changed not only the lives of the Reimer family but also psychologists' beliefs about the concept of gender.

As recounted in John Colapinto's book *As Nature Made Him: The Boy Who Was Raised as a Girl* (2000), Janet and Ron investigated whether Bruce should undergo sexual reassignment and be raised as a girl. Previous sexual reassignment cases had involved intersexed children, who were born with ambiguous genitals (genitals that had characteristics of both male and female organs). The process of gender reassignment had never been attempted on a child born with clearly male genitals. The Reimers contacted the world-renowned (and controversial) sexologist John Money, at Johns Hopkins University. Money convinced them that sexual reassignment was the best course of action for Bruce's psychological well-being. Bruce was castrated (his testes were removed) when he was 22 months old. He was renamed Brenda and raised as a girl (**Figure 9.27**). Throughout the 1970s and 1980s, media accounts and psychology textbooks recounted the story as demonstrating that Brenda was happy and well adjusted and that gender was the result of socialization rather than biology. Unfortunately, Colapinto's analysis indicates that Brenda's sexual reassignment was a failure from the start.

Brenda's life can be described as tumultuous at best, hellish at worst. Although her parents let her hair grow long, dressed her in feminine colors and clothing styles, and encouraged her to play with other girls, by all accounts Brenda was not comfortable or happy being a girl. She was teased incessantly for her roughness and aggressiveness. Brenda grew even more uncomfortable after receiving hormones at age 11 to initiate the development of secondary sexual characteristics. The development of breasts that felt foreign to who she was inside resulted in intense embarrassment and horror for Brenda that did not fade with time.

FIGURE 9.27 Brian and Bruce Reimer
This photo shows Brian and Bruce (Brenda) Reimer as children. Only his short haircut distinguishes Brian as the boy. The fact that they were identical twins made the situation ideal for studying the effects of culture on gender identity.

As the years passed, Janet and Ron were finally forced to consider that Brenda was not—nor would ever truly be—a girl. After 15 years of family and peer problems and intense psychological troubles, Brenda was told the truth about what had happened. A flood of emotions welled up within her, but the most overwhelming feeling was relief. As Brenda later recalled, "Suddenly it all made sense why I felt the way I did. I wasn't some sort of weirdo. I wasn't crazy."

FIGURE 9.28 David (Bruce) Reimer This photo shows David (Bruce) living as a man.

Brenda immediately decided to return to being male. She stopped hormone therapy. She changed her name to David, which she chose because of the biblical story of David and Goliath. New surgical techniques allowed physicians to provide David with a functional artificial penis that could be used for sexual intercourse. At age 23, he met and married a woman with three children, and for many years he lived an apparently happy family life (**Figure 9.28**).

After a while, however, David's marriage failed. A series of financial setbacks, along with the death of his twin brother, led him to become despondent. David killed himself in May 2004 at age 38. Most psychologists believe the stress of being a boy raised as a girl contributed to identity problems that troubled him throughout his adult life.

The lesson from David's life is that gender identity is not shaped solely by whether one has a penis or not or whether a person is treated as a boy or as a girl. The biological aspects of gender come from many sources, the most important of which is brain chemistry. Even though David did not have testicles to generate hormones, hormones still circulated in his infant brain to masculinize his sense of gender identity, or sense of truly being a boy. In the 1960s, people generally favored environmental explanations for most differences between males and females. In hindsight, it seems clear that changing the appearance of a child's genitals, injecting the child with hormones, or treating the child as belonging to a certain gender will not turn that person from a boy into a girl or vice versa.

Instead, gender identity begins very early in prenatal development. It results from a complex cascade of hormones, changes in brain structure and function, and intrauterine environmental forces (Swaab, 2004). In short, biology has a strong effect on whether people identify as female, male, or transgender. A *transgendered* person was born with one biological sex but feels that her or his true gender identity is that of the other sex. This condition is also thought to originate during prenatal brain development (Swaab, 2004).

Researchers are only beginning to understand the dynamic systems that make a person feel that a specific gender reflects who he or she is on the inside. Today, gender is thought to be much more fluid than it used to be conceptualized, with a continuum of traits and behaviors considered quite normal, ranging from extremely "masculine" to extremely "feminine." And many cultures have ideas about gender that go beyond the "male/female" dichotomy, to include a third gender and those who are above gender categorization or can change gender over time (Roscoe, 2000).

For example, Pakistani Hijras are transgendered women (those who are born men but feel they are really women; **Figure 9.29**). In the seventeenth and eighteenth centuries, Hijras traditionally were respected members of the Pakistani emperors' courts. Today they serve mainly as wedding dancers, and they experience much hatred and discrimination for their non–gender-conforming appearance and behavior. Hijra life can be very difficult in a conservative society such as Pakistan. In 2010, however, the Pakistani government implemented legislation to ensure human rights for Hijras.

FIGURE 9.29 Transgender In the Punjab province of Pakistan, a Hijra is preparing herself before going to dance.

The impact of cultural influences on gender roles and gender schemas cannot be overstated. Culture shapes much of who each of us is as we develop a full sense of identity during adolescence. Culture also determines whether each person's identity will be accepted or maligned. In addition to a gender identity, each adolescent—especially each teen of color—must work to establish an ethnic identity.

In a country such as the United States, the process of forming a racial or ethnic identity can be particularly complicated. Because of prejudice and discrimination and the accompanying barriers to economic opportunities, children of ethnic minorities often face challenges with regard to the development of their ethnic identities. Children entering middle childhood have acquired an awareness of their ethnic identities to the extent that they know the labels and attributes that the dominant culture applies to their ethnic groups. Many researchers believe that during middle childhood and adolescence, children in ethnic minority groups often engage in additional processes aimed at ethnic identity formation (Phinney, 1990). The factors that influence these processes vary widely among individuals and groups.

Consider a child of Mexican immigrants. This child may struggle to live successfully in both a traditional Mexican household and a Westernized American neighborhood and school. The child may have to serve as a "cultural broker" for his or her family, perhaps translating materials sent home from school, calling insurance companies to ask about policies for his or her parents, and handling more adultlike responsibilities than other children the same age. In helping the family adjust to a very stressful life as immigrants in a foreign country, the child may feel additional pressures but may also develop important skills in communication, negotiation, and caregiving (Cooper, Denner, & Lopez, 1999).

Even for people of color from the United States, it can be quite challenging to persevere in the face of racism and discrimination while also trying to succeed in the dominant school system and work environment (Spencer, Fegley, & Harpalani, 2003). When a child successfully negotiates these tasks and forms a strong sense of identity related to both her or his own group and the majority culture, the child has developed a *bicultural identity*. That is, the child strongly identifies with two cultures and seamlessly combines a sense of identity with both groups (Vargas-Reighley, 2005). A bicultural individual who is able to develop a bicultural identity is likely to be happier, better adjusted, and have fewer problems in adult social and economic roles than will a bicultural individual who identifies strongly with only one culture to the exclusion of recognizing the other aspects of who he or she is. Parents, teachers, and spiritual and community leaders play key roles in teaching young people the values of their specific cultures in order to help them formulate healthy ethnic identities.

Given that adolescents are undergoing pubertal changes, brain development and the resultant emotional highs and lows, gender and ethnic identity development, and myriad social role expectations, it is impressive that so many teenagers are able to negotiate a pathway to a stable identity. Part of this process includes breaking away from childhood beliefs by questioning and challenging parental and societal ideas (Erikson, 1968).

Three major changes generally cause adolescents to question who they are: Their physical appearances transform, leading to shifts in self-image; their cognitive abilities grow more sophisticated, increasing the tendency for introspection; and they receive heightened societal pressure to prepare for the future (in particular, to make career choices), prompting exploration of real and hypothetical boundaries. In exploring boundaries, teenagers may investigate alternative belief systems and subcultures. They may wonder what they would be like if they were raised in other cultures, by other parents, or in other historical times. They may shift between various peer groups and try out different activities, hobbies, and musical styles. As teenagers move away from spending all their time with parents and toward a peer-oriented lifestyle, parents continue to shape adolescents' development, but peers also play an important role in identity development.

Peers and Parents Help Shape the Sense of Self

THE IMPORTANCE OF PEERS Developmental psychologists increasingly recognize the importance of peers in shaping identity (**Figure 9.30**). Children, regardless of their cultures, tend to spend much of their time interacting with other children, usually playing in various ways. In developmental terms, attention to peers begins at the end of the first year of life, when infants begin to imitate other children, smile, and make vocalizations and other social signals to their peers (Brownell & Brown, 1992). Attention to peers may then continue throughout life. For example, people learn how to behave from their friends. When people behave appropriately, their friends provide social rewards. When people behave inappropriately, their friends provide social punishments.

In developing their identities, children and adolescents compare their strengths and weaknesses with those of their peers. For example, as part of the search for identity, teenagers form friendships with others whose values and worldviews are similar to their own. Adolescents use peer groups to help them feel a sense of belonging and acceptance. They also draw on peer groups as resources for social support and identity acceptance. Despite wide differences in the experiences of teenagers around the world, adolescent peer groups tend to be described by a fairly small set of stereotypical names: jocks, brains, loners, druggies, nerds, and other not-so-flattering designations.

Outside observers tend to quickly place teenagers who dress or act a certain way into groupings, called *cliques*. Members of cliques are thought to exhibit the same personality traits and be interested in the same activities. Individuals are seen as virtually interchangeable, and community members may respond to all youths from that group in similar ways (Urberg, Degirmencioglue, Tolson, & Halliday-Scher, 1995). The teenagers, however, may not see themselves as part of homogeneous groups of peers. In fact, they may see themselves as completely unique and individual, separate from anyone else, or they may see themselves as connected to a small subset of close friends (**Figure 9.31**).

Adolescent identity development is thus shaped by the perceptions of adults, the influences of peers, and the teen's own active exploration of the world. Keep in mind that even though peers become the primary concern for many teenagers, the importance of parental support and guidance does not wane with age.

THE IMPORTANCE OF PARENTS The impact of parents versus peers on young people has become a controversial topic in developmental psychology. People often describe individuals as "coming from a good home" or as having "fallen in with the wrong crowd." These clichés reflect the importance placed on both parents and peers in influencing an individual.

Much research has confirmed that parents have substantial influence throughout an individual's life. Significantly, researchers have emphasized that neither the peer group nor the family can be assigned the primary role in a child's social development. Instead, the two contexts play complementary roles. B. Bradford Brown and colleagues (1993) have argued that parents' influence can be direct or indirect. Parents contribute to specific individual behaviors. They also affect social development indirectly by influencing the choices the child makes about

FIGURE 9.30 Peers and Identity Peers play an important role in each adolescent's development of a sense of identity.

FIGURE 9.31 Cliques and Individuality Outside observers would tend to place these young men into a single clique, "punks," and would tend to react to them all in similar ways. Each adolescent, however, might view himself as individualistic.

what kind of clique to join. In observations of 695 young people from childhood through adolescence, Robert Cairns and Beverly Cairns (1994) found that parents and teachers played a major role in realigning social groups so they were consistent with family norms.

Important support for the significance of child/parent interaction comes from the New York Longitudinal Study, begun in 1956 by Stella Chess and Alexander Thomas. The study ran for six years, assessing 141 children from 85 middle- to upper-middle-class families. Chess and Thomas (1984) pinpointed the most important factor in determining a child's social development: the fit between the child's biologically based temperament or personality and the parents' behaviors.

For instance, most parents find it frustrating to raise a difficult child who tends to have negative moods and a hard time adapting to new situations. Parents who openly demonstrate their frustration with their child's behavior or insist on exposing the child to conflict often unwittingly encourage negative behaviors. If the child is extremely uneasy about entering a new setting, pushing the child can lead to behavioral problems. If the child is very distractible, forcing him or her to concentrate for long periods may lead to emotional upset.

In this study and many others, parents who responded to a difficult child calmly, firmly, patiently, and consistently tended to have the most positive outcomes. Such parents tend not to engage in self-blame for their child's negative behaviors, and they manage to cope with their own frustration with and disappointment in their child. Chess and Thomas also noted that overprotectiveness can encourage a child's anxiety in response to a new situation, thereby escalating the child's distress. Ultimately, then, the best style of parenting is dynamic and flexible, and it takes into account the parents' personalities, the child's temperament, and the particular situation (Steinberg, 2001).

Adolescence is a period of increased conflict between parents and their teenage children. For most families, however, this conflict leads to minor annoyances and not to feelings of hopelessness or doom. Research shows that such conflict actually helps adolescents develop many important skills, including negotiation, critical thinking, communication, and the development of empathy (Holmbeck, 1996). In fact, even though adolescents and their parents may argue and it may seem to parents that their children are not listening, across cultures parents have incredible influence over the development of their children's values and sense of autonomy (Feldman & Rosenthal, 1991).

Other research has shown that parents have multiple influences on their children's attitudes, values, and religious beliefs (Bao, Whitbeck, Hoyt, & Conger, 1999). Children learn about the world in part from the attitudes expressed by their parents, such as the belief in a higher power or even prejudices regarding certain groups of people. Especially nurturing parents tend to raise children who experience more social emotions, such as appropriate guilt, perhaps because the parents encourage an empathic attitude toward others. Parents also help determine the neighborhoods in which their children live, the schools they attend, and the extracurricular activities that provide exercise and stimulation. All of these choices are likely to influence the child subtly and not so subtly.

Thus, for example, parents who ensure their children spend minimal time on television and video games, regularly go on family hikes, and participate in various sports may have children who are more physically fit than those who plunk their children down in front of the television for hours per day. Of course, nature might contribute to these differences as well: Athletic people might possess genes that promote fitness and pass them along to their children, who might respond positively to being active because they have a genetic predisposition to liking exercise and benefiting from it. As shown throughout this book, biological and environmental influences interact to produce behavior at all stages of the life span.

Summing Up

How Do We Progress from Childhood to Adolescence?

Erik Erikson argued that the most important psychosocial challenge for adolescents was to find a clear sense of identity, or who they are in comparison with others in their community. How people develop a sense of identity is influenced by the biological changes of puberty, complex brain changes, parenting experiences, peer groups, and cultural beliefs. One of the most important aspects of identity development is gender identity. Even young children classify themselves on the basis of biological sex, but how they come to understand the cultural meaning of being a boy or a girl is largely determined through their socialization into gender roles, in which children adopt behaviors viewed as appropriate for their sex. Adolescents struggle for identity by questioning social values and personal goals, as they try to figure out who they are and what they want to become. Ethnic identity is also an important discovery for teenagers attempting to figure out who they are in light of the struggles their group may face within the dominant culture. When children and adolescents are supported in their attempts at autonomy and their burgeoning identities are validated, they can develop into successful adults much more easily than when their home lives are characterized by chaos, stress, harsh punishment, or too many transitions. Adolescents continue to need support and guidance from attachment figures, peers, and community members, despite their often argumentative and emotional dispositions.

Measuring Up

1. Which of the following statements is true regarding adolescent development?

   a. The fully mature frontal cortex of the brain drives adolescents' risk-taking behaviors.
   b. The timing of puberty's onset is determined by the individual's genes.
   c. Family conflict during adolescence has many developmental advantages for teens.
   d. A teen of color will have the worst developmental outcome if he or she develops a bicultural identity.

2. The case study of Bruce/Brenda Reimer shows that _____.

   a. gender identity has a strong biological component
   b. gender identity depends almost completely on the way a child is raised
   c. it is fairly easy to teach children they are girls when biologically they are boys or to teach them they are boys when biologically they are girls
   d. changing a child's name after the child has learned her or his name can cause problems with gender identity

For many years, developmental psychologists focused on childhood and adolescence, as if most important aspects of development occurred by age 20. In recent decades, researchers working in a wide range of fields have demonstrated that important changes occur physiologically, cognitively, and socioemotionally throughout adulthood and into old age. Therefore, many contemporary psychologists consider development from a life span perspective, trying to understand how mental activity and social relations change over the entire course of life. Such research shows that we should not equate growing old with despair. In fact, many positive things happen as we grow older. Although aging is associated with cognitive and physical decline, it is an important part of life and can be very meaningful. Today, better health, better nutrition, and medical advances enable people to live longer than in previous generations. Understanding old age is becoming especially important, since most Western cultures are experiencing a boom in the aging population.

Adulthood Presents Psychosocial Challenges

Erik Erikson was one of the first researchers to take such a long-range approach to development. Erikson's sixth stage, *intimacy versus isolation,* takes place during young adulthood (see Table 9.1). The psychosocial challenge during this stage involves forming and maintaining committed friendships and romantic relationships. Essentially, it involves finding people with whom to share your life in intimate ways, as opposed to ending up socially isolated. Erikson emphasized the Western value of merging with others while not losing your own sense of identity.

THE SEVEN AGES OF MAN

SLEEPY HAPPY DOPEY

BASHFUL DOC SNEEZY GRUMPY

Recall that in Erikson's theory, earlier stages build up skills that are needed to successfully negotiate subsequent stages. Thus, for Erikson, building a strong sense of identity in adolescence is paramount to being able to form truly intimate relationships with others in adulthood. He argued that if one has no sense of self, it is more difficult to engage in honest, open, emotionally close relationships with others (Erikson, 1980).

Erikson's seventh-stage challenge, *generativity versus stagnation,* takes place during middle age. This stage involves contributing to future generations. Caring for children, being productive in one's career, having regard for others, and being concerned about the future are positive psychosocial actions of this stage. People may analyze how generative they have been. If their children turned out well, their careers were satisfying, and they contributed to their communities, they are more likely to leave middle age with a sense of generativity, or leaving a positive legacy. The opposite of generativity would be stagnation, which would include a feeling that life is going nowhere or is very materialistic and self-centered.

Erikson's last stage, *integrity versus despair,* takes place in old age. Integrity refers to a sense of honesty about oneself and a feeling that one's life has been well lived, so that facing death is neither scary nor depressing. In this stage, older adults reflect on their lives and respond either positively to having had a worthwhile life or with regret and sadness at what has passed. The crisis at this stage can be triggered by events that highlight the mortal nature of human life, such as the death of a spouse or close friend. The crisis can also be triggered by changing social and occupational roles, such as retirement. Resolving these final challenges allows people to come to terms with the reality of death. If an older person has many regrets, lacks close relationships, or is angry about getting older, the person may resolve this conflict with a sense of despair instead of integrity.

According to Erikson, successful adult development includes having intimate relationships with friends and partners, giving back to society, and viewing one's life in a generally positive light, even if there have been many ups and downs or even tragedies. An older person who faces death with a sense of integrity did not necessarily have an easy life, but this psychosocial conflict involves how one *perceives* life, not whether objectively that life was easy or trauma free. In short, Erikson's theory highlights the way people think about life changes and challenges and how they come to resolve the key psychosocial conflicts of each age period. The following sections examine the physical, socioemotional, and cognitive changes that occur during adulthood and how they affect people's quality of life.

Adults Are Affected by Life Transitions

For many young people, college is a magical time of life. Meeting new friends, learning new ideas, and having a good time occur as adolescents emerge as adults. People in their 20s and 30s undergo significant changes as they pursue career goals and make long-term commitments in relationships, as in getting married and raising children. All of these developments correspond to Erikson's idea that we face challenges as we mature through adulthood. In essence, the major challenges of adulthood reflect the need to find meaning in our lives. Part of that search for meaning includes acknowledging, coping with, and playing an active role in the physiological, cognitive, and socioemotional changes of adulthood.

PHYSICAL CHANGES FROM EARLY TO MIDDLE ADULTHOOD Evolutionarily speaking, a 40-year-old is quite old. At the beginning of the twentieth century, the average life expectancy in the United States was 47 years! Our bodies remain on that timetable, ready to reproduce when we reach our teens and peaking in fitness during our 20s. Since 1900, through modern medicine and improvements in hygiene and in food availability, we have increased the average life expectancy by about 30 years. Still, between the ages of 20 and 40, we experience a steady decline in muscle mass, bone density, eyesight, and hearing (Shephard, 1997).

As we approach middle age, we start to notice that we can no longer drink as much alcohol, eat as much unhealthy food, or function on as little sleep as we could in our 20s. We find the "middle-age spread," the accumulating fat around the belly, becomes harder and harder to work off. For these reasons, nutrition, exercise, and a healthy lifestyle are so important in early adulthood. After middle age, it is much harder to get in shape, reduce fat in our arteries, or make our cognitive functioning sharper. The better cognitive, physical, and psychological shape we are in during early adulthood, the fewer significant declines we will see as we age.

As you will learn in the following sections, brain functioning and body health are "use it or lose it" phenomena: We have to keep oxygen and blood flowing by caring for those systems through adequate sleep, proper diet, cognitive stimulation, and at least moderate daily exercise (Shephard, 1997). Unfortunately, as discussed extensively in Chapter 11, we are currently facing an obesity epidemic in

How Can I Satisfy the Need to Belong?

As you learned earlier in this chapter, one of the developmental challenges we all face is learning how to balance isolation and intimacy (see Table 9.1). While maintaining our own identities, we need to form stable and satisfying relationships with our friends, family members, romantic partners, work colleagues, neighbors, and community members. In short, we need to be ourselves but satisfy our fundamental need to belong, a need that persists throughout development (Baumeister & Leary, 1995; **Figure 9.32**). Jennifer Crocker is a research psychologist interested in the ways that motivations influence well-being. Crocker has examined two motivational perspectives, which she calls *egosystem* and *ecosystem*. These perspectives, it turns out, have important implications for our ability to satisfy the need to belong.

People with an *ego*system orientation are motivated to build and maintain other people's impressions of them. Crocker notes, "They focus on proving themselves, demonstrating their desired qualities, validating their worth, and establishing their deservingness. In this framework people prioritize their own perceived needs over those of others" (Crocker, Olivier, & Nuer, 2009, p. 252). Crocker points out that when we are so focused on building and maintaining

FIGURE 9.32 Satisfying the Need to Belong By helping another person, connecting yourself with a sense of community, you might satisfy your fundamental human need to belong to other humans.

others' perceptions of us, we are likely to see our relationships with others as zero-sum propositions. That is, if I win, you lose; if you win, I lose. Crocker's research shows that students who hold these image-related goals became more depressed and anxious during their first semester in college. These goals are also associated with problematic alcohol use (Moeller & Crocker, 2009).

In contrast, people with an *eco*system orientation perceive themselves as interconnected with others. They see the self as part of a system and thus their own circumstances as linked to those of others. These individuals are unlikely to embrace a zero-sum mentality. Rather than thinking, "If you win, I lose," these individuals are likely to think, "We can both benefit from this situation, and I am responsible for working with others to figure out how to make that happen." Crocker characterizes the ecosystem perspective as follows: "With an ecosystem perspective people prioritize the needs of others, not out of virtue or self-sacrifice, but because they understand these connections and consequently care about the well-being of others" (Crocker et al., 2009, p. 254).

Research (reviewed in Crocker et al., 2009) suggests that students who hold ecosystem goals tend to become less depressed and anxious during their first semester in college. Compared with people low on these goals, people high on these goals are more engaged in their courses and more eager to learn from failure. This perspective is also associated with low levels of entitlement and high agreeableness. In a nutshell, people with an ecosystem perspective, compared with those with an egosystem perspective, seem to enjoy a host of positive benefits.

When you consider strategies for cultivating an ecosystem orientation, bear in mind two complicating factors. First, all the research findings on these motivation perspectives discussed so far are correlational. The results enable us to say that egosystem and ecosystem perspectives are associated with some different qualities, but we cannot claim

that these perspectives cause these qualities. It is reasonable to suggest, however, that our motivations are likely to precede actions such as academic work. Second, these two motivational perspectives—egosystem and ecosystem—are not mutually exclusive. Each of us is capable of both modes of being. Some people might rely on one mode more often than the other, and it is likely that some situations trigger particular modes. The trick is to develop a habit of mind that helps us see ourselves as interconnected.

How might you cultivate an ecosystem perspective? Three strategies will help you:

1. **Think and write about your personal values and priorities.** In their research, Crocker, Niiya, and Mischkowski (2008) asked each participant in their experimental condition to spend 10 minutes writing about an important value and explaining why that value was important to him or her. Participants wrote about their relationships, artistic pursuits, morality, pursuit of knowledge, and other topics. Each participant in the control condition spent 10 minutes writing about an unimportant value. The researchers found that after the 10 minutes, the participants in the experimental condition, compared with the participants in the control condition, felt more loving, joyful, giving, empathic, connected, sympathetic, grateful, and so on. Thus writing about one's values, "rather than affirming the self, . . . enables people to transcend the self" (p. 746). This ability to transcend the self is at the heart of the ecosystem perspective.

2. **Articulate goals you have that relate to outcomes for other people.** Then, as you engage in your daily life, ask yourself how tasks you perform support your other-oriented goals (Crocker, 2006). For example, a student interested in studying medicine might say, "I seek to alleviate other people's physical pain." That student might then think about her organic chemistry class as an opportunity to learn something that will help in future work

with patients. This attitude might help the student avoid a concern related to self-image, such as thinking of the class as a tricky barrier that could show the world he or she is not cut out to be a doctor.

3. **Adopt an attitude of gratitude.** For example, you could keep a gratitude journal. Each evening before you go to bed, scan your memory of the day to identify an instance or two where your outcomes were affected positively by another person. The event might be something small, such as when a kind driver made room for you to merge into traffic. It might be something larger, such as when a friend sat with you for hours as you grieved the loss of a loved one. Reflecting on the many ways in which others touch our lives might, at first blush, seem pretty self-focused. After all, we are asking, "What did others do for me?" But we are also identifying and appreciating moments of humanity, moments of connection.

As you work through the Eriksonian challenge of early adulthood, intimacy versus isolation—that is, as you seek to establish stable and fulfilling relationships—try to draw on an ecosystem perspective. We are often told to "look out for number one," and this advice suggests that our self-interests should serve as a primary motivator when we are making decisions and setting goals. The research of Crocker and colleagues suggests that there is wisdom in taking a broader, less self-focused perspective. In fact, this perspective might also help you negotiate the Eriksonian task of middle age: finding a sense of generativity (versus stagnation).

the Western world, where today's generations may be the first to live shorter life spans than their parents' generations did. Health researchers estimate that obesity-related causes will shorten the expected life span by two to five years if we do not start reversing the trends in poor health (Olshansky et al., 2005). One impetus to improving our health can be our life partners or children. The people we share our lives with sometimes motivate us to take care of ourselves.

MARRIAGE In adulthood, people devote a great deal of effort to achieving and maintaining satisfying relationships. Indeed, the vast majority of people around the world marry at some point in their lives or form some type of permanent bond with a relationship partner, although people today marry later in life and the percentage who marry is declining slowly in most industrialized countries.

Research shows that marriage benefits the individuals involved. For example, married people experience increased longevity compared with people who were never married, were divorced, or were widowed (Waite, 1995). According to this study, widowed women lived longer than divorced or never married women but not as long as still married women. Moreover, married men have lower rates of problem drinking and higher levels of income. When people's income rises (such as by combining two salaries through marriage), they are able to live in safer neighborhoods, have better health care, eat better, and so on. Married people typically experience greater happiness and joy and are at less risk for mental illnesses such as depression compared with unmarried people (Robles & Kiecolt-Glaser, 2003). Cohabiting adults, however, are likely to be in worse health than married people.

Studies suggest that men may benefit from marriage because their wives make sure they smoke less, eat more healthily, and go to the doctor. Women serve as the primary social support for their husbands. In fact, the benefits of marriage are more significant for men than for women. Married men report higher sexual and relationship satisfaction than cohabiting and single men, while there is no difference across these same groups of women. Married women report more emotional satisfaction, however, than cohabiting or single women.

Still, marriage is not a cure-all. Unhappily married people are at greater risk for poor health and even mortality. Conflicts within marriage are associated with poor immune functioning. The risk is comparable to that experienced by smokers, those with high blood pressure, and the morbidly obese (Robles & Kiecolt-Glaser, 2003). In general, people who are in unhappy marriages, are separated, or are divorced have many physical and psychological struggles, from depression to physical illness to violent behavior (Carrère, Buehlman, Gottman, Coan, & Ruckstuhl, 2000). Note, though, that these studies are largely correlational. It could be that happy, well-adjusted people are more likely to get married and not that marriage causes good outcomes for people. Or perhaps unhappy, negative people have both health problems and strained marriages.

The good news is that according to national surveys, at any given time, the vast majority of married people report satisfaction with their marriages (**Figure 9.33**). Those reporting the most satisfaction tend to have sufficient economic resources, share decision making, and together hold the view that marriage should be a lifelong commitment (Amato, Johnson, Booth, & Rogers, 2003). Having a successful marriage contributes to a sense of generativity in middle adulthood, as does having children.

HAVING CHILDREN The birth of a first child is a profound event for most couples. In fact, this arrival changes their lives in almost every respect. Responding to an infant's cries and trying to figure out why the child is distressed often cause anxiety and frustration for first-time parents. But new parents also experience great joys. Seeing a baby's first social smile, watching the first few tentative steps, and hearing a child say "Mommy" or "Daddy" provide powerful reinforcement for parents. As a result of such rewards, parents often become immersed in their children's lives. They make sure their children have playmates, expose them to new experiences, and seek ways to make them happy and healthy. Being a parent is central to the self-schemas of many adults.

Research shows that children can strain a marriage, however, especially when time and money are tight. A consistent finding is that couples with children, especially with adolescent children, report less marital satisfaction than those who are childless (Belsky, 1990; Cowan & Cowan, 1988). Philip and Carolyn Cowan, a married couple who are also marriage researchers, have found that many couples do not discuss roles and responsibilities before they have a child. This failure to communicate leads to misunderstandings and feelings of resentment after the birth of the child.

How many couples with children do you know who sat down and decided ahead of time who would do the laundry, wash the car, pay the bills, walk the dog, and wake up for early-morning poopie diaper duty? Most couples feel their love will be enough to make the birth of a baby a blissful time. These couples often receive a rude awakening when they are sleep deprived, agitated, and less than skilled at caring for their new bundle of joy, especially during the first month (Cowan & Cowan, 1988). The Cowans recommend that couples have serious and detailed conversations about all aspects of their lives and how they will approach each task after the baby is born.

Contemporary researchers are trying to find ways to prepare parents for parenthood so the transition does not exert such a strain on the relationship. For example, a husband who expresses great fondness toward his wife and is aware of her feelings and needs early in the marriage is less likely to report a dip in marital satisfaction after the baby arrives. Likewise, a wife who acknowledges and sympathizes with her husband's needs early on is likely to grow closer to her husband after the baby is born. Partners who report their early married life as chaotic or negative early on are more likely to find that having a baby does not bring them closer together or solve their problems, but increases the existing strain. Thus teaching newlyweds or young partners how to communicate and understand each other's needs may not only prevent divorce, but may also allow

(a)

(b)

(c)

FIGURE 9.33 Marriage Across cultures, marriage remains a building block of society. If the statistics hold true, **(a)** this Sami couple in Norway, **(b)** this Amhara couple in Ethiopia, and **(c)** this Hani couple in China will report being happy in their marriages.

the couple to enjoy parenting when their children are young as well as when they grow older and the children leave home (Shapiro, Gottman, & Carrère, 2000).

The Transition to Old Age Can Be Rewarding

In Western societies, people are living much longer, and the number of people over age 85 is growing dramatically. Indeed, it is becoming commonplace for people to live beyond 100. By 2030, more than 1 in 5 Americans will be over age 65, and these older people will be ethnically diverse, well educated, and physically fit. With this "graying" of the population in Western societies, much greater research attention has been paid to the lives of people over age 60.

The elderly contribute much to modern society. For instance, nearly 40 percent of U.S. federal judges are over 65, and they handle about 20 percent of the caseload (Markon, 2001). A 2010 survey found that 12 percent of federal justices are over 80 years old and 11 of the 1,200 judges are in their 90s (Goldstein, 2011). Many older adults work productively well past their 70s. Our view of the elderly is likely to change a great deal as the baby boom generation ages. Consider music stars—such as Bruce Springsteen, Madonna, and the Rolling Stones—who remain popular and vibrant well into their 50s, 60s, and beyond, certainly in defiance of common stereotypes of old people (**Figure 9.34**).

FIGURE 9.34 Changing Views of the Elderly The Rolling Stones, now in their 60s and early 70s, have been making music for nearly 50 years. In your opinion, can senior citizens "rock"? Do older performers such as the Stones qualify as "elderly"? Explain your answer.

DETERIORATION The body and mind, however, start deteriorating slowly at about age 50. Trivial physical changes include the graying and whitening of hair and the wrinkling of skin. Some of the most serious changes affect the brain, whose frontal lobes shrink proportionally more than other brain regions (Cowell et al., 1994). Scientists once believed that cognitive problems such as confusion and memory loss were an inevitable, normal part of aging. They now recognize that most older adults, while remaining alert, do everything a bit more slowly as they grow older.

Older adults who experience a dramatic loss in mental ability often suffer from *dementia*. This brain condition causes thinking, memory, and behavior to deteriorate progressively. Dementia has many causes, including excessive alcohol intake and HIV. For older adults, the major causes are Alzheimer's disease and small strokes that affect the brain's blood supply. After age 70, the risk of dementia increases with each year of life. Approximately 3 percent to 5 percent of people will develop Alzheimer's disease by age 70 to 75, and 6.5 percent will develop the disease after age 85 (Kawas, Gray, Brookmeyer, Fozard, & Zonderman, 2000). It takes about four years for people to progress from mild cognitive impairment to a diagnosis of Alzheimer's (Kawas et al., 2000).

The initial symptoms of Alzheimer's are typically minor memory impairments, but the disease eventually progresses to more serious difficulties, such as forgetting daily routines (**Figure 9.35**). Eventually, the person loses all mental capacities, including memory and language. Many people with Alzheimer's experience profound personality changes.

We do not know the exact cause of Alzheimer's, but evidence suggests there is a genetic predisposition to its development. One gene involved in cholesterol functioning is predictive of Alzheimer's (Corder et al., 1993). In addition, the memory-related neurotransmitter acetylcholine is very

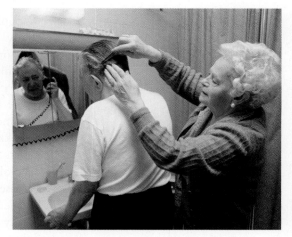

FIGURE 9.35 Impairments from Alzheimer's Disease A woman helps her husband, who is an Alzheimer's patient.

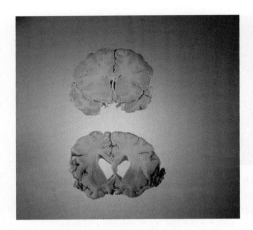

FIGURE 9.36 Damage from Alzheimer's Disease The brain on the bottom shows the ravages of Alzheimer's disease in comparison to the normal brain on top. The holes (ventricles) in the middle of the brain are extremely large, and every section of gray and white matter has lost density.

low in people who suffer from Alzheimer's, and this deficit results in abnormal protein accumulation in the brain (Dineley et al., 2001; **Figure 9.36**).

While some people may have a genetic predisposition to developing dementia of some kind, a predisposition is not a hopeless case. Decades of research show that when people challenge their brains by learning new tasks, working puzzles, reading, remaining socially active, and maintaining physical exercise at least three days per week, their risk of dementia declines significantly (Fratiglioni, Paillard-Borg, & Winblad, 2004; Larson et al, 2006). As you age, playing an active role in your own development can help make adulthood transitions rewarding experiences.

Despite the physical, social, and emotional challenges of aging, most older adults are surprisingly healthy and happy. Except for dementia, older adults have fewer mental health problems, including depression, than younger adults (Jorm, 2000). Indeed, some individuals thrive in old age, especially those with adequate financial resources and good health (Crosnoe & Elder, 2002). Most older adults report being just as satisfied with life, if not more so, than younger adults (Mroczek & Kolarz, 1998).

MEANING People of all ages are concerned with the meaning of life, but meaning often becomes a preoccupation for the elderly. According to the psychologist Laura Carstensen's *socioemotional selectivity theory,* as people grow older they perceive time to be limited, and therefore they adjust their priorities to emphasize emotionally meaningful events, experiences, and goals (Carstensen, 1995; Fung & Carstensen, 2004). For instance, they may choose to spend more time with a smaller group of close friends and avoid new people. They may spend an increasing amount of time reflecting on their lives and sharing memories with family members and friends. As they reminisce about their lives, older adults report more positive emotions than negative ones (Pasupathi & Carstensen, 2003). In essence, older adults want to savor their final years by putting their time and effort into meaningful and rewarding experiences. To the extent that they consider their time well spent, older adults are satisfied and can live their final years gracefully. This result is especially likely if throughout their lives they have worked hard to maintain their physical health, their social ties, and their cognitive capacities.

Cognition Changes as We Age

Cognitive abilities eventually decline with age, but it is difficult to pinpoint exactly what causes the decline. We know that the frontal lobes, which play an important role in working memory and many other cognitive skills, typically shrink as people grow older. One of the most consistent and identifiable cognitive changes is a slowing of mental processing speed. Experiments that test the time it takes to process a sensory input and react with a motor response show an increase in response time as early as an individual's mid-20s (Era, Jokela, & Heikkinen, 1986). This increase in response time becomes larger as the individual ages. Sensory-perceptual changes occur with age and may account for some of the observed decline. For instance, as we age, our sensitivity to visual contrast decreases, so activities such as climbing stairs or driving at night may become more difficult and more dangerous. Sensitivity to sound also decreases with age, especially the ability to tune out background noise. This change may make older people seem confused or forgetful when they simply are not able to hear adequately. And unfortunately, aging also affects memory and intelligence.

MEMORY Older people have difficulty with memory tasks that require the ability to juggle multiple pieces of information at the same time. Tasks in which attention is divided, such as driving while listening to the radio, also prove difficult. Some scientists believe these deficits reflect a decreased ability to store multiple pieces of information in working memory simultaneously (Salthouse, 1992).

Generally speaking, long-term memory is less affected by aging than is working memory. Certain aspects of long-term memory appear to suffer in advanced age, however. Older people often need more time to learn new information, but once they learn it, they use it as efficiently as younger people. The elderly also are better at recognition than at retrieval tasks (Fergus & McDowd, 1987). For example, if the word *cat* is shown to them, they have no trouble recognizing the word if they are asked, "Did you see the word *cat*?" But if they are simply asked what word they saw or whether they saw an animal name, they do not do as well. Consistent with the socioemotional selection theory is the finding that older people show better memory for positive than for negative information (Kennedy, Mather, & Carstensen, 2004). This finding might reflect a tendency to selectively ignore negative events in order to make one's latter years feel more positive and meaningful (Mather & Carstensen, 2003).

As discussed in Chapter 7, the more deeply an item is encoded, the better it is remembered. Do older adults use less efficient strategies for encoding information to be remembered? In an intriguing study, Jessica Logan and colleagues (2002) examined the memory processes of adults in their 20s and adults in their 70s and 80s. As expected, the older adults performed worse than the young adults. They showed less activation in left hemisphere brain areas known to support memory and greater activation in right hemisphere areas that do not aid memory. In a second study, the researchers sought to determine whether the memory deficit could be reduced if they gave the older participants a strategy to improve memorization. To produce deeper encoding, the older participants were asked to classify words as concrete or abstract. Undertaking this classification produced better memory and greater activation of the left frontal regions. These findings suggest that one reason for the decline in memory observed with aging is that older adults tend not to use strategies that facilitate memory. Perhaps, then, cognitive training might be useful for postponing age-related memory deficits. Another reason for declines in working memory is age-related reductions in dopamine activity in the frontal lobes. When researchers blocked dopamine activity in younger adults, they found that performance on a working memory task was similar to that found for older adults (Fischer et al., 2010).

INTELLIGENCE Research has indicated consistently that intelligence, as measured on standard psychometric tests, declines with advanced age. As we age, do we really lose IQ points? Or do older people just have a shorter attention span or lack the motivation to complete such tests?

As discussed in Chapter 8, some researchers have distinguished between fluid intelligence and crystallized intelligence (Horn & Hofer, 1992). Fluid intelligence is the ability to process new general information that requires no specific prior knowledge. Many standardized tests measure this kind of intelligence, as when test takers need to recognize an analogy or arrange blocks to match a picture. Associated with the speed of mental processing, fluid intelligence tends

FIGURE 9.37 Maintaining Health and Happiness
What smart things are these women doing to maintain their health and happiness? How might they further improve their chances? What sorts of factors are beyond their control?

to peak in early adulthood and decline steadily as we age. Crystallized intelligence is based on more specific knowledge—the kind that must be learned or memorized, such as vocabulary, specialized information, or reasoning strategies. This type of intelligence usually increases throughout life. It breaks down only when declines in other cognitive abilities prevent new information from being processed.

The Seattle Longitudinal Study addressed the question of aging's effects on intelligence (Schaie, 1990). The researchers recruited participants between the ages of 25 and 81, and they tracked them over seven years. By testing cognitive abilities such as verbal and mathematical skills, they found that intellectual decline does not occur until people are in their 60s or 70s. Further, people who were healthy and remained mentally active demonstrated less decline. Although memory and the speed of processing may decline, the continued ability to learn new information may mitigate those losses in terms of daily functioning.

Because life expectancies are much longer today than ever before, much more research is likely to be devoted to understanding how people can maintain their cognitive capacities to get the most out of their final years. Moreover, research will continue to examine aging through a more nuanced lens, as contemporary work suggests there may be gender differences in both genetic susceptibility to the negative effects of aging and the level and severity of cognitive impairment late in life (Mortensen & Hogh, 2001).

Thus this chapter ends where it began, with a reminder that all aspects of human development are caused by a complex cascade of influences. These influences include genes, neurotransmitters, family, social ties, culture, and each individual's motivations and actions (**Figure 9.37**). We all play active roles in our own development. We are not passive sponges absorbing our environments, nor are we slaves to our genes. How we experience each phase of the life span depends on our own perceptions, the social support we receive, and the choreographed dance that occurs between nature and nurture.

What Brings Us Meaning in Adulthood?

Scientists now recognize that important changes occur across adulthood. Thus researchers have increasingly been studying humans across the life span, from conception to old age. Erikson proposed that finding intimacy, feeling a sense of meaning or generativity, and achieving integrity or wisdom are three vital tasks to accomplish as we grow older. Adulthood requires people to meet certain challenges, such as facing physical and cognitive changes, getting married, and raising a family. With each of these challenges comes both stress and an opportunity to grow and find meaning in life. Marriage and children can provide social support and comfort, but can also be a source of conflict and stress, depending on the coping skills we use. An overriding theme that emerges from studying life transitions is that people seek meaning in their lives and that they do so increasingly as they age. Thoughtful planning for life transitions, along with reaching out for social support, can make all phases of adult development rewarding. Although older adults are often characterized as feeble and senile, they are for the most part healthy, alert, and vital. Indeed, one of the biggest surprises in recent research is the finding that older people are often more satisfied with their lives than are younger adults. Despite declines in memory and speed of mental processing, people generally maintain their intelligence into very old age, especially if they engage in social and mental activities that help keep their mental skills in shape.

1. Erikson proposed that certain challenges typify the passage through adulthood to old age. Which of the following statements represents these challenges?

    a. As adults, we have the challenge of making a living and caring for our children and other family members.
    b. Across all societies, people have to face the challenge created by a limited life span.
    c. In adulthood, people face the challenge of creating and maintaining close relationships, giving back to society, and responding well to the lives they have lived.
    d. Adults face spiritual challenges that can cause midlife crises and depression.

2. Indicate which of the following statements is true of adult development. Either mark the statement T for true or leave it blank.

    _____ a. Measures of fluid intelligence decline.
    _____ b Marital satisfaction tends to decline after the birth of a child.
    _____ c. Using an egosystem perspective helps us find meaning in adulthood.
    _____ d. The frontal lobes of the brain shrink throughout adulthood.
    _____ e. Physical and mental exercise can decrease the chances of cognitive decline as we age.

2. Options a, b, d, and e are true.

have lived.

relationships, giving back to society, and responding well to the lives they

Answers: 1. c. In adulthood, people face the challenge of creating and maintaining close

StudySpace: Your Place for a Better Grade

Chapter Summary

9.1 What Shapes Us during Childhood?

■ **Development Starts in the Womb:** Many factors in the prenatal environment, such as nutrition and hormones, can affect development. Exposure to teratogens (e.g., drugs, alcohol, viruses) can result in death, deformity, or mental disorders.

■ **Biology and Environment Influence Developmental Milestones:** Infants have many sensory abilities. For example, they can discriminate smells, tastes, and sounds. Infant physical development follows a consistent pattern across cultures, but cultural practices can affect the timing of milestones, such as walking. Dynamic systems theory helps us see how every new development occurs due to complex interactions between biology, environment, and personal agency.

■ **Brain Development Promotes Learning:** Brain development involves both maturation and experience. The brain's plasticity allows changes in the development of connections and in the synaptic pruning of unused neural connections. The timing of experiences necessary for brain development is particularly important in the early years.

■ **Children Develop Attachment and Emotion Regulation:** The emotional bond that develops between a child and a caregiver increases the child's chances of survival. Attachment styles are generally categorized as secure or insecure. Insecure attachment can be avoidant or ambivalent. Secure attachments are related to better adjustment later in life, including good emotion regulation skills and social relationships.

9.2 As Children, How Do We Learn about the World?

■ **Perception Introduces the World:** Experiments using habituation and the preferential-looking technique have revealed infants' considerable perceptual ability. Vision and hearing develop rapidly as neural circuitry develops.

■ **Memory Improves during Childhood:** Infantile memory is limited by a lack of both language ability and autobiographical reference. Source amnesia is common in children. Confabulation, common in young children, may result from underdevelopment of the frontal lobes.

■ **Piaget Emphasized Stages of Development:** Jean Piaget proposed that through interaction with the environment, children develop mental schemas and proceed through stages of cognitive development. In the sensorimotor stage, children experience the world through their senses and develop object permanence. In the preoperational stage, children's thinking is dominated by the appearance of objects rather than by

logic. In the concrete operational stage, children learn the logic of concrete objects. In the formal operational stage, children become capable of abstract, complex thinking.

■ **We Learn from Interacting with Others:** Being able to infer another's mental state is known as theory of mind. Through socialization, children move from egocentric thinking to being able to take another's perspective.

■ **Language Develops in an Orderly Way:** Infants can discriminate phonemes. Language proceeds from sounds to words to telegraphic speech to sentences. According to Noam Chomsky, all human languages are governed by universal grammar, an innate set of relations between linguistic elements. According to Lev Vygotsky, social interaction is the force that develops language. For language to develop, a child must be exposed to it during the sensitive period of the first few months and years of life.

9.3 How Do We Progress from Childhood to Adolescence?

■ **Physical Changes and Cultural Norms Influence the Development of Identity:** The biological changes of puberty affect social and emotional development. Those changes can also be influenced by social events. The adolescent's brain is undergoing important reorganization, which may lead to impulsive or risky behaviors governed by an overactive limbic system and immature frontal cortex. Gender identity develops in children and shapes their behaviors (i.e. gender roles). Gender schemas develop as cognitive representations of appropriate gender characteristics in the culture each person belongs to. Ethnic identity also develops through social forces. A bicultural identity allows a teen of color to feel connected to his or her own culture as well as the dominant culture.

■ **Peers and Parents Help Shape the Sense of Self:** Social comparisons help shape children's identity development. Based on feedback from peer groups and the larger community, teens develop a sense of belonging. Adults may view teens as belonging to homogeneous cliques, but teens emphasize their own individuality. Research shows that parents influence many areas of adolescents' lives, including religiosity, morality, identity, and how children experience emotions. Parents who use flexible parenting styles that respond to children's temperamental characteristics often have well-adjusted teens.

9.4 What Brings Us Meaning in Adulthood?

■ **Adulthood Presents Psychosocial Challenges:** Erikson believed that people develop throughout the life span. He theorized that each stage of life presents important social issues to be resolved. For adults, building intimacy with others, finding a sense of generativity, and facing the end of life with integrity are key challenges.

- **Adults are Affected by Life Transitions:** Adults experience many physical changes. Weight gain, poor diet, and lack of exercise become challenges to face if we do not adopt a healthy lifestyle in early adulthood. Marriage is a typical life transition for most adults and can provide a sense of security, health, and happiness. Married couples who understand each other's needs can adjust positively to the birth of a child, which can be a stressful transition for many.

- **The Transition to Old Age Can Be Rewarding:** As the population in many Western societies ages, more research is being done on aging, which inevitably brings physical and mental changes. Dementia has various causes, including Alzheimer's disease. Most older adults are healthy, remain productive, and become selective about their relationships and activities.

- **Cognition Changes as We Age:** Short-term memory, particularly when attention is divided or tasks are complex, is affected by aging. Crystallized intelligence increases; fluid intelligence declines in old age as processing speed declines. Being mentally active and socially engaged preserves cognitive functioning.

Key Terms

accommodation, p. 385
assimilation, p. 385
attachment, p. 374
concrete operational
    stage, p. 387
conventional level, p. 391
developmental
    psychology, p. 366

dynamic systems
    theory, p. 370
formal operational
    stage, p. 388
gender identity, p. 401
gender roles, p. 401
gender schemas, p. 401
infantile amnesia, p. 383

insecure attachment, p. 377
object permanence, p. 386
postconventional
    level, p. 391
preconventional
    level, p. 391
preoperational
    stage, p. 386

secure attachment, p. 377
sensitive periods, p. 373
sensorimotor
    stage, p. 386
synaptic pruning, p. 372
telegraphic speech, p. 394
teratogens, p. 368
theory of mind, p. 390

Practice Test

1. A 1-week-old infant normally can _____.
   a. differentiate between sweet and nonsweet tastes
   b. display social smiles
   c. grasp a caregiver's finger
   d. make eye contact
   e. orient toward loud sounds
   f. recognize his or her name
   g. roll over from stomach to back
   h. see a caregiver across the room
   i. turn his or her head toward the smell of the mother's breast milk
   j. turn toward a nipple near his or her mouth

2. Which of the following statements best summarizes the key finding from Harry Harlow's study of infant rhesus monkeys?
   a. Contact with "mothers" who provided food promoted a sense of security.
   b. Contact with "mothers" who provided food promoted normal social development.
   c. Contact with comforting "mothers" promoted a sense of security.
   d. Contact with comforting "mothers" promoted normal social development.

3. A 9-month-old child watches as three cubes are covered by a panel, then as three more cubes appear to move behind the panel. Once the panel is lifted, only three cubes appear. Which of the following statements describes the infant's likely reaction?
   a. The infant quickly will lose interest in the screen.
   b. The infant will try to grab the three remaining cubes.
   c. The infant will stare at the researcher's face.
   d. The infant will stare at the three remaining cubes for a relatively long time.

4. Imagine reading a young child a story. In the story, Schuyler calls Emma a mean name. Emma retaliates by biting Schuyler. You ask the child what she thinks about the fact that Emma bit Schuyler. Three possible responses appear below. Label each as typical of one of the levels of moral reasoning described by Kohlberg: preconventional, conventional, or postconventional.
   a. "Emma better not bite again if she doesn't want to get bitten back!"
   b. "Even if someone hurts us, it's never okay to hurt them back."
   c. "It is wrong to bite people. Emma is going to get a time out."

The answer key for the Practice Tests can be found at the back of the book. It also includes answers to the green caption questions.

10

Emotion and Motivation

IN HIS EARLY 30s, ELLIOT BEGAN SUFFERING from severe headaches. He was happily married, a good father, and doing well professionally. His headaches increased until he could no longer concentrate, so he went to see his doctor. As it turned out, a tumor the size of a small orange was growing behind Elliot's eyes (**Figure 10.1**). The tumor grew, forcing his frontal lobes upward into the top of his skull. When a group of skilled surgeons removed the noncancerous tumor, they could not avoid removing some of the surrounding frontal lobe tissue. At first, the surgery appeared to be a great success. Elliot's physical recovery was quick, and he continued to be a reasonable, intelligent, and charming man with a superb memory. But Elliot changed in a way that baffled his friends and family: He no longer experienced emotion.

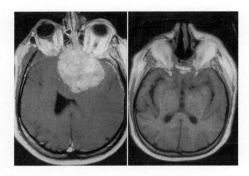

FIGURE 10.1 Tumor in the Prefrontal Cortex Elliot suffered from a brain tumor behind his eye. The brain scan on the left shows a similarly placed tumor in another patient (the light-gray mass is the tumor). On the right is a follow-up brain scan, taken two years after the tumor was removed.

The neurologist Antonio Damasio was asked to examine Elliot to find out whether his emotional problems were caused by the surgery. Damasio noted, "I never saw a tinge of emotion in my many hours of conversation with him: no sadness, no impatience, no frustration with my incessant and repetitious questioning" (Damasio, 1994, p. 45). Even when Damasio's research team showed Elliot a series of disturbing pictures, such as images of severely injured bodies, they observed no emotional reactions from him. Elliot was not oblivious to his loss of emotion. He knew the pictures were disturbing and believed that before the surgery he would have had an emotional response, but now he felt nothing.

Elliot's life fell apart. The absence of emotions sabotaged his ability to make rational decisions, even about trivial things. He lost his job. Against his family's advice, he entered a doomed business venture with a sleazy character and lost all his savings. He divorced, remarried, and then quickly divorced again. Before the surgery, he had been a caring and compassionate man. After it, he became detached from his problems. He could not learn from his mistakes. In fact, he reacted to the events in his life as if they were happening to someone he was not very connected to. Ultimately, while Elliot's brain surgery had left his intellect intact, it robbed him of his ability to function as a member of society.

Elliot apparently suffered impairments in both emotion and motivation: He just did not care. Imagine living without feelings or aspirations to make something of yourself. What sort of life would that be? How profoundly do your feelings affect what you think and do? ■

emotion Feelings that involve subjective evaluation, physiological processes, and cognitive beliefs.

10.1 How Do We Experience Emotions?

Almost everyone has an intuitive sense of what *emotion* means. Still, the term is difficult to define precisely. The terms *emotion* and *mood* are often used interchangeably in everyday language, but it is useful to distinguish between them. Emotions are immediate, specific responses to environmental events, such as how a person feels about being cut off in traffic or about receiving a gift. Emotions typically interrupt whatever is happening, or they trigger changes in thought and behavior. By contrast, moods are diffuse, long-lasting emotional states. Rather than interrupting what is happening, they influence thought and behavior. Often people who are in good or bad moods have no idea why they feel the way they do. Thus moods refer to people's vague senses that they feel certain ways. Think of the difference this way: Getting cut off in traffic can make a person feel irritation (emotion), but for no apparent reason a person can feel irritable (mood).

For psychologists, **emotion** (sometimes called *affect*) refers to feelings that involve subjective evaluation, physiological processes, and cognitive beliefs. In exploring emotion, the following sections focus on those three components. They discuss the *subjective experience,* or the feelings that accompany an emotion; the *physical changes,* such as increases in heart rate, in skin temperature, and in brain activation; and the *cognitive appraisals,* people's beliefs and understandings about why they feel the way they do.

Emotions Have a Subjective Component

We experience emotions subjectively. In other words, we know we are experiencing emotions because we *feel* them. For this reason, we refer to our emotions as feelings. The intensity of emotional reactions varies: Some people report many distinct emotions every day, whereas others report only infrequent and minor emotional reactions.

People who are overemotional or underemotional tend to have psychological problems. For example, some overemotional people suffer from *mood disorders,* such as depression or panic attacks. People with mood disorders can experience such strong emotions that they become immobilized. At the other extreme, some people suffer from *alexithymia.* This disorder causes people to not experience the subjective components of emotions. Elliot, the patient discussed in the chapter opener, had alexithymia as a result of his brain surgery. One cause of alexithymia is that the physiological messages associated with emotions do not reach the brain centers that interpret emotion. Damage to certain brain regions, especially the prefrontal cortex, is associated with a loss of emotion's subjective component.

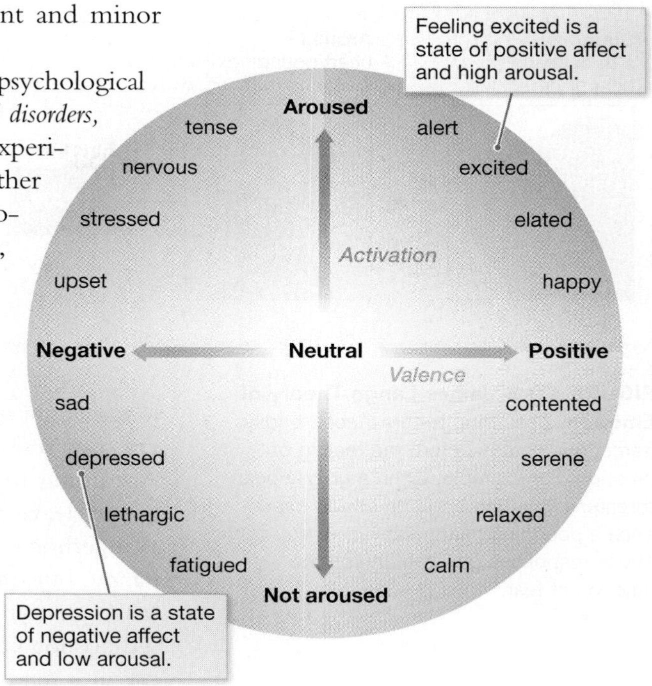

DISTINGUISHING BETWEEN TYPES OF EMOTIONS How many emotions does a person experience? How are different emotions related to one another? Many theorists about emotion distinguish between primary and secondary emotions. This approach is conceptually similar to viewing color as consisting of primary and secondary hues. Basic or **primary emotions** are evolutionarily adaptive, shared across cultures, and associated with specific physical states. They include anger, fear, sadness, disgust, happiness, and possibly surprise and contempt. **Secondary emotions** are blends of primary emotions. They include remorse, guilt, submission, shame, and anticipation. To see the difference between the two types of emotion, imagine that your boyfriend or girlfriend reports feeling neglected by you. Your initial emotional response might be a primary one: anger at being accused, because you did not mean to neglect your companion. Your second emotional response might also be primary: sadness at being accused, because you inadvertently hurt your companion. Your anger and sadness might then combine into a secondary emotion: guilt, because through neglect you brought pain to someone you care about.

One approach to understanding the experience of emotion is the *circumplex model.* On the circumplex map, emotions are arranged in a circle. At the center of the circle is the intersection of two core dimensions of affect: *Valence* indicates how negative or positive emotions are. *Activation* indicates how *arousing* they are (Russell, 1980; **Figure 10.2**). **Arousal** is a generic term used to describe physiological activation (such as increased brain activity) or increased autonomic responses (such as quickened heart rate, increased sweating, or muscle tension). Psychologists have debated the names of dimensions and the whole idea of naming dimensions, but circumplex models have proved useful as a basic taxonomy, or classification system, of mood states (Barrett, Mesquita, Ochsner, & Gross, 2007).

NEGATIVE AFFECT AND POSITIVE AFFECT As David Watson and colleagues (1999) have pointed out, negative affect and positive affect are independent. We can even experience both kinds of emotions simultaneously. Consider the bittersweet feeling of being both happy and sad, as you might feel when remembering good times with someone who has died. In one study, research participants reported feeling happy and sad after moving out of their dormitories, after graduating from college, and after seeing the movie *Life Is Beautiful* (in which a good-natured

Feeling excited is a state of positive affect and high arousal.

Depression is a state of negative affect and low arousal.

FIGURE 10.2 Circumplex Map of Emotion How do you feel while reading this chapter? Consider the valence and activation of your emotion right now and plot your current state on this map.

primary emotions Emotions that are evolutionarily adaptive, shared across cultures, and associated with specific physical states; they include anger, fear, sadness, disgust, happiness, and possibly surprise and contempt.

secondary emotions Blends of primary emotions; they include remorse, guilt, submission, and anticipation.

arousal Physiological activation (such as increased brain activity) or increased autonomic responses (such as increased heart rate, sweating, or muscle tension).

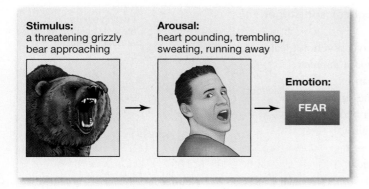

FIGURE 10.3 James-Lange Theory of Emotion According to this theory, bodily perception comes before the feeling of emotion. For example, when a grizzly bear threatens you, you begin to sweat, experience a pounding heart, and run (if you can). These responses generate in you the emotion of fear.

father tries to protect his son in a Nazi prison camp; Larsen, McGraw, & Cacioppo, 2001). Neurochemical evidence supports the idea that positive affect and negative affect are independent. Positive activation states appear to be associated with an increase in dopamine, whereas negative activation states appear to be associated with an increase in norepinephrine (for explanations of neurochemistry, see Chapter 3, "Biology and Behavior").

As you probably know from experience, both negative and positive emotional states can produce crying. Perhaps you have cried tears of *sadness* while watching a movie. Perhaps you have cried tears of *joy* when you finally achieved some long-sought goal (see Figure 4.7). There have been many theories about why we cry, but researchers have not discovered the function of crying (Karpas, 2009). According to the best available evidence, crying results mainly when negative events leave us unable to respond behaviorally to the emotions we are feeling (Vingerhoets, Bylsma, & Rottenberg, 2009). Yes, we sometimes cry when we are happy, but often this kind of crying occurs because the event also makes us a bit sad (e.g., crying at graduation, when you are leaving your friends behind) or when we do not know what to do or say in the situation. For example, a man might cry in a tender moment because he is unable to express his happiness in a more appropriate way. In addition, crying may relieve stress through activation of the parasympathetic nervous system (Hendricks, Rottenberg, & Vingerhoets, 2007). Finally, by bringing sympathy and social support from others, crying might serve an important social function.

Emotions Have a Physiological Component

JAMES-LANGE THEORY Common sense suggests that emotions lead to physical changes. We feel angry or sad or embarrassed, and our bodies respond. But in 1884, William James argued that it was just the opposite. James asserted that a person's interpretation of the physical changes in a situation leads that person to feel an emotion. As he put it, "We feel sorry because we cry, angry because we strike, afraid because we tremble, [it is] not that we cry, strike, or tremble because we are sorry, angry, or fearful" (1884, p. 190). James believed that physical changes occur in distinct patterns that translate directly into specific emotions. Around the same time, a similar theory was independently proposed by the physician and psychologist Carl Lange. According to what is called the *James-Lange theory of emotion,* we perceive specific patterns of bodily responses, and as a result of that perception we feel emotion (**Figure 10.3**).

According to much of the scientific evidence, physical reactions are not specific enough to fully explain the subjective experiences of emotions (Cacioppo, Berntson, Larsen, Poehlmann, & Ito, 2000). Recently, however, studies using brain imaging have found that different primary emotions produce different patterns of brain activation (Vytal & Hamann, 2010). These results support James's theory.

FACIAL FEEDBACK HYPOTHESIS One implication of the counterintuitive James-Lange theory is that if you mold your facial muscles to mimic an emotional state, you activate the associated emotion. In other words, facial expressions trigger the experience of emotions, not the other way around. In 1963, Silvan Tomkins proposed this idea as the *facial feedback hypothesis.* Eleven years later, James Laird tested the idea by having people hold a pencil between their teeth or with their mouths in a way that produced a smile or a frown (**Figure 10.4**). When participants rated cartoons, those in a posed smile found the cartoons the funniest.

Further support comes from the results of studies by Paul Ekman and colleagues (1983), who asked professional actors to portray anger, distress, fear, disgust, joy, and surprise. Physiological changes recorded during the actors' portrayals differed for various emotions. Heart rate changed little with surprise, joy, and disgust, but it increased with distress, fear, and anger. Anger was also associated with higher skin temperature, whereas the other emotions resulted in little change in skin temperature. These results give some support to James's theory that specific patterns of physical changes are the basis for emotional states.

CANNON-BARD THEORY In 1927, the physiologist Walter B. Cannon noted that the human mind and the human body do not experience emotions at the same speed. The mind is quick to experience emotions. The body is much slower, taking at least a second or two to respond. Cannon also noted that many emotions produce similar bodily responses. The similarities make it too difficult for people to determine quickly which emotion they are experiencing. For instance, anger, excitement, and sexual interest all produce similar changes in heart rate and blood pressure. Cannon, along with Philip Bard, proposed that the mind and body experience emotions independently. According to the *Cannon-Bard theory of emotion,* the information from an emotion-producing stimulus is processed in subcortical structures. As a result, we experience two separate things at roughly the same time: an emotion and a physical reaction (**Figure 10.5**).

THE AMYGDALA In 1937, James Papez proposed that many subcortical brain regions were involved in emotion. Fifteen years later, Paul MacLean expanded this list and called it the *limbic system.* (As discussed in Chapter 3, the limbic system consists of brain structures that border the cerebral cortex.) We now know that many brain structures outside the limbic system are involved in emotion and that many limbic structures are not central to emotion per se. For instance, the hippocampus is important mostly for memory, and the hypothalamus is important mostly for motivation. Thus the term *limbic system* is used mainly in a rough, descriptive way rather than as a means of directly linking brain areas to specific emotional functions. For understanding emotion, the two most important brain regions are the amygdala and the prefrontal cortex (**Figure 10.6a**).

The amygdala processes the emotional significance of stimuli, and it generates immediate emotional and behavioral reactions (Phelps, 2006). According to Joseph LeDoux (2007), the processing of emotion in the amygdala is a circuit that has developed over the course of evolution to protect animals from danger. LeDoux (1996, 2007) has established the amygdala as the brain structure most important for emotional learning, as in the development of classically conditioned fear responses (see Chapter 6, "Learning"). People with damage to the amygdala show fear when confronted with dangerous objects, but they do not develop conditioned fear responses to objects associated with dangerous objects. Suppose that study participants receive an electric shock each time they see a picture of a blue square. Normally these participants will develop a conditioned response—indicated by greater physiological arousal—when they see the blue square. But people with damage to the amygdala do not show classical conditioning of these fear associations.

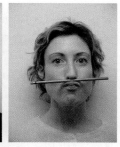

FIGURE 10.4 Facial Feedback Hypothesis According to this hypothesis, a person's facial expression triggers that person's experience of emotion. Even the forced alteration of a person's facial expression can change that person's experience of emotion. **Which of these women is more likely to report feeling happy? Why? To test these results, hold a pen or pencil in these positions and reflect on your feelings.**

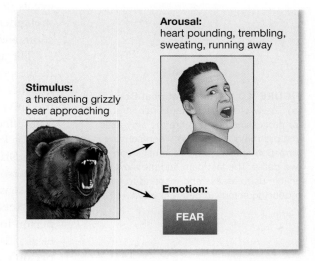

Stimulus: a threatening grizzly bear approaching

Arousal: heart pounding, trembling, sweating, running away

Emotion: FEAR

FIGURE 10.5 Cannon-Bard Theory of Emotion According to this theory, emotion and physical reaction happen together. For example, when a grizzly bear threatens you, you simultaneously feel afraid, begin to sweat, experience a pounding heart, and run (if you can).

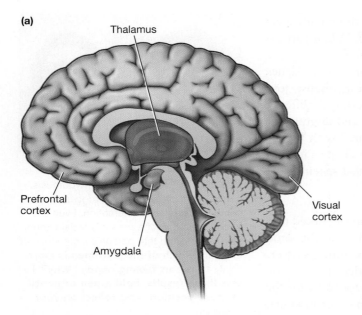

(a)

Thalamus

Prefrontal cortex

Amygdala

Visual cortex

(b)

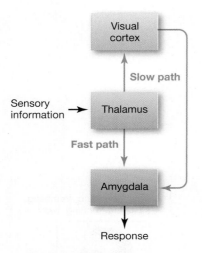

Visual cortex

Slow path

Sensory information → Thalamus

Fast path

Amygdala

Response

FIGURE 10.6 The Emotional Brain
(a) The two most important brain structures for processing emotion are the amygdala and prefrontal cortex. **(b)** When sensory information reaches the thalamus, it can take two paths. The fast path and the slow path enable us to assess and respond to emotion-producing stimuli in different ways.

Consider S.P., a patient who first showed signs of neurological impairment around age 3 and later was diagnosed with epilepsy (Anderson & Phelps, 2000). At age 48, a portion of her amygdala was removed to reduce the frequency of her seizures. The surgery was reasonably successful, and S.P. retained most of her intellectual faculties. She has a normal IQ, has taken college courses, and performs well on standardized tests of visual attention. She does not show fear conditioning, however. While S.P. can tell you that the blue square is associated with shock, her body shows no physiological evidence of having acquired the fear response.

Information reaches the amygdala along two separate pathways. The first path is a "quick and dirty" system that processes sensory information nearly instantaneously. Recall from Chapter 5 that, with the exception of smell, all sensory information travels to the thalamus before going on to other brain structures and the related portions of the cortex. Thus, along this fast path, sensory information travels quickly through the thalamus to the amygdala for priority processing (**Figure 10.6b**). The second path is somewhat slower, but it leads to more deliberate and more thorough evaluations. Along this slow path, sensory material travels from the thalamus to the cortex (i.e., the visual cortex or the auditory cortex), where the information is scrutinized in greater depth before it is passed along to the amygdala. Theorists believe that the fast system prepares animals to respond to a threat in case the slower pathway confirms the threat (LeDoux, 2000).

As noted in Chapter 7, emotional events are especially likely to be stored in memory. The amygdala plays a role in this process. Brain imaging studies have shown that emotional events are likely to increase activity in the amygdala, and that increased activity is likely to improve long-term memory for the event (Cahill et al., 2001; Hamann, Ely, Grafton, & Kilts, 1999). Researchers believe that the amygdala modifies how the hippocampus consolidates memory, especially memory for fearful events (Phelps, 2004, 2006). In short, thanks to the amygdala, emotions such as fear strengthen memories. This adaptive mechanism enables us to remember harmful situations and thus potentially avoid them.

The amygdala also plays another role in the processing of emotions. It is involved in the perception of social stimuli, as when we decipher the emotional meanings of other people's facial expressions. For instance, fMRI studies demonstrate that the amygdala is especially sensitive to the intensity of fearful faces (Dolan, 2000). This effect occurs even if a face is flashed so quickly on a screen that participants do not know they have seen it (Whalen et al., 1998). Perhaps surprisingly, the amygdala reacts more when a person observes a face displaying fear than when the person observes a face displaying anger. On the surface this difference makes little sense, because a person looking at you angrily is likely to be more dangerous. According to some researchers, the greater activity of the amygdala when a person looks at a frightened face is due to the ambiguity of the situation (Whalen et al., 2001). In other words, the perceiver feels like the recipient of the other person's anger—no ambiguity there. But the perceiver may not be sure what the other person fears. The amygdala also responds to other emotional expressions, even happiness. Generally, however, the effect is greatest for fear. One study showed that the amygdala can be activated even by neutral facial expressions, but this effect occurs only in people who are chronically anxious (Somerville, Kim, Johnstone, Alexander, & Whalen, 2004).

Given that the amygdala is involved in processing the emotional content of facial expressions, it is not surprising that social impairments result when the amygdala is damaged. Those with damage to the amygdala often have difficulty evaluating the intensity of fearful faces. They do not have difficulty, however, in judging the intensity of other facial expressions, such as happiness. One study suggests that those with damage to the amygdala can tell a smile from a frown but that they fail to use information within facial expressions to make accurate interpersonal judgments (Adolphs, Tranel, & Damasio, 1998). For instance, they have difficulty using photographs to assess people's trustworthiness—a task most people can do easily (Adolphs, Sears, & Piven, 2001; **Figure 10.7**). They also tend to be unusually friendly with people they do not know. This extra friendliness might result from a lack of the normal mechanisms for caution around strangers and for the feeling that some people should be avoided.

FIGURE 10.7 Try for Yourself: Evaluate Facial Expressions

Which of these people would you trust?

Results: Most people would say the person on the right looks more trustworthy.

Conclusion: The person on the left appears shifty-eyed and avoids our gaze, and therefore he looks less trustworthy. People with certain brain injuries cannot detect how trustworthy people are from facial expressions such as these.

THE PREFRONTAL CORTEX Some evidence suggests that the left and right frontal lobes are affected by different emotions. In a series of studies, Richard Davidson (2000) found that greater activation of the right prefrontal cortex is associated with negative affect, whereas greater activation of the left hemisphere is associated with positive affect. This pattern is known as *cerebral asymmetry*.

People also can be dominant in one hemisphere of their frontal lobes, and that dominant hemisphere can bias their emotions. Those who tend to move their eyes to the right are left-hemisphere dominant, and those who move their eyes to the left are right-hemisphere dominant. Researchers assess hemispherical dominance by asking participants a series of questions about how they might feel in an emotional situation (such as being anxious). A study of responses to film clips found that people who were left-hemisphere dominant showed the most positive response to pleasant scenes, whereas those who were right-hemisphere dominant showed the most negative response to unpleasant scenes. People who tend to be depressed show greater activity in the right frontal lobe when shown the same film clips, mainly because the left frontal lobe does not seem to respond normally (Davidson, Pizzagalli, Nitschke, & Putnam, 2002).

Emotions Have a Cognitive Component

SCHACHTER-SINGER TWO-FACTOR THEORY The social psychologists Stanley Schachter and Jerome Singer (1962) have proposed a *two-factor theory of emotion*. According to this theory, a situation evokes a physiological response, such as arousal, and a cognitive interpretation, or *emotion label*. When people experience arousal,

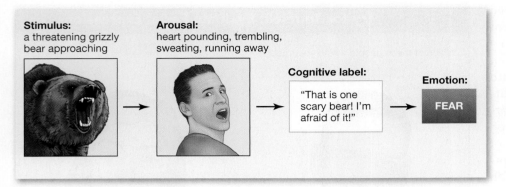

Stimulus:
a threatening grizzly
bear approaching

Arousal:
heart pounding, trembling,
sweating, running away

Cognitive label:
"That is one
scary bear! I'm
afraid of it!"

Emotion:
FEAR

FIGURE 10.8 Schachter-Singer Two-Factor Theory According to this theory, a person experiences physiological changes, applies a cognitive label to explain those changes, and translates that label into an emotion. For example, when a grizzly bear threatens you, you begin to sweat, experience a pounding heart, and run (if you can). You then label those bodily actions as responses to the bear. As a result, you know you are experiencing fear.

they initiate a search for its source (**Figure 10.8**). The search for a cognitive explanation is often quick and straightforward, since a person generally recognizes the event that led to his or her emotional state. What happens when the situation is more ambiguous? According to the two-factor theory, whatever the person believes caused the emotion will determine how the person labels the emotion.

Schachter and Singer devised an ingenious experiment to test the two-factor theory. First, the participants, all of whom were male, were injected with either a stimulant or a placebo. The stimulant was adrenaline, which produced symptoms such as sweaty palms, increased heart rate, and shaking. Some of the participants who received adrenaline were told that the drug they took would make them feel aroused. The other participants were not told anything about the drug's effects. Finally, each participant was left to wait with a confederate of the experimenter. The confederate, also male, was working with the experimenter and behaved according to the research plan. In the euphoric condition, each participant was exposed to a confederate who was in a great mood, played with a hula hoop, and made paper airplanes. In the angry condition, each participant was seated in a room with a confederate. But both the participant and the confederate were asked to fill out a long questionnaire that asked them very intimate, personal questions, such as "With how many men (other than your father) has your mother had extramarital relationships?" (To make the question even more insulting, the choices were 4 or fewer, 5 to 9, or 10 or more.) The confederate became increasingly angry as he filled out the questionnaire. Finally, he ripped it up and stormed out of the room.

When participants received adrenaline but were told how their bodies would respond to the drug, they had an easy explanation for their arousal. They attributed it to the adrenaline, not to the situation. In contrast, when participants received adrenaline but were not given information about its effects, they were just as aroused as the informed group, but they did not know why. They looked to the environment to explain or label their bodies' responses (sweating palms, increased heart rate, and shaking). Participants in the no-explanation group reported that they felt happy when they waited with the euphoric confederate and that they felt less happy when they waited with the angry confederate. While they attributed their feelings to what was happening in the environment, participants in the informed group did not (**Figure 10.9**). Those in the placebo condition responded in between the two adrenaline conditions, depending on how aroused they were by the confederate.

WE CAN MISATTRIBUTE THE SOURCES OF OUR EMOTIONAL STATES One interesting implication of the two-factor theory is that physical states caused by a situation can be attributed to the wrong emotion. When people misidentify the source of their arousal, it is called *misattribution of arousal*.

In one exploration of this phenomenon, researchers tried to see whether people could feel romantic attraction through misattribution (Dutton & Aron, 1974). Each participant, a heterosexual male, was asked to cross either of two bridges over the Capilano River, in British Columbia. One was a narrow suspension bridge with a low rail that swayed 230 feet above raging, rocky rapids. The other was a sturdy modern bridge just above the river. At the middle of the bridge, an attractive female research assistant approached the man and interviewed him. She gave him her phone number and offered to explain the results of the study at a later date if he was interested. According to the two-factor theory of emotion, the less stable bridge would produce arousal (sweaty palms, increased heart rate), which could be misattributed as attraction to the interviewer. Indeed, men interviewed on the less stable bridge were more likely to call the interviewer and ask her for a date (**Figure 10.10**).

FIGURE 10.9 Scientific Method: Testing the Schachter-Singer Two-Factor Theory

Hypothesis: Whatever a person believes caused an emotion will determine how the person experiences and labels the emotion.

Research Method:

1 Participants were injected with a stimulant (adrenaline) or a placebo.

2 Informed participants in the adrenaline condition were told the drug they were given might make them feel shaky, cause their hearts to beat faster, and make their faces feel flushed. All of these bodily activities are side effects of taking adrenaline. Uninformed participants were not told anything about the drug's effects.

3 In the euphoric condition, each participant was exposed to a confederate who was in a great mood, played with a hula hoop, and made paper airplanes.

In the angry condition, each participant was seated with a confederate. Both the participant and the confederate were asked to fill out a questionnaire that asked very insulting questions, such as a question that implied their mothers had cheated on their fathers. The confederate became angry, tore up the questionnaire, and stormed out of the room.

4 The experimenters coded behavioral indicators of euphoria, such as joining in the fun. They also coded behavioral indicators of anger, such as agreeing with the angry confederate. In addition, participants were asked about their emotional states, such as whether they felt happy or angry.

Euphoric condition

Angry condition

Results: When participants received the adrenaline and were told how their bodies would respond to the drug, they had an easy explanation for their arousal. They attributed it to the adrenaline, not to the situation. In contrast, when participants received adrenaline but were not given information about its effects, they looked to the environment to explain or label their bodies' responses.

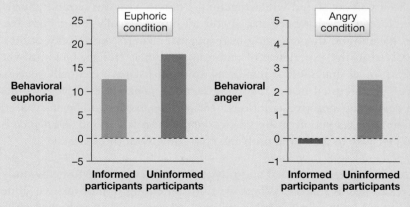

When uninformed participants waited with the euphoric confederates, they displayed behavioral indicators of euphoria (see left-side graph). They also reported feeling happy. When uninformed participants waited with the angry confederates, they displayed behavioral indicators of anger (see right-side graph). They also reported feeling angry. These results happened because the uninformed participants attributed their feelings to what was happening in the environment. Informed participants did not react in the same ways or make the same attributions. For example, in the angry condition, their behavioral indicators of anger decreased.

Conclusion: Feelings of arousal can be attributed to events in the environment, thereby shaping people's emotions.

Source: Schachter, S., & Singer, J. (1962). Cognitive, social, and physiological determinants of emotional state. *Psychological Review, 69*, 379–399.

FIGURE 10.10 Misattribution of Arousal Men who walked across this narrow and scary bridge over the Capilano River displayed more attraction to the female experimenter on the bridge than did men who walked across a safer bridge.

Can you think of a possible confound affecting this study? What about initial differences between the men who chose to cross the less stable bridge and those who chose the safer bridge? Perhaps men who were more likely to take risks were more likely to choose a scary bridge *and* to call for a date. The general idea—that people can misattribute arousal for affection—has been supported in other studies, however.

Excitation transfer is a similar form of misattribution. Here, residual physiological arousal caused by one event is transferred to a new stimulus. For example, in the period after exercise, the body slowly returns to its baseline state. Residual arousal symptoms include an elevated heart rate. After a few minutes, most people will have caught their breath and may not realize their bodies are still aroused. During this interim period, they are likely to transfer the residual excitation from the exercise to any event that occurs. This response has a practical application: On your next date, you might suggest seeing a movie that you think will produce arousal, such as a tearjerker or an action film. Perhaps the person you are out with will misattribute residual arousal to you!

We Regulate Our Emotional States

Emotions can be disruptive and troublesome. Negative feelings can prevent us from behaving as we would like to, but so can positive feelings. While driving, have you ever felt so angry about a past event that you could not concentrate on the road? Or have you ever felt so excited about an upcoming event that you were unable to study for an exam? In our daily lives, circumstances often require us to harness our emotional responses, but doing so is not easy. How do you mask your expression of disgust when you are obligated by politeness to eat something you dislike? How do you force yourself to be nice about losing a competition that really matters to you?

James Gross (1999) outlined various strategies people use to regulate their emotions. Some of these strategies help us prevent or prepare for events, and some of them help us deal with events after they occur. For instance, we try to put ourselves in certain situations and to avoid other situations. If you want to feel romantic when proposing to your girlfriend, you are better off proposing in a quiet, intimate bistro than in a fast-food joint; if you want to avoid feeling jealous of your sister's athletic skill, you could choose not to attend her soccer, basketball, and softball games; and so on. We also help manage our emotional states by focusing our attention on certain aspects of situations. For example, if you are afraid of flying, you can distract yourself from your anxiety by helping the woman next to you entertain her restless toddler. It is also possible to directly alter our emotional reactions to events by reappraising those events in more neutral terms. So if you get scared while watching a movie, you can remind yourself that the whole spectacle has been staged and no one is actually being hurt. Recent studies have found that engaging in reappraisal changes the activity of brain regions involved in the experience of emotion (Ochsner, Bunge, Gross, & Gabrieli, 2002). Not all strategies for regulating emotional states are equally successful, however. As discussed in the following sections, *humor* is a simple, effective method of regulating negative emotions. *Thought suppression* and *rumination* are two common mistakes people make when trying to regulate mood. *Distraction* is, overall, the best way to avoid the problems that come with those mistakes.

HUMOR Humor has many mental and physical health benefits. Most obviously, humor increases positive affect. When we find something humorous, we smile, laugh, and enter a state of pleasurable, relaxed excitation. Research shows that laughter stimulates endocrine secretion, improves the immune system, and stimulates the release of hormones, dopamine, serotonin, and endorphins. When people laugh, they experience rises in circulation, blood pressure, skin temperature, and heart rate, along with a decrease in pain perception. All of these responses are similar to those resulting from physical exercise, and they are considered beneficial to short-term and long-term health.

People sometimes laugh in situations that do not seem very funny, such as funerals or wakes. According to one theory, laughing in these situations helps people distance themselves from their negative emotions, and it strengthens their connections to other people. In one study on the topic, Dacher Keltner and George Bonanno (1997) interviewed 40 people who had recently lost a spouse. The researchers found that genuine laughter during the interview was associated with positive mental health and fewer negative feelings, such as grief. It was a way of coping with a difficult situation.

THOUGHT SUPPRESSION AND RUMINATION Through thought suppression, people attempt to not feel or respond to the emotion at all. Daniel Wegner and colleagues (1990) have demonstrated that trying to suppress negative thoughts is extremely difficult. In fact, doing so often leads to a *rebound effect,* in which people think more about something after suppression than before. For example, people who are dieting and try to not think about tasty foods end up thinking about them more than if they had tried to engage in another activity as a way of not thinking about food.

Rumination involves thinking about, elaborating, and focusing on undesired thoughts or feelings. This response prolongs the mood, and it impedes successful mood regulation strategies, such as distracting oneself or focusing on solutions for the problem (Lyubomirsky & Nolen-Hoeksema, 1995).

DISTRACTION Distraction involves doing something other than the troubling activity or thinking about something other than the troubling thought. By thus absorbing attention, distraction temporarily helps people stop focusing on their problems.

Some distractions backfire, however. People may change their thoughts but end up thinking about other problems. Or they may engage in maladaptive behaviors. For example, as noted in Chapter 5, people sometimes try to escape self-awareness by overeating or binge drinking. To temporarily escape your problems, you might try watching a movie that captures your attention. Choose a movie that will not remind you of your troubled situation. Otherwise, you might simply find yourself wallowing in mental anguish. (For more suggestions on dealing with your day-to-day problems and stresses, see Chapter 11, "Health and Well-Being.")

Summing Up

How Do We Experience Emotions?

Emotions are often classified as primary emotions, which are similar across cultures and have an evolutionarily adaptive purpose, or secondary emotions, which are blends of primary emotions. Emotions have a valence (positive or negative) and a level of activation (level of arousal). The three main theories of emotion differ in their relative emphases on subjective experience, physiological changes, and cognitive interpretation. The James-Lange theory states that specific patterns of physical changes give rise to the perception of associated emotions. The Cannon-Bard theory proposes that two separate pathways, physical changes and subjective experience, occur at the same time. The Schachter-Singer two-factor theory emphasizes the combination of generalized physiological arousal and cognitive appraisals in determining specific emotions. Research has demonstrated that the amygdala and prefrontal cortex play particularly important roles in our experience of emotion. The amygdala processes the emotional significance of stimuli and generates immediate emotional and behavioral reactions; it is associated with emotional learning, memory of emotional events, and the interpretation of facial expressions of emotion. The right and left prefrontal cortices are associated with negative and positive affect, respectively. Consistent with the Schachter-Singer two-factor theory, research has shown that we often misattribute the causes of our emotions, seeking environmental explanations for our feelings. People use various strategies to regulate their emotions. The best methods for regulating negative affect include humor and distraction.

Measuring Up

For each of the three main theories of emotions—James-Lange, Cannon-Bard, and Schachter-Singer two-factor—select all the descriptive statements and examples that apply. Some answers may apply to more than one theory.

Descriptive statements:

1. Our emotions follow from our bodily responses.

2. Our cognitive responses to situations are important in determining our emotions.

3. Bodily responses are an important part of how we label emotions.

4. Excitation transfer is incompatible with this theory of emotion.

Examples:

a. If you sing a happy song, you will feel happy.

b. If you want someone to fall in love (not necessarily stay in love) with you, you should choose an exciting activity, such as snowboarding or rock climbing.

c. Smiling during a painful procedure, such as a painful injection, will put you in a better mood.

d. You feel angry and then notice your heart is beating fast.

Answers: For James-Lange, 1, 3, a, and c apply. For Cannon-Bard, 3, 4, and d apply. For Schachter-Singer two-factor, 1, 2, 3, and b apply.

How Are Emotions Adaptive?

Learning Objectives

- Review research on the cross-cultural universality of emotional expressions.
- Define display rules.
- Discuss the impact of emotions on decision making and self-regulation.
- Discuss the interpersonal functions of guilt and embarrassment.

Over the course of human evolution, we have developed ways of responding to environmental challenges. In solving our adaptive problems, our minds have drawn on our emotions. Negative and positive experiences have guided our species to behaviors that increase the probability of our surviving and reproducing. In other words, emotions are adaptive because they prepare and guide successful behaviors, such as running when you are about to be attacked by a dangerous animal. Emotions provide information about the importance of stimuli to personal goals, and then they prepare people for actions aimed at achieving those goals (Frijda, 1994). A *goal* is a desired outcome, usually associated with some specific object (such as tasty food) or some future behavioral intention (such as getting into a doctoral program in psychology).

Facial Expressions Communicate Emotion

In his 1872 book *Expression of Emotion in Man and Animals,* Charles Darwin argued that expressive aspects of emotion are adaptive because they communicate how we are feeling. People interpret facial expressions of emotion to predict other people's behavior. Facial expressions provide many clues about whether our behavior is pleasing to others or whether it is likely to make them reject, attack, or cheat us. Thus facial expressions, like emotions themselves, provide adaptive information.

The two main areas of the face, eyes and mouth, both convey emotional information. In a classic study, Knight Dunlap (1927) demonstrated that the mouth better conveys emotion than the eyes, especially for positive affect. The eyes are extremely important in communicating emotion, however. If people are presented with pictures of just eyes or just mouths and asked to identify the emotion expressed, they are more accurate when using the eyes (Baron-Cohen, Wheelwright, & Jolliffe, 1997). But if the whole face is presented at once, the mouth appears to be most important in determining how people perceive the emotional expression (Kontsevich & Tyler, 2004).

Much of the research on facial expression is conducted by showing people isolated faces. Yet in the real world faces appear in contexts that provide cues as to what emotion a person is experiencing. In an intriguing study, researchers showed identical facial expressions in different contexts and found that the context profoundly altered how people interpreted the emotion (Aviezer et al., 2008; **Figure 10.11**).

FACIAL EXPRESSIONS ACROSS CULTURES Darwin argued that the face innately communicates emotions to others and that these communications are understandable by all people, regardless of culture. Paul Ekman and colleagues (1969) tested this hypothesis in Argentina, Brazil, Chile, Japan, and the United States. In each country, participants viewed photographs of posed emotional expressions and then were asked to identify the emotional responses. In all five countries, the participants recognized the expressions as anger, fear, disgust, happiness, sadness, and surprise. Because people in these countries had extensive exposure to each other's cultures, however, learning and not biology could have been responsible for the cross-cultural agreement. To control for that potential confound, the researchers then traveled to a remote area in New Guinea. The natives there had little exposure to outside cultures and received only minimal formal education. Nonetheless, the study participants were able to identify the emotions seen in the photos fairly well, although agreement was not quite as high as in other cultures. The researchers also asked participants in New Guinea to display certain facial expressions, and they found that evaluators from other countries identified the expressions at a level better than chance (Ekman & Friesen, 1971; **Figure 10.12**).

Subsequent research has found general support for cross-cultural congruence in identifying some facial expressions; support is strongest for happiness and weakest for fear and disgust (Elfenbein & Ambady, 2002). Some scholars believe the results of these cross-cultural studies may be biased by cultural differences in the use of emotion words and by the way people are asked to identify emotions (Russell, 1994). Overall, however, the evidence indicates that some facial expressions are universal. Therefore, they probably have a biological basis.

Would you expect the physical expression of pride to be biologically based or culturally specific? The psychologist Jessica Tracy has found that young children can recognize when a person feels pride and that isolated populations with

(a)

(b)

FIGURE 10.11 Contextual Effects on Categorizing Emotional Expression Research participants were shown images such as these and asked to categorize them as showing anger, fear, pride, sadness, disgust, surprise, or happiness. **(a)** This photo pairs a sad face with a sad posture. When the face appeared in this context, most participants categorized the expression as sad. **(b)** This photo pairs the same sad face with a fearful posture. When the face appeared in this context, most participants categorized the expression incorrectly, as fearful.

FIGURE 10.12 Scientific Method: Ekman's Study of Facial Expressions across Cultures

Hypothesis: The face innately communicates emotions to others. These communications are understandable by all people, regardless of culture.

Research Method:

1. In the second part of this study, participants in New Guinea were photographed displaying certain facial expressions. For example, they were asked to look like they had come across a rotting pig or like one of their children had died.

2. Participants from other countries were asked to identify the emotions being expressed by the New Guineans.

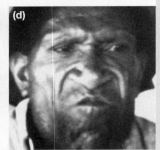

Results: People across cultures largely agreed on the meaning of different facial expressions. The examples here are **(a)** happiness, **(b)** sadness, **(c)** anger, and **(d)** disgust.

Conclusion: Recognition of facial expressions may be universal and therefore biologically based.

Source: Ekman, P., & Friesen, W. V. (1971). Constants across cultures in the face and emotion. *Journal of Personality and Social Psychology, 17*, 124–129.

minimal Western contact also accurately identify the physical signs, which include smiling face, raised arms, expanded chest, and torso pushed out (Tracy & Robins, 2008). Tracy and David Matsumoto (2008) examined pride responses among those competing in judo matches in the 2004 Olympic and Paralympic Games, in which sighted and blind athletes from 37 nations competed. After victory, the behaviors displayed by sighted and blind athletes were very similar. This finding suggests that pride responses are innate rather than learned by observing them in others (**Figure 10.13**).

Display Rules Differ across Cultures and between the Sexes

Thus basic emotions, such as pride, seem to be expressed similarly across cultures. The situations in which people display emotions differ substantially, however. **Display rules** govern how and when people exhibit emotions. These rules are learned through socialization, and they dictate which emotions are suitable to given situations. Differences in display rules help explain cultural stereotypes, such as the loud and obnoxious Americans, the cold and bland British, and the warm and

display rules Rules learned through socialization that dictate which emotions are suitable to given situations.

emotional Italians. Display rules also may explain why the identification of facial expressions is much better within cultures than between cultures (Elfenbein & Ambady, 2002).

From culture to culture, display rules tend to be different for women and men. In particular, the rules for smiling and crying differ between the sexes. It is generally believed that women display emotions more readily, frequently, easily, and intensely (Plant, Hyde, Keltner, & Devine, 2000). The evidence suggests that this belief is true—except perhaps for emotions related to dominance, such as anger (LaFrance & Banaji, 1992). Thus men and women may vary in their emotional expressiveness for evolutionary reasons: The emotions most closely associated with women are related to caregiving, nurturance, and interpersonal relationships. The emotions associated with men are related to dominance, defensiveness, and competitiveness.

While women may be more likely to display many emotions, they do not necessarily experience them more intensely. Although there is strong evidence that women report more-intense emotions, this finding might reflect societal norms about how women are supposed to feel (Grossman & Wood, 1993). Perhaps because of differences in upbringing in modern Western society, women tend to be better than men at articulating their emotions (Feldman Barrett, Lane, Sechrest, & Schwartz, 2000).

Ultimately, do sex differences in emotional expression reflect learned patterns of behaviors or biologically based differences? Nature and nurture work together here, so it is difficult—often impossible—to distinguish their effects.

Emotions Serve Cognitive Functions

For a long time, psychologists considered cognitive processes as separate from emotional processes. Researchers studied decision making, memory, and so on, as if people were evaluating the information from a purely rational perspective. Yet our immediate affective responses arise quickly and automatically. They color our perceptions at the very instant we notice an object. As Robert Zajonc put it, "We do not just see 'a house': We see a *handsome* house, an *ugly* house, or a *pretentious* house" (1980, p. 154). These instantaneous evaluations subsequently guide decision making, memory, and behavior. Therefore, psychologists now generally acknowledge that it is unrealistic to try to separate emotion from cognition (Phelps, 2006).

As Chapter 8 emphasizes, everyday cognition is far from cold and rational. Our decisions and judgments are affected by our feelings. For example, when people are in good moods, they tend to be persistent and to find creative, elaborate responses to challenging problems (Isen, 1993). When people are pursuing goals, positive feelings signal that they are making satisfactory progress and thereby encourage additional effort.

DECISION MAKING Would you rather go rock climbing in the Alps or attend a performance by a small dance troupe in Paris? In considering this question, did you think rationally about all the implications of either choice? Or did you flash on how you would feel in either situation? Emotions influence our decision making in different ways. For example, we anticipate our future emotional states, which then serve as a source of information and a guide in decision making. In this way, we are able to make decisions more quickly and more efficiently. And in the face of complex, multifaceted situations, emotions serve as heuristic guides: They provide feedback for making quick decisions (Slovic, Finucane, Peters, & MacGregor, 2002). There is a major drawback, however, to the effect of emotion

(a)

(b)

FIGURE 10.13 **Pride Expressions** In response to victory in separate judo matches, **(a)** a sighted athlete and **(b)** a congenitally blind athlete expressed their pride through similar behaviors. Because such similarities occur across cultures, the physical expression of pride appears to be biologically based.

Recognizing and Correcting for Belief Persistence in Your Own Thinking and in That of Others

A primary reason the United States declared war on Iraq in March 2003 was the suspicion that the Iraqi government had active programs for developing weapons of mass destruction (WMDs). The assertion that Iraq had WMDs was immediately controversial. In fact, it sparked a 15-month investigation by the Iraq Survey Group, organized by the Pentagon and the Central Intelligence Agency (CIA). On September 30, 2004, Charles Duelfer of the CIA submitted a much-publicized report (often referred to as the Duelfer Report), which concluded that Iraq had neither WMDs nor significant programs for developing them.

Despite the Duelfer Report's findings and previous statements that expressed similar conclusions, however, an October 2004 survey found that among supporters of President George W. Bush, many "continued to believe that Iraq had actual WMD (47%) or a major program for developing them (25%)" (Program on International Policy Attitudes, 2004, p. 1). According to that same survey, supporters of John Kerry, the 2004 Democratic presidential candidate, believed that Iraq had neither the weapons nor the program.

How might we explain the difference in perceptions between Bush and Kerry supporters in the face of information such as that presented in the Duelfer Report? Bush supporters likely were demonstrating *belief persistence,* sometimes called *my side bias*. Both terms refer to the tendency to hold on to previous ideas even when presented with evidence that the belief is questionable or just plain wrong. In fact, people tend to believe information consistent with the side of an issue they already believe true. One study of belief persistence found that once participants had generated their own explanations for their beliefs, they were resistant to information discrediting the beliefs they had just explained (Davies, 1997).

With practice and the desire to make the most-informed decisions possible, you can become aware of this pervasive bias. You can be more open to examining all sides of an issue fairly and altering your beliefs when the evidence supports the change. To reduce the effects of belief persistence, you should deliberately seek evidence that disconfirms your belief (**Figure 10.14**).

List your thesis (A) and its opposite, or antithesis (B).	Supply at least one or two reasons supporting each position, provide evidence for each reason, and evaluate the strength of each piece of evidence.	Supply at least one or two reasons contradicting each position, provide evidence for each reason, and evaluate the strength of each piece of evidence.
	Supporting Reasons and Evidence	Contradicting Reasons and Evidence
A. There is overwhelming evidence that Iraq has WMDs.	1. Strength: 2. Strength:	1. Strength: 2. Strength:
B. There is not enough evidence to prove that Iraq has WMDs.	1. Strength: 2. Strength:	1. Strength: 2. Strength:

FIGURE 10.14 Examining Evidence

on decision making. As discussed in the opening of Chapter 8, recent or particularly vivid events have an especially strong influence on behavior. For instance, after hearing about a plane crash, you might decide to cancel your airline reservation. This effect can occur even if the news does not change your outward belief about the likelihood that your own plane will crash. Risk judgments are strongly influenced by current feelings, and when emotions and cognitions are in conflict, emotions typically have the stronger impact on decisions (Loewenstein, Weber, Hsee, & Welch, 2001).

According to the *affect-as-information* theory, posited by Norbert Schwarz and Gerald L. Clore (1983), we use our current moods to make judgments and appraisals, even if we do not know the sources of our moods. For instance, Schwarz and Clore asked people to rate their overall life satisfaction. To answer this question, people potentially must consider a multitude of factors, including situations, expectations, personal goals, and accomplishments. As the researchers noted, however, in arriving at their answers people did not labor through all these elements but instead seemed to rely on their current moods. People in good moods rated their lives as satisfactory, whereas people in bad moods gave lower overall ratings. Likewise, people's evaluations of plays, of lectures, of politicians, and even of strangers are influenced by their moods. Their moods, meanwhile, are influenced by the day of the week, the weather, their health, and so on. If people are made aware of the sources of their moods (as when the researcher suggests that a good mood might be caused by the bright sunshine), their feelings have less influence over their judgments.

SOMATIC MARKERS Antonio Damasio has suggested that reasoning and decision making are guided by the emotional evaluation of an action's consequences. In his influential book *Descartes' Error* (1994), Damasio sets forth the *somatic marker theory*. According to this theory, most self-regulatory actions and decisions are affected by bodily reactions called **somatic markers.**

Have you ever had a queasy feeling in your stomach when you looked over the edge of a tall building? For Damasio, the term *gut feeling* can be taken almost literally. When you contemplate an action, you experience an emotional reaction based partly on your expectation of the action's outcome. Your expectation is influenced by your history of performing either that action or similar actions. For example, to the extent that driving fast has led to speeding tickets, which made you feel bad, you may choose to slow down when you see a speed limit sign. Hence somatic markers may guide us to engage in adaptive behaviors.

Damasio has found that patients such as Elliot (discussed in the opening of this chapter), who have damage to the middle of the prefrontal region, often are insensitive to somatic markers. When this region is damaged, people still can recall information, but it has lost most of its affective meaning. They might be able to describe their current problems or talk about the death of a loved one, but they do so without experiencing any of the emotional pain that normally accompanies such thoughts. As a result, these people tend not to use past outcomes to regulate future behavior. For instance, in studies using a gambling task, patients who had damage to their frontal lobes continued to follow a risky strategy: They selected a card from a stack that had rare big rewards but frequent bad losses. This strategy had proved faulty in previous trials, but as the patients contemplated selecting a card from the risky deck, they failed to show the more typical response of increased arousal. That is, the somatic marker that would tell most people that something is a bad idea is absent among those with frontal lobe damage.

somatic markers Bodily reactions that arise from the emotional evaluation of an action's consequences.

Emotions Strengthen Interpersonal Relations

Because humans are social animals, many emotions involve interpersonal dynamics. We feel hurt when teased, angry when insulted, happy when loved, and proud when complimented. In interacting with others, we use emotional expressions as powerful nonverbal communications. Although English alone includes over 550 words that refer to emotions (Averill, 1980), we can communicate our emotions quite well without verbal language. For example, because infants cannot talk, they must communicate their needs largely through nonverbal actions and emotional expressions. At birth, infants are capable of expressing joy, interest, disgust, and pain. By 2 months of age, they can express anger and sadness. By 6 months, they can express fear (Izard & Malatesta, 1987). The social importance of emotional expressions can be seen even in 10-month-old infants, who have been found to smile more while their mothers are watching (Jones, Collins, & Hong, 1991). Nonverbal displays of emotions signal inner states, moods, and needs.

For most of the twentieth century, however, psychologists paid little attention to interpersonal emotions. Guilt, embarrassment, and the like were associated with Freudian thinking and therefore not studied in mainstream psychological science. Theorists have since reconsidered interpersonal emotions in view of humans' evolutionary need to belong to social groups. Given that survival was enhanced for those who lived in groups, those who were expelled would have been less likely to survive and pass along their genes. According to this view, people were rejected primarily because they drained group resources or threatened group stability. The fundamental need to belong indicates that people will be sensitive to anything that might lead them to be kicked out of the group, and social emotions may reflect reactions to this possibility. Thus social emotions may be important for maintaining social bonds.

GUILT STRENGTHENS SOCIAL BONDS Guilt is a negative emotional state associated with anxiety, tension, and agitation. The experience of guilt rarely makes sense outside the context of interpersonal interaction. For instance, the typical guilt experience occurs when someone feels responsible for another person's negative affective state. Thus when we believe that something we did directly or indirectly harmed another person, we experience feelings of anxiety, tension, and remorse, feelings that can be labeled as guilt. Guilt occasionally can arise even when we do not feel personally responsible for others' negative situations (e.g, survivor guilt, the guilt felt by people who survive incidents—accidents or catastrophes—in which others have died).

Although excessive feelings of guilt may have negative consequences, guilt is not entirely negative. One theoretical model of guilt outlines its benefits to close relationships. Roy Baumeister and colleagues (1994) contend that guilt protects and strengthens interpersonal relationships in three ways. First, feelings of guilt discourage people from doing things that would harm their relationships, such as cheating on their partners. Feelings of guilt also encourage behaviors that strengthen relationships, such as phoning one's parents regularly. Second, displays of guilt demonstrate that people care about their relationship partners, thereby affirming social bonds. Third, guilt is a tactic that can be used to manipulate others. Guilt is especially effective when people hold power over us and it is difficult to get them to do what we want. For instance, you might try to make your boss feel guilty so you do not have to work overtime. Children may use guilt to get adults to buy them presents or grant them privileges.

Evidence indicates that socialization is more important than biology in determining specifically how children experience guilt. A longitudinal study involving identical and fraternal twins examined the impact of socialization on the development of various negative emotions (Zahn-Waxler & Robinson, 1995). The study found that all the negative emotions showed considerable genetic influence, but guilt was unique in being highly influenced by social environment. With age, the influence on guilt of a shared environment became stronger, whereas the evidence for genetic influences disappeared. Perhaps surprisingly, parental warmth is associated with greater guilt in children. This finding suggests that feelings of guilt arise in healthy and happy relationships. As children become citizens in a social world, they develop the capacity to empathize, and they subsequently experience feelings of guilt when they transgress against others.

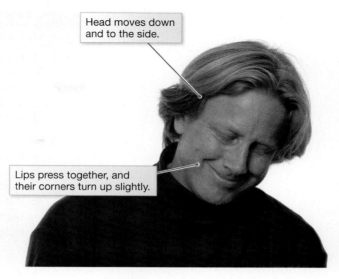

Head moves down and to the side.

Lips press together, and their corners turn up slightly.

FIGURE 10.15 Embarrassment In this photo, the psychologist Dacher Keltner is demonstrating the classic facial signals of embarrassment.

EMBARRASSMENT AND BLUSHING A person is likely to feel embarrassed after violating a cultural norm, losing physical poise, being teased, or experiencing a threat to his or her self-image (Miller, 1996). Some theories of embarrassment suggest that it rectifies interpersonal awkwardness and restores social bonds. Embarrassment represents submission to and affiliation with the social group. It also represents recognition of the unintentional social error. Research supports these propositions in showing that individuals who look embarrassed after wrongdoing elicit from onlookers more sympathy, more forgiveness, more amusement, and more laughter (Cupach & Metts, 1990; **Figure 10.15**). Like guilt, embarrassment may reaffirm close relationships after wrongdoing.

The writer Mark Twain once said, "Man is the only animal that blushes. Or needs to." Darwin, in his 1872 book, called blushing the "most peculiar and the most human of all expressions," thereby separating it from emotional responses he deemed necessary for survival. Recent theory and research suggests that blushing occurs when people believe others view them negatively and that blushing communicates a realization of interpersonal errors. This nonverbal apology is an appeasement that elicits forgiveness in others, thereby repairing and maintaining relationships (Keltner & Anderson, 2000).

Summing Up

How Are Emotions Adaptive?

Emotions are adaptive because they bring about states of behavioral readiness. The evolutionary basis for emotions is supported by research on cross-cultural congruence in the display and recognition of some emotional expressions. Display rules are learned through socialization and dictate which emotions are suitable to given situations. Across cultures, display rules differ for females and males. Emotions influence decision making, serving as heuristic guides for quick decisions, and give rise to somatic markers that facilitate self-regulation. Emotions that are interpersonal in nature—for example, guilt and embarrassment—are particularly important for the maintenance and repair of close interpersonal relationships.

10.3 How Does Motivation Energize, Direct, and Sustain Behavior?

Emotions are a primary source of motivation. After all, we seek events, activities, and objects that make us feel good, and we avoid events, activities, and objects that make us feel bad. Together, motivation and emotion make things happen (both words are from the Latin *movere,* "to move").

Theories of motivation seek to answer questions such as *Where do needs come from? How are goals established? How are motives converted into action?* You might translate such general questions into more-concrete ones, such as *What inspires you to get up in the morning? Why do you choose to eat what you do? Does being in a sexual relationship interest you, or do you not think about it very much?*

Most of the general theories of motivation emphasize four essential qualities of motivational states. First, motivational states are *energizing,* or stimulating. They activate behaviors—that is, they cause animals to do something. For instance, the desire for fitness might motivate you to get up and go for a run on a cold morning. Second, motivational states are *directive.* They guide behaviors toward satisfying specific goals or specific needs. Hunger motivates you to eat; thirst motivates you to drink; pride (or fear or many other feelings) motivates you to study for exams. Third, motivational states help animals *persist* in their behavior until they achieve their goals or satisfy their needs. Hunger gnaws at you until you find something to eat; a desire to win drives you to practice foul shots until you succeed. Fourth, most theories agree that motives differ in *strength,* depending on internal and external forces. Thus, for psychologists, **motivation** refers to factors that energize, direct, or sustain behavior. This section looks at a wide range of factors that, to different degrees, motivate people's behaviors.

motivation Factors that energize, direct, or sustain behavior.

Multiple Factors Motivate Behavior

What do we really need to do to stay alive? For one, we have to satisfy our biological needs. We all *need* air, food, and water to survive. But satisfying our basic biological needs is not enough to live a fully satisfying life. We also have social needs, including the need for achievement and the need to be with others. People *need* other people, although our preferences to be solitary or social vary. A **need,** then, is a state of deficiency, which can be either biological (e.g., water) or social (e.g., to be with other people). Either way, needs lead to goal-directed behaviors. Failure to satisfy a particular need leads to psychosocial or physical impairment.

In the 1940s, Abraham Maslow proposed an influential "need theory" of motivation. Maslow believed that people are driven by many needs, which he arranged into a **need hierarchy (Figure 10.16)**. He placed survival needs (such as hunger and thirst) at the base of the hierarchy, believing they had to be satisfied first. He placed personal growth needs at the pinnacle. To experience personal growth, he believed, people must fulfill their biological needs, feel safe and secure, feel loved, and have a good opinion of themselves.

Maslow's theory is an example of *humanistic psychology*. This school views people as striving toward personal fulfillment. From this perspective, human beings are unique among animals because we continually try to improve ourselves. Humanists focus on the *person* in motivation. For example, it is the person who desires food, not the person's stomach. A state of **self-actualization** occurs when someone achieves his or her personal dreams and aspirations. A self-actualized person is living up to his or her potential and therefore is truly happy. Maslow writes, "A musician must make music, an artist must paint, a poet must write, if he is ultimately to be at peace with himself. What a man *can* be, he *must* be" (Maslow, 1968, p. 46).

Maslow's need hierarchy has long been embraced in education and business, but it lacks empirical support. Self-actualization might or might not be a requirement for happiness, but the ranking of needs is not as simple as Maslow suggests. For instance, some people starve themselves in hunger strikes to demonstrate the importance of their personal beliefs. Others, who have satisfied their physiological and security needs, prefer to be left alone. Maslow's hierarchy, therefore, is more useful as an indicator of what *might* be true about people's behaviors than of what actually *is* true about them.

DRIVES AND INCENTIVES What motivates us to satisfy our needs? A **drive** is a psychological state that, by creating arousal, motivates an organism to satisfy a need. A particular drive encourages behaviors that will satisfy a particular need. To experience one of your own needs and a drive in response to it, see **Figure 10.17.**

"What do you think . . . should we get started on that motivation research or not?"

need A state of biological or social deficiency.

need hierarchy Maslow's arrangement of needs, in which basic survival needs must be met before people can satisfy higher needs.

self-actualization A state that is achieved when one's personal dreams and aspirations have been attained.

drive A psychological state that, by creating arousal, motivates an organism to satisfy a need.

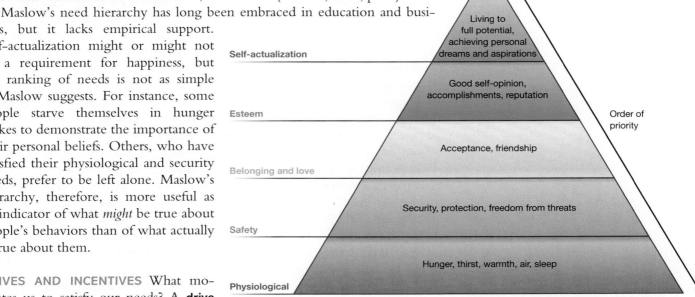

Self-actualization — Living to full potential, achieving personal dreams and aspirations

Esteem — Good self-opinion, accomplishments, reputation

Belonging and love — Acceptance, friendship

Safety — Security, protection, freedom from threats

Physiological — Hunger, thirst, warmth, air, sleep

Order of priority

FIGURE 10.16 Need Hierarchy According to Maslow's hierarchy of needs, humans must satisfy basic needs (such as for food and water) before they can address higher needs (such as for achievement).

FIGURE 10.17 Try for Yourself: Needs and Drives

Hold your breath as long as you can.

Results: Eventually, you will breathe, satisfying your need for oxygen. Before that, after a minute or so of not breathing, you probably will start feeling a strong sense of urgency, even anxiety. This state of arousal is a drive. Needs create drives that motivate specific behaviors, as diagrammed below with other examples.

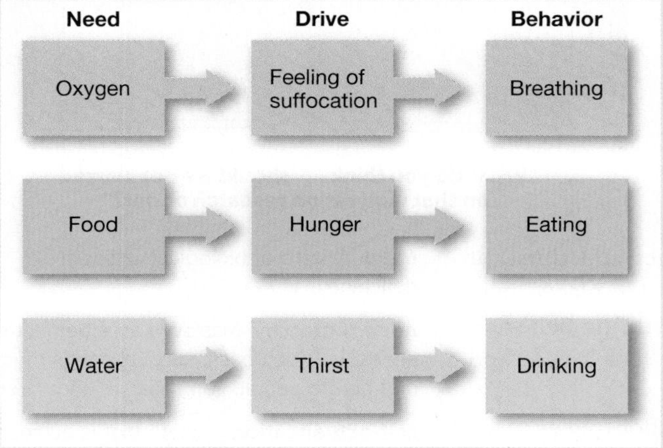

Need	Drive	Behavior
Oxygen	Feeling of suffocation	Breathing
Food	Hunger	Eating
Water	Thirst	Drinking

homeostasis The tendency for bodily functions to maintain equilibrium.

incentives External objects or external goals, rather than internal drives, that motivate behaviors.

For biological states such as thirst or hunger, basic drives help animals maintain steadiness, or *equilibrium*. In the 1920s, Walter Cannon coined the term **homeostasis**, which means the tendency for bodily functions to maintain equilibrium. A good analogy is a home heating and cooling system controlled by a thermostat. The thermostat is set to some optimal level, or *set-point*. That hypothetical state indicates homeostasis. If the actual temperature is different from the set-point, the furnace or air conditioner operates to adjust the temperature (**Figure 10.18**).

Similarly, the human body regulates a set-point of around 37°C (98.6°F). When people are too warm or too cold, brain mechanisms (particularly the hypothalamus) initiate responses such as sweating (to cool the body) or shivering (to warm the body). At the same time, people become motivated to perform behaviors such as taking off or putting on clothes. Models like this, in which the body responds to negative feedback, are useful for describing various basic biological processes, among them eating, fluid regulation, and sleep.

Building on Cannon's work, Clark Hull (1943) proposed that when an animal is deprived of some need (such as water, sleep, or sex), a drive increases in proportion to the amount of deprivation. The hungrier you are, the more driven you are to find food. The drive state creates arousal, which encourages you to do something to reduce the drive, such as having a late-night snack. Although the initial behaviors the animal engages in are arbitrary, any behavior that satisfies a need is reinforced and therefore is more likely to recur. Over time, if a behavior consistently reduces a drive, it becomes a *habit*. The likelihood that a behavior will occur is due to drive and habit.

Suppose you feel the need to forget your troubles. To satisfy that need, you feel driven to distract yourself, so you go to YouTube and watch videos of cute animals. Watching those videos makes you forget your troubles, and that outcome reinforces further video viewing. Over time, you might develop the habit of watching cute animal videos, especially when you are stressed.

Drive states push us to reduce arousal, but we are also pulled toward certain things in our environments. **Incentives** are external objects or external goals, rather than internal drives, that motivate behaviors. For example, getting a good grade on an exam is an incentive for studying hard.

Even forces outside our conscious awareness can provide incentives for us to behave in particular ways. For example, smokers sometimes develop cravings for cigarettes after watching people smoke on-screen. In some cases, the viewers have not even consciously registered that the on-screen figures are smoking (Wagner et al., 2011). As discussed in Chapter 4, subliminal cues influence behavior, even though they appear so quickly that people cannot report what they saw. Researchers from France and England found that study participants worked harder for a larger financial reward—in this case, a subliminally presented pound coin versus a real penny coin—even when they were unable to report how much money was at stake (Pessiglione et al., 2007). Likewise, pairing a positive word, such as *good*, with a subliminal cue, such as the word *exert*, led people to squeeze a lever harder than when the cue was presented without the positive word (Aarts, Custers, & Marien, 2008). Preschool children who were exposed to food advertising ate 45 percent more snack foods than did preschool children who did not see the advertising (Harris, Bargh, & Brownell, 2009).

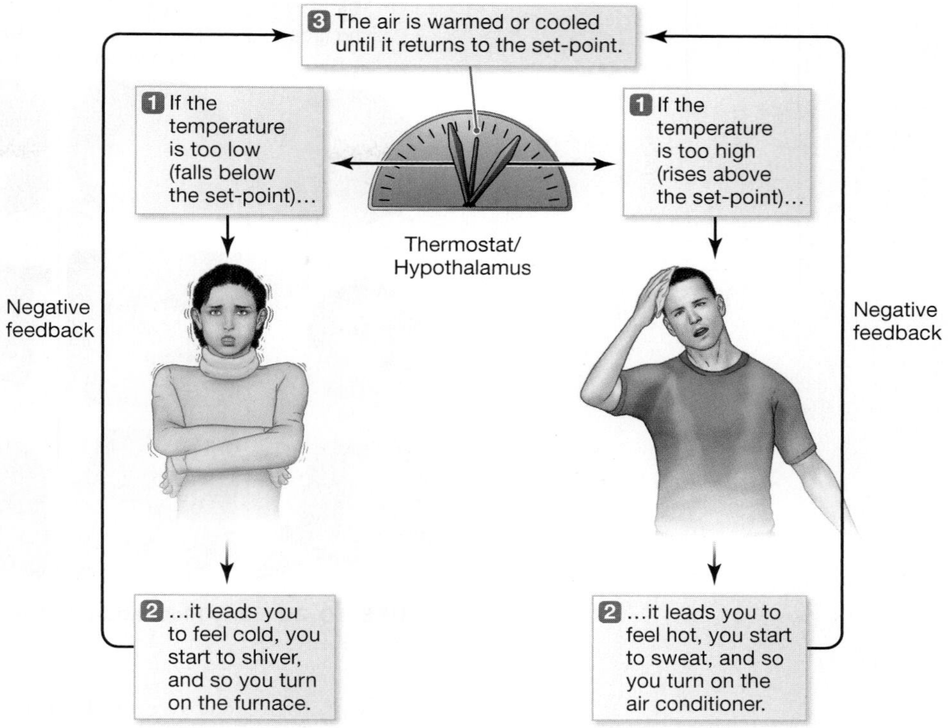

AROUSAL AND PERFORMANCE Because drives motivate behavior by creating arousal, you might think that more arousal will lead to more motivation and thus to better performance. Consider, however, the **Yerkes-Dodson law** (named after the two researchers who formulated it, in 1908). This psychological principle dictates that performance increases with arousal up to an optimal point and then decreases with increasing arousal. A graph of this relationship is shaped like an inverted U (**Figure 10.19**). As the Yerkes-Dodson law predicts, students perform best on exams when feeling moderate anxiety. Too little anxiety can make them inattentive or unmotivated, while too much anxiety can interfere with their thinking ability. Likewise, athletes have to pump themselves up for their events, but they can fall apart under too much stress.

All of us function better with some arousal. In other words, motivation does not always lower tension and arousal. Instead, each of us is motivated to seek an optimal level of arousal, the level of arousal we most prefer. Too little, and we are bored; too much, and we are overwhelmed. We choose stimulating, exciting, or even frightening activities—those that arouse us and absorb our attention. As discussed further in Chapter 13, however, we differ in how stimulating, exciting, frightening, or pleasurable we want those activities to be.

PLEASURE Sigmund Freud proposed that drives are satisfied according to the *pleasure principle,* which drives people to seek pleasure and avoid pain. This idea is central to many theories of motivation. Originating with the ancient Greeks, the concept of *hedonism* refers to humans' desire for pleasantness. We do things that feel good. If something feels good, we do it again. Sexual activity is a good example of hedonism. Even though sex is crucial for the survival of the species, people engage in a variety of sexual behaviors even when they do not want to reproduce.

The idea that pleasure motivates behavior helps us understand a criticism of biological drive theories (such as Clark Hull's). If biological drives explain all behaviors, why do animals engage in behaviors that do not necessarily satisfy biological needs? These behaviors, such as eating dessert when you are not hungry, commonly occur because they are pleasurable. From an evolutionary perspective, positive and negative motivations are adaptive. For instance, the motivations to seek out food, sex, and companionship are typically associated with pleasure, whereas the avoidance of dangerous animals is negatively motivated because of the association with pain (Watson, Wiese, Vaidya, & Tellegen, 1999). A good example of this principle is the finding that

3 The air is warmed or cooled until it returns to the set-point.

1 If the temperature is too low (falls below the set-point)...

1 If the temperature is too high (rises above the set-point)...

Thermostat/ Hypothalamus

Negative feedback

Negative feedback

2 ...it leads you to feel cold, you start to shiver, and so you turn on the furnace.

2 ...it leads you to feel hot, you start to sweat, and so you turn on the air conditioner.

FIGURE 10.18 A Negative-Feedback Model of Homeostasis

Yerkes-Dodson law The psychological principle that performance increases with arousal up to an optimal point, after which it decreases with increasing arousal.

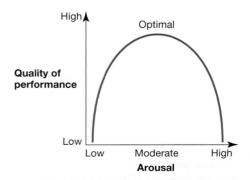

FIGURE 10.19 Graph of the Yerkes-Dodson Law According to this law, performance increases with arousal until an optimal point (here the top of the curve). After that point, arousal interferes with performance.

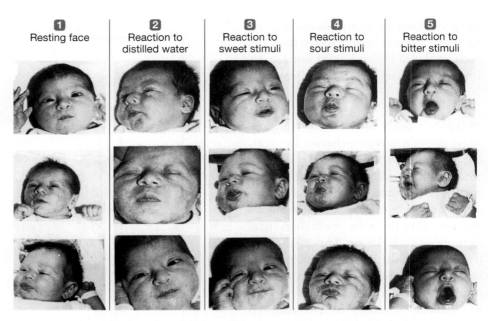

| **1** Resting face | **2** Reaction to distilled water | **3** Reaction to sweet stimuli | **4** Reaction to sour stimuli | **5** Reaction to bitter stimuli |

FIGURE 10.20 Early Motivation As these photos reveal, even newborns prefer sweet tastes to bitter ones.

animals prefer to eat sweets. Infants given sweet solutions seem to find them pleasurable, as revealed by their facial expressions (Steiner, 1977; **Figure 10.20**). Sweetness usually indicates that food is safe to eat. By contrast, most poisons and toxins taste bitter, so it is not surprising that animals avoid bitter tastes.

Some Behaviors Are Motivated for Their Own Sake

Pleasure can be associated with the satisfaction of biological needs and the performance of adaptive behaviors. Such activities are directed toward **extrinsic motivation:** an external goal, a reward, the reduction of a drive. For example, you work to earn a paycheck. Many of the activities people find most satisfying, however—such as reading a good novel, solving crossword puzzles, or listening to music—seem to fulfill no obvious purpose other than enjoyment. Such activities are directed toward **intrinsic motivation:** value or pleasure removed from an apparent external goal. Intrinsically motivated behaviors are performed for their own sake. They simply are enjoyable.

Some intrinsically motivated activities may satisfy our natural curiosity and creativity. After playing with a new toy for a long time, children start to lose interest and will seek out something new. Playful exploration is characteristic of all mammals and especially primates. For example, as Harry Harlow and colleagues have shown, monkeys have a strong exploratory drive. They will work hard, without an external reward, to solve relatively complex puzzles (Harlow, Harlow, & Meyer, 1950). One function of play is that it helps us learn about the objects in an environment. This outcome clearly has survival value, since knowing how things work allows us to use those objects for more serious tasks.

Similarly, many of us are driven toward creative pursuits. Whether we are visiting an art museum or creating artwork ourselves, we may do so simply because we enjoy activities that allow us to express our creativity. *Creativity* is the tendency to generate ideas or alternatives that may be useful in solving problems, communicating, and entertaining ourselves and others (Franken, 1988). Although many creative pursuits are not adaptive solutions, creativity is an important factor in solving adaptive problems.

extrinsic motivation Motivation to perform an activity because of the external goals toward which that activity is directed.

intrinsic motivation Motivation to perform an activity because of the value or pleasure associated with that activity, rather than for an apparent external goal or purpose.

SELF-DETERMINATION THEORY AND SELF-PERCEPTION THEORY As discussed in Chapter 6, a basic principle of learning theory is that rewarded behaviors increase in frequency. You might expect that rewarding intrinsically motivated behaviors would reinforce them. Surprisingly, consistent evidence suggests that extrinsic rewards can undermine intrinsic motivation. In a classic study, Mark Lepper and colleagues allowed children to draw with colored marking pens (Lepper, Greene, & Nisbett, 1973). Most children find this activity intrinsically motivating. One group of children was extrinsically motivated to draw by being led to expect a "good player award." Another group of children was rewarded unexpectedly following the task. A third group was neither rewarded nor led to expect a reward. During a subsequent free-play period, children who were expecting an extrinsic reward spent much less time playing with the pens than did the children who were never rewarded or the children who received an unexpected reward. The first group of children responded as though it was their job to draw with the colored pens. In other words, why would they play with the pens for free when they were used to being paid? There are two theoretical explanations:

According to *self-determination theory,* people are motivated to satisfy needs for competence, relatedness to others, and autonomy, which is a sense of personal control. Self-determination theory argues that extrinsic rewards may reduce intrinsic value because such rewards undermine people's feeling that they are choosing to do something for themselves. In contrast, feelings of autonomy and competence make people feel good about themselves and inspire them to do their most creative work (Deci & Ryan, 1987).

According to *self-perception theory,* people are seldom aware of their specific motives. Instead, they draw inferences about their motives according to what seems to make the most sense (Bem, 1967). Suppose someone gives you a big glass of water. After drinking the whole thing, you exclaim, "Wow, I must have been thirsty!" You believe you were thirsty because you drank the whole glass, even though you were unaware of any physical sensations of thirst. When people cannot come up with obvious external explanations for their behaviors—such as that they acted with the expectation of being rewarded or to satisfy a biological drive—they conclude that they simply like the behaviors. Rewarding people for engaging in an intrinsic activity, however, gives them an alternative explanation for engaging in it. They performed the behavior not just for fun but because of the reward. Therefore, without the reward, they have no reason to engage in the behavior. The reward has replaced the goal of pure pleasure.

We Set Goals to Achieve

So far, this discussion has focused on motivation to fulfill short-term goals, such as satisfying our hunger or spending a pleasurable afternoon. But we have long-term aspirations as well. What motivates us to fulfill those goals? For instance, what would you like to be doing 10 years from now? What things about yourself would you change?

In the 1930s, the personality psychologist Henry Murray proposed 27 basic *psychosocial needs,* including the needs for power, autonomy, achievement, and play. The study of psychosocial needs has yielded important insights into what motivates human behavior. A key insight is that people are especially motivated to achieve personal goals. *Self-regulation* of behavior is the process by which people change their behavior to attain personal goals.

Recognizing When Psychological Reactance May Be Influencing Your Thinking

FIGURE 10.21 Reverse Psychology
Which of these promotional offers conveys more urgency? How is the urgency of each offer related to the potential reward?

Imagine you are thinking about declaring your college major. You have enjoyed your classes in English and computer science, and you cannot decide which field to choose. You discuss the decision with your parents, who insist that you major in computer science because it will lead to better job opportunities after college. They even hint that they are not willing to help pay your tuition if you do not major in the field they prefer. How would this conversation make you feel about the two majors? Would it make the English major seem more attractive? In general, when another person tells you not to do or have something, does that very something become more desirable? Scientific studies and daily experience show that, for most of us, it does.

Psychological reactance is a motivational state aroused when our feelings of personal freedom are threatened (Woller, Buboltz, & Loveland, 2007). Often, we act in ways to regain that freedom, trying to obtain whatever is being withheld. You may be familiar with the common notion of reverse psychology, which is based on psychological reactance. For example, you might play hard to get if you want someone to be romantically interested in you. Similarly, a company might advertise a product as available only to a select few, thus making consumers eager to buy it so they are not left out (**Figure 10.21**).

Why is recognizing psychological reactance a critical thinking skill? This motivational state often affects how we make choices. We can be influenced even when, in fact, there is no reason to prefer an alternative just because it has been denied. By noticing if your thinking has been influenced by this potentially irrelevant variable, you will find it easier to make better-informed and more-rational choices.

Good goals motivate people to work hard. But what is a good goal? According to an influential theory developed by the organizational psychologists Edwin Locke and Gary Latham (1990), challenging—but not overly difficult—and specific goals are best. Challenging goals encourage effort, persistence, and concentration. In contrast, goals that are too easy or too hard can undermine motivation and therefore lead to failure. Dividing specific goals into concrete steps also leads to success. If you are interested in running the Boston Marathon, for instance, your first goal might be gaining the stamina to run 1 mile. When you can run a mile, you can set another goal and thus build up to running the 26-mile marathon. Focusing on concrete, short-term goals facilitates achieving long-term goals.

SELF-EFFICACY AND THE ACHIEVEMENT MOTIVE Albert Bandura argued that people's personal expectations for success play an important role in motivation.

For instance, if you believe studying hard will lead to a good grade on an exam, you will be motivated to study. *Self-efficacy* is the expectancy that your efforts will lead to success. This expectancy helps mobilize your energies. If you have low self-efficacy—that is, if you do not believe your efforts will pay off—you may be too discouraged even to study. People with high self-efficacy often set challenging goals that lead to success. Sometimes, however, people whose self-views are inflated set goals they cannot possibly achieve. Again, goals that are challenging but not overwhelming usually are most conducive to success.

People differ in how insistently they pursue challenging goals. The *achievement motive* is the desire to do well relative to standards of excellence. Compared with those low in achievement need, students high in achievement need sit closer to the front of classrooms, score higher on exams, and obtain better grades in courses relevant to their career goals (McClelland, 1987). Students with high achievement need are more realistic in their career aspirations than are students low in achievement need. Those high in achievement need set challenging but attainable personal goals, while those low in achievement need set extremely easy or impossibly high goals.

DELAYED GRATIFICATION One common challenge in self-regulation is postponing immediate gratification in the pursuit of long-term goals. For example, students who want to be accepted to graduate school often have to stay home and study while their friends are out having fun. In a series of studies, the developmental psychologist Walter Mischel gave children the choice of waiting to receive a preferred toy or food item or having a less preferred toy or food item right away (Mischel, Shoda, & Rodriguez, 1989). Mischel found that some children are better at delaying gratification than other children are. In addition, the ability to delay gratification is predictive of success in life. Children able to delay gratification at age 4 were rated 10 years later as being more socially competent and better able to handle frustration. The ability to delay gratification in childhood has been found to predict higher SAT scores and better school grades. A recent study from New Zealand found that related measures of self-control in childhood predicted physical health, substance dependence, personal finances, and criminal offending outcomes at age 32 (Moffitt et al., 2011).

In Mischel's now-classic studies, how did some children manage to delay gratification? Given the choice between eating one marshmallow right away or two after several minutes, some 4-year-olds waited and engaged in strategies to help them not eat the marshmallow while they waited. One strategy was simply ignoring the tempting item rather than looking at it. On average, older children were better at delaying gratification. Some of them covered their eyes or looked away. Very young children tended to look directly at the item they were trying to resist, making the delay especially difficult. A related strategy was self-distraction, through singing, playing games, or pretending to sleep. The most successful strategy involved what Mischel and his colleague Janet Metcalfe refer to as turning *hot cognitions* into *cold cognitions*. This strategy involves mentally transforming the desired object into something undesired. In one study, children reported imagining a tempting pretzel as a brown log or imagining marshmallows as clouds (**Figure 10.22**). Hot cognitions focus on the rewarding, pleasurable aspects of objects. Cold cognitions focus on conceptual or symbolic meanings. Metcalfe and Mischel (1999) proposed that this hot/cold distinction is based on how the brain processes the information. As

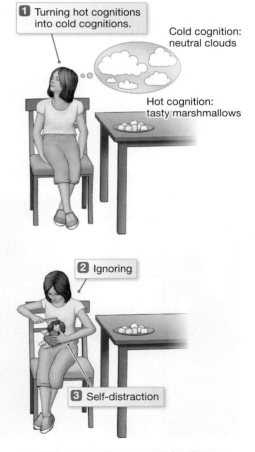

1 Turning hot cognitions into cold cognitions.

Cold cognition: neutral clouds

Hot cognition: tasty marshmallows

2 Ignoring

3 Self-distraction

FIGURE 10.22 Techniques for Delaying Gratification How do each of these three techniques help a person delay gratification?

need to belong theory The theory that the need for interpersonal attachments is a fundamental motive that has evolved for adaptive purposes.

discussed in Chapter 3, subcortical brain regions such as the amygdala and the nucleus accumbens are important for motivating behavior. The prefrontal cortex performs cold-cognitive processes, such as the control of thought and of behavior. Thus, as the result of an evolutionary advance, the prefrontal cortex helps us make choices that may optimize survival.

We Have a Need to Belong

Over the course of human evolution, our ancestors who lived with others were more likely to survive and pass along their genes. Children who stayed with adults (and resisted being left alone) were more likely to survive until their reproductive years because the adults would protect and nurture them. Similarly, adults capable of developing long-term, committed relationships were more likely to reproduce and to have offspring who survived to reproduce. Effective groups shared food, provided mates, and helped care for offspring, including orphans. Some survival tasks (such as hunting large mammals or looking out for predatory enemies) were best accomplished by group cooperation. It therefore makes great sense that, over the millennia, humans have committed to living in groups. Roy Baumeister and Mark Leary (1995) formulated the **need to belong theory,** which states that the need for interpersonal attachments is a fundamental motive that has evolved for adaptive purposes.

MAKING AND KEEPING FRIENDS The need to belong theory explains how easily most people make friends (**Figure 10.23**). Societies differ in their types of groups, but all societies have some form of group membership (Brewer & Caporael, 1990). Not belonging to a group increases a person's risk for various adverse consequences, such as illnesses and premature death (Cacioppo, Hughs, Waite, Hawkley, & Thisted, 2006). Such ill effects suggest that the need to belong is a basic motive driving behavior, just as hunger drives people to seek food and avoid dying from starvation.

If humans have a fundamental need to belong, they ought to have mechanisms for detecting whether they are included in particular groups (MacDonald & Leary, 2005). In other words, given the importance of being a group member, people need to be sensitive to signs that the group might kick them out. Indeed, evidence indicates that people feel anxious when facing exclusion from their social groups. Further, people who are shy and lonely tend to worry most about social evaluation and pay much more attention to social information (Gardner, Pickett, Jefferis, & Knowles, 2005). The take-home message is that just as a lack of food causes hunger, a lack of social contact causes emptiness and despair. In the movie *Cast Away,* Tom Hanks's character becomes stranded on a deserted island and has such a strong need for companionship that he begins carrying on a friendship with a volleyball he calls Wilson (named for the manufacturer, whose name is on the ball). As noted by the film reviewer Susan Stark (2000), this volleyball convinces us that "human company, as much as shelter, water, food and fire, is essential to life as most of us understand it."

FIGURE 10.23 Making Friends College provides many opportunities for making friends. First-year students often make lifelong friendships within days of arriving on campus.

ANXIETY AND AFFILIATION Do you like to be around other people when you are anxious, or do you prefer to avoid them? In a classic study, the social psychologist Stanley Schachter (1959) manipulated anxiety levels and then measured how much the participants, all female, preferred to be around others. The participants in these studies thought they were taking part in a routine psychological study. "Dr. Zilstein," a serious- and cold-looking man with a vaguely European accent, greeted them at the lab. After explaining that he was from the neurology and psychiatric school, the doctor said the study involved measuring "the physiological effects of electric shock." Zilstein told the participants he would hook them up to some electrical equipment and then administer electric current to their skin. Those in the low-anxiety condition were told the shocks would be painless—no more than a tickle. Those in the high-anxiety condition were told: "These shocks will hurt; they will be painful. As you can guess, if we're to learn anything that will really help humanity, it is necessary that our shocks be intense. These shocks will be quite painful, but, of course, they will do no permanent damage." As you might imagine, the participants who heard this speech were quite fearful and anxious.

Zilstein then said he needed time to set up his equipment, so there would be a 10-minute period before the shocks began. At that point, the participants were offered a choice: They could spend the waiting time alone or with others. This choice was the critical dependent measure. After the choice was made, the experiment was over. No one received a shock. Schachter found that increased anxiety led to increased affiliative motivations: Those in the high-anxiety condition were much more likely to want to wait with other people (**Figure 10.24**).

Thus misery appears to love company. But does misery love just any company? A further study revealed that high-anxiety participants wanted to wait only with other high-anxiety participants, not with people who supposedly were waiting just to see their research supervisors. So misery loves miserable company, not just any company.

Why do people in a stressful situation prefer to be around other people in the same situation? According to Schachter, other people provide information that helps us evaluate whether we are acting appropriately. According to Leon Festinger's *social comparison theory* (1954), we are motivated to have accurate information about ourselves and others. We compare ourselves with those around us to test and validate personal beliefs and emotional responses. The effect occurs especially when the situation is ambiguous and we can compare ourselves with people relatively similar to us.

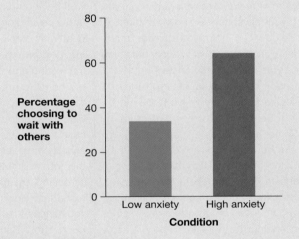

FIGURE 10.24 Scientific Method: Schachter's Study on Anxiety and Affiliation

Hypothesis: Feeling anxious makes people want to be with others.

Research Method:

1 The participants, all female, were told they would be hooked up to equipment that would administer electric current to their skin.

2 Some participants were told the shocks would be painless. Others were told the shocks would be quite painful.

3 All participants were then asked if, while the experiment was being set up, they wanted to wait alone or with others.

Results: The participants who were told the shocks would be painful (the high-anxiety condition) were much more likely to want to wait with others.

Conclusion: Increased anxiety led to increased motivation to be with others, at least for females.

Source: Schachter, S. (1959). *The psychology of affiliation.* Stanford, CA: Stanford University Press.

How Might Psychology Influence My Working Life?

What type of career do you hope to have? Do you view a job as basically a way to pay the bills and do the things you really like to do? Or do you have a very strong interest or career goals that you want to pursue (**Figure 10.25**)? Do you perhaps even have a calling, a greater purpose that might bring meaning and enrichment to yourself and others? Which matters more to you, job satisfaction or material reward? How will you balance your personal life and your career?

Psychology can help you answer questions such as these. It can even help you motivate yourself to begin answering them!

Like many college students, you may be struggling to find a career you hope will be satisfying. Selecting a career path is rarely easy. Sometimes, people who have been toiling in corporate or professional jobs have midlife crises in which they realize that their jobs fail to bring them any meaningful satisfaction. Such situations may result when people focus on making money rather than on finding the right job that will allow them to be the type of person, spouse, parent, or community member they want to be. Career counselors often advise people to follow their passions rather than the wishes of parents or family members. You do not necessarily need a specific plan, but you must be honest with yourself: Assess your strengths and weaknesses and try to develop a general idea of the kind of career you can pursue effectively and are likely to find fulfilling.

The "right career" will probably provide more than just material rewards. It will bring you a sense of accomplishment and purpose. It will help you feel that you contribute to society and that other people recognize you for doing so. It will bring meaning to your life and help you grow as a person and become better able to fulfill your goals in life.

One of the central challenges for employers is keeping their employees motivated to work hard. Employees who are highly mo-

tivated are more likely to enjoy their jobs and feel that their work is meaningful. Many companies hire psychologists to assist them in finding, training, retaining, and motivating employees. These psychologists are trained in industrial and organizational psychology (called *I-O psychology*). The mission of this branch of psychology is to apply findings from psychological science to work settings. Ultimately, the goal is to enhance human well-being and performance. Key challenges in I-O psychology include helping employers deal with employees fairly, helping employers design jobs so that workers find them interesting and satisfying, and helping workers be more productive.

One of the first tasks of I-O psychologists is to help employers hire workers who have the necessary skills, abilities, and personality characteristics needed to perform the job well. Many employers use various screening measures—such as personality tests, interviews, and even tests for illegal substances—to try to make sure they make good hires. But I-O psychologists are also concerned that the hiring process treats people from diverse backgrounds fairly. For instance, I-O psychologists use tests that do not favor people from certain cultures or backgrounds.

How much preparation have you done, or are you planning to do, for job interviews? Many employers place a great deal of emphasis—too much emphasis—on interviews. How you perform in an interview will not be a particularly good predictor of whether you will be effective in the job. Factors such as your likability, physical attractiveness, and assertiveness may obscure your potential weaknesses. Accordingly, I-O psychologists have developed more-structured ways to evaluate employees. For example, they try to identify specific personality traits that match the requirements of the job, or they test for specific knowledge and experience. In other words, the nature of a particular interview will play a large part

in determining how "well" you do. Prepare for your interviews, but do not turn yourself into an interviewing machine.

In addition to helping ensure that employees are good fits for their jobs and particular work situations, I-O psychologists help develop training programs to ensure that workers have the skills they need to succeed at their jobs. They also design programs to encourage workers to be more productive. Finally, I-O psychologists help employers develop formal methods to determine appropriate promotions and raises or to evaluate whether a worker ultimately must be fired.

An important finding in I-O psychology is that satisfied workers are the best workers. Another is that people will work hardest when their jobs are meaningful and when they feel they have some control over what they do. For instance, when workers have a say in decision making, they tend to be more willing to follow the decisions made. Programs that encourage employees to suggest improvements, that give them part ownership, or that involve them in important decisions are associated with greater em-

FIGURE 10.25 Career Options Waitperson and businessperson seem to be very different parts of the workforce. Either job can be a good choice or bad choice, however, depending on the person's interests, circumstances, and long-term goals. Likewise, either job might be a means to an end. It is possible that this waitperson and these businesspeople are making money to pay the bills while pursuing or dreaming of other careers.

ployee satisfaction. Similarly, companies that are family friendly, perhaps offering flexible scheduling or on-site day care, often have the most satisfied employees.

Of course, we live in difficult economic times. Jobs are not plentiful. Circumstances sometimes limit our options or present unexpected career paths, even when we have our sights set on particular fields. In addition, when it comes to making career choices, some of us have more options than others do. Still, the findings from I-O psychology can help you sort through your options. If you can figure out what type of work situation would bring you the most career satisfaction, you will have taken a major step toward motivating yourself in the workplace.

Summing Up

How Does Motivation Energize, Direct, and Sustain Behavior?

Motivation energizes, directs, and sustains behavior. Maslow described a hierarchy of needs: People first must satisfy lower needs, such as hunger and thirst, then safety needs, which are followed by social needs, esteem needs, and self-actualization needs. Needs arise from states of biological or social deficiency; drives are psychological states that create arousal and motivate behaviors to satisfy needs. Our drives help us maintain homeostasis—that is, equilibrium of our bodily functions. The Yerkes-Dodson law suggests that each of us prefers an optimal level of arousal. If we are underaroused or overaroused, our performance will suffer. In contrast to activities that are extrinsically motivated or directed toward an external reward, we often engage in activities that are intrinsically motivating or enjoyable. Providing people with extrinsic rewards can undermine their intrinsic motivation. With respect to setting and achieving goals, research suggests that challenging and specific goals are best. People who are high in self-efficacy and have a high achievement motive are more likely to set challenging but attainable goals for themselves. Moreover, people who are able to delay gratification are more likely to report successful outcomes later in life. According to need to belong theory, people have a fundamental need for interpersonal attachments. This need explains the ease with which we make friends, our sensitivity to social exclusion, the adverse feelings we experience in the absence of social contact, and our efforts to affiliate with others when anxious.

Measuring Up

1. Arrange the levels of Maslow's need hierarchy in the correct order, with lowest needs at the bottom, and then match each example with the correct level.

    Needs:
    a. belonging and love
    b. self-actualization
    c. physiological needs
    d. esteem
    e. safety

    Examples:
    1. You are sleep deprived.
    2. You are being physically threatened by a bully.
    3. You are about to take an exam in a class you are failing.
    4. You have just moved to a new city, where you know few people.
    5. You are an accomplished poet engaged in writing a new book of poems.

Learning Objectives

- Discuss the impact of time, taste, and cultural learning on eating behavior.
- Identify neural structures associated with eating.
- Describe the glucostatic and lipostatic theories of eating.
- Discuss the role that hormones play in regulating eating behavior.

10.4 What Motivates Eating?

One of life's greatest pleasures is eating, and we do a lot of it. Most people in industrialized countries consume between 80,000 and 90,000 meals during their lives—more than 40 tons of food! Everyone needs to eat to survive, but eating involves much more than simply survival. Around the globe, special occasions often involve elaborate feasts, and much of the social world revolves around eating.

Common sense dictates that most eating is controlled by hunger and *satiety*. That is, people eat when they feel hungry and stop eating when they are full. Some people, however, eat a lot even when they are not hungry. Others avoid eating even though they are not full. What complex interactions between biology, cultural influences, and cognition determine our eating behavior?

Time and Taste Set the Stage

Eating is greatly affected by learning. Consider that most people eat lunch at approximately the same time—somewhere between noon and 2 PM. On a physiological level, this practice makes little sense because people differ greatly in their metabolic rates, the amounts they eat for breakfast, and the amounts of fat they have stored for long-term energy needs. We generally do not eat because we have deficient energy stores. We eat because we have been classically conditioned to associate eating with regular mealtimes. The clock indicating mealtime is much like Pavlov's metronome: It leads to various anticipatory responses that motivate eating behavior and prepare the body for digestion. For instance, an increase in insulin promotes glucose use and increases short-term hunger signals. The sight and smell of tasty foods can have the same effect. Just thinking about treats—freshly baked bread, pizza, a decadent dessert—may initiate bodily reactions that induce hunger.

A main factor that motivates eating is flavor—not just good-tasting food but a variety of flavors. Animals, including humans, will stop eating relatively quickly if they have just one type of food to eat, but they will continue eating if presented with a different type of food. Thus they tend to eat much more when various foods are available than when only one or two types of food are available (**Figure 10.26**). One reason animals eat more when presented with a variety of foods is that they quickly grow tired of any one flavor. This phenomenon is called

FIGURE 10.26 The Impact of Variety on Eating Behavior Under what circumstances do you tend to eat more than usual? Under what circumstances do you eat less? How does variety influence your eating behavior?

sensory-specific satiety. Apparently, the region of the frontal lobes that is involved in assessing the reward value of food exhibits decreased activity when the same food is eaten over and over but increased activity when a new food is presented (Rolls, 2007). This increased activity, in encouraging people to continue eating, may explain people's behavior during celebration feasts. For example, on Thanksgiving, Americans notoriously overstuff themselves. They cannot imagine eating another bite of turkey, yet they often can find room for a piece—or two—of pumpkin pie to finish the meal. From an evolutionary perspective, sensory-specific satiety may be advantageous because animals that eat many types of food are more likely to satisfy nutritional requirements and thus to survive than are animals that rely on a small number of foods. In addition, eating large meals may have been adaptive when the food supply was scarce or unpredictable.

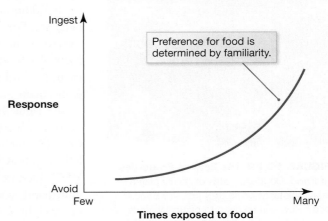

FIGURE 10.27 Tasty Treats Crickets are a popular snack among Cambodians. Would you eat the fried cricket being offered by this vendor in Phnom Penh? Why or why not?

Culture Plays a Role

Would you eat a bat? In the Seychelles, bat is a delicacy. (It tastes something like chicken.) What we will eat has little to do with logic and everything to do with what we believe is food. Some of the most nutritious foods are not eaten in North America because they are viewed as disgusting. For instance, fried termites, a favorite in Zaire, have more protein than beef does. Spiders and other insects are nutritious and in many countries are eaten as tasty treats (**Figure 10.27**). At the same time, people from other cultures might be nauseated by some of the favorite foods in North America, such as pizza and ice cream. Even when people are starving to death, they will refuse to eat perfectly nutritious substances. In Naples in 1770, people died because they were suspicious of the potatoes sent to relieve their famine. In Ireland during the potato famine (1845–52), many people died because they refused to eat corn sent from America. In Bengal in 1943, 3 million people died despite being supplied with wheat, which they rejected because it was not familiar as food.

What people will eat is determined by a combination of personal experience and cultural beliefs. Infants have an inborn preference for sweets, but they can learn to like just about anything. Generally, familiarity determines food preferences (**Figure 10.28**). The avoidance of unfamiliar foods makes great sense because unfamiliar foods may be dangerous or poisonous, so avoiding them is adaptive for survival (Galef & Whiskin, 2000). Getting children to like new foods often involves exposing them to small amounts at a time until they grow accustomed to the taste. Infants and toddlers also learn to try foods by observing their parents and siblings. Children are much more likely to eat a new food offered by their mothers than the same food offered by a friendly stranger. This behavior, too, makes great sense from an evolutionary standpoint. After all, if Mom eats something, it must be safe to eat.

Of course, what a mother or father prefers to eat is determined by his or her own upbringing and experiences. Therefore, families tend to like specific types of food. Ethnic differences in food preference often continue when a family moves to a new country. Although people often enjoy novel ethnic foods, in their regular diets most people prefer the foods of their own culture. As Paul Rozin (1996) points out, cultural rules govern which

FIGURE 10.28 The Impact of Culture on Eating Behavior As this graph illustrates, animals, including humans, tend to like the food they know. They tend to avoid unfamiliar food.

[Graph: vertical axis labeled "Response" with "Ingest" at top and "Avoid" at bottom; horizontal axis labeled "Times exposed to food" with "Few" at left and "Many" at right. A curve rises from bottom-left to upper-right. Callout: "Preference for food is determined by familiarity."]

foods are appropriate in different contexts. For example, most people in North America like chocolate and french fries, but few people like them combined. Local norms for what to eat and how to prepare it—guidelines that Rozin calls *cuisine*—reinforce many food preferences. Moreover, religious and cultural values often tell people which foods to avoid: Kosher Jews eat beef but not pork, and Hindus eat pork but not beef. Taboos on certain types of food may have been adaptive in the past because those foods were likely to contain harmful bacteria. Many food taboos and preferences are idiosyncratic, however, and have nothing to do with avoiding harm. They simply reflect an evolved group preference for specific foods, prepared and eaten in certain ways. Culturally transmitted food preferences powerfully affect the foods we eat.

Brain Structures, Homeostasis, and Hormones Direct the Action

NEURAL PROCESSES The hypothalamus (see Figure 3.18) is the brain structure that most influences eating. Although it does not act alone to elicit eating, the hypothalamus integrates the various inhibitory and excitatory feeding messages, and it organizes behaviors involved in eating. In the first half of the twentieth century, research revealed that, depending on the specific area injured, damage to the hypothalamus dramatically changes eating behavior and body weight. One of the first observations occurred in 1939, when researchers discovered that patients with tumors of the hypothalamus became obese.

To examine whether obesity could be induced in animals of normal weight, researchers selectively damaged specific hypothalamic regions in rats. When the middle, or *ventromedial,* region of the hypothalamus (*VMH*) is damaged, rats eat great quantities of food. This condition, *hyperphagia,* causes the rats with VMH damage to grow extremely obese. In contrast, when the outer, or *lateral,* region of the hypothalamus (*LH*) is damaged, rats eat far less than normal. This condition, *aphagia,* leads to weight loss and eventual death unless the rat is force-fed. The idea that VMH signals fullness and LH signals hunger is too simplistic, however. Instead, the hypothalamus monitors various hormones and nutrients and operates to maintain a state of homeostasis.

In addition, brain structures other than the hypothalamus are involved in eating behavior. For instance, a region of the prefrontal cortex processes taste cues such as sweetness and saltiness (Rolls, 2007). Such cues indicate the potential reward value of particular foods. The craving triggered by seeing tasty food is associated with activity in the limbic system (Volkow, 2007). As discussed in Chapter 3, the limbic system is the main brain region involved in reward (**Figure 10.29**). Damage to this system or the right frontal lobes sometimes produces *gourmand syndrome,* in which people become obsessed with the quality and variety of food and how food is prepared. One 48-year-old man suffered a stroke, grew preoccupied with food, and eventually left his job as a political correspondent to become a food critic (Regard & Landis, 1997). Despite their fascination with fine food and its preparation, those who have gourmand syndrome are not obsessed with eating. They do not necessarily become overweight. Their obsession seems to center on the reward properties of food.

INTERNAL SENSATIONS For a long time, scientists believed eating was a classic homeostatic system. In other words, as discussed earlier, some sort of detector in the hypothalamus would notice deviations from the set-point and would signal that an animal should start or stop eating. But where did the hunger signals come

FIGURE 10.29 The Reward Properties of Food Do these plates of "finely plated" food look tasty, or do they just strike you as odd? How you respond to particular kinds of food is of course related to what kinds of food you are used to. It is also partly biological. If you are experiencing cravings at the sight of these plates, your reaction is related to activity in your limbic system, the main brain region involved in reward.

from? The search for energy-depletion detectors has led scientists from the stomach to the bloodstream to the brain.

Contractions and distensions of the stomach can make the stomach growl. Over the past century, however, research has established that these movements are relatively minor determinants of hunger and eating. Indeed, people who have had their stomachs removed continue to report being hungry. Other research has pointed to the existence of receptors in the bloodstream that monitor levels of vital nutrients. The *glucostatic theory* proposes that the bloodstream is monitored for its glucose levels. Because glucose is the primary fuel for metabolism and is especially crucial for neuronal activity, it makes sense for animals to become hungry when they are deficient in glucose. Similarly, the *lipostatic theory* proposes a set-point for body fat. In this scenario, when an animal loses body fat, hunger signals motivate eating and a return to the set-point.

HORMONAL ACTIVITY The hormone *leptin* is involved in fat regulation. Leptin is released from fat cells as more fat is stored. Leptin travels to the hypothalamus, where it acts to inhibit eating behavior. Some evidence indicates that leptin might affect the reward properties of food and make it less appetizing (Farooqi et al., 2007). Because leptin acts slowly, however, it takes considerable time after eating before leptin levels change in the body. Therefore, leptin may be more important for long-term body fat regulation than for short-term eating control. Animals lacking the gene necessary to produce leptin become extremely obese, and injecting leptin into these animals leads to a rapid loss of body fat (Friedman & Halaas, 1998).

The hormone *ghrelin* originates in the stomach. It surges before meals, then decreases after people eat, so it may play an important role in triggering eating (Abizaid, 2009; Higgins, Gueorguiev, & Korbonits, 2007). When people lose weight, an increase in ghrelin motivates additional eating in a homeostatic fashion (Zorrilla et al., 2006).

How much any hormone contributes to human obesity is unclear. Considerable research is under way to find out whether manipulating hormones can help prevent or treat obesity. As you will learn in Chapter 11, many factors—from genes to culture to bad eating habits—contribute to obesity. You will also learn why most people who diet have trouble losing weight and keeping it off.

Summing Up

What Motivates Eating?

Eating is strongly affected by learning. Through classical conditioning, we associate eating with regular mealtimes. Moreover, what we eat is greatly influenced by cultural rules regarding which foods are appropriate to eat in different contexts. Sensory-specific satiety is a mechanism that has evolved in animals to encourage the consumption of foods that contain diverse nutrients; we quickly grow tired of any single flavor. A number of neural structures are associated with eating behavior, including the frontal lobes, the hypothalamus, the prefrontal cortex, and the limbic system. Two theories have been proposed to explain eating behavior: glucostatic theory and lipostatic theory. Glucostatic theory maintains that eating is under the control of receptors in the bloodstream that monitor levels of glucose—our primary metabolic fuel. Lipostatic theory asserts that eating is regulated to maintain a body fat set-point. Two hormones have been found to be of central importance to our eating behavior: leptin and ghrelin. Leptin is associated with long-term body fat regulation, whereas ghrelin motivates eating behavior.

10.5 What Motivates Sexual Behavior?

Sexual desire has long been recognized as one of humanity's most durable and powerful motivators. Most human beings have a significant desire for sex, but sex drives vary substantially among individuals and across circumstances. Variation in sexual frequency can be explained by individual differences and by society's dominating influence over how and when individuals engage in sexual activity.

For much of the history of psychological science, the study of sex was taboo. The idea that women were motivated to have sex was almost unthinkable. Many theorists even believed women were incapable of *enjoying* sex. In the 1940s, the pioneering work of Alfred Kinsey and his colleagues provided—for the times—shocking evidence that women's sexual attitudes and behaviors were in many ways similar to those of men. In Kinsey's surveys of thousands of Americans, he found that more than half of both men and women reported premarital sexual behavior, that masturbation was common in both sexes, that women enjoyed orgasms, and that homosexuality was much more common than most people believed. Very little was known about human sexuality when Kinsey began his work, and Kinsey's approach exemplified psychology's empirical nature. His surveys were controversial, but Kinsey showed a deep respect for collecting data as a way of answering a research question. More than 50 years later, we know a great deal more about sexual behavior, but the topic still makes many people uncomfortable. Public discussion of sexual activity is rare, except perhaps on the Web, talk radio, and daytime television shows. This section examines what psychological science has learned about the motivation for sex.

Biology Influences Sexual Behavior

Kinsey's research during the 1940s demonstrated how little most people knew about human sexual behavior. Despite his eye-opening contributions, ignorance about the physiology of sex persisted into the 1960s, when William Masters and Virginia Johnson began laboratory studies of sexual behavior. Their sample was somewhat biased, in that only people willing to be filmed while having intercourse or masturbating served as research participants. Nonetheless, Masters and Johnson gained considerable insight into the physiology of human sexual behavior. The most enduring contribution of their research was the identification of the **sexual response cycle**. This predictable pattern of physical and psychological responses consists of four stages (**Figure 10.30**).

The *excitement phase* occurs when people contemplate sexual activity or begin engaging in behaviors such as kissing and touching in a sensual manner. During this stage, blood flows to the genitals, and people report feelings of arousal. For men, the penis begins to become erect. For women, the clitoris becomes swollen, the vagina expands and secretes fluids, and the nipples enlarge.

As excitement continues into the *plateau phase,* pulse rate, breathing, and blood pressure increase, as do the various other signs of arousal. For many people, this stage is the frenzied phase of sexual activity. Inhibitions are lifted, and passion takes control.

The plateau phase culminates in the *orgasm phase*. This stage consists of involuntary muscle contractions throughout the body, dramatic increases in breathing and heart rate, rhythmic contractions of the vagina for women, and ejaculation of semen for men. For healthy males, orgasm nearly always occurs. For females, orgasm is more variable. When it occurs, however, women and men report nearly identical pleasurable sensations.

Following orgasm, there is a dramatic release of sexual tension and a slow return to a normal state of arousal. In this stage, the *resolution phase,* the male enters a refractory period. During this period, he is temporarily unable to maintain an erection or have an orgasm. The female does not have such a refractory period and may experience multiple orgasms with short resolution phases between each one. Again, the female response is more variable than the male response.

HORMONES As discussed in Chapter 3, hormones are involved in producing and terminating sexual behaviors. In nonhuman animals, hormones profoundly influence sexual activity. In many species, females are sexually receptive only when

sexual response cycle A four-stage pattern of physiological and psychological responses during sexual activity.

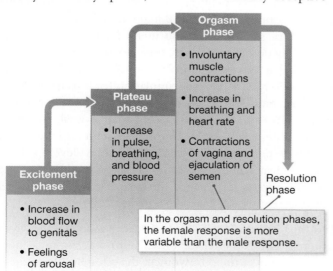

FIGURE 10.30 Diagram of the Sexual Response Cycle

fertile, and estrogen is believed to control reproductive behaviors. Estrogen appears to play only a small role in human female sexuality, but hormones affect human sexual behavior in two ways. First, as discussed in Chapter 9, they influence physical development of the brain and body during puberty. Second, hormones influence sexual behavior through motivation. That is, they activate reproductive behavior.

As noted in Chapter 3, sex hormones are released from the gonads (testes and ovaries), and females and males have some amount of all the sex hormones. But males have a greater quantity of androgens than females do, and females have a greater quantity of estrogens and progesterone. Androgens are apparently much more important for reproductive behavior than estrogens are, at least for humans. In men and women, testosterone—a type of androgen—is involved in sexual functioning (Sherwin, 2008). Males need a certain amount of testosterone to be able to engage in sex, but they do not perform better if they have more testosterone. The availability of testosterone, not large quantities of it, apparently drives male sexual behavior. The more testosterone women have, the more likely they are to have sexual thoughts and desires—although normal females have relatively low levels of testosterone (Meston & Frohlich, 2000). Adolescent females with higher than average testosterone levels for their age are more likely to engage in sexual intercourse (Halpern, Udry, & Suchindran, 1997).

Another important hormone in men and women is *oxytocin,* which is released during sexual arousal and orgasm. (As you will see in Chapter 11, oxytocin also is associated with trust.) Some researchers believe oxytocin may promote feelings of love and attachment between partners; it also seems to be involved in social behavior more generally (Bartels & Zeki, 2004).

Given the important role of the hypothalamus in controlling the release of hormones into the bloodstream, it is no surprise that the hypothalamus is the brain region considered most important for stimulating sexual behavior. Studies have shown that damaging the hypothalamus in rats interrupts sexual behavior, although which damaged brain area has the greatest effect differs slightly for males and females.

NEUROTRANSMITTERS Neurotransmitters can affect various aspects of the sexual response. For instance, dopamine receptors in the limbic system are involved in the physical experience of pleasure, and dopamine receptors in the hypothalamus stimulate sexual activity (Pfaus, 2009). Serotonin also is implicated in sexual behavior. The most common pharmacological treatments for depression enhance serotonin function, but they seriously reduce sexual interest, especially for women. Small doses of drugs that enhance serotonin are also useful for treating premature ejaculation. Researchers currently do not know why these effects occur.

One chemical that acts as a neurotransmitter in the brain and is critical for sexual behavior is *nitric oxide.* Sexual stimulation leads to nitric oxide production. The increased nitric oxide promotes blood flow to both the penis and the clitoris and subsequently plays an important role in sexual arousal, especially penile erections. When this system fails, males cannot maintain an erection. Various drugs that enhance this system, such as Viagra, have been developed to treat erectile disorders. It is not clear whether such drugs can be used to treat women's sexual disorders, but they appear to enhance the sexual experience for healthy women (Caruso, Intelisano, Farina, Di Mari, & Agnello, 2003).

VARIATIONS ACROSS THE MENSTRUAL CYCLE Women differ from men in how the hypothalamus controls the release of sex hormones. In men, hormones are released at the same rate over time. In women, the release of hormones varies according to a cycle that repeats itself approximately every 28 days: the menstrual cycle.

Research has found only minimal evidence that women's sexual behavior varies across the menstrual cycle. Recent evidence indicates, however, that women may process social information differently, depending on whether they are in a fertile phase of the cycle. For instance, researchers used a computer program to alter masculinity and femininity in male faces (Penton-Voak et al., 1999). They found that, compared with preferences expressed in other phases of the menstrual cycle, during ovulation heterosexual women preferred the more masculine faces. In another study, in which heterosexual women watched videotapes of men, women who were ovulating rated self-assured men as more desirable potential sex partners, but women who were not ovulating did not (Gangestad, Simpson, Cousins, Garver-Apgar, & Christensen, 2004). These studies add to a growing literature that suggests women evaluate men differently across the menstrual cycle. The everyday effects of these differences on women, and on the men they interact with, are unknown.

(a)

VISUAL EROTIC STIMULATION Some brain imaging studies indicate that viewing erotica activates reward regions in the brain, such as various limbic structures. This effect is greatest for men who have higher levels of testosterone (Stoleru et al., 1999). As noted in Chapter 3, Hamann and colleagues (2004) found that when men and women viewed sexually arousing stimuli, such as film clips of sexual activity or pictures of opposite-sex nudes, men showed more activation of the amygdala. This activation, the authors suggest, increases the arousal caused by the stimuli. Men are more likely than women to report visual erotic stimulation as pleasurable (Herz & Cahill, 1997), but this finding might simply mean that erotica is generally produced more for men's interests than for women's. Research has shown that women prefer erotica produced specifically for women, which tends to emphasize more of the emotional factors of sexual interaction. One study found that although both sexes prefer viewing erotic movies aimed at their own sex, men were aroused by both types of movies (Janssen, Carpenter, & Graham, 2003). Finally, one brain imaging study found that women's reactions to viewing erotica varied according to the phases of their menstrual cycles (Gizewski et al., 2006).

(b)

Cultural Scripts and Cultural Rules Shape Sexual Interactions

In the movies, sexual relationships often start when one attractive young person meets another by chance. They spend some exciting time together, an attraction develops, and sexual behavior ensues—often within a day or two. In real life, however, the course of action is often quite different. For one thing, most people rely on social networks to meet their sex partners. In addition, people generally do not fall into bed together as fast as they do in the movies. Most people know someone a long time before having sex. But the depiction of sexual behavior in movies and other media shapes beliefs and expectations about what sexual behaviors are appropriate and when they are appropriate.

Sexual scripts are cognitive beliefs about how a sexual episode should be enacted (for a discussion of scripts, see Chapter 8, "Thinking and Intelligence"). For instance, the sexual script indicates who should make the first move, whether the other person should resist, the sequence of sexual acts, and even how the partners should act afterward (**Figure 10.31**). In Westernized societies, the sexual script involves initial flirtation through nonverbal actions, the male initiating physical contact, the female controlling whether sexual activity takes place, and refusals typically being verbal and direct (Berscheid & Regan, 2005). The scripts differ in many places in the world, such as in countries where arranged marriages are common.

(c)

FIGURE 10.31 Sexual Scripts Sexual scripts influence behaviors such as **(a)** flirting, **(b)** pursuing romantic interest, and **(c)** dating.

REGULATING SEXUAL BEHAVIOR The sexual revolution of the late twentieth century significantly changed sexual behaviors in many countries. Most of the changes in sexual behaviors must be attributed to changes in cultural pressures and cultural expectations. Although sexual customs and norms vary across cultures, all known cultures have some form of sexual morality. This universality indicates the importance to society of regulating sexual behavior. For example, one well-known pattern of regulating sexual behavior is the *double standard*. This unwritten law stipulates that certain activities (such as premarital or casual sex) are morally and socially acceptable for men but not for women. Cultures may seek to restrain and control sex for various reasons, including maintaining control over the birthrate, helping establish paternity, and reducing conflicts.

SEX DIFFERENCES IN SEXUAL BEHAVIOR A noticeable and consistent finding in nearly all measures of sexual desire is that men, on average, have a higher level of sexual motivation than women do. There are, of course, many individual exceptions. Research studies have found that, in general, men masturbate more frequently than women, want sex earlier in the relationship, think and fantasize about sex more often, spend more time and money (and other resources) in the effort to obtain sex, desire more different sexual activities, initiate sex more and refuse sex less, and rate their own sex drives as stronger than women's (Baumeister, Catanese, & Vohs, 2001). In one study, researchers asked college-age men and women how many sex partners they ideally would like to have in their lives, if they were unconstrained by fears about disease, social pressures, and the like (Miller & Fishkin, 1997). Most women wanted one or two partners. Men's average answer was several dozen. A study of more than 16,000 people from 10 major regions around the world found that the greater male motivation for sexual activity and sexual variety occurs in all cultures (Schmitt et al., 2003).

The relative influence of nature and culture on sexual motivation may vary with gender. Roy Baumeister's (2000) term *erotic plasticity* refers to the extent that sex drive can be shaped by social, cultural, and situational factors. Evidence suggests that women have higher erotic plasticity than men. A woman's sexuality may evolve and change throughout her adult life, whereas a man's desires remain relatively constant (except for a gradual decline with age). Women's sexual desires and behaviors depend significantly on social factors such as education and religion, whereas men's sexuality shows minimal relationships to such influences.

To account for these differences, the evolutionary psychologist David Buss has proposed the **sexual strategies theory** (Buss & Schmitt, 1993). From this perspective, throughout human history males and females have faced different adaptive problems. One result is that women differ from men in how they maximize the passing along of their genes to future generations. Women's basic strategy is intensive care of a relatively small number of infants. Their commitment is to nurture offspring rather than simply maximize production. Once a woman is pregnant, additional matings are of no reproductive use. Once she has a small child, an additional pregnancy can put her current offspring at risk. Thus biological mechanisms ensure spacing between children. For example, nursing typically makes ovulation less likely to occur. On purely reproductive grounds, men have no such sexual interludes. For them, all matings may have a reproductive payoff. They bear few of the personal costs of pregnancy, and their fertility is unaffected by getting a woman pregnant.

According to the sexual strategies theory, women are more likely to be more cautious about having sex because having offspring is a much more intensive commitment for them than it is for men. Indeed, there is evidence that women are much less willing than men to have sex with someone they do not know well. In

sexual strategies theory A theory that maintains that women and men have evolved distinct mating strategies because they faced different adaptive problems over the course of human history. The strategies used by each sex maximize the probability of passing along their genes to future generations.

one study of 96 university students, a stranger approached a person of the opposite sex and said, "I have been noticing you around campus. I find you attractive. Would you go to bed with me tonight?" Each stranger was somewhere between mildly unattractive and moderately attractive. Not one woman said yes to the stranger's request, but three-quarters of the men agreed to the request (**Figure 10.32**). Indeed, the men were less likely to agree to go on a date with the stranger than they were to agree to have sex with her (Clark & Hatfield, 1989).

In another study, people were asked how long a couple should be together before it is acceptable for them to have sexual intercourse, given mutual desire. Women tend to think couples should be together for at least a month or more before sex is appropriate. Men tend to believe that even after relatively short periods of acquaintanceship, such as on the first or second date, sex is acceptable (Buss & Schmitt, 1993).

MATE PREFERENCES What do men and women want in their mates? It is perhaps easier to say what they do not want. In seeking mates, both sexes avoid certain characteristics, such as insensitivity, bad manners, loudness or shrillness, and the tendency to brag about sexual conquests (Cunningham, Barbee, & Druen, 1996).

According to sexual strategies theory, however, men and women should differ in what they desire in mates. Both men and women should seek attractive partners, because relative youth and beauty imply potential fertility. Because women are limited in the number of offspring they can produce, they should be choosier in selecting mates. Therefore, women should seek men who can provide resources that will help them successfully nurture their children. In essence, men should care mainly about looks because looks imply fertility, whereas women should also be concerned about indications that their mates will be good fathers. Is there any scientific support for these ideas?

According to a study of 92 married couples in 37 cultures, women generally prefer men who are considerate, honest, dependable, kind, understanding, fond of children, well liked by others, good earners, ambitious, career oriented, from a good family, and fairly tall. By contrast, men tend to value good looks, cooking skills, and sexual faithfulness. Above all, women value a good financial prospect more than men do. In all 37 cultures, women tend to marry older men, who often are more settled and financially stable (Buss, 1989). In short, males and females differ in the relative emphases they place on social status and physical appearance, at least for long-term relationships. In one study, men and women reported kindness and intelligence as necessary in their selection of mates, but their views of status and attractiveness differed. For the average woman seeking a long-term mate, status was a necessity and good looks were a luxury. In contrast, men viewed physical attractiveness as a necessity rather than a luxury in mate selection (Li, Bailey, Kenrick, & Linsenmeier, 2002).

This is not to say that women do not care about attractiveness. Women's preference for status over attractiveness depends on several factors. For example, is the relationship short term or long term? Looks are more important in the short term. Does the woman perceive herself as attractive? Women who view themselves as very attractive appear to want it all—status and good looks (Buss & Shackelford, 2008). In general, both men and women value physical attractiveness highly, but their relative emphases conform to evolutionary predictions.

The evolutionary account of human mating is controversial. Some researchers believe that behaviors shaped by evolution have little impact on contemporary relationships. We must consider two important factors. First, the modern era is a tiny fraction of human evolutionary history. The modern mind resides in

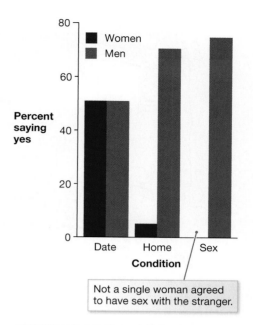

Not a single woman agreed to have sex with the stranger.

FIGURE 10.32 Sexual Behaviors and Responses Men and women were propositioned by a stranger of the opposite sex. Both sexes were equally likely to accept a date. Men were much more willing than women to agree to have sex or to go home with the stranger.

"I'm rich, you're thin. Together, we're perfect."

a Stone Age brain, solving adaptive problems that have faced our species for thousands of years. Thus remnants of behaviors that were adaptive in prehistoric times may linger even if they are not adaptive in contemporary society. Second, however, is that natural selection bestows biological urges as well as a strong sensitivity to cultural and group norms. In other words, instinctive behaviors are constrained by social context. The frontal lobes work to inhibit people from breaking social rules, which are determined largely by culture.

The current social context differs greatly from that of millions of years ago, and human mating strategies are influenced by these contemporary norms. For example, from a biological view, it might seem advantageous for humans to reproduce as soon as they are able. But many contemporary cultures discourage sexual behavior until people are older and better able to care for their offspring. The critical point is that human behavior emerges to solve adaptive problems. To some degree, the modern era introduces new adaptive challenges based on societal standards of conduct. These standards shape the context in which men and women view sexual behavior as desirable and appropriate.

We Differ in Our Sexual Orientations

Why are some people homosexual and others heterosexual? Homosexual behavior has been noted in various forms throughout recorded history. From an evolutionary perspective, homosexuality appears to make little sense. Exclusive homosexuality would not lead to reproduction and therefore would not survive in the gene pool. Many theories of sexual orientation have emerged, but none has received conclusive support. One evolutionary theory is that lesbians and gays often act as "spare" parents to their siblings' offspring. In this way, they might ensure the continuation of family genes. Of course, many gays and lesbians are parents, sometimes from earlier marriages and sometimes through artificial insemination or adoption.

In the nineteenth and much of the twentieth century, at least in Western cultures, homosexuality was regarded as deviant and abnormal, a psychological disorder. Until 1973, psychiatrists officially viewed homosexuality as a mental illness. Classic psychoanalytic theories of sexual orientation emphasized the importance of parenting practices. Families with a domineering mother and a submissive father were thought to cause the children to identify with the opposite-sex parent (e.g., a boy with his mother). Such identification translated into a sexual attraction toward the gender opposite of their identification—that is, a same-sex attraction. The overwhelming majority of studies, however, have found little or no evidence that how parents treat their children has anything to do with sexual orientation. Likewise, no other environmental factor has been found to account for homosexuality. So does biology determine sexual orientation?

BIOLOGICAL FACTORS Remember that when we ask whether something is biological, we really are talking about the relative contributions of biological factors compared with those of environmental factors. Every behavior results from biological processes, such as gene expression, that are themselves influenced by events in environment.

One approach to examining the extent to which biological factors contribute to sexual orientation explores the effect of hormones. Early theorists speculated that lesbians had higher levels of testosterone and gay males had higher levels of estrogen, but those speculations were wrong. The levels of circulating hormones do not differ between heterosexual and homosexual same-sex individuals. Rather, the best available evidence suggests that exposure to hormones, especially androgens, in the prenatal environment might play some role in sexual orientation (Mustanski, Chivers, & Bailey, 2002). For example, because of a mother's medical condition, some females are exposed to higher than normal levels of androgens during prenatal development. These females often have masculine characteristics, at birth and throughout life. Later in life, they are more likely to report being lesbians. An intriguing finding is that compared with straight males, gay males are more likely to have older male siblings. One explanation is that the mother's body develops an immune reaction during pregnancy with a male and that subsequent immune responses alter the level of hormones in the prenatal environment when the mother becomes pregnant with another male (Blanchard & Ellis, 2001; Bogaert, 2006). But most males with older brothers are not gay, so why would this response affect only some males?

A second approach to understanding the biological contribution to sexual orientation is through genetics. The idea that gene expression might be involved in sexual orientation is supported by a study using fruit flies. Researchers found that altering the expression of a single "master" gene reversed the sexual orientations of male and female flies (Demir & Dickson, 2005). But what about in humans? In 1993, the biologist Dean Hamer reported finding a link between a marker on the X chromosome and sexual orientation in males, and the media quickly dubbed the marker "the gay gene." Other researchers have failed to find any specific genes for sexual orientation. Is homosexuality inherited? Twin studies have provided some support for the idea of a genetic component to homosexuality, particularly for males. As discussed in Chapter 3, identical twins are most similar in genetic makeup, but they also are likely to have had similar environments, and it is difficult to pull apart these two types of contributions. In a review of previous studies, Mustanski and colleagues (2002) report the heritability of homosexuality as being greater for males than for females but with a significant genetic component for both. It remains unclear how human sexual orientation might be encoded in the genes.

Some research suggests the hypothalamus may be related to sexual orientation. In postmortem examinations, the neuroscientist Simon LeVay (1991) found that an area of the hypothalamus that typically differs between men and women was only half as large in gay men as in straight men. In fact, the size of this area in gay men was comparable to its size in straight women. Likewise, in a recent brain imaging study, straight males showed greater activation of the hypothalamus when they sniffed a female pheromone (a hormonal secretion that travels through the air) than they did when they sniffed a male pheromone, whereas straight females showed greater activation when they sniffed a male pheromone rather than a female pheromone (Savic, Berglund, & Lindström, 2005). Gay men showed a pattern more similar to that of women than of straight men: greater activation of the hypothalamus in response to the male pheromone.

Although intriguing, both of these studies can be criticized on the grounds that correlation does not equal causation. That is, a size difference or activation difference in any one part of the brain cannot establish whether this area determines sexual orientation, whether being heterosexual or homosexual results in changes to brain structure or function, or whether a third variable is responsible for all these effects. For instance, some researchers believe that the size of the hypothalamus is determined by prenatal exposure to androgens. Thus although these studies' findings are suggestive, evidence currently is insufficient to establish a causal connection between brain regions and sexual orientation. Considered together,

Brent Sims,
Joseph Taravella

John Brullo

Brent Alan Sims and Dr. Joseph Robert Taravella celebrated their partnership last evening at the Waldorf-Astoria in New York. The Rev. Dr. Susan Corso, a nondenominational Christian minister, led a ceremony of commitment.

Mr. Sims (above, left), is 36. He works in New York as the vice president for finance and administration in the national advertising sales division of Fox television stations. He graduated from the University of Texas and received an M.B.A. from Southern Methodist University. Mr. Sims uses the surname of his mother and stepfather, Sandra and Loyd Sims of Lindale, Tex., who retired as the owners of a Western Auto store in Dumas.

Eva Ogielska,
Paul Zei

Dr. Eva Marya Ogielska and Dr. Paul Cameron Zei were married yesterday at the Compass Rose Gardens in Bodega Bay, Calif. The Rev. Nancy Hargis, a non-denominational minister, performed the ceremony.

The couple, both 32, met at Stanford University, where the bride earned a Ph.D. in neuroscience and the bridegroom a medical degree and a Ph.D. in molecular and cellular physiology.

The bride is to become an associate in September at Foley Hoag, a Boston law firm. She graduated cum laude from Brandeis and received a law degree from the University of California at Berkeley.

She is the daughter of Sophia and Andrew Ogielski

FIGURE 10.33 Sexual Orientation These gay and straight wedding announcements illustrate the complexity of contemporary society. Society is coming to mirror the complexity of the factors underlying humans' sexual orientation.

the evidence is consistent that biological processes play some role in sexual orientation. The question is how and when biology contributes, and to what degree.

BIOLOGY AND ENVIRONMENTAL FACTORS Many psychologists believe it is likely that multiple biological and environmental processes affect a person's sexual orientation in subtle ways. Daryl Bem (1996) has proposed that feeling different from opposite-sex peers or same-sex peers predicts later sexual orientation. Homosexuals report preferring the leisure activities of their opposite-sex peers, and Bem believes this tendency may be due to biological differences in temperament. Children tend to play in same-sex groups, so boys and girls often are segregated. Regarding sexual orientation, Bem believes people are attracted to what is different. The difference creates arousal, and this arousal is the essence of sexual attraction—in Bem's words, "the exotic becomes erotic." Because the opposite sex is different, it becomes attractive; so most girls are attracted to boys, and vice versa. To some children, however, peers of their own sex seem different; so members of the same sex ultimately become erotic. Bem's model is interesting because it is based on the idea of initial biological differences in temperament but then proposes that the social environment shapes what is sexually attractive. Although the theory is supported by anecdotal evidence, so far no concrete evidence supports it. But how can researchers ever really test such theories in humans? What evidence is needed to conclude whether sexual orientation is determined or chosen?

STABILITY OF SEXUAL ORIENTATION Although there are Web reports of effective homosexual conversion therapies, there is little empirical evidence that these programs do any more than suppress behavior. No good evidence exists that sexual orientation can be changed through therapy. Moreover, being with people whose sexual orientation differs from yours does not change your sexual orientation. In some cultures and subcultures, people may engage in same-sex behaviors for a period and then revert to heterosexual behaviors. In jail, for example, men and women often engage in same-sex relationships but do not consider themselves homosexuals. For reasons such as these, few psychologists or physicians believe sexual orientation—as opposed simply to sexual activity—is a choice or that it can be changed. Modern society, too, is increasingly acknowledging homosexuals' rights to express their sexuality: Canada, Spain, Norway, Sweden, South Africa, Portugal, and an increasing number of states in the United States allow gays and lesbians to marry, and other places around the world recognize same-sex relationships in varying ways. In some ways, the contemporary world is catching up with human history. Homosexuals have always existed, whether or not they were free to be themselves (**Figure 10.33**).

Summing Up

What Motivates Sexual Behavior?

Pioneering research by Alfred Kinsey launched the study of human sexual behavior and shattered many myths regarding men's and women's sexual lives. Masters and

Johnson identified four stages in the sexual response cycle that are very similar for men and women: excitement, plateau, orgasm, and resolution. Hormones influence the development of secondary sex characteristics during puberty and motivate sexual behavior. Testosterone and oxytocin have been found to be particularly important determinants of sexual behavior. Neurotransmitters, including dopamine, serotonin, and nitric oxide, have also been found to influence sexual functioning. Sexual behavior is constrained by sexual scripts: socially determined beliefs regarding the appropriate behaviors for men and women to engage in during sexual interactions. Research has demonstrated that, on average, men have a higher level of sexual motivation and engage in more sexual activity than women do. Men and women look for similar qualities in potential partners, but men are more concerned about a potential partner's attractiveness, and women are more concerned with a potential partner's status. These differences in relative importance may be due to the different adaptive problems the sexes faced over the course of human evolutionary history. Many theories have been proposed to explain sexual orientation. For example, researchers have suggested that prenatal hormone exposure, genes, and functional differences in the hypothalamus may influence sexual orientation. Although evidence has emerged to support each of these theories, the data are correlational and cannot be used to make causal inferences. Indeed, many psychologists believe that multiple biological and environmental factors determine sexual orientation.

Measuring Up

1. Arrange the stages of the human sexual response cycle in order, and match each stage with its description.

    Stages: plateau, excitement, resolution, orgasm
    a. increasing signs of arousal, including increases in blood pressure and in breathing rate
    b. contractions of the vagina for women and ejaculation of semen for men
    c. swelling of genitals in response to blood flow
    d. return to prestimulation state

2. Identify whether each of the following statements about human sexual behavior best describes a biological, cultural, or evolutionary perspective. Some statements may describe more than one perspective.
    a. Researchers have found that women prefer masculine-looking faces more during ovulation than in other phases of the menstrual cycle.
    b. Across 37 cultures, women preferred men who could earn a good living, and men rated a future mate's physical attractiveness as more important than women did.
    c. Across religious groups and in different countries, there are differences in women's willingness to engage in premarital sex.
    d. Women tend to prefer erotica that is more relationship oriented than men do.
    e. Many drugs used for depression also reduce sex drive, especially in women.
    f. Male sex function requires a minimal level of androgens.
    g. In general, men have higher levels of sexual motivation than women do.

Answers: 1. excitement—c; plateau—a; orgasm—b; resolution—d.
2. a. biological and evolutionary; b. evolutionary; c. cultural; d. cultural and evolutionary; e. biological; f. biological; g. biological and evolutionary.

Chapter Summary

10.1 How Do We Experience Emotions?

■ **Emotions Have a Subjective Component:** Primary emotions are evolutionarily adaptive and are universal across cultures. They include anger, fear, sadness, disgust, happiness, and possibly surprise and contempt. Secondary emotions are blends of the primary emotions. Emotions may be described using two dimensions: valence and activation. Negative affect and positive affect are independent.

■ **Emotions Have a Physiological Component:** The James–Lange theory of emotion maintains that we perceive patterns of bodily responses and, as a result of our perceptions, experience emotion. The Cannon–Bard theory of emotion maintains that the mind and body experience emotion independently. Consistent with both theories, studies have demonstrated that emotions are associated with changes in bodily states. Research points to important roles of the amygdala and the prefrontal cortex in the production and experience of emotion.

■ **Emotions Have a Cognitive Component:** According to the Schachter–Singer two-factor theory of emotion, emotions involve a physiological component and a cognitive component or interpretation. The interpretation determines the emotion that we feel. Misattribution of arousal occurs when people misidentify the source of their arousal. Excitation transfer occurs when residual arousal caused by one event is transferred to a new stimulus.

■ **We Regulate Our Emotional States:** We use various strategies to regulate or manage our emotional states. Humor and distraction are effective strategies for regulating negative affect, whereas rumination and thought suppression are not effective strategies for regulating negative affect.

10.2 How Are Emotions Adaptive?

■ **Facial Expressions Communicate Emotion:** Facial expressions of emotion are adaptive because they communicate how we feel. Across cultures, there are some expressions of emotion that are universally recognized. These include happiness, sadness, anger, and pride.

■ **Display Rules Differ across Cultures and between the Sexes:** Display rules are learned through socialization and dictate how and when people express emotions. Females express emotions more readily, frequently, easily, and intensely than males, possibly as a consequence of display rules.

■ **Emotions Serve Cognitive Functions:** We use our emotions as a guide when making decisions. Indeed, emotions often serve as heuristic guides, enabling quick decisions to be made. Somatic marker theory maintains that we use our bodily reactions to emotional events to regulate our behaviors. That is, we interpret our body's responses and use that information to help make decisions.

■ **Emotions Strengthen Interpersonal Relations:** Emotions facilitate the maintenance and repair of social bonds. Guilt serves several functions. For example, it discourages people from engaging in actions that may harm their relationships and encourages people to engage in actions that will strengthen their relationships. Embarrassment rectifies interpersonal awkwardness and restores social bonds after a social error or wrongdoing has been committed.

10.3 How Does Motivation Energize, Direct, and Sustain Behavior?

■ **Multiple Factors Motivate Behavior:** Motives activate, direct, and sustain behaviors that will satisfy a need. Needs create arousal, and the response to being aroused is a drive to satisfy the need. Maslow's hierarchy proposes five needs: physiological, safety, belonging and love, esteem, and self-actualization needs. *Homeostasis* refers to the body's attempts to maintain a state of equilibrium. The Yerkes-Dodson law states that a person performs best when his or her level of arousal is neither too low nor too high.

■ **Some Behaviors Are Motivated for Their Own Sake:** Behaviors that are extrinsically motivated are directed toward the achievement of an external goal. Behaviors that are intrinsically motivated fulfill no obvious purpose. They are performed simply because they are pleasurable. Extrinsic rewards decrease intrinsic motivation because they decrease our experience of autonomy and competence or because the reward replaces the goal of pleasure.

■ **We Set Goals to Achieve:** Challenging and specific goals are most likely to lead to success. People who are high in self-efficacy and have a high need to achieve are more likely to set challenging but attainable goals. Moreover, those who are able to delay gratification as they work toward their goals are more likely to be successful. Several strategies facilitate delayed gratification, including distraction and the use of cold cognitions rather than hot cognitions.

■ **We Have a Need to Belong:** Humans have a fundamental need to belong. Evolutionary theorists maintain that this need provided a survival advantage to our ancestors. Our need to belong facilitates the development of friendships, makes us sensitive to social exclusion, and produces feelings of emptiness and despair in the absence of other people. When we are anxious, we seek out similar others. Other people provide information that helps us determine if we are acting appropriately.

10.4 What Motivates Eating?

- **Time and Taste Set the Stage:** Eating is greatly affected by learning. Through classical conditioning, we associate eating with regular mealtimes. Having a variety of flavors results in more eating. Sensory-specific satiety refers to our tendency to eat less when there is little variety in our food choices.

- **Culture Plays a Role:** Culture determines what a person considers edible. Researchers have found that infants have an innate preference for sweet tastes, but children can learn to like most foods—particularly those foods offered by family members.

- **Brain Structures, Homeostasis, and Hormones Direct the Action:** The hypothalamus is the brain structure most closely identified with eating. Rats whose ventromedial hypothalami were damaged experienced hyperphagia. That is, they consumed huge quantities of food. By contrast, rats whose lateral hypothalami were damaged exhibited aphagia. That is, they stopped eating to the point of death. Other structures that influence our eating behavior include a region of the frontal lobes (sensory-specific satiety, processing of taste cues) and the limbic system (cravings). Blood glucose monitors, set-point sensors for body fat, and the hormones leptin and ghrelin also play important roles in determining how much we eat.

10.5 What Motivates Sexual Behavior?

- **Biology Influences Sexual Behavior:** The four stages of the human sexual response cycle are excitement, plateau, orgasm, and resolution. Testosterone and oxytocin influence the sexual behavior of both women and men. Among the neurotransmitters that affect sexual functioning among women and men are dopamine, serotonin, and nitric oxide. Although women's sexual behavior does not appear to vary across the menstrual cycle, some data show that heterosexual women's preferences for masculine-looking and self-assured men increases during ovulation.

- **Cultural Scripts and Cultural Rules Shape Sexual Interactions:** Sexual scripts are beliefs about how women and men should behave in sexual relationships. Sexual scripts are socially determined and differ across cultures. The double standard is one means by which sexual behavior is regulated in many cultures; it allows men greater sexual latitude than it allows women. Research has demonstrated that, around the world, men exhibit greater motivation for sexual activity and sexual variety than women. According to sexual strategies theory, women and men have evolved distinct mating strategies to maximize their reproductive potential. For example, women tend to be more selective in choosing partners because their investments in pregnancy and child care are intensive. In contrast, men are less selective in choosing partners because they are not required to invest as much in potential offspring. In addition, women tend to seek men who are good providers for their children because good providers will increase the likelihood that the women's offspring will survive. In contrast, men tend to seek attractive women because attractiveness suggests fertility.

- **We Differ in Our Sexual Orientations:** A number of biological theories of sexual orientation have been proposed. In particular, theories have implicated prenatal hormone exposure, genes, and the hypothalamus in determining sexual orientation. Although research has emerged to support these theories, the data are largely correlational, precluding causal statements. Many contemporary researchers maintain that both biological and environmental factors influence sexual orientation.

Key Terms

arousal, p. 423
display rules, p. 434
drive, p. 441
emotion, p. 422
extrinsic motivation, p. 444

homeostasis, p. 442
incentives, p. 442
intrinsic motivation, p. 444
motivation, p. 440
need, p. 441

need hierarchy, p. 441
need to belong theory, p. 448
primary emotions, p. 423
secondary emotions, p. 423
self-actualization, p. 441

sexual response cycle, p. 457
sexual strategies theory, p. 460
somatic markers, p. 437
Yerkes-Dodson law, p. 443

Practice Test

1. Students enrolled in a difficult class are preparing to give end-of-term presentations, which will count 50 percent toward their final grades. Which student below is likely to perform the best?

   a. Ahn is not at all stressed about the presentation. He has done well all semester and is confident he will do just fine this time around, too. He puts together his slides a week before the due date and then reviews the talk a few hours before giving the presentation.

   b. Sonya is somewhat anxious about this presentation. She knows her stuff but recognizes how much is riding on the quality of this presentation. This anxious energy motivates her to polish her slides and practice her talk.

   c. Marcus is very stressed about this presentation. A bad evaluation on the presentation will ruin his grade for the class, which in turn will ruin his strong GPA. He decides to spend every waking moment preparing the talk, working late into the night and sometimes dreaming about the presentation.

2. Which neurotransmitter is *not* implicated in the sexual response?
   a. dopamine
   b. GABA
   c. nitric oxide
   d. serotonin

The answer key for the Practice Tests can be found at the back of the book. It also includes answers to the green caption questions.

Health and Well-Being

WAS GARY STOCKLAUFER TOO FAT TO BE A PARENT? He was a happily married man, a state-certified foster parent, and the adoptive father of a great son. When his cousin was unable to raise Max, the cousin's baby son, Stocklaufer and his wife stepped in as the child's foster parents. After three months, they filed the paperwork to adopt their cherished foster son. A judge in Missouri, who also presided over Stocklaufer's earlier adoption, said no. The judge cited Stocklaufer's weight—at the time, between 500 and 600 pounds—as the reason for the denial. Apart from his weight, the Stocklaufers were healthy, but the judge reasoned that Mr. Stocklaufer was likely to develop a serious disease and die at a young age because he was obese (**Figure 11.1**).

When asked about the case, the judge responded that he was required to consider the welfare and best interests of the child. The National Association to Advance Fat Acceptance (NAAFA),

FIGURE 11.1 Gary Stocklaufer Stocklaufer is shown here weighing over 500 pounds. Shortly after this photograph was taken, he underwent surgery to help him lose weight.

Learning Objectives

- Discuss the goals of health psychology.

- Describe the biopsychosocial model of health.

- Identify behaviors that contribute to the leading causes of death in industrialized societies.

- Describe the placebo effect.

health psychology A field that integrates research on health and on psychology; it involves the application of psychological principles to promote health and well-being.

well-being A positive state that includes striving for optimal health and life satisfaction.

asking whether "fat = poor parenting," established a legal defense fund for Stocklaufer. Ultimately, the case was appealed, and the judge reversed his earlier ruling because Stocklaufer had lost over 200 pounds following gastric bypass surgery.

Stocklaufer's case is only one of many similar stories in which fat people were denied the right to adopt. Is it reasonable to consider someone's weight when deciding something as important as adoption? Since body weight has a substantial genetic component, should a potential parent be held accountable for his or her weight? Would it make a difference if we could show that the potential parent's obesity was caused by factors beyond the person's control? Would a judge be acting in the children's best interests if he or she ruled that people who smoke cannot adopt children? What about people with diabetes or other conditions associated with a reduced life span? In considering health and well-being, this chapter will examine individual differences and individuals' rights. ■

11.1 Can Psychosocial Factors Affect Health?

People often think about health and wellness in biological and medical terms. They are therefore surprised to learn that their behaviors and attitudes affect their health. The traditional medical model emphasizes disease states and the treatments, including drugs, designed to rid us of disease. According to this model, people are passive recipients of disease and of the medical treatments designed to return them to health after illness. The underlying idea in the traditional medical model is that health professionals know best and thus maintain control over what happens to the patient. Psychologists—and, increasingly, many medical professionals—take a more holistic and active approach to health and well-being. They believe our behaviors and attitudes are critical in keeping us healthy, helping us regain health following illness, and helping us achieve well-being. As you will learn in this chapter, a healthy lifestyle goes a long way toward promoting health and preventing disease.

Health psychology, one of psychology's many subdisciplines, is an area of study that integrates research on health and on psychology. This field was launched nearly three decades ago, when psychologists, physicians, and other health professionals came to appreciate the importance of lifestyle factors to physical health. Health psychologists apply their knowledge of psychological principles to promote health and well-being, instead of thinking about health merely as the absence of disease.

Well-being is a positive state in which we feel our best. To achieve this state, we need to strive for optimal health and life satisfaction. To achieve optimal health, we need to actively participate in health-enhancing behaviors. Health and well-being is a growing area of psychology, and some psychologists provide health services and conduct research on the health outcomes of different behaviors and emotions. Some psychologists, recognizing the importance of behavioral and psychological variables in health, integrate their practices with medical professionals in a wide range of health contexts, such as diabetes, cardiology, and rehabilitation.

Psychologists who study health and well-being rely on the research methods of psychology to understand the interrelationship between thoughts (health-related cognitions), actions, and physical and mental health. Researchers address issues such as ways to help people lead healthier lives. They study how our behavior and social systems affect our health and how ethnic and sex differences influence health outcomes. Health psychologists also study the inverse of these relationships: how health-related behaviors and health outcomes affect our actions, thoughts, and emotions. Health psychology is necessarily an interdisciplinary field that combines theories and research from the various areas of health studies and of psychology.

The Biopsychosocial Model of Health Incorporates Multiple Perspectives for Understanding and Improving Health

How can a person's personality or thoughts or behaviors affect his or her health? To answer this question, you need to understand the **biopsychosocial model.** This model "views health and illness as the product of a combination of factors including biological characteristics (e.g., genetic predisposition), behavioral factors (e.g., lifestyle, stress, health beliefs), and social conditions (e.g., cultural influences, family relationships, social support)" (American Psychological Association, Health Psychology Division 38, n.d.). Research that integrates these levels of analysis helps to identify strategies that may help prevent disease and promote health.

As shown in **Figure 11.2,** our thoughts and actions affect the environments we choose to interact with, and those environments, in turn, affect the biological underpinnings of our thoughts and actions. To understand how this continuous loop operates in real life, suppose you are genetically predisposed to be anxious. You learn that one way to reduce your anxiety is to eat comfort foods such as mashed potatoes, macaroni and cheese, and ice cream. If you consume these foods in excess, you may gain weight and eventually become overweight. Overweight people often find that exercise is not very pleasant. If their extra weight makes even moderate exercise difficult, they may decrease their physical activity. That decrease would slow down their metabolism. The slower metabolism would cause them to gain weight. The circle would repeat. Additional examples of the interplay between biological, social, and psychological factors are presented elsewhere in this chapter.

The biopsychosocial model is central to understanding the difference between the traditional medical model and the approach taken by health psychologists. In the traditional model, the individual is passive. For health psychologists, the individual's thoughts, feelings, and behaviors are central to understanding and improving health.

Behavior Contributes to the Leading Causes of Death

Are you an anxious flyer? Are you afraid of being killed in a shark attack? Does the thought of eating a hamburger terrorize you? Like many people, you may be at least somewhat anxious about flying. You may (surreptitiously) look around for nearby sharks whenever you wade into the ocean. Most likely you do not find a hamburger terrifying. According to the statistics about the leading causes of death, however, you probably are fearing the wrong things. A statistical expert in the field of aviation who is also a professor at MIT explained the risk of death from flying this way: "It's once every

FIGURE 11.2 The Biopsychosocial Model This model illustrates how health and illness result from a combination of factors.

19,000 years—and that is only provided the person flew on an airplane once a day for 19,000 years!" (Barnett, quoted in "The six most feared," 2005, 5). Other researchers have estimated that 1 in 13 million passengers dies in an airplane crash. If you have read Chapter 8, you know that in the months following the September 11, 2001, terrorist attack in the United States, many people avoided flying. Instead, they preferred what they believed to be the safety of driving. Yet, as described more fully in Chapter 8, the number of people who died in automobile accidents because they chose to drive instead of fly after the attacks far exceeded the number of people who were killed in the attacks.

According to data from the U.S. National Center for Health Statistics (Xu, Kochanek, Murphy, & Tejada-Vera, 2010), people are most likely to die from causes that stem from their own behaviors, which they can learn to modify. For example, the most common cause of death in the United States in 2007 was heart disease, which was responsible for about 25 percent of the nearly 2.5 million deaths that year. Obesity, lack of exercise, smoking, high-fat diets, and, as you will learn later in this chapter, certain personality traits contribute to this cause of death. Those who suffer from heart disease are not always to blame for their conditions, because heart disease also occurs in easygoing people who lead healthy lives. But all of us can change our behaviors in ways that may reduce the likelihood of heart disease or postpone it until late in life.

Accidents are another leading cause of death. Most of us think about accidents as being beyond our control, but many accidents are avoidable. For accidents that are not avoidable, we can reduce the probability (e.g., by driving safely) and reduce the resulting injury (e.g., by wearing seat belts). Additional causes of death—accidental or not—include risky sexual behavior (AIDS is 100 percent preventable), the use of illegal drugs, the illegal use of legal drugs, and the use of firearms. It is easy to understand how our behaviors literally can kill us.

Even more sobering are the data regarding behaviors of both teenagers and young adults (Miniño, 2010). In this age group, almost half (48 percent) of all deaths are due to accidents, mostly car accidents. Homicides are the second leading cause of death (13 percent), closely followed by suicide (11 percent). It is a paradox of modern life that in the transition period between childhood and young adulthood, most people are at their strongest and in their best physical health, yet they sometimes make bad decisions that can have disastrous outcomes.

Lifestyle behaviors that begin in childhood and the teen years may decrease health or even lead to death. For example, although relatively few teens die from heart disease, poor eating habits ("You want fries with that burger?") contribute to heart disease later in life. Violence, accidents, obesity, lack of exercise, risky sexual behaviors, the use and abuse of drugs—all these negative factors are associated strongly with young people.

In your great-grandparents' generation, and even more so in their parents' generation, the leading causes of death were childbirth, infectious diseases, and accidents. Thanks to advances in medicine and living conditions, the first two items on this list are rarely fatal in modern societies. Hunger and malnutrition, like disease, remain tragic realities in developing countries, but most industrialized countries have made great progress in feeding their populations. The abundance of cheap, tasty food has brought new health problems to the developed world, however. As the interrelated biopsychosocial model makes clear, good and bad behaviors influence environments, and environments in turn influence the good and bad biological bases of behaviors.

Identifying Regression to the Mean

Think about a time when you had a cold or flu. Did you wait until you felt very ill before you started taking medicine or before you made an appointment to see a physician? If so, you are like most people, who seek medical help only when their symptoms are bad. Usually when you are sick, you will get better no matter what you do. That is, eventually you will return to your usual state of not feeling sick. If you wait until you are very sick to get medical help, then often almost anything you do, including nothing at all, will be followed with feeling better. Because you went to the doctor, however, you might credit the doctor with making you feel better.

For any range of events, a more extreme event (in this case, feeling very sick) will tend to be followed by an event closer to the average or mean (in this case, feeling okay). This principle is true for statistical reasons, and it operates in almost every situation. The phenomenon being described is called *regression to the mean*.

Regression to the mean can be a difficult concept to understand and recognize because most of us usually have other explanations for why we returned to more normal states. Consider a golfer who repeatedly plays on the same course for years. Over the years, the golfer usually shoots around par (his or her average score for the given course). One day, the golfer shoots five under par (does better than usual). How do you think this person is likely to do the next time she or he plays? In all likelihood, the person would score closer to par. Now suppose the same golfer has a bad day and shoots five over par. Trying now to correct the problem, the golfer slightly changes his or her swing. Sure enough, the next time the golfer's score is back around par. But now the golfer attributes the better performance to the change in swing. The real reason for the better performance is probably regression to the mean. The golfer has simply experienced a normal day rather than a bad one

As presented in the biopsychosocial model, our thoughts—in this case, the ways we explain both why we get sick and how we get well—are a critical determinant of how we take care of our health. Such thoughts often direct our behaviors, which in turn affect the biological underpinnings of health and well-being.

Remember: An extreme event will most likely be followed by a less extreme event. If you are aware of this principle, regression to the mean, you are less likely to believe an unrelated factor is responsible for the return to a more normal state (**Figure 11.3**).

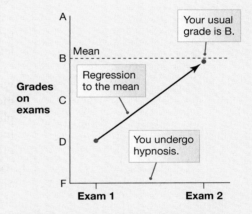

FIGURE 11.3 Identifying Regression to the Mean Suppose you study as usual for an exam. Just by bad luck, the professor asks questions you cannot answer, so you get a very low grade. If you study as usual for the next exam, you are likely (but not guaranteed) to get a grade closer to your usual grades. If you study as usual but also go to a hypnotist to help calm your anxiety for the next exam, what will most likely happen? What factors would explain the result? (Hint: On the realities of hypnosis, see the Critical Thinking Skill in Chapter 4, "Sensation and Perception.")

Placebos Can Be Powerful Medicine

Suppose you feel sick and go to a doctor, but the doctor does not take your complaint seriously. To keep you happy, the doctor prescribes, unknown to you, "sugar pills." You, believing the pills will work because the doctor said they would, feel better. Stories like this one usually end with a good laugh about how gullible and foolish the patient is. In this story, the pills act as placebos. That is, they have no apparent physiological effect on the health condition for which they are prescribed.

placebo effect An improvement in health following treatment with a placebo—that is, with a drug or treatment that has no apparent physiological effect on the health condition for which it was prescribed.

Scientists often study a drug or treatment by comparing it with a placebo. As described in Chapter 2, research participants typically are assigned at random to either an experimental group or a control group. In this case, the experimental group would receive the drug or treatment, and the control group would receive a placebo. Ideally, everything about the two groups is as similar as possible. If the treatment consists of a large blue pill or weekly injections or dietary restrictions, the placebo group would take a large blue pill or receive weekly injections or follow different dietary restrictions. For the placebo group, however, the pill might be made of sugar, the injections might deliver only water, and the diet might restrict foods believed to be unrelated to the treatment. Would you guess that some participants get well with only placebos? In fact, they do. This improvement in health, attributed to the inert drug or bogus treatment, is called the **placebo effect.**

The validity of the placebo effect is complicated. After all, statistically speaking, most people's illnesses will improve even without treatment (see "Critical Thinking Skill: Identifying Regression to the Mean"). Even a few people with presumably terminal illnesses seem to beat the odds. But do not assume that when you are ill you will always have statistics on your side. For example, you cannot determine how long a minor illness might take to improve, or what complications it might produce if left untreated, or whether it is in fact the beginning of a major illness. When you are suffering, seek appropriate treatment. When you are well, take preventive measures.

For a placebo to improve health, the participant must believe it will. The person who receives the placebo must not know that, for example, the pills are chemically inert. Indeed, as discussed further in Chapter 15, the placebos that produce minor physical reactions that people associate with drug effects—such as having a dry mouth—produce the strongest placebo effects. Have you ever gone to a doctor's office feeling very sick—and noticed that as soon as the doctor said your problems were not serious, you immediately felt so relieved that you started feeling better? Some portion of the placebo effect is attributable to decreased anxiety, which creates various psychological changes that can reduce pain and help recovery from an illness. But the placebo effect clearly is more than a reduction in anxiety. We cannot separate the effects of our minds from those of our bodies, because they are seamlessly the same. The placebo effect is "all in the head," but the effect is real—all of our thoughts and feelings are in our heads. Thus the placebo effect is gaining new respect now that psychologists have a better understanding of its biological bases.

As discussed in Chapter 4, pain is more than just a sensory experience. How much pain people feel depends on many variables, including context (e.g., being on a battlefield versus being at home), expectations (i.e., feeling anxious or calm about a potentially painful experience), and thoughts about the pain (e.g., imagining it as less unpleasant). When people are calmer, their pain is less intense, so an important part of getting well lies in finding ways to reduce anxiety. Placebos can reduce pain perception when people believe they will (Wager, 2005). Brain imaging shows that when patients have positive expectations about a placebo, the neural processes involved in responding to it are similar to the ones activated in response to a biologically active treatment (Benedetti, Mayberg, Wagner, Stohler, & Zubieta, 2005). Consider drugs that interfere with the body's natural method of reducing pain. These drugs also make pain relievers or placebos equally ineffective (Amanzio & Benedetti, 1999). This result indicates that the body has responded in the same way to the pain relievers and to the placebos.

The placebo effect is a good example of the biopsychosocial model at work. The belief that a medication will work is a psychological factor, and it affects the body in ways similar to those of medications, or treatments, with known biological effects. These effects occur within a social context that determines if, when, and

Recognizing Placebo Effects When Evaluating Treatment Claims

Placebo effects can occur in many health contexts. Critical thinkers need to watch out for these effects in various settings.

Suppose you are participating in a study. The researchers tell you that your room is being infused with an odorless substance that will make you feel better. Each day, the researchers ask you to write about how you feel that day and whether you feel better than you did the previous day. If you believe their claim about the odorless substance, you probably will feel a little better each day. You might attribute this subjective judgment about how you feel to the odorless chemical you supposedly are breathing.

In fact, we fall for such false claims all the time. Consider this advertisement for copper bracelets, which is paraphrased only slightly:

> For hundreds of years people have worn copper bracelets to relieve pain from arthritis. This folklore belief has persisted, and copper bracelets continue to be popular. These bracelets promote close contact between the copper and your wrist.

The advertisement does not say that copper bracelets relieve arthritis pain. The bracelets do not have this effect, and explicitly saying they do could lead to legal problems. But what do people remember after reading this advertisement? They remember reading that copper bracelets are good for arthritis. Many people wear copper bracelets and believe the bracelets provide some relief for their arthritis pain (**Figure 11.4**). You might ask if it matters as long as people feel less pain. Yes, it matters, because people who fall for phony treatments often avoid medical care. Ultimately, medical care can provide greater pain relief than people receive from these placebo bracelets. In addition, people are paying for treatments that do not really treat their health problem.

A believer in copper bracelets might ask: If it really does not work, then why do I feel better? No one believes he or she will fall for a placebo. It can be difficult to acknowledge that much of how we feel—but by no means all of it—is influenced by our beliefs.

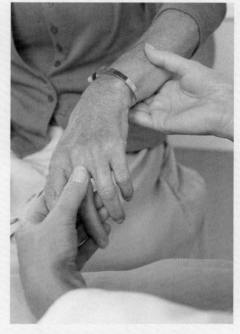

FIGURE 11.4 Recognizing Placebo Effects Many people believe copper and zinc increase circulation. The idea appeals to those suffering from conditions such as arthritis, but any relief people feel from such "treatments" might be only a placebo effect.

how much the body will respond to the placebo. In the study of health and well-being, it can be difficult to separate psychological, biological, and social influences. A holistic approach considers all these elements of health.

Summing Up

Can Psychosocial Factors Affect Health?

Health psychology integrates research on health and on psychology. The biopsychosocial model of health and illness posits the interaction of biological variables (such as genetic predispositions), behavioral variables (such as lifestyle, stress, and beliefs), and social variables (such as cultural beliefs about diseases and social support). The leading causes of serious illness and death in modern industrialized societies are, at least in part, behavioral. Behaviors such as overeating, not exercising, and smoking contribute in large measure to the development of heart disease, which is the leading cause of death in the United States. Among teens and young adults, accidents, homicide, and suicide are the leading causes of death. In fact, almost half of all deaths in this age range are due to accidents, many of them preventable. Placebos can powerfully affect health. Research suggests that placebos affect our neural processes in ways that are similar to biologically active treatments.

Measuring Up

1. Of the following possibilities, select one way that our behaviors contribute to reduced health.
   a. We can make unhealthy choices, such as eating a poor diet and smoking.
   b. We can have genetic predispositions to obesity.
   c. We can refuse to be in any research that has a placebo control group.
   d. Our beliefs in a placebo can result in neural activity similar to the neural activity that results from biologically active treatments.
   e. Our personalities cannot be controlled, so they cannot affect our health behaviors.
   f. By being too passive, we allow other people to take advantage of us, often to the detriment of our health.

2. Which of the following statements exemplifies the biopsychosocial model?
   a. The heart is a biological organ that we cannot control directly, so we rely on other people to affect the health of our hearts.
   b. By engaging in healthy behaviors, we can strengthen our immune systems.
   c. Reckless people exist in every society in the world, so behaviors related to accidents are not likely to be affected by culture.
   d. That hostile people cannot change their personalities proves that biology influences health.

Answers: 1. a. We can make unhealthy choices, such as eating a poor diet and smoking. 2. b. By engaging in healthy behaviors, we can strengthen our immune systems.

Learning Objectives

- Define stress.
- Describe the hypothalamic-pituitary-adrenal axis.
- Discuss sex differences in responses to stressors.
- Describe the general adaptation syndrome.
- Discuss the association between personality traits and health.
- Distinguish between emotion-focused coping and problem-focused coping.
- Define hardiness.

11.2 How Do We Cope with Stress?

Stress is a basic component of our daily lives (**Figure 11.5**). However, stress does not exist objectively, out in the world. Instead, it results directly from the ways we think about events in our lives. For example, some students respond to final exams as extremely stressful and often get sick at exam time, whereas other students perceive the same finals as mere inconveniences. When researchers study stress, then, what are they studying?

Stress is a pattern of behavioral, psychological, and physiological responses to events that match or exceed an organism's ability to respond in a healthy way. A **stressor** is an environmental event or stimulus that threatens an organism. A stressor elicits a **coping response,** which is any response an organism makes to avoid, escape from, or minimize an aversive stimulus. When too much is expected of us or when events are worrisome or scary, we perceive a discrepancy between the demands of the situation and the resources of our biological, psychological, and social systems. That discrepancy might be real, or we might be imagining it. In general, positive and negative life changes are stressful. Think about the stresses of going to college, getting a job, marrying, being fired, losing a parent, winning a major award, and so on. The greater the number of

FIGURE 11.5 **Stress in Everyday Life**
How do you cope with the stress in your life? What makes your strategies effective?

changes, the greater the stress, and the more likely it is that the stress will affect our physiological states.

Stress is often divided into two types: *Eustress* is the stress of positive events. For example, you might experience eustress when you are admitted to the college you really want to attend or when you are preparing for a party you are looking forward to. *Distress, also called duress,* is the stress of negative events. For example, you might experience distress when you are late for an important meeting and become trapped in traffic or when you are helping a loved one deal with a serious illness.

Most people use the term *stress* only in referring to negative events, but both distress and eustress put strains on our bodies. Different levels of stress are optimal for different people. It is essential for each of us to develop a sense of how much stress we can handle comfortably. That information can help us recognize the effects of stress on our individual mental, physical, and emotional well-being. It can also help us make life choices, such as the type of career to pursue.

Psychologists typically think of stressors as falling into two categories: major life stressors and daily hassles. *Major life stressors* are changes or disruptions that strain central areas of people's lives. Major life stressors include choices made by individuals, not just things that happen to them. For instance, some parents report that having their first child is one of the most joyful—but also one of the most taxing—experiences of their lives. Nonetheless, research has shown that unpredictable and uncontrollable catastrophic events (such as floods, earthquakes, or wars) are especially stressful. To avoid serious health problems, combat soldiers and others in prolonged stressful situations often must use combinations of strategies to cope with the stress of their situations.

Daily hassles are small, day-to-day irritations and annoyances, such as driving in heavy traffic, dealing with difficult people, or waiting in line. Daily hassles are stressful, and their combined effects can be comparable to the effects of major life changes. Because these low-level irritations are ubiquitous, they pose a threat to coping responses by slowly wearing down personal resources. Studies that ask people to keep diaries of their daily activities find consistently that the more intense and frequent the hassles, the poorer the physical and mental health of the participant. People may habituate to some hassles but not to others. For example, conflicts with other people appear to have a cumulative detrimental effect

stress A pattern of behavioral, psychological, and physiological responses to events, when the events match or exceed the organism's ability to respond in a healthy way.

stressor An environmental event or stimulus that threatens an organism.

coping response Any response an organism makes to avoid, escape from, or minimize an aversive stimulus.

hypothalamic-pituitary-adrenal (HPA) axis The biological system responsible for the stress response.

fight-or-flight response The physiological preparedness of animals to deal with danger.

on health and well-being. Living in poverty or in a crowded, noisy, or polluted place also can have cumulative detrimental effects on health and well-being.

Stress Has Physiological Components

Researchers have a good understanding of the biological mechanisms that underlie the stress response. A stressor activates a complex chain of events, in what is known as the **hypothalamic-pituitary-adrenal (HPA) axis.**

As shown in **Figure 11.6,** stress begins in the brain with the perception of some stressful event. For our very distant ancestors, the event might have been the sight of a predator approaching at a rapid clip. For us, it is more likely to be an approaching deadline, a stack of unpaid bills, a fight, an illness, and so on. In the HPA axis, the hypothalamus sends a chemical message to the pituitary gland (a major gland located just below the brain). In turn, the pituitary gland secretes the hormone ACTH (short for adrenocorticotropic hormone). ACTH travels through the bloodstream and eventually reaches the adrenal glands (located near the kidneys). The adrenal glands then secrete cortisol. In turn, cortisol increases the amount of glucose in the bloodstream. The adrenal glands also release norepinephrine and epinephrine, which activate the sympathetic nervous system, increasing blood pressure, heart rate, and other sympathetic responses (see Chapter 3, "Biology and Behavior"). All of these actions help the body prepare to respond to the stressor. For example, the response might consist of fighting an attacker.

Because hormones have long-lasting effects, stress affects organs after the stressor has been removed. Studies of stress show that, in human and nonhuman animals, excessive stress disrupts working memory, an effect that is especially noticeable when the demands on working memory are high (Oei, Everaerd, Elzinga, Van Well, & Bermond, 2006). Chronic stress has also been associated with long-term memory impairments: Cortisol damages neurons in brain areas such as the hippocampus, which is important for storing long-term memories (Sapolsky, 1994). Stress also interferes with the ability to retrieve information from long-term memory (Diamond, Fleshner, Ingersoll, & Rose, 1996).

There Are Sex Differences in How We Respond to Stressors

From an evolutionary perspective, the ability to deal effectively with stressors is important to survival and reproduction. The physiological and behavioral responses that accompany stress help mobilize resources to deal with danger. The physiologist Walter Cannon coined the term **fight-or-flight response** to describe the physiological preparation of animals to deal with an attack (**Figure 11.7**). Within seconds or minutes, this response to a stressor allows the organism to direct all energy to dealing with the threat at hand. Thus the HPA axis was an efficient system for our ancestors because it results in increased energy. Our ancestors needed that energy for either outrunning a charging predator or standing their ground and fighting it. (Either response causes further stress.) The physical reaction includes increased heart rate, re-

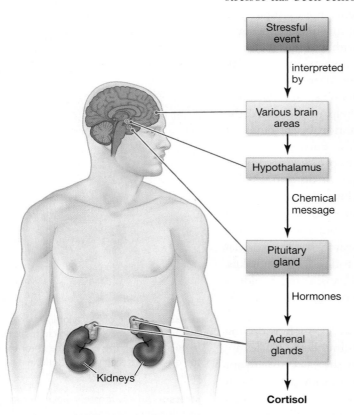

FIGURE 11.6 Hypothalamic-Pituitary-Adrenal (HPA) Axis A stressful event will set off a complex chain of responses in the body.

distribution of the blood supply from skin and viscera (digestive organs) to muscles and brain, deepening of respiration, dilation of the pupils, inhibition of gastric secretions, and an increase in glucose released from the liver. At the same time, less critical autonomic activities such as food digestion, which can occur after the stressor is removed, are postponed. (The autonomic system is described in more detail in Chapter 3.)

The generalizability of the fight-or-flight response has been questioned by Shelley Taylor and colleagues (Tayor, 2006; Taylor et al., 2002). They argue that because the vast majority of human and nonhuman animal research has been conducted using males (females represent fewer than 1 in 5 of the participants), the results have distorted the scientific understanding of responses to stress. The exclusion of females from these early studies has many possible explanations. For example, researchers often use rats in studies of heart disease that cannot be conducted with humans because the research might increase participants' risk of heart disease, and most rat studies use male rats to avoid complications that may be caused by female hormonal cycles. Similarly, most researchers have avoided using women in their studies of responses to stress because female menstrual patterns might make women more difficult to study. That is, women's responses could be mediated by (influenced by) fluctuations in circulating hormones that vary over the menstrual cycle. The result is a sex inequality in laboratory stress studies. This research bias can blind us to the fact that women and men often respond differently to stressors.

Taylor and colleagues argue that, in very general terms, females respond to stress by protecting and caring for their offspring, as well as by forming alliances with social groups to reduce risks to individuals, including themselves. They coined the phrase **tend-and-befriend response** to describe this pattern (**Figure 11.8**). Tend-and-befriend responses make sense from an evolutionary perspective. Females typically bear a greater responsibility for the care of offspring, and responses that protect their offspring as well as themselves would be maximally adaptive. When a threat appears, quieting the offspring and hiding may be more effective means of avoiding harm than trying to flee while pregnant or with a clinging infant. Furthermore, females who selectively affiliate with others, especially other females, might acquire additional protection and support.

The tend-and-befriend stress response is an excellent example of how thinking about psychological mechanisms in view of their evolutionary significance may lead us to question long-standing assumptions about how the mind works. Females who respond to stress by nurturing and protecting their young and by forming alliances with other females apparently have a selective advantage over those who fight or flee, and thus these behaviors would pass to future generations.

Oxytocin, a hormone important for mothers in bonding to newborns, is produced in the hypothalamus and released into the bloodstream through the pituitary gland. Recent research has shown that oxytocin levels tend to be high for women, but not men, who are socially distressed. Although oxytocin exists naturally in men and women, it seems especially important in women's stress response. Thus it provides a possible biological basis for the tend-and-befriend response to stress exhibited (mainly) by women (Taylor, 2006). A great deal of research currently is being conducted on the role of oxytocin during stress responses. According to one recent hypothesis, it is possible that the release of oxytocin during social stress encourages women to affiliate with, or befriend, others (Taylor, Saphire-Bernstein, & Seeman, 2010).

FIGURE 11.7 Fight-or-Flight Response This response is an organism's tendency to prepare for dealing with a stressor. Here the man on the left appears to be the aggressor and the man on the right appears to be holding himself in readiness. If the man on the left strikes, the man on the left will need to respond, such as by fighting or fleeing.

FIGURE 11.8 Tend-and-Befriend Response This response is females' tendency to care for offspring and gather in social groups. Here women guide a group of schoolchildren.

tend-and-befriend response Females' tendency to protect and care for their offspring and form social alliances rather than flee or fight in response to threat.

oxytocin A hormone that is important for mothers in bonding to newborns and may encourage affiliation during social stress.

immune system The body's mechanism for dealing with invading microorganisms, such as allergens, bacteria, and viruses.

general adaptation syndrome A consistent pattern of responses to stress that consists of three stages: alarm, resistance, and exhaustion.

The General Adaptation Syndrome Is a Bodily Response to Stress

In the early 1930s, the endocrinologist Hans Selye began studying the physiological effects of sex hormones by injecting rats with hormones from other animals. Surmising that the foreign hormones must have caused these changes, Selye conducted further tests. He tried different types of chemicals, and he even physically restrained the animals to create stressful situations. Selye found that each manipulation produced roughly the same pattern of physiological changes: enlarged adrenal glands, decreased levels of *lymphocytes* (specialized white blood cells) in the blood, and stomach ulcers. The decreased lymphocytes result from damaged lymphatic structures—that is, from damage to part of the **immune system.** Together, the enlarged adrenal glands, damage to the immune system, and stomach ulcers reduce the organism's potential ability to resist additional stressors. Selye concluded that these responses are the hallmarks of a *nonspecific stress response.* He called this pattern the **general adaptation syndrome.**

The general adaptation syndrome consists of three stages: alarm, resistance, and exhaustion (**Figure 11.9**). The *alarm stage* is an emergency reaction that prepares the body to fight or flee. That is, physiological responses, such as release of cortisol and epinephrine, are aimed at boosting physical abilities while reducing activities that make the organism vulnerable to infection after injury. In this stage, the body is most likely to be exposed to infection and disease, so the immune system kicks in and the body begins fighting back. During the *resistance stage,* the defenses prepare for a longer, sustained attack against the stressor. Immunity to infection and disease increases somewhat as the body maximizes its defenses. When the body reaches the *exhaustion stage,* a variety of physiological and immune systems fail. Body organs that were already weak before the stress are the first to fail.

THE IMMUNE SYSTEM One of Selye's central points was that stress alters the functions of the immune system. Normally, when foreign substances such as viruses, bacteria, or allergens enter the body, the immune system launches into action to destroy the invaders. Stress interferes with this natural process. The field of *psychoneuroimmunology* studies the response of the body's immune system to psychological variables. More than 300 studies have demonstrated that short-term

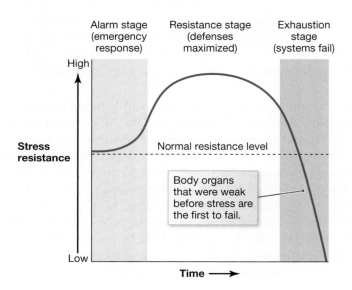

FIGURE 11.9 The General Adaptation Syndrome Selye described three stages of physiological response to stress. As shown here, the body may progress from alarm to resistance to exhaustion.

stress boosts the immune system, whereas chronic stress weakens it, leaving the body less able to deal with infection (Segerstrom & Miller, 2004).

The detrimental effects of long-term stress on physical health are due partly to decreased lymphocyte production. This decrease renders the body less capable of warding off foreign substances. In a particularly clear demonstration that stress affects the immune system, Sheldon Cohen and colleagues (1991) paid healthy volunteers to have cold viruses swabbed into their noses. Those who reported the highest levels of stress before being exposed to the cold viruses developed worse cold symptoms and higher viral counts than those who reported being less stressed (**Figure 11.10**). (Surprisingly, behaviors such as smoking, maintaining a poor diet, and not exercising had very small effects on the incidence of colds.) Apparently, when the underlying physiological basis of the stress response is activated too often or too intensely, the function of the immune system is impaired, and the probability and severity of ill health increase (Herbert & Cohen, 1993; McEwen, 2008).

In a study that looked specifically at the effects of desirable and undesirable events on the immune system, participants kept daily diaries for up to 12 weeks (Stone et al., 1994). In the diaries, they recorded their moods and the events in their lives. They rated the events as desirable or undesirable. Each day, the participants took an antigen, a substance (in this case a protein from a rabbit) that their immune systems recognized as a threat and therefore formed antibodies against. Then the participants provided saliva samples so the researchers could examine their antibody responses. The more desirable events a participant reported, the greater the antibody production. Similarly, the more undesirable events reported, the weaker the antibody production. The effect of a desirable event on antibodies lasted for two days. These and subsequent findings provide substantial evidence that perceived stress influences the immune system. Although short-term stressors appear to boost immune responses, chronic stress, especially when associated with changes in social roles or identity (such as becoming a refugee, losing a job, or getting divorced), has the greatest impact on the immune system (Segerstrom & Miller, 2004).

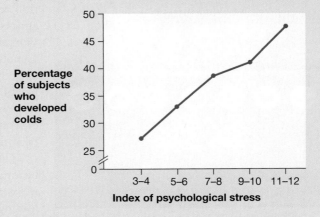

FIGURE 11.10 Scientific Method: Cohen's Study of Stress and the Immune System

Hypothesis: Stress affects health.

Research Method: Researchers swabbed the noses of healthy volunteers with cold viruses.

Results: Participants who reported higher levels of stress before being exposed to the cold viruses developed worse cold symptoms.

Conclusion: The functioning of the immune system can be impaired when a stress response is activated.

Source: Cohen, S., Tyrrell, D. A. J., & Smith, A. P. (1991). Psychological stress and susceptibility to the common cold. *New England Journal of Medicine, 325*, 606–612.

Stress Affects Health

Stress hormones are essential to normal health, but over the long term they negatively affect health. In addition to altering the function of the immune system, stress hormones are associated with problems such as increased blood pressure, cardiac disease, diabetes, declining sexual interest, and dwarfism in children (caused by the suppression of growth hormones). People who have very stressful jobs—such as air traffic controllers, combat soldiers, and firefighters—tend to have many health problems that presumably are due partly to the effects of chronic stress. There is overwhelming evidence that chronic stress, especially psychosocial stress, is associated with the initiation and progression of a wide variety of diseases, from cancer to AIDS to cardiac disease (Cohen, Janicki-Deverts, & Miller, 2007; McEwen & Gianaros, 2011; Thoits, 2010). In addition, many people cope with stress by engaging in damaging behaviors. For instance, the number one reason

FIGURE 11.11 Heart Disease To increase people's awareness of this growing problem, countries, cities, and local agencies employ public service campaigns like this one.

Type A behavior pattern A pattern of behavior characterized by competitiveness, achievement orientation, aggressiveness, hostility, restlessness, impatience with others, and inability to relax.

that problem drinkers give for abusing alcohol is to cope with distress in their lives. When people are stressed, they drink, smoke cigarettes, eat junk food, use drugs, and so on (Baumeister, Heatherton, & Tice, 1994). As discussed later in this chapter, most of the major health problems in industrialized societies are partly attributable to unhealthful behaviors, many of which occur when people feel stressed.

HEART DISEASE Coronary heart disease is the leading cause of death for adults in the industrialized world. According to a World Health Organization report in 2011, each year more than 7 million people die from heart attacks (**Figure 11.11**). Even though the rate of heart disease is lower in women than in men, heart disease is the number one killer of women. Genetics is among the many factors that determine heart disease, but two extremely important determinants are health behaviors and a small number of personality traits related to the way people respond to stress. Later, this chapter will discuss three major risk factors for heart disease: lack of exercise, obesity, and smoking. This section is concerned with the way personality traits can affect the heart.

The heart pumps nearly 2,000 gallons of blood each day, on average beating more than 100,000 times. A vast network of blood vessels carries oxygen and nutrients throughout the body. As people age, the arteries leading from the heart become narrow due to the buildup of fatty deposits, known as plaque. This narrowing makes it more difficult for the heart to pump blood and leads to coronary heart disease. When pieces of plaque break off from the wall of a blood vessel, blood clots form around the plaque and interrupt blood flow. If a clot blocks a blood vessel that feeds the heart, the blockage causes a heart attack. If a clot blocks a vessel that feeds the brain, the blockage causes a stroke.

Stress and negative emotions increase the risk of coronary heart disease (Albus, 2010; Sirois & Burg, 2003). Being stressed or feeling negative emotions can cause heart problems in two ways. First, people often cope with these states through behaviors that are bad for health, such as overeating, drinking excessively, or smoking. Second, over time, stress causes wear and tear on the heart, making the heart more likely to fail. Chronic stress leads to overstimulation of the sympathetic nervous system, causing higher blood pressure, constriction of blood vessels, elevated levels of cortisol, increased release of fatty acids into the bloodstream, and greater buildup of plaque on arteries; each of these conditions contributes to heart disease. For these reasons, people who tend to be stressed out are more likely to have heart disease than are people who tend to be laid-back.

One of the earliest tests of the hypothesis that personality affects coronary heart disease was conducted by the Western Collaborative Group, in San Francisco (Rosenman et al., 1964). In 1960, this group of physicians began an 8½-year study. The participants were 3,500 men from northern California who were free of heart disease at the start of the study. The men were screened annually for established risk factors such as high blood pressure, accelerated heart rate, and high cholesterol. Their overall health practices were assessed. Personal details—such as education level, medical and family history, income, and personality traits—also were assessed.

The results indicated that a set of personality traits predicted heart disease. This set of traits is now known as the **Type A behavior pattern.** Type A describes people who are competitive, achievement oriented, aggressive, hostile, impatient, and time-pressed (feeling hurried, restless, unable to relax). Men who exhibited these traits were much more likely to develop coronary heart disease than were those who exhibited the **Type B behavior pattern.** Type B describes non-competitive, relaxed, easygoing, accommodating people. In fact, this study found that a Type A personality was as strong a predictor of heart disease as was high blood pressure, high cholesterol, or smoking (Rosenman et al., 1975). Although the initial work was done only with men, more-recent research shows that these conclusions apply to women as well (Knox, Weidner, Adelman, Stoney, & Ellison, 2004; Krantz & McCeney, 2002).

Over the past 50 years, research has found that the original list of traits was too broad and that only certain components of the Type A behavior pattern are related to heart disease. For example, researchers have found that the most toxic factor on the list is hostility (Williams, 1987). Hot-tempered people who are frequently angry, cynical, and combative are much more likely to die at an early age from heart disease (Eaker, Sullivan, Kelly-Hayes, D'Agostino, & Benjamin, 2004). Indeed, having a high level of hostility while in college predicts greater risk for heart disease later in life (Siegler et al., 2003). But there is considerable evidence that negative emotional states not on the list, especially depression, also predict heart disease (Miller, Freedland, Carney, Stetler, & Banks, 2003). Of course, having a heart condition might *make* people hostile and depressed. Still, having a hostile personality and being depressed also predicted the worsening of heart disease, so causes and effects might be connected in a vicious cycle. In contrast, optimistic people tend to be at lower risk for heart disease (Maruta, Colligan, Malinchoc, & Offord, 2002). Learning to manage both stress and anger improves outcomes for those who have heart disease (Sirois & Burg, 2003). Later in this chapter, you will find many suggestions for managing stress.

How might negative personality traits combine to promote coronary heart disease? Being hostile, angry, or depressed can cause heart problems in two ways. First, as already noted, people often cope with their problems through behavioral strategies that are bad for health, and negative personality traits can increase people's problems — another vicious cycle. But negative personality traits also can produce direct physiological effects on the heart.

Think back to a time when you were very angry with someone. How did it feel to be so angry? Your body responded by increasing your heart rate, shutting down digestion, moving more blood to your muscles. In short, your body acted as though you were preparing to fight or run away. You may have seen someone turn red with anger or start to shake. People with hostile personalities frequently experience such physiological responses, and these responses take a toll on the heart. Chronic hostility can lead to the same physical symptoms as chronic stress. Over time, then, being hostile or angry causes wear and tear on the heart, making the heart more likely to fail.

Numerous studies have identified the biological pathways that lead from being angry and hostile to developing heart disease. As you might expect, the repeated cascade of bodily responses in hostile and angry individuals affects more than just the health of their hearts. Other bodily organs suffer as well. Researchers investigated whether an association existed between hostility and chronic pulmonary disease or early indicators that pulmonary disease was developing (Jackson, Kubzansky, Cohen, Jacobs, & Wright, 2007). Chronic pulmonary disease, a progressive condition in which airflow to the lungs is reduced, is a serious health risk in itself and a contributor to coronary heart disease. Even among the young, healthy participants in this study, higher levels of hostility were related to several measures of reduced pulmonary functioning.

Type B behavior pattern A pattern of behavior characterized by noncompetitive, relaxed, easygoing, and accommodating behavior.

TYPE Z BEHAVIOR

The evidence across multiple studies with different indices of disease and markers for the early development of disease is clear: Hostile, angry people are at greater risk for serious diseases and earlier death than are those with more optimistic and happier personalities. This conclusion appears to be universal. For example, a cross-cultural comparative study conducted with Japanese and non-Japanese college students replicated the association of anger and impatience with a wide range of health symptoms for students from all ethnic and cultural groups (Nakano & Kitamura, 2001).

Coping Is a Process

We all experience stressful events. To deal effectively with the stressors in our lives, we use cognitive appraisals that link feelings with thoughts. Cognitive appraisals enable us to think about and manage our feelings more objectively. Richard Lazarus (1993) conceptualized a two-part appraisal process: We use **primary appraisals** to decide whether stimuli are stressful, benign, or irrelevant. When we decide that stimuli are stressful, we use **secondary appraisals** to evaluate response options and choose coping behaviors. Such cognitive appraisals also affect our perceptions of potential stressors and our reactions to stressors in the future. In other words, making cognitive appraisals can help us prepare for stressful events. Coping that occurs before the onset of a future stressor is called *anticipatory coping*. For example, when parents are planning to divorce, they sometimes rehearse how they will tell their children.

TYPES OF COPING Susan Folkman and Richard Lazarus (1988) have grouped coping strategies into two general categories: In **emotion-focused coping,** a person tries to prevent an emotional response to the stressor. That is, the person adopts strategies, often passive, to numb the pain. Such strategies include avoidance, minimizing the problem, trying to distance oneself from the outcomes of the problem, or engaging in behaviors such as eating or drinking. For example, if you are having difficulty at school, you might avoid the problem by skipping class, minimize the problem by telling yourself school is not all that important, distance yourself from the outcome by saying you can always get a job if college does not work out, or overeat and drink alcohol to dull the pain of the problem. These strategies do not solve the problem or prevent it from recurring in the future. By contrast, **problem-focused coping** involves taking direct steps to solve the problem: generating alternative solutions, weighing their costs and benefits, and choosing between them. In this case, if you are having academic trouble, you might think about ways to alleviate the problem, such as arranging for a tutor or asking for an extension for a paper. Given these alternatives, you could consider how likely a tutor is to be helpful, discuss the problem with your professors, and so on. People adopt problem-focused behaviors when they perceive stressors as controllable and are experiencing only moderate levels of stress. Conversely, emotion-focused behaviors may enable people to continue functioning in the face of uncontrollable stressors or high levels of stress.

The best way to cope with stress depends on personal resources and on the situation. Most people report using both emotion-focused coping and problem-focused coping. Usually, emotion-based strategies are effective only in the short run. For example, if your partner is in a bad mood and is giving you a hard time, just ignoring him or her until the mood passes can be the best option. In contrast, ignoring your

primary appraisals Part of the coping process that involves making decisions about whether a stimulus is stressful, benign, or irrelevant.

secondary appraisals Part of the coping process during which people evaluate their response options and choose coping behaviors.

emotion-focused coping A type of coping in which people try to prevent having an emotional response to a stressor.

problem-focused coping A type of coping in which people take direct steps to confront or minimize a stressor.

partner's drinking problem will not make it go away, and eventually you will need a better coping strategy. Problem-focused coping strategies work, however, only if the person with the problem can do something about the situation.

In one study that tested the best way to cope with an extremely threatening situation (Strentz & Auerbach, 1988), 57 airline workers were held hostage for four days by five "terrorists." Even though the participants volunteered to be hostages and knew their captors were actually FBI agents, the situation was very realistic and extremely stressful. Half the participants had been trained to use emotion-based coping, and half had been trained to use problem-based coping. Can you predict which type of coping worked better? The emotion-based participants experienced less stress because they assumed any resistance they offered would just put them in greater danger. In other words, their best coping strategy was to remain calm. Problem-focused coping would have been ineffective in this scripted situation. In contrast, on September 11, 2001, the passengers on the hijacked United Airlines Flight 93 knew that three other planes had been crashed by terrorists that morning (see the opening of Chapter 8, "Thinking and Intelligence"). Assuming their hijackers also planned to crash Flight 93, these passengers knew they had an equal or better chance of surviving if they resisted. Some of them decided they had nothing to lose, chose a problem-based coping strategy, and fought back against the hijackers (**Figure 11.12**).

Susan Folkman and Judith Moskowitz (2000) have demonstrated that, in addition to problem-focused coping, two strategies can help people use positive thoughts to deal with stress. Both strategies involve *positive reappraisal*. Using this cognitive process, a person focuses on possible good things in his or her current situation. That is, the person looks for the proverbial silver lining. One strategy is to make *downward comparisons*, comparing oneself to those who are worse off. This kind of comparison has been shown to help people cope with serious illnesses. *Creation of positive events* is a strategy of giving positive meaning to ordinary events. For example, if you were diagnosed with diabetes, you could focus on how having diabetes would force you to eat a healthy diet and exercise regularly (positive reappraisal). You could recognize that diabetes is not as serious as heart disease (downward comparison). You could take joy in everyday activities (creation of positive events). For example, riding a bike, watching the sun set, or savoring a recent compliment might help you focus on the positive aspects of your life and deal with your negative stress.

INDIVIDUAL DIFFERENCES IN COPING People differ widely in their perceptions of how stressful life events are. Some people seem *stress resistant* because they are so capable of adapting to life changes by viewing events constructively. Suzanne Kobasa (1979) has named this personality trait *hardiness*. According to Kobasa, hardiness has three components: *commitment, challenge,* and *control*. People high in hardiness are committed to their daily activities, view threats as challenges or as opportunities for growth, and see themselves as being in control of their lives. People low in hardiness typically are alienated, fear or resist change, and view events as being under external control. Numerous studies have found that people high in hardiness report fewer negative responses to stressful events. In a laboratory experiment in which participants were given difficult cognitive tasks, people high in hardiness exhibited physiological changes that indicated active coping. Moreover, a questionnaire completed immediately after the tasks revealed that, in response to

FIGURE 11.12 Flight 93 This film still is from *United 93* (2006), a dramatic re-creation of events on the fourth hijacked plane on 9/11. Here passengers discuss their options after learning about the crashes of the three other planes. **If you had been one of these passengers, what type of coping strategy would you have used? What past cognitive appraisals would have led to your choice?**

the stressor, participants high in hardiness increased the number of positive thoughts they had about themselves.

Generally, some people are more resilient than others, better able to cope in the face of adversity (Block & Kremen, 1996). When faced with hardships or difficult circumstances, resilient individuals bend without breaking, allowing them to bounce back quickly when bad things happen. Those who are highest in resilience are able to use their emotional resources flexibly to meet the demands of stressful situations (Bonanno, 2004). In a study involving brain imaging, participants received one cue if they were about to see a threatening picture and a different cue if they were about to see a neutral picture (Waugh, Wager, Fredrickson, Noll, & Taylor, 2008). Sometimes, however, the threat cue was followed by a neutral picture rather than a threatening picture. In resilient individuals, there was increased activity in brain regions associated with anxiety only when threatening pictures appeared, regardless of the cue. In individuals low in resilience, there was heightened brain activity following the cue, whether the picture was threatening or not. Not only do those high in resilience show emotional flexibility, but they also recover from threats more quickly than do those low in resilience (Tugade & Fredrickson, 2004).

Can resilience be taught? Some researchers believe that people can become more resilient by following concrete steps (Algoe & Fredrickson, 2011). The steps in this process include coming to understand when particular emotions are adaptive, learning specific techniques for regulating both positive and negative emotions, and working to build healthy social and emotional relations with others.

FAMILY-FOCUSED INTERVENTIONS AND AUTONOMY At some point in life, many of us will suffer from a medical condition such as cancer, asthma, arthritis, heart disease, or AIDS. Perhaps our loved ones will suffer from chronic illness or chronic pain. One of the most stressful events in life is dealing with illness or pain. Although including family members in the treatment plan for a chronically ill person might seem important, research shows that including family members in a treatment plan is often not effective (Martire & Schulz, 2007). A major problem in enlisting family members is that the patient may feel as though family members are controlling his or her life rather than providing assistance. As previously discussed, being in control of essential decisions in one's life is a central component of hardiness. A common theme in the psychological literature is that this kind of control reduces stress and promotes well-being (Karasek & Theorell, 1990).

Family interventions can be beneficial, however, when family members promote the patient's autonomy. Some behaviors that seem to help when a family member has a chronic illness include (1) motivating the patient to make his or her own health and life choices and to carry out the activities of everyday living, (2) modeling healthy behaviors, (3) providing rewards, and (4) pointing out the positive consequences of caring for one's illness (Martire & Schulz, 2007). For example, family members might prepare food for the patient or help the patient practice relaxation techniques. By providing motivation, encouragement, and emotional support, families can also assist the patient in adjusting to life with the illness.

How Can I Avoid Getting Sick after Final Exams?

Many students feel ambivalent about the end of a semester. On the one hand, semester's end means a welcomed break from studies, more time to spend with friends and family, and more time to sleep. On the other hand, to make it to that break, students must first survive the stress of final exams. After successfully navigating finals week, many students feel run-down or get sick. Because they are nursing colds, viruses, or worse, they find themselves unable to fully enjoy all the perks of their much needed vacations. Why do so many students get sick right around final exams? What can you do to avoid that problem?

As decades of research have made clear, stress impairs immune function (Segerstrom & Miller, 2004). Brief stressors, including final examination periods, decrease the ability of our white blood cells (Kiecolt-Glaser & Glaser, 1991) and natural killer cells (Kang, Coe, McCarthy, & Ershler, 1997) to fight off infection. Our bodies even heal more slowly when we are stressed than when we are not stressed (Kiecolt-Glaser, Page, Marucha, MacCullum, & Glaser, 1998).

Adding insult to injury, the immune systems of those of us who tend to be particularly anxious (Maes et al., 2002) or who are already juggling a bunch of other daily hassles (Marshall, Agarwal, Lloyd, Cohen, Henninger, & Morris, 1998) tend to be especially vulnerable. Some of the behaviors that stressed-out college students may engage in—such as smoking cigarettes, drinking alcohol, and skipping sleep—further exacerbate the problem (Glaser & Kiecolt-Glaser, 2005).

In a nutshell, stress can wreak havoc on your immune system. To assess your current stress level, complete the Perceived Stress Scale (**Figure 11.13**). Note your current score. Then, at different points in the semester, complete the scale again. Compare your subsequent scores. Chances are good that, as the semester draws to a close,

---

FIGURE 11.13 Try for Yourself: The Perceived Stress Scale

This scale is one tool researchers use to assess stress among study participants. The 10 questions ask about your feelings and thoughts. Use the scale provided to indicate how often you felt or thought a certain way.

To compute your stress score, answer all 10 questions. Then reverse-code your responses to questions 4, 5, 7, and 8. That is, for those four questions, change 0s to 4s, 1s to 3s, 3s to 1s, and 4s to 0s (2s will remain 2s). Then add together all 10 answers.

| 0 = never | 1 = almost never | 2 = sometimes | 3 = fairly often | 4 = very often |

___ 1. In the last month, how often have you been upset because of something that happened unexpectedly?

___ 2. In the last month, how often have you felt that you were unable to control the important things in your life?

___ 3. In the last month, how often have you felt nervous and "stressed"?

___ 4. In the last month, how often have you felt confident about your ability to handle your personal problems?

___ 5. In the last month, how often have you felt that things were going your way?

___ 6. In the last month, how often have you found that you could not cope with all the things that you had to do?

___ 7. In the last month, how often have you been able to control irritations in your life?

___ 8. In the last month, how often have you felt that you were on top of things?

___ 9. In the last month, how often have you been angered because of things that were outside of your control?

___ 10. In the last month, how often have you felt difficulties were piling up so high that you could not overcome them?

SOURCE: Cohen, Kamarck, & Mermelstein, 1993.

---

your score will increase. Be mindful of shifts in your stress. When you notice an increase in stress, engage in stress-reducing behaviors. While it is not practical to abolish stress from our lives, we can take steps to minimize our stress and, along the way, to protect our immune systems. If at any point your stress score is higher than you would like, take some of these steps to lower it:

1. **Get enough sleep.** Even though you could use a couple more hours in the day, stealing those hours from your sleep affects your experience of stress and makes you less able to fight off illness. Try to get 8 hours of sleep every night.

2. **Exercise.** Getting even a little bit of exercise a couple times a week helps boost your mood and decrease stress.

3. **Eat healthfully.** Do not skip meals, but skip junk food. Make good decisions about what goes into your body.

4. **Meditate.** Engage in a little relaxation or meditation every day. For instructions on performing concentrative meditation and mindfulness meditation, see Figure 5.21.

5. **Connect.** Social support is another stress-busting tool, so make time for your friends. You might be tempted to put your friendships on hold during finals week, feeling you need to seclude

(continued)

yourself to get in all the studying you will need to ace your exams. Instead, see if you can make your stress-busting efforts a social pursuit.

You might be wondering: How am I supposed to sleep 8 hours a night, exercise, eat, meditate, connect daily, study, complete projects, *and* take exams? First, not all these suggestions for reducing stress will appeal to everyone. Pick the techniques you will find most restorative. Second, think creatively about how to combine these activities. For example, take a brisk walk around campus before heading into the dining hall. Take that walk with a friend, then sit down together to talk over a dinner of leafy greens, whole grains, and broiled fish. Take your books or laptop to a park to study, then take a 15-minute break to meditate in the sun. Third, do these things in moderation. Shoot for at least 20 minutes per day of nonsleep stress busting. That translates to just 140 minutes out of over 10,000 minutes during the week. Your health—and your ability to enjoy an illness-free break after finals—is worth 1.4 percent of your time!

Summing Up

How Do We Cope with Stress?

Stress occurs when people feel overwhelmed by the challenges they face. The term refers to a pattern of behavioral, psychological, and physiological responses to events, when the events match or exceed the individual's ability to respond in an adaptive way. Stressors include major life changes as well as daily hassles. The hypothalamic-pituitary-adrenal axis refers to the biological events that occur when we encounter a stressor. The hypothalamus sends a signal to the pituitary gland, which causes the adrenal gland to release hormones (such as cortisol, norepinephrine) into the bloodstream. Research suggests that when confronted by a stressor, females are more likely to tend and befriend, whereas males are more likely to fight or flee. Hans Selye's general adaptation syndrome identifies three stages of physiological coping: alarm, resistance, and exhaustion. Individuals who are hostile or depressed are more susceptible to heart disease, presumably due to the impact of frequent physiological responses that adversely affect the heart. Cognitive appraisals of potential stressors and the coping strategies that we use (emotion-focused coping strategies versus problem-focused coping strategies) can alleviate our experience of stress or minimize its harmful effects. Hardy people handle stress well because they are committed to and actively engage in what they do, they see obstacles as challenges to overcome, and they believe that they can control events in their lives. A sense of autonomy and control reduces stress and promotes well-being.

Measuring Up

1. Match each stage in the general adaptation syndrome—alarm, resistance, and exhaustion—with one of the following examples.
   a. After years of responding to tight deadlines at work, the executive developed several medical problems that required hospitalization.
   b. When Myrtle returned home and found a stranger in her living room, her heart began pounding rapidly.
   c. As the hurricane lashed the shore, nearby residents struggled to keep themselves safe.

11.3 What Behaviors Affect Mental and Physical Health?

The previous sections looked at how stress affects the body and how people cope with stress. This section looks at the effects of stress on behavior. Before the twentieth century, most people died from infections and from diseases transmitted person to person. But the last century saw a dramatic shift in the leading causes of mortality. According to a 2011 United States Census Bureau report, people now are most likely to die from heart disease, cancer, strokes, lung disease, and accidents. All of these causes of death are at least partially outcomes of lifestyle. Daily habits such as smoking, poor eating, alcohol use, and lack of exercise contribute to nearly every major cause of death in developed nations (Smith, Orleans, & Jenkins, 2004). Stress plays an important role in motivating each of these health-threatening behaviors. For example, a study of more than 12,000 people from Minnesota found that high stress was associated with heavier smoking, less-frequent exercise, and greater intake of fat (Ng & Jeffrey, 2003).

Obesity Results from a Genetic Predisposition and Overeating

Obesity is a major health problem with physical and psychological consequences. There is no precise definition of obesity. People are considered obese, however, if they are more than 20 percent over ideal body weight, as indicated by various mortality studies. One measure of obesity widely used in research is **body mass index (BMI)**, a ratio of body weight to height. **Figure 11.14** shows how to calculate BMI and how to interpret the value obtained. Understanding obesity requires a multilevel approach that examines behavior, underlying biology, cognition (how we think about food and obesity), and the societal context that makes cheap and tasty food readily available. In fact, obesity is an ideal example of the biopsychosocial model of health presented earlier in the chapter. As you read about obesity, keep in mind the linkages between genetic predispositions, thoughts, feelings, and behaviors as well as the continuous loop through which these variables cycle.

Learning Objectives

- Discuss the causes and consequences of obesity.
- Review evidence to support the set-point regulation of body weight.
- Contrast restrained and unrestrained eaters.
- Compare and contrast anorexia nervosa and bulimia nervosa.
- Discuss the causes and consequences of smoking.
- Review the benefits of regular exercise.
- Discuss ethnic differences in health behaviors.

body mass index (BMI) A ratio of body weight to height, used to measure obesity.

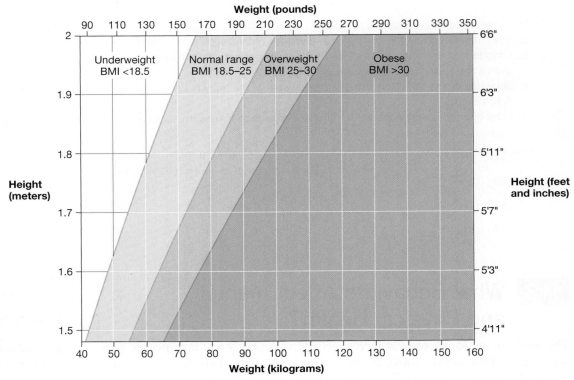

FIGURE 11.14 Determining Body Mass Index To determine your own BMI, find the point at which your weight and height meet on the graph. Beyond or below the optimal normal range, you are at greater risk for health problems.

In Western nations, there has been a rather dramatic increase in obesity. For example, according to nationally representative samples, obesity rates have increased dramatically in the United States, from fewer than 15 percent of the population meeting the criteria for obesity in 1980 to more than 33 percent meeting those criteria in 2008 (Flegal, Carroll, Ogden, & Curtis, 2010). Indeed, the numbers are even higher for racial and ethnic minorities, with nearly half of African American women (49.6 percent) and of Mexican American women (45.1 percent) classified as obese. Extreme obesity (having a BMI over 40), which was almost unheard of in 1960, now characterizes more than 1 in 20 Americans (Ogden & Carroll, 2010; **Figure 11.15**). Likewise, the percentage of obese children has quadrupled since the 1960s. This is not just a problem in the United States. According to the World Health Organization, obesity has doubled around the globe since 1980 (WHO, 2011). Given the numerous health consequences associated with obesity, there has been a great interest in understanding why people are gaining weight and what might be done to reverse this trend.

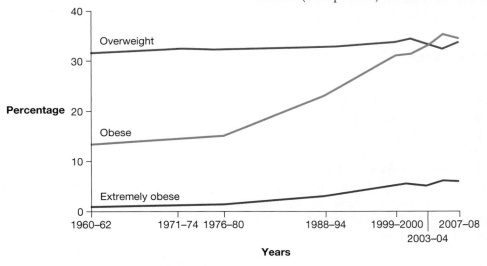

FIGURE 11.15 Trends in Overweight, Obesity, and Extreme Obesity This graph shows the trends in overweight, obesity, and extreme obesity among adults aged 20–74 in the United States, 1960–2008.

One factor that contributes to obesity is overeating, which some people are especially likely to do when stressed (Heatherton & Baumeister, 1991). Scientists do not know why some people can control how much they eat and others cannot. Some nonscientists believe that those who overeat are lazy or unmotivated. The truth is that obese people typically try multiple diets and other "cures" for fat, but dieting is a notoriously ineffective means of achieving permanent weight loss (Aronne, Wadden, Isoldi, & Woodworth, 2009). Most individuals who lose weight through dieting eventually regain the weight; often, they gain back more than they lost.

The availability of food is one factor in the maintenance of weight. For instance, rats that normally maintain a steady body weight when eating one type of food eat huge amounts and become obese when they are presented with a variety of high-calorie foods, such as chocolate bars, crackers, and potato chips (Sclafani & Springer, 1976; **Figure 11.16**). Humans show the same effect, eating much more when various foods are available than when only one or two types of food are available (Epstein, Robinson, Roemmich, Marusewski, & Roba, 2010; Raynor & Epstein, 2001). People also eat more when portions are larger (Rolls, Roe, & Meengs, 2007). In addition, overweight people show more activity in reward regions of the brain when they look at good-tasting foods than do normal-weight individuals (Rothemund et al., 2007). Together, these findings suggest that, in industrialized nations, the increase in obesity over the past few decades is partly explained by two factors: the sheer variety of high-calorie foods and the large portions served in many restaurants.

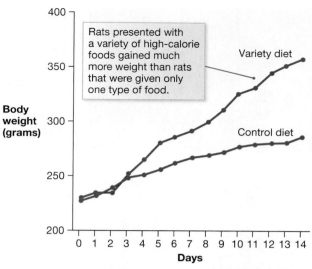

FIGURE 11.16 **The Impact of Variety on Eating Behavior** As shown in this graph, rats will become obese if given ample opportunity.

GENETIC INFLUENCE A trip to the local mall or anyplace families gather reveals one obvious fact about body weight: Obesity tends to run in families. Indeed, various family and adoption studies indicate that approximately half the variability in body weight can be considered the result of genetics (Klump & Culbert, 2007). One of the best and largest studies, carried out in Denmark during the 1980s, found that the BMI of adopted children was strongly related to the BMI of their biological parents and not at all to the BMI of their adoptive parents (Sorensen, Holst, Stunkard, & Skovgaard, 1992). Studies of identical and fraternal twins provide even stronger evidence of the genetic control of body weight. As discussed in Chapter 3, heritability refers to the proportion of variability, in a population, attributed to genetic transmission of a trait from parents to their offspring. Estimates of the heritability of body weight range from 60 percent to 80 percent. Moreover, the similarity between the body weights of identical twins does not differ for twins raised together versus twins raised apart (Bouchard & Pérusse, 1993; Wardle, Carnell, Haworth, & Plomin, 2008). This finding suggests that genetics has far more effect on body weight than environment has.

If genes primarily determine body weight, why has the percentage of Americans who are obese doubled over the past few decades? Albert Stunkard, a leading researcher on human obesity, points out that genetics determines whether a person *can* become obese, but environment determines whether that person *will* become obese (Stunkard, 1996). In an important study conducted by the geneticist Claude Bouchard, identical twins were overfed by approximately 1,000 calories a day for 100 days (Bouchard, Tremblay et al., 1990). Most of the twins gained some weight, but there was great variability among pairs in how much they gained (ranging from 4.3 kilograms to 13.3 kilograms, or 9.5 pounds to 29.3 pounds). Further, within the twin pairs there was a striking degree of similarity in how much weight they gained and in which parts of the body they stored the fat. Some of the twin pairs were especially likely to put on weight. Thus genetics determines sensitivity to environmental influences. Genes predispose some

(a)

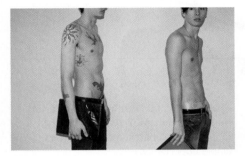

(b)

(c)

FIGURE 11.17 Variations in Body Image (a) In some places, people find larger body shapes more desirable. Consider these welcoming women on the island of Fatu Hiva, in French Polynesia. **(b, c)** By contrast, consider the skinniness embodied by these models in the United States.

people to obesity in environments that promote overfeeding, such as contemporary industrialized societies. Many genes are involved in obesity, as might be expected for such a complex condition: More than 300 genetic markers or genes have been identified as playing some role (Snyder et al., 2004).

THE STIGMA OF OBESITY As already noted, obesity is associated with a significant number of medical problems. It also can give rise to various psychological problems, primarily because of the extreme stigma associated with being overweight. In most Western cultures, obese individuals are viewed as less attractive, less socially adept, less intelligent, and less productive than their normal-weight peers (Dejong & Kleck, 1986). Moreover, perceiving oneself as overweight is linked to depression, anxiety, and low self-esteem (Stice, 2002). Bear in mind, however, that researchers cannot randomly assign people to conditions related to weight, depression, anxiety, or self-esteem. Therefore, most of the obesity research with human participants is correlational. For example, we can note links between being overweight and having low self-esteem, but we cannot say that one factor causes the other.

Not all cultures stigmatize obesity (Hebl & Heatherton, 1998). In some developing countries, such as many African nations, being obese is a sign of being upper class. Obesity may be desirable in developing countries because it helps prevent some infectious diseases, reduces the likelihood of starvation, and is associated with having more successful births. It may also serve as a status symbol in developing countries. That is, obesity may indicate that one can afford to eat luxuriously. In Pacific Island countries such as Tonga and Fiji, being obese is a source of personal pride, and dieting is uncommon (**Figure 11.17a**).

In most industrialized cultures, food is generally abundant. Therefore, being overweight is associated with lower socioeconomic status, especially for women. The upper classes in Western cultures have a clear preference for very thin body types, as exemplified in fashion magazines (**Figure 11.17b**). The typical woman depicted by the fashion industry is 5 feet 11 inches tall and weighs approximately 110 pounds (**Figure 11.17c**). In other words, the standard represented by models is 7 inches taller and 55 pounds lighter than the average woman in the United States. Such extreme thinness represents a body weight that is difficult, if not impossible, for most people to achieve. Indeed, women report holding body weight ideals that are not only lower than average weight but also lower than what men find attractive (Fallon & Rozin, 1985).

Such standards contribute to society's negative attitudes toward overweight people. According to Bettye Travis, the former president of the National Association to Advance Fat Acceptance (NAAFA), fat people are "one of the last marginal groups that are still targeted. . . . [I]t is still OK to make fun of fat people" (cited in Stewart, 2007, p. B7). After a lifetime of both shame and failed attempts to lose weight, she learned to say "the f word": *fat*. NAAFA exists to help fat people fight "size discrimination," as in being denied the right to be an adoptive parent (see the opening of this chapter). NAAFA members do not oppose attempts to lose weight, nor do they dispute the research indicating serious health risks for people who are obese. But after experiencing repeated disappointments with diets, they realize that they are likely to always be fat and that they must learn to accept themselves and to educate society about obesity. Given the rise in obesity in industrialized countries around the world, especially in the United States, the organization may see its membership grow. Even many obese people stigmatize obese people, however. Obese people with a prejudice against obesity may not want to join a group that advocates "fat acceptance."

RESTRICTIVE DIETING DOES NOT WORK Most diets fail primarily because of the body's natural defense against weight loss (Kaplan, 2007). Body weight is regulated around a set-point determined primarily by genetic influence. Consider two examples. In 1966, several inmates at a Vermont prison were challenged to increase their body weight by 25 percent (Sims et al., 1968). For six months, these inmates consumed more than 7,000 calories a day, nearly double their usual intake. If each inmate was eating about 3,500 extra calories a day (the equivalent of seven large cheeseburgers), simple math suggests that each should have gained approximately 170 pounds over the six months. In reality, few inmates gained more than 40 pounds, and most lost the weight when they went back to normal eating. Those who did not lose the weight had family histories of obesity.

At the other end of the spectrum, researchers have investigated the short-term and long-term effects of semistarvation (Keys, Brozek, Henschel, Mickelsen, & Taylor, 1950). During World War II, more than 100 men volunteered to take part in this study as an alternative to military service. Over six months, the participants lost an average of 25 percent of their body weight. Most found this weight reduction very hard to accomplish, and some had great difficulty losing more than 10 pounds. The men underwent dramatic changes in emotions, motivation, and attitudes toward food. They became anxious, depressed, and listless; they lost interest in sex and other activities; and they became obsessed with eating. Many of these outcomes are similar to those experienced by people with eating disorders.

Although it is possible to alter body weight, the body responds to weight loss by slowing down the metabolism and using less energy. Therefore, after the body has been deprived of food, it needs less food to maintain a given body weight. Likewise, weight gain occurs much faster in previously starved animals than would be expected by caloric intake alone. In addition, repeated alterations between caloric deprivation and overfeeding have been shown to have cumulative metabolic effects. That is, each time an animal is placed on caloric deprivation, the animal's metabolic functioning and weight loss become slower than they were the previous time. Each time overfeeding resumes, the animal's weight gain occurs more rapidly (Brownell, Greenwood, Stellar, & Shrager, 1986). This pattern might explain why "yo-yo dieters" tend to become heavier over time.

In addition, body weight is socially contagious. One study found that close friends of the same sex tend to be similar in body weight (Christakis & Fowler, 2007). This study also found that even when close friends live far apart from each other, if one friend is obese, the other one is likely to be obese as well. Studies of the social transmission of obesity suggest that it is not eating the same meals or cooking together that is critical. Instead, it is the implicit agreement on what body weight is acceptable or normal (**Figure 11.18**). If many of your close friends are obese, implicitly you learn that obesity is normal. Thus subtle communications can affect how we think and act when we eat. Such findings illustrate a main theme of this book: We are not aware of many of the psychological influences on our thoughts, behaviors, and attitudes.

RESTRAINED EATING Janet Polivy and Peter Herman (1985) characterize some chronic dieters as *restrained eaters*. According to Polivy and Herman, restrained eaters are prone to excessive eating in certain situations. These bouts of overeating may be occasional or not so occasional. For instance, if restrained eaters believe they have eaten high-calorie foods, they abandon their diets. Their mindsets become, "I've blown my diet, so I might as well just keep eating." Many restrained eaters diet through the workweek. On the weekend, when they are faced with increased food temptations and at the same time are in less structured

FIGURE 11.18 Body Weight Is Socially Contagious Friends tend to influence one another's sense of what body weight is appropriate.

environments, they lose control. In one study, restrained eaters and unrestrained eaters each consumed a large milk shake (Demos, Kelley, & Heatherton, 2011). When the restrained eaters then viewed pictures of appetizing food, there was increased activity in the brain regions connected with reward. By contrast, when the unrestrained eaters viewed the same pictures, the reward activity in their brains was reduced. Presumably, the milk shake had satisfied the unrestrained eaters. Thus the reward systems in the brains of restrained eaters seem to encourage additional eating after the eaters break their diets. Being under stress also leads restrained eaters to break their diets (Heatherton, Herman, & Polivy, 1991).

Binge eating by restrained eaters depends on their *perceptions* of whether they have broken their diets. Dieters can eat 1,000-calorie Caesar salads and believe their diets are fine. But if they eat 200-calorie chocolate bars, they feel their diets are ruined and they become disinhibited. Becoming disinhibited means that, after first inhibiting their eating, they lose the inhibition. In short, the problem for restrained eaters is that they rely on cognitive control of food intake: Rather than eating according to internal states of hunger and satiety, restrained eaters eat according to rules, such as time of day, number of calories, and type of food. If they feel that food is healthy, whether it is or not, they eat more of it (Provencher, Polivy, & Herman, 2009). Such patterns are likely to break down when dieters eat high-calorie foods or feel distressed. Getting restrained eaters back in touch with internal motivational states is one goal of sensible approaches to dieting.

DISORDERED EATING When dieters fail to lose weight, they often blame their lack of willpower. They may vow to redouble their efforts on the next diet. Repeated dietary failures may have harmful and permanent physiological and psychological consequences. In physiological terms, weight-loss and weight-gain cycles alter the dieter's metabolism and may make future weight loss more difficult. Psychologically, repeated failures diminish satisfaction with body image and damage self-esteem. Over time, chronic dieters tend to feel helpless and depressed. Some eventually engage in more extreme behaviors to lose weight, such as taking drugs, fasting, exercising excessively, or purging. For a vulnerable individual, chronic dieting may promote the development of a clinical eating disorder. The two most common eating disorders are *anorexia nervosa* and *bulimia nervosa* (Wiseman, Harris, & Halmi, 1998).

Individuals with **anorexia nervosa** have an excessive fear of becoming fat. As a result, they refuse to eat. Anorexia most often begins in early adolescence. Although it was once believed that this disorder mainly affected upper-middle-class and upper-class Caucasian girls, there is evidence that race and class are no longer defining characteristics of eating disorders (Polivy & Herman, 2002). This change might have come about because media images of a thin ideal have permeated all corners of society in the United States. Although many adolescent girls strive to be thin, fewer than 1 in 100 meet the clinical criteria of anorexia nervosa (**Table 11.1**). These criteria include both objective measures of thinness and psychological characteristics that indicate an abnormal obsession with food and body weight. Those who have anorexia view themselves as fat despite being at least 15 percent to 25 percent underweight. Issues of food and weight pervade their lives, controlling how they view themselves and how they view the world. Initially, the results of self-imposed starvation may draw favorable comments from others. But as the anorexic approaches her emaciated ideal, family and friends usually become concerned. In many cases, medical attention is required to prevent death from starvation. Anorexia is difficult to treat,

anorexia nervosa An eating disorder characterized by an excessive fear of becoming fat and thus a refusal to eat.

TABLE 11.1 Diagnostic Criteria for Anorexia Nervosa and Bulimia Nervosa

Criteria for Anorexia Nervosa	Criteria for Bulimia Nervosa
A. Refusal to maintain body weight at or above a minimum normal for age and height (e.g., weight loss leading to maintenance of body weight less than 85 percent of that expected; or failure to make expected weight gain during period of growth, leading to body weight less than 85 percent of that expected).	A. Recurrent episodes of binge eating. An episode of binge eating is characterized by both of the following: (1) Eating, in a discrete period (e.g., within any 2-hour period), an amount of food that is definitely larger than most people would eat during a similar period of time and under similar circumstances. (2) A sense of lack of control over eating during the episode (e.g., a feeling that one cannot stop eating or control what or how much one is eating).
B. Intense fear of gaining weight or becoming fat, even though underweight.	B. Recurrent inappropriate compensatory behavior in order to prevent weight gain, such as self-induced vomiting; misuse of laxatives, diuretics, enemas, or other medications; fasting; or excessive exercise.
C. Disturbance in the way in which one's body weight or shape is experienced, undue influence of body weight or shape on self-evaluation, or denial of the seriousness of the current low body weight.	C. The binge eating and inappropriate compensatory behaviors both occur, on average, at least twice a week for three months.
D. In postmenarcheal females, amenorrhea (the absence of at least three consecutive menstrual cycles).	D. Self-evaluation is unduly influenced by body shape and weight.

SOURCE: *American Psychiatric Association*, 2000a.

since patients maintain the belief that they are overweight or not as thin as they would like to be, even when they are severely emaciated. This dangerous disorder causes a number of serious health problems, in particular a loss of bone density, and about 15 percent to 20 percent of those with anorexia eventually die from the disorder—they literally starve themselves to death (American Psychiatric Association, 2000b).

Individuals with **bulimia nervosa** alternate between dieting and binge eating. Bulimia often develops during late adolescence. Approximately 1 percent to 2 percent of women in high school and college meet the definitional criteria for bulimia nervosa. These women tend to be of average weight or slightly overweight. They regularly binge-eat, feel their eating is out of control, worry excessively about body weight issues, and engage in one or more compensatory behaviors, such as self-induced vomiting, excessive exercise, or the abuse of laxatives. Whereas anorexics cannot easily hide their self-starvation, binge-eating behavior tends to occur secretly. When ordering large quantities of food, bulimics pretend they are ordering for a group. They often hide the massive quantities of food they buy for binges. They try to vomit quietly or seek out little-used bathrooms to avoid being heard while they vomit. Although bulimia is associated with serious health problems, such as dental and cardiac disorders, it is seldom fatal (Keel & Mitchell, 1997).

bulimia nervosa An eating disorder characterized by dieting, binge eating, and purging.

(a)

(b)

FIGURE 11.19 Smoking Is a Global Phenomenon (a) These men are smoking in Tiananmen Square, in Beijing, China. **(b)** These smokers belong to the Mentawi people, a seminomadic hunter-gatherer tribe in the coastal and rain forest regions of Indonesia.

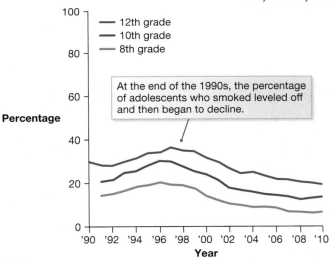

At the end of the 1990s, the percentage of adolescents who smoked leveled off and then began to decline.

FIGURE 11.20 Adolescents and Smoking This graph shows the percentages of adolescents who smoked in the given years.

A disorder similar to bulimia is *binge-eating disorder.* People with this disorder engage in binge eating at least twice weekly, but they do not purge. Many people with binge-eating disorder are obese. Compared to bulimia, binge-eating disorder is more common among males and ethnic minorities, and it tends to start at later ages (Wilfley, Bishop, Wilson, & Agras, 2007). Although bulimia and binge-eating disorder share many common features—differing most notably in that only bulimics purge—many researchers believe the two are distinct disorders (Striegel-Moore & Franco, 2008).

Eating disorders tend to run in families. Like obesity, these disorders are due partly to genetics. The incidence of eating disorders in the United States increased into the 1980s (Keel, Baxter, Heatherton, & Joiner, 2007). This increase suggests that when people have genetic predispositions for eating disorders, they will tend to develop the disorders if they live in societies with an abundance of food. Bulimia seems to be more culture bound, meaning that there are large cultural variations in its incidence. Anorexia is prevalent in all societies that have abundant food.

Smoking Is a Leading Cause of Death

Despite overwhelming evidence that smoking cigarettes leads to premature death, millions around the globe continue to light up (Carmody, 1993). According to the World Health Organization (2008), increasing numbers of people are smoking in low-income countries, and 5.4 million deaths are caused by tobacco every year. Thirty percent of all smokers worldwide are in China; 10 percent are in India; and an additional 25 percent come from Indonesia, Russia, the United States, Japan, Brazil, Bangladesh, Germany, and Turkey combined (**Figure 11.19**). The Centers for Disease Control and Prevention reported that in 2009, about 1 in 5 American adults was a current smoker. Smoking is blamed for more than 440,000 deaths per year in the United States and decreases the typical smoker's life by more than 12 years (Centers for Disease Control and Prevention, 2010a).

Most smokers begin in childhood or early adolescence. In the 1990s, every day nearly 5,000 Americans aged 11 to 17 smoked their first cigarette (Gilpin, Choi, Berry, & Pierce, 1999). About half of these young smokers will likely continue smoking into adulthood, and one-third of those will die from smoking (United States Department of Health and Human Services, 2001). Fortunately, after an increase in the 1990s, there has been a dramatic reduction in adolescent smoking over the last decade (Johnston, O'Malley, Bachman, & Schulenberg, 2011; **Figure 11.20**). Regular smoking dropped from approximately 13 percent to 7 percent, with a 33 percent drop in the number of adolescents who even try smoking (Centers for Disease Control and Prevention, 2010c).

Smoking causes numerous health problems, including heart disease, respiratory ailments, and various cancers. Cigarette smoke also causes health problems for nonsmoking bystanders, and this finding has led to bans on smoking in many public and private places. Smokers also endure scoldings from physicians, and loved ones, concerned for their health and welfare. Besides spending money on cigarettes, smokers pay significantly more for life insurance and health insurance. Why do they continue to smoke? Why does anyone start?

STARTING SMOKING It is hard to imagine any good reason to start smoking. First attempts at smoking often involve a great deal of coughing, watering eyes, a terrible taste in the mouth, and feelings of nausea. So why do kids persist? Most researchers point to powerful social influences as the leading cause of adolescent smoking (Chassin, Presson, & Sherman, 1990; **Figure 11.21**). Research has demonstrated that adolescents are more likely to smoke if their parents or friends smoke (Hansen et al., 1987). They often smoke their first cigarettes in the company of other smokers, or at least with the encouragement of their peers. Moreover, many adolescent smokers appear to show a false consensus effect: They overestimate the number of adolescent and adult smokers (Sherman, Presson, Chassin, Corty, & Olshavsky, 1983). Adolescents who incorrectly believe that smoking is common may take it up to fit in with the crowd.

Other studies have pointed to the potential meaning of "being a smoker" as having a powerful influence. For instance, research has shown that smokers are viewed as having positive qualities such as being tough, sociable, and good with members of the opposite sex. Children take up smoking partially to look "tough, cool, and independent of authority" (Leventhal & Cleary, 1980, p. 384). Thus smoking may be one way for adolescents to enhance their self-images as well as their public images (Chassin et al., 1990). As discussed in Chapter 6, adolescents imitate models through observational learning. Smokers on television and in movies are often portrayed in glamorous ways that appeal to adolescents (**Figure 11.22**). Researchers in Germany found that the more German children aged 10 to 16 watched popular North American movies that depicted smoking, the more likely they were to try smoking (Hanewinkel & Sargent, 2008). By the 12th grade, 50 percent to 70 percent of adolescents in the United States have had some experience with tobacco products (Centers for Disease Control and Prevention, 2010c; Mowery, Brick, & Farrelly, 2000). Of course, it is hard to look tough while gasping and retching; so while most adolescents try one or two cigarettes, most do not become regular smokers. Still, many of the experimenters go on to smoke on a regular basis (Baker, Brandon, & Chassin, 2004).

Over time, casual smokers become addicted. It is now widely acknowledged that the drug nicotine, in tobacco, is of primary importance in motivating and maintaining smoking behavior (Fagerström & Schneider, 1989; United States Department of Health and Human Services, 2004). Once the smoker becomes "hooked" on nicotine, going without cigarettes will lead to unpleasant withdrawal symptoms, including distress and heightened anxiety (Russell, 1990). Some people appear especially susceptible to nicotine addiction, perhaps because of genetics (Sabol et al., 1999). Nicotine may lead to increased activation of dopamine neurons, which can have a rewarding effect. (The functions of dopamine neurons are discussed further in Chapter 3, "Biology and Behavior.")

Exercise Has Physical, Emotional, and Cognitive Benefits

Because physical exercise helps control appetite, control metabolism, and burn calories, it is an essential element of any weight control program. In general, the more people exercise, the better their physical and mental health. Scientists do

FIGURE 11.21 Social Influence and Smoking Cigarette companies have employed "authorities" and other role models to encourage smoking. As this 1950s advertisement illustrates, they even touted the fact that doctors used particular brands.

FIGURE 11.22 Glamorous Portrayals of Smoking The enormously popular AMC series *Mad Men* is set in and around the advertising business of the early 1960s. The show has become famous and infamous for its portrayals of "adult" activities, such as drinking, having sex, and smoking.

not know exactly how exercise exerts all of its positive effects. It makes people feel good because they know the exercise is good for them. It helps people build self-confidence and cope with stress. It affects neurotransmitter systems involved in reward, motivation, and emotion. It also enhances both neurogenesis, the growth of new neurons and neural connections, and synaptogenesis, the production of synaptic connections.

Research clearly shows the benefits of exercise on almost every aspect of our lives, including enhanced memory and enhanced cognition (Harburger, Nzerem, & Frick, 2007). Aerobic exercise—the kind that temporarily increases breathing and heart rate—promotes neurogenesis (Carmichael, 2007). The additional neurons created through exercise result in a larger brain, and the brain region that experiences the most growth is the hippocampus. As discussed in Chapter 3, the hippocampus is important for memory and cognition. Aerobic exercise is also especially good for cardiovascular health; it lowers blood pressure and strengthens the heart and lungs (Lesniak & Dubbert, 2001). As little as 10 minutes of exercise can promote feelings of vigor and enhance mood, although at least 30 minutes of daily exercise is associated with the most positive mental state (Hansen, Stevens, & Coast, 2001). In fact, there is compelling evidence that exercise can contribute to positive outcomes for the clinical treatment of depression (Craft & Perna, 2004), as well as being beneficial in the treatment of addiction and alcoholism (Read & Brown, 2003).

Still, unlike societies throughout most of human history, modern society allows people to exert little physical energy. People drive to work, take elevators, spend hours watching remote-controlled television, spend even more hours online, use various labor-saving devices, and complain about not having time to exercise. Once people are out of shape, it is difficult for them to start exercising regularly.

Fortunately, it is never too late to start exercising and receiving its positive benefits. In one study, sedentary adults between the ages of 60 and 79 were randomly assigned to either six months of aerobic training (such as running or fast dancing) or six months of a nonaerobic control group (Colcombe et al., 2006). Participants in aerobic training significantly increased their brain volume, including both white (myelinated) and gray matter. The nonaerobic control group experienced no comparable changes. In another study, older adults were assigned randomly to either three months of aerobic exercise or three months of a nonaerobic control group (Emery, Kiecolt-Glaser, Glaser, Malarkey, & Frid, 2005). All the participants agreed to have small cuts made on their bodies so the researchers could study whether aerobic exercise hastened the time it took for the wounds to heal. The wounds of the aerobic group took an average of 29.2 days to heal, whereas those of the nonaerobic group took an average of 38.9 days to heal. Besides faster healing time, the aerobic group had better cardiorespiratory (heart and lung) fitness. In another study, older adults with memory problems were randomly assigned to an exercise group (three hours a week for two weeks) or to a control group (Lautenschlager et al., 2008). The participants in the exercise group improved in their overall cognition, including memory. The control group showed no changes. The researchers concluded that exercise reduces cognitive decline in older adults with moderate memory problems.

There Are Ethnic Differences in Health Behaviors

Worldwide, racial and ethnic groups have large disparities in health. For example, in the United States, the life expectancy for children born in 2007 varies as follows: 75.9 years for white males, 80.8 years for white females, 70 years for African American males, and 76.8 years for African American females (Centers for Disease Control and Prevention, 2010b, Table 22). The reasons that racial and ethnic groups experience differences in their health include genetics, access to affordable health care, and cultural factors. *Acculturation*—the extent to which individuals assimilate the customs, values, beliefs, and behaviors of the mainstream culture—is an important variable in understanding why different groups have disparate health behaviors and health outcomes.

Consider that in the United States, the mainstream culture has traditionally been represented by European Americans. Compared with European Americans, Hispanics and African Americans have higher obesity rates and higher rates of sedentary behavior (Center for Disease Control and Prevention, 2002). What factors explain this disparity? According to a study of health behaviors in U.S. college students (Despues & Friedman, 2007), African Americans and Hispanics are less likely to smoke or drink alcohol than are European Americans and Asian Americans. African Americans, Hispanics, and Asian Americans, however, are all less likely to exercise, eat fruit, or go to a dentist than are European Americans. Additionally, in each "minority" group, those who are more acculturated tend to be more like the European Americans in their health behaviors.

Such important differences in health behaviors among ethnic groups have long-term consequences for people's health and expected life spans (**Figure 11.23**). Thus researchers seek to understand how culture influences behaviors and how behaviors alter underlying biology. Each level of analysis provides a piece of the intricate puzzle that determines health and well-being.

Note, however, that not all healthy behaviors are associated with acculturation to the mainstream society. People might want to keep the healthy behaviors associated with their own ethnic groups while adopting the healthy behaviors of other groups. For instance, researchers have found that Latinos are less likely to drink and smoke than non-Latinos (Perez-Stable, Marin, & Marin, 1994). The longer they live in the United States, however, the more likely Latinos are to engage in unhealthy behaviors, as they come to drink more, smoke more, and are more likely to become obese (Abraido-Lanza, Chao, & Florez, 2005). By contrast, some cultural factors that are more pronounced among Latinos, such as the high value placed on childbearing (Poma, 1983) and the emotional support provided by the community (Anderson et al., 1981), appear to provide an important health buffer.

FIGURE 11.23 The Longest-Living People The Japanese tend to live very long lives. Their longevity is no doubt due to a combination of genetics and behavior. Pictured here are 99-year-old Matsu and 91-year-old Taido, both of Ogimi Village.

Health Can Be Maintained by Stopping Bad Habits

Many people struggle to improve their health by curbing their bad habits. How likely are people to control their health-related behaviors, such as eating too much, smoking, and not exercising enough? Consider obesity. For weight-loss programs to be successful, individuals need to make permanent lifestyle changes that include altering eating habits, increasing exercise, eliminating food cues, enlisting family members to help, and, for some, taking prescription drugs and undergoing surgery. Although it is far from easy, and most people do not succeed, some people manage to lose excess weight and maintain a healthy weight.

Gary Stocklaufer, discussed at the opening of this chapter, is one of the many obese people who have had surgery to reduce their stomachs and prevent them from overeating because they could not lose weight with diet and exercise. Many other obese people have turned to drugs to help them lose weight. There are no get-thin-quick medications, however. All the available medications require exercise and healthy eating to bring about weight loss. People who are not obese but want to shed extra pounds can join support groups to help them exercise more and eat better. In fact, some people have lost weight and kept it off by adopting healthy lifelong habits.

Similarly, cigarette smokers need orchestrated efforts for their best chances at stopping smoking. These efforts often include nicotine patches to assist with the withdrawal symptoms, avoiding places where other people smoke, and substituting behaviors that are healthier than smoking. Like other addicts, smokers may need to "hit rock bottom" before realizing they have to do something about their behavior. The psychologist David Premack discusses a case study of a man who quit smoking because of something that happened as he was picking up his children at the city library:

> A thunderstorm greeted him as he arrived there; and at the same time a search of his pockets disclosed a familiar problem: he was out of cigarettes. Glancing back at the library, he caught a glimpse of his children stepping out in the rain, but he continued around the corner, certain that he could find a parking space, rush in, buy the cigarettes and be back before the children got seriously wet. (Premack, 1970)

For the smoker, it was a shocking vision of himself "as a father who would actually leave the kids in the rain while he ran after cigarettes." According to Premack, the man quit smoking on the spot.

Summing Up

What Behaviors Affect Mental and Physical Health?

The leading causes of death in industrialized societies are influenced by lifestyle choices. Excessive eating, smoking, and lack of exercise contribute to most major causes of death in developed nations. Excessive eating is most likely to occur when a variety of high-calorie foods are available and larger portions are served. Although obesity is largely influenced by genetic makeup, excessive eating may also contribute to obesity. In addition to the adverse health consequences of obesity, individuals who are obese face substantial social stigma. Restrictive dieting is relatively ineffective in accomplishing weight loss because body weight is regulated at a set-point. Restrained eating also tends to be ineffective because restrained eaters are prone to overeating when they believe they have broken their diets. In extreme cases, individuals may develop an eating disorder—for example, anorexia nervosa or bulimia nervosa—as a consequence of their efforts to control their weight and body shape. Smoking continues to be a major health concern. Individuals typically begin smoking in adolescence as a consequence of social influences or in an effort to exhibit the positive qualities sometimes associated with smokers (such as being tough and independent). Exercise is one of the best things people can do for their health. Regular physical activity improves memory and cognition, enhances emotional experiences, and strengthens the heart and lungs. Racial and ethnic groups exhibit health disparities, some of which can be attributed to differences in their health behaviors. As groups acculturate to the mainstream culture, they tend to adopt the health behaviors of that culture—whether those behaviors have positive or negative outcomes for health. For changes in health behaviors to be successful, individuals need to incorporate those behaviors into permanent lifestyle changes.

Measuring Up

1. Why do restrictive diets rarely work in reducing obesity?
   a. Obese people usually cheat when they are on restrictive diets.
   b. The body learns to conserve calories, so restrictive dieting may lead ultimately to greater weight gain.
   c. We do not know enough about foods' caloric contents to determine good diets.

2. How does exercise affect the brain?
   a. Exercise improves muscles and lungs, but does not affect the brain.
   b. As revealed in MRI brain scans, excessive exercise can cause an aversion to physical activity.
   c. People already in good physical shape show no brain effects, and those in poor physical shape show an enlargement in the areas corresponding to motor control.
   d. Exercise causes the growth of new neurons and new neural connections, especially in brain areas associated with memory and cognition.

Answers: 1. b. The body learns to conserve calories, so restrictive dieting may lead ultimately to greater weight gain. 2. d. Exercise causes the growth of new neurons and new neural connections, especially in brain areas associated with memory and cognition.

Can a Positive Attitude Keep Us Healthy?

Positive Psychology Emphasizes Well-Being

Psychologists from the humanist school of thought focused on what is positive in the human experience. Abraham Maslow, Carl Rogers, and Erik Erikson were among the early pioneers in the field of positive psychology, although it was not known by that title then. These early humanist psychologists enjoyed the greatest success in the decades from 1950 to 1970. Other schools of thought, especially cognitive perspectives, then took the leading roles in psychology. Since the 1990s, positive psychology has enjoyed a tremendous comeback as psychologists have begun to use the methods of science to study humanity's positive aspects. The *positive psychology* movement was launched by the clinical psychologist Martin Seligman (Seligman & Csikszentmihalyi, 2000). Seligman and others have encouraged the scientific study of qualities such as faith, values, creativity, courage, and hope. The earliest emphasis in positive psychology was on understanding what makes people authentically happy. If you have read Chapter 2, then you might be wondering how the term *happiness* is operationalized. According to positive psychologists, happiness has three components: (1) positive emotion and pleasure, (2) engagement in life, and (3) a meaningful life (Seligman, Steen, Park, & Peterson, 2005). For example, college students high in authentic happiness might experience pleasure when interacting with other students (component 1), might be actively engaged in class discussions and course readings (component 2), and might find meaning in how the material influences their lives (component 3; **Figure 11.24**). More recently, Seligman has promoted a shift away from focusing on happiness to a greater emphasis on overall well-being. In his book *Flourish* (2011), Seligman argues that a truly successful life involves not only happiness (i.e., pleasure, engagement, and meaning), but also good relationships and a history of accomplishment.

The new positive psychology emphasizes the strengths and virtues that help people thrive. Its primary aim is an understanding of psychological well-being.

Learning Objectives

- Discuss the goals of positive psychology.
- Describe the health benefits of positive affect, social support, marriage, trust, and spirituality.

FIGURE 11.24 Try for Yourself: How to Be Happier

Research shows that with relatively short interventions, people can become happier. These effects occur in the short run. The long-term effects of the interventions are unknown.

Here are some suggestions based on research findings about happiness. You can try these activities for yourself to test their effects.

1. In the next week, write a letter of gratitude and deliver it in person to someone who has been kind to you but whom you have never thanked.
2. Once a week, write down three things that went well that day and explain why they went well.
3. Tell a friend about a time when you did your very best, and then think about the strengths you displayed. Review this story every night for the next week.
4. Imagine yourself 10 years in the future as your best possible self, as having achieved all your most important goals. Describe in writing what your life is like and how you got there.
5. Keep a journal in which you write about the positive aspects of your life. Reflect on your health, freedom, friends, and so on.
6. Act like a happy person. Sometimes just going through the motions of being happy will create happiness.

Result: Data suggest that each of these activities can enhance a person's happiness (Lyubomirsky, King, & Diener, 2005). Activities such as these are called "shotgun interventions" because they are fast acting, cover a broad range of behaviors, have relatively large effects for such a small investment, and pose little risk.

For instance, Ed Diener (2000) has found that well-being varies across cultures. According to Diener, the wealthiest countries often have the highest levels of satisfaction. This finding fits well with Maslow's proposal that people need to satisfy basic needs such as food, shelter, and safety before they can address self-esteem needs (**Figure 11.25**). Michele Tugade and Barbara Fredrickson (2004) have found that people who are resilient, who can bounce back from negative events, experience positive emotions even when under stress. According to the *broaden-and-build theory,* positive emotions prompt people to consider novel solutions to their problems. Thus resilient people tend to draw on their positive emotions in dealing with setbacks or negative life experiences (Fredrickson, 2001).

Being Positive Has Health Benefits

Earlier in this chapter, you read about the negative health consequences of negative emotions, especially hostility and stress. You may have wondered about the flip side of this relationship: Are positive emotions and well-being associated with good health (**Figure 11.26**)?

To address this question, researchers asked more than 1,000 patients in a large medical practice to fill out questionnaires about their emotional traits (Richman et al., 2005). The questionnaires included scales that measured positive emotions (hope and curiosity) and negative emotions (anxiety and anger). Two years after receiving the questionnaires, the researchers used the patients' medical files to determine if there was a relationship between these emotions and three broad types of diseases: hypertension, diabetes, and respiratory tract infections. Higher levels of hope were associated with reduced risk of these medical diseases, and higher levels of curiosity were associated with reduced risk of hypertension and diabetes. Therefore, the answer is: Yes, in general, positive emotions can predict better health.

Satisfaction with Life Scale

Using the 1–7 scale below, indicate your agreement with each item by placing the appropriate number on the line preceding that item. Be open and honest in your responding. Then add the five numbers to determine your overall life satisfaction.

7 = strongly agree
6 = agree
5 = slightly agree
4 = neither agree nor disagree

3 = slightly disagree
2 = disagree
1 = strongly disagree

_____ In most ways, my life is close to my ideal.
_____ The conditions of my life are excellent.
_____ I am satisfied with my life.
_____ So far, I have gotten the important things I want in life.
_____ If I could live my life over, I would change almost nothing.

31–35 extremely satisfied
26–30 satisfied
21–25 slightly satisfied
20   neutral

15–19 slightly dissatisfied
10–14 dissatisfied
 5–9   extremely dissatisfied

Result: The Satisfaction with Life Scale has been found to reliably and validly assess a person's general satisfaction in life.

SOURCE: Pavot and Diener, 1993.

Indeed, research reveals that having a positive affect, or being generally positive, has multiple beneficial effects on the immune system (Marsland, Pressman, & Cohen, 2007). People with a positive affect show enhanced immune system functioning and greater longevity than their less positive peers (Dockray & Steptoe, 2010; Xu & Roberts, 2010). For example, they have fewer illnesses after exposure to cold germs and flu viruses (Cohen, Alper, Doyle, Treanor, & Turner, 2006). Thus, across multiple studies and types of measures, positive emotions are related to considerable health benefits.

Social Support Is Associated with Good Health

Social interaction is beneficial for physical and mental health. People high in well-being tend to have strong social networks and are more socially integrated than are those lower in well-being (Smith, Langa, Kabeto, & Ubel, 2005). People with larger social networks (more people they interact with regularly) are less likely to catch colds (Cohen, Doyle, Skoner, Rabin, & Gwaltney, 1997). Apparently, people who have more friends also live longer than those who have fewer friends. A study that used a random sample of almost 7,000 adults found that people with smaller social networks were more likely to die during the nine-year period between assessments than were people with more friends (Berkman & Syme, 1979). Men with fewer friends were 2.3 times more likely to die than comparable men with more friends. Women with fewer friends were 2.8 times more likely to die than comparable women with more friends. Social support was independent of other factors, such as stated health at the time of the first contact, obesity, smoking, socioeconomic status, and physical activity. In addition, ill people who are socially isolated are likely to die sooner than ill people who are well connected to others (House, Landis, & Umberson, 1988). This

FIGURE 11.26 **Positivity** Laughing clubs, such as this one in India, believe in laughter as therapy and a way to keep in shape. **Does the theory behind these clubs seem valid enough to test scientifically? What information in this chapter leads you to think so? What does your own experience suggest?**

effect may be related to the association between chronic loneliness and numerous psychological and health problems (Cacioppo & Patrick, 2008). Indeed, accumulating evidence indicates that loneliness predicts both physical illness and mortality (Hawkley & Cacioppo, 2010).

Social support helps people cope and maintain good health in two basic ways. First, people with social support experience less stress overall. Consider single parents who have to juggle job and family demands. The lack of a partner places more demands on them, thus increasing their likelihood of feeling stressed. Therefore, social support can take tangible forms, such as providing material help or assisting with daily chores. To be most effective, however, social support needs to imply that people care about the recipient of the support. Knowing that other people care can lessen the negative effects of stress. The **buffering hypothesis** proposes that when others provide emotional support, the recipient is better able to cope with stressful events (Cohen & Wills, 1985). Examples of emotional support include expressions of caring and willingness to listen to another person's problems.

MARRIAGE CAN BE GOOD FOR YOUR HEALTH The research on social support shows clearly that positive relationships are good for health. Marriage is generally people's most intimate and long-lasting supportive relationship, and it has many health advantages. Most of these theories focus on the ways that marital partners can support each other. For example, each member of the couple can help the other deal with stress or assist in meeting life's demands. Married people may also influence their partners' healthful behavior by encouraging them to eat properly, to get exercise, and so on.

In an international study of marriage and well-being, involving more than 59,000 people from 42 countries, researchers found that marriage's effect on well-being was fairly similar in all the countries studied despite their diversity (Diener, Gohm, Suh, & Oishi, 2000). Not only were there cross-cultural similarities in response to marriage, but men and women derived approximately equal benefits from marriage. One small difference between countries was the finding that the benefits of being married compared with being divorced were slightly higher in collectivist countries. Collectivist countries emphasize the common good and group values rather than individual achievement. (Countries considered collectivist in the study included China, South Korea, Nigeria, Turkey, and Brazil. Individualist countries included the United States, Great Britain, the Netherlands, Canada, and Switzerland.) Being single leads to greater mortality for both women and men. (Data on the relationship between marital status and health are shown in **Figure 11.27.**)

Comparable data are not available for gays or lesbians who are married or in long-term, marriage-like relationships. It is reasonable to expect, however, that homosexuals would receive the same beneficial effects as heterosexuals. A recent study compared straight and gay and lesbian couples in long-term, committed relationships (Roisman, Clausell, Holland, Fortuna, & Elieff, 2008). All the couples were indistinguishable in terms of self-reports on the quality of the relationship, partner reports on the quality of the relationship, and various physiological indicators of health. The one exception was that the lesbian couples worked more cooperatively on laboratory tasks than did the straight or gay couples.

Marriage is not a panacea for ill health, however. Troubled marriages are associated with increased stress, and unmarried people can be happier than people in bad marriages. In a study that categorized newlyweds based on observed interactions, couples who fought more and showed more hostility toward each

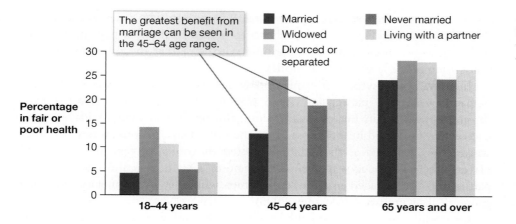

The greatest benefit from marriage can be seen in the 45–64 age range.

Married
Widowed
Divorced or separated
Never married
Living with a partner

Percentage in fair or poor health

18–44 years   45–64 years   65 years and over

FIGURE 11.27 Relationship between Marriage and Health These data come from the National Health Interview Surveys in the United States from 1999 to 2002.

other exhibited decreased immune system activity in the 24 hours after conflict (Kiecolt-Glaser, Malarkey, Chee, & Newton, 1993). Janice Kiecolt-Glaser and Ronald Glaser (1988) found that people with troubled marriages and people going through a divorce or bereavement all had compromised immune systems.

TRUSTING OTHERS IS ASSOCIATED WITH BETTER HEALTH An important feature of healthy relationships is that partners trust one another. Given that social relationships are critical for health, it should be clear that trust is essential for psychological and physical health. In fact, various sources of data suggest that trust is associated with better health and a longer life. This relationship was supported in a study of more than 160,000 people from every state in the United States. Each participant responded to the question *Most people can't be trusted. Do you agree or disagree with this statement?* In each state, as the percentage of respondents who believed most people cannot be trusted increased, so did the percentage who reported that their health was fair to poor (Kawachi, Kennedy, & Glass, 1999; **Figure 11.28**).

The hormone oxytocin appears to increase trust. In an experimental study on the relationship between oxytocin and trust, participants played a monetary exchange game (Uvnas-Moberg, 1998). In studies of this kind, participants are given money by the experimenter and then choose how much to give to another person. The experimenter then increases the amount of money received by the

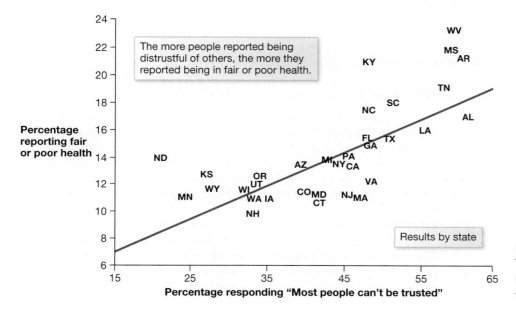

The more people reported being distrustful of others, the more they reported being in fair or poor health.

Percentage reporting fair or poor health

Results by state

Percentage responding "Most people can't be trusted"

FIGURE 11.28 Relationship between Trust and Health More than 160,000 people in the United States were asked if they agreed that most people cannot be trusted.

second person—say, by four or five times. The person who receives the money then chooses whether, or how much, to give back to the first person. Thus, to make the most money, the first person has to trust that the other person will share some of the larger pool of money.

In this study, oxytocin or a placebo was sprayed into the noses of the participants while the participants were playing. (Receptors for oxytocin exist throughout the brain but especially along the olfactory passages.) Players who had oxytocin sprayed in their noses gave the other players more money. In other words, they behaved as though they trusted the other players more than did players who had placebos sprayed in their noses. Oxytocin is also released when participants are engaged in trust relationships while playing monetary exchange games (Zak, Kurzban, & Matzner, 2005).

One way that oxytocin might increase both trust and well-being is by increasing social bonds. Recall from earlier in this chapter that oxytocin has been implicated as critical to the tend-and-befriend response. This phenomenon describes people's tendency to respond to stress by attending to their social relationships. As discussed in Chapter 9, oxytocin is involved in attachments between mothers and their children. It is also released when people feel empathy toward others, and it is involved in feelings of love (Panksepp, 1992).

Spirituality Contributes to Well-Being

In many studies, people who are religious report greater feelings of well-being than do people who are not religious. According to David Myers (2000), religious people are better at coping with crises in their lives. Their religious beliefs serve as a buffer against hard knocks. On a daily basis, religious beliefs can help people achieve and maintain well-being through the social and physical support provided by faith communities. Many religions support healthy behaviors, such as avoiding alcohol and tobacco. Some religions place eating restrictions on less healthful foods such as pork, fatty meats, or caffeine. From their faith, people also derive meaning and purpose in their lives. The positive effects are not associated with any single religion, however. The benefits come from a sense of spirituality that occurs across religions (**Figure 11.29**). As Rabbi Harold Kushner notes, people need to feel they are "something more than just a momentary blip in the universe" (quoted in Myers, p. 64).

FIGURE 11.29 Spirituality and Well-Being A sense of spirituality can have positive effects on well-being. That sense does not have to be connected with a particular religion.

Summing Up

Can a Positive Attitude Keep Us Healthy?

Positive psychology is concerned with the scientific study of the strengths and virtues that contribute to psychological well-being. A number of studies have shown that people who are positive are healthier and live longer than their more negative counterparts. Social support and being socially integrated in a group are also protective health factors, because concerned others provide material and emotional support. Research has shown that marriages that are low in conflict are associated with better health for both partners. Trust is another factor that is associated with better health and longer life. The hormone oxytocin has been implicated in the experience of trust. Spirituality also contributes to better health due to the support that people receive from their faith communities, the health behaviors that are promoted by religions, and the sense of meaning that can be derived from religious beliefs.

1. Which of the following statements explains how researchers concluded that oxytocin causes people to be more trusting?
   a. Infants secrete oxytocin when they are being nursed, causing them to bond with their mothers.
   b. Oxytocin levels were found to be highest among people living in countries where people generally distrust each other.
   c. Across the United States, there was a linear relationship between oxytocin levels and reports of good health.
   d. When researchers sprayed oxytocin in the noses of people playing the trust game, the players acted in a more trusting way than did the placebo control group.

2. What aspects of social support are most important in creating a positive effect on health?
   a. The support needs to come from family members because of the genetic basis of this effect.
   b. It is more important to know many people than it is to interact with them regularly.
   c. It is most important that people around you genuinely care about your well-being.
   d. It is most important that the people providing social support be religious because they can share in your spirituality.

Answers: 1. d. When researchers sprayed oxytocin in the noses of people playing the trust game, the players acted in a more trusting way than did the placebo control group. 2. c. It is most important that people around you genuinely care about your well-being.

11.5 Action Plan for Health and Well-Being

Taking Care of Mind and Body

Over the last three decades, psychologists have learned much about the complex relations between stress, behavior, and health. Fifty years ago, people did not know that smoking is so unhealthy, that saturated fats and other dietary factors contribute to cardiovascular disease, or that being under prolonged stress can damage the body. We now know that, to be healthy, people need to cope with stress, regulate their emotions, and control their daily habits. The following strategies will enhance your health and well-being. Are you willing to adopt them and take control of your life?

- **Eat natural foods.** Food fads come and go, but the basic rules never change: Eat a varied diet that emphasizes natural foods. Whole grains, fruits, and vegetables should be the major parts of that diet, but various animal products, such as poultry or other lean meats, can also be part of it. Avoid processed foods and fast foods. Avoid foods containing trans-fatty acids and other artificial types of fat that prolong store shelf life.

- **Watch portion size.** Eat a varied diet in moderation, and eat only when you are hungry. Eating small snacks between meals may prevent you from becoming too hungry and overeating at your next meal. Remember that many prepared foods are sold in large portions, which encourage over-eating. Over time, the extra calories from large portions may contribute to obesity.

- **Drink alcohol in moderation, if at all.** Some research indicates that one glass of wine per day, or similar quantities of other alcohol-containing drinks, may have cardiovascular benefits (Klatsky, 2009). But excessive alcohol consumption can cause serious health problems, including alcoholism, liver problems, some cancers, heart disease, and immune system deficiencies.

- **Keep active.** Exercise is an excellent daily strategy for keeping stress in check. Four times a week or more, engage in at least a half hour of moderate physical activity. Ignore the saying *no pain, no gain,* because pain may actually deter you from exercising over the long run. Start with moderate exercise that will not leave you breathless, and gradually increase the intensity. Look for other ways to be active, such as taking the stairs or walking to work or school.

- **Do not smoke.** This recommendation may seem obvious, yet many college students and other adults begin smoking each year. Smoking eventually produces undesirable physical effects for all smokers, such as a hacking cough, unpleasant odor, bad breath, some cancers, and death at a younger age.

- **Practice safe sex.** Sexually transmitted diseases (STDs) affect millions of people worldwide—including college students. Many new HIV cases are occurring among those under age 25, who are infected through heterosexual or homosexual activity. Despite the devastating consequences of some STDs, many young adults engage in risky sexual practices, such as not using condoms, and they are especially likely to do so when using alcohol or other drugs. Ways to avoid STDs include condom use or abstinence.

- **Learn to relax.** Daily hassles and stress can cause many health problems. For example, conditions such as insomnia can interfere with your ability to function. By contrast, relaxation exercises can help soothe the body and mind. Seek help from trained counselors who can teach you these methods, such as using biofeedback to measure your physiological activity so you can learn to control it. You might also try a relaxing activity, such as yoga.

- **Learn to cope.** Negative events are a part of life. Learn strategies for assessing them realistically and seeing what might be positive about them as well as accepting the difficulties they pose. You can learn strategies for dealing with stressors: seeking advice or assistance, attempting new solutions, distracting yourself with more pleasant thoughts or activities, reinterpreting situations humorously, and so on. Find out which strategies work best for you. The important thing is not to allow stress to consume your life.

- **Build a strong support network.** Friends and family can help you deal with much of life's stress, from daily frustrations to serious catastrophes. Avoid people who encourage you to act in unhealthy ways or are threatened by your efforts to be healthy. Instead, find people who share your values, who understand what you want from life, who can listen and provide advice, assistance, or simply encouragement. Trusting others is a necessary part of social support, and it is associated with positive health outcomes.

- **Consider your spiritual life.** If you have spiritual beliefs, try incorporating them into your daily living. Benefits can accrue from living a meaningful life and from experiencing the support provided by faith communities.

- **Try some of the happiness exercises.** The exercises suggested in Figure 11.24 to enhance happiness include low-risk activities such as expressing gratitude and imagining your "best possible self." By focusing on positive events—and more positive explanations of troubling ones—you may become a happier person.

Chapter Summary

11.1 Can Psychosocial Factors Affect Health?

■ **The Biopsychosocial Model of Health Incorporates Multiple Perspectives for Understanding and Improving Health:** The biopsychosocial model describes the reciprocal and multiple influences of biological factors (e.g., genetic predispositions), behavioral factors (e.g., lifestyle), and social factors (e.g., social support) on health. In contrast to the traditional medical model, this model maintains that people are active participants in determining their health outcomes.

■ **Behavior Contributes to the Leading Causes of Death:** The leading causes of death in industrialized societies are influenced by our behaviors. Lifestyle variables—such as overeating, poor diet, smoking, and lack of exercise—contribute to heart disease, the leading cause of death in the United States. Teenagers and young adults are most likely to die from accidents, homicide, and suicide. These causes of death are often preventable.

■ **Placebos Can Be Powerful Medicine:** Placebos can have powerful effects on health and well-being. A placebo is effective, however, only if the person taking it believes in its ability to improve health. Research suggests that placebos may activate the same neural processes as biologically active (nonplacebo) treatments.

11.2 How Do We Cope with Stress?

■ **Stress Has Physiological Components:** Stressful events cause a cascade of physiological events—specifically, the release of hormones from the hypothalamus, the pituitary gland, and the adrenal glands. Stress-related hormones (e.g., cortisol, norepinephrine) circulate through the bloodstream, affecting organs throughout the body.

■ **There Are Sex Differences in How We Respond to Stressors:** Women and men respond somewhat differently to stress. Women are more likely to tend and befriend, whereas men are more likely to fight or flee. Evolutionary psychology maintains that these distinct responses emerged as a consequence of the distinct challenges faced by women and men in our ancestral environment. Research suggests that the hormone oxytocin may play a role in the tend-and-befriend response.

■ **The General Adaptation Syndrome Is a Bodily Response to Stress:** Selye outlined the general adaptation syndrome. This syndrome consists of the steps by which the body responds to stress. The initial response, alarm, is followed by resistance. If the stressor continues, the final response is exhaustion.

■ **Stress Affects Health:** Excessive stress negatively affects health. Stress is associated with the occurrence of a wide variety of diseases, including heart disease. Heart disease is the leading cause of death of adults in the industrialized world. Individuals who are hostile or depressed are more likely to develop heart disease than those who are not.

■ **Coping Is a Process:** We engage in cognitive appraisal of potential stressors. We may use emotion-focused and problem-focused coping strategies. Problem-focused coping strategies tend to be more effective for controllable stressors and under conditions of moderate stress. Emotion-focused coping strategies tend to be more effective for uncontrollable stressors and under conditions of high stress. Individuals who are hardy are more stress resilient. Having a sense of autonomy and control reduces the experience of stress and increases well-being.

11.3 What Behaviors Affect Mental and Physical Health?

■ **Obesity Results from a Genetic Predisposition and Overeating:** In industrialized countries around the world, an increasing number of people are obese. Obesity results from a combination of a genetic predisposition and overeating. Restrictive diets rarely help obese people lose weight because weight is regulated around a set-point. Similarly, restrictive eating tends to fail because restrictive eaters are susceptible to overeating when they believe they have broken their diets. Extreme efforts to control weight and body shape may result in the onset of either anorexia nervosa or bulimia nervosa.

■ **Smoking Is a Leading Cause of Death:** Smoking contributes to heart disease, cancer, and many other deadly diseases. People typically begin smoking as children or adolescents as a consequence of social influences or in an effort to display the positive characteristics that we associate with smokers (e.g., tough, independent).

■ **Exercise Has Physical, Emotional, and Cognitive Benefits:** Exercise has positive effects on the heart and lungs. In addition, exercise has been shown to improve memory, enhance mood, and speed healing. Research has demonstrated that exercise can reduce cognitive decline in older adults.

■ **There Are Ethnic Differences in Health Behaviors:** Racial and ethnic differences in health behaviors can explain some of the disparities in health outcomes. As groups become more acculturated to the mainstream culture, they tend to adopt the health behaviors of that culture, positive and negative.

■ **Health Can Be Maintained by Stopping Bad Habits:** For changes in health behaviors to be successful, individuals need to incorporate those behaviors into permanent lifestyle changes.

11.4 Can a Positive Attitude Keep Us Healthy?

- **Positive Psychology Emphasizes Well-Being:** Positive psychology has its origins in the work of humanist psychologists. The early emphasis of this field was happiness. Today, positive psychologists emphasize the strengths and virtues associated with psychological well-being.

- **Being Positive Has Health Benefits:** According to a range of evidence, there are health benefits to having a positive, optimistic outlook.

- **Social Support Is Associated with Good Health:** Social support is critical to good health because when others care about

us, they provide material and emotional support. Research has demonstrated enhanced well-being and reduced mortality among individuals who are in good marriages. Trust in others is critical to psychological and physical health. Oxytocin is secreted during trusting encounters and is involved in infant/parent attachments and love relationships.

- **Spirituality Contributes to Well-Being:** Spirituality contributes to a sense of well-being. Members of religious groups derive social and physical support from their faith communities. Many religions support healthy behaviors, and faith provides meaning to people's lives.

Key Terms

anorexia nervosa, p. 494
biopsychosocial model, p. 471
body mass index (BMI), p. 489
buffering hypothesis, p. 504
bulimia nervosa, p. 495
coping response, p. 476
emotion-focused coping, p. 484

fight-or-flight response, p. 478
general adaptation syndrome, p. 480
health psychology, p. 470
hypothalamic-pituitary-adrenal (HPA) axis, p. 478
immune system, p. 480
oxytocin, p. 479

placebo effect, p. 474
primary appraisals, p. 484
problem-focused coping, p. 484
secondary appraisals, p. 484
stress, p. 476
stressor, p. 476
tend-and-befriend response, p. 479

Type A behavior pattern, p. 482
Type B behavior pattern, p. 483
well-being, p. 470

Practice Test

1. Which of the following statements most accurately represents health psychologists' current understanding of illness?
   a. Illness is totally under our own control. We can stay healthy simply by making healthy decisions.
   b. Illness is a matter of luck. If our bodies are destined to become ill, we're out of luck.
   c. When a person has a family history of heart disease, breast cancer, or diabetes, the person's genetic predisposition guarantees that she or he will develop the illness.
   d. Genetic predispositions to some diseases exist. But living healthily can help reduce the chance of developing a disease.

2. The correct answer to the previous question is consistent with the _____ of health and illness.
   a. biomedical model
   b. biopsychosocial model
   c. moral model
   d. self-efficacy model

3. Latasha is normally an engaged and satisfied employee. For a few months, she becomes very dissatisfied, grumpy, and uninterested in her job. Shortly after participating in a weekend-long seminar about the secrets of success, Latasha begins enjoying her work again. Which of the following attributions for her improved satisfaction at work best reflects the concept of regression to the mean?

   a. "Well, I figured I couldn't stay in that funk forever. Things eventually had to start looking up again."
   b. "That seminar was amazing! Things are really starting to go my way now that I know the secret to success."
   c. "I'm so glad my boss moved to another department. Now that she's gone, things are looking up."
   d. "Everything started going better once I changed my negative attitude."

4. Individuals who are hardy _____. (Choose all that apply.)
   a. are committed to daily activities
   b. are optimistic
   c. have access to financial resources
   d. have many close friends
   e. see challenges as opportunities for growth
   f. see themselves as able to control their own lives

5. Which of the following statements are true?
   a. Our bodies have natural defenses against weight loss that limit dieting's effectiveness.
   b. Body weight seems to be determined largely by a set-point.
   c. Dieters who lose and regain weight repeatedly tend to become heavier over time.
   d. Exercise is an essential element of any weight control program.

The answer key for the Practice Tests can be found at the back of the book. It also includes answers to the green caption questions.

Social Psychology

WHAT WAS WRONG WITH THE GUARDS at Abu Ghraib? This prison in Iraq, now named the Baghdad Central Prison, will always be remembered as the site of disgusting abuses of power. During 2003, the first year of the Iraq War, American soldiers brutalized Iraqi detainees at Abu Ghraib. The soldiers raped prisoners, threatened them with dogs, beat them with objects such as broom handles and chairs, stripped them, placed them in humiliating positions such as lying on top of each other naked, and forced them to perform or simulate oral sex and masturbation (**Figure 12.1a**).

(a)

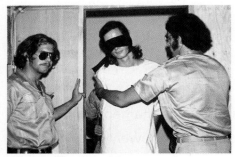

(b)

FIGURE 12.1 When Good People Go Bad (a) Were soldier-guards at Abu Ghraib who harassed, threatened, and tortured prisoners just a few "bad apples," or were they normal people reacting to an extreme situation? Why do you think so? (b) In the Stanford prison study, student-guards took on their roles with such vigor that the study was ended early because of concerns for the well-being of the "guards" and the "prisoners." If this study were conducted at your school today, what would you predict the results to be? What knowledge of people, and specifically of your peers, is your answer based on?

According to the international treaties called the Geneva Conventions and their Additional Protocols, prisoners of war should be treated with respect and dignity. Even amid the horrors of war, we expect the military to behave in a civilized and professional manner. When the news media began to reveal the abuse at Abu Ghraib, and especially when photographs of the guards' actions appeared on the Web, outrage and condemnation of the deplorable conduct followed. U.S. government officials stressed that these were isolated incidents carried out by a small group of wayward soldiers. The idea that only a few troubled individuals were responsible for abusing prisoners is bizarrely comforting. Somehow we are relieved to know that their deviant behavior does not reflect on ordinary people. Surely most of us would not inflict such pain on prisoners, many of whom were just teenagers, young men, and women rounded up for questioning. Or would we?

How do we explain the guards' actions at Abu Ghraib, whether or not the guards were ordered to perform them? The case of Abu Ghraib challenges many commonsense notions about human nature and forces us to consider questions about humanity's dark side. People humiliate, beat, rape, torture, and murder others. Is something wrong with these people?

According to social psychologists, nothing typically is wrong with people such as the guards at Abu Ghraib. Rather, they are probably normal people caught up in overwhelming situations that shape their actions. A number of situational elements are likely to have influenced the guards' behavior. These elements included an unclear chain of command and a diffusion of responsibility. Moreover, people typically are obedient to authority, especially in times of war. Also, the working conditions at Abu Ghraib promoted aggression: Some of the soldiers had expected to be in Iraq a short time, working in traffic control. Instead, they were stationed in an overcrowded prison. Before the war, that prison had a notorious reputation as a torture chamber under the regime of the Iraqi dictator, Saddam Hussein. Now, as guards, the soldiers were working long hours six or seven days a week, in extremely hot temperatures, and frequently under mortar attack. Finally, during wartime, people are especially likely to view the world as consisting of "us" and "them." Members of the enemy group are dehumanized: viewed as being all the same, often as evil and inferior. All of these factors contributed to the mistreatment of prisoners at Abu Ghraib.

In a classic study that illuminates the forces at work in situations such as Abu Ghraib, the psychologists Philip Zimbardo and Chris Haney had male Stanford undergraduates play the roles of prisoners and guards in a mock prison (Haney, Banks, & Zimbardo, 1973). The students, who had all been screened and found to be psychologically stable, were randomly assigned to their roles. What happened was unexpected and shocking. Within days, the "guards" became brutal and sadistic. They constantly harassed the "prisoners," forcing them to engage in meaningless and tedious tasks and exercises. Although the study was scheduled to last two weeks, it became necessary to stop it after only six days. The Stanford prison study demonstrated the speed at which apparently normal college students could be transformed into the social roles they were playing. Similarly, the guards at Abu Ghraib believed it was their job to "soften up" the prisoners for interrogation, and their actions were strikingly similar to those of the Stanford participants (**Figure 12.1b**).

Would you beat up or humiliate someone simply because you were ordered to do so or were in a situation where others were doing so? Or would you defy authority and resist peer pressure? ■

12.1 How Do We Form Our Impressions of Others?

Learning Objectives

- Identify the goals of social psychology.
- Discuss the role that nonverbal behavior plays in impression formation.
- Define the fundamental attribution error and the actor/observer discrepancy.
- Describe the functions and self-fulfilling effects of stereotypes.
- Distinguish between prejudice and discrimination.
- Distinguish between ingroups and outgroups.
- Discuss strategies to inhibit stereotypes and reduce prejudice.

When people act brutally and sadistically, we assume they are brutal and sadistic. We neglect to consider the situation in which they have acted brutally and sadistically. We do not assess how much power the situation had in shaping the behavior. If we acknowledge the power of the situation, we are not suggesting that individual traits are unimportant. Nor are we saying that people are not responsible for their behavior. We are recognizing, however, that many behaviors become more understandable within particular contexts.

Humans are social animals who live in a highly complex world. At any moment, hundreds of millions of people are talking with friends, forming impressions of strangers, arguing with family members, even falling in love with potential mates. Our regular interactions with others—even imagined others, even online "avatars"—shape who we are and how we understand the world. Social psychology is concerned with how people influence other people's thoughts, feelings, and actions. Because almost every human activity has a social dimension, research in social psychology covers expansive and varied territory: how we perceive and understand others, how we function in groups, why we hurt or help people, why we fall in love, why we stigmatize and discriminate against certain people. In this chapter, you will learn the basic principles of how people interact with each other. You will see that research in social psychology provides insights into situations such as Abu Ghraib. The research reveals that humans are not inherently flawed or evil. They are distinct individuals who are powerfully influenced by social context.

Over the course of human evolution, one fact has remained constant: Because we are social animals, we live in groups. Groups provide security from predators and from competing groups. They provide mating opportunities. They provide assistance in hunting food and gathering it. At the same time, members within a group may compete for food and for mates. Mechanisms have therefore evolved for distinguishing members of one's own group from members of other groups, as well as for detecting dangers from within the group, such as deception, coercion, and infidelity. In fact, we constantly are required to make social judgments. We assess whether people are friends or foes, potential mates or potential challengers, honest or dishonest, trustworthy or unreliable, and so on. We also automatically classify people into social categories, and doing so can have major implications for how we treat them. As social psychologists have shown, our long-term evaluations of people are heavily influenced by our first impressions.

Nonverbal Actions and Expressions Affect Our First Impressions

When someone walks toward you, you make a number of quick judgments. For example, do you know the person? Does the person pose danger? Do you want to know the person better? How you initially feel will be determined mostly by the person's nonverbal behavior. Facial expressions, gestures, mannerisms, and movements are all examples of **nonverbal behavior,** sometimes referred to as *body language* (**Figure 12.2**).

FIGURE 12.2 Reading Nonverbal Behavior People's body language affects our impressions of the people and their situations. **What does this picture suggest about this couple? Which details support your impressions?**

nonverbal behavior The facial expressions, gestures, mannerisms, and movements by which one communicates with others.

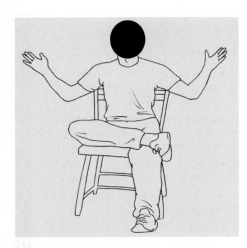

FIGURE 12.3 Nonverbal Cues from Body Shape After watching a 10-second clip of a figural outline such as this one, participants correctly guessed the figure's sexual orientation at a better-than-chance rate. In other words, thin slices of behavior can be sufficient cues for us to form general impressions about people.

How much can be learned from nonverbal behavior? Nalini Ambady and Robert Rosenthal have found that people can make accurate judgments based on only a few seconds of observation. They refer to such quick views as *thin slices of behavior.* Thin slices of behavior are powerful cues for impression formation. For instance, videotapes of judges giving instructions to juries reveal that a judge's nonverbal actions can predict whether a jury will find the defendant guilty or not guilty. Judges, perhaps unconsciously, may indicate their beliefs about guilt or innocence through facial expressions, tones of voice, and gestures. In one study, the participants viewed soundless 30-second film clips of college teachers lecturing (Ambady & Rosenthal, 1993). The participants were asked to rate the lecturers' teaching ability. Based solely on nonverbal behaviors, the participants' ratings corresponded very highly with the ratings given by the instructors' students.

One important nonverbal cue is how people walk, known as *gait.* Gait provides information about affective state. People with a bounce in their step, who walk along swinging their arms, are seen as happy. By contrast, people who scurry along, taking short steps while stooped over, are perceived as hostile. Those taking long strides with heavy steps are perceived to be angry. In an intriguing study, researchers found that participants accurately judged sexual orientation at a better-than-chance rate after watching a 10-second silent video or a dynamic figural outline of someone walking or gesturing (Ambady, Hallahan, & Conner, 1999; **Figure 12.3**). For perceivers, the primary cue for sexual orientation is how much the person's body shape and body motion match those of the gender-typical male or female (Johnson, Gill, Reichman, & Tassinary, 2007).

FACIAL EXPRESSIONS The first thing we notice about another person is usually the face. When human babies are less than an hour old, they prefer to look at and will track a picture of a human face rather than a blank outline of a head (Morton & Johnson, 1991). The face communicates information such as emotional state, interest, and distrust. For example, people use their eyes to indicate anger, to flirt, or to catch the attention of a passing waiter.

Eye contact is important in social situations, though how we perceive it depends on our culture. People from Western cultures tend to seek eye contact when they speak to someone. If the other person does not meet their eyes, they might assume, perhaps incorrectly, that the person is embarrassed, ashamed, or lying, whereas they tend to view a person who looks them in the eyes as truthful and friendly. For this reason, people wearing sunglasses are often described as cold and aloof, and police officers sometimes wear sunglasses partly to seem intimidating. In other groups, such as certain Native American tribes, making direct eye contact, especially with the elderly, is considered disrespectful.

We Make Attributions about Others

We constantly try to explain other people's motives, traits, and preferences. Why did she say that? Why is he crying? Why does she study so hard? And so on. **Attributions** are people's explanations for events or actions, including other people's behavior. We are motivated to draw inferences in part by a basic need for both order and predictability. The world can be a dangerous place in which many unexpected things happen. We prefer to think that things happen for reasons and that therefore we can anticipate future events. For instance, you might expect that if you study for an exam, you will do well on it.

attributions People's explanations for why events or actions occur.

Sometimes a violent act, such as a rape or murder, appears to be senseless. In such cases, people often make attributions about the victim, such as "she deserved it" or "he provoked it." Attributions of this kind are part of the *just world hypothesis*. From this perspective, victims must have done something to justify what happened to them. For example, people might apply the just world hypothesis to the events at Abu Ghraib. They might say that the Iraqi detainees must have done something that led them to be arrested. Therefore, the detainees were responsible for the abuse they received. Perhaps they even deserved the abuse. It is simply easier to believe that the prisoners, not the guards, must have been guilty of criminal actions. Such attributions make the mistreatment seem more understandable and more justified. They make the world seem safer and saner.

ATTRIBUTIONAL DIMENSIONS   In any situation, there are dozens of plausible explanations for specific outcomes. For example, doing well on a test could be due to brilliance, luck, intensive studying, the test's being unexpectedly easy, or a combination of factors. Fritz Heider, the originator of attribution theory, drew an essential distinction between two types of attributions. **Personal attributions** are also known as *internal* or *dispositional attributions*. These explanations refer to things within people, such as abilities, moods, or efforts. **Situational attributions** are also known as *external attributions*. These explanations refer to outside events, such as luck, accidents, or the actions of other people. Bernard Weiner (1974) noted that attributions can vary on other dimensions. For example, attributions can be stable over time (permanent) or unstable (temporary). They can be controllable or uncontrollable. Consider that the weather is situational, unstable, and uncontrollable. How would you classify good study habits?

ATTRIBUTIONS ABOUT THE SELF   In making attributions about our own behavior, we tend to have a self-serving bias. We attribute our failures to situational, unstable, or uncontrollable factors in a way that casts us in a positive light. Essentially, we attribute our failures to temporary aspects of situations that are not our fault. In contrast, we attribute our successes to personal, permanent factors in a way that gives us credit for doing well. For example, if you fail a test, you may blame your poor performance on your not getting enough sleep or on the professor's creating a bad exam. But if you do well on a test, you may attribute that good performance to your being smart.

Weiner's theory has been used to explain psychological states such as depression. As you will see in Chapters 13 and 14, people suffering from depression attribute their failures to their own incompetence. They believe their incompetence is permanent.

ATTRIBUTIONAL BIAS   When explaining other people's behavior, we tend to overemphasize the importance of personality traits and underestimate the importance of situation. This tendency is so pervasive that it has been called the **fundamental attribution error.** Theorists such as Fritz Heider and Harold Kelley have described people as intuitive scientists who try to draw inferences about others and make attributions about events. Unlike objective scientists, however, people tend to be systematically biased when they process social information. That is, they make self-serving attributions that are consistent with their pre-existing beliefs, and they generally fail to take into account that other people are influenced by social circumstances (**Figure 12.4**).

personal attributions Explanations that refer to people's internal characteristics, such as abilities, traits, moods, or efforts.

situational attributions Explanations that refer to external events, such as the weather, luck, accidents, or other people's actions.

fundamental attribution error In explaining other people's behavior, the tendency to overemphasize personality traits and underestimate situational factors.

FIGURE 12.4 Fundamental Attribution Error Since 1984, Alex Trebek has hosted the enormously popular television game show *Jeopardy!* Here Trebek converses with three contestants on the show. Viewers exhibit the fundamental attribution error when they assume Trebek must be very smart because he knows so much information. Trebek may indeed be very smart. But when viewers develop this belief based on his performance on the show, they neglect to take into account that he knows the questions and the answers because writers have provided them on cards.

Edward Jones originated the idea of the fundamental attribution error during the 1960s. He called it the *correspondence bias* to emphasize our tendency to expect the behaviors of others to correspond with our own beliefs and personalities. In contrast, according to Jones, when we make attributions about ourselves, we tend to focus on situations rather than on our personal dispositions. This error, in conjunction with the fundamental attribution error, leads to the *actor/observer discrepancy*. This term refers to two tendencies: When interpreting our own behavior, we tend to focus on situations. When interpreting other people's behavior, we tend to focus on dispositions. For instance, we tend to attribute our own lateness to external factors, such as traffic or competing demands. We tend to attribute other people's lateness to personal characteristics, such as laziness or lack of organization.

According to a meta-analysis of 173 studies, we most often fall prey to the actor/observer discrepancy when we are interpreting negative events (Malle, 2006; Malle, Knobe, & Nelson, 2007). That is, as mentioned earlier, when things go wrong for us, we are most likely to attribute the result to outside forces. When things go wrong for other people, however, we are most likely to attribute the result to the people's dispositions.

Is the fundamental attribution error really fundamental? That is, does it occur across cultures, or do attributional styles differ between Eastern cultures and Western cultures? As discussed in Chapter 1, people in Eastern cultures tend to be more holistic in how they perceive the world. They see the forest rather than individual trees. On average, people in Eastern cultures use much more information when making attributions than do people in Western cultures, and they are more likely to believe that human behavior is the outcome of both personal and situational factors (Choi, Dalal, Kim-Prieto, & Park, 2003; Miyamoto & Kitayama, 2002). Although Easterners are more likely than Westerners to take situational forces into account, however, they still tend to favor personal information over situational information when making attributions about others (Choi, Nisbett, & Norenzayan, 1999). Thus, in interpreting behavior, cultures tend not to differ in whether they emphasize personal factors. Instead, cultures differ in how much they emphasize the situation.

Stereotypes Are Based on Automatic Categorization

Do all Italians have fiery tempers? Do all Canadians like hockey? Can white women rap? We hold beliefs about groups because they allow us to answer these sorts of questions quickly (**Figure 12.5**). As discussed in Chapter 8, such beliefs are stereotypes. That is, they are cognitive schemas that help us organize information about people on the basis of their membership in certain groups. Mental shortcuts are forms of heuristic thinking: They enable us to make quick decisions. Stereotypes are mental shortcuts that allow for easy, fast processing of social information. Stereotyping occurs automatically and, in most cases, outside of our awareness.

In and of themselves, stereotypes are neutral. They simply reflect efficient cognitive processes. Indeed, some stereotypes are based in truth: Men tend to be more violent than women, and women tend to be more nurturing than men. These statements are true on average, however. Not all men are violent, nor are all women nurturing.

We construct and use categories of this kind for two basic reasons: to streamline our formation of impressions and to deal with the limitations inherent in mental processing. That is, because of limited mental resources, we cannot scrutinize every person we encounter. Rather than consider each person as unique and unpredictable, we categorize people as belonging to

(a)

(b)

FIGURE 12.5 Stereotypes (a) Would this photo, of fans at a 2010 Olympic Gold Medal Hockey game between Canada and the United States, lead you to think that all Canadians like hockey? (b) Would this photo lead you to think that all women in Canada look like the Canadian singer Céline Dion? What do the differences between these photos and between your responses to them tell you about stereotypes?

Identifying and Avoiding the Actor/Observer Discrepancy

An important part of critical thinking is understanding the ways that we assign causes to behaviors. As discussed above, we assign causes to our own behaviors and to the behaviors of others. In keeping with the actor/observer discrepancy, we have two strong tendencies: We see other people's actions as caused by individual attributes, as in "She failed the quiz because she is stupid." We see our own actions as caused by circumstances, as in "I failed the quiz because I was tired."

With a little attention, you will begin to see people around you making such attributions. During a political campaign, listen to the way the various candidates explain their own behaviors and those of their opponents. This bias is especially noticeable when a candidate says or does something controversial. For example, a candidate who has changed her or his position on an important policy issue is likely to claim that she or he did so for situational reasons. Perhaps the candidate will say he or she lacked access to certain information when making the initial statement. If a candidate's opponent has changed position on an issue, the candidate is likely to attribute this opponent's change of stance to a lack of firm convictions or another personality flaw.

It is easier to recognize the actor/observer discrepancy in other people's thinking than in your own. Still, once you are aware of this bias, it becomes easier to avoid it. Consider the following scenario: If you have a quick encounter with someone who seems rude or inattentive, do you immediately think, "Wow, what a nasty person"? Now turn the situation around: Suppose a troubling family problem has made you late for class. As you rush across campus, someone stops you and asks a question. How likely is it that you will think, "Can't this person see I'm busy?" Might you be somewhat rude and inattentive? Yet you might feel justified in behaving this way because of your immediate situation. By learning to recognize the actor/observer discrepancy in your own thinking, you will be able to judge other people's behaviors more fairly. You will also be able to take more responsibility for your own behaviors.

particular groups. We hold knowledge about the groups in long-term memory. For example, we might automatically categorize others on the basis of clothing or hairstyles. Once we have put others into particular categories, we will have beliefs about the others based on stereotypes about the particular categories. That is, stereotypes affect the formation of impressions (Kunda & Spencer, 2003). Consider the stereotype that men are more likely than women to be famous. As a result of this stereotype, we are more likely to falsely remember a male name than a female name as that of a famous person (Banaji & Greenwald, 1995; this misremembering, the false fame effect, is discussed further in Chapter 7, "Attention and Memory").

Once we form stereotypes, we maintain them by a number of processes. As schematic structures, stereotypes guide attention toward information that confirms the

stereotypes and away from disconfirming evidence. Our memories are also biased to match stereotypes. These biases lead to illusory correlations in which we believe that relationships exist when they do not.

Suppose a mixed-race college class includes only a few black students. One of the black students performs poorly, but the rest perform well. If the instructor relates the poor performance to that student's blackness, the instructor may be confirming a false belief that performance is related to race. Similarly, one type of behavior might be perceived in different ways so it is consistent with a stereotype. Thus a white man's success may be attributed to hard work and determination, whereas a black man's success may be attributed to one or more outside factors, such as luck or affirmative action. A lawyer described as aggressive and a construction worker described as aggressive conjure up different images. Moreover, when we encounter someone who does not fit a stereotype, we put that person in a special category rather than alter the stereotype. This latter process is known as *subtyping*. Thus a racist who believes blacks are lazy may categorize a superstar such as LeBron James or Beyoncé as an exception to the rule rather than as evidence for the invalidity of the stereotype. Forming a subtype that includes successful blacks allows the racist to maintain the stereotype that most blacks are unsuccessful.

SELF-FULFILLING EFFECTS How does being treated as a member of a stereotyped group affect a person? Stereotypes that are initially untrue can become true. **Self-fulfilling prophecy** is people's tendency to behave in ways that confirm their own or others' expectations.

In the 1960s, the psychologist Robert Rosenthal and a school principal, Lenore Jacobsen, conducted one of the most impressive early examinations of this process. As part of their study, elementary school students took a test that supposedly identified some of them as being especially likely to show large increases in IQ during the school year. These students were labeled *bloomers*. Teachers were given a list of the bloomers in their classes. At the end of the year, standardized testing revealed that the bloomers showed large increases in IQ. As you might have guessed, the bloomers had been chosen at random rather than through the test. Therefore, their increases in IQ seemed to have resulted from the extra attention and encouragement provided by the teachers. The teachers' expectations turned into reality.

Of course, negative stereotypes can become self-fulfilling as well. When teachers expect certain students to fail, they might subtly, however unconsciously, undermine those students' self-confidence or motivation (McKown & Weinstein, 2008). For instance, offering unwanted help, even with the best intentions, can send the message that the teacher does not believe the students have what it takes to succeed.

In another study, each male participant engaged in a phone conversation with a woman about a potential date (Snyder, Tanke, & Berscheid, 1977). Each man saw a photo he believed was of the woman he was speaking with, but the women did not know the men were seeing photos. The photos were not actually of the women participating in the study. Instead, they were of attractive or unattractive women who had earlier agreed to allow their photos to be used in the research. The men who thought the women they talked with were

self-fulfilling prophecy People's tendency to behave in ways that confirm their own expectations or other people's expectations.

attractive rated the women as more sociable, poised, and humorous than did men who thought they were talking with unattractive women. Perhaps this finding is not surprising. In addition, however, a separate group of men and women listened to the women's side of the conversation but did not see photos, nor did they know which women were thought to be attractive by the other participants. Those participants also rated the women believed to be attractive in more positive terms!

How did this happen? Some of the women interacted with men who believed they were attractive. Some of the women interacted with men who believed they were unattractive. When the women interacted with the men who found them attractive, the women behaved more pleasantly than did the women who interacted with the men who found them unattractive. In short, the men's *behavior* helped confirm the stereotypes by bringing out behaviors in the women associated with our perceptions of what attractive and unattractive people are like. As emphasized so often throughout this book, our thoughts and behaviors are influenced by events that we are not consciously aware of.

Yet another example of how expectations can affect performance is stereotype threat. As discussed in Chapter 8, stereotype threat affects any group for which there is a negative stereotype (Steele & Aronson, 1995). For instance, when women are asked to indicate if they are male or female and then tested on their math ability, they tend to perform more poorly than when they are not initially reminded of their sex (Shih, Pittinsky, & Ambady, 1999). Stereotype threat may partly explain the underlying disparity between the numbers of men and women in science careers.

Over the past decade, stereotype threat has been among the most studied topics in social psychology. Researchers have sought to understand what causes this effect and how to prevent it. A recent review of the literature identified three interrelated mechanisms as producing decreased performances following threat: First, physiological stress affects people's prefrontal functioning. Second, people tend to think about their performances, and this thinking distracts them from the tasks. Third, people attempt to suppress negative thoughts and emotions, and this suppression requires a great deal of effort (Schmader, Johns, & Forbes, 2008). In each of these examples, people's beliefs about how others viewed them altered their behaviors in ways that confirmed the stereotypes. These effects occurred even though the people had no conscious knowledge of the influences.

Stereotypes Can Lead to Prejudice

Stereotypes may be positive, neutral, or negative. When they are negative, stereotypes lead to prejudice and discrimination. **Prejudice** involves negative feelings, opinions, and beliefs associated with a stereotype. **Discrimination** is the inappropriate and unjustified treatment of people as a result of prejudice. Prejudice and discrimination are responsible for much of the conflict and warfare around the world. Within nearly all cultures, some groups of people are treated negatively because of prejudice. Over the last half century, social psychologists have studied the causes and consequences of prejudice, and they have tried to find ways to reduce its destructive effects.

Why do stereotypes so often lead to prejudice and discrimination? Various researchers have theorized that only certain types of people are prejudiced, that people treat others as scapegoats to relieve the tensions of daily living, and that people discriminate against others to protect their own self-esteem. One explanation, consistent with the theme that the mind is adaptive, is that evolution has led to two processes that produce prejudice and discrimination: We tend to favor

prejudice Negative feelings, opinions, and beliefs associated with a stereotype.

discrimination The inappropriate and unjustified treatment of people as a result of prejudice.

FIGURE 12.6 Ingroup/Outgroup Bias
People tend to identify strongly with the groups to which they belong. Here, during the semifinal match of the 2011 Men's World Hockey Championships, players from Sweden (in the yellow and blue uniforms) fight with players from the Czech Republic.

our own groups over other groups, and we tend to stigmatize those who pose threats to our groups.

INGROUP/OUTGROUP BIAS We are powerfully connected to the groups we belong to. We cheer them on, fight for them, and sometimes are even willing to die for them. Those groups to which we belong are *ingroups;* those to which we do not belong are *outgroups* (**Figure 12.6**).

Our group memberships are an important part of our social identities, and they contribute to each group member's overall sense of self-esteem. As discussed in Chapter 6, when people participate in conditioning experiments in which aversive stimuli are paired with members of their own racial group or members of a different racial group, they more easily associate the negative stimuli with outgroup members (Olsson, Ebert, Banaji, & Phelps, 2005). This finding suggests that people are predisposed to be wary of others who do not belong to their own groups. Presumably, this predisposition has developed because outgroup members have been more dangerous over the course of human evolution.

The separation of people into ingroup and outgroup members appears to occur early in development. Researchers have found that Caucasian 6-year-olds show as much racial bias as Caucasian adults (Baron & Banaji, 2006). As noted in Chapter 4, we are better able to remember the faces of people of our own race than the faces of people of other races, likely beacause we are most often exposed to members of our own race. Researchers have found that 3-month-old Caucasian infants in the United Kingdom recognize faces from their own group as well as they recognize faces from other groups (African, Middle Eastern, and Chinese). By 6 months of age, however, the infants recognize only Caucasian and Chinese faces, and by 9 months they recognize only Caucasian faces (Kelly et al., 2007).

Once we categorize others as ingroup or outgroup members, we treat them accordingly. For instance, due to the *outgroup homogeneity effect,* we tend to view outgroup members as less varied than ingroup members. UCLA students may think Berkeley students are all alike, but when they think about UCLA students, they cannot help but notice the wide diversity of student types. Of course, for Berkeley students, the reverse is true about UCLA students and themselves.

The consequence of categorizing people as ingroup or outgroup members is **ingroup favoritism.** That is, we are more likely to distribute resources to ingroup members than to outgroup members. In addition, we are more willing to do favors for ingroup members or to forgive their mistakes or errors. The power of group membership is so strong that people exhibit ingroup favoritism even if the groups are determined by arbitrary processes.

Henri Tajfel and John Turner (1979) randomly assigned volunteers to two groups, using meaningless criteria such as flipping a coin. Participants were then given a task in which they divided up money. Not surprisingly, they gave more money to their ingroup members, but they also tried to prevent the outgroup members from receiving any money. These effects occurred even when the participants were told that the basis of group membership was arbitrary and that giving money to the outgroup would not affect how much money their own group obtained.

Why do people value members of their own groups? We can speculate that over the course of human evolution, personal survival has depended on group survival. Those who work together to keep resources within their group and deny resources to outgroup members have a selective advantage over those who are willing to share with the outgroup. This advantage becomes especially important when groups are competing for scarce resources.

ingroup favoritism The tendency for people to evaluate favorably and privilege members of the ingroup more than members of the outgroup.

In addition, women show a much greater automatic ingroup bias toward other women than men do toward other men (Rudman & Goodwin, 2004). Although men generally favor their ingroups, they fail to do so when the category is sex. Rudman and Goodwin speculate that both men and women depend on women for nurturing and that both are threatened by male violence. Moreover, women can freely express their affection for their female friends. Men appear to be less comfortable doing so for their male friends, perhaps because it might threaten their sexual identities.

STEREOTYPES AND PERCEPTION So far, the discussion of stereotypes has focused on beliefs and behavior. What does social psychology have to say about perception itself?

Research has shown that stereotypes can influence basic perceptual processes. In two experiments that demonstrated this influence, white participants looked at pictures of either tools or guns and were asked to classify them as quickly as possible (Payne, 2001). Immediately before seeing a picture, the participants briefly were shown a picture of a white face or a black face. They were told that the face was being shown to signal that either a gun or a tool would appear next. Being shown a black face led the participants to identify guns more quickly and to mistake tools for guns (**Figure 12.7**). In another study, in which over 90 percent of

---

FIGURE 12.7 **Scientific Method: Payne's Experiments on Stereotypes and Perception**

Hypothesis: Stereotypes can influence basic perceptual processes.

Research Method:

1 White participants were shown a picture of a white face or a picture of a black face.

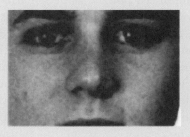

2 Immediately after viewing a picture of a face, participants were shown a picture of an object and asked to classify it as a gun or a tool as quickly as possible.

Results: Participants primed by seeing black faces identified guns more quickly and mistook tools for guns.

Conclusion: Stereotypes affect perception.

Source: Payne, B. K. (2001). Prejudice and perception: The role of automatic and controlled processes in misperceiving a weapon. *Journal of Personality and Social Psychology, 81,* 181–192.

the participants were white, found that the reverse is also true: Priming people with pictures of weapons (e.g., guns and knives) leads them to pay greater attention to pictures of black faces than to pictures of white faces (Eberhardt, Goff, Purdie, & Davies, 2004).

Using a virtual reality simulation, Greenwald, Oakes, and Hoffman (2003) required each participant in a study to play the role of a police officer. On each trial, the participant had to respond as three things appeared: When a criminal was holding a gun, the participant needed to click a computer mouse to shoot the criminal. When a fellow police officer was holding a gun, the participant needed to press the space bar. When a civilian was holding a neutral object, the participant needed to do nothing. In some trials, the criminal holding a gun was a white male and the police officer holding a gun was a black male. In the other trials, these pairings were reversed. Whatever their assigned roles in the study, blacks were more likely to be incorrectly shot. These shootings occurred, in part, because the participants were more likely to identify as weapons the objects held by the blacks. Fortunately, evidence suggests special computerized training—in which race is unrelated to the presence of a weapon—can help police officers avoid racial bias in deciding when to shoot (Plant & Peruche, 2005). Research compared police officers who received this training with community members who had not. In simulated decisions to shoot or not shoot blacks and whites, the police officers were much less likely to shoot unarmed people and were equally likely to shoot armed blacks and whites (Correll et al., 2007). The community members were more likely to shoot unarmed black targets. Thus training seems to be able to override the effects of stereotypes.

INHIBITING STEREOTYPES Most people do not consider themselves prejudiced, and many are motivated to avoid stereotyping others. Yet according to many researchers who study social cognition, categorization and stereotyping occur automatically, without people's awareness or intent (Bargh & Ferguson, 2000).

Patricia Devine (1989) has made the important point that people can override the stereotypes they hold and act in nondiscriminatory ways. For instance, most people in North America know the negative stereotypes associated with African Americans. When a nonblack North American encounters a black person, the information in the stereotypes becomes cognitively available. According to Devine, people low in prejudice override this automatic activation and act in a nondiscriminatory fashion. While some automatic stereotypes alter how we perceive and understand the behavior of those we stereotype, simply categorizing people does not necessarily lead to mistreating them.

Indeed, numerous studies have shown that we can consciously alter our automatic stereotyping (Blair, 2002). For instance, Dasgupta and Greenwald (2001) found that presenting positive examples of admired black individuals (e.g., Denzel Washington) produced more-favorable responses toward African Americans. In another study, training people to respond counter-stereotypically—as in having them press a "no" key when they saw an elderly person paired with a stereotype of the elderly—led to reduced automatic stereotyping in subsequent tasks (Kawakami, Dovidio, Moll, Hermsen, & Russin, 2000). Telling people their test scores indicate that they hold negative stereotypes can motivate people to correct their beliefs, and the worse they feel about holding those beliefs, the harder they try not to be biased (Monteith, 1993).

In everyday life, however, inhibiting stereotyped thinking is difficult and requires self-control (Monteith, Ashburn-Nardo, Voils, & Czopp, 2002). The challenge comes, in part, from the need for the frontal lobes to override the emotional responses associated with amygdala activity. As discussed throughout this book, the frontal lobes are important for controlling both thoughts and behavior, whereas the amygdala is involved in detecting potential threats. In one brain imaging study, the amygdala became activated when white participants were briefly shown pictures of black faces (Cunningham et al., 2004). In this context, the amygdala activity may indicate that the participants' immediate responses to black faces were negative. If the faces were presented longer, however, the frontal lobes became active and the amygdala response decreased. Thus the frontal lobes appear to have overridden the immediate reaction.

Cooperation Can Reduce Prejudice

Can the findings of social psychology be used to reduce prejudice? Can they be used to encourage peace? Since the 1950s, social psychologists have worked with politicians, activists, and others in numerous attempts to alleviate the hostility and violence between factions. Beliefs about ethnic groups are embedded deeply in cultural and religious values, however, and it is extraordinarily difficult to change such beliefs. Around the world, groups clash over disputes that predate the births of most of the combatants. Sometimes people cannot even remember the original sources of particular conflicts. Yet recall the earthquakes and tsunamis in Japan in 2011, when thousands of people were killed, or the devastating earthquake in Haiti in 2010, when hundreds of thousands of people were killed and millions were left homeless (**Figure 12.8**). The international responses to these tragedies show that people respond to outgroup members in need. In working together toward a greater purpose, people can overcome intergroup hostilities.

Social psychology may be able to suggest strategies for promoting intergroup harmony and producing greater tolerance for outgroups. The first study to suggest so was conducted in the 1950s by Muzafer Sherif and colleagues (1961). Sherif arranged for 22 well-adjusted and intelligent white fifth-grade boys from Oklahoma City to attend a summer camp at a lake. The boys did not know each other. Before arriving at camp, they were divided into two groups that were essentially the same. During the first week, each group lived in a separate camp on a different side of the lake. Neither group knew that the other group existed.

The next week, over a four-day period, the groups competed in an athletic tournament. They played games such as tug-of-war, football, and softball, and the stakes were high. The winning team would receive a trophy, individual medals, and appealing prizes. The losers would receive nothing. The groups named themselves the Rattlers and the Eagles. Group pride was extremely strong, and animosity between the groups quickly escalated. The Eagles burned the Rattlers' flag, and the Rattlers retaliated by trashing the Eagles' cabin. Eventually, confrontations and physical fights had to be broken up by the experimenters. All the typical signs of prejudice emerged, including the outgroup homogeneity effect and ingroup favoritism.

Phase 1 of the study was complete. Sherif had shown how easy it was to make people hate each other: Simply divide them into groups and have the groups compete, and prejudice and mistreatment will result. Phase 2 of the study then explored whether the hostility could be undone.

Sherif first tried what made sense at the time: simply having the groups come in contact with each another. This approach failed miserably. The hostilities were too strong, and skirmishes continued. Sherif reasoned that if competition led to hostility, then cooperation should reduce hostility. The experimenters created situations in which members of both groups had to cooperate to achieve necessary goals. For instance, the experimenters rigged a truck to break down. Getting the truck moving required all the boys to pull together. In an ironic twist,

FIGURE 12.8 Global Cooperation After the earthquake in Haiti in 2010, workers from around the world assisted efforts to rebuild the country. Dealing with a natural catastrophe can help people overcome their differences.

the boys had to use the same rope they used earlier in the tug-of-war. When they succeeded, a great cheer arose from the boys, with plenty of backslapping all around. After a series of tasks that required cooperation, the walls between the two sides broke down, and the boys became friends across the groups. Among strangers, competition and isolation created enemies. Among enemies, cooperation created friends (**Figure 12.9**).

Research over the past four decades has indicated that only certain types of contact between hostile groups is likely to reduce prejudice and discrimination. Shared *superordinate* goals—goals that require people to cooperate—reduce hostility between groups. People who work together to achieve a common goal often break down subgroup distinctions as they become one larger group (Dovidio et al., 2004). For example, athletes on multiethnic teams often develop positive feelings toward other ethnicities. In addition, other strategies have been shown to reduce prejudice. For example, bilingual instruction in schools leads to less ingroup favoritism among elementary school children (Wright & Tropp, 2005). Prejudice can also be reduced through explicit efforts to train people about stereotypical associations. For example, participants who practice associating women and counter-stereotypical qualities (e.g., strength, dominance) are more likely than a control group to choose to hire women (Kawakami, Dovidio, & van Kamp, 2005).

JIGSAW CLASSROOM The programs that most successfully bring groups together involve person-to-person interaction. A good example is the social psychologist Eliot Aronson's jigsaw classroom, which he developed with his students in the 1970s. In this program, students work together in mixed-race or mixed-sex groups in which each member of the group is an expert on one aspect of the assignment. For instance, when studying Mexico, one group member might focus on the country's geography, another on its history, and so on. The various geography experts

---

FIGURE 12.9 Scientific Method: Sherif's Study of Competition and Cooperation

Hypothesis: Just as competition between groups promotes prejudice and hostility, so cooperation between groups can promote harmony.

Research Method:

1 In Phase 1 of the experiment, boys from two summer camps were pitted against each other in athletic competitions:

2 In Phase 2, the boys from the two camps were required to work together as one group to achieve common goals.

Results: At first, competition created tension and hostility. After a series of cooperative efforts, the boys began to make friends across groups.

Conclusion: When shared goals require cooperation across group lines, hostility can decrease between the groups.

Source: Sherif, M., Harvey, O. J., White, B. J., Hood, W. R., & Sherif, C. W. (1961). *Intergroup cooperation and competition: The Robbers Cave experiment*. Norman, OK: University Book Exchange.

from each group get together and master the material. They then return to their own groups and teach the material to their team members. In other words, each group member cooperates outside the group and within the group. More than 800 studies of the jigsaw classroom have demonstrated that it leads to more-positive treatment of other ethnicities and that students learn the material better and perform at higher levels. According to Aronson, children in jigsaw classrooms grow to like each other more and develop higher self-esteem than do children in traditional classrooms. The lesson is clear: Communal work toward superordinate goals can reduce prejudice and benefit all the workers.

Summing Up

How Do We Form Our Impressions of Others?

Social interaction requires us to form impressions of others. We are highly sensitive to nonverbal information (e.g., gait, facial expression, eye contact), and we can develop accurate impressions of others on the basis of very thin slices of behavior. We also are motivated to figure out what causes other people to behave the way they do. We often make biased attributions. When interpreting our own behavior, we tend to focus on the situation. When interpreting other people's behavior, we tend to focus on the people's dispositions. This tendency is called the fundamental attribution error. Together, these two biases result in the actor/observer discrepancy. Stereotypes result from the normal cognitive process of categorization and may be positive, neutral, or negative. Stereotypes may be self-fulfilling, as has been demonstrated by research on stereotype threat. Negative stereotypes can lead to prejudice (negative feelings, opinions, and beliefs) and discrimination (inappropriate and unjustified treatment of others as a result of prejudice). We tend to develop prejudices and engage in discrimination against outgroup members—that is, members of groups to which we do not belong. In contrast, we tend to display ingroup favoritism toward ingroup members—that is, members of groups to which we belong. A number of strategies have been identified to inhibit stereotypes and reduce prejudice. These strategies include presenting people with positive information about members of negatively stereotyped groups and requiring members of different groups to work cooperatively toward superordinate goals.

Measuring Up

1. Max was arrested for driving while under the influence of alcohol. Label each of the following statements as an example of personal attribution, situational attribution, or fundamental attribution error.
   a. Max says, "Nobody would give me a ride home. I couldn't sleep at the bar, so I had to get home. I had no other option."
   b. Max's friend says, "Max should know better, but he is a selfish and irresponsible jerk."

2. Label each of the following statements as an example of stereotyping, prejudice, or discrimination.
   a. "People from New York are loud and obnoxious."
   b. "What can I say, I just don't like people from New York."
   c. Walter tells a joke that makes fun of people from New York.

- Explain how attitudes are formed.
- Identify characteristics of attitudes that are predictive of behavior.
- Distinguish between explicit and implicit attitudes.
- Describe cognitive dissonance theory.
- Identify factors that influence the persuasiveness of messages.
- Describe the elaboration likelihood model.

12.2 How Do Attitudes Guide Behavior?

You probably have feelings, opinions, and beliefs about particular racial and ethnic groups. In the same way, you have feelings, opinions, and beliefs about yourself, your friends, your favorite television program, and so on. These feelings, opinions, and beliefs are called **attitudes.** Such evaluations of objects, of events, or of ideas are central to social psychology. Attitudes are shaped by social context, and they play an important role in how we evaluate and interact with other people.

We have attitudes about all sorts of things. For example, we consider trivial and mundane matters, such as which deodorant works best. We form positions on grand issues, such as politics, morals, and religion—that is, the core beliefs and values that define who we are as human beings. Some attitudes we are aware of, but others we do not even know we hold. Some attitudes are simple, but others are complex and involve multiple components. If you like eating ice cream but believe ice cream is bad for your health, your attitude toward ice cream qualifies as complex. If you are horrified by an abuse of power but feel pity for the people who have abused their power, your attitude toward the horrific situation also qualifies as complex. This section considers how both simple and complex attitudes affect our daily lives.

We Form Attitudes through Experience and Socialization

Throughout life, we encounter new things. Those things can be objects, people, or situations. When we hear about things, read about them, or experience them directly, we learn about them and perhaps explore them. Through this process, we gain information that shapes our attitudes. Generally, people develop negative attitudes about new things more quickly than they develop positive attitudes about them (Fazio, Eisner, & Shook, 2004).

We talk about acquiring a taste for foods that we did not like originally, such as coffee or sushi. How do we come to like something that we could not stand the first time we were exposed to it? Typically, the more we are exposed to something, the more we tend to like it. In a classic set of studies, Robert Zajonc (1968, 2001) exposed people to unfamiliar items a few times or many times. Greater exposure to the item, and therefore greater familiarity with it, caused people to have more-positive attitudes about the item. This process is called the *mere exposure effect.* For example, when people are presented with normal photographs of themselves and the same images reversed, they tend to prefer the reversed versions. Why would this be the case? The reversed images correspond to what people see when they look in the mirror (**Figure 12.10**). Their friends and family members prefer the true photographs, which correspond to how they view the people.

Because our associations between things and their meanings can change, our attitudes can be conditioned (for a full discussion of conditioning, see Chapter 6, "Learning"). Advertisers often use classical conditioning: When we see a celebrity paired with a product, we tend to develop more-positive attitudes about the product. After conditioning, a formerly neutral stimulus (e.g., a deodorant) triggers the same attitude response as the paired object (e.g., Brad Pitt if he were to endorse a deodorant). Operant conditioning also shapes attitudes: If you are rewarded with good grades each time you study, you will develop a more positive attitude toward studying.

FIGURE 12.10 The Mere Exposure Effect If he is like most people, U.S. president Barack Obama will prefer **(right)** his mirror image to **(left)** his photographic image. There is nothing wrong the photographic image. President Obama will simply be more familiar with the mirror image.

attitudes People's evaluations of objects, of events, or of ideas.

Attitudes are also shaped through socialization. Caregivers, peers, teachers, religious leaders, politicians, and media figures guide our attitudes about many things. For example, teenagers' attitudes about clothing styles and music, about behaviors such as smoking and drinking alcohol, and about the latest celebrities are heavily influenced by their peers' beliefs. Society instills many of our basic attitudes, including which things are edible. For instance, many Hindus do not eat beef, whereas many Jews do not eat pork. Would you eat a worm? Most Westerners would find it disgusting. But in some cultures, worms are a delicacy.

Behaviors Are Consistent with Strong Attitudes

In general, the stronger and more personally relevant the attitude, the more likely it is to predict behavior. The strong and personally relevant nature of the attitude will lead the person to act the same across situations related to that attitude. It will also lead the person to defend the attitude. For instance, someone who grew up in a strongly Democratic household, especially one where derogatory comments about Republicans were expressed frequently, is more likely to register as a Democrat and vote Democratic than someone who grew up in a more politically neutral environment. Moreover, the more specific the attitude, the more predictive it is. For instance, your attitudes toward recycling are more predictive of whether you take your soda cans to a recycling bin than are your general environmental beliefs. Attitudes formed through direct experience also tend to predict behavior better. Consider parenthood. No matter what kind of parent you think you will be, by the time you have seen one child through toddlerhood, you will have formed very strong attitudes about child-rearing techniques. These attitudes will predict how you approach the early months and years of your second child.

From moment to moment, the way that you rear your second child will also depend on your memory. How easily can you retrieve from memory your attitudes about child rearing? *Attitude accessibility* refers to the ease or difficulty that a person has in retrieving an attitude from memory. This accessibility predicts behavior consistent with the attitude. Russell Fazio (1995) has shown that easily activated attitudes are more stable, predictive of behavior, and resistant to change. Thus the more quickly you recall that you like your psychology course, the more likely you are to attend lectures and read the textbook.

Attitudes Can Be Explicit or Implicit

How do you know your attitude about something? Recall from Chapter 5 that access to our mental processes is limited and that unconscious processes can influence behavior. Our conscious awareness of our attitudes can be limited because of several factors, such as our desire to believe we hold positive attitudes about certain racial groups, but our actions can reveal our less positive attitudes (Nosek, Hawkins, & Frazier, 2011). Most people in contemporary society say that they view African Americans positively and that they are not prejudiced. Yet earlier in life they may have learned societal stereotypes of African Americans that are at odds with their expressed beliefs. These unconscious attitudes can reveal themselves through subtle responses, such as feeling more apprehensive when a black person walks behind them at night than when a white person does.

Over the last 15 years, researchers have demonstrated that attitudes can be *explicit* or *implicit* and that these different attitudes have different effects on

FIGURE 12.11 **Try for Yourself: Implicit Association Test**

At the Web site for Project Implicit® (https://implicit.harvard.edu/implicit/), you can try your hand at various association tests on topics such as age, race, and gender.

After answering questions or responding to certain words and images, you will receive your results and information about the preferences of others.

behavior. **Explicit attitudes** are those you know about and can report to other people. If you say you like bowling, you are stating your explicit attitude toward it. Anthony Greenwald and Mahzarin Banaji (1995) have noted that our many **implicit attitudes** influence our feelings and behaviors at an unconscious level. We access implicit attitudes from memory quickly, with little conscious effort or control. In this way, implicit attitudes function like implicit memories. As discussed in Chapter 7, implicit memories make it possible for us to perform actions, such as riding a bicycle, without thinking through all the required steps. Similarly, you might purchase a product endorsed by a celebrity even though you have no conscious memory of having seen the celebrity use the product. The product might simply look familiar to you. Some evidence suggests that implicit attitudes involve brain regions associated with implicit rather than explicit memory (Lieberman, 2000).

In assessing implicit attitudes, researchers use indirect means, as they do in assessing implicit memories. For example, they observe participants' behaviors rather than soliciting self-reports from the participants. Consider the 2008 presidential election, when many observers wondered how attitudes about blacks would affect people's willingness to vote for Barack Obama. People higher in self-reported (explicit) prejudice were indeed less likely to vote for Obama. In addition, however, people who reported low levels of prejudice but whose scores on an implicit measure indicated negative attitudes about blacks were also less likely to vote for Obama (Payne et al., 2010). For this second group of people, their implicit attitudes were better predictors of behavior than their explicit attitudes.

One method researchers use to assess implicit attitudes is a reaction time test called the Implicit Association Test (IAT; Greenwald, McGhee, & Schwartz, 1998). The IAT measures how quickly a person associates concepts or objects with positive or negative words (**Figure 12.11**). Responding more quickly to the association *female = bad* than to *female = good* indicates your implicit attitude about females. A meta-analysis of more than 100 studies found that, in socially sensitive situations in which people might not want to admit their real attitudes, the IAT is a better predictor of behavior than are explicit self-reports (Greenwald, Poehlman, Uhlmann, & Banaji, 2009).

Discrepancies Lead to Dissonance

Generally, we expect attitudes to guide behavior. We expect people to vote for candidates they like and to avoid eating foods they do not like. What happens when people hold conflicting attitudes? In 1957, the social psychologist Leon Festinger answered that question by proposing the theory of **cognitive dissonance** (**Figure 12.12**).

According to this theory, dissonance — a lack of agreement — occurs when there is a contradiction between two attitudes or between an attitude and a behavior. For example, people experience cognitive dissonance when they smoke even though they know that smoking might kill them. A basic assumption of cognitive dissonance theory is that dissonance causes anxiety and tension. Anxiety and tension cause displeasure. Displeasure motivates people to reduce dissonance. Generally, people reduce dissonance by changing their attitudes or behaviors. They sometimes also rationalize or trivialize the discrepancies.

explicit attitudes Attitudes that a person can report.

implicit attitudes Attitudes that influence a person's feelings and behavior at an unconscious level.

cognitive dissonance An uncomfortable mental state due to a contradiction between two attitudes or between an attitude and a behavior.

Dissonance theory provides important insights into many perplexing behaviors. Consider the American soldiers who served as prison guards at Abu Ghraib. Their treatment of prisoners likely was dissonant from their views on how people generally should be treated. In such poorly run, overcrowded wartime prisons, guards commonly develop extremely negative attitudes about their prisoners, even viewing them as subhuman. Although these changes in attitude might resolve dissonance for the guards, it encourages mistreatment of the prisoners. The following sections examine how dissonance affects attitudes and behavior.

POSTDECISIONAL DISSONANCE According to cognitive dissonance theory, dissonance arises when a person holds positive attitudes about different options but has to choose one of the options. For example, a person might have trouble deciding which college to attend. The person might narrow the choice to two or three alternatives and then have to choose. *Postdecisional dissonance* then motivates the person to focus on one school's—the chosen school's—positive aspects and the other schools' negative aspects. This effect occurs automatically, with minimal cognitive processing, and apparently without awareness. Indeed, even patients with long-term memory loss may show postdecisional effects for past choices, even if the patients do not consciously recall which items they chose (Lieberman, Ochsner, Gilbert, & Schacter, 2001).

INSUFFICIENT JUSTIFICATION In one of the original dissonance studies, each participant performed an extremely boring task for an hour (Festinger & Carlsmith, 1959). The experimenter then paid the participant $1 or $20 to lie and tell the next participant that the task was really interesting, educational, and worthwhile. Nearly all the participants subsequently provided the false information. Later, under the guise of a different survey, the same participants were asked how worthwhile and enjoyable the task had actually been. You might think that those paid $20 remembered the task as more enjoyable, but just the opposite happened. Participants who had been paid $1 rated the task much more favorably than those who had been paid $20.

According to the researchers, this effect occurred because those paid $1 had insufficient monetary justification for lying. Therefore, to justify why they went along with the lie, they changed their attitudes about performing the dull experimental task. Those paid $20 had plenty of justification for lying, since $20 was a large amount of money in 1959 (roughly equivalent to $150 today), so they did not experience dissonance and did not have to change their attitudes about the task (**Figure 12.13**). As this research shows, one way to get people to change their attitudes is to change their behaviors first, using as few incentives as possible. For example, as discussed in Chapter 10, giving children rewards for drawing creatively with colored pens undermines how much they subsequently use the pens.

JUSTIFYING EFFORT So far, the discussion of people's attitudes has focused on changes in individual behavior. What about group-related behavior? Consider the extreme group-related behaviors of initiation rites. On college campuses, administrators impose rules and penalties to discourage hazing, yet some fraternities and sororities continue to do it. The groups require new recruits to undergo embarrassing or difficult rites of passage because these endurance tests make membership in the group seem much more valuable. The tests also make the group more cohesive.

FIGURE 12.12 Leon Festinger Festinger's theory of cognitive dissonance was an important influence on research in experimental social psychology.

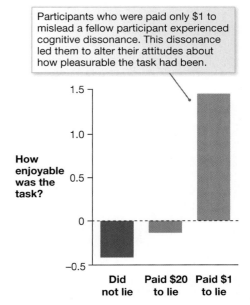

Participants who were paid only $1 to mislead a fellow participant experienced cognitive dissonance. This dissonance led them to alter their attitudes about how pleasurable the task had been.

FIGURE 12.13 Cognitive Dissonances In Festinger's dissonance study, participants performed an extremely boring task and then reported to other participants how enjoyable it was. Some participants were paid $20 to lie, and some were paid $1.

FIGURE 12.14 Justifying Effort In early 2008, the University of Maryland removed the Delta Sigma chapter of the Delta Tau Delta fraternity from the College Park campus. Photos such as this one revealed that the fraternity's hazing included abusive alcohol consumption and mental, emotional, and physical duress. **How do you suspect the pledges justified their willingness to undergo mistreatment? What attitudes, feelings, and behaviors might they have used, consciously or unconsciously?**

persuasion The active and conscious effort to change an attitude through the transmission of a message.

To test these ideas, Eliot Aronson and Judson Mills (1959) required women to undergo a test to see if they qualified to take part in a research study. Some women had to read a list of obscene words and sexually explicit passages in front of the male experimenter. In the 1950s, this display was very difficult for many women and took considerable effort. A control group read a list of milder words, such as *prostitute*. Participants in both conditions then listened to a boring and technical presentation about mating rituals in lower animals. Women who read the embarrassing words reported that the presentation was much more interesting, stimulating, and important than did the women who read the milder words.

As this research shows, when people put themselves through pain, embarrassment, or discomfort to join a group, they experience a great deal of dissonance. After all, they typically would not choose to be in pain, embarrassed, or uncomfortable. Yet they made such a choice. They resolve the dissonance by inflating the importance of the group and their commitment to it. This justification of effort helps explain why people are willing to subject themselves to humiliating experiences such as hazing (**Figure 12.14**). More tragically, it may help explain why people who give up connections to families and friends to join cults or to follow enigmatic leaders are willing to die rather than leave the groups. If they have sacrificed so much to join a group, people believe, the group must be extraordinarily important.

Attitudes Can Be Changed through Persuasion

A number of forces other than dissonance can conspire to change attitudes. We are bombarded by television advertisements; lectures from parents, teachers, and physicians; pressure from peers; public service announcements; politicians appealing for our votes; and so on. **Persuasion** is the active and conscious effort to change an attitude through the transmission of a message. In the earliest scientific work on persuasion, Carl Hovland and colleagues (1953) emphasized that persuasion is most likely to occur when people pay attention to a message, understand it, and find it convincing. In addition, the message must be memorable, so its impact lasts over time.

Various factors affect the persuasiveness of a message (Petty & Wegener, 1998). Such factors include the *source* (who delivers the message), the *content* (what the message says), and the *receiver* (who processes the message). Sources who are both attractive and credible are the most persuasive. Thus television ads for medicines and medical services often feature very attractive people playing the roles of physicians. Even better, of course, is when a drug company ad uses a spokesperson who is both attractive *and* an actual doctor. Credibility and persuasiveness may also be heightened when the receiver perceives the source as similar to himself or herself.

Of course, the arguments in the message are also important for persuasion (Greenwald, 1968). Strong arguments that appeal to our emotions are the most persuasive. Advertisers also use the mere exposure effect, repeating the message over and over in the hope that multiple exposures will lead to increased persuasiveness. For this reason, politicians often make the same statements over and over during campaigns. Those who want to persuade (including, of course, politicians) also have to decide whether to deliver one-sided arguments or to consider both sides of particular issues. One-sided arguments work best when the audience is on the speaker's side or is gullible. With a more skeptical crowd, speakers who acknowledge both sides but argue that one is superior tend to be more persuasive than those who completely ignore the opposing view.

According to Richard Petty and John Cacioppo's **elaboration likelihood model** (1986), persuasive communication leads to attitude change in two fundamental ways (**Figure 12.15**). When people are motivated to process information and are able to process that information, persuasion takes the *central route*. That is, people are paying attention to the arguments, considering all the information, and using rational cognitive processes. This route leads to strong attitudes that last over time and that people actively defend. When people are either not motivated to process information or are unable to process it, persuasion takes the *peripheral route*. That is, people minimally process the message. This route leads to more-impulsive action, as when a person decides to purchase a product because a celebrity has endorsed it or because of how an advertisement makes the person feel. Peripheral cues, such as the attractiveness or status of the person making the argument, influence what attitude is adopted. Attitudes developed through the peripheral route are weaker and more likely to change over time.

elaboration likelihood model A theory of how persuasive messages lead to attitude changes.

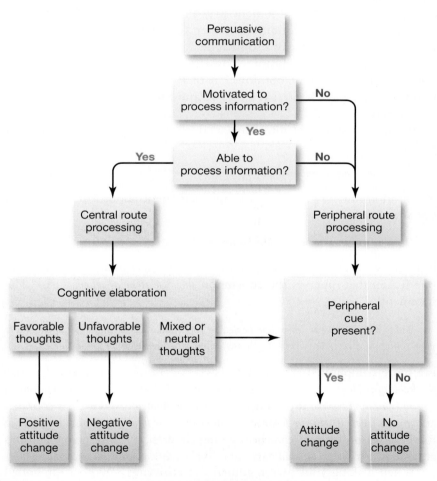

FIGURE 12.15 The Elaboration Likelihood Model (left) When people are motivated and able to consider information, they process it via the central route. As a result, their attitude changes reflect cognitive elaboration. **(right)** When people are either not motivated or not able to consider information, they process it via the peripheral route. As a result, their attitude changes reflect the presence or absence of shallow peripheral cues. For example, as a result of peripheral processing, people may be persuaded because the person making an argument is attractive or a celebrity.

Making Sound Arguments

Rhetorical arguments appear in much of the information we consume, from tweets to this textbook. What is a rhetorical argument? *Rhetoric* is the art of speaking or writing as a means of communication or persuasion. In studying this form of verbal art, scholars have created a specialized vocabulary. For example, in everyday language, the word *argument* refers to a dispute between people. In terms of rhetoric, the same word has a different and more precise meaning: An argument consists of one or more statements, called reasons or premises, used to support a conclusion. In other words, the presenter of an argument seeks to persuade the listener or reader that the conclusion is true or probably true.

What does an argument consist of? An argument must have a conclusion and reasons, but these components do not have to appear in a particular order. The argument may include a qualifier: a constraint or restriction on the conditions under which the conclusion is supported. The argument may also include a counterargument: reasons that run counter to the conclusion. You strengthen your argument by acknowledging alternative opinions. In that way, you show that various points of view have been taken into account in reaching the argument's conclusion.

Because an argument must have a conclusion and reasons, a statement such as

Psychology is my favorite subject.

is not an argument. It is just a simple statement about a preference. A statement such as

Get plenty of exercise because it helps relieve stress.

is a simple argument. It includes a conclusion *(Get plenty of exercise)* and one reason that supports the conclusion *(because it helps relieve stress).* The statement

Young children love to learn from books, so you should develop the habit of reading to your young child every day, even if you are feeling tired from work or family life.

is a more complicated argument. It has a conclusion *(so you should develop the habit of reading to your young child every day).* It has a reason *(Young children love to learn from books).* It has a qualifier *(Young children).* And it has a counterargument *(even if you are feeling tired from work or family life).* That is, being tired is a reason for not reading to young children, but it is included in this argument in a way that makes it seem like a weak counterargument.

When making your own arguments or analyzing arguments presented to you, you must consider the strengths of the reasons that support the conclusion. You must also consider the strengths of the arguments that run counter to the conclusion. You need to combine this information to determine if the overall support for the conclusion is strong, medium, weak, or nonexistent. To assess the argument's overall strength, you need to take into account everything you know about good research and about critical thinking. Assessing arguments in this way is not about making everyone think the same. Instead, it is about focusing on important information and becoming a better thinker.

Suppose you want to address the relationship between media and violence (see the discussions in Chapter 6, "Learning"). Specifically, you want to argue that playing violent video games increases aggressiveness. You would first gather reasons that support the conclusion. You would then gather counter-reasons against that same conclusion. Some reasons, for and against, would be stronger than others. For example, one piece of evidence that supports the conclusion might be a large and well-controlled scientific study. Say the study found that teenage boys who play violent video games are more likely to push people after playing these games. In contrast, suppose you and your friends spend hours every week playing violent video games and yet none of you are aggressive. You could list this "finding" as a reason that runs counter to the conclusion. The results from the study would provide strong support for the conclusion. Your personal experience would be weak evidence against the conclusion. (It would be weak because it is anecdotal. For more information on the weakness of anecdotal evidence, see the discussion of ESP in Chapter 4, "Sensation and Perception.")

Making sound arguments is an essential critical thinking skill. If you develop the habit of systematically listing reasons and counter-reasons, weighing the strength of each reason, and listing qualifiers, you will have greater confidence in the conclusions you come to. You will also be more persuasive in convincing people to agree with your conclusions (**Figure 12.16**).

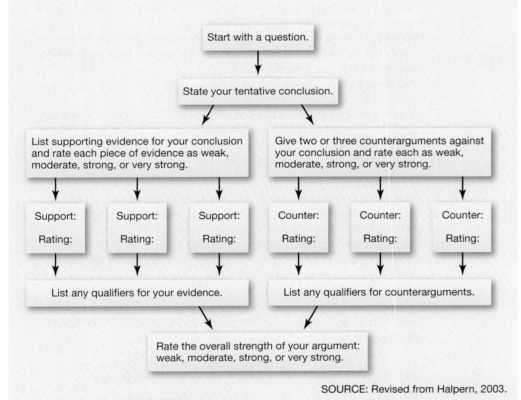

SOURCE: Revised from Halpern, 2003.

FIGURE 12.16 Argument Template When you are constructing an argument, you can use this template to make sure you have all the parts you need to make the strongest possible argument. When you are evaluating someone else's argument, you can use this template to make sure the parts of the argument fit together accurately.

How Do Attitudes Guide Behavior?

Attitudes are evaluations of objects, of events, or of ideas. They are formed through direct experience and socialization, and they best predict behavior when they are strong, personally relevant, specific, formed through personal experience, and easily accessible. Explicit attitudes are those that we are aware of and can report, whereas implicit attitudes operate at an unconscious level. In socially sensitive situations, implicit attitudes are a better predictor of behavior than explicit attitudes are. Discrepancies between attitudes, or between attitudes and behavior, lead to cognitive dissonance. People reduce dissonance by changing their attitudes or behaviors or by rationalizing or trivializing the discrepancy. Persuasion is the active and conscious effort to change attitudes through transmission of a message. According to the elaboration likelihood model, persuasive messages can change attitudes in two ways: In central route processing, people think carefully about the issues. In peripheral route processing, people process the message to a lesser extent and rely more on cues such as the attractiveness of the person giving the message. Compared with peripheral route processing, central route processing leads to stronger attitudes, which are more likely to persist over time.

Measuring Up

1. Identify the attitude formation(s) or change process(es) described in each of the following examples. Choose from cognitive dissonance, conditioning, mere exposure effect, persuasion, and socialization.
   a. Miwa returns home from her first day of kindergarten. She tells her parents, "I don't like my teacher." A few weeks later, her parents hear Miwa talking about how much she likes her teacher.
   b. Arnie always wears his seat belt because his parents taught him to when he was a child.
   c. Given the choice between a Coke or a Pepsi, Manish chooses a Coke. Later that night, he watches his favorite TV show and realizes that Coca-Cola is one of its sponsors.
   d. Sam proclaims her love of coffee to her date. Later, the couple goes to a café. Although Sam is really craving an Italian soda, she orders a coffee.

2. For each of the following scenarios, indicate whether the attitude is likely to predict the subsequent behavior. In a few words, explain why or why not.
   a. Badu somewhat agrees that it is important to vote. Later, a friend asks Badu if he would like to go to the polling place with him.
   b. When asked how she feels about eating fast food, Brooke immediately looks disgusted and proclaims, "Ick!" Later, a friend asks her to grab lunch at a popular fast food joint.
   c. Zane writes a blog entry advocating fair treatment for all people. Later, a friend asks Zane to attend a protest supporting an increase in the wages earned by migrant farm workers.

Answers: 1. a. mere exposure; b. persuasion and socialization; c. conditioning; d. cognitive dissonance. 2. a. No, attitude is not strong; b. Yes, attitude is strong and highly accessible; c. No, attitude lacks specificity.

12.3 How Do Others Influence Us?

We humans have an overriding motivation to fit in with the group. One way we try to fit in is by presenting ourselves positively. We display our best behavior and try not to offend others. We also conform to group norms, obey commands made by authorities, and are easily influenced by others in our social groups. In fact, the desire to fit in with the group and avoid being ostracized is so great that under some circumstances we willingly engage in behaviors we otherwise would condemn. As noted throughout this chapter, the power of the social situation is much greater than most people believe—and this truth is perhaps the single most important lesson from social psychology.

Groups Influence Individual Behavior

SOCIAL FACILITATION The first social psychology experiment was conducted in 1897. Through that experiment, Norman Triplett showed that bicyclists pedal faster when they ride with other people than when they ride alone. They do so because of **social facilitation.** That is, the presence of others enhances performance. Social facilitation also occurs in other animals, including horses, dogs, rats, birds, fish, and even cockroaches.

Robert Zajonc (1965) proposed a model of social facilitation that involves three basic steps (**Figure 12.17**). According to Zajonc, all animals are genetically predisposed to become aroused by the presence of others of their own species. Why? Others are associated with most of life's rewards and punishments. Zajonc then invokes Clark Hull's well-known learning principle: Arousal leads animals to emit a dominant response, that is, the response most likely to be performed in the situation. In front of food, for example, the dominant response is to eat. Zajonc's model expands on Triplett's, predicting that social facilitation can enhance or impair performance. If the dominant response is relatively easy, then the presence of others will enhance performance. If the dominant response is more difficult, the presence of others will impair performance. These effects help explain why crowds of spectators bother professional golfers less than they bother novice golfers. The professionals practice so often that hitting a good shot is their dominant response. Therefore, the professionals may be even more likely to hit well in the presence of spectators.

SOCIAL LOAFING In some cases, people work less hard when in a group than when working alone. This effect is called **social loafing.** It occurs when people's efforts are pooled so that individuals do not feel personally responsible for the group's output. In a classic study, six blindfolded people wearing headphones were told to shout as loudly as they could. Some were told they were shouting alone. Others were told they were shouting with other people. Participants did not shout as loudly when they believed that others were shouting as well (Latané, Williams, & Harkins, 1979). When people know that their individual efforts can be monitored, however, they do not engage in social loafing. Thus if a group is working on a project, each person must feel personally responsible for some component of the project for everyone to exert maximum effort (Williams, Harkins, & Latané, 1981).

DEINDIVIDUATION People sometimes lose their individuality when they become part of a group. **Deindividuation** occurs when people are not self-aware and

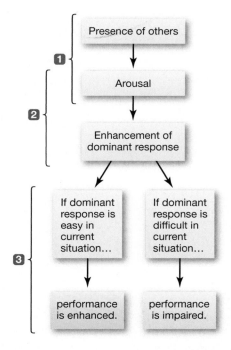

FIGURE 12.17 Zajonc's Model of Social Facilitation According to this model, the mere presence of others leads to increased arousal. The arousal favors the dominant response (the response most likely to be performed in the particular situation). If the dominant response is easy, performance is enhanced. If the dominant response is difficult, performance suffers.

social facilitation When the mere presence of others enhances performance.

social loafing The tendency for people to work less hard in a group than when working alone.

deindividuation A state of reduced individuality, reduced self-awareness, and reduced attention to personal standards; this phenomenon may occur when people are part of a group.

therefore are not paying attention to their personal standards. As you will see in Chapter 13, self-awareness typically causes people to act in accordance with their values and beliefs. When self-awareness disappears, so do restraints. Deindividuated people often do things they would not do if they were alone or self-aware. A good example is crowd behavior. Most of us like to think we would try to help a person who was threatening suicide. But people in crowds often fail to intercede in such situations. Disturbingly, they also sometimes egg the person on, yelling "Jump! Jump!" to someone teetering on a ledge.

People are especially likely to become deindividuated when they are aroused and anonymous and when responsibility is diffused. Rioting by fans, looting following disasters, and other mob behaviors are the products of deindividuation. Recall the Stanford prison study, mentioned at the beginning of this chapter. The study had to be stopped after just six days because the students became so immersed in their roles that many "guards" acted brutally and many "prisoners" became listless and apathetic. The situation was powerful enough to radically alter people's behavior through a process of deindividuation. Most militaries around the world require each of their members to have a standard haircut and an identical uniform because people who look similar are more likely to conform and respond to orders—including orders to commit acts of violence against an enemy. Not all deindividuated behavior is so serious, of course. Gamblers in crowded casinos, fans doing the wave, and people dancing the funky chicken while inebriated at a wedding are most likely in deindividuated states. Accordingly, in these situations, people act in ways they would avoid if they were self-aware (**Figure 12.18**).

GROUP DECISION MAKING Social psychologists have shown that being in a group influences decision making in complex ways. For instance, in the 1960s, James Stoner found that groups often make riskier decisions than individuals do. Stoner identified this phenomenon as the *risky-shift effect*. It accounts for why children in a group may try something dangerous that none of them would have tried alone. But sometimes groups become more cautious. Subsequent research has demonstrated that the initial attitudes of group members determine if the group becomes riskier or more cautious. If most of the group members are somewhat cautious, then the group becomes even more cautious. This process is known as *group polarization* (Myers & Lamm, 1976). For example, when a jury discusses a case, the discussion tends to make individual jurors believe more strongly in their initial opinions about a defendant's guilt or innocence. When groups make decisions, they usually choose the course of action that was initially favored by the majority of individuals in the group. Through mutual persuasion, the decision making individuals come to agreement.

Sometimes group members are particularly concerned with maintaining the group's cohesiveness. Therefore, for the sake of cordiality, the group may end up making a bad decision. In 1972, the social psychologist Irving Janis coined the term *groupthink* to describe this extreme form of group polarization. Contemporary examples of groupthink include the decision to launch the space shuttle *Challenger* despite the clear evidence of a problem with a part; choices made by President Bill Clinton and his advisers following the allegations of his affair with Monica Lewinsky, a sequence of events that ultimately led to his impeachment; and the second Bush administration's decision to go to war with Iraq over weapons of mass destruction that did not exist, as later investigations showed (see "Critical Thinking Skill: Recognizing and Correcting for Belief Persistence in Your Own Thinking and in That of Others," in Chapter 10).

FIGURE 12.18 Deindividuation Here, deindividuated fans are doing the "wave" during a University of Oklahoma game against the University of Miami. **What are some potentially positive aspects of deindividuation? What are some potentially negative aspects of it? Describe a situation in which you experienced deindividuation. Were your experiences positive, negative, or both?**

Groupthink typically occurs when a group is under intense pressure, is facing external threats, and is biased in a particular direction. The group does not carefully process all the information available to it, dissension is discouraged, and group members assure each other they are doing the right thing. To prevent groupthink, leaders must refrain from expressing their opinions too strongly at the beginning of discussions. The group should be encouraged to consider alternative ideas, either by having someone play devil's advocate or by purposefully examining outside opinions. Carefully going through alternatives and weighing the pros and cons of each can help people avoid groupthink (**Figure 12.19**).

Of course, a group can make a bad decision even without falling victim to groupthink. Others factors, such as political values, can bias a group's decision making. The main point behind the concept of groupthink is that group members sometimes go along with bad decisions to protect group harmony.

We Conform to Others

Another powerful form of social influence is **conformity.** Why do we conform, altering our behaviors or opinions to match those of others or to match what is expected of us? Social psychologists have identified two primary reasons that we conform: *Normative influence* occurs when we go along with the crowd to avoid looking foolish. *Informational influence* occurs when we assume that the behavior of the crowd

conformity The altering of one's behaviors and opinions to match those of other people or to match other people's expectations.

FIGURE 12.19 Try for Yourself: Working Effectively in Groups

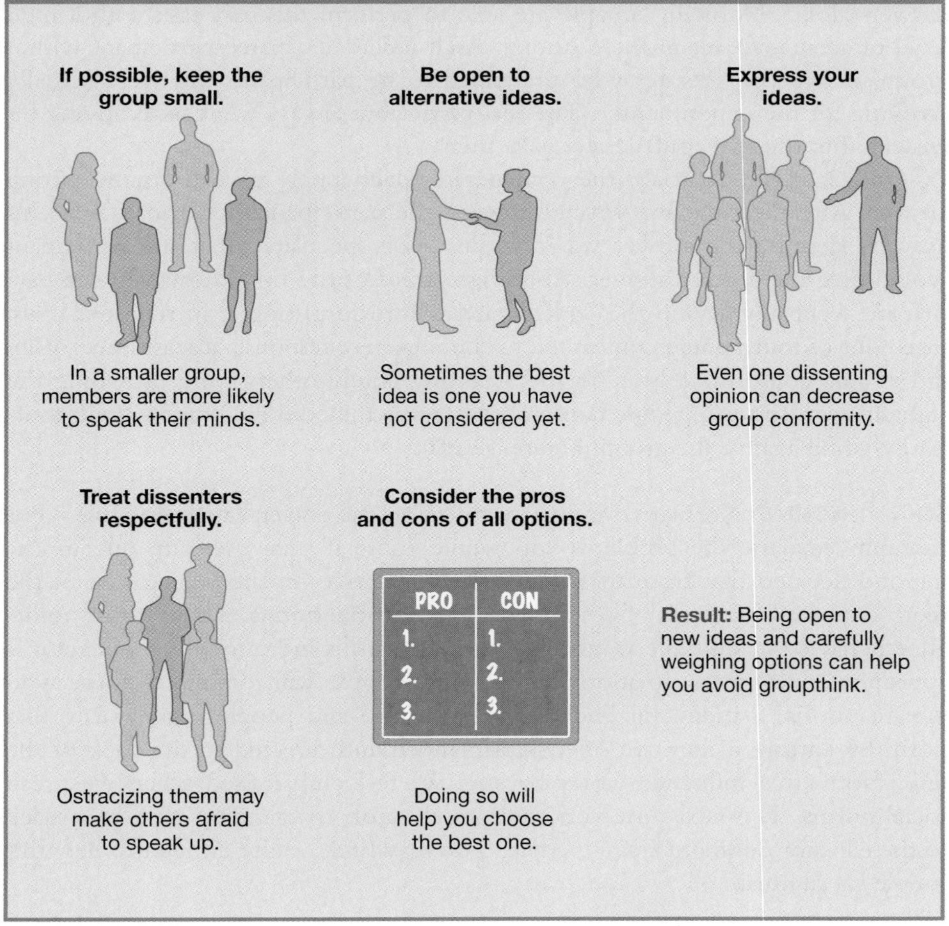

If possible, keep the group small.

In a smaller group, members are more likely to speak their minds.

Be open to alternative ideas.

Sometimes the best idea is one you have not considered yet.

Express your ideas.

Even one dissenting opinion can decrease group conformity.

Treat dissenters respectfully.

Ostracizing them may make others afraid to speak up.

Consider the pros and cons of all options.

PRO	CON
1.	1.
2.	2.
3.	3.

Doing so will help you choose the best one.

Result: Being open to new ideas and carefully weighing options can help you avoid groupthink.

represents the correct way to respond. Suppose you are in a train station. You turn a corner and see a mass of people running for the exit. You might join them if you suspect they are exiting for a good reason. In situations such as this potential emergency, other people's actions provide information about the right thing to do.

In the 1930s, Muzafer Sherif became one of the first researchers to demonstrate the power of conformity in social judgment. Sherif's studies relied on the *autokinetic effect*. Through this perceptual phenomenon, a stationary point of light appears to move when viewed in a totally dark environment. This effect occurs because we have no frame of reference and therefore cannot correct for small eye movements. Sherif asked participants who were alone in a room to estimate how far the light moved. Individual differences were considerable: Some saw the light move only an inch or two, whereas others saw it move 8 inches or more.

In the second part of the study, Sherif put two or more participants in the room and had them call out their estimates. Although there were initial differences, participants very quickly revised their estimates until they agreed. They relied on the information provided by others to base their estimates. In ambiguous situations, people often compare their reactions with the reactions of others to judge what is the correct course of action.

Solomon Asch (1955) speculated that Sherif's results probably occurred because the autokinetic effect is a subjective visual illusion. If there were objective perceptions, Asch thought, participants would not conform. To test his hypothesis, Asch assembled male participants for a study of visual acuity. In the 18 trials, the participants looked at a reference line and three comparison lines. They decided which of the three comparison lines matched the reference line and said their answers aloud. Normally, people are able to perform this easy task with a high level of accuracy. But in these studies, Asch included a naive participant with a group of five confederates who pretended to be participants but were actually working for the experimenter. The real participant always went sixth, giving his answer after the five confederates gave theirs.

On 12 of the 18 trials, the confederates deliberately gave the same wrong answer. After hearing five wrong answers, the participant then had to state his answer. Because the answer was obvious, Asch speculated that the participant would give the correct answer. About one-third of the time, however, the participant went along with the confederates. More surprisingly, in repeated trials, three out of four people conformed to the incorrect response at least once. Why did people conform? It was not because they knew others were providing the right answer. Instead, people conformed because they did not want to look foolish by going against the group (**Figure 12.20**).

SOCIAL NORMS Normative influence relies on the societal need for rules. For example, imagine the problems you would cause if you woke up one morning and decided that from then on you would drive on the wrong side of the road. Expected standards of conduct are called **social norms.** These norms influence behavior in multiple ways. For example, norms indicate which behavior is appropriate in a given situation and also how people will respond to those who violate norms. Standing in line is a social norm, and people who violate that norm by cutting in line are often reprimanded and directed to the back of the line. Normative influence works because we feel embarrassed when we break social norms. The next time you enter an elevator, try standing with your back to the elevator door and facing people. You may find it quite difficult to defy this simple social norm.

social norms Expected standards of conduct, which influence behavior.

FIGURE 12.20 **Scientific Method: Asch's Study on Conformity to Social Norms**

Hypothesis: Conformity would not take place if there were objective perceptions.

Research Method:

1 A naive participant joined a group of five other participants. The five others were confederates, secretly in league with the researcher. Each participant was asked to look at a reference line **(left)** and then say out loud which of three comparison lines matched it **(right)**.

Reference line   Comparison lines

2 On 12 of the 18 trials, the five confederates deliberately gave the wrong answer.

The real participant, in the middle, hears the answer given by the confederates.

He has a hard time believing their wrong answers.

But he starts to doubt his own eyes.

Results: When confederates gave false answers first, 3/4 of the real participants conformed by giving the wrong answer at least once.

Conclusion: People tend to conform to social norms, even when those norms are obviously wrong.

Source: Asch, S. E. (1955). Opinions and social pressure. *Scientific American, 193*, 31–35.

Research consistently has demonstrated that people tend to conform to social norms. This effect can be seen outside the laboratory as well: Adolescents conform to peer pressure to smoke; jury members go along with the group rather than state their own opinions; people stand in line to buy tickets. But when do people reject social norms? In a series of follow-up studies, Asch (1956) and others identified factors that decrease the chances of conformity. One factor is group size. When there are only one or two confederates, a naive participant usually does not conform. When the confederates number three or more, the participant conforms. Conformity seems to level off at a certain point, however. Subsequent research has found that even groups as large as 16 do not lead to greater conformity than groups of 7.

Asch found that lack of unanimity is another factor that diminishes conformity. If even one confederate gives the correct answer, conformity to the group norm decreases a great deal. Any dissent from majority opinion can diminish the influence of social norms. But dissenters are typically not treated well by groups. Stanley Schachter (1951) conducted a study in which a group of students debated the fate of a juvenile delinquent, Johnny Rocco. A confederate deviated from the group judgment of how Johnny should be treated. When it became clear that the confederate would not be persuaded by group sentiment, the group began to ostracize him. When group members subsequently were given the opportunity to reduce group size, they consistently rejected the "deviant" confederate.

The bottom line is that groups enforce conformity, and those who fail to go along are rejected. The need to belong, including the anxiety associated with the fear of social exclusion, gives a group powerful influence over its members. Indeed, a brain imaging study was done that used a conformity test similar to Asch's (Berns et al., 2005). Some participants gave answers that did not conform to the group's incorrect answer. In the dissenting participants' brains, there was activity in the amygdala that might have represented a fear response.

SOCIAL NORMS MARKETING Can the power of social norms be harnessed to modify behavior in positive ways? Across North America, universities have tried to use social norms marketing to reduce binge drinking on campus. For example, they have attempted to correct misperceptions regarding peer drinking. Proponents have put up posters with messages such as "Most students have fewer than four drinks when they party." Unfortunately, social norms marketing may inadvertently increase drinking among light drinkers, whose behavior is also susceptible to social norms (Russell, Clapp, & Dejong, 2005). Students who usually have only one drink might interpret the posters as suggesting that the norm is to have two or three drinks, and they might adjust their behavior accordingly. One team of researchers demonstrated that simply providing descriptive norms (i.e., the frequency of behavior) can cause this sort of backfire effect. They found that adding a message that the behavior is undesirable might help prevent social norms marketing from increasing the behavior it is meant to reduce (Schultz, Nolan, Cialdini, Goldstein, & Griskevicius, 2007).

We Are Compliant

Often people influence our behavior simply by asking us to do things. If we do the requested thing, we are exhibiting **compliance.** A number of factors increase compliance. For instance, Joseph Forgas (1998) has demonstrated that a person in a good mood is especially likely to comply. This tendency may be the basis for "buttering up" others when we want things from them. In addition, according to Robert Cialdini (2008), people often comply with requests because they fail to pay attention. Wanting to avoid conflict, they follow a standard mental shortcut: They respond without fully considering their options. Thus if you give people a reason for a request, they will be much more likely to comply, even if the reason makes little sense.

People can use a number of powerful strategies to influence others to comply. Consider the *foot-in-the-door effect:* If people agree to a small request, they become more likely to comply with a large and undesirable request. Jonathan Freedman and Scott Fraser (1966) asked homeowners to allow a large, unattractive "DRIVE CAREFULLY" sign to be placed on their front lawns. As you might imagine, fewer than one in five people agreed to do so. Other homeowners, however, were first asked to sign a petition that supported legislation intended to reduce traffic accidents. A few weeks later, these same people were approached about having the large sign placed on their lawns, and more than half agreed. Once people commit to a course of action, they behave in ways consistent with that course.

compliance The tendency to agree to do things requested by others.

The opposite influence technique is the *door in the face:* People are more likely to agree to a small request after they have refused a large request. After all, the second request seems modest in comparison, and the people want to seem reasonable. As you might have encountered, salespeople often use this technique. Another favorite tactic among salespeople is the *low-balling strategy.* Here a salesperson offers a product—for example, a car—for a very low price. Once the customer agrees, the salesperson may claim that the manager did not approve the price or that there will be additional charges. Whatever the reason, someone who has already agreed to buy a product will often agree to pay the increased cost.

We Are Obedient to Authority

One of the most famous and most disturbing psychology experiments was conducted in the early 1960s by Stanley Milgram. Milgram wanted to understand why apparently normal German citizens willingly obeyed orders to injure or kill innocent people during World War II (**Figure 12.21**). Milgram was interested in the determinants of *obedience.* That is, he wanted to find out which factors influence people to follow orders given by an authority.

Imagine yourself as a participant in Milgram's experiment. You have agreed to take part in a study on learning. On arriving at the laboratory, you meet your fellow participant, a 60-year-old grandfatherly type. The experimenter describes the study as consisting of a teacher administering electric shocks to a learner engaged in a simple memory task that involves word pairs. Your role as the teacher is determined by an apparently random drawing of your name from a hat. On hearing that he may receive electric shocks, the learner reveals that he has a heart condition and expresses minor reservations. The experimenter says that although the shocks will be painful, they will not cause permanent tissue damage. You help the experimenter take the learner to a small room and hook him up to the electric shock machine. You then proceed to a nearby room and sit at a table in front of a large shock generator with switches that will deliver from 15 volts to 450 volts. Each voltage level carries a label, and the labels range from "slight" to "danger—severe shock" to, finally, an ominous "XXX" (which apparently does not mean three kisses!).

You perform your task. Each time the learner makes a mistake, you give him a shock. With each subsequent error, you increase the voltage. When you reach 75 volts, over the intercom you hear the man yelp in pain. At 150 volts, he screams, bangs on the wall, and demands that the experiment be stopped. At the experimenter's command, you apply additional, stronger shocks. The learner is clearly in agony. Each time you say you are quitting and try to stop the experiment, the experimenter replies, "The experiment requires that you continue," "It is essential that you go on," "There is no other choice; you must go on!" So you do. At 300 volts, the learner refuses to answer any more questions. After 330 volts, the learner is silent. All along you have wanted to leave, and you severely regret participating in the study. You might have killed the man, for all you know.

FIGURE 12.21 Stanley Milgram Milgram, pictured here with his infamous shock generator, demonstrated that average people will obey even hideous orders given by an authority figure.

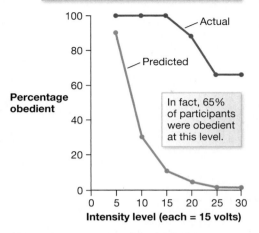

The overall prediction was that fewer than 1/10 of a percent of participants in the Milgram experiments would obey completely and provide the maximum level of shock.

In fact, 65% of participants were obedient at this level.

FIGURE 12.22 Predicting the Results Psychiatrists, college sophomores, middle-class adults, and both graduate students and professors in the behavioral sciences offered predictions about the results of Milgram's experiments. Their predictions were incorrect.

Does this scenario sound crazy to you? If you really were the teacher, at what level would you stop administering the shocks? Would you quit as soon as the learner started to complain? Would you go up to 450 volts? Before conducting the experiment, Milgram asked various people for predictions. These people predicted that most participants would go no higher than 135 volts. They felt that fewer than one in a thousand participants would administer the highest level of shock. But that is not what happened. What did happen changed how people viewed the power of authority.

Almost all the participants tried to quit. Nearly two-thirds, however, completely obeyed all the experimenter's directives (**Figure 12.22**). The majority were willing to administer 450 volts to an older man with a heart condition (actually a confederate). These findings have been replicated by Milgram and others around the world. The conclusion of these studies is that ordinary people can be coerced into obedience by insistent authorities. This effect occurs even when what the people are coerced into doing goes against the way they usually would behave. At the same time, these results do not mean all people are equally obedient. Indeed, some aspects of personality seem related to being obedient, such as the extent to which people are concerned about how others view them (Blass, 1991). As discussed in the next chapter, both situation and personality influence behavior.

Surprised by the results of his study, Milgram next studied ways to reduce obedience. He found that some situations produced less compliance. For instance, if the teacher could see or had to touch the learner, obedience decreased. When the experimenter gave the orders over the telephone and thus was more removed from the situation, obedience dropped dramatically.

Throughout these studies, Milgram was highly concerned with his participants' mental states. In systematic debriefings, he carefully revealed the true nature of the experiments to the participants, and he made sure that the teachers met the confederate learners and that the teachers could see that the learners were not hurt in any way. Milgram (1974) also followed his participants over time to ensure that they experienced no long-term negative effects. Actually, many people were glad they had participated. They felt they had learned something about themselves and about human nature. Most of us assume that only sadistic miscreants would willingly inflict injury on others when ordered to do so. Milgram's research, and studies that followed up on it, demonstrated that ordinary people may do horrible things when ordered to do so by an authority (**Figure 12.23**). Although some people have speculated that these results would not be true today, a recent replication found that 70 percent of the participants were obedient up to the maximum voltage in the experiment (Burger, 2009).

Recall the discussion at the opening of this chapter, about the prison guards at Abu Ghraib. All the background data available on those soldiers suggests they were ordinary people. Investigators have not determined exactly what the guards were ordered to do. Still, a number of social factors likely played prominent roles in the mistreatment of the Abu Ghraib prisoners. These contributing factors would have included deindividuation, social facilitation, inappropriate norms, and conformity. As noted earlier, all of us need to be aware of situational influences when we evaluate our own behavior and that of others. We need to be especially vigilant about situational influences when our core beliefs and values are at risk.

FIGURE 12.23 **Scientific Method: Milgram's Shock Experiments on Obedience**

Hypothesis: People are obedient to authority figures.

Research Method:

1 In one condition, each participant was instructed to "shock," from another room, a participant (learner). The learner was secretly in league with the experimenter.

2 In another condition, each participant was instructed to touch and "shock" a learner sitting next to the participant. In both conditions, the experimenter would instruct the participant to give the learner increasingly severe shocks.

3 After the experiment, each participant was introduced to the confederate learner and could see that the learner had not been harmed.

Results: In the first condition, almost all the participants tried to quit, but nearly 2/3 obeyed the experimenter's directives. In the "touch" condition, fewer than 1/3 of the participants obeyed the experimenter's orders.

Conclusion: Most people will obey even hideous orders given by insistent authority figures, but this willingness is lessened when people are made more personally responsible.

Source: Milgram, S. (1974). *Obedience to authority: An experimental view*. New York: Harper & Row.

Summing Up

How Do Others Influence Us?

We are influenced greatly by social situations. Social psychologists have identified a number of phenomena that demonstrate the influence of the group on the individual. These phenomena include social facilitation (improved performance of relatively easy tasks in the presence of others), social loafing (working less hard when in a group than when alone), deindividuation (loss of individuality, of self-awareness, and of attention to personal standards, when in a group), group polarization (adopting the initial opinions of the group more strongly through mutual persuasion), and groupthink (agreeing to bad decisions to maintain group harmony). Other forms of social influence include conformity, compliance, and obedience. We conform when we alter our behaviors or opinions to match those of others or their expectations. Conformity is influenced by group size and unanimity. We comply when we agree to the requests of others. Compliance is influenced by mood and by strategies such as the foot-in-the-door and door-in-the-face techniques. We obey when we follow orders given by an authority. Obedience is influenced by personality and by proximity to the authority figure.

12.4 When Do We Harm or Help Others?

Although obedience can lead people to commit horrible acts, the need to belong to a group also can lead us to acts of altruism and of generosity. Events of the last few years have revealed the human capacities for harming and helping others. We have seen terrorists killing civilians at points around the globe. As noted earlier in this chapter, we have also seen people being kind, compassionate, and giving in response to natural disasters. Similarly, members of the group Doctors Without Borders travel to dangerous regions to care for those in need. This tension between our aggressive and altruistic sides is at the core of who we are as a species. Psychologists working at all levels of analysis have provided much insight into the roles that nature and nurture play in these fundamental human behaviors.

Many Factors Can Influence Aggression

Aggression can be expressed through countless behaviors. These behaviors all involve the intention to harm someone else. Among nonhuman animals, aggression often occurs in the context of fighting over a mate or defending territory from intruders. In the latter case, just the threat of aggressive action may be sufficient to dissuade. Among humans, physical aggression is common among young children but relatively rare in adults. Adults' aggressive acts more often involve words, or other symbols, meant to threaten, intimidate, or emotionally harm others. Aggression can be considered across the levels of analysis, from basic biology to cultural context.

aggression Any behavior that involves the intention to harm someone else.

BIOLOGICAL FACTORS The biology of aggression has largely been studied in nonhuman animals. Research has shown that stimulating certain brain regions or altering brain chemistry can lead to substantial changes in behavior. Stimulating or damaging the septum, amygdala, or hypothalamus regions in the brain leads to corresponding changes in the level of aggression displayed. For example, stimulating a cat's amygdala with an electric probe causes the animal to attack, whereas damaging the amygdala leads to passive behavior. In 1937, the researchers Heinrich Klüver and Paul Bucy produced a striking behavioral change by removing the amygdalas of normally very aggressive rhesus monkeys. Following the surgery, the monkeys were tame, friendly, and easy to handle. They began to approach and explore objects they normally feared, such as snakes. They also showed unusual oral behavior: They put anything within reach into their mouths, including snakes, matches, nails, dirt, and feces. The behavior associated with damage to this region is now referred to as *Klüver-Bucy syndrome*.

In terms of brain chemistry, several lines of evidence suggest that serotonin is especially important in the control of aggressive behavior (Caramaschi, de Boer, & Koolhaus, 2007). In a study using monkeys, drugs that enhance the activity of serotonin lowered aggression, whereas those that interfere with serotonin increased aggression (Raleigh, McGuire, Brammer, Pollack, & Yuwiler, 1991; **Figure 12.24**). In humans, low levels of serotonin have been associated with aggression in adults and hostility and disruptive behavior in children (Kruesi et al., 1992). In a large sample of men from New Zealand, low levels of serotonin were associated with violence but not with criminal acts in general (Moffitt et al., 1998). Additionally, postmortem examinations of suicide victims have revealed extremely low levels of serotonin. Suicide may seem very different from aggression, but many psychologists believe suicide and violence toward others are manifestations of the same aggressive tendencies. Indeed, low levels of serotonin were found among those who had killed themselves violently (such as by shooting themselves) but not among those who had done so nonviolently (such as by taking drug overdoses; Asberg, Shalling, Traskman-Bendz, & Wagner, 1987).

Decreased levels of serotonin may interfere with good decision making in the face of danger or of social threat. For instance, monkeys with the lowest levels of serotonin are the least socially skilled (Higley et al., 1996). This lack

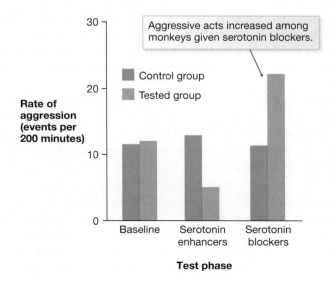

FIGURE 12.24 Serotonin and Aggression Male vervet monkeys were given either serotonin enhancers or serotonin blockers. The results suggest serotonin is important in the control of aggressive behavior.

frustration-aggression hypothesis The extent to which people feel frustrated predicts the likelihood that they will act aggressively.

FIGURE 12.25 Frustration-Aggression Hypothesis Frustration generally leads to aggression. For example, road rage is most likely to occur where traffic is heavy and drivers feel frustrated.

of social competence often leads the other monkeys to attack and kill them. Monkeys with low serotonin are also likely to pick fights with much larger monkeys. Do these findings have implications for humans? Possibly. In one study, participants given a drug that enhances serotonin activity were found to be less hostile and more cooperative over time, compared with the control group (Knutson et al., 1998).

SITUATIONAL FACTORS In the 1930s, John Dollard and colleagues proposed the first major psychological model of aggression. According to their **frustration-aggression hypothesis,** the extent to which people feel frustrated predicts the likelihood that they will be aggressive. The more people's goals are blocked, the greater their frustration and therefore the greater their aggression. For example, slow traffic is frustrating. If the traffic impedes you from getting somewhere you really want or need to go, you may feel especially frustrated. If another driver then cuts in front of you, you may feel especially angry and perhaps make an aggressive hand gesture, shout, or otherwise express yourself (**Figure 12.25**).

According to Leonard Berkowitz's *cognitive-neoassociationistic* model (1990), frustration leads to aggression by eliciting negative emotions. Similarly, any situation that induces negative emotions—such as being insulted, afraid, overly hot, or in pain—can trigger physical aggression even if it does not induce frustration. Berkowitz proposed that negative emotion leads to aggression because it primes cognitive knowledge associated with aggression. In other words, negative events activate thoughts related to fighting or escaping, and those thoughts prepare a person to act aggressively. Whether someone behaves aggressively depends on the situational context. If the situation also cues violence—for example, if the person has recently watched a violent movie or been in the presence of weapons—the person is more likely to act aggressively.

SOCIAL AND CULTURAL FACTORS An evolutionary approach to aggression would call for similar patterns of aggressive behavior to exist in all human societies. After all, if aggression provided a selective advantage for human ancestors, it should have done so for all humans. But the data show that violence varies dramatically across cultures and even within cultures at different times. For example, over the course of 300 years, Sweden went from being one of the most violent nations on Earth to being one of the most peaceable. This cultural change did not correspond with a change in the gene pool. Moreover, murder rates are far higher in some countries than in others (**Figure 12.26**). And analysis of crime statistics in the United States reveals that physical violence is much more prevalent in the South than in the North. Aggression may be part of human nature, but society and culture influence people's tendencies to commit acts of physical violence.

Some cultures may be violent because they subscribe to a *culture of honor.* In this belief system, men are primed to protect their reputations through physical aggression. Men in the southern United States, for example, traditionally were (and perhaps still are) raised to be ready to fight for their honor and to respond aggressively to personal threats. To determine whether southern males are more likely to be aggressive than northern males, researchers at the University of Michigan conducted a series of studies (Cohen, Nisbett, Bowdle, & Schwarz, 1996). In each study, a male participant had to walk down a narrow hallway. The participant had to pass a filing cabinet, where a male confederate was blocking the hallway. As the participant tried to edge past the confederate, the confederate responded angrily and insulted the participant. Compared with participants raised

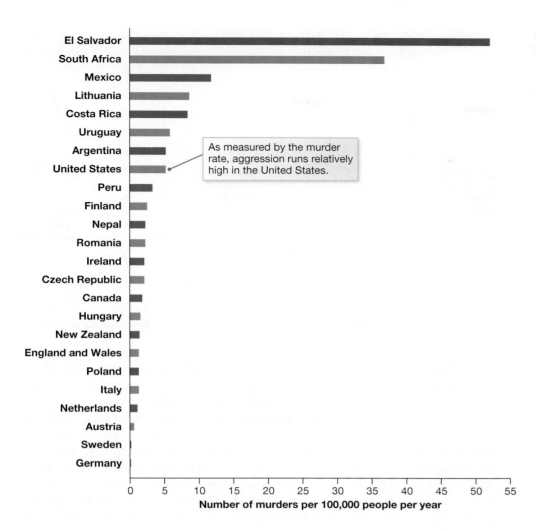

FIGURE 12.26 Aggression Varies across Cultures The numbers in this chart are the most recent available, from 2008. They come from the United Nations Office on Drugs and Crime (n.d.).

As measured by the murder rate, aggression runs relatively high in the United States.

Number of murders per 100,000 people per year

in the North, those raised in the South became more upset and were more likely to feel personally challenged. They were more physiologically aroused (measured by cortisol and testosterone increases), more cognitively primed for aggression, and more likely to act in an aggressive and dominant manner for the rest of the experiment. For instance, in another part of the studies, participants raised in the South shook a new confederate's hand much more vigorously than the participants raised in the North did (**Figure 12.27**).

The culture-of-honor theory of violence supports Bandura's social learning theory. According to this theory, as discussed in Chapter 6, much aggressive behavior is learned through vicarious social observation of both reward and punishment. Bandura's theory also suggests that our attitudes toward violence are determined by our societies' cultural norms.

Steroids May Play a Role in Some Violent Behavior

In August 1991, a 16-year-old boy, Jamie Fuller, killed his 14-year-old girlfriend, Amy Carnevale. Fuller reportedly was angry that, the day before, Carnevale had gone to the beach with some other boys. He repeatedly stabbed her and then dumped her body in a pond. According to the prosecutors who tried him for murder, Fuller was a troubled youth who had planned the killing for months and discussed it with his friends. Afterward, he even bragged about the killing. According

FIGURE 12.27 **Aggressive Responses to Insults** These graphs show some of the results from studies at the University of Michigan.

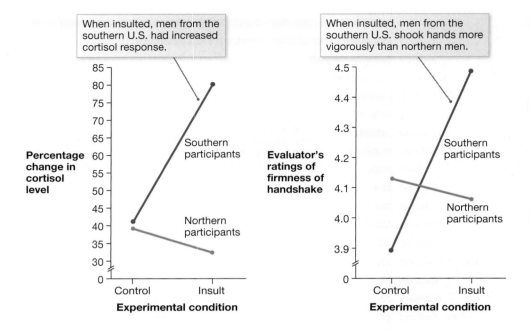

When insulted, men from the southern U.S. had increased cortisol response.

When insulted, men from the southern U.S. shook hands more vigorously than northern men.

Percentage change in cortisol level

Southern participants

Northern participants

Control   Insult

Experimental condition

Evaluator's ratings of firmness of handshake

Southern participants

Northern participants

Control   Insult

Experimental condition

to the defense attorneys, however, Fuller had been taking steroids at the time of the crime, and the effects of steroids caused him to become enraged and lose control. Such violent outbursts produced by steroids have been called "roid rage."

The particular steroid that Fuller ingested was a synthetic form of the male sex hormone testosterone, which enhances muscle growth. As discussed in Chapter 3, steroids are banned in most sports, but some athletes use them to become stronger, faster, and more competitive. Steroid use is reputedly widespread in sports such as weight lifting. As the cases of Barry Bonds and Mark McGuire indicate, it also occurs in baseball. There is little doubt that steroids can enhance performance, but can they create killers? Given that the steroid Fuller was taking was a synthetic form of testosterone, is there any evidence that testosterone itself is associated with aggression?

Males have more testosterone than females, and males carry out the vast majority of aggressive and violent acts. Boys play more roughly than girls at an early age. They become especially aggressive during early adolescence, a time when their levels of testosterone rise 10-fold (Mazur & Booth, 1998). Consider, however, that these increases in testosterone in boys coincide with other maturational changes that promote aggression, such as physical growth.

The overall picture suggests only a modest correlation between testosterone and human aggression. Particularly aggressive men, such as violent criminals, and particularly physical athletes, such as hockey players, have been found to have higher levels of testosterone than other males (Dabbs & Morris, 1990). This relationship, however, is not large, and it is unclear how testosterone is linked to greater aggressiveness. There is evidence that testosterone may increase aggression because it reduces the activity of brain circuits that control impulses (Mehta & Beer, 2010).

Testosterone changes may be the result—rather than the cause—of aggressive behavior. That is, the situation may change testosterone levels. A number of studies have shown that testosterone rises just prior to athletic competition. Testosterone remains high for the winners of competitive matches and drops lower for the losers. Even those who simply watch a competition can be affected. Hockey players who watched a replay of a former victory by their team showed increased testosterone (Carré & Putnam, 2010). Even fans are affected. Testosterone increased in Brazilian television viewers who watched Brazil beat Italy in the 1994 World Cup soccer tournament, but decreased in Italian television viewers (Bernhardt, Dabbs, Fielden, & Lutter, 1998). These results suggest that testosterone might not play a direct role in aggression, but rather may be related to social dominance, the results of having greater power and status (Mazur & Booth, 1998; Mehta, Jones, & Josephs, 2008). If this finding is true, the question then is how feelings of dominance are related to aggression.

Taking large doses of some steroids might increase testosterone to such a level that the hormone produces an extreme need for dominance and control. This need, in turn, would provoke violent behavior when a male is challenged (Carré, McCormick, & Hariri, 2011). Jamie Fuller had been a skinny, introverted teen who often was picked on by bigger kids. After he took steroids for many months, his appearance and personality changed dramatically: He gained some 30 pounds of muscle and became more socially assertive, as well as increasingly short-tempered and belligerent. According to testimony by the psychiatrist Harrison Pope, steroids caused these changes in Jamie Fuller. Pope claimed that there had been a number of case studies of steroid users becoming extremely violent. Athletes themselves report becoming more aggressive and even committing violent crimes after steroid use. In self-report studies, those who admit taking large quantities of steroids also report experiencing grandiose beliefs and frenzied mental states and engaging in reckless and aggressive behavior. Should we believe these anecdotal reports? Might the athletes simply be repeating what they have heard or using this possible link to excuse their aggressive actions?

It is important to remember that correlation does not prove causation. In self-report studies, researchers cannot determine whether it is the steroids or some other factor that is responsible for aggressive outbursts. Perhaps the social environment of athletes encourages aggressive behavior. After all, emotionally intense practices and demanding coaches cannot be discounted. Alternatively, perhaps male athletes who are susceptible to violence or who have other psychological problems are more likely to use steroids to enhance athletic performance (Yates, Perry, & Murray, 1992). Pope and colleagues found that weight lifters who used steroids were much more likely to be substance abusers, as was Fuller, than those who had never taken steroids (Kanayama, Pope, Cohane, & Hudson, 2003). Which causes which?

An effective research strategy to understand the effect of steroids is to administer randomly either steroids or placebos to research participants, without anyone knowing which participants received which, and then examine changes in mood and behavior. Pope and colleagues (2000) conducted such a double-blind study and found that those participants who took steroids experienced overall increases in aggression and frenzied emotions. But they also found that these effects were highly variable, with 16 percent of the participants showing quite dramatic changes and the remainder showing minimal effects. One limitation of this kind of research is that it is unethical to give research participants the massive doses of steroids that athletes often take, since serious health consequences are associated with such use. Maybe if higher doses were used, all of the participants would have shown increased aggression. It is impossible to know. But the preponderance of evidence suggests that chronic high doses of steroids may promote aggressive outbursts, at least among some users. Still, does this conclusion sufficiently explain why Jamie Fuller killed Amy Carnevale? The actual trial jury rejected the steroid defense. Fuller was convicted and sentenced to life in prison (**Figure 12.28**).

FIGURE 12.28 Fact or Fiction? Five years after Jamie Fuller murdered Amy Carnevale, the incident inspired a made-for-television movie called *No One Would Tell*. Fred Savage played a high school athlete named Bobby Tennison, and Candace Cameron played his girlfriend/victim, Stacy Collins.

Many Factors Can Influence Helping Behavior

People inflict harm on one another in many situations, but they also behave in **prosocial** ways. That is, they act for the benefit of others. Prosocial behaviors include doing favors, offering assistance, paying compliments, subjugating egocentric desires or needs, resisting the temptation to insult or throttle another person, or simply being pleasant and cooperative. By providing benefits to others, prosocial behaviors promote positive interpersonal relationships. Group living, in which people necessarily engage in prosocial behaviors such as sharing and cooperating, may be a central human survival strategy. After all, a group that works well together is a strong group, and belonging to a strong group benefits the individual members.

Why are humans prosocial? Theoretical explanations range from selflessness to selfishness and from the biological to the philosophical. For instance, Daniel Batson and colleagues (Batson et al., 1988; Batson, Turk, Shaw, & Klein, 1995) argue that prosocial behaviors are motivated by empathy, in which people share other people's emotions. Conversely, Robert Cialdini and colleagues (1987; also Maner et al., 2002) argue that most prosocial behaviors have selfish motives, such as wanting to manage one's public image or relieve one's negative mood. Others have proposed that people have an inborn tendency to help others. Consider that young infants become distressed when they see other infants crying (Zahn-Waxler & Radke-Yarrow, 1990). Generally, children's early attempts to soothe other children are ineffective. For instance, they tend initially to comfort themselves rather than the other children. Still, this empathic response to other people's suffering suggests that prosocial behavior is hardwired in us.

Altruism is the providing of help when it is needed, without any apparent reward for doing so. The fact that people help others, and even risk personal safety to do so, may seem contrary to evolutionary principles. After all, those who protect themselves first would appear to have an advantage over those who risk their lives to help others. During the 1960s, the geneticist William Hamilton offered an answer to this riddle. Hamilton proposed that natural selection occurs at the genetic level rather than at the individual level.

As discussed in Chapter 1, the "fittest" animals pass along the most genes to future generations. These animals increase the chances of passing along their genes by helping ensure that their offspring survive. Hamilton's concept of *inclusive fitness* describes the adaptive benefits of transmitting genes rather than focusing on individual survival. According to this model, people are altruistic toward those with whom they share genes. This phenomenon is known as *kin selection*. A good example of kin selection occurs among insects, such as ants and bees. In these species, workers feed and protect the egg-laying queen, but they never reproduce. By protecting the group's eggs, they maximize the number of their common genes that will survive into future generations (Dugatkin, 2004).

Of course, animals sometimes help nonrelatives. For example, dolphins and lions will look after orphans within their own species. Similarly, a person who jumps into a lake to save a drowning stranger is probably not acting for the sake of genetic transmission. To help explain altruism toward nonrelatives, Robert Trivers (1971) proposed the idea of *reciprocal helping*. According to Trivers, one animal helps another because the other may return the favor in the future. Consider grooming, in which primates take turns cleaning each other's fur: "You scratch my back, and I'll scratch yours." For reciprocal helping to be adaptive, benefits must outweigh costs. Indeed, people are less likely to help others when the costs of doing so are high. Reciprocal helping is also much more likely to

prosocial Tending to benefit others.

altruism The providing of help when it is needed, without any apparent reward for doing so.

occur among animals, such as humans, that live in social groups because their species survival depends on cooperation. Thus, as discussed earlier, people are more likely to help members of their ingroups than to help members of outgroups. From an evolutionary perspective, then, altruism confers benefits. When an animal acts altruistically, the animal may increase the chances that its genes will be transmitted. The altruistic animal may also increase the likelihood that other members of the social group will reciprocate when needed.

Some Situations Lead to Bystander Apathy

In 1964, a young woman named Kitty Genovese was walking home from work in a relatively safe area of New York City. An assailant savagely attacked her for half an hour, eventually killing her. At the time, a newspaper reported that none of the 38 witnesses to the crime tried to help or called the police (**Figure 12.29**). As you might imagine, most people who followed the story were outraged that 38 people could sit by and watch a brutal murder. That story appears to have been wrong, however. None of the few witnesses was in a position to observe what was happening to Genovese (Manning, Levine, & Collins, 2007).

Yet the idea of 38 silent witnesses prompted researchers to undertake important research on how people react in emergencies. Shortly after the Genovese murder, the social psychologists Bibb Latané and John Darley examined situations that produce the **bystander intervention effect.** This term refers to the failure to offer help by those who observe someone in need. Common sense might suggest that the more people there are who are available to help, the more likely it is that a victim will be helped. Latané and Darley made the paradoxical claim, however, that a person is less likely to offer help if other bystanders are around.

To test their theory, Latané and Darley conducted studies in which people were placed in situations that indicated they should seek help. In one of the first situations, male college students were in a room, filling out questionnaires (Latané & Darley, 1968). Pungent smoke started puffing in through the heating vents. Some participants were alone. Some were with two other naive participants. Some were with two confederates, who noticed the smoke, shrugged, and continued filling out their questionnaires. When participants were on their own, most went for help. When three naive participants were together, however, few initially went for help. With the two calm confederates, only 10 percent of participants went for help in the first 6 minutes (**Figure 12.30**). The other 90 percent "coughed, rubbed their eyes, and opened the window—but they did not report the smoke" (p. 218). In subsequent studies, people were confronted with mock crimes, apparent heart attack victims in subway cars, and people passed out in public places. The experimenters obtained similar results each time. The bystander intervention effect, also called *bystander apathy,* has been shown to occur in a wide variety of contexts. Even divinity students, while rushing to give a lecture on the Good Samaritan, failed to help a person in apparent need of medical attention (Darley & Batson, 1973).

Years of research have indicated four major reasons for the bystander intervention effect. First, a diffusion of responsibility occurs. In other words, bystanders expect other bystanders to help. Thus the greater the number of people who

FIGURE 12.29 Kitty Genovese Based on what you have read about Genovese's murder so far, would you say she was the victim of bystander apathy?

bystander intervention effect The failure to offer help by those who observe someone in need.

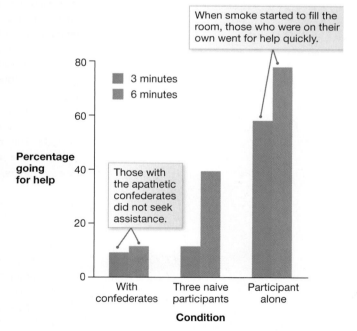

FIGURE 12.30 The Bystander Intervention Effect In Latané and Darley's experiments, participants waited with two apathetic confederates, with two other naive participants, or alone. This chart records the participants' reactions to smoke filling the room.

witness someone in need of help, the less likely it is that any of them will step forward. Second, people fear making social blunders in ambiguous situations. All the laboratory situations had some degree of ambiguity, and people may have worried that they would look foolish if they sought help that was not needed. There is evidence that people feel less constrained from seeking help as the need for help becomes clearer. In the Genovese murder case, the few witnesses found the situation unclear and therefore might have been reluctant to call the police. Third, people are less likely to help when they are anonymous and can remain so. Therefore, if you need help, it is often wise to point to a specific person and request his or her help by saying something like, "You, in the red shirt, call an ambulance!" Fourth, people weigh two factors: How much harm do they risk to themselves by helping? What benefits might they have to forgo if they help? Imagine you are walking to a potentially dull class on a beautiful day. Right in front of you, someone falls down, twists an ankle, and needs transportation to the nearest clinic. You probably would be willing to help. Now imagine you are running to a final exam that counts for 90 percent of your grade. In this case, you probably would be much less likely to offer assistance.

Summing Up

When Do We Harm or Help Others?

Aggression is a fundamental human behavior. With respect to biological factors, research suggests that the amygdala and serotonin levels are especially important in the control of aggressive behavior. With respect to situational factors, research suggests that any situation that elicits negative emotion—including frustration—increases the likelihood that people will act aggressively. This effect may occur because negative emotion primes aggressive thoughts. With respect to sociocultural factors, research suggests that societies that subscribe to a culture of honor are prone to higher levels of violence. Research has demonstrated a modest correlation between testosterone and aggression. Moreover, steroid use may contribute to aggressive outbursts, at least in some users. The evolutionary perspective maintains that altruistic behavior is selfishly motivated. That is, we help others to pass on common genes or to increase the likelihood that others will reciprocate help when we need it. The bystander intervention effect occurs when people fail to help someone in need. This phenomenon is most likely to occur when we are among other bystanders, are in ambiguous situations, can remain anonymous, and perceive risk in helping others.

Measuring Up

1. Indicate whether each of the following statements supports a biological, situational, or sociocultural explanation for aggression.
   a. Drugs that enhance serotonin activity decrease aggressive behaviors.
   b. If some people recently watched a violent movie, they will more likely act aggressively.
   c. Levels and types of violence vary across cultures.
   d. Levels and types of violence vary within cultures across time.
   e. Physical violence is more prevalent in the southern United States than in the northern United States.
   f. Postmortem examinations of people who committed suicide reveal extremely low serotonin levels.

g. Removing the amygdala in a rhesus monkey tames this normally aggressive creature.

h. Stimulating a cat's amygdala with an electric shock causes the animal to attack.

i. The more an individual's goals are blocked, the greater his or her frustration and aggression.

2. For each of the following scenarios, indicate whether the individuals are likely to evidence bystander apathy. Briefly explain why or why not.

a. A college student is in an academic building late one Friday afternoon, when almost everyone has gone home for the weekend. She sees one of her professors lying in the hallway; his breathing is shallow, and he is grasping his chest.

b. A driver hurrying to a meeting sees a man hovering over a woman sitting on a park bench. The man is shaking his fist violently, and the woman is looking up at him with terror in her eyes.

c. College students are walking across campus after a night on the town. They come across a person who appears to be homeless, curled up on the sidewalk. His eyes and mouth are open, but he does not seem alert.

Answers: 1. a, f, g,—biological; b, i—situational; c, d, e—sociocultural. 2. a. no (no ambiguity, no opportunity to diffuse responsibility, no anonymity); b. yes (high cost-benefit ratio, driver can remain anonymous, opportunity for diffusion of responsibility); c. yes (situation is ambiguous, opportunity for diffusion of responsibility).

12.5 What Determines the Quality of Relationships?

Learning Objectives

- Identify factors that influence interpersonal attraction.
- Distinguish between passionate and companionate love.
- Discuss the function of idealization in romantic relationships.
- Identify interpersonal styles and attributional styles that contribute to relationship dissatisfaction and dissolution.

Our involvements with others sometimes lead to relationships. Here the term *relationships* refers to connections with friends and romantic partners. You might expect that studying relationships would be a high priority for psychologists. But until the last decade or so, psychologists have paid little attention to how people select either their friends or their romantic partners. After all, it is difficult to develop rigorous experiments to test complex and fuzzy concepts such as love. Some people think this mysterious state is more appropriate for consideration by poets than by scientists. Researchers have made considerable progress, however, in identifying the factors that lead us to form relationships (Berscheid & Regan, 2005). Many of these findings consider the adaptive value of forming lasting affiliative bonds with others. As discussed in Chapter 10, humans have a strong need for social contact, and various factors influence how people select mates. This section considers the factors that determine the quality of human relationships: how friendships develop, why people fall in love, why romantic relationships sometimes fail, and how people can work to sustain their romantic relationships. As you will see, many of the same principles are involved in choosing our friends and choosing our lovers.

Situational and Personal Factors Influence Friendships

Psychologists have discovered a number of factors that promote friendships. In 1950, Leon Festinger, Stanley Schachter, and Kurt Back examined friends in a college dorm. Because room assignments were random, the researchers were able to examine the effects of proximity on friendship. *Proximity* here simply means how often people come into contact. The researchers found that the more often students come into contact, the more likely they are to become friends. Indeed, friendships often form among people who belong to the same groups, clubs, and so on.

Proximity might have its effects because of familiarity: People like familiar things more than unfamiliar ones. In fact, humans generally fear anything novel. This phenomenon is known as *neophobia*. By contrast, as discussed earlier, when we are repeatedly exposed to something, we tend to like the thing more over time. This effect—the mere exposure effect—has been demonstrated in hundreds of studies that have used various objects, including faces, geometric shapes, Chinese characters, and nonsense words (Zajonc, 2001). Familiarity can also breed contempt rather than liking. The more we get to know a person, the more aware we become of how different that person is from us (Norton, Frost, & Ariely, 2007). And we tend to prefer people who are similar to us.

BIRDS OF A FEATHER Birds of a feather really do flock together. People similar in attitudes, values, interests, backgrounds, and personalities tend to like each other. In high school, people tend to be friends with those of the same sex, race or ethnicity, age, and year in school. College roommates who are most similar at the beginning of the school year are most likely to become good friends (Neimeyer & Mitchell, 1988). The most successful romantic couples also tend to be the most physically similar, a phenomenon called the *matching principle* (Bentler & Newcomb, 1978; Caspi & Herbener, 1990). Of course, people can and do become friends with, become romantic partners with, and marry people of other races, people who are much older or younger, and so on. Such friendships and relationships tend to be based on other important similarities, such as values, education, and socioeconomic status.

PERSONAL CHARACTERISTICS People tend to especially like those who have admirable personality characteristics and who are physically attractive. This tendency holds true whether people are choosing friends or lovers. In a now-classic study, Norman Anderson (1968) asked college students to rate 555 trait descriptions by how much they would like others who possessed those traits. As you might guess from the earlier discussion of who is rejected from social groups, people dislike cheaters and others who drain group resources. Indeed, as shown in **Table 12.1,** the least likable characteristics are dishonesty, insincerity, and lack of personal warmth. Conversely, people especially like those who are kind, dependable, and trustworthy. Generally, people like those who have personal characteristics valuable to the group. For example, people like those whom they perceive to be competent or reliable much more than those they perceive to be incompetent or unreliable. People who seem overly competent or too perfect make others feel uncomfortable or inadequate, however, and small mistakes can make a person seem more human and therefore more likable. In one study, a highly competent person who spilled a cup of coffee on himself was rated more highly than an equally competent person who did not perform this clumsy act (Helmreich, Aronson, & LeFan, 1970).

PHYSICAL ATTRACTIVENESS What determines physical attractiveness? Some standards of beauty, such as preferences for particular body types, appear to change over time and across cultures. Nevertheless, how people rate attractiveness

TABLE 12.1 The Ten Most Positive and Most Negative Personal Characteristics

Most Positive	Most Negative
Sincere	Unkind
Honest	Untrustworthy
Understanding	Malicious
Loyal	Obnoxious
Truthful	Untruthful
Trustworthy	Dishonest
Intelligent	Cruel
Dependable	Mean
Open-Minded	Phony
Thoughtful	Liar

SOURCE: Anderson (1968).

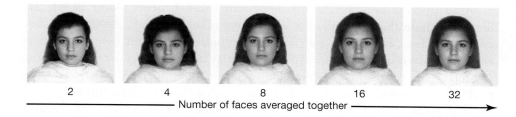

2 4 8 16 32
Number of faces averaged together ⟶

FIGURE 12.31 "Average" Is Attractive The more faces that are averaged together, the more attractive people find the outcome. The face on the right, a combination of 32 faces, typically is rated most attractive.

is generally consistent across all cultures (Cunningham, Roberts, Barbee, Druen, & Wu, 1995).

In a cleverly designed study of what people find attractive, Langlois and Roggman (1990) used a computer program to combine (or "average") various faces without regard to individual attractiveness. They found that as more faces were combined, participants rated the "averaged" faces as more attractive (**Figure 12.31**). People may view averaged faces as attractive because of the mere exposure effect. In other words, average faces may be more familiar than unusual faces (**Figure 12.32**). Other researchers contend that although averaged faces might be attractive, averaged *attractive* faces are rated more favorably than averaged *unattractive* faces (Perrett, May, & Yoshikawa, 1994).

Most people find symmetrical faces more attractive than asymmetrical ones. This preference may be adaptive, because a lack of symmetry could indicate poor health or a genetic defect. There are no racial differences in the extent to which faces are symmetrical, but biracial people tend to have more-symmetrical facial features and correspondingly are rated as more attractive than those who are uniracial (Phelan, 2006). It does not seem to matter which two races are involved in the genetic makeup.

FIGURE 12.32 Try for Yourself: Which Average Is More Attractive?

Which face do you find most attractive?

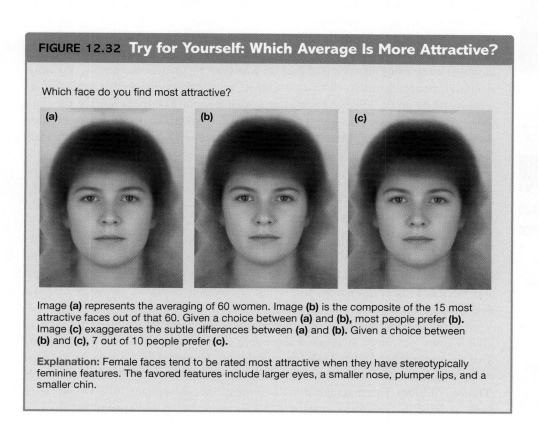

(a) (b) (c)

Image **(a)** represents the averaging of 60 women. Image **(b)** is the composite of the 15 most attractive faces out of that 60. Given a choice between **(a)** and **(b)**, most people prefer **(b)**. Image **(c)** exaggerates the subtle differences between **(a)** and **(b)**. Given a choice between **(b)** and **(c)**, 7 out of 10 people prefer **(c)**.

Explanation: Female faces tend to be rated most attractive when they have stereotypically feminine features. The favored features include larger eyes, a smaller nose, plumper lips, and a smaller chin.

Attractiveness can bring many important social benefits: Most people are drawn to those they find physically attractive (Langlois et al., 2000). Attractive people are less likely to be perceived as criminals; are given lighter sentences when convicted of crimes; are typically rated as happier, more intelligent, more sociable, more capable, more gifted, more successful, and less socially deviant; are paid more for doing the same work; and have greater career opportunities. These findings point to what Karen Dion and colleagues (1972) dubbed the *"what is beautiful is good"* stereotype.

The preference for attractiveness begins early. Children as young as 6 months prefer to look at attractive faces, and young children prefer attractive over unattractive playmates (Rubenstein, Kalakanis, & Langlois, 1999). Even mothers treat attractive children differently from unattractive children. In one study, researchers observed more than 100 mothers feeding and playing with their just-born babies (while still in the hospital) and then again three months later (Langlois, Ritter, Casey, & Sawin, 1995). Mothers of attractive infants were much more affectionate and playful than mothers of unattractive children. In fact, mothers of unattractive children attended to other people more than to their own infants. Mothers of attractive infants also expressed slightly more positive attitudes about their infants than did mothers of unattractive infants.

Given such preferential treatment, do attractive people actually possess characteristics consistent with the "what is beautiful is good" stereotype? The evidence on this issue is mixed. Attractive people tend to be more popular, more socially skilled, and healthier, but they are not necessarily smarter or happier (Feingold, 1992). Among studies of college students, the correlation between objective ratings of attractiveness and other characteristics appears small. In one study, multiple judges objectively rated the attractiveness of the participants. The researchers did not find any relation between appearance and grades, number of personal relationships, financial resources, or just about anything (Diener, Wolsic, & Fujita, 1995). In addition, attractive people are similar to less attractive people in intelligence, life satisfaction, and self-esteem. Why does having all the benefits of attractiveness not lead to greater happiness? Possibly, attractive people learn to distrust attention from others, especially romantic attention (Reis et al., 1982). They assume that people like them simply for their looks. Because they believe that good things happen to them primarily because they are good-looking, attractive people may come to feel insecure. After all, looks can change or fade with age.

Love Is an Important Component of Romantic Relationships

As already noted, psychologists have long neglected the study of love. Thanks to the pioneering work of Elaine Hatfield and Ellen Berscheid, researchers now can use scientific methods to examine this important interpersonal bond. Hatfield and Berscheid have drawn an important distinction between *passionate love* and *companionate love.*

Passionate love is a state of intense longing and sexual desire. This kind of love is often portrayed stereotypically in movies and on television. In passionate love, people fall head over heels for each other. They feel an overwhelming urge to be together. When they are together, they are continually aroused sexually (**Figure 12.33a**). Brain imaging studies show that passionate love is associated with activity in dopamine reward systems, the same systems involved in drug

FIGURE 12.33 Passionate versus Companionate Love (a) The arts tend to focus on passionate love. Consider this image from the 2010 movie *Blue Valentine,* starring Ryan Gosling and Michelle Williams. **(b)** Some romances, however, depict the development of companionate love. Contrast the *Blue Valentine* shot with this image from the 2010 movie *Love and Other Drugs* (2010), starring Jake Gyllenhaal and Anne Hathaway.

addiction (Fisher, Aron, & Brown, 2006; Ortigue, Bianchi-Demicheli, Hamilton, & Grafton, 2007).

People experience passionate love early in relationships. In most enduring relationships, passionate love evolves into companionate love (Sternberg, 1986). Companionate love is a strong commitment to care for and support a partner. This kind of love develops slowly over time because it is based on friendship, trust, respect, and intimacy (**Figure 12.33b**).

One theory of love is based on attachment theory. As discussed in Chapter 9, infants can form different levels of attachment with their parents. According to Cindy Hazan and Phillip Shaver (1987), adult relationships also vary in their attachment styles. Romantic relationships are especially likely to vary in terms of attachment. The attachment style a person has as an adult appears to be related to how the person's parents treated her or him as a child (Fraley & Shaver, 2000). People who believe their parents were warm, supportive, and responsive report having secure attachments in their relationships. They find it easy to get close to others and do not fear being abandoned. Just under 60 percent of adults report having this attachment style (Mickelson, Kessler, & Shaver, 1997). Roughly the remaining 40 percent have insecure attachments. For example, people who believe their parents were cold and distant report having avoidant attachments. They find it hard to trust or depend on others, and they are wary of those who try to become close to them. Relationship partners make them uncomfortable. About 25 percent of adults report having this attachment style. People whose parents treated them inconsistently—sometimes warm and sometimes not—have ambivalent attachments. These people are best described as clingy. They worry that people do not really love them and are bound to leave them. About 11 percent of adults report having this attachment style. These findings are based partly on people's recollections of how their parents treated them, however. It is possible that people's memories in this area are distorted.

Love Is Fostered by Idealization

According to the Irish playwright George Bernard Shaw, "Love is a gross exaggeration of the difference between one person and everybody else." Is there any truth in Shaw's cynical remark?

Researchers have argued that there is. Sandra Murray, John Holmes, and Dale Griffin reasoned that people who fall in love and maintain that love tend to be biased toward positive views of their partners. This bias enables the lovers to reconcile two conflicting thoughts: "I love my partner" and "My partner sometimes does things that drive me crazy!" After all, people in love relationships often have to make accommodations for one another's failures.

Suppose your romantic partner has annoying habits, such as frequently arriving late or always leaving dirty dishes around your home. Or suppose your partner behaves in an unlovable way, such as becoming angry and kicking the wall, growing very overweight, or losing money in a get-rich-quick scheme. According to Murray and colleagues, paying attention to your partner's flaws or placing too much importance on your partner's occasional failure should make it very difficult to remain in love. If, however, you hold positive illusions about your partner, you should encounter fewer conflicting thoughts. So you might think of your partner's anger as reflecting how "he is in touch with his feelings," his increasing girth as a sign that "he knows how to enjoy life," and his botched investments as indications that "he's trying his best to provide his

How Can Psychology Help My Romantic Relationship Thrive?

Some couples seem loving and supportive. We look at them and think, "That's the kind of relationship I'd like to have someday!" Other couples seem downright mean to each other. We look at them and think, "That relationship seems so toxic! Why are they even together?" What different factors help create these healthy and unhealthy relationships? How can their successes and failures help you create a healthy relationship that will thrive?

Over the past two decades, a number of psychologists have conducted research on healthy and unhealthy relationships. Among the foremost of these researchers is John Gottman. To understand what predicts marital outcomes, Gottman (1998) has studied thousands of married couples. In *Why Marriages Succeed or Fail . . . and How You Can Make Yours Last* (1994), Gottman outlines numerous differences between couples who are happy and those who are not.

Based on his research, Gottman believes that if a couple has about five positive interactions for every negative one, chances are good that the relationship will be stable. If the interactions fall below this level, the couple may be headed for a breakup. If there are as many negatives as positives in a relationship, the prognosis is pretty bleak. Therefore, the task for any couple is to seek opportunities for positive feelings and interactions within the relationship. According to Gottman and others, the same principles apply to all long-term, committed relationships, heterosexual or homosexual:

1. **Show interest in your partner.** Listen to him or her describe the events of the day. Pay attention while he or she is speaking, and maintain eye contact. Try to be empathetic: Show you really understand and can feel what your partner is feeling. Such empathy and understanding cannot be faked. To convey that you understand your partner's feelings, say things like "That must have been really annoying."
2. **Be affectionate.** You can show love in very quiet ways, such as simply touching the person once in a while. Reminisce about happy times together. Appreciate the benefits of the relationship. When

a couple talk about the joys of their relationship, they tend to be happier with the relationship. Such conversation can include comparing the partnership favorably with the partnerships of other people.
3. **Show you care.** Try to do spontaneous things such as buying flowers or calling your partner at an unexpected time just to see how he or she is doing (**Figure 12.34a**). Such actions let your partner know you think about him or her, even when you are not together. When we are dating people, we flirt with them, give them compliments, and display our best manners. Being in a committed relationship does not mean you do not have to do any of these things. Be nice to your partner and try to make him or her feel that you value your mutual companionship. Praise your partner whenever possible. In turn, he or she will feel free to act in kind, which will help you feel good about yourself. Positivity begets positivity.
4. **Spend quality time together.** It is easy for a couple to drift apart and develop separate lives. Find time to explore

family with new opportunities." You should thus have an easier time keeping the love going.

To investigate this hypothesis, Murray and colleagues (1996) investigated partners' perceptions of each other. Their study included couples who were dating and married couples. The results were consistent with their predictions. Those people who loved their partners the most also idealized their partners the most. That is, they viewed their partners in the most unrealistically positive terms compared with how they viewed other people *and* compared with how their partners viewed themselves. Those people with the most positively biased views of their partners were more likely to still be in the relationships with their partners several months later than were those people with more "realistic" views of their partners. A little idealization appears to buffer a relationship against the ugly truths that might threaten it.

(a) **(b)**

FIGURE 12.34 Principles for a Committed Relationship Positive interactions help keep a relationship stable. **(a)** A thoughtful gesture is one way to show your partner you care. **(b)** Doing activities you both enjoy is one way to spend quality time together.

joint interests, such as hobbies or other activities (**Figure 12.34b**). Partners should pursue independent interests, but having some activities and goals in common helps bring a couple closer. In fact, research shows that, when a couple engage in novel and exciting activities, the couple's relationship satisfaction increases (Aron, Norman, Aron, McKenna, & Heyman, 2000). Having fun together is an important part of any relationship. Share private jokes, engage in playful teasing, be witty, have adventures. Enjoy each other.

5. **Maintain loyalty and fidelity.** Outside relationships can threaten an intimate partnership. Believing your partner is emotionally or physically involved with another person can pose harm to even the healthiest relationship, as can being distrustful or jealous for no reason. At their core, relationship partners have to trust each other. Anything that threatens that basic sense of trust will harm the relationship. When relationship partners disparage attractive or threatening alternatives, the partners are better able to remain faithful (Rusbult & Buunk, 1993).

6. **Learn how to handle conflict.** Many people believe that conflict is a sign of a troubled relationship and that couples who never fight must be the happiest, but these ideas are not true. Fighting, especially when it allows grievances to be aired, is one of the healthiest things a couple can do for their relationship. Conflict is inevitable in any serious relationship, but resolving conflict positively is the key to happiness as a couple. Do not avoid conflict or pretend you have no serious issues. Rather, calm down, try to control your anger, and avoid name-calling, sarcasm, or excessive criticism; if you're unable to do so in the heat of the moment, call for a time-out. Return to the discussion when you both feel ready to engage respectfully. Validate your partner's feelings and beliefs even as you express your own feelings and beliefs. Look for areas of compromise.

Much of this advice may seem like common sense. However, many couples lose sight of how to express their love and commitment. Partners can get so caught up in everything else in their lives, from work to stress about exams to worries about family, that it becomes easier to focus on what is wrong in a relationship than on what is right. When that happens, the relationship has taken a wrong turn. To make a relationship stronger, partners must put considerable effort into recognizing and celebrating all that is good about the relationship. Those affirming experiences make relationships succeed.

Staying in Love Can Require Work

Passion typically fades over time. The long-term pattern of sexual activity within relationships shows a rise and then a decline. Typically, for a period of months or even years, the two people experience frequent, intense desire for one another. They have sex as often as they can arrange it. Past that peak, however, their interest decreases in having sex with each other. For example, from the first year of marriage to the second, frequency of sex declines by about half. After that, the frequency continues to decline, but it does so more gradually. In addition, people typically experience less passion for their partners over time. Unless people develop other forms of satisfaction in their romantic relationships—such as friendship, social support, and intimacy—the loss of passion leads to dissatisfaction and often to the eventual dissolution of the relationship (Berscheid & Regan, 2005).

Perhaps unsurprisingly, then, relatively few marriages meet the blissful ideals that newlyweds expect. Many contemporary Western marriages fail. In North America, approximately half of all marriages end in divorce or separation, often within the first few years. In addition, many couples who do not get divorced live together unhappily. Some "partners" exist in a constant state of tension or as strangers sharing a home. They take each other for granted, openly criticize each other, and take out their frustrations on each other by being cruel or cold. The social psychologist Rowland Miller notes that "married people are meaner to each other than they are to total strangers" (1997, p. 12).

DEALING WITH CONFLICT Even in the best relationships, some conflict is inevitable. Couples continually need to resolve strife. Confronting and discussing important problems is clearly an important aspect of any relationship. The way a couple deals with conflict often determines whether the relationship will last.

John Gottman (1994) describes four interpersonal styles that typically lead couples to discord and dissolution. These maladaptive strategies are *being overly critical, holding the partner in contempt* (i.e., having disdain, lacking respect), *being defensive,* and *mentally withdrawing from the relationship.* Gottman humorously uses the phrase *Four Horsemen of the Apocalypse* to reflect the serious threats that these patterns pose to relationships. For example, when one partner voices a complaint, the other partner responds with his or her own complaint(s). The responder may raise the stakes by recalling all of the other person's failings. People use sarcasm and sometimes insult or demean their partners. Inevitably, any disagreement, no matter how small, escalates into a major fight over the core problems. Often, the core problems center around a lack of money, a lack of sex, or both.

When a couple is more satisfied with their relationship, the partners tend to express concern for each other even while they are disagreeing. They manage to stay relatively calm and try to see each other's point of view. They may also deliver criticism lightheartedly and playfully (Keltner, Young, Heerey, Oemig, & Monarch, 1998). In addition, optimistic people are more likely to use cooperative problem solving; as a result, optimism is linked to having satisfying and happy romantic relationships (Assad, Donnellan, & Conger, 2007; Srivastava, McGonigal, Richards, Butler, & Gross, 2006).

ATTRIBUTIONAL STYLE AND ACCOMMODATION Happy couples also differ from unhappy couples in *attributional style,* or how one partner explains the other's behavior (Bradbury & Fincham, 1990). Happy couples make partner-enhancing attributions. That is, they overlook bad behavior or respond constructively, a process called *accommodation* (Rusbult & Van Lange, 1996). In contrast, unhappy couples make distress-maintaining attributions: They view each other in the most negative ways possible. Essentially, happy couples attribute good outcomes to each other, and they attribute bad outcomes to situations. Unhappy couples attribute *good* outcomes to situations, and they attribute *bad* outcomes to each other. For example, if a couple is happy and one partner brings home flowers as a gift, the other partner reflects on the gift-giver's generosity and sweetness. If a couple is unhappy and one of the partners brings home flowers as gift, the other partner wonders what bad deed the first partner is making up for. Above all, then, viewing your partner in a positive light—even to the point of idealization—may be key to maintaining a loving relationship.

What Determines the Quality of Relationships?

Many factors increase interpersonal attraction. These factors include proximity, similarity, admirable personality characteristics, and physical attractiveness. We find "averaged" faces and symmetrical faces to be most attractive. Physically attractive people experience many social benefits, but they do not report greater happiness. In the context of romantic love, researchers distinguish between passionate love and companionate love. Passionate love is characterized by intense longing and sexual desire. Companionate love is characterized by commitment and support. Passion typically fades over time, but the development of friendship, of support, and of intimacy over time contributes to the stability of romantic relationships. Love is fostered through the idealization of one's partner. That is, people who love their partners the most also idealize their partners the most. Research has demonstrated that there are four maladaptive styles of managing interpersonal conflict in relationships: being overly critical, holding one's partner in contempt, being defensive, and mentally withdrawing. In addition, research has shown that attributional style influences relationship satisfaction. In particular, attributing positive outcomes to one's partner and negative outcomes to situational factors and making partner-enhancing attributions increase relationship satisfaction.

1. Label each of the following characteristics as an attribute of passionate love or companionate love.
   a. a longing to be together
   b. associated with dopamine reward systems
   c. based on friendship
   d. develops slowly over time
   e. strong commitment to care for and support one's partner
   f. typified by sexual desire
   g. typified by trust and respect

2. For each of the following situations, select the comment that, according to empirical findings, indicates a lasting relationship.

Situation 1: Chris finds a receipt in Sam's pocket for a $200 pair of pants. Because they are on a tight budget, this expense angers Chris. Chris confronts Sam about the expense.
   a. Sam replies, "It seems only fair that I get to treat myself when you have your $70-a-month gym membership."
   b. Sam replies, "I understand why you're upset. I really do need a new pair of pants, but I don't need a $200 pair of pants, so I'll return these tomorrow and get a less expensive pair."

Situation 2: Jordan and Jane receive a letter from the Internal Revenue Service saying they owe $3,000 in back taxes because of an error in the documents their accountant filed a few years ago.
   a. Jordan notes, "The accountant made this error, and now we have to come up with the money to pay for it! Well, good thing we've been saving."
   b. Jordan notes, "Didn't you say you reviewed those documents? Next time, you have to be more careful."

Answers: 1. Choices a, b, f are attributes of passionate love; c, d, e, g are attributes of companionate love.
2. Situation 1—b; Situation 2—a.

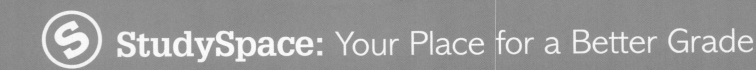
Chapter Summary

12.1 How Do We Form Our Impressions of Others?

■ **Nonverbal Actions and Expressions Affect Our First Impressions:** Nonverbal behavior, sometimes referred to as body language, is interpreted quickly and provides valuable information. Important nonverbal cues include gait, facial expression, and eye contact.

■ **We Make Attributions about Others:** We use personal dispositions and situational factors to explain other people's behavior. The fundamental attribution error occurs when personal attributions are favored over situational attributions in explaining other people's behavior. Our tendency to make personal attributions when explaining other people's behavior and situational attributions when explaining our own behavior is referred to as the actor/observer discrepancy.

■ **Stereotypes Are Based on Automatic Categorization:** Stereotypes are cognitive schemas that allow for fast, easy processing of social information. Self-fulfilling prophecies occur when people behave in ways that confirm their own or other people's expectations. Stereotype threat is a self-fulfilling prophecy in which people behave in ways that confirm negative stereotypes of their group.

■ **Stereotypes Can Lead to Prejudice:** Prejudice occurs when the feelings, opinions, and beliefs associated with a stereotype are negative. Prejudice can lead to discrimination, the inappropriate and unjustified treatment of others. We show a preference for members of ingroups versus members of outgroups. Stereotypes may be inhibited—for instance, by presenting people with positive examples of negatively stereotyped groups.

■ **Cooperation Can Reduce Prejudice:** Sharing superordinate goals that require cooperation can lead to reduced prejudice and discrimination.

12.2 How Do Attitudes Guide Behavior?

■ **We Form Attitudes through Experience and Socialization:** Attitudes are evaluations of objects, of events, or of ideas. Attitudes are influenced by familiarity (the mere exposure effect) and may be shaped by conditioning and socialization.

■ **Behaviors Are Consistent with Strong Attitudes:** Attitudes that are strong, personally relevant, specific, formed through personal experience, and easily accessible are most likely to affect behavior.

■ **Attitudes Can Be Explicit or Implicit:** Implicit attitudes operate at an unconscious level. Implicit attitudes may differ from explicit

attitudes, or those attitudes that we are consciously aware of and can report. In situations that are socially sensitive, implicit attitudes tend to predict behavior better than explicit attitudes do.

■ **Discrepancies Lead to Dissonance:** A contradiction between attitudes or between an attitude and a behavior produces cognitive dissonance. This state is characterized by anxiety, tension, and displeasure. People reduce dissonance by changing their attitudes or behaviors, or by rationalizing or trivializing the discrepancies.

■ **Attitudes Can Be Changed through Persuasion:** Persuasion involves the use of a message to actively and consciously change an attitude. According to the elaboration likelihood model, persuasion through the central route (which involves careful thought about the message) produces stronger and more persistent attitude change than persuasion through the peripheral route (which relies on peripheral cues, such as the attractiveness of the person making the argument).

12.3 How Do Others Influence Us?

■ **Groups Influence Individual Behavior:** The presence of others can improve performance (social facilitation) or result in decreased effort (social loafing). Loss of individuality and self-awareness (deindividuation) can occur in groups. Group decisions can become extreme (group polarization), and poor decisions may be made to preserve group harmony (groupthink).

■ **We Conform to Others:** Conformity occurs when we alter our behavior or opinions to match the behaviors, opinions, or expectations of others. Conformity increases when we are in a large group and the group demonstrates unanimity.

■ **We Are Compliant:** Compliance occurs when we agree to the requests of others. Compliance increases when we are in a good mood or are subjected to tactics such as the foot-in-the-door, door-in-the-face, and low-balling techniques.

■ **We Are Obedient to Authority:** Obedience occurs when we follow the orders of an authority. As demonstrated by Milgram's famous study, people may inflict harm on others if ordered to do so by an authority. Individuals who are concerned about others' perceptions of them are more likely to be obedient. Obedience decreases with greater distance from the authority.

12.4 When Do We Harm or Help Others?

■ **Many Factors Can Influence Aggression:** Aggression is influenced by biological, situational, and sociocultural factors. The amygdala and the neurotransmitter serotonin have been implicated in aggressive behavior. Situations that elicit negative emotions—including frustration—increase the likelihood of aggression. In societies that advocate a culture of honor, people are more likely to exhibit violence.

- **Steroids May Play a Role in Some Violent Behavior:** Research has demonstrated a modest correlation between testosterone and aggression. Steroids may promote aggressive behavior, at least in some users.

- **Many Factors Can Influence Helping Behavior:** Prosocial behaviors maintain social relations. Altruism toward kin members increases the likelihood of passing on common genes. Altruism toward nonrelatives increases the likelihood that others will reciprocate help when we need it.

- **Some Situations Lead to Bystander Apathy:** The bystander intervention effect occurs when we fail to help others in need. This effect is most likely to occur when other bystanders are present and we experience diffusion of responsibility; when a situation is unclear and we fear making social blunders; when we are anonymous; and when we perceive greater risk than benefit to helping others.

12.5 What Determines the Quality of Relationships?

- **Situational and Personal Factors Influence Friendships:** People are attracted to individuals that they have frequent contact with, with whom they share similar attributes, who possess admirable characteristics, and who are physically attractive.

- **Love Is an Important Component of Romantic Relationships:** Passionate love is characterized by intense longing and sexual desire. Companionate love is characterized by commitment and support. In successful romantic relationships, passionate love tends to evolve into companionate love.

- **Love Is Fostered by Idealization:** Romantic relationships may be more resilient when partners view each other in unrealistically positive terms.

- **Staying in Love Can Require Work:** How a couple deals with conflict influences the stability of their relationship. Being overly critical, holding a partner in contempt, being defensive, and mentally withdrawing are maladaptive strategies for coping with interpersonal conflict. Couples that attribute positive outcomes to each other and negative outcomes to situational factors and make partner-enhancing attributions report higher levels of marital happiness.

Key Terms

aggression, p. 546
altruism, p. 552
attitudes, p. 528
attributions, p. 516
bystander intervention effect, p. 553
cognitive dissonance, p. 530
compliance, p. 542
conformity, p. 539
deindividuation, p. 537

discrimination, p. 521
elaboration likelihood model, p. 533
explicit attitudes, p. 530
frustration-aggression hypothesis, p. 548
fundamental attribution error, p. 517
implicit attitudes, p. 530
ingroup favoritism, p. 522
nonverbal behavior, p. 515
personal attributions, p. 517

persuasion, p. 532
prejudice, p. 521
prosocial, p. 552
self-fulfilling prophecy, p. 520
situational attributions, p. 517
social facilitation, p. 537
social loafing, p. 537
social norms, p. 540

Practice Test

1. Some of the following statements illustrate cognitive or behavioral outcomes of stereotyping. As appropriate, label those statements as examples of illusory correlation, ingroup favoritism, outgroup homogeneity, or self-fulfilling prophecy. Not all response options will apply.
   a. A first-year college student states, "Students at our college are so unique! Each person has his or her own passions and aptitudes."
   b. A professor mistakenly comments to a colleague, "The athletes in my class always seem to ask for extensions on their homework; none of my other students ever ask for extensions."
   c. A senior at College A tells her friend, "Whatever you do, don't go to parties at College B. They all drink way too much, and the guys can't keep their hands off the women at their parties."

2. Dorm A and Dorm B have a long-standing rivalry. Recently, the rivalry has intensified, resulting in destructive acts to property and harassment of outgroup members. A couple of students from each dorm encourage the students to get together to brainstorm possible strategies for easing the tension. According to the ideas presented in this chapter, which suggestion would be most effective?
   a. "Let's hold a series of dorm dinners. Dorm A can invite people from Dorm B over one week, and Dorm B can invite people from Dorm A over the following week."
   b. "Since people in Dorm A are such strong math students, we could have Dorm A offer math tutoring to students from Dorm B."
   c. "The administration should hold a meeting with the dorm presidents to let them know that funding for dorm activities will be cut unless the interdorm tension subsides."
   d. "We can hold an all-campus competition, where teams of dorms would compete for prizes. Dorm A and Dorm B could be on one team; Dorm C and Dorm D could be on the other team."

The answer key for the Practice Tests can be found at the back of the book. It also includes answers to the green caption questions.

13

Personality

SIX YEARS AGO, MARC (NOT HIS REAL NAME) BROKE UP WITH THE WOMAN he had been dating for almost a decade. Internet dating was a growing phenomenon, but Marc was determined not to try it. He would find someone the old-fashioned way: by going out into the world and pursuing his interests. After all, he did not know exactly what qualities he was looking for in a companion. Mainly, he wanted someone who *was not* his ex-girlfriend. He lived in New York City, where he worked 9 to 5. Somewhere in the city, he hoped, he would meet a woman who enjoyed city life as much as he did. Where better to find a like-minded person than at a concert, a museum, a park, or a cultural event? In other words, Marc wanted to find someone by being himself. He was not interested in selling some version of himself on the Web.

Since the emergence of Internet dating in the 1990s, more and more people have been searching online for romantic partners and lifelong mates. According to a survey conducted by the Pew Foundation, nearly one-third of Americans know someone who has used an online dating site, and one in six adults knows someone who has been in a long-term relationship with someone she or he met online (Madden & Lenhart, 2006).

After a few months of being on his own, Marc heard success stories about couples who had met online. Friends encouraged him to give it a shot. He decided to try.

Months of bizarre encounters followed. After an email exchange, a first date usually involved sitting across a table from a relative stranger. You spread your wares across the table and wondered if the other person would be interested. You had spent decades creating this version of yourself, and in a matter of minutes someone had the opportunity to reject it outright: "Sorry, this doesn't seem like a match."

Just when Marc was fed up and ready to take a break from online dating, he visited the usual site and saw a photo of a stylish-looking woman. In her profile, she described qualities he found appealing. For example, among the items this woman could not live without were "cool sneakers" and "possibility." She sounded fun and positive and open, not like the tough-talking, guarded women he had been meeting. None of those women had really seemed to want to be in a relationship.

For about a month, Marc and Christine (also not her real name) carried on a sometimes entertaining, sometimes emotionally fraught email exchange. Finally, they met on a rainy Sunday. He liked the cute way she removed her hood before stepping inside the bar. She liked his smile.

Like Marc, Christine was fed up with online dating by that rainy Sunday. Despite his sometimes too-blunt emails, she decided to give this guy a try because he seemed more promising than the duds, doormats, and domineering characters she had been meeting. Christine tends to be more analytical than Marc, and she had a clearer sense of the characteristics she was looking for: a self-sufficient, trustworthy man with his own ideas.

In looking for life partners, Christine and Marc had their parents as models. Both sets of parents had held their marriages together, through good times and bad, over many decades. When we choose romantic partners, describe our friends and enemies, or try to understand ourselves, we rely on the notion of *personality*. But how does personality work? Are we really the same person across situations, or do we act differently at different times? Marc and Christine are both only children. They exhibit stereotypical tendencies of only children, such as self-centeredness. They also avoid the stereotypes, such as by being emotionally expressive. They alternate between introversion and extraversion. Each prefers to work alone, but each can become the catalyst for conversation at a party, a meeting, or some other gathering.

From observing their parents and themselves, Christine and Marc know very well that our personalities come from the combination of our genes and our experiences. Photos from early childhood show them expressing many of the same traits—the stubbornness, the dramatic flair—that each exhibits today (**Figure 13.1**). Still, during their six years together, Marc and Christine have brought out each other's best qualities. Marc thrives emotionally because he has someone to devote himself to. Because Christine accepts him for who he is, he knows that the work of being himself has paid off. Christine is less prone to letting her melancholic streak build up into a wall between herself and others. Because her boyfriend is also her best friend, she feels confident enough to present her best self to the world.

Where does personality come from? Can we change our personalities? Can other people change them for us? ■

(a)

(b)

FIGURE 13.1 Made for Each Other?
(a) This boy, determined to be himself even in the presence of a professional photographer, grew up to be "Marc." (b) This girl, playing her own version of Wonder Woman with earrings, grew up to be "Christine."

13.1 How Have Psychologists Studied Personality?

Learning Objectives

- Describe the major approaches to the study of personality.
- Identify theorists associated with the major approaches to the study of personality.
- Define key terms associated with the major approaches to the study of personality.

People obviously differ in many ways: Some are hostile, some are nurturing, some are withdrawn. This chapter explores how people differ. Because humans are so complex, the discussion of personality brings together a host of topics from across psychology. These topics include nature and nurture, intrapsychic dramas and interpersonal dynamics. The picture that emerges is a familiar one in psychology: Personality is a combination of how we are born, which forces are in our environments, and what we decide to be. In addition to examining those factors, this chapter considers how much a person's behavior tells us about his or her personality.

People constantly try to figure out other people—to understand why they behave in certain ways and to predict their behavior. In fact, many students take psychology courses partly because they want to know what makes other people tick. One challenge of figuring out people is that they may act differently in different situations.

For psychologists, **personality** consists of the characteristic thoughts, emotional responses, and behaviors that are relatively stable in an individual over time and across circumstances. Personality psychologists explore the influence of culture, learning, biology, and cognition. Some personality psychologists are most interested in understanding *whole persons*. That is, they take one person and try to understand as much as possible about that person as an individual. Other personality psychologists study how individual characteristics, such as self-esteem or shyness, influence behavior. For instance, they want to know how people with low self-esteem differ from those with high self-esteem. Their interest is in how the particular characteristic influences behavior. Each characteristic is a **personality trait:** a dispositional tendency to act in a certain way over time and across circumstances.

Personality is not just a list of traits, however. Gordon Allport, a leading personality researcher, gave a classic scientific definition of personality: "the dynamic organization within the individual of those psychophysical systems that determine [the individual's] characteristic behavior and thought" (1961, p. 28; **Figure 13.2**). This definition includes many of the concepts most important to a contemporary understanding of personality. The notion of *organization* indicates that personality is a coherent whole. This organized whole is *dynamic* in that it is goal seeking, sensitive to particular contexts, and adaptive to the person's environment. By emphasizing *psychophysical systems,* Allport brought together two ideas: He highlighted the psychological nature of personality, and he recognized that personality arises from basic biological processes. In addition, his definition stresses that personality causes people to have *characteristic* behaviors and thoughts (and feelings). In other words, people do and think and feel things relatively consistently over time.

Understanding personality as both dynamic and consistent may be one of humankind's oldest quests. In fact, the word *personality* comes from the Latin word *persona,* meaning "mask." In ancient Greek and Roman theater, actors performed their roles wearing masks. Each mask represented a separate personality. Since antiquity, many theories have been proposed to explain such basic differences between individuals. During the twentieth century, psychologists approached the study of personality from a number of different theoretical perspectives. Psychologists' views on personality were based on their individual theoretical orientations. For example,

personality The characteristic thoughts, emotional responses, and behaviors that are relatively stable in an individual over time and across circumstances.

personality trait A characteristic; a dispositional tendency to act in a certain way over time and across circumstances.

FIGURE 13.2 Gordon Allport In 1937, Allport published the first major textbook of personality psychology. His book defined the field. He also championed the study of individuals and established traits as a central concept in personality research.

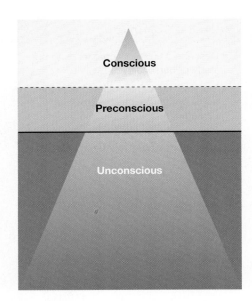

FIGURE 13.3 Levels of Consciousness
Sigmund Freud theorized that mental activity occurred in these three zones. He believed that much of human behavior was influenced by unconscious processes.

psychodynamic theory Freudian theory that unconscious forces determine behavior.

id In psychodynamic theory, the component of personality that is completely submerged in the unconscious and operates according to the pleasure principle.

psychodynamic theorists believed unconscious forces determined personality. Humanists emphasized personal growth and self-understanding. Behaviorists believed that personality resulted from histories of reinforcement. Cognitively oriented psychologists focused on how thought processes affected personality. Contemporary psychologists are primarily interested in *trait approaches* and the biological basis of personality *traits*. The following sections consider these various theoretical perspectives.

Psychodynamic Theories Emphasize Unconscious and Dynamic Processes

As discussed in Chapter 1, Sigmund Freud was a physician. Freud developed many ideas about personality by observing patients he was treating for psychological disturbances. For example, some of Freud's patients suffered from paralysis that had no apparent physical cause. Freud came to believe their problems were *psychogenic,* caused by psychological rather than physical factors. From his clinical work, Freud developed his **psychodynamic theory** of personality. The central premise of this theory is that unconscious forces—such as wishes, desires, and hidden memories—determine behavior. Many of Freud's ideas are controversial and not well supported by scientific research, but his theories had an enormous influence over psychological thinking for much of the early history of the field.

UNCONSCIOUS CONFLICTS For Freud, the powerful forces that drive behavior were often in conflict. A key aspect of his thinking was that we are typically unaware of those forces or their conflicts. For instance, you might unknowingly want to steal an object you desire. That impulse would conflict with your implicit knowledge that you could get in trouble for the theft or that society considers theft a crime. Freud believed that our conscious awareness was only a small fraction of our mental activity. That is, conscious awareness represented the proverbial tip of the iceberg, with most mental processes buried under the surface (**Figure 13.3**).

According to this model, the *conscious* level consists of the thoughts that we are aware of. The *preconscious* level consists of content that is not currently in awareness but that could be brought to awareness. This level is roughly analogous to long-term memory. The *unconscious* level contains material that the mind cannot easily retrieve. These hidden memories, wishes, desires, and motives are often in conflict. The conflicts between them produce anxiety or other psychological discomfort. To protect us from this distress, these forces and their conflicts are not accessible. Sometimes, however, this information leaks into consciousness. As discussed in Chapter 5, for example, we may accidentally reveal a hidden motive when uttering a Freudian slip. Think of someone introducing herself or himself to an attractive person by saying, "Excuse me, I don't think we've been properly seduced," instead of "properly introduced." For Freud, these slips were not accidents. Instead, they offered a glimpse into unconscious conflicts that determine behavior. Likewise, both the content of a person's dreams and jokes the person told indicated individual conflicts that reflected the person's personality.

A STRUCTURAL MODEL OF PERSONALITY Freud also proposed a model of how personality is organized. In this model, personality consists of three interacting structures, and these structures vary in their access to consciousness.

The first structure, the **id,** exists at the most basic level: completely submerged in the unconscious. The id operates according to the pleasure principle, which directs us to seek pleasure and to avoid pain. Freud called the force that drives the pleasure principle the *libido.* Although today the term *libido* has a sexual connotation, Freud used it to refer more generally to the energy that promotes pleasure seeking. In other words, the libido acts on impulses and desires. The id is like an infant, crying to be fed whenever hungry, held whenever anxious. The second structure, the **superego,** acts as a brake on the id. Largely unconscious, the superego develops in childhood and is the internalization of parental and societal standards of conduct. It is a rigid structure of morality, or conscience. The third structure, the **ego,** mediates between the id and the superego. That is, the ego tries to satisfy the wishes of the id while being responsive to the dictates of the superego. The ego operates according to the *reality principle,* which involves rational thought and problem solving. Some aspects of the ego's operations are open to conscious awareness. For example, the ego allows us to delay gratification so that the wishes of the id can be realized while accommodating the rules of the superego. According to psychodynamic theory, unique interactions of the id, ego, and superego produce individual differences in personality.

Conflicts between the id and the superego lead to anxiety. The ego then copes with anxiety through various **defense mechanisms:** unconscious mental strategies that the mind uses to protect itself from distress. (Several common defense mechanisms are listed in **Table 13.1.**) For instance, people often *rationalize* their behavior by blaming situational factors over which they have little control. Perhaps you have told your parents or your friends that you did not call them because you were too busy studying for an exam? Finding good excuses keeps people from feeling bad and can also prevent others from feeling angry toward them.

Much of the theoretical work on defense mechanisms can be credited to Freud's daughter, Anna Freud (1936; **Figure 13.4**). Over the past 40 years, psychological research has provided considerable support for the existence of many

superego In psychodynamic theory, the internalization of societal and parental standards of conduct.

ego In psychodynamic theory, the component of personality that tries to satisfy the wishes of the id while being responsive to the dictates of the superego.

defense mechanisms Unconscious mental strategies that the mind uses to protect itself from distress.

TABLE 13.1 Common Defense Mechanisms

Mechanism	Definition	Example
Denial	Refusing to acknowledge source of anxiety	Ill person ignores medical advice
Repression	Excluding source of anxiety from awareness	Person fails to remember an unpleasant event
Projection	Attributing unacceptable qualities of the self to someone else	Competitive person describes others as supercompetitive
Reaction formation	Warding off an uncomfortable thought by overemphasizing its opposite	Person with unacknowledged homosexual desires makes homophobic remarks
Rationalization	Concocting a seemingly logical reason or excuse for behavior that might otherwise be shameful	Person cheats on taxes because "everyone does it"
Displacement	Shifting the attention of emotion from one object to another	Person yells at children after a bad day at work
Sublimation	Channeling socially unacceptable impulses into constructive, even admirable, behavior	Sadist becomes a surgeon or dentist

FIGURE 13.4 Anna Freud Anna Freud studied defense mechanisms and contributed to the understanding of children's development.

of the defense mechanisms (Baumeister, Dale, & Sommers, 1998). According to contemporary researchers, however, these mechanisms do not relieve unconscious conflict over libidinal desires. Instead, defense mechanisms protect self-esteem. For instance, reaction formation occurs when a person wards off an uncomfortable thought about the self by embracing the opposite thought. In one study of reaction formation in men, the participants were asked to express their views on homosexuality (Adams, Wright, & Lohr, 1996). Then they watched videos that depicted homosexual sex. The men who had expressed the most negative views of homosexuality showed greater physiological arousal when watching the videos than did men who were more accepting of homosexuality. These findings suggest that repression of homosexual impulses might lead to reaction formation. The reaction consists of homophobia.

PSYCHOSEXUAL DEVELOPMENT An important component of Freudian thinking is the idea that early childhood experiences have a major impact on the development of personality. Freud believed that children unconsciously aim to satisfy libidinal urges to experience pleasure. In their pursuit of these satisfactions, children go through developmental stages that correspond to the different urges. These developmental stages are called **psychosexual stages.**

In each psychosexual stage, libido is focused on one of the *erogenous zones:* the mouth, the anus, or the genitals. The *oral stage* lasts from birth to approximately 18 months. During this time, infants seek pleasure through the mouth. Because hungry infants experience relief when they breast-feed, they come to associate pleasure with sucking. When children are 2 to 3 years old, they enter the *anal stage*. During this time, toilet training—learning to control the bowels—leads them to focus on the anus. From age 3 to 5, children are in the *phallic stage*. That is, they direct their libidinal energies toward the genitals. Children often discover the pleasure of rubbing their genitals during this time, although they have no sexual intent per se. The phallic stage is followed by a brief *latency stage*. During this time, children suppress libidinal urges or channel them into doing schoolwork or building friendships. Finally, in the *genital stage,* adolescents and adults attain mature attitudes about sexuality and adulthood. They center their libidinal urges on the capacities to reproduce and to contribute to society.

One of the most controversial Freudian theories applies to children in the phallic stage. According to Freud, children desire an exclusive relationship with the opposite-sex parent. For this reason, children consider the same-sex parent a rival, and they develop hostility toward that parent. In boys, this phenomenon is known as the *Oedipus complex*. It is named after the Greek character Oedipus, who unknowingly killed his father and married his mother. Freud believed that children develop unconscious wishes to kill the one parent in order to claim the other parent. Children resolve this conflict by repressing their desires for the opposite-sex parent and identifying with the same-sex parent. That is, they take on many of that parent's values and beliefs. This theory was mostly applicable to boys. Freud's theory for girls was more complex and even less convincing. Few data support either theory.

According to Freud, progression through these psychosexual stages profoundly affects personality. For example, some people become *fixated* at a stage during which they receive excessive parental restriction or indulgence. Those fixated at the oral stage develop *oral personalities*. They continue to seek pleasure through the mouth, such as by smoking. They are also excessively needy. Those fixated at the anal phase may have *anal-retentive personalities*. They are stubborn and highly regulating. Anal fixation may arise from overly strict toilet training or excessively rule-based child rearing.

psychosexual stages According to Freud, developmental stages that correspond to distinct libidinal urges; progression through these stages profoundly affects personality.

PSYCHODYNAMIC THEORY SINCE FREUD Sigmund Freud is the thinker most closely identified with psychodynamic theory, but a number of influential scholars have modified Freud's ideas in their own psychodynamic theories. While rejecting aspects of Freudian thinking, they have embraced the notion of unconscious conflict. These *neo-Freudians* include Carl Jung, Alfred Adler, and Karen Horney. For instance, Adler and Horney strongly criticized Freud's view of women, finding many of his ideas misogynistic. Consider that the phallic stage of development is named for the male sex organ, although Freud used this label for both female and male development. Many neo-Freudians rejected Freud's emphasis on sexual forces. Adler viewed the primary conflict as based on fears of inadequacy, which he called the *inferiority complex*. Horney focused on a fear of abandonment. In her view, this fear resulted from the child's relationship with the mother.

Contemporary neo-Freudians focus on social interactions, especially children's emotional attachments to their parents or primary caregivers. This focus is embodied in *object relations theory*. According to this theory, a person's mind and sense of self develop in relation to others in the particular environment. "Objects" are real others in the world, and how the person relates to these others shapes the person's personality.

Psychologists largely have abandoned psychodynamic theories. After all, Freud's central premises cannot be examined through accepted scientific methods. Today, Freud has to be understood in the context of his time and the methods he had at his disposal. He was an astute observer of behavior and a creative theorist. His observations and ideas continue to affect personality psychology and have framed much of the research in personality over the last century (Hines, 2003; Westen, 1998).

Humanistic Approaches Emphasize Integrated Personal Experience

By the early 1950s, most psychological theories of personality were heavily deterministic. That is, theorists viewed personality and behavioral characteristics as arising from forces beyond a person's control. For example, Freudians had believed that personality is determined by unconscious conflicts. Behaviorists such as B. F. Skinner argued that personality is based on response tendencies, which are determined by patterns of reinforcement (see Chapter 6, "Learning").

Against this backdrop, a new view of personality emerged: **Humanistic approaches** emphasize personal experience, belief systems, the uniqueness of the human condition, and the inherent goodness of each person. They propose that we seek to fulfill our potential for personal growth through greater self-understanding. This process is referred to as *self-actualization*. Abraham Maslow's theory of motivation is an example. As discussed in Chapter 10, Maslow believed that the desire to become self-actualized is the ultimate human motive.

The most prominent humanistic psychologist was Carl Rogers (**Figure 13.5**). Rogers introduced a *person-centered approach* to understanding personality and human relationships. That is, he emphasized people's subjective understandings of their lives. In the therapeutic technique Rogers advocated, the therapist would create a supportive and accepting environment. The therapist and the client would deal with the client's problems and concerns as the client understood them.

Rogers's theory highlights the importance of how parents show affection for their children and how parental treatment affects personality development. Rogers speculated that most parents provide love and support that is conditional: The parents love their children as long as the children do what the parents want them to do. Parents who disapprove of their children's behavior may withhold their

humanistic approaches Approaches to studying personality that emphasize how people seek to fulfill their potential through greater self-understanding.

FIGURE 13.5 Carl Rogers Rogers was one of the founders of humanistic psychology. His approach emphasized people's subjective understandings of their lives.

love. As a result, children quickly abandon their true feelings, dreams, and desires. They accept only those parts of themselves that elicit parental love and support. Thus people lose touch with their true selves in their pursuit of positive regard from others. To counteract this effect, Rogers encouraged parents to raise their children with *unconditional positive regard*. That is, parents should accept and prize their children no matter how the children behave. Parents might express disapproval of children's bad behavior, but at the same time they should express their love for the children. According to Rogers, a child raised with unconditional positive regard would develop a healthy sense of self-esteem and would become a *fully functioning person*.

Personality Reflects Learning and Cognition

Behavioral psychologists such as B. F. Skinner rejected the idea that personality is the result of internal processes. Instead, behaviorists viewed personality mainly as learned responses to patterns of reinforcement. Over time, however, psychologists became dissatisfied with strict models of learning theory. They began to incorporate cognition into the understanding of personality. For instance, the early cognitive theorist George Kelly (1955) emphasized how we view and understand our circumstances. He referred to such views and understandings as *personal constructs:* personal theories of how the world works. Kelly believed that we view the world as if we were scientists—constantly testing our theories by observing ongoing events, then revising those theories based on what we observe. According to Kelly, personal constructs develop through our experiences and represent our interpretations and explanations for events in our social worlds.

Julian Rotter (1954) built further on the cognitive approach. Rotter introduced the idea that behavior is a function of two things: our *expectancies* for reinforcement and the *values* we ascribe to particular reinforcers. Suppose you are deciding whether to study for an exam or go to a party. You probably will consider the likelihood that studying will lead to a good grade. You will consider how much that grade matters. Then you will weigh those two considerations against two others: the likelihood that the party will be fun and the extent to which you value having fun (**Figure 13.6**).

Rotter also proposed that people differ in how much they believe their efforts will lead to positive outcomes. People with an *internal locus of control* believe they bring about their own rewards. People with an *external locus of control* believe rewards—and therefore their personal fates—result from forces beyond their control. These generalized beliefs affect individuals' psychological adjustment.

The incorporation of cognition into learning theories led to the development of *cognitive-social theories* of personality. These theories emphasize how personal beliefs, expectancies, and interpretations of social situations shape behavior and personality. For instance, Albert Bandura (1977) argued that our mental capacities interact with our environments to influence our behavior. Mental capacities include beliefs, thoughts, and expectations. For Bandura, as discussed in Chapter 10, one important determinant of behavior is self-efficacy. This term refers to how much we believe we can achieve specific outcomes. Moreover, as discussed in Chapter 6, Bandura proposed that we may develop expectancies partly through observational learning. For example, we may notice that other people are rewarded for acting in certain ways and punished for acting in different ways.

One of the most influential yet controversial cognitive-social theorists has been Walter Mischel. According to Mischel's *cognitive-affective personality system*

FIGURE 13.6 Expectancies and Value According to Julian Rotter, what series of thoughts might a student go through while deciding whether to stay in and study or go out to a party? What role would positive reinforcement play in those thoughts?

(*CAPS*), our personalities often fail to predict our behavior across different circumstances (Mischel & Shoda, 1995). Instead, our responses are influenced by how we perceive a given situation, our affective (emotional) responses to the situation, our skills in dealing with challenges, and our anticipation of the outcomes of our behavior (**Figure 13.7**).

For example, do you tend to make a good impression when you walk into a room? If so, you might walk into a party expecting to make a good impression. But what if your social experiences have been very different? Suppose you tend to be awkward and shy in social situations. In that case, you might walk into that same party expecting to be rejected. Consider also the personality style *defensive pessimism,* which has been studied by Julie Norem and Nancy Cantor. Defensive pessimists expect to fail and therefore enter test situations with dread. By contrast, optimists enter test situations with high expectations. Yet pessimists and optimists tend to perform similarly on exams (Norem, 1989). These two personality styles reflect different motivational strategies: Pessimists expect the worst so they can be relieved when they succeed. Optimists focus on positive outcomes.

The CAPS model and other cognitive-social theories of personality also emphasize *self-regulatory capacities.* This term refers to our relative ability to set personal goals, evaluate our progress, and adjust our behavior accordingly. Indeed, many personality psychologists believe that motives and strivings—such as those for achievement, power, or intimacy—are an essential aspect of personality (Snyder & Cantor, 1998). According to these views, then, what is personality? Personality represents behavior that emerges from the interaction of three factors: our interpretations of our social worlds, our beliefs about how we will affect our social situations, and our beliefs about how we will be affected *by* our social situations.

Trait Approaches Describe Behavioral Dispositions

Psychodynamic and humanistic approaches seek to explain the mental processes that shape personality. According to these theories, the same underlying processes occur in everyone, but individuals differ because they experience different conflicts, are treated differently by their parents, and so on. Other approaches to personality focus more on description than explanation. For example, in describing a friend, you probably would not delve into unconscious conflicts. Instead, you would describe your friend as a certain type. You might say, "Jessica is such an introvert" or "Yuen is a free spirit."

Personality types are discrete categories of people. We fill in gaps in our knowledge about individuals with our beliefs about the behaviors and dispositions associated with these types. *Implicit personality theory* is the study of two tendencies related to personality types: We tend to assume that certain personality characteristics go together. Because of that assumption, we tend to make predictions about people based on minimal evidence. For example, we might think that introverts dislike parties, like solitary activities such as reading, and are sensitive. We might think that free spirits choose unusual occupations, speak their minds, and are fun to be around.

Many personality psychologists are concerned with traits in addition to types. As discussed earlier, traits are behavioral dispositions that endure over time and across situations. Traits exist on a continuum, so that most people fall toward the middle and relatively few people fall at the extremes. Thus, for example, people range from being very introverted to very extraverted, but most are somewhere

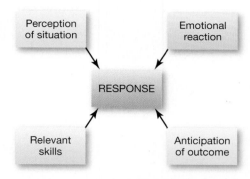

FIGURE 13.7 CAPS Model Mischel and Shoda proposed this model to account for cognitive-social influences on behavior. What does this model indicate about the relationship between personality traits and behavior?

personality types Discrete categories of people based on personality characteristics.

in the middle. The **trait approach** to personality focuses on how individuals differ in personality dispositions, such as sociability, cheerfulness, and aggressiveness (Funder, 2001).

How many traits are there? Early in his career, Gordon Allport, along with his colleague Henry Odbert, counted the dictionary words that could be used as personality traits. They found nearly 18,000. During the 1950s, the researcher Raymond Cattell set out to ascertain the basic elements of personality. Cattell believed that statistical procedures would enable him to take the scientific study of personality to a higher level and perhaps to uncover the basic structure of personality. He asked participants to fill out personality questionnaires that presented a number of trait items, which he had reduced from the larger set produced by Allport and Odbert. Cattell then performed *factor analysis,* grouping items according to their similarities. For instance, he grouped all the terms that referred to friendliness: *nice, pleasant, cooperative,* and so on. Through factor analysis, Cattell (1965) identified 16 basic dimensions of personality. These dimensions included intelligence, sensitivity, dominance, and self-reliance. Cattell gave many of the dimensions rather unusual names to avoid confusion with everyday language, but most personality psychologists no longer use these terms.

EYSENCK'S HIERARCHICAL MODEL In the 1960s, the psychologist Hans Eysenck further reduced the number of basic traits. Eysenck proposed a hierarchical model of personality (**Figure 13.8**). The basic structure of this model begins at the *specific response level* (**Figure 13.9**). Specific responses are observed behaviors. For instance, a person might buy an item because it is on sale. Suppose that person generally has a hard time resisting items that are on sale. If the person repeats that behavior occasionally, the buying of sale items exists at the *habitual response level.* If a person behaves the same way on many occasions, the person is characterized as possessing a trait. Traits such as impulsiveness and sociability can be viewed as components of *superordinate traits.* Eysenck proposed that there are three superordinate traits: introversion/extraversion, emotional stability, and psychoticism.

The term *introversion/extraversion* was coined by the psychoanalyst Carl Jung. It refers to how shy, reserved, and quiet a person is or, alternatively, how sociable, outgoing, and bold the person is. As discussed later in this chapter, Eysenck believed that this dimension reflects differences in biological functioning. *Emotional stability* refers to how much a person's moods and emotions change. A person low in emotional stability is considered *neurotic.* A neurotic person experiences frequent and dramatic mood swings, especially toward negative emotions, compared with a person who is more stable. In addition, a neurotic person often feels anxious, moody, and depressed. The person generally holds a very low opinion of himself or herself. *Psychoticism* is a mix of aggression, impulse control, and empathy. A person high in psychoticism is more aggressive, impulsive, and self-centered than a person low in psychoticism. The term *psychoticism* implies a level of psychopathology that Eysenck did not intend. More-recent conceptions of this superordinate trait call it *constraint.* According to this sense of the trait, people range from restrained to disinhibited (Watson & Clark, 1997).

THE BIG FIVE In the last 30 years or so, many personality psychologists have embraced the **five-factor theory.** This theory identifies five basic personality traits (McCrae & Costa, 1999). These traits have emerged from factor analyses performed by personality researchers. The so-called *Big Five* are *openness to experience,*

FIGURE 13.8 Hans Eysenck Eysenck proposed an influential model of personality. He was also one of the leading proponents of the idea that personality is rooted in biology.

trait approach An approach to studying personality that focuses on how individuals differ in personality dispositions.

five-factor theory The idea that personality can be described using five factors: openness to experience, conscientiousness, extraversion, agreeableness, and neuroticism.

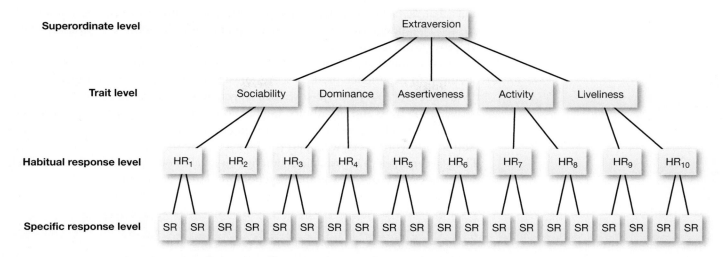

FIGURE 13.9 Eysenck's Hierarchical Model of Personality This chart shows how Eysenck's hierarchical model applies to a single trait, extraversion. As shown here, extraversion is a superordinate trait. It is made up of sociability, dominance, assertiveness, activity, and liveliness. Each of these subordinate traits is made up of habitual responses and specific responses.

conscientiousness, extraversion, agreeableness, and *neuroticism* (**Figure 13.10**). For each factor, there is a continuum from low to high. In addition, as in Eysenck's model, each factor is a higher-order trait that is made up of interrelated lower-order traits. For instance, conscientiousness is determined by how careful and organized a person is. Agreeableness reflects the extent to which a person is trusting and helpful. A person high in openness to experience is imaginative and independent, whereas a person low in this basic trait is down-to-earth and conformist.

Considerable evidence supports the five-factor theory (John, 1990). The Big Five emerge across cultures, among adults and children, even when vastly different questionnaires assess the factors. The same five factors appear whether people rate themselves or are rated by others. Furthermore, people's "scores" on the Big Five traits have been shown to predict a wide variety of different behaviors (Paunonen & Ashton, 2001). Their scores have also have been shown to predict people's satisfaction with their jobs, their marriages, and life generally (Heller, Watson, & Ilies, 2004). Some cross-cultural differences emerge, however. For example, interpersonal relatedness, or harmony, is not an important trait in Western cultures. But personality studies conducted in China have shown that interpersonal relatedness is an important trait there (Cheung et al., 2001; Cheung, Cheung, & Leung, 2008). One possible explanation for this difference is that many Chinese live in densely populated areas. Therefore, getting along with others may be more essential in China than in societies where people live farther apart.

Some researchers have questioned whether the five-factor theory really clarifies personality. After all, the factor terms are descriptive rather than explanatory, and reducing all of human personality to five dimensions ignores individual subtleties. The theory is valuable, however, as an organizational structure for the vast number of

FIGURE 13.10 The Big Five Personality Factors The acronym *OCEAN* is a good way to remember these terms.

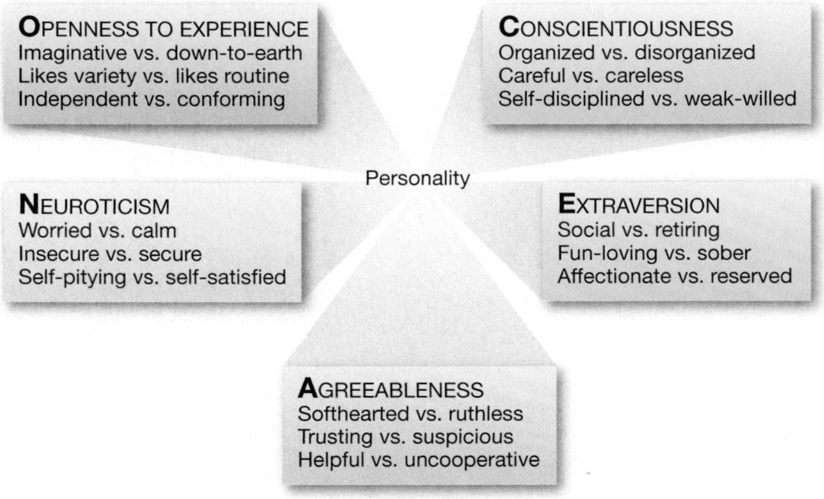

OPENNESS TO EXPERIENCE
Imaginative vs. down-to-earth
Likes variety vs. likes routine
Independent vs. conforming

CONSCIENTIOUSNESS
Organized vs. disorganized
Careful vs. careless
Self-disciplined vs. weak-willed

Personality

NEUROTICISM
Worried vs. calm
Insecure vs. secure
Self-pitying vs. self-satisfied

EXTRAVERSION
Social vs. retiring
Fun-loving vs. sober
Affectionate vs. reserved

AGREEABLENESS
Softhearted vs. ruthless
Trusting vs. suspicious
Helpful vs. uncooperative

traits that describe personality. By providing a common descriptive framework, the Big Five integrate and invigorate the trait approach (John & Srivastava, 1999). Moreover, the factors uniquely predict certain outcomes. For instance, conscientiousness predicts grades in college but not scores on standardized tests, whereas openness to experience predicts scores on standardized tests but not grades (Noftle & Robins, 2007). These particular effects may occur because of connections between the traits and the results: Highly conscientious people tend to work very hard, and this characteristic matters for grades. People who are high in openness tend to use words very well, and this characteristic matters for achievement tests. Thus factors exist at more than a descriptive level. Today, the Big Five approach dominates much of the way that psychologists study personality.

Summing Up

How Have Psychologists Studied Personality?

Varied approaches have emerged within psychology to understand the ways in which people are similar to and different from one another. The psychodynamic approach maintains that unconscious forces determine behavior. This approach distinguishes between three components of personality: the id, the superego, and the ego. According to this approach, progression through psychosexual stages during childhood shapes personality. Humanistic theories emphasize personal experience, belief systems, individual uniqueness, and the inherent goodness of each person. According to these theories, personality reflects our efforts to fulfill our potential for personal growth through greater self-understanding. Early learning theories emphasized patterns of reinforcement. Later theories incorporated diverse cognitive factors, including personal constructs, expectancies, values, and self-regulatory capacities. Trait theories describe personality on the basis of behavioral dispositions, focusing on how individuals differ. Eysenck's theory maintains that there are three biologically based higher-order traits: introversion/extraversion, emotional stability, and psychoticism. The dominant trait theory today is the Big Five. This theory identifies five higher-order traits: openness to experience, conscientiousness, extraversion, agreeableness, and neuroticism.

Measuring Up

1. Indicate which theorists are associated with each of the following four approaches to studying personality: psychodynamic, humanistic, type and trait, and learning and cognition.
   a. Abraham Maslow
   b. Albert Bandura
   c. Anna Freud
   d. Carl Jung
   e. Carl Rogers
   f. B. F. Skinner
   g. George Kelly
   h. Julian Rotter
   i. Hans Eysenck
   j. Karen Horney
   k. Raymond Cattell
   l. Sigmund Freud
   m. Walter Mischel

2. Indicate which concepts are associated with each of the four approaches to studying personality (see question 1).
   a. defense mechanisms
   b. id, ego, superego
   c. describing how individuals differ from one another
   d. locus of control
   e. people seeking to fulfill their potential for personal growth through greater self-understanding
   f. personal beliefs, expectations, and interpretations of social situations shaping personality
   g. personality traits
   h. personality types
   i. self-efficacy
   j. sexual instincts
   k. the Big Five
   l. unconditional positive regard
   m. unconscious forces influencing behavior

Answers: 1. psychodynamic—b, j, m; humanistic—e, l; type and trait—c, g, h, k; learning and cognition—b, f, g, h, m.
2. psychodynamic—a, b, j, m; humanistic—e, l; type and trait—c, g, h, k; learning and cognition—d, f, i.

13.2 How Is Personality Assessed, and What Does It Predict about People?

Personality researchers do not agree on the best method for assessing personality. Its three aspects—thoughts, feelings, and behaviors—need to be considered in any assessment. Psychologists measure personality by having people report on themselves, by asking people's friends or relatives to describe them, or by watching how people behave. Each method has strengths and limitations. This section considers how psychologists assess personality and how the different methods influence our understanding of individuals.

Personality Refers to Both Unique and Common Characteristics

Allport divided the study of personality into two approaches. **Idiographic approaches** are person-centered. They focus on individual lives and how various characteristics are integrated into unique persons. **Nomothetic approaches** focus on characteristics that are common among all people but that vary from person to person. In other words, idiographic approaches use a different metric for each person. Nomothetic approaches use the same metric to compare all people.

Idiographic approaches assume all individuals are unique. Suppose each person in your psychology class identified 10 personality traits that described himself or herself. If your instructor compiled a list of everyone's traits, some of the traits would overlap. Other traits would probably apply to just one person in the class.

Learning Objectives

- Distinguish between idiographic and nomothetic approaches to the study of personality.
- Distinguish between projective and objective measures of personality.
- Discuss the accuracy of observers' personality judgments.
- Define situationism and interactionism.
- Distinguish between strong situations and weak situations.
- Discuss cultural and sex differences in personality.

idiographic approaches Person-centered approaches to studying personality; they focus on individual lives and how various characteristics are integrated into unique persons.

nomothetic approaches Approaches to studying personality that focus on how common characteristics vary from person to person.

FIGURE 13.11 Adolf Hitler In his personality analysis of Hitler, Henry Murray (1943) stated that the German leader was impotent in heterosexual relations and had engaged in a homosexual relationship. Murray's report predicted Hitler's suicide.

After all, people like to be unique, so they tend to choose traits that distinguish themselves from other people. These *central traits* are especially important for how individuals define themselves. In contrast, people consider *secondary traits* less personally descriptive or not applicable. As you can imagine, certain traits are central for some people and secondary for others. You might define yourself in terms of how bold you are, but someone else might not consider boldness a very relevant part of her or his self-definition. In general, central traits are more predictive of behavior than are secondary traits.

Researchers who use idiographic approaches often examine case studies of individuals through interviews or biographical information. The personality psychologist Henry Murray pioneered this approach. For example, Murray was one of the many scholars who have tried to account for Adolf Hitler's behavior in Nazi Germany by studying Hitler's early childhood experiences, his physical stature, and his personal motivations (**Figure 13.11**). This type of study emphasizes the idea that personality unfolds over the life course as people react to their particular circumstances.

Another idiographic approach considers a human life as a narrative. To study personality, narrative psychologists pay attention to the stories people tell about themselves. According to Dan McAdams (1999, 2001), each person weaves a *life story*. The life story integrates self-knowledge into a coherent whole. In other words, the individual creates *personal myths* that bind together past events and future possibilities into one life story. These myths, whether true or not, help the individual make sense of the world and find meaning in life.

Nomothetic approaches focus on common traits rather than individual uniqueness. Researchers in this tradition compare people by measuring traits such as agreeableness or disagreeableness. For example, they might give participants a questionnaire that lists 100 personality traits and have the participants rate themselves on each trait, using a scale of 1 to 10. From the nomothetic perspective, individuals are unique because of their unique combinations of common traits. The five-factor theory, discussed earlier, is an example of a nomothetic approach. That is, it looks at how all people vary on five basic personality traits.

Researchers Use Projective and Objective Methods to Assess Personality

As mentioned earlier, researchers use numerous methods to assess personality. The possibilities range from observer reports to self-reports to clinical interviews. In addition, the way researchers choose to measure personality depends to a great extent on their theoretical orientations. For instance, trait researchers use personality descriptions, whereas humanistic psychologists use more holistic approaches. At the broadest level, assessment procedures can be grouped into *projective measures* and *objective measures*.

PROJECTIVE MEASURES According to psychodynamic theory, personality is influenced by unconscious conflicts. **Projective measures** explore the unconscious by having people describe or tell stories about ambiguous stimulus items. The general idea is that people will project their mental contents onto the ambiguous items. Through these projections, according to the theory, people will reveal hidden aspects of personality such as motives, wishes, and unconscious conflicts. Many such procedures are used to assess psychopathology, but many of them have been criticized for being too subjective and insufficiently validated. One of the best-known projective measures is the *Rorschach inkblot test*. In this procedure,

projective measures Personality tests that examine unconscious processes by having people interpret ambiguous stimuli.

a person looks at an apparently meaningless inkblot and describes what it appears to be. How a person describes the inkblot is supposed to reveal unconscious conflicts and other problems. The Rorschach does a poor job of diagnosing specific psychological disorders, however, and it finds many normal adults and children to be psychologically disturbed (Wood, Garb, Lilienfeld, & Nezworski, 2002).

One classic projective measure used by personality psychologists is the *Thematic Apperception Test (TAT)*. In the 1930s, Henry Murray and Christiana Morgan developed the TAT to study achievement motivation. In this test, a person is shown an ambiguous picture and is asked to tell a story about it (**Figure 13.12**). Scoring of the story is based on the motivational schemes that emerge, because the schemes are assumed to reflect the storyteller's personal motives. Indeed, the TAT has been useful for measuring motivational traits—especially those related to achievement, power, and affiliation—and therefore it continues to be used in contemporary research (McClelland, Koestner, & Weinberger, 1989). If used properly, the TAT reliably predicts how interpersonally dependent people are (Bornstein, 1999). For example, this test predicts how likely people are to seek approval and support from others.

FIGURE 13.12 Thematic Apperception Test Vintage pictures of this type are used in the TAT.

OBJECTIVE MEASURES **Objective measures** of personality are straightforward assessments. They usually involve self-report questionnaires or observer ratings. Measuring only what the raters believe or observe, they make no pretense of uncovering hidden conflicts or secret information. Personality researchers use these objective measures to compare people's responses and assess how much the answers predict behavior. A questionnaire might target a specific trait, such as how much excitement a person seeks out of life. More often, an objective measure will include a large inventory of traits. For example, the *NEO Personality Inventory* consists of 240 items, which are designed to assess the Big Five personality factors (Costa & McCrae, 1992).

Although some personality tests are called objective, they require people to make subjective judgments. As discussed in Chapter 2, self-reports can be affected by desires to avoid looking bad and by biases in self-perception. In addition, it can be difficult for researchers to compare self-reported objective measures directly, because individual respondents do not have objective standards to rate themselves against. For example, two individuals reporting a 5 on a 7-point shyness scale may not be equally shy because the term can mean different things to different people.

objective measures Relatively direct assessments of personality, usually based on information gathered through self-report questionnaires or observer ratings.

One technique for assessing traits is the *California Q-Sort*. In this procedure, each participant is given 100 cards that have statements printed on them. The participant is asked to sort the cards into nine piles according to how accurately the statements describe the person. The piles represent categories that range from "not at all descriptive" to "extremely descriptive" (**Figure 13.13**). A participant may place only so many cards in each pile. Fewer cards are allowed at the extreme ends of the scale. Because the participant must pile most of the cards in the moderately descriptive categories, the Q-Sort has a built-in procedure for identifying those traits that people view as most central. The Q-Sort, like most objective measures, can also be used by observers. For example, parents, teachers, therapists, and friends can sort the cards to describe the person being evaluated.

Researchers have also developed a number of objective measures that assess how personality emerges in daily life. For example, Matthias Mehl and James Pennebaker (Mehl, Pennebaker, Crow, Dabbs, & Price, 2001) created the

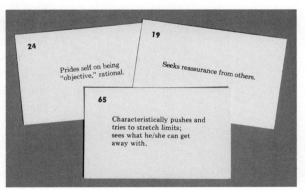

FIGURE 13.13 California Q-Sort These are three of the cards a participant sorts when taking the Q-Sort assessment. How well does the statement on each card describe you?

electronically activated record (EAR). This device unobtrusively tracks a person's real-world moment-to-moment interactions. As the wearer goes about her or his daily life, the EAR picks up snippets of conversations and other auditory information. People quickly get used to wearing the EAR and have no idea when it is recording. Through a study using the device, researchers found that the stereotype that women talk more than men is false; women and men use an average of 16,000 words per day (Mehl, Vazire, Ramirez-Esparza, Slatcher, & Pennebaker, 2007). According to another study using the device, the happiest people have the most social interactions, and they also have more substantive conversations (as opposed to small talk) in their daily interactions (Mehl, Vazire, Holleran, & Clark, 2010). The EAR has also been used to show that self-reports on the Big Five traits predict real-world behavior (Mehl, Gosling, & Pennebaker, 2006). According to this study, extraverts talk more and spend less time alone; agreeable people swear less often; conscientious people attend class more often; neurotic people spend more time arguing; and people open to experience spend more time in restaurants, bars, and coffee shops. Likewise, people high in narcissism are more outgoing but less agreeable, skip class more often, and use sexual words more often (Holtzman, Vazire, & Mehl, 2010).

Other aspects of the environment can also be used to predict personality. Consider whether you keep your bedroom tidy or messy, warm or cold. In his book *Snoop,* Sam Gosling (2008) notes that each person's personality leaks out in many situations, such as through a Facebook profile (Back et al., 2010), a personal Web page (Vazire & Gosling, 2004), and the condition of a bedroom or office (Gosling, Ko, Mannarelli, & Morris, 2002). In each case, study participants who viewed public information about other people were able to form reasonably accurate impressions of how those people rated themselves on the Big Five personality traits.

Observers Show Accuracy in Trait Judgments

People might be able to judge our personalities by looking at our bedrooms and Facebook profiles, but how well do they really know us? Imagine that you often feel shy in new situations, as many people do. Would others know that shyness is part of your personality? Some shy people force themselves to be outgoing to mask their feelings, so their friends might have no idea that they feel shy. Other people react to their own fear of social situations by remaining quiet and aloof, so observers might believe them to be cold, arrogant, and unfriendly. Ultimately, how well do observers' personality judgments predict others' behavior?

An important study by David Funder (1995) found a surprising degree of accuracy for trait judgments under certain circumstances. For instance, a person's close acquaintances may predict the person's behavior more accurately than the person does. In some studies, friends predicted assertiveness and other behaviors better than the person's own ratings did (Kolar, Funder, & Colvin, 1996; Vazire & Mehl, 2008). This effect may occur because our friends actually observe how we behave in situations. While we are in those situations, we may be preoccupied with evaluating other people and therefore fail to notice how we behave. Another possibility is that our subjective perceptions may diverge from our objective behaviors. In either case, the study implies that there is a disconnect between how people view themselves and how they behave. Not surprisingly, evidence indicates that people come to know others better over time, as they witness others' behavior across different circumstances; thus we are more accurate in predicting a close friend's behavior than in predicting the behavior of a mere acquaintance (Biesanz, West, & Millevoi, 2007).

Simine Vazire (2010; Vazire & Carlson, 2011) has compared the accuracy of people's self-judgments with the accuracy of how their friends describe them. The comparative accuracy depends on whether the traits are observable and whether the people being rated are motivated to view themselves positively on the traits. Vazire argues that people have blind spots about aspects of their personalities because they want to feel good about themselves. This tendency is particularly true for highly evaluative traits, such as creativity. On highly evaluative traits—which by definition are traits that people care about—people are biased when judging themselves (biases in self-perception are discussed later in this chapter). Thus people are more accurate in rating themselves for traits that are hard to observe and less prone to bias because they are neutral. For instance, a person might be accurate in knowing whether he or she is anxious or optimistic, because those traits are associated with feelings that can be ambiguous to observers. Friends might be more accurate in knowing whether the person is talkative or charming, because the behaviors associated with those traits are easy to observe. Vazire's key insight is that a trait easy to observe but also highly meaningful to people, such as creativity, is more likely to be judged accurately by friends than by the person with the trait (**Figure 13.14**).

People Sometimes Are Inconsistent

Imagine again that you are shy. Are you shy in all situations? Probably not. Shy people tend to be most uncomfortable in new situations in which they are being evaluated. They usually are not shy around family and close friends. In 1968, Walter

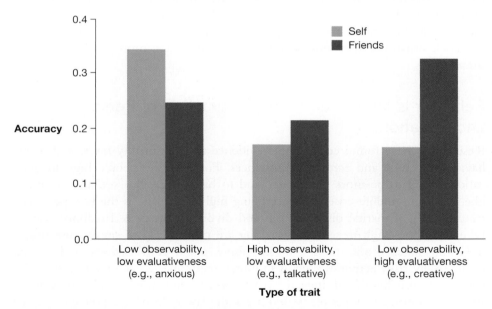

FIGURE 13.14 Self-Rating and Friends' Rating for Different Traits In judgments of personality traits, how accurate are people's self-ratings versus their friends' ratings? This chart, based on the data from the Vazire (2010) study, shows the average accuracy scores for three types of traits. As shown on the left, self-ratings tend to be more accurate than friends' ratings for traits that are low in both observability and evaluativeness. As shown in the middle, friends' ratings tend to be more accurate than self-ratings for traits that are high in observability and low in evaluativeness. As shown on the right, friends' ratings tend to be especially accurate for traits that are low in observability and high in evaluativeness.

situationism The theory that behavior is determined more by situations than by personality traits.

Mischel dropped a bombshell on the field of personality by proposing that behaviors are determined more by situations than by personality traits. This idea has come to be called **situationism.** For evidence, Mischel referred to studies in which people who were dishonest in one situation were completely honest in another. Suppose a student is not totally honest with a professor in explaining why a paper is late. That student probably is no more likely to steal or to cheat on taxes than is a student who admits to oversleeping. Mischel's critique of personality traits caused considerable rifts between social psychologists, who emphasize situational forces, and personality psychologists, who focus on individual dispositions. After all, the most basic definition of personality holds that it is relatively stable across situations and circumstances. If Mischel was correct and there was relatively little stability, the whole concept of personality seemed empty.

As you might expect, there was a vigorous response to Mischel's critique. The discussion has come to be called the *person/situation debate*. Personality researchers argued that how much a trait predicts behavior depends on three factors: the *centrality* of the trait, the *aggregation* of behaviors over time, and the *type* of trait being evaluated. People tend to be more consistent in their central traits than in their secondary traits, since the former are most relevant to them. In addition, if behaviors are averaged across many situations, personality traits are more predictive of behavior. Shy people may not be shy all the time, but on average they are shy more than people who are not shy. Moreover, people who report being shy in college continue to report being shy many years later, so the trait of shyness seems to be stable. Some traits, such as honesty, are more likely to be consistent across situations. Other traits, such as shyness, might vary depending on the situation. Finally, some people may be more consistent than others. Consider the trait of self-monitoring, which involves being sensitive to cues of situational appropriateness. People high in *self-monitoring* alter their behavior to match the situation, so they exhibit low levels of consistency. By contrast, people low in self-monitoring are less able to alter their self-presentations to match situational demands, so they tend to be much more consistent across situations.

Behavior Is Influenced by the Interaction of Personality and Situations

Researchers have found considerable evidence that personality traits predict behavior over time and across circumstances. For instance, people high in neuroticism tend to be more depressed, tend to have more illnesses, and are more likely to have midlife crises. Indeed, being highly neurotic is the best personality predictor of marital dissatisfaction and divorce (Karney & Bradbury, 1995). Likewise, those high in sensation seeking are more likely to smoke, use drugs, have sex, watch erotic movies, be impulsive, begin conversations, and engage in physically risky activities such as mountain climbing (Zuckerman, 2007). Yet people are also highly sensitive to social context, and most people conform to situational norms. Few people would break the law in front of a police officer or drive on the wrong side of the road just because they felt like it. Situations such as these, where there are strong external influences, dictate behavior irrespective of personality.

Situational influences can be subtle. Consider your own behavior. You may reveal different aspects of your personality during your interactions with different people. Your goals for social interaction change. The potential consequences of your actions also change. For example, your family may be more tolerant of your bad moods than your friends are. Thus you may feel freer to express your bad moods around your family.

Situations differ in how much they constrain the expression of personality (Kenrick & Funder, 1991). Suppose one person is highly extraverted, aggressive, and boisterous. A second person is shy, thoughtful, and restrained. At a funeral, these two people might display similar or even nearly identical behavior. At a party, the same two people would most likely act quite differently. Personality psychologists differentiate between *strong situations* and *weak situations*. Strong situations (e.g., elevators, religious services, job interviews) tend to mask differences in personality because of the power of the social environment. Weak situations (e.g., parks, bars, one's house) tend to reveal differences in personality (**Figure 13.15**). Most trait theorists are **interactionists.** That is, they believe that behavior is determined jointly by situations and underlying dispositions.

People also affect their social environments, however. First, people choose their situations. Introverts tend to avoid parties or other situations in which they might feel anxious, whereas extraverts seek out social opportunities. Once people are in situations, their behavior affects those around them. Some extraverts may draw people out and encourage them to have fun, whereas others might act aggressively and turn people off. Some introverts might create an intimate atmosphere that encourages people to open up and reveal personal concerns, whereas others might make people uncomfortable and anxious. A reciprocal interaction occurs between the person and the social environment so that they simultaneously influence each other. The important point is that personality reflects a person's underlying disposition, the activation of the person's goals in a particular situation, and the activation of the person's emotional responses in the pursuit of those goals.

(a)

(b)

FIGURE 13.15 Strong and Weak Situations (a) A strong situation, such as a funeral, tends to discourage displays of personality. **(b)** A weak situation, such as hanging out with friends, tends to let people behave more freely.

There Are Cultural and Sex Differences in Personality

How similar are people around the world? Certainly there are stereotypes about people from different countries, as well as about men and women. But is there any truth to these stereotypes? Does scientific evidence document differences in personality between cultures or between women and men?

Studying cultural differences in personality presents many challenges. As noted in Chapter 2, cross-cultural research can be difficult when language is a central component of what is being studied. Recall from Chapter 1 that people from Eastern cultures tend to think in terms of relations with other people, whereas those from Western cultures tend to think in terms of independence. People from Eastern cultures might therefore interpret a question about personality traits as referring to their family or group. People from Western cultures might interpret the same question as referring to them alone. Making comparisons across cultures also requires the use of standardized questionnaires that are reliably translated so that the questions clearly refer to the same personality trait in all cultures and all respondents interpret the questions in the same way. Another problem involves sampling: Often researchers use convenience samples, such as the college students who are taking the researchers' classes at the time of the study. In different countries, however, different types of people may go to college or university. Thus apparent cultural differences result from examining different types of people in the different cultures.

Recognizing these issues, one research team conducted a careful investigation of personality differences across 56 nations (Schmitt, Allik, McCrae, & Benet-Martinez, 2007). They found that the Big Five personality traits are valid

interactionists Theorists who believe that behavior is determined jointly by situations and underlying dispositions.

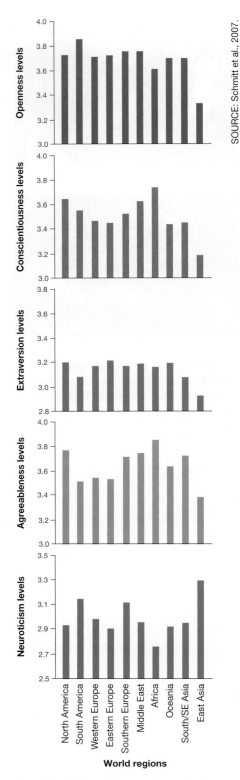

SOURCE: Schmitt et al., 2007.

FIGURE 13.16 Cross-Cultural Research on Personality Traits A team of more than 120 scientists investigated the Big Five personality traits around the world, from Argentina to Zimbabwe. This chart presents some of their findings.

across all the countries. This finding supports the argument that the Big Five are universal for humans. The investigators found modest differences in those traits across the 56 nations, however. People from East Asia (e.g., Japan, China, Korea) rated themselves comparatively lower than other respondents on extraversion, agreeableness, and conscientiousness, and they rated themselves comparatively higher on neuroticism (**Figure 13.16**). By contrast, respondents from countries in Africa rated themselves as more agreeable, more conscientious, and less neurotic than people from most other countries rated themselves. These ratings might have reflected differences, however, in cultural norms for saying good and bad things about oneself. People from East Asian countries might simply be the most modest.

Research findings have made clear that self-reports often do not match cultural stereotypes about the respondents. One team of researchers examined typical beliefs about the personality characteristics of people from 49 cultures (Terracciano et al., 2005). The researchers then compared those ratings to self-reports and observer reports of people from those cultures. There was little correspondence. For instance, Canadians were widely believed to be relatively low in neuroticism and high in agreeableness, yet self-reports by Canadians did not support this pattern. Canadians reported themselves to be just as neurotic and disagreeable as people from other cultures. Steven Heine and colleagues (2008) have argued that national reputations may be accurate and that self-reports might be biased by individuals' comparisons of themselves with their national reputations.

To understand this idea, imagine that everyone in Country X works extremely hard and is always on time. People in Country Y work only when the urge strikes them. Therefore, the people in Country X are high in conscientiousness compared with the people in Country Y. Meanwhile, an individual in Country X and an individual in Country Y may be equally conscientious. Compared with their fellow citizens in their respective countries, however, the person in Country X may feel average, whereas the person in Country Y may feel far above average. Thus people can view the same behavior differently, depending on how they compare themselves with others. In other words, maybe Canadians really are especially agreeable, and it is simply hard to notice one person's agreeableness around all those other agreeable Canadians.

What about sex? Are the stereotypes about men and women accurate? Women and men are much more similar than different in terms of personality, but the differences between them largely support the stereotypes. That is, across various studies, women typically report and are rated as being more empathic and agreeable than men, but also as being somewhat more neurotic and concerned about feelings. By contrast, men tend to report and are rated as being more assertive (Costa, Terracciano, & McCrae, 2001; Feingold, 1994; Maccoby & Jacklin, 1974).

Of particular interest is how sex differences emerge across cultures. You might guess that the more egalitarian and developed a society, the more similarity between the sexes would be observed. After all, if we treat boys and girls equally, we might expect them to turn out to be more similar than they would if we treated them differently. Thus it is puzzling to discover that sex differences in personality are largest in societies in North America and Europe, which provide more equal opportunities and treatment than many other societies, and smallest in Asian and African communities (Costa et al., 2001; Guimond et al., 2007; Schmitt, Realo, Voracek, & Allik, 2008). One theory to explain this pattern is that prosperous, developed societies that emphasize women's rights to education and to work allow for greater personal expression of individuality (Schmitt et al., 2008). Still, why might differences between females and males emerge when people can express themselves freely?

According to the social psychologist Serge Guimond (2008), people in individualist cultures—such as within Western Europe and North America—tend to compare themselves against other groups. Thus women in such cultures describe themselves in ways that differentiate them from men, thereby creating gender differences in personality. From this perspective, the apparent cultural differences in the sex gap result from cultural differences in how people compare themselves rather than from any genuine cultural differences. As you will see later in this chapter, however, some evidence suggests that certain sex differences in personality emerge during early childhood.

Summing Up

How Is Personality Assessed, and What Does It Predict about People?

Idiographic approaches to the study of personality are person-centered, focusing on individual lives and each person's unique characteristics. In contrast, nomothetic approaches to the study of personality are concerned with individual variation in characteristics that are common among all people. Personality may be assessed through projective or objective measures. Projective measures (such as the Rorschach inkblot test and the Thematic Apperception Test) explore unconscious processes by having people interpret ambiguous stimuli. Objective measures (such as the California Q-Sort) assess what raters believe. People are relatively good at assessing other people's personality traits. In fact, there is some evidence that observers might be better at predicting other people's behavior than people are at predicting their own behavior. Traits that are readily observable and meaningful to people tend to be judged more accurately by others than by ourselves. Situationism maintains that behavior is determined more by situations than by personality dispositions. Interactionism maintains that behavior is determined by both situations and our dispositions. Most trait theories adopt an interactionist view. Situations differ in how much they constrain behavior: Strong situations mask differences in personality, and weak situations reveal differences in personality. The structure of personality is stable across cultures, although self-reports concerning some traits differ across cultures. These differences may be attributed to biases in self-report. Sex differences in personality are consistent with common sex stereotypes. Sex differences are greater in more egalitarian and developed societies, reflecting the greater tendency among individualists to compare themselves to others.

Measuring Up

1. Match the strengths and limitations listed below to the following assessment methods: California Q-Sort, NEO Personality Inventory, Rorschach inkblot test, Thematic Apperception Test. (Each method may be associated with multiple strengths and multiple limitations.)

Strengths:

a. Can be completed by an individual or by observers who evaluate that individual.

b. Supposed to reveal hidden aspects of personality.

c. Effectively measures motivational states.

d. Offers a built-in procedure for identifying traits perceived to be most central to the rater.

Limitations:

e. Can be biased by the rater's desire to avoid looking bad.

f. Does a poor job of diagnosing psychological disorders.

g. Many normal individuals who take this test are misdiagnosed as being psychologically disturbed.

2. For each scenario, indicate which person is most likely to engage in the behavior described, and explain why in a sentence.

Scenario 1: The two people described below each have a birthday party. After the party, who is more likely to follow through on his plan to send thank-you cards to the guests? Why?

a. Chad describes himself as highly conscientious; moreover, he says his conscientiousness is vital to who he is.

b. Malik takes the NEO Personality Inventory. He is a little surprised by the results, which indicate he is highly conscientious.

Scenario 2: The two people described below are each engaged in conversations with total strangers. Which person is most likely to give an honest answer when asked, "How are you doing?" Why?

a. Hayley is in an office conference room, talking with the boss's administrative assistant while waiting for the boss to arrive for Hayley's interview.

b. Roxanne is at a bar talking to the bartender while sipping her drink.

Answers: 1. California Q-Sort—a, d, e; NEO Personality Inventory—a, e; Rorschach inkblot test—b, f, g; Thematic Apperception Test—b, c.
2. Scenario 1—a, because conscientiousness is centrally important to Hayley's personality; Scenario 2—b, because a bar is a weak situation and thus less likely to dictate behavior.

- Review research assessing personality traits among nonhuman animals.

- Summarize the results of twin studies and adoption studies as those results pertain to personality.

- Identify the genetic basis of novelty seeking, neuroticism, and agreeableness.

- Identify distinct temperaments.

- Discuss the neurobiological basis of extraversion/introversion.

- Summarize the results of research on personality stability across time.

13.3 What Are the Biological Bases of Personality?

Where does personality come from? In his theory of psychosexual stages, Freud emphasized early childhood experiences. Rogers believed that unconditional positive regard leads to positive mental health. Most people assume that how a child is treated—by parents, guardians, peers, and so on—will substantially affect that child's personality and subsequent development. As discussed earlier, both sex and culture influence personality. So what role does biology play? Is each person born with certain predispositions? How do the workings of the body, including those of the brain, affect the development of personality?

Over the past few decades, evidence has emerged that biological factors—such as genes, brain structures, and neurochemistry—play an important role in determining personality. Of course, these factors are all affected by experience. As discussed in Chapter 3, every cell in the body contains the genome, or master recipe, that provides detailed instructions for physical processes. Gene expression—whether the gene is turned off or on—underlies all psychological activity. Ultimately, genes have their effects only if they are expressed. Environment determines when or if gene expression happens. In terms of personality, genetic makeup may predispose certain traits or characteristics, but whether these genes are expressed depends on the unique circumstances that each child faces during development. For instance, as noted in Chapter 3, children with a certain gene variation were found to be more likely to become violent criminals as adults if they were abused during childhood. An important theme throughout this book is that nature and nurture work together to produce individuals; this theme holds particularly true for personality.

Animals Have Personalities

If you have ever owned a pet, you probably felt that your pet had a distinct personality. For most of the history of psychological science, your intuition would have been regarded skeptically. That is, psychologists would have assumed that you were projecting your own sense of personality onto your pet. When considering the question of whether animals have personalities, some psychologists now think in terms of the principles of evolution. That is, humans and other animals evolved as they solved occasionally similar adaptive challenges. Therefore, some continuity exists across species. This view raises the possibility that animals, across circumstances, might display consistent individual differences in behaviors, and those individual differences might reflect underlying biological bases of personality (Gosling, 2001). But how do psychologists determine an animal's personality?

Sam Gosling studied the behavior of a group of 34 spotted hyenas (Gosling, 1998). From his findings, Gosling created a personality scale that consisted of 44 traits applicable to both humans and hyenas. Four observers who knew hyenas well used the scale independently to rate the animals. Agreement among the raters was as high as is typically found in personality studies of humans, and this result suggests that the raters could assess the hyenas reliably. Using factor analysis, Gosling found that the traits clustered into five factors. These factors were not exactly the same as the Big Five, but rough similarities existed between humans and hyenas in traits related to agreeableness, neuroticism, and openness to experience. Hyenas showed no evidence of a conscientiousness factor. Extraversion seemed to exist in the hyenas mainly in the form of assertiveness, and this finding makes sense given that hyenas form dominance hierarchies (**Figure 13.17**).

Gosling and Oliver John (1999) summarized the findings of 19 studies that assessed multiple personality traits in nonhuman animals. The studies involved modestly large samples of household pets, monkeys and other primates, pigs, donkeys, aquatic animals, and other species. Gosling and John found evidence that traits similar to extraversion, neuroticism, and agreeableness could be seen in most species. Only chimpanzees showed any signs of conscientiousness, however. This finding may not be surprising, since chimps are humans' closest relatives.

Do these judgments of personality in animals reflect true variations, or are they just stereotypes of certain species or breeds (**Figure 13.18**)? To test whether differences in personality traits among animals exist and can be measured, Gosling and colleagues (2003) examined personality judgments for domestic dogs. They compared those judgments to judgments made for humans. Gosling asked each dog owner to rate his or her animal and also to provide the name of a

"I could cry when I think of the years I wasted accumulating money, only to learn that my cheerful disposition is genetic."

FIGURE 13.17 Scientific Method: Gosling's Study of Personality in Animals

Hypothesis: Nonhuman animals can be described in terms of basic personality traits.

1 The researchers defined 44 traits and asked four observers to rate 34 spotted hyenas on each trait.

2 Through factor analysis, the 44 traits were clustered into five principal dimensions:

ASSERTIVENESS   CURIOSITY

EXCITABILITY   HUMAN-DIRECTED
              AGREEABLENESS

SOCIABILITY

Results: The four judges' ratings showed as much agreement as in most personality studies of humans. The five personality dimensions could not be accounted for by other factors, such as sex or age.

Conclusion: The finding that hyenas can reliably be described in terms of personality traits lends support for further personality research on nonhuman animals.

Source: Gosling, S. D. (1998). Personality dimensions in spotted hyenas (*Crocuta crocuta*). *Journal of Comparative Psychology, 112,* 107–118.

(a)

(b)

FIGURE 13.18 Do Dogs Have Personalities? Which is friendlier, (a) a golden retriever or (b) a rottweiler? How might you test your hypothesis?

friend who knew the dog well enough to rate it. Independent judges also assessed the behavior of the dog while it played in a park and performed a wide array of tasks. The dogs were assessed on four personality factors that corresponded roughly to openness to experience, extraversion, agreeableness, and neuroticism. The findings generally indicated that the ratings of the dogs were consistent over time, that the judges agreed, and that the trait behaviors displayed by the dogs corresponded to ratings of those traits made by independent judges. This study suggests that dogs' personalities can be rated with impressive accuracy. Thus animals show clear evidence of basic personality traits. This evidence suggests that the traits are biologically based and passed along through genes.

Personality Is Rooted in Genetics

There is overwhelming evidence that nearly all personality traits have a genetic component (Plomin & Caspi, 1999). One of the earliest studies to document the heritability of personality was conducted by James Loehlin and Robert Nichols (1976). The researchers examined similarities in personality in more than 800 pairs of twins. Across a wide variety of traits, identical twins proved much more similar than fraternal twins. As discussed in Chapter 3, this pattern reflects the actions of genes, since identical twins share nearly the same genes, whereas fraternal twins do not. Numerous twin studies subsequently have found that genetic influence accounts for approximately half the variance

(40 percent to 60 percent) between individuals in personality traits, including the Big Five, as well as in specific attitudes that reflect personality traits, such as attitudes toward the death penalty, abortion on demand, and enjoying roller coaster rides (Olson, Vernon, Harris, & Jang, 2001). Further, the genetic basis of these five traits has been shown to be the same across cultures (Yamagata et al., 2006). These patterns persist whether the twins rate themselves or whether friends, family, or trained observers rate them (**Figure 13.19**).

Of course, identical twins might receive more-similar treatment than other siblings, and that treatment might explain the similarities in personality. The best evidence refuting this idea was obtained by Thomas Bouchard and colleagues (1990). As described in Chapter 3, these researchers studied twins raised apart. They found that these twins are often as similar as, or even more similar than, twins raised together. One possible explanation for this finding is that parents strive to bring out individual strengths in each twin so that each feels unique and special. Thus parenting style may foster differences rather than similarities. If this explanation is correct, we might expect stronger correlations between personality traits for older twins than for younger twins, since the effects of parenting would diminish over time. And indeed, identical twins become more alike as they grow older. By contrast, siblings and fraternal twins do not.

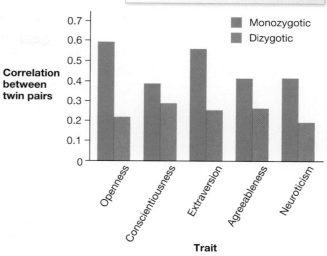

For each Big Five trait, the correlations for monozygotic twins were higher than for dizygotic twins.

FIGURE 13.19 Correlations in Twins
Researchers examined correlations between 123 pairs of identical (monozygotic) twins and 127 pairs of fraternal (dizygotic) twins in Vancouver, Canada. This chart summarizes some of their findings.

ADOPTION STUDIES Further evidence for the genetic basis of personality comes from adoption studies. Say that two children who are not biologically related are raised in the same household as adopted siblings. Those two children tend to be no more alike in personality than any two strangers randomly plucked off the street (Plomin & Caspi, 1999). Moreover, the personalities of adopted children bear no significant relationship to those of the adoptive parents. Together these findings suggest that parenting style may have relatively little impact on personality. In fact, current evidence suggests that parenting style has much less impact than has long been assumed. For instance, studies typically find small correlations in personality between biological siblings or between children and their biological parents. These correlations are still larger than for adopted children. In other words, the similarities in personality between biological siblings and between children and their biological parents seem to have some genetic component.

Why, then, are children raised together in the same household (who are not identical twins) so different? One explanation is that the lives of siblings diverge as they establish friendships outside the home. Even though the siblings are raised in the same home, their environments differ as a function of age and the fact that they have younger or older sisters or brothers and their parents respond to each of them differently. Siblings' personalities slowly grow apart as their initial differences become magnified through their interactions with the world.

Although the small correlations in personality among siblings might imply that parenting style has little effect, this does not mean that parents are unimportant (see Chapter 9, "Human Development"). David Lykken (2000), a leading behavioral genetics researcher, has argued that children raised with inadequate parenting are not socialized properly and therefore are much more likely to become delinquent or to display antisocial behavior. Thus a minimum level of parenting is crucial, but the particular style of parenting may not have a major impact on personality.

ARE THERE SPECIFIC GENES FOR PERSONALITY? Research has revealed genetic components for particular behaviors, such as viewing television or getting divorced, and even for specific attitudes, such as feelings about capital punishment or appreciation of jazz (Tesser, 1993). These findings do not mean, of course, that genes lurking in our DNA determine the amount or types of television we watch. Instead, genes predispose us to have certain personality traits. Those personality traits are associated with behavioral tendencies. In most cases, researchers note the influence of multiple genes that interact independently with the individual's environment to produce general dispositions. For example, genes and environment together might result in a person's preferring indoor activities to outdoor pursuits.

There is growing evidence, however, that genes can be linked with some specificity to personality traits. For instance, a gene that regulates one particular dopamine receptor has been associated with novelty seeking (Cloninger, Adolfsson, & Svrakic, 1996; Ekelund, Lichtermann, Jaervelin, & Peltonen, 1999). The theory is that people with one form of this gene are deficient in dopamine. As a result, these people seek out novel experiences to increase the release of dopamine. Research on neuroticism and agreeableness implicates a gene that regulates serotonin, although the effect is not large (Jang et al., 2001). These genes and perhaps thousands of others contribute to specific traits that combine to influence a person's overall personality and sense of psychological well-being (Weiss, Bates, & Luciano, 2008).

According to David Lykken and colleagues (1992), it may be that each chance aggregation of genes produces a unique individual. These researchers provide the analogy of a poker hand received by a child. Say that the child's mother has dealt the 10 and king of hearts and the child's father has dealt the jack, queen, and ace of hearts. Although neither parent alone has dealt a meaningful hand, together they have passed on a royal flush. Of course, some people receive winning hands and others receive difficult hands to play. The point is that each person's personality reflects the genetic hand dealt jointly by both of that person's parents. Moreover, each person experiences different circumstances that may cause the selective expression of certain genes. Given the complexity of most personalities, the complexity of their underlying physiology is hardly surprising. As psychologists gain a greater understanding of the human genome, they are likely to continue identifying how specific genes interact with environment to produce various aspects of personality.

Temperaments Are Evident in Infancy

Genes work by affecting biological processes. Since genes influence personality, it makes sense that genes help produce biological differences in personality. These differences are called **temperaments**: general tendencies to feel or act in certain ways. Temperaments are broader than personality traits. Life experiences may alter personality traits, but temperaments represent the innate biological structures of personality.

Arnold Buss and Robert Plomin (1984) have argued that three personality characteristics can be considered tempera-

"Oh, he's cute, all right, but he's got the temperament of a car alarm."

ments. *Activity level* is the overall amount of energy and of behavior a person exhibits. For example, some children race around the house, others are less vigorous, and still others are slow paced. *Emotionality* describes the intensity of emotional reactions. For example, children who cry often or easily become frightened, as well as adults who quickly anger, are likely to be high in emotionality. Finally, *sociability* refers to the general tendency to affiliate with others. People high in sociability prefer to be with others rather than to be alone. These temperaments have been linked to people's propensities to move to new locations. A study of migration patterns in Finland found that people who scored high on sociability were more likely to migrate to urban areas and were more likely to migrate to places that were quite distant from their hometowns. Those people who had high activity levels were more likely, in general, to migrate to a new location, regardless of that location. And finally, those who were high in emotionality were likely to migrate to places that were close to their hometowns (Jokela, Elovainio, Kivimaki, & Keltikangas-Jarvinen, 2008). According to Buss and Plomin, these three temperamental styles are the main personality factors influenced by genes. Indeed, evidence from twin studies, adoption studies, and family studies indicates a powerful effect of heredity on these core temperaments.

As discussed earlier, reliable differences exist between males and females in terms of personality traits, at least within Western cultures. How early do these differences emerge? Do temperament differences exist between girls and boys? A meta-analysis found robust gender differences in temperament in early childhood (Else-Quest, Hyde, Goldsmith, & Van Hulle, 2006). Girls demonstrated stronger abilities to control their attention and resist their impulses. Boys were more physically active and experienced more high-intensity pleasure, such as in rough-and-tumble play. However, there were no temperamental differences in negative emotions, such as being angry or neurotic, during childhood.

LONG-TERM IMPLICATIONS OF TEMPERAMENTS To what extent do infant temperaments predict adult personality? Recent research has documented compelling evidence that early childhood temperaments significantly influence behavior and personality structure throughout a person's development (Caspi, 2000). As discussed in Chapter 3, researchers investigated the health, development, and personalities of more than 1,000 people born during a one-year period (Caspi et al., 2002). These individuals were examined approximately every two years. Most of them (97 percent) remained in the study through their 21st birthdays. At 3 years of age, they were classified into temperamental types based on examiners' ratings. The classification at age 3 predicted personality structure and a variety of behaviors in early adulthood. For instance, inhibited children were much more likely, as adults, to be anxious, to become depressed, to be unemployed, to have less social support, and to attempt suicide (**Figure 13.20**). These findings suggest that early childhood temperaments may be good predictors of later behaviors.

The extent to which people are shy in adolescence and adulthood has been linked to early differences in temperament. Research has shown that children as young as 6 weeks of age can be identified as likely to be shy (Kagan & Snidman, 1991). Approximately 15 percent to 20 percent of newborns react to new situations or strange objects by becoming startled and distressed, crying, and vigorously moving their arms and legs. The developmental psychologist Jerome Kagan refers to these children as *inhibited,* and he views this characteristic as biologically determined. Showing signs of inhibition at 2 months of age predicts later parental reports that the children are shy at 4 years of age, and such children are likely to be shy well into their teenage years. The biological evidence suggests that the

temperaments Biologically based tendencies to feel or act in certain ways.

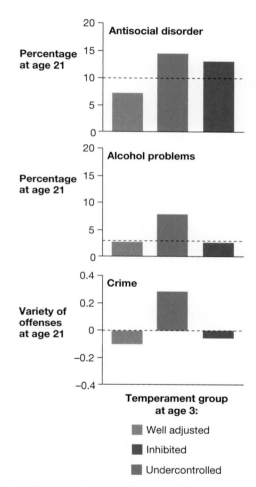

Temperament group at age 3:
■ Well adjusted
■ Inhibited
■ Undercontrolled

FIGURE 13.20 Predicting Behavior
Researchers investigated the personality development of more than 1,000 people. As shown in these graphs, the individuals judged undercontrolled at age 3 were later more likely to be antisocial, to have alcohol problems, and to be criminals than those judged either well adjusted or inhibited. In each graph, the dotted line indicates the average for the entire sample.

amygdala—the brain region involved in emotional responses, especially fear—is involved in shyness.

Although shyness has a biological component, it has a social component as well. Approximately one-quarter of behaviorally inhibited children are not shy later in childhood (Kagan, 2011). This development typically occurs when parents create supportive and calm environments in which children can deal with stress and novelty at their own paces. But these parents do not completely shelter their children from stress, so the children gradually learn to deal with their negative feelings in novel situations. Moreover, shyness varies across cultures. For example, shyness is quite common in Japan and less common in Israel (Zimbardo, 1990). Such social and cultural factors highlight the interplay between nature and nurture.

Personality Is Linked to Specific Neurophysiological Mechanisms

In each child, genes act to produce temperaments. The resulting temperaments affect how the child responds to and shapes her or his environment. In turn, the child's environment and temperaments interact to shape the child's personality. But what is the exact role of genetic predispositions in producing personality? That is, what neurophysiological mechanisms are linked to personality?

Some theories focus on the biological processes that produce the thoughts, emotions, and behaviors that make up personality. From this perspective, differences between personalities may reflect differences in the relative activation of different biological systems (Canli, 2006). Most research on the neurobiological underpinnings of personality has explored the dimension of extraversion/introversion.

AROUSAL AND EXTRAVERSION/INTROVERSION The intellectual founder of the modern biological approach to personality was Hans Eysenck. Eysenck believed that differences in cortical arousal produce the behavioral differences between extraverts and introverts. Cortical arousal, or alertness, is regulated by the *ascending reticular activating system (ARAS)*. As discussed in Chapters 3 and 5, the brain stem contains networks of neurons that are known collectively as the reticular formation. The reticular formation projects up into the cerebral cortex. It affects alertness and is also involved in inducing and terminating the different stages of sleep. Eysenck proposed that the system of reticular activation differs between extraverts and introverts. He noted that extraverts seem constantly to seek additional arousal. For example, extraverts tend to enjoy going to parties or meeting new people. By contrast, introverts seem to avoid arousal. They prefer solitary, quiet activities, such as reading.

As discussed in Chapter 10, each person prefers to operate—and operates best—at some optimal level of arousal. Eysenck proposed that the resting levels of the ARAS are higher for introverts than for extraverts. Extraverts typically are below their optimal levels. In other words, extraverts are chronically under-aroused. To operate efficiently, they have to find arousal, so they impulsively seek out new situations and new emotional experiences. Introverts typically are above their optimal levels of arousal. Because they do not want any additional arousal, they prefer quiet solitude with few stimuli. If you are an introvert, a noisy environment will distract you. If you are an extravert, quiet places will bore you. Consistent with Eysenck's theory, research has demonstrated that extraverts perform better in noisy settings (Geen, 1984).

If introverts are chronically more aroused than extraverts, they ought to be more sensitive to stimuli at all levels of intensity. Generally, introverts do appear more sensitive. For example, they experience pain more intensely than extraverts do. They also experience sourness more intensely: They salivate more when lemon juice is placed on their tongues than extraverts do. Evidence for baseline differences in arousal has been more difficult to produce. That is, the visible biological difference between introverts and extraverts appears to be their level of arousability, or how much they react to stimuli. As you might have guessed, introverts are more arousable.

BEHAVIORAL ACTIVATION AND INHIBITION SYSTEMS   A number of theorists have offered refinements to Eysenck's initial work that reflect a more current understanding of how the brain functions. The various theories have some common features. For example, each theory differentiates between approach learning and avoidance learning. Jeffrey Gray (1987) incorporated this distinction in his approach/inhibition model of the relation between learning and personality. Gray proposed that personality is rooted in two motivational functions: the *behavioral approach system* and the *behavioral inhibition system*. These functions have evolved to help organisms respond efficiently to reinforcement and punishment. In Gray's model, the **behavioral approach system (BAS)** consists of the brain structures that lead organisms to approach stimuli in pursuit of rewards. This is the *"go" system*. The *"stop" system* is known as the **behavioral inhibition system (BIS).** Because it is sensitive to punishment, the BIS inhibits behavior that might lead to danger or pain (**Figure 13.21**).

According to Gray, extraverts have a stronger BAS than BIS. For this reason, extraverts are more influenced by rewards than by punishments. Indeed, extraverts tend to act impulsively in the face of strong rewards, even following punishment (Patterson & Newman, 1993). Introverts have a more active BIS. Their chronic anxiety often leads them to avoid social situations in which they anticipate possible negative outcomes. Different brain regions involved in emotion and reward underlie BIS/BAS systems (DeYoung & Gray, 2009). Gray's model has been particularly useful for understanding personality differences in impulsivity and risk-taking, such as when people act impulsively or take risks while drinking or using drugs (Franken, Muris, & Georgieva, 2006).

We still have much to learn about the biological bases of personality. Only with recent advances in technology have researchers started to explore personality's genetic and brain correlates. Imaging research, for example, has shown that each of the Big Five personality traits is associated with different brain regions (DeYoung et al., 2010). Moreover, brain activity may also depend on genes. In one study of people who possess a particular form of a serotonin gene associated with greater fearfulness and negativity, participants showed greater amygdala activity when looking at pictures of human faces with emotional expressions than did participants with the other form of the gene (Hariri et al., 2002). Using brain imaging and gene data together may become a powerful new way to assess the biological basis of personality (Green et al., 2008). We can anticipate many exciting new discoveries relevant to personality and temperament as a result of the advances in biological research (DeYoung, 2010).

behavioral approach system (BAS) The brain system involved in the pursuit of incentives or rewards.

behavioral inhibition system (BIS) The brain system that is sensitive to punishment and therefore inhibits behavior that might lead to danger or pain.

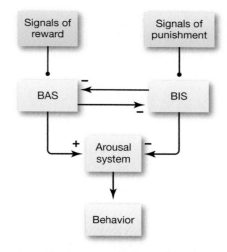

FIGURE 13.21 Behavioral Approach System and Behavioral Inhibition System As depicted in this diagram, signals of potential reward are processed by the behavioral approach system. Signals of potential punishment are processed by the behavioral inhibition system. Based on the information each system receives, the BAS activates behavior and the BIS inhibits behavior. The activation or inhibition comes about partly through the influence of the BAS or BIS on how the person feels, such as her or his state of arousal.

Personality Is Adaptive

The human genome has been shaped over the course of evolution. In fact, it continues to be shaped by evolution. Through the processes of natural selection and sexual selection, adaptive characteristics have spread through the gene pool and have occurred in increasing numbers from generation to generation. Thus we might expect that personality traits useful for survival and reproduction have been favored. For example, it is easy to imagine how being competitive has enabled individuals to obtain great rewards or to enjoy increased value in their social groups. In addition, traits provide important information about desirable and undesirable qualities in mates. Through observing behavior, we come to know whether potential mates are conscientious, agreeable, neurotic, and so on. David Buss (1999) has argued that the Big Five personality traits emerged as foundational because each one provides important information regarding mate selection.

Another possible explanation for individual differences is related to the skills possessed by members of groups. Namely, groups whose members possess diverse skills have a selective advantage over groups whose members have a limited

CRITICAL THINKING SKILL

Avoiding Single-Cause Explanations

Imagine you are talking to two people who are brother and sister. The brother explains that he is a terrible spendthrift because he grew up very poor. His sister explains that she is thrifty, to the point of being cheap, because she grew up very poor. In other words, they provide the same explanation for opposite behaviors. Although most of us understand that differences between people result from multiple causal factors, we often act as though single explanations are correct (Nisbett and Ross, 1980).

Most people prefer single explanations that confirm their preexisting biases. (See the discussion of confirmation bias in Chapter 8, "Thinking and Intelligence," and see the discussion of belief persistence in Chapter 10, "Emotion and Motivation.") For example, people who have never received welfare—assistance from the government for basic necessities—are likely to describe welfare recipients as lazy. People on welfare might explain that they need the help because they have been unlucky or because a weak economy does not provide enough job opportunities. (Notice that these single explanations also reflect the actor/observer discrepancy bias, discussed in Chapter 12, "Social Psychology." The actor/observer discrepancy bias is the tendency to explain other people's behavior as caused by their own actions and to view one's own behavior as caused by external events.)

Consider the debate over why men or women constitute the majority in different occupations (e.g., women in nursing and clerical jobs, men in the building trades and architecture). Most people argue from the standpoint of either nature or nurture, even though they admit that both must be important. Similarly, individuals usually are on welfare for multiple reasons, such as insufficient education, poverty in childhood, limited access to good jobs, and poor health. Whenever you hear people claiming single causes for complex phenomena, or when you find yourself starting to do so, remember to consider multiple causes instead (**Figure 13.22**).

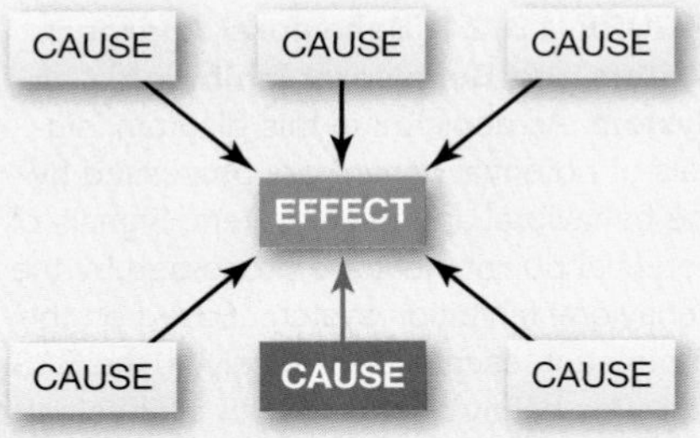

FIGURE 13.22 Cause(s) and Effect
Be sure to consider multiple causes of a phenomenon, not just the one that jumps out at you.

number of skills (Caporael, 2001). Consider the trait of novelty seeking. Having group members who seek out and explore new territory might lead to the discovery of new resources, such as an abundant food supply. Novelty seekers expose themselves to greater risks, however, and the group would suffer if all its members followed this strategy. Therefore, it is to the group's advantage to have cautious members as well. Cautious individuals may enhance the group in other ways, perhaps by being more considerate or providing social support. The diversity of skills thus makes the success of the group more likely. And, of course, members of successful groups are all more likely to survive and reproduce and thus transmit their genes to future generations.

Personality Traits Are Stable over Time

The Jesuits have a maxim: *Give me a child until he is seven, and I will show you the man.* This proverbial saying is the thesis of Michael Apted's *Up* series of documentary films (see Figure 2.5). Through the series, Apted follows the development of a group of British people. Each participant has been interviewed at ages 7, 14, 21, 28, 35, 42, and 49. A striking aspect of these films is the apparent stability of personality over time. For example, the boy interested in the stars and science becomes a professor of physics. The boy who finds his childhood troubling and confusing develops an apparent schizoaffective personality. The reserved, well-mannered, upper-class girl at age 7 grows into the reserved, well-mannered woman in her pastoral retreat at age 35. Are people really so stable? Childhood temperaments may predict behavioral outcomes in early adulthood, but what about change during adulthood? Clinical psychology is based on the belief that people can and do change important aspects of their lives. They exert considerable energy trying to change. They attend self-help groups, read self-help books, pay for therapy sessions, and struggle to make changes in their lives. But how much can people really change?

How we define the essential features of personality has tremendous implications for whether personality is fixed or changeable. Continuity over time and across situations is inherent in the definition of *trait,* and most research finds personality traits to be remarkably stable over the adult life span (Heatherton & Weinberger, 1994). For instance, over many years the relative rankings of individuals on each of the Big Five personality traits remain stable (McCrae & Costa, 1990). A meta-analysis of 150 studies—through which a total of nearly 50,000 participants had been followed for at least one year—found strong evidence for stability in personality (Roberts & Friend-DelVecchio, 2000). The rank orderings of individuals on any personality trait were quite stable over long periods across all age ranges. Stability was lowest for young children, however, and highest for those over age 50 (**Figure 13.23**). This finding suggests that personality changes somewhat in childhood but becomes more stable by middle age. In 1890, the psychologist William James wrote: "For most of us, by age 30, the character has set like plaster and will never soften again" (p. 12b). According to the meta-analysis, James was right that personality becomes set, but it appears to happen a little later than age 30.

AGE-RELATED CHANGE Stability in rank ordering means that individuals stay the same as compared with others. Researchers have asked an additional question about the stability of personality traits, however: Might all people change in personality as they grow older, while retaining their relative rankings? For instance, do people always become wiser and more cautious as they get older? In general,

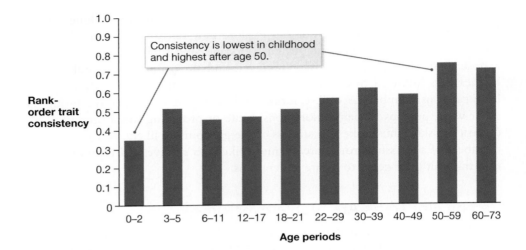

FIGURE 13.23 The Stability of Personality This graph shows the levels of consistency of the study participants' personalities. Participants ranged in age from newborn to 73.

people become less neurotic, less extraverted, and less open to new experiences. They also tend to become more agreeable and more conscientious (Srivastava, John, Gosling, & Potter, 2003). These effects are not large, but they are consistent (Roberts, Walton, & Viechtbauer, 2006). Moreover, the pattern holds in different cultures (McCrae et al., 2000; **Figure 13.24**). These findings suggest that age-related changes in personality occur independently of environmental influences and therefore that personality change itself may be based in human physiology. Indeed, the extent of personality change is more similar in monozygotic twins than in dizygotic twins, and this finding indicates that personality change has a genetic component (McGue, Bacon, & Lykken, 1993).

CHARACTERISTIC ADAPTATIONS In their research on potential change in personality, Robert McCrae and Paul Costa (1999) emphasize an important distinction. They separate basic tendencies of personality from characteristic adaptations (**Figure 13.25**). *Basic tendencies* are dispositional traits determined largely by biological processes. As such, they are very stable. *Characteristic adaptations* are adjustments to situational demands. Such adaptations tend to be somewhat consistent because they are based on skills, habits, roles, and so on. But changes in behavior produced by characteristic adaptations do not indicate changes in basic tendencies. Consider

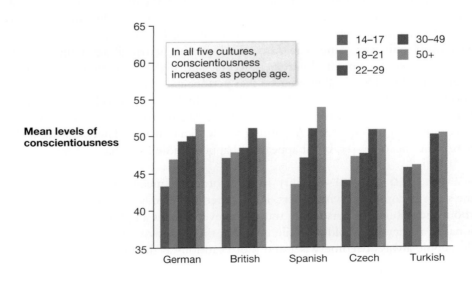

FIGURE 13.24 Conscientiousness at Different Ages in Five Cultures Note that bars are missing from this graph because data were not available for the 14–17 age group in Spain and the 22–29 age group in Turkey.

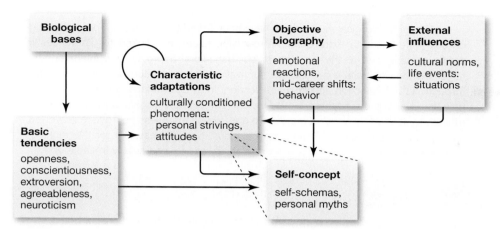

FIGURE 13.25 McCrae and Costa's Model of Personality As shown on the left side of this model, basic tendencies are biologically based. As represented by the complications in the middle and on the right, characteristic adaptations are influenced by basic tendencies and by situations. The arrows indicate some of the ways in which the different components of personality interact. **According to this model, do basic tendencies change across situations? Does objective biography (observable behavior) change? If change occurs in either case, what factors can influence that change?**

a highly extraverted woman. In her youth, she may go to parties frequently, be a thrill seeker, and have multiple sexual partners. In her old age, she will be less likely to do these things, but she may have many friends and enjoy traveling. Although the exact behaviors differ, they reflect the core basic tendency of extraversion.

Overall, then, personality appears to be relatively stable, especially among adults. Because personality is determined partly by biological mechanisms, some changes in personality are tied to changes in biological makeup. Indeed, damage to certain brain regions is associated with dramatic changes in personality. Recall the story of the railroad worker Phineas Gage (described in Chapter 3, "Biology and Behavior") and the story of Elliot (described in Chapter 10, "Emotion and Motivation"). In these cases and many others, damage to the frontal lobes produced changes in personality, such as increased extraversion, impulsiveness, moodiness, and socially inappropriate behavior (Stuss, Gow, & Hetherington, 1992). The brain develops well into early adulthood, and the pace of brain development may explain the greater evidence of personality change before age 30. At the same time, people's environments tend to be relatively stable, especially after early adulthood. People tend to have successive jobs with the same status level and tend to marry people whose attitudes and personalities are similar to their own. It is likely that the stability of situations contributes to the stability of personality.

Summing Up

What Are the Biological Bases of Personality?

Research has provided evidence of basic personality traits in nonhuman animals. These findings suggest that the traits are biologically based. Evidence from behavioral genetics—in particular, twin studies and adoption studies—has demonstrated that personality has a substantial genetic component. In fact, genes may account for approximately half of the variance between individuals in personality traits. For example, research has implicated a gene associated with dopamine levels in novelty seeking and a gene associated with serotonin levels in neuroticism and agreeableness. Temperaments, biologically based personality tendencies, are evident in early childhood and have long-term implications for adult behavior. Activity level, emotionality, and sociability have been identified as temperaments.

Neurophysiological mechanisms have been linked to personality. For instance, individual differences in extraversion/introversion have been linked to differences in cortical arousal and to the strength of our behavioral approach and inhibition systems. Personality traits that facilitate survival and reproduction have been favored through natural selection and sexual selection. Individual differences within a group may be advantageous to the group's survival. The biological basis of personality contributes to its stability across time. As we age, we become less neurotic, extraverted, and open but more agreeable and conscientious. Nevertheless, our relative rankings on the Big Five personality traits remain relatively stable, particularly in adulthood.

Measuring Up

1. Which of the following statements are true regarding the relationship between environment, genes, personality traits, and temperaments? Select all that apply.
   a. Environment interacts with personality traits to shape temperaments.
   b. Environment interacts with temperaments to shape personality traits.
   c. Genes act to produce temperaments.
   d. Temperaments affect how each child responds to and shapes his or her environment.
   e. The influence of genes on temperaments and on personality traits changes over the life span.

2. Which of the following findings support biological bases of personality?
   a. Children as young as 6 weeks of age can be classified as evidencing specific temperaments (Kagan & Snidman, 1991).
   b. Factor analysis reveals five basic personality traits (McCrae & Costa, 1999).
   c. Personality traits can predict academic outcomes, including scores on standardized tests and grades in college (Noftle & Robins, 2007).
   d. Changes in personality as people age occur the same across all cultures (McCrae et al., 2000).
   e. Siblings who are adopted (and not biologically related) and raised in the same household are no more alike in personality than random strangers (Plomin & Caspi, 1999).
   f. Twin studies suggest that 40 percent to 60 percent of the variance between individuals in personality traits can be accounted for by genetics.

Answers: 1. Choices b, c, and d are true. 2. Choices a, d, f, and g support biological bases.

Learning Objectives

- Differentiate between self awareness, self-schema, the working self-concept, and self-esteem.

- Review theories of self-esteem.

- Discuss research findings regarding the association between self-esteem and life outcomes.

- Identify strategies people use to maintain positive self-views.

- Discuss cultural differences in the self-concept and the use of self-serving biases.

13.4 How Do We Know Our Own Personalities?

In the previous sections, the subject was people's personalities generally. The central question was *What must we know to know a person well?* In considering our own personalities, we can rephrase that question as *What must we know to know ourselves well?* This section examines how we process information about ourselves and how that processing shapes our personalities.

Each of us has a notion of something we call the "self." Still, the self is difficult to define. We can say that each person's sense of self involves the person's mental representations of personal experiences. Those representations include both memories and perceptions of what is going on at any particular moment during the person's life. The self also encompasses the person's thought processes, physical body, and conscious awareness of being separate from others and unique. This sense of self is a unitary experience, continuous over time and space. For example, when you wake up in the morning, you do not have to figure out who you are (even if you sometimes have to figure out where you are, such as when you are on vacation).

Our Self-Concepts Consist of Self-Knowledge

Write down 20 answers to the question *Who am I?* The information in your answers is part of your *self-concept,* which is everything you know about yourself (**Figure 13.26**). For example, answers commonly given by college students include gender, age, student status, interpersonal style (e.g., shy, friendly), personal characteristics (e.g., moody, optimistic), and body image. But how would thinking of yourself as shy or optimistic or overweight affect how you feel and function from day to day? Many psychologists view the self-concept as a cognitive knowledge structure. This structure guides your attention to information relevant to you and helps you adjust to your environment. If you think of yourself as shy, you might avoid a raucous party. If you believe yourself to be optimistic, you might easily bounce back from a poor grade in organic chemistry. Look back at the 20 answers you provided above. Then think of some concrete examples of how those ideas about yourself have influenced your thoughts or behaviors. In performing this exercise, you have begun the process of exploring your self-awareness.

SELF-AWARENESS William James and the sociologist George Herbert Mead were two of the first modern thinkers to consider the nature of the self. James and Mead each differentiated between the self as the knower ("I") and the self as the object that is known ("me"). As the knower, the self is the subject doing the thinking, feeling, and acting. It is involved in executive functions such as choosing, planning, and exerting control. By contrast, psychologists now call the self that is known the *objectified self.* The objectified self is the knowledge the subject holds about itself, such as its best and worst qualities. The sense of self as the object of attention is the psychological state known as *self-awareness.* Through self-awareness, the "I" thinks about the "me."

What are the consequences of being self-aware? In 1972, the psychologists Shelley Duval and Robert Wicklund introduced the theory of objective self-awareness. According to this theory, self-awareness leads people to act in accordance with the values and beliefs they hold. For instance, one study showed that when college students are given the opportunity to cheat, they are less likely to do so if they are sitting in front of mirrors (Diener & Wellborn, 1976). Perhaps seeing their own faces reminds them that they do not value cheating. As discussed in Chapter 10, a discrepancy between a personal standard and a goal can motivate a behavior that reduces the discrepancy. In this example, the personal standard would be not cheating. The goal would be passing the test. What behaviors immediately occur to you as reducing the discrepancy? (Hint: Studying was at the top of your list, right?)

FIGURE 13.26 Sense of Self Each of us has a self-concept. One component of that sense is physical appearance.

The psychologist Tory Higgins (1987) studied how standards, goals, and the discrepancies between them affect behavior. According to Higgins's *self-discrepancy theory,* an individual's awareness of differences between personal standards and goals leads to strong emotions. The emotions might differ, depending on the person's perceptions of the discrepancies. For example, suppose your personal standard is to work hard. Your goal is to do well in school. Because you do not study enough, however, you fail a class. The emotions you feel as a result of your failure will depend on your perspective. If you blame yourself for being lazy, you might feel disappointed, frustrated, and depressed. By contrast, if you think about how *your parents* will feel about your failure, you might feel anxious and guilty because your parents will not view you as hardworking.

From studies of patients with brain injuries, we know that self-awareness is highly dependent on normal development of the frontal lobes. People with damage to the frontal lobes tend to be only minimally self-reflective. They seldom report daydreaming or other types of introspection. They also often show a lack of interest in or knowledge about their disorders. Such individuals are not completely unaware of themselves, but they do not find information about the self personally significant.

The neuropsychologist Donald Stuss (1991) reported on a highly intelligent patient who had a tumor removed from his frontal lobes. Subsequently, the patient had difficulty at work and became extremely unproductive, even though his intelligence and knowledge about the world were intact. As noted in Chapter 3, people with damage to the frontal lobes often have social and motivational impairments. These impairments may interfere with job performance. Despite 18 months of therapy, this patient continued to do poorly on the job, but he could not recognize that he had a problem. When asked to role-play the situation as if he were the boss, he quickly recognized the problem and made an appropriate recommendation. Namely, he recommended that the worker (himself) be put on a disability pension. When asked to evaluate himself from his own subjective perspective, however, he disagreed with the recommendation he had just made. Dramatic examples such as this one show the types of distortion that frontal lobe patients may experience in processing information about the self.

SELF-SCHEMA Picture yourself at a loud, crowded party. You can barely hear yourself speak. When someone across the room mentions your name, however, you hear it clearly above the noise. As discussed in Chapter 7, psychologists refer to effects of this kind as the cocktail party phenomenon. These effects occur because each person processes information about himself or herself deeply, thoroughly, and automatically. The information becomes part of the person's *self-schema.*

According to Hazel Markus (1977), the self-schema is the cognitive aspect of the self-concept. That description might seem intimidating, but it simply means that the self-schema consists of an integrated set of memories, beliefs, and generalizations about the self. The set can be viewed as a network of interconnected knowledge about the self (**Figure 13.27**).

The self-schema helps each of us perceive, organize, interpret, and use information about the self. It also helps each of us filter information so that we are likely to notice things that are self-relevant, such as our own names. Examples of our behavior, and aspects of our personalities, that are important to us become prominent in our self-schemas. For instance, being a good athlete or a good student may be a major component of your self-schema, whereas having few cavities probably is not.

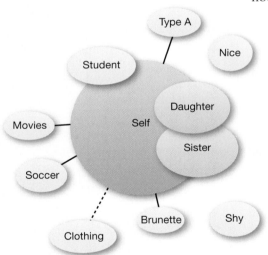

FIGURE 13.27 Self-Schema As this example illustrates, the self-schema consists of interrelated knowledge about the self. Here the concepts that overlap with the self—student, daughter, and sister—are most strongly related to the self. Concepts connected to self with a solid line—Type A, movies, soccer, and brunette—are not quite as strongly related to self-knowledge. Clothing, connected to self with a dotted line, is connected more weakly. Concepts with no connecting lines do not relate to the self.

Thus when asked if you are ambitious, you can answer without sorting through occasions in which you did or did not act ambitiously. Your self-schema summarizes the relevant past information.

Meanwhile, your self-schema may lead you to have enhanced memory for information that you process in reference to yourself. Tim Rogers and colleagues (1977) showed that when a person processes trait adjectives self-referentially, the person is likely to recall the words better than comparable words processed only for their general meanings. Suppose you are asked, "What does the word *honest* mean?" If you are later asked to recall the word you were asked about, you might or might not recall *honest*. Now suppose the initial question is, "Does the word *honest* describe you?" When asked later, you will be more likely to remember the word.

What brain activity is involved in this effect? Researchers typically find that when people process information about themselves, there is activity in the middle of the frontal lobes (Gillihan & Farah, 2005; Kelley et al., 2002; **Figure 13.28**). For example, this brain region is more active when we answer questions about ourselves (e.g., "Are you honest?") than when we answer questions about other people (e.g., "Is your mother honest?"). The greater the activation of this area during the self-referencing, the more likely the person is to remember the item later during a surprise memory task (Macrae, Moran, Heatherton, Banfield, & Kelley, 2004). As discussed earlier, damage to the frontal lobes tends to reduce or eliminate self-awareness. Activation of the frontal lobes clearly seems to be important for processing information about the self (Heatherton, 2011).

WORKING SELF-CONCEPT Psychologists refer to the immediate experience of the self as the *working self-concept*. This experience is limited to the amount of personal information that can be processed cognitively at any given time. Because the working self-concept includes only part of the vast array of self-knowledge, the sense of self varies from situation to situation. Suppose your self-concept includes the traits *fun-loving* and *intelligent*. At a party, you might think of yourself as fun-loving *rather than* intelligent. In other words, your self-descriptions vary. They depend on which memories you retrieve, which situation you are in, which people you are with, and your role in that situation.

When people consider who they are or think about different features of their personalities, they often emphasize characteristics that make them distinct from others. Think back to your 20 responses to the question *Who am I?* Which answers stressed your similarity to other people or membership in a group? Which ones stressed your differences from other people, or at least from the people immediately around you? Respondents are especially likely to mention features such as ethnicity, gender, or age if the respondents differ in these respects from other people around them at the moment (**Figure 13.29**). For example, Canadians are more likely to note their nationality if they are in Boston than if they are in Toronto. Because the working self-concept guides behavior, this tendency implies that Canadians are also more likely to feel and act like "Canadians" when in Boston than when in Toronto. Most people have optimal levels of distinctiveness, however, since generally they want to avoid standing out too much from the crowd.

Perceived Social Regard Influences Self-Esteem

North American culture has been obsessed with self-esteem since at least the 1980s. At a basic level, *self-esteem* is the evaluative aspect of the self-concept. In other words, self-esteem indicates a person's emotional response to contemplating

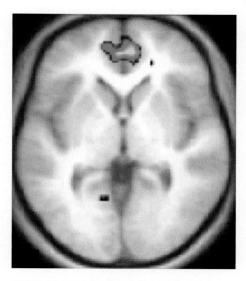

FIGURE 13.28 The Self and Frontal Lobe Activity This brain scan comes from the 2002 study by Kelley and colleagues. The colored area is the brain area that was active when people made trait judgments about themselves.

FIGURE 13.29 Working Self-Concept When considering themselves or their personalities, people are especially likely to mention characteristics that distinguish them from other people. For example, when working with a group of women, an African American man might be most aware of his maleness. When working with a group of Caucasians, he might emphasize his being African American.

personal characteristics: "Am I worthy or unworthy?" "Am I good or bad?" Although self-esteem is related to self-concept, people can objectively believe positive things about themselves without liking themselves very much. Conversely, people can like themselves very much, and therefore have high self-esteem, even when objective indicators do not support such positive self-views.

Many theories assume that people's self-esteem is based on how they believe others perceive them. This view is known as *reflected appraisal*. When people internalize the values and beliefs expressed by important people in their lives, they adopt those attitudes (and related behaviors) as their own. Consequently, people come to respond to themselves in ways that are consistent with how others respond to them. From this perspective, when an important figure rejects, ignores, demeans, or devalues a person, the person is likely to experience low self-esteem.

SOCIOMETER THEORY In a novel and important account of self-esteem, Mark Leary and colleagues (1995) have proposed that self-esteem is a mechanism for monitoring the likelihood of social exclusion. This theory assumes that, as discussed in Chapter 12, humans have a fundamental, adaptive need to belong. For most of human evolution, those who belonged to social groups have been more likely to survive and reproduce than those who were excluded and left to survive on their own. When people behave in ways that increase the likelihood that they will be rejected, they experience a reduction in self-esteem. Thus self-esteem is a **sociometer,** an internal monitor of social acceptance or rejection (**Figure 13.30**).

When a person's sociometer indicates a low probability of rejection, the person will tend to experience high self-esteem. As long as the probability of rejection remains low, the person will probably not worry about how he or she is perceived by others. When a person's sociometer indicates the imminent possibility of rejection, the person will tend to experience low self-esteem. Therefore the person will be highly motivated to manage his or her public image. Abundant evidence supports the sociometer theory, including the consistent finding that low self-esteem is highly correlated with social anxiety (Leary, 2004; Leary & MacDonald, 2003). Recall, though, that even high correlation does not prove causation.

SELF-ESTEEM AND DEATH ANXIETY One provocative theory proposes that self-esteem is related to humans' anxiety over their mortality (Greenberg, 2008; Greenberg, Solomon, & Pyszczynski, 1997; Pyszczynski, Greenberg, Solomon, Arndt, & Schimel, 2004). According to *terror management theory,* self-esteem gives meaning to people's lives. In this way, self-esteem protects people from the horror associated with knowing they eventually will die. People counter their fears of mortality by creating a sense of symbolic immortality through contributing to their culture and upholding its values. From this cultural perspective, self-esteem develops from a person's belief that he or she is living up to criteria valued within the culture. Accordingly, people sometimes exaggerate their personal importance in attempts to buffer anxiety about inevitable death. Research has demonstrated that reminding people of their mortality leads them to act in ways that enhance their self-esteem (Goldenberg, McCoy, Pyszczynski, Greenberg, & Solomon, 2000). Likewise, encountering information that threatens people's self-esteem and their cultural values leads people to think about death more (Schimel, Hayes, Williams, & Jahrig, 2007).

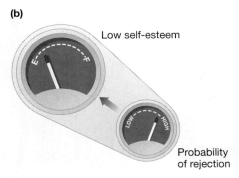

(a)

High self-esteem

Probability of rejection

(b)

Low self-esteem

Probability of rejection

FIGURE 13.30 Sociometers According to sociometer theory, self-esteem is the gauge that measures the extent to which a person believes he or she is being included in or excluded from a social group. **(a)** If the probability of rejection seems low, the person's self-esteem will tend to be high. **(b)** If the probability of rejection seems high, the person's self-esteem will tend to be low.

Resisting Appeals to Snobbery

Choosy mothers choose Jif.
Inquiring minds want to know.
L'Oreal: Because you're worth it.
When you care enough to send the very best.

What unites these advertising slogans? Each one appeals to snobbery. Appeals to snobbery effectively play on people's desire to perceive themselves (and be perceived by others) as superior. For example, people want to be sophisticated, intelligent, stylish, wealthy, and educated. Consumers may be flattered by the suggestion that they are among the select few who can appreciate a particular product (**Figure 13.31**). The messages are not always verbal. An appeal to snobbery might be conveyed through images, such as when well-dressed, attractive people are portrayed in luxurious homes. On television, the radio, and the Web, sound effects, background music, or actors' accents can subtly suggest wealth, high social class, and advanced education.

Not all appeals to snobbery have an economic objective, however. Political advertisements often convey messages about the type of people who support a certain political candidate or party. Of course, intelligent and hardworking people would never be fooled by the opposing candidate's rhetoric! The message is that if you belong to (or want to belong to) this group of people, you will support the candidate being advertised.

With practice, you will recognize when a persuasive message is trying to play on your desire to be better than others. The next time you watch television or leaf through a magazine, look for advertisements that make appeals based on consumers' snobbery. How do the advertisers convey their messages? What desired traits do they associate with their product? Most important, if you buy this product, will it make you feel smarter, trendier, or classier than everyone else, or will you be falling prey to clever advertising?

FIGURE 13.31 An Appeal to Snobbery
This billboard is advertising a residential development in Dubai. The slogan presents housing as more than just a place to live. Here, housing is also a lifestyle: "designer living."

SELF-ESTEEM AND LIFE OUTCOMES With such emphasis placed on self-esteem within Western culture, you might expect that having high self-esteem is the key to life success. The evidence from psychological science, however, indicates that self-esteem may be less important than is commonly believed. After reviewing several hundred studies, Roy Baumeister and colleagues (Baumeister, Campbell, Krueger, & Vohs, 2003, 2005) found that although people with high self-esteem report being much happier, self-esteem is weakly related to objective life outcomes. People with high self-esteem who consider themselves smarter, more attractive, and better liked do not necessarily have higher IQs and are not necessarily thought of more highly by others. Many people with high self-esteem are successful in their careers, but so are many people with low self-esteem. While a small relationship exists between self-esteem and some outcomes, such as academic success, it is possible that success causes high self-esteem. That is, people might have higher self-esteem because they have done well in school.

In fact, there may even be some downsides to having very high self-esteem. Violent criminals commonly have very high self-esteem; indeed, some people become violent when they feel that others are not treating them with an appropriate level of respect (Baumeister, Smart, & Boden, 1996). School bullies also often have high self-esteem (Baumeister et al., 2003). When people with high self-esteem believe their abilities have been challenged, they may act in ways that cause other people to dislike them (Heatherton & Vohs, 2000; Vohs & Heatherton, 2004). For example, the sense of needing to prove their worth might lead people to become antagonistic or boastful. Ultimately, having high self-esteem seems to make people happier, but it does not necessarily lead to successful social relationships or life success.

One personality trait associated with inflated self-esteem is *narcissism*. The term comes from Greek mythology, in which Narcissus rejected the love of others and fell in love with his own reflection in a pond. In the psychological sense of narcissism, self-centered people view themselves in grandiose terms, feel entitled to special treatment, and are manipulative (Bosson et al., 2008). Because narcissists' greatest love is for the self, they tend to have poor relations with others (Campbell, Bush, Brunell, & Shelton, 2005). They become angry when challenged (Rhodewalt & Morf, 1998). They abuse people who do not share their lofty opinions of themselves (Bushman & Baumeister, 1998; Twenge & Campbell, 2003). They are unfaithful (Campbell, Foster, & Finkel, 2002).

You might be interested to learn that a meta-analysis found increasing narcissism among American college students between 1979 and 2006 (Twenge, Konrath, Foster, Campbell, & Bushman, 2008). The researchers point to a few possible contributing factors: programs aimed at increasing self-esteem among young schoolchildren (such as having them sing songs about how they are special), grade inflation that makes students feel more capable than they might really be, and a rise in the use of self-promotion Web sites such as Facebook and MySpace. A different team of researchers was unable to replicate the results of this meta-analysis, however, and there is controversy regarding what the findings mean (Trzesniewski, Donnellan, & Roberts, 2008).

We Use Mental Strategies to Maintain Our Views of Self

Most people show favoritism to anything associated with themselves. For example, people consistently prefer their belongings to things they do not own (Beggan, 1992). People even prefer the letters of their own names, especially their initials, to other letters (Koole, Dijksterhuis, & van Knippenberg, 2001; **Figure 13.32**). Sometimes these positive views of the self seem inflated. For instance, 90 percent of adults claim they are better-than-average drivers, even if they have been hospitalized for injuries caused by car accidents in which they were one of the drivers involved (Guerin, 1994; Svenson, 1981). Similarly, when the College Entrance Examination Board surveyed more than 800,000 college-bound seniors, not a single senior rated herself or himself as below average, whereas a whopping 25 percent rated themselves in the top 1 percent (Gilovich, 1991). Most people describe themselves as above average in nearly every way, and psychologists refer to this phenomenon as the *better-than-average effect* (Alicke, Klotz, Breitenbecher, Yurak, & Vredenburg, 1995). People with high self-esteem are especially likely to exhibit this effect.

According to Shelley Taylor and Jonathan Brown (1988), most people have positive illusions—overly favorable and unrealistic beliefs—in at least three domains. First, most people continually experience the better-than-average effect. Second, they unrealistically perceive their personal control over events. For example, some

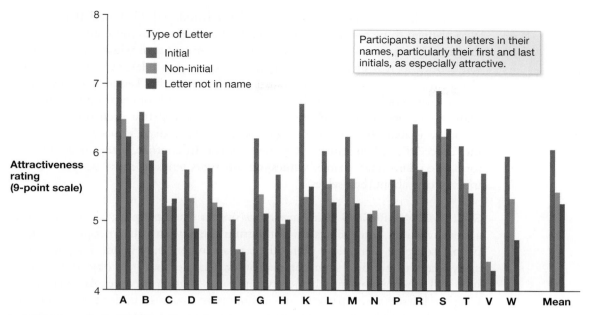

FIGURE 13.32 Favoritism This graph shows the study participants' ratings of the letters of the alphabet.

fans believe they help their favorite sports teams win if they attend games or wear their lucky jerseys. Third, most people are unrealistically optimistic about their personal futures. They believe they probably will be successful, marry happily, and live long lives. Positive illusions can be adaptive when they promote optimism in meeting life's challenges. Alternatively, positive illusions can lead to trouble when people overestimate their skills and underestimate their vulnerabilities.

Life is filled with failure, rejection, and disappointment, yet most people feel pretty good about themselves. How do people maintain such positive views? Psychologists have cataloged a number of unconscious strategies that help people maintain a positive sense of self. Among the most common are *self-evaluative maintenance, social comparisons,* and *self-serving biases.* As you read the following discussions, bear in mind that psychologists do not necessarily endorse these strategies.

SELF-EVALUATIVE MAINTENANCE Abraham Tesser (1988) notes that self-esteem can be affected by how people perform, how relevant their performances are to their self-concepts, and how their performances compare with those of significant people around them. According to the theory of *self-evaluative maintenance,* people can feel threatened when someone close to them outperforms them on a task that is personally relevant. If you had a twin brother who shared your aspiration to be a world-class chef, his brilliant success at cooking would have important implications for how you felt about yourself. To maintain your sense of self-esteem, Tesser argues, you would either distance yourself from the relationship or select a different aspiration. Of course, if your twin brother excels at something you do not find relevant, you might bask in the glow of reflected glory and experience a boost in self-esteem based on your relationship. Indeed, self-evaluative maintenance causes people to exaggerate or publicize their connections to winners and to minimize or hide their relations to losers.

In some situations, people will feel good about themselves when they encounter someone who is doing much better than they are on a relevant dimension.

For example, Penelope Lockwood and Ziva Kunda (1997) found that students who planned to be teachers or accountants rated themselves more positively when they read about a high-achieving teacher or accountant than when they read about someone who was successful in a domain that was not relevant to them. At first glance, this finding seems to contradict those reported by Tesser. The key difference is that people feel good about themselves as a result of comparing themselves with "superstars" in their chosen fields when they feel that such successful performance is attainable for them. If people can believe that "someday, that will be me," successful others can be very inspirational. In contrast, if the successful performance seems unattainable, witnessing superstars tends to make people feel that much worse about themselves.

SOCIAL COMPARISONS *Social comparison* occurs when people evaluate their own actions, abilities, and beliefs by contrasting them with other people's. That is, people compare themselves with others to see where they stand. They are especially likely to perform such comparisons when they have no objective criteria, such as knowing how much money represents a good income. As discussed in Chapter 10, social comparisons are an important means of understanding our actions and emotions. In general, people with high self-esteem make downward comparisons. That is, they contrast themselves with people deficient to them on relevant dimensions. People with low self-esteem tend to make upward comparisons. They contrast themselves with people superior to them. People also use a form of downward comparison when they recall their own pasts: They often view their current selves as better than their former selves (Wilson & Ross, 2001; **Figure 13.33**). These findings suggest that viewing ourselves as better than others or as better than we used to be makes us feel good about ourselves. But people who constantly compare themselves with others who do better may confirm their negative self-feelings.

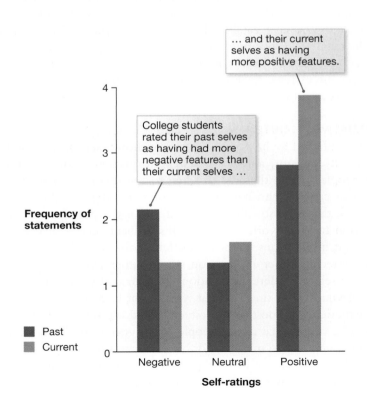

FIGURE 13.33 Rating the Self across Time This graph shows the results of Wilson and Ross's 2001 study.

SELF-SERVING BIASES People with high self-esteem tend to take credit for success but blame failure on outside factors. Psychologists refer to this tendency as the **self-serving bias.** For instance, students who do extremely well on exams often explain their performance by referring to their skills or hard work. Those who do poorly might describe the test as an arbitrary examination of trivial details. People with high self-esteem also assume that criticism is motivated by envy or prejudice. Indeed, members of groups prone to discrimination (e.g., the disabled; ethnic minorities) tend to have high self-esteem. According to a theory proposed by Jennifer Crocker and Brenda Major (1989), members of these groups maintain positive self-esteem by taking credit for success and blaming negative feedback on prejudice. Thus if they succeed, the success is due to personal strengths and occurs despite the odds. If they fail, the failure is due to external factors and unfair obstacles.

Over the last 40 years, psychologists have documented many ways that people show bias in thinking about themselves compared with how they think about others (Campbell & Sedikides, 1999). In thinking about our failures, for example, we compare ourselves with others who did worse, we diminish the importance of the challenge, we think about the things we are really good at, and we bask in the reflected glory of both family and friends. The overall picture suggests we are extremely well equipped to protect our positive beliefs about ourselves. Some researchers have even argued that self-serving biases reflect healthy psychological functioning (Mezulis, Abramson, Hyde, & Hankin, 2004; Taylor & Brown, 1988). Recall the earlier discussion of narcissism, however. This trait reflects more of a disorder of personality than healthy functioning.

There Are Cultural Differences in the Self

An important way in which people differ in self-concept is whether they view themselves as fundamentally separate from or connected to other people. For example, as noted in Chapter 1, Westerners tend to be independent and autonomous, stressing their individuality. Easterners tend to be more interdependent, stressing their sense of being part of a collective. Harry Triandis (1989) notes that some cultures (e.g., in Japan, Greece, Pakistan, China, and some regions of Africa) emphasize the collective self more than the personal self. Collectivist cultures emphasize connections to family, to social groups, and to ethnic groups; conformity to societal norms; and group cohesiveness. Individualist cultures (e.g., in northern and western Europe, Australia, Canada, New Zealand, and the United States) emphasize rights and freedoms, self-expression, and diversity. For example, in the United States, people dress differently from one another, cultivate personal interests, and often enjoy standing out from the crowd. In Japan, people tend to dress more similarly and respect situational norms. When an American family goes to a restaurant, each person usually orders what he or she prefers. When a family goes to a restaurant in China, all the people at the table share multiple dishes.

Hazel Markus and Shinobu Kitayama (1991) have noted that people in collectivist cultures have *interdependent self-construals*. In other words, these people's self-concepts are determined to a large extent by their social roles and personal relationships (**Figure 13.34**). As children, they are raised to follow group norms and to be obedient to parents, teachers, and other people in authority. They are expected to find their proper place in society and not to challenge or complain about their status. By contrast, people in individualist cultures have *independent self-construals*. Parents and teachers encourage children to be self-reliant and to pursue personal success, even at the expense of interpersonal relationships. Thus children's senses of

self-serving bias The tendency for people to take personal credit for success but blame failure on external factors.

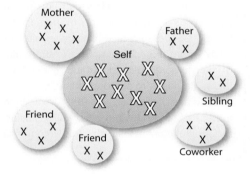

(a) Individualist

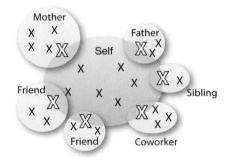

(b) Collectivist

FIGURE 13.34 Cultural Differences in Self-Construals Self-construals differ across cultures. **(a)** In individualist cultures, the most important elements of a person's self-construal tend to reside within the person. **(b)** In collectivist cultures, the most important elements of a person's self-construal tend to reside in areas where the person's sense of self is connected with others.

Do Personalities Matter in Roommate Relationships?

If you live on campus, you may think of your residence hall as your home or at least your home away from home. You probably spend a good deal of time studying, sleeping, relaxing, and socializing in the comfy confines of your 200-square-foot dorm room. And if you are like the majority of residential college students, you share your room with at least one roommate.

Positive roommate relationships can be a highlight of the college experience and can provide a foundation for lifelong friendships. Unfortunately, negative roommate relationships can add significant stress to the college experience and can even disrupt the mental health and academic performance of the students involved. How can you use a psychological understanding of personality to help ensure a positive roommate relationship? There are no guarantees in the realm of interpersonal relating, but the research on this topic points to some useful advice.

Carli and colleagues (1991) examined the association between personality similarity and relationship satisfaction among 30 college roommate pairs. The roommates had been randomly assigned to live together during the fall of their freshman year. After living together for six months, they completed self-report inventories. The researchers found that personality similarity between roommates was positively correlated with both relationship satisfaction and intent to live together the following year. That is, students liked their roommates when they were similar to those roommates.

Does this mean that personality similarity causes relationship satisfaction? Not necessarily. But two factors point to that possibility. First, personality tends to be stable over time. It is unlikely that having a strong relationship with someone like a roommate would lead to a change in your personality. Second, these roommates had been randomly assigned to live together. Therefore, we cannot reject the results of this study as reflecting the possibility that people *choose* to live with people they like (and with whom they are alike).

What do the results of this study mean for you? When it comes time to select a roommate, look for someone who is similar to you, especially on the characteristics that are most important to you. If you really like routine, you might find it grating if your roommate insists on rearranging your furniture once a month or throws impromptu TV-viewing parties in the middle of the week. Likewise, if you are a trusting soul and do not mind sharing your belongings with your roommate, you might bristle at a suspicious roommate who runs a strip of masking tape down the center of the room to delineate your respective spaces.

Preference for—and comfort with—a tidy versus a messy living space is not a personality trait in the same way that openness or agreeableness is a personality trait. This preference is certainly an individual difference worth paying attention to, however. Ogletree and colleagues (2005) found that a third of their college-age participants reported experiencing roommate conflict related to the cleanliness of their living space. Over a quarter of the students were dissatisfied with their roommates' housecleaning habits, and

---

self are based on their feelings of being distinct from others. Note, however, that within these broad patterns there is variability. Some people in individualist cultures have interdependent self-construals, and some people in collectivist cultures have independent self-construals.

CULTURE AND SELF-SERVING BIAS Psychologists generally have viewed the self-enhancing bias as a universal human trait (Sedikides & Gregg, 2008). In other words, self-enhancement may be as much a part of human nature as eating is. Although people suffering from depression might fail to show the effect, the assumption is that most healthy, functioning individuals show robust self-enhancement. Steven Heine and colleagues (1999) have argued, however, that the self-serving bias may be more common in Western cultures than in Eastern cultures (**Figure 13.35**). After all, Western cultures emphasize individuality. Believing that someone is an especially talented individual presupposes that some people are better than others. Such an attitude is not acceptable in Eastern cultures. There, the group is special, not the individual. The question of whether self-serving bias is universal has led to lively debate among psychologists.

nearly half had talked with their roommates about these habits on multiple occasions. A fifth of the students had changed their living situations because of these sorts of concerns at some point during the preceding three years!

Thus it is a good idea to ask potential roommates about their cleanliness preferences. You have at least three options for figuring out how a potential roommate compares with you on this and other valued dimensions. You can ask the potential roommate, you can ask her or his previous roommates, or you can rely on your own observations. **Table 13.2** offers some questions you might wish to ask of roommate candidates. In fact, many colleges and universities ask students to complete personality questionnaires before matching roommates in dorms. You might already have responded to questions like these as part of your application for residence. In that case, if the system has worked, you and your roommate might already be a good fit.

Understandably, you might feel a bit intrusive asking these sorts of questions of a potential roommate. You should, of course, be tactful in your approach. Remember, though, that you are doing yourself and your potential roommate a favor by addressing these issues before you commit to living together. Individuals differ in their relationship-interdependent self construal—that is, their tendency to think about themselves in terms of their relationships with close others (Cross, Bacon, & Morris, 2000). College students who are "high relationals" tend to self-disclose more personal information to their roommates than do "low relationals" (Gore, Cross, & Morris, 2006). The roommates of high relationals, in turn, report feeling more favorably about the relationships. Ultimately, they too share more personal information about themselves. That is, one person's self-construal (a part of personality) can help shape another person's self-disclosure. If your sense of self is very much informed by your relationships, you might naturally share personal information with a new roommate. In the long run, doing so can help create the very sort of relationship you tend to value.

(a)

(b)

FIGURE 13.35 Individualist versus Collectivist Cultures (a) Western cultures tend to highlight individual success. (b) Eastern cultures tend to value those who fall in line with the masses.

In one study (Endo & Meijer, 2004), American students and Japanese students were asked to list as many of their own successes and failures as they could. The Americans showed a bias for listing successes. The Japanese students listed failures and successes equally. In addition, the Americans used outside forces to explain failure, but the Japanese students used outside forces to explain success. Indeed, Markus and Kitayama (1991) have argued that in Asian cultures, self-criticism is more the social norm than self-promotion is. The overall evidence supports the view that people in individualist cultures are more concerned with self-enhancement than those in collectivist, particularly Asian, cultures (Heine, 2003). For example, in a meta-analysis involving more than 500 studies, people in Western cultures showed a much larger self-serving bias than those in Eastern cultures (Mezulis et al., 2004).

Might these differences reflect cultural rules about publicly admitting positive self-views? Perhaps people in the East engage in strategic self-enhancement, but they are just more modest in public. In studies using anonymous reporting, however—where presumably there is less call for modesty—Easterners continue to show a low level of self-serving bias (Heine, 2003). At the same time, indirect evidence using an implicit measure indicates that people from China and Japan show a positivity bias—a tendency to see themselves as better than others—equivalent to that of Americans (Yamaguchi et al., 2007). As discussed in Chapter 12, implicit attitude assessment is useful for situations in which people are hesitant to make explicit reports. In this case, the research finding suggests that although Easterners value themselves just as much as Westerners, they are hesitant to admit it.

According to another perspective, self-enhancement is universal, but the traits people focus on to achieve it vary across cultures (Brown & Kobayashi, 2002; Sedikides, Gaertner, & Toguchi, 2003). Thus when the culture emphasizes personal achievement, people self-enhance as individuals. When the culture emphasizes group achievement, people self-enhance as group members. In yet another complication, however, some research reveals a pattern that contradicts these findings. Namely, people in Eastern cultures are more critical of their groups compared with people in Western cultures (Heine & Lehman, 1999). East Asians often are especially self-critical in aspects of life that are important to them (Heine, Kitayama, & Hamamura, 2007).

The debate goes on, but why? Does it really matter if the self-serving bias is universal? The universality matters, in part, because it relates to how culture shapes the sense of self (Heine, 2005; Sedikides et al., 2003). How much do *you* believe people really differ around the world in terms of self-enhancement? Is it more important to be respected by others or to feel good about yourself no matter what others think? Might people in Eastern cultures feel better about themselves when they demonstrate that they are modest and self-effacing, whereas Westerners feel better when they can show they are successful? What function does self-enhancement serve in different cultures?

How Do We Know Our Own Personalities?

Everything a person knows about herself or himself constitutes the person's self-concept. Self-awareness is characterized by the experience of the self as an object of attention. When a person is especially aware of himself or herself as an object, the person is more likely to behave according to his or her personal standards and beliefs. The self-schema is the cognitive aspect of the self-concept. It helps each of us process self-relevant information efficiently and quickly. The working self-concept refers to each person's immediate experience of the self and varies from situation to situation. Self-esteem is the evaluative component of the self-concept. Several theories have been proposed to explain the basis of self-esteem, including sociometer theory (self-esteem is a mechanism for monitoring the likelihood of social exclusion) and terror management theory (self-esteem gives meaning to our lives and reduces anxiety over our mortality). Although self-esteem is associated with happiness, it is only weakly related to objective life outcomes. We employ numerous unconscious strategies to maintain positive self-views, including self-evaluative maintenance, social comparisons, and self-serving biases. Research has found cultural differences in how the self is construed: Collectivist cultures emphasize the interdependent self, and individualist cultures emphasize the independent self. The tendency to engage in self-serving biases may be less common in collectivist cultures than in individualist cultures.

Measuring Up

1. Imagine that while browsing the shelves of a local bookstore, you discover a series of books about self-esteem. Which of the following three theoretical perspectives is most likely addressed in each book: self-evaluation maintenance theory, sociometer theory, or terror management theory?
   a. *Protecting Your Self-Esteem When Your Best Friend Is Better at Everything*
   b. *Anxious about Your Inevitable Death? Self-Esteem Can Help*
   c. *Feeling Bad about Feeling Left Out: What Your Self-Esteem Is Trying to Tell You*

2. Sort the following list of attributes into two groups: those more often evidenced in collectivist cultures and those more often evidenced in individualist cultures.
   a. emphasis on the collective self
   b. emphasis on the personal self
   c. encouragement to pursue personal success, even at the expense of interpersonal relationships
   d. fundamental separation of people
   e. inherent connection between people
   f. less variation in how people dress
   g. particular concern with self-enhancement
   h. emphasis on obedience to authority
   i. emphasis on self-reliance
   j. self-concepts determined largely by social roles and by personal relationships
   k. self-criticism more normative than self-promotion
   l. greater tendency to respect situational norms

Answers: 1. a. self-evaluation maintenance theory; b. terror management theory; c. sociometer theory. 2. collectivist cultures—a, e, f, h, j, k, l; individualist cultures—b, c, d, g, i.

Chapter Summary

13.1 How Have Psychologists Studied Personality?

■ **Psychodynamic Theories Emphasize Unconscious and Dynamic Processes:** Freud believed that unconscious forces determine behavior. He argued that personality consists of three structures: the id, the superego, and the ego. The ego mediates between the id and the superego, using defense mechanisms to reduce anxiety due to conflicts between the id and the superego. Freud proposed that we pass through five stages of psychosexual development and that these stages shape our personalities. In contrast to Freud, neo-Freudians have focused on relationships—in particular, children's emotional attachments to their parents.

■ **Humanistic Approaches Emphasize Integrated Personal Experience:** Humanistic theories emphasize our experiences, beliefs, and inherent goodness. According to these theories, we strive to realize our full potential. Rogers's person-centered approach suggests that unconditional positive regard in childhood enables people to become fully functioning.

■ **Personality Reflects Learning and Cognition:** Through interaction with the environment, people learn patterns of responding that are guided by their personal constructs, expectancies, and values. Self-efficacy, the extent to which people believe they can achieve specific outcomes, is an important determinant of behavior. The cognitive-affective personality system (CAPS) emphasizes self-regulatory capacities—that is, people's ability to set personal goals, evaluate their progress, and adjust their behavior accordingly.

■ **Trait Approaches Describe Behavioral Dispositions:** Personality type theories focus more on description than on explanation. Trait theorists assume that personality is a collection of traits or behavioral dispositions. According to Eysenck's model of personality, there are three biologically based higher-order personality traits: introversion/extraversion, emotional stability, psychoticism. Each of these traits encompasses a number of lower-order traits. Five-factor theory maintains that there are five higher-order personality traits: openness to experience, conscientiousness, extraversion, agreeableness, and neuroticism.

13.2 How Is Personality Assessed, and What Does It Predict about People?

■ **Personality Refers to Both Unique and Common Characteristics:** Idiographic approaches are person-centered. They focus on individual lives and each person's unique characteristics. Nomothetic approaches assess individual variation in characteristics that are common among all people.

■ **Researchers Use Projective and Objective Methods to Assess Personality:** Projective measures assess unconscious processes by having people interpret ambiguous stimuli. Objective measures are relatively direct measures of personality, typically involving the use of self-report questionnaires or observer ratings.

■ **Observers Show Accuracy in Trait Judgments:** Close acquaintances may better predict a person's behavior than the person can. Acquaintances are particularly accurate when judging traits that are readily observable and meaningful.

■ **People Sometimes Are Inconsistent:** Mischel proposed the notion of situationism. According to this theory, situations are more important than traits in predicting behavior.

■ **Behavior Is Influenced by the Interaction of Personality and Situations:** Interactionism maintains that behavior is determined by both situations and our dispositions. Strong situations mask differences in personality, whereas weak situations reveal differences in personality. Most trait theories adopt an interactionist view.

■ **There Are Cultural and Sex Differences in Personality:** Cross-cultural research suggests that the Big Five personality factors are universal among humans. Sex differences in personality are consistent with common sex stereotypes. For example, women report being more empathic than men, and men report being more assertive than women.

13.3 What Are the Biological Bases of Personality?

■ **Animals Have Personalities:** Research on a wide variety of animal species has shown that animals have distinct personality traits that correspond roughly to the Big Five in humans.

■ **Personality Is Rooted in Genetics:** The results of twin studies and adoption studies suggest that 40 percent to 60 percent of personality variation is the product of genetic variation. Personality characteristics are influenced by multiple genes. These genes interact with the environment to produce general dispositions. Novelty seeking has been linked to a gene associated with dopamine levels, and neuroticism and agreeableness have been linked to a gene associated with serotonin levels.

■ **Temperaments Are Evident in Infancy:** Temperaments are biologically based personality tendencies. They are evident in early childhood and have long-term implications for adult behavior. Researchers have identified activity level, emotionality, and sociability as temperaments.

■ **Personality Is Linked to Specific Neurophysiological Mechanisms:** Extraversion/introversion has been linked to differences in cortical arousal. Cortical arousal is regulated by the ascending reticular activating system. Extraversion/introversion has also been linked to the strength of our behavioral approach and inhibition systems. These systems are sensitive to reward and punishment, respectively.

- **Personality Is Adaptive:** Personality traits that facilitate survival and reproduction have been favored through natural selection and sexual selection. Individual differences result in diverse skills within a group and are advantageous to the group's survival.

- **Personality Traits Are Stable over Time:** With increasing age, scores on neuroticism, extraversion, and openness decrease. Scores on agreeableness and conscientiousness increase. Relative rankings on the Big Five personality traits remain stable, particularly in adulthood.

13.4 How Do We Know Our Own Personalities?

- **Our Self-Concepts Consist of Self-Knowledge:** Self-awareness is characterized by the experience of the self as an object. The self-schema is the cognitive aspect of the self-concept. The working self-concept is the immediate experience of the self at any given time.

- **Perceived Social Regard Influences Self-Esteem:** Self-esteem is the evaluative component of the self-concept. According to sociometer theory, our need to belong influences self-esteem. According to terror management theory, death anxiety influences self-esteem. Self-esteem is associated with happiness. Self-esteem is only weakly correlated with objective life outcomes, however.

- **We Use Mental Strategies to Maintain Our Views of Self:** Positive illusions of self are common. We employ numerous unconscious strategies to maintain positive views of ourselves, including self-evaluative maintenance, social comparisons, and self-serving biases.

- **There Are Cultural Differences in the Self:** People from collectivist cultures (e.g., Asian and African countries) tend to have interdependent self-concepts. People from individualist cultures (e.g., the United States, Canada) tend to have independent self-concepts. The tendency to engage in self-serving biases may be less common among collectivists than individualists, or they may differ on which dimensions they are biased.

Key Terms

behavioral approach system (BAS), p. 595

behavioral inhibition system (BIS), p. 595

defense mechanisms, p. 571

ego, p. 571

five-factor theory, p. 576

humanistic approaches, p. 573

id, p. 570

idiographic approaches, p. 579

interactionists, p. 585

nomothetic approaches, p. 579

objective measures, p. 581

personality, p. 569

personality trait, p. 569

personality types, p. 575

projective measures, p. 580

psychodynamic theory, p. 570

psychosexual stages, p. 572

self-serving bias, p. 609

situationism, p. 584

sociometer, p. 604

superego, p. 571

temperaments, p. 592

trait approach, p. 576

Practice Test

1. Your psychology instructor asks the students in your class to form groups of five and then take turns answering the question *What do we need to know about you to truly know you?* The people in your group give the following answers; label each as representative of psychodynamic approaches, humanistic theory, type and trait perspectives, or learning and cognition perspectives.
   a. "To know me, you would have to ask me questions about myself. I took a survey once that said I am an extremely intuitive introvert."
   b. "To know me, you need to know how I've responded in the past and what I think about the world."
   c. "To know me, you would have to figure out a way to peer into my unconscious. There's so much I can't even know about myself; I'm not sure you could ever really know me."
   d. "To know me, you would have to know about my hopes and aspirations. I seek to become the best person I can be."

2. June asks people to watch a 5-minute recording of a play in which two characters find themselves in a dangerous situation. Then she asks her research participants to write an ending to the story, which she codes to reveal features of each participant's personality. This proposed measure of personality can best be described as _____ and _____.
   a. idiographic; projective
   b. nomothetic; projective
   c. idiographic; objective
   d. nomothetic; objective

3. Which of the following statements might explain why our close acquaintances sometimes are better able to predict our behaviors than we are? Select all that apply.
   a. Our ego defense mechanisms prevent us from knowing our true personalities and thus undermine our abilities to accurately predict our own behaviors.
   b. Predictions of our own behaviors may be biased in favor of our subjective perceptions (how we *think* we act) rather than our objective behaviors (how we *do* act).
   c. We tend to pay more attention to others than to ourselves and thus fail to notice our own behavior; others notice how we behave and are better able to predict our future behaviors.

The answer key for the Practice Tests can be found at the back of the book. It also includes answers to the green caption questions.

14

Psychological Disorders

BORN IN ITALY AND RAISED IN CANADA, the actor Tony Rosato became famous as a star of *Second City Television (SCTV,* a Canadian sketch comedy show) and *Saturday Night Live* (**Figure 14.1**). For his role in the television drama *Night Heat,* he was nominated for a Canadian broadcasting industry award in 1989. But in 2005, Rosato's world fell apart. He developed the strange belief that his wife, Leah, and their infant had been replaced by imposters. He was arrested for repeatedly complaining

FIGURE 14.1 Tony Rosato The Canadian actor Tony Rosato was well known for his zany portraits of comic characters. His psychological disorder is no laughing matter.

to the police about the "imposters" and for criminally threatening Leah and the child. According to an expert psychiatrist, Rosato was suffering from a quite rare psychological disorder called Capgras syndrome.

Capgras is named after the French psychiatrist who first described it. A person with the syndrome can be otherwise perfectly lucid. The person believes, however, that a family member or friend has been replaced by an identical-looking imposter. This disorder is often associated with schizophrenia or a brain injury.

Researchers obtained insights into the peculiar symptoms of Capgras by studying a 30-year-old Brazilian man, D.S., who developed Capgras after receiving a head injury in a traffic accident (Hirstein & Ramachandran, 1997). When asked why he thought his father was an imposter, D.S. replied, "He looks exactly like my father, but he really isn't. He's a nice guy, but he isn't my father, Doctor." D.S. did not believe his father was an imposter when he spoke with him on the phone. The belief occurred only when he could see his father. A series of tests showed that D.S. could recognize faces normally. He also could tell the differences between emotions. What he lacked was the ability to link an emotional response to a familiar face. For those with Capgras, somehow the normal emotions we feel when we see a loved one are absent. This lack of feeling leads people with Capgras to conclude that the relatives they encounter are not really their loved ones.

Given that Capgras syndrome had caused Tony Rosato so many problems, you might expect that he accepted the diagnosis with relief. Instead, however, he denied having mental health problems and refused treatment. He remained in jail until 2009, when he finally agreed to take antipsychotic medication that helped him deal with his condition. He then was released. Reportedly, he is back with his family and trying to resurrect his career.

Rosato's case raises many questions about psychological disorders (also called mental disorders). For example, when does it become clear that a person has a psychological disorder rather than just personal problems? Is it ethical to treat a person who denies having a severe problem? Is it fair to put someone with a severe psychological problem in prison rather than in a hospital?

Learning Objectives

- Describe the multiaxial classification system of the *Diagnostic and Statistical Manual of Mental Disorders*.
- Identify assessment methods for psychological disorders.
- Describe the diathesis-stress model.
- Identify biological, psychological, and cognitive-behavioral causes of psychological disorders.
- Discuss sex differences and cultural differences in psychological disorders.

14.1 How Are Psychological Disorders Conceptualized and Classified?

Over the course of history, people have struggled with how best to understand **psychopathology.** This term means, literally, sickness or disorder of the mind. From the writings of Aristotle to those of Freud, accounts exist of people suffering from various forms of psychopathology. The earliest views of psychopathology explained apparent "madness" as resulting from possession by demons or evil spirits. The ancient Babylonians believed a demon called Idta caused madness. Similar examples of demonology can be found among the ancient Chinese, Egyptians, and Greeks. This view of psychopathology continued into the Middle Ages. At that time, there was greater emphasis on possession having resulted from the wrath of God for some sinful moral transgression. During any of these periods, someone like Tony Rosato might have been persecuted and subjected to an array of methods to cast out his demons. Such "treatments" included exorcism, bloodletting, and the forced ingestion of magical potions.

In the latter half of the Middle Ages and into the Renaissance, people with psychopathology were removed from society so they would not bother others. In the 1700s, Rosato likely would have been left in an understaffed, overcrowded mental institution called an asylum. Even there, the small staff would have made little attempt to understand Rosato's disorder and even less of an attempt to treat him. Indeed, people housed in asylums were often chained up and lived in incredibly filthy conditions, treated more like nonhuman animals than humans.

As far back as ancient Greece, some people had a sense that there was a physical basis to psychopathology. Hippocrates (c. 460–377 BCE), often credited as the founder of modern medicine, classified psychopathologies into *mania, melancholia,* and *phrenitis,* the latter characterized by mental confusion. Hippocrates believed that such disorders resulted from the relative amount of "humors," or bodily fluids, a person possessed (Maher & Maher, 1994). For instance, having too much black bile led to *melancholia,* or extreme sadness and depression. From this term, we get the word *melancholy,* which we often use to describe people who are sad. The idea that bodily fluids cause mental illness was abandoned long ago, however. Increasingly throughout the nineteenth and twentieth centuries, psychopathology was viewed more as a medical condition than as a demonic curse caused by sin. During the last 200 years, recognition has grown that psychopathology reflects dysfunction of the body, particularly of the brain.

At various points in recent history, researchers and clinicians would have focused on environmental factors that contributed to Tony Rosato's psychological disorder. For example, was Rosato abused as a child? Although environmental factors are important, we now understand that biology plays a critical role in many psychological disorders, especially disorders such as Capgras or schizophrenia. Indeed, an important lesson in this chapter is that environment and biology interact to produce psychological disorders. As noted throughout the book, it is meaningless to state that a condition is caused by just biology or just environment. Both factors affect all psychological disorders to some extent.

Psychopathology Is Different from Everyday Problems

Psychological disorders are common around the globe, in all countries and all societies. These disorders account for the greatest proportion of disability in developed countries, surpassing even cancer and heart disease (Centers for Disease Control and Prevention, 2011). Indeed, about 1 in 4 Americans over age 18 has a diagnosable mental disorder in a given year (Kessler, Chiu, Demler, & Walters, 2005a). About 1 in 5 American adults receives treatment over any two-year period (Kessler et al., 2005b). Nearly 1 in 2 Americans will have some form of mental disorder at some point in life, most commonly a mood disorder (such as depression), an impulse control disorder (such as hyperactivity and problems paying attention), an anxiety disorder, or a substance abuse disorder (Kessler & Wang, 2008).

Of course, mental disorders range in severity. Only about 7 percent of the U.S. population is severely affected, and this group also tends to suffer from multiple mental disorders (Kessler et al., 2005a). For example, at a given time, someone might be anxious and depressed and also abuse drugs or alcohol. There are also enormous sex differences in psychopathology: Some disorders are much

psychopathology Sickness or disorder of the mind.

more common in women (such as depression and anxiety disorders), and other disorders are much more common in men (such as antisocial personality disorder and autism). These sex differences likely reflect biology *and* culture. That is, the sexes may differ in their predispositions to mental disorders, but cultural values influence how often different disorders are diagnosed for women and for men.

Who among us has not felt exceedingly sad on occasion or has not felt anxious when contemplating some difficult challenge? In fact, drawing the line between a normal emotional experience and a mental disorder can be a difficult challenge. After all, different people respond to events differently, and the level of personal suffering is hard to measure objectively. When a psychological problem disrupts a person's life and causes significant distress over a long period, the problem is considered a disorder rather than the normal low points of everyday life.

As you read this chapter, you may realize that you have experienced some of the symptoms of many psychological disorders. Even if particular symptoms seem to describe you (or anyone you know) perfectly, resist the urge to make a diagnosis. Just like medical students who worry they have every disease they learn about, you need to guard against overanalyzing yourself and others. At the same time, what you learn in this chapter and the next (on treating disorders) may help you understand the mental health problems you or others might experience.

PSYCHOLOGICAL DISORDERS ARE MALADAPTIVE How do you know if someone has a psychological disorder? It can be challenging to decide if a given behavior is caused by psychopathology. Keep in mind that behavior, especially unusual behavior, always must be reviewed in the context of the situation. A woman running through the streets screaming, sobbing, and grabbing and hugging people might have some form of mental disorder—or she might be celebrating because she just won the lottery. Many behaviors considered normal in one setting may be considered deviant in other settings. For example, some tribes in Africa spread feces in their hair as part of rituals. Some Native American and East Asian cultures consider it a great honor to hear the voices of spirits. In urban America, the former would be seen as deviant behavior and the latter as evidence of auditory hallucinations.

In determining whether behavior represents psychopathology, it is important to consider certain criteria: (1) Does the person act in a way that deviates from cultural norms for acceptable behavior? (2) Is the behavior maladaptive? That is, does the behavior interfere with the person's ability to respond appropriately in different situations? For example, a person who is afraid to leave the house may avoid feeling anxious by staying inside, and that behavior might prevent the person from working, having a social life, or both. (3) Is the behavior self-destructive, does it cause the individual personal distress, or does it threaten other people in the community? (4) Does the behavior cause discomfort and concern to others, thus impairing a person's social relationships?

Because it is hard to draw the line between normal and abnormal, psychopathology increasingly is defined as thoughts, and behaviors, that are maladaptive rather than deviant. For example, people concerned about germs may wash their hands more than average and therefore be deviant, but that behavior may be beneficial in many ways and therefore adaptive—after all, it is the best way of avoiding contagious disease. The same behavior, however, can be maladaptive when people cannot stop until they have washed their hands raw. Indeed, the diagnostic criteria for all the major disorder categories stipulate that the symptoms of the disorder must interfere with at least one aspect of the person's life, such as work, social relations, or self-care. This component is critical in determining whether a given behavior or set of behaviors represents a mental disorder or is simply unusual.

Psychological Disorders Are Classified into Categories

There are clear advantages to categorizing psychological disorders. To fully understand any disorder, psychologists need to investigate its **etiology:** the factors that contribute to its development. They also need to investigate possible treatments. Grouping disorders into meaningful categories begins the investigative process. For this reason, researchers and clinicians have struggled for many years with how best to categorize mental disorders. In the late 1800s, the psychiatrist Emil Kraepelin recognized that not all patients with mental disorders suffer from the same disorder (**Figure 14.2**). Kraepelin identified mental disorders on the basis of groups of symptoms that occur together. For instance, he separated disorders of mood from disorders of cognition. He called the latter disorder *dementia praecox*. It is now better known as *schizophrenia* and is discussed fully in this chapter and the next one.

The idea of categorizing mental disorders systematically was not officially adopted until 1952, when the American Psychiatric Association published the first edition of the *Diagnostic and Statistical Manual of Mental Disorders (DSM)*. Since then, the *DSM* has undergone several revisions. It remains the standard in psychology and psychiatry. The early versions focused on the presumed causes of mental disorders. Beginning with the *DSM-III,* in 1980, there was a return to classifying psychopathology based on observable symptoms.

In the current edition, disorders are described in terms of observable symptoms. A patient must meet specific criteria to receive a particular diagnosis. In addition, a patient does not receive a single label. Instead, the patient is classified through a **multiaxial system.** Detailed in **Table 14.1,** this system is based on the realization that various factors affect mental health. Diagnoses include evaluations on five dimensions, also known as axes. They are (1) major clinical disorders, including depression, schizophrenia, and anxiety disorders; (2) mental retardation, which consists of longstanding problems in intellectual functioning, and personality disorders, which are maladaptive personality traits that typically persist across

etiology Factors that contribute to the development of a disorder.

multiaxial system The system used in the *DSM;* it calls for assessment along five axes that describe important mental health factors.

FIGURE 14.2 Emil Kraepelin Kraepelin was one of the first researchers to propose a classification system for mental disorders.

TABLE 14.1 *DSM-IV-TR* Multiaxial Classification System	
Axis I	Clinical disorders and other conditions that may be a focus of clinical attention (e.g., schizophrenia, mood disorders, anxiety disorders, sexual and gender disorders, sleep disorders, eating disorders)
Axis II	Mental retardation and personality disorders (e.g., antisocial personality disorder, paranoid personality disorder, borderline personality disorder)
Axis III	General medical conditions that may be relevant to mental disorders (e.g., cancer, epilepsy, obesity, Parkinson's disease, Alzheimer's disease)
Axis IV	Psychosocial and environmental problems that might affect the diagnosis, treatment, and prognosis of mental disorders (e.g., unemployment, divorce, legal problems, homelessness, poverty, parental overprotection)
Axis V	Global assessment of functioning (social, psychological, and occupational), rated on a scale from 1 to 100, with 1 representing danger of hurting self or others and 100 meaning superior functioning in a wide range of areas

SOURCE: American Psychiatric Association, 2000a.

Recognizing When Categories Represent Continuous Dimensions

Can a woman be "a little bit" pregnant? Most people would agree that pregnancy is an all-or-none state and that a woman who is a few days pregnant is every bit as pregnant as a woman in her ninth month.

Many other categories are not so cut and dried. Is a person honest or dishonest? Smart or unintelligent? Good-looking or unattractive? Like these, most categories represent points along a continuum. Most dimensions in life (e.g., hot/cold, day/night) do not represent absolute differences. The same is true for mental health versus mental disorders: A diagnosis of a mental disorder indicates membership in a category, but the underlying dimension is continuous.

Suppose your neighbor is diagnosed with an anxiety disorder. This news means that a mental health practitioner, such as a clinical psychologist, has decided that your neighbor's symptoms of anxiety are beyond what is considered normal. This label, or diagnosis, carries the understanding that to alleviate the symptoms, your neighbor needs psychotherapy or medication. The label lumps your neighbor with all people who share the diagnosis. The severity of the disorder can range, however, from just slightly more anxious than normal to extremely anxious in a way that interferes with daily living. You cannot know from the diagnosis exactly where your neighbor falls along the continuum (**Figure 14.3**).

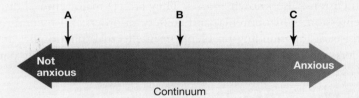

FIGURE 14.3 Recognizing When Categories Represent Continuous Dimensions How should a clinician classify a person at point A? A person at point B? A person at point C? What do your answers reveal about the classification of psychological disorders?

the life span—either mental retardation or personality disorders may or may not be involved in an Axis I disorder; (3) medical conditions that may contribute to a person's psychological functioning; (4) psychosocial problems, such as legal, financial, or family problems; and (5) global or overall assessment of how well the person is functioning based on a 100-point scale, from persistent "danger of hurting self or others" to "superior functioning" with no symptoms. Diagnosing a patient on all five axes provides a more complete picture of the person than simply assigning a clinical category. The text was revised in 2000, and it is now known as the *Diagnostic and Statistical Manual of Mental Disorders Fourth Edition* (Text Revision), or *DSM-IV-TR*.

One problem with the *DSM* approach is that it implies that a person either has a mental disorder or does not, an either/or evaluation known as a *categorical approach* (Bernstein, 2011). That is, the diagnosis is categorical, and a person is either in the category or not. This approach fails to capture differences in the severity of a disorder.

An alternative type of evaluation, called a *dimensional approach,* is to consider mental disorders along a continuum in which people vary in degree rather than in kind. For example, people vary in how much they are suffering from depression. If a person began suffering from depression a tiny bit more, that person would not suddenly meet the formal criteria for depression. A dimensional approach recognizes that many mental disorders are extreme versions of normal feelings, such as the normal experiences of depression or anxiety.

Another problem with the current *DSM* is that people seldom fit neatly into the precise categories provided. For example, anxiety and depression often go together even though the *DSM-IV-TR* treats them as separate disorders. Thus a person who is both anxious and depressed may be diagnosed with two disorders. A dual diagnosis offers no advantages in terms of treatment.

DSM-V is due out in May 2013. As a result of empirical research, the revisers are considering a number of major changes. In particular, this next version of the manual may use broader categories of disorders and recognize the substantial overlap between similar disorders. Thus similar disorders will be clustered together and considered to range across a spectrum of impairment. For example, autism spectrum disorders (discussed later) range from mild to severe social impairments. And the DSM-V will pay greater attention to how people with personality disorders function in their daily lives rather than to the specific types of disorders those people might have.

Psychological Disorders Must Be Assessed

Physical disorders often can be detected by medical tests, such as blood tests or biopsies. Determining whether a person has a mental disorder is not as straightforward. Clinical psychologists often work like detectives, tracking down information from sources that include self-reports, observations, and interviews. The process of examining a person's mental functions and psychological health is known as **assessment.** The primary goal of assessment is to make a *diagnosis* so that appropriate treatment can be provided. The course and probable outcome, or *prognosis,* will depend on the particular mental disorder that is diagnosed. Therefore, a correct diagnosis will help the patient and perhaps the patient's family understand what the future might bring.

Assessment does not stop with diagnosis, however. Ongoing assessment helps mental health workers understand whether specific situations might cause a worsening of the disorder, whether progress is being made in treatment, and other factors that might help in understanding unique aspects of a given case (**Figure 14.4**).

The method of initial assessment sometimes depends on how a person comes into contact with mental health workers. When the person has severe symptoms, the initial meeting often takes place in an emergency room. The patient may exhibit confusion, memory problems, or other mental impairments. In response to this condition, mental health workers may administer a *mental status exam* to provide a snapshot of the patient's psychological functioning. This exam involves behavioral observations: evaluations of the person's personal grooming, ability to make eye contact, tremors or twitches, mood, speech, thought content, and memory. For example, a patient who arrives agitated and in a

assessment In psychology, examination of a person's mental state to diagnose possible psychological disorders.

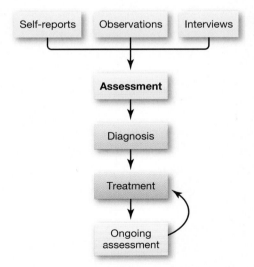

FIGURE 14.4 Assessing a Patient
Clinical psychologists examine a person's mental functions and psychological health to diagnose a mental disorder and determine an appropriate treatment. This flowchart shows the factors that lead to treatment.

disheveled state and wearing excess layers of clothing is more likely to suffer from schizophrenia than from an anxiety disorder. The mental status exam is also useful for determining whether the mental impairments are due to a psychological condition or an acute physical condition, such as stroke or head injury.

Most symptoms of psychological problems develop over fairly long periods. Frequently, a person seeking help for such problems is encouraged to see a mental health professional by family members or by a physician. A psychologist's first step in an assessment is to ask the person about current symptoms and about recent experiences that might be causing distress. For example, if the person is feeling depressed, the psychologist is likely to ask whether he or she recently has experienced some sort of loss. In this *clinical interview,* the interviewer's skills determine the quantity and value of information obtained. A good interviewer expresses empathy, builds rapport quickly, is nonjudgmental and trusting, and supports the client's efforts to find out what is wrong and how it might be addressed.

STRUCTURED VERSUS UNSTRUCTURED INTERVIEWS Since the beginning of modern psychology, most interviews have been *unstructured.* That is, the topics of discussion vary as the interviewer probes different aspects of the person's problems. The interview is guided by the clinician's past experiences, his or her observations of the client, and the types of problems that are most likely. Unstructured interviews are highly flexible. Indeed, no two unstructured interviews are likely to elicit identical information from the same patient. Unstructured interviews are also overly dependent on the interviewer's skills.

In *structured interviews,* clinicians ask standardized questions in the same order each time. The patient's answers are coded according to a predetermined formula, and the diagnosis is based on the specific patterns of responding. The most commonly used structured interview is the *Structured Clinical Interview for DSM (SCID),* through which diagnoses are made according to *DSM* criteria (Spitzer, Williams, Gibbon, & First, 1992). The SCID begins with general questions, such as *What kind of work do you do?* It proceeds to questions about the client's symptoms, such as about their frequency and severity. The SCID is also valuable for treatment and research, because the results obtained from one group of patients will likely apply to other patients diagnosed with the same disorder.

OBSERVATION AND TYPES OF TESTING A psychological assessor often can gain valuable information simply by observing the client's behavior. For instance, a client who avoids eye contact during an examination might suffer from social anxiety or have an attention deficit disorder. A client whose eyes dart around nervously may feel paranoid. Behavioral assessments often are useful with children, as in observing their interactions with others or seeing whether they can sit still in a classroom.

Another source of information regarding psychopathology is psychological testing. Chapter 13 provides examples of these types of tests for assessing personality. Of the thousands of psychological tests available to clinicians, some are for specific mental disorders, such as the widely used *Beck Depression Inventory* (Beck, Steer, & Brown, 1996; Beck, Ward, Mendelson, Mock, & Erbaugh, 1961). Other measures assess both a broad range of mental disorders and general mental health.

The most widely used questionnaire for psychological assessment is the *Minnesota Multiphasic Personality Inventory (MMPI).* Developed during the 1930s, the MMPI was updated in the 1990s for language changes. The latest version consists of 567 true/false items that assess emotions, thoughts, and behaviors. The MMPI has 10 clinical scales (e.g., paranoia, depression, mania, hysteria). Using these scales, the assessor generates a profile that may indicate whether the client has a particular mental disorder.

As discussed in Chapter 2, there is a common problem with all self-report assessments, such as the MMPI. Namely, to make a favorable impression, respondents sometimes distort the truth or lie outright. To avoid detection of a mental disorder, a test taker might be evasive or defensive. To look especially troubled, another test taker might untruthfully lean toward negative items. To counter such response biases, the MMPI includes validity scales in addition to the clinical scales. The validity scales measure the probability that respondents are being less than truthful when taking the test.

Recall from Chapter 2 that one type of validity refers to the extent that a dependent variable measures what it is supposed to measure. The MMPI includes a variety of questions that are used to judge whether the person's answers accurately reflect the respondent's true thoughts and behaviors. For instance, a person might try to present himself or herself too positively by agreeing with a large number of items such as "I always make my bed" and "I never tell lies." A high score on this category would indicate an attempt to present a perfectly positive image. Fabrications of this kind are known as *faking good*. Even if the test taker is not responding in this way consciously, the scoring of answers on the other items must take into account the positivity bias in responses. Other validity scales examine whether the test taker answers similar questions in the same manner each time and whether he or she responds "true" to items that are extremely rare or to an especially large number of negative items. Fabrications of this kind are known as *faking bad,* or pretending that one is more ill or disabled than is true.

Although tests such as the MMPI are used widely in psychological assessment, they are seldom the sole source of information. Indeed, most clinicians do not diagnose until they have consistent results from psychological tests and structured interviews. In addition, although in North America the MMPI generally has been a reliable and valid assessment tool, it has been criticized as inappropriate for use in other countries or among groups such as the poor, the elderly, and racial minorities. The problem here is that scores considered "normal" on the MMPI are based on studies in which such people were inadequately represented.

Another assessment method is neuropsychological testing. In this method, the client performs actions such as copying a picture; drawing a design from memory; sorting cards that show various stimuli into categories based on size, shape, or color; placing blocks into slots on a board while blindfolded; and tapping fingers rapidly (**Figure 14.5**). Each task requires an ability such as planning, coordinating, or remembering. By highlighting actions that the client performs poorly, the assessment might indicate problems with a particular brain region. For instance, people who have difficulty switching from one rule to another for categorizing objects, such as sorting by shape rather than by color, may have impairments in the frontal lobes. Subsequent assessment with MRI or PET (brain imaging techniques discussed in Chapter 2, "Research Methodology") might indicate brain damage caused by a tumor or by an injury.

EVIDENCE-BASED ASSESSMENT A key question is whether psychological assessments provide information that is useful for treating psychological disorders. Many popular methods of assessment, such as projective tests, have not been shown to be helpful in predicting the kinds of treatments that are useful. Moreover, individual clinicians often choose assessment procedures based on their subjective beliefs and training rather than based on scientific studies. For instance,

FIGURE 14.5 Neuropsychological Testing The assessment depicted here uses a neuropsychological test to examine mental function. In this timed test, a researcher watches a client fit wooden blocks into a corresponding template to test for signs of Alzheimer's disease.

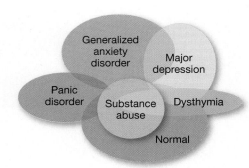

FIGURE 14.6 Comorbidity As this diagram illustrates, psychological disorders commonly overlap. For instance, substance abuse is common across psychological disorders, and people with depression often also have anxiety disorders.

diathesis-stress model A diagnostic model that proposes that a disorder may develop when an underlying vulnerability is coupled with a precipitating event.

family systems model A diagnostic model that considers symptoms within an individual as indicating problems within the family.

sociocultural model A diagnostic model that views psychopathology as the result of the interaction between individuals and their cultures.

cognitive-behavioral approach A diagnostic model that views psychopathology as the result of learned, maladaptive thoughts and beliefs.

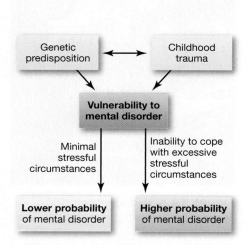

FIGURE 14.7 Diathesis-Stress Model of the Onset of Mental Disorders How does this model illustrate how nature and nurture work together in the onset of mental disorders?

some use their clinical judgment rather than any formal method, such as a structured interview based on *DSM* criteria, to make a diagnosis.

Evidence-based assessment is an approach to clinical evaluation in which research guides the evaluation of mental disorders, the selection of appropriate psychological tests and neuropsychological methods, and the use of critical thinking in making a diagnosis (Hunsley & Mash, 2007; Joiner, Walker, Pettit, Perez, & Cukrowicz, 2005). For instance, scientific research indicates that many mental disorders occur together. This state is known as *comorbidity* (**Figure 14.6**). Research also indicates that people who are depressed often have substance abuse disorders. Therefore, an evidence-based assessment approach would indicate that people found to be depressed should also be assessed for comorbid conditions, such as substance abuse.

Psychological Disorders Have Many Causes

Psychologists do not completely agree about the causes of most mental disorders. Still, some factors are thought to play important developmental roles. As discussed throughout this book, both nature and nurture matter, and it is futile to try to identify biology or environment as solely responsible for a given disorder. The **diathesis-stress model** (presented as a flowchart in **Figure 14.7**) provides one way of thinking about the onset of mental disorders (Monroe & Simons, 1991).

In this model, an individual can have an underlying vulnerability or predisposition (known as *diathesis*) to a mental disorder. This diathesis can be biological, such as a genetic predisposition to a specific disorder, or it can be environmental, such as childhood trauma. The vulnerability may not be sufficient to trigger a mental disorder, but the addition of stressful circumstances can tip the scales. If the stress level exceeds an individual's ability to cope, the symptoms of mental disorder will occur. In this view, a family history of mental disorder suggests vulnerability rather than destiny.

BIOLOGICAL FACTORS The biological perspective focuses on how physiological factors, such as genetics, contribute to psychological disorders (Kandel, 1998). Chapter 3 describes how comparing the rates of mental disorders between identical and fraternal twins and studying individuals who have been adopted have revealed the importance of genetic factors (Kendler, Prescott, Myers, & Neale, 2003; Krueger, 1999). Other biological factors also influence the development and course of mental disorders. The fetus is particularly vulnerable. There is evidence that some mental disorders may arise from prenatal problems, such as malnutrition, exposure to toxins, and maternal illness (Salum, Polanczyk, Miguel, & Rohde, 2010). Similarly, during childhood and adolescence, environmental toxins and malnutrition can put an individual at risk for mental disorders. All of these biological factors may contribute to mental disorders because of their effects on the central nervous system. Evidence is emerging that neurological dysfunction contributes to the expression of many mental disorders.

The recent use of imaging to identify brain regions associated with psychopathology has allowed researchers to generate hypotheses about the types of subtle deficits that might be associated with different mental disorders (Reichenberg & Harvey, 2007). Structural imaging has revealed differences in brain anatomy, perhaps due to genetics, between those with mental disorders and those without. Functional neuroimaging is currently at the forefront of research into the neurological components of mental disorders: PET and fMRI have revealed brain regions that may function differently in individuals with mental disorders (**Figure 14.8**).

Another source of insights into neural dysfunction has been research on the role of neurotransmitters in mental disorders. In some cases, medications have been developed based on what is known about the neurochemistry of mental disorders. In other cases, however, the unexpected effects of medications have led to discoveries about the neurotransmitters involved in mental disorders.

Again, biological factors often reflect the vulnerabilities that occur in individuals. Situational factors often play prominent roles in the expression of mental disorders. As the diathesis-stress model reminds us, single explanations (nature *or* nurture, rather than nature *and* nurture) are seldom sufficient for understanding mental disorders.

PSYCHOLOGICAL FACTORS The first edition of the *DSM* was influenced heavily by Freudian psychoanalytic theory. Freud believed that mental disorders were mostly due to unconscious conflicts, often sexual in nature, that dated back to childhood. Consistently with this perspective, the first edition of the *DSM* described many disorders as reactions to environmental conditions or as involving various defense mechanisms. Although Freud made important historical contributions in shaping psychology, most of his theories—particularly his theories on the causes of mental health disorders—have not stood the test of time. Psychological factors clearly play an important role, however, in the expression and treatment of mental disorders.

Indeed, thoughts and emotions are shaped by environment and can profoundly influence behavior, including disordered behavior. Not only traumatic events but also less extreme circumstances, such as constantly being belittled by a parent, can have long-lasting effects. The **family systems model** proposes that an individual's behavior must be considered within a social context, particularly within the family (Kazak, Simms, & Rourke, 2002). Problems that arise within an individual are manifestations of problems within the family (Goodman & Gotlib, 1999). Thus developing a profile of an individual's family interactions can be important for understanding the factors that may be contributing to the disorder. A profile can also be important for determining whether the family is likely to be helpful or detrimental to the client's progress in therapy.

Similarly, the **sociocultural model** views psychopathology as the result of the interaction between individuals and their cultures. For example, disorders such as schizophrenia appear to be more common among the lower socioeconomic classes (**Figure 14.9**). From the sociocultural perspective, these differences in occurrence are due to differences in lifestyles, in expectations, and in opportunities between classes. There may be biases in people's willingness to ascribe disorders to different social classes, however. Eccentric behavior among the wealthy elite might be tolerated or viewed as amusing. The same behaviors observed among those living in poverty might be taken as evidence of mental disorders. Moreover, people who develop schizophrenia may have trouble finding work and so experience financial problems because of their disorder.

COGNITIVE-BEHAVIORAL FACTORS The central principle of the **cognitive-behavioral approach** is that abnormal behavior is learned (Butler, Chapman, Forman, & Beck, 2006). As discussed in Chapter 6, through classical conditioning an unconditioned stimulus produces an unconditioned response. For example, a loud noise produces a startled response. A neutral stimulus paired with this unconditioned stimulus can eventually by itself produce a similar response. As was the case with Little Albert, if a child is playing with a fluffy white rat and is frightened by a loud noise, the white rat alone can later cause fear in the child. In fact, this process is how John B. Watson, the founder of behaviorism, demonstrated that many fears are learned rather than innate.

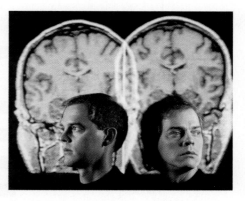

FIGURE 14.8 Biological Factors in Mental Disorders Although these men are twins, the one on the right has schizophrenia and the one on the left does not. In the MRI of the twin with schizophrenia, note the larger ventricles (these fluid-filled cavities appear dark in the image). This same pattern has emerged in the study of other twin pairs in which one has schizophrenia and the other does not. Thus the brain may be deteriorating over time for those with schizophrenia, and this finding tells us that biological factors may be important for understanding schizophrenia.

FIGURE 14.9 Sociocultural Model of Psychopathology According to the sociocultural model, psychopathology results from the interaction between individuals and their cultures. This homeless man with schizophrenia lives on the streets in Notting Hill, a fashionable area of London.

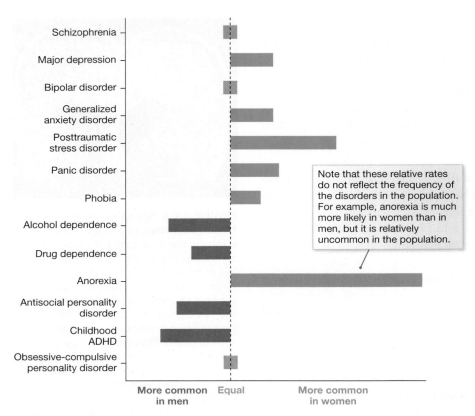

Note that these relative rates do not reflect the frequency of the disorders in the population. For example, anorexia is much more likely in women than in men, but it is relatively uncommon in the population.

FIGURE 14.10 Sex Differences in Mental Disorders The bars in this graph represent how common particular mental disorders are for men and for women.

Proponents of strict behaviorism argue that mental disorders result from classical and operant conditioning. Strict behaviorists originally defined behavior as overt and observable actions, but later this view was challenged. According to the revised cognitive-behavioral perspective, thoughts and beliefs are types of behavior and can be studied empirically. The premise of this approach is that thoughts can become distorted and produce maladaptive behaviors and maladaptive emotions. In contrast to the psychologists who subscribe to the psychoanalytic perspective, cognitive-behavioral psychologists believe that thought processes are available to the conscious mind.

Individuals are aware of, or easily can be made aware of, the thought processes that give rise to maladaptive emotions and behaviors.

SEX DIFFERENCES IN MENTAL DISORDERS Some mental disorders, such as schizophrenia and bipolar disorder, are equally likely in the sexes (**Figure 14.10**). Other disorders vary between the sexes. For example, dependence on alcohol is much more likely in males, whereas anorexia is much more likely in females. The reasons for these differences are both biological and environmental.

One way of categorizing mental disorders is to divide them into two major groups: *Internalizing disorders* are characterized by negative emotions, and they can be grouped into categories that reflect the emotions of distress and fear. These disorders include major depression, generalized anxiety disorder, and panic disorder. *Externalizing disorders* are characterized by disinhibition. These disorders include alcoholism, conduct disorders, and antisocial behavior (**Figure 14.11**). In general, the disorders associated with internalizing are more prevalent in females, and those associated with externalizing are more prevalent in males (Krueger & Markon, 2006).

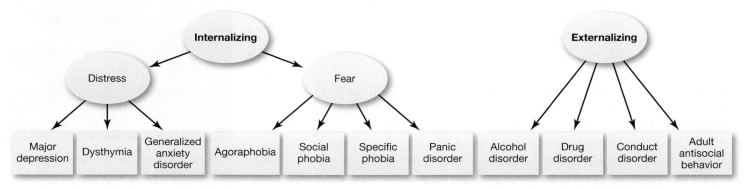

SOURCE: Krueger & Markon, 2006.

FIGURE 14.11 Internalizing and Externalizing Model of Mental Disorders This diagram divides mental disorders into two basic categories, internalizing and externalizing. It also divides internalizing disorders into those related to fear and those related to distress.

CULTURE AND MENTAL DISORDERS Increasingly, psychologists and other mental health professionals are recognizing the importance of culture on many aspects of our lives. Most mental disorders show both universal and culture-specific symptoms. That is, the disorders may be very similar around the world, but they still reflect cultural differences. A disorder with a strong biological component will tend to be more similar across cultures. A disorder heavily influenced by learning, context, or both is more likely to differ across cultures. For example, depression is a major mental health problem around the world, but the manifestations of depression differ by culture.

Since the 1994 edition, the *DSM* has included a section on *culture-bound syndromes*. These disorders occur mainly in specific cultures or regions. (**Table 14.2** presents examples of culture-bound disorders; **Figure 14.12** depicts another

FIGURE 14.12 Suchi-Bai Disorder
Suchi-bai disorder occurs in Bengal, India, and is particularly common in Hindu widows. This disorder involves an excessive concern for cleanliness. The sufferer might change out of her street clothes when indoors, wash money, hop while walking to avoid dirt, wash furniture, and remain immersed in a holy river. Here a widow washes herself in an ashram. In India, widows are often discriminated against and blamed for the deaths of their husbands.

TABLE 14.2 Culture-Bound Syndromes

Name	Definition and Location
Amok	A sudden outburst of explosive and assaultive violence preceded by a period of social withdrawal and apathy (Southeast Asia, Philippines)
Ataque de nervios	Uncontrollable shouting and/or crying; verbal and physical aggression; heat in chest rising to head; feeling of losing control; occasional amnesia for experience (Caribbean Latinos and South American Latinos)
Hwa-byung	Acute panic, fear of death, fatigue, loss of appetite, palpitations, lump in upper stomach (Korea)
Kuro (shook yong)	Intense fear following perception that one's genitals (men/women) or breasts (women) are withdrawing into one's body; shame if perception is associated with immoral sexual activity (Chinese populations in Hong Kong and Southeast Asia)
Phii pob	Belief that one is possessed by a spirit; numbness of limbs, shouting, weeping, confused speech, shyness (Thailand)
Susto (espanto)	Strong sense of fear that one has lost one's soul; accompanied by loss of appetite, weight loss, skin pallor, fatigue, lethargy, extensive thirst, untidiness, and withdrawal (Latinos in South and Central America, Mexico; Latino migrants to North America)
Taijin kyofusho	Intense fear of interpersonal relations; belief that parts of the body give off offensive odors or displease others (Japan)
Tawatl ye sni	Total discouragement; preoccupation with death, ghosts, spirits; excessive drinking, suicidal thoughts and attempts (Sioux Indians)
Uquamairineq	Hypnotic states, disturbed sleep, and occasional hallucinations (Native Alaskans: Inuit, Yuit)
Wendigo psychosis	An insatiable desire or craving to consume human flesh along with a worry about turning into a cannibal and consuming others (Algonquian)

example.) Clinicians and researchers need to be sensitive to cultural issues to avoid making mistakes in their diagnoses and treatments (Marsella & Yamada, 2007). Cultural factors can be critical in determining how a disorder is expressed and how an individual will respond to different types of therapies.

Summing Up

How Are Psychological Disorders Conceptualized and Classified?

Because psychopathology takes many forms, psychological disorders are difficult to define and categorize. The behavioral manifestations vary widely, but people diagnosed with these disorders have two things in common: Their behavior deviates from cultural norms and is maladaptive. The *DSM* adopts a multiaxial system to describe mental health. The five axes are major clinical disorders, mental retardation and personality disorders, medical conditions, psychosocial problems, and global assessment. Clinical assessments may include interviews, behavioral assessments, psychological tests, and neuropsychological tests. Each of these assessments provides clinicians with insight into a person's mental functions and psychological health. The diathesis-stress model suggests that psychological disorders result from an underlying vulnerability coupled with a stressful, precipitating event. The causes of most mental disorders are unknown and may result from complex interactions between psychological, biological, and cognitive-behavioral factors. In general, females are more likely to suffer from internalizing disorders, such as major depression and generalized anxiety disorder. Males are more likely to suffer from externalizing disorders, such as alcoholism and conduct disorder. Most psychological disorders show both universal and culture-specific symptoms. Disorders that are largely biologically determined tend to be more similar across cultures than disorders that are strongly influenced by learning and context. The *DSM* includes a number of culture-bound disorders—that is, disorders that occur in specific cultures or regions.

Measuring Up

1. Indicate whether each of the following scenarios is best described as a mental status exam, a structured interview, an unstructured interview, a behavioral test, a psychological test, or a neuropsychological test.
   a. A child psychologist asks a young client to study a series of words and then to list the words immediately afterward; memory for the words is assessed again later in the session.
   b. A social worker at a homeless shelter conducts systematic behavioral observations of new clients as they register for services.
   c. The staff member in charge of assessing the mental health status of recently incarcerated persons asks the same series of questions of each new inmate.

2. While at a conference on mental disorders, you attend a symposium titled *Understanding the Origins of Mental Health*. Excerpts from three of the presentations appear below. Match each excerpt with one of the etiological models discussed in this chapter: diathesis-stress model, biological model,

family systems model, sociocultural model, and cognitive-behavioral approach. (Not all the models will have matches.)

a. "By understanding the mechanisms by which neurotransmitters affect behavior and cognition and emotion, we gain insight into the underlying causes of mental illness."

b. "Children are not raised in vacuums; they are raised in families. Therefore, to understand the origins of mental illness, we must understand the dynamics of the client's family."

c. "Some individuals are predisposed—whether as a function of their biology or of their past experiences—to develop psychological disorders. Stressful circumstances amplify these predispositions, making the individual more likely to evidence symptoms of psychopathology."

Answers: 1. a. a neuropsychological test (given the emphasis on memory, a brain function); b. mental status exam; c. structured interview. 2. a. biological; b. family systems model; c. diathesis-stress model.

Can Anxiety Be the Root of Seemingly Different Disorders?

Learning Objectives

■ Distinguish between anxiety disorders.

■ Identify cognitive, situational, and biological factors that contribute to anxiety disorders.

What does the fear of spiders have in common with the need to repeatedly check that the stove is turned off? They are both manifestations of anxiety disorders. Anxiety itself is normal and even useful. It can prepare us for upcoming events and motivate us to learn new ways of coping with life's challenges. Being anxious about tests reminds us to keep up with our homework and study. Likewise, being slightly anxious when meeting new people helps us avoid doing bizarre things and making bad impressions. For some people, however, anxiety can become debilitating and can interfere with every aspect of life. *Anxiety disorders* are characterized by excessive anxiety in the absence of true danger. It is normal to be anxious in stressful or threatening situations. It is abnormal to feel strong chronic anxiety without cause.

There Are Different Types of Anxiety Disorders

More than 1 in 4 Americans will have some type of anxiety disorder during their lifetimes (Kessler & Wang, 2008). Those suffering from anxiety disorders feel anxious, tense, and apprehensive. They are often depressed and irritable because they cannot see any solution to their anxiety. Constant worry can make falling asleep and staying asleep difficult, and attention span and concentration can be impaired. By continually arousing the autonomic nervous system, chronic anxiety also causes bodily symptoms such as sweating, dry mouth, rapid pulse, shallow breathing, increased blood pressure, and increased muscular tension. Chronic arousal can also result in hypertension, headaches, and intestinal problems and can even cause illness or tissue damage.

Because of their high levels of autonomic arousal, people who suffer from anxiety disorders also exhibit restless and pointless motor behaviors. Exaggerated startle response is typical, and behaviors such as toe tapping and excessive fidgeting are common. Problem solving and judgment may suffer as well. Research has shown that chronic stress can produce atrophy in the hippocampus, a brain structure involved in learning and memory (McEwen, 2008). Because chronic stress can damage the body, including the brain, it is very important to identify and effectively treat disorders that involve chronic anxiety. Different anxiety disorders share some emotional, cognitive, somatic, and motor symptoms, even though the behavioral manifestations of these disorders are quite different (Barlow, 2002).

PHOBIC DISORDER As discussed in Chapter 6, a phobia is a fear of a specific object or situation. Of course, some fear can be a good thing. As an adaptive force, fear can lead us to avoid potential dangers, such as poisonous snakes and rickety bridges. In phobias, however, the fear is exaggerated and out of proportion to the actual danger.

Phobias are classified based on the object of the fear. *Specific phobias*, which affect about 1 in 8 people, involve particular objects and situations. Common specific phobias include fear of snakes (ophidiophobia), fear of enclosed spaces (claustrophobia), and fear of heights (acrophobia). (**Table 14.3** lists some unusual specific phobias.) Another common specific phobia is fear of flying. Even though the odds of dying in a plane crash, compared with a car crash, are extraordinarily small, some people find flying terrifying. For those who need to travel frequently for their jobs, a fear of flying can cause significant impairment in daily living.

Social phobia is a fear of being negatively evaluated by others. This specific phobia is sometimes called *social anxiety disorder*. It includes fears of public speaking, speaking up in class, meeting new people, and eating in front of others. About 1 in 8 people will experience social phobia at some point in their life-

TABLE 14.3 **Some Unusual Specific Phobias**
• **Arachibutyrophobia:** fear of peanut butter sticking to the roof of one's mouth
• **Automatonophobia:** fear of ventriloquists' dummies
• **Barophobia:** fear of gravity
• **Dextrophobia:** fear of objects at the right side of the body
• **Geliophobia:** fear of laughter
• **Gnomophobia:** fear of garden gnomes
• **Hippopotomonstrosesquippedaliophobia:** fear of long words
• **Ochophobia:** fear of being in a moving automobile
• **Panophobia:** fear of everything
• **Pentheraphobia:** fear of mothers-in-law
• **Triskaidekaphobia:** fear of the number 13

times, and around 7 percent are experiencing social phobia at any given time (Ruscio et al., 2008). It is one of the earliest forms of anxiety disorder to develop, often beginning around age 13. The more social fears a person has, the more likely he or she is to develop other disorders, particularly depression and substance abuse problems. Indeed, assessment must consider the overlap between social phobia and related disorders to make an informed diagnosis (Stein & Stein, 2008; **Figure 14.13**).

GENERALIZED ANXIETY DISORDER The anxiety in phobic disorders has a specific focus. By contrast, the anxiety in **generalized anxiety disorder (GAD)** is diffuse and always present. People with this disorder are constantly anxious and worry incessantly about even minor matters (Sanderson & Barlow, 1990). They even worry about being worried! Because the anxiety is not focused, it can occur in response to almost anything, so the sufferer is constantly on the alert for problems. This hypervigilance results in distractibility, fatigue, irritability, and sleep problems, as well as headaches, restlessness, light-headedness, and muscle pain. Just under 6 percent of the United States population is affected by this disorder at some point in their lives, though women are diagnosed more often than men (Kessler et al., 1994; Kessler & Wang, 2008).

POSTTRAUMATIC STRESS DISORDER (PTSD) When people experience severe stress or emotional trauma—such as having a serious accident, being raped, fighting in active combat, or surviving a natural disaster—they often have negative reactions long after the danger has passed. In severe cases, people develop **posttraumatic stress disorder (PTSD),** a serious mental health disorder that involves frequent and recurring unwanted thoughts related to the trauma, including nightmares, intrusive thoughts, and flashbacks. The lifetime prevalence of PTSD is around 7 percent, with women being more likely to develop the disorder (Kessler et al., 2005b).

generalized anxiety disorder (GAD)
A diffuse state of constant anxiety not associated with any specific object or event.

posttraumatic stress disorder (PTSD)
A mental disorder that involves frequent nightmares, intrusive thoughts, and flashbacks related to an earlier trauma.

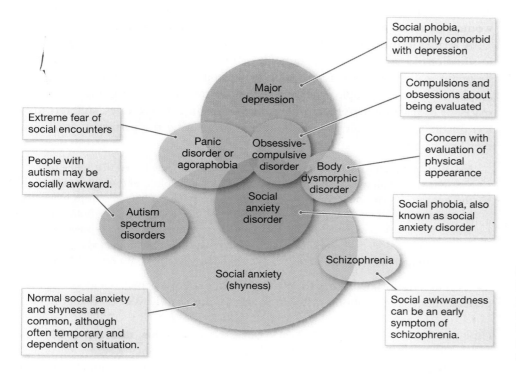

Social phobia, commonly comorbid with depression

Compulsions and obsessions about being evaluated

Concern with evaluation of physical appearance

Social phobia, also known as social anxiety disorder

Social awkwardness can be an early symptom of schizophrenia.

Extreme fear of social encounters

People with autism may be socially awkward.

Normal social anxiety and shyness are common, although often temporary and dependent on situation.

Major depression

Panic disorder or agoraphobia

Obsessive-compulsive disorder

Body dysmorphic disorder

Social anxiety disorder

Autism spectrum disorders

Social anxiety (shyness)

Schizophrenia

FIGURE 14.13 Comorbidity of Social Phobia As this diagram illustrates, social phobia is comorbid with many other psychological disorders. If a patient is suffering from social phobia, all of these disorders need to be considered to make an accurate and complete diagnosis.

An opportunity to study susceptibility to PTSD came about because of a tragedy at Northern Illinois University in 2008. On the campus, in front of many observers, a lone gunman killed five people and wounded 21. Among a sample of female students, those with certain genetic markers related to serotonin functioning were much more likely to show PTSD symptoms in the weeks after the shooting (Mercer et al., 2011) This finding suggests that some individuals may be more at risk than others for developing PTSD after exposure to a stressful event.

Those with PTSD often have chronic tension, anxiety, and health problems, and they may experience memory and attention problems in their daily lives. PTSD involves an unusual problem in memory—the inability to forget. PTSD is associated with an attentional bias, such that people with PTSD are hypervigilant to stimuli associated with their traumatic events. For instance, soldiers with combat-induced PTSD show increased physiological responsiveness to pictures of troops, sounds of gunfire, and even words associated with combat. Exposure to stimuli associated with past trauma leads to activation of the amygdala (Rauch, van der Kolk, Fisler, & Alpert, 1996). It is as if the severe emotional event is "overconsolidated," burned into memory (see Chapter 7 for a discussion of consolidation of memory).

PANIC DISORDER **Panic disorder** consists of sudden, overwhelming attacks of terror. The attacks seemingly come out of nowhere, or they are cued by external stimuli or internal thought processes. Panic attacks typically last for several minutes, during which the person may begin to sweat and tremble; feels his or her heart racing, feels short of breath; feels chest pain; and may feel dizzy and light-headed, with numbness and tingling in the hands and feet. People experiencing panic attacks often feel that they are going crazy or that they are dying, and those who suffer from persistent panic attacks attempt suicide much more frequently than those in the general population (Fawcett, 1992; Korn et al., 1992; Noyes, 1991). People who experience panic attacks during adolescence are especially likely to develop other anxiety disorders—such as PTSD (after a traumatic event) and generalized anxiety disorder—in adulthood (Goodwin et al., 2004). Panic disorder affects an estimated 3 percent of the population in a given year, and women are twice as likely to be diagnosed as men (Kessler & Wang, 2008).

A related disorder is **agoraphobia.** People with this specific phobia fear being in situations in which escape is difficult or impossible (e.g., being in a crowded shopping mall). Their fear is so strong that being in such situations causes panic attacks. As a result, people who suffer from agoraphobia avoid going into open spaces or to places where there might be crowds. In extreme cases, sufferers may feel unable to leave their homes. In addition to fearing the particular situations, they fear having a panic attack in public:

> Ms. Watson began to dread going out of the house alone. She feared that while out she would have an attack and would be stranded and helpless. She stopped riding the subway to work out of fear she might be trapped in a car between stops when an attack struck, preferring instead to walk the 20 blocks between her home and work. She also severely curtailed her social and recreational activities—previously frequent and enjoyed—because an attack might occur, necessitating an abrupt and embarrassing flight from the scene. (Spitzer, Skodol, Gibbon, & Williams, 1983)

This description demonstrates the clear links between panic attacks and agoraphobia. Indeed, agoraphobia without panic is quite rare (Kessler & Wang, 2008).

OBSESSIVE-COMPULSIVE DISORDER **Obsessive-compulsive disorder (OCD)** involves frequent intrusive thoughts and compulsive actions (Kessler & Wang, 2008). Affecting 1 percent to 2 percent of the population, OCD is more common

panic disorder An anxiety disorder that consists of sudden, overwhelming attacks of terror.

agoraphobia An anxiety disorder marked by fear of being in situations in which escape may be difficult or impossible.

obsessive-compulsive disorder (OCD) An anxiety disorder characterized by frequent intrusive thoughts and compulsive actions.

in women than men, and it generally begins in early adulthood (Robins & Regier, 1991; Weissman et al., 1994). *Obsessions* are recurrent, intrusive, and unwanted thoughts or ideas or mental images. They often include fear of contamination, of accidents, or of one's own aggression (**Figure 14.14**). *Compulsions* are particular acts that the OCD patient feels driven to perform over and over again. The most common compulsive behaviors are cleaning, checking, and counting. For instance, a person might continually check to make sure a door is locked, because of an obsession that his or her home might be invaded, or a person might engage in superstitious counting to protect against accidents, such as counting the number of telephone poles while driving.

Those with OCD anticipate catastrophe and loss of control. However, as opposed to those who suffer from other anxiety disorders—who fear what might happen to them—those with OCD fear what they might do or might have done. Checking is one way to calm the anxiety:

"Is the Itsy Bitsy Spider obsessive-compulsive?"

> While in reality no one is on the road, I'm intruded with the heinous thought that I *migh*t have hit someone . . . a human being! God knows where such a fantasy comes from. . . . I try to make reality chase away this fantasy. I reason, "Well, if I hit someone while driving, I would have *felt* it." This brief trip into reality helps the pain dissipate . . . but only for a second. . . . I start ruminating, "Maybe I did hit someone and didn't realize it. . . . Oh my God! I might have killed somebody! I have to go back and check." (Rapoport, 1990, pp. 22–27)

Anxiety Disorders Have Cognitive, Situational, and Biological Components

The behavioral manifestations of anxiety disorders can be quite different, but anxiety disorders share some causal factors (Barlow, 2002). These factors can be divided into three groups: cognitive, situational, and biological.

COGNITIVE COMPONENTS When presented with ambiguous or neutral situations, anxious individuals tend to perceive them as threatening, whereas nonanxious individuals assume they are nonthreatening (Eysenck, Mogg, May, Richards, & Matthews, 1991; **Figure 14.15**). Anxious individuals also focus excessive attention on perceived threats (Rinck, Reinecke, Ellwart, Heuer, & Becker, 2005). They thus recall threatening events more easily than nonthreatening events, exaggerating their perceived magnitude and frequency.

SITUATIONAL COMPONENTS As discussed in Chapter 6, monkeys develop a fear of snakes if they observe other monkeys responding to snakes fearfully. Similarly, a person could develop a fear of flying by observing another person's fearful reaction to the closing of cabin doors. Such a fear might then generalize to other enclosed spaces, resulting in claustrophobia.

BIOLOGICAL COMPONENTS As noted in Chapter 13, children who have an inhibited temperamental style are usually shy and tend to avoid unfamiliar people and novel objects. These inhibited children are more likely to develop anxiety disorders later in life (Fox, Henderson, Marshall, Nichols, & Ghera, 2005). They are especially at risk for developing social phobia (Biederman et al., 2001).

In one study, adults received brain scans while viewing pictures of familiar faces and of novel faces (Schwartz, Wright, Shin, Kagan, & Rauch, 2003). One group

FIGURE 14.14 Howie Mandel The comedian Howie Mandel is a diagnosed sufferer of obsessive-compulsive disorder. Like many people with OCD, Mandel suffers from mysophobia, or the fear of germs. His trademark shaved head helps him with this problem, as it makes him feel cleaner. Mandel even built a second, sterile house, to which he can retreat if he feels he might be contaminated by anyone around him. Here Mandel promotes his autobiography, *Here's the Deal: Don't Touch Me* (2009), in which he "comes clean" about suffering from OCD and other disorders.

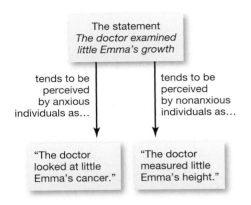

The statement
The doctor examined little Emma's growth

tends to be perceived by anxious individuals as...

tends to be perceived by nonanxious individuals as...

"The doctor looked at little Emma's cancer."

"The doctor measured little Emma's height."

FIGURE 14.15 Anxiety Disorders As this example illustrates, anxious individuals tend to perceive ambiguous situations as threatening.

of these adults had been categorized as inhibited before age 2. The other group had been categorized as uninhibited before age 2. Compared with the uninhibited group, the inhibited group showed greater activation of the amygdala—a brain region involved when people are threatened—while viewing the novel faces. That is, after the passage of so many years, the inhibited group still seemed to show a threat response to novel faces. This finding suggests that some aspects of childhood temperament are preserved in the adult brain (**Figure 14.16**).

CAUSES OF OBSESSIVE-COMPULSIVE DISORDER To understand how anxiety disorders result from several different factors, it is helpful to consider the multiple factors that cause obsessive-compulsive disorder.

A paradoxical aspect of OCD is that people are aware that their obsessions and compulsions are irrational, yet they are unable to stop them. One explanation is that the disorder results from conditioning. In the person with OCD, anxiety is somehow paired to a specific event, probably through classical conditioning. As a result, the person engages in behavior that reduces anxiety and therefore is reinforced through operant conditioning. This reduction of anxiety is reinforcing and increases the person's chance of engaging in that behavior again.

Suppose you are forced to shake hands with a man who has a bad cold. You have just seen him wiping his nose with his right hand. Shaking that hand might cause you to be anxious or uncomfortable because you do not want to get sick. As soon as the pleasantries are over, you run to the bathroom and wash your hands. You feel relieved. You have now paired hand-washing with a reduction in anxiety, thus increasing the chances of hand-washing in the future (**Figure 14.17**). If you develop OCD, however, the compulsive behavior will reduce your anxiety only temporarily, so you will need to perform the behavior over and over.

FIGURE 14.16 Scientific Method: Inhibition and Social Anxiety

Hypothesis: People who had an inhibited temperamental style as children are more likely to show signs of social anxiety later in life.

Research Method:

1 Adults received brain scans while viewing pictures of familiar faces and of novel faces. One group of these adults had been categorized as inhibited before age 2. The other group had been categorized as uninhibited before age 2.

2 Two regions of the brain were more activated by novel faces. These areas were the amygdala (marked "Amy" in the brain scan below) and the occipito-temporal cortex (marked "OTC"). The amygdala is normally active when people are threatened. The occipitotemporal cortex is normally active when people see faces, whether the faces are novel or familiar.

Results: Compared with the uninhibited group, the inhibited group showed greater activation of the amygdala while viewing novel faces. That activation indicated that, when seeing novel faces, the inhibited group showed greater brain activity associated with threat.

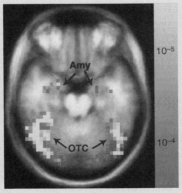

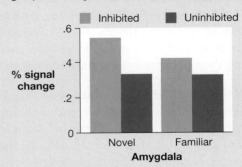

Conclusion: The results suggest that some aspects of childhood temperament are preserved in the adult brain. In particular, biological factors seem to play an important role in social anxiety.

Source: Schwartz, C. E., Wright, C. I., Shin, L. M., Kagan, J., & Rauch, S. L. (2003, June 20). Inhibited and uninhibited infants "grown up": Adult amygdalar response to novelty. *Science, 300,* 1952–1953.

There is also good evidence that the etiology of OCD is in part genetic (Crowe, 2000). Indeed, various behavioral genetics methods, such as twin studies, have shown that OCD runs in families. The specific mechanism has not been identified, but the OCD-related genes appear to control the neurotransmitter glutamate (Pauls, 2008). As noted in Chapter 3, glutamate is the major excitatory transmitter in the brain, causing increased neural firing.

Brain imaging has provided some evidence regarding which brain systems are involved in OCD. The caudate, a brain structure involved in suppressing impulses, is smaller and has structural abnormalities in people with OCD (Baxter, 2000). Moreover, brain imaging studies show abnormal activity in the caudates of people with OCD compared with the caudates of controls (Maia, Cooney, & Peterson, 2008). Because the caudate is involved in impulse suppression, dysfunction in this region may result in the leak of impulses into consciousness. The prefrontal cortex, which is involved in conscious control of behavior, then becomes overactive in an effort to compensate (Whiteside, Port, & Abramowitz, 2004; Yucel et al., 2007). As discussed in Chapter 15, deep brain electrical stimulation of the caudate has been successful in alleviating the symptoms of OCD, providing additional evidence that this brain structure is involved in OCD (Aouizerate et al., 2004).

There is also growing evidence that OCD can be triggered by environmental factors. In particular, a streptococcal infection apparently can cause a severe form of OCD in some young children. Originally identified in 1998 by Susan Swedo and her colleagues at the National Institute of Mental Health, this syndrome strikes virtually overnight. The affected children suddenly display odd symptoms of OCD, such as engaging in repetitive behaviors, developing irrational fears and obsessions, and having facial tics. Researchers have speculated that an auto-immune response damages the caudate, thereby producing the symptoms of OCD (Snider & Swedo, 2004). Treatments that enhance the immune system have been found to diminish the symptoms of OCD in children with this syndrome. Why some children are susceptible to this autoimmune response is unknown.

Most likely, biological and cognitive-behavioral factors interact to produce the symptoms of OCD. First a dysfunctional caudate allows impulses to enter consciousness. Then these impulses give rise to the obsessions of OCD. The prefrontal cortex becomes overactive in an attempt to compensate. As a result, associations are established between obsessions and behaviors that reduce the anxiety arising from the obsessions. These behaviors thus become compulsions through conditioning. Nature (biology) and nurture (cognition, situation) together result in the disorder.

FIGURE 14.17 OCD Cycle This flowchart illustrates the operations of conditioning for the example given in the text. Classical conditioning (step 1) and operant conditioning (steps 2 and 3) reinforce behavior. Continued reinforcement may contribute to a person's developing OCD (step 4).

Summing Up

Can Anxiety Be the Root of Seemingly Different Disorders?

Anxiety disorders are characterized by excessive anxiety in the absence of true danger. Common anxiety disorders include phobic disorder, generalized anxiety disorder, posttraumatic stress disorder, panic disorder, and obsessive-compulsive disorder. Although the behavioral manifestations of these disorders differ, they share many emotional, cognitive, somatic, and motor symptoms. The anxiety associated with these disorders results from cognitive factors (such as paying excessive attention to perceived threats), situational factors (such as observing another individual's fearful reaction), and biological factors (such as temperamental style). These factors interact to produce obsessive-compulsive disorder. These interactions illustrate that nature and nurture influence the development of this condition.

14.3 Are Mood Disorders Extreme Manifestations of Normal Moods?

Our moods color every aspect of our lives. When we are happy, the world seems like a wonderful place, and we are filled with boundless energy. When we are sad, we view the world in a decidedly less rosy light, feeling hopeless and isolated. Few of us, however, experience these symptoms day after day until they disrupt our ability to work, learn, and play. It is easy to imagine how periods of sadness can interfere with daily life. In addition, however, we need to understand that periods of excessive elation can also be devastating.

There Are Two Categories of Mood Disorders

Mood disorders, also called *affective disorders,* are classified into two categories. Although some of their characteristics overlap, the two categories represent fundamentally different disorders. Both kinds reflect extreme emotions: *Depressive disorders* feature persistent and pervasive feelings of sadness. *Bipolar disorders* involve radical fluctuations in mood.

DEPRESSIVE DISORDERS Depressive disorders can be major or less severe. To be diagnosed with **major depression** according to *DSM* criteria, a person must have one of two symptoms: depressed (often irritable) mood or loss of interest in pleasurable activities for at least two weeks. In addition, the person must have other symptoms, such as appetite and weight changes, sleep disturbances, loss of energy, difficulty concentrating, feelings of self-reproach or guilt, and frequent thoughts of death, perhaps by suicide. The following excerpt is from a case study of a 56-year-old woman diagnosed with depression:

> She described herself as overwhelmed with feelings of guilt, worthlessness, and hopelessness. She twisted her hands almost continuously and played nervously with her hair. She stated that her family would be better off without her and that she had considered taking her life by hanging herself. She felt that after death she would go to hell, where she would experience eternal torment, but that this would be a just punishment. (Andreasen, 1984, p. 39)

Feelings of depression are relatively common, but only long-lasting episodes that impair a person's life are diagnosed as mood disorders. Major depression affects about 6 percent to 7 percent of Americans in a given 12-month period, whereas approximately 16 percent of Americans will experience major depression at some point in their lives (Kessler & Wang, 2008). Although major depression varies in severity, those who receive a diagnosis are highly impaired by the condition, and it tends to persist over several months for them, often lasting for years (Kessler, Merikangas, & Wang, 2007). Women are nearly twice as likely to be diagnosed with major depression as men are (Kessler et al., 2003).

Unlike major depression, **dysthymia** is of mild to moderate severity. This kind of depression is not severe enough to merit a diagnosis of major depression. That is, people with dysthymia may have many of the same symptoms as people with major depression, but those symptoms are less intense. People diagnosed with dysthymia—approximately 2 percent to 3 percent of the population—must have a depressed mood most of the day, more days than not, for at least 2 years. Periods of dysthymia last from 2 to 20 or more years, although the typical duration is about 5 to 10 years. Because the depressed mood is so long-lasting, some psychologists consider it a personality disorder rather than a mood disorder.

The distinctions between a depressive personality, dysthymic disorder, and major depression are unclear. In keeping with a dimensional view of mental disorders, these states may be points along a continuum rather than distinct disorders. One research finding in support of this view is that dysthymia often precedes major depression (Lewinsohn, Allen, Seeley, & Gotlib, 1999; Lewinsohn, Rodhe, Seeley, & Hops, 1991).

THE ROLES OF CULTURE AND GENDER IN DEPRESSIVE DISORDERS Depression is so prevalent that it is sometimes called the common cold of mental disorders. In its most severe form, depression is the leading cause of disability in the United States and worldwide (Worley, 2006). The stigma associated with this disorder has especially dire consequences in developing countries, where people do not take advantage of the treatment options because they do not want to admit to being depressed. Depression is the leading risk factor for suicide, which claims approximately a million lives annually around the world and is among the top three causes of death for people between 15 and 35 years of age (Insel & Charney, 2003). One way to combat the stigma of mental disorders is to focus attention on their high incidence and to educate more people about effective treatments (discussed in Chapter 15, "Treatment of Psychological Disorders"; **Figure 14.18**).

major depression A disorder characterized by severe negative moods or a lack of interest in normally pleasurable activities.

dysthymia A form of depression that is not severe enough to be diagnosed as major depression.

For more information talk to your doctor

FIGURE 14.18 Informing the Public Television ads may help "normalize" the treatment of mental disorders. The more we hear about talking to doctors about our problems, the more inclined we may be to visit doctors when problems arise.

bipolar disorder A mood disorder characterized by alternating periods of depression and mania.

Gender also plays a role in the incidence of depression. Across multiple countries and contexts, twice as many women as men suffer from depression (Üstün, Ayuso-Mateos, Chatterji, Mathers, & Murray, 2004). In fact, suicide is the leading cause of death among young women in India and China (Khan, 2005), and the highest rates of depression are found in women in developing countries, with especially high rates reported for women in rural Pakistan (Mumford, Saeed, Ahmad, Latif, & Mubbashar, 1997).

Why are the rates of depression so much higher for women than men? Some researchers have theorized that women's multiple roles in most societies—as wage earners and family caregivers—cause stress that results in increased incidence of depression; but other researchers have pointed out the health benefits of having multiple roles, such as wife, mother, and employee (Barnett & Hyde, 2001). Thus it is not multiple roles per se but more likely overwork and lack of support that contribute to the high rate of depression in women. Research in India, Brazil, and Chile shows that low income, lack of education, and difficult family relationships contribute to mental disorders in women (Blue & Harpham, 1996).

Furthermore, men present symptoms in ways that are more in line with the male gender role. For example, when men are distressed, they are more likely to abuse alcohol and other drugs and engage in violent and risky behaviors, including unsafe sexual practices, because having a disorder can make men feel as though they are admitting to weakness (Doyal, 2001). One theory is that women respond to stressful events by internalizing their feelings, which leads to depression and anxiety, whereas men externalize with alcohol, drugs, and violence (Holden, 2005).

BIPOLAR DISORDER We all experience variations in moods. Our normal fluctuations from sadness to exuberance seem minuscule, however, compared with the extremes experienced by people with **bipolar disorder.** This disorder previously was known as manic depression, because those who are diagnosed with the disorder have periods of major depression but also experience episodes of mania.

Manic episodes are characterized by elevated mood, increased activity, diminished need for sleep, grandiose ideas, racing thoughts, and extreme distractibility. During episodes of mania, heightened levels of activity and euphoria often result in excessive involvement in pleasurable but foolish activities. People may engage in sexual indiscretions, buying sprees, risky business ventures, and similar "out of character" behaviors that they regret once the mania has subsided.

Whereas some sufferers of bipolar disorder experience true manic episodes, others may experience less extreme mood elevations. These *hypomanic episodes* are often characterized by heightened creativity and productivity. They can be extremely pleasurable and rewarding. In fact, they are not too disruptive in people's lives.

Bipolar disorder is much less common than depression. The lifetime prevalence for any type is estimated at around 4 percent (Kessler & Wang, 2008). In addition, whereas depression is more common in women, bipolar disorder is equally prevalent in women and men. Bipolar disorder emerges most commonly during late adolescence or early adulthood.

FIGURE 14.19 Kay Redfield Jamison Jamison was able to overcome her crippling bipolar disorder to succeed as a teacher, researcher, and author.

A CASE STUDY OF BIPOLAR DISORDER The psychology professor Kay Redfield Jamison acknowledged her own struggles with bipolar disorder in her award-winning memoir, *An Unquiet Mind* (1995; **Figure 14.19**). Her work has helped shape the study of the disorder, and her 1990 textbook, coauthored with Frederick Goodwin, is considered the standard for the field (Goodwin & Jamison, 1990).

In *An Unquiet Mind,* Jamison details how as a child she was intensely emotional and occasionally obsessive. When she was 17, she had her first serious bout of what she describes as psychotic, profoundly suicidal depression. Jamison experienced deepening swings from nearly psychotic exuberance to paralyzing depression throughout her undergraduate years. In 1975, after obtaining her Ph.D. in clinical psychology, she joined the UCLA Department of Psychiatry, where she directed the Affective Disorders Clinic.

Within months after she began this job, her condition deteriorated dramatically. She began hallucinating and feared that she was losing her mind. This state so terrified her that she sought out a psychiatrist, who quickly diagnosed her as having manic-depressive disorder (i.e, bipolar disorder) and prescribed a drug called lithium. (For more information about lithium and other treatments for bipolar disorder, see Chapter 15, "Treatment of Psychological Disorders.")

One of the unfortunate side effects of lithium is that it blunts positive feelings. People with bipolar disorder experience profoundly enjoyable highs during their manic phases. Even though these patients know that lithium helps them, they often resent the drug and refuse to take it. Although lithium has helped Jamison, she also credits the psychological support of her psychiatrist, as well as the support of her family and friends.

Jamison has made the point that lithium can rob people of creative energy. In her book *Touched with Fire* (1993), she asks whether lithium would have dampened the genius of those major artists and writers who may have had mood disorders, such as Michelangelo, Vincent van Gogh, Georgia O'Keeffe, Emily Dickinson, and Ernest Hemingway. Jamison demonstrates the strong association between bipolar disorder and artistic genius, and she raises the disturbing question of whether eradicating the disorder would rob society of much great art. Jamison embodies this irony: Her early career benefited from the energy and creativity of her manic phases even as her personal life was threatened by devastating depression.

Mood Disorders Have Biological, Situational, and Cognitive Components

Mood disorders can be devastating. The sadness, hopelessness, and inability to concentrate that characterize major depression can result in the loss of jobs, of friends, and of family relationships. Because of this disorder's profound effects, particularly the danger of suicide, much research has focused on understanding the causes of major depression and treating it. People with bipolar disorder are also at risk for suicide. In addition, errors in judgment during manic episodes can have devastating effects.

BIOLOGICAL COMPONENTS Studies of twins, of families, and of adoptions support the notion that depression has a genetic component. Although there is some variability among studies, *concordance rates* (i.e., the percentage who share the same disorder) between identical twins are generally around two to three times higher than rates between fraternal twins (Levinson, 2006). The genetic contribution to depression is somewhat weaker than the genetic contribution to schizophrenia or to bipolar disorder (Belmaker & Agam, 2008). Twin studies reveal that the concordance for bipolar disorder in identical twins is more than 70 percent, versus only 20 percent in fraternal, or dizygotic, twins (Nurnberger, Goldin, & Gershon, 1994).

In the 1980s, the Amish community was involved in a genetic research study. The Amish were an ideal population for this sort of research because they keep good genealogical records and few outsiders marry into the community. In addition, substance abuse is virtually nonexistent among Amish adults, so mental disorders are easier to detect. The research results revealed that bipolar disorder ran in a limited number of families and that all of those afflicted had a similar genetic defect (Egeland et al., 1987).

Genetic research suggests, however, that the hereditary nature of bipolar disorder is complex and not linked to just one gene. Current research focuses on identifying several genes that may be involved. In addition, it appears that in families with bipolar disorder, successive generations have more-severe disorders and earlier ages of onset (McInnis et al., 1993; Petronis & Kennedy, 1995). Research on this pattern of transmission may help reveal the genetics of the disorder, but the specific nature of the heritability of bipolar disorder remains to be discovered.

The existence of a genetic component implies that biological factors are involved in depression. In fact, there is much evidence that major depression involves a deficiency of one or more monoamines. (As discussed in Chapter 3, monoamines are neurotransmitters that regulate emotion and arousal and motivate behavior.) For instance, medications that increase the availability of norepinephrine, a monoamine, may help alleviate depression. Medications that decrease levels of this neurotransmitter can cause symptoms of depression. Medications such as Prozac are known as *selective serotonin reuptake inhibitors (SSRIs)*. SSRIs selectively increase another monoamine, serotonin, and there is increased interest in understanding the role of this neurotransmitter in mood disorders (Barton et al., 2008; SSRIs and other medications are discussed in Chapter 15).

In addition, studies of brain function have suggested that certain neural structures may be involved in mood disorders. Damage to the left prefrontal cortex can lead to depression, but damage to the right hemisphere does not. The brain waves of people with depression show low activity in the left prefrontal cortex (Allen, Coan, & Nazarian, 2004), irrespective of their current mood (Stewart, Coan, Towers, & Allen, 2011). Interestingly, this pattern persists in patients who have been depressed but are currently in remission (Henriques & Davidson, 1990). The pattern may therefore be a biological marker of a predisposition to depression.

Biological rhythms also have been implicated in depression. Depressed patients enter REM sleep more quickly and have more of it. In fact, one symptom of depression is excessive sleeping and tiredness. In addition, many people show a cyclical pattern of depression, depending on the season. This condition, *seasonal affective disorder (SAD)*, results in periods of depression that correspond to the shorter days of winter in northern latitudes.

SITUATIONAL COMPONENTS Situational factors also play a role in depression. A number of studies have implicated life stressors in many cases of depression (Hammen, 2005). Particularly relevant for depression is interpersonal loss, such as the death of a loved one or a divorce (Paykel, 2003). Depression is especially likely in the face of multiple negative events (Brown & Harris, 1978), and patients with depression often have experienced negative life events during the year before the onset of their depression (Dohrenwend, Shrout, Link, Skodol, & Martin, 1986).

How an individual reacts to stress, however, can be influenced by interpersonal relationships, which play an extremely important role in depression (Joiner, Coyne, & Blalock, 1999). Regardless of any other factors, relationships contribute to the development of depression, alter people's experiences when depressed, and ultimately may be damaged by the constant needs of the person with depression. Many people report negative reactions to people with depression, perhaps because of their frequent complaining. Over time, people may avoid interactions with those suffering from depression, thus initiating a downward spiral by making the sufferers even more depressed (Dykman, Horowitz, Abramson, & Usher, 1991). By contrast, a person who has a close friend or group of friends is less likely to become depressed when faced with stress. This protective factor is not related to the number of friends. It is related to the quality of the friendships. One good friend is more protective than a large number of casual acquaintances.

COGNITIVE COMPONENTS Finally, cognitive processes play a role in depression. The psychologist Aaron Beck has hypothesized that people with depression think negatively about themselves ("I am worthless"; "I am a failure"; "I am ugly"), about their situations ("everybody hates me"; "the world is unfair"), and about the future ("things are hopeless"; "I can't change"). Beck refers to these negative thoughts about self, situation, and the future as the *cognitive triad* (Beck, 1967, 1976; Beck, Brown, Seer, Eidelson, & Riskind, 1987; Beck, Rush, Shaw, & Emery, 1979; **Figure 14.20**).

People with depression blame misfortunes on personal defects while seeing positive occurrences as the result of luck. People who are not suffering from depression do the opposite. Beck also notes that people with depression make errors in logic. For example, they overgeneralize based on single events, magnify the seriousness of bad events, think in extremes (such as believing they should either be perfect or not try), and take responsibility for bad events that actually have little to do with them.

A second cognitive model of depression is based on **learned helplessness** (Seligman, 1974, 1975). "Learned helplessness" means that people come to see themselves as unable to have any effect on events in their lives. The psychologist Martin Seligman based this model on years of animal research. When animals are placed in aversive situations they cannot escape (such as receiving unescapable shock), the animals eventually become passive and unresponsive. They end up lacking the motivation to try new methods of escape when given the opportunity. Similarly, people suffering from learned helplessness come to expect that bad things will happen to them and believe they are powerless to avoid negative events. The *attributions,* or explanations, they make for negative events refer to personal factors that are stable and global, rather than to situational factors that are temporary and specific. This attributional pattern leads people to feel hopeless about making positive changes in their lives (Abramson, Metalsky, & Alloy, 1989). According to the scientific evidence, dysfunctional cognitive patterns are a cause rather than a consequence of depression.

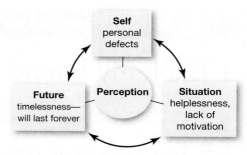

FIGURE 14.20 Cognitive Triad According to Beck, people suffering from depression perceive themselves, their situations, and the future negatively. These perceptions influence each other and contribute to the disorder.

learned helplessness A cognitive model of depression in which people feel unable to control events in their lives.

I Think My Friend Might Be Suicidal. What Should I Do?

Many people contemplate suicide at some point in their lives. Tragically, as of 2007, suicide was the third leading cause of death among Americans 10 to 24 years old (American Association of Suicidology, 2011). As a result, many college students will be or have been touched by suicide. Perhaps you know someone who died by suicide. Perhaps a friend of yours talks about wanting to die. Or maybe you have considered taking your own life. Understanding the risk factors associated with suicide is an important step toward preventing suicide. Knowing where and how to find support can save lives.

In his book *Why People Die by Suicide* (2005), the clinical psychologist Thomas Joiner considers two key questions about suicide: Who *wants* to commit suicide? And who *can* commit suicide? In answering the first question, Joiner argues that "people desire death when two fundamental needs are frustrated to the point of extinction" (p. 47). The first of these fundamental needs is the need to belong, to feel connected with others. We all want to have positive interactions with others who care about us. If we do not perceive those things in our lives, our need to belong is thwarted. The second of these fundamental needs is the need for competence. We all want to be capable agents in the world. If we do not perceive ourselves as able to do the things we think we should be able to do, our need for competence is thwarted. Joiner says that when the need to belong and the need for competence are frustrated, we desire death.

But as Joiner points out, just because a person wants to commit suicide does not mean she or he will be able to do so. Evolution has hardwired us with a tremendously strong self-preservation instinct. What makes a person able to endure the tremendous physical pain or overwhelming psychological fear many of us would experience if we tried to kill ourselves? Joiner presents a straightforward answer: practice. He writes that "those prone to serious suicidal behav-ior have reached that status through a process of exposure to self-injury and other provocative experiences" (pp. 85–86) and "when people get used to dangerous behavior . . . the groundwork for catastrophe is laid" (p. 48). For example, a person who drives recklessly, engages in self-cutting, and/or experiments with drugs is more practiced at self-harm than someone who does not engage in any of these behaviors. Thus the person who engages in dangerous behavior is more likely to have the capacity to carry out lethal self-injury.

Take a look at **Figure 14.21**. The larger oval represents the people in the world who desire suicide. These individuals perceive themselves to be burdens on others and do not perceive themselves as having frequent and positive interactions with others who care about them. The smaller oval represents the people who, over time, have developed the ability to lethally injure themselves. The overlap between the ovals represents a small fraction of the people who want to commit suicide and are able to do so. It also represents, conversely, the small fraction of the people who are well practiced at endangering themselves and want to die. Again, Joiner posits that the individuals who are *most* at risk of dying by suicide both want to do so and are able to do so.

Of course, like so many other topics you have learned about in this book, suicide is a very complex psychological phenomenon. Perhaps you have heard that suicide tends to run in families or that everyone who commits suicide has a mental illness. Indeed, the data support a genetic risk factor for suicide (Roy, 1992), and the majority of people who commit suicide seem to suffer from mental illness (Cavanagh, Carson, Sharpe, & Lawrie, 2003). How do these factors figure into Joiner's model? He points out: "Genes, neurobiology, impulsivity, childhood adversity, and mental disorders are interconnected strands that converge and influence whether people acquire the ability for lethal self-injury, feel a burden on others, and fail to feel they belong" (Joiner, 2005, p. 202). In other words, many factors might lead someone to want to commit suicide. In addition, many factors might prompt someone to arm himself or herself with the ability to endure self-harm.

With such risk factors in mind, we can now turn to the important question of what to do if you think a friend might be suicidal. First and foremost, take suicidal threats seriously. Second, get help. Someone who is considering suicide should be screened by a trained professional. Contact a counselor at your school, ask a religious leader for help, or speak to someone at the National Suicide Prevention Lifeline: 1-800-273-TALK (8255). These individuals can help you get your friend the support he or she needs. Third, let your friend know you care.

Remember, suicide risk is particularly high when people do not feel a sense of connection with others and when they feel a lack of competence. You can remind the suicidal person that you value your relationship, that you care about her or his well-being, that

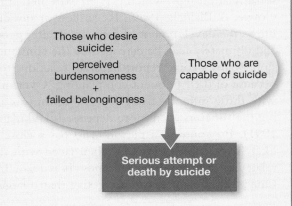

FIGURE 14.21 The Risk of Suicide: Desire + Capability = Attempt? According to Joiner, the individuals who are *most* at risk of dying by suicide both want to do so and are able to do so.

you would be devastated if that person were no longer in your life. These forms of support can challenge the suicidal person's sense that she or he lacks belongingness. To challenge the person's perceived incompetence, you can remind your friend about the reasons you admire her or him, or you can ask for help on a project or issue you are genuinely struggling with.

And remember, suicide is forever. The problems that prompt a person to feel suicidal, however, are often temporary. If you ever find yourself or a friend feeling that suicide offers the best way out of an overwhelming or hopeless situation, know that other options exist. You or your friend might not be able to see those options right away. Reach out to someone who can help you or your friend see the ways out of current problems and into the future.

Summing Up

Are Mood Disorders Extreme Manifestations of Normal Moods?

Everyone experiences both extreme moods and fluctuations in mood. However, mood disorders are different from normal variations in mood. These disorders disrupt a person's ability to function, interfering with daily life. Although major depression and bipolar disorder are both described as mood disorders and share certain characteristics, they are distinctly different disorders. Major depression is characterized by depressed mood or a loss of interest in pleasurable activities, among other symptoms. Due to social stigma, depression is often left untreated in developing countries. Depression is more common among females than among males, with the highest rates among women in developing countries. Bipolar disorder is characterized by alternating periods of depression and mania. During periods of mania, heightened levels of activity and euphoria may result in pleasurable but foolish behavior. Research suggests that both depression and bipolar disorder are influenced by genes. Other biological factors (such as neurotransmitter levels, frontal lobe functioning, biological rhythms) have been implicated in the occurrence of depression. Situational factors (such as poor relationships) and cognitive factors (such as the cognitive triad and learned helplessness) also contribute to the occurrence of depression.

Measuring Up

1. Indicate whether each of the symptoms and causes listed below is associated with major depression.
   a. appetite changes
   b. disorder caused partly by dysfunctional cognitive patterns
   c. disorder caused partly by life stressors
   d. excessive involvement in pleasurable activities
   e. difficulty concentrating
   f. heightened creativity and heightened productivity
   g. hereditary component
   h. loss of interest in pleasurable activities
   i. racing thoughts
   j. risk factor for suicide
   k. sleep disturbances
   l. typified by extreme emotion

2. Which of the following statements represent dysfunctional cognitive patterns believed to cause depression? If a statement is an example of dysfunctional cognition, briefly describe why.
   a. "I didn't make the soccer team. I fail at everything."
   b. "I didn't get a raise because I was late to work a number of times over the past quarter."
   c. "There's nothing I can do about the fact that my boss is so mean to me."
   d. "This assignment is really hard. I need to see my instructor during office hours."

What Are Dissociative Disorders?

Learning Objectives

- Describe dissociative amnesia, dissociative fugue, and dissociative identity disorder.
- Identify possible causes of dissociative identity disorder.
- Discuss the current controversy regarding dissociative identity disorder.

As noted in Chapter 5, we sometimes get lost in our thoughts or daydreams, even to the point of losing track of what is going on around us. Many of us have had the experience of forgetting what we are doing while in the middle of an action ("Why was I headed to the kitchen?"). When we wake up in an unfamiliar location, we may momentarily be disoriented and not know where we are. In other words, our thoughts and experiences can become dissociated, or split, from the external world.

Dissociative disorders are extreme versions of this phenomenon. These disorders involve disruptions of identity, of memory, or of conscious awareness (Kihlstrom, 2005). The commonality among dissociative disorders is the splitting off of some parts of memory from conscious awareness. Dissociative disorders are believed to result from extreme stress. That is, the person with a dissociative disorder has split off a traumatic event in order to protect the self. Some researchers believe that people prone to dissociative disorders are also prone to PTSD (Cardeña & Carlson, 2011).

Dissociative Amnesia and Fugue Involve Loss of Memory

In *dissociative amnesia,* a person forgets that an event happened or loses awareness of a substantial block of time. For example, the person with this disorder may suddenly lose memory for personal facts, including his or her identity and place of residence. These memory failures cannot be accounted for by ordinary forgetting (such as momentarily forgetting where you parked your car) or by the effects of drugs or alcohol.

Consider the case of Dorothy Joudrie, from Calgary, Canada. In 1995, after suffering years of physical abuse from her husband, Joudrie shot her husband six times. Her husband survived, and he described her behavior during the shooting as very calm, as if she were detached from what she was doing. When the police arrived, however, Joudrie was extremely distraught. She had no memory of the shooting and told the police that she simply found her husband shot and lying on the garage floor, at which time she called for help. Joudrie was found not criminally responsible for her actions because of her dissociative state (Butcher, Mineka, & Hooley, 2007).

dissociative disorders Mental disorders that involve disruptions of identity, of memory, or of conscious awareness.

The rarest and most extreme form of dissociative amnesia is *dissociative fugue*. The disorder involves a loss of identity. In addition, it involves travel to another location (the French word *fugue* means "flight") and sometimes the assumption of a new identity. The fugue state often ends suddenly, with the person unsure how she or he ended up in unfamiliar surroundings. Typically, the person does not remember events that occurred during the fugue state.

Recall the case of Jeff Ingram, who developed retrograde amnesia, a form of dissociative amnesia (see Figure 7.24). After Ingram found himself in Denver not knowing who he was, his fiancée brought him home to Washington state. Ingram did not recognize his fiancée's face, but she felt familiar to him, as did his home.

Dissociative Identity Disorder Is a Controversial Diagnosis

Dissociative identity disorder (DID) was formerly called *multiple personality disorder*. This condition consists of the occurrence of two or more distinct identities in the same individual. Consider the strange case of Billy Milligan, who in 1978 was found innocent of robbery and rape charges on the grounds that he had dissociative identity disorder. Milligan clearly committed the robberies and rapes, but his lawyers successfully argued that he had multiple personalities and that different ones committed the crimes. Therefore, Billy could not be held responsible.

In his book *The Minds of Billy Milligan* (1981), Daniel Keyes describes the 24 separate personalities sharing the body of 26-year-old Billy Milligan. One is Arthur, who at age 22 speaks with a British accent and is self-taught in physics and biology. He reads and writes fluent Arabic. Eight-year-old David is the keeper of the pain. Anytime something physically painful happens, David experiences it. Christene is a 3-year-old dyslexic girl who likes to draw flowers and butterflies. Regan is 23 and Yugoslavian; speaks with a marked Slavic accent; and reads, writes, and speaks Serbo-Croatian. He is the protector of the "family" and acknowledges robbing his victims, but he denies raping them. Adalana, a 19-year-old lesbian who writes poetry, cooks, and keeps house for the others, later admitted to committing the rapes.

After his acquittal, Milligan spent close to a decade in various mental hospitals. In 1988, psychiatrists declared that Milligan's 24 personalities had merged into one and that he was no longer a danger to society. Milligan was released and reportedly has lived quietly since then. Many people respond to reports such as this with astonishment and incredulity, believing that people such as Milligan must be faking. To judge the facts, we need to examine what is known about his condition and how it is diagnosed.

Most people diagnosed with DID are women who report being severely abused as children. According to the most common theory of DID, children cope with abuse by pretending it is happening to someone else. They enter a trancelike state in which they dissociate their mental states from their physical bodies. Over time, this dissociated state takes on its own identity. Different identities develop to deal with different traumas. Often the identities have periods of amnesia, and sometimes only one identity is aware of the others. Indeed, diagnosis often occurs only when a person has difficulty accounting for large chunks of his or her day. The separate identities usually differ substantially, such as in gender identity, sexual orientation, age, language spoken, interests, physiological profiles, and patterns of brain activation (Reinders et al., 2003). Even their handwritings can differ (**Figure 14.22**).

dissociative identity disorder (DID) The occurrence of two or more distinct identities in the same individual.

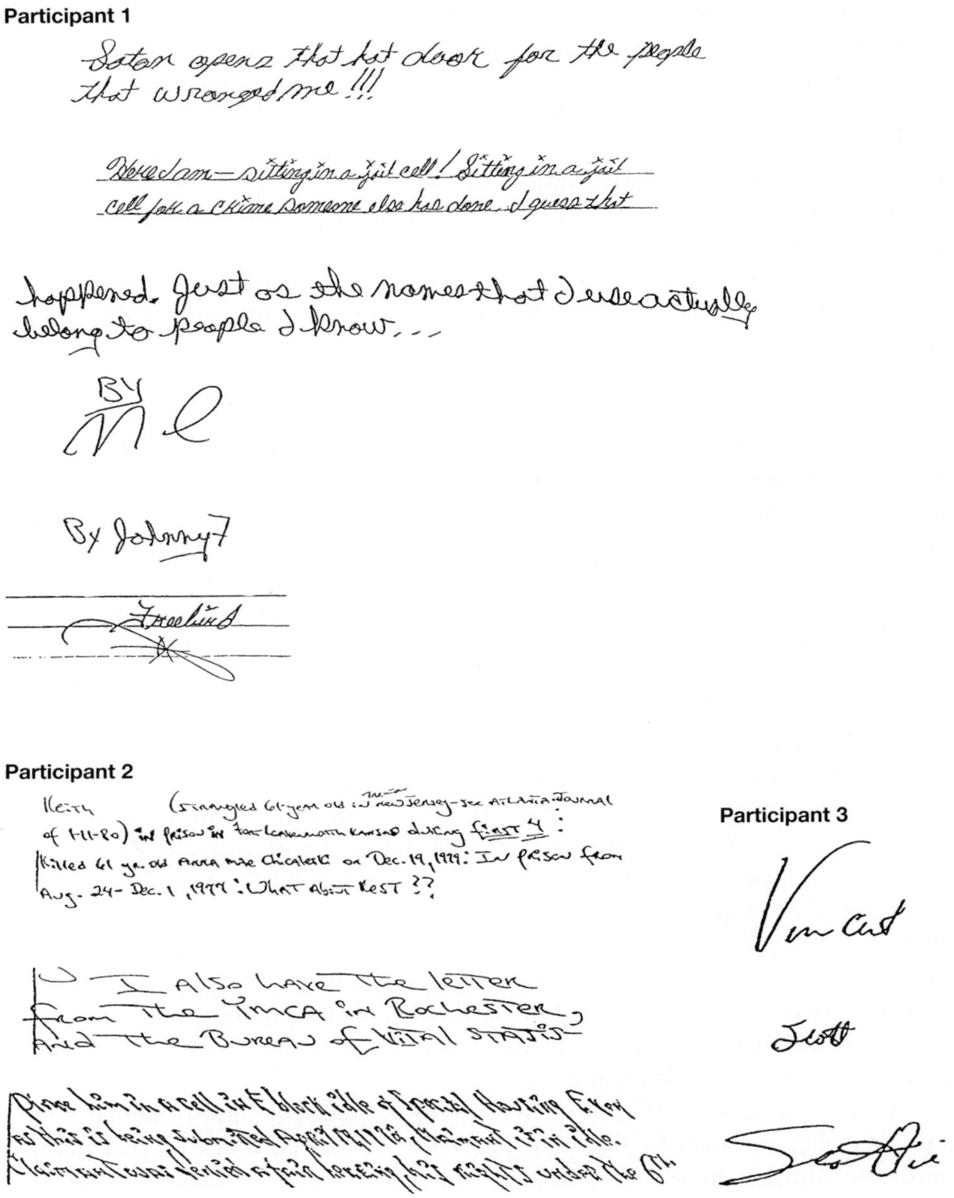

FIGURE 14.22 Handwriting Samples of Three People Diagnosed with Dissociative Identity Disorder When researchers studied 12 murderers diagnosed with DID, writing samples from 10 of the participants revealed markedly different handwriting in each of their identities. Here handwriting samples from three of the participants show different identities expressing themselves.

Participant 1

Participant 2

Participant 3

Despite this evidence, many researchers remain skeptical about whether DID is a genuine mental disorder or whether it exists at all (Kihlstrom, 2005). Moreover, some people may have ulterior motives for claiming DID. A diagnosis of DID often occurs after someone has been accused of committing a crime. This timing raises the possibility that people are pretending to have multiple identities to avoid conviction. Other skeptics point to the sharp rise in reported cases as evidence that the disorder might not be real or that it is diagnosed far too often.

Before the 1980s, this disorder was reported only sporadically. Famous cases include the women portrayed in the 1957 movie *The Three Faces of Eve* (Thigpen & Cleckley, 1954) and the 1976 movie *Sybil* (Schreiber, 1974). In the 1990s, the number of cases skyrocketed into the tens of thousands, particularly in the United States. Moreover, those displaying the disorder went from having two or three identities to having several dozen or even hundreds. What can explain these changes? Some of these patients may have developed DID after seeing therapists who believed strongly in the disorder. Indeed, in most cases, those diagnosed as having DID were unaware of their other identities until after many therapy sessions. The 1980s and 1990s saw a surge of therapists who believed that childhood trauma frequently was repressed and that it needed to be uncovered during treatment. These therapists tended to use hypnosis, and they might have suggested DID symptoms to the patients they were assessing while the patients were hypnotized.

Independent reports have verified, however, that at least some patients with DID were abused. Physical or sexual abuse can cause psychological problems, including distortions of consciousness. Ultimately, how can we know whether a diagnosis of DID is valid? As mentioned earlier, most often there is no objective, definitive test for diagnosing a mental disorder. It can be difficult to tell if a person is faking, has come to believe what a therapist said, or has a genuine mental disorder.

Summing Up

What Are Dissociative Disorders?

Dissociative disorders involve disruptions of identity, of memory, or of conscious awareness. Dissociative amnesia involves forgetting that an event happened or losing awareness of a substantial block of time. Dissociative fugue involves a loss of identity. Dissociative identity disorder involves the occurrence of two or more distinct identities in the same individual. Dissociative identity disorder is believed to emerge as a consequence of severe abuse—through repeated dissociation, different identities develop to cope with different traumas. Dissociative identity disorder remains a controversial diagnosis for two reasons: The condition is often diagnosed after someone has been accused of a crime, and a sharp rise in reported cases has occurred in recent years.

Measuring Up

1. Which of the following statements about fugue are true?
   a. It is a form of dissociative amnesia.
   b. It involves a loss of identity.
   c. It is also referred to as dissociative identity disorder.
   d. It may occur as a result of alcohol or drug abuse.
   e. It occurs concurrently with posttraumatic stress disorder.

2. Some researchers are skeptical about the validity of dissociative identity disorder because _____.
   a. its rates have dropped sharply in recent years
   b. it is often diagnosed after an individual has been accused of a crime
   c. those diagnosed with dissociative identity disorder are often unaware of their condition
   d. dissociative identity disorder often occurs with other mental disorders

Answers: 1. a. It is a form of dissociative amnesia.; b. It involves a loss of identity.
2. b. It is often diagnosed after an individual has been accused of a crime.

schizophrenia A psychological disorder characterized by a split between thought and emotion; it involves alterations in thoughts, in perceptions, or in consciousness.

positive symptoms Symptoms of schizophrenia that are marked by excesses in functioning, such as delusions, hallucinations, and disorganized speech or behavior.

negative symptoms Symptoms of schizophrenia that are marked by deficits in functioning, such as apathy, lack of emotion, and slowed speech and movement.

14.5 What Is Schizophrenia?

The term *schizophrenia* literally means "splitting of the mind." The psychological disorder **schizophrenia** is characterized by a split between thought and emotion (**Figure 14.23**). In popular culture, schizophrenia is often confused with dissociative identity disorder, or split personality, but the two disorders are unrelated. With DID, the "self" is split. Schizophrenia is a *psychotic disorder,* meaning it involves alterations in thought, in perceptions, or in consciousness. The essence of schizophrenia is a disconnection from reality, which is referred to as *psychosis*.

According to current estimates, between 0.5 percent and 1.0 percent of the population has schizophrenia (Tandon, Keshavan, & Nasrallah, 2008). A meta-analysis of 188 studies from 46 countries found similar rates for men and women, roughly 4 to 7 per 1,000 people (Saha, Chant, Welham, & McGrath, 2006). These researchers also found that the rate of schizophrenia was slightly lower in developing nations. Interestingly, the prognosis is better in developing than in developed cultures (Kulhara & Chakrabarti, 2001). Perhaps there is more tolerance for symptoms or greater sympathy for unusual or different people in developing countries.

Not all cases of schizophrenia are identical, and the disorder has distinct subtypes. Clinicians and researchers rely on lists of symptoms to diagnose these various subtypes of schizophrenia (**Table 14.4**).

Schizophrenia Has Positive and Negative Symptoms

For the victim and for the family, schizophrenia is arguably the most devastating mental disorder. It is characterized by a combination of motor, cognitive, behavioral, and perceptual abnormalities. These abnormalities result in impaired social, personal, or vocational functioning or in some combination of these impairments. Some researchers have grouped these characteristics into two categories: **Positive symptoms** are excesses. They are not positive in the sense of being good or desirable. Instead, they are additional. **Negative symptoms** are deficits in functioning.

FIGURE 14.23 Schizophrenia In the 2001 film *A Beautiful Mind,* Russell Crowe plays the real-life Princeton mathematics professor and Nobel laureate John Forbes Nash. Nash has suffered from schizophrenia.

TABLE 14.4 *DSM-IV-TR* **Subtypes of Schizophrenia**

Subtype	Characteristics
Paranoid type	Preoccupation with delusions or auditory hallucinations; little or no disorganized speech, disorganized or catatonic behavior, or inappropriate or flat affect
Disorganized type	Disorganized speech, disorganized behavior, and inappropriate or flat affect are prominent, but catatonic-type criteria are not met; delusions or hallucinations may be present but only in fragmentary or noncoherent form
Catatonic type	At least two of the following: extreme motor immobility, purposeless excessive motor activity, extreme negativism (motionless resistance to all instructions) or mutism (refusing to speak), peculiar or bizarre voluntary movement, echolalia
Undifferentiated type	Does not fit any of the subtypes above, but meets the symptom criteria for schizophrenia
Residual type	Has experienced at least one episode of schizophrenia, but currently does not have prominent positive symptoms (delusions, hallucinations, disorganized speech or behavior); however, continues to show negative symptoms and a milder variation of positive symptoms (odd beliefs, eccentric behavior)

SOURCE: American Psychiatric Association, 2000a.

POSITIVE SYMPTOMS OF SCHIZOPHRENIA One of the positive (i.e., excessive) symptoms most commonly associated with schizophrenia is **delusions.** Delusions are false beliefs based on incorrect inferences about reality. (Common types of delusions are listed in **Table 14.5.**) Delusional people persist in their beliefs despite evidence that contradicts those beliefs. Although Tony Rosato suffered from Capgras rather than schizophrenia, his belief, discussed in the opening of this chapter, that his wife and child had been replaced by imposters is an example of a delusion. The persistence of this belief in spite of clear evidence to the contrary is a good example of how people with psychological disorders can deny reality because their cognitive processes misinform them about what is real and what is not.

Delusions are characteristic of schizophrenia regardless of the culture, but the type of delusion can be influenced by cultural factors (Tateyama et al., 1993). When the delusions of German and Japanese patients with schizophrenia were compared, the two groups had similar rates of *delusions of grandeur,* believing themselves much more powerful and important than they really were. The two groups differed significantly, however, for other types of delusions. The German patients had delusions that involved guilt and sin, particularly as these concepts related to religion. By contrast, the Japanese patients had *delusions of harassment,* such as the belief that they were being slandered by others. The types of delusions that people with schizophrenia have can also be affected by current events:

> In summer, 1994, mass media in the U.S. reported that North Korea was developing nuclear weapons. At that time, in New York, a middle-age woman with schizophrenia told me that she feared a Korean invasion. In fall, 1995, during a psychiatric interview a young woman with psychotic disorder told me that she had secret connections with the United Nations, the Pope, and O. J. Simpson, and they were helping her. The celebration of the 50th Anniversary of the United Nations, the visit of the Pope to the U.S., and the O. J. Simpson criminal trial were the highly publicized events in the United States at that time. (Sher, 2000, p. 507)

The other positive symptom most commonly associated with schizophrenia is **hallucinations.** Hallucinations are false sensory perceptions that are experienced without an external source. Frequently auditory, they can also be visual, olfactory, or somatosensory:

> I was afraid to go outside and when I looked out of the window, it seemed that everyone outside was yelling, "kill her, kill her.". . . Things continued to get worse. I imagined that I had a foul body odor and I sometimes took up to six showers a day. I recall going to the grocery store one day, and I imagined that the people in the store were saying "Get saved, Jesus is the answer." (O'Neal, 1984, pp. 109–110)

Auditory hallucinations are often accusatory voices. These voices may tell the person with schizophrenia that he or she is evil or inept, or they may command the person to do dangerous things. Sometimes the person hears a cacophony of sounds with voices intermingled.

The cause of hallucinations remains unclear. Neuroimaging studies suggest, however, that hallucinations are associated with activation in areas of the cortex that process external sensory stimuli. For example, auditory hallucinations accompany increased activation in brain areas that are activated in normal subjects when they engage in inner speech (Stein & Richardson, 1999). This finding has led to speculation that auditory hallucinations might be caused by a difficulty in distinguishing normal inner speech (i.e., the type we all engage in) from external sounds. People with schizophrenia need to learn to ignore the voices in their heads, but doing so is extremely difficult and sometimes impossible.

TABLE 14.5	Delusions and Associated Beliefs
Persecution	Belief that others are persecuting, spying on, or trying to harm them
Reference	Belief that objects, events, or other people have particular significance to them
Grandeur	Belief that they have great power, knowledge, or talent
Identity	Belief that they are someone else, such as Jesus Christ or the president of the United States
Guilt	Belief that they have committed a terrible sin
Control	Belief that their thoughts and behaviors are being controlled by external forces

delusions False beliefs based on incorrect inferences about reality.

hallucinations False sensory perceptions that are experienced without an external source.

Loosening of associations is another characteristic associated with schizophrenia. Here the individual shifts between seemingly unrelated topics as he or she speaks, making it difficult or impossible for a listener to follow the speaker's train of thought:

> They're destroying too many cattle and oil just to make soap. If we need soap when you can jump into a pool of water, and then when you go to buy your gasoline, my folks always thought they could get pop, but the best thing to get is motor oil, and money. May as well go there and trade in some pop caps and, uh, tires, and tractors to car garages, so they can pull cars away from wrecks, is what I believed in. (Andreasen, 1984, p. 115)

More-extreme cases involve *clang associations:* the stringing together of words that rhyme but have no other apparent link. Such strange speaking patterns make it very difficult for people with schizophrenia to communicate (Docherty, 2005).

Another common symptom of schizophrenia is **disorganized behavior.** People exhibiting this symptom might wear multiple layers of clothing even on hot summer days, walk along muttering to themselves, alternate between anger and laughter, or pace and wring their hands as if extremely worried.

People who have *catatonic schizophrenia* might mindlessly repeat words they hear, a behavior called *echolalia.* They might remain immobilized in one position for hours, with a rigid, masklike facial expression and their eyes staring into the distance. Catatonic behavior may be an extreme fear response, akin to how animals respond to sudden dangers—the person is literally "scared stiff" (Moskowitz, 2004).

NEGATIVE SYMPTOMS OF SCHIZOPHRENIA A number of behavioral deficits associated with schizophrenia result in patients' becoming isolated and withdrawn. People with schizophrenia often avoid eye contact and seem apathetic. They do not express emotion even when discussing emotional subjects. Their speech is slowed, they say less than normal, and they use a monotonous tone of voice. Their speech may be characterized by long pauses before answering, failure to respond to a question, or inability to complete an utterance after initiating it. There is often a similar reduction in overt behavior: Patients' movements may be slowed and their overall amount of movement reduced, with little initiation of behavior and no interest in social participation. These symptoms, though less dramatic than delusions and hallucinations, can be equally serious. Negative symptoms are more common in men than in women (Raesaenen, Pakaslahti, Syvaelahti, Jones, & Isohanni, 2000). They are associated with a poorer prognosis.

Although the positive symptoms of schizophrenia can be dramatically reduced or eliminated with antipsychotic medications, the negative symptoms often persist. Because negative symptoms are more resistant to medications, researchers have speculated that positive and negative symptoms have different organic causes. Since positive symptoms respond to a class of medications (known as *antipsychotics*) that act on neurotransmitter systems, these symptoms are thought to result from neurotransmitter dysfunction. In contrast, negative symptoms may be associated with abnormal brain anatomy, since structural brain deficits are not affected by changes in neurochemistry. The apparent differences in biological causality lead some researchers to believe that schizophrenia with negative symptoms is in fact a separate disorder from schizophrenia with positive symptoms (Messias et al., 2004).

Schizophrenia Is Primarily a Brain Disorder

The etiology of schizophrenia is complex and not well understood. Early theories attributed this disorder to the patients' mothers. According to these theories, the mothers simultaneously accepted and rejected their children. This contradictory behavior caused the children to develop schizophrenia. Schizophrenia runs in families, how-

loosening of associations A speech pattern among some people with schizophrenia in which their thoughts are disorganized or meaningless.

disorganized behavior Acting in strange or unusual ways, including strange movement of limbs, bizarre speech, and inappropriate self-care, such as failing to dress properly or bathe.

ever, and it is clear that genetics plays a role in the development of the disorder (**Figure 14.24**). If one twin develops schizophrenia, the likelihood of the other twin's succumbing is almost 50 percent if the twins are identical but only 14 percent if the twins are fraternal. If one parent has schizophrenia, the risk of a child's developing the disease is 13 percent. If, however, both parents have schizophrenia, the risk jumps to almost 50 percent (Gottesman, 1991). Yet the genetic component of schizophrenia represents a predisposition rather than destiny. If schizophrenia were caused solely by genetics, concordance in identical twins would approach 100 percent.

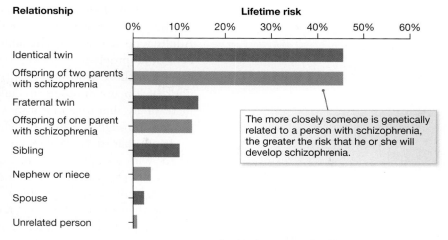

FIGURE 14.24 Genetics and Schizophrenia

People with schizophrenia have rare mutations of their DNA about three to four times more often than healthy individuals do, especially in genes related to brain development and to neurological function (Walsh et al., 2008). These mutations may result in abnormal brain development, which might lead to schizophrenia. No single gene causes schizophrenia. Instead, it is likely that multiple genes contribute in subtle ways to the expression of the disorder. Each of at least two dozen candidate genes might modestly influence the development of schizophrenia (Gottesman & Hanson, 2005).

Schizophrenia is primarily a brain disorder (Walker, Kestler, Bollini, & Hochman, 2004). As seen in imaging that shows the structure of the brain, the ventricles are enlarged in people with schizophrenia (see Figure 14.8). In other words, actual brain tissue is reduced. Moreover, greater reductions in brain tissue are associated with more negative outcomes (Mitelman, Shihabuddin, Brickman, Hazlett, & Buchsbaum, 2005), and longitudinal studies show continued reductions over time (Ho et al., 2003; van Haren et al., 2011). This reduction of tissue occurs in many regions of the brain, especially the frontal lobes and medial temporal lobes. In addition, as seen in imaging that shows the functioning of the brain, activity is typically reduced in the frontal and temporal regions in people with schizophrenia (Barch, Sheline, Csernansky, & Snyder, 2003). Given that abnormalities occur throughout many brain regions in people with schizophrenia, some researchers have speculated that schizophrenia is more likely a problem of connection between brain regions than the result of diminished or changed functions of any particular brain region (Walker et al., 2004).

One possibility is that schizophrenia results from abnormality in neurotransmitters. Since the 1950s, scientists have believed that dopamine may play an important role. Drugs that block dopamine activity decrease symptoms, whereas drugs that increase the activity of dopamine neurons increase symptoms. There is now also evidence that a number of other neurotransmitter systems are involved. More recently, researchers have suggested that schizophrenia might involve abnormalities in the glial cells that make up the myelin sheath (Davis et al., 2003; Moises & Gottesman, 2004). Such abnormalities would impair neurotransmission throughout the brain.

If schizophrenia is a brain disorder, when do these brain abnormalities emerge? Because schizophrenia is most often diagnosed when people are in their 20s or 30s, it is hard to assess whether brain impairments occur earlier in life. There is evidence that some neurological signs of schizophrenia can be observed long before the disorder is diagnosed. Elaine Walker and colleagues (2004) have analyzed home movies taken by parents whose children later developed schizophrenia. Compared with their siblings, those who developed the disorder displayed unusual social behaviors, more-severe negative emotions, and motor disturbances. All of these differences often went unnoticed during the children's early years.

One study followed a group of children at risk for developing psychopathology because their parents suffered from a mental disorder (Amminger et al., 1999). Adults who developed schizophrenia were much more likely to have displayed behavioral problems as children—such as fighting or not getting along with others—than those who developed mood disorders or drug abuse problems or did not develop any disorders in adulthood. Children at risk for schizophrenia display increasingly abnormal motor movements, such as strange facial expressions, as they progress through adolescence (Mittal, Neumann, Saczawa, & Walker, 2008).

In another study, Walker and colleagues followed a group of children, ages 11 to 13, with a high genetic risk of schizophrenia (Schiffman et al., 2004). These children were videotaped eating lunch in 1972. Those who later developed schizophrenia showed greater impairments in social behavior and motor functioning than those who developed other mental disorders or those who developed no problems. Another team of researchers followed 291 high-risk youths (average age 16) over 2.5 years (Cannon et al., 2008). These psychologists determined that five factors predicted the onset of psychotic disorders: a family history of schizophrenia, greater social impairment, higher levels of suspicion/paranoia, a history of substance abuse, and higher levels of unusual thoughts. When youths had two or three of the first three factors, nearly 80 percent of them developed full-blown psychosis. Studies such as these suggest that schizophrenia develops over the life course but that obvious symptoms often emerge by late adolescence. Hints of future problems may even be evident in young children.

Environmental Factors Influence Schizophrenia

Since genetics does not account fully for the onset and severity of schizophrenia, other factors must also be at work. In those at risk for schizophrenia, environmental stress seems to contribute to its development (Walker et al., 2004). One study looked at adopted children whose biological mothers were diagnosed with schizophrenia (Tienari et al., 1990, 1994). If the adoptive families were psychologically healthy, none of the children became psychotic. If the adoptive families were severely disturbed, 11 percent of the children became psychotic and 41 percent had severe psychological disorders. More generally, growing up in a dysfunctional family may increase the risk of developing schizophrenia for those who are genetically at risk (Tienari et al., 2004; **Figure 14.25**).

Some researchers have theorized that the increased stress of urban environments can trigger the onset of the disorder, since being born or raised in an urban area approximately doubles the risk of developing schizophrenia later in life (Torrey, 1999). Others have speculated that some kind of *schizovirus* exists. If so, the close quarters of a big city increases the likelihood of the virus spreading. In support of the virus hypothesis, some researchers have reported finding antibodies in the blood of people with schizophrenia that are not found in those without the disorder (Waltrip et al., 1997). Moreover, people with schizophrenia are more likely to have been born during late winter and early spring (Mednick, Huttunen, & Machon, 1994; Torrey, Torrey, & Peterson, 1977). Consider that mothers of children born in late winter and early spring were in their second trimester of pregnancy during flu season. Retrospective studies suggest that the mothers of people with schizophrenia are more likely than other mothers to have contracted influenza during this critical period (Limosin, Rouillon, Payan, Cohen, & Strub, 2003; Mednick et al., 1994). During the second trimester, a great deal of fetal brain development occurs. At that time, trauma or pathogens can interfere with the organization of brain regions.

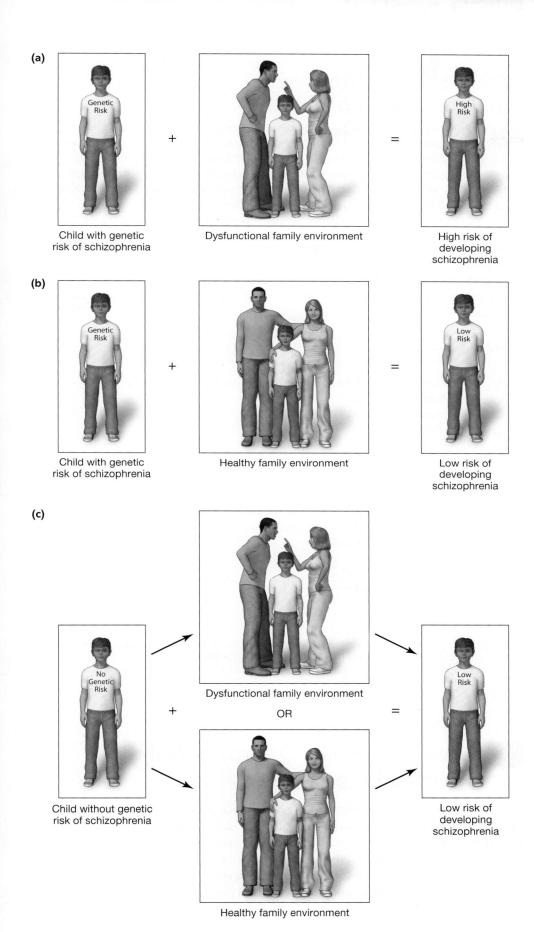

(a)

Child with genetic
risk of schizophrenia

+

Dysfunctional family environment

=

High risk of
developing
schizophrenia

(b)

Child with genetic
risk of schizophrenia

+

Healthy family environment

=

Low risk of
developing
schizophrenia

(c)

Child without genetic
risk of schizophrenia

+

Dysfunctional family environment

OR

Healthy family environment

=

Low risk of
developing
schizophrenia

FIGURE 14.25 Dysfunctional Environment and Schizophrenia **(a)** If a child has a genetic risk for schizophrenia and is raised in a dysfunctional family environment, that child will have a high risk of developing schizophrenia. **(b)** By contrast, if the child has a genetic risk for schizophrenia but is raised in a healthy family environment, that child will have a low risk of developing the disorder. **(c)** Finally, if the child has *no* genetic risk of developing schizophrenia, the child will have a low risk of developing the disorder whether the child is raised in a dysfunctional family environment or a healthy family environment.

What Is Schizophrenia?

Schizophrenia is characterized by a split between thought and emotion. The positive symptoms associated with schizophrenia reflect excesses. These symptoms include delusions, hallucinations, and disorganized speech. The negative symptoms of schizophrenia reflect deficits. These symptoms include apathy, lack of emotion, and slowed speech. Research suggests that schizophrenia is largely a biological disorder. Twin, adoption, and family studies have highlighted the critical role of genetics in the development of schizophrenia, and recent advances in genetic analysis have indicated that multiple genes may contribute to this disorder. In addition, research has shown that schizophrenia is associated with abnormalities in brain anatomy and neurotransmitters. In addition to the biological factors that contribute to schizophrenia, most researchers agree that environmental factors play a role. In particular, environmental stressors such as dysfunctional family dynamics, urban stress, and exposure to pathogens may contribute to the genesis of schizophrenia.

Measuring Up

1. Indicate whether each of the following phenomena is a negative or a positive symptom of schizophrenia.
   a. social withdrawal
   b. flat affect
   c. delusions
   d. hallucinations
   e. slowed motor movement
   f. loosening of associations

2. Indicate whether each of the following phenomena is a biological or an environmental factor contributing to schizophrenia.
   a. abnormalities in brain function
   b. abnormalities in brain structure
   c. family members' mental health
   d. hereditary predisposition
   e. stress

Answers: 1. a. negative; b. negative; c. positive; d. positive; e. negative; f. positive. 2. a. biological; b. biological; c. environmental; d. biological; e. environmental.

14.6 Are Personality Disorders Truly Mental Disorders?

As discussed in Chapter 13, personality reflects each person's unique response to his or her environment. Although individuals change somewhat over time, the ways they interact with the world and cope with events are fairly fixed by the end of adolescence. For example, some people interact with the world in maladaptive and inflexible ways. When this style of interaction is long-lasting and causes problems in work and in social situations, it becomes a *personality disorder*.

All of us are likely to exhibit symptoms of personality disorders. At times we might be indecisive, self-absorbed, or emotionally unstable. In fact, true personality disorders are relatively common, affecting just under 1 in 10 people (Lenzenweger, Lane, Loranger, & Kessler, 2007). People with personality disorders consistently behave in maladaptive ways, show a more extreme level of maladaptive behavior, and experience more personal distress and more problems as a result of their behavior.

Personality Disorders Are Maladaptive Ways of Relating to the World

The other disorders discussed in this chapter are classified on Axis I of Table 14.1. Personality disorders are classified on Axis II, along with mental retardation. Personality disorders and mental retardation are grouped together because they usually last throughout the life span, with no expectation of significant change.

Personality disorders generally are divided into three groups, as listed in **Table 14.6.** Disorders in the first group are characterized by odd or eccentric behavior. *Paranoid, schizoid,* and *schizotypal* personality disorders make up this group. People with these disorders are often reclusive and suspicious, and they have difficulty

---

TABLE 14.6 Personality Disorders and Associated Characteristics

Odd or Eccentric Behavior

Paranoid	Tense, guarded, suspicious; holds grudges
Schizoid	Socially isolated, with restricted emotional expression
Schizotypal	Peculiarities of thought, appearance, and behavior that are disconcerting to others; emotionally detached and isolated

Anxious or Fearful Behavior

Avoidant	Easily hurt and embarrassed; few close friends; sticks to routines to avoid new and possibly stressful experiences
Dependent	Wants others to make decisions; needs constant advice and reassurance; fears being abandoned
Obsessive-compulsive	Perfectionistic; overconscientious; indecisive; preoccupied with details; stiff; unable to express affection

Dramatic, Emotional, or Erratic Behavior

Histrionic	Seductive behavior; needs immediate gratification and constant reassurance; rapidly changing moods; shallow emotions
Narcissistic	Self-absorbed; expects special treatment and adulation; envious of attention to others
Borderline	Cannot stand to be alone; intense, unstable moods and personal relationships; chronic anger; drug and alcohol abuse
Antisocial	Manipulative, exploitative; dishonest; disloyal; lacking in guilt; habitually breaks social rules; childhood history of such behavior; often in trouble with the law

SOURCE: Adapted from American Psychiatric Association, 2000a.

forming personal relationships because of their strange behavior and aloofness. As you might expect, people with personality disorders in this category show some similarities to people with schizophrenia, but their symptoms are far less severe.

Disorders in the second group are characterized by anxious or fearful behavior. *Avoidant, dependent,* and *obsessive-compulsive* personality disorders make up this group. These disorders share some characteristics of anxiety disorders such as social phobia or generalized anxiety disorder. However, the personality disorders in this second group are different from anxiety disorders in that they refer more to general ways of interacting with others and of responding to events. For instance, a person with an obsessive-compulsive personality disorder may be excessively neat and orderly. The person might always eat the same food at precisely the same time or perhaps read a newspaper in a particular order each time. This pattern becomes problematic only when it interferes with the person's life, as in making it impossible to travel or to maintain relationships.

Disorders in the third group are characterized by dramatic, emotional, or erratic behaviors. *Histrionic, narcissistic, borderline,* and *antisocial* personality disorders make up this group. Borderline and antisocial personality disorders have been the focus of much research, and they are considered in more detail in the following sections.

In modern clinical practice, personality disorders are controversial for several reasons. First, personality disorders appear to be extreme versions of normal personality traits, demonstrating the continuum between what is considered normal versus abnormal. For example, indecisiveness is characteristic of obsessive-compulsive personality disorder, but the *DSM* does not define the degree to which someone must be indecisive to be diagnosed as obsessive-compulsive. Second, there is overlap among the traits listed as characteristic of different personality disorders, so the majority of people diagnosed with one personality disorder also meet the criteria for another (Clark, 2007). This overlap suggests that the categories may not be mutually exclusive and that fewer types of personality disorders may exist than are listed in the *DSM.* Also, some aspects of personality disorders are less stable over time than has been assumed. For this reason, the personality disorders section in *DSM-V* will reflect a substantial revision. It is likely that there will be a reduction in the number of categories and an increased focus on the degree of impairment in personal functioning.

Personality disorders may not seem to affect daily life as much as do some of the Axis I disorders (clinical diagnoses) discussed in this chapter, such as schizophrenia or bipolar disorder. Although people with personality disorders do not hallucinate or experience radical mood swings, however, their ways of interacting with the world can have serious consequences. The following in-depth consideration of borderline personality disorder and antisocial personality disorder illustrates the devastating effect of these disorders on the individual, family and friends, and society.

Borderline Personality Disorder Is Associated with Poor Self-Control

Borderline personality disorder is characterized by disturbances in identity, in affect, and in impulse control. This disorder was officially recognized as a diagnosis in 1980. The term *borderline* was initially used because these patients were considered on the border between normal and psychotic (Knight, 1953). As presented in **Table 14.7,** the wide variety of clinical features of this disorder reflects its

borderline personality disorder A personality disorder characterized by disturbances in identity, in affect, and in impulse control.

TABLE 14.7 Clinical Features of Borderline Personality Disorder

A person having at least five of these characteristics might be considered to have borderline personality disorder.

1. Employment of frantic efforts to avoid real or imagined abandonment

2. Unstable and intense interpersonal relationships

3. Persistent and markedly disturbed, distorted, or unstable sense of self (e.g., a feeling that one doesn't exist or that one embodies evil)

4. Impulsiveness in such areas as sex, substance abuse, crime, and reckless driving

5. Recurrent suicidal thoughts, gestures, or behavior

6. Emotional instability, with periods of extreme depression, irritability, or anxiety

7. Chronic feelings of emptiness

8. Inappropriate intense anger or lack of control of anger (e.g., loss of temper, recurrent physical fights)

9. Transient, stress-related paranoid thoughts or severe dissociative symptoms

SOURCE: American Psychiatric Association, 2000a.

complexity. Approximately 1 percent to 2 percent of adults meet the criteria for borderline personality disorder, and the disorder is more than twice as common in women as in men (Lenzenweger et al., 2007; Swartz, Blazer, George, & Winfield, 1990; Torgerson, Kringlen, & Cramer, 2001).

People with borderline personality disorder seem to lack a strong sense of self. They cannot tolerate being alone and have an intense fear of abandonment. Because they desperately need an exclusive and dependent relationship with another person, they can be very manipulative in their attempts to control relationships, as shown in the following example:

> A borderline patient periodically rented a motel room and, with a stockpile of pills nearby, would call her therapist's home with an urgent message. He would respond by engaging in long conversations in which he "talked her down." Even as he told her that she could not count on his always being available, he became more wary of going out evenings without detailed instructions about how he could be reached. One night the patient couldn't reach him due to a bad phone connection. She fatally overdosed from what was probably a miscalculated manipulation. (Gunderson, 1984, p. 93)

In addition to problems with identity, borderline individuals have affective disturbances. Emotional instability is paramount. Episodes of depression, anxiety, anger, irritability, or some combination of these states can last from a few hours to a few days. Shifts from one mood to another usually occur with no obvious precipitating cause. Consider the therapist Molly Layton's description of her patient Vicki:

> She had chronic and debilitating feelings of emptiness and paralyzing numbness, during which she could only crawl under the covers of her bed and hide. On these days, she was sometimes driven to mutilate her thighs with scissors. Although highly accomplished as a medical student and researcher, who had garnered many grants and fellowships, she would sometimes panic and shut down in the middle of a project, creating unbearable pressures on herself to finish the work. While she longed for intimacy and friendship, she was disablingly shy around men. (Layton, 1995, p. 36)

The third hallmark of borderline personality disorder is impulsivity, which may explain the much higher rate of the disorder in prison populations (Conn et al., 2010). This characteristic can include sexual promiscuity, physical fighting, and binge eating and purging. As was the case with Vicki, however, self-mutilation is most commonly associated with this disorder. Cutting and burning of the skin are typical, as well as a high risk for suicide. Some evidence indicates that those with borderline personality disorder have diminished capacity in the frontal lobes, which normally help control behavior (Silbersweig et al., 2007).

In addition, patients with borderline personality disorder often show sleep abnormalities characteristic of depression. One possible reason that borderline personality disorder and affective disorders such as depression may be linked is that both appear to involve the neurotransmitter serotonin. Evidence has linked low serotonin levels to the impulsive behavior seen in borderline personality disorder (Skodol et al., 2002).

Borderline personality disorder may also have an environmental component, as a strong relationship exists between the disorder and trauma or abuse (Lieb, Zanarini, Schmahl, Linehan, & Bohus, 2004). Some studies have reported that 70 percent to 80 percent of patients with borderline personality disorder have experienced physical or sexual abuse or observed some kind of extreme violence. Other theories implicate early interactions with caretakers. Borderline patients may have had caretakers who did not accept them or were unreliable or unavailable. The constant rejection and criticism made it difficult for the individuals to learn to regulate emotions and understand emotional reactions to events (Linehan, 1987). An alternative theory is that caregivers encouraged dependence, preventing each of the individuals in their charge from adequately developing a sense of self. As a result, the individuals became overly sensitive to others' reactions: If rejected by others, they reject themselves.

Antisocial Personality Disorder Is Associated with a Lack of Empathy

In the 1800s, the term *psychopath* was coined to describe people who seem willing to take advantage of and to hurt others without any evidence of concern or of remorse (Koch, 1891). In his classic book *The Mask of Sanity* (1941), the psychiatrist Hervey Cleckley described characteristics of psychopaths from his clinical experience. For example, such individuals could be superficially charming and rational; be insincere, unsocial, and incapable of love; lack insight; and be shameless. In 1980, the *DSM* dropped the label *psychopath,* which was seen as pejorative, and adopted the term **antisocial personality disorder (APD).** This change has led to confusion because *psychopath* is still widely used to refer to a related but not identical type of personality disorder as defined by the *DSM*. There are plans to reconcile the two terms in the *DSM-V*.

APD is the catchall diagnosis for individuals who behave in socially undesirable ways, such as breaking the law, being deceitful and irresponsible, and feeling a lack of remorse for their behavior. People with this disorder tend to be hedonistic, seeking immediate gratification of wants and needs without any thought of others. Note that all criminals do not fall into this category.

Psychopaths display more extreme behaviors than those with APD. They also tend to have other personality characteristics not found in those with APD, such as glibness, a grandiose sense of self-worth, shallow affect, and cunning/manipulativeness. They are pathological in their degree of callousness and are particularly dangerous. For instance, one study of murderers found that those

antisocial personality disorder (APD)
A personality disorder marked by a lack of empathy and remorse.

with psychopathic tendencies nearly always kill intentionally. They want to gain something, such as money, sex, or drugs. People without psychopathic tendencies are much more likely to commit murder impulsively, when provoked or angry (Woodworth & Porter, 2002). Psychopaths fit the stereotype of cold-blooded killers. Infamous examples include Dennis Rader (the BTK strangler) and Gary Gilmore (**Figure 14.26**). In 1977, Gilmore was executed for the murder he describes here:

> I went in and told the guy to give me the money. I told him to lay on the floor and then I shot him. I then walked out and was carrying the cash drawer with me. I took the money and threw the cash drawer in a bush and I tried to push the gun in the bush, too. But as I was pushing it in the bush, it went off and that's how come I was shot in the arm. It seems like things have always gone bad for me. It seems like I've always done dumb things that just caused trouble for me. I remember when I was a boy I would feel like I had to do things like sit on a railroad track until just before the train came and then I would dash off. Or I would put my finger over the end of a BB gun and pull the trigger to see if a BB was really in it. Sometimes I would stick my finger in water and then put my finger in a light socket to see if it would really shock me. (Spitzer et al., 1983, pp. 66–68)

ASSESSMENT AND CONSEQUENCES It is estimated that between 1 percent and 4 percent of the population has antisocial personality disorder (Compton, Conway, Stinson, Colliver, & Grant, 2005). People with this condition who also show more-extreme psychopathic traits are less common (Lenzenwegger et al., 2007). It is much more common in men than in women (Robins & Regier, 1991).

Much of what psychologists know about the traits associated with antisocial personality disorder was discovered by the psychologist Robert Hare (1993). Hare also developed many of the assessment tools to identify people with psychopathic tendencies. He and colleagues have shown that the disorder is most apparent in late adolescence and early adulthood, and it generally improves around age 40 (Hare, McPherson, & Forth, 1988), at least for those without psychopathic traits. According to the diagnostic criteria, APD cannot be diagnosed before age 18, but the person must have displayed antisocial conduct before age 15. This stipulation ensures that only those with a lifetime history of antisocial behaviors can be diagnosed with antisocial personality disorder. They also must meet other criteria, such as repeatedly performing illegal acts, repeatedly lying or using aliases, and showing reckless disregard for their own safety or the safety of others. Because many such individuals are quite bright and highly verbal, they can talk their way out of bad situations. In any event, punishment seems to have very little effect on them (Lykken, 1957, 1995), and they often repeat the problem behaviors a short time later.

Perhaps as much as 50 percent of the prison population meets the criteria for antisocial personality disorder (Hare, 1993; Widiger & Corbitt, 1995). Because of the prevalence of the disorder in the prison population, much of the research on antisocial personality disorder has been conducted in this setting. One researcher, however, came up with an ingenious way of finding research participants outside of prison. She put the following advertisement in a counterculture newspaper: "Wanted: charming, aggressive, carefree people who are impulsively irresponsible but are good at handling people and at looking after number one. Send name, address, phone, and short biography proving how interesting you are to . . ." (Widom, 1978, p. 72). Seventy-three people responded, and about one-third of them met the criteria for antisocial

FIGURE 14.26 Gary Gilmore after His Arrest Under the *DSM-IV-TR*, Gilmore would have been given a diagnosis of antisocial personality disorder. He also showed psychopathic traits.

FIGURE 14.27 American Psychopath In the 2000 movie *American Psycho,* Christian Bale plays Patrick Bateman, who appears to be a suave man-about-town, a successful professional, and a serial killer. The movie, like the Bret Easton Ellis novel it is based on, raises questions about the connections between a slick presentation of self, a knack for making and spending money, and psychopathy.

personality disorder. These individuals were then interviewed and given a battery of psychological tests. Their characteristics proved very similar to those of prisoners diagnosed with antisocial personality disorder, except that the group that responded to the ad had avoided imprisonment. Indeed, these findings fit Cleckly's view of people with psychopathic traits as often being charming and intelligent. Lacking remorse, willing to lie or cheat, and lacking empathy, some psychopaths manage to be successful professionals and to elude detection for crimes they may commit. Their psychopathic traits may even provide advantages in some occupations, such as business and politics (**Figure 14.27**).

THE ETIOLOGY OF ANTISOCIAL PERSONALITY DISORDER Various physiological abnormalities may play a role in antisocial personality disorder. In 1957, David Lykken reported that psychopaths do not become anxious when they are subjected to aversive stimuli. He and other investigators have continued this line of work, showing that such individuals do not seem to feel fear or anxiety (Lykken, 1995).

Electroencephalogram (EEG) examinations have demonstrated that criminals who meet the criteria for antisocial personality disorder have slower alpha-wave activity (Raine, 1989). This finding indicates a lower overall level of arousal. It is possible that low arousal prompts people with APD to engage in sensation-seeking behavior. In addition, because of low arousal, these individuals do not learn from punishment because they do not experience punishment as particularly aversive. This pattern of reduced psychophysiological response in the face of punishment also occurs in adolescents at risk for developing psychopathy (Fung et al., 2005).

There is also evidence of amygdala abnormalities in those with antisocial tendencies, such as having a smaller amygdala and being less responsive to negative stimuli (Blair, 2003; Marsh et al., 2011). Deficits in frontal lobe functioning have also been found and may account for the lack of forethought and the inability to consider the implications of actions, both characteristic of antisocial personality disorder (Seguin, 2004).

Genetic and environmental factors appear to play roles in antisocial personality disorder. Genetics may be more important for psychopathy, however. Identical twins have a higher concordance of criminal behavior than do fraternal twins (Lykken, 1995), although the research just cited did not rule out the role of a shared environment. A study of 14,000 adoptions found that adopted male children have a higher rate of crime if their biological fathers have criminal records (Mednick, Gabrielli, & Hutchings, 1987). In addition, the greater the criminal record of the biological father, the more likely it is that the adopted son will engage in criminal behavior.

Although genes may be at the root of antisocial behaviors and psychopathy, factors such as low socioeconomic status, dysfunctional families, and childhood abuse may also be important. Indeed, malnutrition at age 3 has been found to predict antisocial behavior at age 17 (Liu, Raine, Venables, & Mednick, 2004). An enrichment program for children that included a structured nutrition component was associated with less criminal and antisocial behavior 20 years later (Raine, Mellingen, Liu, Venables, & Mednick, 2003). This finding raises the possibility that malnutrition or other, similar environmental factors might contribute to the development of antisocial personality disorder.

Are Personality Disorders Truly Mental Disorders?

Personality disorders are diagnosed along Axis II of the *DSM*. Personality disorders are distinct from Axis I disorders—that is, major clinical disorders—in that they persist across the life span with no expectation of significant change. Ten personality disorders, clustered in three groups, are identified in the *DSM:* paranoid, schizoid, schizotypal, avoidant, dependent, obsessive-compulsive, histrionic, narcissistic, borderline, and antisocial. Borderline personality disorder is characterized by disturbances in identity, in affect, and in impulse control. Research has shown that people with this disorder often have diminished frontal lobe capacity, low levels of serotonin, and a history of abuse or rejection by caregivers. Those with antisocial personality disorder engage in socially undesirable behavior, are hedonistic and impulsive, and lack empathy for others. This disorder is associated with lower levels of arousal, a smaller amygdala, and deficits in frontal lobe functioning. Twin and adoption studies suggest that genes play a role in antisocial personality disorder. However, environmental factors (such as low socioeconomic status, dysfunctional families, abuse, and malnutrition) also contribute to the development of this disorder.

The DSM-IV-TR groups together seemingly different disorders—such as borderline personality disorder, antisocial personality disorder, and mental retardation. What features of these disorders justify this grouping? Check all that apply.

   a. They last throughout the life span.
   b. They likely will change with appropriate intervention.
   c. There is no expectation of significant change.
   d. These are all clinical disorders.

Answers: a. They last throughout the life span. c. There is no expectation of significant change.

14.7 Should Childhood Disorders Be Considered a Unique Category?

In his classic text on the classification of mental disorders, published in 1883, Emil Kraepelin did not mention childhood disorders. The first edition of the *DSM,* published 70 years later, essentially considered children small versions of adults. Consequently, the manual did not consider childhood disorders separately from adulthood disorders. The current version of the manual responds to the belief that cognitive, emotional, and social abilities should be considered in the context of the individual's developmental state. As a result, the *DSM* has a category in Axis I called "disorders usually first diagnosed in infancy, childhood, or adolescence." This category includes a wide range of disorders. Some of these conditions—such as reading disorders and stuttering—affect only circumscribed

autistic disorder A developmental disorder characterized by deficits in social interaction, by impaired communication, and by restricted interests.

areas of a child's world. Other conditions—such as autistic disorder, attention deficit hyperactivity disorder, and others listed in **Table 14.8**—affect every aspect of a child's life. Some of these disorders, such as autistic disorder, usually do not get better over time. Others, such as attention deficit hyperactivity disorder, usually do improve over time.

All of the disorders in this category should be considered within the context of normal childhood development. Some symptoms of childhood mental disorders are extreme manifestations of normal behavior or are actually normal behaviors for children at an earlier developmental stage. For example, bedwetting is normal for 2-year-olds but not for 10-year-olds. Other behaviors, however, deviate significantly from normal development. Two disorders of childhood, autism and attention deficit hyperactivity, are explored here as illustrations.

Autistic Disorder Involves Social Deficits

Autistic disorder, or autism, is characterized by deficits in social interaction, by impaired communication, and by restricted interests (Volkmar, Chawarska, & Klin, 2005). The disorder was first described in 1943, by the psychiatrist and physician Leo Kanner. Struck by the profound isolation of some children, Kanner coined the term *early infantile autism*.

Approximately 3 to 6 children out of 1,000 show signs of autistic disorder, and males with autism outnumber females with autism 3 to 1 (Muhle, Trentacoste, & Rapin, 2004). From 1991 to 1997, there was a dramatic increase—of

TABLE 14.8 Childhood Disorders	
Disorder	**Description**
Attention deficit hyperactivity disorder	A pattern of hyperactive, inattentive, and impulsive behavior that causes social or academic impairment
Autistic disorder	Characterized by unresponsiveness; impaired language, social, and cognitive development; and restricted and repetitive behavior
Elimination disorders	The repeated passing of feces or urination in inappropriate places by children from whom continence should be expected
Learning disorders	Marked by substantially low performance in reading, mathematics, or written expression with regard to what is expected for age, amount of education, and intelligence
Mental retardation	Characterized by below-average intellectual functioning (IQ lower than 70) and limited adaptive functioning that begins before age 18
Selective mutism	Failure to speak in certain social situations, despite the ability to speak in other situations; interferes with social or academic achievement
Tourette's disorder	Recurrent motor and vocal tics that cause marked distress or impairment and are not related to a general medical condition

SOURCE: Based on American Psychiatric Association, 2000a.

556 percent—in the number of children diagnosed with autism (Stokstad, 2001). This increase was likely due to a greater awareness of symptoms by parents and physicians and a willingness to apply the diagnosis to a wider spectrum of behaviors (Rutter, 2005). For example, a study of all children born between 1983 and 1999 in Western Australia found that the apparent increase in the diagnosis of autistic disorder was due to changes in how it was diagnosed as well as an increase in funding for psychological services for children showing signs of autism (Nassar et al., 2009). In other words, the notion that autism is epidemic overstates reality. In fact, there are several serious problems with studies that claim huge increases in cases of autism (Gernsbacher, Dawson, & Goldsmith, 2005). Recognizing how changing criteria may alter diagnosis rates underscores the value of critical thinking in understanding important health issues.

Autism varies in severity, from mild social impairments to severe social and intellectual impairments. As a result, some psychologists prefer the term *autism spectrum disorders,* which covers the range of symptoms of autistic disorder. High-functioning autism is called *Asperger's syndrome,* named after the pediatrician who first described it. A child with Asperger's has normal intelligence but deficits in social interaction. These deficits reflect an underdeveloped theory of mind. As discussed in Chapter 9, theory of mind is both the understanding that other people have mental states and the ability to predict their behavior accordingly.

Perhaps the most famous person with Asperger's is Temple Grandin, an accomplished scientist who now designs humane slaughterhouse facilities (Grandin, 1995). Although extremely intelligent, Grandin has great difficulty understanding the subtle social motives and the behaviors of other people, and she finds it easier to relate to nonhuman animals. She understands the environment from an animal's point of view, and this understanding enables her to design facilities that are calming for the animals. The HBO movie *Temple Grandin* (2010) accurately depicted her story.

(a)

CORE SYMPTOMS OF AUTISM Children with severe autism are seemingly unaware of others. As babies, they do not smile at their caregivers, do not respond to vocalizations, and may actively reject physical contact with others. Children with autism do not establish eye contact and do not use their gazes to gain or direct the attention of those around them. One group of researchers had participants view video footage of the first birthdays of children with autism to see if characteristics of autism could be detected before the children were diagnosed (Osterling & Dawson, 1994). By considering only the number of times a child looked at another person's face, the participants correctly classified the children as autistic or normal 77 percent of the time (**Figure 14.28**).

Deficits in communication are the second major cluster of behaviors characteristic of autism. Such deficits are evident by 14 months of age among children who subsequently are diagnosed with autism (Landa, Holman, & Garrett-Mayer, 2007). Children with autism show severe impairments in verbal and nonverbal communication. Even if they vocalize, it is often not with any intent to communicate. Children with autism who develop language usually exhibit odd speech patterns. One such pattern is echolalia, mentioned earlier as a symptom of catatonia. Echolalia involves the mindless repetition of words or phrases that someone else has spoken. The repeater may imitate the first speaker's intonation or may use a high-pitched monotone. Another odd speech pattern is *pronoun reversal,* in which children with autism replace "I" with "you." This pattern may be related to echolalia, but children who do not have autism also reverse pronouns occasionally as they learn language. For example, a preschooler might say "pick you up" when she or

(b)

FIGURE 14.28 Scenes from Videotapes of Children's Birthday Parties (a) This child focused more on objects than on people. The child was later diagnosed with autism. **(b)** This child focused appropriately on objects and on people. The child developed normally.

FIGURE 14.29 Toddler Viewer with Autism As shown in these combined video images from a 1994 study of autism, a 2-year-old with autism will focus on the unimportant details in the scene rather than on the social interaction.

Area focused on by a 2-year-old with autism.

he wants to be picked up. Even if children with autism cease being echolalic, their pronoun confusion often persists beyond the years of basic language learning. Those who develop functional language also often interpret words literally, use language inappropriately, and lack verbal spontaneity.

A third category of deficits includes restricted activities and interests. Children with autism appear oblivious to people around them, but they are acutely aware of their surroundings. Although most children automatically pay attention to the social aspects of a situation, those with autism may focus on seemingly inconsequential details (Klin, Jones, Schultz, & Volkmar, 2003; **Figure 14.29**).

Any changes in daily routine or in the placement of furniture or of toys are very upsetting for children with autism. Once they are upset, the children can become extremely agitated or throw tantrums. In addition, the play of children with autism tends to be repetitive and obsessive, with a focus on objects' sensory aspects. They may smell and taste objects, or they may spin and flick them for visual stimulation. Similarly, their own behavior tends to be repetitive, with strange hand movements, body rocking, and hand flapping. Self-injury is common, and some children must be forcibly restrained to keep them from hurting themselves.

AUTISM IS PRIMARILY A BIOLOGICAL DISORDER Kanner, one of the first scientists to study autism, believed the disorder was innate in some children but exacerbated by cold and unresponsive mothers, whom he called "ice box mothers" or "refrigerator mothers." He described the parents of children with autism as insensitive, meticulous, introverted, and highly intellectual. This view is given little credence today, as it is now well established that autism is the result of biological factors. For example, there is evidence for a genetic component to autistic disorder. A number of studies have found concordance rates in twins to be as high as 90 percent for identical twins and 10 percent for dizygotic twins (Bailey et al., 1995; Hyman, 2008; Steffenburg et al., 1989). These findings should not lead us to overstate the genetic contribution, however. A study using a large sample of twins and more-contemporary diagnostic criteria found somewhat lower concordance rates for identical twins and somewhat higher concordance rates for dizygotic twins (Hallmayer et al., 2011). This finding tells us that although autism is heritable, environmental or other factors are also important.

In addition to autism being heritable, it also appears that gene mutations may play a role. An international study compared 996 children with autism to 1,287 control children and found a number of rare gene abnormalities (Pinto et al., 2010). These rare genetic mutations involve cells having an abnormal number of copies of DNA segments. An independent study of over 1,000 individuals with autism spectrum disorders who had an unaffected sibling found that these gene mutations were much more common in the children with autistic disorder (Levy et al., 2011). The gene mutations may affect the way neural networks are formed during childhood development (Gilman et al., 2011).

Research into the causes of autism also points to prenatal and/or neonatal events that may result in brain dysfunction. The brains of children with autism grow unusually large during the first two years of life, and then growth slows until age 5 (Courchesne et al., 2007; Courchesne, Redcay, & Kennedy, 2004).

The brains of children with autism also do not develop normally during adolescence (Amaral, Schumann, & Nordahl, 2008). Researchers are investigating genetic factors, such as gene mutations, and nongenetic factors that might explain this overgrowth/undergrowth pattern.

Some recent work suggests that exposure to antibodies in the womb may affect brain development. Investigators found abnormal antibodies in the blood of the mothers of 11 percent of children with autism but not in a large sample of mothers with healthy children or mothers of children with other developmental disorders (Braunschweig et al., 2008). Following up on this study, the psychologist David Amaral and colleagues injected four pregnant rhesus monkeys with the antibodies from the mothers of children with autism. All the offspring of these monkeys demonstrated unusual behaviors characteristic of autism, such as repetitive movements and hyperactive limb movements (Martin et al., 2008). None of the offspring of monkeys injected with normal antibodies from mothers of healthy children showed this unusual behavior.

In addition, there is evidence that the brains of people with autism have faulty wiring in a large number of areas (Minshew & Williams, 2007). Some of those brain areas are associated with social thinking, and others might support attention to social aspects of the environment (Minshew & Keller, 2010).

One line of research examined the possibility that those with autism have impairments in the mirror neuron system. (Recall from Chapter 6 that mirror neurons are involved in observational learning and are activated when we watch other people performing actions.) This connection between mirror neurons and autism was suggested by an imaging study that found weaker activation in the mirror neuron system for those with autism than for those without (Dapretto et al., 2006). Other researchers, however, have not found impairments in mirror neuron activity for gestures and movements (Dinstein et al., 2010; Southgate & Hamilton, 2008). What might these apparently contradictory findings mean?

It is possible that impairments in the mirror neuron system prevent the person with autism from understanding the *why* of actions, not the *what* of actions (Rizzolatti & Fabbri-Destro, 2010). For example, suppose that the person with autism knows that another person is lifting a pair of scissors. The person with autism may have little insight into what the person intends to do with the scissors.

Attention Deficit Hyperactivity Disorder Is a Disruptive Impulse Control Disorder

Suppose you are a child who exhibits hyperactivity. At home, you might have difficulty remembering not to trail your dirty hand along the clean wall as you run from the front door to the kitchen. While playing games with your peers, you might spontaneously change the rules. At school, you might ask what you are supposed to do immediately after the teacher has presented detailed instructions to the entire class. You might make warbling noises or other strange sounds that inadvertently disturb anyone nearby. You might seem to have more than your share of accidents: for example, knocking over the tower your classmates are erecting, spilling your juice, or tripping over the television cord while retrieving the family cat—and thereby disconnecting the set in the middle of the Super Bowl (Whalen, 1989).

Symptoms such as these can seem humorous in the retelling, but the reality is a different story. Children with **attention deficit hyperactivity disorder (ADHD)** are restless, inattentive, and impulsive. They need to have directions repeated and

attention deficit hyperactivity disorder (ADHD) A disorder characterized by restlessness, inattentiveness, and impulsivity.

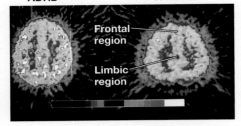

Person without ADHD **Person with a history of ADHD**

Frontal region

Limbic region

White indicates the highest level of activation.

FIGURE 14.30 ADHD and the Brain
The brain image of a person with a history of ADHD shows less overall activation (at the red and white levels), especially in the frontal and limbic regions.

rules explained over and over. Although these children are often friendly and talkative, they can have trouble making and keeping friends because they miss subtle social cues and make unintentional social mistakes. Many of these symptoms are exaggerations of typical toddler behavior, and thus the line between normal and abnormal behavior is hard to draw. Estimates of the prevalence of ADHD vary widely. The best available evidence for children in the United States is that 11 percent of boys and 4 percent of girls have the disorder (Bloom & Cohen, 2007).

THE ETIOLOGY OF ADHD The causes of this disorder are unknown. One of the difficulties in pinpointing the etiology is that ADHD is most likely a heterogeneous disorder. In other words, the behavioral profiles of children with ADHD vary, so the causes of the disorder most likely vary as well. Children with ADHD may be more likely than other children to come from disturbed families. Factors such as poor parenting and social disadvantage may contribute to the onset of symptoms, as is true for all mental disorders. Still, ADHD clearly has a genetic component: Concordance is estimated at 55 percent in identical twins and 32 percent in dizygotic twins (Goodman & Stevenson, 1989; Sherman, McGue, & Iacono, 1997).

In an early imaging study, Alan Zametkin and colleagues (1990) found that adults who had been diagnosed with ADHD in childhood had reduced metabolism in brain regions involved in the self-regulation of motor functions and of attentional systems (**Figure 14.30**). These researchers theorized that the connection between the frontal lobes and the limbic system is impaired in ADHD patients. In fact, the symptoms of ADHD are similar to those seen in patients with frontal lobe damage: problems with planning, sustaining concentration, using feedback, and thinking flexibly. Other imaging studies have found that when adolescents with ADHD perform tasks that require them to inhibit motor responses, greater impairments in performance on the tasks are associated with abnormal activation of prefrontal regions (Schulz et al., 2004).

Researchers have also demonstrated differences in the basal ganglia in the brains of some ADHD patients (Aylward, Reiss, Reader, & Singer, 1996; Castellanos, Giedd, Eckberg, & Marsh, 1998; Fillipek et al., 1997). Because this structure is involved in regulating motor behavior and impulse control, dysfunction in the basal ganglia could contribute to the hyperactivity characteristic of ADHD.

ADHD ACROSS THE LIFE SPAN Children generally are not given diagnoses of ADHD until they enter structured settings in which they must conform to rules, get along with peers, and sit in their seats for long periods. In the past, these things happened when children entered school, between ages 5 and 7. Now, with the increasing prevalence of structured day care settings, the demands on children to conform are occurring much earlier.

According to longitudinal studies, children do not outgrow ADHD by the time they enter adulthood (McGough & Barkley, 2004). Adults with ADHD symptoms, about 4 percent of the population (Kessler et al., 2006), may struggle academically and vocationally. They generally reach a lower-than-expected socioeconomic level and change jobs more frequently than other adults (Bellak & Black, 1992; Mannuzza et al., 1991). At the same time, many adults with ADHD learn how to adapt to their condition, such as by reducing distractions while they work (**Figure 14.31**).

FIGURE 14.31 Living with ADHD Paula Luper, of North Carolina, was diagnosed with ADHD in elementary school. Here, as a senior in high school, she is taking a quiz in the teachers lounge to avoid distraction.

Should Childhood Disorders Be Considered a Unique Category?

Until recently, children were considered small versions of adults, and mental disorders in children were classified according to adult categories. Currently, disorders in children are considered in the context of normal development. In some cases, mental disorders identified in childhood have lasting impacts on the individual, and the problems apparent early in life continue throughout maturation. This outcome is clearly the case for autism. This condition is characterized by impaired social interaction, deficits in communication, and restricted interests. Research suggests that autism is heritable. Causes of autism include gene mutations, unusual patterns of brain growth, exposure to unusual antibodies in the womb, faulty brain wiring, and impairments in mirror neuron activity. ADHD is characterized by restlessness, inattentiveness, and impulsivity. Environmental and genetic factors contribute to the development of ADHD. Abnormalities associated with the frontal lobes, limbic system, and basal ganglia have been identified in individuals with ADHD.

Measuring Up

1. Children with autism exhibit deficits in which of the following categories?

    a. awareness of other people
    b. communication
    c. desire for changes in environment
    d. impulsivity
    e. activities and interests

2. Compared with people without ADHD, people with ADHD show _____ activation in the _____ of the brain.

    a. less; frontal lobes and limbic regions
    b. less; temporal lobes and Broca's area
    c. more; frontal lobes and limbic regions
    d. more; temporal lobes and Broca's area

Answers: 1. a. awareness of other people; b. communication; e. activities and interests. 2. a. less; frontal lobes and limbic regions.

Visit StudySpace to access free review materials, such as:

■ complete study outlines   ■ vocabulary flashcards of all key terms   ■ additional chapter review quizzes

Chapter Summary

14.1 How Are Psychological Disorders Conceptualized and Classified?

■ **Psychopathology Is Different from Everyday Problems:** Psychological disorders are common in all societies. Psychological disorders differ from everyday problems. Individuals with psychological disorders behave in ways that deviate from cultural norms and that are maladaptive.

■ **Psychological Disorders Are Classified into Categories:** The *Diagnostic and Statistical Manual of Mental Disorders* is a multiaxial system for diagnosing psychological disorders. The five axes used for the evaluation of mental health are major clinical disorders, mental retardation and personality disorders, medical conditions, psychosocial problems, and global assessment.

■ **Psychological Disorders Must Be Assessed:** Assessment is the process of examining a person's mental functions and psychological health to make a diagnosis. Assessment is accomplished through interviews, behavioral observations, psychological testing, and neuropsychological testing.

■ **Psychological Disorders Have Many Causes:** The diathesis-stress model suggests that mental health problems arise from a vulnerability coupled with a stressful precipitating event. Psychological disorders may arise from biological factors, psychological factors, or cognitive behavioral factors. Females are more likely than males to exhibit internalizing disorders (such as major depression and generalized anxiety disorder). Males are more likely than females to exhibit externalizing disorders (such as alcoholism and conduct disorders). Most mental disorders show some universal symptoms, but the *DSM* recognizes a number of culture-bound mental health problems.

14.2 Can Anxiety Be the Root of Seemingly Different Disorders?

■ **There Are Different Types of Anxiety Disorders:** Phobias are exaggerated fears of specific stimuli. Generalized anxiety disorder is diffuse and omnipresent. Posttraumatic stress disorder involves frequent and recurring nightmares, intrusive thoughts, and flashbacks related to an earlier trauma. Panic attacks cause sudden overwhelming terror and may lead to agoraphobia. Obsessive-compulsive disorder involves frequent intrusive thoughts and compulsive behaviors.

■ **Anxiety Disorders Have Cognitive, Situational, and Biological Components:** Cognitive, situational, and biological factors contribute to the onset of anxiety disorders. This is well illustrated by obsessive-compulsive disorder, which is influenced by conditioning and genetics and may be induced in children exposed to a streptococcal infection that causes autoimmune damage to the brain.

14.3 Are Mood Disorders Extreme Manifestations of Normal Moods?

■ **There Are Two Categories of Mood Disorders:** Mood disorders include major depression and bipolar disorder. Major depression is characterized by a number of symptoms, including depressed mood and a loss of interest in pleasurable activities. Depression is more common in females than in males and is most common among women in developing countries. Bipolar disorder is characterized by depression and manic episodes—that is, episodes of increased activity and euphoria.

■ **Mood Disorders Have Biological, Situational, and Cognitive Components:** Both depression and bipolar disorder are, in part, genetically determined. The biological factors implicated in depression are neurotransmitter (MAO, serotonin) levels, frontal lobe functioning, and biological rhythms. Poor interpersonal relations and maladaptive cognitions—including the cognitive triad and learned helplessness—also contribute to depression.

14.4 What Are Dissociative Disorders?

■ **Dissociative Amnesia and Fugue Involve Loss of Memory:** Dissociative amnesia involves forgetting that an event happened or losing awareness of a substantial block of time. Dissociative fugue is a type of dissociative amnesia that involves a loss of identity.

■ **Dissociative Identity Disorder Is a Controversial Diagnosis:** Also called multiple personality disorder, dissociative identity disorder involves two or more identities within one person. It is believed to result from severe abuse—through dissociation, individuals develop distinct identities to cope with different traumas. Dissociative identity disorder is a controversial diagnosis. Skeptics note that the condition is often diagnosed after someone has been accused of a crime and may reflect the faking of symptoms. Also, in recent years, there has been a sharp rise in reported cases, possibly as a consequence of therapists suggesting symptoms of dissociative identity disorder to their patients.

14.5 What Is Schizophrenia?

■ **Schizophrenia Has Positive and Negative Symptoms:** Positive symptoms include excesses, such as delusions and hallucinations. Negative symptoms are deficits in functioning, such as apathy and lack of emotion.

■ **Schizophrenia Is Primarily a Brain Disorder:** The brains of people with schizophrenia have larger ventricles and less brain mass, with reduced frontal and temporal lobe activation. A variety of neural structural and neurochemical abnormalities exist as well.

- **Environmental Factors Influence Schizophrenia:** The stress of dysfunctional family dynamics and urban environments may trigger the onset of schizophrenia. Exposure to pathogens may also contribute to the development of this disorder.

14.6 Are Personality Disorders Truly Mental Disorders?

- **Personality Disorders Are Maladaptive Ways of Relating to the World:** The *DSM* identifies 10 personality disorders clustered in three groups. Paranoid, schizoid, and schizotypal comprise the odd and eccentric cluster; avoidant, dependent, and obsessive-compulsive comprise the anxious and fearful cluster; histrionic, narcissistic, borderline, and antisocial comprise the dramatic, emotional, and erratic cluster.

- **Borderline Personality Disorder Is Associated with Poor Self-Control:** Borderline personality disorder involves disturbances in identity, in affect, and in impulse control. Borderline personality disorder is associated with reduced frontal lobe capacity, low levels of serotonin, and a history of trauma and abuse.

- **Antisocial Personality Disorder Is Associated with a Lack of Empathy:** Antisocial personality disorder is characterized by socially undesirable behavior, hedonism, sensation seeking, and a lack of remorse. Antisocial personality disorder is associated with lower levels of arousal, a smaller amygdala, and deficits in frontal lobe functioning. Both genetics and environment seem to contribute to the development of this condition.

14.7 Should Childhood Disorders Be Considered a Unique Category?

- **Autistic Disorder Involves Social Deficits:** Autism emerges in infancy and is marked by impaired social functioning and communication and restricted interests. Autism is heritable and may result from genetic mutations. Autism has been linked to abnormal brain growth, exposure to antibodies in utero, faulty brain wiring, and mirror neuron impairment.

- **Attention Deficit Hyperactivity Disorder Is a Disruptive Impulse Control Disorder:** Children with ADHD are restless, inattentive, and impulsive. The causes of ADHD may include environmental factors such as poor parenting and social disadvantages; genetic factors; and brain abnormalities, particularly with regard to activation of the frontal lobes, limbic system, and basal ganglia. ADHD continues into adulthood, presenting challenges to academic work and to career pursuits.

Key Terms

agoraphobia, p. 634
antisocial personality disorder (APD), p. 660
assessment, p. 623
attention deficit hyperactivity disorder (ADHD), p. 667
autistic disorder, p. 664
bipolar disorder, p. 640
borderline personality disorder, p. 658

cognitive-behavioral approach, p. 627
delusions, p. 651
diathesis-stress model, p. 626
disorganized behavior, p. 652
dissociative disorders, p. 646
dissociative identity disorder (DID), p. 647
dysthymia, p. 639
etiology, p. 621

family systems model, p. 627
generalized anxiety disorder (GAD), p. 633
hallucinations, p. 651
learned helplessness, p. 643
loosening of associations, p. 652
major depression, p. 639
multiaxial system, p. 621
negative symptoms, p. 650

obsessive-compulsive disorder (OCD), p. 634
panic disorder, p. 634
positive symptoms, p. 650
posttraumatic stress disorder (PTSD), p. 633
psychopathology, p. 618
schizophrenia, p. 650
sociocultural model, p. 627

Practice Test

1. Which of the following questions would a clinician ask to determine whether a behavior represents psychopathology? Select all that apply.
   a. Does the behavior deviate from cultural norms?
   b. Is the behavior causing the individual personal distress?
   c. Is the behavior maladaptive?
   d. Is the behavior unusual?
   e. Is the behavior upsetting to members of the client's social network?

2. Two students visit the campus health center. Student A describes feeling constantly fearful and anxious. Student B describes feeling persistently agitated and often exhibiting violent outbursts. Student A's symptoms are consistent with an _____ disorder, which is more common in _____; student Bs symptom's are consistent with an _____ disorder, which is more common in _____. Choose from the following pairs of words to fill in the blanks.
   a. externalizing, females; internalizing, males
   b. externalizing, males; internalizing, females
   c. internalizing, females; externalizing, males
   d. internalizing, males; externalizing, females

The answer key for the Practice Tests can be found at the back of the book. It also includes answers to the green caption questions.

Treatment of Psychological Disorders

DENNIS WAS A 31-YEAR-OLD INSURANCE SALESMAN. One day, while shopping in a mall with his fiancée, Dennis suddenly felt very sick. His hands began to shake, his vision became blurred, and he felt a great deal of pressure in his chest. He began to gasp and felt weak all over. All of this was accompanied by a feeling of overwhelming terror. Without stopping to tell his fiancée what was happening, he ran from the store and sought refuge in the car. He opened the windows and lay down, and he started to feel better in about 10 minutes. Later, Dennis explained to his

FIGURE 15.1 Panic Attacks The stress of being in a crowd can bring on a panic attack in someone who has an anxiety disorder.

fiancée what had happened. Because he had experienced this sort of attack before, he revealed, he would often avoid shopping malls and places like them.

At the urging of his fiancée, Dennis agreed to see a psychologist. During his first several treatment sessions, Dennis downplayed his problems, clearly concerned that others might think him crazy. After a few sessions, it became clear that he had a long history of anxiety problems. The incidents dated back to his college days, when he often "choked" on exams. As Dennis entered a classroom, his palms would get sweaty, his mouth would get dry, and his breathing would become rapid. Some professors had been sympathetic, but Dennis's grades suffered, and he was placed on academic probation. He ended up leaving college early to take the sales job. Dennis's problems with anxiety continued, although they varied in severity. He coped largely by avoiding any situation that made him anxious, such as anywhere that involved crowds. Once Dennis had revealed this history, the therapist explained that Dennis was experiencing panic attacks (**Figure 15.1**).

Dennis told the therapist he was not interested in drug treatment because he had been given tranquilizers in the past for anxiety and he did not like the way they made him feel. He also believed that taking medication was an artificial "crutch." Dennis had read about cognitive-behavioral therapy and was interested in trying it to address his problems. Fortunately, he had found a therapist with the appropriate expertise to help him.

The therapist believed Dennis's problems were the result of vulnerability to stress combined with thoughts and behaviors that exacerbated anxiety. The first step in performing cognitive-behavioral therapy was therefore relaxation training. This training would give Dennis a strategy to use when he became anxious and tense.

The next step was to modify his maladaptive thought patterns. Dennis kept a diary for several weeks to identify situations in which his distorted thoughts might be producing anxiety, such as meeting with prospective clients. Before meeting with a client, Dennis would become extremely anxious because he felt it would be catastrophic if he were unable to make the sale. With his therapist's help, Dennis came to recognize that being turned down by a client was difficult but manageable and that it was unlikely to have a long-term impact on his career.

The final phase of treatment was to address Dennis's avoidance of situations that he associated with panic attacks. Dennis and his therapist constructed a hierarchy of increasingly stressful situations. The first was an easy situation, involving a short visit to a department store on a weekday morning, when it would not be too crowded. Dennis's fiancée accompanied him so that he would feel less vulnerable. After completing this task, he moved on to increasingly difficult situations, using relaxation techniques as necessary to control his anxiety.

After six months, therapy was discontinued. Dennis's anxiety levels were significantly reduced, and he was able to get himself to relax when he did become tense. In addition, he had not experienced a panic attack during that period and was no longer avoiding situations he previously had found stressful (Oltmanns, Martin, Neale, & Davison, 2009). ∎

15.1 How Are Psychological Disorders Treated?

Learning Objectives

- Distinguish between forms of psychotherapy.
- Describe the major categories of psychotropic drugs.
- Identify alternative biological treatments for mental disorders.
- Distinguish between specialized mental health practitioners.

Chapter 14 discussed various psychological disorders, including ones like Dennis's. This chapter explores the basic principles of therapy and describes the various treatment approaches to specific disorders.

At this time, there are no instant cures for psychological disorders. They need to be managed over time through treatment that helps alleviate symptoms so people can function in their daily lives. Scientific research has produced tremendous advances in ways of treating many psychological disorders. The choice of treatment depends on the type and severity of symptoms as well as on the diagnosis. As you will learn throughout this chapter, most mental disorders can be treated in more than one way. Often, however, a particular method is more successful than others for a specific disorder.

Psychologists use two basic categories of techniques to treat mental disorders: psychological and biological. The generic name given to formal psychological treatment is **psychotherapy.** The particular techniques used may depend on the practitioner's training, but all forms of psychotherapy involve interactions between practitioner and client. These interactions are aimed at helping the client understand his or her symptoms and problems and providing solutions for them.

Biological therapies reflect medical approaches to illness and to disease. In other words, these therapies are based on the notion that mental disorders result from abnormalities in neural and bodily processes. For example, the client (sometimes referred to as the patient in medical settings) might be experiencing an imbalance in a specific neurotransmitter or a malfunction in a particular brain region. Biological treatments range from drugs to electrical stimulation of brain regions to surgical intervention. *Psychopharmacology,* the use of medications that affect brain or body functions, can be particularly effective for some disorders, at least on a short-term basis. One limitation of biological therapies, however, is that long-term success may require the person to continue treatment. Sometimes, treatment continues indefinitely. Moreover, nonbiological treatments may prove more effective for some disorders over the long term. For many disorders, the recent focus has been on combining biological therapies with other approaches to find the best treatment for each patient.

As outlined in Chapter 14, psychologists have proposed a number of theories to account for psychopathology. Some of these theories are about general issues, such as the role of learning or cognition in all psychological disorders. Other theories are specific to a particular disorder, such as the theory that certain types of thought patterns underlie depression. Each theory includes treatment strategies that are based on the theory's assumptions about the causes of mental disorders. Researchers are continually gaining better understandings of the etiologies (i.e., causes) of particular mental disorders. These understandings do not always lead to further insights, however, into how best to treat the disorders. For example, autism clearly is caused by biological factors, but this knowledge has not led to any significant advances in therapies for the disorder. In fact, as discussed later in this chapter, the best available treatment for autism is based on behavioral, not biological, principles. Likewise, in a situation where the patient's loss of a parent has led to clinical depression, drugs might be useful for treatment, at least in the short term. The therapist might favor this biological treatment for this particular patient even though the depression was caused by the situation, not by biological factors.

psychotherapy The generic name given to formal psychological treatment.

biological therapies Treatment based on medical approaches to illness and to disease.

Psychotherapy Is Based on Psychological Principles

Regardless of the treatment provider's theoretical perspective, psychotherapy generally is aimed at changing patterns of thought or of behavior. The ways in which such changes are brought about can differ dramatically, however. It has been estimated that there are more than 400 approaches to treatment (Kazdin, 1994). Many therapists follow an *eclectic* approach, using a variety of techniques that seem appropriate for a given client. The following discussion highlights the major components of the most common approaches, and it describes how therapists use these methods to treat specific mental disorders.

One factor known to affect the outcome of therapy is the relationship between the therapist and the client. This connection is true partly because a good relationship can foster an expectation of receiving help (Miller, 2000; Talley, Strupp, & Morey, 1990). Most people in the mental health field use the curative power of client expectation to help their patients achieve success in therapy. This approach is not limited to psychological disorders, however. A good relationship with a service provider is important for any aspect of physical or mental health.

PSYCHODYNAMIC THERAPY FOCUSES ON INSIGHT One of the first people to develop psychological treatments for mental disorders was Sigmund Freud. Freud believed that such disorders were caused by prior experiences, particularly early traumatic experiences. Along with Josef Breuer, he pioneered the method of psychoanalysis.

In early forms of psychoanalysis, the client would lie on a couch while the therapist sat out of view (**Figure 15.2**). This method was meant to reduce the client's inhibitions and allow freer access to unconscious thought processes. Treatment involved uncovering unconscious feelings and drives that, Freud believed, gave rise to maladaptive thoughts and behaviors. Techniques included *free association* and *dream analysis*. In free association, the client would say whatever came to mind and the therapist would look for signs of unconscious conflicts, especially where the client appeared resistant to discussing certain topics. In dream analysis, the therapist would interpret the hidden meaning of the client's dreams (see the discussion in Chapter 5, "Consciousness").

The general goal of psychoanalysis is to increase the client's awareness of his or her own unconscious psychological processes and how these processes affect daily functioning. By gaining **insight** of this kind, the client is freed from these unconscious influences. According to psychoanalysis, the client's symptoms diminish as a result of reducing unconscious conflicts. (Note that this use of the term *insight*—to mean an understanding of one's own psychological processes—is different from its use in Chapter 8. There, *insight* means the sudden solution of a problem.)

Psychotherapists later reformulated some of Freud's ideas, and these later adaptations are known collectively as *psychodynamic therapy*. In using this approach, a therapist aims to help a patient examine the patient's needs, defenses, and motives as a way of understanding why the patient is distressed. Most proponents of the psychodynamic perspective today continue to embrace Freud's "talking therapy." They have replaced the couch with a chair, however, and the talking tends to be more conversational.

Some features of contemporary psychodynamic therapy include exploring the client's avoidance of distressing thoughts, looking for recurring themes and patterns in thoughts and feelings, discussing early

FIGURE 15.2 Psychoanalysis in Freud's Office As part of the treatment process, Freud sat behind his desk (partly visible in the lower left corner). His clients lay on the couch, facing away from him. **What would you say are the potential benefits of this arrangement? What are the potential drawbacks?**

insight The goal of psychoanalysis; a patient's awareness of his or her own unconscious psychological processes and how these processes affect daily functioning.

LASSIE! GET HELP!!

traumatic experiences, focusing on interpersonal relations and childhood attachments, emphasizing the relationship with the therapist, and exploring fantasies, dreams, and daydreams (Shedler, 2010). Some of these features, such as focusing on patterns in thoughts and feelings and focusing on interpersonal relationships, are common to most forms of psychotherapy, and thus they do not distinguish psychodynamic therapy from other types of treatment (Tryon & Tryon, 2011).

During the past few decades, the use of psychodynamic therapy has become increasingly controversial. Traditional psychodynamic therapy is expensive and time consuming, sometimes continuing for many years. There is some evidence that this therapy has promise for certain disorders, such as borderline personality disorder (Gibbons, Crits-Chistoph, & Hearon, 2008). There is only weak evidence, however, for its effectiveness in treating most psychological disorders. As mentioned throughout this textbook, there is minimal empirical evidence for much of Freudian theorizing, and therefore it is not surprising that treatments based on those theories are largely ineffective.

A new approach to psychodynamic therapy consists of offering fewer sessions and focusing more on current relationships than on early-childhood experiences. Therapists who use this approach do not necessarily accept all of Freud's ideas, but they do believe that people have underlying conflicts that need to be resolved, such as their relations with other people. Proponents argue that this short-term psychodynamic therapy can be useful for treating certain disorders, including depression, eating disorders, and substance abuse (Leichsenring, Rabung, & Leibing, 2004). But the dropout rates in these studies are extremely high (Winfried & Hofmann, 2008). In addition, it is not clear whether the psychodynamic aspects are superior to other brief forms of therapy, such as simply talking about personal problems to a caring therapist. The opportunity to talk about one's problems to someone who will listen plays a role in all therapeutic relationships.

HEALTH BENEFITS OF TALKING AND EXPRESSING EMOTION Can expressing your emotions improve your health? To address this question, James Pennebaker and colleagues conducted a series of studies (Pennebaker, Barger, & Tiebout, 1989; Pennebaker, Mayne, & Francis, 1997). They asked participants to write about or talk about emotional events. The events that participants chose to examine ranged from childhood incest and the horrors of the Holocaust to less traumatic events, such as not being included in a social event. Repeatedly, the researchers found positive health effects for people who disclosed these emotional events (**Figure 15.3**). In one study, college students randomly assigned to write about an emotional event visited the university health center fewer times than students assigned to write about other topics, even though there were no group differences in how often the students visited the health center before participating in the study (Pennebaker & Beall, 1986).

As discussed in Chapter 11, Pennebaker has explored the healing power of talking about one's problems. When people reveal intimate and highly emotional material, they go into an almost trancelike state. The pitch of their voices goes down, their rates of speech speed up, and they lose track of time and place. Subsequent research has revealed that talking or writing about emotionally charged events reduces blood pressure, muscle tension, and skin conduction during the disclosure and immediately thereafter (Pennebaker, 1990, 1995). Even e-mailing about emotional topics can have a positive influence on health (Sheese, Brown, & Graziano, 2004). Over the long term, writing about emotional events

FIGURE 15.3 Emotional Disclosure
Holocaust survivors may find comfort in talking with others about their experiences. The survivors above, siblings Hilda Shlick and Simon Glasberg, are holding a picture of their parents.

improves immune function, even in people with HIV (Petrie, Fontanilla, Thomas, Booth, & Pennebaker, 2004). One way talking about troubling events may help individuals is that it may help them reinterpret the events in less threatening ways. As you will learn, such reinterpretation is a central component of many cognitive therapies.

HUMANISTIC THERAPIES FOCUS ON THE WHOLE PERSON As noted in Chapter 13, the humanistic approach to personality emphasizes personal experience and the individual's belief systems. The goal of humanistic therapy is to treat the person as a whole, not as a collection of behaviors or a repository of repressed thoughts.

One of the best-known humanistic therapies is **client-centered therapy.** Developed by the psychologist Carl Rogers, this approach encourages people to fulfill their individual potentials for personal growth through greater self-understanding. A key ingredient of client-centered therapy is to create a safe and comforting setting for clients to access their true feelings. Therapists strive to be empathic, to take the client's perspective, and to accept the client through unconditional positive regard. Instead of directing the client's behavior or passing judgment on the client's actions or thoughts, the therapist helps the client focus on his or her subjective experience. Often, a client-centered therapist will use *reflective listening,* in which the therapist repeats the client's concerns to help the person clarify his or her feelings. Although relatively few practitioners follow the tenets of humanistic theory strictly, many techniques advocated by Rogers are used currently to establish a good therapeutic relationship between practitioner and client.

One form of treatment, *motivational interviewing,* uses a client-centered approach over a very short period (such as one or two interviews). Motivational interviewing has proved a valuable treatment for drug and alcohol abuse, as well as for increasing both healthy eating habits and exercise (Burke, Arkowitz, & Menchola, 2003). William Miller (2000), the psychologist who developed the technique, attributes the outstanding success of this brief form of empathic therapy to the warmth expressed by the therapist toward the client.

COGNITIVE AND BEHAVIORAL THERAPIES TARGET THOUGHTS AND BEHAVIORS Many of the most successful therapies involve trying to change people's cognition and behavior directly. Whereas insight-based therapies consider maladaptive behavior the result of an underlying problem, behavioral and cognitive therapies treat the thoughts and behaviors as the problem. For example, the therapist will not be particularly interested in why a person has come to fear elevators, such as if childhood traumas produced the fear. Instead, the therapist is interested in helping the client overcome the fear. In therapy, thoughts and behaviors are targeted directly.

The premise of **behavior therapy** is that behavior is learned and therefore can be unlearned through the use of classical and operant conditioning. As discussed in Chapter 6, behavior modification is based on operant conditioning. It is a method of helping people to learn desired behaviors and unlearn unwanted behaviors. Desired behaviors are rewarded (rewards might include small treats or praise). Unwanted behaviors are ignored or punished (punishments might include groundings, time-outs, or the administration of unpleasant tastes). Many treatment centers use token economies, in which people earn tokens for good behavior and can trade the tokens for rewards or privileges.

client-centered therapy An empathic approach to therapy; it encourages people to fulfill their individual potentials for personal growth through greater self-understanding.

behavior therapy Treatment based on the premise that behavior is learned and therefore can be unlearned through the use of classical and operant conditioning.

For a desired behavior to be rewarded, however, the client first must exhibit the behavior. A therapist can use *social skills training* to elicit desired behavior. When a client has particular interpersonal difficulties, such as with initiating a conversation, she or he learns appropriate ways to act in specific social situations. The first step is often *modeling,* in which the therapist acts out an appropriate behavior. Recall from Chapter 6 that we learn many behaviors by observing others perform them. In modeling, the client is encouraged to imitate the displayed behavior, rehearse it in therapy, and later apply the learned behavior to real-world situations. The successful use of newly acquired social skills is itself rewarding and encourages the continued use of those skills.

Cognitive therapy is based on the theory that distorted thoughts can produce maladaptive behaviors and emotions. Treatment strategies that modify these thought patterns should eliminate the maladaptive behaviors and emotions. A number of approaches to cognitive therapy have been proposed. For example, Aaron T. Beck has advocated **cognitive restructuring** (**Figure 15.4**). Through this approach, a clinician seeks to help a client recognize maladaptive thought patterns and replace them with ways of viewing the world that are more in tune with reality (**Figure 15.5**). Albert Ellis, another major thinker in this area, has introduced *rational-emotive therapy.* Through this approach, a therapist acts as a teacher, explaining the client's errors in thinking and demonstrating more-adaptive ways to think and behave.

In cognitive therapy and rational-emotive therapy, maladaptive behavior is assumed to result from individual belief systems and ways of thinking rather than from objective conditions. By contrast, *interpersonal therapy* focuses on circumstances—namely, relationships the client attempts to avoid. This approach integrates cognitive therapy with psychodynamic insight therapy (Markowitz & Weissman, 1995). Interpersonal therapy developed out of psychodynamic ideas on how people relate to one another, but it uses cognitive techniques that help people gain more-accurate insight into their social relationships. Because interpersonal functioning is seen as critical to psychological adjustment, treatment focuses on helping clients explore their interpersonal experiences and express their emotions (Blagys & Hilsenroth, 2000).

To help prevent relapse of psychological disorders following treatment, John Teasdale and colleagues (2000) developed *mindfulness-based cognitive therapy.* The principle behind this method is that people who recover from depression continue to be vulnerable to faulty thinking when they experience negative moods. For instance, they may be prone to negative, ruminative thinking. Mindfulness-based cognitive theory is based on principles derived from mindfulness meditation, which originated from Eastern meditation and yoga practices. This therapy has two goals: to help clients become more aware of their negative thoughts and feelings at times when they are vulnerable and to help them learn to disengage from ruminative thinking through meditation. A recent review of studies using this method to prevent recurrence of major depression found that it is quite effective (Piet & Hougaard, 2011).

Cognitive-behavioral therapy (CBT) incorporates techniques from cognitive therapy and behavior therapy. CBT tries to correct the client's faulty cognitions and to train the client to engage in new behaviors. Suppose the client has social phobia—a fear of being viewed negatively by others. The therapist will encourage the client to examine other people's reactions to the client. The aim is to help the client understand how his or her appraisals of other people's reactions might

FIGURE 15.4 Aaron T. Beck Beck is one of the pioneers of cognitive therapy for mental disorders, especially depression.

cognitive therapy Treatment based on the idea that distorted thoughts produce maladaptive behaviors and emotions; treatment strategies attempt to modify these thought patterns.

cognitive restructuring A therapy that strives to help patients recognize maladaptive thought patterns and replace them with ways of viewing the world that are more in tune with reality.

cognitive-behavioral therapy (CBT) A therapy that incorporates techniques from cognitive therapy and behavior therapy to correct faulty thinking and change maladaptive behaviors.

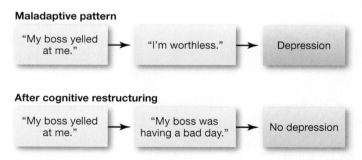

Maladaptive pattern

"My boss yelled at me." → "I'm worthless." → Depression

After cognitive restructuring

"My boss yelled at me." → "My boss was having a bad day." → No depression

FIGURE 15.5 Cognitive Restructuring Through this technique, a therapist helps a client learn to replace maladaptive thought patterns with more-realistic, positive ones. **How does cognitive restructuring reflect the basic principles of cognitive therapy?**

exposure A cognitive-behavioral therapy technique that involves repeated exposure to an anxiety-producing stimulus or situation.

1 The little girl in the white shirt (on the right) has a phobia about dogs.

2 She is encouraged to approach a dog that scares her.

3 From this mild form of exposure she learns that the dog is not dangerous, and she overcomes her fear.

FIGURE 15.6 Exposure Exposure is a common feature of many cognitive-behavioral therapies. In this sequence, a little girl gradually overcomes her fear of dogs by slowly increasing her level of exposure to a dog.

be inaccurate. At the same time, the therapist will teach the client social skills. CBT is perhaps the most widely used version of psychotherapy, and it is one of the most effective forms of psychotherapy for many types of psychological disorders, especially anxiety disorders and mood disorders (Deacon & Abramowitz, 2004; Hollon, Thase, & Markowitz, 2002).

Many cognitive-behavioral therapies for psychological disorders include an **exposure** component. Through this technique, the client is exposed repeatedly to the anxiety-producing stimulus or situation (**Figure 15.6**). The theory behind exposure is based on classical conditioning. Therefore, it reflects the behavioral aspect of cognitive-behavioral therapy.

When an individual avoids either stimuli or situations out of fear, the person experiences reductions in anxiety that reinforce the avoidance behavior. Repeated exposure to a feared stimulus increases the client's anxiety. If the client is not permitted to avoid the stimulus, however, the client's avoidance response is eventually extinguished. In this case, the treatment is known as *exposure and response prevention*. This form of treatment is highly effective for obsessive-compulsive disorder.

A gradual form of exposure therapy is *systematic desensitization*. In this method, the therapist exposes the client to increasingly anxiety-producing situations by having the client imagine them and then teaching the client to relax at the same time. You will learn later that exposure and systematic desensitization are reliable treatments for many phobias. It can even be tried at home for mild cases, as long as the person with the phobia can control how quickly and how close she or he comes to the feared object.

GROUP THERAPY BUILDS SOCIAL SUPPORT Group therapy rose in popularity after World War II. Because of the many different stresses related to the war, more people needed therapy than there were therapists available to treat them. Therapists came to realize that in some instances group therapy offers advantages over individual therapy. The most obvious benefit is cost: Group therapy is often significantly less expensive than individual treatment. In addition, the group setting provides an opportunity for members to improve their social skills and learn from one another's experiences.

Group therapies vary widely in the types of clients enrolled in the group, the duration of treatment, the theoretical perspective of the therapist running the group, and the group size—although some practitioners believe around eight clients is the ideal number. Many groups are organized around a particular type of problem (e.g., sexual abuse) or around a particular type of client (e.g., adolescents). Many groups continue over long periods, with some members leaving and others joining the group at various intervals. Depending on the approach favored by the therapist, the group may be highly structured, or it may be a more loosely organized forum for discussion. Behavioral and cognitive-behavioral groups usually are highly structured, with specific goals and techniques designed to modify the thought and behavior patterns of group members. This type of group has been effective for disorders such as bulimia and obsessive-compulsive disorder. In contrast, less structured groups usually focus on increasing insight and providing social support. In fact, the social support that group members can provide each other is one of the most beneficial aspects of this type of therapy. As a result, group therapy is often used to augment individual psychotherapy.

FAMILY THERAPY FOCUSES ON THE FAMILY CONTEXT The therapy a client receives is of course an important element in treating a mental disorder. The client's family often plays an almost equally important role.

According to a *systems approach,* an individual is part of a larger context. Any change in individual behavior will affect the whole system. This effect is often clearest within the family. Each person in a family plays a particular role and interacts with the other members in specific ways. Over the course of therapy, the way the individual thinks, behaves, and interacts with others may change. Such changes can profoundly affect the family dynamics. For instance, an alcoholic who gives up drinking may start to criticize other members of the family when they drink. In turn, the family members might provide less support for the client's continuing abstinence. After all, if the family members do not have drinking problems, they might resent the comments. If they do have drinking problems, they might resist the comments because they do not want to give up drinking.

Family attitudes are often critical to long-term prognoses. For this reason, some therapists insist that family members be involved in therapy when practical, except when including them is impossible or would be counterproductive. All the family members involved in therapy are together considered the client. For instance, suppose a child's defiant behavior has led to conflict between the parents, who disagree about how to respond to the child (**Figure 15.7**). In this case, the treatment will involve not only working on the child's behavior, but also helping the parents learn to resolve their parenting disagreements.

There is also evidence that helping families provide appropriate social support leads to better therapy outcomes and reduces relapses for individuals in treatment. The key is the type of family involvement. For instance, studies have documented the importance of attitudes expressed by family members toward people with schizophrenia. In this context, **expressed emotion** is a pattern of negative actions by a client's family members. The pattern includes making critical comments about the client, being hostile toward the client, and being emotionally overinvolved (e.g., being overprotective, pitying, or having an exaggerated response to the client's disorder). The level of expressed emotion from family members corresponds to the relapse rate for patients with schizophrenia (Hooley & Gotlib, 2000), and relapse rates are highest if the client has a great deal of contact with the family.

Jill Hooley (2007) notes that expressed emotion predicts relapse in many countries, ranging from Australia to Denmark to China to Iran. The patterns of expressed emotion that affect relapse differ across those countries and their cultures, however, in part because behaviors such as emotional overinvolvement are more acceptable in some cultures. In turn, culture affects the relationship between expressed emotion and relapse. For example, patients with schizophrenia are more likely to relapse when they belong to hostile families in India than when they belong to hostile families in Japan. By contrast, patients with schizophrenia are more likely to relapse when they belong to emotionally overinvolved families in Japan than when they belong to emotionally overinvolved families in India.

Culture Can Affect the Therapeutic Process

Societal definitions of both psychological health and psychological disorders are central to the treatments used in psychotherapy. Culture has multiple influences on the way psychological disorders are expressed, which people with psychological disorders are likely to recover, and people's willingness to seek help. Depression, anxiety, alcoholism, and other psychological disorders can be debilitating

FIGURE 15.7 Family Therapy The actions, reactions, and interactions of family members can become important topics during therapy.

expressed emotion A pattern of negative actions by a client's family members; the pattern includes critical comments, hostility directed toward the client by family members, and emotional overinvolvement.

FIGURE 15.8 Cultural Effects on Therapy A psychologist counsels a young victim of the massive earthquake in the Sichuan province in China, 2008.

for anyone, but when a stigma is associated with any of these disorders, the problems are exacerbated because people will often then suffer in silence, failing to get the psychotherapy that can help them.

Psychotherapy is accepted to different extents in different countries. Some countries, such as China, have relatively few psychotherapists. Many of those countries are seeing a growing demand, as the last two decades or so of economic expansion have brought increasingly stressful lifestyles and an awareness of the mental health problems that come with them.

In 2008, the massive earthquake in China's Sichuan Province demonstrated a new acceptance of psychotherapy in that region. At first, mental health workers rushed in to assist the survivors. But it is critical to understand cultural beliefs about psychotherapy to deliver it effectively, and few of the displaced and grieving Chinese showed up for mental health services offered under the banner "Earthquake Psychological Health Station." Because of traditional cultural beliefs, many Chinese distrust emotional expression and avoid seeking help for depression, anger, or grief (Magnier, 2008). Despite such cultural stigmas against getting help for mental disorders, the Chinese government then sent large numbers of psychotherapists into the region to provide culturally sensitive assistance for coping with the earthquake's aftermath (**Figure 15.8**). (You will learn later in this chapter that simply encouraging venting following disasters can backfire and cause a worsening of emotional problems.)

The Indian government is recognizing that psychological disorders, such as depression, can be as debilitating as malaria and other physical diseases and that the economic consequences of psychological disorders are enormous. In one program in India, a corps of health counselors was trained to screen for psychological disorders whenever someone entered a medical office. Because of the stigma of mental disorders, terms such as *mental illness, depression,* and *anxiety* were avoided; instead, terms such as *tension* and *strain* were used to communicate mental health problems (Kohn, 2008).

Culture also plays a critical role in determining the availability, use, and effectiveness of different types of psychotherapy for various cultural and ethnic groups living within any country. Psychotherapy and definitions of psychological health are based on the dominant cultural paradigm. Beverly Greene (2007) describes the problem this way: "Women, people of color, people with disabilities, members of sexual minority groups, and people who are poor have all been unfairly stigmatized and have suffered to a greater or lesser extent because of the way psychology has defined what is normal" (p. 47). She urges psychotherapists not to gloss over or deny differences in the life experiences of people from different racial, ethnic, and cultural backgrounds in the United States, such as how they are affected by discrimination. Anderson Franklin (2007) makes a similar point in terms of African American men. Early in psychotherapy, most clients and therapists avoid the complex issues at the intersection of race and gender. They act as though the mental disorders of African American men are no different from those of white American men. According to Franklin, African American men's experiences differ in multiple ways that have a cumulative effect on mental disorders, and these differences must be addressed early in therapy.

Another study explored the way Muslim religious beliefs can influence the outcomes of psychotherapy (Ali, Liu, & Humedian, 2004). Religious minorities in any society need to find healthy ways to reaffirm their faith and deal with discrimination. Psychotherapy can be helpful in this regard if therapists have a fundamental understanding of their clients' culture and can modify their own style and type of therapy to be more culturally appropriate. At the same time, some Western psychotherapists are adopting practices from other cultures to enhance treatment. For example, as described earlier, an Eastern form of meditation is used to help people avoid relapsing after their major depression is treated.

Medication Is Effective for Certain Disorders

Drugs have proved effective for treating some psychological disorders. Their use is based on the assumption that psychological disorders result from imbalances in specific neurotransmitters or because receptors for those neurotransmitters are not functioning properly. Drugs that affect mental processes are called **psychotropic medications.** They act by changing brain neurochemistry. For example, they inhibit action potentials, or they alter synaptic transmission to increase or decrease the action of particular neurotransmitters (see Chapter 3, "Biology and Behavior").

Most psychotropic medications fall into three categories: *anti-anxiety drugs, antidepressants,* and *antipsychotics.* Note, however, that sometimes drugs from one category are used to treat a disorder from another category, such as using an anti-anxiety drug to treat depression. One reason for this is comorbidity. For example, as discussed in Chapter 14, a substantial number of people suffering from depression also meet diagnostic criteria for an anxiety disorder. Another reason is that in most cases there is insufficient evidence about why a particular drug is effective in reducing symptoms of a psychological disorder. That is, many questions remain about how brain chemistry is related to psychological disorders, and many drug treatments have been based on trial-and-error clinical trials in which different drugs have been tried to see if they reduce symptoms.

Anti-anxiety drugs, commonly called *tranquilizers,* are used for the short-term treatment of anxiety. One class of anti-anxiety drugs is benzodiazepines (such as Xanax and Ativan). These drugs increase the activity of GABA, the most pervasive inhibitory neurotransmitter. Although benzodiazepines reduce anxiety and promote relaxation, they also induce drowsiness and are highly addictive. They should therefore be used sparingly.

The second class of psychotropic medications is the **antidepressants.** These drugs are primarily used to treat depression. However, they are often used for other disorders, particularly anxiety disorders. *Monoamine oxidase (MAO) inhibitors* were the first antidepressants to be discovered. Monoamine oxidase is an enzyme that breaks down serotonin in the synapse. MAO inhibitors therefore stop this process and result in more serotonin being available in the synapse. These drugs also raise levels of norepinephrine and dopamine. A second category of antidepressant medications is the *tricyclic antidepressants,* named after their core molecular structure of three rings. These drugs inhibit the reuptake of certain neurotransmitters, resulting in more of each neurotransmitter being available in the synapse. More recently, *selective serotonin reuptake inhibitors (SSRIs)* have been introduced; the best-known is Prozac. These drugs inhibit the reuptake of serotonin, but they act on other neurotransmitters to a significantly lesser extent. (**Figure 15.9** depicts the way SSRIs work.)

Some critics have charged that SSRIs are too often used to treat people who are sad and have low self-esteem but who are not clinically depressed. Such widespread prescribing of SSRIs is a problem because, like all drugs, SSRIs have side effects. For example, SSRIs can lead to sexual dysfunction. At the same time, SSRIs have been valuable for a variety of disorders. Therefore, when the use of SSRIs is being considered, the potential side effects should be weighed against the potential benefits.

psychotropic medications Drugs that affect mental processes.

anti-anxiety drugs A class of psychotropic medications used for the treatment of anxiety.

antidepressants A class of psychotropic medications used for the treatment of depression.

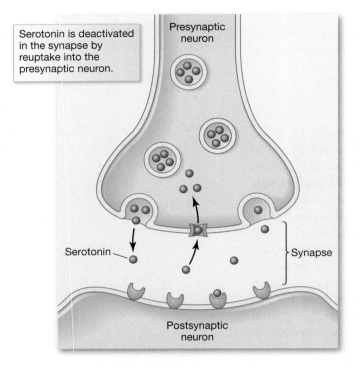

Serotonin is deactivated in the synapse by reuptake into the presynaptic neuron.

Presynaptic neuron

Serotonin

Synapse

Postsynaptic neuron

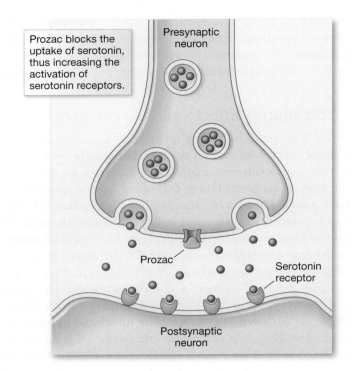

Prozac blocks the uptake of serotonin, thus increasing the activation of serotonin receptors.

Presynaptic neuron

Prozac

Serotonin receptor

Postsynaptic neuron

FIGURE 15.9 Selective Serotonin Reuptake Inhibitors SSRIs, such as Prozac, work by blocking reuptake of serotonin into the presynaptic neuron. In this way, they allow serotonin to remain in the synapse, where its effects on postsynaptic receptors are prolonged. The greater amount of serotonin in the synapse helps alleviate depression.

antipsychotics A class of psychotropic medications used for the treatment of schizophrenia and other disorders that involve psychosis.

The third class of psychotropic medications is **antipsychotics.** Also known as *neuroleptics,* antipsychotics are used to treat schizophrenia and other disorders that involve psychosis. These drugs reduce symptoms such as delusions and hallucinations. Traditional antipsychotics bind to dopamine receptors, thus blocking the effects of dopamine. Antipsychotics are not always effective, however, and they have significant side effects that can be irreversible. One such side effect is *tardive dyskinesia,* the involuntary twitching of muscles, especially in the neck and face. Moreover, these drugs are not useful for treating the negative symptoms of schizophrenia, such as apathy and social withdrawal (see Chapter 14, "Psychological Disorders").

Clozapine, one of the newer antipsychotics, is significantly different. Clozapine acts on dopamine receptors, but it also acts on serotonin, norepinephrine, acetylcholine, and histamine receptors. Many patients who do not respond to the other antipsychotics improve on clozapine. This drug can cause serious problems with white blood cells, however, as will be discussed later. Even newer drugs, such as Risperdal and Zyprexa, are used widely because they are safer than clozapine. Still, as discussed later, these drugs may not be as effective as clozapine.

Other drugs used to treat mental disorders do not fall into traditional categories. Many of them are used as mood stabilizers. *Lithium* is the most effective treatment for bipolar disorder, although the neural mechanisms of how it works are unknown. Drugs that prevent seizures, called *anticonvulsants,* can also stabilize moods in bipolar disorder.

Alternative Biological Treatments Are Used in Extreme Cases

Not all people are treated successfully with psychotherapy or medication or both combined. These people are called treatment resistant. To alleviate their disorders, they may attempt alternative biological methods. Such alternatives include brain surgery, the use of magnetic fields, and electrical stimulation. All of these methods are used to alter brain function. These treatments often are used as last resorts because they are more likely to have serious side effects than psychotherapy or medication will. Many early efforts reflected crude attempts to control disruptive behavior. More-recent approaches reflect a growing understanding of the brain mechanisms that underlie various psychological disorders.

As discussed in Chapter 1, for many centuries people have recognized that the brain is involved with the mind, including the mind's abnormalities. From locations as varied as France and Peru, scientists have found numerous prehistoric skulls in which our ancestors made holes (**Figure 15.10**). Many of the holes were healed over to some extent, indicating that the recipients survived for years after their procedures. Such surgery, *trepanning*, may have been used to let out evil spirits believed to be causing unusual behavior. In parts of Africa and the Pacific, various groups still practice trepanning as a treatment for epilepsy, headaches, and symptoms of mental disorders.

FIGURE 15.10 Prehistoric Skull with Holes Made by Our Ancestors A skull at the Archaeological Museum in Cusco, Peru, bears the marks of a cranial surgical operation performed by the Incas.

Early in the twentieth century, medical researchers went beyond cutting holes in the skull to manipulating the brain. One of the earliest formal procedures used on patients with severe mental illness was *psychosurgery*, in which areas of the frontal cortex were selectively damaged. These prefrontal lobotomies were used to treat severe mental disorders, including schizophrenia, major depression, and anxiety disorders. To understand such drastic measures, we need to appreciate that treatment for mental disorders had made almost no progress before the 1950s. Patients were simply restrained and warehoused in institutions for their entire lives. In this climate of medical desperation, various risky procedures were explored.

electroconvulsive therapy (ECT) A procedure that involves administering a strong electrical current to the patient's brain to produce a seizure; it is effective for some cases of severe depression.

Although some brain surgeries were performed as early as the 1880s, Egas Moniz generally is credited with bringing the practice to the attention of the medical world in the 1930s. His surgical procedure, later known as prefrontal lobotomy, involved severing nerve-fiber pathways in the prefrontal cortex (see Figure 3.24). After patients received lobotomies, they were often listless and had flat affect (on a similar state, see the discussion of Elliot at the opening of Chapter 10, "Emotion and Motivation"). Moreover, the procedure often impaired many important mental functions, such as abstract thought, planning, motivation, and social interaction. With the development of effective pharmacological treatments in the 1950s, the use of lobotomy was discontinued. Nowadays some brain surgery is used for mental disorders, but it involves small regions of the brain and typically is performed only as a last resort.

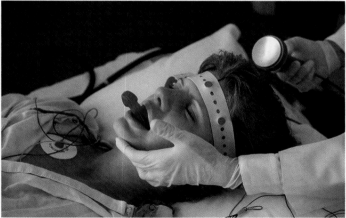

ELECTROCONVULSIVE THERAPY **Electroconvulsive therapy (ECT)** involves placing electrodes on a patient's head and administering an electrical current strong enough to produce a seizure (**Figure 15.11**). This procedure was developed in Europe in the 1930s and tried on the first human in 1938. In the 1950s and 1960s, it was commonly used to treat some psychological disorders, including schizophrenia and depression.

The general public has a very negative view of ECT. Ken Kesey's 1962 novel *One Flew over the Cuckoo's Nest,* as well as the award-winning 1975 film version, did a great deal to expose the abuses in mental health care and graphically depicted ECT as well as the tragic effects of lobotomy. Although care for the mentally ill is still far from perfect, many reforms have been implemented. ECT now generally occurs under anesthesia, with powerful muscle relaxants to eliminate motor convulsions and confine the seizure to the brain. As you will

FIGURE 15.11 Electroconvulsive Therapy A woman being prepared for ECT has a soft object placed between her teeth to prevent her from swallowing her tongue. ECT is most commonly used to treat severe depression that has not been responsive to medication or psychotherapy.

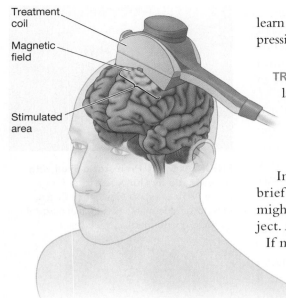

FIGURE 15.12 **Transcranial Magnetic Stimulation** In TMS, current flows through a wire coil placed over the scalp where a brain area is to be stimulated. The stimulation interrupts neural function in that region. TMS is used mainly to treat severe depression.

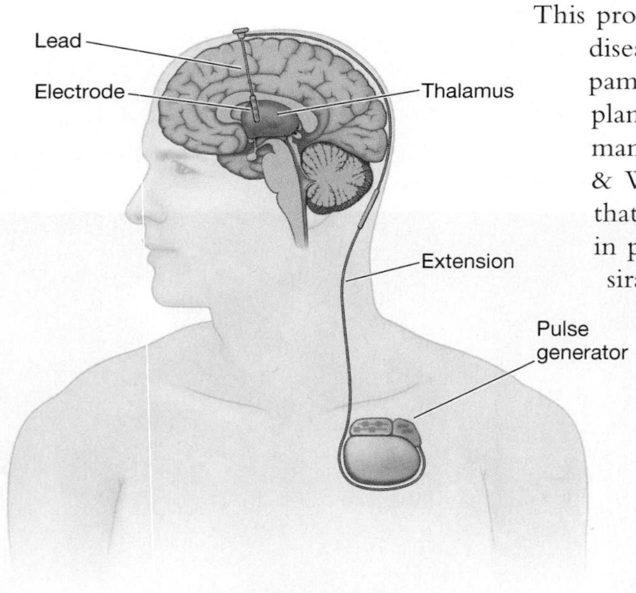

FIGURE 15.13 **Deep Brain Stimulation** In DBS, an electrical generator placed just under the skin below the collarbone sends out continuous stimulation to the implanted electrodes. DBS is used for a variety of medical conditions (such as Parkinson's disease), OCD, and major depression.

learn later in the chapter, ECT is particularly effective for some cases of severe depression, but there are some risks to its use.

TRANSCRANIAL MAGNETIC STIMULATION During transcranial magnetic stimulation (TMS), as discussed in Chapter 2, a powerful electrical current produces a magnetic field (about 40,000 times Earth's magnetic field). When rapidly switched on and off, this magnetic field induces an electrical current in the brain region directly below the coil, thereby interrupting neural function in that region (**Figure 15.12**).

In *single-pulse TMS,* the disruption of brain activity occurs only during the brief period of stimulation. For instance, a pulse given over a motor region might interfere with a person's ability to reach smoothly toward a target object. A pulse given over the speech region may disrupt speaking momentarily. If multiple pulses of TMS occur over extended time, the procedure is known as *repeated TMS.* Here the disruption can last beyond the period of direct stimulation. Researchers are investigating the therapeutic potential of this procedure in treating mental disorders; as noted later in this chapter, TMS may be useful for depression (Loo & Mitchell, 2005; Padberg & George, 2009).

DEEP BRAIN STIMULATION One of the most dramatic new techniques for treating severe mental disorders is *deep brain stimulation (DBS).* This technique involves surgically implanting electrodes deep within the brain. Mild electricity is then used to stimulate the brain at an optimal frequency and intensity, much the way a pacemaker stimulates the heart (**Figure 15.13**).

This procedure was first widely used to treat the symptoms of Parkinson's disease. As discussed in Chapter 3, Parkinson's is a disorder of the dopamine system and causes problems with movement. Electrodes implanted into motor regions of the brains of Parkinson's patients reverse many of the movement problems associated with the disease (DeLong & Wichmann, 2008). The success of DBS for Parkinson's is so great that it is now the treatment of choice for many patients. This is true, in part, because the drugs used to treat Parkinson's often cause undesirable side effects, such as increased involuntary movements. By contrast, DBS has few side effects and a low complication rate, as is typical of any minor surgical procedure. Given DBS's tremendous success in treating Parkinson's—with more than 75,000 people worldwide receiving this treatment (Shah et al., 2010)—DBS is being tested for treating other disorders, including mental disorders. As you will learn, DBS might be especially valuable for treating severe OCD and depression.

Therapies Not Supported by Scientific Evidence Can Be Dangerous

Just as we need to use critical thinking to recognize and avoid flawed science, we also need to recognize and avoid therapies with no scientific basis to confirm they are effective. As the next section will discuss, most psychologists recommend treatments that careful empirical research has shown to be effective (Kazdin, 2008). Unfortunately, many available therapies have no scientific basis.

Such therapies include ones in which people reenact their own births, scream, or have their body parts manipulated (**Figure 15.14**).

Some treatments widely believed to be effective are actually counterproductive. These programs include encouraging people to describe their experiences following major trauma, such as an earthquake, scaring adolescents away from committing crimes by exposing them to prisoners or tough treatments, having police officers run drug education programs such as DARE, and using hypnosis to recover painful memories. These methods not only lack adequate evidence but also may produce results opposite to those intended (Hines, 2003; Lilienfeld, 2007). That is, people debriefed after natural disasters are slightly more likely to develop posttraumatic stress disorder than those who are not debriefed, teens in "scared straight" programs show an increase in conduct problems, children in DARE programs are more likely to drink alcohol and smoke cigarettes than children who do not attend such programs, and hypnosis can produce false memories (as discussed in Chapter 7, "Attention and Memory").

In addition, many self-help books make questionable claims. Consider *Make Anyone Fall in Love with You in 5 Minutes* or *Three Easy Steps for Having High Self-Esteem*. It is important to recognize the difference between evidence-based psychotherapies and "alternative," or "fringe," therapies because the latter can prevent people from getting effective treatment and may even be dangerous. In one tragic case, a 10-year-old girl died from suffocation after being wrapped in a blanket for 70 minutes during a supposed therapy session to simulate her own birth, an untested and unscientific method being used to correct the child's unruly behavior (Lowe, 2001). The people conducting the session were unlicensed, not having passed the tests that certify knowledge about psychotherapy.

A Variety of Providers Can Assist in Treatment for Psychological Disorders

As noted in Chapter 14, nearly half of all Americans meet *DSM-IV-TR* criteria for a psychological disorder at some point in their lives, with 25 percent of the population meeting criteria within any given year (Kessler & Wang, 2008). A dizzying array of providers offer treatment. The providers range from those with limited training (e.g., former addicts who provide peer counseling) to those with advanced degrees in psychopathology and its treatment. In addition to mental health specialists, regular health care providers (e.g., internists, pediatricians), human-service workers (e.g., school counselors), and volunteers (e.g., self-help groups) also assist people with psychological disorders. No matter who administers the therapy, however, most of the techniques used have emerged from psychological laboratories.

As summarized in **Table 15.1,** the major types of specialized mental health practitioners include the following:

- *Clinical psychologists* typically have a doctoral degree. The graduate training for a Ph.D. takes four to six years, and it emphasizes the design and analysis of research and the use of treatments that have empirical support. Many clinical psychologists work in academic or hospital settings, where many of them conduct research in addition to providing treatment.

  A relatively new training program in clinical psychology leads to the Psy.D. This program emphasizes clinical skills over research and is meant for those who intend to provide direct mental health services. Clinical

FIGURE 15.14 John Lennon, Yoko Ono, and Primal Scream Therapy The late former Beatle John Lennon and his wife, the artist Yoko Ono, are probably the most famous people to have undergone scream therapy. They undertook this treatment for about four months in 1970. After ending the treatment early, Lennon said that he found it helpful but unnecessary—that he knew himself better than the therapist could. Later that year, Lennon released his first major solo album, *John Lennon/Plastic Ono Band.* Many of the lyrics reflected the memories and feelings Lennon reportedly dealt with during the therapy. On intense songs such as "Mother," his singing included full-throated screams. Regardless of such artistic inspiration, there is no scientific evidence that scream therapy has any beneficial effect.

psychologists typically are not able to prescribe medications, although efforts are under way to give them such privileges. In New Mexico and Louisiana, clinical psychologists with specialized training in psychoactive drugs can prescribe medications; similar legislation is being proposed elsewhere in the United States (McGrath, 2010).

- *Psychiatrists* have a medical degree (MD) and three to four additional years of specialized training in residency programs. They often work in hospitals or in private practice. Psychiatrists are the only mental health practitioners legally authorized to prescribe drugs in most of the United States.

- *Counseling psychologists* often have a Ph.D. in counseling psychology. They typically deal with problems of adjustment and life stress that do not involve mental illness, such as stress related to scholastic, marital, and occupational problems. Most colleges have staff members who specialize in problems common to students, such as test anxiety, learning disorders, sleep problems, and family issues.

- *Psychiatric social workers* most often have a master's degree in social work (MSW) and specialized training in mental health care. In addition to working with patients in psychiatric hospitals, they may visit people in their homes and address problems arising from the home environments. Their work might include helping clients receive appropriate resources from social and community agencies.

- *Psychiatric nurses* typically have a bachelor's degree in nursing (BSN) and special training in the care of mentally ill patients. They often work in hospitals or in residential treatment programs that specialize in serious mental illness.

- *Paraprofessionals* have limited advanced training, do not need a degree, and usually work under supervision. They assist those with mental health problems in the challenges of daily living. For example, they may work in crisis intervention, pastoral counseling, or community outreach programs, or they may supervise clients of residential treatment programs.

TABLE 15.1 The Major Types of Specialized Mental Practitioners

Specialty	Degree	Placement
Clinical psychologists	Ph.D. or Psy.D.	Academic or hospital settings
Psychiatrists	Medical degree (MD)	Hospitals or private practice
Counseling psychologists	Ph.D.	Schools/colleges (counselors, academic settings) Private practice
Psychiatric social workers	Master's in social work (MSW)	Psychiatric hospitals, house calls
Psychiatric nurses	Bachelor's in nursing (BSN)	Hospitals or residential treatment programs
Paraprofessionals	Limited advanced training	Outreach programs, residential treatment programs

Choosing the right therapist is difficult but extremely important for ensuring successful treatment. The right therapist must have the appropriate training and experience for the specific mental disorder, and the person seeking help must believe the therapist is trustworthy and caring. The initial consultation should make the person feel at ease and hopeful that his or her psychological problem can be resolved. If not, the person should seek another therapist. The ability to prescribe medication should play only a minor role in the choice of therapist, since almost all practitioners have arrangements with physicians who can prescribe medications. It is more important to find someone who is both empathic and experienced in the methods known to be effective in treating specific mental disorders. And it is most important that individuals not feel hopeless in their struggles with mental health problems. They should seek help just as they would for any illness or injury. College students usually have access to low-cost or free therapies at their schools. Most communities have sliding-free, low-cost, or free facilities to help people who do not have insurance coverage.

One of the central problems with treating psychological disorders is that there simply are not enough people available to provide traditional one-on-one psychotherapy to all who need it. After all, there are only around 700,000 mental health service providers in the United States (Hoge et al., 2007), and if one-quarter of the population has a disorder, then approximately 75 million people could benefit from treatment. Accordingly, a number of programs have been developed to broaden the reach of treatment (Kazdin & Blase, 2011). For instance, telephone hotlines, where trained volunteers help people in crisis, can serve a useful role in helping people deal with psychological issues.

Advances in technology have provided methods for providing treatment to those who are not physically present. *Technology-based treatments* use minimal contact with therapists and rely on smartphones, computer programs, or the Internet to provide some form of psychological treatment. For instance, smartphones can provide applications that allow clients to keep track of their moods and mental states, and they can provide specific exercises that people can use to deal with what they are thinking and feeling. These methods appear to be especially useful

CRITICAL THINKING SKILL

Avoiding the Sunk Costs Fallacy

Suppose you are in therapy with someone who has a good reputation and was highly recommended to you by a good friend or your family physician. You have been meeting with this therapist once a week for the last three months. Despite this sizable commitment of both time and money, you do not feel you are doing any better or that the therapist is committed to helping you lessen your problem. Would you reason that since you have already spent so much time and money working with this therapist you should continue, or would you look for a new therapist?

If you stick with a therapist simply because of what you have invested, you are demonstrating the "sunk costs" fallacy. The time and money spent are gone, and you cannot get them back. Future actions cannot be justified by thinking about prior, or "sunk," costs. This fallacy can occur in various settings, so it is important to learn how to recognize and avoid such thinking. Instead, the decision should rest on what the best option is at this point.

How Do I Find a Therapist Who Can Help Me?

College students are sometimes apprehensive about seeking therapeutic support for dealing with life stressors or psychological problems. That apprehension is understandable. After all, stepping into a stranger's office and disclosing your personal thoughts and feelings is not easy (**Figure 15.15**). Nor is it easy to admit—to yourself or others—that you need extra support. If you decide the time has come, knowing how to find a therapist can quell some of the apprehension you might be feeling. The questions and answers below address issues commonly on the minds of therapy-seeking college students:

How do I know if I need therapy? Many times family members, friends, professors, or physicians encourage college students to seek help for psychological problems. For example, if a student complains about feeling tired all the time, a doctor might ask if the student has been under stress or feeling sad. These conditions might indicate that the person is suffering from depression and could be helped by a therapist. Of course, sometimes a student knows he or she has a psychological problem and does not need encouragement to seek out a therapist. For example, a student who struggles night after night to fall asleep because of constant worry about academic performance might seek help for dealing with anxiety.

You need not be 100 percent certain that you need therapy before seeking it out. You can think of the first couple of sessions as a trial period to help you figure out if therapy might be a valuable tool in your situation.

What kind of issues can therapists help with? According to the psychologist Katherine Nordal, an executive director at the American Psychological Association, "Psychologists [and other therapists] work with clients who are looking for help in making lifestyle and behavior changes that lead to better physical and mental health. Psychologists [and other therapists] can help people learn to cope with anxiety or depression, deal with stressful situations, overcome addictions, manage chronic illnesses, both physical and psychological, and break past barriers that might prevent them from reaching their goals" (American Psychological Association, 2010). In other words, therapists can help clients deal with various issues, ranging from acute stressors (e.g., preparing to move across the country for graduate school) to chronic concerns (e.g., managing generalized anxiety disorder).

How do I find a therapist who is a good fit with me and my needs? Most college campuses have counselors who can direct students to appropriate treatment providers. In addition, you can ask friends, teachers, and clergy members if they can recommend someone in your area. And organizations such as the American Psychological Association host referral services, many of which are free and Web-based.

But just because you have the name and phone number of a therapist does not mean she or he will be a good fit for you. To make that determination, you will want to do some information gathering up front. First, what are your preferences? Do you think you would be more comfortable working with someone who is the same gender as you? Or with someone from a similar cultural background? Second, it is a good idea to ask the therapist about her or his level of experience helping people with your particular problem (e.g., depression, procrastination, coming out to your parents). Third, pay attention to your comfort level as you interact with the therapist during the first session or two. It is critical that you find a therapist who is trustworthy and caring. The initial consultation should make you feel at ease and hopeful that your issue can be resolved.

If you do not feel a connection with one therapist, seek another. In other words, it might take more than one try for you to find someone you want to work with. This effort will be well spent. Ultimately, the rapport you feel with your therapist will be a key indicator of therapeutic success. Choosing the right

FIGURE 15.15 Meeting with a Therapist The relationship between client and therapist is necessarily intimate. A person with some sort of problem meets with a professional who seeks to offer help. If the relationship succeeds, the trust that develops between the client and the therapist will be a major component of that success.

therapist can be difficult, but it is extremely important for ensuring successful treatment.

Will my therapist prescribe medication? Typically, only psychiatrists (medical doctors with special training in treating psychological disorders; see "A Variety of Providers Can Assist in Treatment for Psychological Disorders") are legally permitted to prescribe medication (though the laws vary by state). That said, almost all therapists have arrangements with physicians who can prescribe medications, including psychotropic drugs, if necessary. The question of the ability to prescribe medication should play only a minor role in the choice of therapist. It is more important to find someone who strikes you as empathic and who is experienced in the effective treatments for your problem.

Remember, therapy involves a kind of relationship. Just as you would not expect every first date to be a love connection, do not expect every therapist to be a good fit for you. Finding someone you connect with is a worthwhile goal.

For more information, visit the American Psychological Association's Web page about therapy: http://apa.org/topics/therapy/index. aspx for treating problems with addiction, including drug abuse, pathological gambling, and smoking (Newman, Szkodny, Llera, & Przeworski, 2011). For example, the Web site ModeratedDrinking.com assists people who are dealing with alcohol problems. A study that randomly assigned problem drinkers to a control group or a Web-based treatment at ModeratedDrinking.com found that the program led to improved long-term outcomes in days abstaining from alcohol, although it was mainly effective for those who were not heavy drinkers (Hester, Delaney, & Campbell, 2011). Internet-based and computer-based cognitive-behavioral therapy are also successful for the treatment of anxiety disorders, including panic disorder (Schmidt & Keough, 2011).

The Internet provides a growing number of resources for those dealing with life problems on their own. The Web sites of the American Psychological Association (www.apa.org) and the National Institute of Mental Health (www.nimh.nih.gov) offer additional information about choosing mental health practitioners.

Summing Up

How Are Psychological Disorders Treated?

Psychotherapy refers to formal psychological treatment—that is, treatment aimed at changing thought and behavior. There are many forms of psychotherapy. Psychodynamic therapy provides people with insight. Humanistic therapies foster growth through self-understanding. Behavior therapies change maladaptive behaviors. Cognitive therapies change maladaptive thought patterns. Group therapies vary widely, but generally they are inexpensive, develop participants' social skills, and provide social support to participants. Family therapy focuses on family dynamics, adopting a systems approach to psychotherapy. An individual's cultural background can be an important determinant of whether she or he will seek therapy and what type of therapy is most likely to be effective. Psychopharmacology is based on the idea that maladaptive behavior results from neurological dysfunction, and psychotropic medications are therefore aimed at correcting imbalances of neurotransmitters in the brain. Categories of psychotropic medications include anti-anxiety drugs, antidepressants, and antipsychotics. When traditional treatments fail, alternative biological methods may be used, including ECT, TMS, and DBS. Therapies not supported by empirical research can be ineffective and sometimes dangerous. There are many types of specialized practitioners who assist people with psychological disorders, including clinical psychologists, psychiatrists, counseling psychologists, psychiatric social workers, psychiatric nurses, and paraprofessionals. In choosing among these different types of psychotherapists, the client needs to find someone she or he can trust and with whom she or he can establish a productive therapeutic relationship.

Measuring Up

1. Identify the psychotherapeutic orientation each of the following scenarios typifies. Response options include client-centered therapy, cognitive-behavioral therapy, group therapy, and psychodynamic therapy.
   a. Allen seeks therapy to help him cope with social anxiety and panic attacks. During a review of Allen's thought records from the previous week, Allen's therapist says, "Allen, I see you had one panic attack last week during one of your attempts to socialize. On a scale of 0 to 10 in severity, you rated the panic attack an 8. Tell me about the thoughts you had just before and during the attack. This will help us understand what triggered your panic attack."
   b. During a therapy session, Carlos's therapist says, "Carlos, you've described feeling angry toward your wife when she asks how you're dealing with your

father's death. I sensed frustration and anger toward me when I asked you about his death just a moment ago. Usually anger covers more uncomfortable feelings, like hurt, pain, and anguish. If you put your anger aside for a moment, what emotion comes to the surface?"

   c. Following Parin's expression of despair that his girlfriend broke up with him, his therapist responds empathically by saying, "Parin, you feel devastated knowing your love for her was not enough to keep the two of you together. I am sorry you are experiencing so much pain."

2. Identify the disorder most commonly treated with each medication. Response options are anxiety, depression, and schizophrenia.
   a. antipsychotics
   b. selective serotonin reuptake inhibitors
   c. tranquilizers

Answers: 1. a. cognitive-behavioral therapy; b. psychodynamic therapy; c. client-centered therapy.
2. a. schizophrenia; b. depression; c. anxiety.

Learning Objective

■ Identify the treatments that are most effective for specific psychological disorders

15.2 What Are the Most Effective Treatments?

Research over the past three decades has shown that certain types of treatments are particularly effective for specific types of mental disorders (Barlow, 2004). Outcomes are influenced by the interaction of client and therapist, so it is difficult to make comparisons across disorders and therapists. Nonetheless, some treatments have empirical support for use with specific disorders. Other treatments do not have empirical support. Moreover, the scientific study of treatment indicates that although some mental disorders are quite easily treated, others are not. For instance, highly effective treatments exist for anxiety disorders, mood disorders, and sexual dysfunction, but few treatments for alcoholism are superior to the natural course of recovery that many people undergo without psychological treatment (Seligman, Walker, & Rosenhan, 2001). People who experience depression following the death of a loved one usually feel better with the passage of time. That is, people often resolve personal problems on their own without psychological treatment. Because people tend to enter therapy when they experience crises, they often show improvements no matter what therapy they receive. (For information on the tendency of conditions to improve over time, see "Critical Thinking Skill: Identifying Regression to the Mean," in Chapter 10.)

Effectiveness of Treatment Is Determined by Empirical Evidence

The only way to know whether a treatment is valid is to conduct empirical research that compares the treatment with a control condition, such as receiving helpful information or having supportive listeners (Kazdin, 2008). In keeping with good scientific principles, client-participants should be randomly assigned to conditions. The use of *randomized clinical trials* is one of the hallmarks of good research to establish whether a particular treatment is effective. Recall from Chapter 2 that randomization helps to ensure that groups are comparable and also controls for many potential confounds.

David Barlow (2004), a leading researcher on anxiety disorders, points out that findings from medical studies often lead to dramatic changes in treatment practice. Barlow provides the example of the sharp downturn in the use of hormone replacement therapy in postmenopausal women following evidence that this treatment causes cardiovascular and neurological problems. Similarly, within a year after evidence emerged that arthroscopic knee surgery did not produce better outcomes than sham surgery (in which there was no actual procedure), use of the knee surgery declined dramatically. Such developments reflect the increasing importance of *evidence-based treatments* in medicine. Barlow argues that psychological disorders should always be treated in ways that scientific research has shown to be effective. He prefers the term *psychological treatments* to distinguish evidence-based treatment from the more generic term *psychotherapy,* which refers to any form of therapy.

There is some debate regarding the most appropriate methods and criteria used to assess clinical research (e.g., Benjamin, 2005; Westen, Novotny, & Thompson-Brenner, 2004). As Barlow notes, however, three features characterize psychological treatments. First, treatments vary according to the particular mental disorder and the client's specific psychological symptoms. Just as treatment for asthma differs from that for psoriasis, treatments for panic disorder are likely to differ from those for bulimia nervosa. Second, the techniques used in these treatments have been developed in the laboratory by psychologists, especially behavioral, cognitive, and social psychologists. Third, no overall grand theory guides treatment. Instead, treatment is based on evidence of its effectiveness. The following sections examine the evidence to find the treatments of choice for some of the most common mental disorders.

Treatments That Focus on Behavior and on Cognition Are Superior for Anxiety Disorders

Treatment approaches to anxiety disorders have had mixed success. In the era when Freudian psychoanalytic theory governed the classification of mental disorders, anxiety disorders were thought to result from repressed sexual and aggressive impulses. This underlying cause, rather than specific symptoms, was of interest to the therapist. Ultimately, psychoanalytic theory did not prove useful for treating anxiety disorders. The accumulated evidence suggests that cognitive-behavioral therapy works best to treat most adult anxiety disorders (Hofmann & Smits, 2008).

Anxiety-reducing drugs are also beneficial in some cases. With drugs, however, there are risks of side effects and, after drug treatment is terminated, the risk of relapse. For instance, tranquilizers work in the short term for generalized anxiety disorder, but they do little to alleviate the source of anxiety and are addictive. Therefore, they are not used much today. Antidepressant drugs that block the reuptake of both serotonin and norepinephrine have been effective for treating generalized anxiety disorder (Hartford et al., 2007; Nicolini et al., 2008). As with all drugs, the effects may be limited to the period during which the drug is taken. By contrast, the effects of cognitive-behavioral therapy persist long after treatment (Hollon, Stewart, & Strunk, 2006).

SPECIFIC PHOBIAS As discussed in Chapter 14, specific phobias are characterized by the fear and avoidance of particular stimuli, such as heights, blood, and spiders. Learning theory suggests these fears are acquired either through experiencing a trauma or by observing similar fear in others. Most phobias, however, apparently develop in the absence of any particular precipitating event. Although learning theory cannot completely explain the development of phobias, behavioral techniques are the treatment of choice.

One of the classic methods used to treat phobias is a form of behavior therapy known as systematic desensitization, mentioned earlier. The client first makes a *fear hierarchy:* a list of situations in which fear is aroused, in ascending order. The example in **Table 15.2** is from a client's therapy to conquer a fear of heights in order to go mountain climbing. The next step is relaxation training, in which the client learns to alternate muscular tension with muscular relaxation and to use relaxation techniques. Exposure therapy is often the next step. While the client is relaxed, she or he is asked to imagine or enact scenarios that become progressively more upsetting. New scenarios are not presented until the client is able to maintain relaxation at the previous levels. The theory behind this technique is that the relaxation response competes with and eventually replaces the fear response. Evidence indicates that it is exposure to the feared object rather than the relaxation that extinguishes the phobic response. Thus many contemporary practitioners leave out the relaxation component.

To expose clients without putting them in danger, practitioners may use *virtual environments,* sometimes called *virtual reality.* Computers can simulate the environments and the feared objects (**Figure 15.16**). There is substantial evidence that exposure to these virtual environments can reduce fear responses (Rothbaum et al., 1999).

Used along with the behavioral methods, some cognitive strategies have also proved useful for the treatment of phobia. If the client is not aware that the particular fear is irrational, therapy is likely to begin by increasing his or her awareness of the thought processes that maintain the fear of the stimulus.

Brain imaging data indicate that successful treatment with cognitive-behavioral therapy alters the way the brain processes the fear stimulus. In one study, research participants suffering from severe spider phobia received brain scans while looking at pictures of spiders (Paquette et al., 2003). The participants whose treatment had been successful showed decreased activation in a frontal brain region involved in the regulation of emotion. These findings suggest that psychotherapy effectively "rewires" the brain and, therefore, that both psychotherapy and medication affect the underlying biology of mental disorders.

Pharmacological treatments for phobias sometimes include tranquilizers. These drugs can help people handle immediate fears. As soon as the drugs wear off, however, the fears return. Studies have suggested that SSRIs might be useful for social

TABLE 15.2 Anxiety Hierarchy	
Degree of fear	**Situation**
5	I'm standing on the balcony of the top floor of an apartment tower.
10	I'm standing on a stepladder in the kitchen to change a lightbulb.
15	I'm walking on a ridge. The edge is hidden by shrubs and treetops.
20	I'm sitting on the slope of a mountain, looking out over the horizon.
25	I'm crossing a bridge 6 feet above a creek. The bridge consists of an 18-inch-wide board with a handrail on one side.
30	I'm riding a ski lift 8 feet above the ground.
35	I'm crossing a shallow, wide creek on an 18-inch-wide board, 3 feet above water level.
40	I'm climbing a ladder outside the house to reach a second-story window.
45	I'm pulling myself up a 30-degree wet, slippery slope on a steel cable.
50	I'm scrambling up a rock, 8 feet high.
55	I'm walking 10 feet on a resilient, 18-inch-wide board, which spans an 8-foot-deep gulch.
60	I'm walking on a wide plateau, 2 feet from the edge of a cliff.
65	I'm skiing an intermediate hill. The snow is packed.
70	I'm walking over a railway trestle.
75	I'm walking on the side of an embankment. The patch slopes to the outside.
80	I'm riding a chair lift 15 feet above the ground.
85	I'm walking up a long, steep slope.
90	I'm walking up (or down) a 15-degree slope on a 3-foot-wide trail. On one side of the trail the terrain drops down sharply; on the other side is a steep upward slope.
95	I'm walking on a 3-foot-wide ridge. The trail slopes on one side are more than 25 degrees steep.
100	I'm walking on a 2-foot-wide ridge. The trail slopes on either side are more than 25 degrees.

phobia. Indeed, in one comprehensive study, researchers found that both Prozac and cognitive-behavioral therapy were equally effective in treating social phobia (Davidson et al., 2004). After 14 weeks, symptoms exhibited by participants in the study did not differ. Those taking Prozac, however, had more physical complaints, such as lack of sexual interest. Thus cognitive-behavioral therapies are the treatments of choice for phobia.

PANIC DISORDER Like Dennis, whose condition was described in the chapter opener, many of us sometimes experience symptoms of a panic attack. We react to these symptoms in different ways. Some shrug off the symptoms. Others interpret heart palpitations as the beginnings of a heart attack or hyperventilation as a sign of suffocation. Panic disorder has multiple components, and each symptom may require a different treatment. This clinical observation is supported by the finding that imipramine, a tricyclic antidepressant, prevents panic attacks but does not reduce the anticipatory anxiety that occurs when people fear they might have an attack. To break the learned association between the physical symptoms and the feeling of impending doom, cognitive-behavioral therapy can be effective, as in Dennis's case.

An important psychotherapeutic method for treating panic disorder is based on cognitive therapy. When people feel anxious, they tend to overestimate the probability of danger. Thus they potentially contribute to their rising feelings of panic. Cognitive restructuring addresses ways of reacting to the symptoms of a panic attack. First, the client identifies his or her specific fears, such as having a heart attack or fainting. The client then estimates how many panic attacks he or she has experienced. The therapist helps the client assign percentages to specific fears and then compare these numbers with the actual number of times the fears have been realized. For example, a client might estimate that she fears having a heart attack during 90 percent of her panic attacks and fainting during 85 percent of her attacks. The therapist can then point out that the actual rate of occurrence was zero. In fact, people do not faint during panic attacks. The physical symptoms of a panic attack, such as having a racing heart, are the opposite of fainting.

Even if clients recognize the irrationality of their fears, they often still suffer panic attacks. From a cognitive-behavioral perspective, the attacks continue because of a conditioned response to the trigger (e.g., shortness of breath). The goal of therapy is to break the connection between the trigger symptom and the resulting panic. This break can be made by exposure treatment. For example, the therapist might induce feelings of panic—perhaps by having the client breathe in and out through a straw to bring about hyperventilation or by spinning the client rapidly in a chair. Whatever the method, it is done repeatedly to induce habituation and then extinction.

In the treatment of panic attacks, cognitive-behavioral therapy appears to be as effective as or more effective than medication (Schmidt & Keough, 2011). For example, David Barlow and colleagues (2000) found that in the short term, cognitive-behavioral therapy alone and imipramine alone were more effective than a placebo for treating panic disorder. Moreover, cognitive-behavioral therapy and imipramine did not differ in results. Six months after treatment had ended, however, those who received psychotherapy were less likely to relapse than those who had taken medication. These results support the conclusion that cognitive-behavioral therapy is the treatment of choice for panic disorder. For those who have panic disorder with agoraphobia, the fear of being in open spaces, the combination of CBT and drugs is better than either treatment alone (Starcevic, Linden, Uhlenhuth, Kolar, & Latas, 2004).

FIGURE 15.16 Using Virtual Environments to Conquer Fear
Computer-generated images can simulate feared environments or social interactions. For example, the client can *virtually* stand on the edge of a very tall building or *virtually* fly in an aircraft. The clients can conquer the virtual environment before taking on the feared situation in real life.

OBSESSIVE-COMPULSIVE DISORDER As discussed in Chapter 14, obsessive-compulsive disorder (OCD) is a combination of recurrent intrusive thoughts (obsessions) and behaviors that an individual feels compelled to perform over and over (compulsions). There is evidence that OCD is partly genetic and appears to be related to Tourette's syndrome, a neurological disorder characterized by motor and vocal tics. This evidence convinced many practitioners that people with OCD would respond to drug treatment. Traditional antianxiety drugs are completely ineffective for OCD, however.

When SSRIs were introduced to treat depression, they were particularly effective in reducing the obsessive components of some depressions. For example, they helped reduce the constant feelings of worthlessness experienced by people when they suffer from depression. We do not know the reasons for these effects. As a result of the initial success, however, SSRIs were tried with patients suffering from OCD and were found to be effective (Rapoport, 1989, 1991). The drug of choice for OCD is clomipramine, a potent serotonin reuptake inhibitor. It is not a true SSRI, since it blocks reuptake of other neurotransmitters as well, but its strong enhancement of the effects of serotonin appears to make it effective for OCD.

Cognitive-behavioral therapy is also effective for OCD (Franklin & Foa, 2011). The two most important components of behavioral therapy for OCD are exposure and response prevention. The client is directly exposed to the stimuli that trigger compulsive behavior, but is prevented from engaging in the behavior. This treatment derives from the theory that a particular stimulus triggers anxiety and that performing the compulsive behavior reduces the anxiety. For example, a client might compulsively wash his or her hands after touching a doorknob, using a public telephone, or shaking hands with someone (**Figure 15.17**). In exposure and response-prevention therapy, the client would be required to touch a doorknob and then would be instructed not to wash his or her hands afterward. As with exposure therapy for panic disorder, the goal is to break the conditioned link between a particular stimulus and a compulsive behavior. Some cognitive therapies are also useful for OCD, such as helping the client recognize that most people occasionally experience unwanted thoughts and compulsions. In fact, unwanted thoughts and compulsions are a normal part of human experience.

In the 1990s, researchers imaged the brains of patients with OCD who were being treated either with Prozac or with cognitive-behavioral therapy. Patients in both treatment groups showed the same changes in neural activity (Baxter et al., 1992; Schwartz, Stoessel, Baxter, Martin, & Phelps, 1996). Recall the findings, discussed earlier, that the treatment for a spider phobia led to changes in brain activity. These studies provide further evidence that psychotherapies in which people reinterpret their fears and change their behaviors can in fact change the way their brains function.

How does drug treatment compare with cognitive-behavioral therapy for OCD? In one study, the use of exposure and response prevention proved superior to the use of clomipramine, the drug of choice for OCD, although both were better than a placebo (Foa et al., 2005; **Figure 15.18**). Cognitive-behavioral therapy may thus be a more effective way of treating OCD than medication, especially over the long term (Foa et al., 2005). There is evidence that, at a minimum, adding CBT to SSRI treatment may improve outcomes (Simpson et al., 2008). Therefore, many practitioners recommend the combination of these treatments (Franklin & Foa, 2011).

One exciting possibility is that deep brain stimulation (DBS) may be an effective treatment for those with OCD who have not found relief from CBT or medications. Early studies used psychosurgery to remove brain regions thought to contribute to OCD. There were promising outcomes, and these surgical interventions

FIGURE 15.17 Obsessive Ritual Hand washing is one OCD ritual.

involved much less damage than earlier methods, such as lobotomy. Still, brain surgery is inherently a risky therapy because it is irreversible. Deep brain stimulation offers new hope.

Consider the case of Mr. A., a 56-year-old man suffering from a severely debilitating case of OCD that had lasted for more than four decades. Mr. A. had a number of obsessions about body parts and about gastrointestinal functioning. His compulsions included repetitive movements and dietary restrictions. Researchers implanted DBS electrodes into the caudate, an area of the brain abnormal among people with OCD. DBS was very effective for Mr. A., who showed significant remission from symptoms after six months of treatment. After more than two years, Mr. A. continued to have stunning improvements in psychological functioning and the quality of his daily living (Aouizerate et al., 2004).

Since 2000, four separate research teams from the United States and Europe, including the group who treated Mr. A., have been exploring the use of DBS for severe cases of OCD. These teams are targeting brain regions identified as problematic in OCD, such as the caudate and surrounding regions. DBS leads to a clinically significant reduction of symptoms and increased daily functioning in about two-thirds of those receiving treatment (Greenberg et al., 2008). Although this method remains exploratory, it holds great promise for helping those who have not benefited from other forms of treatment.

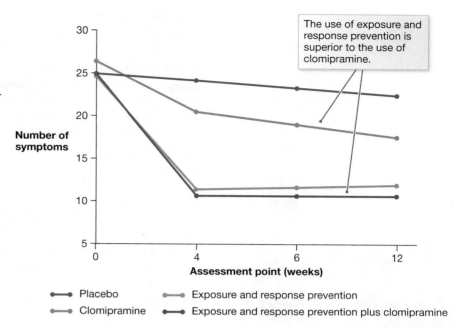

FIGURE 15.18 Treatments for Obsessive-Compulsive Disorder
Treatments for OCD include the drug clomipramine, exposure, and response prevention. This graph shows how, in the 2005 study by Foa and colleagues, the numbers of symptoms changed over a period of 12 weeks. With each type of treatment, rates of success are different.

Many Effective Treatments Are Available for Depression

As discussed in Chapter 14, depression is characterized by low mood or loss of interest in pleasurable activities. This condition is one of the most widespread mental disorders among adolescents and adults, and it has become more common over the past few decades (Hollon et al., 2002). Fortunately, scientific research has validated a number of effective treatments. There is no "best" way to treat depression. Many approaches are available, and ongoing research is determining which type of therapy works best for which types of individuals.

PHARMACOLOGICAL TREATMENT In the 1950s, tuberculosis was a major health problem in the United States, particularly in urban areas. A common treatment was iproniazid. This drug reduced bacteria associated with tuberculosis in patients' saliva. It also stimulated patients' appetites, increased their energy levels, and gave them an overall sense of well-being. In 1957, researchers who had noted iproniazid's effect on mood reported preliminary success in using it to treat depression. In the following year, nearly half a million patients suffering from depression were given the drug.

Iproniazid is an MAO inhibitor. MAO inhibitors can be toxic because of their effects on various physiological systems. Patients taking these drugs must avoid ingesting any substances containing tyramine, an amino acid found in various foods, including red wine, cured meats, and aged cheeses. The interaction of an MAO inhibitor and tyramine can result in severe, sometimes lethal elevations in blood pressure. In addition, the interaction of an MAO inhibitor with particular prescription and over-the-counter medications can be fatal. As a result of these complications, MAO inhibitors are generally reserved for patients who do not respond to other antidepressants.

Tricyclics, another type of antidepressant, were also identified in the 1950s. One of these—imipramine, developed as an antihistamine—was found effective in relieving clinical depression. This drug and others like it act on neurotransmitters as well as on the histamine system. Tricyclics are extremely effective antidepressants. Because of their broad-based action, however, they have a number of unpleasant side effects. For example, they can result in drowsiness, weight gain, sweating, constipation, heart palpitations, dry mouth, or any combination of such problems.

The discovery of these early antidepressants was largely serendipitous. Subsequently, researchers began to search for antidepressants that did not affect multiple physiological and neurological systems and so would not have such troublesome side effects. In the 1980s, researchers developed Prozac. This SSRI does not affect histamine or acetylcholine. Therefore, it has none of the side effects associated with the tricyclic antidepressants, although it occasionally causes insomnia, headache, weight loss, and sexual dysfunction. Because they have fewer serious side effects than MAO inhibitors, Prozac and other SSRIs began to be prescribed more frequently. A number of other drug treatments for depression have also been validated. For example, bupropion (brand name Wellbutrin) affects many neurotransmitter systems, but it has fewer side effects for most people than other drugs. Unlike most antidepressants, bupropion does not cause sexual dysfunction. Unlike SSRIs, bupropion is an ineffective treatment for panic disorder and OCD.

Researchers have attempted to determine how particular types of patients will respond to antidepressants. Still, physicians often must resort to a trial-and-error approach in treating patients who are experiencing depression. No single drug stands out as being most effective. There is some evidence that tricyclics might be beneficial for the most serious forms of depression, especially for hospitalized patients (Anderson, 2000). SSRIs are generally considered first-line medications because they have the fewest serious side effects (Olfson et al., 2002). Often the decision of which drug to use depends on the patient's overall medical health and the possible side effects of each medication.

"*Before Prozac, she loathed company.*"

CRITICAL THINKING SKILL

Recognizing Sources of Bias in Drug Research

The arrival of Prozac on the market, in 1987, led to a dramatic shift in the treatment of depression (**Figure 15.19**). Nowadays, most people who experience depression are first treated by a medical doctor. The doctor is likely to prescribe an antidepressant rather than refer the patient to a psychotherapist. An estimated 1 in 10 Americans over age 6 takes antidepressant medication (Angell, 2011).

Concern is growing that the increased use of antidepressants (and other pharmacological treatments for psychological disorders) may be overly due to the marketing pressures of the drug industry. Critics charge that promotions by drug companies have given doctors an inflated sense of the evidence for the effectiveness of pharmacological treatment.

One area of great concern is that much of the research conducted on the effectiveness of drug treatments is paid for by the pharmaceutical industry. That is, a drug company will pay a researcher to examine the effectiveness of its drug. Such payments can represent a conflict of interest because the researcher may be motivated, even unconsciously, to obtain findings that please the company. After all, the researcher probably wants to obtain future funding from the company. Recall from Chapter 2 that experimenter bias can affect research outcomes. For this reason, many scientific journals require investigators to declare any financial interests they have in the research.

There are also biases in the literature on the effectiveness of drug therapy (Turner, Matthews, Linardatos, Tell, & Rosenthal, 2008). In science, it is much easier to publish positive results—those that indicate treatment success—than negative results. Moreover, drug companies are much more likely to publicize studies that show their drugs are effective than those that do not. How can researchers tell whether published studies present a different story than unpublished studies? The psychologist Irving Kirsch found a way to answer that question.

In approving a new drug, the U.S. Food and Drug Administration (FDA) requires drug companies to submit all clinical studies they have conducted regardless of whether those findings were ever published. Kirsch and colleagues (2008) used a Freedom of Information Act request to obtain all placebo-controlled studies of the most widely used antidepressants. Of the 42 studies they obtained, most had negative results. Overall, placebos were 80 percent as effective as antidepressants, and the change in ratings on a standard report of depressive symptoms showed that improvement on drugs compared with placebos was modest at best.

Thus a look at all the data raises questions about whether drug company claims about the highly effective nature of drug treatments for depression are supported by empirical research. The drug companies focus on the studies that show their drugs work. This fact may lead those who prescribe or take the medications to overestimate how much the drugs will help alleviate psychological disorders, such as depression.

FIGURE 15.19 Antidepressants on the Market This advertisement is a sample of the claims made for the antidepressant Zoloft.

QUESTIONS ABOUT PHARMACOLOGICAL TREATMENT The use of antidepressants is based on the belief that depression (like other psychological disorders) is caused by an imbalance in neurotransmitters or problems with neural receptors. Recently, a number of critics have challenged this view, arguing that there is no evidence to suggest that people with depression had abnormal brain functioning before drug treatment (Angell, 2011). Indeed, faulty logical reasoning may be at play.

Yes, drugs such as SSRIs seem to help symptoms of depression. This success has been viewed as evidence that depression is caused by an abnormality in serotonin function. As a critical thinker, you probably recognize that this connection is not good proof. After all, when you have a cold, you might take a medication that treats your runny nose. Doing so does not prove that your cold was caused by your runny nose. Thus antidepressants may help treat the symptoms of depression without having any influence on the underlying cause.

Moreover, other critics have questioned whether antidepressants are more effective than placebos in treating depression. According to published studies, approximately 60 percent to 70 percent of patients who take antidepressants experience relief from their symptoms, compared with about 30 percent who respond to placebos. Such findings indicate that although there are placebo effects in the treatment of depression, antidepressants seem to lead to greater improvement. Remember, though, that placebo effects are a component of all therapeutic outcomes. For a treatment to work, the patient must believe that the treatment will work, and simply believing so seems to lead to improvement. Active placebos, those that produce some side effects (such as a dry mouth), are more likely to produce therapeutic gains than placebos that do not produce any side effects (Kirsch, 2011). Why would this finding come about? The placebos' side effects suggest to the client-participants that they are receiving real drugs! So when antidepressants are compared with active placebos, the benefits of antidepressants are more modest. Only drug trials that involve individuals with severe depression show clear benefits of drugs over placebos, in part because people with severe depression show less response to placebo treatments (Kirsch et al., 2008).

There is evidence that placebo treatment for depression leads to changes in brain activity (Leuchter, Cook, Witte, Morgan, & Abrams, 2002). In this study, 38 percent of participants receiving placebos showed improvement in depressive symptoms and increased activity in the prefrontal cortex. This pattern of brain activation was different from that observed for participants receiving antidepressants. Thus placebo treatments appear to be associated with changes in neurochemistry and to alleviate symptoms for some people. Placebos may work by giving people hope that they will feel better. This positive expectancy may then alter brain activity.

The take-home message here is that placebos can have powerful effects on the symptoms of depression. The exception is the most severe cases, where the use of medications seems warranted. One recent meta-analysis suggests that for minor depression—when patients experience psychological suffering and other symptoms of depression but do not meet *DSM* criteria for major depression—drug treatment is no more effective than a placebo (Barbui, Cipriani, Patel, Ayuso-Mateos, & van Ommeren, 2011). This finding does not mean that drugs or placebos do not work. Instead, both drugs and placebos help people who are suffering from depression.

COGNITIVE-BEHAVIORAL TREATMENT Not all patients benefit from antidepressant medications. In addition, some patients cannot or will not tolerate the side effects. Fortunately, cognitive-behavioral therapy is just as effective as antidepressants in treating depression (Hollon et al., 2002). From a cognitive perspective, people who become depressed do so because of automatic, irrational thoughts. According to the cognitive distortion model developed by Aaron Beck, depression is the result of a cognitive triad of negative thoughts about oneself, the situation, and the future (see Figure 14.23). The thought patterns of people with depression differ from the thought patterns of people with anxiety disorders. That is, people with anxiety disorders worry about the future. People with depression think about how they have failed in the past, how poorly they are dealing with the present situation, and how terrible the future will be.

The goal of the cognitive-behavioral treatment of depression is to help the client think more adaptively. This change is intended to improve mood and behavior. The specific treatment is adapted to the individual client, but some general principles apply to this type of therapy. Clients may be asked to recognize and record negative thoughts (**Figure 15.20**). Thinking about situations in a negative way can become automatic, and recognizing these thought patterns can be difficult. Once the patterns are identified and monitored, the clinician can help the client recognize other ways of viewing the same situation that are not so dysfunctional.

Cognitive-behavioral therapy can be effective on its own, but combining it with antidepressant medication can be more effective than either one of these approaches alone (McCullough, 2000). In addition, the response rates and remission rates of the combined-treatment approach are extremely good (Keller et al., 2000; Kocsis et al., 2003). The issue is not drugs versus psychotherapy. The issue is which treatment provides—or which treatments provide—relief for each individual. For instance, drug treatment may be the most effective option for clients who are suicidal, in acute distress, or unable to commit to regular attendance with a therapist. For most clients, especially those who have physical problems such as liver impairment or cardiac problems, psychotherapy may be the treatment of choice because it is long-lasting and does not have the side effects associated with medications (Hollon et al., 2006).

FIGURE 15.20 Try for Yourself: Recording Thoughts

Patients in cognitive-behavioral therapy may be asked to keep a record of their automatic thoughts. This example comes from a person suffering from depression.

Date	Event	Emotion	Automatic thoughts
April 4	Boss seemed annoyed.	Sad, anxious, worried	Oh, what have I done now? If I keep making him angry, I'm going to get fired.
April 5	Husband didn't want to make love.	Sad	I'm so fat and ugly.
April 7	Boss yelled at another employee.	Anxious	I'm next.
April 9	Husband said he's taking a long business trip next month.	Sad, defeated	He's probably got a mistress somewhere. My marriage is falling apart.
April 10	Neighbor brought over some cookies.	A little happy, mostly sad	She probably thinks I can't cook. I look like such a mess all the time. And my house was a disaster when she came in!

A log of such events and reactions to those events can help identify patterns in thinking.

Try keeping a log of your own reactions to certain situations, and see if you can identify patterns in your thinking.

As with other mental disorders, treatment of depression with psychotherapy leads to changes in brain activation similar to those observed for drug treatments (Brody et al., 2001). One study found that although psychotherapy and drugs involved the same brain regions, activity in those regions was quite different during the two treatments (Goldapple et al., 2004). This finding suggests that psychotherapy and drugs operate through different mechanisms.

ALTERNATIVE TREATMENTS In patients with seasonal affective disorder (SAD), episodes of depression are most likely to occur during winter. A milder form of SAD has been called the winter blues. The rate of these disorders increases with latitude (**Figure 15.21**). Many of these patients respond favorably to *phototherapy,* which involves exposure to a high-intensity light source for part of each day (**Figure 15.22**).

For some patients with depression, regular aerobic exercise can reduce the symptoms and prevent recurrence (Pollock, 2004). Aerobic exercise may reduce depression because it releases endorphins. These neurotransmitters are chemically related to norepinephrine, a neurotransmitter implicated in depression. As discussed in Chapter 5, the release of endorphins can cause an overall feeling of well-being (a feeling runners sometimes experience as "runner's high"). Aerobic exercise may also regularize bodily rhythms, improve self-esteem, and provide social support if people exercise with others. Patients with depression, however, may have difficulty finding the energy and motivation to begin an exercise regimen.

Electroconvulsive therapy (ECT) is a very effective treatment for those who are severely depressed and do not respond to conventional treatments (Hollon et al., 2002). For a number of reasons, ECT might be preferable to other treatments for depression. Antidepressants can take weeks to be effective, whereas ECT works quickly. For a suicidal patient, waiting several weeks for relief can literally be deadly. In addition, ECT may be the treatment of choice for depression in pregnant women, since there is no evidence that the seizures harm the developing fetus. Many psychotropic medications, in contrast, can cause birth defects. Most important, ECT has proved effective in patients for whom other treatments have failed.

FIGURE 15.21 Incidence of Seasonal Affective Disorder As shown by this map, incidence of SAD varies by latitude.

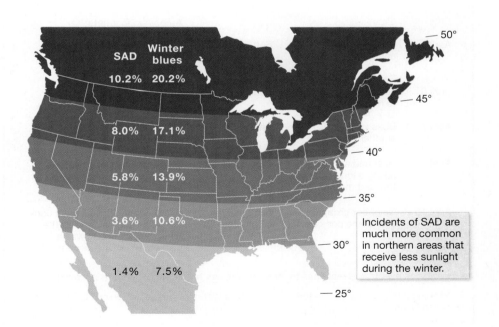

SAD | Winter blues

10.2% 20.2%

8.0% 17.1%

5.8% 13.9%

3.6% 10.6%

1.4% 7.5%

Incidents of SAD are much more common in northern areas that receive less sunlight during the winter.

ECT does, however, have some serious limitations, including a high relapse rate (often necessitating repeated treatments) and memory impairments (Fink, 2001). In most cases, memory loss is limited to the day of ECT treatment, but some patients experience substantial permanent memory loss (Donahue, 2000). Some centers perform unilateral ECT over only the hemisphere not dominant for language, a treatment that seems to reduce memory disruption (Papadimitriou, Zervas, & Papakostas, 2001).

A series of studies has demonstrated that transcranial magnetic stimulation (TMS) over the left frontal regions results in a significant reduction in depression (Chistyakov et al., 2004; George, Lisanby, & Sackheim, 1999; George et al., 1995; Pascual-Leone, Catala, & Pascual-Leone, 1996). Because TMS does not involve anesthesia or have any major side effects (other than headache), it can be administered outside hospital settings. It is not likely, however, that TMS will ever completely replace ECT. The two methods may act via different mechanisms and may therefore be appropriate for different types of patients. The long-term value of TMS is that it is effective even for those who have not responded to treatment with antidepressants (Fitzgerald et al., 2003). In October 2008, TMS was approved by the FDA for the treatment of major depression in patients who are not helped by traditional therapies.

FIGURE 15.22 Phototherapy One treatment for SAD is phototherapy. In this method, the patient sits in front of strong lighting for several hours each day to reduce symptoms.

DEEP BRAIN STIMULATION As with obsessive-compulsive disorder, DBS might be valuable for treating severe depression when all other treatments have failed. In 2003, Helen Mayberg and colleagues became the first to try out this novel treatment. Mayberg's earlier research had pointed to an area of the prefrontal cortex as abnormal in depression. Following the logic of using DBS for Parkinson's, neurosurgeons inserted electrodes into this brain region in six patients suffering from severe depression (Mayberg et al., 2005; McNeely, Mayberg, Lozano, & Kennedy, 2008). The results were stunning for four of the patients. In fact, some of them felt relief as soon as the switch was turned on. For all four, it was as if a horrible noise had stopped and a weight had been lifted, as if they had emerged into a more beautiful world (Dobbs, 2006; Ressler & Mayberg, 2007; **Figure 15.23**).

Several studies have been done of using DBS for treatment-resistant depression, and each time at least half of the clients benefited from this treatment (Bewernick et al., 2010; Malone et al., 2009). One study followed 20 patients for three to six years and found that about two-thirds showed long-lasting benefits from DBS (Kennedy et al., 2011). These studies demonstrate that DBS is useful for helping clients lead more productive lives. For instance, in the study just mentioned, only 10 percent of the client-participants were able to work or engage in meaningful activities outside the house (e.g., volunteering) before DBS, whereas two-thirds were able to do so after DBS.

DBS differs from other treatments in that researchers can relatively straightforwardly alter the electrical current, without the patients knowing, to demonstrate that the DBS is responsible for improvements in psychological functioning. Research using DBS to treat severe depression is now under way at a number of sites around the globe. In France, researchers used DBS in two patients who had both OCD and major depression. Stimulation of electrodes placed in the caudate relieved symptoms of OCD but not depression, whereas stimulation of electrodes in the nucleus accumbens alleviated symptoms of depression but not OCD (Aouizerate et al., 2009).

GENDER ISSUES IN TREATING DEPRESSION As noted in Chapter 14, women are twice as likely to be diagnosed with depression as men are. Some portion of this difference relates to high rates of domestic and other violence against women,

FIGURE 15.23 Scientific Method: Mayberg's Study of DBS for Depression

Hypothesis: Deep brain stimulation of an area of the prefrontal cortex may alleviate depression.

Research Method:

1 A pair of small holes were drilled into the skulls of six participants.

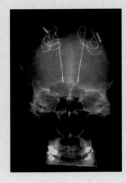

2 A pulse generator was attached under the collarbone, connecting to electrodes that passed through the holes in the skull to a specific area of the prefrontal cortex.

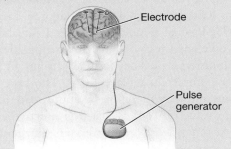

Electrode

Pulse generator

Results: Some participants reported relief as soon as the electrodes were switched on, and 2/3 of the participants felt significantly better within months.

Conclusion: DBS may be an especially effective method for patients resistant to other treatments.

Source: Mayberg, H. S., Lozano, A. M., Voon, V., McNeely, H. E., Seminowicz, D., Hamani, C., et al. (2005). Deep brain stimulation for treatment-resistant depression. *Neuron, 45,* 651–660.

reduced economic resources, and inequities at work (American Psychological Association, 2007). Women are also the primary consumers of psychotherapy. The American Psychological Association therefore has published *Guidelines for Psychological Practice with Girls and Women* (2007). These guidelines remind therapists to be aware of gender-specific stressors, such as the way work and family interact to place additional burdens on women and the biological realities of reproduction and of menopause. The guidelines also point out that women of color, lesbians, and women with disabilities are often stereotyped in ways that signal disregard for the choices they have made and the challenges they face. All of these factors can interfere with the therapeutic process.

Problems also exist in the treatment of depression in men. Men's reluctance to admit to depression and even greater reluctance to seek appropriate therapy have been described as "a conspiracy of silence that has long surrounded depression in men" (Brody, 1997). Two prominent men—Mike Wallace, a journalist and television news anchor, and the late William Styron, a Pulitzer Prize–winning author—have talked openly about their battles with depression (**Figure 15.24**). Wallace describes it this way: "The sunshine means nothing to you at all. The seasons, friends, good food mean nothing. All you focus on is yourself and how bad you feel." Styron writes: "In severe depression, the entire body and spirit of a person is in a state of shipwreck, of desolate lostness. Nothing animates the body or spirit. It's a total wipeout" (both quoted in Brody, 1997, paragraphs 2–3). Public statements from such well-respected men may help break the silence surrounding depression in men and increase the number of men who seek psychotherapy. One goal is to help men stop masking their depression with alcohol, isolation, and irritability. Any of these retreats from the social world may be a symptom of unacknowledged depression.

Lithium Is Most Effective for Bipolar Disorder

Major depression and bipolar disorder are both disorders of mood, but they are fundamentally different and require different treatments. In bipolar disorder, as discussed in Chapter 14, mood cycles between mania and depression. This condition is one of the few mental disorders for which there is a clear optimal treatment: psychotropic medications, especially the mood stabilizer lithium (Geddes, Burgess, Hawton, Jamison, & Goodwin, 2004). In one study, only about 20 percent of patients maintained on lithium experienced relapses (Keller & Baker, 1991).

As with the uses of other psychotropic drugs, the discovery of lithium for the treatment of bipolar disorder was serendipitous. In 1949, the researcher John Cade found that the urine of manic patients was toxic to guinea pigs. He believed that a toxin—specifically, uric acid—might be causing the symptoms of mania. If so, once the uric acid was removed from the body through the urine, the symptoms would diminish (a solution that would explain why the patients were not always manic). When he gave lithium urate, a salt in uric acid, to the guinea pigs, however, it proved nontoxic. To his surprise, it protected them against the toxic effects of the manic patients' urine and also sedated them. He next tried lithium salts on himself. When he was assured of their safety, he gave the salts to 10 hospitalized manic patients. All the patients recovered rapidly.

The mechanisms by which lithium stabilizes mood are not well understood, but the drug seems to modulate neurotransmitter levels, balancing excitatory and inhibitory activities (Jope, 1999). Lithium has unpleasant side effects, however, including thirst, hand tremors, excessive urination, and memory problems. The side effects often diminish after several weeks on the drug. Because lithium works better on mania than on depression, patients often are treated with both lithium and an antidepressant. SSRIs are preferable to other antidepressants because they are less likely to trigger episodes of mania (Gijsman, Geddes, Rendell, Nolen, & Goodwin, 2004). Anticonvulsive medications, more commonly used to reduce seizures, also can stabilize mood and may be effective for intense bipolar episodes.

As with all psychological disorders, compliance with drug therapy can be a problem for various reasons. For example, patients may skip doses or stop taking the medications completely in an effort to reduce the drugs' side effects. In these situations, cognitive-behavioral therapy can help increase compliance with medication regimens (Miller, Norman, & Keitner, 1989). Patients with bipolar disorder also may stop taking their medications because they miss the "highs" of their hypomanic and manic phases. Psychological therapy can help patients accept their need for medication and understand the impact their disorder has on them and on those around them.

Pharmacological Treatments Are Superior for Schizophrenia

In the early 1900s, Freud's psychoanalytic theory and treatments based on it were widely touted as the answer to many mental disorders. Even Freud, however, admitted that his techniques were effective only for what he termed "neuroses" and were unlikely to benefit patients with more-severe psychotic disorders, such as schizophrenia. Because psychotic patients were difficult to handle and even more difficult to treat, they generally were institutionalized in large mental hospitals. By 1934, according to estimates, the physician-to-patient ratio in such institutions in New York State was less than 1 to 200.

(a)

(b)

FIGURE 15.24 Men Who Have Broken the Conspiracy of Silence Men are much less likely than women to admit that they have suffered from depression. Two famous men who were willing to break this conspiracy of silence are **(a)** Mike Wallace, a news correspondent best-known for his work on the television show *60 Minutes,* whose depression began after accusations of libel and a related lawsuit; **(b)** William Styron, best-known as the author of the novel *The Confessions of Nat Turner* (1967), the novel *Sophie's Choice* (1979), and the memoir *Darkness Visible* (1990), which chronicled his bouts of depression.

In this undesirable situation, the staff and administration of mental hospitals were willing to try any inexpensive treatment that had a chance of decreasing the patient population or that at least might make the inmates more manageable. Brain surgery, such as prefrontal lobotomy, was considered a viable option for patients with severe mental disorders. Moniz initially reported that the operation was frequently successful (see the earlier section "Alternative Biological Treatments Are Used in Extreme Cases"). It soon became evident to him that patients suffering from anxiety or depression benefited most from the surgery. Patients with schizophrenia did not seem to improve following the operation. Fortunately, as noted earlier, the introduction of psychotropic medications in the 1950s eliminated the use of lobotomy.

PHARMACOLOGICAL TREATMENTS Since the sixteenth century, extracts from dogbane, a toxic herb, had been used to calm highly agitated patients. The critical ingredient was isolated in the 1950s and named *reserpine*. When given to patients with schizophrenia, reserpine not only had a sedative effect. It also was an effective antipsychotic, reducing the positive symptoms of schizophrenia, such as delusions and hallucinations. Shortly afterward, a synthetic version of reserpine was created that had fewer side effects. This drug, *chlorpromazine,* acts as a major tranquilizer. It reduces anxiety, sedates without inducing sleep, and decreases the severity and frequency of the positive symptoms of schizophrenia. Later, another antipsychotic, *haloperidol,* was developed that was chemically different and had less of a sedating effect than chlorpromazine.

Haloperidol and chlorpromazine revolutionized the treatment of schizophrenia and became the most frequently used treatment for this disorder. Patients with schizophrenia who had been hospitalized for years were able to walk out of mental institutions and live independently. These antipsychotics have drawbacks, however. For example, the medications have little or no impact on the negative symptoms of schizophrenia. In addition, they have significant side effects. Chlorpromazine sedates patients, can cause constipation and weight gain, and causes cardiovascular damage. Haloperidol does not cause these symptoms, but both drugs have significant motor side effects that resemble symptoms of Parkinson's disease: immobility of facial muscles, trembling of extremities, muscle spasms, uncontrollable salivation, and a shuffling walk. Tardive dyskinesia—as discussed earlier, involuntary movements of the lips, tongue, face, legs, or other parts of the body—is another devastating side effect of these medications and is irreversible once it appears. Despite these side effects, haloperidol and chlorpromazine were the only available options.

The late 1980s saw the introduction of *clozapine*. This drug is significantly different from previous antipsychotic medications in a number of ways. First, it acts on receptors for dopamine, serotonin, norepinephrine, acetylcholine, and histamine. Second, it is beneficial in treating the negative as well as the positive symptoms of schizophrenia (**Figure 15.25**). Many patients who had not responded to the previously available neuroleptics improved on clozapine. Third, no signs of Parkinson's symptoms or of tardive dyskinesia appeared in any of the patients taking the drug. Clozapine has fewer side effects than chlorpromazine or haloperidol, but its side effects are serious: seizures, heart arrhythmias, and substantial weight gain. Of even greater concern is that clozapine can cause a fatal reduction in white blood cells. Although the risk of this problem is low, patients taking the drug must have frequent blood tests. The cost of the blood tests, in addition to the high cost of the medication, has made this drug treatment prohibitively expensive for many patients.

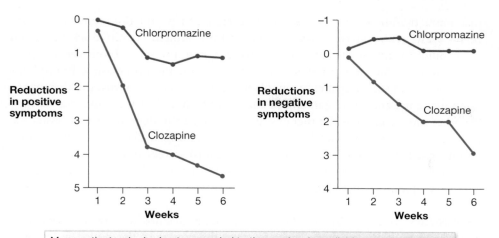

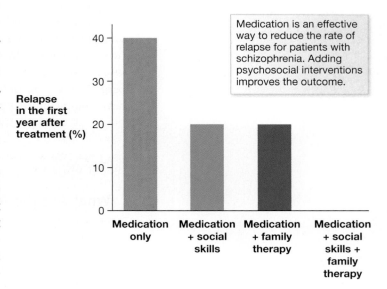

FIGURE 15.25 **The Effectiveness of Clozapine** These graphs compare the effects, in representative cases, of using either clozapine or chlorpromazine to treat patients with schizophrenia.

Many patients who had not responded to the previously available neuroleptics found that clozapine reduced the positive and negative symptoms of schizophrenia.

Other medications similar to clozapine in structure, pharmacology, and effectiveness have been introduced that do not reduce white blood cell counts. These are Risperdal and Zyprexa, which along with clozapine are called *second-generation antipsychotics* (sometimes they are called *atypical antipsychotics* to differentiate them from the typical drugs that had been used previously). These drugs are now the first line of defense in the treatment of schizophrenia (Walker, Kestler, Bollini, & Hochman, 2004), although clozapine is typically reserved for more-severe cases because of its more-serious side effects. An analysis of 11 studies of a total of 2,769 patients found that these second-generation antipsychotics have about one-fifth the risk of producing tardive dyskinesia as first-generation drugs (Correll, Leucht, & Kane, 2004).

PSYCHOSOCIAL TREATMENTS Medication is essential in the treatment of schizophrenia. Without it, patients may deteriorate, experiencing more-frequent and more-severe psychotic episodes. When antipsychotic drugs became available, other types of therapies for schizophrenia were virtually dismissed. It became clear over time, however, that although medication effectively reduces delusions and hallucinations, it does not substantially affect patients' social functioning. Thus antipsychotic drugs fall short of being a cure. The drugs must be combined with other treatments to help people lead productive lives.

For example, *social skills training* is an effective way to address some deficits in patients with schizophrenia (**Figure 15.26**). These patients can benefit from intensive training in regulating affect, recognizing social cues, and predicting the effects of their behavior in social situations. With intensive long-term training, patients with schizophrenia can generalize the skills learned in therapy to other social environments. Also, when self-care skills are deficient, behavioral interventions can focus on areas such as grooming and bathing, management of medications, and financial planning. Training in specific cognitive skills, such as in modifying thinking patterns and in coping with auditory hallucinations, has been less effective.

Aaron Beck has proposed that an intensive form of cognitive-behavioral therapy (CBT) is effective for treating schizophrenia (Beck & Rector, 2005). Beck believes

Medication is an effective way to reduce the rate of relapse for patients with schizophrenia. Adding psychosocial interventions improves the outcome.

FIGURE 15.26 **The Effectiveness of Antipsychotic Medications, Social Skills Training, and Family Therapy** This graph shows the relapse rates, in representative cases, of using different methods—alone or in combination—to treat patients with schizophrenia.

that brain dysfunction gives rise to disordered beliefs and disordered behaviors. In his view, schizophrenia may arise partly from limited cognitive resources and an inability to inhibit the intrusion of inappropriate thoughts. From this perspective, delusions and hallucinations reflect biased information processing. In CBT for schizophrenia, much initial effort involves getting the client to trust the therapist as nonjudgmental and understanding of the client's outlook. Over time, the therapy becomes more formal as the therapist helps the client understand how stressful life circumstances contribute to disordered thoughts and how alternative explanations might exist for delusions and hallucinations. Initial studies using CBT for schizophrenia indicate that it is more effective than other psychological treatments in reducing symptoms such as delusions and hallucinations.

PROGNOSIS IN SCHIZOPHRENIA Most patients diagnosed with schizophrenia experience multiple psychotic episodes over the course of the disorder. In some patients, the disorder apparently progresses. Each schizophrenic episode lays the groundwork for increasingly severe symptoms in the future. Thus it is in the best interest of the patient to treat the disorder early and aggressively.

Most patients with schizophrenia improve over time. One long-term study that followed participants for an average of 32 years showed that between half and two-thirds were recovered or had experienced considerable improvement in functioning on follow-up (Harding, Zubin, & Strauss, 1987). No one knows why most people with schizophrenia apparently improve as they grow older. Perhaps they find a treatment regimen most effective for them, or perhaps changes in the brain that occur with aging somehow result in fewer psychotic episodes. Dopamine levels may decrease with age, and this decrease may be related to the improvement in symptoms.

The prognosis for patients with schizophrenia depends on factors that include age of onset, gender, and culture. People diagnosed later in life tend to have a more favorable prognosis than people who experience their first symptoms during childhood or adolescence (McGlashan, 1988). Women tend to have better prognoses than men do (Hambrecht, Maurer, Hafner, & Sartorius, 1992), perhaps because schizophrenia in women tends to appear later than in men. Culture also plays a role in prognosis. In developing countries, schizophrenia often is not so severe as in developed countries (Jablensky, 1989; Leff, Sartorius, Jablensky, Korten, & Ernberg, 1992). This difference may arise because more-extensive family networks in developing countries provide more support for patients with schizophrenia.

Summing Up

What Are the Most Effective Treatments?

Evidence-based treatments should be used for psychological disorders. Psychological treatments differ from psychotherapy in that they vary according to the particular disorder being treated, are developed in labs by psychologists, and are not guided by an overall grand theory. Cognitive and behavioral therapies—including cognitive restructuring, systematic desensitization, exposure, and response prevention—are particularly effective in the treatment of anxiety disorders. Drug treatments are also effective in the treatment of panic disorder and OCD. For severe cases of OCD, research suggests that DBS may be effective in alleviating symptoms. Among the treatment strategies for depression are antidepressants, cognitive-behavioral therapy, exercise, electroconvulsive therapy, transcranial magnetic stimulation, and deep brain stimulation. Sex differences in the incidence of depression have led to the development of specific guidelines for psychotherapy that remind therapists of gender-specific factors associated with the experience, recognition, and treatment of psychological disorders. Lithium is a mood stabilizer that is effective in the treatment of bipolar disorder. Drugs are recommended for the treatment of schizophrenia. However, the most effective treatment for schizophrenia involves the use of both drugs and psychosocial interventions. Social skills training, behavioral interventions, and cognitive skills training have been found to be effective in reducing relapse rates for schizophrenia. The prognosis for individuals with schizophrenia is more favorable for those who are diagnosed later in life, for females, and for those who live in developing countries.

Measuring Up

Indicate whether cognitive-behavioral therapy, drug therapy, or a combination of the two is the recommended treatment for each disorder listed.

    a. bipolar disorder
    b. depression
    c. generalized anxiety disorder
    d. obsessive-compulsive disorder
    e. panic disorder
    f. phobias
    g. schizophrenia

Answers: Drug therapy is most effective for choices a, g; cognitive-behavioral therapy is most effective for c, d, e, f; a combination of drug therapy and cognitive-behavioral therapy is most effective for b.

15.3 Can Personality Disorders Be Treated?

Learning Objective

- Discuss therapeutic approaches for borderline personality disorder and antisocial personality disorder.

As discussed in Chapter 14, not much is known about the causes of personality disorders, such as borderline personality disorder and antisocial personality disorder. Likewise, little is known about how best to treat personality disorders. There is a growing literature of case studies that describe treatment approaches for these disorders, but few large, well-controlled studies have been undertaken.

The one thing about personality disorders that most therapists agree on is that they are notoriously difficult to treat. Individuals with personality disorders who are in therapy are usually also being treated for an Axis I disorder, such as OCD or depression. The Axis I disorder is typically the problem for which the patient sought therapy in the first place. People rarely seek therapy for personality disorders, because one hallmark of these disorders is that patients see the environment rather than their own behavior as the cause of their problems. This outlook often makes individuals with personality disorders very difficult to engage in therapy.

Dialectical Behavior Therapy Is Most Successful for Borderline Personality Disorder

FIGURE 15.27 Marsha Linehan The psychologist Marsha Linehan pioneered the therapeutic technique DBT. Linehan has recently "come out" as having experienced the kind of psychological disorder this technique is used to treat.

The impulsivity, emotional disturbances, and identity disturbances characteristic of borderline personality disorder make it very challenging to provide therapy for the people affected. Traditional psychotherapy approaches have been largely unsuccessful, so therapists have attempted to develop approaches specific to borderline personality disorder.

The most successful treatment approach to date for borderline personality disorder was developed by the psychologist Marsha Linehan in the 1980s (**Figure 15.27**). Two decades earlier, as a young woman, Linehan had suffered from extreme social withdrawal, physical self-destructiveness, and recurrent suicidality (Carey, 2011). Institutionalized and diagnosed as schizophrenic, she was locked in a seclusion room, treated with various medications, given Freudian analysis, and treated with electroshock. Eventually, after being released from the hospital with little hope of surviving, Linehan learned to accept herself rather than striving for some impossible ideal. This "radical acceptance," as she puts it, enabled Linehan to function. She earned her Ph.D. in psychology with the goal of helping people who are chronically self-destructive or even suicidal. Linehan's **dialectical behavior therapy (DBT)** combines elements of the behavioral and cognitive treatments with a mindfulness approach based on Eastern meditative practices (Lieb, Zanarini, Schmahl, Linehan, & Bohus, 2004). All patients are seen in both group and individual sessions, and the responsibilities of the patient and the therapist are made explicit.

Therapy proceeds in three stages. In the first stage, the therapist targets the patient's most extreme and dysfunctional behaviors. Often these are self-cutting and threats of suicide or suicide attempts. The focus is on replacing these behaviors with more-appropriate ones. The patient learns problem-solving techniques and more-effective ways of coping with his or her emotions. In this stage, the person is taught to control attention so that the person focuses on the present. Strategies for controlling attention are based on mindfulness meditation. In the second stage, the therapist helps the patient explore past traumatic experiences that may be at the root of emotional problems. In the third stage, the therapist helps the patient develop self-respect and independent problem solving. This stage is crucial because patients with borderline personality disorder depend heavily on others for support and validation. These patients must be able to generate the appropriate attitudes and necessary skills themselves, or they are likely to revert to their previous behavior patterns.

The symptoms experienced by individuals with borderline personality disorder can border on psychosis or resemble depression. As a result, researchers previously believed these patients would develop a disorder such as schizophrenia or depression. Studies that have followed individuals with borderline personality disorder over time, however, have demonstrated that their symptoms remain relatively unchanged (Plakun, Burkhardt, & Muller, 1985). The only patients that show long-term improvement are borderline patients of a high socioeconomic level who receive intensive treatment; these individuals demonstrate improved interpersonal relationships and often achieve full-time employment (Stone, Stone, & Hurt, 1987). In the remainder of patients with borderline personality disorder, interpersonal and occupational problems are the norm. Substance abuse is common, and many patients attempt suicide multiple times.

Therapeutic approaches targeted at borderline personality disorder, such as DBT, may improve the prognosis for these patients. Studies have demonstrated

dialectical behavior therapy (DBT) A form of therapy used to treat borderline personality disorder.

that patients undergoing DBT are more likely to remain in treatment and less likely to be suicidal than are patients in other types of therapy (Linehan, Armstrong, Suarez, Allmon, & Heard, 1991; Linehan, Heard, & Armstrong, 1993). SSRIs are often prescribed along with DBT to treat feelings of depression.

Antisocial Personality Disorder Is Extremely Difficult to Treat

Treating patients with borderline personality disorder can be very difficult. Treating those with antisocial personality disorder often seems impossible. These patients lie without thinking twice about it, care little for other people's feelings, and live for the present without consideration of the future. All these factors make development of a therapeutic relationship and motivation for change remote possibilities at best. Individuals with this disorder are often more interested in manipulating their therapists than in changing their own behavior. Therapists working with these patients must be constantly on guard.

THERAPEUTIC APPROACHES FOR ANTISOCIAL PERSONALITY DISORDER Numerous treatment approaches have been tried for antisocial personality disorder (and the related but not identical disorder *psychopathy*). Because individuals with antisocial personality disorder apparently have diminished cortical arousal, stimulants have been prescribed to normalize arousal levels. There is evidence that these drugs are beneficial in the short term but not the long term. Anti-anxiety drugs may lower hostility levels somewhat, and lithium has shown promise in treating the aggressive, impulsive behavior of violent criminals who are psychopathic. Overall, however, psychotropic medications have not been effective in treating this disorder.

Similarly, traditional psychotherapeutic approaches seem of little use in treating antisocial personality disorder. Behavioral and cognitive approaches have had somewhat more success. Behavioral approaches reinforce appropriate behavior. They ignore or punish inappropriate behavior in an attempt to replace maladaptive behavior patterns with behavior patterns that are more socially appropriate. This approach seems to work best when the therapist controls reinforcement, the client cannot leave treatment, and the client is part of a group. Individual therapy sessions rarely produce any change in anti social behavior. Clearly, the behavioral approach cannot be implemented on an outpatient basis, since the client will receive reinforcement for his or her antisocial behavior outside of therapy and can leave treatment at any time. For these reasons, therapy for this disorder is most effective in a residential treatment center or a correctional facility.

Cognitive approaches have been tried for antisocial personality disorder. Aaron Beck and colleagues (1990) have conceptualized this disorder as a series of faulty cognitions. The individual with antisocial personality disorder believes her or his desire for something justifies any actions she or he takes to attain it. The person believes those actions will not have negative consequences or, if they do, that these consequences are not important. The person also believes he or she is always right and what others think is unimportant. Therapy therefore focuses on making the client aware of these beliefs and challenging their validity. Therapists try to demonstrate that the client can meet his or her goals more easily by following the rules of society than by trying to get around them, as in the following example (Beck et al., 1990):

Therapist: How well has the "beat-the-system" approach actually worked out for you over time?

Brett: It works great . . . until someone catches on or starts to catch on. Then you have to scrap that plan and come up with a new one.

Therapist: How difficult was it, you know, to cover up one scheme and come up with a new one?

Brett: Sometimes it was really easy. There are some real pigeons out there.

Therapist: Was it always easy?

Brett: Well, no. Sometimes it was a real bitch. . . . Seems like I'm always needing a good plan to beat the system.

Therapist: Do you think it's ever easier to go with the system instead of trying to beat it in some way?

Brett: Well, after all that I have been through, I would have to say yes, there have been times that going with the system would have been easier in the long run. . . . But . . . it's such a challenge to beat the system. It feels exciting when I come up with a new plan and think I can make it work.

This dialogue illustrates both the cognitive approach and why these clients are so difficult to work with. Even if they know what they are doing is wrong, they do not care. They live for the thrill of getting away with something.

PROGNOSIS FOR ANTISOCIAL PERSONALITY DISORDER The prognosis that patients with antisocial personality disorder will change their behaviors as a result of therapy is poor. This conclusion is especially true for patients with psychopathic traits. Some of the more recently developed cognitive techniques show promise, but no good evidence indicates that they produce long-lasting or even real changes. Fortunately for society, individuals with antisocial personality disorder but without psychopathy typically improve after age 40 (**Figure 15.28**).

The reasons for this improvement are unknown, but it may be due to a reduction in biological drives. Alternative theories suggest these individuals may gain insight into their self-defeating behaviors or may just get worn out and be unable to continue their manipulative ways. The improvement, however, is mainly in the realm of antisocial behavior. The underlying egocentricity, callousness, and manipulativeness can remain unchanged (Harpur & Hare, 1994), especially for those who are psychopathic. In fact, although criminal acts decrease among those with antisocial personality disorder after age 40, more than half of the individuals with psychopathic traits continue to be arrested after age 40 (Hare, McPherson, & Forth, 1988). Thus although some aspects of their behavior mellow with age, psychopaths remain rather indifferent to traditional societal norms.

Because of the limited effectiveness of therapy for this disorder, time and effort may be better spent in prevention. *Conduct disorder* is a childhood condition known to be a precursor to antisocial personality disorder. Some of the environmental and developmental risk factors for conduct disorder have been identified. Focusing on these factors may reduce the likelihood that a child with conduct disorder will grow up to have antisocial personality disorder.

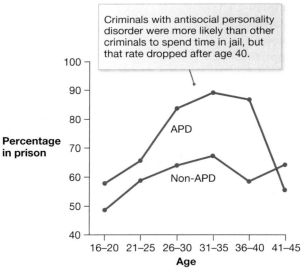

Criminals with antisocial personality disorder were more likely than other criminals to spend time in jail, but that rate dropped after age 40.

FIGURE 15.28 Antisocial Personality Disorder For this longitudinal study, the percentage of participants in prison during each five-year period is shown. **What factors do you think might lead to the improvement in behavior of middle-aged patients with APD?**

15.4 How Should Childhood Disorders and Adolescent Disorders Be Treated?

It is estimated that in the United States at least 12 percent to 20 percent of children and adolescents suffer from mental disorders (Leckman et al., 1995; Merikangas et al., 2010). Each person's experiences and development during early life are critically important to that person's mental health in adulthood. Problems not addressed during childhood or adolescence may persist into adulthood. Most theories of human development regard children and adolescents as more malleable than adults and therefore more amenable to treatment. Thus childhood disorders and adolescent disorders should be the focus of research into etiology, prevention, and treatment. To illustrate the issues involved in treating disorders of early life, this section considers treatment approaches for adolescent depression, ADHD, and autism.

The Use of Medication to Treat Adolescent Depression Is Controversial

Adolescent depression is a serious problem. Recently, approximately 8 percent of the U.S. population ages 12 to 17 reported experiencing within the last year a major depressive episode that met *DSM* criteria (SAMHSA, 2011;

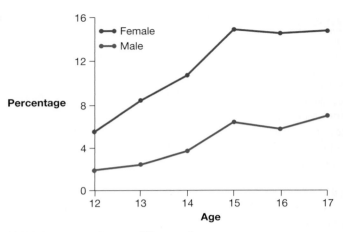

FIGURE 15.29 Rates of Depression in Teenagers This graph shows results from the National Survey on Drug Use and Health undertaken by the Substance Abuse and Mental Health Services Administration (SAMHSA), a branch of the U.S. Department of Health and Human Services. The lines chart the rates of major depressive episodes and treatments among adolescents in 2009.

Figure 15.29). Untreated adolescent depression is associated with drug abuse, dropping out of school, and suicide. In the United States, approximately 5,000 teenagers kill themselves each year, making it the third leading cause of death for that age group (Arias, MacDorman, Strobino, & Guyer, 2003). For many years, depression in children and adolescents was ignored or viewed as a typical part of growing up. Only about one-third of adolescents with psychological disorders receive any form of treatment (Merikangas et al., 2011). The percentage is even lower for adolescents from racial and ethnic minorities (Cummings & Druss, 2010). Understandably, then, many mental health professionals reacted favorably to the initial use of SSRIs, such as Prozac, to treat adolescent depression. Studies had found tricyclic antidepressants ineffective and the side effects potentially dangerous for adolescents, but the first studies using SSRIs found them effective and safe (e.g., Emslie et al., 1997).

Shortly after SSRIs were introduced as treatments for adolescent depression, some mental health researchers raised concerns that the drugs might cause some adolescents to become suicidal (Jureidini et al., 2004). These concerns arose partly from findings that SSRIs cause some adults to feel restless, impulsive, and suicidal. Following a report by one drug company of an increase in suicidal thoughts among adolescents taking its product, the FDA asked all drug companies to analyze their records for similar reports. An analysis of reports on more than 4,400 children and adolescents found that about twice as many of those taking SSRIs reported having suicidal thoughts (4 percent) as those taking a placebo (2 percent). None of the children or adolescents committed suicide. Given evidence of increased thoughts of suicide, the FDA voted in 2004 to require manufacturers to add to their product labels a warning that antidepressants increase the risk of suicidal thinking and suicidal behavior in children and adolescents and that physicians prescribing these drugs to young people suffering from depression need to balance risk with clinical need. Physicians were also advised to watch their young patients closely, especially in the first few weeks of treatment. Suddenly many parents were wondering whether SSRIs were safe for their children.

Many questions about SSRIs and young people need to be answered. First, are SSRIs effective for young people? If so, are they more effective than other treatments? Second, do these drugs cause suicidal feelings, or are young people with depression likely to feel suicidal whether or not they take medication? Finally, how many children and adolescents would be suicidal if their depression was left untreated?

TADS The Treatment for Adolescents with Depression Study (TADS, 2004) was an ambitious research program supported by the U.S. National Institutes of Health. TADS provided clear evidence that the SSRI Prozac is effective in treating adolescent depression.

The study examined 439 patients ages 12 to 17 who had suffered from depression for an average of 40 weeks before the study began. Participants were assigned randomly to a type of treatment and followed for 12 weeks. The results indicated that 61 percent of participants taking Prozac showed improvement in symptoms, compared with 43 percent receiving cognitive-behavioral therapy and 35 percent taking a placebo. The group receiving Prozac and CBT did best (71 percent improved). This latter finding is consistent with the findings of studies using adult participants. In short, combining drugs and psychotherapy often produces the strongest results for treating depression.

Three years after the initial TADS study, a 36-week follow-up study was done of the TADS treatment sample (March et al., 2007). The combined group had the best outcomes (86 percent improvement). Improvement with CBT alone (81 percent) was similar to that with Prozac alone (81 percent; **Figure 15.30**).

In terms of suicidality, the results were more mixed. All treatment groups experienced a reduction in thoughts of suicide compared with the baseline. Participants in the Prozac group, however, were twice as likely to have serious suicidal thoughts or intentions compared with those undergoing other treatments. Of the seven adolescents who attempted suicide during the study, six were taking Prozac. The greater risk of suicidal thoughts or events continued through 36 weeks. Critics of adolescents receiving drugs point out that these findings are consistent with other studies showing a risk from SSRIs (Antonuccio & Burns, 2004).

FIGURE 15.30 **Scientific Method: The Treatment for Adolescents with Depression Study (TADS)**

Hypothesis: Prozac is the most effective method for treating adolescent depression.

Research Method:

1 Patients aged 12 to 17 were randomly assigned to a type of treatment and followed it for 12 weeks.

2 Some of the patients were given Prozac, some cognitive-behavioral therapy, some a placebo, and some Prozac and cognitive-behavioral therapy together.

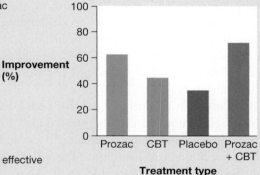

Results: The group that received Prozac and CBT did best. In a follow-up study of the TADS treatment sample, the combined group continued to have the best outcomes. Improvement with CBT alone was similar to that with Prozac alone.

Conclusion: Both CBT and Prozac are effective in treating adolescent depression.

Sources:

Treatment for Adolescents with Depression Study (TADS) Team. (2004). Fluoxetine, cognitive-behavioral therapy, and their combination for adolescents with depression: Treatment for adolescents with depression study (TADS) randomized controlled trial. *Journal of the American Medical Association, 292*, 807–820.

March, J. S., Silva, S., Petrycki, S., Curry, J., Wells, K., Fairbank, J., et al. (2007). The Treatment for Adolescents With Depression Study (TADS): Long-term effectiveness and safety outcomes. *Archives of General Psychiatry, 64*, 1132–1143.

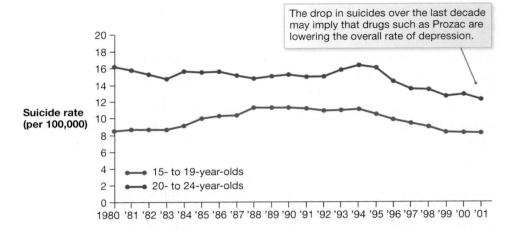

FIGURE 15.31 Declining Suicide Rates This graph depicts the declining suicide rates among people from ages 15 to 24 during a 20-year period. **What other factors, in addition to medication, might have led to this decrease?**

The drop in suicides over the last decade may imply that drugs such as Prozac are lowering the overall rate of depression.

Suicide rate (per 100,000)

● 15- to 19-year-olds
● 20- to 24-year-olds

1980 '81 '82 '83 '84 '85 '86 '87 '88 '89 '90 '91 '92 '93 '94 '95 '96 '97 '98 '99 '00 '01

FURTHER THOUGHTS ON TREATMENT APPROACHES A few things should be kept in mind in analyzing the use of SSRIs for adolescent depression. In the TADS study, suicide attempts were quite uncommon (7 of 439 patients). This result is consistent with the FDA finding that about 4 percent of adolescents taking Prozac will become suicidal. Moreover, only a small number of the 5,000 adolescents who kill themselves each year are taking antidepressants of any kind. The question is whether the millions of children who take antidepressants experience more benefits than risks.

Note that the suicide rates have dropped since the use of SSRIs became widespread (**Figure 15.31**). The greater the increase in the number of SSRI prescriptions for adolescents within a region, the greater the reduction in teenage suicides (Olfson, Shaffer, Marcus, & Greenberg, 2003). Thus not providing SSRIs to adolescents may raise the suicide rate (Brent, 2004).

According to some researchers, the relative success of psychotherapy for teenage depression makes it a better treatment choice. Indeed, considerable evidence shows that psychotherapy is effective on its own (Mufson et al., 2004) and also enhances drug treatment. Psychological treatments such as interpersonal psychotherapy are successful as well (Hollon et al., 2002). But getting adolescents to comply with psychotherapy can be challenging. Psychotherapy is also time consuming and expensive, and many health insurance companies provide only minimal support (Rifkin & Rifkin, 2004). In addition, it is unrealistic to expect there to be sufficient resources to provide psychotherapy to all adolescents who need it in the near future.

By contrast, it is relatively easy for pediatricians and family physicians to prescribe drugs. Unfortunately, the prescribing of such medications by general practitioners can be problematic because these individuals do not have training in treating psychological disorders. Thus although prescribing drugs without CBT might be cost-effective (Domino et al., 2008), it may not be in the best interests of adolescents with depression.

Children with ADHD Can Benefit from Various Approaches

There is some dispute about whether attention deficit hyperactivity disorder is a mental disorder or simply a troublesome behavior pattern that children eventually outgrow. Some people diagnosed with ADHD as children grow out of it. Many more, however, suffer from the disorder throughout adolescence and adulthood. These individuals are more likely to drop out of school and to reach a lower socioeconomic level than expected. They show continued patterns of inattention, of impulsivity, and of hyperactivity, and they are at increased risk for other psychiatric disorders (Wilens, Faraone, & Biederman, 2004). Because of this somewhat bleak long-term prognosis, effective treatment early in life may be of great importance.

PHARMACOLOGICAL TREATMENT OF ADHD The most common treatment for ADHD is a central nervous system stimulant, such as *methylphenidate*. This drug is most commonly known by the brand name Ritalin. (A time-release version of this methylphenidate is called Concerta.) Ritalin's actions are not fully understood, but the drug may affect multiple neurotransmitters, particularly dopamine. Another drug used to treat ADHD is Adderall, which combines two other stimulants. The behavior of children with ADHD might suggest that their brains are overactive, and it may seem surprising that a stimulant would improve their symptoms. In fact, functional brain imaging shows that children with ADHD have underactive brains. Their hyperactivity may raise their arousal levels.

At appropriate doses, central nervous system stimulants such as Ritalin and Adderall decrease overactivity and distractibility. They increase attention and the ability to concentrate. Children on these drugs experience an increase in positive behaviors and a decrease in negative behaviors (**Figure 15.32**). They are able to work more effectively on a task without interruption and are less impulsive. It is likely that these improvements in behavior have contributed to the large number of children who take this medication. Parents often feel pressured by school

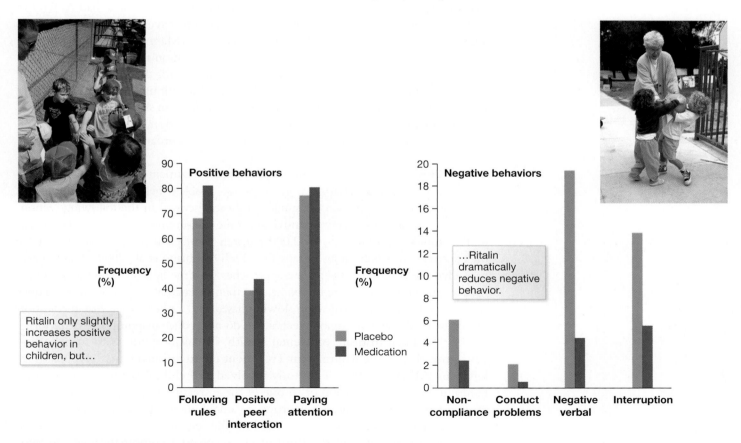

FIGURE 15.32 The Effects of Ritalin These graphs compare the effects of Ritalin on the positive and negative symptoms of ADHD.

systems to medicate children who have ongoing behavior problems, and parents often pressure physicians to prescribe Ritalin because its effects can make home life much more manageable. Studies have shown that children taking Ritalin are happier, more adept socially, and somewhat more successful academically, although the effects on academic performance are modest (Chronis, Jones, & Raggi, 2006; Van der Oord et al., 2008). These children also interact more positively with their parents, perhaps because they are more likely to comply with requests.

One study measured Ritalin's effects on the behavior of children playing baseball (Pelham et al., 1990). Children with ADHD who were taking the medication would assume the ready position in the outfield and could keep track of the game. Children with ADHD who were not taking the drug would often throw or kick their mitts even while the pitch was in progress.

The medication has its drawbacks, however. Side effects include sleep problems, reduced appetite, body twitches, and the temporary suppression of growth (Rapport & Moffitt, 2002; Schachter, Pham, King, Langford, & Moher, 2001). There is evidence that the short-term benefits of stimulants may not be maintained over the long term. In addition, because stimulants affect everyone who takes them, there is a very real risk of abuse, with numerous cases of children and adolescents buying and selling drugs such as Ritalin and Adderall. One study found that nearly 8 percent of college students had taken a nonprescribed stimulant in the past 30 days and 60 percent reported knowing students who misused stimulants (Weyandt et al., 2009). Indeed, a controversial issue is whether using stimulants to treat children with attention deficit hyperactivity disorder may increase the risk that they will develop substance abuse problems as adults. Two recent studies have demonstrated that substance abuse problems are common among those who have had ADHD in childhood, but having taken Ritalin does not seem to have increased or decreased adult rates of substance abuse (Biederman et al., 2008; Mannuzza et al., 2008).

Perhaps most important, some children on medication may see their problems as beyond their control. They may not feel responsible for their behaviors and may not learn coping strategies they will need if they discontinue their medication or if it ceases to be effective. Most therapists believe medication should be supplemented by psychological therapies, such as behavior modification. Some therapists even urge that medication be replaced by other treatment approaches when possible.

BEHAVIORAL TREATMENT OF ADHD Behavioral treatment of ADHD aims to reinforce positive behaviors and ignore or punish problem behaviors. The difficulties with this treatment approach are similar to those discussed in the following section, on autism. Treatment is very intensive and time consuming. A recent meta-analysis of 174 studies consisting of over 2,000 research participants found clear support for the effectiveness of behavioral therapy for ADHD (Fabiano et al., 2009). Many therapists advocate combining behavioral approaches with medication. The medication is used to gain control over the behaviors, and then behavioral modification techniques can be taught and the medication slowly phased out. Others argue that medication should be used only if behavioral techniques do not reduce inappropriate behaviors.

The National Institute of Mental Health, in collaboration with teams of investigators, began the Multimodal Treatment of Attention-Deficit Hyperactivity Disorder (MTA) in 1992. The study involved 579 children, who were assigned randomly to a control group or to one of three treatment groups. The treatment groups lasted 14 months. One group received medical management (usually treatment with a stimulant such as Ritalin), the second group received intensive behavioral treatment, and the third group received a combination of the two. Follow-up studies a year later revealed that the children receiving medication and those receiving a combination of medication and behavioral therapy had greater improvement in their ADHD symptoms than did those in the behavioral treatment group (Jensen et al., 2001, 2005). Children who received medication and behavioral therapy showed a slight advantage in areas such as social skills, academics, and parent-child relations over those who received only medication.

After three years, however, the advantage of the medication therapy was no longer significant. The children who received behavioral therapy improved over the three years, whereas those who received medication improved quickly but then tended to regress over the three years (Jensen et al., 2007). These findings reinforce the key point here: Medications may be important in the short term, but psychological treatments may produce superior outcomes that last.

Children with Autism Benefit from Structured Behavioral Treatment

The treatment of children with autism presents unique challenges to mental health professionals. The core symptoms of autism—impaired communication, restricted interests, and deficits in social interaction—make these children particularly difficult to work with. They often exhibit extreme behaviors as well as forms of self-stimulation, such as hand waving, rocking, humming, and jumping up and down. Although these behaviors must be reduced or eliminated before progress can occur in other areas, doing so is difficult because effective reinforcers are hard to find. Normal children respond positively to social praise and small prizes, but children with autism often are oblivious to these rewards. In some cases, food is the only effective reinforcement in the initial stages of treatment.

Another characteristic of children with autism is an overselectivity of attention. This tendency to focus on specific details while ignoring others interferes with generalizing learned behavior to other stimuli and situations. For example, a child who learns to set the table with plates may not know what to do when presented with bowls instead. Generalization of skills must be explicitly taught. For this reason, structured therapies are more effective for these children than are unstructured interventions, such as play therapy (in which the therapist tries to engage the child in conversation while the child plays with toys).

BEHAVIORAL TREATMENT FOR AUTISM As noted earlier, autism clearly is caused by biological factors, but this knowledge has not led to any significant advances in therapies for the disorder. Indeed, one of the best-known and perhaps most effective treatments for children with autism was developed by Ivar Lovaas and his colleagues. The program, **applied behavioral analysis (ABA),** is based on principles of operant conditioning: Behaviors that are reinforced should increase in frequency. Behaviors that are not reinforced should diminish (**Figure 15.33**). There is evidence that this method can be used successfully to treat autism (Warren et al., 2011), particularly if treatment is started early in life (Vismara & Rogers, 2010).

This very intensive approach requires a minimum of 40 hours of treatment per week. In Lovaas's study, preschool-age children with autism were treated by teachers and by their parents, who received specific training. After more than two years of ABA treatment, the children had gained about 20 IQ points on average and most of them were able to enter a normal kindergarten program (Lovaas, 1987). In contrast, IQ did not change in a comparable control group of children who did not receive any treatment. A group of children who received 10 hours of treatment per week fared no better than the control group. Initiating treatment at a younger age also yielded better results, as did involving the parents

applied behavioral analysis (ABA) An intensive treatment for autism, based on operant conditioning.

FIGURE 15.33 Applied Behavioral Analysis This form of treatment involves intensive interaction between children with autism and their teachers and parents.

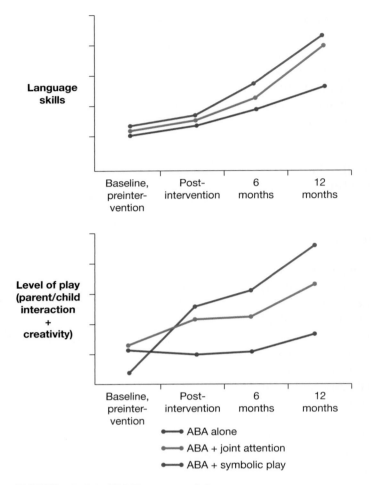

Language skills

Level of play (parent/child interaction + creativity)

Baseline, preinter-vention | Post-intervention | 6 months | 12 months

— ABA alone
— ABA + joint attention
— ABA + symbolic play

FIGURE 15.34 ABA Treatment, Joint Attention, and Symbolic Play At the start of this study, the children were 3 or 4 years old. All the children received ABA treatment. Children receiving only ABA treatment were the control condition. In addition, some children received training in maintaining joint attention, and some children received training in symbolic play. Both of these combinations led to better language skills, greater parent/child play interaction, and greater creativity in play than did ABA alone.

and having at least a portion of the therapy take place in the home. Children with better language skills before entering treatment had better outcomes than those who were mute or echolalic (repeating whatever they heard).

Recent studies have shown that other tasks can improve ABA treatment. One study found that teaching children to engage in joint attention during ABA treatment, such as by having the parent or teacher imitate the child's actions and work to maintain eye contact, improved language skills significantly over ABA treatment alone (Kasari, Paparella, Freeman, & Jahromi, 2008). In another condition, children received instruction in symbolic play. Examples of symbolic play include imagining something, such as a doll driving a car, or pretending that one object respresents another. Instruction in symbolic play also led to increased language use, greater parent/child play, and greater creativity in play (**Figure 15.34**)

Lovaas's ABA program has some drawbacks. The most obvious is the time commitment, because the therapy is very intensive and lasts for years. Parents essentially become full-time teachers for their child with autism. The financial and emotional drains on the family can be substantial. If the family includes other children, they may feel neglected or jealous because of the amount of time and energy expended on the child with autism.

BIOLOGICAL TREATMENT FOR AUTISM There is good evidence that autism is caused by brain dysfunction. Many attempts have been made to use this knowledge to treat the disorder. It is easy to find compelling case studies of children who have benefited from alternative treatment approaches. When the treatments are assessed in controlled studies, however, there is little or no evidence that most are effective.

One approach involves selective serotonin reuptake inhibitors. SSRIs have been tried as a treatment for autism for two reasons. First, SSRIs such as Prozac reduce compulsions in patients with obsessive-compulsive disorder, and autism involves compulsive and repetitive behavior. Second, there is evidence that children with autism have abnormal serotonin functioning. A review of pharmacological studies found that SSRIs are not helpful for treating the symptoms of autism and actually may increase agitation (McPheeters et al., 2011). However, the review also found that antipsychotics, such as Risperdal, appear to reduce repetitive behaviors associated with self-stimulation. Unfortunately, antipsychotics have side effects, such as weight gain.

The important role of oxytocin in social behavior has been discussed throughout this textbook (see, for example, the discussion in Chapter 11, "Health and Well-Being," of the relationship between oxytocin and affiliation). Given oxytocin's role in social relations, some researchers have speculated that oxytocin plays a role in autism. The first finding is that a deficit in oxytocin may be related to some of the behavioral manifestations of autism. Mice lacking oxytocin behave normally, except that they cannot recognize other mice or their mother's scent; a single dose of oxytocin cures them (Ferguson et al., 2000). In human studies, researchers have found that administering a nasal spray containing oxytocin leads people to make more eye contact, feel increased trust in others, and better infer emotions from other people's facial expressions (Ross & Young, 2009).

The question is whether oxytocin can improve social functioning in people with autism. In one study, adults with autism who received injections of oxytocin showed a dramatic improvement in their symptoms (Novotny et al., 2000). In another study, high-functioning adults with autism were injected with oxytocin. Then they performed a social cognition task in which they listened to spoken sentences (e.g., "The boy went to the store") and had to identify the speaker's emotional tone. The participants who received oxytocin were better able to tell if the sentence was read in an angry, sad, happy, or indifferent tone than were the participants who received the placebo (Hollander et al., 2007). Oxytocin injections seem particularly useful for reducing repetitive behaviors (e.g., repeating the same phrase), questioning, inappropriate touching, and self-injury (Green & Hollander, 2010; Hollander et al., 2003). These findings are promising, but researchers need to do much more work before we can conclude that oxytocin is an empirically validated treatment for autism.

At this point, the neurobiology of autism is not well understood. Attempts to use psychopharmacology to treat the disorder have led to some improvements in behavior, but much remains to be learned.

PROGNOSIS FOR CHILDREN WITH AUTISM Despite a few reports of remarkable recovery from autism, the long-term prognosis is poor. A follow-up study of men in their early 20s revealed that they continued to show the ritualistic self-stimulating behavior typical of autism. In addition, nearly three-quarters had severe social difficulties and were unable to live and work independently (Howlin, Mawhood, & Rutter, 2000). Several factors affect the prognosis. Although therapists once believed the prognosis was particularly poor for children whose symptoms were apparent before age 2 (Hoshino et al., 1980), possibly only the most severe cases of autism were diagnosed that early before public recognition of the disorder increased.

Early diagnosis clearly allows for more effective treatments (National Research Council, 2001). Still, severe cases—especially those involving notable cognitive deficiencies—are less likely to improve with treatment. Early language ability is associated with better outcome (Howlin et al., 2000), as is higher IQ. Children with autism have difficulty generalizing from the therapeutic setting to the real world, and this limitation severely restricts their social functioning (Handleman, Gill, & Alessandri, 1988). A higher IQ may mean a better ability to generalize learning and therefore a better overall prognosis.

A CASE STUDY OF CHILDHOOD AUTISM To understand how autism affects families and how treatment can be beneficial, consider the following case study. John O'Neil, a deputy editor at the *New York Times,* has described what it is like to be the parent of a child with autism (O'Neil, 2004). O'Neil's son James had been an easy baby. As a toddler, he began to show signs of being "different." He seemed to have difficulty looking his parents in the eye and did not display a strong sense of connection. James indicated little interest in objects, even toys, that were given or shown to him. Instead, he repeated behaviors to the point of harming himself. For example, he pulled his cowboy boots on and off until his feet were raw. He responded to loud noises by crying.

James's behavior really started to deteriorate when he was 2½, following the arrival of a baby brother and a move to a new house. His parents assumed he was overwhelmed, but the director of James's new preschool noticed the telltale signs of autism. On her recommendation, a professional assessed James and determined that he had autism. During the first visit to a speech therapist, James's mother learned just how much her son needed treatment: He had forgotten his name.

The discovery of James's autism follows a familiar pattern. Most diagnoses of autism are made by age 3, but the disorder can be detected earlier if parents or pediatricians know what to look for. Many children who will develop autism show abnormal social behavior in infancy. Other signs include staring at objects for long periods and not reaching developmental milestones, such as speaking. Sometimes autism appears to strike suddenly in an otherwise normally developing child. The child simply withdraws from social contact, stops babbling, and may become self-abusive. Parents and pediatricians who notice such symptoms of autism in a child may write them off as quirks or feel that the child is just a little slow to develop. Luckily for James, the preschool staff recommended a professional evaluation because of his unusual behavior. The earlier treatment begins, the better the prognosis.

On finding out that treatments for autism exist, the O'Neils were relieved. But then they heard the bad news: Treatment is expensive, difficult, and time consuming—as noted earlier, the recommended amount of treatment is over 40 hours per week. Most versions of treatment are based on Lovaas's ABA therapy. This program requires parents and teachers to spend hours helping the child with autism learn basic skills, such as saying his or her name. Using operant conditioning to reward even small behaviors, parents and teachers teach the child each task as a series of simple steps. They watch the child repeat the same behaviors over and over for hours on end. They attempt to actively engage the child's attention in highly structured activities.

As is the case in many school districts, resources were insufficient for James to receive full treatment in school. His mother, a physician, gave up her full-time position to set up a home-based program for James. He spent up to 8 hours every day performing tasks that most children would find extremely boring, such as repeatedly imitating the therapist's placing two blocks next to each other or touching her nose. James's day might begin with physical activities to strengthen coordination and build body awareness. After this exercise period, he would take a snack break, during which appropriate social behaviors were reinforced and language skills were stressed. Each part of the day was designed to work on James's problem areas. Along the way, progress was charted to guide subsequent sessions. At one point, James's language skills clearly had to improve if he was going to be able to attend mainstream school. Encouraged by being given any treat he asked for, James learned to talk.

He started school with the assistance of one of his full-time instructors, who attended class with him. Despite some rocky moments, James made tremendous progress. He still had problems in some areas, such as reading comprehension, math, attention, and social skills. He did not understand why he suffered from a disorder and why other kids did not. But James triumphed. Perhaps his biggest accomplishment was making friends with a classmate named Larry (**Figure 15.35**).

Why, O'Neil speculates, was Larry attracted to James as a friend? Perhaps they shared a love of potty humor, or perhaps they were similarly warm and enthusiastic. One day, O'Neil overheard the two friends engaged in silly conversation, telling stupid jokes and gossiping about their "girlfriends." In that moment, O'Neil realized just how many of his dreams for James had been realized.

FIGURE 15.35 James O'Neil At the time of this photo, James **(center)** was 8 years old. At left is his friend Larry, also 8. At right is James's brother Miles, 6.

Summing Up

How Should Childhood Disorders and Adolescent Disorders Be Treated?

Depression is a relatively common and serious problem among adolescents. Using drugs such as Prozac to treat depression in adolescents is controversial. Although these drugs are effective in managing symptoms, they have a slight risk of increasing suicidal thoughts. Research suggests that combining drugs and psychotherapy is most effective in treating depression. Medications such as Ritalin can be quite effective in treating children with ADHD. However, side effects (such as sleep problems, reduced appetite, and body twitches) are associated with the use of this type of medication. Recent research suggests that, in the long term, behavioral therapy may be more effective for the treatment of ADHD than the use of psychotropic drugs. At present, the most effective treatment for autism is structured and intensive behavioral therapy. Applied behavioral analysis is an intensive treatment for autism that is based on the principles of operant conditioning. A biological treatment for autism has not been identified. Initial research findings suggest that oxytocin may prove helpful in the treatment of autism.

Measuring Up

Label each point below as an argument either for or against the practice of prescribing SSRI medications to adolescents with depression.

- **a.** Depressed adolescents taking SSRIs report having suicidal thoughts twice as often as depressed adolescents not taking SSRIs.
- **b.** Many depressed adolescents improve when taking SSRIs.
- **c.** Psychotherapy alone is an effective treatment option.
- **d.** SSRIs are widely available.
- **e.** SSRIs offer a relatively inexpensive treatment.
- **f.** Suicide rates have dropped since the use of SSRIs became widespread.

Answers: Choices b, d, e, and f support the use of SSRIs in treating adolescent depression. Choices a and c argue against the use of SSRIs in this population.

Chapter Summary

15.1 How Are Psychological Disorders Treated?

■ **Psychotherapy Is Based on Psychological Principles:** Psychotherapy is the generic name for formal psychological treatment. Psychodynamic treatment focuses on insight and uncovering unconscious conflicts. Humanistic approaches focus on the person as a whole, encouraging personal growth through self-understanding. Behavioral approaches focus on modifying maladaptive behaviors. Cognitive approaches restructure thinking. Group therapy is cost-effective, improves social skills, and provides support. Family therapy adopts a systems approach, seeing the individual as part of a larger context.

■ **Culture Can Affect the Therapeutic Process:** Culture influences the expression of psychological disorders, recovery from psychological disorders, and willingness to seek psychotherapy. In some cultures, mental health problems and psychotherapy are highly stigmatized, preventing people from seeking help. Psychologists must be prepared to provide culturally sensitive assistance to people from different cultural backgrounds with different belief systems.

■ **Medication Is Effective for Certain Disorders:** Psychotropic medications change neurochemistry. Anti-anxiety drugs increase GABA activity. Antidepressants affect serotonin availability. Antipsychotics block the effects of dopamine, reducing positive symptoms.

■ **Alternative Biological Treatments Are Used in Extreme Cases:** When traditional treatments are not successful, alternative treatments are used. These include psychosurgery, electroconvulsive therapy, transcranial magnetic stimulation, and deep brain stimulation.

■ **Therapies Not Supported by Scientific Evidence Can Be Dangerous:** Increasingly, psychologists are turning to evidence-based practices. Some treatment approaches that have no credible evidence to support their use have proved detrimental, and all may prevent or delay a patient from receiving effective evidence-based therapy.

■ **A Variety of Providers Can Assist in Treatment for Psychological Disorders:** A variety of specialized mental health practitioners exist. These specialists include clinical psychologists, psychiatrists, counseling psychologists, psychiatric social workers, psychiatric nurses, and paraprofessionals. The providers differ in their training and work in diverse settings.

15.2 What Are the Most Effective Treatments?

■ **Effectiveness of Treatment Is Determined by Empirical Evidence:** Randomized clinical trials should be used to assess the effectiveness of treatments for psychological disorders. Psychological treatments vary according to the particular disorder being addressed, are based on techniques developed in the lab by psychologists, and are not guided by a single, overall grand theory.

■ **Treatments That Focus on Behavior and on Cognition Are Superior for Anxiety Disorders:** Behavioral methods—in particular, systematic desensitization and exposure—alleviate specific phobias. Cognitive restructuring, coupled with exposure, is effective in treating panic disorder. Obsessive-compulsive disorder (OCD) responds to medications that block serotonin reuptake and to exposure and response prevention. Deep brain stimulation holds promise for the treatment of severe cases of OCD.

■ **Many Effective Treatments Are Available for Depression:** Pharmacological treatments include MAO inhibitors, tricyclics, and SSRIs. Cognitive behavioral treatments target distorted cognitions—in particular, the cognitive triad. Alternative therapies include exercise, electroconvulsive therapy, transcranial magnetic stimulation, and deep brain stimulation. Sex differences in rates of depression have resulted in the development of specific guidelines for treatment.

■ **Lithium Is Most Effective for Bipolar Disorder:** Lithium has been found to be most effective in stabilizing mood among bipolar patients. This drug has considerable side effects, however. Psychological therapy can help support compliance with drug treatment.

■ **Pharmacological Treatments Are Superior for Schizophrenia:** First-generation antipsychotic medications are most effective for reducing the positive symptoms of schizophrenia. Tardive dyskinesia and other side effects are common with these older antipsychotic drugs. Clozapine acts specifically on neurotransmitter receptors and reduces positive and negative symptoms, with fewer side effects. Drug therapy is most effective when combined with psychosocial treatment. The prognosis for patients depends on factors such as age of onset, gender, and culture.

15.3 Can Personality Disorders Be Treated?

■ **Dialectical Behavior Therapy Is Most Successful for Borderline Personality Disorder:** DBT combines elements of behavioral, cognitive, and psychodynamic therapy. Therapy proceeds in three stages. First, the most extreme behaviors are targeted and replaced with more appropriate behaviors. Next, the therapist explores past traumatic events. Finally, the therapist helps the patient develop self-respect and independence.

■ **Antisocial Personality Disorder Is Extremely Difficult to Treat:** Psychotherapeutic approaches have not proved effective for treating antisocial personality disorder. Behavioral and cognitive approaches have been more effective, primarily in a controlled residential treatment environment. Generally, the prognosis is poor. Focusing on prevention by addressing conduct disorder in childhood may be the best strategy.

15.4 How Should Childhood Disorders and Adolescent Disorders Be Treated?

- **The Use of Medication to Treat Adolescent Depression Is Controversial:** The use of SSRIs, such as Prozac, in the treatment of depression in adolescents is increasingly common. SSRIs may lead to increased suicidality, but the available evidence indicates that such medications may have more benefits than costs. Cognitive-behavioral treatment is also effective in the treatment of depression, particularly when combined with drug treatment.

- **Children with ADHD Can Benefit from Various Approaches:** Ritalin, despite its side effects, is an effective pharmacological treatment for ADHD. Research has provided support for the effectiveness of behavioral therapy in the treatment of ADHD, with behavioral therapy resulting in better long-term outcomes than medication therapy.

- **Children with Autism Benefit from Structured Behavioral Treatment:** Structured behavioral treatment has proved effective in improving the symptoms of autism. Applied behavioral analysis—an intensive treatment based on the principles of operant conditioning—has been used successfully in the treatment of autism. A biological treatment for autism has not been identified, but treatment with oxytocin holds promise.

Key Terms

anti-anxiety drugs, p. 683
antidepressants, p. 683
antipsychotics, p. 684
applied behavioral analysis (ABA), p. 719
behavior therapy, p. 678
biological therapies, p. 675

client-centered therapy, p. 678
cognitive-behavioral therapy (CBT), p. 679
cognitive restructuring, p. 679
cognitive therapy, p. 679

dialectical behavior therapy (DBT), p. 710
electroconvulsive therapy (ECT), p. 685
exposure, p. 680
expressed emotion, p. 681

insight, p. 676
psychotherapy, p. 675
psychotropic medications, p. 683

Practice Test

1. Which of the following statements are true regarding how culture can affect the therapeutic process?
   a. Culture can influence people's willingness to seek help.
   b. Culture can influence the expression of mental disorders.
   c. Definitions of mental health are consistent across cultures.
   d. Strategies for assessing mental illness are consistent across cultures.
   e. The extent to which mental illness is stigmatized varies by culture.

2. Barlow advocates distinguishing between psychological treatments and general talk therapy. Which of the following attributes characterize psychological treatments?
   a. Treatments should be based on evidence of their effectiveness.
   b. Treatments should be appropriate for the particular disorders.
   c. Specific techniques for treatment should be developed in the laboratory by psychologists.
   d. Treatments should be guided by grand theories.

3. Dialectical behavior therapy takes place in three stages. Place the descriptions of the three stages below in the correct order.
   a. The therapist helps the client explore past traumatic experiences that may be at the root of emotional problems.
   b. The therapist helps the patient develop self-respect and independent problem solving.
   c. The therapist works with the client to replace the most dysfunctional behaviors with more appropriate behaviors.

4. During his early adult years, Joshua was diagnosed with antisocial personality disorder. Joshua is now 40. Over the coming years, his friends and family will likely see a decrease in which of the following behaviors? Select all that apply.
   a. Joshua's lack of remorse for hurting others' feelings.
   b. Joshua's tendency to feel entitled to special treatment.
   c. Joshua's tendency to get into fistfights.

5. Three-year-old Marley recently received a diagnosis of autism. Which of the following are true about her likely treatment?
   a. Many individuals will need to be involved in Marley's treatment, including parents, teachers, and mental health practitioners.
   b. Marley's treatment is likely to strain family dynamics and family finances.
   c. Marley's treatment will focus largely on using social praise and small gifts to reinforce desired behavior.
   d. Marley's treatment will need to be highly structured.
   e. Marley's treatment will require a minimum of 20 hours per week and will likely last for two to three months.

The answer key for the Practice Tests can be found at the back of the book. It also includes answers to the green caption questions.

GLOSSARY

absentmindedness The inattentive or shallow encoding of events.

accommodation The process by which we create a new schema or drastically alter an existing schema to include new information that otherwise would not fit into the schema.

accuracy The extent to which an experimental measure is free from error.

acetylcholine (ACh) The neurotransmitter responsible for motor control at the junction between nerves and muscles; also involved in mental processes such as learning, memory, sleeping, and dreaming.

acquisition The gradual formation of an association between the conditioned and unconditioned stimuli.

action potential The neural impulse that passes along the axon and subsequently causes the release of chemicals from the terminal buttons.

activation-synthesis theory A theory of dreaming; this theory proposes that the brain tries to make sense of random brain activity that occurs during sleep by synthesizing the activity with stored memories.

adaptations In evolutionary theory, the physical characteristics, skills, or abilities that increase the chances of reproduction or survival and are therefore likely to be passed along to future generations.

additive color mixing A process of color mixing that occurs when different wavelengths of light interact within the eye's receptors; a psychological process.

aggression Any behavior that involves the intention to harm someone else.

agonists Drugs that enhance the actions of neurotransmitters.

agoraphobia An anxiety disorder marked by fear of being in situations in which escape may be difficult or impossible.

all-or-none principle The principle whereby a neuron fires with the same potency each time, although frequency can vary; a neuron either fires or not—it cannot partially fire.

altruism The providing of help when it is needed, without any apparent reward for doing so.

amnesia A deficit in long-term memory, resulting from disease, brain injury, or psychological trauma, in which the individual loses the ability to retrieve vast quantities of information from long-term memory.

amygdala A brain structure that serves a vital role in our learning to associate things with emotional responses and in processing emotional information.

analogical representations Mental representations that have some of the physical characteristics of objects; they are analogous to the objects.

anorexia nervosa An eating disorder characterized by an excessive fear of becoming fat and thus a refusal to eat.

antagonists Drugs that inhibit the actions of neurotransmitters.

anterograde amnesia A condition in which people lose the ability to form new memories.

anti-anxiety drugs A class of psychotropic medications used for the treatment of anxiety.

antidepressants A class of psychotropic medications used for the treatment of depression.

antipsychotics A class of psychotropic medications used for the treatment of schizophrenia and other disorders that involve psychosis.

antisocial personality disorder (APD) A personality disorder marked by a lack of empathy and remorse.

applied behavioral analysis (ABA) An intensive treatment for autism, based on operant conditioning.

arousal Physiological activation (such as increased brain activity) or increased autonomic responses (such as increased heart rate, sweating, or muscle tension).

assessment In psychology, examination of a person's mental state to diagnose possible psychological disorders.

assimilation The process by which we place new information into an existing schema.

attachment A strong emotional connection that persists over time and across circumstances.

attention deficit hyperactivity disorder (ADHD) A disorder characterized by restlessness, inattentiveness, and impulsivity.

attitudes People's evaluations of objects, of events, or of ideas.

attributions People's explanations for why events or actions occur.

audition Hearing; the sense of sound perception.

autistic disorder A developmental disorder characterized by deficits in social interaction, by impaired communication, and by restricted interests.

autonomic nervous system (ANS) A component of the peripheral nervous system; it transmits sensory signals and motor signals between the central nervous system and the body's glands and internal organs.

availability heuristic Making a decision based on the answer that most easily comes to mind.

axon A long narrow outgrowth of a neuron by which information is transmitted to other neurons.

basal ganglia A system of subcortical structures that are important for the production of planned movement.

behavior modification The use of operant-conditioning techniques to eliminate unwanted behaviors and replace them with desirable ones.

behavioral approach system (BAS) The brain system involved in the pursuit of incentives or rewards.

behavioral inhibition system (BIS) The brain system that is sensitive to punishment and therefore inhibits behavior that might lead to danger or pain.

behaviorism A psychological approach that emphasizes the role of environmental forces in producing behavior.

behavior therapy Treatment based on the premise that behavior is learned and therefore can be unlearned through the use of classical and operant conditioning.

binocular depth cues Cues of depth perception that arise from the fact that people have two eyes.

binocular disparity A depth cue; because of the distance between a person's eyes, each eye receives a slightly different retinal image.

biological therapies Treatment based on medical approaches to illness and to disease.

biopsychosocial model A model of health that integrates the effects of biological, behavioral, and social factors on health and illness.

bipolar disorder A mood disorder characterized by alternating periods of depression and mania.

blindsight A condition in which people who are blind have some spared visual capacities in the absence of any visual awareness.

blocking The temporary inability to remember something that is known.

body mass index (BMI) A ratio of body weight to height, used to measure obesity.

borderline personality disorder A personality disorder characterized by disturbances in identity, in affect, and in impulse control.

bottom-up processing A hierarchical model of pattern recognition in which data are relayed from one level of mental processing to the next, always moving to a higher level of processing.

brain stem An extension of the spinal cord; it houses structures that control functions associated with survival, such as breathing, swallowing, vomiting, urination, and orgasm.

Broca's area A small portion of the left frontal region of the brain, crucial for the production of language.

buffering hypothesis The idea that other people can provide direct emotional support in helping individuals cope with stressful events.

bulimia nervosa An eating disorder characterized by dieting, binge eating, and purging.

bystander intervention effect The failure to offer help by those who observe someone in need.

case studies A research method that involves the intensive examination of unusual people or organizations.

cell body Site, in the neuron, where information from thousands of other neurons is collected and integrated.

central nervous system (CNS) The brain and the spinal cord.

central tendency A measure that represents the typical response or the behavior of a group as a whole.

cerebellum A large, convoluted protuberance at the back of the brain stem; it is essential for coordinated movement and balance.

cerebral cortex The outer layer of brain tissue, which forms the convoluted surface of the brain.

change blindness A failure to notice large changes in one's environment.

chromosomes Structures within the cell body that are made up of DNA. DNA consists of genes.

chunking Organizing information into meaningful units to make it easier to remember.

circadian rhythms The regulation of biological cycles into regular patterns.

classical conditioning (Pavlovian conditioning) A type of learned response; a neutral object comes to elicit a response when it is associated with a stimulus that already produces that response.

client-centered therapy An empathic approach to therapy; it encourages people to fulfill their individual potentials for personal growth through greater self-understanding.

cognition Mental activity that includes thinking and the understandings that result from thinking.

cognitive-behavioral approach A diagnostic model that views psychopathology as the result of learned, maladaptive thoughts and beliefs.

cognitive-behavioral therapy (CBT) A therapy that incorporates techniques from cognitive therapy and behavior therapy to correct faulty thinking and change maladaptive behaviors.

cognitive dissonance An uncomfortable mental state due to a contradiction between two attitudes or between an attitude and a behavior.

cognitive map A visual/spatial mental representation of an environment.

cognitive neuroscience The study of the neural mechanisms (mechanisms involving the brain, nerves, and nervous tissue) that underlie thought, learning, and memory.

cognitive psychology The study of how people think, learn, and remember.

cognitive restructuring A therapy that strives to help patients recognize maladaptive thought patterns and replace them with ways of viewing the world that are more in tune with reality.

cognitive therapy Treatment based on the idea that distorted thoughts produce maladaptive behaviors and emotions; treatment strategies attempt to modify these thought patterns.

compliance The tendency to agree to do things requested by others.

concept A mental representation that groups or categorizes objects, events, or relations around common themes.

concrete operational stage The third stage in Piaget's theory of cognitive development; during this stage, children begin to think about and understand logical operations, and they are no longer fooled by appearances.

conditioned response (CR) A response to a conditioned stimulus; a response that has been learned.

conditioned stimulus (CS) A stimulus that elicits a response only after learning has taken place.

cones Retinal cells that respond to higher levels of illumination and result in color perception.

confabulation The unintended false recollection of episodic memories.

conformity The altering of one's behaviors and opinions to match those of other people or to match other people's expectations.

confound Anything that affects a dependent variable and may unintentionally vary between the experimental conditions of a study.

consciousness One's subjective experience of the world, resulting from brain activity.

consolidation A process by which immediate memories become lasting (or long-term) memories.

continuous reinforcement A type of learning in which the desired behavior is reinforced each time it occurs.

control group A comparison group; the participants in a study that receive no intervention or receive an intervention that is unrelated to the independent variable being investigated.

conventional level Middle stage of moral development; at this level, strict adherence to societal rules and the approval of others determine what is moral.

convergence A cue of binocular depth perception; when a person views a nearby object, the eye muscles turn the eyes inward.

coping response Any response an organism makes to avoid, escape from, or minimize an aversive stimulus.

cornea The clear outer covering of the eye.

correlational studies A research method that examines how variables are naturally related in the real world, without any attempt by the researcher to alter them or assign causation between them.

critical thinking Systematically evaluating information to reach reasonable conclusions.

cross-sectional studies A research method that compares participants in different groups (e.g., young and old) at the same time.

cryptomnesia A type of misattribution that occurs when a person thinks he or she has come up with a new idea, yet has only retrieved a stored idea and failed to attribute the idea to its proper source.

crystallized intelligence Intelligence that reflects both the knowledge one acquires through experience and the ability to use that knowledge.

culturally sensitive research Studies that take into account the role that culture plays in determining thoughts, feelings, and actions.

culture The beliefs, values, rules, and customs that exist within a group of people who share a common language and environment and that are transmitted through learning from one generation to the next.

data Objective observations or measurements.

decision making Attempting to select the best alternative among several options.

declarative memory The cognitive information retrieved from explicit memory; knowledge that can be declared.

deductive reasoning Using general rules to draw conclusions about specific instances.

defense mechanisms Unconscious mental strategies that the mind uses to protect itself from distress.

defining attribute model A way of thinking about concepts: A category is characterized by a list of features that determine if an object is a member of the category.

deindividuation A state of reduced individuality, reduced self-awareness, and reduced attention to personal standards; this phenomenon may occur when people are part of a group.

delusions False beliefs based on incorrect inferences about reality.

dendrites Branchlike extensions of the neuron that detect information from other neurons.

dependent variable In an experiment, the variable that is affected by the manipulation of the independent variable.

descriptive statistics Statistics that summarize the data collected in a study.

descriptive studies A research method that involves observing and noting the behavior of people or other animals to provide a systematic and objective analysis of the behavior.

developmental psychology The study of changes, over the life span, in physiology, cognition, emotion, and social behavior.

dialectical behavior therapy (DBT) A form of therapy used to treat borderline personality disorder.

diathesis-stress model A diagnostic model that proposes that a disorder may develop when an underlying vulnerability is coupled with a precipitating event.

directionality problem A problem encountered in correlational studies; the researchers find a relationship between two variables, but they cannot determine which variable may have caused changes in the other variable.

discrimination The inappropriate and unjustified treatment of people as a result of prejudice.

disorganized behavior Acting in strange or unusual ways, including strange movement of limbs, bizarre speech, and inappropriate self-care, such as failing to dress properly or bathe.

display rules Rules learned through socialization that dictate which emotions are suitable to given situations.

dissociative disorders Mental disorders that involve disruptions of identity, of memory, or of conscious awareness.

dissociative identity disorder (DID) The occurrence of two or more distinct identities in the same individual.

dizygotic twins Also called *fraternal twins;* twin siblings that result from two separately fertilized eggs and therefore are no more similar genetically than nontwin siblings.

dominant gene A gene that is expressed in the offspring whenever it is present.

dopamine A monoamine neurotransmitter involved in motivation, reward, and motor control over voluntary movement.

dreams Products of an altered state of consciousness in which images and fantasies are confused with reality.

drive A psychological state that, by creating arousal, motivates an organism to satisfy a need.

dynamic systems theory The view that development is a self-organizing process, where new forms of behavior emerge through consistent interactions between a biological being and his or her cultural and environmental contexts.

dysthymia A form of depression that is not severe enough to be diagnosed as major depression.

eardrum A thin membrane that marks the beginning of the middle ear; sound waves cause it to vibrate.

ego In psychodynamic theory, the component of personality that tries to satisfy the wishes of the id while being responsive to the dictates of the superego.

elaboration likelihood model A theory of how persuasive messages lead to attitude changes.

electroconvulsive therapy (ECT) A procedure that involves administering a strong electrical current to the patient's brain to produce a seizure; it is effective for some cases of severe depression.

electroencephalograph (EEG) A device that measures electrical activity in the brain.

emotion Feelings that involve subjective evaluation, physiological processes, and cognitive beliefs.

emotional intelligence (EI) A form of social intelligence that emphasizes the abilities to manage, recognize, and understand emotions and use emotions to guide appropriate thought and action.

emotion-focused coping A type of coping in which people try to prevent having an emotional response to a stressor.

encoding The processing of information so that it can be stored.

encoding specificity principle The idea that any stimulus that is encoded along with an experience can later trigger memory for the experience.

endocrine system A communication system that uses hormones to influence thoughts, behaviors, and actions.

endorphins Neurotransmitters involved in natural pain reduction and reward.

epinephrine A monoamine neurotransmitter responsible for bursts of energy after an event that is exciting or threatening.

episodic memory Memory for one's personal past experiences.

etiology Factors that contribute to the development of a disorder.

evolutionary theory A theory presented by the naturalist Charles Darwin; it views the history of a species in terms of the inherited, adaptive value of physical characteristics, of mental activity, and of behavior.

exemplar model A way of thinking about concepts: All members of a category are examples (exemplars); together they form the concept and determine category membership.

experiment A study that tests causal hypotheses by measuring and manipulating variables.

experimental groups Treatment groups; the participants in a study that receive the intervention.

experimenter expectancy effect Actual change in the behavior of the people or nonhuman animals being observed that is due to the expectations of the observer.

explicit attitudes Attitudes that a person can report.

explicit memory The system underlying conscious memories.

exposure A cognitive-behavioral therapy technique that involves repeated exposure to an anxiety-producing stimulus or situation.

expressed emotion A pattern of negative actions by a client's family members; the pattern includes critical comments, hostility directed toward the client by family members, and emotional overinvolvement.

external validity The degree to which the findings of an experiment can be generalized outside the laboratory.

extinction A process in which the conditioned response is weakened when the conditioned stimulus is repeated without the unconditioned stimulus.

extrinsic motivation Motivation to perform an activity because of the external goals toward which that activity is directed.

family systems model A diagnostic model that considers symptoms within an individual as indicating problems within the family.

fight-or-flight response The physiological preparedness of animals to deal with danger.

five-factor theory The idea that personality can be described using five factors: openness to experience, conscientiousness, extraversion, agreeableness, and neuroticism.

fixed schedule A schedule in which reinforcement is provided after a specific number of occurrences or a specific amount of time.

flashbulb memories Vivid episodic memories for the circumstances in which people first learned of a surprising, consequential, or emotionally arousing event.

fluid intelligence Intelligence that reflects the ability to process information, particularly in novel or complex circumstances.

forgetting The inability to retrieve memory from long-term storage.

formal operational stage The final stage in Piaget's theory of cognitive development; during this stage, teenagers can think abstractly, and they can formulate and test hypotheses through deductive logic.

fovea The center of the retina, where cones are densely packed.

framing The effect of presentation on how information is perceived.

frontal lobes Regions of the cerebral cortex—at the front of the brain—important for movement and higher-level psychological processes associated with the prefrontal cortex.

frustration-aggression hypothesis The extent to which people feel frustrated predicts the likelihood that they will act aggressively.

functionalism An approach to psychology concerned with the adaptive purpose, or function, of mind and behavior.

functional magnetic resonance imaging (fMRI) An imaging technique used to examine changes in the activity of the working human brain.

fundamental attribution error In explaining other people's behavior, the tendency to overemphasize personality traits and underestimate situational factors.

GABA Gamma-aminobutyric acid; the primary inhibitory transmitter in the nervous system.

gender identity Personal beliefs about whether one is male or female.

gender roles The characteristics associated with males and females because of cultural influence or learning.

gender schemas Cognitive structures that reflect the perceived appropriateness of male and female characteristics and behaviors.

general adaptation syndrome A consistent pattern of responses to stress that consists of three stages: alarm, resistance, and exhaustion.

general intelligence (g) The idea that one general factor underlies intelligence.

generalized anxiety disorder (GAD) A diffuse state of constant anxiety not associated with any specific object or event.

genes The units of heredity that help determine the characteristics of an organism.

genotype The genetic constitution of an organism, determined at the moment of conception.

Gestalt theory A theory based on the idea that the whole of personal experience is different from simply the sum of its constituent elements.

glutamate The primary excitatory transmitter in the nervous system.

gonads The main endocrine glands involved in sexual behavior: in males, the testes; in females, the ovaries.

gustation The sense of taste.

habituation A decrease in behavioral response after repeated exposure to a nonthreatening stimulus.

hallucinations False sensory perceptions that are experienced without an external source.

haptic sense The sense of touch.

health psychology A field that integrates research on health and on psychology; it involves the application of psychological principles to promote health and well-being.

heritability A statistical estimate of the extent to which variation in a trait within a population is due to genetic factors.

heuristics Shortcuts (rules of thumb or informal guidelines) used to reduce the amount of thinking that is needed to make decisions.

hippocampus A brain structure that is associated with the formation of memories.

homeostasis The tendency for bodily functions to maintain equilibrium.

hormones Chemical substances, released from endocrine glands, that travel through the bloodstream to targeted tissues; the tissues are subsequently influenced by the hormones.

humanistic approaches Approaches to studying personality that emphasize how people seek to fulfill their potential through greater self-understanding.

hypnosis A social interaction during which a person, responding to suggestions, experiences changes in memory, perception, and/or voluntary action.

hypothalamic-pituitary-adrenal (HPA) axis The biological system responsible for the stress response.

hypothalamus A brain structure that is involved in the regulation of bodily functions, including body temperature, blood pressure, and blood glucose levels; it also influences our basic motivated behaviors.

hypothesis A specific prediction of what should be observed if a theory is correct.

id In psychodynamic theory, the component of personality that is completely submerged in the unconscious and operates according to the pleasure principle.

idiographic approaches Person-centered approaches to studying personality; they focus on individual lives and how various characteristics are integrated into unique persons.

immune system The body's mechanism for dealing with invading microorganisms, such as allergens, bacteria, and viruses.

implicit attitudes Attitudes that influence a person's feelings and behavior at an unconscious level.

implicit memory The system underlying unconscious memories.

incentives External objects or external goals, rather than internal drives, that motivate behaviors.

independent variable In an experiment, the variable that is manipulated by the experimenter to examine its impact on the dependent variable.

inductive reasoning Using specific instances to draw conclusions about general rules.

infantile amnesia The inability to remember events from early childhood.

inferential statistics A set of procedures used to make judgments about whether differences actually exist between sets of numbers.

ingroup favoritism The tendency for people to evaluate favorably and privilege members of the ingroup more than members of the outgroup.

insecure attachment The attachment style for a minority of infants; the infant may exhibit insecure attachment through various behaviors, such as avoiding contact with the caregiver, or by alternating between approach and avoidance behaviors.

insight (1) The sudden realization of a solution to a problem. (2) The goal of psychoanalysis; a patient's awareness of his or her own unconscious psychological processes and how these processes affect daily functioning.

insomnia A disorder characterized by an inability to sleep.

institutional review boards (IRBs) Groups of people responsible for reviewing proposed research to ensure that it meets the accepted standards of science and provides for the physical and emotional well-being of research participants.

intelligence The ability to use knowledge to reason, make decisions, make sense of events, solve problems, understand complex ideas, learn quickly, and adapt to environmental challenges.

intelligence quotient (IQ) An index of intelligence computed by dividing a child's estimated mental age by the child's chronological age, then multiplying this number by 100.

interactionists Theorists who believe that behavior is determined jointly by situations and underlying dispositions.

internal validity The extent to which the data collected in a study address the research hypothesis in the way intended.

interneurons One of the three types of neurons; these neurons communicate only with other neurons.

interpreter A term specific to the left hemisphere; refers to the left hemisphere's attempts to make sense of actions and ongoing events.

interval schedule A schedule in which reinforcement is available after a specific unit of time.

intrinsic motivation Motivation to perform an activity because of the value or pleasure associated with that activity, rather than for an apparent external goal or purpose.

introspection A systematic examination of subjective mental experiences that requires people to inspect and report on the content of their thoughts.

iris The colored muscular circle on the surface of the eye; it changes shape to let in more or less light.

kinesthetic sense Perception of the positions in space and movements of our bodies and our limbs.

latent content According to Sigmund Freud, what a dream symbolizes; the material that is disguised in a dream to protect the dreamer from confronting a conflict directly.

latent learning Learning that takes place in the absence of reinforcement.

law of effect Thorndike's general theory of learning: Any behavior that leads to a "satisfying state of affairs" is likely to occur again, and any behavior that leads to an "annoying state of affairs" is less likely to occur again.

learned helplessness A cognitive model of depression in which people feel unable to control events in their lives.

learning A relatively enduring change in behavior, resulting from experience.

longitudinal studies A research method that studies the same participants multiple times over a period of time.

long-term memory The relatively permanent storage of information.

long-term potentiation (LTP) The strengthening of a synaptic connection, making the postsynaptic neurons more easily activated.

loosening of associations A speech pattern among some people with schizophrenia in which their thoughts are disorganized or meaningless.

magnetic resonance imaging (MRI) A method of brain imaging that produces high-quality images of the brain.

major depression A disorder characterized by severe negative moods or a lack of interest in normally pleasurable activities.

manifest content According to Sigmund Freud, the plot of a dream; the way a dream is remembered.

mean A measure of central tendency that is the arithmetic average of a set of numbers.

median A measure of central tendency that is the value in a set of numbers that falls exactly halfway between the lowest and highest values.

meditation A mental procedure that focuses attention on an external object or on a sense of awareness.

meme A unit of knowledge transmitted within a culture.

memory The nervous system's capacity to acquire and retain skills and knowledge.

memory bias The changing of memories over time so that they become consistent with current beliefs or attitudes.

mental age An assessment of a child's intellectual standing compared with that of same-age peers; determined by comparing the child's test score with the average score for children of each chronological age.

mental sets Problem solving strategies that have worked in the past.

meta-analysis A "study of studies" that combines the findings of multiple studies to arrive at a conclusion.

mind/body problem A fundamental psychological issue: Are mind and body separate and distinct, or is the mind simply the physical brain's subjective experience?

mirror neurons Neurons that are activated when one observes another individual engage in an action and when one performs the action that was observed.

mnemonics Learning aids, strategies, and devices that improve recall through the use of retrieval cues.

mode A measure of central tendency that is the most frequent score or value in a set of numbers.

modeling The imitation of behavior through observational learning.

monocular depth cues Cues of depth perception that are available to each eye alone.

monozygotic twins Also called *identical twins;* twin siblings that result from one zygote splitting in two and therefore share the same genes.

motivation Factors that energize, direct, or sustain behavior.

motor neurons One of the three types of neurons; these efferent neurons direct muscles to contract or relax, thereby producing movement.

multiaxial system The system used in the *DSM;* it calls for assessment along five axes that describe important mental health factors.

multiple intelligences The idea that there are different types of intelligence that are independent of one another.

myelin sheath A fatty material, made up of glial cells, that insulates the axon and allows for the rapid movement of electrical impulses along the axon.

narcolepsy A sleep disorder in which people experience excessive sleepiness during normal waking hours, sometimes going limp and collapsing.

naturalistic observation A type of descriptive study in which the researcher is a passive observer, making no attempt to change or alter ongoing behavior.

natural selection In evolutionary theory, the idea that those who inherit characteristics that help them adapt to their particular environments have a selective advantage over those who do not.

nature/nurture debate The arguments concerning whether psychological characteristics are biologically innate or acquired through education, experience, and culture.

need A state of biological or social deficiency.

need hierarchy Maslow's arrangement of needs, in which basic survival needs must be met before people can satisfy higher needs.

need to belong theory The theory that the need for interpersonal attachments is a fundamental motive that has evolved for adaptive purposes.

negative punishment The removal of a stimulus to decrease the probability of a behavior's recurring.

negative reinforcement The removal of a stimulus to increase the probability of a behavior's being repeated.

negative symptoms Symptoms of schizophrenia that are marked by deficits in functioning, such as apathy, lack of emotion, and slowed speech and movement.

neurons The basic units of the nervous system; cells that receive, integrate, and transmit information in the nervous system. They operate through electrical impulses, communicate with other neurons through chemical signals, and form neural networks.

neurotransmitters Chemical substances that carry signals from one neuron to another.

nodes of Ranvier Small gaps of exposed axon, between the segments of myelin sheath, where action potentials are transmitted.

nomothetic approaches Approaches to studying personality that focus on how common characteristics vary from person to person.

nonverbal behavior The facial expressions, gestures, mannerisms, and movements by which one communicates with others.

norepinephrine A monoamine neurotransmitter involved in states of arousal and awareness.

objective measures Relatively direct assessments of personality, usually based on information gathered through self-report questionnaires or observer ratings.

object permanence The understanding that an object continues to exist even when it cannot be seen.

observational learning The acquisition or modification of a behavior after exposure to at least one performance of that behavior.

observational techniques A research method of careful and systematic assessment and coding of overt behavior.

observer bias Systematic errors in observation that occur because of an observer's expectations.

obsessive-compulsive disorder (OCD) An anxiety disorder characterized by frequent intrusive thoughts and compulsive actions.

obstructive sleep apnea A disorder in which a person, while asleep, stops breathing because his or her throat closes; the condition results in frequent awakenings during the night.

occipital lobes Regions of the cerebral cortex, at the back of the brain, important for vision.

olfaction The sense of smell.

olfactory bulb The brain center for smell, located below the frontal lobes.

olfactory epithelium A thin layer of tissue, within the nasal cavity, that contains the receptors for smell.

operant conditioning (instrumental conditioning) A learning process in which the consequences of an action determine the likelihood that it will be performed in the future.

oxytocin A hormone that is important for mothers in bonding to newborns and may encourage affiliation during social stress.

panic disorder An anxiety disorder that consists of sudden, overwhelming attacks of terror.

parallel processing Processing multiple types of information at the same time.

parasympathetic division A division of the autonomic nervous system; it returns the body to its resting state.

parietal lobes Regions of the cerebral cortex, in front of the occipital lobes and behind the frontal lobes, important for the sense of touch and for conceptualizing the spatial layout of an environment.

partial reinforcement A type of learning in which behavior is reinforced intermittently.

partial-reinforcement extinction effect The greater persistence of behavior under partial reinforcement than under continuous reinforcement.

participant observation A type of descriptive study in which the researcher is actively involved in the situation.

perception The processing, organization, and interpretation of sensory signals; it results in an internal representation of the stimulus.

perceptual constancy Correctly perceiving objects as constant in their shape, size, color, and lightness, despite raw sensory data that could mislead perception.

peripheral nervous system (PNS) All nerve cells in the body that are not part of the central nervous system. The peripheral nervous system includes the somatic and autonomic nervous systems.

persistence The continual recurrence of unwanted memories.

personal attributions Explanations that refer to people's internal characteristics, such as abilities, traits, moods, or efforts.

personality The characteristic thoughts, emotional responses, and behaviors that are relatively stable in an individual over time and across circumstances.

personality trait A characteristic; a dispositional tendency to act in a certain way over time and across circumstances.

personality types Discrete categories of people based on personality characteristics.

persuasion The active and conscious effort to change an attitude through the transmission of a message.

phenotype Observable physical characteristics, which result from both genetic and environmental influences.

phobia An acquired fear that is out of proportion to the real threat of an object or of a situation.

pituitary gland A gland located at the base of the hypothalamus; it sends hormonal signals to other endocrine glands, controlling their release of hormones.

placebo effect An improvement in health following treatment with a placebo—that is, with a drug or treatment that has no apparent physiological effect on the health condition for which it was prescribed.

plasticity A property of the brain that allows it to change as a result of experience, drugs, or injury.

population Everyone in the group the experimenter is interested in.

positive punishment The administration of a stimulus to decrease the probability of a behavior's recurring.

positive reinforcement The administration of a stimulus to increase the probability of a behavior's being repeated.

positive symptoms Symptoms of schizophrenia that are marked by excesses in functioning, such as delusions, hallucinations, and disorganized speech or behavior.

positron emission tomography (PET) A method of brain imaging that assesses metabolic activity by using a radioactive substance injected into the bloodstream.

postconventional level Highest stage of moral development; at this level, decisions about morality depend on abstract principles and the value of all life.

posttraumatic stress disorder (PTSD) A mental disorder that involves frequent nightmares, intrusive thoughts, and flashbacks related to an earlier trauma.

preconventional level Earliest level of moral development; at this level, self-interest and event outcomes determine what is moral.

prefrontal cortex The frontmost portion of the frontal lobes, especially prominent in humans; important for attention, working memory, decision making, appropriate social behavior, and personality.

prejudice Negative feelings, opinions, and beliefs associated with a stereotype.

preoperational stage The second stage in Piaget's theory of cognitive development; during this stage, children think symbolically about objects, but they reason based on intuition and superficial appearance rather than logic.

primary appraisals Part of the coping process that involves making decisions about whether a stimulus is stressful, benign, or irrelevant.

primary emotions Emotions that are evolutionarily adaptive, shared across cultures, and associated with specific physical states; they include anger, fear, sadness, disgust, happiness, and possibly surprise and contempt.

proactive interference When prior information inhibits the ability to remember new information.

problem-focused coping A type of coping in which people take direct steps to confront or minimize a stressor.

problem solving Finding a way around an obstacle to reach a goal.

procedural memory A type of implicit memory that involves motor skills and behavioral habits.

projective measures Personality tests that examine unconscious processes by having people interpret ambiguous stimuli.

prosocial Tending to benefit others.

prospective memory Remembering to do something at some time in the future.

prototype model A way of thinking about concepts: Within each category, there is a best example—a prototype—for that category.

psychological science The study of mind, brain, and behavior.

psychoanalysis A method developed by Sigmund Freud that attempts to bring the contents of the unconscious into conscious awareness so that conflicts can be revealed.

psychodynamic theory Freudian theory that unconscious forces determine behavior.

psychopathology Sickness or disorder of the mind.

psychosexual stages According to Freud, developmental stages that correspond to distinct libidinal urges; progression through these stages profoundly affects personality.

psychotherapy The generic name given to formal psychological treatment.

psychotropic medications Drugs that affect mental processes.

pupil The small opening in the eye; it lets in light waves.

random assignment Placing research participants into the conditions of an experiment in such a way that each participant has an equal chance of being assigned to any level of the independent variable.

ratio schedule A schedule in which reinforcement is based on the number of times the behavior occurs.

reactivity When the knowledge that one is being observed alters the behavior being observed.

reasoning Using information to determine if a conclusion is valid or reasonable.

receptors In neurons, specialized protein molecules on the postsynaptic membrane; neurotransmitters bind to these molecules after passing across the synaptic cleft.

recessive gene A gene that is expressed only when it is matched with a similar gene from the other parent.

reconsolidation Neural processes involved when memories are recalled and then stored again for later retrieval.

reinforcer A stimulus that follows a response and increases the likelihood that the response will be repeated.

reliability The extent to which a measure is stable and consistent over time in similar conditions.

REM sleep The stage of sleep marked by rapid eye movements, dreaming, and paralysis of motor systems.

replication Repetition of an experiment to confirm the results.

representativeness heuristic Placing a person or object in a category if that person or object is similar to one's prototype for that category.

Rescorla-Wagner model A cognitive model of classical conditioning; it states that the strength of the CS-US association is determined by the extent to which the unconditioned stimulus is unexpected or surprising.

research A scientific process that involves the systematic and careful collection of data.

response performance A research method in which researchers quantify perceptual or cognitive processes in response to a specific stimulus.

resting membrane potential The electrical charge of a neuron when it is not active.

restructuring A new way of thinking about a problem that aids its solution.

retina The thin inner surface of the back of the eyeball; it contains the photoreceptors that transduce light into neural signals.

retrieval The act of recalling or remembering stored information when it is needed.

retrieval cue Anything that helps a person (or a nonhuman animal) recall information stored in long-memory.

retroactive interference When new information inhibits the ability to remember old information.

retrograde amnesia A condition in which people lose past memories, such as memories for events, facts, people, or even personal information.

reuptake The process whereby a neurotransmitter is taken back into the presynaptic terminal buttons, thereby stopping its activity.

rods Retinal cells that respond to low levels of illumination and result in black-and-white perception.

sample A subset of a population.

scatterplot A graphical depiction of the relationship between two variables.

schemas Cognitive structures that help us perceive, organize, process, and use information.

schizophrenia A psychological disorder characterized by a split between thought and emotion; it involves alterations in thoughts, in perceptions, or in consciousness.

scientific method A systematic procedure of observing and measuring phenomena (observable things) to answer questions about *what* happens, *when* it happens, *what* causes it, and *why*; involves a dynamic interaction between theories, hypotheses, and research.

secondary appraisals Part of the coping process during which people evaluate their response options and choose coping behaviors.

secondary emotions Blends of primary emotions; they include remorse, guilt, submission, and anticipation.

secure attachment The attachment style for a majority of infants; the infant is confident enough to play in an unfamiliar environment as long as the caregiver is present and is readily comforted by the caregiver during times of distress.

selection bias In an experiment, unintended differences between the participants in different groups.

self-actualization A state that is achieved when one's personal dreams and aspirations have been attained.

self-fulfilling prophecy People's tendency to behave in ways that confirm their own expectations or other people's expectations.

self-report methods Methods of data collection in which people are asked to provide information about themselves, such as in questionnaires or surveys.

self-serving bias The tendency for people to take personal credit for success but blame failure on external factors.

semantic memory Memory for knowledge about the world.

sensation The sense organs' detection of external stimuli, their responses to the stimuli, and the transmission of these responses to the brain.

sensitive periods Time periods when specific skills develop most easily.

sensitization An increase in behavioral response after exposure to a threatening stimulus.

sensorimotor stage The first stage in Piaget's theory of cognitive development; during this stage, infants acquire information about the world through their senses and motor skills. Reflexive responses develop into more deliberate actions through the development and refinement of schemas.

sensory adaptation A decrease in sensitivity to a constant level of stimulation.

sensory memory A memory system that very briefly stores sensory information in close to its original sensory form.

sensory neurons One of the three types of neurons; these afferent neurons detect information from the physical world and pass that information along to the brain.

serial position effect The ability to recall items from a list depends on order of presentation, with items presented early or late in the list remembered better than those in the middle.

serotonin A monoamine neurotransmitter important for a wide range of psychological activity, including emotional states, impulse control, and dreaming.

sexual response cycle A four-stage pattern of physiological and psychological responses during sexual activity.

sexual strategies theory A theory that maintains that women and men have evolved distinct mating strategies because they faced different adaptive problems over the course of human history. The strategies used by each sex maximize the probability of passing along their genes to future generations.

shaping A process of operant conditioning; it involves reinforcing behaviors that are increasingly similar to the desired behavior.

short-term memory A memory storage system that briefly holds a limited amount of information in awareness.

signal detection theory (SDT) A theory of perception based on the idea that the detection of a faint stimulus requires a judgment—it is not an all-or-none process.

situational attributions Explanations that refer to external events, such as the weather, luck, accidents, or other people's actions.

situationism The theory that behavior is determined more by situations than by personality traits.

social facilitation When the mere presence of others enhances performance.

social loafing The tendency for people to work less hard in a group than when working alone.

social norms Expected standards of conduct, which influence behavior.

social psychology The study of how people are influenced by their interactions with others.

sociocultural model A diagnostic model that views psychopathology as the result of the interaction between individuals and their cultures.

sociometer An internal monitor of social acceptance or rejection.

somatic markers Bodily reactions that arise from the emotional evaluation of an action's consequences.

somatic nervous system A component of the peripheral nervous system; it transmits sensory signals and motor signals between the central nervous system and the skin, muscles, and joints.

sound wave A pattern of changes in air pressure during a period of time; it produces the percept of a sound.

source amnesia A type of amnesia that occurs when a person shows memory for an event but cannot remember where he or she encountered the information.

source misattribution Memory distortion that occurs when people misremember the time, place, person, or circumstances involved with a memory.

split brain A condition in which the corpus callosum is surgically cut and the two hemispheres of the brain do not receive information directly from each other.

spontaneous recovery A process in which a previously extinguished response reemerges after the presentation of the conditioned stimulus.

standard deviation A statistical measure of how far away each value is, on average, from the mean.

stereotypes Cognitive schemas that allow for easy, fast processing of information about people based on their membership in certain groups.

stereotype threat Apprehension about confirming negative stereotypes related to one's own group.

stimulus discrimination A differentiation between two similar stimuli when only one of them is consistently associated with the unconditioned stimulus.

stimulus generalization Learning that occurs when stimuli that are similar but not identical to the conditioned stimulus produce the conditioned response.

storage The retention of encoded representations over time.

stream of consciousness A phrase coined by William James to describe each person's continuous series of ever-changing thoughts.

stress A pattern of behavioral, psychological, and physiological responses to events, when the events match or exceed the organism's ability to respond in a healthy way.

stressor An environmental event or stimulus that threatens an organism.

structuralism An approach to psychology based on the idea that conscious experience can be broken down into its basic underlying components.

subliminal perception The processing of information by sensory systems without conscious awareness.

substance P A neurotransmitter involved in pain perception.

subtractive color mixing A process of color mixing that occurs within the stimulus itself; a physical, not psychological, process.

suggestibility The development of biased memories from misleading information.

superego In psychodynamic theory, the internalization of societal and parental standards of conduct.

symbolic representations Abstract mental representations that do not correspond to the physical features of objects or ideas.

sympathetic division A division of the autonomic nervous system; it prepares the body for action.

synapse The site at which chemical communication occurs between neurons.

synaptic cleft The gap between the axon of a "sending" neuron and the dendrites of a "receiving" neuron; it contains extracellular fluid.

synaptic pruning A process whereby the synaptic connections in the brain that are frequently used are preserved, and those that are not used are lost.

synesthesia Cross-sensory experience (e.g., a visual image has a taste).

taste buds Sensory organs in the oral cavity that contain the receptors for taste.

telegraphic speech The tendency for toddlers to speak using rudimentary sentences that are missing words and grammatical markings but follow a logical syntax and convey a wealth of meaning.

temperaments Biologically based tendencies to feel or act in certain ways.

temporal lobes Regions of the cerebral cortex—below the parietal lobes and in front of the occipital lobes—important for processing auditory information, for memory, and for object and face perception.

tend-and-befriend response Females' tendency to protect and care for their offspring and form social alliances rather than flee or fight in response to threat.

teratogens Environmental agents that harm the embryo or fetus.

terminal buttons Small nodules, at the ends of axons, that release chemical signals from the neuron into the synapse.

thalamus The gateway to the brain; it receives almost all incoming sensory information before that information reaches the cortex.

theory A model of interconnected ideas or concepts that explains what is observed and makes predictions about future events.

theory of mind The term used to describe the ability to explain and predict another person's behavior as a result of recognizing her or his mental state.

thinking The mental manipulation of representations of information (i.e., of objects we encounter in our environments).

third variable problem A problem that occurs when the researcher cannot directly manipulate variables; as a result, the researcher cannot be confident that another, unmeasured variable is not the actual cause of differences in the variables of interest.

top-down processing A hierarchical model of pattern recognition in which information at higher levels of mental processing can also influence lower, "earlier" levels in the processing hierarchy.

trait approach An approach to studying personality that focuses on how individuals differ in personality dispositions.

transcranial magnetic stimulation (TMS) The use of strong magnets to briefly interrupt normal brain activity as a way to study brain regions.

transduction A process by which sensory receptors produce neural impulses when they receive physical or chemical stimulation.

transience Forgetting over time.

Type A behavior pattern A pattern of behavior characterized by competitiveness, achievement orientation, aggressiveness, hostility, restlessness, impatience with others, and inability to relax.

Type B behavior pattern A pattern of behavior characterized by noncompetitive, relaxed, easygoing, and accommodating behavior.

unconditioned response (UR) A response that does not have to be learned, such as a reflex.

unconditioned stimulus (US) A stimulus that elicits a response, such as a reflex, without any prior learning.

unconscious The mental processes that operate below the level of conscious awareness.

variability In a set of numbers, how widely dispersed the values are from each other and from the mean.

variable Something in the world that can vary and that a researcher can measure.

variable schedule A schedule in which reinforcement is applied at different rates or at different times.

vestibular sense Perception of balance.

vicarious learning Learning the consequences of an action by watching others being rewarded or punished for performing the action.

well-being A positive state that includes striving for optimal health and life satisfaction.

working memory An active processing system that keeps different types of information available for current use.

Yerkes-Dodson law The psychological principle that performance increases with arousal up to an optimal point, after which it decreases with increasing arousal.

REFERENCES

Aarts, H., Custers, R., & Marien, H. (2008). Preparing and motivating behavior outside of awareness. *Science, 319,* 1639.

Abizaid, A. (2009). Ghrelin and dopamine: New insights on the peripheral regulation of appetite. *Journal of Neuroendocrinology, 21,* 787–793.

Abraido-Lanza, A. F., Chao, M. T., & Florez, K. R. (2005). Do healthy behaviors decline with greater acculturation? Implications for the Latino mortality paradox. *Social Science and Medicine, 61,* 1243–1255.

Abramson, L. Y., Metalsky, G., & Alloy, L. (1989). Hopelessness depression: A theory-based subtype of depression. *Psychological Review, 96,* 358–372.

Ackerman, P. L., Beier, M. E., & Boyle, M. O. (2005). Working memory and intelligence: The same or different constructs? *Psychological Bulletin, 131,* 30–60.

Adair, J., & Kagitcibasi, C. (1995). Development of psychology in developing countries: Factors facilitating and impeding its progress. *International Journal of Psychology, 30,* 633–641.

Adams, H. E., Wright, L. W., & Lohr, B. A. (1996). Is homophobia associated with homosexual arousal? *Journal of Abnormal Psychology, 105,* 440–445.

Adams, R. B., Jr., Gordon, H. L., Baird, A. A., Ambady, N., & Kleck, R. E. (2003, June 6). Effects of gaze on amygdala sensitivity to anger and fear faces. *Science, 300,* 1536–1537.

Adolphs, R. (2003). Cognitive neuroscience of human social behavior. *Nature Reviews Neuroscience, 1,* 165–178.

Adolphs, R., Gosselin, F., Buchanan, T. W., Tranel, D., Schyns, P., & Damasio, A. R. (2005). A mechanism for impaired fear recognition after amygdala damage. *Nature, 433,* 68–72.

Adolphs, R., Sears, L., & Piven, J. (2001). Abnormal processing of social information from faces in autism. *Journal of Cognitive Neuroscience, 13,* 232–240.

Adolphs, R., Tranel, D., & Damasio, A. R. (1998). The human amygdala in social judgment. *Nature, 393,* 470–474.

Agawu, K. (1995). *African rhythm: A northern ewe perspective.* Cambridge, UK: Cambridge University Press.

Ainsworth, M. D. S., Blehar, M. C., Waters, E., & Wall, S. (1978). *Patterns of attachment: A psychological study of the strange situation.* Hillsdale, NJ: Lawrence Erlbaum.

Albus, C. (2010). Psychological and social factors in coronary heart disease. *Annals of Medicine, 42,* 487–494.

Algoe, S. B., & Fredrickson, B. L. (2011). Emotional fitness and the movement of affective science from lab to field. *American Psychologist, 66,* 35–42.

Ali, S. R., Liu, W. M., & Humedian, M. (2004). Islam 101: Understanding the religion and therapy implications. *Professional Psychology Research and Review, 35,* 635–642.

Alicke, M. D., Klotz, M. L., Breitenbecher, D. L., Yurak, T. J., & Vredenburg, D. S. (1995). Personal contact, individuation, and the better-than-average effect. *Journal of Personality and Social Psychology, 68,* 804–825.

Alicke, M. D., LoSchiavo, F. M., Zerbst, J., & Zhang, S. (1997). The person who outperforms me is a genius: Maintaining perceived competence in upward social comparisons. *Journal of Personality and Social Psychology, 73,* 781–789.

Allen, J. B., Coan, J. A., & Nazarian, M. (2004). Issues and assumptions on the road from raw signals to metrics of frontal EEG asymmetry in emotion. *Biological Psychology, 67,* 183–218.

Allport, G. W. (1954). *The nature of prejudice* (8th ed.). Oxford, UK: Addison-Wesley.

Allport, G. W. (1961). *Pattern and growth in personality.* New York: Holt, Rinehart & Winston.

Amanzio, M., & Benedetti, F. (1999). Neuropharmacological dissection of placebo analgesia: Expectation-activated opioid systems versus conditioning-activated specific subsystems. *Journal of Neuroscience, 19,* 484–494.

Amaral, D. G., Schumann, C. M., & Nordahl, C. W. (2008). Neuroanatomy of autism. *Trends in Neurosciences, 3,* 137–45.

Amato, P. R., Johnson, D. R., Booth, A., & Rogers, S. J. (2003). Continuity and change in marital quality between 1980 and 2000. *Journal of Marriage and Family, 65,* 1–22.

Ambady, N., Hallahan, M., & Conner, B. (1999). Accuracy of judgments of sexual orientation from thin slices of behavior. *Journal of Personality and Social Psychology, 77,* 538–547.

Ambady, N., & Rosenthal, R. (1993). Half a minute: Predicting teacher evaluations from thin slices of nonverbal behavior and physical attractiveness. *Journal of Personality and Social Psychology, 64,* 431–441.

American Academy of Pediatrics, Committee on Drugs. (1998). Neonatal drug withdrawal. *Pediatrics, 10,* 1079–1088.

American Association of Suicidology. (2011). *Youth suicidal behavior* [Fact sheet]. Retrieved from http://www.suicidology.org/c/document_library/get_file?folderId=232&name=DLFE-335.pdf

American Psychiatric Association. (2000a). *Diagnostic and statistical manual of mental disorders* (4th ed., text revision). Washington, DC: Author.

American Psychiatric Association. (2000b). Practice guidelines for the treatment of patients with eating disorders (revised). *American Journal of Psychiatry, 157* (Suppl.), 1–39.

American Psychological Association. (2007, February). *Guidelines for psychological practice with girls and women.* Retrieved from http://www.apa.org/practice/guidelines/girls-and-women.pdf

American Psychological Association (2010, May 13). *Dr. Katherine C. Nordal on How to Find a Therapist.* Retrieved from http://apa.org/news/press/releases/2010/05/locate-a-therapist.aspx

American Psychological Association, Health Psychology Division 38. (n.d.). *What is health psychology?* Retrieved August 4, 2008, from http://www.health-psych.org

Amiraian, D. E., & Sobal, J. (2009). Dating and eating. Beliefs about dating foods among university students. *Appetite, 53*(2), 226–232. doi:10.1016/j.appet.2009.06.012

Amminger, G. P., Pape, S., Rock, D., Roberts, S. A., Ott, S. L., Squires-Wheeler, E., et al. (1999). Relationship between childhood behavioral disturbance and later schizophrenia in the New York high-risk project. *American Journal of Psychiatry, 156*, 525–530.

Anderson, A. K., Christoff, K., Stappen, I., Panitz, D., Ghahremani, D. G., Glover, G., et al. (2003). Dissociated neural representations of intensity and valence in human olfaction. *Nature Neuroscience, 6*, 196–202.

Anderson, A. K., & Phelps, E. A. (2000). Expression without recognition: Contributions of the human amygdala to emotional communication. *Psychological Science, 11*, 106–111.

Anderson, C. A., Berkowitz, L., Donnerstein, E., Huesmann, L. R., Johnson, J., Linz, D., et al. (2003). The influence of media violence on youth. *Psychological Science in the Public Interest, 4*, 81–110.

Anderson, I. M. (2000). Selective serotonin reuptake inhibitors versus tricyclic antidepressants: A meta-analysis of efficacy and tolerability. *Journal of Affective Disorders, 58*, 19–36.

Anderson, N. H. (1968). Likableness ratings of 555 personality-trait words. *Journal of Personality and Social Psychology, 9*, 272–279.

Anderson, R., Lewis, S. Z., Gichello, A. L., Aday, L. A., & Chiu, G. (1981). Access to medical care among the Hispanic population of the Southwestern United States. *Journal of Health and Social Behavior, 22*, 78–89.

Anderson, S. W., Bechara, A., Damasio, H., Tranel, D., & Damasio, A. R. (1999). Impairment of social and moral behavior related to early damage in human prefrontal cortex. *Nature Neuroscience, 2*, 1032–1037.

Andreasen, N. C. (1984). *The broken brain: The biological revolution in psychiatry.* New York: Harper & Row.

Angell, M. (2000, June 23). The epidemic of mental illness: Why? *The New York Review of Books.* Retrieved from http://www.nybooks.com

Antonuccio, D., & Burns, D. (2004). Adolescents with depression [Letter to the editor]. *Journal of the American Medical Association, 292*, 2577.

Aouizerate, B., Cuny, E., Bardinet, E., Yelnik, J., Martin-Guehl, C., Rotge, J. Y., et al. (2009). Distinct striatal targets in treating obsessive-compulsive disorder and major depression. *Journal of Neurosurgery, 111*, 775–779.

Aouizerate, B., Cuny, E., Martin-Guehl, C., Guehl, D., Amieva, H., Benazzouz, A., et al. (2004). Deep brain stimulation of the ventral caudate nucleus in the treatment of obsessive-compulsive disorder and major depression: Case report. *Journal of Neurosurgery, 101*, 574–575.

Araneta, M. R. G., Schlanger, K. M., Edmonds, L. D., Destiche, D. A., Merz, R. D., Hobbs, C. A., & Gray, G. G. (2003). Prevalence of birth defects among infants of Gulf War veterans in Arkansas, Arizona, California, Georgia, Hawaii, and Iowa, 1989–1993. *Birth Defects Research, 67*, 246–260.

Arias, E., MacDorman, M. F., Strobino, D. M., & Guyer, B. (2003). Annual summary of vital statistics: 2002. *Pediatrics, 112*, 1215–1230.

Aron, A., Norman, C. C., Aron, E. N., McKenna, C., & Heyman, R. E. (2000). Couples' shared participation in novel and arousing activities and experienced relationship quality. *Journal of Personality and Social Psychology, 78*(2), 273–284. doi:10.1037/0022-3514.78.2.273

Aronne, L. J., Wadden, T., Isoldi, K. K., & Woodworth, K. A. (2009). When prevention fails: Obesity treatment strategies. *American Journal of Medicine, 122*(4 Suppl 1), S24–S32.

Aronson, E., & Mills, J. (1959). The effects of severity of initiation on liking for a group. *Journal of Abnormal and Social Psychology, 59*, 177–181.

Asberg, M., Shalling, D., Traskman-Bendz, L., & Wagner, A. (1987). Psychobiology of suicide, impulsivity, and related phenomena. In H. Y. Melzer (Ed.), *Psychopharmacology: The third generation of progress* (pp. 655–668). New York: Raven Press.

Asch, S. E. (1955). Opinions and social pressure. *Scientific American, 193*, 31–35.

Asch, S. E. (1956). Studies of independence and conformity: A minority of one against a unanimous majority. *Psychological Monographs, 70*, Whole No. 416.

Assad, L. K., Donnellan, M. B., & Conger, R. D. (2007). Optimism: An enduring resource for romantic relationships. *Journal of Personality and Social Psychology, 93*, 285–297.

Austin, E. J., Saklofske, D. H., & Mastoras, S. M. (2010). Emotional intelligence, coping and exam-related stress in Canadian undergraduate students. *Australian Journal of Psychology, 62*, 42–50.

Austin, M. P., Hadzi-Pavlovic, D., Leader, L., Saint, K., & Parker, G. (2005). Maternal trait anxiety, depression, and life event stress in pregnancy: Relationship with infant temperament. *Early Human Development, 81*, 183–190.

Averill, J. R. (1980). A constructivist view of emotion. In R. Plutchik & H. Kellerman (Eds.), *Theories of emotion* (pp. 305–339). New York: Academic Press.

Aviezer, H., Hassin, R. R., Ryan, J., Grady, C., Susskind, J., Anderson, A., et al. (2008). Angry, disgusted, or afraid? Studies on the malleability of emotion perception. *Psychological Science, 19*, 724–732.

Axelsson, J., Sundelin, T., Ingre, M., Van Someren, E. J. W., Olsson, A., & Lekander, M. (2010). Beauty sleep: Experimental study on the perceived health and attractiveness of sleep deprived people. *British Journal of Medicine, 341.* Retrieved December 10, 2010, from http://www.bmj.com/content/341/bmj.c6614.abstract

Aylward, E. H., Reiss, A. L., Reader, M. J., & Singer, H. S. (1996). Basal ganglia volumes in children with attention-deficit hyperactivity disorder. *Journal of Child Neurology, 11*, 112–115.

Baars, B. (1988). *A cognitive theory of consciousness.* Cambridge, UK: Cambridge University Press.

Babson, K. A., Trainor, C. D., Feldner, M. T., & Blumenthal, H. (2010). A test of the effects of acute sleep deprivation on general and specific self-reported anxiety and depressive symptoms: An experimental extension. *Journal of Behavior Therapy and Experimental Psychiatry, 41*, 297–303.

Back, M. D., Stopfer, J. M., Vazire, S., Gaddis, S., Schmukle, S. C., Egloff, B., & Gosling, S. D. (2010). Facebook profiles reflect actual personality not self-idealization. *Psychological Science, 21*, 372–374.

Baddeley, A.D., & Hitch, G. (1974). Working memory. In G. H. Bower (Ed.), *The psychology of learning and motivation: Advances in research and theory* (Vol. 8, pp. 47–89). New York: Academic Press.

Baddeley, A. D. (2002). Is working memory still working? *European Psychologist, 7*, 85–97.

Bailey, A., Le Couteur, A., Gottesman, I., Bolton, P., Simonoff, E., Yuzda, E., et al. (1995). Autism as a strongly genetic disorder: Evidence from a British twin study. *Psychological Medicine, 25*, 63–78.

Baillargeon, R. (1987). Object permanence in 3½ and 4½ month old infants. *Developmental Psychology, 23*, 655–664.

Baillargeon, R. (1995). Physical reasoning in infancy. In M. S. Gazzaniga (Ed.), *The cognitive neurosciences* (pp. 181–204). Cambridge, MA: MIT Press.

Baillargeon, R., Li, J., Ng, W., & Yuan, S. (2009). A new account of infants' physical reasoning. In A. Woodward & A. Needham (Eds.), *Learning and the infant mind* (pp. 66–116). New York: Oxford University Press.

Baker, T. B., Brandon, T. H., & Chassin, L. (2004). Motivational influences on cigarette smoking. *Annual Review of Psychology, 55*, 463–491.

Baldwin, D. A. (1991). Infants' contribution to the achievement of joint reference. *Child Development, 62*, 875–890.

Baldwin, D. A., & Baird, J. A. (2001). Discerning intentions in dynamic human action. *Trends in Cognitive Sciences, 5*, 171–178.

Baler, R. D., & Volkow, N. D. (2006). Drug addiction: The neurobiology of disrupted self-control. *Trends in Molecular Medicine, 12*(12), 559–566.

Ballantyne, J. C., & LaForge, K. S. (2007). Opioid dependence and addiction during opioid treatment of chronic pain. *Pain, 129*, 235–255.

Balthazard, C. G., & Woody, E. Z. (1992). The spectral analysis of hypnotic performance with respect to 'absorption.' *International Journal of Clinical and Experimental Hypnosis, 40*, 21–43.

Baltimore, D. (2001). Our genome unveiled. *Nature, 409*, 814–816.

Banaji, M. R., & Greenwald, A. G. (1995). Implicit gender stereotyping in judgments of fame. *Journal of Personality and Social Psychology, 68*, 181–198.

Bandura, A. (1977). *Social learning theory*. Englewood Cliffs, NJ: Prentice-Hall.

Bandura, A., Ross, D., & Ross, S. (1961). Transmission of aggression through imitation of aggressive models. *Journal of Abnormal and Social Psychology, 66*, 3–11.

Bandura, A., Ross, D., & Ross, S. (1963). Vicarious reinforcement and imitative learning. *Journal of Abnormal and Social Psychology, 67*, 601–607.

Bao, W. N., Whitbeck, L. B., Hoyt, D. R., & Conger, R. D. (1999). Perceived parental acceptance as a moderator of religious transmission among adolescent boys and girls. *Journal of Marriage and Family, 61*, 362–374.

Barbui, C., Cipriani, A., Patel, V., Ayuso-Mateos, J., & van Ommeren, M. (2011). Efficacy of antidepressants and benzodiazepines in minor depression: Systematic review and meta-analysis. *British Journal of Psychiatry, 198*, 11–16.

Barch, D. M., Sheline, Y. I., Csernansky, J. G., & Snyder, A. Z. (2003). Working memory and prefrontal cortex dysfunction: Specificity to schizophrenia compared with major depression. *Biological Psychiatry, 53*, 376–384.

Bargh, J. A. (2006). What have we been priming all these years? On the development, mechanisms, and ecology of nonconscious social behavior. *European Journal of Social Psychology, 36*(147), 168.

Bargh, J. A., & Chartrand, T. L. (1999). The unbearable automaticity of being. *American Psychologist, 54*, 462–479.

Bargh, J. A., Chen, M., & Burrows, L. (1996). Automaticity of social behavior: Direct effects of trait construct and stereotype activation on action. *Journal of Personality and Social Psychology, 71*, 230–244.

Bargh, J. A., & Ferguson, M. J. (2000). Beyond behaviorism: On the automaticity of higher mental processes. *Psychological Bulletin, 126*, 925–945.

Bargh, J. A., & Morsella, E. (2008). The unconscious mind. *Perspectives on Psychological Science, 3*, 73–79.

Barlow, D. H. (2002). *Anxiety and its disorders: The nature and treatment of anxiety and panic* (2nd ed.). New York: Guilford Press.

Barlow, D. H. (2004). Psychological treatments. *American Psychologist, 59*, 869–878.

Barlow, D. H., Gorman, J. M., Shear, M. K., & Woods, S. W. (2000). Cognitive-behavioral therapy, imipramine, or their combination for panic disorder: A randomized controlled trial. *Journal of the American Medical Association, 283*, 2529–2536.

Barnett, R. C., & Hyde, J. S. (2001). Women, men, work, and family: An expansionist theory. *American Psychologist, 56*, 781–796.

Baron, A. S., & Banaji, M. R. (2006). The development of implicit attitudes. *Psychological Science, 17*, 53–58.

Baron-Cohen, S., Wheelwright, S., & Jolliffe, T. (1997). Is there a "language of the eyes"? Evidence from normal adults and adults with autism or Asperger syndrome. *Visual Cognition, 4*, 311–332.

Barr, A. M., Panenka, W. J., MacEwan, G. W., Thornton, A. E., Lang, D. J., Honer, W. G., et al. (2006). The need for speed: An update on methamphetamine addiction. *Journal of Psychiatry & Neuroscience, 31*(5), 301–313.

Barrett, L. F., Mesquita, B., Ochsner, K. N., & Gross, J. J. (2007). The experience of emotion. *Annual Review of Psychology, 58*, 373–403.

Bartels, A., & Zeki, S. (2004). The neural correlates of maternal and romantic love. *Neuroimage, 21*, 1155–1166.

Bartels, J., Andreasen, D., Ehirim, P., Mao, H., Seibert, S., Wright, E. J., et al. (2008). Neurotrophic electrode: Method of assembly and implantation into human motor speech cortex. *Journal of Neuroscience Methods, 174*, 168–176.

Barton, D. A., Esler, M. D., Dawood, T., Lambert, E. A., Haikerwal, D., Brenchley, C., et al. (2008). Elevated brain serotonin turnover in patients with depression: Effect of genotype and therapy. *Archives of General Psychiatry, 65*, 38–46.

Bartoshuk, L. M. (2000). Comparing sensory experiences across individuals: Recent psychophysical advances illuminate genetic variation in taste perception. *Chemical Senses, 25*, 447–460.

Batson, C. D., Dyck, J. L., Brandt, J. R., Batson, J. G., Powell, A. L., McMaster, M. R., et al. (1988). Five studies testing two new egoistic alternatives to the empathy-altruism hypothesis. *Journal of Personality and Social Psychology, 55*, 52–77.

Batson, C. D., Turk, C. L., Shaw, L. L., & Klein, T. (1995). Information function of empathic emotion: Learning that we value the other's welfare. *Journal of Personality and Social Psychology, 68*, 300–313.

Baumeister, R. F. (1991). *Escaping the self: Alcoholism, spirituality, masochism, and other flights from the burden of selfhood*. New York: Basic Books.

Baumeister, R. F. (2000). Gender differences in erotic plasticity: The female sex drive as socially flexible and responsive. *Psychological Bulletin, 126,* 347–374.

Baumeister, R. F., Campbell, J. D., Krueger, J. I., & Vohs, K. D. (2003). Does high self-esteem cause better performance, interpersonal success, happiness, or healthier lifestyles? *Psychological Science in the Public Interest, 4,* 1–44.

Baumeister, R. F., Campbell, J. D., Krueger, J. I., & Vohs, K. D. (2005, January). Exploding the self-esteem myth. *Scientific American, 292,* 84–91.

Baumeister, R. F., Catanese, K. R., & Vohs, K. D. (2001). Is there a gender difference in strength of sex drive? Theoretical views, conceptual distinctions, and a review of the relevant literature. *Social Psychology Review, 5,* 242–273.

Baumeister, R. F., Dale, K., & Sommers, K. L. (1998). Freudian defense mechanisms and empirical findings in modern social psychology: Reaction formation, projection, displacement, undoing, isolation, sublimation, and denial. *Journal of Personality, 66,* 1081–1124.

Baumeister, R. F., Heatherton, T. F., & Tice, D. (1994). *Losing Control: How and Why People Fail at Self-Regulation.* San Diego: Academic Press.

Baumeister, R. F., & Leary, M. R. (1995). The need to belong: Desire for interpersonal attachments as a fundamental human motivation. *Psychological Bulletin, 117*(3), 497–529. doi:10.1037/0033-2909.117.3.497

Baumeister, R. F., & Masicampo, E. J. (2010). Conscious thought is for facilitating social and cultural interactions: How mental simulations serve the animal–culture interface. *Psychological Review, 117,* 945–971.

Baumeister, R. F., Masicampo, E. J., & Vohs, K. D. (2011). Do conscious thoughts cause behavior? *Annual Review of Psychology, 62,* 331–361.

Baumeister, R. F., Smart, L., & Boden, J. M. (1996). Relation of threatened egotism to violence and aggression: The dark side of high self-esteem. *Psychological Review, 103,* 5–33.

Baumeister, R. F., Stillwell, A. M., & Heatherton, T. F. (1994). Guilt: An interpersonal approach. *Psychological Bulletin, 115,* 243–267.

Baumgartner, T., Lutz, K., Schmidt, C. F., & Jäncke, L. (2006). The emotional power of music: How music enhances the feeling of affective pictures. *Brain Research 1075*(1), 151–164.

Bäuml, K. T., & Samenieh, A. (2010). The two faces of memory retrieval. *Psychological Science, 21,* 793–795.

Baumrind, D., Larzelere, R. E., & Cowan, P. A. (2002). Ordinary physical punishment: Is it harmful? Comment on Gershoff (2002). *Psychological Bulletin, 128,* 580–589.

Baxter, L. R. (2000). Functional imaging of brain systems mediating obsessive-compulsive disorder. In D. S. Charney, E. J. Nestler, & B. S. Bunney (Eds.), *Neurobiology of mental illness* (pp. 534–547). New York: Oxford University Press.

Baxter, L. R., Schwartz, J. M., Bergman, K. S., Szuba, M. P., Guze, B., Mazziota, J. C., et al. (1992). Caudate glucose metabolic rate changes with both drug and behavior therapy for obsessive-compulsive disorder. *Archives of General Psychiatry, 49,* 681–689.

Baydala, L., Rasmussen, C., Birch, J., Sherman, J., Wikman, E., Charchun, J., et al. (2009). Self-beliefs and behavioural development as related to academic achievement in Canadian Aboriginal children. *Canadian Journal of School Psychology, 24,* 19–33.

Beck, A. T. (1967). *Depression: Clinical, experimental and theoretical aspects.* New York: Harper & Row.

Beck, A. T. (1976). *Cognitive therapy and the emotional disorders.* New York: International Universities Press.

Beck, A. T., Brown, G., Seer, R. A., Eidelson, J. L., & Riskind, J. H. (1987). Differentiating anxiety and depression: A test of the cognitive content-specificity hypothesis. *Journal of Abnormal Psychology, 96,* 179–183.

Beck, A. T., Freeman, A., & Associates. (1990). *Cognitive therapy of personality disorders.* New York: Guilford Press.

Beck, A. T., & Rector, N. A. (2005). Cognitive approaches to schizophrenia: Theory and therapy. *Annual Review of Clinical Psychology, 1,* 577–606.

Beck, A. T., Rush, A. J., Shaw, B., & Emery, G. (1979). *Cognitive therapy of depression.* New York: Guilford Press.

Beck, A. T., Steer, R. A., & Brown, G. K. (1996). *Beck depression inventory manual.* San Antonio, TX: The Psychological Corporation.

Beck, A. T., Ward, C. H., Mendelson, M., Mock, J., & Erbaugh, J. (1961). An inventory for measuring depression. *Archives of General Psychiatry, 4,* 561–571.

Beck, H. P., Levinson, S., & Irons, G. (2009). Finding Little Albert: A journey to John B. Watson's infant laboratory. *American Psychologist, 64,* 605–614.

Becker, D. V., Kenrick, D. T., Neuberg, S. L., Blackwell, K. C., & Smith, D. M. (2007). The confounded nature of angry men and happy women. *Journal of Personality and Social Psychology, 92,* 179–190.

Beggan, J. K. (1992). On the social nature of nonsocial perception: The mere ownership effect. *Journal of Personality and Social Psychology, 62,* 229–237.

Beggs, J. M., Brown, T. H., Byrne, J. H., Crow, T., LeDoux, J. E., LeBar, K., et al. (1999). Learning and memory: Basic mechanisms. In M. J. Zigmond, F. E. Bloom, S. C. Landis, J. L. Roberts, & L. R. Squire (Eds.), *Fundamentals of neuroscience* (pp. 1411–1454). San Diego, CA: Academic Press.

Behne, T., Carpenter, M., Call, J., & Tomasello, M. (2005). Unwilling versus unable: Infants' understanding of intentional action. *Developmental Psychology, 41,* 328–337.

Bellak, L., & Black, R. B. (1992). Attention-deficit hyperactivity disorder in adults. *Clinical Therapeutics, 14,* 138–147.

Belmaker, R. H., & Agam, G. (2008). Major depressive disorder. *New England Journal of Medicine, 358,* 55–68.

Belsky, J. (1990). Children and marriage. In F. D. Fincham & T. N. Bradbury (Eds.), *The psychology of marriage: Basic issues and applications* (pp. 172–200). New York: Guilford Press.

Belsky, J., Houts, R. M., & Fearon, R. M. P. (2010). Infant attachment security and the timing of puberty: Testing an evolutionary hypothesis. *Psychological Science, 21,* 1195–1201.

Bem, D. J. (1967). Self-perception: An alternative explanation of cognitive dissonance phenomena. *Psychological Review, 74,* 183–200.

Bem, D. J. (1996). Exotic becomes erotic: A developmental theory of sexual orientation. *Psychological Review, 103,* 320–335.

Bem, D. J. (2011). Feeling the future: Experimental evidence for anomalous retroactive influences on cognition and affect. *Journal of Personality and Social Psychology, 100*(3), 407–425.

Bem, D. J., & Honorton, C. (1994). Does psi exist? Replicable evidence for an anomalous process of information transfer. *Psychological Bulletin, 115,* 4–18.

Bem, S. L. (1981). Gender schema theory: A cognitive account of sex typing.

Bender, H. L., Allen, J. P., McElhaney, K. B., Antonishak, J., Moore, C. M., Kelly, H. O., et al. (2007). Use of harsh physical discipline and developmental outcomes in adolescence. *Development and Psychopathology, 19*, 227–242.

Benedetti, F., Mayberg, H. S., Wagner, T. D., Stohler, C. S., & Zubieta, J. K. (2005). Neurobiological mechanisms of the placebo effect. *Journal of Neuroscience, 25*, 10390–10402.

Benedetti, F., Serretti, A., Colombo, C., Campori, E., Barbini, B., di Bella, D., et al. (1999). Influence of a functional polymorphism within the promoter of the serotonin transporter gene on the effects of total sleep deprivation in bipolar depression. *American Journal of Psychiatry, 156*, 1450–1452.

Benjamin, L. T. (2005). A history of clinical psychology as a profession in America (and a glimpse at its future). *Annual Review of Clinical Psychology, 1*, 1–30.

Bentler, P.M., & Newcomb, M. D. (1978). Longitudinal study of marital success and failure. *Journal of Consulting and Clinical Psychology, 46*, 1053–1070.

Berkman, L. F., & Syme, S. L. (1979). Social networks, host resistance, and mortality: A nine-year follow-up study of Alameda County residents. *American Journal of Epidemiology, 109*, 186–204.

Berkowitz, L. (1990). On the formation and regulation of anger and aggression: A cognitive-neoassociationistic analysis. *American Psychologist, 45*, 494–503.

Bernhardt, P. C., Dabbs, J. M., Fielden, J. A., & Lutter, C. D. (1998). Testosterone changes during vicarious experiences of winning and losing among fans at sporting events. *Physiology & Behavior, 65*, 59–62.

Berns, G. S., Chappelow, J., Zink, C. F., Pagnoni, G., Martin-Skurski, M. E., & Richards, J. (2005). Neurobiological correlates of social conformity and interdependence during mental rotation. *Biological Psychiatry, 58*, 245–253.

Bernstein, C.A. (2011). Meta-structure in DSM-5 process. *Psychiatric News, 46*, 7.

Berridge, K. C., Ho, C. Y., Richard, J. M., & DiFeliceantonio, A. G. (2010). The tempted brain eats: Pleasure and desire circuits in obesity and eating disorders. *Brain Research, 1350*, 43–64.

Berscheid, E., & Regan, P. (2005). *The psychology of interpersonal relationships*. New York: Prentice-Hall.

Betancourt, H., & Lopez, S. R. (1993). The study of culture, ethnicity, and race in American psychology. *American Psychologist, 48*, 629–637.

Bewernick, B. H., Hurlemann, R., Matusch, A., Kayser, S., Grubert, C., Hadrysiewicz, B., et al. (2010). Nucleus accumbens deep brain stimulation decreases ratings of depression and anxiety in treatment-resistant depression. *Biological Psychiatry, 67*, 110–116.

Bickerton, D. (1998). The creation and re-creation of language. In C. B. Crawford & D. L. Krebs (Eds.), *Handbook of evolutionary psychology: Ideas, issues, and applications* (pp. 613–634). Mahwah, NJ: Erlbaum.

Bidell, T. R., & Fischer, K. W. (1995). Between nature and nurture: The role of agency in the epigenesis of intelligence. In R. Sternberg & E. Grigorenko (Eds.), *Intelligence: Heredity and environment*. New York: Cambridge University Press.

Biederman, J., Hirshfeld-Becker, D. R., Rosenbaum, J. F., Herot, C., Friedman, D., Snidman, N., et al. (2001). Further evidence of association between behavioral inhibition and social anxiety in children. *American Journal of Psychiatry, 158*, 1673–1679.

Biederman, J., Monuteaux, M. C., Spencer, T., Wilens, T. E., Macpherson, H. A., & Faraone, S. V. (2008). Stimulant therapy and risk for subsequent substance use disorders in male adults with ADHD: A naturalistic controlled 10-year follow-up study. *American Journal of Psychiatry, 165*, 597–603.

Biesanz, J., West, S. G., & Millevoi, A. (2007). What do you learn about someone over time? The relationship between length of acquaintance and consensus and self-other agreement in judgments of personality. *Journal of Personality and Social Psychology, 92*, 119–135.

Bjorklund, D. F. (2007). *Why Youth is Not Wasted on the Young: Immaturity in Human Development*. Malden, MA: Blackwell.

Blagys, M. D., & Hilsenroth, M. J. (2000). Distinctive feature of short-term psychodynamic-interpersonal psychotherapy: A review of the comparative psychotherapy process literature. *Clinical Psychology: Science and Practice, 7*, 167–188.

Blair, I. V. (2002). The malleability of automatic stereotypes and prejudice. *Personality and Social Psychology Review, 6*, 242–261.

Blair, R. J. (2003). Neurobiological basis of psychopathy. *British Journal of Psychiatry, 182*, 5–7.

Blakemore, C. (1983). *Mechanics of the mind*. Cambridge, UK: Cambridge University Press.

Blakemore, S. J., & Choudhury, S. (2006). Development of the adolescent brain: Implications for executive function and social cognition. *Journal of Child Psychology and Psychiatry, 47*, 296–312. doi: 10.1111/j.1469-7610.2006.01611.x

Blakemore, S. J., Wolpert, D. M., & Frith, C. D. (1998). Central cancellation of self-produced tickle sensation. *Nature Neuroscience, 1*, 635–640.

Blakeslee, S. (2001, April 10). A reason we call our cheddar cheese "sharp" and shirts "loud." *The New York Times*. Retrieved from http://www.nytimes.com

Blanchard, R., & Ellis, L. (2001). Birth weight, sexual orientation, and the sex of preceding siblings. *Journal of Biosocial Science, 33*, 451–467.

Blass, T. (1991). Understanding behavior in the Milgram obedience experiment: The role of personality, situations, and their interactions. *Journal of Personality and Social Psychology, 60*, 398–413.

Block, J., & Kremen, A. M. (1996). IQ and ego-resiliency: Conceptual and empirical connections and separateness. *Journal of Personality and Social Psychology, 70*(2), 349–361.

BloodAlcoholContent.Org. (2007–2010). Measuring BAC. Retrieved October 29, 2010, from http://bloodalcoholcontent.org/measuringbac.html

Bloom, B., & Cohen, R. A. (2007). Summary health statistics for U. S. children: National health interview survey, 2006 (Vital and Health Statistics, Series 10, No. 234). Hyattsville, MD: Centers for Disease Control and Prevention.

Blue, I., & Harpham, T. (1996). Urbanization and mental health in developing countries. *Current Issues in Public Health, 2*, 181–185.

Bogaert, A. F. (2006). Biological versus nonbiological older brothers and men's sexual orientation. *Proceedings of the National Academy of Sciences, USA, 103*, 10771–10774.

Bohlin, G., Hagekull, B., & Rydell, A. M. (2000). Attachment and social functioning: A longitudinal study from infancy to middle childhood. *Social Development, 9*, 24–39. doi: 10.1111/1467-9507.00109

Bolles, R. C. (1970). Species-specific defense reactions and avoidance learning. *Psychological Review, 77*, 32–48.

Bonanno, G. A. (2004). Loss, trauma, and human resilience: Have we underestimated the human capacity to thrive after extremely aversive events? *American Psychologist, 59*(1), 20–28.

Bootzin, R. R., & Epstein, D. R. (2011). Understanding and treating insomnia. *Annual Review of Clinical Psychology, 7,* 435–458.

Bornstein, R. F. (1999). Criterion validity of objective and projective dependency tests: A meta-analytic assessment of behavioral prediction. *Psychological Assessment, 11,* 48–57.

Bosson, J. K., Lakey, C. E., Campbell, W. K., Zeigler-Hill, V., Jordan, C. H., & Kernis, M. H. (2008). Untangling the links between narcissism and self-esteem: A theoretical and empirical review. *Social and Personality Psychology Compass, 2,* 1415–1439.

Bouchard, C., & Pérusse, L. (1993). Genetics of obesity. *Annual Review of Nutrition, 13,* 337–354.

Bouchard, C., Tremblay, A., Despres, J. P., Nadeau, A., Lupien, J. P., Theriault, G., et al. (1990). The response to long-term overfeeding in identical twins. *New England Journal of Medicine, 322,* 1477–1482.

Bouchard, T. J., Jr., Lykken, D. T., McGue, M., Segal, N. L., & Tellegen, A. (1990, October 12). Sources of human psychological differences: The Minnesota study of twins reared apart. *Science, 250,* 223–228.

Bouton, M. E. (1994). Context, ambiguity, and classical conditioning. *Current Directions in Psychological Science, 3,* 49–53.

Bouton, M. E., Westbrook, R. F., Corcoran, K. A., & Maren, S. (2006). Contextual and temporal modulation of extinction: Behavioral and biological mechanisms. *Biological Psychiatry, 60,* 352–360.

Bower, A. (2001). Attractive models in advertising and the women who loathe them: The implications of negative affect for spokesperson effectiveness. *Highly Journal of Advertising, 30,* 51–63.

Bowlby, J. (1982). Attachment and loss: Retrospect and prospect. *American Journal of Orthopsychiatry, 52,* 664–678.

Brackett, M. A., Rivers, S. E., & Salovey, P. (2011). Emotional intelligence: Implications for personal, social, academic, and workplace settings. *Social and Personality Psychology Compass, 5,* 88–103.

Bradbury, T. N., & Fincham, F. D. (1990). Attributions in marriage: Review and critique. *Psychological Bulletin, 107,* 3–33.

Bransford, J. D., & Johnson, M. K. (1972). Contextual prerequisites for understanding: Some investigations of comprehension and recall. *Journal of Verbal Learning and Verbal Behavior, 11,* 717–726. (Reprinted and modified in *Human memory,* p. 305, by E. B. Zechmeister & S. E. Nyberg, Eds., 1982, Pacific Grove, CA: Brooks Cole.)

Braunschweig, D., Ashwood, P., Krakowiak, P., Hertz-Picciotto, I., Hansen, R., Croen, L. A., et al. (2008). Autism: Maternally derived antibodies specific for fetal brain proteins. *Neurotoxicology, 29,* 226–231.

Breedlove, S. M., Rosenzweig, M. R., & Watson, N. V. (2007). *Biological psychology* (5th ed.). Sunderland, MA: Sinauer Associates.

Breland, K., & Breland, M. (1961). The misbehavior of organisms. *American Psychologist, 16,* 681–684.

Brent, D. A. (2004). Antidepressants and pediatric depression: The risk of doing nothing. *New England Journal of Medicine, 351,* 1598–1601.

Brewer, M. B., & Caporael, L. R. (1990). Selfish genes vs. selfish people: Sociobiology as origin myth. *Motivation and Emotion, 14,* 237–243.

Brigham, J. C., & Malpass, R. S. (1985). The role of experience and contact in the recognition of faces of own- and other-races persons. *Journal of Social Issues, 41,* 139–155.

Brody, A. L., Saxena, S., Stoessel, P., Gillies, L. A., Fairbanks, L. A., Alborzian, S., et al. (2001). Regional brain metabolic changes in patients with major depression treated with either paroxetine or interpersonal therapy: Preliminary findings. *Archives of General Psychiatry, 58,* 631–640.

Brody, J. E. (1997, December 30). Personal health: Despite the despair of depression, few men seek treatment. *The New York Times.* Retrieved from http://www.nytimes.com

Brody, N. (1992). *Intelligence.* San Diego, CA: Academic Press.

Bromley, S. M., & Doty, R. L. (1995). Odor recognition memory is better under bilateral than unilateral test conditions. *Cortex, 31,* 25–40.

Brown, A. S. (1991). A review of the tip-of-the-tongue phenomenon. *Psychological Bulletin, 109,* 204–223.

Brown, B. B., Mounts, N., Lamborn, S. D., & Steinberg, L. (1993). Parenting practices and peer group affiliations in adolescence. *Child Development, 64,* 467–482.

Brown, G. W., & Harris, T. O. (1978). *Social origins of depression: A study of psychiatric disorders in women.* New York: Free Press.

Brown, J. D., & Kobayashi, C. (2002). Self-enhancement in Japan and America. *Asian Journal of Social Psychology, 5,* 145–168.

Brown, R. (1973). Development of the first language in the human species. *American Psychologist, 28,* 97–106. doi: 10.1037/h0034209

Brown, R., & Kulik, J. (1977). Flashbulb memories. *Cognition, 5*(1), 73–99.

Brown, R., & McNeill, D. (1966). The "tip-of-the-tongue" phenomenon. *Journal of Verbal Learning and Verbal Behavior, 5,* 325–337.

Brownell, C. A., & Brown, E. (1992). Peers and play in infants and toddlers. In V. Van Hasselt & M. Hersen (Eds.), *Handbook of social development: A lifespan perspective* (pp. 183–200). New York: Plenum Press.

Brownell, K. D., Greenwood, M. R. C., Stellar, E., & Shrager, E. E. (1986). The effects of repeated cycles of weight loss and regain in rats. *Physiology & Behavior, 38,* 459–464.

Bruce, V., & Young, A. (1986). Understanding face recognition. *British Journal of Psychology, 77,* 305–327.

Bruck, M. L., & Ceci, S. (1993). Amicus brief for the case of State of New Jersey v. Michaels. Presented by Committee of Concerned Social Scientists. Supreme Court of New Jersey Docket No. 36, 633. (Reprinted in *Psychology, Public Policy and Law, 1,* 1995, 272–322.)

Bruder, C. E., Piotrowski, A., Gijsbers, A. A., Andersson, R., Erickson, S., de Ståhl, T. D., et al. (2008). Phenotypically concordant and discordant monozygotic twins display different DNA copy-number-variation profiles. *American Journal of Human Genetics, 82,* 763–771.

Burger, J. M. (2009). Replicating Milgram: Would people still obey today? *American Psychologist, 64,* 1–11.

Burke, B. L., Arkowitz, H., & Menchola, M. (2003). The efficacy of motivational interviewing: A meta-analysis of controlled clinical trials. *Journal of Consulting and Clinical Psychology, 71,* 843–861.

Bush, E. C., & Allman, J. M. (2004). The scaling of frontal cortex in primates and carnivores. *Proceedings of the National Academy of Sciences, USA, 101,* 3962–3966.

Bushman, B. J., & Baumeister, R. F. (1998). Threatened egotism, narcissism, self-esteem, and direct and displaced aggression: Does self-love or self-hate lead to violence? *Journal of Personality and Social Psychology, 75,* 219–229.

Bushman, B. J., & Huesmann, L. R. (2001). Effects of televised violence on aggression. In D. G. Singer & J. L. Singer (Eds.), *Handbook of children and the media* (pp. 223–254). Thousand Oaks, CA: Sage.

Buss, A. H., & Plomin, R. (1984). *Temperament: Early developing personality traits.* Hillsdale, NJ: Erlbaum.

Buss, D. M. (1989). Sex differences in human mate preferences: Evolutionary hypotheses tested in 37 cultures. *Behavioral and Brain Sciences, 12,* 1–49.

Buss, D. M. (1995). Psychological sex differences: Origins through sexual selection. *American Psychologist, 50,* 164–168. doi: 10.1037/0003-066X.50.3.164

Buss, D. M. (1999). Human nature and individual differences: The evolution of human personality. In L. A. Pervin & O. P. John (Eds.), *Handbook of personality: Theory and research* (pp. 31–56). New York: Guilford Press.

Buss, D. M., & Schmitt, D. P. (1993). Sexual strategies theory: An evolutionary perspective on human mating. *Psychological Review, 100,* 204–232.

Buss, D. M., & Shackelford, T. K. (2008). Attractive women want it all: Good genes, investment, parenting indicators, and commitment. *Evolutionary Psychology, 6,* 134–146.

Butcher, J. N., Mineka, S., & Hooley, J. M. (2007). *Abnormal psychology* (13th ed.). Boston: Allyn and Bacon.

Butler, A. C., Chapman, J. E., Forman, E. M., & Beck, A. T. (2006). The empirical status of cognitive-behavioral therapy: A review of meta-analyses. *Clinical Psychology Review, 26,* 17–31.

Byers-Heinlein, K., Burns, T. C., & Werker, J. F. (2010). The roots of bilingualism in newborns. *Psychological Science, 21,* 343–348.

Cacioppo, J. T., Berntson, G. G., Larsen, J. T., Poehlmann, K. M., & Ito, T. A. (2000). The psychophysiology of emotion. In M. Lewis & R. J. M. Haviland-Jones (Eds.), *The handbook of emotions* (2nd ed., pp. 173–191). New York: Guilford Press.

Cacioppo, J. T., Hughes, M. E., Waite, L. J., Hawkley, L. C., & Thisted, R. A. (2006). Loneliness as a specific risk factor for depressive symptoms: Cross sectional and longitudinal analyses. *Psychology and Aging, 21,* 140–151.

Cacioppo, J. T., & Patrick, W. (2008). *Loneliness: Human nature and the need for social connection.* New York: Norton.

Cahill, L., Haier, R. J., White, N. S., Fallon, J., Kilpatrick, L., Lawrence, C., et al. (2001). Sex-related difference in amygdala activity during emotionally influenced memory storage. *Neurobiology of Learning and Memory, 75,* 1–9.

Cahill, L., Prins, B., Weber, M., & McGaugh, J. L. (1994). Beta-adrenergic activation and memory for emotional events. *Nature, 371,* 702–704.

Cahn, B. R., & Polich, J. (2006). Meditation states and traits: EEG, ERP, and neuroimaging studies. *Psychological Bulletin, 132,* 180–211.

Cairns, R. B., & Cairns, B. D. (1994). *Lifelines and risks: Pathways of youth in our times.* Cambridge, UK: Cambridge University Press.

Campbell, W. K., Bush, C. P., Brunell, A. B., & Shelton, J. (2005). Understanding the social costs of narcissism: The case of tragedy of the commons. *Personality and Social Psychology, 31,* 1358–1368.

Campbell, W. K., Foster, C. A., & Finkel, E. J. (2002). Does self-love lead to love for others? A story of narcissistic game playing. *Journal of Personality and Social Psychology, 83,* 340–354.

Campbell, W. K., & Sedikides, C. (1999). Self-threat magnifies the self-serving bias: A meta-analytic integration. *Review of General Psychology, 3,* 23–43.

Canli, T. (2006). *Biology of personality and individual differences.* New York: Guilford Press.

Cannon, T. D., Cadenhead, K., Cornblatt, B., Woods, S. W., Addington, J., Walker, E., et al. (2008). Prediction of psychosis in youth at high clinical risk: A multisite longitudinal study in North America. *Archives of General Psychiatry, 65,* 28–37.

Cannon, W. B. (1927). The James-Lange theory of emotion: A critical examination and an alternative theory. *American Journal of Psychology 39,* 106–124.

Caporael, L. R. (2001). Evolutionary psychology: Toward a unifying theory and a hybrid science. *Annual Review of Psychology, 52,* 607–628.

Caramaschi, D., de Boer, S. F., & Koolhaas, J. M. (2007). Differential role of the 5-HT receptor in aggressive and non-aggressive mice: An across-strain comparison. *Physiology & Behavior, 90,* 590–601.

Cardeña, E., & Carlson, E. (2011). Acute stress disorder revisited. *Annual Review of Clinical Psychology, 7,* 245–267.

Carey, B. (2011, June 23). Expert on mental illness reveals her own fight. *The New York Times.* Retrieved from http://newyorktimes.com

Carli, L. L., Ganley, R., & Pierce-Otay, A. (1991). Similarity and satisfaction in roommate relationships. *Personality and Social Psychology Bulletin, 17*(4), 419–426. doi:10.1177/0146167291174010

Carmichael, M. (2007, March 26). Stronger, faster, smarter. *Newsweek, 149*(13). Retrieved from http://www.newsweek.com

Carmody, T. P. (1993). Nicotine dependence: Psychological approaches to the prevention of smoking relapse. *Psychology of Addictive Behaviors, 7,* 96–102.

Carnagey, N. L., Anderson, C. A., & Bartholow, B. D. (2007). Media violence and social neuroscience: New questions and new opportunities. *Current Directions in Psychological Science, 16,* 178–182.

Carnagey, N. L., Anderson, C. A., & Bushman, B. J. (2007). The effect of video game violence on physiological desensitization to real-life violence. *Journal of Experimental Social Psychology, 43,* 489–496.

Caro, T. M., & Hauser, M. D. (1992). Is there teaching in nonhuman animals? *Quarterly Journal of Biology, 67,* 151–174.

Carré, J. M., McCormick, C. M., & Hariri, A. R. (2011, in press). The social neuroendocrinology of human aggression. *Psychoneuroendocrinology.*

Carré, J. M., & Putnam, S. K. (2010). Watching a previous victory produces an increase in testosterone among elite hockey players. *Psychoneuroendocrinology, 35,* 475–479.

Carrère, S., Buehlman K. T., Gottman, J. M., Coan, J. A., & Ruckstuhl, L. (2000). Predicting marital stability and divorce in newlywed couples. *Journal of Family Psychology, 14,* 42–58.

Carstensen, L. L. (1995). Evidence for a life-span theory of socioemotional selectivity. *Current Directions in Psychological Science, 4,* 151–156.

Carter, C. S. (2003). Developmental consequences of oxytocin. *Physiology & Behavior, 74,* 383–397.

Caruso, S., Intelisano, G., Farina, M., Di Mari, L., & Agnello, C. (2003). The function of sildenafil on female sexual pathways: A double-blind, cross-over, placebo-controlled study. *European Journal of Obstetrics & Gynecology and Reproductive Biology, 110,* 201–206.

Case, R. (1992). The role of the frontal lobes in development. *Brain and Cognition, 20,* 51–73.

Casey, B. J., Jones, R. M., & Somerville, L. H. (2011). Braking and accelerating of the adolescent brain. *Journal of Research in Adolescence, 21,* 21–33.

Caspi, A. (2000). The child is father of the man: Personality continuities from childhood to adulthood. *Journal of Personality and Social Psychology, 78,* 158–172.

Caspi, A., & Herbener, E. S. (1990). Continuity and change: Assortative marriage and the consistency of personality in adulthood. *Journal of Personality and Social Psychology, 58,* 250–258.

Caspi, A., McClay, J., Moffit, T. E., Mill, J., Martin, J., Craig, I. W., et al. (2002). Role of genotype in the cycle of violence in maltreated children. *Science, 29,* 851–854.

Castellanos, F. X., Giedd, J. N., Eckberg, P., & Marsh, W. L. (1998). Quantitative morphology of the caudate nucleus in attention deficit hyperactivity disorder. *American Journal of Psychiatry, 151,* 1791–1796.

Cattell, R. B. (1965). *The scientific analysis of personality.* London: Penguin.

Cattell, R. B. (1971). *Abilities: Their structure, growth, and action.* Boston: Houghton Mifflin.

Cavanagh, J. O., Carson, A. J., Sharpe, M. M., & Lawrie, S. M. (2003). Psychological autopsy studies of suicide: A systematic review. *Psychological Medicine: A Journal of Research in Psychiatry and the Allied Sciences, 33*(3), 395–405.

Ceci, S. J. (1999). Schooling and intelligence. In S. J. Ceci & W. M. Williams (Eds.), *The nature-nurture debate: The essential readings* (pp. 168–175). Oxford, UK: Blackwell.

CensusScope. (2000). *Multiracial profile: United States.* Retrieved from http://www.censusscope.org/us/chart_multi.html

Centers for Disease Control and Prevention. (1999, November 17). A report of the Surgeon General: Physical activity and health. Retrieved from http://www.cdc.gov/nccdphp/sgr/adults.htm

Centers for Disease Control and Prevention, National Center for Health Statistics. (2002, October 8). *HHS news: Obesity still on the rise, new data show* [Press release.]. Retrieved from http://www.cdc.gov/nchs/PRESSROOM/02news/obesityonrise.htm

Centers for Disease Control and Prevention, National Center on Birth Defects and Developmental Disabilities. (2004, July). *Fetal alcohol syndrome: Guidelines for referral and diagnosis.* Retrieved from http://www.cdc.gov/ncbddd/fas/publications/FAS_guidelines_ accessible.pdf

Centers for Disease Control and Prevention. (2010a). How tobacco smoke causes disease: The biology and behavioral basis for smoking-attributable disease: A Report of the Surgeon General.

Centers for Disease Control and Prevention, National Center for Health Statistics. (2010b). [Table 22, Life expectancy at birth, at 65 years of age, and at 75 years of age, by race and sex: United States, selected years 1900–2007]. *Health, United States, 2010.* Retrieved from http://www.cdc.gov/nchs/data/hus/hus10.pdf#022

Centers for Disease Control and Prevention. (2010c). Accessed at http://www.cdc.gov/HealthyYouth/yrbs/pdf/us_tobacco_combo.pdf

Centers for Disease Control and Prevention. (2011). Mental illness surveillance among adults in the United States. *Morbidity and Mortality Weekly Report, 60*(3), 1–32.

Cepeda, N. J., Pashler, H., Vul, E., Wixted, J. T., & Rohrer, D. (2006). Distributed practice in verbal recall tasks: A review and quantitative synthesis. *Psychological Bulletin, 132,* 354–380.

Chabas, D., Taheri, S., Renier, C., & Mignot, E. (2003). The genetics of narcolepsy. *Annual Review of Genomics & Human Genetics, 4,* 459–483.

Chabris, C. (1999). Prelude or requiem for the "Mozart effect"? *Nature, 400,* 826–827.

Chambers, D. W. (1983). Stereotypic images of the scientist: The draw-a-scientist test. *Science Education, 67,* 255–265.

Chase, V. D. (2006). *Shattered nerves: How science is solving modern medicine's most perplexing problem.* Baltimore: The Johns Hopkins University Press.

Chase, W. G., & Simon, H. A. (1973). Perception in chess. *Cognitive Psychology, 4,* 55–81.

Chassin, L., Presson, C. C., & Sherman, S. J. (1990). Social psychological contributions to the understanding and prevention of adolescent cigarette smoking. *Personality and Social Psychology Bulletin, 16,* 133–151.

Cherry, E. C. (1953). Some experiments on the recognition of speech, with one and two ears. *Journal of the Acoustical Society of America, 25,* 975–979.

Chesher, G., & Greeley, J. (1992). Tolerance to the effects of alcohol. *Alcohol, Drugs, and Driving, 8,* 93–106.

Chess, S., & Thomas, A. (1984). *Origins and evolution of behavior disorders: From infancy to early adult life.* Cambridge, MA: Harvard University Press.

Cheung, F. M., Cheung, S. F., & Leung, F. (2008). Clinical utility of the cross-cultural (Chinese) personality assessment inventory (CPAI-2) in the assessment of substance use disorders among Chinese men. *Psychological Assessment, 20,* 103–113.

Cheung, F. M., Leung, K., Zhang, J. X, Sun, H. F., Gan, Y. G., Song, W. Z, et al. (2001). Indigenous Chinese personality constructs: Is the five-factor model complete? *Journal of Cross-Cultural Psychology, 32,* 407–433.

Chiao, J. Y., Iidaka, T., Gordon, H. L., Nogawa, J., Bar, M., Aminoff, E., et al. (2008). Cultural specificity in amygdala response to fear faces. *Journal of Cognitive Neuroscience, 20*(12), 2167–2174.

Chistyakov, A. V., Kaplan, B., Rubichek, O., Kreinin, I., Koren, D., Feinsod, M., et al. (2004). Antidepressant effects of different schedules of repetitive transcranial magnetic stimulation vs. clomipramine in patients with major depression: Relationship to changes in cortical excitability. *International Journal of Neuropsychopharmacology, 8,* 223–233.

Choi, I., Dalal, R., Kim-Prieto, C., & Park, H. (2003). Culture and judgment of causal relevance. *Journal of Personality and Social Psychology, 84,* 46–59.

Choi, I., Nisbett, R. E., & Norenzayan, A. (1999). Causal attribution across cultures: Variation and universality. *Psychological Bulletin, 125,* 47–63.

Choleris, E., Gustafsson, J. A., Korach, K. S., Muglia, L. J., Pfaff, D. W., & Ogawa, S. (2003). An estrogen-dependent four-gene micronet regulating social recognition: A study with oxytocin and estrogen receptor-alpha and -beta knockout mice. *Proceedings of the National Academy of Sciences, USA, 100,* 6192–6197.

Christakis, N. A., & Fowler, J. H. (2007). The spread of obesity in a large social network over 32 years. *New England Journal of Medicine, 357,* 370–379.

Christianson, S. (1992). Emotional stress and eyewitness memory: A critical review. *Psychological Bulletin, 112,* 284–309.

Chronis, A. M., Jones, H. A., & Raggi, V. L. (2006). Evidence-based psychosocial treatments for children and adolescents with attention-deficit/hyperactivity disorder. *Clinical Psychology Review, 26,* 486–502.

Chun, M. M., Golomb, J. D., & Turk-Browne, N. B. (2011). A taxonomy of external and internal attention. *Annual Review of Psychology, 62,* 73–101.

Cialdini, R. B. (2008). *Influence: Science and prejudice* (5th ed.). Boston: Allyn & Bacon.

Cialdini, R. B., Shaller, M., Houlihan, D., Arps, K., Fultz, J., & Beaman, A. L. (1987). Empathy-based helping: Is it selflessly or selfishly motivated? *Journal of Personality and Social Psychology, 52,* 749–758.

Cicchetti, D., Rogosh, F. A., & Toth, S. (1998). Maternal depressive disorder and contextual risk: Contributions to the development of attachment insecurity and behavior problems in toddlerhood. *Development and Psychopathology, 10,* 283–300.

Clark, L. A. (2007). Assessment and diagnosis of personality disorder: Perennial issues and an emerging reconceptualization. *Annual Review of Psychology, 58,* 227–257.

Clark, R. D., & Hatfield, E. (1989). Gender differences in receptivity to sexual offers. *Journal of Psychology and Human Sexuality, 2,* 39–55.

Clark, S. E., & Wells, G. L. (2008). On the diagnosticity of multiple-witness identifications. *Law and Human Behavior, 32,* 406–422.

Cleckley, H. M. (1941). *The mask of sanity: An attempt to reinterpret the so-called psychopathic personality.* St. Louis: Mosby.

Cloninger, C., Adolfsson, R., & Svrakic, N. (1996). Mapping genes for human personality. *Nature and Genetics, 12,* 3–4.

Cohen, D., Nisbett, R. E., Bowdle, B. F., & Schwarz, N. (1996). Insult, aggression, and the southern culture of honor: An "experimental ethnography." *Journal of Personality and Social Psychology, 70,* 945–960.

Cohen, G. L., Garcia, J., Apfel, N., & Master, A. (2006). Reducing the racial achievement gap: A social-psychological intervention. *Science, 313,* 1307–1310.

Cohen, S., Alper, C. M., Doyle, W. J., Treanor, J. J., & Turner, R. B. (2006). Positive emotional style predicts resistance to illness after experimental exposure to rhinovirus or influenza A virus. *Psychomatic Medicine, 68,* 809–815.

Cohen, S., Doyle, W. J., Skoner, D. P., Rabin, B. S., & Gwaltney, J. M. J. (1997). Social ties and susceptibility to the common cold. *Journal of the American Medical Association, 277,* 1940–1944.

Cohen, S., Janicki-Deverts, D., & Miller, G. E. (2007). Psychological stress and disease. *Journal of the American Medical Assocation, 298,* 1685–1687.

Cohen, S., Kamarck, T., & Mermelstein, R. (1983). A global measure of perceived stress. *Journal of Health and Social Behavior, 24,* 386–396.

Cohen, S., Tyrrell, D. A. J., & Smith, A. P. (1991). Psychological stress and susceptibility to the common cold. *New England Journal of Medicine, 325,* 606–612.

Cohen, S., & Wills, T. A. (1985). Stress, social support, and the buffering hypothesis. *Psychological Bulletin, 98,* 310–357.

Cohn, J. F., & Tronick, E. Z. (1983). Three month old infants' reaction to simulated maternal depression. *Child Development, 54,* 185–193.

Colapinto, J. (2000). *As nature made him: The boy who was raised as a girl.* New York: HarperCollins.

Colcombe, S. J., Erickson, K. I., Scalf, P., Kim, J., Prkash, R., McAuley, E., et al. (2006). Aerobic exercise training increases brain volume in aging humans. *Journal of Gerontology: Medical Sciences, 61A,* 1166–1170.

Compton, W. M., Conway, K. P., Stinson, F. S., Colliver, J. D., & Grant, B. F. (2005). Prevalence, correlates, and comorbidity of DSM-IV antisocial personality syndromes and alcohol and specific drug use disorders in the United States: Results from the national epidemiologic survey on alcohol and related conditions. *Journal of Clinical Psychiatry, 66,* 677–685.

Conn, C., Warden, R., Stuewig, R., Kim, E., Harty, L., Hastings, M., & Tangney, J. P. (2010). Borderline personality disorder among jail inmates: How common and how distinct? *Corrections Compendium, 35,* 6–13.

Conrad, A., Wilhelm, F. H., Roth, W. T., Spiegel, D., & Taylor, C. B. (2008). Circadian affective, cardiopulmonary, and cortisol variability in depressed and nondepressed individuals at risk for cardiovascular disease. *Journal of Psychiatric Research, 42,* 769–777.

Conway, A. R. A., Kane, M. J., Bunting, M. F., Hambrick, D. Z., Wilhelm, O., & Engle, R. W. (2005). Working memory span tasks: A methodological review and user's guide. *Psychonomic Bulletin & Review, 12,* 769–786.

Conway, A. R. A., Kane, M. J., & Engle, R. W. (2003). Working memory capacity and its relation to general intelligence. *Trends in Cognitive Sciences, 7,* 547–552.

Conway, M. A., Anderson, S. J., Larsen, S. F., Donnelly, C. M., McDaniel, M. A., McClelland, A. G. R., et al. (1994). The formation of flashbulb memories. *Memory and Cognition, 22,* 326–343.

Conway, M., & Ross, M. (1984). Getting what you want by revising what you had. *Journal of Personality and Social Psychology, 47,* 738–748.

Cook, G. I., Marsh, R. L., Clark-Foos, A., & Meeks, J. T. (2007, February). Learning is impaired by activated intentions. *Psychonomic Bulletin and Review, 14,* 101–106.

Cook, M., & Mineka, S. (1989). Observational conditioning of fear to fear-relevant versus fear-irrelevant stimuli in rhesus monkeys. *Journal of Abnormal Psychology, 98,* 448–459.

Cooke, S. F., & Bliss, T. V. P. (2006). Plasticity in the human central nervous system. *Brain: A Journal of Neurology, 129,* 1659–1673.

Cooney, J., & Gazzaniga, M. S. (2003). Neurological disorders and the structure of human consciousness. *Trends in Cognitive Sciences, 7,* 161–165.

Cooper, C. R., Denner, J., & Lopez, E. M. (1999). Cultural brokers: Helping Latino children on pathways toward success. *The Future of Children, 9,* 51–57.

Corder, E. H., Saunders, A. M., Strittmatter, W. J., Schmechel, D. E., Gaskell, P. C., Small, G. W., et al. (1993). Gene dose of apolipoprotein E type 4 allele and the risk of Alzheimer's disease in late onset families. *Science, 261,* 921–923.

Coren, S. (1996). Daylight savings time and traffic accidents. *New England Journal of Medicine, 334,* 924.

Correll, C. U., Leucht, S., & Kane, J. M. (2004). Lower risk for tardive dyskinesia associated with second-generation antipsychotics: A systematic review of 1-year studies. *American Journal of Psychiatry, 161,* 414–425.

Correll, J., Park, B., Judd, C. M., Wittenbrink, B., Sadler, M. S., & Keesee, T. (2007). Across the thin blue line: Police officers and racial bias in the decision to shoot. *Journal of Personality and Social Psychology, 92,* 1006–1023.

Cosmides, L., & Tooby, J. (1997). *Evolutionary psychology: A primer.* Retrieved May 24, 2002, from http://www.psych.ucsb.edu/research/cep/primer.html

Cosmides, L., & Tooby, J. (2000). The cognitive neuroscience of social reasoning. In M. S. Gazzaniga (Ed.), *The new cognitive neurosciences* (pp. 1259–1270). Cambridge, MA: MIT Press.

Costa, P. T., & McCrae, R. R. (1992). *Revised NEO Personality Inventory (NEO-PI-R) and NEO Five-Factor Inventory (NEO-FFI) professional manual.* Odessa, FL: Psychological Assessment Resources.

Costa, P. T., Terracciano, A., & McCrae, R. R. (2001). Gender differences in personality traits across cultures: Robust and surprising findings. *Journal of Personality and Social Psychology, 81*, 322–331.

Courchesne, E., Pierce, K., Schumann, C. M., Redcay, E., Buckwalter, J. A., Kennedy, D. P., et al. (2007). Mapping early brain development in autism. *Neuron, 56*, 399–413.

Courchesne, E., Redcay, E., & Kennedy, D. P. (2004). The autistic brain: Birth through adulthood. *Current Opinion in Neurology, 17*, 489–496.

Cowan, C. P., & Cowan, P. A. (1988). Who does what when partners become parents? Implications for men, women, and marriage. In R. Palkovitz & M. B. Sussman (Eds.), *Transitions to parenthood* (pp. 105–132). New York: The Haworth Press.

Cowell, P. E., Turetsky, B. E., Gur, R. C., Grossman, R. I., Shtasel, D. L., & Gur, R. E. (1994). Sex differences in aging of the human frontal and temporal lobes. *Journal of Neuroscience, 14*, 4748–4755.

Craft, L. L., & Perna, F. M. (2004). The benefits of exercise for the clinically depressed. *Journal of Clinical Psychiatry, 6*, 104–111.

Craik, F. I. M., & Lockhart, R. S. (1972). Levels of processing: A framework for memory research. *Journal of Verbal Learning and Verbal Behavior, 11*, 671–684.

Crawford, H. J., Corby, J. C., & Kopell, B. (1996). Auditory event-related potentials while ignoring tone stimuli: Attentional differences reflected in stimulus intensity and latency responses in low and highly hypnotizable persons. *International Journal of Neuroscience, 85*, 57–69.

Crocker, J. (2006, June). *Time for your life and your goals.* Workshop sponsored by the Junior Scholars Professional Development Task Force, presented at the biannual meeting of the Society for the Psychological Study of Social Issues, Long Beach, CA.

Crocker, J., & Major, B. (1989). Social stigma and self-esteem: The self-protective properties of stigma. *Psychological Review, 96*, 608–630.

Crocker, J., Niiya, Y., & Mischkowski, D. (2008). Why does writing about important values reduce defensiveness? Self-affirmation and the role of positive other-directed feelings. *Psychological Science, 19*(7), 740–747. doi:10.1111/j.1467-9280.2008.02150.x

Crocker, J., Olivier, M., & Nuer, N. (2009). Self-image goals and compassionate goals: Costs and benefits. *Self and Identity, 8*(2–3), 251–269. doi:10.1080/15298860802505160

Crosnoe, R., & Elder, G. H., Jr. (2002). Successful adaptation in the later years: A life-course approach to aging. *Social Psychology Quarterly, 65*, 309–328.

Cross, S. E., Bacon, P. L., & Morris, M. L. (2000). The relational-interdependent self-construal and relationships. *Journal of Personality and Social Psychology, 78*(4), 791–808. doi:10.1037/0022-3514.78.4.791

Crowe, R. R. (2000). Molecular genetics of anxiety disorders. In D. S. Charney, E. J. Nestler, & B. S. Bunney (Eds.), *Neurobiology of mental illness* (pp. 451–462). New York: Oxford University Press.

Csikszentmihalyi, M. (1990). *Flow: The psychology of optimal experience.* New York: Harper & Row.

Csikszentmihalyi, M. (1999). If we are so rich, why aren't we happy? *American Psychologist, 54*, 821–827.

Cummings, J. R., & Druss, B. G. (2010). Racial/ethnic differences in mental health service use among adolescents with major depression. *Journal of the American Academy of Child & Adolescent Psychiatry, 50*, 160–170.

Cunningham, M. R., Barbee, A. P., & Druen, P. B. (1996). Social allergens and the reactions they produce: Escalation of annoyance and disgust in love and work. In R. M. Kowalski (Ed.), *Aversive interpersonal behaviors* (pp. 189–214). New York: Plenum Press.

Cunningham, M. R., Roberts, A. R., Barbee, A. P., Druen, P. B., & Wu, C. (1995). Their ideas of beauty are, on the whole, the same as ours: Consistency and variability in the cross-cultural perception of female physical attractiveness. *Journal of Personality and Social Psychology, 68*, 261–279.

Cunningham, W. A., Johnson, M. K., Raye, C. L., Gatenby, J. C., Gore, J. C., & Banaji, M. R. (2004). Separable neural components in the processing of black and white faces. *Psychological Science, 15*, 806–813.

Cupach, W. R., & Metts, S. (1990). Remedial processes in embarrassing predicaments. In J. Anderson (Ed.), *Communication yearbook* (pp. 323–352). Newbury Park, CA: Sage.

Curtiss, S. (1977). *Genie: A psycholinguistic study of a modern day "wild child."* New York: Academic Press.

Cvetkovic-Lopes, V., Bayer, L., Dorsaz, S., Maret, S., Pradervand, S., Dauvilliers, Y., et al. (2010). Elevated Tribbles homolog 2-specific antibody levels in narcolepsy patients. *Journal of Clinical Investigation, 120*, 713–719.

Dabbs, J. M., & Morris, R. (1990). Testosterone, social class, and antisocial behavior in a sample of 4462 men. *Psychological Science, 1*, 209–211.

Dalton, M. A., Bernhardt, A. M., Gibson, J. J., Sargent, J. D., Beach, M. L., Adachi-Mejia, A. M., Titus-Ernstoff, L. T., & Heatherton, T. F. (2005). "Honey, have some smokes." Preschoolers use cigarettes and alcohol while role playing as adults. *Archives of Pediatrics & Adolescent Medicine, 159*, 854–859.

Damasio, A. R. (1994). *Descartes' error.* New York: Avon Books.

Damasio, H., Grabowski, T., Frank, R., Galaburda, A. M., & Damasio, A. R. (1994, May 20). The return of Phineas Gage: Clues about the brain from the skull of a famous patient. *Science, 264*, 1102–1105.

Dapretto, M., Davies, M. S., Pfeifer, J. H., Scott, A. A., Sigman, M., Bookheimer, S. Y., & Iacoboni, M. (2006). Understanding emotions in others: Mirror neuron dysfunction in children with autism spectrum disorders. *Nature Neuroscience, 9*, 28–30.

Darley, J. M., & Batson, C. D. (1973). "From Jerusalem to Jericho": A study of situational and dispositional variables in helping behavior. *Journal of Personality and Social Psychology, 27*, 100–108.

Darwin, C. (1859). *On the origin of species by means of natural selection, or the preservation of favoured races in the struggle for life.* London: John Murray.

Darwin, C. R. (1872). *The expression of the emotions in man and animals.* London: John Murray.

Dasgupta, A. G., & Greenwald, A. G. (2001). Exposure to admired group members reduces automatic intergroup bias. *Journal of Personality and Social Psychology, 81*, 800–814.

Davidson, J. R., Foa, E. B., Huppert, J. D., Keefe, F. J., Franklin, M. E., Compton, J. S., et al. (2004). Fluoxetine, comprehensive cognitive behavioral therapy, and placebo in generalized social phobia. *Archives of General Psychiatry, 61*, 1005–1013.

Davidson, R. J. (2000). Affective style, psychopathology, and resilience: Brain mechanisms and plasticity. *American Psychologist, 55*, 1196–1214.

Davidson, R. J., Pizzagalli, D., Nitschke, J. B., & Putnam, K. M. (2002). Depression: Perspectives from affective neuroscience. *Annual Review of Psychology, 53*, 545–574.

Davidson Ward, S. L., Bautisa, D., Chan, L., Derry, M., Lisbin, A., Durfee, M., et al. (1990). Sudden infant death syndrome in infants of drug abusing mothers. *Journal of Pediatrics, 117*, 876–887.

Davies, M. F. (1997). Belief persistence after evidential discrediting: The impact of generated versus provided explanations on the likelihood of discredited outcomes. *Journal of Experimental Social Psychology, 33*, 561–578.

Davis, K. L., Stewart, D. G., Friedman, J. I., Buchsbaum, M., Harvey, P. D., Hof, P. R., et al. (2003). White matter changes in schizophrenia: Evidence for myelin-related dysfunction. *Archives of General Psychiatry, 60*, 443–456.

Davis, M. (1997). Neurobiology of fear responses: The role of the amygdala. *Journal of Neuropsychological and Clinical Neuroscience, 9*, 382–402.

Deacon, B. J., & Abramowitz, J. S. (2004). Cognitive and behavioral treatments for anxiety disorders: A review of meta-analytic findings. *Journal of Clinical Psychology, 60*, 429–441.

DeAngelis, T. (2008). Psychology's growth careers. *Monitor on Psychology, 39*, 64.

Deary, I. J. (2000). *Looking down on human intelligence*. New York: Oxford University Press.

Deary, I. J. (2001). *Intelligence: A very short introduction*. New York: Oxford University Press.

Deary, I. J., Batty, G. D., Pattie, A., & Gale, C. R. (2008). More intelligent, more dependable children live longer: A 55-year longitudinal study of a representative sample of the Scottish nation. *Psychological Science, 19*, 874–880.

Deary, I. J., & Der, G. (2005). Reaction time explains IQ's association with death. *Psychological Science, 16*, 64–69.

DeCasper, A. J., & Fifer, W. P. (1980, June 6). Of human bonding: Newborns prefer their mothers' voices. *Science, 208*, 1174–1176.

DeCasper, A. J., & Spence, M. J. (1986). Prenatal maternal speech influences newborns' perception of speech sounds. *Infant Behavior and Development, 9*, 133–150.

deCharms, R. C., Maeda, F., Glover, G. H, Ludlow, D., Pauly, J. M., Soneji, D., et al. (2005). Control over brain activation and pain learned by using real-time functional MRI. *Proceedings of the National Academy of Sciences, USA, 102*, 18626–18631.

Deci, E. L., & Ryan, R. M. (1987). The support of autonomy and the control of behavior. *Journal of Personality and Social Psychology, 53*, 1024–1037.

Decyk, B. N. (1994).Using examples to teach concepts. In *Changing college classrooms: New teaching and learning strategies for an increasingly complex world* (pp. 39–63). San Francisco: Jossey Bass.

Dehaene, S., Changeux, J. P., Naccache, L., Sackur, J., & Sergent, C. (2006). Conscious, preconscious, and subliminal processing: A testable taxonomy. *Trends in Cognitive Sciences, 10*, 204–211.

Dejong, W., & Kleck, R. E. (1986). The social psychological effects of overweight. In C. P. Herman, M. P. Zanna, & E. T. Higgins (Eds.), *Physical appearance, stigma and social behavior: The Ontario Symposium* (pp. 65–87). Hillsdale, NJ: Erlbaum.

De Lisi, R., & Staudt, J. (1980). Individual differences in college students' performance on formal operations tasks. *Journal of Applied Developmental Psychology, 1*, 201–208. doi: 10.1016/0193-3973(80)90009-X

DeLong, M. R., & Wichmann, T. (2008). *The expanding potential of deep brain stimulation: The 2008 progress report on brain research*. New York: Dana Foundation.

Demerouti, E. (2006). Job characteristics, flow, and performance: The moderating role of conscientiousness. *Journal of Occupational Health Psychology, 11*(3), 266–280.

Demir, E., & Dickson, B. J. (2005). Fruitless: Splicing specifies male courtship behavior in drosophila. *Cell, 121*, 785–794.

Demos, K. D., Kelley, W. M., Heatherton, T. F. (2011). Dietary restraint violations influence reward responses in the nucleus accumbens and amygdala. *Journal of Cognitive Neuroscience, 23*(8), 1952–1963.

Despues, D., & Friedman, H. S. (2007). Ethnic differences in health behaviors among college students. *Journal of Applied Social Psychology, 37*, 131–142.

Devine, P. G. (1989). Stereotypes and prejudice: Their automatic and controlled components. *Journal of Personality and Social Psychology, 56*, 5–18.

de Wijk, R. A., Schab, F. R., & Cain, W. S. (1995). Odor identification. In F. R. Schab (Ed.), *Memory for odors* (pp. 21–37). Mahwah, NJ: Erlbaum.

DeYoung, C. G. (2010). Personality neuroscience and the biology of traits. *Social and Personality Psychology Compass, 4*, 1165–1180.

DeYoung, C. G., & Gray, J. R. (2009). Personality neuroscience: Explaining individual differences in affect, behavior, and cognition. In P. J. Corr & G. Matthews (Eds.), *The Cambridge handbook of personality psychology* (pp. 323–346). New York: Cambridge University Press.

DeYoung, C. G., Hirsh, J. B., Shane, M. S., Papademetris, X., Rajeevan, N., & Gray, J. R. (2010). Testing predictions from personality neuroscience: Brain structure and the big five. *Psychological Science, 21*, 820–828.

Diamond, D. M., Fleshner, M., Ingersoll, N., & Rose, G. (1996). Psychological stress impairs spatial working memory: Relevance to electro-physiological studies of hippocampal function. *Behavioural Brain Research, 62*, 301–307.

Dickson, P. R., & Vaccarino, F. J. (1994). GRF-induced feeding: Evidence for protein selectivity and opiate involvement. *Peptides, 15*(8), 1343–1352.

Diener, E. (2000). Subjective well-being: The science of happiness and a proposal for a national index. *American Psychologist, 55*, 34–43.

Diener, E., Gohm, C. L., Suh, E., & Oishi, S. (2000). Similarity of the relations between marital status and subjective well-being. *Journal of Cross-Cultural Psychology, 31*, 419–436.

Diener, E., & Wellborn, M. (1976). Effect of self-awareness on antinormative behavior. *Journal of Research in Personality, 10*, 107–111.

Diener, E., Wolsic, B., & Fujita, F. (1995). Physical attractiveness and subjective well-being. *Journal of Personality and Social Psychology, 69*, 120–129.

Dijksterhuis, A. (2004). Think different: The merits of unconscious thought in preference development and decision making. *Journal of Personality and Social Psychology, 87*, 586–598.

Dijksterhuis, A., & Aarts, H. (2010). Goals, attention, and (un)conscious. *Annual Review of Psychology, 61*, 467–490.

Dijksterhuis, A., & Nordgren, L. F. (2006). A theory of unconscious thought. *Perspectives on Psychological Science, 1*, 95–109.

Dijksterhuis, A., & van Knippenberg, A. (1998). The relation between perception and behavior, or how to win a game of Trivial Pursuit. *Journal of Personality and Social Psychology, 74*, 865–877.

Dineley, K. T., Westerman, M., Bui, D., Bell, K., Ashe, K. H., & Sweatt, J. D. (2001). β-amyloid activates the mitogen-activated protein kinase cascade via hippocampal α7 nicotinic acetylcholine receptors: In vitro and in vivo mechanisms related to Alzheimer's Disease. *The Journal of Neuroscience, 21*, 4125–4133.

Dinstein, I., Thomas, C., Humphreys, K., Minshew, N., Behrmann, M., & Heeger, D. J. (2010). Normal movement selectivity in autism. *Neuron, 66*, 461–469.

Dion, K., Berscheid, E., & Walster, E. (1972). What is beautiful is good. *Journal of Personality and Social Psychology, 24*, 285–290.

Diotallevi, M. (2008). Testimonials versus evidence. *Canadian Medical Association Journal, 179*, 449.

Dobbs, D. (2006, August/September). Turning off depression. *Scientific American Mind*, 26–31.

Docherty, N. M. (2005). Cognitive impairments and disordered speech in schizophrenia: Thought disorder, disorganization, and communication failure perspectives. *Journal of Abnormal Psychology, 114*, 269–278.

Dockray, A., & Steptoe, A. (2010). Positive affect and psychobiological process. *Neuroscience and Biobehavioral Reviews, 35*, 69–75.

Dohrenwend, B. P., Shrout, P. E., Link, B. G., Skodol, A. E., & Martin, J. L. (1986). Overview and initial results from a risk factor study of depression and schizophrenia. In J. E. Barrett (Ed.), *Mental disorders in the community: Progress and challenge* (pp. 184–215). New York: Guilford Press.

Dolan, R. J. (2000). Emotion processing in the human brain revealed through functional neuroimaging. In M. S. Gazzaniga (Ed.), *The new cognitive neurosciences* (pp. 115–131). Cambridge, MA: MIT Press.

Domhoff, G. W. (2003). *The scientific study of dreams: Neural networks, cognitive development, and content analysis*. Washington, DC: American Psychological Association.

Domino, M. E., Burns, B. J., Silva, S. G., Kratochvil, C. J., Vitiello, B., Reinecke, M. A., et al. (2008). Cost-effectiveness of treatments for adolescent depression: Results from TADS. *American Journal of Psychiatry, 165*, 588–596.

Domjan, M. (2003). *Principles of learning and behavior* (5th ed.). Belmont, CA: Thomson/Wadsworth.

Donahue, A. B. (2000). Electroconvulsive therapy and memory loss: A personal journey. *Journal of ECT, 16*, 133–143.

Dovidio, J. F., ten Vergert, M., Stewart, T. L., Gaertner, S. L., Johnson, J. D., Esses, V. M., et al. (2004). Perspective and prejudice: Antecedents and mediating mechanisms. *Personality and Social Psychology Bulletin, 30*, 1537–1549.

Doyal, L. (2001). Sex, gender, and health: The need for a new approach. *British Medical Journal, 323*, 1061–1063.

Drews, F. A., Pasupathi, M., & Strayer, D. L. (2008). Passenger and cell phone conversations in simulated driving. *Journal of Experimental Psychology: Applied, 14*, 392–400.

Drosopoulos, S., Schulze, C., Fischer, S., & Born, J. (2007). Sleep's function in the spontaneous recovery and consolidation of memories. *Journal of Experimental Psychology: General 136*(2), 169–183.

Duckworth, A. L., & Seligman, M. E. P. (2005). Self-discipline outdoes IQ in predicting academic performance of adolescents. *Psychological Science, 16*, 939–944.

Dugatkin, L. A. (2004). *Principles of animal behavior*. New York: Norton.

Dunbar, R. I. M., Baron, R., Frangou, A., Pearce, E., van Leeuwen, E. J. C., Stow, J., Partridge, G., MacDonald, I., Barra, V., & van Vugt, M. (2011). Social laughter is correlated with elevated pain threshold. *Proceedings of the Royal Society Biological Sciences*.

http://rspb.royalsocietypublishing.org/content/early/2011/09/19/rspb.2011.1373

Duncan, J., Burgess, P., & Emslie, H. (1995). Fluid intelligence after frontal lobe lesions. *Neuropsychologia, 33*, 261–268.

Duncker, K. (1945). On problem solving. *Psychological Monographs, 58*(5, Whole No. 70).

Dunlap, K. (1927). *The role of eye-muscles and mouth-muscles in the expression of the emotions*. Worcester, MA: Clark University Press.

Durante, K. M., Li, N. P., & Haselton, M. G. (2008). Changes in women's choice of dress across the ovulatory cycle: Naturalistic and laboratory task-based evidence. *Personality and Social Psychology Bulletin, 34*, 1451–1460.

Dutton, D. G., & Aron, A. P. (1974). Some evidence for heightened sexual attraction under conditions of high anxiety. *Journal of Personality and Social Psychology, 30*, 510–517.

Duval, S., & Wicklund, R. A. (1972). *A theory of objective self-awareness*. New York: Academic Press.

Dykman, B. M., Horowitz, L. M., Abramson, L. Y., & Usher, M. (1991). Schematic and situational determinants of depressed and nondepressed students' interpretation of feedback. *Journal of Abnormal Psychology, 100*, 45–55.

Eacott, M. J. (1999). Memory for the events of early childhood. *Current Directions in Psychological Science, 8*, 46–49.

Eagly, A. H., Karau, S. J., & Makhijani, M. G. (1995). Gender and the effectiveness of leaders: A meta-analysis. *Psychological Bulletin, 117*, 125–145.

Eaker, E. D., Sullivan, L. M., Kelly-Hayes, M., D'Agostino, R. B., Sr., & Benjamin, E. J. (2004). Anger and hostility predict the development of atrial fibrillation in men in the Framingham Offspring Study. *Circulation, 109*, 1267–1271.

Eberhardt, J. L., Goff, P. A., Purdie, V. J., & Davies, P. G. (2004). Seeing black: Race, crime, and visual processing. *Journal of Personality and Social Psychology, 87*, 876–893.

Ecker, U. K. H., Lewandowsky, S., Oberauer, K., & Chee, A. E. H. (2010). The components of working memory updating: An experimental decomposition and individual differences. *Journal of Experimental Psychology: Learning, Memory, and Cognition, 36*, 170–189.

Egeland, J. A., Gerhard, D. S., Pauls, D. L., Sussex, J. N., Kidd, K. K., Allen, C. R., et al. (1987). Bipolar affective disorders linked to DNA markers on chromosome 11. *Nature, 325*, 783–787.

Eich, J. E., Weingartner, H., Stillman, R. C., & Gillin, J. C. (1975). State-dependent accessibility of retrieval cues in the retention of a categorized list. *Journal of Verbal Learning and Verbal Behavior, 14*, 408–417.

Einstein, G. O., & McDaniel, M. A. (2005). Prospective memory. Multiple retrieval processes. *Current Directions in Psychological Science, 14*, 286–290.

Eisenberg, N. (2000). Emotion, regulation, and moral development. *Annual Review of Psychology, 51*, 665–697.

Eisenberg, N. (2002). Empathy-related emotional responses, altruism, and their socialization. In R. J. Davidson and A. Harrington (Eds.), *Visions of compassion: Western scientists and Tibetan Buddhists examine human nature* (pp. 131–164). New York: Oxford University Press.

Ekelund, J., Lichtermann, D., Jaervelin, M., & Peltonen, L. (1999). Association between novelty seeking and type 4 dopamine receptor gene in a large Finnish cohort sample. *American Journal of Psychiatry, 156*, 1453–1455.

Ekman, P., & Friesen, W. V. (1971). Constants across cultures in the face and emotion. *Journal of Personality and Social Psychology, 17*, 124–129.

Ekman, P., Levenson, R. W., & Friesen, W. V. (1983, September 16). Autonomic nervous system activity distinguishes among emotions. *Science, 221*, 1208–1210.

Ekman, P., Sorenson, E. R., & Friesen, W. V. (1969, April 4). Pan-cultural elements in facial displays of emotions. *Science, 164*, 86–88.

Elfenbein, H. A., & Ambady, N. (2002). On the universality of cultural specificity of emotion recognition: A meta-analysis. *Psychological Bulletin, 128*, 203–235.

Else-Quest, N., Hyde, J. S., Goldsmith, H. H., & Van Hulle, C. A. (2006). Gender differences in temperament: A meta-analysis. *Psychological Bulletin, 132*, 33–72.

Emery, C. F., Kiecolt-Glaser, J. K., Glaser, R., Malarkey, W. B., & Frid, D. J. (2005). Exercise accelerates wound healing among healthy older adults: A preliminary investigation. *Journals of Gerontology, 60A*(11), 1432–1436.

Emslie, G. J., Rush, A. J., Weinberg, W. A., Kowatch, R. A., Hughes, C. W., Carmody, T., et al. (1997). A double-blind, randomized, placebo-controlled trial of fluoxetine in children and adolescents with depression. *Archives of General Psychiatry, 54*, 1031–1037.

Endo, Y., & Meijer, Z. (2004). Autobiographical memory of success and failure experiences. In Y. Kashima, Y. Endo, E. S. Kashima, C. Leung, & J. McClure (Eds.), *Progress in Asian social psychology* (Vol. 4, pp. 67–84). Seoul, Korea: Kyoyook-Kwahak-Sa Publishing.

Engle, R. W., & Kane, M. J. (2004). Executive attention, working memory capacity, and a two-factor theory of cognitive control. In B. Ross (Ed.), *The psychology of learning and motivation* (pp. 145–199). New York: Elsevier.

Engle, R. W., Tuholski, S. W., Laughlin, J. E., & Conway, A. R. A. (1999). Working memory, short-term memory, and general fluid intelligence: A latent variable approach. *Journal of Experimental Psychology: General, 128*, 309–331.

Engwall, M., & Duppils, G. S. (2009). Music as a nursing intervention for postoperative pain: A systematic review. *Journal of Perianesthesia Nursing, 24*, 370–383.

Enns, J. (2005). *The thinking eye, the seeing brain*. New York: Norton.

Epstein, L. H., Robinson, J. L., Roemmich, J. N., Marusewski, A. L., & Roba, L. G. (2010). What constitutes food variety? Stimulus specificity of food. *Appetite, 54*, 23–29.

Era, P., Jokela, J., & Heikkinen, E. (1986). Reaction and movement times in men of different ages: A population study. *Perceptual and Motor Skills, 63*, 111–130.

Erikson, E. H. (1968). *Identity: Youth and crisis*. New York: Norton.

Erikson, E. H. (1980). *Identity and the life cycle*. New York: Norton.

Eriksson, P. S., Perfilieva, E., Bjork-Eriksson, T., Alborn, A. M., Nordborg, C., Peterson, D. A., et al. (1998). Neurogenesis in the adult human hippocampus. *Nature Medicine, 4*, 1313–1317.

Erk, S., Spitzer, M., Wunderlich, A. P., Galley, L., & Walter, H. (2002). Cultural objects modulate reward circuitry. *Neuroreport, 13*(18), 2499–2503.

Eron, L. D. (1987). The development of aggressive behavior from the perspective of a developing behaviorism. *American Psychologist, 42*, 435–442.

Espie, C. A. (2002). Insomnia: Conceptual issues in the development, persistence, and treatment of sleep disorders in adults. *Annual Review of Psychology, 53*, 215–243.

Eysenck, M. W., Mogg, K., May, J., Richards, A., & Matthews, A. (1991). Bias in interpretation of ambiguous sentences related to threat in anxiety. *Journal of Abnormal Psychology, 100*, 144–150.

Fabiano, G. A., Pelham, W. E., Coles, E. K., Gnagy, E. M., Chronis-Tuscano, A., & O'Connor, B. C. (2009). A meta-analysis of behavioral treatments for attention-deficit/hyperactivity disorder. *Clinical Psychology Review, 29*, 129–140.

Fagerström, K. O., & Schneider, N. G. (1989). Measuring nicotine dependence: A review of the Fagerström tolerance questionnaire. *Journal of Behavioral Medicine, 12*, 159–181.

Fallon, A. E., & Rozin, P. (1985). Sex differences in perceptions of desirable body shape. *Journal of Abnormal Psychology, 94*, 102–105.

Fantz, R. L. (1966). Pattern discrimination and selective attention as determinants of perceptual development from birth. In A. H. Kidd & L. J. Rivoire (Eds.), *Perceptual development in children* (pp. 143–173). New York: International Universities Press.

Farah, M. J. (1996). Is face recognition "special"? Evidence from neuropsychology. *Behavioural Brain Research, 76*, 181–189.

Farah, M. J., Betancourt, L., Shera, D. M., Savage, J. H., Giannetta, J. M., Malmud, E. K., et al. (2008). Environmental stimulation, parental nurturance and cognitive development in humans. *Developmental Science, 11*, 793–801.

Farah, M. J., Shera, D. M., Savage, J. H., Betancourt, L., Giannetta, J. M., Brodsky, N. L., et al. (2006). Childhood poverty: Specific associations with neurocognitive development. *Brain Research, 1110*, 166–174.

Farb, N. A., Anderson, A. K., Mayberg, H., Bean, J., McKeon, D., & Segal, Z. V. (2010). Minding one's emotions: Mindfulness training alters the neural expression of sadness. *Emotion, 10*, 25–33.

Farb, N. A., Segal, Z. V., Mayberg, H., Bean, J., McKeon, D., Fatima, Z., et al. (2007). Attending to the present: Mindfulness meditation reveals distinct neural modes of self-reference. *Social Cognitive and Affective Neuroscience, 2*, 313–322.

Farooqi, I. S., Bullmore, E., Keogh, J., Gillard, J., O'Rahilly, S., & Fletcher, P. C. (2007, September 7). Leptin regulates striatal regions and human eating behavior. *Science, 317*, 1355.

Fawcett, J. (1992). Suicide risk factors in depressive disorders and in panic disorders. *Journal of Clinical Psychiatry, 53*, 9–13.

Fazio, R. H. (1995). Attitudes as object-evaluation associations: Determinants, consequences, and correlates of attitude accessibility. In R. E. Petty & J. A. Krosnick (Eds.), *Attitude strength: Antecedents and consequences* (pp. 247–282). Hillsdale, NJ: Erlbaum.

Fazio, R. H., Eisner, J. R., & Shook, N. J. (2004). Attitude formation through exploration: Valence asymmetries. *Journal of Personality and Social Psychology, 87*, 293–311.

Feingold, A. (1992). Good-looking people are not what we think. *Psychological Bulletin, 111*, 304–341.

Feingold, A. (1994). Gender differences in personality: A meta-analysis. *Psychological Bulletin, 116*, 429–456.

Feldman, R., Weller, A., Zagoory-Sharon, O., & Levine, A. (2007). Evidence for a neuroendocrinological foundation of human affiliation: Plasma oxytocin levels across pregnancy and the post-partum period predict mother-infant bonding. *Psychological Science, 18*, 965–970.

Feldman, S. S., & Rosenthal, D. A. (1991). Age expectations of behavioural autonomy in Hong Kong, Australian and American youth: The Influence of family variables and adolescents' values. *International Journal of Psychology, 26*, 1–23.

Feldman Barrett, L., Lane, R. D., Sechrest, L., & Schwartz, G. E. (2000). Sex differences in emotional awareness. *Personality and Social Psychology Bulletin, 26*, 1027–1035.

Fergus, I., & McDowd, J. M. (1987). Age differences in recall and recognition. *Journal of Experimental Psychology: Learning, Memory, and Cognition, 13*, 474–479. doi: 10.1037/0278-7393.13.3.474

Ferguson, J. N., Young, L. J., Hearn, E. F., Matzuk, M. M., Insel, T. R., & Winslow, J. T. (2000). Social amnesia in mice lacking the oxytocin gene. *Nature Neuroscience, 25*, 284–288.

Ferguson, T. J., & Stegge, H. (1995). Emotional states and traits in children: The case of guilt and shame. In J. P. Tangney & K. W. Fischer (Eds.), *Self-conscious emotions* (pp. 174–197). New York: Guilford Press.

Fernald, A. (1989). Intonation and communicative intent in mothers' speech to infants: Is the melody the message? *Child Development, 60*, 1497–1510.

Fernberger, S. W. (1943). Edwin Burket Twitmyer 1873–1943. *Psychological Review 50*(3), 345–349. doi: 10.1037/h0063068

Ferrari, P. F., Gallese, V., Rizzolatti, G., & Fogassi, L. (2003). Mirror neurons responding to the observation of ingestive and communicative mouth actions in the monkey ventral premotor cortex. *European Journal of Neuroscience, 17*, 1703–1714.

Ferrari, P. F., Visalberghi, E., Paukner, A., Fogassi, L., Ruggiero, A., & Suomi, S. (2006). Neonatal imitation in rhesus macaques. *PLoS Biology, 4*, 1501–1508.

Ferry, G. (Writer/Broadcaster). (2002, 12 & 19 November). Hearing colours, eating sounds. *BBC Radio 4, Science.* Retrieved from BBC, http://www.bbc.co.uk/radio4/science/hearingcolours.shtml

Festinger, L. (1954). A theory of social comparison processes. *Human Relations, 7*, 117–140.

Festinger, L. (1987). A personal memory. In N. E. Grunberg, R. E. Nisbett, J. Rodin, & J. E. Singer (Eds.), *A distinctive approach to psychological research: The influence of Stanley Schachter* (pp. 1–9). New York: Erlbaum.

Festinger, L., & Carlsmith, J. M. (1959). Cognitive consequences of forced compliance. *Journal of Abnormal and Social Psychology, 58*, 203–210.

Festinger, L., Riecken, H. W., & Schachter, S. (1956). *When prophecy fails.* Minneapolis: University of Minnesota Press.

Festinger, L., Schachter, S., & Back, K. W. (1950). *Social pressures in informal groups.* New York: Harper.

Fibiger, H. C. (1993). Mesolimbic dopamine: An analysis of its role in motivated behavior. *Seminars in Neuroscience, 5*, 321–327.

Fillipek, P. A., Semrud-Clikeman, M., Steingard, R. J., Renshaw, P. F., Kennedy, D. N., & Biederman, J. (1997). Volumetric MRI analysis comparing subjects having attention-deficit hyperactivity disorder with normal controls. *Neurology, 48*, 589–600.

Finger, S. (1994). *Origins of neuroscience.* Oxford, UK: Oxford University Press.

Fink, M. (2001). Convulsive therapy: A review of the first 55 years. *Journal of Affective Disorders, 63*, 1–15.

Fischer, C., Hatzidimitriou, G., Wlos, J., Katz, J., & Ricaurte, G. (1995). Reorganization of ascending 5-HT axon projections in animals previously exposed to the recreational drug (+/−)3,4-methylene-dioxymethamphetamine (MDMA, "ecstasy"). *Journal of Neuroscience, 15*, 5476–5485.

Fischer, H., Nyberg, L., Karlsson, S., Karisson, P., Brehmer, Y., Rieckmann, A., et al. (2010). Simulating neurocognitive aging: Effects of dopaminergic antagonist on brain activity during working memory. *Biological Psychiatry, 67*, 575–580.

Fischer, K. (1980). A theory of cognitive development: The control and construction of hierarchies of skills. *Psychological Review, 87*, 477–531.

Fisher, H. E., Aron, A., & Brown, L. L. (2006). Romantic love: A mammalian brain system for mate choice. *Philosophical Transactions of the Royal Society of London, 361B*, 2173–2186.

Fitzgerald, P. B., Brown, T. L., Marston, N. A., Daskalakis, Z. J., De Castella, A., & Kulkarni, J. (2003). Transcranial magnetic stimulation in the treatment of depression: A double-blind, placebo-controlled trial. *Archives of General Psychiatry, 60*, 1002–1008.

Fixx, J. F. (1978). *Solve it.* New York: Doubleday.

Flegal, K. M., Carroll, M. D., Ogden, C. L., & Curtin, L. R. (2010). Prevalence and trends in obesity among U.S. adults, 1999–2008. *Journal of the American Medical Association, 303*(3), 235–41.

Flynn, J. R. (1981). The mean IQ of Americans: Massive gains 1932 to 1978. *Psychological Bulletin, 95*, 29–51.

Flynn, J. R. (1987). Massive IQ gains in 14 nations: What IQ tests really measure. *Psychological Bulletin, 101*, 171–191.

Flynn, J. R. (2007, October/November). Solving the IQ puzzle. *Scientific American Mind*, 24–31.

Foa, E. B., Liebowitz, M. R., Kozak, M. J., Davies, S., Campeas, R., Franklin, M. E., et al. (2005). Randomized, placebo-controlled trial of exposure and ritual prevention, clomipramine, and their combination in the treatment of obsessive-compulsive disorder. *American Journal of Psychiatry, 162*, 151–161.

Foer, Joshua. (2011, February 20). Secrets of a mind-gamer: How I trained my brain and became a world-class memory athlete. *The New York Times Magazine.* Retrieved from http://www.nytimes.com

Foley, K. M. (1993). Opioids. *Neurologic Clinics, 11*, 503–522.

Folkman, S., & Lazarus, R. S. (1988). Coping as a mediator of emotion. *Journal of Personality and Social Psychology, 54*, 466–475.

Folkman, S., & Moskowitz, J. T. (2000). Positive affect and the other side of coping. *American Psychologist, 55*, 647–654.

Forgas, J. P. (1998). Asking nicely: Mood effects on responding to more or less polite requests. *Personality and Social Psychology Bulletin, 24*, 173–185.

Fost, N. (1989). Maternal-fetal conflicts: Ethical and legal considerations. *Annals of the New York Academy of Sciences, 56*, 248–254.

Fox, N. A., Henderson, H. A., Marshall, P. J., Nichols, K. E., & Ghera, M. M. (2005). Behavioral inhibition: Linking biology and behavior within a developmental framework. *Annual Review of Psychology, 56*, 235–262.

Fraley, R. C., & Shaver, P. R. (2000). Adult romantic attachment: Theoretical developments, emerging controversies, and unanswered questions. *Review of General Psychology, 4*, 132–154.

Frangou, S., Chitins, X., & Williams, S. C. (2004). Mapping IQ and gray matter density in healthy young people. *Neuroimage, 23*, 800–805.

Frank, C. K., & Temple, E. (2009). Cultural effects on the neural basis of theory of mind. *Progress in Brain Research, 178,* 213–223.

Franken, I. H. A., Muris, P., & Georgieva, I. (2006). Gray's model of personality and addiction. *Addictive Behaviors, 31,* 399–403.

Franken, R. E. (1998). *Human motivation.* Pacific Grove, CA: Brooks Cole.

Frankl, V. E. (1959). *Man's search for meaning.* New York: Simon & Schuster.

Franklin, A. J. (2007). Gender, race and invisibility in psychotherapy with African American men. In J. C. Muran (Ed.), *Dialogues on difference: Studies of diversity in the therapeutic relationship* (pp. 117–131). Washington, DC: American Psychological Association.

Franklin, M. E., & Foa, E. B. (2011, April). Treatment of obsessive compulsive disorder. *Annual Review of Clinical Psychology, 7,* 229–243.

Fratiglioni, L., Paillard-Borg, S., & Winblad, B. (2004). An active and socially integrated lifestyle in late life might protect against dementia. *Lancet Neurology, 3,* 343–353.

Fredrickson, B. L. (2001). The role of positive emotions in positive psychology: The broaden-and-build theory of positive emotions. *American Psychologist, 56,* 218–226.

Freedman, J. L. (1984). Effects of television violence on aggression. *Psychological Bulletin, 96,* 227–246.

Freedman, J. L., & Fraser, S. C. (1966). Compliance without pressure: The foot-in-the-door technique. *Journal of Personality and Social Psychology, 4,* 196–202.

Freud, A. (1936). *The ego and the mechanisms of defense.* New York: International Universities Press.

Friedman, J. M., & Halaas, J. (1998). Leptin and the regulation of body weight in mammals. *Nature, 395,* 763–770.

Frijda, N. H. (1994). Emotions are functional, most of the time. In P. Ekman & R. J. Davidson (Eds.), *The nature of emotion: Fundamental questions, Vol. 4. Series in affective science* (pp. 112–122). New York: Oxford University Press.

Funder, D. C. (1995). On the accuracy of personality judgment: A realistic approach. *Psychological Review, 102,* 652–670.

Funder, D. C. (2001). Personality. *Annual Review of Psychology, 52,* 197–221.

Fung, H. H., & Carstensen, L. L. (2004). Motivational changes in response to blocked goals and foreshortened time: Testing alternatives to socioemotional selectivity theory. *Psychology and Aging, 19,* 68–78.

Fung, M. T., Raine, A., Loeber, R., Lynam, D. R., Steinhauer, S. R., Venables, P. D., et al. (2005). Reduced electrodermal activity in psychopathy-prone adolescents. *Journal of Abnormal Psychology, 114,* 187–196.

Galanter, E. (1962). Contemporary psychophysics. In R. Brown (Ed.), *New directions in psychology.* New York: Holt, Rinehart & Winston.

Galef, B. G., Jr., & Whiskin, E. E. (2000). Social influences on the amount eaten by Norway rats. *Appetite, 34,* 327–332.

Gallup. (1995). *Disciplining children in America: A Gallup poll report.* Princeton, NH: Author.

Gangestad, S. W., Simpson, J. A., Cousins, A. J., Garver-Apgar, C. E., & Christensen, P. N. (2004). Women's preferences for male behavioral displays change across the menstrual cycle. *Psychological Science, 15,* 203–207.

Garcia, J., & Koelling, R. A. (1966). Relation of cue to consequence in avoidance learning. *Psychonomic Science, 4,* 123–124.

Gardner, H. (1983). *Frames of mind: The theory of multiple intelligences.* New York: Basic Books.

Gardner, W. L., Pickett, C. L., Jefferis, V., & Knowles, M. (2005). On the outside looking in: Loneliness and social monitoring. *Personality and Social Psychology Bulletin, 31,* 1549–1560.

Garlick, D. (2002). Understanding the nature of the general factor of intelligence: The role of individual differences in neural plasticity as an explanatory mechanism. *Psychological Review, 109,* 116–136.

Garoff-Eaton, R. J., Slotnick, S. D., & Schacter, D. L. (2006). Not all false memories are created equal: The neural basis of false recognition. *Cerebral Cortex, 16,* 1645–1652.

Garon, N., Bryson, S. E., & Smith, I. M. (2008). Executive function in preschoolers: A review using an integrative framework. *Psychological Bulletin, 134,* 31–60.

Gawryluk, J. R., D'Arcy, R. C., Connolly, J. F., & Weaver, D. F. (2010). Improving the clinical assessment of consciousness with advances in electrophysiological and neuroimaging techniques. *BioMed Central Neurology, 10*(11). doi:10.1186/1471-2377-10-11

Gazzaniga, M. S. (2000). Cerebral specialization and interhemispheric communication: Does the corpus callosum enable the human condition? *Brain, 123,* 1293–1326.

Geddes, J. R., Burgess, S., Hawton, K., Jamison, K., & Goodwin, G. M. (2004). Long-term lithium therapy for bipolar disorder: Systematic review and meta-analysis of randomized controlled trials. *American Journal of Psychiatry, 161,* 217–222.

Geen, R. G. (1984). Preferred stimulation levels in introverts and extraverts: Effects on arousal and performance. *Journal of Personality and Social Psychology, 46,* 1303–1312.

Gentile, D. A., Saleem, M., & Anderson, C. A. (2007). Public policy and the effects of media violence on children. *Social Issues and Policy Review, 1,* 15–51.

George, M. S., Lisanby, S. H., & Sackheim, H. A. (1999). Transcranial magnetic stimulation: Applications in neuropsychiatry. *Archives of General Psychiatry, 56,* 300–311.

George, M. S., Wassermann, E. M., Williams, W. A., Callahan, A., Ketter, T. A., Basser, P., et al. (1995). Daily repetitive transcranial magnetic stimulation (rTMS) improves mood in depression. *Neuroreport, 6,* 1853–1856.

Gergely, G., & Csibra, G. (2003). Teleological reasoning in infancy: The naïve theory of rational action. *Trends in Cognitive Sciences, 7,* 287–292.

Gernsbacher, M. A., Dawson, M., & Goldsmith, H. H. (2005). Three reasons not to believe in an autism epidemic. *Current Directions in Psychological Science, 14,* 55–58.

Gershoff, E. T. (2002). Parental corporal punishment and associated child behaviors and experiences: A meta-analytic and theoretical review. *Psychological Bulletin, 128,* 539–579.

Gershon, E. S., Berrettini, W. H., & Goldin, L. R. (1989). Mood disorders: Genetic aspects. In H. I. Kaplan & B. J. Sadock (Eds.), *Comprehensive textbook of psychiatry* (5th ed.). Baltimore: Williams & Wilkins.

Geula, C., & Mesulam, M. (1994). Cholinergic systems and related neuropathological predilection patterns in Alzheimer disease. In R. D. Terry, R. Katzman, & K. Bick (Eds.), *Alzheimer disease* (pp. 263–291). New York: Raven Press.

Gibbons, M. B. C., Crits-Christoph, P., & Hearon, B. (2008). The empirical status of psychodynamic therapies. *Annual Review of Clinical Psychology, 4,* 93–108.

Gick, M. L., & Holyoak, K. J. (1983). Schema induction and analogical transfer. *Cognitive Psychology, 15,* 1–38.

Giedd, J. N., Castellanos, F. X., Rajapakse, J. C., Vaituzis, A. C., & Rapoport, J. L. (1997). Sexual dimorphism of the developing human brain. *Progress in Neuro-Psychopharmacology & Biological Psychiatry, 21*(8), 1185–1201.

Gigerenzer, G. (2004). Dread risk, September 11, and fatal traffic accidents. *Psychological Science, 15*, 286–287.

Gijsman, H. J., Geddes, J. R., Rendell, J. M., Nolen, W. A., & Goodwin, G. M. (2004). Antidepressants for bipolar depression: A systematic review of randomized, controlled trials. *American Journal of Psychiatry, 161*, 1537–1547.

Gilbert, D. T., Giesler, R. B., & Morris, K. A. (1995). When comparisons arise. *Journal of Personality and Social Psychology, 69*, 227–236.

Gilbert, D. T., Morewedge, C. K., Risen, J. L., & Wilson, T. D. (2004). Looking forward to looking backward: The misprediction of regret. *Psychological Science, 15*, 346–350.

Gilbert, D. T., Pinel, E. C., Wilson, T. D., Blumberg, S. J., & Wheatley, T. (1998). Immune neglect: A source of durability bias in affective forecasting. *Journal of Personality and Social Psychology, 75*, 617–638.

Gilbert, D. T., & Wilson, T. D. (2007, September). Prospection: Experiencing the future. *Science, 317*, 1351–1354.

Gillihan, S. J, & Farah, M. J. (2005). Is self special? A critical review of evidence from experimental psychology and cognitive neuroscience. *Psychological Bulletin, 131*, 76–97.

Gillogley, K. M., Evans, A. T., Hansen, R. L., Samuels, S. J., & Batra, K. K. (1990). The perinatal impact of cocaine, amphetamine, and opiate use detected by universal intrapartum screening. *American Journal of Obstetrics and Gynecology, 163*, 1535–1542.

Gilman, S. R., Iossifov, I., Levy, D., Ronemus, M., Wigler, M., & Vitkup, D. (2011). Rare de novo variants associated with autism implicate a large functional network of genes involved in formation and function of synapses. *Neuron, 70*, 898–907.

Gilovich, T. (1991). *How we know what isn't so: The fallibility of human reason in everyday life.* New York: The Free Press.

Gilpin, E. A., Choi, W. S., Berry, C., & Pierce, J. P. (1999). How many adolescents start smoking each day in the United States? *Journal of Adolescent Health, 25*, 248–255.

Gizewski, E. R., Krause, E., Karama, S., Baars, A., Senf, W., & Forsting, M. (2006). There are differences in cerebral activation between females in distinct menstrual phases during viewing of erotic stimuli: A fMRI study. *Experimental Brain Research, 174*, 101–108.

Gladwell, M. (2005). *Blink: The power of thinking without thinking.* New York: Little, Brown.

Glaser, R. & Kiecolt-Glaser, J. K. (2005). Stress-induced immune dysfunction: Implications for health. *Nature Reviews, 5*, 243–251.

Godden, D. R., & Baddeley, A. D. (1975). Context-dependent memory in two natural environments: On land and underwater. *British Journal of Psychology, 66*, 325–331.

Golby, A. J., Gabrieli, J. D. E., Chiao, J. Y., & Eberhardt, J. L. (2001). Differential responses in the fusiform region to same-race and other-race faces. *Nature Neuroscience, 4*, 845–850.

Goldapple, K., Segal, Z., Garson, C., Lau, M., Bieling, P., Kennedy, S., et al. (2004). Modulation of cortical-limbic pathways in major depression: Treatment-specific effects of cognitive behavior therapy. *Archives of General Psychiatry, 61*, 34–41.

Goldenberg, J. L., McCoy, S. K., Pyszczynski, T., Greenberg, J., & Solomon, S. (2000). The body as a source of self-esteem: The effects of mortality salience on identification with one's body, interest in sex, and appearance monitoring. *Journal of Personality and Social Psychology, 79*, 118–130.

Goldstein, J. (2011, January 18). Life tenure for federal judges raises issues of senility, dementia. *ProPublica: Journalism in the Public Interest.* Retrieved from http://www.propublica.org/article/life-tenure-for-federal-judges-raises-issues-of-senility-dementia

Goldstein, R. Z., Craig, A. D. B., Bechara, A., Garavan, H., Childress, A. R., Paulus, M. P., & Volkow, N. D. (2009). The neurocircuitry of impaired insight in drug addiction. *Trends in Cognitive Science, 13*, 372–380.

Gong, Q., Sluming, V., Mayes, A., Keller, S., Barrick, T., Cezayirli, E., et al. (2005). Voxel-based morphometry and stereology provide convergent evidence of the importance of medial prefrontal cortex for fluid intelligence in healthy adults. *Neuroimage, 25*, 1175–1186.

Gonzales, R., Mooney, L., & Rawson, R. A. (2010). The methamphetamine problem in the United States. *Annual Review of Public Health, 31*, 385–398.

Goodale, M. A., & Milner, A. D. (1992). Separate visual pathways for perception and action. *Trends in Neuroscience, 15*, 22–25.

Goodall, G. (1984). Learning due to the response-shock contingency in signaled punishment. *Quarterly Journal of Experimental Psychology, 36*, 259–279.

Goodman, R., & Stevenson, J. (1989). A twin study of hyperactivity-II. The aetiological role of genes, family relationships, and perinatal adversity. *Journal of Child Psychology and Psychiatry, 30*, 691–709.

Goodman, S. H., & Gotlib, I. H. (1999). Risk for psychopathology in the children of depressed mothers: A developmental model for understanding mechanisms of transmission. *Psychological Review, 106*, 458–490.

Goodwin, D. W., Powell, B., Bremer, D., Hoine, H., & Stern, J. (1969, March 21). Alcohol and recall: State dependent effects in man. *Science, 163*, 1358.

Goodwin, F. K., & Jamison, K. R. (1990). *Manic-depressive illness.* New York: Oxford University Press.

Goodwin, R. D., Lieb, R., Hoefler, M., Pfister, H., Bittner, A., Beesdo, K., et al. (2004). Panic attack as a risk factor for severe psychopathology. *American Journal of Psychiatry, 161*, 2207–2214.

Gopnik, A., & Graf, O. (1988). Knowing how you know: Young children's ability to identify and remember the sources of their beliefs. *Child Development, 59*, 1366–1371.

Gore, J. S., Cross, S. E., & Morris, M. L. (2006). Let's be friends: Relational self-construal and the development of intimacy. *Personal Relationships, 13*(1), 83–102. doi:10.1111/j.1475-6811.2006.00106.x

Gosling, S. D. (1998). Personality dimensions in spotted hyenas (*Crocuta crocuta*). *Journal of Comparative Psychology, 112*, 107–118.

Gosling, S. D. (2001). From mice to men: What can we learn about personality from animal research? *Psychological Bulletin, 127*, 45–86.

Gosling, S. D. (2008). *Snoop: What your stuff says about you.* New York: Basic Books.

Gosling, S. D., & John, O. P. (1999). Personality dimension in non-human animals: A cross-species review. *Current Directions in Psychological Science, 8*, 69–75.

Gosling, S. D., Ko, S. J., Mannarelli, T., & Morris, M. E. (2002). A room with a cue: Judgments of personality based on offices and bedrooms. *Journal of Personality and Social Psychology, 82*, 379–398.

Gosling, S. D., Kwan, V. S. Y., & John, O. P. (2003). A dog's got personality: A cross-species comparative approach to evaluating personality judgments. *Journal of Personality and Social Psychology, 85,* 1161–1169.

Gosselin, P., & Larocque, C. (2000). Facial morphology and children's categorization of facial expressions and emotions: A comparison between Asian and Caucasian faces. *Journal of Genetic Psychology, 161,* 346–358.

Gottesman, I. I. (1991). *Schizophrenia genesis: The origins of madness.* New York: Freeman.

Gottesman, I. I., & Hanson, D. R. (2005). Human development: Biological and genetic processes. *Annual Review of Psychology, 56,* 263–286.

Gottfredson, L. S. (2004a). Intelligence: Is it the epidemiologists' elusive "fundamental cause" of social class inequalities in health? *Journal of Personality and Social Psychology, 86,* 174–199.

Gottfredson, L. S. (2004b, Summer). Schools and the g factor. *The Wilson Quarterly, 28*(3), 35–45.

Gottfredson, L. S., & Deary, I. J. (2004). Intelligence predicts health and longevity: But why? *Current Directions in Psychological Science, 13,* 1–4.

Gottman, J. (1994). *Why marriages succeed or fail . . . and how you can make yours last.* New York: Simon & Schuster.

Gottman, J. M. (1998). Psychology and the study of marital processes. *Annual Review of Psychology, 49,* 169–197.

Gould, E., & Tanapat, P. (1999). Stress and hippocampal neurogenesis. *Biological Psychiatry, 46,* 1472–1479.

Graf, P., & Schacter, D. L. (1985). Implicit and explicit memory for new associations in normal and amnesic subjects. *Journal of Experimental Psychology: Learning, Memory and Cognition, 13,* 45–53.

Graf, P., & Uttl, B. (2001). Prospective memory: A new focus for research. *Consciousness and Cognition, 10,* 437–450.

Grandin, T. (1995). *Thinking in pictures: And other reports from my life with autism.* New York: Doubleday.

Granot, D., & Mayseless, O. (2001). Attachment security and adjustment to school in middle childhood. *International Journal of Behavioral Development, 25,* 530–541. doi: 10.1080/01650250042000366 000

Gray, J. R., & Thompson, P. M. (2004). Neurobiology of intelligence: Science and ethics. *Nature Reviews Neuroscience, 5,* 471–482.

Gray, J. A. (1987). *The psychology of fear and stress* (2nd ed.). Cambridge: Cambridge University Press.

Green, A. E., Munafò, M. R., DeYoung, C. G., Fossella, J. A., Fan, J., & Gray, J. R. (2008). Using genetic data in cognitive neuroscience: From growing pains to genuine insights. *Nature Reviews Neuroscience, 9,* 710–720.

Green, D. M., & Swets, J. A. (1966). *Signal detection theory and psychophysics.* New York: Wiley.

Green, J. J., & Hollander, E. (2010). Autism and oxytocin: New developments in translational approaches to therapeutics. *Neurotherapeutics, 7,* 250–257.

Greenberg, B. D., Gabriels, L. A., Malone, D. A., Jr., Rezai, A. R., Friehs, G. M., Okun, M. S., et al. (2008). Deep brain stimulation of the ventral internal capsule/ventral striatum for obsessive-compulsive disorder: Worldwide experience. *Molecular Psychiatry.* Advance online publication. Retrieved May 20, 2008. doi: 10.1038/mp.2008.55

Greenberg, J. (2008). Understanding the vital human quest for self-esteem. *Perspectives on Psychological Science, 3,* 48–55.

Greenberg, J., Solomon, S., & Pyszczynski, T. (1997). Terror management theory of self-esteem and cultural worldviews: Empirical assessments and conceptual refinements. In M. P. Zanna (Ed.), *Advances in Experimental Social Psychology* (Vol. 29, pp. 61–136). New York: Academic Press.

Greene, B. (2007). How difference makes a difference. In J. C. Muran (Ed.), *Dialogues on difference: Studies of diversity in the therapeutic relationship* (pp. 47–63). Washington, DC: American Psychological Association.

Greenwald, A. G. (1992). New look 3: Reclaiming unconscious cognition. *American Psychologist, 47,* 766–779.

Greenwald, A. G., & Banaji, M. R. (1995). Implicit social cognition: Attitudes, self-esteem, and stereotypes. *Psychological Review, 102,* 4–27.

Greenwald, A. G., McGhee, D., & Schwartz, J. (1998). Measuring individual differences in implicit cognition: The implicit association test. *Journal of Personality and Social Psychology, 74,* 1464–1480.

Greenwald, A. G., Oakes, M. A., & Hoffman, H. (2003). Targets of discrimination: Effects of race on responses to weapons holders. *Journal of Experimental Social Psychology, 39,* 399–405.

Greenwald, A. G., Poehlman, T. A., Uhlmann, E., & Banaji, M. R. (2009). Understanding and using the Implicit Association Test: III. Meta-analysis of predictive validity. *Journal of Personality and Social Psychology, 97,* 17–41.

Greitemeyer, T. (2009). Effects of songs with prosocial lyrics on prosocial behavior: Further evidence and a mediating mechanism. *Personality and Social Psychology Bulletin, 35*(11), 1500–1511.

Grill-Spector, K., Knouf, N., & Kanwisher, N. (2004). The fusiform face area subserves face perception, not generic within-category identification. *Nature Neuroscience, 7,* 555–562.

Groebel, J. (1998). *The UNESCO global study on media violence: A joint project of UNESCO, the world organization of the Scout movement and Utrecht University, the Netherlands. Report Presented to the Director General of UNESCO.* Paris: UNESCO.

Gross, J. J. (1999). Emotion and emotion regulation. In L. A. Pervin & O. P. John (Eds.), *Handbook of personality: Theory and research* (2nd ed., pp. 525–552). New York: Guilford Press.

Grossman, L. (2005, January 24). Grow up? Not so fast. *Time, 165,* 42–53.

Grossman, M., & Wood, W. (1993). Sex differences in intensity of emotional experience: A social role interpretation. *Journal of Personality and Social Psychology, 65,* 1010–1022.

Gruber, S. A., Silveri, M. M., & Yurgelun-Todd, D. A. (2007). Neuropsychological consequences of opiate use. *Neuropsychological Review, 17,* 299–315.

Gruenewald, P. J., Millar, A. B., Treno, A. J., Yang, Z., Ponicki, W. R., & Roeper, P. (1996). The geography of availability and driving after drinking. *Addiction, 91,* 967–983.

Gruzelier, J. H. (2000). Redefining hypnosis:Theory, methods, and integration. *Contemporary Hypnosis, 17,* 51–70.

Guenther, F. H., Brumberg, J. S., Wright, E. J., Nieto-Castanon, A., Tourville, J. A., et al. (2009). A wireless brain-machine interface for real-time speech synthesis. *PLoS ONE, 4*(12), e82128.

Guerin, B. (1994). What do people think about the risks of driving? Implications for traffic safety interventions. *Journal of Applied Social Psychology, 24,* 994–1021.

Guerri, C. (2002). Mechanisms involved in central nervous system dysfunctions induced by prenatal ethanol exposure. *Neurotoxicity Research, 4*(4), 327–335.

Guimond, S. (2008). Psychological similarities and differences between women and men across cultures. *Social and Personality Psychology Compass, 2*, 494–510.

Guimond, S., Branscombe, N. R., Brunot, S., Buunk, A. P., Chatard, A., Desert, M., et al. (2007). Culture, gender, and the self: Variations and impact of social comparison processes. *Journal of Personality and Social Psychology, 92*, 1118–1134.

Gunderson, J. G. (1984). *Borderline personality disorder*. Washington, DC: American Psychiatric Press.

Gur, R. C., & Gur, R. E. (2004). Gender differences in the functional organization of the brain. In M. J. Legato (Ed.), *Principles of gender-specific medicine* (pp. 63–70). Amsterdam: Elsevier.

Haier, R. J., Jung, R. E., Yeo, R. A., Head, K., & Alkire, M. T. (2005). The neuroanatomy of general intelligence: Sex matters. *Neuroimage, 25*, 320–327.

Halligan, P. W., & Marshall, J. C. (1998). Neglect of awareness. *Consciousness and Cognition, 7*, 356–380.

Hallmayer, J., Cleveland, S., Torres, A., Phillips, J., Cohen, B., Torigoe, T., Miller, J., Fedele, A., Collins, J., Smith, K., Lotspeich, L., Croen, L. A., Ozonoff, S., Lajonchere, C., Grether, J. K., & Risch, N. (2011). Genetic heritability and shared environmental factors among twin pairs with autism. *Archives of General Psychiatry,* doi:10.1001/archgenpsychiatry.2011.76, e-pub ahead of print.

Halpern, C. T., Udry, J. R., & Suchindran, C. (1997). Testosterone predicts initiation of coitus in adolescent females. *Psychosomatic Medicine, 59*, 161–171.

Halpern, D. F. (2000). *Sex differences in cognitive abilities* (3rd ed.). Mahwah, NJ: Erlbaum.

Halpern, D. F. (2003). *Thought and knowledge: An introduction to critical thinking* (4th ed.). Mahwah, NJ: Erlbaum.

Halpern, D. F., Benbow, C., Geary, D., Gur, D., Hyde, J., & Gernsbacher, M. A. (2007). The science of sex-differences in science and mathematics. *Psychological Science in the Public Interest, 8*, 1–51.

Hamann, S. B., Ely, T. D., Grafton, D. T., & Kilts, C. D. (1999). Amygdala activity related to enhanced memory for pleasant and aversive stimuli. *Nature Neuroscience, 2*, 289–293.

Hamann, S., Herman, R. A., Nolan, C. L., & Wallen, K. (2004). Men and women differ in amygdala response to visual sexual stimuli. *Nature Neuroscience, 7*, 411–416.

Hambrecht, M., Maurer, K., Hafner, H., & Sartorius, N. (1992). Transnational stability of gender differences in schizophrenia: Recent findings on social skills training and family psychoeducation. *Clinical Psychology Review, 11*, 23–44.

Hamilton, N. A., Gallagher, M. W., Preacher, K. J., Stevens, N., Nelson, C. A., Karlson, C., et al. (2007). Insomnia and well-being. *Journal of Consulting and Clinical Psychology, 75*, 939–946.

Hammen, C. (2005). Stress and depression. *Annual Review of Clinical Psychology, 1*, 293–319.

Hancock, P. J., Bruce, V., & Burton, A. M. (2000). Recognition of unfamiliar faces. *Trends in Cognitive Sciences, 4*, 330–337.

Handleman, J. S., Gill, M. J., & Alessandri, M. (1988). Generalization by severely developmentally disabled children: Issues, advances, and future directions. *Behavior Therapist, 11*, 221–223.

Hanewinkel, R., & Sargent, J. D. (2008). Exposure to smoking in internationally distributed American movies and youth smoking in Germany: A cross-cultural cohort study. *Pediatrics, 121*, 108–117.

Haney, C., Banks, C., & Zimbardo, P. (1973). Interpersonal dynamics in a simulated prison. *International Journal of Criminology and Penology, 1*, 69–97.

Hansen, C. J., Stevens, L. C., & Coast, J. R. (2001). Exercise duration and mood state: How much is enough to feel better? *Health Psychology, 20*, 267–275.

Hansen, W. B., Graham, J. W., Sobel, J. L., Shelton, D. R., Flay, B. R., & Johnson, C. A. (1987). The consistency of peer and parental influences on tobacco, alcohol, and marijuana use among young adolescents. *Journal of Behavioral Medicine, 10*, 559–579.

Haque, A. (2004). Psychology from Islamic perspective: Contributions of early Muslim scholars and challenges to contemporary Muslim psychologists. *Journal of Religion & Health, 43*(4), 357–377.

Harburger, L. L., Nzerem, C. K., & Frick, K. M. (2007). Single enrichment variables differentially reduce age-related memory decline in female mice. *Behavioral Neuroscience, 121*(4), 679–688.

Harding, C. M., Zubin, J., & Strauss, J. S. (1987). Chronicity in schizophrenia: Fact, partial fact, or artifact? *Hospital and Community Psychiatry, 38*, 477–486.

Hare, R. D. (1993). *Without conscience: The disturbing world of the psychopaths among us.* New York: Pocket Books.

Hare, R. D., McPherson, L. M., & Forth, A. E. (1988). Male psychopaths and their criminal careers. *Journal of Consulting and Clinical Psychology, 56*, 710–714.

Hariri, A. R., Mattay, V. S., Tessitore, A., Kolachana, B., Fera, F., Goldman, D., et al. (2002, July 19). Serotonin transporter genetic variation and the response of the human amygdala. *Science, 297*, 400–403.

Harlow, H. F., & Harlow, M. K (1966). Learning to love. *American Scientist, 54*, 244–272.

Harlow, H. F., Harlow, M. K., & Meyer, D. R. (1950). Learning motivated by a manipulation drive. *Journal of Experimental Psychology, 40*, 228–234.

Harpur, T. J., & Hare, R. D. (1994). Assessment of psychopathy as a function of age. *Journal of Abnormal Psychology, 103*, 604–609.

Harris, J. L., Bargh, J. A., & Brownell, K. D. (2009). Priming effects of television food advertising on eating behavior. *Health Psychology, 28*, 404–413.

Hartford, J., Kornstein, S., Liebowitz, M., Pigott, T., Russell, J., Detke, M., et al. (2007). Duloxetine as an SNRI treatment for generalized anxiety disorder: Results from a placebo and active-controlled trial. *International Clinical Psychopharmacology, 22*, 167–174.

Hauk, O., Johnsrude, I., & Pulvermüller, F. (2004). Somatotopic representation of action words in human motor and premotor cortex. *Neuron, 41*, 301–307.

Hawkley, L., & Cacioppo, J. T. (2010). Loneliness matters: A theoretical and empirical review of consequences and mechanisms. *Annals of Behavioral Medicine, 40*, 218–227.

Hayne, H. (2004). Infant memory development: Implications for childhood amnesia. *Developmental Review, 24*, 33–73. doi: 10.1016/j.dr.2003.09.007

Hazan, C., & Shaver, P. R. (1987). Romantic love conceptualized as an attachment process. *Journal of Personality and Social Psychology, 52*, 511–524.

Heatherton, T. F. (2011). Neuroscience of self and self-regulation. *Annual Review of Psychology, 62*, 363–390.

Heatherton, T. F., & Baumeister, R. F. (1991). Binge eating as escape from self-awareness. *Psychological Bulletin, 110*, 86–108.

Heatherton, T. F., Herman, C. P., & Polivy, J. (1991). Effects of physical threat and ego threat on eating behavior. *Journal of Personality and Social Psychology, 60*, 138–143.

Heatherton, T. F., & Vohs, K. D. (2000). Interpersonal evaluations following threats to self: Role of self-esteem. *Journal of Personality and Social Psychology, 78*, 725–736.

Heatherton, T. F., & Weinberger, J. L. (1994). *Can personality change?* Washington, DC: American Psychological Association.

Hebl, M. R., & Heatherton, T. F. (1998). The stigma of obesity in women: The difference is black and white. *Personality and Social Psychology Bulletin, 24*, 417–426.

Heine, S. J. (2003). An exploration of cultural variation in self-enhancing and self-improving motivations. In V. Murphy-Berman & J. J. Berman (Eds.), *Nebraska symposium on motivation: Vol. 49. Cross-cultural differences in perspectives on the self* (pp. 101–128). Lincoln: University of Nebraska Press.

Heine, S. J. (2005). Where is the evidence for pancultural self-enhancement? A reply to Sedikides, Gaertner, & Toguchi. *Journal of Personality and Social Psychology, 89*, 531–538.

Heine, S. J., Buchtel, E., & Norenzayan, A. (2008). What do cross-national comparisons of self-reported personality traits tell us? The case of conscientiousness. *Psychological Science, 19*, 309–313.

Heine, S. J., & Hamamura, T. (2007). In search of East Asian self-enhancement. *Personality and Social Psychology Review, 11*, 4–27.

Heine, S. J., Kitayama, S., & Hamamura, T. (2007). The inclusion of additional studies yields different conclusions: A reply to Sedikides, Gaertner, & Vevea (2005), Journal of Personality and Social Psychology. *Asian Journal of Social Psychology, 10*, 49–58.

Heine, S. J., Lehman, D. R., Markus, H. R., & Kitayama, S. (1999). Is there a universal need for positive self-regard? *Psychological Review, 106*, 766–794.

Heine, S. J., & Lehman, D. R. (1999). Culture, self-discrepancies, and self-satisfaction. *Personality and Social Psychology Bulletin, 25*, 915–925.

Heine, S. J., Lehman, D. R., Markus, H. R., & Kitayama, S. (1999). Is there a universal need for positive self-regard? *Psychological Review, 106*, 766–794.

Heller, D., Watson, D., & Ilies, R. (2004). The role of person versus situation in life satisfaction: A critical examination. *Psychological Bulletin, 130*, 574–600.

Helmreich, R., Aronson, E., & LeFan, J. (1970). To err is humanizing sometimes: Effects of self-esteem, competence, and a pratfall on interpersonal attraction. *Journal of Personality and Social Psychology, 16*, 259–264.

Hendricks, M., Rottenberg, J., & Vingerhoets, A. J. (2007). Can the distress-signal and arousal-reduction views of crying be reconciled? Evidence from the cardiovascular system. *Emotion, 7*, 458–463.

Henrich, J., Heine, S. J., & Norenzayan, A. (2010). The weirdest people in the world? *Behavioral and Brain Sciences, 33*, 61–83, 111–135. doi:10.1017/S0140525X0999152X

Henriques, J. B., & Davidson, R. J. (1990). Regional brain electrical asymmetries discriminate between previously depressed and healthy control subjects. *Journal of Abnormal Psychology, 99*, 22–23.

Herbert, T. B., & Cohen, S. (1993). Stress and immunity in humans: A meta-analytic review. *Psychosomatic Medicine, 55*, 364–379.

Herdener, M., Esposito, F., di Salle, F., Boller, C., Hilti, C. C., et al. (2010). Musical training induces functional plasticity in human hippocampus. *Journal of Neuroscience, 30*(4), 1377–1384.

Hering, E. (1964). *Outlines of a theory of the light sense* (L. M. Hurvich & D. Jameson, Trans.). Cambridge, MA: Harvard University Press. (Original work published 1878).

Herrnstein, R. J., & Murray, C. (1994). *The bell curve: Intelligence and class structure in American life*. New York: Free Press.

Herz, R. S., & Cahill, E. D. (1997). Differential use of sensory information in sexual behavior as a function of gender. *Human Nature, 8*, 275–285.

Hester, R. K., Delaney, H. D., & Campbell, W. (2011). ModerateDrinking.com and moderation management: Outcomes of a randomized clinical trail with non-dependent problem drinkers. *Journal of Consulting and Clinical Psychology, 79*, 215–234.

Hickok, G. (2009). Eight problems for the mirror neuron theory of action understanding in monkeys and humans. *Journal of Cognitive Neuroscience, 21*, 1229–1243.

Higgins, E. T. (1987). Self-discrepancy: A theory relating self and affect. *Psychological Review, 94*, 319–340.

Higgins, L. T., & Zheng, M. (2002). An introduction to Chinese psychology—Its historical roots until the present day. *The Journal of Psychology, 136*(2), 225–239.

Higgins, S. C., Gueorguiev, M., & Korbonits, M. (2007). Ghrelin, the peripheral hunger hormone. *Annals of Medicine, 39*, 116–136.

Higley, J. D., Mehlman, P.T., Higley, S. B., Fernald, B., Vickers, J., Lindell, S. G., et al. (1996). Excessive mortality in young free-ranging male nonhuman primates with low cerebrospinal fluid 5-hydroxyindoleacetic acid concentrations. *Archives of General Psychiatry, 53*, 537–543.

Hilgard, E. R., & Hilgard, J. R. (1975). *Hypnosis in the relief of pain*. Los Altos, CA: Kaufmann.

Hill, S. E., & Durante, K. M. (2009). Do women feel worse to look their best? Testing the relationship between self-esteem and fertility status across the menstrual cycle. *Personality and Social Psychology Bulletin, 35*, 1592–1601.

Hines, T. (2003). *Pseudoscience and the paranormal*. Amherst, NY: Prometheus.

Hirst, W., Phelps, E. A., Buckner, R. L., Budson, A. E., Cuc, A., Gabrieli, J. D. E., et al. (2009). Long-term memory for the terrorist attack of September 11: Flashbulb memories, event memories, and the factors that influence their retention. *Journal of Experimental Psychology: General, 138*, 161–176.

Hirstein, W., & Ramachandran, V. S. (1997). Capgras syndrome: a novel probe for understanding the neural representation of the identity and familiarity of persons. *Proceedings of the Royal Society B (Biological Sciences), 264*, 437–444.

Ho, B. C., Andreasen, N. C., Nopoulos, P., Arndt, S., Magnotta, V., & Flaum, M. (2003). Progressive structural brain abnormalities and their relationship to clinical outcome: A longitudinal magnetic resonance imaging study early in schizophrenia. *Archives of General Psychiatry, 60*, 585–594.

Hobson, J. A. (2009). REM sleep and dreaming: Towards a theory of protoconsciousness. *Nature Reviews Neuroscience, 10*, 803–814.

Hobson, J. A., & McCarley, R. (1977.) The brain as a dream state generator: An activation-synthesis hypothesis of the dream process. *American Journal of Psychiatry, 134*, 1335–1348.

Hobson, J. A., Pace-Schott, E. F., & Stickgold, R. (2000). Consciousness: Its vicissitudes in waking and sleep. In M. S. Gazzaniga (Ed.), *The new cognitive neurosciences* (pp. 1341–1354). Cambridge, MA: MIT Press.

Hockley, W. E. (2008). The effect of environmental context on recognition memory and claims of remembering. *Journal of Experimental Psychology: Learning, Memory, and Cognition, 34*, 1412–1429.

Hofmann, S. G., & Smits, J. A. J. (2008). Cognitive-behavioral therapy for adult anxiety disorders: A meta-analysis of randomized placebo-controlled trials. *Journal of Clinical Psychiatry, 69*, 621–632.

Hogan, M. J., Parker, J. D., Wiener, J., Watters, C., Wood, L. M., & Oke, A. (2010). Academic success in adolescence: Relationships among verbal IQ, social support and emotional intelligence. *Australian Journal of Psychology, 62*, 30–41.

Hoge, M. A., Morris, J. A., Daniels, A. S., Stuart, G. W., Huey, L. Y., & Adams, N. (2007). *An action plan for behavioral health workplace development*. Washington, DC: U.S. Department of Health and Human Services.

Holden, C. (2005, June 10). Sex and the suffering brain. *Science, 308*, 1574.

Holland, P. C. (1977). Conditioned stimulus as a determinant of the form of the Pavlovian conditioned response. *Journal of Experimental Psychology: Animal Behavior Processes, 3*, 77–104.

Hollander, E., Bartz, J., Chaplin, W., Phillips, A., Sumner, J., Soorya, L., et al. (2007). Oxytocin increases retention of social cognition in autism. *Biological Psychiatry, 61*, 498–503.

Hollander, E., Novotny, S., Hanratty, M., Yaffe, R., DeCaria, C. M., Aronowitz, B. R., et al. (2003). Oxytocin infusion reduces repetitive behaviors in adults with autistic and Asperger's disorders. *Neuropsychopharmacology, 28*, 193–198.

Hollis, K. L. (1997). Contemporary research on Pavlovian conditioning: A "new" functional analysis. *American Psychologist, 52*, 956–965.

Hollon, S. D., Stewart, M. O., & Strunk, D. (2006). Enduring effects for cognitive behavior therapy in the treatment of depression and anxiety. *Annual Review of Psychology, 57*, 285–315.

Hollon, S. D., Thase, M. E., & Markowitz, J. C. (2002). Treatment and prevention of depression. *Psychological Science in the Public Interest, 3*, 39–77.

Holmbeck, G. N. (1996). A model of family relational transformations during the transition to adolescence: Parent-adolescent conflict and adaptation. In J. A. Graber, J. Brooks-Gunn, & A. C. Petersen (Eds.), *Transitions through Adolescence* (pp. 67–200). Mahwah, NJ: Lawrence Erlbaum.

Holstein, S. B., & Premack, D. (1965). On the different effects of random reinforcement and presolution reversal on human concept-identification. *Journal of Experimental Psychology, 70*(3), 335–337.

Holtzman, N. S., Vazire, S., & Mehl, M. R. (2010). Sounds like a narcissist: Behavioral manifestations of narcissism in everyday life. *Journal of Research in Personality, 44*, 478–484.

Hooley, J. (2007). Expressed emotion and relapse of psychopathology. *Annual Review of Clinical Psychology, 3*, 329–352.

Hooley, J. M., & Gotlib, I. H. (2000). A diathesis-stress conceptualization of expressed emotion and clinical outcome. *Applied and Preventive Psychology, 9*, 135–152.

Horn, J. L. (1968). Organization of abilities and the development of intelligence. *Psychological Review, 75*, 242–259.

Horn, J. L., & Hofer, S. M. (1992). Major abilities and development in the adult period. In R. J. Sternberg & C. A. Berg (Eds.), *Intellectual development* (pp. 44–99). New York: Cambridge University Press.

Horn, J. L., & McArdle, J. J. (2007). Understanding human intelligence since Spearman. In R. Cudeck & R. C. MacCallum (Eds.), *Factor analysis at 100: Historical developments and future directions* (pp. 205–247). Mahwah, NJ: Erlbaum.

Hoshino, Y., Kumashiro, H., Yashima, Y., Tachibana, R., Watanabe, M., & Furukawa, H. (1980). Early symptoms of autism in children and their diagnostic significance. *Japanese Journal of Child and Adolescent Psychiatry, 21*, 284–299.

Hothersall, D. (1995). *History of psychology*. New York: McGraw-Hill.

House, J. S., Landis, K. R., & Umberson, D. (1988, July 29). Social relationships and health. *Science, 241*, 540–545.

Hovland, C. I., Janis, I. L., & Kelley, H. H. (1953). *Communication and persuasion: Psychological studies of opinion change*. New Haven, CT: Yale University Press.

Howlin, P., Mawhood, L., & Rutter, M. (2000). Autism and developmental receptive language disorder—A follow-up comparison in early adult life. II: Social, behavioural, and psychiatric outcomes. *Journal of Child Psychology and Psychiatry and Allied Disciplines, 41*, 561–578.

Hubel, D. H., & Wiesel, T. N. (1962). Receptive fields, binocular interaction, and functional architecture in the cat's visual cortex. *Journal of Physiology* (London), *160*, 106–154.

Huesmann, L. R. (1998). The role of social information processing and cognitive schemas in the acquisition and maintenance of habitual aggressive behavior. In R. G. Geen & E. Donnerstein (Eds.), *Human aggression: Theories, research, and implications for policy* (pp. 73–109). New York: Academic Press.

Hughes, H. C. (1999). *Sensory exotica*. Cambridge, MA: MIT Press.

Hull, C. L. (1943). *Principles of behavior: An introduction to behavior theory*. New York: D. Appleton-Century.

Hull, J. G., & Bond, C. F. (1986). Social and behavioral consequences of alcohol consumption and expectancy: A meta-analysis. *Psychological Bulletin, 99*, 347–360.

Hulse, G. K., Milne, E., English, D. R., & Holman, C. D. J. (1998). Assessing the relationship between maternal opiate use and ante-partum haemorrhage. *Addiction, 93*, 1553–1558.

Hunsley, J., & Mash, E. J. (2007). Evidence-based assessment. *Annual Review of Clinical Psychology, 3*, 29–51.

Hyde, J. S. (2005). The gender similarities hypothesis. *American Psychologist, 60*, 581–592. doi: 10.1037/0003-066X.60.6.581

Hyman, I. E., & Pentland, J. (1996). The role of mental imagery in the creation of false childhood memories. *Journal of Memory and Languages, 35*, 101–117.

Hyman, S. E. (2008). A glimmer of light for neuropsychiatric disorders. *Nature, 455*, 890–893.

Ikier, S., Tekcan, A. I., Gülgöz, S., & Küntay, A. (2003). Whose life is it anyway? Adoption of each other's autobiographical memories by twins. *Applied Cognitive Psychology, 17*, 237–247.

Ilan, A. B., Smith, M. E., & Gevins, A. (2004). Effects of marijuana on neurophysiological signals of working and episodic memory. *Psychopharmacology, 176*, 214–222.

Insel, T. R., & Young, L. J. (2001). The neurobiology of attachment. *Nature Reviews Neuroscience, 2*, 129–136.

Insel, T. R., & Charney, D. S. (2003). Research on major depression. *Journal of the American Medical Association, 289*, 3167–3168.

Isen, A. M. (1993). Positive affect and decision making. In M. Lewis & J. M. Haviland (Eds.), *Handbook of emotions* (pp. 261–277). New York: Guilford Press.

Ishigami, Y., & Klein, R. M. (2009). Is a handsfree phone safer than a handheld phone? *Journal of Safety Research, 40*, 157–164.

Ivanovic, D. M., Leiva, B. P., Perez, H. T., Olivares, M. G., Diaz, N. S., Urrutia, M. S., et al. (2004). Head size and intelligence, learning, nutritional status and brain development: Head, IQ, learning, nutrition and brain. *Neuropsychologia, 42*, 1118–1131.

Iyengar, S. S., & Lepper, M. R. (2000). When choice is demotivating: Can one desire too much of a good thing? *Journal of Personality and Social Psychology, 79*, 995–1006.

Izard, C. E., & Malatesta, C. Z. (1987). Perspectives on emotional development. In J. Osofsky (Ed.), *Handbook of infant development* (pp. 494–554). New York: Wiley.

Jablensky, A. (1989). Epidemiology and cross-cultural aspects of schizophrenia. *Psychiatric Annals, 19*, 516–524.

Jackson, B., Kubzansky, L. D., Cohen, S., Jacobs, D. R., Jr., & Wright, R. J. (2007). Does harboring hostility hurt? Associations between hostility and pulmonary function in the coronary artery risk development in (young) adults (CARDIA) Study. *Health Psychology, 26*(3), 333–340.

Jackson, S. A., Thomas, P. R., Marsh, H. W., & Smethurst, C. J. (2001). Relationships between flow, self-concept, psychological skills, and performance. *Journal of Applied Sport Psychology, 13*, 129–153.

Jacoby, L. L., Kelley, C., Brown, J., & Jasechko, J. (1989). Becoming famous overnight: Limits on the ability to avoid unconscious influences of the past. *Journal of Personality and Social Psychology, 56*, 326–338.

Jacoby, L. L., & Witherspoon, D. (1982). Remembering without awareness. *Canadian Journal of Psychology, 32*, 300–324.

James, William. (1884). What is an emotion? *Mind, 9*, 188–205.

James, W. (1890). *The principles of psychology.* New York: Henry Holt.

Jamieson, G. A. (2007). *Hypnosis and conscious states: The cognitive neuroscience perspective.* New York: Oxford University Press.

Jamison, K. R. (1993). *Touched with fire: Manic-depressive illness and the artistic temperament.* New York: Simon & Schuster.

Jamison, K. R. (1995). *An unquiet mind.* New York: Vintage Books.

Janata, P. (2009). The neural architecture of music-evoked autobiographical memories. *Cerebral Cortex, 19*, 2579–2594.

Jang, K. L., Hu, S., Lively, W. J., Angleitner, A., Riemann, R., Ando, J., et al. (2001). Covariance structure of neuroticism and agreeableness: A twin and molecular genetic analysis of the role of the serotonin transporter gene. *Journal of Personality and Social Psychology, 81*, 295–304.

Janssen, E., Carpenter, D., & Graham, C. A. (2003). Selecting films for sex research: Gender differences in erotic film preference. *Archives of Sexual Behavior, 32*, 243–251.

Jencks, C. (1979). *Who gets ahead? The determinants of economic success in America.* New York: Basic Books.

Jensen, A. R. (1998). *The g factor: The science of mental ability.* Westport, CT: Praeger.

Jensen, P. S., Arnold, L. E., Swanson, J. M., Vitiello, B., Abikoff, H. B., Greenhill, L. L., et al. (2007). 3-year follow-up of the NIMH MTA study. *Journal of the American Academy of Child and Adolescent Psychiatry, 46*, 989–1002.

Jensen, P. S., Garcia, J. A., Glied, S., Crowe, M., Foster, M., Schlander, M., et al. (2005). Cost-effectiveness of ADHD treatments: Findings from the multimodal treatment study of children with ADHD. *American Journal of Psychiatry, 162*, 1628–1636.

Jensen, P. S., Hinshaw, S. P., Swanson, J. M., Greenhill, L. L., Conners, C. K., Arnold, L. E., et al. (2001). Findings from the NIMH multimodal treatment study of ADHD (MTA): Implications and applications for primary care providers. *Journal of Developmental and Behavioral Pediatrics, 22*, 60–73.

Jiang, Y., Sheikh, K., & Bullock, C. (2006). Is there a sex or race difference in stroke mortality? *Journal of Stroke and Cerebrovascular Disease 15*(5), 179–186.

John, O. P. (1990). The "Big Five" factor taxonomy: Dimensions of personality in the natural language and in questionnaires. In L. A. Pervin & O. P. John (Eds.), *Handbook of personality: Theory and research* (pp. 66–100). New York: Guilford Press.

John, O. P., & Srivastava, S. (1999). The Big Five trait taxonomy: History, measurement, and theoretical perspectives. In L. A. Pervin & O. P. John (Eds.), *Handbook of personality: Theory and research* (2nd ed., pp. 102–138). New York: Guilford Press.

Johns, F., Schmader, T., & Martens, A. (2005). Knowing is half the battle—Teaching stereotype threat as a means of improving women's math performance. *Psychological Science, 16*, 175–179.

Johnson, D. L., Wiebe, J. S., Gold, S. M., Andreasen, N. C., Hichwa, R. D., Watkins, G. L., et al. (1999). Cerebral blood flow and personality: A positron emission tomography study. *American Journal of Psychiatry, 156*, 252–257.

Johnson, K. L., Gill, S., Reichman, V., & Tassinary, L. G. (2007). Swagger, sway, and sexuality: Judging sexual orientation from body motion and morphology. *Journal of Personality and Social Psychology, 93*, 321–334.

Johnson, W., Jung, R. E., Colom, R., & Haier, R. J. (2008). Cognitive abilities independent of IQ correlate with regional brain structure. *Intelligence, 36*, 18–28.

Johnston, L. D., O'Malley, P. M., Bachman, J. G., & Schulenberg, J. E. (2011). *Monitoring the future national results on adolescent drug use: Overview of key findings, 2010.* Ann Arbor: Institute for Social Research, University of Michigan.

Joiner, T. E. (2005). *Why people die by suicide.* Cambridge, MA: Harvard University Press.

Joiner, T. E., Coyne, J. C., & Blalock, J. (1999). On the interpersonal nature of depression: Overview and synthesis. In T. E. Joiner & J. C. Coyne (Eds.), *The interactional nature of depression: Advances in interpersonal approaches* (pp. 3–19). Washington, DC: American Psychological Association.

Joiner, T. E., Jr., Walker, R. L., Pettit, J. W., Perez, M., & Cukrowicz, K. C. (2005). Evidence-based assessment of depression in adults. *Psychological Assessment, 17*, 267–277.

Jokela, M., Elovainio, M., Kivimaki, M., & Keltikangas-Jarvinen, L. (2008). Temperament and migration patterns in Finland. *Psychological Science, 19*, 831–837.

Jokela, M., Elovainio, M., Singh-Manoux, A., & Kivimäki, M. (2009). IQ, socioeconomic status, and early death. *Psychosomatic Medicine, 71*, 322–328.

Jones, M. C. (1924). A laboratory study of fear: The case of Peter. *The Pedagogical Seminary, 31*, 308–315.

Jones, S. S., Collins, K., & Hong, H. (1991). An audience effect on smile production in 10-month-old infants. *Psychological Science, 2*, 45–49.

Jope, R. S. (1999). Anti-bipolar therapy: Mechanism of action of lithium. *Molecular Psychiatry, 4,* 117–128.

Jorm, A. F. (2000). Does old age reduce the risk of anxiety and depression?: A review of epidemiological studies across the adult life span. *Psychological Medicine, 30,* 3011–3022. doi: 10.1017/S0033291799001452

Jureidini, J. N., Doecke, C. J., Mansfield, P. R., Haby, M., Menkes, D. B., & Tonkin, A. L. (2004). Efficacy and safety of antidepressants for children and adolescents. *British Medical Journal, 328,* 879–883.

Kagan, J. (2011). Three lessons learned. *Perspectives in Psychological Science, 6,* 107–113.

Kagan, J., & Snidman, N. (1991). Infant predictors of inhibited and uninhibited profiles. *Psychological Science, 2,* 40–44.

Kahneman, D. (2007, July 20–22). *A short course in thinking about thinking. A master class by Danny Kahneman.* [Online video.] Retrieved from *Edge, The Third Culture,* at http://www.edge.org/3rd_culture/kahneman07/kahneman07_index.html/

Kahneman, D., & Tversky, A. (1972). Subjective probability: A study of representativeness. *Cognitive Psychology, 3,* 430–454.

Kahneman, D., & Tversky, A. (1984). Choices, values, and frames. *American Psychologist, 39,* 341–350.

Kalechstein, A. D., De La Garza II, R., Mahoney III, J. J., Fantegrossi, W. E., & Newton, T. F. (2007). MDMA use and neurocognition: A meta-analytic review. *Psychopharmacology, 189,* 531–537.

Kallio, S., & Revonsuo, A. (2003). Hypnotic phenomena and altered states of consciousness: A multi-level framework of description and explanation. *Contemporary Hypnosis, 20,* 111–164.

Kamara, S., Colom, R., Johnson, W., Deary, I., Haier, R., Waber, D., et al., and the Brain Development Cooperative Groups. (2011). Cortical thickness correlates of specific cognitive performance accounted for by the general factor of intelligence in healthy children aged 6 to 18. *Neuroimage, 55*(4), 1443–1453. doi:10.1016/j.neuroimage.2011.01.016

Kanayama, G., Pope, H. G., Cohane, G., & Hudson, J. L. (2003). Risk factors for anabolic-steroid use among weightlifters: A case-control study. *Drug and Alcohol Dependence, 71,* 77–86.

Kanazawa, S. (2004). General intelligence as a domain-specific adaptation. *Psychological Review, 111,* 512–523.

Kandall, S. R., & Gaines, J. (1991). Maternal substance use and subsequent sudden infant death syndrome (SIDS) in offspring. *Neurotoxicology and Teratology, 13,* 235–240.

Kandel, E. R. (1998). A new intellectual framework for psychiatry. *American Journal of Psychiatry, 155,* 457–469.

Kandel, E. R., Schwartz, J. H., & Jessell, T. M. (1995). *Essentials of neural science and behavior.* Norwalk, CT: Appleton & Lange.

Kane, M. J., Hambrick, D. Z., & Conway, A. R. (2005). Working memory capacity and fluid intelligence are strongly related constructs: Comment on Ackerman, Beier, and Boyle (2005). *Psychological Bulletin, 131,* 66–71.

Kang, D. H., Coe, C. L., McCarthy, D. O., & Ershler, W. B. (1997). Immune responses to final exams in healthy and asthmatic adolescents. *Nursing Research, 46,* 12–19.

Kanwisher, N., Tong, F., & Nakayama, K. (1998). The effect of face inversion on the human fusiform face area. *Cognition, 68,* 1–11.

Kaplan, R. M. (2007). Should Medicare reimburse providers for weight loss interventions? *American Psychologist, 62,* 217–219.

Kappenberg, E. S., & Halpern, D. F. (2006). Kinship center attachment questionnaire: Development of a caregiver-completed attachment measure for children under six years of age. *Educational and Psychological Measurement, 66,* 852–873.

Kapur, S. E., Craik, F. I. M., Tulving, E., Wilson, A. A., Houle, S., & Brown, G. R. (1994). Neuroanatomical correlates of encoding in episodic memory: Levels of processing effects. *Proceedings of the National Academy of Sciences, USA, 91,* 2008–2011.

Karasek, R. A., & Theorell, T. (1990). *Healthy work: Stress, productivity, and the reconstruction of working life.* New York: Basic Books.

Karney, B. R., & Bradbury, T. N. (1995). The longitudinal course of marital quality and stability: A review of theory, methods, and research. *Psychological Bulletin, 118,* 3–34.

Karpas, A. (2009). Mysterious tears: The phenomenon of crying from the perspective of social neuroscience. In T. Fögen (Ed.), *Tears in the Graeco-Roman world* (pp. 419–437). Berlin, Germany: De Gruyter.

Karpicke, J. D., & Blunt, J. R. (2011). Retrieval practice produces more learning than elaborative studying with concept mapping. *Science, 331,* 772–775.

Kasari, C., Paparella, T., Freeman, S., & Jahromi, L. B. (2008). Language outcomes in autism: Randomized comparison of joint attention and play interventions. *Journal of Counseling and Clinical Psychology, 76,* 125–137.

Kawachi, I., Kennedy, B., & Glass, R. (1999). Social capital and self-rated health: A contextual analysis. *American Journal of Public Health, 89*(8), 1187–1193.

Kawakami, K., Dovidio, J. F., Moll, J., Hermsen, S., & Russin, A. (2000). Just say no (to stereotyping): Effects of training in the negation of stereotypic associations on stereotype activation. *Journal of Personality and Social Psychology, 78,* 871–888.

Kawakami, K., Dovidio, J. F., & van Kamp, S. (2005). Kicking the habit: Effects of nonstereotypic association training and correction processes on hiring decisions. *Journal of Experimental Social Psychology, 41,* 68–75.

Kawas, C., Gray, S., Brookmeyer, R., Fozard, J., & Zonderman, A. (2000). Age-specific incidence rates of Alzheimer's disease: The Baltimore longitudinal study of aging, *Neurology, 54,* 2072–2077.

Kay, K. N., Naselaris, T., Prenger, R. J., & Gallant, J. L. (2008). Identifying natural images from human brain activity. *Nature, 452,* 352–355.

Kazak, A., Simms, S., & Rourke, M. (2002). Family systems practice in pediatric psychology. *Journal of Pediatric Psychology, 27,* 133–143.

Kazdin, A. E. (1994). Methodology, design, and evaluation in psychotherapy research. In A. E. Bergin & S. L. Garfield (Eds.), *International handbook of behavior modification and behavior change* (4th ed., pp. 19–71). New York: Wiley.

Kazdin, A. E. (2008). Evidence-based treatment and practice: New opportunities to bridge clinical research and practice, enhance the knowledge base, and improve patient care. *American Psychologist, 63,* 146–159.

Kazdin, A. E., & Benjet, C. (2003). Spanking children: Evidence and issues. *Current Directions in Psychological Science, 12,* 99–103.

Kazdin, A. E., & Blase, S. L. (2011). Rebooting psychotherapy research and practice to reduce the burden of mental illness. *Perspectives in Psychological Science, 6,* 21–37.

Keane, M. (1987). On retrieving analogues when solving problems. *Quarterly Journal of Experimental Psychology, 39A,* 29–41.

Keel, P. K., Baxter, M. G., Heatherton, T. F., & Joiner, T. E. (2007). A 20-year longitudinal study of body weight, dieting, and eating disorder symptoms. *Journal of Abnormal Psychology, 116*, 422–432.

Keel, P. K., & Mitchell, J. E. (1997). Outcome in bulimia nervosa. *American Journal of Psychiatry, 154*, 313–321.

Keller, J., & Bless, H. (2008). Flow and regulatory compatibility: An experimental approach to the flow model of intrinsic motivation. *Personality and Social Psychology Bulletin, 34*, 196–209.

Keller, M. B., & Baker, L. A. (1991). Bipolar disorder: Epidemiology, course, diagnosis, and treatment. *Bulletin of the Menninger Clinic, 55*, 172–181.

Keller, M. B., McCullough, J. P., Klein, D. N., Arnow, B., Dunner, D. L., Gelenberg, A. J., et al. (2000). A comparison of nefazodone, a cognitive behavioral analysis system of psychotherapy, and their combination for the treatment of chronic depression. *New England Journal of Medicine, 342*, 1462–1470.

Kelley, W. T., Macrae, C. N., Wyland, C., Caglar, S., Inati, S., & Heatherton, T. F. (2002). Finding the self? An event-related fMRI study. *Journal of Cognitive Neuroscience, 14*, 785–794.

Kellman, P. J., Spelke, E. S., & Short, K. R. (1986). Infant perception of object unity from translatory motion in depth and vertical translation. *Child Development, 57*, 72–86.

Kelly, D. J., Quinn, P. C., Slater, A., Lee, K., Ge, L., & Pascalis, O. (2007). The other-race effect develops during infancy: Evidence of perceptual narrowing. *Psychological Science, 18*, 1084–1089.

Kelly, G. A. (1955). *The psychology of personal constructs.* New York: Norton.

Keltner, D., & Anderson, C. (2000). Saving face for Darwin: The functions and uses of embarrassment. *Current Directions in Psychological Science, 9*, 187–192.

Keltner, D., & Bonanno, G. A. (1997). A study of laughter and dissociation: Distinct correlates of laughter and smiling during bereavement. *Journal of Personality and Social Psychology, 73*, 687–702.

Keltner, D., Young, R. C., Heerey, E. A., Oemig, C., & Monarch, N. D. (1998). Teasing in hierarchical and intimate relations. *Journal of Personality and Social Psychology, 75*, 1231–1247.

Kendler, K. S., Prescott, C. A., Myers, J., & Neale, M. C. (2003). The structure of genetic and environmental risk factors for common psychiatric and substance use disorders in men and women. *Archives of General Psychiatry, 60*, 929–937.

Kennedy, Q., Mather, M., & Carstensen, L. L. (2004). The role of motivation in the age-related positivity effect in autobiographical memory. *Psychological Science, 15*, 208–214.

Kennedy, S. H., Giacobbe, P., Rizvi, S., Placenza, F. M., Nishikawa, Y., Mayberg, H. S., & Lozano, A. M. (2011). Deep brain stimulation for treatment-resistant depression: Follow-up after 3 to 6 years. *American Journal of Psychiatry, 168*, 502–510.

Kenrick, D. T., & Funder, D. C. (1991). The person-situation debate: Do personality traits really exist? In V. J. Derlega, B. A. Winstead, & W. H. Jones (Eds.), *Personality: Contemporary theory and research* (pp. 149–174). Chicago: Nelson Hall.

Kenrick, D. T., Montello, D. R., Gutierres, S. E., & Trost, M. R. (1993). Effects of physical attractiveness on affect and perceptual judgments: When social comparison overrides social reinforcement. *Personality and Social Psychology Bulletin, 19*, 195–199.

Kessler, R. C., Adler, L., Barkley, R., Biederman, J., Conners, C. K., Demler, O., et al. (2006). The prevalence and correlates of adult ADHD in the United States: Results from the national comorbidity survey replication. *American Journal of Psychiatry, 163*, 716–723.

Kessler, R. C., Berglund, P., Demler, O., Jin, R., Koretz, D., Merikangas, K., et al. (2003). The epidemiology of major depressive disorder: Results from the national comorbidity survey replication (NCS-R). *Journal of the American Medical Association, 289*, 3095–3105.

Kessler, R. C., Chiu, W. T., Demler, O., & Walters, E. E. (2005a). Prevalence, severity, and comorbidity of twelve-month DSM-IV disorders in the national comorbidity survey replication (NCS-R). *Archives of General Psychiatry, 62*, 617–627.

Kessler, R. C., Demler, O., Frank, R. G., Olfson, M., Pincus, M. A., Walters, E. E., et al. (2005b). Prevalence and treatment of mental disorders, 1990 to 2003. *New England Journal of Medicine, 352*, 2515–2523.

Kessler, R. C., McGonagle, K. A., Zhao, S., Nelson, C. B., Hugh, M., Eshleman, S., et al. (1994). Lifetime and 12-month prevalence of DSM-III-R psychiatric disorders in the United States: Results from the national comorbidity study. *Archives of General Psychiatry, 51*, 8–19.

Kessler, R. C., Merikangas, K. R., & Wang, P. S. (2007). Prevalence, comorbidity, and service utilization for mood disorders in the United States at the beginning of the twenty-first century. In S. NolenHoeksema, T. Cannon, & T. Widiger (Eds.), *Annual review of clinical psychology: Vol. 3* (pp. 137–158). Palo Alto, CA: Annual Reviews.

Kessler, R. C., Sonnega, A., Bromet, E., Hughes, M., & Nelson, C. B. (1995). Posttraumatic stress disorder in the national comorbidity survey. *Archives of General Psychiatry, 52*, 1048–1060.

Kessler, R. C., & Wang, P. S. (2008). The descriptive epidemiology of commonly occurring mental disorders in the United States. *Annual Review of Public Health, 29*, 115–129.

Keyes, Daniel. (1981). *The minds of Billy Milligan.* New York: Random House.

Keys, A., Brozek, J., Henschel, A. L., Mickelsen, O., & Taylor, H. L. (1950). *The biology of human starvation.* Minneapolis: University of Minnesota Press.

Khan, M. M. (2005). Suicide prevention and developing countries. *Journal of the Royal Society of Medicine, 98*, 459–463.

Kiecolt-Glaser, J. K., & Glaser, R. I. (1988). Immunological competence. In E. A. Blechman & K. D. Brownell (Eds.), *Handbook of behavioral medicine for women* (pp. 195–205). Elmsford, NY: Pergamon Press.

Kiecolt-Glaser, J. K., & Glaser, R. I (1991). Stress and immune function in humans. In Ader, R., Felten, D., and Cohen, N. (Eds.), *Psychoneuroimmunology II* (pp. 849–867). San Diego: Academic Press.

Kiecolt-Glaser, J. K., Malarkey, W. B., Chee, M., & Newton, T. (1993). Negative behavior during marital conflict is associated with immunological down-regulation. *Psychosomatic Medicine, 55*, 395–409.

Kiecolt-Glaser, J. K., Page, G. G., Marucha, P. T., MacCullum, R. C., & Glaser, R. (1998). Psychological influences on surgical recovery: Perspectives from psychoneuroimmunology. *American Psychologist, 53*, 1209–1218.

Kihlstrom, J. F. (1985). Hypnosis. *Annual Review of Psychology, 36*, 385–418.

Kihlstrom, J. F. (2005). Dissociative disorder. *Annual Review of Clinical Psychology, 1*, 227–253.

Kihlstrom, J. F., & Eich, E. (1994). Altering states of consciousness. In D. Druckman & R. A. Bjork (Eds.), *Learning, remembering, and believing: Enhancing performance* (pp. 207–248). Washington, DC: National Academy Press.

Kilbride, J. E., Robbins, M. C., & Kilbride, P. L. (1970). The comparative motor development of Bagandan, American white, and American black infants. *American Anthropologist, 72*, 1422–1428.

Kim, J. B., Zaehres, H., Wu, G., Gentile, L., Ko, K., Sebastiano, V., et al. (2008). Pluripotent stem cells induced from adult neural stem cells by reprogramming with two factors. *Nature, 454*, 646–650.

Kim, J. J., & Jung, M. W. (2006). Neural circuits and mechanisms involved in Pavlovian fear conditioning: A critical review. *Neuroscience & Biobehavioral Reviews, 30*(2), 188–202.

Kim, S. J., Lyoo, I. K., Hwang, J., Chung, A., Hoon Sung, Y., Kim, J., et al. (2006). Prefrontal grey-matter changes in short-term and long-term abstinent methamphetamine abusers. *The International Journal of Neuropsychopharmacology, 9*, 221–228.

Kimura, D. (1999). *Sex and Cognition.* Cambridge, MA: MIT Press.

Kirsch, I. (2011, June). The placebo effect has come of age. *The Journal of Mind-Body Regulation, 1*(2), 106–109.

Kirsch, I., Deacon, B. J., Huedo-Medina, T. B., Scoboria, A., Moore, T. J., & Johnson, B. T. (2008). Initial severity and antidepressant benefits: A metaanalysis of data submitted to the Food and Drug Administration. *PLoS Medicine, 5*: e45. doi:10.1371

Kirsch, I., & Lynn, S. J. (1995). The altered state of hypnosis: Changes in the theoretical landscape. *American Psychologist, 10*, 846–858.

Klatsky, A. (2009). Alcohol and cardiovascular health. *Physiology and Behavior, 100*, 76–81.

Klauer, M. H., Musch, J., & Naumer, B. (2000). On belief bias in syllogistic reasoning. *Psychological Review, 107*, 852–884.

Klin, A., Jones, W., Schultz, R., & Volkmar, F. (2003). The enactive mind, or from actions to cognition: Lessons from autism. *Philosophical Transactions of the Royal Society of London, 358B*, 345–360.

Klump, K. L., & Culbert, K. M. (2007). Molecular genetic studies of eating disorders: Current status and future directions. *Current Directions in Psychological Science, 16*, 37–41.

Kluver, H., & Bucy, P. C. (1937). Psychic blindness and other symptoms following bilateral temporal lobectomy in rhesus monkeys. *American Journal of Physiology, 119*, 352–353.

Knight, R. (1953). Borderline states. *Bulletin of the Menninger Clinic, 17*, 1–12.

Knox, S. S., Weidner, G., Adelman, A., Stoney, C. M., & Ellison, R. C. (2004). Hostility and physiological risk in the national heart, lung, and blood institute family heart study. *Archives of Internal Medicine, 164*, 2442–2447.

Knutson, B., Fong, G. W., Adams, C. M., Varner, J. L., & Hommer, D. (2001). Dissociation of reward anticipation and outcome with event-related fMRI. *NeuroReport, 12*, 3683–3687.

Knutson, B., Wolkowitz, O. M., Cole, S. W., Chan, T., Moore, E. A., Johnson, R. C., et al. (1998). Selective alteration of personality and social behavior by serotonergic intervention. *American Journal of Psychiatry, 155*, 373–379.

Kobasa, S. C. (1979). Personality and resistance to illness. *American Journal of Community Psychology, 7*, 413–423.

Koch, J. L. (1891). *Die psychopathischen Minderwertigkeiten.* Ravensburg, Germany: Maier.

Kocsis, J. H., Rush, A. J., Markowitz, J. C., Borian, F. E., Dunner, D. L., Koran, L. M., et al. (2003). Continuation treatment of chronic depression: A comparison of nefazodone, cognitive behavioral analysis system of psychotherapy, and their combination. *Psychopharmacology Bulletin, 37*, 73–87.

Koelsch, S., Offermanns, K., & Franzke, P. (2010). Music in the treatment of affective disorders: A new method for music-therapeutic research. *Music Perception, 27*(4), 307–316.

Koh, K., Joiner, W. J., Wu, M. N., Yue, Z., Smith, C. J., Sehgal, A. (2008). Identification of SLEEPLESS, a sleep-promoting factor. *Science, 321*, 372–376.

Kohlberg, L. (1984). *Essays on moral development: Vol. 2. The psychology of moral development.* San Francisco: Harper & Row.

Köhler, W. (1925). *The mentality of apes.* New York: Harcourt Brace.

Kohn, D. (2008, March 11). Cases without borders: Psychotherapy for all. *The New York Times.* Retrieved from http://www.nytimes.com

Kolar, D. W., Funder, D. C., & Colvin, C. R. (1996). Comparing the accuracy of personality judgments by the self and knowledgeable others. *Journal of Personality, 64*, 311–337.

Kontsevich, L. L., & Tyler, C. W. (2004). What makes Mona Lisa smile? *Vision Research, 44*, 1493–1498.

Koole, S. L., Dijksterhuis, A., & van Knippenberg, A. (2001). What's in a name: Implicit self-esteem and the automatic self. *Journal of Personality and Social Psychology, 80*, 669–685.

Korn, M. L., Kotler, M., Molcho, A., Botsis, A. J., Grosz, D., Chen, C., et al. (1992). Suicide and violence associated with panic attacks. *Biological Psychiatry, 31*, 607–612.

Kosslyn, S. M. (2007). *Clear and to the point: 8 principles for compelling PowerPoint presentations.* New York: Oxford University Press.

Kosslyn, S. M., & Koenig, O. (1995). *Wet mind: The new cognitive neuroscience.* New York: Free Press.

Kosslyn, S. M., Thompson, W. L., Constantine-Ferrando, M. F., Alpert, N. M., & Spiegel, D. (2000). Hypnotic visual illusion alters color processing in the brain. *American Journal of Psychiatry, 157*, 1279–1284.

Kosslyn, S. M., Thompson, W. L., Kim, I. J., & Alpert, N. M. (1995). Topographical representations of mental images in primary visual cortex. *Nature, 378*, 496–493.

Kowalski, P., & Taylor, A. K. (2004). Ability and critical thinking as predictors of change in students' psychological misconceptions. *Journal of Instructional Psychology, 31*, 297.

Kozorovitskiy, Y., & Gould, E. (2004). Dominance hierarchy influences adult neurogenesis in the dentate gyrus. *Journal of Neuroscience, 24*, 6755–6759.

Kramer, M. S., Aboud, F., Mironova, E., Vanilovich, I., Platt, R. W., & Matush, L., et al. (2008). Breastfeeding and child cognitive development: New evidence from a large randomized trial. *Archives of General Psychiatry, 65*, 578–584.

Krantz, D. S., & McCeney, M. K. (2002). Effects of psychological and social factors on organic disease: A critical assessment of research on coronary heart disease. *Annual Review of Psychology, 53*, 341–369.

Krendl, A. C., Richeson, J. A., Kelley, W. M., & Heatherton, T. F. (2008). The negative consequences of threat: An fMRI investigation of the neural mechanisms underlying women's underperformance in math. *Psychological Science, 19*, 168–175.

Kringelbach, M. L., & Berridge, K. C. (2009). Toward a functional neuroanatomy of pleasure and happiness. *Trends in Cognitive Sciences, 13*, 479–487.

Krueger, R. F. (1999). The structure of common mental disorders. *Archives of General Psychiatry, 56*, 921–926.

Krueger, R. F., & Markon, K. E. (2006). Understanding psychopathology: Melding behavior genetics, personality, and quantitative psychology to develop an empirically based model. *Current Directions in Psychological Science, 15*, 113–117.

Kruesi, M. J., Hibbs, E. D., Zahn, T. P., Keysor, C. S., Hamburger, S. D., Bartko, J. J., et al. (1992). A 2-year prospective follow-up study of children and adolescents with disruptive behavior disorders. Prediction by cerebrospinal fluid 5-hydroxyindoleacetic acid, homovanillic acid, and autonomic measures. *Archives of General Psychiatry, 49*, 429–435.

Krulwich, R. (2007). Sweet, sour, salty, bitter . . . and umami. *NPR: Krulwich on Science*. Retrieved November 14, 2008, from http://www.npr.org/templates/story/story.php?storyId=15819485

Kuhl, P. K. (2004). Early language acquisition: Cracking the speech code. *Nature Reviews Neuroscience, 5*, 831–843.

Kuhl, P. K. (2006). Is speech learning "gated" by the social brain? *Developmental Science, 10*, 110–120.

Kuhl, P. K., Stevens, E., Hayashi, A., Deguchi, T., Kiritani, S., & Iverson, P. (2006). Infants show a facilitation effect for native language phonetic perception between 6 and 12 months. *Developmental Science, 9*, F13–F21.

Kuhl, P. K., Tsao, F. M., & Liu, H. M. (2003). Foreign-language experience in infancy: effects of short-term exposure and social interaction on phonetic learning. *Proceedings of the National Academy of Sciences, USA, 100*, 9096–9101.

Kuhn, C., Swartzwelder, S., & Wilson, W. (2003). *Buzzed: The straight facts about the most used and abused drugs from alcohol to ecstasy* (2nd ed.). New York: Norton.

Kulhara, P., & Chakrabarti, S. (2001). Culture and schizophrenia and other psychotic disorders. *Psychiatric Clinics of North America, 24*, 449–464.

Kuncel, N. R., Hezlett, S. A., & Ones, D. S. (2004). Academic performance, career potential, creativity, and job performance: Can one construct predict them all? *Journal of Personality and Social Psychology, 86*, 148–161.

Kunda, Z., & Spencer, S. J. (2003). When do stereotypes come to mind and when do they color judgment? A goal-based theoretical framework for stereotype activation and application. *Psychological Bulletin, 129*, 522–544.

Kyllonen, P. C., & Christal, R. E. (1990). Reasoning ability is (little more than) working-memory capacity?! *Intelligence, 14*, 389–433.

LaFrance, M. L., & Banaji, M. (1992). Toward a reconsideration of the gender-emotion relationship. In M. Clarke (Ed.), *Review of personality and social psychology* (pp. 178–201). Beverly Hills, CA: Sage.

Lager, A., Bremberg, S., & Vågerö, D. (2009). The association of early IQ and education with mortality: 65 year longitudinal study in Malmö, Sweden. *British Medical Journal, 339*(b5282). doi:10.1136/bmj.b582.

Laird, J. D. (1974). Self-attribution of emotion: The effects of expressive behavior on the quality of emotional experience. *Journal of Perspectives in Social Psychology, 29*, 475–486.

Lambert, T. J., Fernandez, S. M., & Frick, K. M. (2005). Different types of environmental enrichment have discrepant effects on spatial memory and synaptophysin levels in female mice. *Neurobiology of Learning and Memory, 83*, 206–216.

Lamm, C., Batson, C. D., & Decety, J. (2007). The neural substrate of human empathy: Effects of perspective-taking and cognitive appraisal. *Journal of Cognitive Neuroscience, 19*, 42–58.

Landa, R., Holman, K., & Garrett-Mayer, E. (2007). Social and communication development in toddlers with early and later diagnosis of autism spectrum disorders. *Archives of General Psychiatry, 64*, 853–864.

Langlois, J. H., Kalakanis, L., Rubenstein, A. J., Larson, A., Hallam, M., & Smoot, M. (2000). Maxims or myths of beauty? A meta-analytic and theoretical review. *Psychological Bulletin, 126*, 390–423.

Langlois, J. H., Ritter, J. M., Casey, R. J., & Sawin, D. B. (1995). Infant attractiveness predicts maternal behaviors and attitudes. *Developmental Psychology, 31*, 464–472.

Langlois, J. H., & Roggman, L. A. (1990). Attractive faces are only average. *Psychological Science, 1*, 115–121.

Larsen, J. T., McGraw, A. P., & Cacioppo, J. T. (2001). Can people feel happy and sad at the same time? *Journal of Personality and Social Psychology, 81*, 684–696.

Larson, E. B., Wang, L., Bowen, J. D., McCormick, W. C., Teri, L., Crane, P., & Kukull, W. (2006). Exercise is associated with reduced risk for incident dementia among persons 65 years of age and older. *Annals of Internal Medicine, 144*, 73–81.

Latané, B., & Darley, J. M. (1968). Group inhibition of bystander intervention in emergencies. *Journal of Personality and Social Psychology, 10*, 215–221.

Latané, B., Williams, K., & Harkins, S. G. (1979). Many hands make light the work: The causes and consequences of social loafing. *Journal of Personality and Social Psychology, 37*, 822–832.

Laureys, S. (2007, May). Eyes open, brain shut. *Scientific American, 296*, 84–89.

Lautenschlager, N. T., Cox, K. L., Flicker, L., Foster, J. K., van Bockxmeer, F. M., Xiao, J., et al. (2008). Effect of physical exercise on cognitive function in older adults at risk for Alzheimer disease. *Journal of the American Medical Association, 300*, 1027–1037.

Layton, M. (1995, May/June). Emerging from the shadows. *Family Therapy Networker*, 35–41.

Lazarus, R. S. (1993). From psychological stress to the emotions: A history of changing outlooks. *Annual Review of Psychology, 44*, 1–21.

Leary, M. R. (2004). The function of self-esteem in terror management theory and sociometer theory: Comment on Pyszczynski et al. *Psychological Bulletin, 130*, 478–482.

Leary, M. R., & MacDonald, G. (2003). Individual differences in self-esteem: A review and theoretical integration. In M. R. Leary & J. P. Tangney (Eds.), *Handbook of self and identity* (pp. 401–418). New York: Guilford Press.

Leary, M. R., Tambor, E. S., Terdal, S. K., & Downs, D. L. (1995). Self-esteem as an interpersonal monitor: The sociometer hypothesis. *Journal of Personality and Social Psychology, 68*, 518–530.

Leckman, J. F., Elliott, G. R., Bromet, E. J., Campbell, M., Cicchetti, D., Cohen, D. J., et al. (1995). Report card on the national plan for research on child and adolescent mental disorders: The midway point. *Archives of General Psychiatry, 34*, 715–723.

LeDoux, J. E. (1996). *The emotional brain: The mysterious underpinnings of emotional life*. New York: Simon & Schuster.

LeDoux, J. E. (2000). Emotion circuits in the brain. *Annual Review of Neuroscience, 23*, 155–184.

LeDoux, J. E. (2002). *Synaptic self*. New York: Viking.

LeDoux, J. E. (2007). The amygdala. *Current Biology, 17*, R868–R874.

Lee, P. A. (1980). Normal ages of pubertal events among American males and females. *Journal of Adolescent Health Care, 1*, 26–29. doi: 10.1016/S0197-0070(80)80005-2.

Leff, J., Sartorius, N., Jablensky, A., Korten, A., & Ernberg, G. (1992). The international pilot study of schizophrenia: Five-year follow-up findings. *Psychological Medicine, 22*, 131–145.

Lehrner, J. P. (1993). Gender differences in long-term odor recognition memory: Verbal versus sensory influences and the consistency of label use. *Chemical Senses, 18*, 17–26.

Leichsenring, F., Rabung, S., & Leibing, E. (2004). The efficacy of short-term psychodynamic psychotherapy in specific psychiatric disorders: A meta-analysis. *Archives of General Psychiatry, 61*, 1208–1216.

Leigh, B. C., & Schafer, J. C. (1993). Heavy drinking occasions and the occurrence of sexual activity. *Psychology of Addictive Behaviors, 7*, 197–200.

Leigh, B. C., & Stacy, A. W. (2004). Alcohol expectancies and drinking in different age groups. *Addiction, 99*, 215–217.

Lenzenweger, M. F., Lane, M. C., Loranger, A. W., & Kessler, R. C. (2007). DSM-IV personality disorders in the national comorbidity survey replication. *Biological Psychiatry, 62*, 553–564.

Lepper, M. R., Greene, D., & Nisbett, R. E. (1973). Undermining children's intrinsic interest with extrinsic reward: A test of the "overjustification" hypothesis. *Journal of Personality and Social Psychology, 28*, 129–137.

Lesniak, K. T., & Dubbert, P. M. (2001). Exercise and hypertension. *Current Opinion in Cardiology, 16*, 356–359.

Leuchter, A. F., Cook, I. A., Witte, E. A., Morgan, M., & Abrams, M. (2002). Changes in brain function of depressed subjects during treatment with placebo. *American Journal of Psychiatry, 159*, 122–129.

LeVay, S. (1991, August 30). A difference in hypothalamic structure between heterosexual and homosexual men. *Science, 253*, 1034–1037.

Leventhal, H., & Cleary, P. D. (1980). The smoking problem: A review of research and theory in behavioral risk modification. *Psychological Bulletin, 88*, 370–405.

Levin, J. M., Ross, M. H., Mendelson, J. H., Kaufman, M. J., Lange, N., et al. (1998). Reduction in BOLD fMRI response to primary visual stimulation following alcohol ingestion. *Psychiatry Research, 82*(3), 135–146.

Levinson, D. F. (2006). The genetics of depression: A review. *Biological Psychiatry, 60*, 84–92.

Levitin, D. J. (2006). *This is your brain on music: The science of a human obsession.* New York: Dutton/Penguin.

Levitin, D. J., & Menon, V. (2003). Musical structure in "language" areas of the brain: A possible role for Brodmann Area 47 in temporal coherence. *NeuroImage, 20*, 2142–2152.

Levy, D., Ronemus, M., Yamrom, B., Lee, Y., Leotta, A., Kendall, J., et al. (2011). Rare de novo and transmitted copy-number variation in autistic spectrum disorders. *Neuron, 70*, 886–897.

Lewin, C., & Herlitz, A. (2002). Sex differences in face recognition: Women's faces make the difference. *Brain and Cognition, 50*, 121–128.

Lewinsohn, P. M., Allen, N. B., Seeley, J. R., & Gotlib, I. H. (1999). First onset versus recurrence of depression: Differential processes of psychosocial risk. *Journal of Abnormal Psychology, 108*, 483–489.

Lewinsohn, P. M., Rodhe, P. D., Seeley, J. R., & Hops, H. (1991). Comorbidity of unipolar depression: I. Major depression with dysthymia. *Journal of Abnormal Psychology, 98*, 107–116.

Lewontin, R. C. (1976). Race and intelligence. In N. J. Block & G. Dworkin (Eds.), *The IQ controversy.* New York: Pantheon Books.

Li, N. P., Bailey, J. M., Kenrick, D. T., & Linsenmeier, J. A. W. (2002). The necessities and luxuries of mate preferences: Testing the tradeoffs. *Journal of Personality and Social Psychology, 82*, 947–955.

Lieb, K., Zanarini, M. C., Schmahl, C., Linehan, M. M., & Bohus, M. (2004). Borderline personality disorder. *Lancet, 364*, 453–461.

Lieberman, M. D. (2000). Intuition: A social cognitive neuroscience approach. *Psychological Bulletin, 126*, 109–137.

Lieberman, M. D., Ochsner, K. N., Gilbert, D. T., & Schacter, D. L. (2001). Do amnesiacs exhibit cognitive dissonance reduction? The role of explicit memory and attention in attitude change. *Psychological Science, 121*, 135–140.

Lilienfeld, S. O. (2007). Psychological treatments that cause harm. *Perspectives on Psychological Science, 2*, 53–67.

Limosin, F., Rouillon, F., Payan, C., Cohen, J., & Strub, N. (2003). Prenatal exposure to influenza as a risk factor for adult schizophrenia. *Acta Psychiatrica Scandinavica, 107*, 331–335.

Lindemann, B. (2001). Receptors and transduction in taste. *Nature, 413*, 219–225.

Linehan, M. M. (1987). Dialectical behavior therapy for borderline personality disorder: Theory and method. *Bulletin of the Menninger Clinic, 51*, 261–276.

Linehan, M. M., Armstrong, H. E., Suarez, A., Allmon, D., & Heard, H. (1991). Cognitive behavioral treatment of chronically parasuicidal borderline patients. *Archives of General Psychiatry, 48*, 1060–1064.

Linehan, M. M., Heard, H., & Armstrong, H. E. (1993). Naturalistic follow-up of a behavioral treatment for chronically parasuicidal borderline patients. *Archives of General Psychiatry, 50*, 971–974.

Liu, J., Raine, A., Venables, P. H., & Mednick, S. A. (2004). Malnutrition at age 3 years and externalizing behavior problems at ages 8, 11, and 17 years. *American Journal of Psychiatry, 161*, 2005–2013.

Ljungberg, T., Apicella, P., & Schultz, W. (1992). Responses of monkey dopamine neurons during learning of behavioral reactions. *Journal of Neurophysiology, 67*, 145–163.

Lledo, P. M., Gheusi, G., & Vincent, J. D. (2005). Information processing in the mammalian olfactory system. *Physiological Review, 85*, 281–317.

Locke, E. A., & Latham, G. P. (1990). *A theory of goal setting and task performance.* Englewood Cliffs, NJ: Prentice-Hall.

Lockwood, P., & Kunda, Z. (1997). Superstars and me: Predicting the impact of role models on the self. *Journal of Personality and Social Psychology, 73*, 91–103.

Loehlin, J. C., & Nichols, R. C. (1976). *Heredity, environment, and personality: A study of 850 sets of twins.* Austin: University of Texas Press.

Loewenstein, G. F., Weber, E. U., Hsee, C. K., & Welch, N. (2001). Risk as feelings. *Psychological Bulletin, 127*, 267–286.

Loftus, E. F. (1993). The reality of repressed memories. *American Psychologist, 48*, 518–537.

Loftus, E. F., & Palmer, J. C. (1974). Reconstruction of automobile destruction: An example of the interaction between language and memory. *Journal of Learning and Verbal Behavior, 13*, 585–589.

Loftus, E. F., Miller, D. G., & Burns, H. J. (1978). Semantic integration of verbal information into a visual memory. *Journal of Experimental Psychology: Human Learning and Memory, 4*, 19–31.

Logan, J. M., Sanders, A. L., Snyder, A. Z., Morris, J. C., & Buckner, R. L. (2002). Under-recruitment and nonselective recruitment: Dissociable neural mechanisms associated with aging. *Neuron, 33*, 1–20.

Loggia, M. L., Mogil, J. S., & Bushnell, M. C. (2008). Experimentally induced mood changes preferentially affect pain unpleasantness. *Journal of Pain, 9,* 784–791.

Loo, C. K., & Mitchell, P. B. (2005). A review of the efficacy of transcranial magnetic stimulation (TMS) treatment for depression, and current and future strategies to optimize efficacy. *Journal of Affective Disorders, 88,* 255–267.

Lovaas, O. I. (1987). Behavioral treatment and normal educational and intellectual functioning in young autistic children. *Journal of Consulting and Clinical Psychology, 55,* 3–9.

Lowe, P. (2001, October 12). No prison for Candace's adoptive mom. *Denver Rocky Mountain News,* p. 26A.

Lozano, A. M., Laxton, A. W., Tang-Wai, D. F., McAndrews, M. P., Zumsteg, D., et al. (2010). A phase I trial of deep brain stimulation of memory circuits in Alzheimer's disease. *Annals of Neurology 68*(4), 521–534.

Luauté, J. J., Maucort-Boulch, D. D., Tell, L. L., Quelard, F. F., Sarraf, T. T., Iwaz, J. J., Boisson, D., & Fischer, C. C. (2010). Long-term outcomes of chronic minimally conscious and vegetative states. *Neurology, 75*(3), 246–252. doi:10.1212/WNL.0b013e3181e8e8df

Lubinski, D. (2004). Introduction to the special section on cognitive abilities: 100 years after Spearman's (1904) "'General intelligence,' objectively determined and measured." *Journal of Personality and Social Psychology, 86,* 96–111.

Lubinski, D., & Benbow, C. P. (2000). States of excellence. *American Psychologist, 55,* 137–150.

Luchins, A. S. (1942). Mechanization in problem solving. *Psychological Monographs, 54,* Whole No. 248.

Luria, A. R. (1968). *The mind of a mnemonist.* New York: Avon.

Lykken, D. T. (1957). A study of anxiety in the sociopathic personality. *Journal of Abnormal Social Psychology, 55,* 6–10.

Lykken, D. T. (1995). *The antisocial personalities.* Hillsdale, NJ: Erlbaum.

Lykken, D. T. (2000). The causes and costs of crime and a controversial cure. *Journal of Personality, 68*(3), 560–605.

Lykken, D. T., McGue, M., Tellegen, A., & Bouchard, T. J., Jr. (1992). Emergenesis: Genetic traits that may not run in families. *American Psychologist, 47,* 1565–1577.

Lyubomirsky, S., & Nolen-Hoeksema, S. (1995). Effects of self-focused rumination on negative thinking and interpersonal problem solving. *Journal of Personality and Social Psychology, 69,* 176–190.

Lyubomirsky, S., King, L., & Diener, E. (2005). The benefits of frequent positive affect: Does happiness lead to success? *Psychological Bulletin, 131,* 803–855.

Maccoby, E. E., & Jacklin, C. N. (1974). *The psychology of sex differences.* Stanford, CA: Stanford University Press.

MacDonald, G., & Leary, M. R. (2005). Why does social exclusion hurt? The relationship between social and physical pain. *Psychological Bulletin, 131,* 202–223.

MacKay, D. G. (1973). Aspects of a theory of comprehension, memory and attention. *Quarterly Journal of Experimental Psychology, 25,* 22–40.

Macrae, C. N., Bodenhausen, G. V., & Calvini, G. (1999). Contexts of cryptomnesia: May the source be with you. *Social Cognition, 17,* 273–297.

Macrae, C. N., Moran, J. M., Heatherton, T. F., Banfield, J. F., & Kelley, W. M. (2004). Medial prefrontal activity predicts memory for self. *Cerebral Cortex, 14,* 647–654.

Madden, M., & Lenhart, A. (2006, Mar. 5). Online dating. *Pew Internet & American Life Project.* Retrieved from http://www.pewinternet.org/~/media//Files/Reports/2006/PIP_Online_Dating.pdf.pdf.

Maes, M., Van Gastel, A., Delmeire, L., Kenis, G., Bosmans, E., & Song, C. (2002). Platelet alpha2-adrenoceptor density in humans: Relationships to stress-induced anxiety, psychasthenic constitution, gender and stress-induced changes in the inflammatory response system. *Psychological Medicine, 32,* 919–928.

Magnier, M. (2008, May 26). China quake survivors show signs of post-traumatic stress. *Los Angeles Times,* p. 1.

Maguire, E. A., Spiers, H. J., Good, C. D., Hartley, T., Frackowiak, R. S. J., & Burgess, N. (2003). Navigation expertise and the human hippocampus: A structural brain imaging analysis. *Hippocampus, 13,* 250–259.

Maher, B.A., & Maher, W. R. (1994). Personality and psychopathology: A historical perspective. *Journal of Abnormal Psychology, 103,* 72–77.

Maia, T. V., Cooney, R. E., & Peterson, B. S. (2008). The neural bases of obsessive-compulsive disorder in children and adults. *Developmental Psychopathology, 20,* 1251–1283.

Maier, N. R. F. (1931). Reasoning in humans, II: The solution of a problem and its appearance in consciousness. *Journal of Comparative Psychology, 12,* 181–194.

Malle, B. F., Knobe, J., & Nelson, S. (2007). Actor-observer asymmetries in behavior explanations: New answers to an old question. *Journal of Personality and Social Psychology, 93,* 491–514.

Malle, B. F. (2006). The actor-observer asymmetry in causal attribution: A (surprising) meta-analysis. *Psychological Bulletin, 132,* 895–919.

Malone, D. A., Jr., Dougherty, D. D., Rezai, A. R., Carpenter, L. L., Friehs, G. M., Eskandar, E. N., et al. (2009). Deep brain stimulation of the ventral capsule/ventral striatum for treatment-resistant depression. *Biological Psychiatry, 65,* 267–275.

Maner, J. K., Luce, C. L., Neuberg, S. L., Cialdini, R. B., Brown, S., & Sagarin, B. J. (2002). The effects of perspective taking on motivations for helping: Still no evidence for altruism. *Personality and Social Psychology Bulletin, 28,* 1601–1610.

Manhart, K. (2004, December). The limits of multi-tasking. *Scientific American Mind,* 62–67.

Manning, R., Levine, M., & Collins, A. (2007). The Kitty Genovese murder and the social psychology of helping: The parable of the 38 witnesses. *American Psychologist, 62,* 555–562.

Mannuzza, S., Klein, R. G., Bonagura, N., Malloy, P., Giampino, T. L., & Addalli, K. A. (1991). Hyperactive boys almost grown up. Replications of psychiatric status. *Archives of General Psychiatry, 48,* 77–83.

Mannuzza, S., Klein, R. G., Truong, N. L., Moulton, J. L., III, Roizen, E. R., Howell, K. H., et al. (2008). Age of methylphenidate treatment initiation in children with ADHD and later substance abuse: Prospective follow-up into adulthood. *American Journal of Psychiatry, 165,* 604–609.

March, J. S., Silva, S., Petrycki, S., Curry, J., Wells, K., Fairbank, J., et al. (2007). The Treatment for Adolescents With Depression Study (TADS): Long-term effectiveness and safety outcomes. *Archives of General Psychiatry, 64,* 1132–1143.

Marcus, G. F. (1996). Why do children say "breaked"? *Current Directions in Psychological Science, 5,* 81–85.

Marcus, G. F. (2004). *The birth of the mind.* New York: Basic Books.

Marcus, G. F., Pinker, S., Ullman, M., Hollander, M., Rosen, T. S., & Xu, F. (1992). Overregularization in language acquisition. *Monographs of the Society for Research in Child Development, 57*(4, serial No. 228), 181.

Markon, J. (2001, October 8). Elderly judges handle 20 percent of U. S. caseload. *The Wall Street Journal*, p. A15.

Markowitz, J. C., & Weissman, M. M. (1995). Interpersonal psychotherapy. In E. E. Beckham & W. R. Leber (Eds.), *Handbook of depression* (2nd ed., pp. 376–390). New York: Guilford Press.

Markus, H. R. (1977). Self-schemata and processing information about the self. *Journal of Personality and Social Psychology, 35,* 63–78.

Markus, H. R., & Kitayama, S. (1991). Culture and the self: Implications for cognition, emotion, and motivation. *Psychological Review, 98,* 224–253.

Marlatt, G. A. (1999). Alcohol, the magic elixir? In S. Peele & M. Grant (Eds.), *Alcohol and pleasure: A health perspective* (pp. 233–248). Philadelphia: Brunner/Mazel.

Marsella, A. J., & Yamada, A. M (2007). Culture and psychopathology: Foundations, issues, directions. In S. Kitayama & D. Cohen (Eds.), *Handbook of cultural psychology* (pp. 797–819). New York: Guilford Press.

Marsh, A. A., Finger, E. C., Schechter, J. C., Jurkowitz, I. T. N., Reid, M. E., & Blair, R. J. R. (2011). Adolescents with psychopathic traits report reductions in physiological responses to fear. *Journal of Child Psychology & Psychiatry, 52*(8), 834–841.

Marshall, G. D. J., Agarwal, S. K., Lloyd, C., Cohen, L., Henninger, E. M., & Morris, G. J. (1998). Cytokine dysregulation associated with exam stress in healthy medical students. *Brain, Behavior, and Immunity, 12,* 297–307.

Marsland, A. L., Pressman, S., & Cohen, S. (2007). Positive affect and immune function. *Psychoneuroimmunology, 2,* 761–779.

Martin, L. A., Ashwood, P., Braunschweig, D., Cabanlit, M., Van de Water, J., & Amaral, D. G. (2008). Stereotypes and hyperactivity in rhesus monkeys exposed to IgG from mothers of children with autism. *Brain, Behavior, and Immunity, 22,* 804–805.

Martire, L. M., & Schulz, R. (2007). Involving family in psychosocial interventions for chronic illness. *Current Directions in Psychological Science, 16,* 90–94.

Maruta, T., Colligan, R. C., Malinchoc, M., & Offord, K. P. (2002). Optimism-pessimism assessed in the 1960s and self-reported health status 30 years later. *Mayo Clinic Proceedings, 77,* 748–753.

Maslow, A. (1968). *Toward a psychology of being.* New York: Van Nostrand.

Mather, M., & Carstensen, L. L. (2003). Aging and attentional biases for emotional faces. *Psychological Science, 14,* 409–415.

Mayberg, H. S., Lozano, A. M., Voon, V., McNeely, H. E., Seminowicz, D., Hamani, C., et al (2005). Deep brain stimulation for treatment-resistant depression. *Neuron, 45,* 651–660.

Mayhew, D. R., Brown, S. W., & Simpson, H. M. (2002). *The alcohol-crash problem in Canada: 1999.* Ottawa, Canada: Transport Canada.

Mazur, A., & Booth, A. (1998). Testosterone and dominance in men. *Behavioral and Brain Science, 21,* 353–397.

McAdams, D. P. (1999). Personal narratives and the life story. In L. A. Pervin & O. P. John (Eds.), *Handbook of personality: Theory and research* (2nd ed., pp. 478–500). New York: Guilford Press.

McAdams, D. P. (2001). The psychology of life stories. *Review of General Psychology, 5,* 100–122.

McCabe, D. P., Roediger, H. L., McDaniel, M. A., Balota, D. A., & Hambrick, D. Z. (2010). The relationship between working memory capacity and executive functioning: Evidence for a common executive attention construct. *Neuropsychology, 24,* 222–243.

McCarthy, G., Puce, A., Gore, J. C., & Allison, T. (1997). Face-specific processing in the human fusiform gyrus. *Journal of Cognitive Neuroscience, 9,* 605–610.

McClelland, D. C. (1987). *Human motivation.* New York: Cambridge University Press.

McClelland, D. C., Koestner, R., & Weinberger, J. (1989). How do self-attributed and implicit motives differ? *Psychological Review, 96,* 690–702.

McClintock, M. K. (1971). Menstrual synchrony and suppression. *Nature, 229,* 244–245.

McCrae, R. R., & Costa, P. T., Jr. (1990). *Personality in adulthood.* New York: Guilford Press.

McCrae, R. R., & Costa, P. T., Jr. (1999). A five-factor theory of personality. In L. A. Pervin & O. P. John (Eds.), *Handbook of personality: Theory and research* (2nd ed., pp. 139–153). New York: Guilford Press.

McCrae, R. R., Costa, P. T., Ostendorf, F., Angleitner, A., Hrebickova, M., Avia, M. D., et al. (2000). Nature over nurture: Temperament, personality, and life span development. *Journal of Personality and Social Psychology, 78,* 173–186.

McCullough, J. P. (2000). *Treatment for chronic depression: Cognitive behavioral analysis system of psychotherapy (CBASP).* New York: Guilford Press.

McDaniel, M. A. (2005). Big-brained people are smarter: A meta-analysis of the relationship between in vivo brain volume and intelligence. *Intelligence, 33,* 337–346.

McDaniel, M. A., & Einstein, G. O. (2000). Strategic and automatic processes in prospective memory retrieval: A multiprocess framework. *Applied Cognitive Psychology, 14,* S127–S144.

McEwen, B. S. (2008). Central effects of stress hormones in health and disease: Understanding the protective and damaging effects of stress and stress mediators. *European Journal of Pharmacology, 583,* 174–185.

McEwen, B. S., & Gianaros, P. J. (2011). Stress- and allostatis-induced brain plasticity. *Annual Review of Medicine, 62,* 431–435.

McGlashan, T. H. (1988). A selective review of recent North American long-term follow-up studies of schizophrenia. *Schizophrenia Bulletin, 14,* 515–542.

McGough, J. J., & Barkley, R. A. (2004). Diagnostic controversies in adult attention deficit hyperactivity disorder. *American Journal of Psychiatry, 161,* 1948–1956.

McGrath, R.W. (2010). Prescriptive authority for psychologists. *Annual Review of Clinical Psychology, 6,* 21–47.

McGue, M., Bacon, S., & Lykken, D. T. (1993). Personality stability and change in early adulthood: A behavioral genetic analysis. *Developmental Psychology, 29,* 96–109.

McInnis, M. G., McMahon, F. J., Chase, G. A., Simpson, S. G., Ross, C. A., & DePaulo, J. R. (1993). Anticipation in bipolar affective disorder. *American Journal of Human Genetics, 53,* 385–390.

McKown, C., & Weinstein, R. S. (2008). Teacher expectations, classroom context, and the achievement gap. *Journal of School Psychology, 46,* 235–261.

McNeely, H. E., Mayberg, H. S., Lozano, A. M., & Kennedy, S. H. (2008). Neuropsychological impact of Cg25 deep brain stimulation for treatment-resistant depression: Preliminary results over 12 months. *The Journal of Nervous and Mental Disease, 196,* 405–410.

McNeil, D. G., Jr. (2006, November 23). For rare few, taste is in the ear of the beholder. *The New York Times.* Retrieved from http://www.nytimes.com

McPheeters, M. L., Warren, Z., Sathe, N., Bruzek, J., Krishnaswami, S., et al. (2011). A systematic review of medical treatments for children with autism spectrum disorders. *Pediatrics* (published online April 4).

Meddis, R. (1977). *The sleep instinct*. London: Routledge & Kegan Paul.

Mednick, S. A., Gabrielli, W. F., & Hutchings, B. (1987). Genetic factors in the etiology of criminal behavior. In S. A. Mednick, T. E. Moffitt, & S. A. Stacks (Eds.), *The causes of crime: New biological approaches* (pp. 267–291). New York: Cambridge University Press.

Mednick, S. A., Huttunen, M. O., & Machon, R. A. (1994). Prenatal influenza infections and adult schizophrenia. *Schizophrenia Bulletin, 20*, 263–267.

Medvec, V. H., Madey, S. F., & Gilovich, T. (1995). When less is more: Counterfactual thinking and satisfaction among Olympic medalists. *Journal of Personality and Social Psychology, 69*, 603–610.

Mehl, M. R., Gosling, S. D., & Pennebaker, J. W. (2006). Personality in its natural habitat: Manifestations and implicit folk theories of personality in daily life. *Journal of Personality and Social Psychology, 90*, 862–877.

Mehl, M. R., Pennebaker, J. W., Crow, M. D., Dabbs, J., & Price, J. H. (2001). The electronically activated recorder (EAR): A device for sampling naturalistic daily activities and conversations. *Behavior Research Methods, Instruments, and Computers, 33*, 517–523.

Mehl, M. R., Vazire, S., Holleran, S. E., & Clark, C. S. (2010). Eavesdropping on happiness: Well-being is related to having less small talk and more substantive conversations. *Psychological Science, 21*, 539–541.

Mehl, M. R., Vazire, S., Ramirez-Esparza, N., Slatcher, R. B., & Pennebaker, J. W. (2007). Are women really more talkative than men? *Science, 317*, 82.

Mehler, J., & Bever, T. G. (1967, October 6). Cognitive capacity of very young children. *Science, 158*, 141–142.

Mehta, P. H., & Beer, J. (2010). Neural mechanisms of the testosterone-aggression relation: The role of orbitofrontal cortex. *Journal of Cognitive Neuroscience, 22*, 2357–2368.

Mehta, P. H., Jones, A. C., & Josephs, R. A. (2008). The social endocrinology of dominance: Basal testosterone predicts cortisol changes and behavior following victory and defeat. *Journal of Personality and Social Psychology, 94*, 1078–1093.

Mehu, M., & Dunbar, R. M. (2008). Naturalistic observations of smiling and laughter in human group interactions. *Behaviour, 145*(12), 1747–1780. doi:10.1163/156853908786279619

Melzack, R., & Wall, P. D. (1965). Pain mechanisms: A new theory. *Science, 150*, 971–979.

Melzack, R., & Wall, P. D. (1982). *The challenge of pain*. New York: Basic Books.

Mendez, I., Viñuela, A., Astradsson, A., Mukhida, K., Hallett, P., Robertson, H., et al. (2008). Dopamine neurons implanted into people with Parkinson's disease survive without pathology for 14 years. *Nature Medicine, 14*, 507–509.

Mennella, J. A., Jagnow, C. P., & Beauchamp, G. K. (2001). Prenatal and postnatal flavor learning by human infants. *Pediatrics, 107*, e88.

Mercer, K. B., Orcutt, H. K., Quinn, J. F., Fitzgerald, C. A., Conneely, K. N., Barfield, R. T., Gillespie, C. F., & Ressler, K. J. (2011). Acute and posttraumatic stress symptoms in a prospective gene x environment study of a university campus shooting. *Archives of General Psychiatry*, doi:10.1001/archgenpsychiatry.2011.109, e-pub ahead of print.

Merikangas, K. R., Burstein, M., Swanson, S. A., Avenevoli, S., Cui, L., Benjet, C., et al. (2010). Lifetime prevalence of mental disorders in U.S. adolescents: Results from the national comorbidity survey replication-adolescent supplement (NCS-A). *Journal of the American Academy of Child and Adolescent Psychiatry, 49*, 980–989.

Merikangas, K., He, J., Burstein, M., Swendsen, J., Avenevoli, S., Case, B., et al. (2011). Service utilization for lifetime mental disorders in U.S. adolescents: Results of the National comorbidity survey–adolescent supplement (NCS-A). *Journal of the American Academy of Child and Adolescent Psychiatry, 50*, 32–45.

Messias, E., Kirkpatrick, B., Bromet, E., Ross, D., Buchanan, R. W., Carpenter, W. T., Jr., et al. (2004). Summer birth and deficit schizophrenia: A pooled analysis from 6 countries. *Archives of General Psychiatry, 61*, 985–989.

Meston, C. M., & Frohlich, P. F. (2000). The neurobiology of sexual function. *Archives of General Psychiatry, 57*, 1012–1030.

Metcalfe, J., & Mischel, W. (1999). A hot/cool-system analysis of delay of gratification: Dynamics of willpower. *Psychological Review, 106*, 3–19.

Mezulis, A. H., Abramson, L. Y., Hyde, J. S., & Hankin, B. L. (2004). Is there a universal positivity bias in attributions? A meta-analytic review of individual, developmental, and culture differences in the self-serving attributional bias. *Psychological Bulletin, 130*, 711–747.

Mickelson, K. D., Kessler, R. C., & Shaver, P. R. (1997). Adult attachment in a nationally representative sample. *Journal of Personality and Social Psychology, 73*, 1092–1106.

Milgram, S. (1974). *Obedience to authority: An experimental view*. New York: Harper & Row.

Mill, J. S. (1843). *A system of logic, ratiocinative and inductive: Being a connected view of the principles of evidence and the methods of scientific investigation*. London: John W. Parker.

Miller, G. (2005, July 1). How are memories stored and retrieved? *Science, 309*, 92–93.

Miller, G. E., Freedland, K. E., Carney, R. M., Stetler, C. A., & Banks, W. A. (2003). Cynical hostility, depressive symptoms, and the expression of inflammatory risk markers for coronary heart disease. *Journal of Behavioral Medicine, 26*, 501–515.

Miller, I. W., Norman, W. H., & Keitner, G. I. (1989). Cognitive-behavioral treatment of depressed inpatients: Six- and twelve-month follow-up. *American Journal of Psychiatry, 146*, 1274–1279.

Miller, L. C., & Fishkin, S. A. (1997). On the dynamics of human bonding and reproductive success: Seeking windows on the adapted-for human-environmental interface. In J. Simpson & D. T. Kenrick (Eds.), *Evolutionary social psychology* (pp. 197–236). Mahwah, NJ: Erlbaum.

Miller, R. S. (1996). *Embarrassment: Poise and peril in everyday life*. New York: Guilford Press.

Miller, R. S. (1997). We always hurt the ones we love: Aversive interactions in close relationships. In R. M. Kowalski (Ed.), *Aversive interpersonal behaviors* (pp. 11–29). New York: Plenum Press.

Miller, W. T. (2000). Rediscovering fire: Small interventions, large effects. *Psychology of Addictive Behaviors, 14*, 6–18.

Milton, J., & Wiseman, R. (2001). Does psi exist? Reply to Storm and Ertel (2001). *Psychological Bulletin, 127*, 434–438.

Mineka, S., Davidson, M., Cook, M., & Keir, R. (1984). Observational conditioning of snake fear in rhesus monkeys. *Journal of Abnormal Psychology, 93*, 355–372.

Miniño, A. M. (2010). Mortality among teenagers aged 12–19 years: United States, 1999–2006. NCHS Data Brief, No. 37. U.S. Department of Health and Human Services.

Minshew, N. J., & Keller, T.A. (2010). The nature of brain dysfunction in autism: Functional brain imaging studies. *Current Opinions in Neurology, 23*, 124–130.

Minshew, N. J., & Williams, D. L. (2007). The new neurobiology of autism: Cortex, connectivity, and neuronal organization. *Archives of Neurology, 64*, 945–950.

Mischel, W., & Shoda, Y. (1995). A cognitive-affective system theory of personality: Reconceptualizing situations, dispositions, dynamics, and invariance in personality structure. *Psychological Review, 102*, 246–268.

Mischel, W., Shoda, Y., & Rodriguez, M. L. (1989, May 26). Delay of gratification in children. *Science, 244*, 933–938.

Mitelman, S. A., Shihabuddin, L., Brickman, A. M., Hazlett, E. A., & Buchsbaum, M. S. (2005). Volume of the cingulate and outcome in schizophrenia. *Schizophrenia Research, 72*, 91–108.

Mittal, V. A., Neumann, C., Saczawa, M., & Walker, E. F. (2008). Longitudinal progression of movement abnormalities in relation to psychotic symptoms in adolescents at high risk of schizophrenia. *Archives of General Psychiatry, 65*, 165–171.

Miyake, K. (1993). Temperament, mother-child interaction, and early development. *The Japanese Journal of Research on Emotions, 1*, 48–55.

Miyamoto, Y., & Kitayama, S. (2002). Cultural variation in correspondence bias: The critical role of attitude diagnosticity of socially constrained behavior. *Journal of Personality and Social Psychology, 83*, 1239–1248.

Mobbs, D., Greicius, M. D., Abdel-Azim, E., Menon, V., & Reiss, A. L. (2003). Humor modulates the mesolimbic reward centers. *Neuron, 40*, 1041–1048.

Moeller, S. J., & Crocker, J. (2009). Drinking and desired self-images: Path models of self-image goals, coping motives, heavy-episodic drinking, and alcohol problems. *Psychology of Addictive Behaviors, 23*(2), 334–340. doi:10.1037/a0015913

Moffitt, T. E., Arseneault, L., Belsky, D., Dickson, N., Hancox, R. J., Harrington, H., et al. (2011). A gradient of childhood self-control predicts health, wealth, and public safety. *Proceedings of the National Academy of Sciences*. Advanced publication: www.pnas.org/cgi/doi/10.1073/pnas.1010076108

Moffitt, T. E., Brammer, G. L., Caspi, A., Fawcett, J. P., Raleigh, M., Yuwiler, A., et al. (1998). Whole blood serotonin relates to violence in an epidemiological study. *Biological Psychiatry, 43*, 446–457.

Moises, H. W., & Gottesman, I. I. (2004). Does glial asthenia predispose to schizophrenia? *Archives of General Psychiatry, 61*, 1170.

Moll, J., & de Oliveira-Souza, R. (2007). Moral judgments, emotions and the utilitarian brain. *Trends in Cognitive Sciences, 11*, 319–321, ISSN 1364-6613. doi: 10.1016/j.tics.2007.06.001

Monroe, S. M., & Simons, A. D. (1991). Diathesis-stress theories in the context of life-stress research: Implications for depressive disorders. *Psychological Bulletin, 110*, 406–425.

Monteith, M. J. (1993). Self-regulation of prejudiced responses: Implications for progress in prejudice reduction efforts. *Journal of Personality and Social Psychology, 65*, 469–485.

Monteith, M. J., Ashburn-Nardo, L., Voils, C. I., & Czopp, A. M. (2002). Putting the brakes on prejudice: On the development and operation of cues for control. *Journal of Personality and Social Psychology, 83*, 1029–1050.

Montepare, J. M., & Vega, C. (1988). Women's vocal reactions to intimate and casual male friends. *Personality and Social Psychology Bulletin, 14*, 103–113.

Montgomery, G. H., DuHamel, K. N., & Redd, W. H. (2000). A metaanalysis of hypnotically induced analgesia: How effective is hypnosis? *International Journal of Clinical and Experimental Hypnosis, 48*, 138–153.

Monti, M. M., Vanhaudenhuyse, A., Coleman, M. R., Boly, M., Pickard, J. D., Tshibanda, L., et al. (2010). Willful modulation of brain activity in disorders of consciousness. *New England Journal of Medicine, 362*, 579–589.

Morgan, R. K. (n.d.) *Information for majors*. Retrieved April 23, 2008, from http://homepages.ius.edu/RMORGAN

Morin, C. M., Vallières, A., Guay, B., Ivers, H., Savard, J., Mérette, C., et al. (2009). Cognitive behavioral therapy, singly and combined with medication, for persistent insomnia: A randomized controlled trial. *Journal of the American Medical Association, 301*, 2005–2015.

Morr Serewicz, M., & Gale, E. (2008). First-date scripts: Gender roles, context, and relationship. *Sex Roles, 58*(3–4), 149–164. doi:10.1007/s11199-007-9283-4

Morris, N. M., Udry, J. R., Khan-Dawood, F., & Dawood, M. Y. (1987). Marital sex frequency and midcycle female testosterone. *Archives of Sexual Behavior, 16*, 27–37.

Morrison, A. B., & Chein, J. M. (2011). Does working memory training work? The promise and challenges of enhancing cognition by training working memory. *Psychonomic Bulletin Review, 18*, 46–60.

Morrison, M. (n.d.) *Sports superstitions*. Retrieved November 11, 2008, from http://www.infoplease.com/spot/superstitions1.html

Mortensen, E. L., & Hogh, P. (2001). A gender difference in the association between APOE genotype and age-related cognitive decline. *Neurology, 57*, 89–95.

Mortensen, E. L., Michaelsen, K. F., Sanders, S. A., & Reinisch, J. M. (2002). The association between duration of breastfeeding and adult intelligence. *Journal of the American Medical Association, 287*, 2365–2371.

Morton, J., & Johnson, M. H. (1991). CONSPEC and CONLERN: A two-process theory of infant face recognition. *Psychological Review, 98*, 164–181.

Moscovitch, M. (1995). Confabulation. In D. L. Schacter (Ed.), *Memory distortions: How minds, brains, and societies reconstruct the past* (pp. 226–251). Cambridge, MA: Harvard University Press.

Moskowitz, A. K. (2004). "Scared stiff": Catatonia as an evolutionary-based fear response. *Psychological Bulletin, 111*, 984–1002.

Moskowitz, H., & Fiorentino, D. A. (2000). *Review of the literature on the effects of low doses of alcohol on driving-related skills*. Washington, DC: National Highway Traffic Safety Administration.

Mowery, P. D., Brick, P. D., & Farrelly, M. (2000). Pathways to established smoking: Results from the 1999 national youth tobacco survey (Legacy First Look Report No. 3). Washington, DC: American Legacy Foundation.

Mroczek, D. K., & Kolarz, C. M.(1998). The effect of age on positive and negative affect: A developmental perspective on happiness. *Journal of Personality and Social Psychology, 75*, 1333–1349.

Mufson, L., Dorta, K. P., Wickramaratne, P., Nomura, Y., Olfson, M., & Weissman, M. M. (2004). A randomized effectiveness trial of interpersonal psychotherapy for depressed adolescents. *Archives of General Psychiatry, 61*, 577–584.

Muhle, R., Trentacoste, S. V., & Rapin, I. (2004). The genetics of autism. *Pediatrics, 113*, 472–486.

Mukherjee, R. A. S., Hollins, S., Abou-Saleh, M. T., & Turk, J. (2005). Low levels of alcohol consumption and the fetus. *British Medical Journal, 330*(7488), 375–385.

Mulder, J., Ter Bogt, T. F. M., Raiijmakers, Q. A. W., Nic Gabhainn, S., et al. (2009). The soundtrack of substance abuse: Music preference and adolescent smoking and drinking. *Substance Use & Misuse 44*(4), 514–531.

Mumford, D. B., Saeed, K., Ahmad, I., Latif, S., & Mubbashar, M. H. (1997). Stress and psychiatric disorder in rural Punjab: A community survey. *British Journal of Psychiatry, 170*, 473–478.

Munson, J. A., McMahon, R. J., & Spieker, S. J. (2001). Structure and variability in the developmental trajectory of children's externalizing problems: Impact of infant attachment, maternal depressive symptomatology, and child sex. *Development and Psychopathology, 13*, 277–296.

Murata, M. (2000). Secular trends in growth and changes in eating patterns of Japanese children. *American Journal of Clinical Nutrition, 72*, 1379–1383.

Murray, H. A. (1943.) *Analysis of the Personality of Adolph Hitler: With Predictions of his Future Behavior and Suggestions for Dealing with Him Now and After Germany's Surrender.* Washington, DC: OSS Archives.

Murray, S. L., Holmes, J. G., & Griffin, D. W. (1996). The benefits of positive illusions: Idealization and the construction of satisfaction in close relationships. *Journal of Personality and Social Psychology, 70*, 79–98.

Mustanski, B. S., Chivers, M. L., & Bailey, J. M. (2002). A critical review of recent biological research on human sexual orientation. *Annual Review of Sex Research, 13*, 89–140.

Myers, D. G. (2000). The funds, friends, and faith of happy people. *American Psychologist, 55*, 56–67.

Myers, D. G., & Lamm, H. (1976). The group polarization phenomenon. *Psychological Bulletin, 83*, 602–627.

Nader, K., & Einarsson, E. O. (2010). Memory reconsolidation: An update. *Annals of the New York Academy of Sciences, 1191*(1), 27–41.

Nader, K., Schafe, G. E., & Le Doux, J. E. (2000). Fear memories require protein synthesis in the amygdala for reconsolidation after retrieval. *Nature, 406*, 722–726.

Nakano, K., & Kitamura, T. (2001). The relation of the anger subcomponent of type A behavior to psychological symptoms in Japanese and foreign students. *Japanese Psychological Research, 43*(1), 50–54.

Ziv, N., & Goshen, M. (2006). The effect of 'sad' and 'happy' background music on the interpretation of a story in 5- to 6-year-old children. *British Journal of Music Education 23*, 303–314.

Naqvi, N. H., Rudrauf, D., Damasio, H., & Bechara, A. (2007, January 27). Damage to the insula disrupts addiction to cigarette smoking. *Science, 315*, 531–534.

Nash, M., & Barnier, A. (2008). *The Oxford handbook of hypnosis.* New York: Oxford University Press.

Nassar, N., Dixon, G., Bourke, J., Bower, C., Glasson, E., de Klerk, N., et al. (2009). Autism spectrum disorders in young children: Effect of changes in diagnostic practices. *International Journal of Epidemiology, 38*, 1245–1254.

National Center for Learning Disabilities (2009). *LD at a glance.* Retrieved from http://www.ncld.org/ld-basics/ld-explained/basic-facts/learning-disabilities-at-a-glance

National Highway Traffic Safety Administration. (2009). An examination of driver distraction as recorded in NHSTA databases. DOT HS 811216. September 2009. Retrieved from http://www-nrd.nhtsa.dot.gov/pubs/811216.pdf

National Human Genome Research Institute. (n.d.). *Learning about sickle cell disease.* Retrieved October 12, 2007, from http://www.genome.gov/10001219

National Institute of Drug Abuse. (2006). *NIDA Research Report: Methamphetamine Abuse and Addiction.* (NIH Publication No. 06–4210). Retrieved from http://www.nida.nih.gov/ResearchReports/methamph/methamph.html

National Institute of Drug Abuse. (2010). *MDMA (Ecstasy)* [Fact sheet]. Retrieved from http://teens.drugabuse.gov/facts/facts_xtc1.php

National Research Council, Committee on Educational Interventions for Children with Autism. (2001). *Educating young children with autism.* Washington, DC: National Academy Press.

Neimeyer, R. A., & Mitchell, K. A. (1988). Similarity and attraction: A longitudinal study. *Journal of Social and Personal Relationships, 5*, 131–148.

Neisser, U. (1967). *Cognitive psychology.* New York: Appleton-Century-Crofts.

Neisser, U., Boodoo, G., Bouchard, T. J., Jr., Boykin, A. W., Brody, N., Ceci, S. J., et al. (1996). Intelligence: Knowns and unknowns. *American Psychologist, 51*, 77–101.

Neisser, U., & Harsch, N. (1993). Phantom flashbulbs: False recollections of hearing the news about Challenger. In E. Winograd & U. Neisser (Eds.), *Affect and accuracy in recall: Studies of "flashbulb" memories* (pp. 9–31). New York: Cambridge University Press.

Nelson, G. (1998, April 29). The observatory: You don't have to be a rocket scientist to think like one. *Minneapolis Star Tribune*, p. 14.

Nelson, R. M., & DeBacker, T. K. (2008). Achievement motivation in adolescents: The role of peer climate and best friends. *Journal of Experimental Education, 76*(2), 170–189.

Newman, M. G., Szkodny, L., Llera, S. J., & Przeworski, A. (2011). A review of technology assisted self-help and minimal contact therapies for drug and alcohol abuse and smoking addiction: Is human contact necessary for therapeutic efficacy? *Clinical Psychology Review, 31*(1), 178–186.

Ng, D. M., & Jeffrey, E. W. (2003). Relationships between perceived stress and health behaviors in a sample of working adults. *Health Psychology, 22*, 638–642.

Nicolini, H., Bakish, D., Duenas, H., Spann, M., Erickson, J., Hallberg, C., et al. (2008). Improvement of psychic and somatic symptoms in adult patients with generalized anxiety disorder: Examination from a duloxetine, venlafaxine extended-release and placebo-controlled trial. *Psychological Medicine, 19*, 1–10.

Nisbett, R. E., Peng, K., Choi, I., & Norenzayan, A. (2001). Culture and systems of thought: Holistic versus analytic cognition. *Psychological Review, 108*, 291–310.

Nisbett, R. E., & Ross, L. (1980). *Human inferences: Strategies and shortcomings of social judgment.* Englewood Cliffs, NJ: Prentice-Hall.

Nisbett, R. E., & Wilson, T. D. (1977). Telling more than we can know: Verbal reports on mental processes. *Psychological Review, 84*, 231–259.

Nishino, S. (2007). Narcolepsy: Pathophysiology and pharmacology. *Journal of Clinical Psychiatry, 68*(Suppl. 13), 9–15.

Noftle, E. E., & Robins, R. W. (2007). Personality predictors of academic outcomes: Big five correlates of GPA and SAT scores. *Journal of Personality and Social Psychology, 93*, 116–130.

Norem, J. K. (1989). Cognitive strategies as personality: Effectiveness, specificity, flexibility and change. In D. M. Buss & N. Cantor (Eds.), *Personality psychology: Recent trends and emerging issues* (pp. 45–60). New York: Springer-Verlag.

Norman, K. A., Polyn, S. M., Detre, G. J., & Haxby, J. V. (2006). Beyond mind-reading: Multi-voxel pattern analysis of fMRI data. *Trends in Cognitive Sciences, 10*, 424–423.

Norton, M. I., Frost, J. A., & Ariely, D. (2007). Less is more: The lure of ambiguity, or why familiarity breeds contempt. *Journal of Personality and Social Psychology, 92*, 97–106.

Nosek, B. A., Hawkins, C. B., & Frazier, R. S. (2011). Implicit social cognition: From measures to mechanisms. *Trends in Cognitive Sciences, 15*, 152–159.

Novotny, S. L., Hollander, E., Allen, A., Aronowitz, B. R., DeCaria, C., Cartwright, C., et al. (2000). Behavioral response to oxytocin challenge in adult autistic disorders. *Biological Psychiatry, 47*, 52.

Noyes, R. (1991). Suicide and panic disorder: A review. *Journal of Affective Disorders, 22*, 1–11.

Nurnberger, J. J., Goldin, L. R., & Gershon, E. S. (1994). Genetics of psychiatric disorders. In G. Winokur & P. M. Clayton (Eds.), *The medical basis of psychiatry* (pp. 459–492). Philadelphia: Saunders.

O'Kane, G. O., Kensinger, E. A., & Corkin, S. (2004). Evidence for semantic learning in profound amnesia: An investigation with the patient H. M. *Hippocampus, 14*, 417–425.

O'Leary, S. G. (1995). Parental discipline mistakes. *Current Directions in Psychological Science, 4*, 11–13.

O'Neal, J. M. (1984). First person account: Finding myself and loving it. *Schizophrenia Bulletin, 10*, 109–110.

O'Neil, J. (2004, December 29). Slow-motion miracle: One boy's journey out of autism's grasp. *The New York Times*, p. B8.

O'Neil, S. (1999). Flow theory and the development of musical performance skills. *Bulletin of the Council for Research in Music Education, 141*, 129–134.

O'Toole, A. J., Jiang, F., Abdi, H., & Haxby, J. V. (2005). Partially distributed representations of objects and faces in ventral temporal cortex. *Journal of Cognitive Neuroscience, 17*, 580–590.

Oberauer, K., Schulze, R., Wilhelm, O., & Süß, H. M. (2005). Working memory and intelligence—Their correlation and their relation: Comment on Ackerman, Beier, and Boyle (2005). *Psychological Bulletin, 131*, 61–65.

Obot, I. S., & Room, R. (2005). *Alcohol, gender and drinking problems: Perspectives from low and middle income countries.* Geneva, Switzerland: World Health Organization.

Ochsner, K. N., Bunge, S. A., Gross, J. J., & Gabrieli, J. D. E. (2002). Rethinking feelings: An fMRI study of the cognitive regulation of emotion. *Journal of Cognitive Neuroscience, 14*, 1215–1299.

Oei, N. Y. L., Everaerd, W. T. A. M., Elzinga, B. M., Van Well, S., & Bermond, B. (2006). Psychosocial stress impairs working memory at high loads: An association with cortisol levels and memory retrieval. *Stress, 9*, 133–141.

Ogbu, J. U. (1994). From cultural differences to differences in cultural frames of reference. In P. M. Greenfield & R. R. Cocking (Eds.), *Cross cultural roots of minority child development* (pp. 365–392). Hillsdale, NJ: Erlbaum.

Ogden, C. L., & Carroll, M. (2010). Prevalence of overweight, obesity, and extreme obesity among adults: United States, trends 1976–1980 through 2007–2008. A report of the National Center for Health Statistics. http://www.cdc.gov/NCHS/data/hestat/obesity_adult_07_08/obesity_adult_07_08.pdf/

Ogletree, S. M., Turner, G., Vieira, A., & Brunotte, J. (2005). College living: Issues related to housecleaning attitudes. *College Student Journal, 39*(4), 729–733.

Olanow, C. W., Goetz, C. G., Kordower, J. H., Stoessl, A. J., Sossi, V., Brin, M. F., et al. (2003). A double-blind controlled trial of bilateral fetal nigral transplantation in Parkinson's disease. *Annals of Neurology, 54*, 403–414.

Olds, J. (1962). Hypothalamic substrates of reward. *Psychological Review, 42*, 554–604.

Olds, J., & Milner, P. (1954). Positive reinforcement produced by electrical stimulation of the septal area and other regions of the rat brain. *Journal of Comparative and Physiological Psychology, 47*, 419–428.

Olfson, M., Marcus, S. C., Druss, B., Elinson, L., Tanielian, T., & Pincus, H. A. (2002). National trends in the outpatient treatment of depression. *Journal of the American Medical Association, 287*, 203–209.

Olfson, M., Shaffer, D., Marcus, S. C., & Greenberg, T. (2003). Relationship between antidepressant medication treatment and suicide in adolescents. *Archives of General Psychiatry, 60*, 978–982.

Olshansky, S. J., Passaro, D. J., Hershow, R. C., Layden, J. C., Bruce, A., Brody, J., .& Ludwig, D. S. (2005). A potential decline in life expectancy in the United States in the 21st century. *Journal of Obstetrical & Gynecological Survey, 60*, 450–452.

Olson, J. M., Vernon, P. A., Harris, J. A., & Jang, K. L. (2001). The heritability of attitudes: A study of twins. *Journal of Personality and Social Psychology, 80*, 845–860.

Olson, R., Hogan, L., & Santos, L. (2006). Illuminating the history of psychology: Tips for teaching students about the Hawthorne studies. *Psychology Learning and Teaching, 5*, 110–118.

Olsson, A., Ebert, J. P., Banaji, M. R., & Phelps, E. A. (2005, July 29). The role of social groups in the persistence of learned fear. *Science, 309*, 785–787.

Olsson, A., Nearing, K. I., & Phelps, E. A. (2007). Learning fears by observing others: The neural systems of social fear transmission. *Social Cognitive and Affective Neuroscience Advance Access, 2*, 3–11.

Olsson, A., & Phelps, E. A. (2007). Social learning of fear. *Nature Neuroscience, 10*, 1095–1102.

Oltmanns, T. F., Martin, M. T., Neale, J. M., & Davison, G. C. (2009). *Case studies in abnormal psychology.* Hoboken, NJ: Wiley.

Onishi, K. H., & Baillargeon, R. (2005, April 8). Do 15-month-old infants understand false beliefs? *Science, 308*, 255–258.

Ortigue, S., Bianchi-Demicheli, F., Hamilton, C., & Grafton, S. T. (2007, July). The neural basis of love as a subliminal prime: An event-related functional magnetic resonance imaging study. *Journal of Cognitive Neuroscience, 19*(7), 1218–1230.

Osterling, J., & Dawson, G. (1994). Early recognition of children with autism: A study of first birthday home videotapes. *Journal of Autism and Developmental Disorders, 24*, 247–257.

Ottieger, A. E., Tressell, P. A., Inciardi, J. A., & Rosales, T. A. (1992). Cocaine use patterns and overdose. *Journal of Psychoactive Drugs, 24*, 399–410.

Owen, A. M., Coleman, M. R., Boly, M., Davis, M. H., Laureys, S., & Pickard, J. D. (2006). Detecting awareness in the vegetative state. *Science, 313*, 1402.

Owen, A. M., Hampshire, A., Grahn, J. A., Stenton, R., Dajani, S., Burns, A. S., Howard, R. J., & Ballard, C. G. (2010). Putting brain training to the test. *Nature, 465*(7299), 775–778 doi:10.1038/nature09042

Pack, A.I., & Pien, G.W. (2011). Update on sleep and its disorders. *Annual Review of Medicine, 62*, 447–460.

Padberg, F., & George, M. S. (2009). Repetitive transcranial magnetic stimulation of the prefrontal cortex in depression. *Experimental Neurology, 219*, 2–13.

Pagnoni, G., & Cekic, M. (2007). Age effects on gray matter volume and attentional performance in Zen meditation. *Neurobiology of Aging, 28*, 1623–1627.

Panksepp, J. (1992). Oxytocin effects on emotional processes: Separation distress, social bonding, and relationships to psychiatric disorders. *Annals of the New York Academy of Sciences, 652*, 243–252.

Papadimitriou, G. N., Zervas, I. M., & Papakostas, Y. G. (2001). Unilateral ECT for prophylaxis in affective illness. *Journal of ECT, 17*, 229–231.

Paquette, V., Levesque, J., Mensour, B., Leroux, J. M., Beaudoin, G., Bourgouin, P., et al. (2003). "Change the mind and you change the brain": Effects of cognitive-behavioral therapy on the neural correlates of spider phobia. *Neuroimage, 18*, 401–409.

Pascual-Leone, A., Catala, M. D., & Pascual-Leone, P. A. (1996). Lateralized effect of rapid-rate transcranial magnetic stimulation of the prefrontal cortex on mood. *Neurology, 46*, 499–502.

Pasupathi, M., & Carstensen, L. L. (2003). Age and emotional experience during mutual reminiscing. *Psychology and Aging, 18*, 430–442.

Patterson, B. W. (2004). The "tyranny of the eyewitness." *Law & Psychology Review, 28*, 195–203.

Patterson, C. M., & Newman, J. P. (1993). Reflectivity and learning from aversive events: Toward a psychological mechanism for the syndromes of disinhibition. *Psychological Review, 100*, 716–736.

Patterson, D., & Jensen, M. (2003). Hypnosis and clinical pain. *Psychological Bulletin, 129*(4), 495–521.

Paul-Labrador, M., Polk, D., Dwyer, J. H., Velasquez, I., Nidich, S., Rainforth, M., et al. (2006). Effects of a randomized controlled trial of transcendental meditation on components of the metabolic syndrome in subjects with coronary heart disease. *Archives of Internal Medicine, 166*, 1218–1224.

Pauls, D. L. (2008). The genetics of obsessive compulsive disorder: A review of the evidence. *American Journal of Medical Genetics, 148C*, 133–139.

Paunonen, S. V., & Ashton, M. C. (2001). Big five factors and facets and the prediction of behavior. *Journal of Personality and Social Psychology, 81*, 524–539.

Pavlov, I. P. (1927). *Conditioned reflexes: An investigation of the physiological activity of the cerebral cortex.* (Translated and edited by G. V. Anrep.) London: Oxford University Press; Humphrey Milford.

Pavot, W., & Diener, E. (1993). Review of the satisfaction with life scale. *Psychological Assessment, 5*, 164–172.

Paykel, E. S. (2003). Life events and affective disorders. *Acta Psychiatrica Scandinavica, 108*, 61–66.

Payne, B. K. (2001). Prejudice and perception: The role of automatic and controlled processes in misperceiving a weapon. *Journal of Personality and Social Psychology, 81*, 181–192.

Payne, B. K., Krosnick, J. A., Pasek, J., Lelkes, Y., Akhtar, O., & Tompson, T. (2010) Implicit and explicit prejudice in the 2008 American presidential election. *Journal of Experimental Social Psychology, 46*, 367–374.

Paz-Elizur, T., Krupsky, M., Blumenstein, S., Elinger, D., Schechtman, E., & Livneh, Z. (2003). DNA repair activity for oxidative damage and risk of lung cancer. *Journal of the National Cancer Institute, 95*, 1312–1331.

Pegna, A. J., Khateb, A., Lazeyras, F., & Seghier, M. L. (2005). Discriminating emotional faces without primary visual cortices involves the right amygdala. *Nature Neuroscience, 8*, 24–25.

Pelham, W. E., McBurnett, K., Harper, G. W., Milich, R., Murphy, D. A., Clinton, J., et al. (1990). Methylphenidate and baseball playing in ADHD children: Who's on first? *Journal of Consulting and Clinical Psychology, 58*, 130–133.

Penacoli, J. (2011). "Extra's" Jerry Penacoli to Michael Douglas: Your story inspired me. Retrieved from http://extratv.warnerbros.com/2011/01/extras_jerry_penacoli_to_michael_douglas_your_story_inspired_me.php

Penfield, W., & Jasper, H. (1954). *Epilepsy and the functional anatomy of the human brain.* Boston: Little, Brown.

Pennebaker, J. W. (1990). *Opening up: The healing power of confiding in others.* New York: Morrow.

Pennebaker, J. W. (1995). *Emotion, disclosure, & health.* Washington, DC: American Psychological Association.

Pennebaker, J. W., Barger, S. D., & Tiebout, J. (1989). Disclosure of traumas and health among Holocaust survivors. *Psychosomatic Medicine, 51*(5), 577–589.

Pennebaker, J. W., & Beall, S. K. (1986). Confronting a traumatic event: Toward an understanding of inhibition and disease. *Journal of Abnormal Psychology, 95*, 274–281.

Pennebaker, J. W., Mayne, T. J., & Francis, M. E. (1997). Linguistic predictors of adaptive bereavement. *Journal of Personality and Social Psychology, 72*, 863–871.

Pennisi, E. (2007, December 21). Breakthrough of the year. Human genetic variation. *Science, 318*, 1842–1843.

Penton-Voak, I. S., Perrett, D. I., Castles, D., Burt, M., Koyabashi, T., & Murray, L. K. (1999). Female preference for male faces changes cyclically. *Nature, 399*, 741–742.

Peretz, I. (1996). Can we lose memory for music? A case of music agnosia in a nonmusician. *Journal of Cognitive Neuroscience, 8*, 481–496.

Peretz, I., & Zatorre, R. J. (2005). Brain organization for music processing. *Annual Review of Psychology, 56*, 89–114.

Perez-Stable, E. J., Marin, G., & Marin, B. V. (1994). Behavioral risk factors: Comparison of Latinos and non-Latino whites in San Francisco. *American Journal of Public Health, 84*, 971–976.

Perkins, W. J. (2007, February/March). How does anesthesia work? *Scientific American Mind*, 84.

Perrett, D. I., May, K. A., & Yoshikawa, S. (1994). Facial shape and judgments of female attractiveness. *Nature, 368*, 239–242.

Perry, B. D. (2002). Childhood experience and the expression of genetic potential: What childhood neglect tells us about nature and nurture. *Brain and Mind, 3*, 79–100.

Pessiglione, M., Schmidt, L., Draganski, B., Kalisch, R., Lau, H., Dolan, R. J., et al. (2007, May 11). How the brain translates money into force: A neuroimaging study of subliminal motivation. *Science, 316*, 904–906.

Petitto, L. A. (2000). On the biological foundations of human language. In H. Lane & K. Emmorey (Eds.), *The signs of language revisited* (pp. 447–471). Mahwah, NJ: Erlbaum.

Petitto, L. A., & Seidenberg, M. S. (1979). On the evidence for linguistic abilities in signing apes. *Brain and Language, 8*, 162–183.

Petrie, K. J., Fontanilla, I., Thomas, M. G., Booth, R. J., & Pennebaker, J. W. (2004). Effect of written emotional expression on immune function in patients with human immunodeficiency virus infection: A randomized trial. *Psychosomatic Medicine, 66,* 272–275.

Petronis, A., & Kennedy, J. L. (1995). Unstable genes—Unstable mind? *American Journal of Psychiatry, 152,* 164–172.

Petty, R. E., & Cacioppo, J. T. (1986). *Communication and persuasion: Central and peripheral routes to attitude change.* New York: Springer-Verlag.

Petty, R. E., & Wegener, D. T. (1998). Attitude change: Multiple roles for persuasion variables. In D. T. Gilbert, S. T. Fiske, & G. Lindzey (Eds.), *The handbook of social psychology* (4th ed., pp. 323–390). Boston: McGraw-Hill.

Pezdek, K., & Hodge, D. (1999). Planting false childhood memories in children: The role of event plausibility. *Child Development, 70,* 887–895.

Pfaus, J. G. (2009). Pathways of sexual desire. *Journal of Sex Medicine, 6,* 1506–1533.

Phelan, J. (2006). Foreword. In A. Ziv, *Breeding between the lines: Why inter-racial people are healthier and more attractive.* Lanham, MD: National Book Network.

Phelps, E. A. (2004). Human emotion and memory: Interactions of the amygdala and hippocampal complex. *Current Opinion in Neurobiology, 14,* 198–202.

Phelps, E. A. (2006). Emotion and cognition: Insights from studies of the human amygdala. *Annual Review of Psychology, 57,* 27–53.

Phelps, E. A., Ling, S., & Carrasco, M. (2006). Emotion facilitates perception and potentiates the perceptual benefits of attention. *Psychological Science, 17,* 292–299.

Phinney, J. S. (1990). Ethnic identity in adolescents and adults: Review of research. *Psychological Bulletin, 108,* 499–514.

Piet, J., & Hougaard E. (2011). The effect of mindfulness-based cognitive therapy for prevention of relapse in recurrent major depressive disorder: A systematic review and meta-analysis. *Clinical Psychology Review, 31*(6), 1032–1040. doi 10.1016/j.cpr.2011.05.002

Pilcher, J. J., & Huffcutt, A. I. (1996). Effects of sleep deprivation on performance: A meta-analysis. *Sleep, 19*(4), 318–326.

Pinker, S. (1984). *Language learnability and language development.* Cambridge, MA: Harvard University Press.

Pinker, S. (1994). *The language instinct.* New York: Morrow.

Pinto, D., Pagnamenta, A. T., Klei, L., Anney, R., Merico, D., Regan, R., et al. (2010). Functional impact of global rare copy number variation in autism spectrum disorders. *Nature.* Published online June 9, 2010. doi:10.1038/nature09146

Pitman, R., Sanders, K., Zusman, R., Healy, A., Cheema, F., Lasko, N., et al. (2002). Pilot study of secondary prevention of post-traumatic stress disorder with propranolol. *Biological Psychiatry, 51,* 189–192.

Plakun, E. M., Burkhardt, P. E., & Muller, A. P. (1985). Fourteen-year follow-up of borderline and schizotypal personality disorders. *Comprehensive Psychiatry, 26,* 448–455.

Plant, E. A., Hyde, J. S., Keltner, D., & Devine, P. G. (2000). The gender stereotyping of emotions. *Psychology of Women Quarterly, 24,* 81–92.

Plant, E. A., & Peruche, M. (2005). The consequences of race for police officers' responses to criminal suspects. *Psychological Science, 16,* 180–183.

Plomin, R., & Caspi, A. (1999). Behavioral genetics and personality. In L. A. Pervin & O. P. John (Eds.), *Handbook of personality: Theory and research* (2nd ed., pp. 251–276). New York: Guilford Press.

Plomin, R., & Spinath, F. M. (2004). Intelligence: Genetics, genes, and genomics. *Journal of Personality and Social Psychology, 86,* 112–129.

Polivy, J., & Herman, C. P. (1985). Dieting and bingeing: A causal analysis. *American Psychologist, 40,* 193–201.

Polivy, J., & Herman, C. P. (2002). Causes of eating disorders. *Annual Review of Psychology, 53,* 187–213.

Pollock, K. M. (2004). Exercise in treating depression: Broadening the psychotherapist's role. *Journal of Clinical Psychology, 57,* 1289–1300.

Poma, P. A. (1983). Hispanic cultural influences on medical practice. *Journal of the National Medical Association, 75,* 941–946.

Pope, H. G., Jr., Kouri, E. M., & Hudson, J. I. (2000). Effects of supraphysiologic doses of testosterone on mood and aggression in normal men: A randomized controlled trial. *Archives of General Psychiatry, 57,* 133–140.

Posner, M. I., & DiGirolamo, G. J. (2000). Cognitive neuroscience: Origins and promise. *Psychological Bulletin, 126,* 873–889.

Premack, D. (1959). Toward empirical behavior laws: 1. Positive reinforcement. *Psychological Review, 66*(4), 219–233.

Premack, D. (1970). Mechanisms of self-control. In W. A. Hunt (Ed.), *Learning mechanisms in smoking* (pp. 107–123). Chicago: Aldine.

Prentiss, D., Power, R., Balmas, G., Tzuang, G., & Israelski, D. (2004). Patterns of marijuana use among patients with HIV/AIDS followed in a public health care setting. *Journal of Acquired Immune Deficiency Syndromes, 35*(1), 38–45.

Press, C., Cook, J., Blakemore, S. J., & Kilner, J. (2011). Dynamic properties of the perception-action matching system. *Journal of Neuroscience, 31,* 2792–2800.

Price, D. D., Harkins, S. W., & Baker, C. (1987). Sensory-affective relationships among different types of clinical and experimental pain. *Pain, 28,* 297–307.

Program on International Policy Attitudes (PIPA)/Knowledge Networks Poll. (2004, October 21). *Bush supporters still believe Iraq had WMD or major program, supported al Qaeda* [Press release]. Retrieved from http://www.pipa.org/OnlineReports/Iraq/IraqRealities_Oct04/IraqRealitiesOct04rpt.pdf

Provencher, V., Polivy, J., & Herman, C. P. (2009). Perceived healthiness of food: If it's healthy, you can eat more! *Appetite 2009, 52,* 340–344.

Psychological Review, 88, 354–364. doi: 10.1037/0033-295X.88.4.354

Pyszczynski, T., Greenberg, J., Solomon, S., Arndt, J., & Schimel, J. (2004). Why do people need self-esteem? A theoretical and empirical review. *Psychological Bulletin, 130,* 435–468.

Raesaenen, S., Pakaslahti, A., Syvaelahti, E., Jones, P. B., & Isohanni, M. (2000). Sex differences in schizophrenia: A review. *Nordic Journal of Psychiatry, 54,* 37–45.

Raine, A. (1989). Evoked potentials and psychopathy. *International Journal of Psychopathology, 8,* 1–16.

Raine, A., Mellingen, K., Liu, J., Venables, P., & Mednick, S. A. (2003). Effects of environmental enrichment at ages 3–5 years on schizotypal personality and antisocial behavior at ages 17 and 23 years. *American Journal of Psychiatry, 160,* 1627–1635.

Rainville, P., Duncan, G. H., Price, D. D., Carrier, B., & Bushnell, M. C. (1997, August 15). Pain affect encoded in human anterior cingulate but not somatosensory cortex. *Science, 277,* 968–971.

Rainville, P., Hofbauer, R. K., Bushnell, M. C., Duncan, G. H., & Price, D. D. (2002). Hypnosis modulates activity in brain structures involved in the regulation of consciousness. *Journal of Cognitive Neuroscience, 14,* 887–901.

Raleigh, M. J., McGuire, M. T., Brammer, G. L., Pollack, D. B., & Yuwiler, A. (1991). Serotonergic mechanisms promote dominance in adult male vervet monkeys. *Brain Research, 559,* 181–190.

Ram, S., Seirawan, H., Kumar, S.K., & Clark, G.T. (2010). Prevalence and impact of sleep disorders and sleep habits in the United States. *Sleep Breath, 14,* 63–70.

Ramachandran, V. S., & Hirstein, W. (1998). The perception of phantom limbs: The D. O. Hebb lecture. *Brain, 121,* 1603–1630.

Ramachandran, V. S., & Hubbard, E. M. (2001). Psychophysical investigations into the neural basis of synaesthesia. *Proceedings of the Royal Society of London, 268B,* 979–983.

Ramachandran, V. S., & Hubbard, E. M. (2003, May). Hearing colors, tasting shapes: Color-coded world. *Scientific American, 288*(5), 42–49.

Rampon, C., Jiang, C. H., Dong, H., Tang, Y., Lockhart, D. J., Schultz, P. G., et al. (2000). Effects of environmental enrichment on gene expression in the brain. *Proceedings of the National Academy of Sciences, USA, 97,* 12880–12884.

Ramsden, S. R., & Hubbard, J. A. (2002). Family expressiveness and family emotion coaching: Their role in children's emotion regulation and aggression. *Journal of Abnormal Child Psychology, 30,* 657–667. doi: 10.1023/A:1020819915881

Rapoport, J. L. (1989, March). The biology of obsessions and compulsions. *Scientific American, 260,* 83–89.

Rapoport, J. L. (1990). *The boy who couldn't stop washing: The experience and treatment of obsessive-compulsive disorder.* New York: Penguin.

Rapoport, J. L. (1991). Recent advances in obsessive-compulsive disorder. *Neuropsychopharmacology, 5,* 1–10.

Rapport, M. D., & Moffitt, C. (2002). Attention-deficit/hyperactivity disorder and methylphenidate: A review of the height/weight, cardiovascular, and somatic complaint side effects. *Clinical Psychology Review, 22,* 1107–1131.

Rauch, S. L., van der Kolk, B. A., Fisler, R. E., & Alpert, N. M. (1996). A symptom provocation study of posttraumatic stress disorder using positron emission tomography and script-driven imagery. *Archives of General Psychiatry, 53,* 380–387.

Rauscher, F. H., Shaw, G. L., & Ky, K. N. (1993). Music and spatial task performance. *Nature, 365,* 611.

Raynor, H. A., & Epstein, L. H. (2001). Dietary variety, energy regulation, and obesity. *Psychological Bulletin, 127,* 325–341.

Raz, A., Fan, J., & Posner, M. I. (2005). Hypnotic suggestion reduces conflict in the human brain. *Proceedings of the National Academy of Sciences, USA, 102,* 9978–9983.

Raz, A., Shapiro, T., Fan, J., & Posner, M. I. (2002, December). Hypnotic suggestion and the modulation of Stroop interference. *Archives of General Psychiatry, 59,* 1155–1161.

Read, J. P., & Brown, R. A. (2003). The role of exercise in alcoholism treatment and recovery. *Professional Psychology: Research and Practice, 34,* 49–56.

Reddy, L., Tsuchiya, N., & Serre, T. (2010). Reading the mind's eye: Decoding category information during mental information. *Neuroimage, 50,* 818–825.

Reeves, L. M., & Weisberg, R. W. (1994). The role of content and abstract information in analogical transfer. *Psychological Bulletin, 115,* 381–400.

Regard, M., & Landis, T. (1997). "Gourmand syndrome": Eating passion associated with right anterior lesions. *Neurology, 48,* 1185–1190.

Reichenberg, A., & Harvey, P. D. (2007). Neuropsychological impairments in schizophrenia: Integration of performance-based and brain imaging findings. *Psychological Bulletin, 133,* 833–858.

Reinders, A. A., Nijenhuis, E. R., Paans, A. M., Korf, J., Willemsen, A. T., & den Boer, J. A. (2003). One brain, two selves. *Neuroimage, 20,* 2119–2125.

Reis, D. L., Brackett, M. A., Shamosh, N. A., Kiehl, K. A., Salovey, P., & Gray, J. R. (2007). Emotional intelligence predicts individual differences in social exchange reasoning. *Neuroimage, 35,* 1385–1391.

Reis, H. X, Wheeler, L., Spiegel, N., Kernis, M. H., Nezlek, J., & Perri, M. (1982). Physical attractiveness in social interaction: II. Why does appearance affect social experience? *Journal of Personality and Social Psychology, 43,* 979–996.

Renfrow, P. J., & Gosling, S. D. (2003). The do re mi's of everyday life: The structure and personality correlates of music preferences. *Journal of Personality and Social Psychology, 84,* 1236–1256.

Rescorla, R. (1966). Predictability and number of pairings in Pavlovian fear conditioning. *Psychonomic Science, 4,* 383–384.

Rescorla, R. A., & Wagner, A. R. (1972). A theory of Pavlovian conditioning: Variations in the effectiveness of reinforcement and non-reinforcement. In A. H. Black & W. F. Prokosy (Eds.), *Classical conditioning II: Current research and theory* (pp. 64–99). New York: Appleton-Century-Crofts.

Ressler, K. J., & Mayberg, H. S. (2007). Targeting abnormal neural circuits in mood and anxiety disorders: From the laboratory to the clinic. *Nature Neuroscience, 10,* 1116–1124.

Revonsuo, A. (2000). *Prospects for a scientific research program on consciousness—Neural correlates of consciousness.* Cambridge, MA: MIT Press.

Reyna, C., Brandt, M., & Viki, G. T. (2009). Blame it on hip-hop: Anti-rap attitudes as a proxy for prejudice. *Group Process and Intergroup Relations, 12,* 361–380.

Rhodewalt, F., & Morf, C. C. (1998). On self-aggrandizement and anger: A temporal analysis of narcissism and affective reactions to success and failure. *Journal of Personality and Social Psychology, 74,* 672–685.

Richman, L. S., Kubzansky, L., Maselko, J., Kawachi, I., Choo, P., & Bauer, M. (2005). Positive emotion and health: Going beyond the negative. *Health Psychology, 24*(4), 422–429.

Ridley, M. (2003). *Nature versus nurture: Genes, experience, and what makes us human.* New York: HarperCollins.

Rifkin, A., & Rifkin, W. (2004). Adolescents with depression. *Journal of the American Medical Association, 292,* 2577–2578.

Rinck, M., Reinecke, A., Ellwart, T., Heuer, K., & Becker, E. S. (2005). Speeded detection and increased distraction in fear of spiders: Evidence from eye movements. *Journal of Abnormal Psychology, 114,* 235–248.

Rizzolatti, G., & Arbib, M. A. (1998). Language within our grasp. *Trends in Neuroscience, 21,* 188–194.

Rizzolatti, G., & Craighero, L. (2004). The mirror-neuron system. *Annual Reviews in Neuroscience, 27*, 169–192.

Rizzolatti, G., & Fabbri-Destro, M. (2010). Mirror neurons: From discovery to autism. *Experimental Brain Research, 200*, 223–237.

Rizzolatti, G., Fadiga, L., Gallese, V., & Fogassi, L. (1996). Premotor cortex and the recognition of motor actions. *Cognitive Brain Research, 3*, 131–141.

Roberts, B. W., & Friend-DelVecchio, W. (2000). The rank-order consistency of personality traits from childhood to old age: A quantitative review of longitudinal studies. *Psychological Bulletin, 126*, 3–25.

Roberts, B. W., Walton, K. E., & Viechtbauer, W. (2006). Patterns of mean-level change in personality traits across the life course: A meta-analysis of longitudinal studies. *Psychological Bulletin, 132*, 3–21.

Roberts, D. F. (2000). Media and youth: Access, exposure, and privatization. *Journal of Adolescent Health 27*(Suppl.), 8–14.

Roberts, S. (2006, November 15). A neuroscientist's life's work: Analyzing brains to study structure and cognition. *The New York Times.* Retrieved from http://www.nytimes.com

Robins, L. N., & Regier, D. A. (1991). *Psychiatric disorders in America: The epidemiological catchment areas study.* New York: Free Press.

Robins, L. N., Helzer, J. E., & Davis, D. H. (1975). Narcotic use in Southeast Asia and afterward: An interview study of 898 Vietnam returnees. *Archives of General Psychiatry, 32*, 955–961.

Robinson, T. E., & Berridge, K. C. (1993). The neural basis of drug craving: An incentive-sensitization theory of addiction. *Brain Research Reviews, 18*, 247–291.

Robles, T. F., & Kiecolt-Glaser, J. K. (2003). The physiology of marriage: Pathways to health. *Physiology & Behavior, 79*, 409–416.

Rock, I. (1984). *Perception.* New York: Scientific American Books.

Roediger, H. L., III, & Karpicke, J. D. (2006). The power of testing memory: Basic research and implications for educational practice. *Psychological Science, 1*, 181–210.

Roethlisberger, F. J., & Dickson, W. J. (1939). *Management and the worker: An account of a research program conducted by the Western Electric Company, Hawthorne Works, Chicago.* Cambridge, MA: Harvard University Press.

Rogan, M. T., Stäubli, U. V., & LeDoux, J. E. (1997). Fear conditioning induces associative long-term potentiation in the amygdala. *Nature, 390*, 604–607.

Rogers, T. B., Kuiper, N. A., & Kirker, W. S. (1977). Self-reference and the encoding of personal information. *Journal of Personality and Social Psychology, 35*, 677–688.

Roisman, G. I., Clausell, E., Holland, A., Fortuna, K., & Elieff, C. (2008). Adult romantic relationships as contexts of human development: A multimethod comparison of same-sex couples with opposite-sex dating, engaged, and married dyads. *Developmental Psychology, 44*, 91–101.

Rolls, B. J., Roe, L. S., & Meengs, J. S. (2007). The effect of large portion sizes on energy intake is sustained for 11 days. *Obesity Research, 15*, 1535–1543.

Rolls, E. T. (2007). Sensory processing in the brain related to the control of food intake. *Proceedings of the Nutritional Society, 66*, 96–112.

Rolls, E. T., Burton, M. J., & Mora, F. (1980). Neurophysiological analysis of brain-stimulation reward in the monkey. *Brain Research, 194*, 339–357.

Roscoe, W. (2000). *Changing ones: Third and fourth genders in native North America.* New York: St. Martins Griffin.

Rosenman, R. H., Brand, R. J., Jenkins, C. D., Friedman, M., Straus, R., & Wurm, M. (1975). Coronary heart disease in the Western Collaborative Group Study: Final follow-up experience of 8½ years. *Journal of the American Medical Association, 233*, 872–877.

Rosenman, R. H., Friedman, M., Straus, R., Wurm, M., Kositchek, R., Hahn, W., et al. (1964). A predictive study of heart disease. *Journal of the American Medical Association, 189*(1), 15–22.

Rosenstein, D., & Oster, H. (1988). Differential facial responses to four basic tastes in newborns. *Child Development, 59*, 1555–1568.

Rosenthal, R., & Fode, K. L. (1963). The effect of experimenter bias on the performance of the albino rat. Behavioral Science, 8, 183–189.

Rosenzweig, M. R., Bennett, E. L., & Diamond, M. C. (1972, February). Brain changes in response to experience. *Scientific American, 226*, 22–29.

Ross, H. E., & Young, L. J. (2009). Oxytocin and the neural mechanisms regulating social cognition and affiliative behavior. *Frontiers in Neuroendocrinology, 30*, 534–547.

Rothbaum, B. O., Hodges, L., Alarcon, R., Ready, D., Shahar, F., Graap, K., et al. (1999). Virtual reality exposure therapy for PTSD Vietnam veterans: A case study. *Journal of Traumatic Stress, 12*, 263–271.

Rothemund, Y., Preuschhof, C., Bohner, G., Bauknecht, H. C., Klingebiel, R., Flor, H., et al. (2007). Differential activation of the dorsal striatum by high-calorie visual food stimuli in obese individuals. *Neuroimage, 37*, 410–421.

Rotter, J. B. (1954). *Social learning and clinical psychology.* New York: Prentice-Hall.

Rovee-Collier, C. (1999). The development of infant memory. *Current Directions in Psychological Science, 8*, 80–85.

Rowe, D. C., Chassin, L., Presson, C., & Sherman, S. J. (1996). Parental smoking and the "epidemic" spread of cigarette smoking. *Journal of Applied Social Psychology, 26*, 437–445.

Roy, A. (1992). Are there genetic factors in suicide? *International Review of Psychiatry, 4*, 169–175.

Rozin, P. (1996). Sociocultural influences on human food selection. In E. D. Capaldi (Ed.), *Why we eat what we eat: The psychology of eating* (pp. 233–263). Washington, DC: American Psychological Association.

Rubenstein, A. J., Kalakanis, L., & Langlois, J. H. (1999). Infant preferences for attractive faces: A cognitive explanation. *Developmental Psychology, 35*, 848–855.

Rudman, L. A., & Goodwin, S. A. (2004). Gender differences in automatic in-group bias: Why do women like women more than men like men? *Journal of Personality and Social Psychology, 87*, 494–509.

Rupp, H. A., James, T. W., Ketterson, E. D., Sengelaub, D. R., Janssen, E., & Heiman, J. R. (2009). Neural activation in the orbitofrontal cortex in response to male faces increases during the follicular phase. *Hormones and Behavior, 56*, 66–72.

Rusbult, C. E., & Buunk, B. D. Commitment processes in close relationships: An interdependence analysis. *Journal of Social and Personal Relationships, 10*, 175–204.

Rusbult, C. E., & Van Lange, P. A. M. (1996). Interdependence processes. In E. T. Higgins & A. Kruglanski (Eds.), *Social psychology: Handbook of basic principles* (pp. 564–596). New York: Guilford Press.

Ruscio, A. M., Brown, T. A., Chiu, W. T., Sareen, J., Stein, M. B., & Kessler, R. C. (2008). Social fears and social phobia in the USA: Results from the national comorbidity survey replication. *Psychological Medicine, 35*, 15–28.

Russell, C. A., Clapp, J. D., & Dejong, W. (2005). Done 4: Analysis of a failed social norms marketing campaign. *Health Communication, 17*(1), 57–65.

Russell, J. A. (1980). A circumplex model of affect. *Journal of Personality and Social Psychology, 39,* 1161–1178.

Russell, J. A. (1994). Is there universal recognition of emotion from facial expressions? A review of the cross-cultural studies. *Psychological Bulletin, 115,* 102–141.

Russell, M. A. H. (1990). The nicotine trap: A 40-year sentence for four cigarettes. *British Journal of Addiction, 85,* 293–300.

Russo, N.F., & Denmark, F. L. (1987). Contributions of women to psychology. *Annual Review of Psychology, 38,* 279–298.

Rutgers, A. H., Bakermans-Kranenburg, M. J., van Ijzendoorn, M. H., & van Berckelaer-Onnes, I. A. (2004). Autism and attachment: A meta-analytic review. *Journal of Child Psychology and Psychiatry, 45,* 1123–1134. doi: 10.1111/j.1469-7610.2004.t01-1-00305.x

Rutter, M. (2005). Incidence of autism disorders: Changes over time and their meaning. *Acta Paediatrica, 94,* 2–15.

Rymer, R. (1993). *Genie: A scientific tragedy.* New York: HarperCollins.

Sabol, S. Z., Nelson, M. L., Fisher, C., Gunzerath, L., Brody, C. L., Hu, S., et al. (1999). A genetic association for cigarette smoking behavior. *Health Psychology, 18,* 7–13.

Sacks, O. (1995). *An anthropologist on Mars: Seven paradoxical tales.* New York: Knopf.

Saha, S., Chant, D. C., Welham, J. L., & McGrath, J. J. (2006). The incidence and prevalence of schizophrenia varies with latitude. *Acta Psychiatrica Scandinavica, 114,* 36–39.

Salimpoor, V. N., Benovoy, M., Larcher, K., Dagher, A., & Zatorre, R.J. (2011). Anatomically distinct dopamine release during anticipation and experience of peak emotion to music. *Nature Neuroscience, 14,* 257–262. *doi:*10.1038/nn.2726

Salovey, P., & Grewel, D. (2005). The science of emotional intelligence. *Current Directions in Psychological Science, 14,* 281–286.

Salovey, P., & Mayer, J. D. (1990). Emotional intelligence. *Imagination, Cognition, and Personality, 9,* 185–211.

Salthouse, T. (1992). The information-processing perspective on cognitive aging. In R. Sternberg & C. Berg (Eds.), *Intellectual development* (pp. 261–277). Cambridge, UK: Cambridge University Press.

Salum, G. A., Polanczyk, G. V., Miguel, E. C., & Rohde, L. A. (2010). Effects of childhood development on late-life mental disorders. *Current Opinion in Psychiatry, 23,* 498–503.

SAMHSA (2011). Major depressive episode and treatment among adolescents: 2009. *National Survey on Drug Use and Health.* Accessed at http://www.oas.samhsa.gov/2k11/009/AdolescentDepression.htm

Sanderson, W. C., & Barlow, D. H. (1990). A description of patients diagnosed with DSM-III-R generalized anxiety disorder. *The Journal of Nervous and Mental Disease, 178,* 588–591.

Sapolsky, R. M. (1994). *Why zebras don't get ulcers.* New York: Freeman.

Sargent, J. D., Beach, M. L., Adachi-Mejia, A. M., Gibson, J. J., Titus-Ernstoff, L. T., Carusi, C. P., et al. (2005). Exposure to movie smoking: Its relation to smoking initiation among US adolescents. *Pediatrics, 116,* 1183–1191.

Savic, I., Berglund, H., & Lindström, P. (2005). Brain responses to putative pheromones in homosexual men. *Proceedings of the National Academy of Sciences, USA, 102,* 7356–7361.

Savitz, D. A., Schwingle, P. J., & Keels, M. A. (1991). Influences of paternal age, smoking, and alcohol consumption on congenital anomalies. *Teratology, 44,* 429–440.

Sayette, M. A. (1993). An appraisal-disruption model of alcohol's effects on stress responses in social drinkers. *Psychological Bulletin, 114,* 459–476.

Scarr, S., & McCarthy, K. (1983). How people make their own environments: A theory of genotype l environment effects. *Child Development, 54,* 424–435.

Schab, F. R. (1991). Odor memory: Taking stock. *Psychological Bulletin, 109,* 242–251.

Schachter, H. M., Pham, B., King, J., Langford, S., & Moher, D. (2001). How efficacious and safe is short-acting methylphenidate for the treatment of attention-deficit hyperactivity disorder in children and adolescents? A meta-analysis. *Canadian Medical Association Journal, 165,* 1475–1488.

Schachter, S. (1951). Deviation, rejection, and communication. *Journal of Abnormal Psychology, 46,* 190–207.

Schachter, S. (1959). *The psychology of affiliation.* Stanford, CA: Stanford University Press.

Schachter, S., & Singer, J. (1962). Cognitive, social, and physiological determinants of emotional state. *Psychological Review, 69,* 379–399.

Schacter, D. L. (1996). *Searching for memory: The brain, the mind, and the past.* New York: Basic Books.

Schacter, D. L. (1999). The seven sins of memory: Insights from psychology and cognitive neuroscience. *American Psychologist, 54,* 182–203.

Schacter, D. L. (2001). *The seven sins of memory: How the mind forgets and remembers.* Boston: Houghton Mifflin.

Schacter, D. L., & Tulving, E. (1994). What are the memory systems of 1994? In D. L. Schacter & E. Tulving (Eds.), *Memory systems 1994* (pp. 1–38). Cambridge, MA: MIT Press.

Schaie, K. W. (1990). Intellectual development in adulthood. In J. E. Birren & K. W. Schaie (Eds.), *Handbook of the psychology of aging* (3rd ed., pp. 291–319). New York: Van Nostrand Reinhold.

Schank, R. C., & Abelson, R. P. (1977). *Scripts, plans, goals, and understanding.* Hillsdale, NJ: Erlbaum.

Scheerer, M. (1963). Problem-solving. *Scientific American, 208,* 118–128.

Schiffman, J., Walker, E., Ekstrom, M., Schulsinger, F., Sorensen, H., & Mednick, S. (2004). Childhood videotaped social and neuromotor precursors of schizophrenia: A prospective investigation. *American Journal of Psychiatry, 161,* 2021–2027.

Schiller, D., Monfils, M., Raio, C., Johnson, D., LeDoux, J. E., & Phelps, E. A. (2010). Preventing the return of fear in humans using reconsolidation update mechanisms. *Nature, 463,* 49–54.

Schimel, J., Hayes, J., Williams, T. J., & Jahrig, J. (2007). Is death really the worm at the core? Converging evidence that worldview threat increases death-thought accessibility. *Journal of Personality and Social Psychology, 92,* 789–803.

Schmader, T. (2010). Stereotype threat deconstructed. *Current Directions in Psychological Science, 19,* 14–18.

Schmader, T., Johns, M., & Forbes, C. (2008). An integrated process model of stereotype threat effects on performance. *Psychological Review, 115,* 336–356.

Schmajuk, N. A., Lamoureux, J. A., & Holland, P. C. (1998). Occasion setting: A neural network approach. *Psychological Review, 105,* 3–32.

Schmidt, F. L., & Hunter, J. (2004). General mental ability in the world of work: Occupational attainment and job performance. *Journal of Personality and Social Psychology, 96*, 162–173.

Schmidt, N. B., & Keough, M. E. (2011). Treatment of panic. *Annual Review of Clinical Psychology, 6*, 241–256.

Schmitt, D. P., Alcalay, L., Allik, J., Angleitner, A., Ault, L., Austers, I., et al. (2003). Universal sex differences in the desire for sexual variety: Tests from 52 nations, 6 continents, and 13 islands. *Journal of Personality and Social Psychology, 85*, 85–104.

Schmitt, D. P., Allik, J., McCrae, R. R., & Benet-Martinez, V. (2007). The geographic distribution of big five personality traits: Patterns and profiles of human self-description across 56 nations. *Journal of Cross-Cultural Psychology, 38*, 173–212.

Schmitt, D. P., Realo, A., Voracek, M., & Allik, J. (2008). Why can't a man be more like a woman? *Journal of Personality and Social Psychology, 94*, 168–182.

Schmitz, T. W., De Rosa, E., & Anderson, A. K. (2009). Opposing influences of affective state valence in visual cortical encoding. *Journal of Neuroscience, 29*, 7199–7207.

Schneider, B., & Csikszentmihalyi, M. (2000). *Becoming adult: How teenagers prepare for the world of work*. New York: Basic Books.

Schoenemann, P. T., Sheehan, M. J., & Glotzer, L. D. (2005). Prefrontal white matter volume is disproportionally larger in humans than in other primates. *Nature Neuroscience, 8*, 242–252.

Schreiber, F. R. (1974). *Sybil: The true story of a woman possessed by sixteen personalities*. London: Penguin.

Schultz, P. W., Nolan, J. M., Cialdini, R. B., Goldstein, N. J., & Griskevicius, V. (2007). The constructive, destructive, and reconstructive power of social norms. *Psychological Science, 18*, 429–434.

Schultz, W. (2010). Dopamine signals for reward value and risk: Basic and recent data. *Behavioral and Brain Functions, 6*(24): 1–9.

Schulz, K. P., Fan, J., Tang, C. Y., Newcorn, J. H., Buchsbaum, M. S., Cheung, A. M., et al. (2004). Response inhibition in adolescents diagnosed with attention deficit hyperactivity disorder during childhood: An event-related fMRI study. *American Journal of Psychiatry, 161*, 1650–1657.

Schuur, Diane. (1999, June 14). Heroes and icons: Helen Keller. *Time*. Retrieved from http://www.time.com/time/time100/heroes/profile/keller01.html

Schwartz, B. (2004). *The paradox of choice: Why more is less*. New York: Ecco.

Schwartz, C. E., Wright, C. I., Shin, L. M., Kagan, J., & Rauch, S. L. (2003, June 20). Inhibited and uninhibited infants "grown up": Adult amygdalar response to novelty. *Science, 300*, 1952–1953.

Schwartz, J. M., Stoessel, P. W., Baxter, L. R., Martin, K. M., & Phelps, M. E. (1996). Systematic changes in cerebral glucose metabolic rate after successful behavior modification treatment of obsessive-compulsive disorder. *Archives of General Psychiatry, 53*, 109–113.

Schwartz, S., & Maquet, P. (2002). Sleep imaging and the neuropsychological assessment of dreams. *Trends in Cognitive Sciences, 6*, 23–30.

Schwarz, N., & Clore, G. L. (1983). Mood, misattribution, and judgments of well-being: Informative and directive functions of affective states. *Journal of Personality and Social Psychology, 45*, 513–523.

Scislowska, M. (2007, June 4). Man wakes from 19-year coma to "prettier" Poland. Railway worker is shocked at radical changes. *Associated Press*. Retrieved from http://www.associatedpress.com

Sclafani, A., & Springer, D. (1976). Dietary obesity in adult rats: Similarities to hypothalamic and human obesity syndromes. *Physiology and Behavior, 17*, 461–471.

Sedikides, C., Gaertner, L., & Toguchi, Y. (2003). Pancultural self-enhancement. *Journal of Personality and Social Psychology, 84*, 60–79.

Sedikides, C., & Gregg, A. (2008). Self-enhancement: Food for thought. *Perspectives on Psychological Science, 3*, 102–116.

Sedlmeier, P., & Gigerenzer, G. (1997). Intuitions about sample size: The empirical law of large numbers. *Journal of Behavioral Decision Making, 10*, 33–51.

Seegmiller, J. K., Watson, J. M., & Strayer, D. L. (2011, February 7). Individual differences in susceptibility to inattentional blindness. *Journal of Experimental Psychology: Learning, Memory, and Cognition*. Advance online publication. doi: 10.1037/a0022474

Segerstrom, S. C., & Miller, G. E. (2004). Psychological stress and the human immune system: A meta-analytic study of 30 years of inquiry. *Psychological Bulletin, 130*, 601–630.

Seguin, J. R. (2004). Neurocognitive elements of antisocial behavior: Relevance of an orbitofrontal cortex account. *Brain and Cognition, 55*, 185–197.

Seligman, M. E. P. (1970). On the generality of the laws of learning. *Psychological Review, 77*, 406–418.

Seligman, M. E. P. (1974). Depression and learned helplessness. In R. J. Friedman & M. M. Katz (Eds.), *The psychology of depression: Contemporary theory and research* (pp. 83–113). Washington, DC: V. H. Winston.

Seligman, M. E. P. (1975). *Helplessness: On depression, development, and death*. San Francisco: Freeman.

Seligman, M. E. P. (2011). *Flourish*. New York: Simon & Schuster.

Seligman, M. E. P., & Csikszentmihalyi, M. (2000). Positive psychology: An introduction. *American Psychologist, 55*, 5–14.

Seligman, M. E. P., Steen, T. A., Park, N., & Peterson, C. (2005). Positive psychology progress: Empirical validation of interventions. *American Psychologist, 60*, 410–421.

Seligman, M. E. P., Walker, E. F., & Rosenhan, D. L. (2001). *Abnormal psychology*. New York: Norton.

Shah, R. S., Chang, S., Min, H., Cho, Z., Blaha, C., & Lee, K. H. (2010). Deep brain stimulation: Technology at the cutting edge. *Journal of Clinical Neurology, 6*, 167–182.

Shallice, T., & Warrington, E. (1969). Independent functioning of verbal memory stores. *Quarterly Journal of Experimental Psychology, 22*, 261–273.

Shapiro, A. F., Gottman, J. M., & Carrère, S. (2000). The baby and the marriage: Identifying factors that buffer against decline in marital satisfaction after the first baby arrives. *Journal of Family Psychology, 14*, 59–70. doi: 10.1037/0893-3200.14.1.59

Shedler, J. (2010). The efficacy of psychodynamic psychotherapy. *American Psychologist, 65*, 98–109.

Shedler, J., & Block, J. (1990). Adolescent drug use and psychological health: A longitudinal inquiry. *American Psychologist, 45*, 612–630.

Sheese, B. E., Brown, E. L., & Graziano, W. G. (2004). Emotional expression in cyberspace: Searching for moderators of the Pennebaker disclosure effect via e-mail. *Health Psychology, 23*, 457–464.

Shenkin, S. D., Starr, J. M., & Deary, I. J. (2004). Birth weight and cognitive ability in childhood: A systematic review. *Psychological Bulletin, 130*, 989–1013.

Shephard, R. J. (1997). *Aging, physical activity, and health*. Champaign, IL: Human Kinetics Publishers.

Sher, L. (2000). Sociopolitical events and technical innovations may affect the content of delusions and the course of psychotic disorders. *Medical Hypotheses, 55*, 507–509.

Sherif, M., Harvey, O. J., White, B. J., Hood, W. R., & Sherif, C. W. (1961). *Intergroup cooperation and competition: The Robbers Cave experiment.* Norman, OK: University Book Exchange.

Sherman, D. K., McGue, M. K., & Iacono, W. G. (1997). Twin concordance for attention deficit hyperactivity disorder: A comparison of teacher's and mother's reports. *American Journal of Psychiatry, 154*, 532–535.

Sherman, S. J., Presson, C., Chassin, L., Corty, E., & Olshavsky, R. (1983). The false consensus effect in estimates of smoking prevalence: Underlying mechanisms. *Personality and Social Psychology Bulletin, 9*, 197–207.

Sherwin, B. B. (1988). A comparative analysis of the role of androgen in human male and female sexual behavior: Behavioral specificity, critical thresholds, and sensitivity. *Psychobiology, 16*, 416–425.

Sherwin, B. B. (1994). Sex hormones and psychological functioning in postmenopausal women. *Experimental Gerontology, 29*, 423–430.

Sherwin, B. B. (2008). Hormones, the brain, and me. *Canadian Psychology, 49*, 42–48.

Sherwood, R. A., Keating, J., Kavvadia, V., Greenough, A., & Peters, T. J. (1999). Substance misuse in early pregnancy and relationship to fetal outcome. *European Journal of Pediatrics, 158*, 488–492.

Shettleworth, S. J. (2001). Animal cognition and animal behaviour. *Animal Behaviour, 61*, 277–286.

Shih, M., Pittinsky, T. L., & Ambady, N. (1999). Stereotype susceptibility: Identity salience and shifts in quantitative performance. *Psychological Science, 10*, 80–83.

Siegel, J. M. (2008). Do all animals sleep? *Trends in Neuroscience, 31*, 208–213.

Siegel, S. (1984). Pavlovian conditioning and heroin overdose: Reports by overdose victims. *Bulletin of the Psychonomic Society, 22*, 428–430.

Siegel, S. (2005). Drug tolerance, drug addiction, and drug anticipation. *Current Directions in Psychological Science, 14*(6), 296–300.

Siegel, S., Baptista, M. A. S., Kim, J. A., McDonald, R. V., & Weise-Kelly, L. (2000). Pavlovian psychopharmacology: The associative basis of tolerance. *Experimental and Clinical Psychopharmacology, 8*, 276–293.

Siegel, S., Hinson, R. E., Krank, M. D., & McCully, J. (1982). Heroin "overdose" death: Contribution of drug-associated environmental cues. *Science, 216*, 436–437.

Siegler, I. C., Costa, P. T., Brummett, B. H., Helms, M. J., Barefoot, J. C., Williams, R., et al. (2003). Patterns of change in hostility from college to midlife in the UNC alumni heart study predict high-risk status. *Psychosomatic Medicine, 65*, 738–745.

Sigurdsson, T., Doyère, V., Cain, C. K., & LeDoux, J. E. (2007). Long-term potentiation in the amygdala: A cellular mechanism of fear learning and memory. *Neuropharmacology, 52*, 215–227.

Silber, M., Ancoli-Israel, S., Bonnet, M., Chokroverty, S., Grigg-Damberger, M., Hirshkowitz, M., et al. (2007). The visual scoring of sleep in adults. *Journal of Clinical Sleep Medicine, 3*, 121–131.

Silbersweig, D., Clarkin, J. F., Goldstein, M., Kernberg, O. F., Tuescher, O., Levy, K. N., et al. (2007). Failure of frontolimbic inhibitory function in the context of negative emotion in borderline personality disorder. *American Journal of Psychiatry, 64*, 1832–1841.

Silva, C. E., & Kirsch, I. (1992). Interpretive sets, expectancy, fantasy proneness, and dissociation as predictors of hypnotic response. *Journal of Personality and Social Psychology, 63*, 847–856.

Simner, J., Mulvenna, C., Sagiv, N., Tsakanikos, E., Witherby, S. A., Fraser, C., et al. (2006). Synaesthesia: The prevalence of atypical cross-modal experiences. *Perception, 35*, 1024–1033.

Simon, T. (2003). Photographer's foreword to *The Innocents.* [Electronic version]. Retrieved from http://www.pbs.org/wgbh/pages/frontline/shows/burden/innocents/

Simons, D. J., & Ambinder, M. S. (2005). Change blindness: Theory and consequences. *Current Directions in Psychological Science, 14*, 44–48.

Simons, D. J., & Levin, D. T. (1998). Failure to detect changes to people during a real-world interaction. *Psychonomic Bulletin and Review, 5*, 644–649.

Simpson, H. B., Foa, E. B., Liebowitz, M. R., Ledley, D. R., Huppert, J. D., Cahill, S., et al. (2008). A randomized, controlled trial of cognitive-behavioral therapy for augmenting pharmacotherapy in obsessive-compulsive disorder. *American Journal of Psychiatry, 165*, 621–630.

Simpson, J. A., Collins, A., Tran, S., & Haydon, K. C. (2007). Attachment and the experience and expression of emotions in romantic relationships: A developmental perspective. *Journal of Personality and Social Psychology, 92*, 355–367.

Sims, H. E. A., Goldman, R. F., Gluck, C. M., Horton, E., Kelleher, P., & Rowe, D. (1968). Experimental obesity in man. *Transactions of the Association of American Physicians, 81*, 153–170.

Singer, T., Seymour, B., O'Doherty, J., Kaube, H., Dolan, R. J., & Frith, C. D. (2004, February 20). Empathy for pain involves the affective but not sensory components of pain. *Science, 303*, 1157–1162.

Sirois, B. C., & Burg, M. M. (2003). Negative emotion and coronary heart disease: A review. *Behavior Modification, 27*, 83–102.

Six most feared but least likely causes of death. (2005, July 13). *Be Safe, Live Long & Prosper* [E-newsletter]. Retrieved from http://www.sixwise.com/newsletters/05/07/13/the_six_most_feared_but_least_likely_causes_of_death.htm

Skinner, B. F. (1948). *Walden two.* Indianapolis: Hackett.

Skinner, B. F. (1971). *Beyond freedom and dignity.* New York: Wiley.

Skodol, A. E., Siever, L. J., Livesley, W. J., Gunderson, J. G., Pfohl, B., & Widiger, T. A. (2002). The borderline diagnosis II: Biology, genetics, and clinical course. *Biological Psychiatry, 51*, 951–963.

Slovic, P., Finucane, M., Peters, E., & MacGregor, D. (2002). The affect heuristic. In T. Gilovich, D. Griffin, & D. Kahneman (Eds.), *Heuristics and biases: The psychology of intuitive judgment* (pp. 397–420). New York: Cambridge University Press.

Smith, C., & Lapp, L. (1991). Increases in number of REMs and REM density in humans following an intensive learning period. *Sleep, 14*, 325–330.

Smith, D. M., Langa, K. M., Kabeto, M. U., & Ubel, P. A. (2005). Health, wealth, and happiness: Financial resources buffer subjective well-being after the onset of a disability. *Psychological Science, 16*, 663–664.

Smith, L. B., & Thelen, E. (August, 2003). Development as a dynamic system. *Trends in Cognitive Sciences, 7*, 343–348.

Smith, S. M., Glenberg, A. M., & Bjork, R. A. (1978). Environmental context and human memory. *Memory and Cognition, 6*, 342–353.

Smith, T. W., Orleans, C. T., & Jenkins, C. D. (2004). Prevention and health promotion: Decades of progress, new challenges, and an emerging agenda. *Health Psychology, 23*, 126–131.

Snider, L. A., & Swedo, S. E. (2004). PANDAS: Current status and directions for research. *Molecular Psychiatry, 9*, 900–907.

Snyder, E. E., Walts, B. M., Chagnon, Y. C., Pérusse, L., Weisnagel, S. J., Chagnon, Y. C., et al. (2004). The human obesity gene map: The 2003 update. *Obesity Research, 12*, 369–438.

Snyder, M., & Cantor, N. (1998). Understanding personality and personal behavior: A functionalist strategy. In D. T. Gilbert, S. T. Fiske, & G. Lindzey (Eds.), *Handbook of social psychology* (pp. 635–679). New York: McGraw-Hill.

Snyder, M., Tanke, E. D., & Berscheid, E. (1977). Social perception and interpersonal behavior: On the self-fulfilling nature of social stereotypes. *Journal of Personality and Social Psychology, 35*, 656–666.

Solms, M. (2000). Dreaming and REM sleep are controlled by different brain mechanisms. *Behavioral and Brain Sciences, 23*, 793.

Somerville, L. H., Kim, H., Johnstone, T., Alexander, A. L., & Whalen, P. J. (2004). Human amygdala responses during presentation of happy and neutral faces: Correlations with state anxiety. *Biological Psychiatry, 55*, 897–903.

Sommerville, J. A., & Woodward, A. L. (2005). Pulling out the intentional structure of action: The relation between action processing and action production in infancy. *Cognition, 95*, 1–30.

Sorensen, T., Holst, C., Stunkard, A. J., & Skovgaard, L. T. (1992). Correlations of body mass index of adult adoptees and their biological and adoptive relatives. *International Journal of Obesity and Related Metabolic Disorders, 16*, 227–236.

Southgate, V., & Hamilton, A. F. (2008). Unbroken mirrors: Challenging a theory of autism. *Trends in Cognitive Science, 12*, 225–229.

Spanos, N. P., & Coe, W. C. (1992). A social-psychological approach to hypnosis. In E. Fromm & M. Nash (Eds.), *Contemporary hypnosis research* (pp. 102–130). New York: Guilford Press.

Spearman, C. (1904). "General intelligence," objectively determined and measured. *American Journal of Psychology, 15*, 201–293.

Spencer, M. B., Fegley, S. G., & Harpalani, V. (2003). A theoretical and empirical examination of identity as coping: Linking coping resources to the self processes of African American youth. *Applied Developmental Science, 7*, 181–188.

Spencer, S. J., Steele, C. M., & Quinn, D. M. (1999). Stereotype threat and women's math performance. *Journal of Experimental Social Psychology, 35*, 4–28.

Sperling, G. (1960). The information available in brief visual presentations. *Psychological Monographs, 74*, 1–29.

Spitzer, R. L., Skodol, A. E., Gibbon, M., & Williams, J. B. W. (1983). *Psychopathology, a case book.* New York: McGraw-Hill.

Spitzer, R. L., Williams, J. B., Gibbon, M., & First, M. B. (1992). The structured clinical interview for DSM-III-R (SCID). I: History, rationale, and description. *Archives of General Psychiatry, 49*, 624–629.

Spurr, K. F., Graven, M. A., & Gilbert, R. W. (2008). Prevalence of unspecified sleep apnea and the use of continuous positive airway pressure in hospitalized patients, 2004 national hospital discharge survey. *Sleep and Breathing, 12*, 229–234.

Squire, L. R., & Moore, R. Y. (1979). Dorsal thalamic lesion in a noted case of human memory dysfunction. *Annals of Neurology, 6*, 503–506.

Squire, L. R., Stark, C. E. L., & Clark, R. E. (2004). The medial temporal lobe. *Annual Review of Neuroscience, 27*(27), 279–306.

Srivastava, S., John, O. P., Gosling, S. D., & Potter, J. (2003). Development of personality in early and middle adulthood: Set like plaster or persistent change? *Journal of Personality and Social Psychology, 84*, 1041–1053.

Srivastava, S., McGonigal, K. M., Richards, J. M., Butler, E. A., & Gross, J. J. (2006). Optimism in close relationships: How seeing things in a positive light makes them so. *Personality Processes and Individual Differences, 91*(1), 143–153.

Starcevic, V., Linden, M., Uhlenhuth, E. H., Kolar, D., & Latas, M. (2004). Treatment of panic disorder with agoraphobia in an anxiety disorders clinic: Factors influencing psychiatrists' treatment choices. *Psychiatry Research, 125*, 41–52.

Stark, S. (2000, December 22). "Cast Away" lets Hanks fend for himself. *The Detroit News.* Retrieved from http://www.detnews.com

Steele, C. M., & Aronson, J. (1995). Stereotype threat and the intellectual test performance of African-Americans. *Journal of Personality and Social Psychology, 69*(5), 797–811.

Steeves, J. K., Culham, J. C., Duchaine, B. C., Pratesi, C. C., Valyear, K. F., Schindler, I., et al. (2006). The fusiform face area is not sufficient for face recognition: Evidence from a patient with dense prosopagnosia and no occipital face area. *Neuropsychologia, 4*, 594–609.

Steffenburg, S., Gillberg, C., Helgren, L., Anderson, L., Gillberg, L., Jakobsson, G., et al. (1989). A twin study of autism in Denmark, Finland, Iceland, Norway, and Sweden. *Journal of Child Psychological Psychiatry, 30*, 405–416.

Stein, J., & Richardson, A. (1999). Cognitive disorders: A question of misattribution. *Current Biology, 9*, R374–R376.

Stein, M. B., & Stein, D. J. (2008). Social anxiety disorder. *Lancet, 371*, 1115–1125.

Steinberg, L. (2001). We know some things: Parent–adolescent relationships in retrospect and prospect. *Journal of Research on Adolescence, 11*, 1–19.

Steinberg, L., & Sheffield, A. M. (2001). Adolescent development. *Journal of Cognitive Education and Psychology, 2*, 55–87.

Steiner, J. E. (1977). Facial expressions of the neonate infant indicating the hedonics of food-related chemical stimuli. In J. M. Weiffenbach (Ed.), *Taste and development* (pp. 173–189). Bethesda, MD: National Institutes of Health.

Stellar, J. R., Kelley, A. E., & Corbett, D. (1983). Effects of peripheral and central dopamine blockade on lateral hypothalamic self-stimulation: Evidence for both reward and motor deficits. *Pharmacology, Biochemistry, and Behavior, 18*, 433–442.

Steriade, M. (1992). Basic mechanisms of sleep generation. *Neurology, 42*(Suppl. 6), 9–18.

Sternberg, R. J. (1986). A triangular theory of love. *Psychological Review, 93*, 119–135.

Sternberg, R. J. (1999). The theory of successful intelligence. *Review of General Psychology, 3*, 292–316.

Stewart, J. L., Coan, J. A., Towers, D. N., & Allen, J. J. B. (2011). Frontal EEG asymmetry during emotional challenge differentiates individuals with and without major depressive disorder. *Journal of Affective Disorders, 129*, 167–174.

Stewart, J. Y. (2007, June 4). Bettye Travis, 55; activist for the overweight [Obituary.]. *Los Angeles Times*, p. B7.

Stice, E. (2002). Risk and maintenance factors for eating pathology: A meta-analytic review. *Psychological Bulletin, 128*, 825–848.

Stickgold, R., Whidbee, D., Schirmer, B., Patel, V., & Hobson, J. A. (2000). Visual discrimination task improvement: A multi-step process occurring during sleep. *Journal of Cognitive Neuroscience, 12*, 246–254.

Stokes, M., Thompson, R., Cusack, R., & Duncan, J. (2009). Top-down activation of shape-specific population codes in visual cortex during mental imagery. *Journal of Neuroscience, 29*, 1565–1572.

Stokstad, E. (2001, October 5). New hints into the biological basis of autism. *Science, 294*, 34–37.

Stoleru, S., Gregoire, M. C., Gerard, D., Decety, J., Lafarge, E., Cinotti, L., et al. (1999). Neuroanatomical correlates of visually evoked sexual arousal in human males. *Archives of Sexual Behavior, 28*, 1–21.

Stone, A. A., Neale, J. M., Cox, D. S., Napoli, A., Valdimardottir, H., & Kennedy-Moore, E. (1994). Daily events are associated with a secretory immune response to an oral antigen in men. *Health Psychology, 13*, 440–446.

Stone, M. H., Stone, D. K., & Hurt, S. W. (1987). The natural history of borderline patients treated by intensive hospitalization. *Psychiatric Clinics of North America, 10*, 185–206.

Stone, V. E., Baron-Cohen, S., & Knight, R. T. (1998). Frontal lobe contributions to theory of mind. *Journal of Cognitive Neuroscience, 10*, 640–656.

Strahan, E. J., Spencer, S. J., & Zanna, M. P. (2002). Subliminal priming and persuasion: Striking while the iron is hot. *Journal of Experimental Social Psychology, 38*, 556–568.

Strayer, D. L., & Drews, F. A. (2007). Cell-phone-induced driver distraction. *Current Directions in Psychological Science, 16*, 128–131.

Strayer, D. L., Drews, F. A., & Johnston, W. A. (2003). Cell phone-induced failures of visual attention during simulated driving. *Journal of Experimental Psychology: Applied, 9*, 23–32.

Strentz, T., & Auerbach, S. M. (1988). Adjustment to the stress of simulated captivity: Effects of emotion-focused versus problem-focused preparation on hostages differing in locus of control. *Journal of Personality and Social Psychology, 55*, 652–660.

Striegel-Moore, R. H., & Franko, D. L. (2008). Should binge eating disorder be included in the DSM-V? A critical review of the state of the evidence. *Annual Review of Clinical Psychology, 4*, 305–324.

Stunkard, A. J. (1996). Current views on obesity. *American Journal of Medicine, 100*, 230–236.

Stuss, D. T. (1991). Self, awareness, and the frontal lobes: A neuropsychological perspective. In J. Strauss & G. R. Goethals (Eds.), *The self: Interdisciplinary approaches* (pp. 255–278). New York: Springer-Verlag.

Stuss, D. T., Gow, C. A., & Hetherington, C. R. (1992). "No longer Gage": Frontal lobe dysfunction and emotional changes. *Journal of Consulting and Clinical Psychology, 60*, 349–359.

Süß, H. M., Oberauer, K., Wittman, W. W., Wilhelm, O., & Schulze, R. (2002). Working-memory capacity explains reasoning ability—and a little bit more. *Intelligence, 30*, 261–288.

Sulin, R. A., & Dooling, D. J. (1974). Intrusion of a thematic idea in retention of prose. *Journal of Experimental Psychology, 103*, 255–262.

Sullivan, M. J. L., Thorn, B., Haythornthwaite, J. A., Keefe, F., Martin, M., Bradley, L. A., et al. (2001). Theoretical perspectives on the relation between catastrophizing and pain. *Clinical Journal of Pain, 17*, 52–64.

Super, C. M. (1976). Environmental effects on motor development: The case of African precocity. *Developmental Medicine and Child Neurology, 18*, 561–567.

Surian, L., Caldi, S., & Sperber, D. (2007). Attribution of beliefs by 13-month-old infants. *Psychological Science, 18*, 580–586.

Svenson, O. (1981). Are we all less risky and more skillful than our fellow drivers? *Acta Psychologica, 47*, 143–148.

Swaab, D. F. (2004). Sexual differentiation of the human brain: Relevance for gender identity, transsexualism and sexual orientation. *Gynecological Endocrinology, 19*, 301–312.

Swartz, M. S., Blazer, D., George, L., & Winfield, I. (1990). Estimating the prevalence of borderline personality disorder in the community. *Journal of Personality Disorders, 4*, 257–272.

Tajfel, H., & Turner, J. C. (1979). An integrative theory of intergroup conflict. In W. G. Austin & S. Worchel (Eds.), *The social psychology of intergroup relations* (pp. 33–47). Monterey, CA: Brooks/Cole.

Talarico, J. M., & Rubin, D. C. (2003). Confidence, not consistency, characterizes flashbulb memories. *Psychological Science, 14*, 455–461.

Talley, P. R., Strupp, H. H., & Morey, L. C. (1990). Matchmaking in psychotherapy: Patient-therapist dimensions and their impact on outcome. *Journal of Consulting and Clinical Psychology, 58*, 182–188.

Tandon, R., Keshavan, M. S., & Nasrallah, H. A. (2008). Schizophrenia, "Just the facts." What we know in 2008. 2. Epidemiology and etiology. *Schizophrenia Research, 102*, 1–18.

Tang, Y. P., Wang, H., Feng, R., Kyin, M., Tsien, J. Z. (2001). Differential effects of enrichment on learning and memory function in NR2B transgenic mice. *Neuropharmacology, 41*, 779–790.

Tang, Y. Y., Ma, Y. H., Wang, J. H., Fan, Y. X., Feng, S. G., Lu, Q. L., et al. (2007). Short-term meditation training improves attention and self-regulation. *Proceedings of the National Academy of Sciences, USA, 104*, 17152–17156.

Tangney, J. P., Stuewig, J., & Mashek, D. J. (2007). Moral emotions and moral behavior. *Annual Review of Psychology, 58*, 345–372. doi: 10.1146/annurev.psych.56.091103.070145

Tateyama, M., Asai, M., Kamisada, M., Hashimoto, M., Bartels, M., & Heimann, H. (1993). Comparison of schizophrenic delusions between Japan and Germany. *Psychopathology, 26*, 151–158.

Taylor, S. E. (2006). Tend and befriend: Biobehavioral bases of affiliation under stress. *Current Directions in Psychological Science, 15*, 273–277.

Taylor, S. E., & Brown, J. D. (1988). Illusion and well-being: A social psychological perspective on mental health. *Psychological Bulletin, 103*, 193–210.

Taylor, S. E., Lewis, B. P., Gruenewald, T. L., Gurung, R. A. R., Updegraff, J. A., & Klein, L. C. (2002). Sex differences in biobehavioral responses to threat: Reply to Geary and Flinn. *Psychological Review, 109*, 751–753.

Taylor, S. E., Saphire-Bernstein, S., & Seeman, T. E. (2010). Are plasma oxytocin in women and plasma vasopressin in men biomarkers of distressed pair-bond relationships? *Psychological Science, 21*, 3–7.

Teasdale, J. D., Segal, Z. V., Williams, J. M. G., Ridgeway, V. A., Soulsby, J. M., & Lau, M. A. (2000). Prevention of relapse/recurrence in major depression by mindfulness-based cognitive therapy. *Journal of Consulting and Clinical Psychology, 68*, 615–623.

Teller, D. Y., Morse, R., Borton, R., & Regal, C. (1974). Visual acuity for vertical and diagonal gratings in human infants. *Vision Research, 14*, 1433–1439.

Terracciano, A., Abdel-Khalek, A. M., Ádám, N., Adamovová, L., Ahn, C. K., Ahn, H. N., et al. (2005, October 7). National character does not reflect mean personality trait levels in 49 cultures. *Science, 310*, 96–100.

Tesser, A. (1988). Toward a self-evaluation maintenance model of social behavior. *Advances in Experimental Social Psychology, 21,* 181–227.

Tesser, A. (1993). The importance of heritability: The case of attitudes. *Psychological Review, 100,* 129–142.

Tessler, L. G. (1997). *How college students with learning disabilities can advocate for themselves.* Retrieved from http://www.ldanatl.org/aboutld/adults/post_secondary/print_college.asp

Tettamanti, M., Buccino, G., Saccuman, M. C., Gallese, V., Danna, M., Scifo, P., et al. (2005). Listening to action-related sentences activates fronto-parietal motor circuits. *Journal of Cognitive Neuroscience, 17,* 273–281.

Thigpen, C. H., & Cleckley, H. (1954). A case of multiple personality. *Journal of Abnormal Psychology, 49,* 135–151.

Thoits, P. A. (2010) Stress and health: Major findings and policy implications. *Journal of Health and Social Behavior, 51,* 41–53.

Thompson, P. (1980). Margaret Thatcher: A new illusion. *Perception, 9,* 483–484.

Thompson, P. M., Hayashi, K. M., Simon, S. L., Geaga, J. A., Hong, M. S., Sui, Y., et al. (2004). Structural abnormalities in the brains of human subjects who use methamphetamine. *Journal of Neuroscience, 24,* 6028–6036.

Thompson, W. F., Schellenberg, E. G., & Husain, G. (2001). Arousal, mood, and the Mozart effect. *Psychological Science, 12,* 248–251.

Thorgeirsson, T. E., Geller, F., Sulem, P., Rafnar, T., Wiste, A., Magnusson, K. P., et al. (2008). A variant associated with nicotine dependence, lung cancer and peripheral arterial disease. *Nature, 452,* 638–642.

Tickle, J. J., Sargent, J. D., Dalton, M. A., Beach, M. L., & Heatherton, T. F. (2001). Favorite movie stars, their tobacco use in contemporary movies and its association with adolescent smoking. *Tobacco Control, 10,* 16–22.

Tienari, P., Lahti, I., Sorri, A., Naarala, M., Moring, J., Kaleva, M., et al. (1990). Adopted-away offspring of schizophrenics and controls: The Finnish adoptive family study of schizophrenia. In L. Robins & M. Rutter (Eds.), *Straight and devious pathways from childhood to adulthood* (pp. 365–379). New York: Cambridge University Press.

Tienari, P., Wynne, L. C., Moring, J., Lahti, I., Naarala, M., Sorri, A., et al. (1994). The Finnish adoptive family study of schizophrenia: Implications for family research. *British Journal of Psychiatry, 23*(Suppl.), 20–26.

Tienari, P., Wynne, L. C., Sorri, A., Lahti, I., Laksy, K., Moring, J., et al. (2004). Genotype-environment interaction in schizophrenia spectrum disorder. *British Journal of Psychiatry, 184,* 216–222.

Tiggermann, M., & McGill, B. (2004). The role of social comparison in the effect of magazine advertisements on women's mood and body dissatisfaction. *Journal of Social and Clinical Psychology, 23,* 23–44.

Tipper, C. M., Handy, T. C., Giesbrecht, B., & Kingstone, A. F. (2008). Brain responses to biological relevance. *Journal of Cognitive Neuroscience, 20,* 879–891.

Tollesfson, G. D. (1995). Selective serotonin reuptake inhibitors. In A. F. Schatzberg & C. B. Nemeroff (Eds.), *The American Psychiatric Press textbook of psychopharmacology* (1st ed., pp. 161–182). Washington, DC: American Psychiatric Press.

Tolman, E. C., & Honzik, C. H. (1930). Introduction and removal of reward, and maze performance in rats. *University of California Publications in Psychology, 4,* 257–275.

Tomasello, M. (1999). *The cultural origins of human cognition.* Cambridge, MA: Harvard University Press.

Tombs, S., & Silverman, I. (2004). Pupillometry: A sexual selection approach. *Evolution and Human Behavior, 25,* 221–228.

Tomkins, S. S. (1963). *Affect imagery consciousness: Vol. 2. The negative affects.* New York: Tavistock/Routledge.

Tong, F., Nakayama, K., Vaughan, J. T., & Kanwisher, N. (1998). Binocular rivalry and visual awareness in human extrastriate cortex. *Neuron, 21,* 753–759.

Torgersen, S., Kringlen, E., & Cramer, V. (2001). The prevalence of personality disorders in a community sample. *Archives of General Psychiatry, 58,* 590–596.

Torrey, E. F. (1999). Epidemiological comparison of schizophrenia and bipolar disorder. *Schizophrenia Research, 39,* 101–106.

Torrey, E. F., Torrey, B. B., & Peterson, M. R. (1977). Seasonality of schizophrenic births in the United States. *Archives of General Psychiatry, 34,* 1065–1070.

Tracy, J. L., & Matsumoto, D. (2008). The spontaneous display of pride and shame: Evidence for biologically innate nonverbal displays. *Proceedings of the National Academy of Sciences, USA, 105,* 11655–11660.

Tracy, J. L., & Robins, R. W. (2008). The nonverbal expression of pride: Evidence for cross-cultural recognition. *Journal of Personality and Social Psychology, 94,* 516–530.

Treatment for Adolescents with Depression Study (TADS) Team. (2004). Fluoxetine, cognitive-behavioral therapy, and their combination for adolescents with depression: Treatment for adolescents with depression study (TADS) randomized controlled trial. *Journal of the American Medical Association, 292,* 807–820.

Treffert, D. A., & Christensen, D. D. (2006, June/July). Inside the mind of a savant. *Scientific American Mind,* 50–55.

Treisman, A., & Gelade, G. (1980). A feature-integration theory of attention. *Cognitive Psychology, 12,* 97–136.

Tremblay, P. F., Graham, K., & Wells, S. (2008). Severity of physical aggression reported by university students: A test of the interaction between trait aggression and alcohol consumption. *Personality and Individual Differences, 45*(1), 3–9.

Triandis, H. C. (1989). The self and social behavior in differing cultural contexts. *Psychological Review, 96,* 506–520.

Trivers, R. L. (1971). The evolution of reciprocal altruism. *Quarterly Review of Biology, 46,* 35–57.

Tryon, W. W., & Tryon, G. S. (2011). No ownership of common factors. *American Psychologist, 66,* 151–152.

Trzesniewski, K. H., Donnellan, M. B., & Roberts, R. W. (2008). Is "generation me" really more narcissistic than previous generations? *Journal of Personality, 76,* 903–918.

Tsien, J. Z. (2000, April). Building a brainier mouse. *Scientific American, 282,* 62–68.

Tugade, M. M., & Fredrickson, B. L. (2004). Resilient individuals use positive emotions to bounce back from negative emotional experiences. *Journal of Personality and Social Psychology, 86,* 320–333.

Turner, E. H., Matthews, A. M., Linardatos, B. S., Tell, R. A., & Rosenthal, R. (2008). Selective publication of antidepressant trials and its influence on apparent efficacy. *New England Journal of Medicine, 358,* 252–260.

Twenge, J. M., & Campbell, W. K. (2003). "Isn't it fun to get the respect that we're going to deserve?" Narcissism, social rejection, and aggression. *Personality and Social Psychology Bulletin, 29,* 261–272.

Twenge, J. M., Konrath, S., Foster, J. D., Campbell, K. W., & Bushman, B. J. (2008). Egos inflating over time: A cross-temporal meta-analysis of the narcissistic personality inventory. *Journal of Personality, 76*, 875–902.

U.S. Bureau of Labor Statistics, U.S. Department of Labor. (2009). *Occupational outlook handbook, 2008–2009 edition: psychologists.* Retrieved from http://www.bls.gov/oco/ocos056.htm

Ungerleider, L. G., & Mishkin, M. (1982). Two cortical visual systems. In D. J. Ingle, Mansfield, R. J. W., & M. S. Goodale (Eds.), *The analysis of visual behavior* (pp. 549–586). Cambridge, MA: MIT Press.

United Nations Office on Drugs and Crime. (2009). *World Drug Report 2009.* Vienna, Austria: Author. Retrieved from http://www.unodc.org/unodc/en/data-and-analysis/WDR-2009.html

United Nations Office on Drugs and Crime. (n.d.). Homicide statistics, criminal justice sources—Latest available year (2003–2009). [Data from the Eleventh United Nations Survey of Crime Trends and Operations of Criminal Justice Systems (UN-CTS), 2007–2008]. Retrieved from http://www.unodc.org/unodc/en/data-and-analysis/homicide.html

United States Census Bureau. (2011, September 27). 2012 Statistical abstract: Deaths. Retrieved from http://www.census.gov/compendia/statab/cats/births_deaths_marriages_divorces/deaths.html

United States Department of Health and Human Services. (2001, 8 January). *Preventing disease and death from tobacco use* [Press release]. Retrieved from http://archive.hhs.gov/news/press/2001pres/01fstbco.html

United States Department of Health and Human Services, Office of the Surgeon General (2004, May 27). *The health consequences of smoking: A report of the Surgeon General.* Available from http://www.surgeongeneral.gov/library/smokingconsequences

United States Government. (1990). *Americans with Disabilities Act of 1990, as amended.* Retrieved from http://www.ada.gov/pubs/adastatute08.htm

Upton, N. (1994). Mechanisms of action of new antiepileptic drugs: Rational design and serendipitous findings. *Trends in Pharmacological Sciences, 15*, 456–463.

Urberg, K. A., Degirmencioglue, S. M., Tolson, J. M., & Halliday-Scher, K. (1995). The structure of adolescent peer networks. *Developmental Psychology, 31,* 540–547. doi: 10.1037/0012-1649.31.4.540

Ustün, T. B., Ayuso-Mateos, J. L., Chatterji, S., Mathers, C., & Murray, C. J. (2004). Global burden of depressive disorders in the year 2000. *British Journal of Psychiatry, 184*, 386–392.

Uvnas-Moberg, K. (1998). Oxytocin may mediate the benefits of positive social interaction and emotions. *Psychoneuroendocrinology, 23*, 819–835.

Vallabha, G. K., McClelland, J. L., Pons, F., Werker, J. F., & Amano, S. (2007). Unsupervised learning of vowel categories from infant-directed speech. *Proceedings of the National Academy of Sciences, USA, 104*, 13273–13278.

Van der Oord, S., Prins, P. J. M., Oosterlaan, J., & Emmelkamp, P. M. G. (2008). Efficacy of methylphenidate, psychosocial treatments and their combination in school-aged children with ADHD: A meta-analysis. *Clinical Psychology Review, 28*, 783–800.

van Haren, N. E., Schnack, H. G., Cahn, W., van den Heuvel, M. P., Lepage, C., Collins, L., Evans, A. C., Hulshoff Pol, H. E., & Kahn, R. S. (2011). Changes in cortical thickness during the course of illness in schizophrenia. *Archives of General Psychiatry, 68*, 871–880.

Vargas-Reighley, R. V. (2005). *Bicultural competence and academic resilience among immigrants.* El Paso, TX: LFB Scholarly Publishing.

Vargha-Khadem, F., Gadian, D. G., Watkins, K. E., Connelly, A., Van Paesschen, W., & Mishkin, M. (1997, July 18). Differential effects of early hippocampal pathology on episodic and semantic memory. *Science, 277*, 376–380.

Vazire, S. (2010). Who knows what about a person? The self-other knowledge asymmetry (SOKA) model. *Journal of Personality and Social Psychology, 98*, 281–300.

Vazire, S., & Carlson, E. N. (2011). Others sometimes know us better than we know ourselves. *Current Directions in Psychological Science, 20*, 104–108.

Vazire, S., & Gosling, S. D. (2004). e-perceptions: Personality impressions based on personal websites. *Journal of Personality and Social Psychology, 87*, 123–132.

Vazire, S., & Mehl, M. R. (2008). Knowing me, knowing you: The accuracy and unique predictive validity of self and other ratings of daily behavior. *Journal of Personality and Social Psychology, 95*, 1202–1216.

Ventura, P., Pattamadilok, C., & Fernandes, T. (2008). Schooling in Western culture promotes context-free processing. *Journal of Experimental Child Psychology, 100*(2), 79–88.

Vernon, P. A., Wickett, J. C., Bazana, P. G., Stelmack, R. M., & Sternberg, R. J. (2000). The neuropsychology and psychophysiology of human intelligence. In R. J. Sternberg (Ed.), *Handbook of intelligence* (pp. 245–264). Cambridge, UK: Cambridge University Press.

Vingerhoets, A. J., Bylsma, L. M., & Rottenberg, J. (2009). Crying: A biopsychosocial phenomenon. In T. Fögen (Ed.), *Tears in the Graeco-Roman world* (pp. 439–474). Berlin, Germany: De Gruyter.

Vismera, L., & Rogers, S. (2010). Behavioral treatments in autism spectrum disorders: What do we know? *Annual Review of Clinical Psychology, 6*, 447–468.

Vohs, K. D., & Heatherton, T. F. (2004). Ego threat elicits different social comparison processes among high and low self-esteem people: Implications for interpersonal perceptions. *Social Cognition, 22*, 168–190.

Volkmar, F., Chawarska, K., & Klin, A. (2005). Autism in infancy and early childhood. *Annual Review of Psychology, 56*, 1–21.

Volkow, N. D. (2007, September). This is your brain on food. Interview by Kristin Leutwyler-Ozelli. *Scientific American, 297*, 84–85.

Volkow, N. D., Wang, G. J., & Baler, R. D. (2011). Reward, dopamine, and the control of food intake: Implications for obesity. *Trends in Cognitive Science, 15*, 37–46.

Volkow, N. D., Wang, G. J., Telang, F., Fowler, J. S., Logan, J., Childress, A. R., et al. (2008). Dopamine increases in striatum do not elicit craving in cocaine abusers unless they are coupled with cocaine cues. *Neuroimage, 39*, 1266–1273.

von Neumann, J., & Morgenstern, O. (1947). *Theory of games and economic behavior.* Princeton, NJ: Princeton University Press.

von Restorff, H. (1933). Uber die wirkung von bereichsbildungen im spurenfeld [On the effect of spheres' formations in the trace field]. *Psychologische Forschung, 18*, 299–342.

Vygotsky, L. S. (1978). *Mind in society.* Cambridge, MA: Harvard University Press.

Vytal, K., & Hamann, S. (2010). Neuroimaging support for discrete neural correlates of basic emotions: A voxel-based meta-analysis. *Journal of Cognitive Neuroscience, 22*, 2864–2885.

Wadhwa, P. D., Sandman, C. A., & Garite, T. J. (2001). The neurobiology of stress in human pregnancy: Implications for prematurity and development of the fetal central nervous system. *Progress in Brain Research, 133*, 131–142.

Wager, T. D. (2005). Placebo effects in the brain: Linking mental and physiological processes. *Brain, Behavior, and Immunity, 19*(4), 281–282.

Wagner, D. D., Dal Cin, S., Sargent, J. D., Kelley, W. M., & Heatherton, T. F. (2011). Spontaneous action representation in smokers when watching movie characters smoke. *Journal of Neuroscience, 31*, 894–898.

Waite, L. J. (1995). Does marriage matter? *Demography 32*, 483–507.

Walker, E., Kestler, L., Bollini, A., & Hochman, K. M. (2004). Schizophrenia: Etiology and course. *Annual Review of Psychology, 55*, 401–430.

Walker, M. P., & Stickgold, R. (2006). Sleep, memory, and plasticity. *Annual Review of Psychology, 57*, 139–166.

Walsh, T., McClellan, J. M., McCarthy, S. E., Addington, A. M., Pierce, S. B., Cooper, G. M., et al. (2008, March 27). Rare structural variants disrupt multiple genes in neurodevelopmental pathways in schizophrenia. *Science, 320*, 539–543.

Walton, G. M., & Spencer, S. J. (2009). Latent ability: Grades and test scores systematically underestimate the intellectual ability of negatively stereotyped students. *Psychological Science, 20*, 1132–1139.

Waltrip, R. W., Buchanan, R. W., Carpenter, W. T., Kirkpatrick, B., Summerfelt, A., Breier, A., et al. (1997). Borna disease virus antibodies and the deficit syndrome of schizophrenia. *Schizophrenia Research, 23*, 253–257.

Wamsley, E. J., Tucker, M., Payne, J. D., Benavides, J. A., & Stickgold, R. (2010). Dreaming of a learning task is associated with enhanced sleep-dependent memory consolidation. *Current Biology, 20*(9), 850–855. doi:10.1016/j.cub.2010.03.027

Wardle, J., Carnell, S., Haworth, C. M., & Plomin, R. (2008). Evidence for a strong genetic influence on childhood adiposity despite the force of the obesogenic environment. *American Journal of Clinical Nutrition, 87*, 398–404.

Warren, Z., McPheeters, M., Sathe, N., et al. (2011). A systematic review of early intensive intervention for autism spectrum disorders. *Pediatrics, 127*, e1303–1311.

Watson, D., & Clark, L. A. (1997). Extraversion and its positive emotional core. In R. Hogan, J. Johnson, & S. Briggs (Eds.), *Handbook of personality psychology* (pp. 767–793). San Diego, CA: Academic Press.

Watson, D., Wiese, D., Vaidya, J., & Tellegen, A. (1999). The two general activation systems of affect: Structural findings, evolutionary considerations, and psychobiological evidence. *Journal of Personality and Social Psychology, 76*, 820–838.

Watson, J. B. (1924). *Behaviorism.* New York: Norton.

Watson, J. B., & Rayner, R. (1920). Conditioned emotional reactions. *Journal of Experimental Psychology, 3*, 1–14.

Waugh, C. E., Wager, T. D., Fredrickson, B. L., Noll, D. N., & Taylor, S. F. (2008). The neural correlates of trait resilience when anticipating and recovering from threat. *Social Cognitive and Affective Neuroscience, 3*, 322–332.

Weber, N., & Brewer, N. (2004). Confidence-accuracy calibration in absolute and relative face recognition judgments. *Journal of Experimental Psychology: Applied, 10*, 156–172.

Wegner, D., Shortt, J., Blake, A., & Page, M. (1990). The suppression of exciting thoughts. *Journal of Personality and Social Psychology, 58*, 409–418.

Weiner, B. (1974). *Achievement motivation and attribution theory.* Morristown, NJ: General Learning Press.

Weiss, A., Bates, T. C., & Luciano, M. (2008). Happiness is a personal(ity) thing: The genetics of personality and well-being in a representative sample. *Psychological Science, 19*, 205–210.

Weissman, M. M., Bland, R. C., Canino, G. J., Greenwald, S., Hwu, H. G., Lee, C. K., et al. (1994). The cross national epidemiology of obsessive compulsive disorder. The cross national collaborative group. *Journal of Clinical Psychiatry, 55*, 5–10.

Wells, G. L. (2008). Field experiments on eyewitness identification: Towards a better understanding of pitfalls and prospects. *Law and Human Behavior, 32*, 6–10.

Wells, G. L., Small, M., Penrod, S., Malpass, R. S., Fulero, S. M., & Brimacombe, C. A. E. (1998). Eyewitness identification procedures: Recommendations for lineups and photospreads. *Law and Human Behavior, 22*, 603–647.

Werker, J. F., Gilbert, J. H., Humphrey, K., & Tees, R. C. (1981). Developmental aspects of cross-language speech perception. *Child Development, 52*, 349–355.

West, G. L., Anderson, A. A., Ferber, S., & Pratt, J. (2011, in press). Electrophysiological evidence for biased competition in V1 for fear expressions. *Journal of Cognitive Neuroscience.* doi:10.1162/jocn.2011.21605

West, G., Anderson, A., & Pratt, J. (2009). Motivationally significant stimuli show visual prior entry: Direct evidence for attentional capture. *Journal of Experimental Psychology: Human Perception and Performance, 35*, 1032–1042.

Westen, D. (1998). The scientific legacy of Sigmund Freud: Toward a psychodynamically informed psychological science. *Psychological Bulletin, 124*, 333–371.

Westen, D., Novotny, C. M., & Thompson-Brenner, H. (2004). The empirical status of empirically supported psychotherapies: Assumptions, findings, and reporting in controlled clinical trials. *Psychological Bulletin, 130*, 631–663.

Weyandt, L. L., Janusis, G., Wilson, K., Verdi, G., Paquin, G., Lopes, J., Varejao, M., & Dussault, C. (2009). Nonmedical prescription stimulant use among a sample of college students: Relationships with psychological variables. *Journal of Attention Disorders, 13*, 284-296.

Whalen, C. K. (1989). Attention deficit and hyperactivity disorders. In T. H. Ollendick & M. Herson (Eds.), *Handbook of child psychopathology* (2nd ed., pp. 131–169). New York: Plenum Press.

Whalen, P. J., Rauch, S. L., Etcoff, N. L., McInerney, N. L., Lee, M. B., & Jenike, M. A. (1998). Masked presentations of emotional facial expressions modulate amygdala activity without explicit knowledge. *Journal of Neuroscience, 18*, 411–418.

Whalen, P. J., Shin, L. M., McInerney, S. C. L., Fischer, H., Wright, C. I., & Rauch, S. L. (2001). A functional MRI study of human amygdala responses to facial expressions of fear versus anger. *Emotion, 1*, 70–83.

Wheatley, T., & Haidt, J. (2005). Hypnotic disgust makes moral judgments more severe. *Psychological Science, 16*, 780–784.

Whiteside, S. P., Port, J. D., & Abramowitz, J. S. (2004). A meta-analysis of functional neuroimaging in obsessive-compulsive disorder. *Psychiatry Research, 15*, 69–79.

Widiger, T. A., & Corbitt, E. M. (1995). Are personality disorders well-classified in DSM-IV? In W. J. Lively (Ed.), *The DSM-IV personality disorders* (pp. 103–126). New York: Guilford Press.

Widom, C. S. (1978). A methodology for studying noninstitutionalized psychopaths. In R. D. Hare & D. A. Schalling (Eds.), *Psychopathic behavior: Approaches to research* (pp. 72ff). Chichester, UK: Wiley.

Wierson, M., Long, P. J., & Forehand, R. L. (1993). Toward a new understanding of early menarche: The role of environmental stress in pubertal timing. *Adolescence, 28*, 913–924.

Wiesel, T. N., & Hubel, D. H. (1963). Single-cell responses in striate cortex of kittens deprived of vision in one eye. *Journal of Neurophysiology, 26*, 1003–1017.

Wilens, T. E., Faraone, S. V., & Biederman, J. (2004). Attention-deficit/hyperactivity disorder in adults. *Journal of the American Medical Association, 292*, 619–623.

Wilfley, D. E., Bishop, M., Wilson, G. T., & Agras, W. S. (2007). Classification of eating disorders: Toward DSM-V. *International Journal of Eating Disorders, 40(suppl)*, S123–S129.

Wilke, M., Sohn, J. H., Byars, A. W., & Holland, S. K. (2003). Bright spots: Correlations of gray matter volume with IQ in a normal pediatric population. *Neuroimage, 20*, 202–215

Williams, K., Harkins, S. G., & Latané, B. (1981). Identifiability as a deterrent to social loafing: Two cheering experiments. *Journal of Personality and Social Psychology, 40*, 303–311.

Williams, L. E., & Bargh, J. A. (2008, October 24). Experiences of physical warmth influence interpersonal warmth. *Science, 322*, 606–607.

Williams, R. B., Jr. (1987). Refining the type A hypothesis: Emergence of the hostility complex. *American Journal of Cardiology, 60*, 27J–32J.

Wills, T. A., DuHamel, K., & Vaccaro, D. (1995). Activity and mood temperament as predictors of adolescent substance use: Test of a self-regulation mediational model. *Journal of Personality and Social Psychology, 68*, 901–916.

Wilsnack, R. W., Wilsnack, S. C., & Obot, I. S. (2005). Why study gender, alcohol and culture? In I. S. Obot & R. Room (Eds.), *Alcohol, gender and drinking problems: Perspectives from low and middle income countries* (pp. 1–23). Geneva, Switzerland: World Health Organization.

Wilson, M. A., & McNaughton, B. L. (1994). Reactivation of hippocampal ensemble memories during sleep. *Science, 265*(5172), 676–679.

Wilson, A. E., & Ross, M. (2001). From chump to champ: People's appraisals of their earlier and present selves. *Journal of Personality and Social Psychology, 80*, 572–584.

Wilson, F. A., & Stimpson, J. P. (2010). Trends in fatalities from distracted driving in the United States, 1999 to 2008. *American Journal of Public Health, 100*, 2213–2219.

Wilson, M. A., & McNaughton, B. L. (1994, July 29). Reactivation of hippocampal ensemble memories during sleep. *Science, 265*, 676–679.

Wilson, T. D., & Gilbert, D. T. (2003). Affective forecasting. In M. Zanna (Ed.), *Advances in experimental social psychology* (Vol. 35, pp. 345–411). New York: Elsevier.

Wilson, T. D., & Schooler, J. W. (1991). Thinking too much: Introspection can reduce the quality of preferences and decisions. *Journal of Personality and Social Psychology 60*, 181–192.

Winberg, J., & Porter, R. H. (1998). Olfaction and human neonatal behaviour: Clinical implications. *Acta Paediatrica, 87*, 6–10.

Winfried, R., & Hofmann, S. G. (2008). The missing data problem in meta-analyses. *Archives of General Psychiatry, 65*, 238.

Wise, R. A., & Rompre, P. P. (1989). Brain dopamine and reward. *Annual Review of Psychology, 40*, 191–225.

Wiseman, C. V., Harris, W. A., & Halmi, K. A. (1998). Eating disorders. *Medical Clinics of North America, 82*, 145–159.

Wolfe, J. M., & Horowitz, T. S. (2004). What attributes guide the deployment of visual attention and how do they do it? *Nature Reviews Neuroscience, 5*, 495–501.

Wolford, G. L., Miller, M. B., & Gazzaniga, M. (2000). The left hemisphere's role in hypothesis formation. *Journal of Neuroscience, 20*, 1–4.

Woller, K. M., Buboltz, W. C. J., & Loveland, J. M. (2007). Psychological reactance: Examination across age, ethnicity, and gender. *American Journal of Psychology, 120*(1), 15–24.

Wolpe, J. (1997). Thirty years of behavior therapy. *Behavior Therapy, 28*, 633–635.

Wolraich, M. L., Wilson, D. B., & White, J. W. (1995). The effects of sugar on behavior or cognition in children: A meta-analysis. *Journal of the American Medical Association, 274*, 1617–1621.

Wood, J. M., Garb, H. N., Lilienfeld, S. O., & Nezworski, M. T. (2002). Clinical assessment. *Annual Review of Psychology, 53*, 519–543.

Woodworth, M., & Porter, S. (2002). In cold blood: Characteristics of criminal homicides as a function of psychopathy. *Journal of Abnormal Psychology, 111*, 436–445.

World Health Organization. (2008). *WHO Report on the global tobacco epidemic*. Retrieved from http://www.who.int/tobacco/mpower/en/

World Health Organization. (2011). *The top ten causes of death* [Fact sheet]. Retrieved from http://www.who.int/mediacentre/factsheets/fs310/en/index.html

Worley, H. (2006, June). *Depression: A leading contributor to global burden of disease: Myriad obstacles—particularly stigma—block better treatment in developing countries*. Retrieved November 10, 2008, from http://www.prb.org/Articles/2006/DepressionaLeadingContributortoGlobalBurdenofDisease.aspx

Wright, S. C., & Tropp, L. R. (2005). Language and intergroup contact: Investigating the impact of bilingual instruction on children's intergroup attitudes. *Group Processes and Intergroup Relations, 8*, 309–328.

Xu, J., Kochanek, K. D., Murphy, S. L., & Tejada-Vera, B. (2010). Deaths: Final data for 2007. *National Vital Statistics Reports, 58*, Number 19. U.S. Department of Health and Human Services.

Xu, J., & Roberts, R. E. (2010). The power of positive emotions: It's a matter of life or death—subjective well-being and longevity in a general population. *Health Psychology, 29*, 9–19.

Yamagata, S., Suzuki, A., Ando, J., Ono, Y., Kijima, N., Yoshimura, K., et al. (2006). Is the genetic structure of human personality universal? A cross-cultural twin study from North America, Europe, and Asia. *Journal of Personality and Social Psychology, 90*, 987–998.

Yamaguchi, S., Greenwald, A. G., Banaji, M. R., Murakami, F., Chen, D., Shiomura, K., et al. (2007). Apparent universality of positive implicit self-esteem. *Psychological Science, 18*, 498–500.

Yates, W. R., Perry, P., & Murray, S. (1992). Aggression and hostility in anabolic steroid users. *Biological Psychiatry, 31*, 1232–1234.

Yerkes, R. M., & Dodson, J. D. (1908). The relation of strength of stimulus to rapidity of habit formation. *Journal of Comparative Neurology & Psychology, 18*, 459–482.

Yeshurun, Y., & Sobel, N. (2010). An odor is not worth a thousand words: From multidimensional odors to unidimensional odor objects. *Annual Review of Psychology, 61*, 219–41.

Yoo, S. S., Hu, P. T., Gujar, N., Jolesz, F. A., & Walker, M. P. (2007). A deficit in the ability to form new human memories without sleep. *Nature Neuroscience, 10*, 385–392.

Yucel, M., Harrison, B. J., Wood, S. J., Fornito, A., Wellard, R. M., Pujol, J., et al. (2007). Functional and biochemical alterations of the medial frontal cortex in obsessive-compulsive disorder. *Archives of General Psychiatry, 64*, 946–955.

Yuille, J. C., & Cutshall, J. L. (1986). A case study of eyewitness memory of a crime. *Journal of Applied Psychology, 71*, 291–301.

Zahn-Waxler, C., & Radke-Yarrow, M. (1990). The origins of empathic concern. *Motivation and Emotion, 14*, 107–130.

Zahn-Waxler, C., & Robinson, J. (1995). Empathy and guilt: Early origins of feelings of responsibility. In J. P. Tangney & K. W. Fischer (Eds.), *Self-conscious emotions: The psychology of shame, guilt, embarrassment, and pride* (pp. 143–173). New York: Guilford Press.

Zajonc, R. B. (1965, July 15). Social facilitation. *Science, 149*, 269–274.

Zajonc, R. B. (1968). Attitudinal effects of mere exposure. *Journal of Personality and Social Psychology Monographs, 9*, 1–27.

Zajonc, R. B. (1980). Feeling and thinking: Preferences need no inferences. *American Psychologist, 35*, 151–175.

Zajonc, R. B. (2001). Mere exposure: A gateway to the subliminal. *Current Directions in Psychological Science 10*, 224–228.

Zak, P. J., Kurzban, R., & Matzner, W. T. (2005). Oxytocin is associated with human trustworthiness. *Hormones and Behavior, 48*(5), 522–527.

Zametkin, A. J., Nordahl, T. E., Gross, M., King, A. C., Stemple, W. E., Rumsey, J., et al. (1990). Cerebral glucose metabolism in adults with hyperactivity of childhood onset. *New England Journal of Medicine, 323*, 1361–1366.

Zebian, S., Alamuddin, R., Mallouf, M., & Chatila, Y. (2007). Developing an appropriate psychology through culturally sensitive research practices in the Arab-speaking world: A content analysis of psychological research published between 1950 and 2004. *Journal of Cross-Cultural Psychology, 38*, 91–122.

Zentall, S. S., Sutton, J. E., & Sherburne, L. M. (1996). True imitative learning in pigeons. *Psychological Science, 7*, 343–346.

Zihl, J., von Cramon, D., & Mai, N. (1983). Selective disturbance of movement vision after bilateral brain damage. *Brain, 106*, 313–340.

Zimbardo, P. G. (1990). *Shyness: What it is, what to do about it.* Reading, MA: Addison-Wesley.

Zorrilla, E. P., Iwasaki, S., Moss, J. A., Chang, J., Otsuji, J., Inoue, K., et al. (2006). Vaccination against weight gain. *Proceedings of the National Academy of Sciences, USA, 103*, 13226–13231.

Zuckerman, M. (2007). *Sensation seeking and risky behavior.* Washington, DC: American Psychological Association.

ANSWER KEY FOR CAPTION QUESTIONS AND FOR PRACTICE TESTS

For additional Practice Tests and other review materials, visit StudySpace at http://wwnorton.com/studyspace

CHAPTER 1

Caption Question, p. 4

Answer: In evaluating science-related announcements, most of us first rely on common sense. When news reports pass the common sense test, we might then do research: asking someone with related knowledge, reading a professionally prepared and acknowledged source. One *unreliable* method would be to do a Web search and simply believe whatever information comes up.

Caption Question, p. 5

Answer: Answers will vary. One example: The multimillion-dollar "brain training" industry claims computer mind games improve cognitive function, yet these claims lack empirical support. Improvement seems to be task specific and results from training and practice, not general overall improvement (Owen et al., 2010).

Caption Question, p. 18

Answer: The precise amount of influence that biology exerts on behavior cannot be determined. In a sense, since we cannot separate biology from who we are, every choice we make or action we take is biological. However, as emphasized throughout this book, environment (nurture) is continuously interacting with biology (nature) in making us who we are.

Caption Question, p. 20

Answer: Answers will vary. When considering our ancestors' early evolution, you might think about the development of very basic survival behaviors. When considering more-recent evolution, you might think about the increasing size and complexity of the frontal cortex. This development brought about additional means of survival, namely the greater complexity of humans and of their intelligence.

Practice Test, p. 27

1. **Answer:** c. "I think you'll be surprised by the range of questions psychologists ask about the mind, the brain, and behavior, not to mention the methods they use to answer these questions."

2. **Answers:** a. adaptations; b. survival of the fittest; c. natural selection.

3. **Answers:** a. social; b. biological; c. cultural; d. individual.

4. **Answers:** a. Titchener, Wundt; b. Dewey, James; c. Kohler, Wertheimer; d. Skinner, Watson; e. Köhler, Miller, Tolman; f. Lewin.

5. **Answers:** a. introspection; b. dualism; c. localization; d. stream of consciousness; e. information processing theory.

6. **Answer:** c. "That's great! Psychologists do research to figure out which interventions are most helpful for people with different concerns."

CHAPTER 2

Caption Question, p. 47

Answer: This small sample shows women clustered on the beach. Another small sample might show men clustered. Yet another small sample might show an unrepresentative mixing of women and men. In other words, the smallness of the sample might distort the information available in it. The larger the sample, the greater the chance that the ratio of women to men in the sample will be representative of the beach. In studying the beachgoing ways of women and men, of course, you would want to study more than one beach. The larger your sample of beachgoers, the greater the number of beaches you study, the more likely it will be that your results will be generalizable.

Caption Questions, p. 67

Answer for Figure 2.22: The mean is the most valuable number. Because it is the arithmetic average of all the results, it provides the most generalizable sense of the effect of alcohol on balance. By contrast, the range is based on only the highest and lowest numbers. Therefore it provides the vaguest sense of the results for all the study participants. Note that for any set of data, the mean is always more meaningful when reported with the standard deviation, which expresses the variation in the scores. Note, too, that for this set of data, the mode is not really useful because the frequency is based on only two values (i.e., one more than each individual value). Here the median turns out to be close to the mean, but the median is based on the placement of values rather than their combination.

Answer for Figure 2.23: In general, this relationship is a negative correlation: the greater the level of intoxication, the less ability to balance.

Practice Test, p. 71

1. **Answer:** c. replication.

2. **Answer:** b, because it offers a specific prediction.

3. **Answer:** a, because it is random.

4. **Answer:** c, because it includes experimental and control groups.

5. **Answer:** a, because it uses random assignment.

CHAPTER 3

Caption Question, p. 84

Answer: Answers will vary.

Caption Question, p. 112

Answer: In addition to genetics (nature), environment (nurture) needs to be considered as a factor in the similarities between twins raised apart. What type of environment was each twin raised in, and how might that environment have affected the twin's characteristics? For example, the twins might have been raised apart in highly similar environments. Adoption agencies might tend to place particular kinds of children with particular kinds of parents. Those parents and the communities they live in might tend to have similar values and similar emphases (such as on the merit of being a firefighter). In addition, whether the twins were in similar or different environments, each twin's temperament and physical appearance, both genetically based, might have elicited similar responses from people.

Practice Test, p. 129

1. **Answer:** c. bricks, walls.

2. **Answers:** Choices a, b, and c are true.

3. **Answers:** b. sensory neuron, e. afferent neuron.

4. **Answer:** a. someone who plays computer games requiring the exploration of complex virtual worlds.

CHAPTER 4

Caption Question, p. 137

Answer: Answers will vary about the adjustment time. Kinds of constant stimulation that people must adjust to include flashing lights, machinery noises, and cooking smells. By the way, olfaction appears to have the fastest rate of adaptation.

Caption Question, p. 156

Answer: (a) The blue on the left is brighter because its color is more saturated. The blue on the right is paler because its color is less saturated. (b) The central squares of each pair look different because each square is surrounded by a different color. The brightness of the surrounding color influences your perception of the lightness of the central square.

Caption Question, p. 167

Answer: Context here is the meaning of each word: Your reading of "THE" enables you to see its middle character as an "H." Your reading of "CAT" enables you to see its middle character as an "A." Without the context, each middle character would look the same to you.

Caption Question, p. 170

Answer: Answers will vary. Note that some people are so dominant in one eye that this "crossing" does not occur easily.

Caption Question, p. 171

Answer:

Occlusion: The tree blocks the building behind it.

Relative size: The people at the front of the picture are larger than the people toward the middle and back of the picture.

Familiar size: We know the relative height of men, and we do not assume that the single dark figure is especially small relative to the man in front. Therefore the dark figure must be farther away.

Linear perspective: The lines of the street and of the buildings converge toward the horizon.

Texture gradient: Textures in the foreground are more distinguishable. In the background, as the buildings recede into the distance, textures get denser and blur together.

Position relative to horizon: The figures positioned higher on the page, near the horizon, appear farther away.

Caption Question, p. 175

Answer: When you look at each image, the eye simply collects information about the size of the bearded man. Perspective causes the brain to treat that information differently each time. In (a), the man is farther away, so the brain adjusts his size to make him human size. In (b), the bearded man is on the same frontal plane as the man in the red sweater. Thus the brain does not correct for the bearded man's size. As far as the brain can tell, the bearded man is tiny compared with the man in the sweater.

Practice Test, p. 179

1. **Answer:** a. specialized receptors, thalamus, cortex.

2. **Answer:** c. You can decipher qualitative differences among the instruments because of the involvement of specific sensory receptors, whereas you can make quantitative distinctions—recognizing variations in the notes' intensity—due to the rate of firing of your sensory neurons.

3. **Answer:** b. The intensity of the auditory stimulation does not exceed the minimum threshold needed for you to detect a sensation.

4. **Answers:** a. activated by chemical changes in tissue; e. nonmyelinated axons; f. slow fibers.

5. **Answer:** d. Directing the girl's hand on a quick touching tour of the nearby environment and saying things such as "Feel this tree's rough bark. Touch the grass; it tickles. Feel how smooth this rock is!"

CHAPTER 5

Caption Question, p. 185

Answer: Since this question asks you to imaginatively project yourself into the experience of regaining full consciousness, answers will vary. Note that the few people who emerge from a minimally conscious state do so with severe disabilities (Luauté et al., 2010).

Caption Question, p. 205

Answer: Since this question asks you to evaluate the evidence in the text, answers will vary.

Caption Question, p. 210

Answer: Answers will vary. A case could be made that video games improve eye/hand coordination and even sharpen perception. An opposing case could be made that video games dull perception through sensory overload and that they interfere with person-to-person social interaction.

Caption Question, p. 217

Answer: (a) Patrons such as this woman are physically addicted to smoking. They do not want to step outside the restaurant to smoke, but they are willing to stick their heads and arms through padded holes in the wall. (b) Casinos encourage patrons' "addiction" to gambling through enclosed spaces, bright lights, stimulating sounds, and control of information from the outside environment.

Practice Test, p. 221

1. **Answer:** c. The person in the minimally conscious state shows some degree of brain activity, whereas the person in the persistent vegetative state shows no brain activity.

2. **Answer:** b. Participants in Condition A will be more friendly toward the stranger than will participants in Condition B.

3. **Answer:** a. The participant will say he saw a tire and will draw a car.

4. **Answers:** a. narcolepsy; b. somnambulism; c. insomnia; d. apnea.

5. **Answers:** b. All animals sleep.; c. It is impossible to resist indefinitely the urge to sleep.; e. Animals die when deprived of sleep for extended periods.

6. **Answer:** d. "It's pretty cool that a hypnotist could help those people enter an altered state of consciousness."

7. **Answer:** b. "Lying on your back, rest your hands gently on your abdomen. As you breathe in and out, focus attention on your breath. Notice the rhythmic rise and fall of your abdomen and the slow, deep movement of your chest."

CHAPTER 6

Caption Question, p. 224

Answer: Though answers will vary, today's parenting styles are very different from those of Skinner's time, and people today tend to balk even more at this type of approach.

Caption Question, p. 234

Answer: When an animal learns to avoid food that makes it sick, the animal has a greater chance of surviving. An increased chance of survival gives the animal a greater chance of passing on its genes than the chance of an animal that dies from eating the wrong thing. As the genes of "wiser" and healthier animals are passed along, the species evolves as that much "wiser" and healthier.

Caption Question, p. 236

Answer: The potential misfortunes are unlikely to be supernatural. For example, if you and the cat are in the middle of the road, you might be hit by a car. Or if you try to pet the cat, it might scratch you. If the ladder is not positioned securely, it might fall and hit you. Or you might be so distracted by the ladder that you miss some other peril.

Caption Question, p. 241

Answer: Answers will vary. For example, you might use shaping to teach yourself how to cook an elaborate gourmet meal. How would you begin? Perhaps you need to start with basic skills, such as boiling water to prepare rice. Your next step might be to buy, clean, and slice fresh vegetables. If your recipes call for sauces on those vegetables, you might need to develop sauce-making techniques. Cooking meat or seafood can require specific methods. In learning and layering these abilities, you would be working up to the day when you can put them in the proper order to create a feast.

Caption Question, p. 251

Answer: Answers will vary. However, answers should reflect the fact that memes are units of cultural evolution, influenced in their creation and selection by biological evolution. Biological evolution is slow, and cultural transmission (always predicated on biology) is quick. Macaques learned to enjoy gritless, slightly salty sweet potatoes and passed on this "cultural" food choice. Likewise, we shape and select many behaviors, and those behaviors shape us. For example, the human preference for sweet food has an evolutionary component that then translates into culture-specific representations of candy. Consider Swiss chocolate versus Indonesian durian coconut candy. Milk chocolate may not make as much sense in the hot, humid climate of Indonesia as a candy made from durian fruit and coconut, and durian coconut candy might not taste good to a non-Indonesian Swiss. The human shapes the culture, and the culture shapes the human.

Practice Test, p. 265

1. **Answers:** US is food, UR is going to the food dish to eat the food, CS is the program's theme song, CR is going to the food dish to eat the food when the theme song plays.

2. **Answers:** US is lemon, UR is a pucker, CS is a blue dot, CR is a pucker at the sight of the blue dot.

3. **Answer:** c. The students will experience puckering responses, because of stimulus generalization.

4. **Answer:** b. Eating a box of raisins and experiencing extreme nausea a few hours later.

5. **Answers:** a. positive reinforcement; b. positive punishment; c. negative reinforcement; d. negative punishment (removal of affection).

CHAPTER 7

Caption Question, p. 269

Answer: Computer memory stores whatever information is correctly put into it. Unless the computer is instructed by the user to perform some function on the stored information, the information will remain in the stored form. By contrast, human memory changes the nature of the material it stores. Even without conscious intervention by the rememberer, human memory involves incompleteness, bias, and distortion. And in humans, memory retrieval is sometimes consciously deliberate and other times seemingly random.

Caption Question, p. 272

Answer: Answers will vary. Each of us will have different reasons for wanting to lose or keep particular memories. Eliminating painful parts of the past might make life easier to bear. However, losing a bad memory might end up changing some positive aspect of your personality that is connected to the memory. Losing a bad memory might also cause you to make a related mistake more than once.

Caption Question, p. 274

Answer: At the center of the photo, the woman is looking up, wearing glasses, and wearing a red jacket.

Caption Question, p. 283

Answer: Answers will vary. Successful strategies for remembering might include chunking (e.g., remembering your student ID number in chunks) or mnemonics (e.g., knowing the difference between afferent and efferent neurons by remembering that efferent starts with "e" and so does the word *exit,* so these neurons carry messages away from the CNS).

Practice Test, p. 316

1. **Answer:** a. conjunction task; effortful.

2. **Answer:** d. Anna should use Sarah's name in a sentence.

CHAPTER 8

Caption Question, p. 335

Answer: Answer will vary. It could be that evolution biases us toward gains of resources or toward representations of success. Therefore we perceive loss more acutely as failure to be successful in the acquisition and maintenance of resources.

Caption Question, p. 337

Answer: Answers will vary and may concern job performance, athletics, musical performances, grades, and so on. Your expectations of success or failure may have a direct relationship with your feelings about the outcome of an effort.

Caption Question, p. 338

Answer: Schwartz would recommend that, in making a noncrucial decision such as which variety of Spam to buy, you should not seek to make the absolutely right choice. Instead, you should aim for a reasonable choice that will meet your needs, then focus on the positive aspects of your choice.

Caption Question, p. 347

Answer: Answers will vary. If you agree that the test is not culturally biased, you might argue that the shapes and colors have no cultural meanings in and of themselves. If you disagree, you might argue that, since these colored shapes do not necessarily appear in nature (i.e., without human intervention), their unfamiliarity to some people in some parts of the world might constitute cultural bias. In addition, the type of thinking required to solve a puzzle like this might be emphasized in some cultures more than others and thus give some people a problem-solving advantage.

Caption Question, p. 354

Answer: As the text notes, the overall size and weight of Einstein's brain are unremarkable. Thus the smartest people do not necessarily have the largest brains. The size of Einstein's parietal lobe was larger than average. This finding supports the idea that different kinds of intelligence are related to the sizes of particular brain regions.

Practice Test, p. 363

1. **Answers:** a. All attributes of a category are equally salient.; b. All members of a category fit equally well into that category.; e. Membership within a category is on an all-or-none basis.

2. **Answers:** Option a is most likely; option c is least likely.

3. **Answer:** a. Students will settle into their seats and perhaps glance over the handout. People who already know each other might converse, but they most likely will not discuss the questions.

4. **Answers:** a. inductive; b. deductive; c. deductive; d. inductive; e. inductive.

5. **Answers:** a. framing effect; b. availability heuristic; c. representativeness heuristic.

6. **Answer:** a. achievement, aptitude.

CHAPTER 9

Caption Question, p. 368

Answer: The brain on the right is smaller than the brain on the left and perhaps a bit misshapen, the folds of its cerebral cortex are less elaborate, and its color is different. FAS might have contributed to these aspects of the appearance of the brain on the right.

Caption Question, p. 375

Answer: Imprinting is a biologically timed, biologically determined, and species-specific adaptive process. The ducks are programmed to follow what moves. Attachment is far more complex. Infants develop attachment, but it varies qualitatively based on the interactive dynamic of the infant and mother.

Caption Question, p. 382

Answer: The preferential-looking technique is being used in this test.

Caption Question, p. 391

Answer: Children who like to eat M&M's will tend to be motivated when it comes to determining the number of M&M's. That is, knowing which row has more candies increases the chance that the child will get to eat more candies.

Caption Question, p. 413

Answer: Answers will vary. You might argue that rock music was created as a celebration of youth and that "rocking" requires youthful energy. Alternatively, you might argue that rock is all about spirit and that the Stones still have the spirit of youthful rockers. Then the question is what qualifies a person as elderly—is it chronological age or attitude?

Caption Question, p. 416

Answer: By exercising, socializing, and laughing, these women are increasing their chances of feeling well physically and mentally. Eating right and not consuming harmful things will improve their chances, as will maintaining appropriate weights for their individual body types. In addition, the women should remain mentally active, such as by reading, paying attention to current events, solving problems, and taking in the arts. Since development is always a matter of nature *and* nurture, however, there are biological factors beyond the women's control. Genetics may play a major role in the women's health and longevity.

Practice Test, p. 419

1. **Answers:** a. differentiate between sweet and nonsweet tastes; c. grasp a caregiver's finger; e. orient toward loud sounds; i. turn his or her head toward the smell of the mother's breast milk; j. turn toward a nipple near his or her mouth.

2. **Answer:** c. Contact with comforting "mothers" promoted a sense of security.

3. **Answer:** d. The infant will stare at the three remaining cubes for a relatively long time.

4. **Answers:** a—preconventional; b—postconventional; c—conventional.

CHAPTER 10

Caption Question, p. 423

Answer: Answers will of course vary, but the authors hope your valence and activation are somewhere on the right side of the map.

Caption Question, p. 425

Answer: The woman on the left is more likely to report feeling happy, because she is holding the pen in a way that makes her mouth curve into a smile. The woman on the right is holding the pencil in a way that makes her mouth pucker. Your responses are likely to reflect the ways in which you hold your pen or pencil.

Caption Question, p. 446

Answer: "BUY 1 GET 1 FREE" can be a very attractive offer, especially if you really want the item to begin with. However, "LAST CHANCE TO BUY" conveys special urgency because we are averse to loss. "BUY 1 GET 1 FREE" indicates that the item is in great enough supply that it will be around for a while. "LAST CHANCE TO BUY" indicates that the supply is limited and perhaps running out.

Caption Question, p. 447

Answer: In each case, the person delays gratification by turning his or her attention away from the desired item. Thinking of the item as something similar but undesired turns the thought of the item from hot to cold. Simply ignoring the item, if successful, can remove the hot thought. Self-distraction provides a block between the conscious mind and the hot thought.

Caption Question, p. 452

Answer: Answers will vary, but you might consider factors such as your emotional state, the presence of other people, and the occasion for eating (a special occasion? a celebration? a routine meal?).

Caption Question, p. 453

Answer: Answers will vary, depending on factors such as your palate and adventurousness.

Practice Test, p. 467

1. **Answer:** b. Sonya is somewhat anxious about this presentation. She knows her stuff but recognizes how much is riding on the quality of this presentation. This anxious energy motivates her to polish her slides and practice her talk.

2. **Answer:** b. GABA.

CHAPTER 11

Caption Question, p. 473

Answer: If you study as usual, you are likely to get a grade closer to your usual grades. Regression to the mean is the principle behind this result. The hypnotist might contribute to the result, if you are susceptible to hypnosis and the hypnosis session helps calm your anxiety.

Caption Question, p. 477

Answer: Some of our coping strategies involve solving the problem that has created the stress (e.g., coming up with a plan and schedule for getting a paper done on time). At other times, we try to simply mask the stress by engaging in behaviors that change how we feel (e.g., going to a party instead of studying).

Caption Question, p. 485

Answer: It may be nearly impossible to imagine yourself in that situation. Still, consider that some of the passengers clearly engaged in a secondary appraisal process to develop a plan. They focused on the problem to change the outcome (i.e., not allowing their plane to crash in Washington, D.C.). Could you have done this under the circumstances?

Caption Question, p. 503

Answer: As this chapter emphasizes, a positive attitude can contribute to one's health and well-being. Laughter can be a sign of positivity, but is it, by itself, a means of improving a person's state of mind and physical shape? Psychologists interested in this question have performed experiments to test the effects of laughter. The benefits of laughter are numerous and have an adaptive basis (Dunbar et al., 2011; Mehu & Dunbar, 2008).

Practice Test, p. 511

1. **Answer:** d. Genetic predispositions to some illnesses exist. But living healthily can help reduce the chance of developing a disease.

2. **Answer:** b. biopsychosocial model.

3. **Answer:** a. "Well, I figured I couldn't stay in that funk forever. Things eventually had to start looking up again."

4. **Answers:** a. are committed to daily activities; e. see challenges as opportunities for growth; f. see themselves as able to control their own lives.

5. **Answer:** All the choices are true.

CHAPTER 12

Caption Questions, p. 514

Answers: For (a) and (b), answers will of course vary, depending on each reader's view of the situations, the results, and people.

Caption Question, p. 515

Answer: Body language indicates that the couple is having a disagreement. The woman's right hand is on her hip in a "holding the line" pose. Her left hand is raised in an "oh, please, do not try to make me believe that" gesture. Her upwardly tilted head also indicates disbelief, and she does not seem to be meeting the man's gaze. The man, meanwhile, is stretching out his hands in a gesture of entreaty: "Hey, come on, believe me!" His legs are bent in a way that angles his body toward the woman. His expression suggests mental focus on the matter at hand. At the same time, there is the suggestion of playfulness in both of these people's appearances. Their disagreement might not mean the end of the relationship.

Caption Question, p. 518

Answer: As a critical thinker, you probably would avoid stereotyping all Canadians as hockey fans. After all, is there a country in which *every* person shares an interest? Still, selection bias is on display in this photo: Because it is a photo of hockey fans at an international event, enthusiasm for a particular sport is unmistakably associated with a country's flag and major symbol (hockey = Canada = red maple leaf). This imagery conveys the impression that the sport has particular significance for the national identity. So while you might not stereotype all Canadians as liking hockey, you might associate Canadians with hockey and with patriotism. By contrast, what would the photo of an individual tell you about national identity? You would be on unsteady ground if you were to assert that all Canadians, all Canadian women, all Canadian singers—all anything—share the attributes of Céline Dion. In other words, when you consider the implications of imagery, you need to consider the sample size on display, just as you would consider the sample size in evaluating scientific findings.

Caption Question, p. 532

Answer: If the pledges' behavior matched that of people generally, they justified the hazing as a necessary means of attaining the important goal of joining the fraternity. To justify the importance of that goal, of course, the pledges might have overestimated the importance of belonging to the fraternity.

Caption Question, p. 538

Answer: By uniting the individual with a group, deindividuation can lead to a feeling of belonging. Of course, some groups might be more worth belonging to than other groups are. At its most negative, deindividuation could lead the individual to go along with the group to the point of engaging in behaviors that the individual will regret, such as behaviors that are harmful to the individual or others.

Caption Question, p. 553

Answer: So far, the story might lead you to believe that Genovese was the victim of bystander apathy. After all, how could so many witnesses fail to report the attack? But read on for a fuller understanding of the situation.

Practice Test, p. 565

1. **Answers:** a. ingroup favoritism; b. illusory correlation; c. outgroup homogeneity.

2. **Answer:** d. "We can hold an all-campus competition, where teams of dorms would compete for prizes. Dorm A and Dorm B could be on one team; Dorm C and Dorm D could be on the other team."

CHAPTER 13

Caption Question, p. 574

Answer: The student's thoughts might be something like, "Okay, which is it, stay in and study or go to the party? On the one hand, if I study, I might do better on this test than I did on that last one! On the other hand, if I study, I might miss out on a great time. Chances are good that it'll be a fun party. So, which is more important to me, improving my chances of getting a good grade in this course or having fun tonight? I might hate to admit this, even to myself, but I want to do well in college. Time to study." In this inner monologue, positive reinforcement comes in the form of potential success: a better grade on a test, thus a better grade in the course, thus a better GPA, thus a better chance for success down the line.

Caption Question, p. 575

Answer: The CAPS model indicates that cognitive-social influences can better predict behavior than personality traits can. According to this model, one's response to a situation depends on one's perception of the situation, one's emotional reaction to it, one's relevant skills, and one's anticipation of the outcome. Personality might inform each of those factors, but personality itself does not determine response.

Caption Question, p. 581

Answer: By responding to these statements, you are experiencing one of the ways personality is measured. There are no right responses, as personality varies from person to person.

Caption Question, p. 590

Answer: If dogs have personalities, then it is possible that any answer would have to take into account both the tendency of the particular breeds and individual variation. In other words, do not let these "anecdotal" photos bias your response as to which type of dog is friendlier! Golden retrievers might tend to be friendlier than rottweilers, but an individual golden retriever might be unfriendly and an individual rottweiler might be friendly. Nature and nurture both come into play. To test your hypothesis, you might set up an experiment that would involve safely coming into contact with a number of golden retrievers and a number of rottweilers. You would have to

act the same way in the presence of each dog and measure what you would consider the dog's friendliness.

Practice Test, p. 615

1. **Answers:** a. type and trait; b. learning and cognition; c. psychodynamic; d. humanistic.

2. **Answer:** a. idiographic; projective.

3. **Answers:** b. Predictions of our own behaviors may be biased in favor of our subjective perceptions (how we *think* we act) rather than our objective behaviors (how we *do* act).; c. We tend to pay more attention to others than to ourselves and thus fail to notice our own behavior; others notice how we behave and are better able to predict our future behaviors.

CHAPTER 14

Caption Question, p. 622

Answer: A clinician might note that a person at point A is currently not experiencing anxiety, a person at point B is somewhat anxious or intermittently anxious, and a person at point C is currently very anxious. States of anxiety vary from person to person and from time to time, and their evaluation is always a judgment call on the part of the individual and the clinician. In much the same way, psychological disorders involve continuums: They are generally not all-or-nothing, yes-or-no matters. Evaluation of a patient's symptoms and whether the patient has a particular disorder always involves some investigative work and judgment.

Caption Question, p. 626

Answer: In this model, nature is represented by genetic predisposition, and nurture is represented by childhood trauma. Each of these factors, separately and in combination, can contribute to a person's vulnerability to mental disorder.

Practice Test, p. 671

1. **Answers:** a. Does the behavior deviate from cultural norms?; b. Is the behavior causing the individual personal distress?; c. Is the behavior maladaptive?

2. **Answer:** c. internalizing, females; externalizing, males.

CHAPTER 15

Caption Question, p. 676

Answer: The potential benefits come from the client's position. Because the client is not forced to meet the therapist's gaze, the client might feel less under scrutiny and therefore freer to be honest. Reclining on a presumably soft couch, rather than sitting upright in a comparably harder chair, might also encourage the client to open up about his or her circumstances, feelings, perceptions, and symptoms. One potential drawback is that the position will encourage the client to feel so free that the client drifts into fantasy or drama rather than honesty. Or the client might perceive the therapist as a distant, cut-off authority figure rather than an impartial listener. Too, the therapist might feel distant and cut off rather than able to fully observe the client's facial expressions during their interaction.

Caption Question, p. 679

Answer: Cognitive therapy focuses on distorted thought patterns and how those thought patterns help produce maladaptive behaviors and emotions. By employing cognitive restructuring, the therapist aims to help the client change the thought patterns and thus change the behaviors and emotions. According to this approach, the more realistic and positive the client's thinking, the healthier the client's behaviors and emotions.

Caption Question, p. 712

Answer: As discussed in the paragraphs below, possible contributing factors are a reduction in biological drives during middle age, the patient's gaining of insight into his or her self-defeating behaviors, and the patient's getting too worn out to continue his or her manipulative ways.

Caption Question, p. 716

Answer: In considering the decrease in suicide rates, if we view medication (i.e., the altering of biology) as representing nature, then we also have to ask how nurture might be related. For example, was there an increase in public awareness of teenage suicide, so that young people received more support from their communities? Were the economic conditions at the time on an upturn, so that young people were feeling more upbeat and less stressed out?

Practice Test, p. 725

1. **Answers:** Choices a, b, and e are true.

2. **Answers:** a. Treatments should be based on evidence of their effectiveness.; b. Treatments should be appropriate for the particular disorders.; c. Specific techniques for treatment should be developed in the laboratory by psychologists.

3. **Answer:** The correct order is c, a, b.

4. **Answer:** c. Joshua's tendency to get into fistfights.

5. **Answers:** Choices a, b, and d are likely true.

PERMISSIONS ACKNOWLEDGMENTS

Every effort has been made to contact the copyright holders of the material used in *Psychological Science*. Rights holders of any material not credited should contact Permissions Department, W. W. Norton & Company, Inc., 500 Fifth Avenue, New York, NY 10110 for a correction to be made in the next reprinting of our work.

CHAPTER 1

Opener: Ann Summa/Workbook Stock/Getty Images.

Fig. 1.1: *Time,* January 29, 2007.

Fig. 1.3: © 2010, *Weekly World News,* Bat Boy LLC, All rights reserved.

Fig. 1.4: Hermann J. Knippertz/AP.

Fig. 1.5: Rischgitz/Getty Images.

Fig. 1.6: The Granger Collection, New York.

Fig. 1.7: Imagno/Getty Images.

Fig. 1.8: Bettmann/Corbis.

Fig. 1.9: Archives of the History of American Psychology, University of Akron.

Fig. 1.10: Wikimedia Commons.

Fig. 1.11: From *American Journal of Psychology.* © 1974 by the Board of Trustees of the University of Illinois. Used with permission of the University of Illinois Press.

Fig. 1.12: From *Mind Sights* by Roger N. Shepard. © 1990 by Roger N. Shepard. Henry Holt and Company, LLC.

Fig. 1.13: Archives of the History of American Psychology, University of Akron.

Fig. 1.14: Department of Psychology Archives/McMicken College of Arts and Sciences.

Fig. 1.15: Scott Squire.

Fig. 1.16: Bettmann/Corbis.

Fig. 1.17: Archives of the History of American Psychology, University of Akron.

Fig. 1.18: Courtesy George Miller, Princeton University, © 2001, Pryde Brown Photographs, Princeton, NJ.

Fig. 1.19: Archives of the History of American Psychology, University of Akron.

Fig. 1.20: *Time,* January 28, 2008, cover.

Fig. 1.21: Courtesy Professor Joseph J. Campos, University of California, Berkeley.

Fig. 1.22: *Newsweek,* March 19, 2007.

Fig. 1.23a: Rick Gomez/Corbis.

Fig. 1.23b: Luke Duggleby/OnAsia.

Fig. 1.24(i): SIU/Peter Arnold Images.

Fig. 1.24(ii): © Stockbyte/Alamy.

Fig. 1.24(iii): © Somos Images LLC/Alamy.

Fig. 1.24(iv): Bruno De Hogues/Getty Images.

Fig. 1.25: Levitin, D. J., and Menon, V. (2003).

Cartoon 1.1: © The *New Yorker* Collection 1998/Sam Gross from cartoonbank.com. All Rights Reserved.

Cartoon 1.2: *The Far Side* ® by Gary Larson © 1982 FarWorks, Inc. All Rights Reserved. Used with permission.

CHAPTER 2

Opener: Laura Burke/Corbis.

Fig. 2.1a: Pearl Gabel/*New York Daily News.*

Fig. 2.1b: Jesse Ward/*New York Daily News.*

Fig. 2.3a: Ocean/Corbis.

Fig. 2.3b: Steve Skjold/Photo Edit.

Fig. 2.3c: Ace Stock Limited/Alamy.

Fig. 2.3e: Christy Varonfakis Johnson/Alamy.

Fig. 2.4a: Karl Ammann/Corbis.

Fig. 2.4b: Lawrence S. Sugiyama/University of Oregon.

Fig. 2.5: Courtesy of First Run Features.

Fig. 2.6a: Ocean/Corbis.

Fig. 2.6b: Pauline St. Denis/Corbis.

Fig. 2.8: Peter Arnold, Inc./Alamy.

Fig. 2.11: Corbis/SuperStock.

Fig. 2.12a–b: © Peter Menzel/www.menzelphoto.com.

Fig. 2.13a–b: Roethlisberger, F. J., & Dickson, W. J. (1939). *Management and the worker: An account of a research program conducted by the Western Electric Company, Hawthorne Works, Chicago.* Cambridge, MA: Harvard University Press.

Fig. 2.14a: Richard B. Levine/Newscom.

Fig. 2.14b: Charles Dharapak/AP.

Fig. 2.15a: Janine Wiedel Photolibrary/Alamy.

Fig. 2.15b: John Birdsall/The Image Works.

Fig. 2.15c: JUPITERIMAGES/Creatas/Alamy.

Fig. 2.18a: Mark Burnett/Alamy.

Fig. 2.18b: Richard T. Nowitz/Photo Researchers.

Fig. 2.18c: AJPhoto/Photo Researchers.

Fig. 2.18d: James Cavallini/Photo Researchers.

Fig. 2.18e: Michael Ventura/Alamy.

Fig. 2.18f: WDCN/Univ. College London/Photo Researchers.

Fig. 2.18g: Charles Thatcher/Getty Images.

Fig. 2.18i: Mark Harmel/Alamy.

Fig. 2.18j: Courtesy of Psych Central.

Fig. 2.18k: Marcello Massimini/University of Wisconsin–Madison.

Fig. 2.18l: Dr. K. Singh, Liverpool University/Dr. S. Hamdy & Dr. Q. Aziz, Manchester University.

Fig. 2.19: LOVETTE/REYNOLDS/NIKITIN/SIPA.

Cartoon 2.1: ScienceCartoonsPlus.com.

Cartoon 2.2: Sydney Harris.

Cartoon 2.3: Src. 2005 Sidney Harris from cartoonbanks.com.

CHAPTER 3

Opener: Martin Adolfsson/Gallery Stock.

Fig. 3.2a: © SF Palm/StageImage/The Image Works.

Fig. 3.2b: Brigitte Engl/Redferns/Getty Images.

Fig. 3.3: James Cavallini/Photo Researchers.

Fig. 3.10: Newscom.

Fig. 3.11: Mendez et al. "Simultaneous intrastriatal and intranigral fetal dopaminergic grafts in patients with Parkinson disease: A pilot study, Report of three cases," *J. Neurosurg.*/Volume 96/March 2002.

Fig. 3.12: Philippe Lopez/AFP/Getty Images.

Fig. 3.14a: From Spurzheim, J. (1825). Phrenology, or, the doctrine of the mind and the relations between its manifestations and the body, etc.

Fig. 3.14b: Bettmann/Corbis.

Fig. 3.15a(i): *Nature Reviews Neuroscience 5,* 812–819 (October 2004).

Fig. 3.21b–c: From Penfield, Wilder (1958), *The excitable cortex in conscious man.* Liverpool University Press.

Fig. 3.22: Ramachandran, V. S., and Blakeslee, S., Fig. 6.1, drawing made by a neglect patient, from *Phantoms in the brain.* Copyright © 1998 by V. S. Ramachandran and Sandra Blakeslee. Reprinted by permission of HarperCollins Publishers Inc.

Fig. 3.23a: Collection of Jack and Beverly Wilgus.

Fig. 3.23b: www.hbs.deakin.edu.au/gagepage/pgage.htm.

Fig. 3.23c: Hanna Damasio, © 2004 Massachusetts Medical Society.

Fig. 3.24: Bettmann/Corbis.

Fig. 3.28: Mark Wilson/Getty Images.

Fig. 3.29a: Martin Adolfsson/Gallery Stock.

Fig. 3.29b: Dr. Dennis Kunkel/Getty Images.

Fig. 3.29c: CNRI/Science Photo Library Researchers, Inc.

Fig. 3.30: Ron Edmonds/AP.

Fig. 3.31: CNRI/Science Photo Library Researchers.

Fig. 3.33a–h: Harry B. Clay, Jr.

Fig. 3.34a: David Fox/Oxford Scientific/Photolibrary.

Fig. 3.34b: Dr. David M. Phillips/Visuals Unlimited/Getty Images.

Fig. 3.35a: Tony Freeman/PhotoEdit.

Fig. 3.35b: Bob Sacha.

Fig. 3.36a: © Bob Daemmrich/The Image Works.

Fig. 3.36b: Binda, C., Newton-Vinson, P., Hubalek, F., Edmondson, D. E., Mattevi, A. (2002).

Fig. 3.36c: Robin Nelson/PhotoEdit.

Fig. 3.37: Philippe Garo/Photo Researchers, Inc.

Fig. 3.39: Joan Y. Chiao, Tetsuya Iidaka, Heather L. Gordon, Junpei Nogawa, Moshe Bar, Elissa Aminoff, Norihiro Sadato, and Nalini Ambady, "Cultural Specificity in Amygdala Response to Fear Faces" from *Journal of Cognitive Neuroscience*, 20:12 (December 2008), pp. 2167–2174. Copyright © 2008 by the Massachusetts Institute of Technology. **Photos 3.39a–d:** Courtesy of Ekman & Matsumoto. **Photo 3.39e:** Courtesy of Dr. Joan Chiao.

Fig. 3.41: David Emmite/WORKBOOK.

Fig. 3.42: From Vilayanur S. Ramachandran and Edward M. Hubbard, "Hearing Colors, Tasting Shapes." *Scientific American*, May 2003. Copyright © 2003 Scientific American, Inc. Reproduced with permission. All rights reserved.

Fig. 3.43a–b: Indiana University School of Medicine.

Fig. 3.44: AP Photo.

Cartoon 3.1: Cartoonstock.com.

Cartoon 3.2: © The *New Yorker* Collection 1999/William Haefeli from cartoonbank.com. All Rights Reserved.

CHAPTER 4

Opener: John-Francis Bourke/Getty Images.

Fig. 4.1: Photo courtesy of the New England Historic Genealogical Society (Boston, Mass.).

Fig. 4.6: Jonathan Olley/Getty Images.

Fig. 4.7: George Pimentel/WireImage/Getty Images.

Fig. 4.8: Marcy Maloy/Getty Images.

Fig. 4.9: John-Francis Bourke/Getty Images.

Fig. 4.10a: Steven Errico/Digital Vision/Getty Images.

Fig. 4.10b: Jose Luis Pelaez Inc./Blend Images/Getty Images.

Fig. 4.11: Jochen Sand/agefotostock.

Fig. 4.12: John Bazemore/AP.

Fig. 4.14: Marcos Welsh/agefotostock.

Fig. 4.15: James King-Holmes/Photo Researchers.

Fig. 4.16(ii): Cheyenne Rouse/Getty Images.

Fig. 4.20a–b: © Bjørn Rørslett/NN.

Fig. 4.21b: Figure "Color contrast and color appearance: Brightness constancy and color" from *Vision and Visual Perception*, ed. C.H. Graham (New York: Wiley, 1965). We have made diligent efforts to contact the copyright holder to obtain permission to reprint this selection. If you have information that would help us, please write to us at the address given above.

Fig. 4.25a: Stephen Dalton/NHPA.

Fig. 4.26a: Olveczky et al., 2003, Segregation of Object and Background Motion in Retina. *Nature, 423,* 401–408.

Fig. 4.26b: From Celeste McCollough, "Color adaptation of edge detectors in the human visual system," *Science 149*:1115 (9/3/1965). Reprinted with permission from AAAS.

Fig. 4.26c: Kitaoka, A. "Light of Sweden illusion." Reprinted by permission of Akiyoshi Kitaoka.

Fig. 4.27a–b: Figure 8.4 (a) and (b) from p. 280 of *Psychology* by Peter Gray. © 1991, 1994, 1999 by Worth Publishers. Used with permission.

Fig. 4.27e(i): Figure from Varin, D., "Fenomeni di contrasto e diffusione cromatica," *Rivista di Psicologia 65* (1970).

Fig. 4.27e(ii): Kanizsa, G. "Subjective Contours" from *Scientific American 234*. Copyright © 1976. Reprinted by permission of Jerome Kuhl.

Fig. 4.28: Selfridge, Oliver, "Pattern Recognition and Modern Computers" from *Proceedings of the Western Computer Conference*. Copyright © 1955 by the Association for Computing Machinery, Inc. Reprinted with permission.

Fig. 4.29: A Hawthorne/Arctic Photo.

Fig. 4.30a–b(ii): From McCarthy, G., Price, A., Allison, T. (1997). Face specific processing in the human fusiform gyrus. *Journal of Cognitive Neuroscience, 9I*, 605–610, etc.

Fig. 4.31: Courtesy Peter Thompson, University of York.

Fig. 4.34: Munch, Edvard (1863–1944) © ARS, NY/Scala/Art Resource, NY.

Fig. 4.35: Sartore/Getty Images/*National Geographic*.

Fig. 4.36: Courtesy of Todd Heatherton.

Fig. 4.37a–b: © Exploratorium, www.exploratorium.edu.

Fig. 4.40: Figure from *The Art Pack* by Christopher Frayling, Helen Frayling, and Ron Van der Meer, copyright © 1992 by Singram Company Ltd. The Art Pack copyright © 1992 by Van der Meer Paper Design Ltd. Text copyright © 1992 by Christopher & Helen Frayling. Copyright © 1992 by The Art Pack. Used by permission of Alfred A. Knopf, a division of Random House, Inc.

Fig. 4.41a–b: From *Psychology*, 6th Edition, by Henry Gleitman, Alan J. Fridlund, Daniel Reisberg. Copyright © 2004 by W. W. Norton, etc.

Fig. 4.42: Illustration "Turning Tables" illusion from *Mind Sights* by Roger N. Shepard. Copyright © 1990 by Roger N. Shepard. Reprinted by permission of Henry Holt and Company, LLC.

Cartoon 4.1: © The *New Yorker* Collection, Pat Byrnes from Cartoonbank.com.

Cartoon 4.2: © *Social Signal* 2010. Reprinted by permission. Original cartoon at RobCottingham.com.

CHAPTER 5

Opener: Peter Augustine/Gallery Stock.

Fig. 5.1: Courtesy of Eddie and Erik Ramsey.

Fig. 5.2: Sidney Harris.

Fig. 5.4a: Courtesy Michael Schiavo.

Fig. 5.4b: Bogdan Hrywniak/AFP/Getty Images.

Fig. 5.11: The Photo Works.

Fig. 5.13b: James King-Holmes/Photo Researchers.

Fig. 5.15: PHOTOTAKE Inc./Alamy.

Fig. 5.16: Blickwinkel/Alamy.

Fig. 5.17: Chris Rout/Alamy.

Fig. 5.19: Newscom.

Fig. 5.20: Courtesy Steve G. Jones, Ed.D., Clinical Hypnotherapist.

Fig. 5.21: David Young-Wolff/Getty Images.

Fig. 5.22a–b: "Minding one's emotions" by Farb, Norman A. S.; Anderson, Adam K.; Mayberg, Helen; Bean, Jim; McKeon, Deborah; Segal, Zindel V. *Emotion*. Vol. 10(2), Apr. 2010.

Fig. 5.23: Nathan Benn/Alamy.

Fig. 5.24: Eckehard Schulz/AP.

Fig. 5.26: Kim, S. J., Lyoo, I. K., Hwang, J., Chung, A., Hoon Sung, Y., Kim, J., Kwon, D. H., Chang, K. H., & Renshaw, P. F. (2006).

Fig. 5.27: Multnomah County Sheriff's Office.

Fig. 5.28a–b: 5th edition of the textbook *Biological Psychology: An Introduction to Behavioral, Cognitive, and Clinical Neuroscience,* by Breedlove, Rosenzweig, and Watson (Sinauer Associates).

Fig. 5.30a: Newscom.

Fig. 5.30b: Peter Treanor/Alamy.

Fig. 5.32a: Robert Altman/The Image Works.

Fig. 5.32b: Bettmann/Corbis.

Cartoon 5.1: © Sidney Harris, cartoonbank.com.

Cartoon 5.2: © Sidney Harris.

Cartoon 5.3: 2005 Robert Mankoff, cartoonbank.com. All Rights Reserved.

CHAPTER 6

Opener: Brian Sokol.

Fig. 6.1: Bettmann/Corbis.

Fig. 6.2a: Bettmann/Corbis.

Fig. 6.7a: Psychology Archives—The University of Akron.

Fig. 6.7b: Benjamin Harris, University of New Hampshire

Fig. 6.8: Childress, A. R., Mozey, P. D., McElgin, W., Fitzgerald, J., Revich, M., O'Brien, C. P. (1999).

Fig. 6.9a–b: Lincoln P. Bower.

Fig. 6.10a: Pegaz/Alamy.

Fig. 6.10b: Jonathan Storey/Getty Images.

Fig. 6.12a: Yerkes, Robert M. Manuscripts & Archives, Yale University.

Fig. 6.14a: Nina Leen/*Time*/Pix Images.

Fig. 6.15: AP/Wide World Photos.

Fig. 6.18: Image Source/Getty Images.

Fig. 6.19: Lynn M. Stone/naturepl.com.

Fig. 6.21: F. B. M. deWaal.

Fig. 6.22: Albert Bandura, Dept. of Psychology, Stanford University.

Fig. 6.23: D. Hurst/Alamy.

Fig. 6.24: Susan Mineka, Northwestern University.

Fig. 6.25: Geri Engberg/The Image Works.

Fig. 6.26: © IFC Films/Courtesy Everett Collection.

Fig. 6.27: Courtesy Daniel Miller, Dpt. of Neurology, Carthage College.

Fig. 6.29: Biophoto Associates/Photo Researchers, Inc.

Fig. 6.31: AP/Wide World Photos.

Cartoon 6.1: © The *New Yorker* Collection 1993/Tom Cheney from cartoonbank.com.

CHAPTER 7

Opener: Paul Elledge.

Fig. 7.2: Copyright © Suzanne Corkin, used with permission of The Wylie Agency LLC.

Fig. 7.5: From Wheeler, M. E., Petersen, S. E., & Buckner, R. L. (2000). Memory's echo: Vivid remembering reactivates sensory specific cortex. *Proceedings of the National Academy of Sciences, 97,* 11125–11129.

Fig. 7.6: Photofest.

Fig. 7.7b: Alamy.

Fig. 7.10a–c: Courtesy Daniel J. Simons.

Fig. 7.13: Newscom.

Fig. 7.18a: Bjorn Svensson/Alamy.

Fig. 7.18c: Chris A. Crumley/Alamy.

Fig. 7.19a: David Turnley/Getty Images.

Fig. 7.19b: Newscom.

Fig. 7.20: Michael Blann/Getty Images.

Fig. 7.21: © Asia Images/SuperStock.

Fig. 7.23: Robert E. Klein/AP.

Fig. 7.24a: John Froschauer/AP.

Fig. 7.24b: Photofest.

Fig. 7.25a: Charla Jones/Getstock.com.

Fig. 7.25b: Kennedy Space Center/NASA.

Fig. 7.26: Joe Raedle/Getty Images.

Fig. 7.26c: Tom Stoddart/Getty Images.

Fig. 7.27a–b: AP/Wide World Photos.

Fig. 7.28a–b: From Loftus, Miller, & Burns, 1978. Courtesy Elizabeth Loftus.

Fig. 7.29: Tony Gutierrez/AP.

Fig. 7.32a–b: Peter DaSilva/AP.

Cartoon 7.1: © The *New Yorker* Collection 1998/Mick Stevens from cartoonbank.com.

CHAPTER 8

Opener: Jon Feingersh Photography Inc./Blend Images/Corbis.

Fig. 8.1: Ed Andrieski/AP/Wide World Photos.

Fig. 8.2a: Carmen Taylor/AP.

Fig. 8.2b: Rick Bowmer/AP.

Fig. 8.6: Eysenck, M. W., Figure 8.3, *Cognitive psychology: A student's handbook,* 2nd Edition, Lawrence Erlbaum Associates. Copyright 1990. Reprinted by permission.

Fig. 8.8a: Imagebroker/Alamy.

Fig. 8.8b: Steven Vidler/Eurasia Press/Corbis.

Fig. 8.8c: Warner Bros./Photofest.

Fig. 8.8d: Artisan Entertainment/Photofest.

Fig. 8.9: © Peter Arnold, Inc./Alamy.

Fig. 8.10a: Mario Tama/Getty Images.

Fig. 8.10b: Agencia Estado via AP Images/Wide World Photos.

Fig. 8.11a: © AKG-images/The Image Works.

Fig. 8.11b: Alamy.

Fig. 8.12a: Jeff Greenberg/PhotoEdit.

Fig. 8.12b: Erik Dreyer/Getty Images.

Fig. 8.12c: Corbis.

Fig. 8.13: Dalton, M. A., Bernhardt, A. M., Gibson, J. J., Sargent, J. D., Beach, M. L., Adachi-Mejia, A. M., Titus-Ernstoff, L. T., & Heatherton, T. F. (2005). *Archives of Pediatrics & Adolescent Medicine, 159,* 854–859.

Fig. 8.14a: Imageshop/Alamy.

Fig. 8.14b: © Cultura Limited/SuperStock.

Fig. 8.14c: Alamy.

Fig. 8.14d: © PhotoAlto/SuperStock.

Fig. 8.14e: Glowimages/Getty Images.

Fig. 8.14f: Photodisc/Alamy.

Fig. 8.14g: Photodisc/Getty Images.

Fig. 8.14h: Agency Design Pics Inc./Alamy.

Fig. 8.18a: Mandel Ngan/AFP/Getty Images.

Fig. 8.18b: Mike Coppola/Getty Images.

Fig. 8.19: Adam Butler/AP.

Fig. 8.20a–b: Courtesy Sheena Iyengar. Iyengar, S. S., & Lepper, M. R. (2000). *Journal of Personality and Social Psychology, 79,* 995–1006.

Fig. 8.21: Alamy.

Fig. 8.26: The Granger Collection, New York.

Fig. 8.30a: Reuters New Media Inc./Corbis.

Fig. 8.30b: Duomo/Corbis.

Fig. 8.31a–b: AP/Wide World Photos.

Fig. 8.34: Jim Ross for *The New York Times.*

Fig. 8.35: Dan Kitwood/Getty Images.

Fig. 8.38: From Kristensen and Bjerkedal, "Explaining the relation between birth order and intelligence," *Science 316*:1717 (6/22/2007). Reprinted with permission from AAAS.

Fig. 8.39: Phelan M. Ebenhack/AP.

Cartoon 8.1: © The *New Yorker* Collection 2005/Leo Cullum from cartoonbank.com. All Rights Reserved.

Cartoon 8.2: © The *New Yorker* by Leo Cullum, November 30, 1998. www.cartoonbank.com. All Rights Reserved.

Cartoon 8.3: © The *New Yorker* Collection 2001/David Sipress. www.cartoonbank.com. All Rights Reserved

CHAPTER 9

Opener: Dennis Manarchy/Gallery Stock.

Fig. 9.1: Bettmann/Corbis.

Fig. 9.2a: Dr. Yorgos Nikas/Phototake.

Fig. 9.2b: Petit Format/Photo Researchers.

Fig. 9.2c: Biophoto Associates/Photo Researchers, Inc.

Fig. 9.3: © Bettmann/Corbis.

Fig. 9.4a–b: Courtesy of Sterling K. Clarren, M.D., Clinical Professor of Pediatrics, University of British Columbia Faculty of Medicine.

Fig. 9.6a: Sergio Pitamitz/Marka/agefotostock.

Fig. 9.6b: Panos Pictures.

Fig. 9.6c: Larry Mayer/Billings Gazette/AP.

Fig. 9.6d: Monica Almeida/*The New York Times*/Redux.

Fig. 9.7: From studies conducted by researchers from The ChildTrauma Academy (www.ChildTrauma.org) led by Bruce D. Perry, M.D., Ph.D.

Fig. 9.8: Nina Leen/TimePix/Getty Images.

Fig. 9.9a–b: Nina Leen/Time Life Pictures/Getty Images.

Fig. 9.11: Stock Boston, LLC/Spencer Grant.

Fig. 9.12: Courtesy Velma Dobson, University of Arizona.

Fig. 9.13a–b: Dr. Carolyn Rovee-Collier, Director, Rutgers Early Learning Project.

Fig. 9.14: Bettman/Corbis.

Fig. 9.15a: Sally and Richard Greenhill/Alamy.

Fig. 9.15b: Tom Mareschal/Alamy.

Fig. 9.15c: Alamy.

Fig. 9.15d: Jon Feingersh/Getty Images.

Fig. 9.16a–c: Michael Newman/PhotoEdit.

Fig. 9.20: Alamy.

Fig. 9.21: Ellen Senisi/The Image Works.

Fig. 9.22: Christina Kennedy/Alamy.

Fig. 9.23: Tomas Munita/*The New York Times*/Redux.

Fig. 9.24: Courtesy of Laura-Ann Petitto.

Fig. 9.27: Photo courtesy David Reimer. From Colapinto, John, *As nature made him: The boy who was raised as a girl* (2000), HarperCollins Publishers Inc.

Fig. 9.28: Reuters Newsmedia Inc./Corbis.

Fig. 9.29: Bruno Morandi/Getty Images.

Fig. 9.30: Gale Zucker/Getty Images.

Fig. 9.31: © Peter Turnley/Corbis.

Fig. 9.32: © Heather Bragman/Syracuse Newspapers/The Image Works.

Fig. 9.33a: Alamy.

Fig. 9.33b: R. Matina/agefotostock.

Fig. 9.33c: Alamy.

Fig. 9.34: Chris McGrath/Getty Images.

Fig. 9.35: Stephanie Maze/Corbis.

Fig. 9.36: Corbis.

Fig. 9.37: Getty Images.

Cartoon 9.1: © The *New Yorker* Collection 2003/Donald Reilly from cartoonbank.com. All Rights Reserved.

Cartoon 9.2: © The *New Yorker* Collection 2001/Edward Koren from cartoonbank.com. All Rights Reserved.

Cartoon 9.3: © The *New Yorker* Collection 1994/Sidney Harris from cartoonbank.com. All Rights Reserved.

CHAPTER 10

Opener: Scott Thomas/Corbis.

Fig. 10.1: Bulsara et al., *Neurosurg Focus 13*(4) Article 5, 2002, Figure 1.

Fig. 10.4(i): Courtesy of W. W. Norton & Co., Inc.

Fig. 10.4(ii): Courtesy of W. W. Norton & Co., Inc.

Fig. 10.10: Chris Lisle/Corbis.

Fig. 10.11a–b: Aviezer, H., Hassin, R. R., Ryan, J., Grady, C., Susskind, J., Anderson, A., Moscovitch, M. & Bentin, S.

Fig. 10.12a–d: Ekman (1972–2004).

Fig. 10.13a–b: Tracy & Matsumoto (2008)/Courtesy of Jessica Tracy.

Fig. 10.15: Courtesy of Dacher Keltner.

Fig. 10.20a–o: Jacob E. Steiner, Ph.D., Laboratory of Oral Physiology, The Hebrew University.

Fig. 10.21a–b: Alamy.

Fig. 10.23: Saxpix.com/agefotostock.

Fig. 10.25: Jeff Greenberg/Alamy.

Fig. 10.26: Bob Daemmrich/The Image Works.

Fig. 10.27: Reuters/Corbis.

Fig. 10.29: Simone van den Berg/FeaturePics.

Fig. 10.31: Alex Mares-Manton/agefotostock.

Fig. 10.31b: Seishiro Akiyama/Getty Images.

Fig. 10.31c: Alex Mares-Manton/agefotostock.

Fig. 10.33: Brent Sims, Joseph Taravella, Eva Olielska, and Pail Zei.

Cartoon 10.1: Copyright 205 Bob Zahn from cartoonbank.com.

Cartoon 10.2: © The *New Yorker* collection 1997/Barbara Smaller from cartoonbank.com. All Rights Reserved.

CHAPTER 11

Opener: Laurie Swope/Aurora Photos.

Fig. 11.1: Jim Mahoney/*Dallas Morning News*.

Fig. 11.4: Adam Gault/Photo Researchers.

Fig. 11.5a: Alaska Stock LLC/Alamy.

Fig. 11.5b: Alamy.

Fig. 11.7: Park Street/Photo Edit.

Fig. 11.8: Janine Wiedel Photolibrary/Alamy.

Fig. 11.11: American Heart Association.

Fig. 11.12: The Kobal Collection.

Fig. 11.13: From Sheldon Cohen, Tom Kamarck, and Robin Mermelstein, "A Global Measure of Perceived Stress." *Journal of Health and Social Behavior*, Vol. 24, No. 4 (Dec. 1983), Appendix A. Reprinted by permission of The American Sociological Association.

Fig. 11.17a: Douglas Peebles/photolibrary.

Fig. 11.17b: Eric Johnson/*The New York Times*.

Fig. 11.17c: Stephane Cardinale/People Avenue/Corbis.

Fig. 11.18a: Keith Morris/Alamy.

Fig. 11.18b: nobleIMAGES/Alamy.

Fig. 11.19a: Teh Eng Koon/AFP/Getty Images.

Fig. 11.19b: Travel Ink/Getty Images.

Fig. 11.21: The Granger Collection.

Fig. 11.22: © AMC/Courtesy Everett Collection.

Fig. 11.23: Ana Nance/Redux.

Fig. 14.27: Courtesy of Everett Collection.

Fig. 14.28a–b: From Osterlin, J., & Dawson, G. (1994). Early recognition of children with autism. A study of first birthday home videotapes. *Journal of Autism and Developmental Disorders, 24*, 247–257. Photographs courtesy Geraldine Dawson.

Fig. 14.29(i–ii): Courtesy of Dr. Ami Klin. (2003). The enactive mind from actions to cognition: Lessons from autism. *Philosophical Transactions of the Royal Society.*

Fig. 14.30(i–ii): From Zametkin, A. J., Nordhal, T. E., Gross, M., et al. (1990). Cerebral glucose metabolism in adults with hyperactivity of childhood onset. *New England Journal of Medicine, 323*(0), 1361–1366. Images courtesy of Alan Zametkin, NIH.

Fig. 14.31: JULI/LEONARD/MCT/Landov.

Cartoon 14.1: © The *New Yorker* Collection 2003/Michael Shaw from cartoonbank.com. All Rights Reserved.

CHAPTER 15

Opener: Alex Telfer/Gallery Stock.

Fig. 15.1: Israel Images/Alamy.

Fig. 15.2: Bettmann/Corbis.

Fig. 15.3: Jack Guez/AFP/Getty Images.

Fig. 15.4: Courtesy Barbara A. Marinelli.

Fig. 15.6a–e: © 1983 Erika Stone.

Fig. 15.7: Nancy Sheehan/PhotoEdit.

Fig. 15.8: Barbara Davidson/*Los Angeles Times.*

Fig. 15.10: Daniele Pellegrini/Photo Researchers, Inc.

Fig. 15.11: Will McIntyre/Photo Researchers, Inc.

Fig. 15.14: Harry Goodwin/Rex Features.

Fig. 15.15: Alamy.

Fig. 15.16: Alain Jocard/AFP/Getty Images.

Fig. 15.17: Stockbyte Photography/Veer.

Fig. 15.19: The Advertising Archives.

Fig. 15.22: Pascal Goetheluck/Science Photo Library/Photo Researchers, Inc.

Fig. 15.23: *Scientific American Mind*, p. 31, courtesy of Helen Mayberg, M.D., Professor, Psychiatry and Behavioral Sciences.

Fig. 15.24a: Wide World Photos/AP.

Fig. 15.24b: Ulf Andersen/Getty Images.

Fig. 15.27: Peter Yates/*The New York Times*/REDUX.

Fig. 15.30(i): Najlah Feanny/Corbis.

Fig. 15.30(ii): Michael Newman/PhotoEdit.

Fig. 15.32(i): DMAC/Alamy.

Fig. 15.32(ii): Mary Kate Denny/PhotoEdit.

Fig. 15.33: The Lovaas Institute for Early Intervention.

Fig. 15.34: Kasari, C., Paparella, T., Freeman, S., & Jahromi, L. B. (2008). Language outcomes in autism: Randomized comparison of joint attention and play interventions. *Journal of Counseling and Clinical Psychology, 76*, 125–137.

Fig. 15.35: Richard Perry/*The New York Times.*

Cartoon 15.1: © The *New Yorker* Collection 1989/Danny Shanahan from cartoonbank.com. All Rights Reserved.

Cartoon 15.2: © The *New Yorker* Collection 1993/Lee Lorenz from cartoonbank.com. All Rights Reserved.

NAME INDEX

Page numbers in *italics* refer to illustrations.

Carpenter, M., 390
Carpenter, W. T., Jr., 652, 654
Carrasco, M., 276
Carré, J. M., 551
Carrère, S., 412, 413
Carrier, B., 207
Carroll, M., 490
Carroll, M. D., 490
Carson, A. J., 644
Carstensen, Laura, 414, 415
Carter, C. S., 379
Cartwright, C., 721
Carusi, C. P., 255
Caruso, S., 458
Case, B., 714
Case, R., 388
Casey, B. J., 400
Casey, R. J., 558
Caspi, A., 556, 590, 591, 593
Caspi, Avshalom, 113
Castellanos, F. X., 668
Castles, D., 459
Catala, M. D., 703
Catanese, K. R., 460
Cattell, Raymond, 349, 576
Cavanagh, J. O., 644
CDC, 246, 368, 496, 497, 498–99, 619
Ceci, S. J., 344
Ceci, Stephen, 346, 355, 357, 358, 384
Cekic, M., 208
CensusScope, 108
Cepeda, N. J., 285
Cezayirli, E., 353
Chabas, D., 198
Chabris, Christopher, 5
Chagnon, Y. C., 492
Chakrabarti, S., 650
Chambers, D. W., 324, 402
Chan, L., 368
Chang, S., 686
Changeux, J. P., 185
Chant, D. C., 650
Chao, M. T., 499
Chaplin, W., 721
Chapman, J. E., 626
Chappelow, J., 542
Charchun, J., 360
Charney, D. S., 639
Chartrand, T. L., 2
Chase, G. A., 642
Chase, V. D., 150
Chase, W. G., 282
Chassin, L., 218, 497
Chatard, A., 586

Chatila, Y., 50
Chatterji, S., 640
Chawarska, K., 664
Chee, A. E. H., 282
Chee, M., 505
Cheema, F., 301
Chein, J. M., 282
Chen, C., 634
Chen, D., 612
Cherry, E. C., 275
Chesher, G., 44
Chess, Stella, 406
Cheung, A. M., 668
Cheung, F. M., 577
Cheung, S. F., 577
Chiao, J. Y., 119, 305
Childress, A. R., 217
Chistyakov, A. V., 703
Chitins, X., 353
Chiu, G., 499
Chiu, W. T., 619
Chivers, M. L., 463
Cho, Z., 686
Choi, I., 166, 518
Choi, W. S., 496
Chokroverty, S., 196
Choleris, E., 115
Chomsky, Noam, 395, 396
Choo, P., 502
Choudhury, S., 400
Christakis, N. A., 493
Christensen, D. D., 354
Christensen, P. N., 102, 459
Christianson, S., 304
Christoff, K., 143
Chronis, A. M., 718
Chronis-Tuscano, A., 718
Chun, M. M., 274
Chung, A., 213
Cialdini, R. B., 542
Cialdini, Robert B., 542, 552
Cicchetti, D., 378, 713
Cinotti, L., 459
Cipriani, A., 700
Clapp, J. D., 542
Clark, A. C., 576, 577
Clark, C. S., 582
Clark, G. T., 197
Clark, L. A., 658
Clark, R. D., 461
Clark, R. E., 271
Clark, S. E., 307
Clark-Foos, A., 296
Clarkin, J. F., 660
Clausell, E., 504
Cleary, P. D., 497
Cleckley, H., 648
Cleckley, Hervey, 660, 662

Cleveland, S., 666
Cloninger, C., 592
Clore, G. L., 437
Coan, J. A., 642
Coank, J. A., 412
Coast, J. R., 498
Coe, C. L., 487
Coe, W. C., 206
Cohane, G., 551
Cohen, B., 666
Cohen, D., 548
Cohen, D. J., 713
Cohen, G. L., 360
Cohen, J., 654
Cohen, L., 487
Cohen, R. A., 667
Cohen, S., 481, *481,* 483, *487,* 503, 504
Cohen, Sheldon, 481
Cohn, J. F., 374
Colapinto, John, 402
Colcombe, S. J., 498
Coleman, M. R., 182
Coles, E. K., 718
Colligan, R. C., 483
Collins, A., 379, 553
Collins, Allan, 289
Collins, J., 666
Collins, K., 438
Collins, L., 653
Colliver, J. D., 661
Colom, R., 353
Colombo, C., 200
Colvin, C. R., 582
Compton, J. S., 695
Compton, W. M., 661
Conger, R. D., 406, 562
Conn, C., 660
Conneely, K. N., 634
Connelly, J. F., 184
Conners, C. K., 668, 719
Connor, B., 516
Conway, A. R. A., 282, 348, 352, *353*
Conway, K. P., 661
Conway, M. A., 304
Conway, Martin, 304
Conway, Michael, 303
Cook, G. I., 296
Cook, I. A., 700
Cook, J., 256
Cook, M., 235, 254
Cooke, S. F., 261
Cooney, Jeffrey, 190
Cooney, R. E., 637
Cooper, C. R., 404
Cooper, G. M., 653
Corbett, D., 259
Corbitt, E. M., 661
Corby, J. C., 206
Corcoran, K. A., 230

Corder, E. H., 413
Coren, S., 199
Corkin, Sue, 301
Correll, C. U., 707
Correll, J., 333, 524
Corty, E., 497
Cosmides, Leda, 19
Costa, Paul, 598
Costa, P. T., 483, 581, 586
Costa, P. T., Jr., 576, 597, 598
Courchesne, E., 666
Cousins, A. J., 102, 459
Cowan, C. P., 412
Cowan, P. A., 244, 412
Cowell, P. E., 413
Cox, D. S., 481
Cox, K. L., 498
Coyne, J. C., 643
Craft, L. L., 498
Craig, A. D. B., 217
Craighero, L., 256
Craik, Fergus, 288
Craik, R. I. M., 285
Cramer, V., 659
Crane, P., 414
Crawford, H. J., 206
Cristal, R. E., 352
Crits-Chistoph, P., 677
Crocker, J., 410
Crocker, Jennifer, 609
Croen, L. A., 666
Crosnoe, R., 414
Cross, S. E., 611
Crow, M. D., 581
Crowe, M., 719
Crowe, R. R., 637
Csernansky, J. G., 653
Csibra, G., 390
Csikszentmihalyi, M., 54, 209, 501
Cuc, A., 304
Cui, L., 713
Cukrowicz, K. C., 626
Culbert, K. M., 491
Culham, J. C., 168
Cummings, J. R., 714
Cunningham, M. R., 461
Cunningham, W. A., 525
Cuny, E., 637, 697, 703
Cupach, W. R., 439
Curry, J., 715, *715*
Curtin, L. R., 490
Curtiss, S., 366
Cusack, R., 320
Custers, R., 442
Cutshall, J. L., 307
Cvetkovic-Lopes, V., 198
Czopp, A. M., 524

Dabbs, J., 577
Dabbs, J. M., 550
Dagher, A., 259
D'Agostino, R. B. Sr., 483
Dalal, R., 518
Dal Cin, S., 442
Dale, K., 572
Dalton, M. A., 255, 327, *327*
Damasio, Antonio R., 92, 97, 392, 422, 427, 437
Damasio, H., 97, 217, 392
Daniels, A. S., 689
Danna, M., 256
Dapretto, M., 667
Darby, Joseph, 553
D'Arcy, R. C., 184
Darley, John M., 553
Darwin, Charles, 10, *10,* 228, 239, 433, 439
Darwin, Erasmus, 10
Dasgupta, A. G., 524
Daskalakis, Z. J., 703
Dauvilliers, Y., 198
Davidson, J. R., 695
Davidson, M., 254
Davidson, Richard, 427
Davidson, R. J., 642
Davidson Ward, S. L., 368
Davies, M. F., 436
Davies, M. S., 667
Davies, P. G., 524
Davies, S., 696
da Vinci, Leonardo, 7–8, *8,* 171
Davis, D. H., 218–19
Davis, J. O., 653
Davis, M., 263
Davis, M. H., 182
Davison, G. C., 674
Dawood, M. Y., 102
Dawood, T., 642
Dawson, G., 665
Dawson, M., 665
Deacon, B. J., 680, 699, 700
DeAnglis, T., 25
Deary, I., 353
Deary, Ian J., 348, 351, 352
Deary, I. J., 356
DeCaria, C., 721
DeCasper, Anthony J., 382
De Castella, A., 703
Decety, J., 91, 459
deCharms, R. C., 161
Deci, Edward, 445
Degirmencioglue, S. M., 405
Deguchi, T., 393
Dehaene, S., 185

Freeman, Walter, *97*
Freud, Anna, 571, *571*
Freud, Sigmund, 14, *14,*
16, 17, 33, 203, 225,
383, 443, 569–73, 588,
618, 675–76, *676,* 677,
705
Frick, K., 356
Frick, K. M., 498
Frid, D. J., 498
Friedman, H. S., 499
Friedman, J. I., 653
Friedman, J. M., 455
Friedman, M., 483
Friehs, G. M., 697, 703
Friend-DelVecchio, W.,
597
Friesen, W. V., 433, *434*
Frijda, N. H., 432
Frith, C. D., 91, 146
Frohlich, P. F., 458
Frost, J. A., 556
Fujita, F., 558
Fultz, J., 552
Funder, David, 576, 582,
585
Fung, H. H., 414
Fung, M. T., 662
Furukawa, H., 721

Gabrieli, J. D. E., 304,
305, 430
Gabrielli, W. F., 662
Gabriels, L. A., 697
Gaddis, S., 582
Gaddum, John, 86
Gaertner, L., 612
Gaertner, S. L., 526
Gaines, J., 368
Galaburda, A. M., 97
Gale, C. R., 348
Gale, E., 326
Galef, B. G., Jr., 453
Gall, Franz Joseph, 88
Gallagher, M. W., 197
Gallant, J. L., 185
Gallese, V., 255, 256
Galley, L., 93
Gallup, 244
Galton, Francis, 351
Gan, Y. G., 577
Gangestad, S. W., 102,
459
Ganley, R., 610
Garavan, H., 217
Garb, H. N., 581
Garcia, J., 360
Garcia, J. A., 719
Garcia, John, 234
Gardner, Howard, 349–50
Gardner, W. L., 448

Garite, T. J., 367
Garlick, D., 348
Garoff-Eaton, R. J., 313
Garon, N., 282
Garrett-Mayer, E., 665
Garver-Apgar, C. E., 102,
459
Gaskell, P. C., 413
Gatenby, J. C., 525
Gawryluk, J. R., 184
Gazzaniga, Michael S.,
187, 189, 190, 309
Ge, L., 522
Geaga, J. A., 213
Geary, D., 125, 357
Geddes, J. R., 705
Geen, R. G., 595
Gelade, G., 274
Gelenberg, A. J., 701
Geller, F., 39
Gentile, D. A., 253
Gentile, L., 125
George, L., 659
George, M. S., 686, 703
Georgieva, I., 595
Gerard, D., 459
Gergely, G., 390
Gernsbacher, M. A., 125,
357
Gernsbacher, Morton Ann,
665
Gershoff, E. T., 244
Gershon, E. S., 642
Geula, C., 84
Gevins, A., 212
Ghahremam, D. G., 143
Ghera, M. M., 635
Gheusi, G., 144
Giacobbe, P., 703
Giampino, T. L., 668
Gianaros, P., 481
Giannetta, J. M., 373
Gibbon, M., 624, 634
Gibbons, M. B., 677
Gibson, Eleanor, 13
Gibson, J. J., 255, 327, *327*
Gichello, A. L., 499
Gick, M. L., 342
Giedd, Jay, 124
Giedd, J. N., 668
Giesbrecht, B., 276
Giesler, R. B., 138
Gigerenzer, G., 46
Gigerenzer, Gerd, 318, 319
Gijsbers, A. A., 111
Gijsman, H. J., 705
Gilbert, Daniel, 336
Gilbert, D. T., 138, 336,
531
Gilbert, J. H., 393
Gilbert, R. W., 198

Gill, M. J., 721
Gill, S., 516
Gillard, J., 455
Gillespie, C. F., 634
Gillies, L. A., 702
Gillihan, S. J., 603
Gillogley, K. M., 368
Gilman, S. R., 666
Gilovich, T., 606
Gilovich, Thomas, 336
Gilpin, E. A., 497
Gizewski, E. R., 459
Gladwell, M., 192
Gladwell, Malcolm, 192,
324, 333
Glaser, R., 498
Glaser, R. I., 487
Glaser, Ronald, 505
Glass, R., 505
Glasson, E., 665
Glenberg, A. M., 290
Glied, S., 719
Glotzer, L. D., 95
Glover, G., 143
Glover, G. H., 161
Gnagy, E. M., 718
Godden, D. R., 291, *291*
Goetz, C. G., 85
Goff, P. A., 524
Gohm, C. L., 504
Golby, A. J., 305
Goldapple, K., 702
Goldenberg, J. L., 604
Goldin, L. R., 642
Goldman, D., 595
Goldsmith, H. H., 593,
665
Goldstein, J., 413
Goldstein, M., 660
Goldstein, N. J., 542
Goldstein, R. Z., 217
Goleman, Daniel, 351
Golomb, J. D., 274
Gong, Q., 353
Gonzales, R., 213
Good, C. D., 92
Goodale, M. A., 163
Goodall, Jane, *35,* 243
Goodman, R., 667
Goodman, S. H., 626
Goodwin, D. W., 291
Goodwin, Frederick, 641
Goodwin, G. M., 705
Goodwin, R. D., 634
Goodwin, S. A., 523
Gopnik, A., 384
Gordon, H. L., 119, 168
Gore, J. C., 168, 525
Gore, J. S., 611
Gosling, S. D., 22, 582,
589, 598

Gosselin, F., 92
Gosselin, P., 168
Gotlib, I. H., 626, 639,
681
Gottesman, I. I., 653, 666
Gottfredson, Linda, 345,
348, 350
Gottman, J. M., 412, 413
Gottman, John M., 560,
562
Gould, E., 120
Gould, Elizabeth, 120
Gow, C. A., 599
Graap, K., 694
Grabowski, T., 97
Grady, C., 433
Graf, O., 384
Graf, P., 296
Graf, Peter, 294
Grafton, D. T., 426
Grafton, S. T., 559
Graham, C. A., 459
Graham, J. W., 497
Grandin, T., 665
Granot, D., 378
Grant, B. F., 661
Graven, M. A., 198
Gray, G. G., 369
Gray, Jeffrey, 595
Gray, Jeremy, 355
Gray, J. R., 348, 351, 352,
355, 595
Gray, S., 413
Graziano, W. G., 677
Greeley, J., 44
Green, A. E., 595
Green, D. M., 136
Green, J. J., 721
Greenberg, B. D., 697
Greenberg, J., 604
Greenberg, T., 716
Greene, Beverly, 682
Greene, D., 445
Greenhill, L. L., 719
Greenough, A., 368
Greenwald, A. G., 192,
524, 530, 612
Greenwald, Anthony G.,
519, 524, 530
Greenwald, S., 635
Greenwood, M. R. C.,
493
Gregg, A., 610
Gregoire, M. C., 459
Greicius, M. D., 259
Grether, J. K., 666
Grewel, D., 351
Griffin, D. W., 559, 560
Grigg-Damberger, M., 196
Grill-Spector, K., 168
Griskevicius, V., 542

Groebel, J., 252
Gross, James, 430
Gross, J. J., 423, 430, 562
Gross, M., 667
Grossman, L., 338
Grossman, M., 435
Grossman, R. I., 413
Grosz, D., 634
Gruber, S. A., 214
Grubert, C., 703
Gruenewald, P. J., 38
Gruenewald, T. L., 13, 479
Gruzelier, J. H., 206
Guay, B., 198
Guehl, D., 637, 697
Gueorguiev, M., 455
Guerin, B., 606
Guerri, C., 368
Guimond, S., 586
Guimond, Serge, 587
Gujar, N., 200
Gülgöz, S., 384
Gunderson, J. G., 659
Gunzerath, L., 497
Gur, D., 125, 357
Gur, R. C., 125, 413
Gur, R. E., 125, 413
Gurung, R. A. R., 13, 479
Gustafsson, J. A., 115
Gutierres, S. E., 138
Guyer, B., 714
Guze, B., 696
Gwaltney, J. M. J., 503

Haby, M., 714
Hadrysiewicz, B., 703
Hadzi-Pavlovic, D., 367
Hafner, H., 708
Hagekull, B., 378
Haidt, Jonathan, 205
Haier, R., 353
Haier, Richard, 124
Haier, R. J., 348, 353, 426
Haikerwal, D., 642
Halaas, J., 455
Hallahan, M., 516
Hallberg, C., 693
Hallett, P., 85
Halligan, P. W., 186
Hallmayer, J., 666
Halmi, K. A., 494
Halpern, C. T., 458
Halpern, D. F., 124, 125,
357, 374
Hamamura, T., 54, 612
Hamani, C., 703
Hamann, S., 424, 459
Hamann, S. B., 426
Hamann, Stephan, 92
Hambrecht, M., 708
Hambrick, D. Z., 282, 352

Hamer, Dean, 463
Hamilton, A. F., 667
Hamilton, C., 559
Hamilton, N. A., 197
Hamilton, William, 552
Hammen, C., 642
Hancock, P. J., 168
Hancox, R. J., 447
Handleman, J. S., 721
Handy, T. C., 276
Hanewinkel, R., 497
Haney, C., 514
Hankin, B. L., 609, 612
Hanratty, M., 721
Hansen, C. J., 498
Hansen, R. L., 368
Hansen, W. B., 497
Hanson, D. R., 653
Haque, A., 7
Harburger, L. L., 498
Harding, C. M., 708
Hare, R. D., 661
Hare, Robert D., 712
Hariri, A. R., 551, 595
Harkins, S. G., 537
Harkins, S. W., 207
Harlow, Harry, 375, 376,
    376, 444
Harlow, H. F., 444
Harlow, M. K., 444
Harpalani, V., 404
Harpham, T., 640
Harpur, T. J., 712
Harrington, H., 447
Harris, J. A., 591
Harris, J. L., 443
Harris, T. O., 643
Harris, W. A., 494
Harrison, B. J., 637
Harsch, Nicole, 303
Hartford, J., 693
Hartley, T., 92
Harty, L., 660
Harvey, P. D., 653
Harvey, R. D., 626
Haselton, M. G., 102
Hashimoto, M., 651
Hassin, R. R., 433
Hatfield, E., 461
Hatfield, Elaine, 558
Hatzidimitriou, G., 214
Hauk, O., 256
Hauser, M. D., 254
Hawkins, C. B., 529
Hawkley, L., 504
Hawkley, L. C., 448
Haworth, C. M., 491
Hawton, K., 705
Haxby, J. V., 185
Hayashi, A., 393
Hayashi, K. M., 213

Haydon, K. C., 379
Hayes, J., 604
Hayne, H., 383
Hazan, C., 559
Hazlett, E. A., 653
He, J., 714
Head, K., 348
Healy, A., 301
Heard, H., 711
Hearn, E. F., 720
Hearon, B., 677
Heatherton, T. F., 255,
    327, *327*, 360, 442, 482,
    490, 492, 494, 496, 597,
    603, 606
Hebb, Donald, 120, 260,
    261, 262, 270
Hebl, M. R., 492
Heeger, D. J., 667
Heerey, E. A., 562
Heider, Fritz, 517
Heikkinen, E., 414
Heiman, J. R., 102
Heimann, H., 651
Heine, S. J., 1, 44, 54, 586
Heine, Steven, 21, 586,
    610, 612
Heinrich, J., 1
Heller, D., 577
Helmreich, R., 556
Helms, M. J., 483
Helzer, J. E., 218–19
Henderson, H. A., 635
Hendricks, M., 424
Henninger, E. M., 487
Henrich, J., 44
Henriques, J. B., 642
Henschel, A. L., 493
Herbener, E. S., 556
Herbert, T. B., 481
Hering, E., 153
Herman, C. P., 494
Herman, Peter, 493, 494
Herman, R. A., 92, 459
Hermsen, S., 524
Herrnstein, Richard, 349
Hershow, R. C., 411
Herz, R. S., 459
Hester, R. K., 691
Hetherington, C. R., 599
Heuer, K., 635
Heyman, R. E., 561
Hezlett, S. A., 346
Hickok, G., 256
Higgins, L. T., 7
Higgins, S. C., 455
Higgins, Tory, 602
Higley, J. D., 547
Higley, S. B., 547
Hilgard, E. R., 207
Hilgard, J. R., 207

Hill, S. E., 102
Hilsenroth, M. J., 679
Hines, T., 573, 687
Hinshaw, S. P., 719
Hinson, R. E., 234
Hirsh, J. B., 595
Hirshkowitz, M., 196
Hirst, W., 304
Hirstein, W., 121
Ho, B. C., 653
Hobbs, C. A., 369
Hobson, Alan, 199, 202,
    203–4
Hochman, K. M., 653, 707
Hockley, W. E., 291
Hodge, D., 308
Hodges, L., 694
Hoefler, M., 634
Hof, P. R., 653
Hofbauer, R. K., 206
Hofer, S. M., 415
Hoffman, H., 524
Hofmann, S. G., 677, 693
Hogan, L., 51
Hoge, M. A., 689
Hogh, P., 416
Hoine, H., 291
Holden, C., 640
Holland, A., 504
Holland, P. C., 235, 247
Holland, S. K., 353
Hollander, E., 721
Hollander, M., 394
Holleran, S. E., 582
Hollis, K., 234
Hollis, K. L., 235
Hollon, S. D., 680, 693,
    697, 700, 701, 702, 716
Holman, C. D. J., 368
Holman, K., 665
Holmbeck, G. N., 406
Holmes, J. G., 559, 560
Holst, C., 491
Holtzman, N. S., 582
Holyoak, K. J., 342
Hommer, D., 260
Honer, W. G., 213
Hong, H., 438
Hong, M. S., 213
Honorton, Charles, 157
Hooley, J., 681
Hooley, Jill, 681
Hoon Sung, Y., 213
Hops, H., 639
Horn, J. L., 349, 415
Horney, Karen, 573
Horowitz, L. M., 643
Horowitz, T. S., 274
Hoshino, Y., 721
Hothersall, D., 11
Hougaard, E., 679

Houle, S., 288
Houlihan, D., 552
House, J. S., 503
Houts, R. M., 400
Hovland, Carl, 532
Howell, K. H., 718
Howlin, P., 721
Hoyt, D. R., 406
Hrebickova, M., 598
Hsee, C. K., 437
Hu, P. T., 200
Hu, S., 497
Hubbard, E. M., 122, *122*,
    123
Hubbard, J. A., 373
Hubel, David, 33, 118
Hudson, J. I., 551
Hudson, J. L., 551
Huedo-Medina, T. B.,
    699, 700
Huesmann, L. R., 253
Huey, L. Y., 689
Hugh, M., 633
Hughes, C. W., 714
Hughes, Howard, 156
Hughes, M., 301
Hull, Clark, 442, 443, 537
Hull, Jay, 216
Hulse, G. K., 368
Hulshoff Pol, H. E., 653
Humedian, M., 682
Humphrey, K., 393
Humphreys, K., 667
Hunsley, J., 626
Hunter, J., 346
Huppert, J. D., 695
Hurlemann, R., 703
Hurt, S. W., 710
Husain, G., 5
Hutchings, B., 662
Huttunen, M. O., 654
Hwang, J., 213
Hwu, H. G., 635
Hyde, J., 125, 357
Hyde, J. S., 401, 435, 593,
    609, 612, 640
Hyman, S. E., 384, 666

Iacoboni, M. I., 667
Iacono, W. G., 667
Iidaka, T., 119
Ikier, S., 384
Ilan, A. B., 212
Ilies, R., 577
Inati, S., 603
Inciardi, J. A., 213
Ingersoll, N., 478
Ingre, M., 201
Insel, T. R., 115, 639, 720
Intelisano, G., 458
Iossifov, I., 666

Irons, G., 232
Isen, A. M., 435
Ishigami, Y., 275
Isohanni, M., 652
Isoldi, K. K., 491
Israelski, D., 212
Ito, T. A., 424
Ivanovic, D. M., 353
Ivers, H., 198
Iverson, P., 393
Iyengar, S. S., 337, *337*
Izard, Carroll, 438

Jablensky, A., 708
Jacklin, Carol, 13
Jacklin, C. N., 586
Jackson, B., 483
Jackson, S. A., 209
Jacobs, D. R., 483
Jacobsen, Lenore, 520
Jacoby, Larry, 295, 296
Jaervelin, M., 592
Jagnow, C. P., 142
Jahrig, J., 604
Jahromi, L. B., 720
James, T. W., 102
James, William, 9–10, *9*,
    12, 19, 239, 424, 597,
    601
Jameson, Dorothea, 13
Jamieson, G. A., 205
Jamison, Kay Redfield,
    640–41, 705
Jang, K. L., 591, 592
Janicki-Deverts, D., 481
Janis, Irving, 538
Janssen, E., 102, 459
Janusis, G., 718
Jasechko, J., 296
Jasper, H., 160
Jefferis, V., 448
Jeffrey, E. W., 489
Jencks, C., 346
Jenike, M. A., 426
Jenkins, C. D., 489
Jensen, Arthur, 352, 357,
    358
Jensen, M., 207
Jensen, P. S., 719
Jessell, T. M., 260
Jiang, C. H., 356
Jiang, F., 185
Jiang, Y., 125
Jin, R., 639
John, Oliver, 577, 578
John, O. P., 577, 578, 589,
    598
Johns, M., 359, 360, 521
Johnson, B. T., 699, 700
Johnson, C. A., 496
Johnson, D., 272, 301, 412

Torgerson, S., 659
Torigoe, T., 666
Torres, A., 666
Torrey, B. B., 654
Torrey, E. F., 654
Toth, S., 378405
Towers, D. N., 642
Tracy, Jessica, 433–34
Tracy, J. L., 434
Tran, S., 379
Tranel, D., 92, 392, 427
Traskman-Bendz, L., 547
Travis, Bettye, 492
Treanor, J. J., 503
Treffert, D. A., 354
Treisman, A., 275
Treisman, Anne, 274
Tremblay, A., 491
Treno, A. J., 38
Trentacoste, S. V., 664
Tressel, P. A., 213
Triandis, Harry, 609
Triplett, Norman, 537
Trivers, Robert L., 552
Tronick, E. Z., 374
Tropp, L. R., 526
Trost, M. R., 138
Truong, N. L., 718
Tryon, G. S., 677
Tryon, W. W., 677
Trzesniewski, K. H., 606
Tsao, F. M., 393
Tshibanda, L., 182
Tsien, J. Z., 262, 356
Tsuchiya, N., 320
Tucker, M., 200
Tuescher, O., 660
Tugade, M. M., 486, 502
Tuholski, S. W., 352
Tulving, Endel, 288, 290, 293, 294
Turetsky, B. E., 413
Turk, C. L., 552
Turk-Browne, N. B., 274
Turner, E. H., 699
Turner, G., 610, *611*
Turner, John, 522
Turner, R. B., 503
Tversky, A., 46
Tversky, Amos, 332–35
Twenge, J. M., 606
Twitmyer, Edwin, 227
Tyler, C. W., 433
Tyrrell, D. A., 481, *481*
Tzuang, G., 212

Ubel, P. A., 503
Udry, J. R., 102, 458
Uhlenhuth, E. H., 695
Uhlmann, E., 530
Ullman, M., 394

Umberson, D., 503
Ungerleider, L. G., 163
Updegraff, J. A., 13, 479
Upton, N., 86
Urberg, K. A., 405
USDHHS, 496, 497
Usher, M., 643
Ustün, T. B., 639
Uttl, B., 296
Uvnas-Moberg, Kerstin, 505

Vaccarino, F. J., 103
Vaccaro, D., 218
Vagero, D., 348
Vaidya, J., 423
Vallabha, G. K., 374
Vallières, A., 198
Valyear, K. F., 168
van Berckelaer-Onnes, I. A., 378
van Bockxmeer, F. M., 498
van den Heuvel, M. P., 653
van der Kolk, B. A., 634
Van de Water, J., 667
Van Gastel, A., 487
van Haren, N. E., 653
Vanhaudenhuyse, A., 182
Van Hulle, C. A., 593
van Ijzendoorn, M. H., 378
Vanilovich, I., 356
van Kamp, S., 526
van Knippenberg, A., 2, 193, 606
Van Lange, P. A. M., 562
van Ommeren, M., 700
Van Someren, E. J., 201
Van Well, S., 478
Varejao, M., 718
Vargas-Reighley, R. V., 404
Vargha-Khadem, F., 295
Varner, J. L., 260
Vaughan, J. T., 185
Vazire, S., 582, 583, *583*
Vega, C., 402
Velasquez, I., 208
Venables, P., 662
Venter, J. Craig, *106*
Verdi, G., 718
Vernon, P. A., 353, 591
Vickers, J., 547
Viechtbauer, W., 598
Vieira, A., 610, *611*
Vincent, J. D., 144
Vingerhoets, A. J., 424
Viñuela, A., 85
Visalberghi, E., 254

Vismara, L., 719
Vitiello, B., 716, 719
Vitkup, D., 666
Vohs, J. D., 184
Vohs, K. D., 460, 605, 606
Voils, C. I., 524
Voklow, N. D., 212
Volkman, F, 664
Volkmar, F., 666
Volkow, N. D., 217, 233, 259, 454
von Cramon, D., 173
von Euler, U., 86
von Neumann, John, 332
von Restorff, Hedwig, 304
Voon, V., 703
Voracek, M., 586, 587
Vredenburg, D. S., 606
Vul, E., 285
Vygotsky, Lev, 395–96
Vytal, K., 424

Waber, D., 353
Wadden, T., 491
Wadhwa, P. D., 367
Wager, T. D., 474, 486
Wagner, A., 547
Wagner, Allan, 246
Wagner, D. D., 442
Wagner, T. D., 474
Waite, L. J., 411, 448
Walker, E., 653, 654, 707
Walker, E. F., 653, 654, 692
Walker, M. P., 194, 200
Walker, R. L., 626
Wall, Patrick, 146, 160
Wall, S., 377
Wallen, K., 92, 459
Walraich, M. L., 5
Walsh, T., 653
Walter, H., 93
Walters, E. E., 619, 633
Walton, George, 359, 360
Walton, K. E., 598
Waltrip, R. W., 654
Walts, B. M., 492
Wamsley, E. J., 200
Wang, G. J., 212, 233, 259
Wang, H., 356
Wang, J. H., 208
Wang, L., 414
Wang, P. S., 619, 631, 633, 634, 639, 640, 687
Wang, S.-H., 389
Ward, C. H., 624
Warden, R., 660
Wardle, J., 491
Warrington, E., 284
Washburn, Margaret Flay, 13, *13*

Wassermann, E. M., 703
Watanabe, M., 721
Waters, E., 377
Watson, D., 577
Watson, David, 423, 576
Watson, J. M., 277
Watson, John B., 14, *14*, 59, 224, 225–26, 231–32, 240, 627
Watson, N. V., 102
Waugh, C. E., 486
Weaver, D., 184
Weber, Ernst, 135
Weber, E. U., 437
Weber, M., 301
Weber, N., 309
Wechsler, David, 345
Wegener, D. T., 532
Wegner, Daniel M., 431
Weidner, G., 483
Weinberg, W. A., 714
Weinberger, J. L., 581, 597
Weiner, Bernard, 517
Weinstein, R., 520
Weisberg, R. W., 342
Weise-Kelly, L., 234
Weisnagel, S. J., 492
Weiss, A., 592
Weissman, M. M., 635, 679, 716
Welch, N., 437
Welham, J. L., 650
Wellard, R. M., 637
Wellborn, M., 601
Weller, A., 379
Wells, Gary, 305
Wells, G. L., 307
Wells, K., 715, *715*
Werker, J. F., 374, 393
Wertheimer, Max, 11, 174
West, G., 276
West, S. G., 583
Westbrook, R. F., 230
Westen, D., 573, 693
Westerman, M., 414
Wexler, Nancy, 74
Weyandt, L. L., 718
Whalen, C. K., 667
Whalen, P. J., 92, 168, 426
Wheatley, T., 336
Wheatley, Thalia, 205
Wheeler, L., 558
Wheelwright, S., 433
Whiskin, E. E., 453
Whitbeck, L. B., 406
White, J. W., 5
Whiteside, S. P., 637
WHO, 490, 496
Wichmann, T., 85, 686
Wickett, J. C., 353
Wicklund, Robert, 601

Wickramaratne, P., 716
Widiger, T. A., 661
Widom, C. S., 661
Wierson, M., 400
Wiese, D., 423
Wiesel, Thorsten N., 33, 118
Wigler, M., 666
Wikman, E., 360
Wilens, T. E., 717, 718
Wilfley, D. E., 496
Wilhelm, O., 282, 352
Wilke, M., 353
Williams, D. L., 667
Williams, J. B. W., 624, 634
Williams, J. M. G., 679
Williams, K., 537
Williams, L. E., 3
Williams, R., 483
Williams, R. B., Jr., 483
Williams, S. C., 353
Williams, T. J., 604
Williams, W. A., 703
Wills, T. A., 218, 504
Wilsnack, R. W., 215
Wilsnack, S. C., 215
Wilson, A. A., 288
Wilson, A. E., 608
Wilson, D. B., 5
Wilson, F. A., 274
Wilson, G. T., 496
Wilson, K., 718
Wilson, M. A., 200
Wilson, T. D., 336
Wilson, Timothy, 192, 193, 336
Wilson, W., 212, 214
Winberg, J., 371
Winblad, B., 414
Winfield, I., 659
Winfield, R., 677
Winslow, J. T., 720
Wise, R. A., 258
Wiseman, C. V., 494
Wiseman, R., 157
Wiste, A., 39
Witelson, Sandra, 354
Witherspoon, D., 295
Witte, E. A., 700
Wittenbrink, B., 333, 524
Wittmann, W. W., 352
Wixted, E., 285
Wlos, J., 214
Wolfe, J. M., 274
Wolford, George, 191
Woller, K. M., 446
Wolpe, Joseph, 233
Wolpert, D. M., 146
Wolraich, M. L., 5
Wolsic, B., 558

SUBJECT INDEX

Page numbers in *italics* refer to figures.

American Sign Language, 394
Ames boxes, 172, *172*
amiable skepticism, 4
amnesia, 84, 300–301, *301,* 383–84, 646–47
  childhood, 304
  source, 304
amphetamines, 212, 213, 259
amputation, 121, *121,* 122, 123, 146
amusia, 22
amygdala:
  and basic structure and functions of brain, 91,
    92, 94, *119*
  and emotions, 425–27, *426*
  and fear, 263
  and harming and helping others, 547
  and learning, *233,* 263
  and memory, 270, 271, 301
  and mental disorders, 636, *636,* 662
  and motivation, 448, 459
  and perception, 168–69
  and personality, 594, 595
  and sensation, 143, *145*
  and sexual behavior, 459
  and sleep, 202, *203,* 204
  and social influence, 542
  and stereotypes, 525
analogical representations, 319–20, *319, 320*
analogies, finding appropriate, 342–43
anal phase, 572
anal-retentive personalities, 572
analysis, *see* data, analysis and evaluation of;
    levels of analysis
analytical intelligence, 350
androgens, 101, 102, 458, 463
anecdotal cases, 535
anger, 392, 502, 659, 682
  and depression, 401
  see also hostility
animals:
  communication of, 396
  and mental disorders, 665
  olfactory capabilities of, 142
  personality of, 589–90, *590*
  research on, 59–60, *59, 60*
  and violence, 547, *547*
anonymity, 61
anorexia nervosa, 494–95, *495,* 628, *628*
antagonists, 82, *83*
anterograde amnesia, 301, *301*
anti-anxiety medications, 683, 693, 695, 696,
    711
antibodies, and autism, 667
anticipatory coping, 484
anticonvulsive medications, 684, 705
antidepressant medications, 683, 697–700, 702,
    705
  and placebo effect, 699
antipsychotic medications, 652, 683–84, 706–7,
    707
antisocial personality disorders, 620, 628, *628,*
    658, 660–62, *661,* 709, 711–12, *712*

anxiety:
  and addiction, 216, 217
  and behaviors affecting health, 492, 493, 497,
    502
  and conformity, 542
  and culture, 681
  death, 604
  and health, 502
  and influence of neurotransmission, 86
  and interpersonal relations, 438
  and learning, 231–33, 244, 247
  and mental disorders, 17, 619, 620, 622, 623,
    624, 631–38, *636,* 659
  and motivation, 449, *449*
  and personality, 576, 595
  and scientific foundations of psychology, 17
  and self-knowledge, 604
  separation, 377
  and sleep deprivation, 201
  social, 604
  treatment for, 674, 680, 685, 693–97, 701,
    706
anxious-ambivalent attachment, 377
aphagia, 454
aplysia, 260–61, *260*
applied behavioral analysis (ABA), 719–20, *719,*
    722
appraisals:
  and coping, 484–85
  reflected, 604
Apted, Michael, 597
aptitude, 344, 359
argument, 534–35, *535*
  see also persuasion
arousal:
  and addiction, 217
  and basic structure and functions of brain, 92
  of emotions, 423, *423,* 427–30
  and influence of neurotransmission, 84
  and mental disorders, 632, 662, 711, 717
  and motivation, 441, 443, 457, 459, 464
  and personality, 594–95
  and sexual behavior, 92, 459, 464
  and sleep, 197
  and themes of psychological science, 18
Arthur (case study), 647
ascending reticular activating system (ARAS),
    594
Asch Task, 540
asking approach, 53–55, *54*
Asperger's syndrome, 665
assessment:
  and clinical interview, 623–24
  definition of, 623
  evidence-based, 625–26
  of mental disorders, 620–23, *621*
  of personality, 579–87
  see also specific test
assimilation, 385–86
association, of events, 236
Association for Psychological Science, 13

association networks, 289–90, *290*
associations, loosening of, 652
Ativan, 683
attachment, 373–80, 559
  definition of, 374
attention:
  auditory, 274–75
  definition of, 273
  and intelligence, 352
  and memory, 266–315
  and mental disorders, 619, 710, 719, 720
  overselectivity of, 719
  overview about, 131–32
  visual, 274
  see also attention deficit hyperactivity
    disorder; focusing
attention deficit hyperactivity disorder
    (ADHD), 625, *628,* 664, 667–68, *668,*
    713, 716–19, *717, 720*
attention span, 631
attitude accessibility, 529
attitudes:
  and behavior, 528–36
  change in, 530–35
  definition of, 528
  and emotions, 502, 667–68
  formation of, 528–36
  and health, 501–6
  and social psychology, 528–36
attributions, 515–18, 562, 643
atypical antipsychotics, 707
audition, 148
  see also hearing
auditory attention, 274–75
auditory hallucinations, 651, 707
auditory information, *see* hearing
auditory processing, and levels of analysis, 22
authority, 16, 543–45, *543, 544, 545*
autism, 354, 365, 377, 620, 664–67, *665, 666,*
    675, 713, 719–23, *719*
  and antibodies, 667
  and brain, 666–67
  and IQ, 719, 721
  and mirror neurons, 667
autism spectrum disorders, 623, 665, 666
autokinetic effect, 540
autonomic nervous system (ANS), 98–100, *99,*
    631
autoreception, 82
availability heuristic, 334, *335*
averaging, 45
avoidance behavior, 674, 680
avoidant attachment, 377
avoidant personality disorder, 658
awareness:
  and mental disorders, 646–47
  and perception, 159
  self-, 537–38, 601–2
  and stereotypes, 524
  and study of consciousness, *187*
  and treatment of mental disorders, 694

and mental disorders, 635–36, *636,* 637, 653–54, 663–69, *664,* 712, 713–23
what shapes, 366–73
see also adolescence; parent/child relationship; parenting, style of
Children's Hospital (Los Angeles, California), 366
chimpanzee, Nim Chimpsky, 396
chlorpromazine, 706
Cho, Seung-Hui, *52,* 53
choices, and problem solving, 193, 337–38, *337, 338*
Christene (patient), 647
chromosomes, 105–6, *105,* 109
chronic pulmonary disease, 483
chunking, 282–83, *283,* 284, 288
cigarettes, *see* smoking
circadian rhythms, 194–95, *195,* 199, 200
circumplex model, 423
clang associations, 652
classical conditioning:
    and attitudes, 528
    definition of, 227
    and emotions, 425–26
    and learning, 225, 226–28, *226, 228,* 231–35, *232,* 239–50, 260, 263
    and memory, 271, 295
    and mental disorders, 628, 678, 680
    and motivation, 219
    operant conditioning as different than, 239–50
    and rewards, 260
cleanliness, and roommates (college), 610–11, *611*
Clemens, Roger, 103
client-centered therapy, 678
client-practitioner relationship, 689, 708, 711
clinical interview, 623
clinical psychologists, 687–88
clinical psychology, 24
Clinton, Bill, 538
Clinton, Hillary, *324*
cliques, 405, *405*
clomipramine, 696
closed-ended questions, 53
closure, *166,* 167
clozapine, 684, 706, *707*
coarse coding, 134
Coca-Cola, and cocaine, 213, *213*
cocaine, 82, 212–13, 215, 233, *233,* 259
    and Coca-Cola, 213, *213*
cochlea, 148–50, *149*
cochlear implants, 148–50, *150*
cocktail party effect, 602
cocktail party phenomenon, 275
codeine, 214
coding, *see* encoding
cognition:
    and adulthood, 408
    and aging, 413, 414–16
    and application of psychological science, 5

definition of, 319
and development, 366–73, 384–86, 395, 399
and emotions, 422, 427–30, 435–37
and exercise, 498
and harming and helping others, 548
and health, 470–71
and influence of neurotransmission, 85
information-processing theories of, 15
innate, 389–90
and intelligence, 351–54
and language, 395
and learning, 235–38, 248–49
and mental disorders, 16–17, 632, 635–37, 641–43, *643,* 650
and moral values, 392
and operant conditioning, 248–49
and personality, 570, 574–75
Piaget's stages of development for, 32–33, 384–86, *385*
and research methodology, 32, 55–56
and scientific foundations of psychology, 16–17
and self-knowledge, 601
and sensation, 160, 161
and sleep, 199, 203
and social psychology, 530–32, 548, 601
and treatment of mental disorders, 707, 721
see also cognitive-behavioral therapy; cognitive dissonance; cognitive restructuring; cognitive therapy; decision making; problem solving; representations, mental; schemas; thought/thinking
cognitions, hot/cold, 447–48
Cognitive-Affective Personality System (CAPS), 574–75, *575*
cognitive-behavioral therapy (CBT):
    and sleep, 198
    and treatment of mental disorders, 17, 627–28, 674, 678–81, 694–97, 700–702, *701,* 705, 707, 714
cognitive dissonance, 530–32, *531*
cognitive maps, 248
cognitive-neoassociationistic model, 548
cognitive neuroscience, *15,* 16
cognitive perspective, 235
cognitive psychology, 24
cognitive psychology, and scientific foundations of psychology, 15–16
cognitive restructuring, 679, *679*
cognitive-social theories, of personality, 574–75
cognitive therapy, and treatment of mental disorders, 17, 674, 678–81, 693–97, 710, 711
    see also cognitive-behavioral therapy
cognitive triad, 643
cohort effect, and research methodology, 36
collective self, 609, *611*
College Board Examination Survey, 606
color, 151–56, *153, 155,* 162, 175, 177, 274
coma, 182, *182,* 184
    see also persistent vegetative state

common sense, 8, *8,* 193, 514
communication:
    and adaptation, 20
    of animals, 396
    and basic structure and functions of brain, 93
    and development, 366
    and mental disorders, 664–65, 719, 720
    and nervous system, 75–79, 80
    neuron integration into systems of, 98–104
    and specialization of neurons, 75–79
    and themes of psychological science, 20
    see also language; speech
community, need for, 410–11, *411*
comorbidity, 626, *626,* 633, *633*
companionate love, 558–59, *558*
comparison groups, 40
compensation, and perception, 173
compliance, 542–43, 544
compulsions, *see* obsessive-compulsive disorder
computers:
    brain analogous to, 15–16
    and memory, 279, *280,* 283, *697*
    and PET scans, *57,* 58
    and scientific foundations of psychology, 15
concepts:
    definition of, 321
    and research methodology, 34
    as symbolic representations, 321–24
concordance rates, 641–42, 666, 668
concrete operational stage, 387–88
conditional syllogisms, 330–31
conditioned food aversion, 234–35, 236, *245*
conditioned response (CR), 225–30, 695
conditioned stimulus (CS), 225–30, 234, 263
conditioning:
    and attitudes, 528
    and choosing a practitioner, 687–91, *690*
    and emotions, 425–26
    and learning, 225, 226–30, 263
    and mental disorders, 628, 636, *637*
    second-order, 230
    see also classical conditioning; operant conditioning
conditioning trials, 227
conduct disorder, 712
cones, 151, *152,* 153, *153,* 154, 382
confabulation, 308–10, 384
confidentiality, 60–61, 62
conflict, 562
    and romantic relationships, 561
    and scientific foundations of psychology, 14
conformity, 539–43, *541,* 544
confounds, 40–43
Confucius, 6, 7
conjunction tasks, 274, *275*
conscience, 571
conscientiousness, 577, 578, 586, 589
consciousness:
    and alcohol, 214–17
    altered, 205–19
    definitions of, *182,* 183

consciousness (cont.)
  and drugs, 211–19
  and escapism, 210, 210
  and flow, 209–10
  and hypnosis, 205–7, 205
  and immersion in action/activities, 209–10
  levels of, 598
  and meditation, 207–9, 207
  and memory, 294–95, 296–97
  and mental disorders, 628, 637, 650
  and personality, 570, 570
  and problem solving, 342–43
  and scientific foundations of psychology, 9,
    14
  sleep as altered state of, 195–99
  and split brain, 186–91, 187, 189, 190
  study of, 180–221, 182, 183
  variations in, 185
consolidation process, and memory, 271–72
contact comfort, 366, 375
context-dependent memory, 291, 291
contexts, and emotions, 433, 433
contiguity, and learning, 229, 234–35
continuous reinforcement, 244, 246
control, 146–47, 445, 635, 718
  and research methodology, 34, 40, 42–43
  see also locus of control; self-regulation
convenience sampling, 44, 45, 45, 48
conventional morals, 391
convergence, binocular, 170
cooperation, 525–27, 525, 526
coping:
  and appraisals, 484–85
  and behaviors affecting health, 508
  and exercise, 498
  and individual differences, 485–86
  and mental disorders, 626, 710, 718
  as process, 484–86
  with stress, 476–89, 498, 508
  types of, 484–85
coping response, 476–78
cornea, 150
corpus callosum, 93, 93, 125, 187, 354
correlational studies:
  and ethics, 39–40
  and prediction, 40
  and research methodology, 34, 38–40, 38, 47,
    66–67, 68, 69
  and trauma, 39–40
correlation coefficient, 66, 69
correspondence bias, 518
cortex:
  and basic structure and functions of brain, 93
  and development of brain, 121, 125
  and perception, 168
  reorganization of, 121, 121
  specialization of, 97
  see also cerebral cortex; visual cortex; specific
    cortex
cortical maps, 121
cortisol, 478, 480

counseling psychologists, 24, 688
counterconditioning, 232–34
crack cocaine, 212
cramming, and memory, 285
creative intelligence, 350
creativity:
  definition of, 444
  and motivation, 444
  and scientific foundations of psychology, 10
creole, 396, 396
criminals:
  and mental disorders, 646, 648, 660, 662,
    711, 712
  self-esteem of, 606
critical periods, 118, 373
critical thinking, see thought/thinking, critical
critical trials, 227
cross-cultural studies, 49–50
cross-sectional studies, and research
    methodology, 36, 37
cross-sensory experience, see synesthesia
crowd behavior, 538
cryptomnesia, 305, 305
crystallized intelligence, 349, 353, 415–16
cultural neuroscience, 21
cultural psychology, 24
culture:
  and adaptation, 20–21
  and aging, 413
  and alcohol abuse, 681
  and anxiety, 681
  and behavior, 20–21, 21
  and biology, 399–405
  definition of, 50
  and depression, 681, 682, 683
  and development, 118–19, 366, 369–70,
    371, 392, 393, 395–96, 399–405
  East/West, 20–21, 166
  and eating, 453–54, 453
  and emotions, 433–35, 434, 682
  and euphemisms, 682
  evolution of, 20–21
  and gender, 401
  and harming and helping others, 548–49,
    549
  and identity, 398, 399–405
  and impressions, 518
  and ingroup/outgroup bias, 522–23
  and intelligence, 346–48, 347
  and language, 395–96
  and learning, 251
  and levels of analysis, 21–22
  and memory, 288–89
  and mental disorders, 620, 627, 627, 629–30,
    642, 650, 651, 681–83, 682, 708
  and motivation, 453–54, 459–62
  and nature/nurture debate, 7
  and obesity, 492, 492
  and perception, 166
  and personality, 577, 585–87, 586, 594, 598
  and psychotherapy, 681–83, 682

  and research methodology, 36, 49–50, 49, 54
  and scripts, 325
  and self-knowledge, 604, 609–12
  and self-serving bias, 609–12
  and sensation, 141, 143
  and sexual behavior, 459–62
  and stress, 682
  and themes of psychological science, 20–21,
    21
  and women working, 21
culture-bound syndromes, 629, 629
culture of honor, 548–49, 550
curiosity, 444

"daily hassles" stress, 477
Darwinism, 10
  see also evolution
data:
  analysis and evaluation of, 64–69
  collection of, 49–64
  and research methodology, 31, 33, 34, 64–69
dating:
  and schemas, 326–27
  and scripts, 326–27
  see also romantic relationships
David (patient), 647
deafness, 148–50, 150
death:
  and accidents, 472
  and behavior, 471–72
  and drugs, 472
  homicidal, 472, 548, 549–51
  and lifestyle, 472
  and mental disorders, 639, 692
  see also suicide
death anxiety, 604
debriefing, 61, 62
deception, 61, 62
decision making:
  and amount of thinking, 329
  and emotions, 336, 392, 435–37
  group, 538–39, 539
  and harming and helping others, 547
  and heuristics, 332–38, 435
  and intelligence, 352
  and levels of analysis, 22
  and life transitions, 412
  and moods, 435
  overview about, 317–18, 329
  and problem solving, 329–43
  and reasoning, 329–31, 330
  and scientific foundations of psychology, 15,
    17
  see also problem solving
declarative memory, 294
deductive reasoning, 329–31, 330
deep brain stimulation (DBS), 85, 686, 686,
    697, 703, 704
deep structure, 395
defense mechanisms, 571, 571, 572, 627
defensive pessimism, 575

defining attributes, 321–22, *322*
deindividuation, 537–38, *538,* 544
delayed gratification, 447–48, *447*
delta waves, 196
delusions, 651, *651,* 684, 706, 707, 708
  of grandeur, 651
  of harassment, 651
dementia, 413–14
dementia praecox, 621
demonic possession, 618
demonstration, teaching through, 254–55
dendrites, 77, *77,* 79
Dennis (case study), 673–74
dependence, 217–19, *217,* 658, 659, 660
dependent personality disorder, 658
dependent variables, 40–43, 48
depolarization, 79
depression:
  and addiction, 214
  and adolescence, 713–16, *713*
  and aging, 414
  and anger, 401
  assessment of, 624
  and behaviors affecting health, 492, 493, 498
  causes of, 641–42, *643*
  and culture, 681, 682, 683
  definition of, 697
  and gender, 703–4
  and impressions, 517
  and learning, 247
  major, 639–40
  as mental disorder, 619, 620, 623, 631, 638–43, 659, 660
  and mood, 423
  and nervous system, 84
  and personality, 576
  and race/ethnicity, 704, 714
  and reproduction, 704
  and sexual behavior, 640, 698
  and sleep, 199–200, 201
  and stereotypes, 704
  and suicide, 40
  and teenagers, 401
  treatment for, 675, 679, 683, 685–86, 697–705, 710, 711, 713–16
  and violence, 640, 703
  see also bipolar disorder; moods
depth perception, 169–71, *172,* 381
descriptive statistics, 65, *67*
descriptive studies, and research methodology, 35–38, *35,* 47, 50
desensitization, systematic, 233, 694
despair, versus integrity, 408–9
development, human, 364–420
  and adaptation, 367, 373
  and attachment, 373–80
  and biology, 399–405
  and brain, 366, 368, 371–73, 384, 390–91, 394
  and cognition, 366, 384–86, 395, 399
  and critical learning periods, 373

and culture, 366, 369–70, *371,* 392, 393, 395–96, 399–405
and dynamic systems theory, 370–71, *371*
and environment, 366, 369–71, *371,* 373, 381, 395
and gender, 366, 399–400
and genetics, 366, 367, 373, 376
and how children learn about world, 381–97
and identity, 398–405
and IQ, 367
and isolation, 366, 393
and learning, 371–73, 381–97
and meaning in adulthood, 408–17
and memory, 382–84
and mental disorders, 663, 664, 712, 722
  overview about, 365–66
  parents' role in, 379, 392, 405–7
  and perception, 366, 371, 381–82, 389
  and personality, 572, 593
  Piaget's stages of, 384–86
  prenatal, 367–69
  and scientific foundations of psychology, 15
  and sensitive periods, 373, 375
  and sensory information, 371–72, 381–82, 386
  and what shapes children, 366–73
  see also psychosexual stages; *type of development*
developmental psychology, 24
  definition of, 366–67
D.F. (case study), 163
Diagnostic and Statistical Manual of Mental Disorders (DSM), 621, 622–23, 627, 629, 658, 660, *661,* 663, 687, 713
dialectical behavior therapy (DBT), 710–11, *710*
diathesis, 626
diathesis-stress model, 626, *626,* 627
Dickinson, Emily, 641
diet, restrictive, 472, 493–94
difference threshold, 135–36
Dion, Céline, *518*
directionality problem, 38, 48
discriminability, 177
discrimination, 230, 521, 526, 528, 609, 682
disease:
  and emotions, 502
  and exercise, 498
  and genetics/genes, 110
disordered eating, 494–96
disorganized behavior, 652
display rules, 434–35
dissociative amnesia, 646–47
dissociative disorders, 646–49
dissociative fugue, 647
dissociative identity disorder (DID), 646–49, *648*
  see also multiple personality disorder
dissonance:
  and attitudes, 530–32, *531*
  postdecisional, 531
  see also cognitive dissonance

distance perception, 171–73, *172*
distortion, of memory, 269, 302–13
distractions, *147,* 160–61, 431, 447
distractors, 274
distress (duress), 477
distrust, *see* trust
divorce, 505, 562
DNA (deoxyribonucleic acid), 60, 105–6, *105,* 111, 118, 305, *307,* 592, 653, 666
Doctors Without Borders, 546
dogbane, 706
dominance:
  and emotions, 435
  and testosterone, 551
Doogie Howser mice, 262, *262*
door-in-the-face effect, 543
dopamine:
  and addiction, 212, 213, 214, 217
  and basic structure and functions of brain, 92
  definition of, 84
  and emotions, 424
  functions of, *83,* 84–85, *85*
  and influence of neurotransmission, 84
  and learning, 257–60
  and mental disorders, 653
  and motivation, 458
  and personality, 592
  and rewards, 257–60
  and sexual behavior, 458
  and treatment of mental disorders, 683, 684, 706, 717
dorsal stream, 162
double standard, 460
Douglas, Michael, 336, *336*
dread risks, 318, *318,* 319
dreams:
  and behavioral study of learning, 225
  content of, 203
  definition of, 202
  as evolved threat-rehearsal strategies, 204
  and influence of neurotransmission, 84
  and latent content, 203
  and manifest content, 203
  meaning of, 33, 203
  and mental disorders, 676, 677
  and motor cortex, *203*
  and prefrontal cortex, *203*
  remembering, 203
  and scientific foundations of psychology, 14
  and sleep, 197, 202–4
drives, 441–42, *442,* 676, 712
  see also specific drive
driving study, 54, 275
drugs:
  abuse of, 619, *628,* 640, 654, 678, 691
  addiction to, 217–19, 233–34, *233,* 259
  and children, 218
  as consciousness-altering, 211–19
  and death, 472
  and development, 367, 368

etiology, 621, 675, 713

euphemisms, for mental disorders, 682

eustress, 477

event-related potential (ERP), 58

evidence-based assessment, 625–26

evidence-based treatments, 692–93

evil, 16

evolution:

 of brain, 19–20

 of culture, 20–21

 and emotions, 425, 435

 and harming and helping others, 548, 553

 and impressions, 515

 and ingroup/outgroup bias, 522

 and learning, 234, 242

 and memory, 286

 and menstrual cycle, 400

 and motivation, 461–62

 and personality, 596

 and scientific foundations of psychology, 10

 and sexual behavior, 460, 461–62

 of speech, 256

 and stereotypes, 522

 and stress, 478

 and themes of psychological science, 10, *10,*
  19

evolved threat-rehearsal strategies, dreams as,
 204

examinations, studying for, 310–11

excitation, and nervous system, 79, 80, 86

excitation phase, 457

excitation transfer, 430

executive functions, 601

exemplars, 323–24, *323*

exercise:

 and acculturation, 499

 and behavior modification, 246–47, *247*

 and consciousness, 209

 and health, 472, 482, 489, 497–98, 508

 and life expectancies, 498

 and sleep, 201

 and stress, 482, 508

 as therapy, 702

expectancy, and research methodology, 37

expectations:

 and mental disorders, 627

 and perception, 167–68, *167*

 and personality, 574, *574,* 575

expected utility theory, 332

experience:

 and attitudes, 528

 and development, 366

 and development of brain, 118

 and Gestalt psychology, 12

 and how the brain is divided, 189–91

 and learning, 225, 227

 and memory, 268–69, 279, 286–87, 294–95

 and mental disorders, 676, 678

 and nature/nurture debate, 7

 openness to new, 576, 578

 and perception, 132–33

 and personality, 573–74

 and scientific foundations of psychology, 10,
  12

 and study of consciousness, 184

 see also environment; *type of experience*

experience sampling, 54

experiment, definition of, 40

experimental groups, 40, 42–43, 45

experimental psychology, 8–9, 24

experimental studies:

 and research methodology, 30, 34, 40–43,
  41, 47

 and scientific foundations of psychology,
  8–9, 16

experimenter expectancy effects, 37

explicit attitudes, 529–30

explicit memory, 294–95, *294*

exposure, 680, *680,* 694, 696

exposure and response prevention, 680

expressed emotion, 681

externalizing disorders, 628, *628,* 640

external validity, 44

extinction, 228–30, *229,* 231, 695

extraversion, 577, 586, 589–90

extraverts, 575, 576, 582, 585, 594–95, 599

extrinsic motivation, 444–45

eyes, 118, 150–51

eyewitnesses, 305–7, *305,* 309

face, *see* facial attractiveness; facial expressions;
  facial recognition; fusiform face area

facial attractiveness, 557

facial expressions:

 and basic structure and functions of brain, 92

 and development, 119, 374

 and emotions, 119, *119,* 426–27, *427,* 433–
  34, *433, 439*

 and fear, 119, *119*

 and impression formation, 516

facial feedback hypothesis, 424–25, *425*

facial recognition:

 and basic structure and functions of brain, 94

 and mental disorders, 635–36, *636*

 and perception, 168–69, *168, 169*

 and study of consciousness, 163

factor analysis, 348

faking bad, 625

faking good, 625

false consensus effect, 497

false fame effect, 296, 519

false memories, 307–13

family-focused intervention, 486

family systems model, 627

family therapy, 680–81, *681*

favoritism, *607*

fear, 678

 and adaptation, 19, *19*

 as adaptive, 632

 and brain, 92, 425, 426

 and facial expressions, *119,* 120

 hierarchy of, 694, *694*

and learning, 231–33, 234–35, 244, *253,
 254, 262,* 627, 694

and mental disorders, 17, 635, 662

and relationships, 556

and scientific foundations of psychology, 17

and social influence, 542

and themes of psychological science, 19, *19*

 see also agoraphobia; neophobia; phobias

feature search tasks, *see* visual search tasks

feelings, *see* emotions

fetal alcohol syndrome, 368, *368*

fetal cells, 85, 118, 125

 see also stem cells

fetus, 367, *367, 368*

fight-or-flight response, 478–79, *479,* 480

figure and ground, 165–66

filter theory, 275–76

"fire together, wire together" theory, 120

Fish, Mardy, 336

five-factor theory, 576–78, *577*

 see also Big Five

fixation, 572

fixed interval schedule, 245

fixed schedules, 245, *245*

flashbacks, 633

flashbulb memories, 303–4, *303*

flow, 209–10

fluid intelligence, 349, 353, 415–16

fluoxetine hydrochloride, *see* Prozac

Flynn effect, 357

focusing, 352

Foer, Joshua, 292

Food and Drug Administration (FDA), U.S.,
 148, 699, 703, 714

foot-in-the-door effect, 542

forebrain, 91

forecasting, affective, 336–37

forgetting, 268, 298–302, *301,* 312, 413

formal operation stage, 388

fovea, 151, *152*

Fox, Michael J., 85

framing, 333–35, *333*

 definition of, 333

Franklin, Eileen, *312*

Franklin, George, *312*

fraternal twins, *see* twins, dizygotic

free association, 14, 225, 676

Freudianism, 225, 231, 375, 438, 569–73, *570,*
 627, 693, 710

 and scientific foundations of psychology, 14,
  14, 16

Freudian slips, 193, 570

friendships:

 and development, 405

 and identity, 405, 408

 making and keeping, 448, *448*

 and mental disorders, 668

 and quality of relationships, 555–58

frontal lobes:

 and aging, 413, 414, 415

frontal lobes *(cont.)*
and basic structure and functions of brain, 93, *93*, 94, *187*
and development, 384, 391
and emotions, 393, 421–22, *422*, 437
and intelligence, 353, 355
and learning, 391
and memory, 384, 414
and mental disorders, 625, 637, 653, 660, 662, 668, 685, 694, 703
and motivation, 462
and personality, 599
and self-knowledge, 602, *603*
and sensation, 143
and sexual behavior, 462
and sleep, 202
and stereotypes, 521, 525
and teenagers, 400
see also prefrontal cortex
frustration-aggression hypothesis, 548, *548*
fugue, dissociative, 647
Fuller, Jamie, 549–51, *551*
fully functioning person, 574
functional fixedness, 341
functionalism, 9–10, 17, 19
functional magnetic resonance imaging (fMRI), *57*, *124*, 653
fundamental attribution error, 517, *517*
fusiform face area, 94, *186*, 305
fusiform gyrus, 168, *168*

g, *see* general intelligence
GABA (gamma-aminobutyric acid), *83*, 85–86, 683
Gage, Phineas, 96–97, *96*, 599
Gallup, 244
gambling, 691
gametes, 109
ganglion cells, 151, *152*, 154
gastric bypass surgery, 470, 499
gate-control theory, 146–47, *147*, 160, *160*
Gates, Bill, 350
gateway drugs, 215
gay/gayness, *see* homosexuality
gender:
and alcohol, 215–16
and biology, 402–3
and brain, 92, 123–25, *124*, 401
and careers, 596
and culture, 401
and depression, 703–4
and development, 366, 399–400
and emotions, 435
and environment, 403
and hormones, 124
and identity, 401–4
and impressions, 518–21
and ingroup/outgroup bias, 523
and intelligence, 357
and learning, 235

and mental disorders, 619–20, 628, *628*, 633–34, 639–40, 659, 664, 682, 708
and motivation, 460–61
and personality, 585–87
and psychotherapy, 703–4
roles *325*, 401, 402–3
schemas, 401
and schizophrenia, 628, *628*
and scripts, 324, *325*
and sex characteristics, 400, 402
and sexual behavior, 101–2, 460–61, *461*
and smell, 144
and socialization, 401, 402
and social psychology, 518–21, 523
and stereotypes, *325*
and stress, 478–79
and temperament, 593
gender typed, 402
general adaptation theory, 480–81, *480*
general intelligence, 348–51, 352
generalization, and learning, 230
generalized anxiety disorder, 633
generalized learned behavior, 719, 721
generalizing, 43
genetics/genes:
and adaptation, 10
and adaption, 110
and addictions, 497
and aging, 413–14
as basis of psychological science, 105–17
and behavior, 19, 105, 110–13, 115, 470, 489–92, 493, 497
and brain, 118
definition of, 105
and development, 366, 367, 373, 376
dominant, 107–8, 110
and environment, 105, 107–8, 110–13, *114*, *356*
and harming and helping others, 552
and health, 499
and heredity, 107, *109*
and intelligence, 354–57, *355*
and learning, 235, 262
and mental disorders, 85, 105, 626, 637, 641–42, 653, *653*, 654, 662, 666–67, 668, 696
modification of, 115, *115*
and motivation, 462, 463
mutations of, 10
natural selection at level of, 552
and nature/nurture debate, 7
and obesity, 470, 489–92, 493, 499
and personality, 112–14, 588–89, 590–92, 595, 596, 598
recessive, 107–8, 110
and scientific foundations of psychology, 10
and sensation, 141
and sexual behavior, 462, 463
and smoking, 497
and suicide, 644

and synesthesia, 122, *122*
and themes of psychological science, 19
see also DNA; genotypes; Human Genome Project; phenotypes
Genie (case study), 365–66, *366*, 393
genital stage, 572
genotypes, 107–10, *108*, 111
Genovese, Kitty, 553–54, *553*
Gestalt psychology:
definition of, 11
and learning, 11–12
and perception, 17, 132–33, 164–65, *166*, 167, 174
and scientific foundations of psychology, 11–12, 15, 17
ghrelin, 455
Giffords, Gabrielle, 184
Gilmore, Gary (case study), 661, *661*
glial cells, 77
globalization, 20
global workspace model, 185–86
glucose, 455
glucostatic theory, 455
glutamate, *83*, 86
goals:
achievement of personal, 445–48
and aging, 414
and career choice, 450, *450*
and emotions, 432, 435
and motivation, 445–48
and organization of subgoals, 339
and personality, 575
and problem solving, 338–43
of psychological science, 33
gonads, 101, 458
gourmand syndrome, 454, *454*
Graham, Martha, 350
Grandin, Temple, 665
grasping reflex, 372
gratification, delayed, 447–48, *447*
gray matter, 90, 92, 125
grief, 682
ground, figure and, 165–66
groups:
comparison, 40
control, 40
decision making by, 538–39, *539*
and environment, 357–60
equivalent, 44–45
experimental, 40–43, 45
and genes, 357–60
and harming and helping others, 552
influence on individual behavior of, 537–39
and intelligence, 357–60
polarization in, 538
and scientific foundations of psychology, 16
treatment, 40
see also ingroup/outgroup bias
group therapy, 680, 711
groupthink, 538–39
growth hormone (GH), 103, *103*, 199

growth hormone releasing factor (GRF), 103
Grzebski, Jan, 185, *185*
guilt, 392, 393, 438–39, 639
gustation, *see* taste
gut feelings, 437
Guthrie, Arlo, 74
Guthrie, Woody, 74

habits, 295, 442
habitual response level, 576
habituation, 260–61, 389, 695
Halbrook, Diana, 312
hallucinations, 641, 651, 658, 684, 706, 707, 708
haloperidol, 706
Hamm, Mia, *349*
handwriting, 647, *648*
happiness, 501, 509
    and well-being, 501
haptic sense, 145, *146–47*
    see also touch
hardiness, 485, 486
harming others, 546–55
Harrison, George, 305
Hawthorne effect, 51, *51*
hazing study, 531
head, size of, 353, 354
healing (wounds), and exercise, 498
health:
    and acculturation, 499
    and anger/hostility, 502, 504–5
    and anxiety, 502
    and attitudes, 501–6
    behaviors affecting, 470–72, 489–501
    and cognition, 470–71
    and emotional disclosure, 667–68, *667*
    and emotions, 430–31, 470–71, 502–3
    and general intelligence, 348
    and genes/genetics, 499
    and happiness, 501, *502*, 509
    and homosexual relationships, 504
    and life expectancies, 499, *499*
    and loneliness, 504
    and marriage, 504–5, *505*
    and oxytocin, 505–6
    and personality, 482–83
    and positive psychology, 501–2
    and psychosocial factors, 470–76
    and race/ethnicity, 499
    and resilience, 502
    and social integration, 503–6
    and social support, 503–6
    and spirituality, 506, 509
    and stress, 480–84, *481*, 487–88, 507, 508
    and trust, 505–6, *505*
    and well-being, 468–511
    and writing, 667–68
Health and Human Services Department, U.S.
        (USDHHS), 496, *714*
health psychology, 25, 470
hearing:

and aging, 414
    as basic sensory process, 140, 148–50, *149*
    and basic structure and functions of brain, 94
    and development, 371–72, 382
    and language, 393–94
    and location of sound, 161–62, *162*
    and memory, 271
    and perception, *159*, 161–62
heart disease, 472, 482–84, *482*, 507, 619
Heatherton, James, *172*
Heatherton, Sarah, *172*
hedonism, 443, 660
helping others, 546–55
hemineglect, 94, *96*, 186
Hemingway, Ernest, 641
heredity, 107, *109*, 113
heritability, *109*, 113, 590–92
heroin, 82, 86, 214, 215, 218, *218*, 233
heuristics, 332–38, 435, 518
    definition of, 332
hierarchy:
    of fears, 694, *694*
    model of personality, 576, *577*
    and storage of memory, 290
hippocampus:
    atrophy of, 632
    and basic structure and functions of brain,
        91–92, 94, 355
    and development of brain, 120
    and emotions, 426
    and exercise, 498
    and learning, 261, 262
    and memory, 268, 270, 271, 425, 426
    and mental disorders, 632
    size of, 92, 355
    and sleep, 200
Hippocrates, 619
histamine, 684, 698, 706
histrionic personality, 658
Hitler, Adolf, 580, *580*
HIV, 678
H.M. (case study), 267–68, *268*, 270, 271, 284, 294–95, 301
Holocaust, 667, *667*
homeostasis, 442, *443*, 454
homicidal death, 472, 548, 660–61
    and steroids, 549–51
homosexuality, 456, 462–64, 504, 572, 704
homunculus, 121, 160
honor, culture of, 548–49, *550*
hormone replacement therapy, 693
hormones:
    definition of, 100–101
    and development, 367, 379
    and environment, 400
    and gender, 124, 402, 403
    and motivation, 455, 457–58, 462–63
    and neuron integration into communication
        systems, 100–104
    and sexual behavior, 101–2, 457–58, 462–63
    and stress, 478

and trust, 505–6
    see also specific hormone
hostage study, 485
hostility, 392, 483–84, 504, 525, 526, 569
    see also anger
HPA (hypothalamic-pituitary-adrenal) system,
        478, *478*, 479
human development, *see* development, human
human genome, and themes of psychological
        science, 19
Human Genome Project, 106–7, *106*
    see also genetics/genes
humanistic approach:
    and motivation, 441
    to personality, 573–74, 580
    and scientific foundations of psychology,
        16–17
    and treatment of mental disorders, 678
humor, 430–31
Huntington's disease, 73–74, 92, 125
    as brain disorder, 73–74, *74*
    symptoms of, 74
H.W. (patient), 308–9
hyperactivity disorders, 619
hyperphagia, 454
hyperpolarization, 79
hypertension, 632
hypnosis:
    and brain imaging, *205*, 206
    and consciousness, 205–7
    dissociation theory of, 206, 207
    and dissociative identity disorder (DID), 649
    and memory, 312
    and pain, 206–7
    self-, 207, *207*
    sociocognitive theory of, 206
    theories of, 206
hypnotic analgesia, 206–7
hypomanic episodes, 640
hypothalamus:
    and basic structure and functions of brain, 91
    and body temperature, 442
    and eating, 454, 455
    functions of, 102
    and harming and helping others, 547
    and motivation, 425, 454, 458, 463
    and neuron integration into communication
        systems, 102
    and sexual behavior, 458, 463
    and sleep, 195, *195*
    and stress, 478, 479
    suprachiasmatic nucleus of, 195, *195*
hypotheses, and research methodology,
        31–33

id, 570
idealization, and love, 559–60
identical twins, *see* twins, monozygotic
identity:
    adolescent, 398–405
    bicultural, 404

identity *(cont.)*
   and biology, 399–405
   and culture, 398, 399–405
   and development, 398–405
   and environment, 403
   and friendships, 405–7
   gender, 401–4
   and mental disorders, 646–49, 659, 710
   multiple, 646–49
   and norms, 401–2
   race/ethnicity, 404
   and socialization, 401, 402
   stages of, 366, 408–9
idiographic approach, 579
Ikeda, Kikunae, 140
illusions, 164, *165, 166,* 167, 175, *175*
images, *see* representations, mental
imagination, and mind/body problem, 8
imipramine, 695, 698
imitation, 244, 254–56, *254, 255*
immediate memory, *see* short-term memory
immersion in action/activities, 209–10
immune system, 199, 480–81, *481,* 503, 505,
    508, 637
implicit attitudes, 529–30
implicit attitudes test (IAT), 530, *530*
implicit memory, 294, 295–96, *295,* 530
implicit personality theory, 575
impressions:
   first, 515–16
   formation of, 515–27
imprinting, 375
impulsive control disorders, 619
impulsivity:
   and basic structure and functions of brain, 96
   and brain, 668
   and influence of neurotransmission, 84
   and mental disorders, 637, 658, 660, 662,
    667, 668, 710, 711
   and personality, 576
incentives, 442
inclusive fitness, 552
independent self, 609–10, *611*
independent self-construals, 609, *609*
independent variables, 40, 42–43, 47–48
individual differences, *see* uniqueness, individual
inductive reasoning, 329–31, *330*
industrial and organizational psychology, 450
industrial melanism, 110, *110*
industrial psychologists, 24
infantile amnesia, 384
inferential statistics, 68–69
inferiority complex, 573
influence:
   and conformity, 539–42
   informational, 539
   normative, 539, 540
   social, 537–45
information processing, *see* neurotransmission
information processing model, and memory,
   269–70

information-processing theories, and scientific
   foundations of psychology, 15
informed consent, 61, 62
Ingram, Jeff, *301, 647*
ingroup favoritism, 522, 525, 526
ingroup/outgroup bias, 516, 522–23, *522*
ingroups, 20
inhibiting stereotypes, 524–25
inhibition:
   and eating, 455
   and learning, 595
   and mental disorders, 676
   and nervous system, 79, 80
   and personality, 593–94, 595
innate knowledge, 389–90
inner ear, 148, *149*
Innocence Project, *307*
insecure attachment, 377–79
insight, 339–40, 675, 676, 679, 680, 712
insight learning, 249
insomnia, 197–98
   cognitive-behavioral therapy and, 198
inspection time tasks, 352, *352*
institutional review boards (IRBs), 60, 61
instrumental conditioning, *see* operant
   conditioning
insula, 217
integrity, versus despair, 408–9
intelligence:
   and adaptation, 349
   and aging, 414, 415–16
   and birth weight, 356, *356*
   and brain, 319, 351–54
   cognitive approach to, 351–54
   and culture, 346–48, *347*
   and decision making, 352
   definition of, 344
   and environment, 349, 354–57
   gender and, 357
   and genes, 354–57, *355*
   and group differences, 357–60
   measurement of, 344–60, *344*
   and memory, 268, 295
   and mental disorders, 665, 719, 721
   and Mozart Effect, 5, *5*
   multiple, 349–50, *349, 350*
   overview about, 317–18, 344
   and personality, 576
   and problem solving, 352
   psychometric approach to, 344–60, *344*
   and race, 357–60
   and scientific foundations of psychology, 5,
    15
   and speed of mental processing, 351–52, 416
   testing of, 344–60, 415–16
   and working memory, 352–53
   see also IQ; *type of intelligence*
intelligence quotient, *see* IQ
intentionality, 390
interactionist approach, to personality, 585
interactionists, 585

interactive methods, research, *see* asking
   approach
interdependent self, 609–10, 611, *611*
interdependent self-construals, 609–10, 611,
   611
interference, and memory, 298–99
internalizing disorders, 628, *628,* 640
internal validity, 64
Internet:
   dating, 567–68
   and globalization, 20
interneurons, and nervous system, 76, *76*
interpersonal psychotherapy, 679
interpersonal relations, *see* relationships; support,
   social
interpreter, brain, 189–91, *190,* 205
interval schedules, 245, *245*
intervention, 486
interviews:
   clinical, 623–24, 630
   job, 450
   motivational, 678
   and research methodology, 53
intimacy, versus isolation, 408, 411
intracranial self-stimulation (ICSS), 258–59,
   258
intrinsic motivation, 444–45
introspection, 8–9, 14, 224, 225
introversion/extraversion trait, 576
introverts, 575, 576, 585, 594–95
intrusive thoughts, 633, 635
intuition, 4, 33, 34
ions, 77–79
   see also type of ion
I-O psychology, 450
iproniazid, 697
IQ (intelligence quotient):
   and aging, 415
   and amygdala, 426
   and autism, 719, 721
   and birth weight, 356, *356*
   definition of, 345
   and development, 367
   and environment, 355–57
   and measurement of intelligence, 345–48,
    345
   and memory, 268, 295
   and mental disorders, 719, 721
   and self-fulfilling prophecy, 520
Iran, 25
Iraq, 436, *436*
Iraq War, 513, 517
iris, 150
isolation, 366, 393, 652, 664
   versus intimacy, 408, 411

Jackson, Michael, 303, *303*
Jackson, Randy, *347*
Jackson, Shirley, *350*
Jackson, William, *305*
James, LeBron, 520

Mandel, Howie, *635*
M&M's study, 390, *391*
mania, 619, 705
manic depression, 640–41
manic episodes, 640, 641
manifest content, 203
mantra, 207
marble test, Piaget's, 389, *390*
marijuana, 212, 215, 218, 291
  and chemotherapy, 212
marriage, 409–13, *412,* 504–5, *505,* 562
  and well-being, 504
Masrahi, Yousef Ahmed, *86*
masturbation, 456, 457
matching principle, 556
mates, selection of, 411, 461–62, 464, 596
mathematics, understanding, 389–90
mating selection, 20
maximizing, 338
McCollough effect, *165*
McGuire, Mark, 550
MDMA, 213–14
mean, 66, *67*
media, and violence, 252–53, *253*
medial temporal lobes, 271–72
median, 66, *67*
medications:
  and choosing a practitioner, 688, 689
  and treatment of mental disorders, 17, 642,
    652, 653, 674, 683–84, 693, 695, 697–
    700, 707, 711, 718–19
  see also drugs; psychopharmacology; *type of
    medication or specific medication*
medicine, placebos as, 473–75, 506
meditation, 207–9
  and brain function, 207–9
  concentrative form of, 207, *207*
  and consciousness, 207–9
  mindfulness, 679, 710
  mindfulness form of, 207, *207*
  and sleep, 202
medulla, 90, *90*
melancholia, 619
melatonin, 195
memes, 251, *251*
memory:
  and addiction, 212
  and age regression, 312
  and aging, 413, 415
  altering of, *272,* 301
  and application of psychological science, 4
  and attention, 266–315
  and attitudes, 529
  and brain, 91, 92, 97, 120–21, 267–68, 270–
    72, 295–97, 301, 308–10, 414
  changing/revising, 312
  and childhood, 304
  competitions, 292
  computer analogy of, 279, 283
  and consciousness, 296–97
  and cramming, 285

and culture, 288–89
definition of, 269, 279
and development, 382–84
different systems of, 293–96
distortion of, 269, 302–13
and drugs, 268, 301
and emotions, 301, 303, 426, 437
encoding of, 269–70, *269,* 271, 277, 279–80,
  280, 288, 290–91, 293, 300, 312, 415
and evolution, 286
and exercise, 498
and experience, 268–69, 279, 286–87, *288,*
  294–95
false, 307–13
and forgetting, 268, 298–302, *301,* 312, 413
and hypnosis, 312
and impressions, 519
inaccurate, 384
and influence of neurotransmission, 84, 86
information process model of, 269–70
and intelligence, 268, 295
and learning, 261, 262, 301
and levels of analysis, 22
and levels of processing model, 288
long-term, 426, 518
meaningful, 288
and medial temporal lobes, 271–72
and mental disorders, 625, 703
and mind/body problem, 8
and misattributions, 304–5
network models of, 289–90
number of systems of, 293–94
organization of information in, 281, 282–83,
  287–93
overconsolidation of, 634
overview about, 267–68
and persistence, 301
physical location of, 270–71, *270*
priming of, 3
and race, 305–6
and representations, 321
repressed, 310–12, *312*
retrieval of, 269, 289–92, 297, 298
and scientific foundations of psychology, 15,
  17
and sensation, 143, *145,* 271, 279–81, *280*
and sleep, 197, 199, 200, 201, 203, 271–72
and sleep deprivation, 272
span of, 281–83
storage of, 269, 271–72, 279–80, 284–93,
  298
strategies for improving, 292
and substitution, 282
and themes of psychological science, 18
and transformation, 282
and unconsciousness, 295–96, *295*
see also type or system of memory
Memory Olympics, *283*
memory palace, 292
menopause, *see* menstrual cycle
menstrual cycle, 400, 458–59, 479, 693, 704

and evolution, 400
mental age, 345
mental disorders:
  and adolescence, 662, 713–23, *715*
  and age, 708, 712
  and anxiety, 17
  and anxiety as root of different disorders,
    631–38, *636*
  assessment/diagnosis of, 620–23, *623*
  and behavior, 16, 624, 632, 636, 637, 650,
    652, 666
  and behaviorism, 627–28
  and biology, 17, 84, 626–27, *627,* 632, 635–
    37, 641–43, 654, 666–68
  and brain, 17, 625, 626, 632, 635–36, 642,
    652–55, 662, 667–68, *668,* 683, 685, 694,
    696–97, 700, 703, 706, 720
  and brain stimulation, 686, 697, 703
  categorical approach to, 623
  causes of, 618–19, 626–30, *626,* 675
  and children, 653–54, 663–69, *664,* 712,
    713–23
  and cognition, 17, 632, 635–37, 641–43,
    643, 650, 707, 721
  and comorbidity, 626, *626*
  conceptualization and classification of,
    618–31, *621*
  and conditioning, 628, 636, *637*
  and consciousness, 628, 637, 650
  and continuous dimensions, 622, *622*
  and cost of therapists, 689
  and culture, 620, 627, *627,* 629–30, 642,
    651, 681–83, *682,* 708
  and death/grieving, 692
  and development, 663, 664, 712, 722
  dimensional approach to, 623
  and emotions, 627, 628, 632, 652, 653, 659,
    660, 679
  and environment, 626, 627, 637, 654, *655,*
    660, 662, 668, 688, 712
  and etiology, 621
  euphemisms for, 682
  and experience, 676, 678
  externalizing, 628, *628,* 640
  and gender, 619–20, 628, *628,* 633–34,
    639–40, 659, 664, 682, 708
  and genetics/genes, 85, 105, 626, 637, 641–
    42, 653, *653,* 654, 662, 666–67, 668, 696
  and hypnosis, 649
  and intelligence, 719, 721
  internalizing, 628, *628,* 640
  and magnetic field treatment, 685
  and medications, 642, 652, 653
  and mood, 619, 638–43, 658, 659, 705
  overview about, 617–18, 673–74
  and parents, 666, 668, 717–18, 721–22
  and personality, 639, 646–49, 656–63,
    709–13
  and pregnancy, 654, 666, 667, 702
  and pseudotherapies, 686–87, *687*
  and psychological factors, 627

and psychosurgery, 685, 686, 696, 706
and race/ethnicity, 682
and scientific foundations of psychology, 16–17
and sexual behavior, 640, 660
and situations, 632–33, 635–37, 641–43, 701
and social functioning, 632–33, *633,* 635–36, 652, 665, *665,* 720, 721, 722
and suicide, 644
and testing, 624–25, *625,* 661–62
and thinking/thought, 16
treatment of, 16–17, 672–726
treatment resistant, 684
and unconscious, 627
and violence, 660
see also specific disorder or type of treatment
mental health continuum, *622,* 623
mental health practitioner, choosing a, 687–91, *690*
mental retardation, 368, 657, *664*
mental sets, 341, *341*
mental status exam, 623
mere exposure effect, 528, *528*
Merritte, Douglas, *see* Albert B. (case study)
meta-analysis, *45,* 68–69
metabolism, 455, 493, 497, 668
methamphetamine, 213, *213, 214*
method of loci, 292
methylphenidate, 717
Michelangelo, 641
microsleep, 199
midbrain, 90, *90*
middle ear, 148, *149*
military, 218–19
Miller's Analogy Test, 346
Milligan, Billy (case study), 647
mind:
    adaptivity of, 19
    and behavior, 17
    as blank slate, 226
    and brain, 2, 7–8, 15, 95, 187, 189–91
    development of, 366
    functions of, 10
    and influence of neurotransmission, 84
    and learning, 226
    rational, 8
    representations of, 319–28
    and scientific foundations of psychology, 10, 15, 17
    and situations, 15
    and study of consciousness, 180–221, *182, 183*
    see also mental disorders; mind/body problem; theory of mind
mind/body problem, 7–8
mindfulness-based cognitive therapy, 679
mindfulness meditation, 679, 710
minimally conscious state, 185
Minnesota Multiphasic Personality Inventory (MMPI), 624–25
Minnesota Twin Project, 112

mirror neurons, 255–56
    and autism, 667
misattribution of arousal, 428–30, *430*
misattributions, and memory, 304–5
misattributions, source, 304
misinformation, 306–7, *306*
Miss M. (case study), 195
mistrust, trust versus, 398–99
mnemonics, 292
mode, 66, *67*
modeling, 332, 679
    and imitation, 254–55
ModeratedDrinking.com, 691
Molaison, Henry, *268*
    see also H.M. (case study)
monoamine oxidase (MAO) inhibitors, 113–14, 683, 697
monoamines, 84, 642
    see also specific monoamine
monocular depth perception, 170–71
monosodium glutamate (MSG), 86, 141
moods:
    and application of psychological science, 5
    and cognition, 435
    and decision making, 435
    and emotions, 422, 437, 438
    and exercise, 498
    and influence of neurotransmission, 84, 86
    and levels of analysis, 22
    and memory, 291
    and mental disorders, 423, 619, 638–43, 654, 658, 659, 680, 684, 705
    and personality, 576
    regulation of, 430–31
    and sleep, 199
    see also emotions; *specific disorder*
moral dilemmas, 392
moral values, 392
morphemes, 393
morphine, 86, 214, 218
mothers:
    and mental disorders, 666
    surrogate, 375, *376*
motion:
    aftereffects of, 173
    and perception, 171, 173, *174,* 177
motion parallax, 171, *171*
motivation:
    and adaptive behavior, 444, 462
    and behavior, 440–52
    and behaviors for their own sake, 444–45
    and biology, 463
    and brain, 454, 458, 463
    and career choice, 450, *450*
    and culture, 459–62
    definition and characteristics of, 550
    and development, 375
    and drives, 441–43
    and eating, 452–56, *452*
    and emotion, 420–67
    and environment, 463

and exercise, 499
and gender, 464
and genes, 463
and goals, 445–48
and impressions, 517
and incentives, 442
and intelligence, 346
and needs, 440–41, 448–49
overview about, 421–22
and personality, 573, 575, 581, 595
pleasure as, 443–44, *444*
and self-determination, 445
and self-perception, 445
and self-regulation, 445
and sexual behavior, 456–65
and social influence, 537
and social needs, 448
and social psychology, 517, 521, 524, 537
and stereotypes, 520, 524
and treatment of mental disorders, 678, 711
see also incentives; rewards; *type of motivation*
motivational interviewing, 678
motor functions:
    and brain, 90, *90,* 92, *93,* 94, *95,* 668
    and development, 369
    and memory, 268, 271, 295, *295*
    and mental disorders, 632, 650, 652, 654, 668, 696, 706
    and nervous system, 80, 84
    and sleep, 201
motor memory, *see* procedural memory
motor neurons, 76, *76*
Mozart Effect, 5, *5*
M.P. (case study), 173
Mueller-Lyer illusion, 44
multiaxial system, 621, *621*
Multimodal Treatment of Attention-Deficit Hyperactivity Disorder (MTA), 718
multiple personality disorder, 646–49
    see also dissociative identity disorder
multiple sclerosis, 80
multitasking, 273, 275
Munch, Edvard, *171*
murder, *see* homicidal death
Museum of Tolerance (Los Angeles), 235
music, 5, 22–23
    and negative behaviors, 23
mutations, 110, *110,* 666–67
mutilation, self-, 659, 660
    see also self-abuse
myelination, 146, 371–73, 400
myelin sheath, 77, *78,* 80

narcissistic personality, 582, 606, 658
narcolepsy, 198
National Association to Advance Fat Acceptance (NAAFA), 469, 492
National Center for Learning Disabilities, 127
National Institute of Drug Abuse, 213
National Institute of Mental Health, 637, 690, 718

National Institutes of Health (NIH), 124, 714
National Sleep Foundation, 202
National Suicide Prevention Lifeline, 644
National Survey on Drug Use and Health, *714*
naturalistic observation, 35–36
natural reinforcement, 259
natural selection:
    at gene level, 552
    and harming and helping others, 552
    and motivation, 463
    and personality, 596
    and themes of psychological science, 10
nature-nurture debate, 7, 17, 110–11, 114, 354, 401, 546, 589, 626, *626,* 627
Nazis, 16, 580
needs:
    hierarchy of, *341,* 441
    and motivation, 440–41, *442,* 448–49
    see also type of need
need to belong, 448–49, *448,* 542
negative activation, 423–24, *423*
negative affect, 548
negative feedback model, 442, *443*
negative punishment, 243, *243, 244*
negative reinforcement, 142–43, *243, 244*
negative symptoms, of schizophrenia, 650–52, 706
Nelson, George "Pinky," 42
neo-Freudians, 573
NEO Personality Inventory, 581
neophobia, 556
nervous system:
    and biological basis of psychological science, 75–87
    and development, 367
    and development of brain, 125
    and endocrine system, 100–104, *101*
    and influence of neurotransmission on emotion, thought, and behavior, 80–87
    major divisions of, 98, *99, 100*
    operation of, 75–87
    see also central nervous system; memory; peripheral nervous system
network models, of memory, 289–90
neural networks, 75
neurochemistry:
    and memory, 270, 279
    and mental disorders, 626–27, 637
    and themes of psychological science, 18
    and treatment of mental disorders, 683, 700
neurogenesis, 120
neuroleptics, 684
neuronal firing, *see* action potential
neuronal workspace model, 185
neurons:
    and basic structure and functions of brain, 90
    as basic units of nervous system, 75, *75*
    definition of, 75
    and development, 371–73
    and development of brain, 118, 121
    and eating, 454–55

integration into communication systems of, 98–104
    and intelligence, 356
    and learning, 260–63
    and mental disorders, 642
    mirror, 255–56, 258
    and motivation, 454–55
    and operation of nervous system, 75–87
    and perception, 159, 161, 168
    and personality, 588, 594–96
    and self-knowledge, 602
    and sensation, 133, *134,* 137
    and sleep, 200, 203
    structure of, 77, *77*
neuropsychological testing, 625, *625*
neuroscience, 18
    cultural, 21
neuroscience psychology, 24
neuroses, 705
neuroticism, 576, 577, 584, 586, 589–90, 592
neurotransmission:
    and categories of transmitters, 82–86, *83*
    definition of, 80–81
    and exercise, 498
    influence on emotion, thought, and behavior of, 82–87
    and learning, 259, 261
    and mental disorders, 626–27, 637, 642, 652, 653, 660, 683, 698, 700, 702, 717
    and motivation, 458
    and nervous system, 80–87
    relationship of receptors and, 81–82, *81*
    and sexual behavior, 458
    see also category of transmitter
neutral stimulus, 227
New Guinea study, 433, *434*
New York Longitudinal Study, 406
New Zealand study, 113–14, 547
nicotine, 212, 497
nightmares, 633
Nim Chimpsky (chimpanzee), 396
nitric oxide, 458
NMDA receptors, 262
No Child Left Behind Act, 344
nodes, 289–90
nodes of Ranvier, 77, *78,* 80
nomothetic approach, 579
nonspecific stress response, 480
nonverbal behavior, 515–16, *515*
norepinephrine:
    definition of, 84
    and emotions, 424
    functions of, 84
    and influence of neurotransmission, 84
    and memory, 301
    and mental disorders, 642, 683, 684, 693, 702, 706
normal distribution, 345, *345*
norms:
    and adaptation, 21
    conformity to, 539–43, *541*

and eating, 453–54
    and emotions, 435
    and identity, 401–2
    and motivation, 453–54, 463
    and research methodology, 36
    and sexual behavior, 463
    and social influence, 537, 540–42, 544
    and themes of psychological science, 21
Northern Illinois University, shooting at, 634
nucleus accumbens, 92, 259, *259,* 703
nutrition, and brain, 373

Obama, Barack, *324, 528,* 530
obedience, 16, 543–45, *543, 544, 545*
obesity, 20, 82, 454, 455, 469–70, 471, 472, 482, 489–96, 499
    and brain, 491
object agnosia, 163
objectified self, 601
objective method:
    for personality assessment, 580–82
    and research methodology, 50
object perception, 164–69
object permanence, 386, 388
object relations theory, 573
observation:
    and actor-observer discrepancy, 518, 519
    and learning, 226–27, 251–57, *252,* 574
    naturalistic, 35–36
    participant, 35–36
    and personality, 579, 580, 581, 582–83
    and research methodology, 31, 35–38, 50–52
    and scientific foundations of psychology, 5, 8, 15, 17
    see also eyewitnesses
observational studies, *see* descriptive studies
observer bias, 36, *37*
obsessions, definition of, 635
obsessive-compulsive disorder, 84, 634–35, *635,* 636–37, *637,* 658, 680, 686, *686,* 696–97, *696,* 709, 720
obstructive sleep apnea, 198, *198*
occasion setter, 237
occipital lobe:
    and basic structure and functions of brain, 93–94, *187*
    and perception, *159,* 162
    and sleep, 197
occlusion, 171
odorants, 143, *144*
Oedipus complex, 572
O'Keeffe, Georgia, 641
olfaction, *see* smell
olfactory bulb, 143, *144*
olfactory epithelium, 143, *144*
olfactory hallucinations, 651
Oliver, Jamie, *127*
O'Neil, James, 721–22, *723*
O'Neil, John, 721–22
Ono, Yoko, *687*
open-ended questions, 53, *54*

openness to new experience, 576, 578, 589–90
operant conditioning:
    and attitudes, 528
    and behavior modification, 244–48
    biology's influence on, 248–49
    classical conditioning as different than, 239–50
    cognition's influence on, 248–49
    and learning, 225, 239–50, *239,* 259
    and mental disorders, 628, 636, *637*
    and rewards, 259
    and schedules of reinforcement, 244–48
    and treatment of mental disorders, 678
operational definitions, 34
opiates, 214, 218
opponent-process theory, 153
optical illusions, 172–73, *172*
optic chiasm, 151, *153*
optic nerves, 151, *152, 153,* 154
oral personalities, 572
oral stage, 572
organization, perceptual, 177
organizational psychologists, 24
orgasm, 456, 458
orgasm phase, 457
orienting reflex, 381
orienting response, 237, *237,* 260
ossicles, 148, *149*
Oswald, Lee Harvey, 301
Ouchi, Hajime, *165*
outer ears, 148, *149*
outgroup homogeneity effect, 522, 525
outgroups, 20
overconsolidation, 634
oxytocin, 379–80, 458, 479, 505–6, 720–21

pain:
    and attitudes, 532
    and basic sensory processes, 145–47, *147*
    control of, 160–61
    gate-control theory of, 146–47, *147,* 160, *160*
    and humor, 431
    and hypnosis, 206–7
    and influence of neurotransmission, 86, *86*
    as motivation, 443
    and personality, 595
    phantom, 146
    types of, 146–47, *147*
panic, 423, *633,* 634, 673–74, *674,* 695
paradoxical sleep, *see* REM sleep
parallel processing, 274, *274*
paralysis, 125, 181
paranoid personality, 657
paraprofessionals, 688
parasympathetic division, 99–100, *100*
parent/child relationship:
    and development, 366, 379, 392, 405–7
    and identity, 405–7
    and personality, 572, 573, 591–92
    and social development, 366

see also attachment
parenting:
    and life transitions, 412–13
    style of, 392, *392,* 591–92
parents:
    development role of, 366, 379, 392, 405–7
    and identity, 405–7
    and mental disorders, 666, 668, 717–18, 721–22
    and punishment, 243–44
    and sense of self, 405–7
    see also parent/child relationship; parenting
parietal lobes, 93–94, *159, 187*
Parkinson's disease, 84–85, *85,* 92, 125, 686, 703, 706
partial-reinforcement, 245, 246
partial-reinforcement extinction effect, 246
participant observation, 35–36
passionate love, 558–59, *558*
Pavlovian conditioning, *see* classical conditioning
Pearce, Guy, *301*
Peek, Kim, 354
peer pressure, 514
peers:
    and sense of self, 405, *405*
    see also friendships
"pendulum" experiment, 340
Penny Quiz, *286*
Perceived Stress Scale, 487, *487*
perception:
    and application of psychological science, 4
    basic processes of, 159–76
    and basic sensory processing systems, 157
    and "best" forms, 167
    and bottom-up and top-down processing, 167–68
    and brain, 132–33, *133,* 159–64, 168, 173–75
    and color, 151–56, *153, 155,* 162, 175, 177
    and compensatory factors, 173
    constancies in, 174–75, *175*
    constructive nature of, 135, 164–69
    and culture, 166
    definition of, 132
    depth, 169–71, *172,* 381
    and development, 366, 371, 381–82, 389, *389*
    and discriminability, 177
    distance, 171–73
    and emotions, 426
    and environment, 132, *133*
    and expectations, 167–68, *167*
    and experience, 132–33
    and figure and ground, 165–66
    Gestalt principles of, 17, 164–65, *166,* 167, 174
    and hearing, *159*
    and how we sense the world, 132–33, *133*
    and illusions, 175, *175*
    and location of objects, 169–71

    and mental disorders, 650
    and motion, 171, 173, *174,* 177
    object, 164–69
    and organization, 177
    overview about, 131–32
    and proximity and similarity, 166–67, *166*
    and research methodology, 56
    and salience, 176–77
    and scientific foundations of psychology, 11–12, *11,* 17
    and shape, 175, *175*
    and sixth sense, 157–58
    size, 172–73, *174, 175*
    and smell, 159
    and spatial relationships, 162–63, 169–71
    and stereotypes, 523–24, *523*
    and study of consciousness, *183*
    and survival, 168
    and taste, 159, *159*
    and touch, *159,* 160–61
    and vision, 132, 153, 154, *159,* 162–74
    and what versus where, 163, 168
performance, and motivation, 443
peripheral nervous system (PNS), 75, 98–100, *99*
persistence, and memory, 301
persistent vegetative state, 184–85, *185*
    see also coma
personal attributions, 517, 518
personal constructs, 574
personality:
    and adaptation, 596–97, 598–99, *599*
    and age, 597–98, *598*
    of animals, 589–90, *590*
    assessment of, 579–87
    and behaviorism, 573, 574
    biological basis of, 569, 588–99, *599*
    and brain, 96, *96,* 588, 594, 595, 599
    and cognition, 570, 574–75
    and consciousness, 570
    and culture, 577, 585–87, *586,* 594, *598*
    definition of, 569, 584
    and development, 572, 593
    disorders of, 656–63, *657*
    and emotions, 575, 576
    and environment, 572, 589, 594, 598
    and evolution, 596
    and experience, 573–74, 576, 578
    and gender, 585–87
    and genetics, 112–14, 588–89, 590–92, 595, 596, 598
    and Gestalt psychology, 12
    and health, 482–83
    hierarchical model of, 576, *577*
    how scientists have studied, 569–78
    humanistic approach to, 573–74, 580
    and identity, 406
    and inconsistency, 583–84
    interactionist approach to, 585
    and learning, 574–75, 595

procedural memory, 295–96, *295*

prodigies, 350

progesterone, 458

projective methods, for personality assessment, 580

pronoun reversal, 665–66

propagation, and nervous system, 80

prosocial behavior, 552

prosopagnosia, 168

prospective memory, 296–97, *297*

prospect theory, 335

protein, and genetics/genes, 106

prototypes, 322–23, *322, 323*

proximity and similarity, 166–67

Prozac, 84, 642, 683, 695, 696, 698, 714–15, 716, 720

pseudoinsomnia, 198

pseudotherapies, 686–87, *687*

psychiatric nurses, 688

psychiatric social workers, 688

psychiatrists, 688

psychoactive drugs, 211–14

psychoanalysis:

  and classification of mental disorders, 693

  definition of, 14

  and homosexuality, 463

  and scientific foundations of psychology, 14, *14,* 16–17

  and treatment of mental disorders, 674, 676, *676,* 705

psychobiography, 580

psychodynamic theories:

  of personality, 570–73

  and treatment of mental disorders, 676–77

psychodynamic therapy, definition of, 676

psychographs, 88, *89*

psychological factors, and mental disorders, 627

psychological reactance, 337, *446*

psychological science:

  application of, 3–6

  biological foundations of, 72–129

  and biological revolution, 18–19

  definition of, 2

  genetic foundations of, 105–17

  goals of, 33

  interdisciplinary aspects of, 23

  and levels of analysis, 21–23, *22*

  methods of, 2

  women in, 12–13, *13*

psychological scientists, 2, 3, *3*

psychological testing, 624–25, *625,* 661–62

psychological therapy, 16–17, 693, 706

psychological treatments, versus therapy, 693

psychology:

  biological foundations of, 72–129

  and careers, 450, *450*

  definitions of, 8–9

  reverse, *446*

  scientific foundations of, 6–18

  subfields of, 23–25, *24*

Psychology: Knowledge You Can Use, 62–63, 127, 176–77, 310–11, 487

psychometric approach, to intelligence, 344–60, *344*

psychoneuroimmunology studies, 480

psychopathology, 618–20, 660–62, *661, 662,* 711, 712

psychopharmacology, 675

psychophysics, 135–39

psychophysiological assessment, 56

psychosexual stages, 572, 588

psychosis, 654, 684, 710

  definition of, 650

psychosocial factors, and health, 470–76

psychosocial motives, 445–48

psychosocial therapy, 707–8

psychosurgery, 685, 686, 696, 706

psychotherapy, 675, 676–81, 703–4

  versus psychological treatments, 693

  see also specific technique or method

psychotic disorder, definition of, 650

psychotic disorders, 705, 706

  see also specific disorder

psychotic episodes, 707, 708

psychoticism, 576

psychotropic medications, 683–84, 705, 706, 711

puberty, 399–401, 404, 458

  see also adolescence

punishment:

  definition of, 242, 243

  effectiveness of parental, 244

  and learning, 225, 243, *243*

  and mental disorders, 661, 662

  and parents, 243–44

  and personality, 595

  physical, 244

  as positive or negative, 243, *243*

  and social influence, 537

  and treatment of mental disorders, 678

pupil, 150, *152*

qualia, and study of consciousness, *183*

questions, and research methodology, 53–55, *54*

race/ethnicity:

  and depression, 704, 714

  and exercise, 498–99, 530

  and identity, 404

  and impressions, 520, 524–25

  and intelligence, 357–60

  and memory, 305–6

  and mental disorders, 682

  and perception, 168

  and stereotypes, 520, 523–25

Rader, Dennis, 661

radical acceptance, 710

radical hemispherectomy, 125

Ramsay, Erik, 181–82, *181*

random assignment, 43–47, *45*

random errors, 65

randomized clinical trials, 692

random sampling, 43–47

range, 66, *67*

rapid eye movements, *see* REM sleep

rational-emotive therapy, 679

rationalizing, 571

ratio schedule, 245

reaction formation, 572

reaction times, 55–56, 351

reactivity effect, 51

reality:

  and delusions, 651

  virtual, 694

reality principle, 571

reasoning:

  abstract, 388

  and brain structure and function, 353

  deductive, 329–31, *330*

  definition of, 329

  and emotions, 437

  inductive, 329–31, *330,* 392

  moral, 391–92

  and Piaget's cognitive development stages, 388

  and premises, 329–30

  and problem solving, 329–31, *330*

  see also thought/thinking

rebound effect, 431

recency effect, 283–84, *283*

receptors:

  definition of, 81

  and motivation, 455

  and nervous system, 77, 80–82

  and sensation, 133–36, *134, 140–41,* 143–47, *144–45, 146–47,* 148, *149,* 153, 156

  see also sensation; *type of receptors*

reciprocal helping, 552

recognition:

  and aging, 415

  false, 308

  see also facial recognition

reconsolidation process, and memory, 272

"recreational drugs," 211, 215

reflected appraisal, 604

reflective listening, 678

reflexes, 76, 90, 372, 386

Regan (case study), 647

regression to the mean, 473, *473*

reification, 347

Reimer, Bruce and Brian, 402–3, *402*

Reimer, David (Bruce), *403*

reinforcement:

  absence of, 249

  as conditioning, 242

  and definition of reinforcer, 240

  and learning, 240–48, 259

  natural, 259

  and personality, 573, 574, 595

  as positive or negative, 242–43, *243*

  and potency of reinforcers, 242–43

reinforcement *(cont.)*
  and rewards, 257–60
  schedules of, 244–48, *245*
  successive approximations in, 241
  and treatment of mental disorders, 711, 719
  value of, 574, *574*
  vicarious, 255
  see also rewards
relationships:
  client-practitioner, 689, 708, 711
  and development, 366, 405–7
  and emotions, 435, 438–39
  and Erikson's stage theory of identity, 408
  and learning, 244
  and life transitions, 409–13
  and mental disorders, 643, 658, 659–61, 668, 677, 679
  and personality, 572, 573
  quality of, 555–63
  romantic, 408, 558–59, *558*, 560–61, *561*
  and roommates (college), 610–11
  and treatment of mental disorders, 710
  see also attachment; friendships; parent/child relationship; social interaction
relaxation techniques, 674, 694
  see also meditation
releasing factor, 102
reliability, 64–65, *65*
religion, 506, 509, 682
religious ecstasy, 209, *209*
REM behavior disorder, 198
REM sleep, 197, 198, 200, 202–3, *203*, 642
repeated TMS, 686
replication, 32
representations:
  analogical, 319–20, *319, 320*
  and memory, 288
  mental, 319–28
  and Piaget's cognitive development stages, 384–86
  and problem solving, 340–42
  restructuring, 340–41, 342
  symbolic, 319–20, *319, 320*
representativeness heuristic, 334–35
repressed memories, 310–12, *312*
repression, 312, 572
reproduction:
  and adaptation, 10, 19
  and depression, 704
  and genetic basis of psychological science, 107–10
  and heredity, 107, *109*
  and life transitions, 412
  and motivation, 443, 448, 458
  and personality, 596
  and sexual behavior, 458
  and stress, 478–79
  and themes of psychological science, 10
Rescorla-Wagner model, 236–37, *237*
research methodology, 28–72
  and alternative explanations, 41

and animals, 59–60
and asking approach, 53–55
and averaging, 45
and bias, 31, 33, 36, 44, 54, 698–99
and case studies, 52–53, *52*
and causality, 38, 39, 40–43, 48
and cohort effect, 36
and concepts, 34
and control, 34, 40, 42–43
and correlational studies, 34, 38–40, *38*, 47, 66–67, *68*, 69
and cross-cultural studies, 49–50, *49*
and cross-sectional studies, 36, *37*
and data, 31, 33, 34, 49–69
and descriptive studies, 35–38, *35*, 47
and empirical process, 33
and ethics, 60–63
and experimental studies, 30, 34, 40–43, *45*, 47
and generalizing, 43
and hypotheses, 31–33
and law of large numbers, 47
and longitudinal studies, 36, *36*
and meta-analysis, 68–69
and objectivity, 50
and observation, 31, 35–38, 50–52
overview about, 30
population for, 43–47, 48, 54
and prediction, 31
and questions, 53–55
and scientific inquiry, 31–34
and scientific method, 31–33, *31, 32, 37*
and statistical procedures, 64–69, *65*
and theories, 31–33
and types of studies, 34–48
and unexpected findings, 33
and variables, 38–43
reserpine, 706
resilience, and health, 502
resolution phase, 457
response:
  accuracy of, 56
  bias, *136*, 137
  and scientific foundations of psychology, 14–15
  and sensation, 135–39, *135*
response performance, 55–56, *55*
response-prevention therapy, 696
responsibility:
  diffusion of, 553
  and mental disorders, 718
rest, and sleep, 199
resting membrane potential, 78–79, *78*
restrained eating, 493–94
restrictive dieting, 472, 493–94
restructuring:
  cognitive, 679
  of representations, 340–41, 342
reticular formation, 90
retina, 150–51, *152*, 153, 154, 169–70, *170*, 172, 173, *174*, 175, 382

retrieval, of memory, 269–70, *269, 280, 282,* 289–92, 297, 298
retrieval cues, 289–92
retrieval tasks, and aging, 415
retroactive interference, 299, *299*
retrograde amnesia, 301, *301*
reuptake, 82, 84, 696
reverse psychology, *446*
rewards:
  and attitudes, 531
  biological basis of, 257–60
  and learning, 257–60
  and mental disorders, 678–79
  and motivation, 445
  and personality, 595, 596
  and scientific foundations of psychology, 14–15
  and social influence, 537
  see also incentives
rhetoric, 534
right hemisphere, 151, 168, *168*, 642
risk-benefit ratio, 61
risk judgments, and emotions, 437
risky-shift effect, 538
Risperdal, 684, 707, 720
Ritalin, 717–18, *717*
Robinson, Rebecca, *172*
Rocco, Johnny, 541–42
rods, 151, *152*
"roid rage," 550
role models, 218
Rolling Stones, 413, *413*
romantic relationships, 326–27, 408, 558–59, *558*
  and conflict, 561
  principles of, 560–61, *561*
roommates:
  and cleanliness, 610–11, *611*
  college, 610–11
rooting reflex, 372
Rorschach inkblot test, 580–81
Rosato, Tony, 617–18, *618*, 619
Rousseff, Dilma, *324*
rumination, 431
rumination disorder, *664*
runner's high, 209, 702
Russian newspaper reporter, memory of, 298

sadism, 514, 544
salience, 176–77
salivary reflex, 226–27, *226, 228, 229*
sampling, 42, 43–47, *47, 54*
SAT (Scholastic Aptitude Test), 447
satiety, 84, 452
satisficing, 338
savants, 354
scatterplots, 66, *67*
Schachter-Singer Two-Factor theory of emotion, 427–28, *428, 429, 429*
schemas:
  cognitive, 518, 519

and dating, 326–27
definition of, 288
and development, 384–86
gender, 401
and memory, 288–89
and Piaget's cognitive development stages, 384–86, *384, 385*
and scripts, *325*
self-, 602–3, *602*
and stereotypes, 324, *324*
and thinking/thought, 324–28, *325*
see also stereotypes
Schiavo, Terri, 185, *185*
schizoaffective personality, 597
schizoid personality, 657
schizophrenia, 624, *655*
and Capgras syndrome, 618, 619
and conceptualization and classification of mental disorders, 627, *627*, 650–57, *650, 653*
definition of, 650
and dementia praecox, 621
and gender, 628, *628*
treatment for, 681, 684, 685, 705–8, 710
and virus hypothesis, 654
schizotypal personality, 657
schizovirus hypothesis, 654
school psychologists, 24
scientific inquiry, 31–34
scientific method, 6–18, 31–33, *31, 32, 37*
scripts, 325–27, 459–61, *459*
and dating, 326–27
and schemas, *325*
seasonal affective disorder (SAD), 642, 702, *702, 703*
Seattle Longitudinal Study, 416
secondary appraisals, 484
secondary emotions, 423
secondary reinforcement, 242, 247, 259–60
second-generation antipsychotics, 707
second-order conditioning, 230
secure attachment, 377
seizures, 187, 684, 685, 702, 706
selection bias, 44
see also bias, and research methodology
selective breeding, 107
selective listening, 274–75
selective mutism, *664*
selective permeability, 78–79
selective serotonin reuptake inhibitors (SSRIs), 84, 683, *684*, 693, 694, 696, 698, 705, 714, 716, 720
self:
collective, 609, *611*
independent, 609–10, *611*
interdependent, 609–10, *611, 711*
as knower, 601, *602*
and memory, 268
and mental disorders, 659
mental strategies to main views of, 606–9

objective, 601
sense of, 268, 405–7, 660
self-abuse, 659, 660, 666, 721
self-actualization, 441, 573
self-awareness, 537–38, 601–2
self-care, 707
self-concept, 601–6, *601*
self-construals, 609–10, *609*, 611
self-control, *see* self-regulation
self-determination theory, 445
self-discrepancy theory, 602
self-efficacy, 446–47, 574
self-enhancement, 610–12
self-esteem:
and obesity, 492
and personality, 572, 574
and prejudice/discrimination, 521, 526
and psychological research, 62–63
and relationships, 558
and social regard, 603–6, *604*
and treatment of mental disorders, 683, 702
self-evaluative maintenance, 607–8
self-fulfilling prophecy, 520–21
self-help, 597, 687
self-hypnosis, 207, *207*
self-injury, 710
and autism, 666, 721
and suicide, 644
self-knowledge, 580, 600–613, *602*
self-monitoring, 584
self-mutilation, 659, 660, 710
see also self-abuse
self-perception theory, 445
self-regulation:
and brain, 668
and mental disorders, 658, 668
and motivation, 445
and personality, 575
and stereotypes, 524–25
self-reports, 53–55, *54*, 581, 582, *583*, 586, 625
self-respect, 710
self-schema, 602–3, *602*
self-serving, 607, 609–12
self-serving bias, 519
self-stimulation, 258–59, *258*
semantic memory, 294–95, *294*
sensation:
and adaptation, 137, *137*, 147
and aging, 414
basic processes of, 88, 139–56, *140–41, 144–45, 146–47, 149*
and brain, 132–33, *133, 134*, 139–56, *140–41, 144–45, 146–47, 149*
and cognition, 160
definition of, 132
and development, 371–72, *372*, 386
and emotions, 425
and environment, 137, 148
and experience, 132–33
and genetics, 141

and how we sense the world, 132–39, *133, 134*
internal, 156
and judgment, 138
and learning, 226
and memory, 143, *145*, 271, *271*, 279–81
and nervous system, 77
overview about, 131–32
and sensory thresholds, 135–36, *135*
and sixth sense, 157–58
see also specific sensation
sensation-seeking, 584, 594, 662
sensitive periods, 373, 375
sensitization, 261
sensorimotor stage, 386
sensory coding, 133, *135*
sensory memory, 279–81, *280, 281*
sensory neurons, 76, *76*
sensory-specific satiety, 453
sensory thresholds, 135–36, *135*
separation anxiety, 377
September 11, 2001, 304, 317–18, *318*, 472, 485, *485*
septum, 547
serial position effect, 283, *283*
serotonin:
and addiction, 213
definition of, 84
functions of, *83*, 84
and harming and helping others, 547–48, *547*
and influence of neurotransmission, 84
and mental disorders, 642, 660, 683, 684, 693, 696, 706, 720
and motivation, 458
and personality, 592, 595
and sexual behavior, 458
and sleep, 199
set-points, 442, 455, 493
"seven sins of memory," *299*
sex, *see* gender
sex characteristics, primary and secondary, 400, 402
sexual behavior:
and adaptive behavior, 463
and addiction, 215, 217
and behaviors affecting health, 508
and biology, 457–59, 463
and brain, 91–92, 463
and depression, 640, 698
and endocrine system, 101–2
and environment, 463
and frequency of sex, 558
and gender, 101–2, 460–61, *461*, 464
and hormones, 101–2, 457–58
and love, 561
and mating strategies, 461–62
and mental disorders, 660
and motivation, 443, 456–65
and nervous system, 101–2
and relationships, 558, 561

sexual behavior (cont.)
  and safe sex, 508
  and scientific foundations of psychology, 14
  and sexual orientation, 463–65, *464*
sexual dimorphism, 124
sexual dysfunction, 640, 683, 698
sexual reproduction, *see* reproduction
sexual response cycle, 457, *457*
sexual strategies theory, 461–62
shadowing, 275, *275*
shame, 392
sham surgery, 85, 693
  see also placebo/placebo effect
shape perception, 175, *175*
shaping, 241, *241*
Shiva Fellowship Church Earth Faire, *218*
shock experiments, 543–45, *543, 544, 545*
short-term memory:
  long-term memory distinguished from, 283–84
  as stage of memory, 268–69, *280,* 281–83
shyness, 593–94, 636
sickle-cell disease, 110, *110*
signal-detection theory, 136–37, *136*
sign language, 394–95, *395,* 396
similarity, proximity and, 166–67
Simon, Taryn, 307, *307*
simple models of learning, 260–61, *260*
single-cause explanations, 596, *596*
single-pulse TMS, 686
situationism, 582, 584–85
situations:
  and brain, 15
  and evil, 16
  and harming and helping others, 548, 553–54
  and impressions, 517, 518
  influence on behavior of, 514
  and learning, 16
  and mental disorders, 632–33, 635–37, 641–43
  and personality, 575, 582, 584–85, 594, 598
  and relationships, 555–58
  and research methodology, 35–36
  and scientific foundations of psychology, 16
  and social influence, 544
  and social psychology, 514, 517, 544, 548, 553–58
  strong, 585, *585*
  and treatment of mental disorders, 701
  weak, 585, *585*
sixth senses, 157–58
size perception, 172–73, 174, *175*
skepticism, 4
Skinner, Deborah, 223–24, *224*
Skinner, Yvonne, 223–24
Skinner box, 240–41, *241*
sleep:
  as adaptive behavior, 199–200
  and adenosine, 201
  and alcohol, 201
  as altered state of consciousness, 195–99

amount of, 195
and basic structure and functions of brain, 90
and brain, 194–204, *196*
and caffeine, 201
and cognitive behavioral therapy, 198
deprivation of, *see* sleep deprivation
and development, 370
disorders, 197–99, *198*
and exercise, 201
and meditation, 202
and memory, 201, 271–72
and mental disorders, 631, 633, 639, 640, 642, 660
and moods, 199
and motor functions, 201
and narcolepsy, 198
and nervous system, 84, 117
and obstructive sleep apnea, 198, *198*
purpose of, 195, 199
and restoration, 199–200
SLEEPLESS gene and, 150
and sleep-wake cycles, 103
stages of, 196–97, *196, 197*
what is, 194–204
see also dreams; REM sleep
sleep apnea, 198, *198*
sleep deprivation, 197–200, 201–2, *201*
  and adenosine, 201
  and anxiety, 201
  and caffeine, 201
  and depression, 201
  and exercise, 201
  and meditation, 202
  and memory, 201, 272
sleeper effect, 304
SLEEPLESS gene, 150
sleep spindles, 196
sleepwalking, 199
"slippery slope," 215
slow-wave sleep, 196–97, 200
smell, 91, 142–45, *144–45,* 159, 371
smoking, 39, 217, *217,* 218, 255, *255,* 472, 482, 483, 489, 496–97, *496, 497,* 499, 508, 691
  and children, 218
snobbery, 605
sociability, 593
social anxiety disorder, 632, *633,* 635, *636*
  see also social phobia
social comparisons, 449, 607, 608, *608*
social competence, 548
social development, 366, 373–80, 398–405
social exclusion, 19, 542
social facilitation, 537, *537,* 544
social factors:
  and behavior, 17
  and emotions, 438–39
  and genetic basis of psychological science, 113–14
  and mental disorders, 632–33, 635–36, 652, 665, 720, 721, 722

and scientific foundations of psychology, 17
  see also relationships
social influence, 537–45
social integration, 503–6
social interaction:
  and mental disorders, 652, 665, *665*
  and treatment of mental disorders, 707, 719, 720, 721, 722
  see also relationships
socialization:
  and attitudes, 528–29
  and development, 366
  and emotions, 434, 439
  and gender, 401, 402
  and identity, 401, 402
  and morality, 392
social loafing, 537
socially desirable responding, 54
social multiplier, 355
social needs, and motivation, 448
social norms, 540–42
  see also norms
social phobia, 632–33, *633,* 635, *636,* 679
social psychology, 24
  and adaptation, 552, 607
  and attitudes, 528–36
  and attributions, 515–18, 562
  and cognition, 530–32, 548, 601
  definition of, 514
  and evolution, 522, 548, 553
  and gender, 518–21, 523
  and harming and helping others, 546–55
  and impressions, 515–27
  and motivation, 517, 521, 524, 537
  overview about, 513–14
  and relationships, 555–63
  and scientific foundations of psychology, 15
  and self-knowledge, 600–613
  and situations, 514, 517, 544, 548, 553–58
  and social influence, 547–45
social regard, 603–6
social-skills training, 679, 680, 707, *707,* 722
social support, *see* support, social
sociocognitive theories, of personality, 574–75
sociocultural model, and mental disorders, 627, *627*
socioemotional development, 373
socioemotional selective theory, 414, 415
sociometer theory, 604, *604*
sodium, and nervous system, 78–79, 86
somatic markers, 392, 437
somatic marker theory, 437
somatic nervous system, 98–100, *99*
somatosensory hallucinations, 651
somatosensory homunculus, 94, *95*
somatosensory nerves, 76
somatosensory signals, 99
somnambulism, 199
sound waves, 148, *149*
source amnesia, 304, 384
source misattributions, 304

symbolism, and Piaget's cognitive development stages, 387
sympathetic division, 99–100, *100*
sympathy, 392
synapse/synapses:
    definition of, 77
    and development, 371–73, *372*
    and intelligence, 356
    and learning, 260–61
    and mental disorders, 683
    and nervous system, 77, 80–82, 84, 86
    and termination of synaptic transmission, 82
synaptic cleft, 77, *77,* 81, 82
synaptic pruning, 372
synaptic transmission, 120
synesthesia, 121–23, *121*
synesthetes, 274
syntax, 393, 396
systematic desensitization, 233, 680, 694
systematic errors, 65
systems approach, 681

taboos, 454, 456, 529
tabula rasa, 226
tactile stimulation, 145
talking, and health, 667–68
"talk" psychotherapy, 676, 677–78, 693
    see also psychoanalysis; psychodynamic theories
tardive dyskinesia, 684, 706, 707
taste, 140–42, *140–41, 142, 143,* 159, *159,* 371, 452–53, 454
taste buds, 140, *140, 142*
technology, 2
technology-based treatments, 689–91
teenage brain, 400
teenagers:
    and depression, 401
    and limbic system, 400
teenagers and frontal cortex, 400
telegraphic speech, 394
temperament:
    definition of, 406, 592
    and development, 406
    and gender, 593
    and mental disorders, 636
    and personality, 592–94, *593*
temporal lobes:
    and basic structure and functions of brain, 93–94, *93, 187*
    and memory, 268, *268,* 270–72, 284
    and mental disorders, 653
    and perception, *159,* 161
tend-and-befriend response, 479, *479*
teratogens, 368
terminal buttons, 77, *77,* 82
terrorism, 304, 546
terror management theory, 604
testing:
    aptitude, 344, 359
    intelligence, 351–52, 357–58, 359–60

as measurement of intelligence, 344–60
and mental disorders, 624–25, *625,* 661–62
neuropsychological, 625, *625*
psychological, 624–25, *625,* 661–62
and stress, 487–88
validity of, 345–46
see also type of test
testosterone, 101–2, 458, 459, 463–64
    and aggression, 549–51
    and brain, 550
    and competition, 550–51
    and dominance, 551
    and violence, 550–51
texture gradient, 171
thalamus:
    and basic structure and functions of brain, 91, 92
    and emotions, 426
    and perception, 159, *159,* 160
    and sensation, 132, *141,* 143, *147,* 151
thalidomide, 368
Thatcher, Margaret, 168, *169, 303,* 304
Thatcher illusion, 168, *169*
THC (tetrahydrocannabinol), 212
Thematic Apperception Test (TAT), 581, *581*
theories, and research methodology, 31–33
theory of mind, 390–91, 665
therapists:
    choosing, 687–91, *688, 690*
    client relationship with, 689, 708, 711
    cost of, 689
    manipulation of, 710
theta waves, 196, *196*
thin slices of behavior, 516
third-variable problem, 39, 47
Thompson, Jennifer, 307
thought/thinking:
    abstract, 388
    amount of, 329
    and application of psychological science, 4
    and behavior, 15
    and categorization, 321–24
    critical, 4–6, 42–43, 46–47, 116, 123, 138, *138,* 157–58, 215, 216, 236, 278, 309, 347, 379, 436, 446, 475, 519, 534–35, *535,* 596, 605, 689
    definition of, 319
    influence of neurotransmission on, 82–87
    and mental disorders, 16, 628
    overview about, 317–18
    rational, 571
    and representations, 319–28
    and scientific foundations of psychology, 10, 15, 16
    and structural model of personality, 570–72
    see also cognition; decision making; mind; problem solving; reasoning; representations
threats, 635
thresholds, 135–36, *135*
tickling, 146
tip-of-the-tongue phenomenon, 300

tobacco, and children, *327*
token economies, 247–48
tolerance, 217, 234
top-down processing, 167–68
touch, 145–47, *146–47, 159,* 160–61, 372
Tourette's syndrome, 259, *664, 696*
"Tower of Hanoi" problem, 339, *339*
toxins, and influence of neurotransmission, 82, 84
trait approaches, 570
traits, personality:
    of animals, 589–90, *590*
    as approach for studying personality, 575–78
    assessment of, 580–82, *583,* 586–87
    as behavioral dispositions, 575–78
    central, 580
    consistency of, 569
    definition of, 569
    and hierarchical model, 576, *577*
    and person/situation debate, 584
    secondary, 580
    stability of, 597–99
tranquilizers, 683, 693, 694, 706
transcendental meditation, 208
transcranial magnetic stimulation (TMS), *57,* 59, 686, *686,* 703
    repeated, 686
    single-pulse, 686
transduction:
    and perception, 159
    and sensation, 133, 150
transformation, and memory, 282
transgender, 403, *403*
transience, 298–99
transitions, life, 409–13
transplants, 85, *85*
trauma, 300, 301, 312, 626, 627, 646, 647, 649, 660, 667, 676, 677, 678, 687, 693, 710
    and correlational studies, 39–40
treatment groups, 40
Treatment of Adolescents with Depression Study (TADS), 714–15, *715*
treatment resistant disorders, 684
Trebek, Alex, *517*
trepanning, 685, *685*
tricyclic antidepressants, 683, 695, 698, 714
triggers, and learning, 237
trust, 505–6, *505*
    versus mistrust, 398–99
tumor problem, 342
Twain, Mark, 439
twins:
    dizygotic, 111–12, *112*
    and emotions, 439
    and genetic basis of psychological science, 111–13
    and intelligence, 355
    and mental disorders, 626, *627,* 639, 641–42, 653, *653,* 654, 662, 666, 668
    monozygotic, 111–12, *112*
    and motivation, 463

and obesity, 491
and personality, 590–91, *591,* 598
and sexual behavior, 463
twin studies, 111–13, *112,* 463
two-factor theory, 427–28, *428,* 429, *429*
Type A behavior pattern, 482
Type B behavior pattern, 483
tyramine, 696

unconditional positive regard, 574, 588, 678
unconditioned response (UR), 226–28
unconditioned stimulus (US), 226–28, 233–34, 235–37, 242
unconscious:
   definition of, 14
   as influencing behavior, 192–93
   and memory, 295–96, *295*
   and mental disorders, 627
   and personality, 570–73, *570,* 580
   and scientific foundations of psychology, 14, 17
   smart, 193
   and study of consciousness, 192–93
   and treatment of mental disorders, 676
unexpected findings, 33
UNICEF, 356
unihemispherical sleep, 199
uniqueness, individual, and personality, 579–80, 589
United Nations Office on Drugs and Crime, 211
universal grammar, 395
universality, of self-serving biases, 609
U.S.A. Memory Championships, 292
"use it or lose it" policy, 372
utility, 332

valence, of emotions, 423
validation, 562, 710
validity:
   external, 44
   internal, 64
   and research methodology, 44, 64, *65*
   of tests, 345–46
Valium, 86
Valnord-Kassime, Vionique, 29–30, *30*
values, and personality, 574, *574*
van Gogh, Vincent, 641
variability, 66
variable-ratio schedule, 245, *245,* 246
variables, and research methodology, 34–35, 38–43, 66–67
variable schedules, 245, *245*
variation, 113

ventral stream, 162
vestibular senses, 156
vicarious learning, 255
Vicki (case study), 659
Vicodin, 214
Vietnam War, 218–19, *218*
violence:
   and animal studies, 547
   and depression, 640, 703
   and genetic basis of psychological science, 113–14
   and ingroup/outgroup bias, 525
   and learning, 243, 252–53, *252, 253*
   and media, 252–53, *253,* 535
   and mental disorders, 660
   and steroids, 549–51, *551*
   and testosterone, 550–51
   see also aggression
Virginia Tech University, *52, 53*
virtual environments, 694, *695*
virus hypothesis, 654
vision:
   as basic sensory processing system, 143, 150–56
   and basic structure and functions of brain, 93–94, *93, 188*
   and development, 372, 381–82, *381*
   and Gestalt psychology, 12
   as important source of knowledge, 150
   and learning, 235
   and mental disorders, 666
   and neurons, 134
   and perception, 132, *133,* 134, 153, 154, *159,* 162–74
   and scientific foundations of psychology, 12
   and sleep, 200, 202–3, *203*
   and what versus where, 163
   see also blindsight; visual cortex
visual acuity, 381–82, *382*
visual cortex:
   and basic sensory processes, 151, *153*
   and basic structure and functions of brain, 93–94, *93*
   and development, 382
   and development of brain, 118
   and perception, *159,* 162, 163, 173
visual hallucinations, 651
visual information, and memory, 271, 280
visual search tasks, 274
Viswanathan, Kaavya, *305*
von Restorff effect, 304

Wallace, Mike, 704, *705*
Waller, Patrick, *307*

Warhol, Andy, *350*
Washington, Denzel, 524
waterfall effect, 173
"water lily" problem, 342
Weber's law, 136, 177
Wechsler Adult Intelligence Scale (WAIS), 345, 347
weight, *see* eating; obesity
well-being:
   definition of, 470
   and happiness, 501
   and health, 468–511
   and marriage, 504
   and spirituality, 506, *506*
Wells, H. G., 224
Western Collaborative Group, 482
Wexler, Lenore, 73–74
white matter, 90
whole-language approach, *393*
Wilson, Donald, 85
Wiltshire, Stephen, 354, *354*
withdrawal, 217, 233, 652
women:
   in psychological science, 12–13, *13*
   and sexuality, 456
   working, 21
Woods, Tiger, 255, *358*
working backwards, 342
working memory:
   and basic stages of memory, 281–83
   and brain structure and functions, 352–53
   definition of, 352
   and development, 415
   and intelligence, 352–53, *353*
   and organization of information, 289–90
   and stress, 478
working self-concept, 603, *603*
World Health Organization (WHO), 356, 482, 496
writing, and health, 667–68

Xanax, 683

Yerkes-Dodson law, 443, *443*
yoga, 208, 679
youth, *see* adolescence; children
Yufe, Jack, 112

Zen meditation, 208–9
Zilstein study, 449
Zoloft, *699*
zygotes, 109, 367, *367*
Zyprexa, 684, 707